S0-AIW-357

FEDERAL DOMESTIC OUTLAYS 1983–1990

FEDERAL DOMESTIC OUTLAYS 1983–1990

A DATA BOOK

KENNETH N. BICKERS AND ROBERT M. STEIN

M. E. SHARPE, INC.
ARMONK, NEW YORK
LONDON, ENGLAND

Available in the United Kingdom and Europe from M. E. Sharpe, Publishers, 3 Henrietta Street, London WC2E 8LU.

Library of Congress Cataloging-in-Publication Data

Bickers, Kenneth N., 1960– .
Federal domestic outlays, 1983–1990 : a data book / by Kenneth N. Bickers, Robert M. Stein.
p. cm.
ISBN 0-87332-840-X
1. Grants-in-aid—United States—Statistics. 2. Economic assistance, Domestic—United States—Statistics. I. Stein, Robert M. II. Title.
HJ275.B47 1991
336.1′85—dc20

91-651
CIP

Printed in the United States of America

∞

ED 10 9 8 7 6 5 4 3 2 1

Contents

Acknowledgments

We have received generous assistance and support from many individuals and institutions in completing this data book. A small army of current and former students have worked long and cheerfully on data entry and in the preparation of the tables and figures that are contained in the volume. In particular, we wish to thank Amy Barton, Anthony Carmona, KaLyn Davis, Merrill Davis, Heather Fenstermaker, Ellen Forman, Sharon Koch, and Edward Stewart. Special gratitude is owed to LaVonna Blair and Valerie Heitshusen, the graduate assistants that were responsible for managing many of the day-to-day activities of the project. Ross Goldberg deserves recognition and thanks for his skill and hard work in the final preparation of the volume for publication.

We owe many debts of gratitude to our colleagues at Rice University and elsewhere for their encouragement and advice on this project. John Alford and Ric Stoll have been especially helpful in suggesting solutions to the complications that arose in managing the dozens of data tapes and millions of observations that had to be processed in the course of compiling the information reported in the volume. For their helpful advice and encouragement on the project, we would like to thank Ted Anagnoson, Thomas Anton, David Brady, Joseph Cooper, Keith Hamm, Kenneth Meier, Peter Miezkowski, Mike Rich, Barry Rundquist, and John Witte.

We are also grateful to a number of institutions that have been instrumental in supporting our research. In the early stages of the project, Rice University provided Kenneth Bickers with a Faculty Research Grant to undertake the preliminary stages of the data collection effort. The Rice University Center for the Study of Institutions and Values provided additional funding to the authors to purchase government data tapes. The National Science Foundation (grant number SES-8921109) provided major funding for the project. The Rice University Computer Center, and especially Priscilla Huston, Andrea Martin, David Boyes, and Richard Schafer, provided invaluable technical support and assistance on the project. We would like to thank Robert Brown, Staff Director for the Catalog of Federal Domestic Assistance, and David Kellerman, Director of the Government Division of the U.S. Census Bureau, for their suggestions and assistance in the use of federal data on programmatic expenditures. Finally, we would like to thank Michael Weber of M.E. Sharpe for his support and advice in the preparation of this volume.

Chapter 1

Introduction

1.1 Overview

Everyone no doubt harbors feelings, at least occasionally, that he or she is not receiving benefits from the government in proportion to the tax burden that he or she is bearing. Such feelings are quite natural. Questions of fairness and equity are always at the heart of discussions about the distribution of public benefits and burdens. Elected officials, no less than the public, are sensitive to such questions. In fact, elected officials may be more sensitive to distributional issues. Failure to bring home a "fair share" of government dollars calls into question the performance of elected representatives. Advancement within the legislature and the opportunity to seek higher office typically hinge on being reelected by comfortable margins. At the extreme, inattention to the home district may jeopardize a member's prospects for reelection.

The stakes are particularly high in times of fiscal retrenchment when competition over the public purse intensifies. At such times, increased benefits for some districts come at the expense of others. This was the basic fact underlying federal budgetary politics in the 1980s. Budgetary conflicts will only intensify in the 1990s. Under these conditions, information about the distribution of federal dollars becomes paramount. Unfortunately, to date, detailed information about the distribution of federal dollars has not been readily available or accessible. This volume attempts to address this need by providing extensive information about the distribution of federal domestic outlays across the 435 congressional districts, the 50 states, and the major regions of the United States for the period from 1983 through 1990.

1.2 A brief history of federal data collection efforts

Students of American domestic policy confront a significant obstacle when attempting longitudinal studies of the distribution of federal assistance to congressional districts. Writing in 1980, scholars studying the government's efforts at accounting for its own spending concluded that "the federal government itself has no clear understanding of how much money it spends, where, or in what form" (Anton et al., 1980:12). Those interested in longitudinal studies which span a wide range of substantive policies confront the absence of a reliable time-series on programmatic activities. Under a grant from the National Science Foundation, we have produced a volume which reports the distribution of federal monies to each congressional district for the fiscal years 1983 through 1990. These distributional data are based upon records of the federal government that were available in a comparable form beginning in 1983. These records are contained in the Federal Assistance Awards Data System (FAADS), which is maintained by the Bureau of the Census. FAADS was established in 1981, but underwent significant evolution prior to 1983. The time series reported in this volume covers the years 1983 through 1990. FAADS reports financial awards and obligations to recipients by individual programs. It comprises approximately one million entries per year and is available only on magnetic tape. While FAADS was originally created to improve the flow of information on federal aid to members of Congress and the public, this hope has not been realized.

Unfortunately, even moderately long time-series data on policy decisions at the programmatic level do not exist. What do exist are different pieces of a comprehensive programmatic history of American domestic policy. In most cases, these pieces are time bound and only marginally comparable. In the case of expenditure data, the available data are highly aggregated and void of programmatic and recipient detail. It is important to note, however, that the absence of reliable time-series data on domestic policy activities is neither an accident of history nor the design of any specific government policy. Rather, it reflects the growth and change in the character of federal domestic policy.

Historical studies of American domestic policy should be sensitive to changes in the government's data bases. Scholars must understand the context in which these data were collected. Specifically, different periods in the history of the federal aid system have given to rise to different types of data collections. In each period, the government's data bases have utilized different definitions of outlays, different units and levels of analysis, and have been designed for different purposes. Understanding these differences should enable the researcher to use available data sources effectively and to provide an awareness of the limitations of longitudinal studies of U.S. domestic assistance policy.

The character and scope of American domestic expenditures has undergone a number of significant changes during the history of the Republic. Wright (1988), Anton (1980), Walker (1978), and ACIR (1978) have documented these historical periods. Collectively these authors identify four twentieth-century periods of change: FDR's New Deal, the immediate post-World War II period, Johnson's Great Society, and the Reagan Revolution. Though domestic outlays grew in each of these periods, the nature and scope of growth varied.

The reporting of federal domestic outlays has a history that roughly parallels, but lags behind, changes in national domestic policy. Changes in data collection efforts have typically trailed changes in the size, structure, and character of national domestic policy. When the nation debated new policy initiatives, data adequate to address the issues under debate often were not available.

Wright characterizes the period of American Federalism before the 1930s as a period of conflict and formation (1988:66). This was the period of landmark constitutional conflicts in which state and national interests vied for supremacy. Though McCulloch v. Maryland (1819) awarded the national government significant supremacy in its battles with state governments, this decision did not significantly alter the advantage state and local governments held in domestic policy issues. During the nineteenth and early twentieth century the national government's fiscal role in domestic policy remained modest, relative to state and local governments.

Consistent with the national government's limited role in domestic public policy, efforts to collect information on these activities were minimal. Expenditures for capital projects (dams, rivers, forts, and harbors) were reported in annual congressional appropriations (see Wilson, 1986). Prior to 1916, expenditures by the national government were reported as warrants in the Treasury Department's *Daily Statement of Receipts and Expenditures of the United States*. These figures were based on checks issued by disbursing officers (not budgetary authorizations by Congress) and were reported as aggregates for all federal agencies. The *Daily Statement* was the main source of information on domestic outlays until the conclusion of World War I.

Concurrent with the growth of national responsibilities in the early twentieth century, the federal government in 1902 undertook its first systematic effort to collect data on domestic expenditures. This effort, conducted by the Bureau of Census, and published under the title *Governmental Finances*, provided national grants-in-aid information. These data reported budgetary authorizations, and not the disbursement figures reported in Treasury's *Daily Statement*. Department and agency breakdowns were first reported in 1923.

The collapse of the American economy in the 1930s undermined the fiscal capacity of state and local governments. In order to restore the viability of these governments and the vital services they provided, the federal government created a host of grants-in-aid programs that offered assistance to state and local governments. With these grants-in-aid programs, the federal government subsidized subnational provision of social welfare activities, including programs for old age assistance and aid to dependent children. By 1935 federal domestic outlays had achieved parity with state and local outlays. Thereafter, federal spending for domestic programs quickly outpaced the combined spending of state and local governments (Census, 1975).

The first subnational accounting of federal domestic expenditures was compiled by the Treasury Department beginning in 1930. This report, entitled "Federal Aid to State and Local Governments," was published until 1969 as an appendix to the *Annual Report of the Secretary of the Treasury on the State of Finances*. This report provided aggregate figures for individual states, but the government did not detail outlays by specific agencies or programs. Since the overwhelming majority of monies went to state governments for direct expenditure, there was no need to document the substate distribution of these monies. Beginning in 1969 and lasting until 1981, the Treasury published the *Federal Aids to the States*, which replaced the earlier appendix to the annual Treasury Report. This new publication reported additional detail about the distribution of federal aid to the state level, including agency and some programmatic level authorizations.

The end of the Second World War unleashed an enormous reservoir of monies for domestic spending. The deferred demand for new goods and services resulted in rapid growth in federal domestic spending. Between 1946 and 1961, 21 new grants-in-aid programs were enacted, nearly twice the number created during the New Deal period (ACIR, 1978). Like the New Deal assistance programs, these were largely state-based entitlements. In response to this expansion in federal activity, the Census Bureau in the 1950s began publishing state and substate data on federal aid transfers in the *Census of Governments*. Aggregate figures were reported along with more detailed figures for special categories of aid, including health, hospitals, welfare, roads and highways, education, housing, and a residual "other" category. Initially, these categories exhausted the substantive range of federal domestic aid programs. Anton et al. report, however, that these functional categories have not kept pace with the expansion of the aid system. "Over the years Census has reported more and more federal aid in the 'other' category, making it even more difficult to determine which functional classifications contain precisely which federal programs" (1980:27).

Johnson's landslide victory in 1964 set the stage for a new expansion in the federal domestic agenda. Approximately 150 new federal domestic aid programs were adopted by Congress between 1964 and 1968 (ACIR, 1978). With only temporary exceptions, the expansion in the number of programs continued through the 1970s (Bickers, 1991). The majority of the new programs were project grants, which required extensive applications and were awarded through a competitive selection process. This proliferation of programs and recipients created enormous political opportunities for members of Congress. As John Chubb notes:

> Categorical grants mushroomed in numbers and dollars during the 1960s and 1970s because they fit the political needs of representatives and senators. By their sheer number such grants provide abundant opportunities for legislators for producing discrete benefits for their districts. (1985: 282)

The growth in programs produced corresponding incentives to improve the federal government's information about its own activities. First, members of Congress had an incentive to advertise programs so that potential applicants could gain an awareness of the types of assistance that they were eligible to receive. At the same time, the government was faced with an increasingly large problem of tracking the distribution and use of federal monies.

To fulfill these needs, two new government data bases were created during Great Society: the *Catalog of Federal Domestic Assistance* (CFDA) and the *Geographical Distribution of Federal Funds* (Outlays). First published in 1965, the CFDA provides detailed information on each federal domestic aid program. In the catalog, a program is an activity or function of an agency that provides assistance or benefits to a category of recipients to accomplish a specific purpose. As noted above, the catalog was originally intended to help the government keep track of the plethora of programs created during President Johnson's Great Society, as well as to provide potential recipients with a guide to help in applying for federal aid. Since 1970, the catalog has been issued and updated annually. It documents all programs of the federal government that are intended to provide financial and nonfinancial assistance to domestic constituencies. Information on each program is extensive. In addition to information on the nature of the program, each listing describes application and eligibility requirements, statutory authority, and appropriation levels. Included in the catalog are programs which assist state and local governments, universities, private profit and nonprofit organizations, minority groups, and individual citizens. Forms of financial assistance include loans, loan guarantees, insurance, formula programs, and project grants, as well as direct payments. Forms of nonfinancial assistance include technical assistance by government experts, education, and extensive information systems. The catalog does not include such things as foreign aid, defense procurements contracts, government debt retirement, and federal contracts for items that the government itself consumes, for example, government office buildings, equipment, employee salaries, etc. Also not included are programs that are designed to address a one-time only problem of a particular person or entity. Examples of this type of assistance have included the New York City, Chrysler, Lockheed bailouts. Finally, while domestic assistance programs administered by regular federal agencies are included, those administered by quasi-public agencies, such as the Legal Services Corporation, are not.

Since the catalog continues to be issued annually, it represents the most effective means of longitudinally tracking changes in federal domestic program activity. Moreover, the catalog was the government's first effort to report federal expenditures at the programmatic level within the agencies responsible for their implementation. As noted above, previous publications aggregated "program data into department or functional totals that have little to do with program politics. If the most important component of the American political economy is federal expenditures, understanding that component clearly requires a data system capable of handling federal program decisions" (Anton et al., 1980:18-19). The catalog provides an important ingredient of such a data system.

The CFDA, however, does not address the question of where federal monies flow geographically. In part, the need for distributional information is simply to ensure compliance with program requirements and guidelines. At least as important, however, is the need to keep score of who is winning and who is losing in the competition for federal dollars. Distributional issues are at the heart of most political battles.

The inadequacy of accounting for the distribution of federal domestic outlays peaked in the late 1960s and 1970s, when regional conflict over the distribution of federal resources resembled a second war between the states. At the height of this conflict, Senator Moynihan (Dem.-N.Y.) referred to the attitude of his constituents toward federal resource distribution in the following terms:

> [N]o one much understands it and no one seems responsible for it. New Yorkers sometimes seem to look upon the Federal fisc (sic) in much the manner of a cargo cult. Every so often the great planes fly in, laden with bounty. Then, unpredictably, they fly away, and none can know whether or when they will return (Moynihan, 1979).

In the late 1960s, a system for tracking the distribution of federal outlays was partially provided by the *Geographical Distribution of Federal Funds* (GDFF). The Office of Management and Budget Circular A-84, effective 1967, mandated that all executive departments submit annual reports of "obligations incurred from federal funds in state and local areas" (Anton et al.,1980:19). Agency reports were published in fifty-three volumes: one for each state, one for territories and trusts, and one reporting national totals. Federal obligations were reported for all states, counties, and cities with populations of 25,000 or more persons. Most importantly, outlays were reported by programs as defined by the CFDA. Together with the information in the catalog on individual programs, the GDFF data base provided an accounting of program level disbursements of federal domestic outlays.

Despite the vast improvement over predecessor data bases, the GDFF reports were not without limitations. Outlays are reported only for cities over 25,000 in population, an improvement over previous data bases, but still a constraint on studies of the attributes of all aid recipients. Also, Anton et al. (1980) note that changes in reporting procedures between 1968 and 1974 limit the comparability of these data and thus the length of the available time-series. Some agencies simply did not report program outlays, or were not consistent in what they reported. Only since 1974 were reporting procedures sufficiently stable to sustain a reliable time-series. For programs which provided direct assistance to individuals through state managed programs (e.g., Medicaid, Food Stamps, and AFDC) the disbursement of monies is reported to the county in which the state capital is located. This reporting procedure has been identified as the "pass-through" problem. Pass-through funds are allocated to state governments which in turn are responsible for disbursing the monies to substate recipients. Pass-throughs should not be confused with a state's expenditure of federal funds on behalf of its citizens. In some instances the pass-through of federal funds is prescribed by federal law, while in other instances each state devises its own procedures for distributing federal aid monies to substate recipients. Proration codes published in the GDFF for pass-through programs provide a means of identifying how the monies are allocated among substate recipients. The proration codes, however, provide only a crude means of estimating actual aid disbursements (e.g, per capita allocation to counties, per enrolled student to school districts).

By 1980 another important factor impinged on the operation of federal domestic programs: the Reagan revolution (Chubb and Peterson, 1985). Eager to cut federal domestic spending and to shift greater financial responsibility for these programs to recipients (or at least the states), Reagan pushed through Congress a series of programmatic changes which cut real domestic program spending. These cuts and accompanying structural changes (e.g., grant consolidations) increased conflict over program outlays by making already scarce resources scarcer. The zero-sum quality of competition over dwindling aid transfers increased the need to know where these monies were going. Recall Moynihan's earlier comment about federal aid monies: "they fly away, and none can know whether or when they will return." Accounting for the flow of aid monies had become more than an administrative problem; it had become a political problem. The problem was especially acute for members of Congress who feared that their constituents were being disadvantaged. This fear was exacerbated by the termination of the Community Services Administration, which had produced the GDFF.

With the demise of the GDFF, the government ceased publishing program-by-program data on domestic outlays. The replacement for GDFF is the *Federal Assistance Award Data System* (FAADS), which is compiled by the Bureau of the Census. FAADS is available only on magnetic data tapes, which have been issued quarterly since the last quarter of 1981. The only published volume utilizing FAADS information is the *Consolidated Federal Funds Report* (CFFR), which is issued annually by the Bureau of the Census. The data in CFFR are reported for counties and subcounty areas and represent total agency outlays for a subset of federal agencies. FAADS reports budgetary authorizations and not the actual disbursement of monies. Budgetary authorizations are designated for specific periods (e.g., one year) and in some instances recipients fail to exhaust their authorizations during the designated period. When this occurs FAADS reports a negative sign before the unused amount. In most instances the recipient has failed to comply with programmatic conditions for the authorization of outlays. Simply stated, a negative sign indicates the recipient has failed to spend up to the full authorization level.

FAADS has significant potential beyond what is available in the CFFR. It contains extensive information on aid awards, recipients of the aid, and the programs under which awards are made. FAADS records constitute the underlying data source for the present volume. Programs in FAADS include those listed in the *Catalog of Federal Domestic Assistance*, and are keyed to the same identification codes that are used in the catalog. In most cases, FAADS data are presented as action-by-action records of federal spending awards to particular recipients. For transfer payments to individuals and for other large volume programs (e.g., Social Security, Medicare, Medicaid, Food Stamps), data are presented as aggregate amounts for all recipients in each county area. For the majority of aid programs, the data are presented by individual recipient. Accompanying each record is information on the recipient's geographical location, including state, congressional district, county, city, SMSA, and zip code. These data provide the basis for aggregating awards data at different levels of analysis. Congressional district level data for FAADS were reported first in fiscal year 1983. Prior to 1983, FAADS did not identify the congressional district in which awards were made, making it impossible to construct congressional district level figures for programmatic and agency level outlays that would be directly comparable to the district level data that existed beginning in 1983.

As we have shown, contemporary and historical data bases are shaped largely by the nature of the federal aid system. The absence of data on substate distributions by program prior to 1950 reflects the absence of any significant number of federal aid programs to recipients below the state level. The emergence of data bases with both programmatic and recipient detail reflects the dramatic growth in the number of programs and recipients after 1960. Those interested in studying the targeting capacity of federal aid transfers cannot examine this question at the substate level prior to 1964. The same condition prevails when dealing with the question of programmatic detail. The fact that data bases prior to 1960 reported only agency and department level aggregates reflects both the relatively small number of domestic programs and their concentration within a handful of agencies and departments. The availability of data sources is a function of the character of the aid system in each period. With the advent of the Reagan presidency and the increased pressure to cut federal spending, data bases incorporating programmatic detail and recipient information became available. This volume owes its existence to these new data sources.

1.3 Coding rules and caveats

The chapters that follow this introduction are organized into four parts. Chapter 2 contains histograms for each recipient category, displaying the amounts of money going to each of the four major regions of the country during the 1983-1990 period. Chapter 3 presents tabular data for recipient categories for each congressional district. These tables are designed to allow comparisons of outlays to a congressional district across all recipient categories in a given year. Separate tables are provided for each year of the 1983-1990 period. Chapter 4 presents bar graphs for each of the twelve functional policy categories. These graphs display outlays in each region of the country across the 1983-1990 period. Finally, Chapter 5 reports outlays for the functional policy categories by congressional district. These tables are designed to facilitate comparisons of outlays for each policy category across the 1983-1990 period. Following these chapters are four appendices. Appendix A lists the congressional districts which represent the county in which the state capital is located, and those congressional districts which represent only portions of a county. Appendix B lists the programs included in each recipient category. Appendix C lists the programs included in each functional policy category. Appendix D lists the states that are included in each of the regions of the United States.

This data base is a product of our research agenda. The coding rules and data selection methods reflect our interest in the role of congressional decision making in domestic policy. One of the consequences of this focus is that the basic level of analysis in this volume is the congressional district. However, we have also included outlays for the District of Columbia. The tables and figures in this volume do not include outlays for U.S. protectorates and territories such as Guam, Puerto Rico, and the Virgin Islands.

In interpreting the tables in this volume, it is important to understand some of the characteristics of the data base and the nature of our coding rules. The first concerns the way in which outlays are allocated to congressional districts. As noted above, in most cases, FAADS reports action-by-action outlays, but in a few instances, reports only county aggregates. These county aggregate records pose a coding problem in those situations where counties are represented by more than one member of Congress. The solution adopted here is to apportion outlays to each of these districts based on the proportion of the county's (1980) population that resides in the district. For example, during the 1980s, four congressional districts have encompassed portions of Harris County, Texas. In FAADS, expenditures for Social Security, Aid to Families with Dependent Children, and other high volume programs are not allocated to the four congressional districts representing Harris County, but instead are reported as quarterly aggregates going to the county as a whole. In this volume, such expenditures have been divided among these four districts based on the proportion of the population of Harris County that lives in each of the districts. Consequently, in order to arrive at the total outlays to each district, these expenditures are summed with the outlays going to all of the other counties that are represented, either in whole or in part, by each of the four members of Congress that represent Harris County. The districts that are affected by this coding rule are referenced in Appendix A.

A second limitation of FAADS is how it handles the fact that some federal programs allocate monies to the states to be reallocated to substate recipients. These programs are reported in FAADS as if the money were allocated entirely to the county in which the state capital is located. This poses a difficult problem in determining where the monies are ultimately allocated, since states employ different criteria for distributing funds. The only fully satisfactory solution would be to incorporate each state's decision rules for reallocating the federal monies. In this volume, we follow the convention adopted in FAADS, which is to report these monies as if they were spent in the congressional district or districts which encompass the county containing the state capital. This inflates expenditures to districts that represent state capitals and deflates expenditures to other districts. For this reason, the districts that represent the county in which the state capital is located are referenced in Appendix A.

A third limitation of FAADS is that the funding amounts reported for insurance, loans, guaranteed loans, and other forms of contingent liabilities do not in all cases represent the actual flow of federal funds. In some cases, the amount reported is the appraised value of the properties or assets that are insured or otherwise guaranteed by the government. This is the liability of the government if it were to reimburse all potential claimants for the full amount of their potential losses simultaneously. For example, FAADS reports the value of all properties that are insured under the Flood Insurance program, rather than the actual expenditure amounts paid to compensate victims of flood damage, with the result that this program appears to be larger than Social Security. In other cases, the amount reported is an actual outlay to cover a liability for a specific claim. The failure of FAADS to differentiate between these two types of entries can lead to serious misinterpretation of federal funding amounts. In this volume, our strategy has been to exclude all transactions that involve insurance, direct or guaranteed loans, and other forms of contingent liabilities. Users of this reference volume should be aware, however, that one consequence of this coding rule is that expenditures to cover actual claims for contingent liabilities are excluded along with the value of potential claims against the government. Thus some of the figures in the volume may understate true outlay levels.

The tables in this volume report data separately by recipient categories and by policy categories. The recipient categories include states, cities and towns, counties, special districts, public and private higher education, independent school districts, private profit and nonprofit organizations, small businesses, and individuals. Unfortunately, some of the recipient categories reported in FAADS are not used throughout the eight year time-series included in this volume. Outlays were reported for interstate agencies until 1985, but this expenditure category was dropped in subsequent years. Prior to 1986, outlays to state-supported universities were reported under the category of state government. Outlays were reported separately for state-supported universities beginning only in 1986.

Functional policy categories in this volume include agriculture, business and commerce, community development, disaster prevention and relief, education, employment, labor and training, environmental quality, food and nutrition, health, housing, income security and social services, and transportation. In dollar terms, these policy categories constitute the most important policy areas in the federal government's budget. However, they do not exhaust the government's range of domestic policy activities. The government also devotes considerable resources to such things as economic and social regulation, cultural affairs, legal services, and the preservation of natural resources.

Information on the policy categories into which programs are classified can be obtained from the *Catalog of Federal Domestic Assistance* (CFDA). The CFDA classifies programs into one or more policy categories. It is important to note that many programs serve multiple purposes. For example, food and nutrition programs often have an educational component. Similarly housing programs often provide income security as well as shelter. Rather than attempting to assign programs exclusively to one policy category, we have retained the CFDA's multiple classifications. This means that outlays for some programs are reported in more than one policy category. Comparisons within policy categories are valid. Attempting to sum across policy categories (e.g., health and education) will overestimate the actual amount of monies allocated because the policy categories are not mutually exclusive of one another.

In contrast to the tables that report outlays by policy categories, outlays reported by program recipients are mutually exclusive. While more than one category of recipient may be eligible to receive assistance, FAADS reports outlays to specific recipients. Consequently, a dollar reported as going to one recipient is not reported as going to another. Therefore it is valid to sum across recipient categories to arrive at total outlays for congressional districts, states, or other levels of aggregation.

Finally, due to the availability of only three quarters of data for the 1990 fiscal year at the time that this volume went to press, all figures for 1990 are extrapolated from the first three quarters of the fiscal year. Extrapolations are based on a weighted average of the contribution of the same three quarters over the period from 1987 through 1989, and are statistically adjusted for each recipient category to account for variation in reporting practices by agency and type of recipient. As with any estimates, data for 1990 should be used with caution.

1.4 Conclusion

This volume attempts to accomplish two objectives. The first is to provide a resource that permits useful comparisons of spending categories over time. Second, we have chosen to report domestic outlays at the level of the congressional district because of the centrality of the Congress in the political processes surrounding domestic programs. The choice of this level of analysis is a reflection of the assumption that the districts represented by members of Congress constitute the most basic building block in the creation, maintenance, and expansion of federal programs. Our belief is that a reference volume that reflects the *political* centrality of congressional districts on domestic spending is sorely needed. We hope that others will also find the data included in this volume to be of use.

References

Anton, Thomas, Jerry P. Cawley, and Kevin L. Kramer. 1980. *Moving Money: An Empirical Analysis of Federal Expenditure Patterns*. Cambridge, MA: Oelgeschlager, Gunn and Hain.

Bickers, Kenneth N. 1991 (forthcoming). "The Programmatic Expansion of the U.S. Government," *Western Political Quarterly*.

Chubb, John E. and Paul E. Peterson (eds.). 1985. *The New Direction in American Politics*. Washington, DC: Brookings Institution.

Chubb, John E. 1985. "Federalism and the Bias for Centralization," in John E. Chubb and Paul E. Peterson (eds.). *The New Direction in American Politics*. Washington, DC: Brookings Institution.

Moynihan, Daniel. 1979. "New York State and the Federal Fisc: III Fiscal Year 1978," Washington, DC: U.S. Senate Office of Senator Patrick Moynihan, New York, June 10, 1979.

U.S. Advisory Commission on Intergovernmental Relations. 1978. *Categorical Grants: Their Role and Design*. Washington, DC: U.S. Government Printing Office.

U.S. Bureau of the Census. 1975. *Historical Statistics of the United States, Colonial Times to 1970, Bicentennial Edition, Part 1*, Washington, DC: U.S. Government Printing Office.

Walker, David. *Toward a Functioning Federalism*. 1978. Cambridge, MA: Winthrop.

Wilson, Rick K. 1986. "An Empirical Test of Preferences for the Political Pork Barrel: District Level Appropriations for River and Harbor Legislation, 1899-1913." *American Journal of Political Science*. 30:621-649.

Wright, Deil S. 1988. *Understanding Intergovernmental Relations*, Third Edition, Pacific Grove, CA: Brooks/Cole Publishing Co.

CHAPTER 2

Trends in Federal Outlays to Categories of Recipients for the United States and Major Regions, 1983-1990

Figure 2.1

Total Domestic Outlays for the United States and Regions, 1983-1990

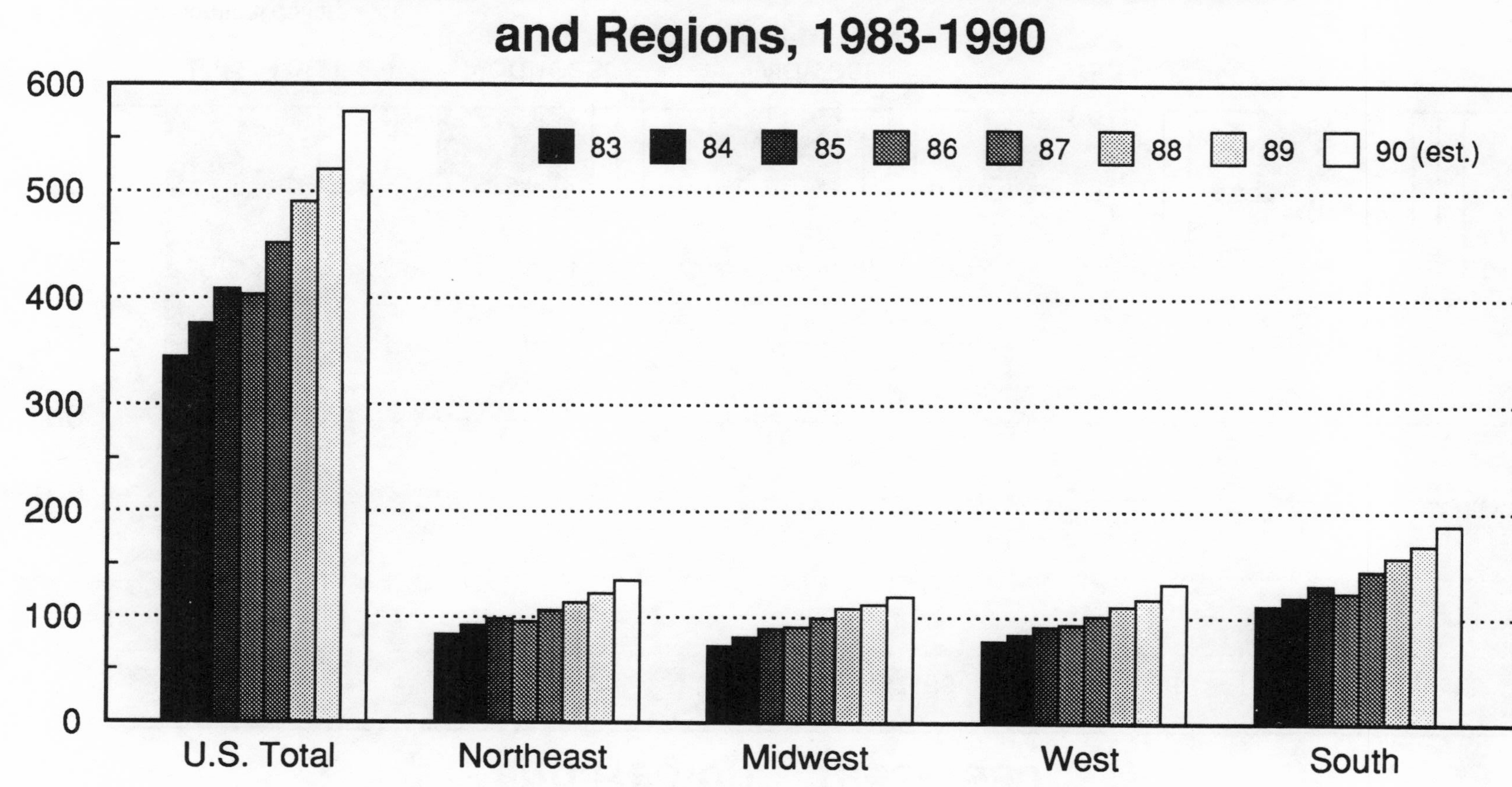

In billions of nominal dollars.
See Appendix B for programs by recipient groups.
See Appendix D for states in each region.

Figure 2.2
Outlays to States and State-Supported Universities for the United States and Regions, 1983-1990

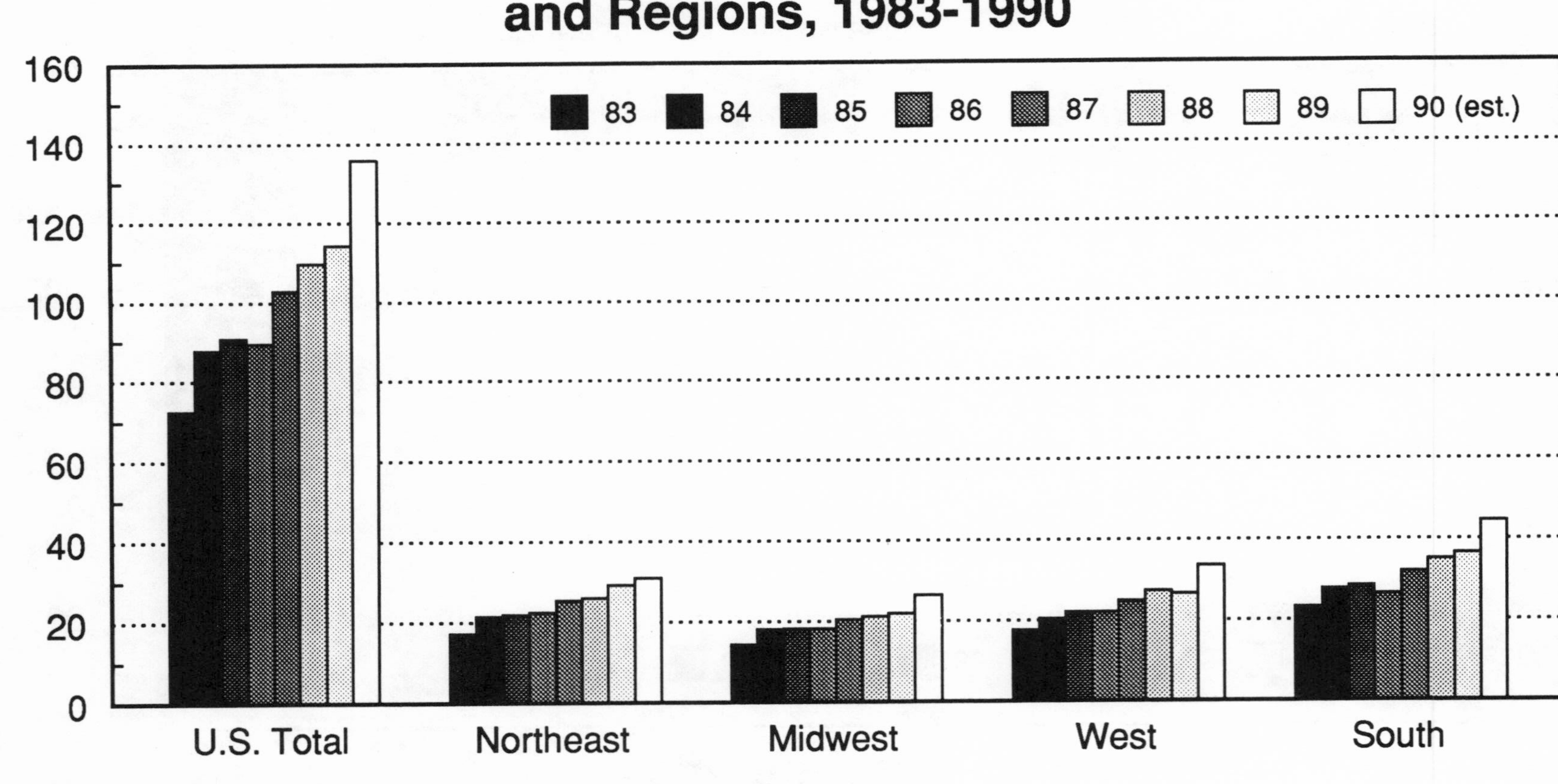

In billions of nominal dollars.
See Appendix B for programs by recipient groups.
See Appendix D for states in each region.

Figure 2.3

Outlays to Cities and Towns for the United States and Regions, 1983-1990

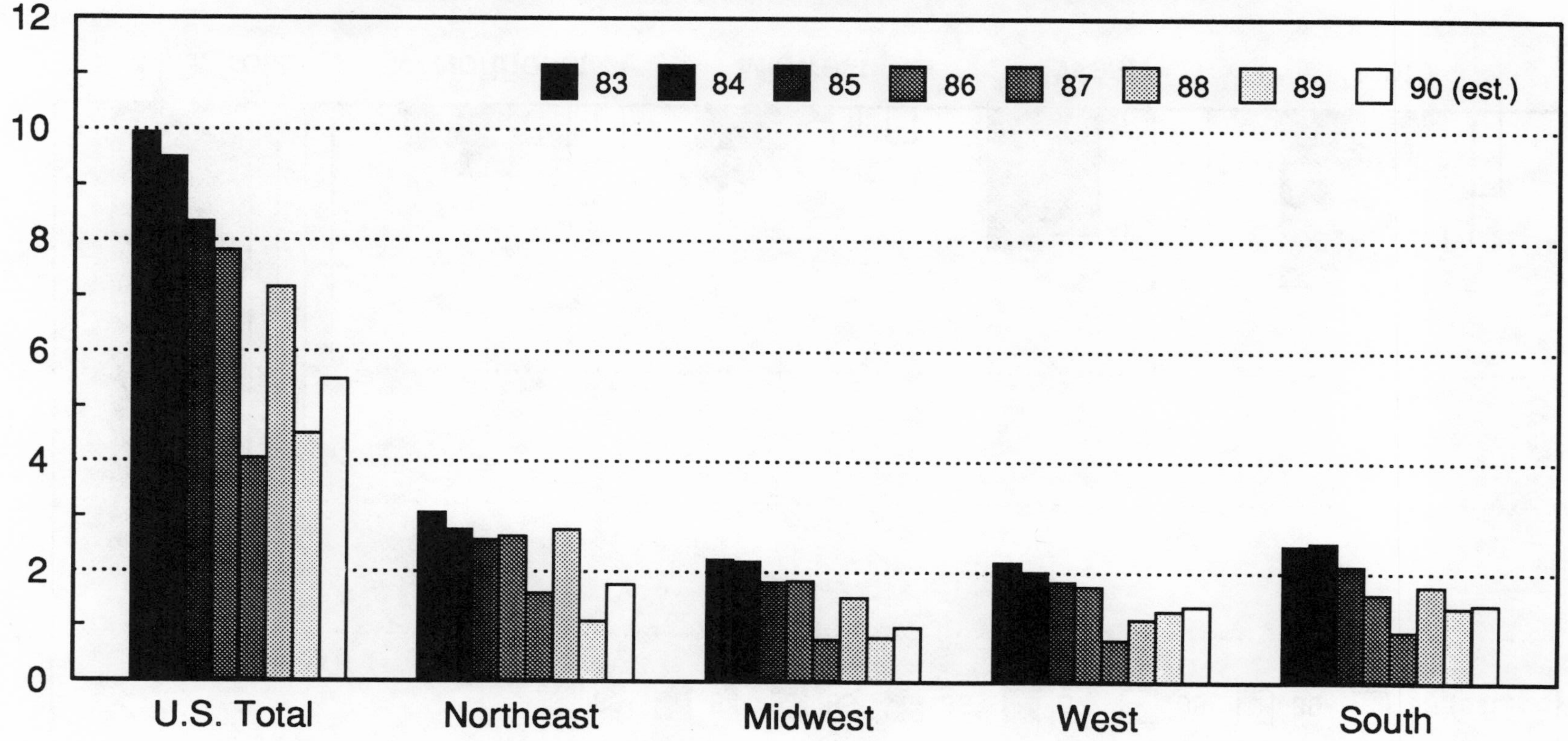

In billions of nominal dollars.
See Appendix B for programs by recipient groups.
See Appendix D for states in each region.

Figure 2.4

Outlays to County Governments for the United States and Regions, 1983-1990

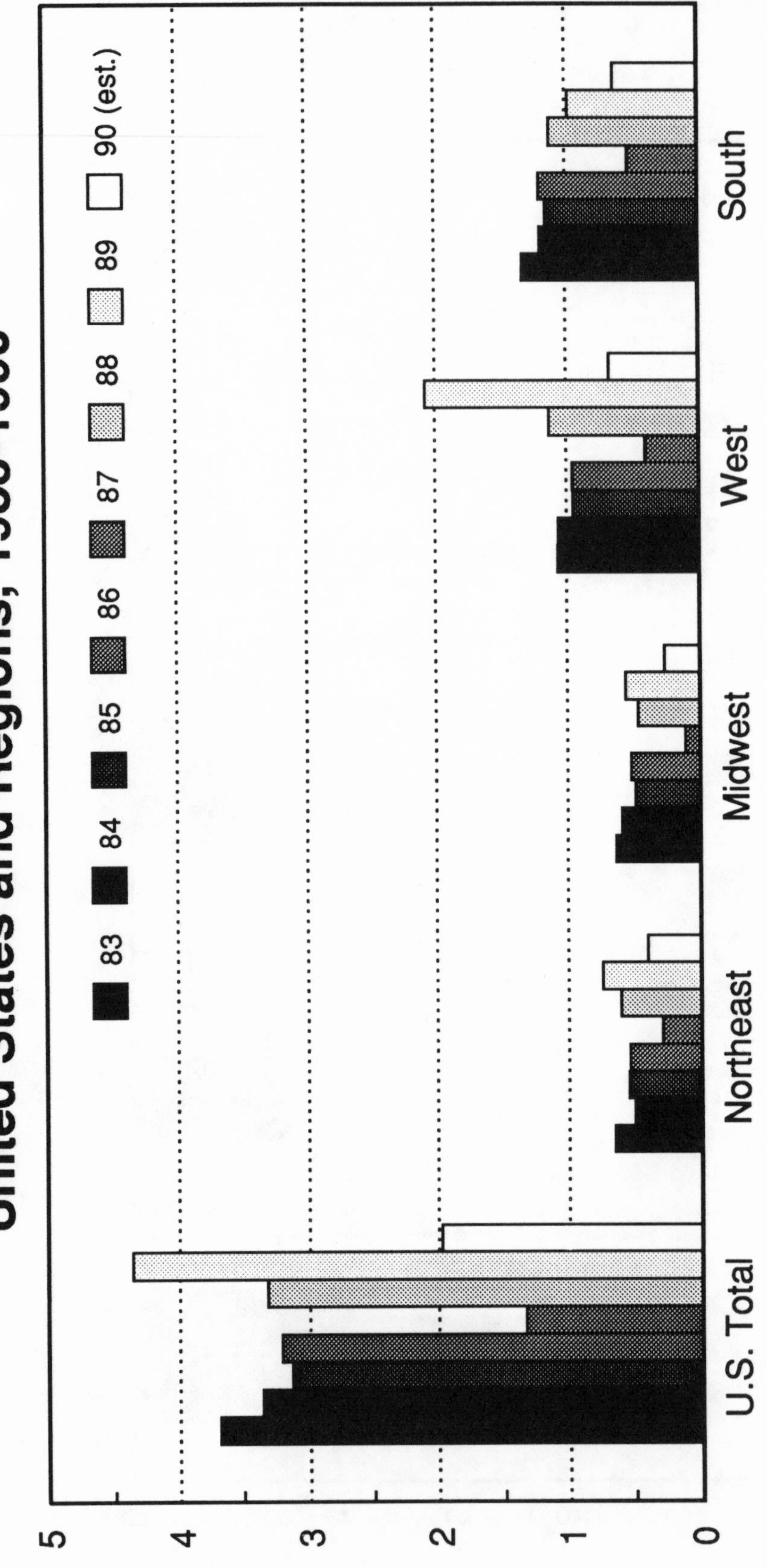

In billions of nominal dollars.
See Appendix B for programs by recipient groups.
See Appendix D for states in each region.

Figure 2.5

Outlays to Special Districts for the United States and Regions, 1983-1990

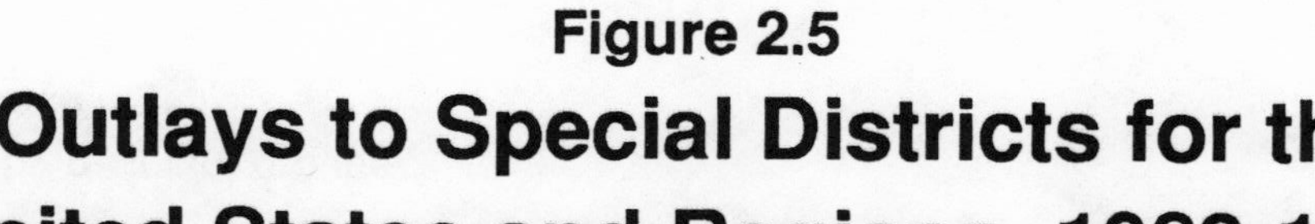

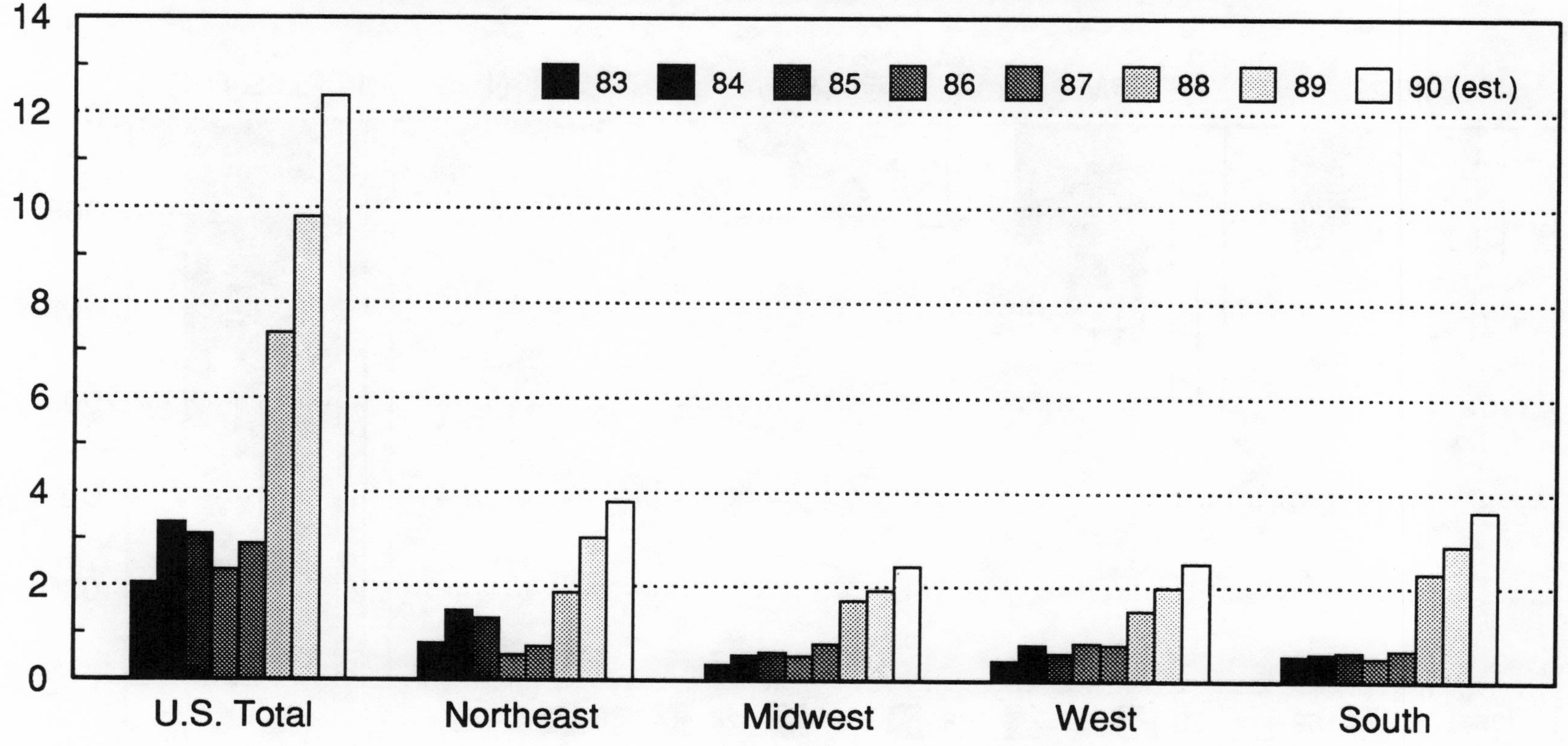

In billions of nominal dollars.
See Appendix B for programs by recipient groups.
See Appendix D for states in each region.

Figure 2.6

Outlays to Independent School Districts for the United States and Regions, 1983-1990

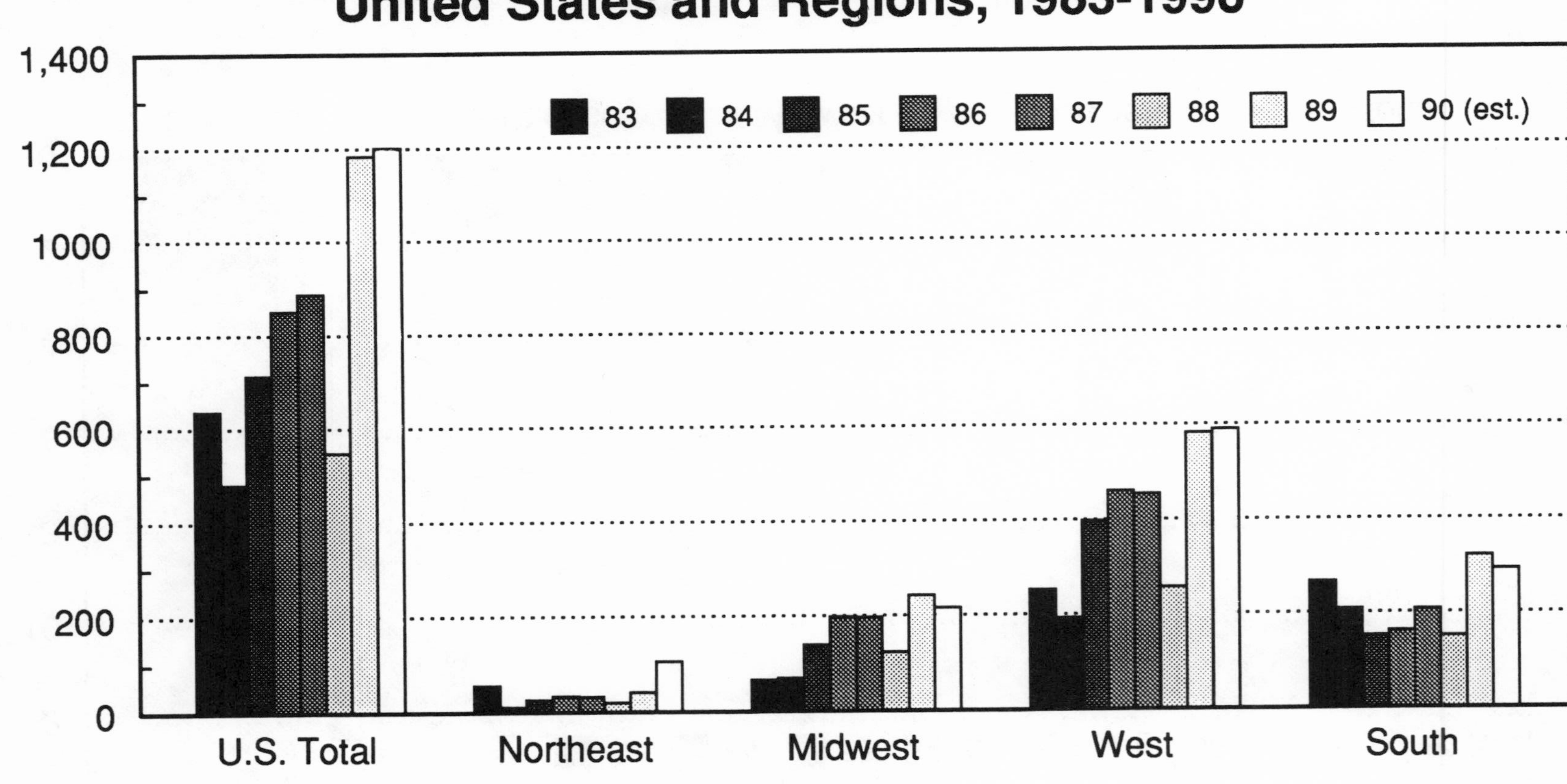

In millions of nominal dollars.
See Appendix B for programs by recipient groups.
See Appendix D for states in each region.

Figure 2.7

Outlays to Indian Tribes for the United States and Regions, 1983-1990

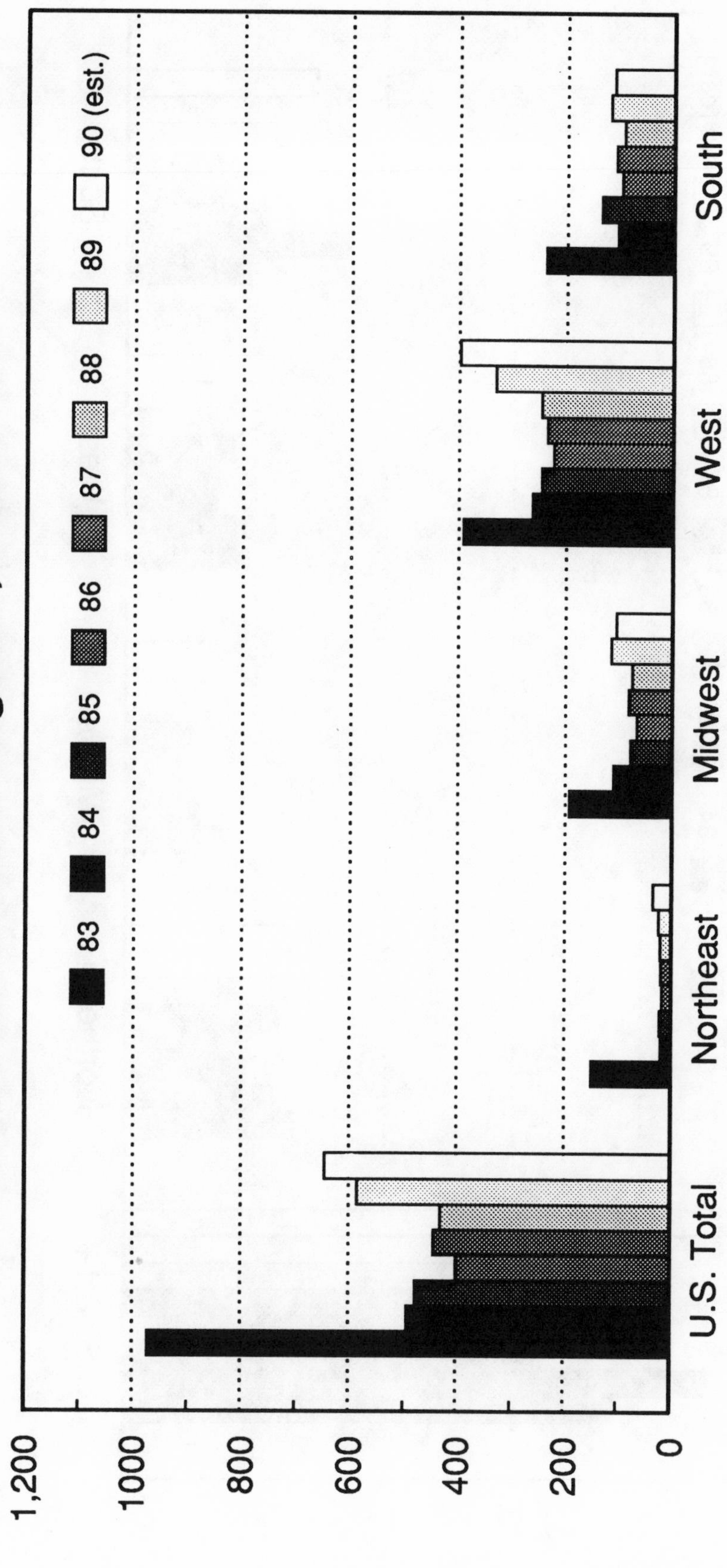

In millions of nominal dollars.
See Appendix B for programs by recipient groups.
See Appendix D for states in each region.

Figure 2.8

Outlays to Nonprofit Agencies for the United States and Regions, 1983-1990

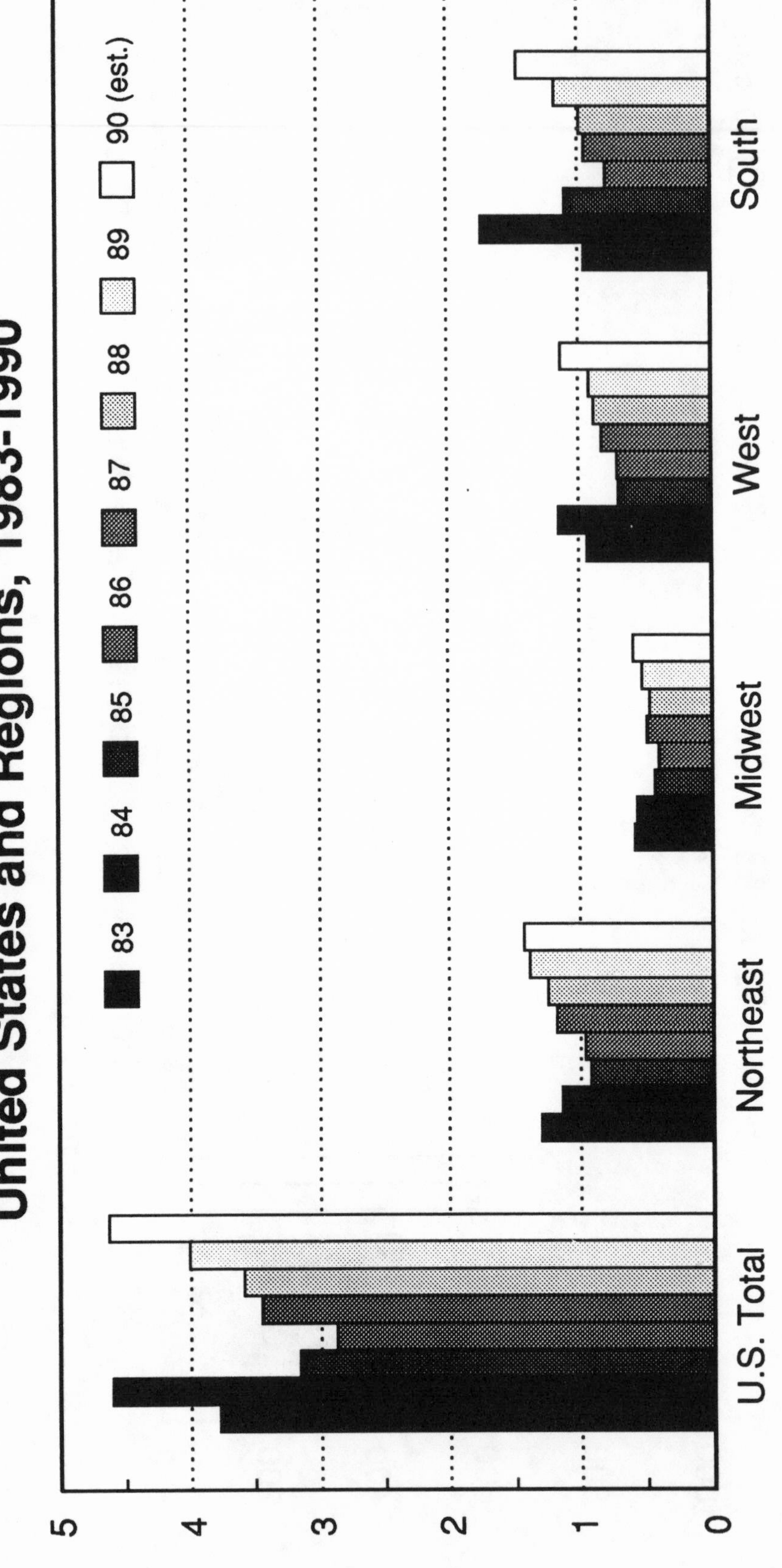

In billions of nominal dollars.
See Appendix B for programs by recipient groups.
See Appendix D for states in each region.

Figure 2.9

Outlays to Private Universities for the United States and Regions, 1983-1990

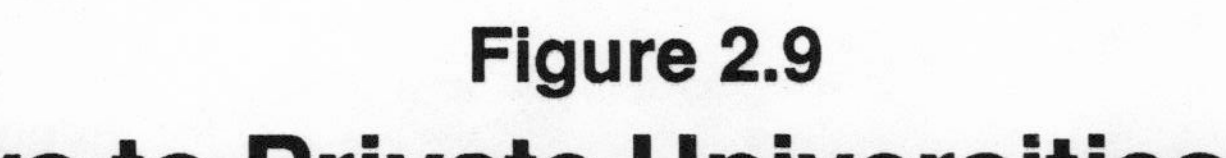

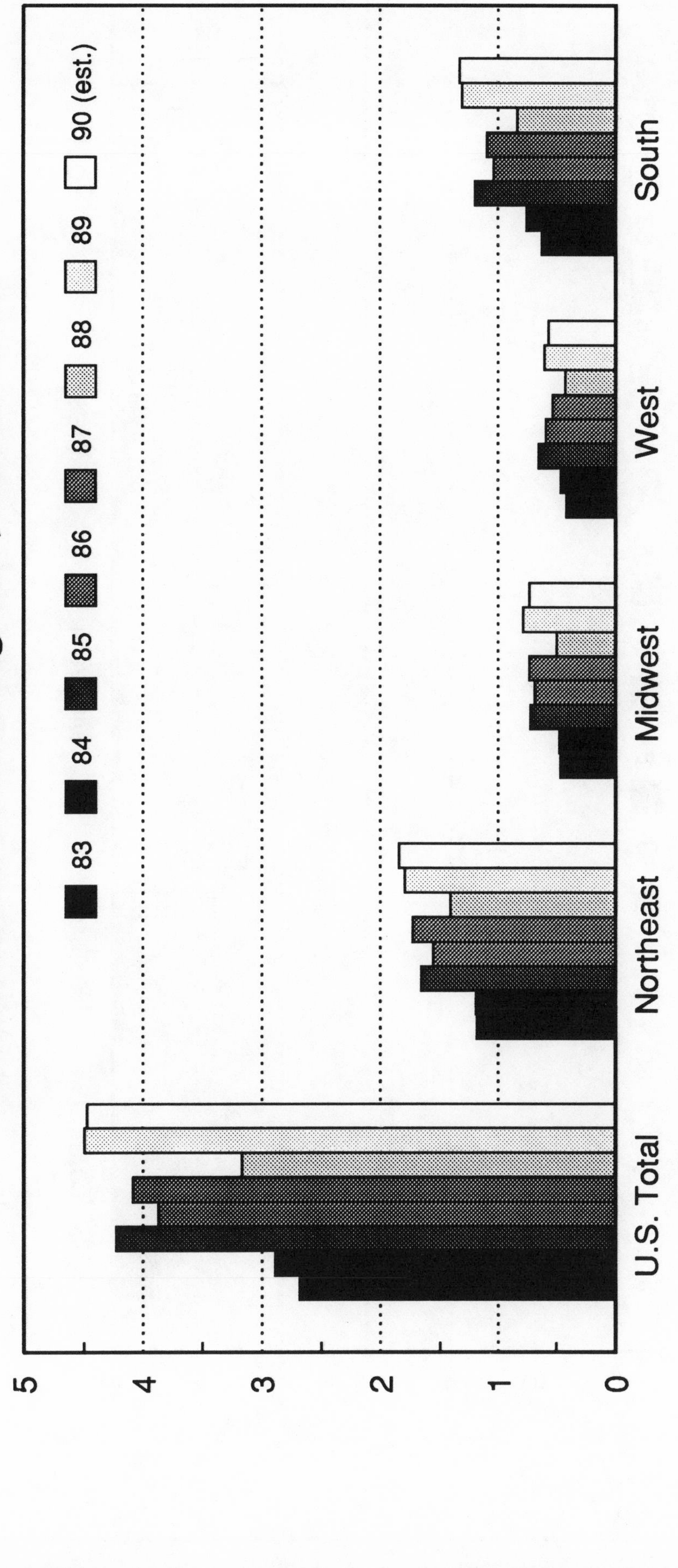

In billions of nominal dollars.
See Appendix B for programs by recipient groups.
See Appendix D for states in each region.

Figure 2.10

Outlays to For-Profit Organizations for the United States and Regions, 1983-1990

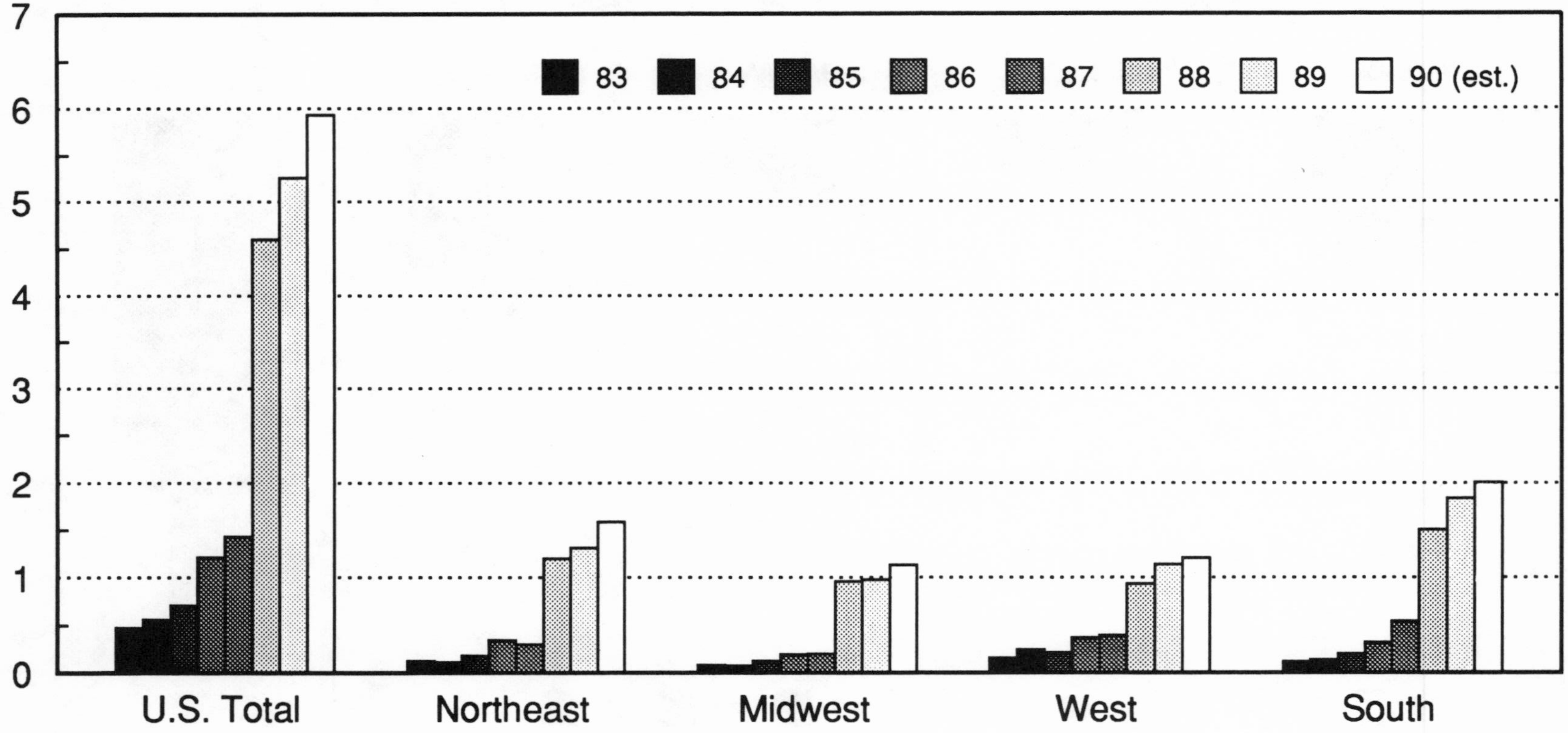

In billions of nominal dollars.
See Appendix B for programs by recipient groups.
See Appendix D for states in each region.

Figure 2.11

Outlays to Small Businesses for the United States and Regions, 1983-1990

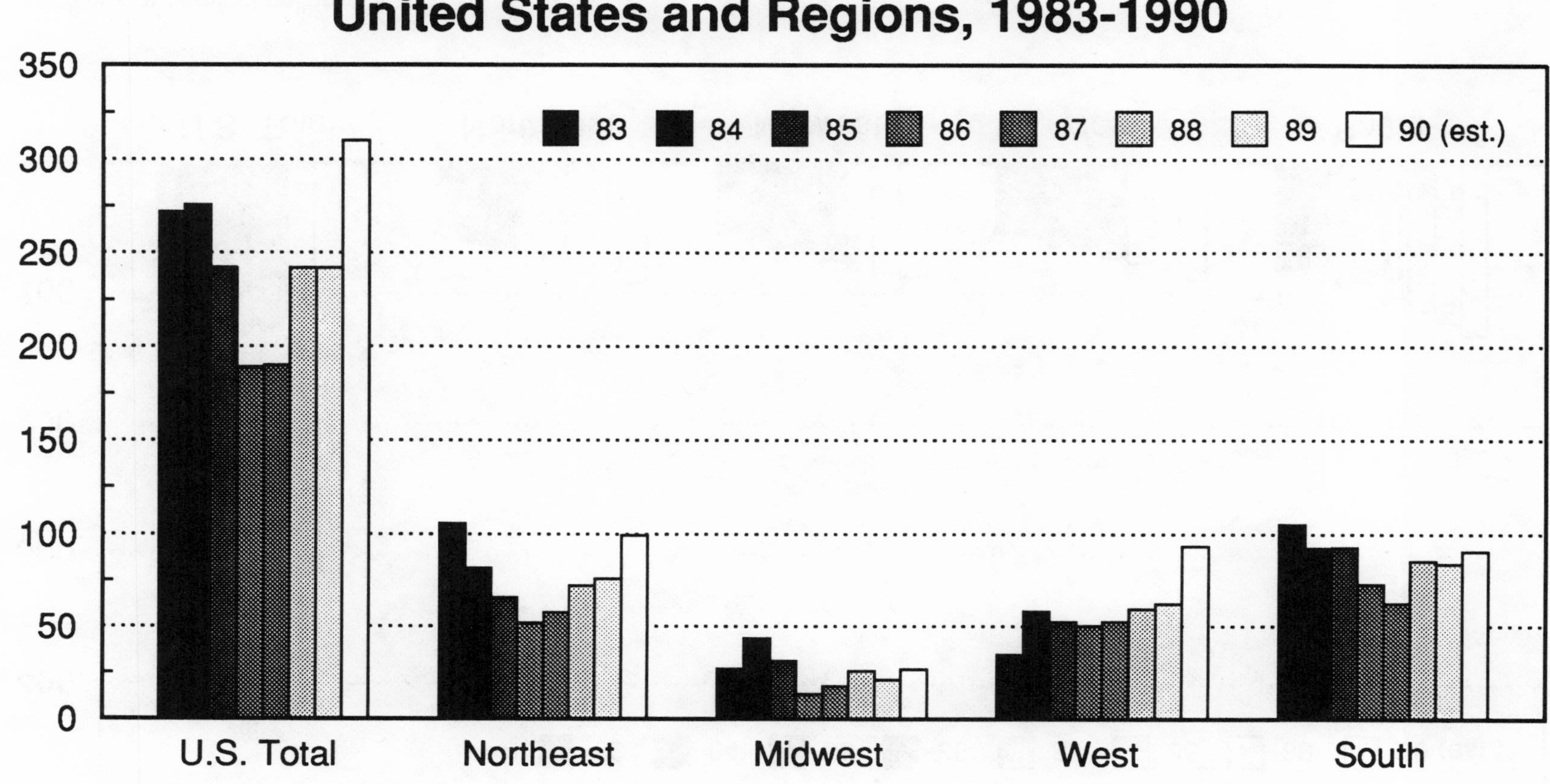

In millions of nominal dollars.
See Appendix B for programs by recipient groups.
See Appendix D for states in each region.

Figure 2.12

Outlays to Individuals for the United States and Regions, 1983-1990

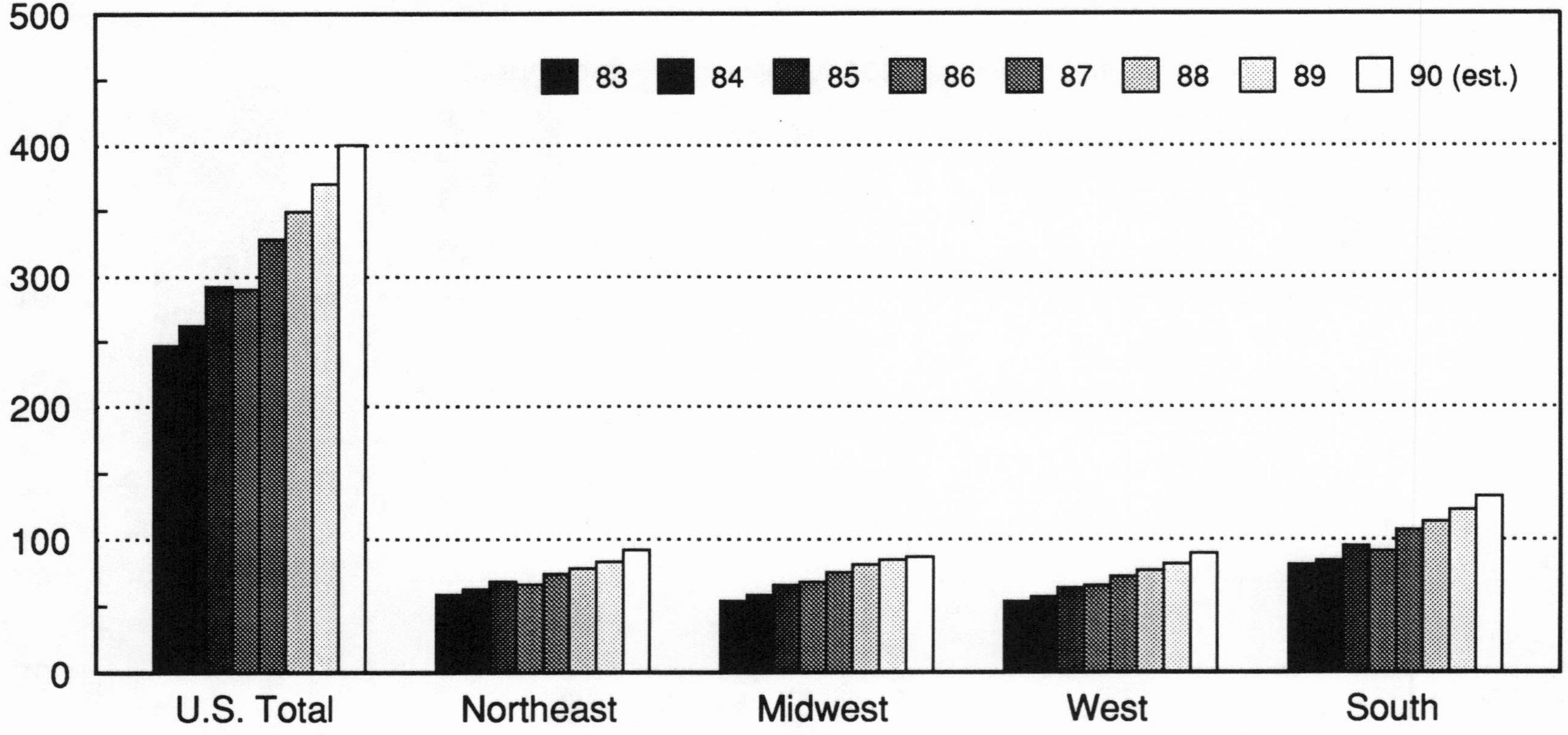

In billions of nominal dollars.
See Appendix B for programs by recipient groups.
See Appendix D for states in each region.

Chapter 3

Federal Outlays to Categories of Recipients by Congressional District, by Year

Table 3.1 Federal Outlays to Categories of Recipients by Congressional District, 1983

District	State Gov't.	Counties	Cities/ Towns	Special Districts	Schools	Interstate Agencies	Indian Tribes	Non-Profits	Private Universities	Individuals	For Profits	Small Businesses	All Others	Total
ALABAMA														
1	49,712,847	4,762,427	14,697,325	3,129,372	24,699	98,506	210,384	8,335,236	577,638	566,202,303	467,589	415,445	1,589,224	650,222,995
2	1,033,229,049	4,734,907	19,409,841	5,778,438	10,952,544	232,873	0	7,269,213	1,408,479	683,205,115	376,433	97,423	1,069,948	1,767,764,263
3	61,084,429	4,222,376	19,706,959	127,463	-49,870	1,565,524	0	4,588,940	7,572,180	560,342,629	761,766	126,280	443,723	660,492,399
4	40,513,593	8,047,606	18,017,220	1,180,446	112,547	0	0	3,079,363	880,817	678,239,041	583,455	37,056	85,056	750,776,200
5	39,666,709	5,010,868	11,047,162	301,034	1,581,536	0	0	3,413,912	3,026,928	511,018,468	681,546	127,569	677,951	576,553,683
6	94,443,537	13,031,505	21,593,654	106,185	66,126	0	0	9,956,330	4,758,529	689,974,807	14,197,632	636,560	2,163,656	850,928,521
7	56,845,275	8,861,862	17,597,943	782,681	78,939	125,430	0	5,025,628	3,117,362	584,464,468	639,097	0	1,003,063	678,541,748
TOTAL	1,375,495,439	48,671,551	122,070,104	11,405,619	12,766,521	2,022,333	210,384	41,668,622	21,341,933	4,273,446,830	17,707,518	1,440,333	7,032,621	5,935,279,808
ALASKA														
TOTAL	307,968,902	8,658,629	75,393,475	579,339	9,582,436	0	21,539,422	24,378,646	102,231	171,046,912	4,827,730	214,850	1,280,046	625,572,61
ARIZONA														
1	284,898,529	8,761,588	39,167,393	1,161,881	1,108,601	0	924,073	8,343,027	801,799	810,845,770	2,162,365	622,934	539,437	1,159,337,397
2	133,888,685	14,022,308	31,065,526	1,261,449	2,153,770	0	9,232,433	7,051,725	945,913	882,112,121	4,844,114	838,032	1,277,387	1,088,693,462
3	14,548,624	2,385,451	4,447,835	1,460,782	2,661,974	0	2,889,885	4,378,922	45,590	324,791,570	954,979	478,663	260,710	359,304,985
4	327,593,232	8,583,803	33,915,092	663,734	13,887,166	0	48,024,705	4,150,062	478,745	723,871,740	1,110,561	194,312	956,112	1,163,429,264
5	15,923,745	6,834,873	8,797,938	0	146,366	0	184,185	327,190	468,570	419,810,493	20,853	152,564	22,680	452,689,457
TOTAL	776,852,816	40,588,023	117,393,784	4,547,846	19,957,877	0	61,255,281	24,250,927	2,740,616	3,161,431,694	9,092,872	2,286,504	3,056,327	4,223,454,565
ARKANSAS														
1	87,486,829	9,702,858	18,032,939	279,202	665,168	0	0	9,911,679	856,586	823,142,739	11,479	38,337	529,520	950,657,336
2	562,133,196	5,947,066	31,453,148	29,653,086	534,025	125,000	30,127	9,746,681	3,368,695	645,194,632	962,565	420,225	504,793	1,290,073,239
3	54,865,744	7,301,001	11,931,382	5,454,540	789,834	600,000	0	2,469,642	1,388,024	724,075,820	2,045,971	5,902	1,972,341	812,900,201
4	75,837,208	7,445,002	14,202,401	195,722	76,094	620,000	0	5,769,422	1,268,809	744,929,813	567,293	-10,414	3,782,574	854,683,924
TOTAL	780,322,977	30,395,927	75,619,870	35,582,550	2,065,121	1,345,000	30,127	27,897,424	6,882,114	2,937,343,004	3,587,308	454,050	6,789,228	3,908,314,700
CALIFORNIA														
1	128,767,533	20,945,091	10,641,311	3,394,589	2,248,559	0	2,385,514	3,639,587	114,021	765,772,036	1,672,971	78,209	368,634	940,028,055
2	89,926,691	16,302,525	9,902,444	877,543	928,673	0	189,655	2,369,288	905,556	776,659,840	1,289,977	600,529	0	899,952,720
3	3,281,193,873	10,433,575	28,544,315	36,638,203	35,422,431	0	2,161,108	13,079,961	169,691	544,179,423	1,798,390	584,364	1,977,180	3,956,182,514
4	526,059,083	15,313,197	9,716,978	1,658,513	19,792,428	0	389,214	22,533,280	184,757	559,322,302	58,472	413,157	-104,304	1,155,337,077
5	136,728,502	-4,677,835	106,154,384	23,613,212	1,034,671	0	20,166,030	8,673,085	760,961	878,754,783	292,678	113,927	529,056	1,172,143,453
6	51,311,012	4,667,732	25,582,922	1,809,730	639,587	0	5,927,558	16,974,402	678,320	502,629,144	228,371	1,287,990	800,099	612,536,868
7	68,298,484	11,930,461	7,781,503	664,360	1,030,187	0	0	1,646,717	156,950	502,911,150	288,245	147,231	354,516	595,209,804
8	178,696,427	10,395,515	26,017,807	5,195,148	953,027	0	50,122	26,388,323	2,106,135	569,934,009	4,612,278	890,667	3,598,523	828,837,981
9	88,739,381	8,460,553	13,083,165	926,743	672,063	0	66,593	463,541	-30,816	588,288,828	343,401	436,295	1,193,479	702,643,226
10	72,261,848	25,736,487	13,134,007	14,906,711	1,017,985	0	207,141	2,739,967	508,488	460,782,593	340,415	258,118	794,379	592,688,137
11	41,582,042	29,674,458	8,570,102	15,813,702	1,145,311	0	3,062	3,093,265	87,622,886	534,752,836	1,764,505	403,496	752,410	725,178,075
12	68,176,321	9,657,104	12,956,486	52,356	1,462,319	0	16,766	19,353,683	15,272,894	450,198,973	3,040,232	594,342	6,537,316	587,318,793
13	58,438,409	11,771,612	11,932,633	7,306,349	1,320,229	0	24,448	5,664,539	15,626,841	400,860,074	1,058,585	359,871	783,040	515,146,631
14	115,685,834	14,724,439	13,125,415	3,478,248	823,132	0	1,141,380	2,801,102	2,778,720	711,999,742	17,563	74,560	1,228,931	867,879,066
15	71,875,535	26,026,085	14,199,827	-60,086	3,310,517	0	3,713	6,929,948	321,001	514,569,185	167,902	344,450	1,712,294	639,400,371
16	71,400,987	18,481,545	18,216,574	2,250,301	3,748,019	0	68,986	6,103,687	689,533	553,318,458	90,195	53,073	3,139,121	677,560,479
17	88,490,581	18,030,203	15,136,943	1,557,318	3,253,289	0	1,392,266	8,092,245	94,362,277	505,396,112	1,176,465	489,388	1,597,874	738,974,961
18	163,900,264	31,293,250	13,908,555	1,697,200	2,737,565	0	2,846,073	1,161,201	-78,737	784,941,975	888,522	0	37,940	1,003,333,807
19	59,170,808	13,929,861	13,007,608	2,614,862	1,711,683	0	215,598	1,328,024	446,984	421,872,194	1,578,606	1,055,876	159,561	517,091,665
20	52,969,058	11,935,298	8,025,814	107,255,955	4,305,102	0	28,833,079	17,251,991	733,568	443,768,080	25,354,052	28,654	1,212,881	701,673,531
21	81,664,414	9,620,643	15,065,776	284,313	193,903	0	66,880	2,495,840	952,674	551,853,739	891,089	97,488	255,317	663,442,076
22	96,039,797	10,015,071	25,871,661	397,626	372,130	0	52,186	3,507,526	20,677,409	572,720,861	2,166,507	96,837	840,774	732,758,385
23	117,654,893	10,242,772	18,843,795	879,556	221,764	0	52,130	126,122,159	3,081,557	531,278,808	962,147	184,368	1,030,790	810,554,740

24	96,278,874	11,448,568	19,292,777	1,435,002	136,738	0	52,121	20,844,945	1,103,576	519,018,372	2,610,658	958,231	736,062	673,915,922
25	100,674,579	15,819,396	23,021,274	1,545,135	925,639	0	52,071	8,039,191	1,047,935	518,526,457	1,013,545	1,040,561	1,477,841	673,183,626
26	84,146,009	8,782,049	16,323,605	405,572	147,053	0	45,761	7,752,869	355,518	455,686,743	683,244	158,584	552,624	575,039,632
27	95,706,620	9,999,704	45,668,817	397,016	136,699	0	52,106	3,616,838	1,263,540	551,415,018	8,650,263	641,579	1,069,143	718,617,343
28	95,887,368	10,143,060	19,379,414	396,959	272,738	0	52,098	3,728,671	81,512,518	526,785,324	1,222,991	467,636	630,039	740,478,816
29	95,332,779	51,484,514	21,297,416	401,872	136,708	0	52,109	2,047,971	686,658	549,023,976	845,965	243,737	857,257	722,410,963
30	97,223,855	10,211,558	138,526,642	4,154,905	1,647,499	0	52,019	1,682,704	750,226	551,134,844	2,203,135	839,910	1,721,550	810,148,849
31	98,028,412	10,273,661	25,786,953	397,296	722,051	0	52,142	2,049,723	5,622,803	565,227,879	1,719,706	157,622	568,898	710,607,148
32	96,446,223	10,038,807	20,376,023	9,248,770	244,629	0	52,309	6,773,038	862,702	532,537,097	759,132	28,140	570,720	677,937,591
33	97,716,863	10,009,936	20,981,303	467,142	598,635	0	52,159	3,838,630	3,197,588	535,267,145	1,124,015	307,037	-254,572	673,305,881
34	97,829,167	10,014,496	23,387,062	469,553	1,293,281	0	52,161	1,523,197	422,749	545,337,951	850,584	647,685	569,105	682,396,992
35	82,482,992	8,203,785	10,546,146	2,383,051	3,073,573	0	1,345,130	800,279	4,669,911	553,517,878	144,704	130,378	3,649	667,301,476
36	283,020,810	16,932,778	11,923,034	3,194,561	6,202,802	0	122,268	10,956,250	103,305	1,021,853,332	-39,511	149,704	5,820,442	1,360,239,774
37	200,090,251	20,248,832	10,016,901	1,310,910	6,113,891	0	659,235	1,527,197	1,856,791	502,119,158	153,865	124,730	399,993	744,621,755
38	33,092,558	7,429,943	8,070,580	-518,917	116,176	0	12,870	3,292,888	224,917	413,100,415	1,341,075	84,061	3,071,540	469,318,105
39	35,172,043	6,761,762	9,951,851	152,702	171,961	0	12,881	445,020	929,555	434,417,457	6,763,846	80,659	505,194	495,364,932
40	43,207,720	10,683,953	11,263,123	1,377,762	967,272	0	12,869	14,792,193	295,037	434,672,916	1,927,435	1,034,035	504,730	520,739,045
41	59,537,115	4,262,102	12,401,327	6,178,332	2,116,967	0	21,626	47,232,772	2,530,765	403,584,929	2,353,975	1,390,597	1,264,623	542,875,128
42	71,896,044	8,742,074	17,656,464	1,546,690	899,907	0	36,767	14,977,269	262,391	499,287,490	1,359,064	766,491	18,713,694	636,144,345
43	86,892,671	8,867,825	18,966,799	3,056,281	4,964,212	0	604,903	87,605,793	637,987	567,569,719	537,136	87,028	1,149,066	780,939,420
44	69,807,520	6,314,643	18,386,920	14,883	1,044,072	0	32,766	5,434,717	436,814	590,183,079	257,471	27,747	1,128,100	693,068,730
45	67,855,377	9,069,999	17,877,846	48,242	2,451,013	0	621,154	5,997,426	508,287	562,152,228	178,701	62,205	1,090,604	667,913,082
TOTAL	7,797,357,630	600,653,088	960,522,299	271,276,173	122,728,089	0	70,309,026	557,372,942	357,323,245	24,959,184,553	86,742,568	18,021,248	70,950,112	35,872,440,973
COLORADO														
1	688,733,266	9,845,886	29,918,543	17,417,166	709,855	369,734	1,012,855	19,990,436	7,464,045	627,294,999	9,560,015	426,261	1,894,152	1,414,637,213
2	57,745,831	4,486,469	9,380,214	3,891,660	517,617	0	133,168	5,552,719	113,777	353,257,984	873,996	626,042	489,610	437,069,086
3	63,081,829	8,443,065	13,099,871	3,213,809	2,675,215	0	2,487,714	5,948,526	219,017	497,568,403	357,439	241,956	1,097,951	598,434,794
4	67,779,203	12,162,067	14,977,706	434,373	67,934	0	0	5,142,759	695,246	492,477,052	84,918	224,570	671,553	594,717,382
5	17,397,297	3,971,386	17,513,726	0	2,928,865	0	0	464,476	1,058,433	257,132,372	1,187,960	215,121	480,568	302,350,204
6	13,385,159	1,676,844	7,924,857	32,264	381,995	0	129,196	1,310,733	0	208,498,587	-178,337	253,604	459,710	233,874,612
TOTAL	908,122,585	40,585,717	92,814,917	24,989,272	7,281,481	369,734	3,762,933	38,409,649	9,550,518	2,436,229,397	11,885,991	1,987,554	5,093,544	3,581,083,292
CONNECTICUT														
1	674,712,967	115,100	25,766,603	23,730,619	7,836,191	0	3,965,738	6,559,025	1,603,068	633,739,133	1,115,100	525,190	1,408,785	1,381,077,519
2	52,944,714	0	11,222,271	196,155	2,586,721	0	431,585	2,905,730	25,595,371	461,561,027	167,388	32,756	2,741,417	560,385,136
3	73,200,827	475,043	55,928,044	475,240	-50,081	0	0	6,239,099	70,228,014	633,894,035	282,934	407,181	3,345,379	844,425,715
4	69,639,822	1,173,760	19,572,940	23,947,575	0	0	0	4,808,784	2,038,444	621,920,095	1,096,233	137,134	5,415,002	749,749,789
5	72,526,769	0	17,023,326	355,352	-11,250	0	33,727	1,322,701	249,164	602,812,492	-32,639	26,482	3,848,490	698,154,613
6	76,603,322	40,112	19,518,238	31,368	0	0	0	831,883	25,160	601,187,132	-110	17,203	195,140	698,449,449
TOTAL	1,019,628,421	1,804,015	149,031,422	48,736,309	10,361,581	0	4,431,050	22,667,221	99,739,221	3,555,113,915	2,628,906	1,145,946	16,954,213	4,932,242,220
DELAWARE														
TOTAL	208,513,408	10,426,906	21,617,946	7,863,639	486,542	282,500	994,900	4,960,970	642,288	631,350,390	267,770	37,404	4,891,780	892,336,443
DISTRICT OF COLUMBIA														
TOTAL	546,320,374	0	65,475,099	6,831,972	115,315,615	207,745	135,195,278	129,517,606	103,002,607	672,673,704	9,809,973	8,750,429	201,489,127	1,994,589,529
FLORIDA														
1	37,799,687	9,461,383	7,987,377	519,840	1,811,567	0	10,000	1,275,486	735,053	523,165,975	248,300	94,225	-17	583,108,875
2	1,656,366,972	9,198,003	18,792,819	11,190,385	-192,639	251,563	73,325	7,410,112	641,541	714,257,932	115,658	89,259	1,319,454	2,419,514,383
3	41,352,156	2,372,270	22,688,894	440,156	1,333,349	0	0	6,200,092	3,735,509	550,726,734	41,973	27,349	4,775,209	633,693,692
4	33,170,903	12,540,403	12,258,716	169,440	354,712	0	0	975,188	5,780,691	892,448,291	102,504	119,820	164,502	958,085,169
5	29,006,030	26,352,862	18,186,278	4,324,239	224,878	0	0	4,992,322	1,011,418	839,677,854	220,191	159,469	1,350,432	925,505,972
6	59,776,043	10,564,641	15,726,490	1,269,793	509,867	0	0	1,625,463	535,398	712,836,084	184,433	160,937	573,804	803,762,954

See Appendix A for a listing of the congressional districts which represent the county in which the state capital is located and congressional districts which represent only portions of a county. See Appendix B for a listing of the programs included in each recipent category.

table continues

Table 3.1 Federal Outlays to Categories of Recipients by Congressional District, 1983 *(continued)*

District	State Gov't.	Counties	Cities/ Towns	Special Districts	Schools	Interstate Agencies	Indian Tribes	Non-Profits	Private Universities	Individuals	For Profits	Small Businesses	All Others	Total
FLORIDA *continued*														
7	45,657,751	28,716,148	16,856,997	675,790	704,513	0	0	3,413,641	2,594,810	661,421,259	2,621,061	1,964,053	926,198	765,552,221
8	29,919,092	12,604,749	13,033,354	950,280	-23,423	0	0	748,360	854,685	1,647,351,191	407,864	186,373	3,391,078	1,709,423,603
9	23,378,291	9,664,714	3,478,436	0	-9,847	0	0	2,354,214	1,292,610	960,776,690	126,953	334,862	461,352	1,001,858,276
10	18,918,127	16,123,042	3,230,116	740,135	242,096	0	290,825	7,061,300	1,068,049	843,068,949	74,725	127,338	2,091,893	893,036,596
11	18,042,598	18,415,946	13,392,512	520,040	169,457	0	2,488	1,210,851	921,094	544,864,615	240,665	110,998	6,902	597,898,167
12	16,391,983	7,844,126	3,349,304	388,754	162,700	0	2,026,137	3,960,379	149,940	804,440,017	255,912	204,085	607,764	839,781,101
13	8,230,739	60,088,610	24,691,650	435,587	243,083	0	301,950	886,660	2,406,157	900,940,810	2,294,930	509,336	276,809	1,001,306,322
14	16,182,451	8,333,498	6,960,199	311,073	1,012,734	0	64,536	2,805,414	7,015,765	983,804,152	870,714	2,008,112	0	1,029,368,648
15	35,522,556	24,970,191	23,256,020	2,116,548	1,080,236	0	203,888	2,545,693	2,557,127	959,128,038	1,283,286	1,089,624	234,750	1,053,987,956
16	20,121,386	5,710,657	7,405,478	-220,760	199,820	0	418,179	1,088,701	160,791	805,057,302	406,123	0	838,073	841,185,750
17	39,684,719	13,113,480	12,352,272	-756,154	684,430	0	10,349	3,755,179	2,025,894	667,001,310	1,089,520	447,975	2,870,592	742,279,567
18	42,775,054	19,786,254	13,401,488	-756,451	684,699	0	10,354	5,100,735	603,202	679,951,653	2,357,066	0	2,901,722	766,815,775
19	36,409,621	13,590,194	10,866,743	-662,786	1,023,086	0	25,713	3,435,393	513,485	623,105,802	737,974	0	2,516,138	691,561,362
TOTAL	2,208,706,161	309,451,171	247,915,142	21,655,909	10,215,319	251,563	3,437,743	60,845,183	34,603,219	15,314,024,659	13,679,852	7,633,815	25,306,654	18,257,726,390
GEORGIA														
1	67,647,289	9,759,727	29,164,626	2,747,703	328,239	0	0	3,322,735	464,686	536,391,935	815,986	287,279	974,107	651,904,312
2	77,608,342	9,331,910	7,209,441	366,852	-71,254	0	0	3,576,820	713,767	554,331,320	207,096	31,327	83,493	653,389,114
3	62,049,673	4,030,703	30,736,918	129,289	442,763	0	0	4,254,387	494,663	516,294,966	139,153	491,672	-97,406	618,966,781
4	571,311,807	12,455,589	6,369,125	13,599,058	52,891	73,845	0	45,208,125	4,510,273	423,987,761	211,411	64,804	6,152,808	1,083,997,498
5	811,487,103	14,582,028	36,497,022	12,659,602	1,154,126	164,390	0	21,569,436	34,095,416	606,462,498	-85,736	537,238	801,620	1,539,924,743
6	49,108,945	6,787,838	6,171,568	1,310,476	34,576	0	0	1,887,048	74,096	455,984,924	548,006	278,760	446,210	522,632,447
7	27,245,919	9,001,658	11,484,843	312,854	26,217	0	0	1,788,976	788,346	457,947,446	-600	10,847	0	508,606,506
8	72,084,987	9,609,784	16,054,942	261,540	-34,780	0	0	4,159,700	2,395,382	558,575,512	260,832	0	1,109,400	664,477,299
9	35,293,754	7,735,615	17,213,172	265,928	0	300,000	0	3,336,535	748,697	506,770,229	53,190	0	0	571,717,120
10	83,098,535	7,817,822	13,675,878	149,002	682,889	0	0	11,441,182	2,956,825	475,095,509	0	0	1,822,175	596,739,817
TOTAL	1,856,936,354	91,112,674	174,577,535	31,802,304	2,615,668	538,235	0	100,544,944	47,242,151	5,091,842,100	2,149,337	1,701,927	11,292,406	7,412,355,636
HAWAII														
1	309,670,883	1,191,732	28,952,448	2,200,183	9,289,671	32,533	776,694	11,659,992	1,150,345	377,059,452	649,208	1,317,587	486,248	744,436,976
2	81,532,752	9,787,138	14,604,512	310,393	0	18,901	0	2,928,762	106,550	425,640,091	43,472	169,816	86,874	535,229,261
TOTAL	391,203,635	10,978,870	43,556,960	2,510,576	9,289,671	51,434	776,694	14,588,754	1,256,895	802,699,543	692,680	1,487,403	573,122	1,279,666,237
IDAHO														
1	249,947,736	7,191,726	16,378,992	7,626,039	545,452	0	2,804,776	11,993,364	1,229,012	507,368,301	110,088	281,443	2,950,684	808,427,613
2	56,521,084	5,217,350	7,934,818	209,778	560,293	0	1,742,568	2,801,220	-2,205	427,735,307	100,645	62,224	155,582	503,038,664
TOTAL	306,468,820	12,409,076	24,313,810	7,835,817	1,105,745	0	4,547,344	14,794,584	1,226,807	935,103,608	210,733	343,667	3,106,266	1,311,466,277
ILLINOIS														
1	100,065,743	4,922,943	72,180,942	67,350,384	0	0	16,513,704	16,833,739	83,292,403	542,112,517	3,432,598	507,003	2,038,993	909,250,968
2	95,554,478	4,932,137	28,762,748	5,123	67,964	0	15,681	2,348,030	672,101	541,805,487	652,480	405,913	159,569	675,381,711
3	96,543,045	4,933,173	29,725,415	131,258	0	0	15,684	1,171,807	963,427	564,627,910	707,543	609,844	159,602	699,588,710
4	49,145,996	3,114,873	18,177,249	2,215	-68,553	0	6,781	2,041,093	355,468	391,516,909	323,050	179,797	68,998	464,863,875
5	95,727,889	4,932,518	37,398,967	420,147	0	0	15,682	3,179,062	1,801,554	576,905,942	4,246,312	42,191	1,237,578	725,907,843
6	45,523,989	5,252,896	32,354,791	25,327,780	84,665	0	29,050,901	19,529,409	572,925	435,579,789	508,540	71,413	59,442	593,916,541
7	104,706,493	13,480,813	34,719,984	5,124	2,256,352	0	59,684	50,639,382	7,773,399	567,905,374	2,866,711	2,795,513	1,171,114	788,379,943
8	95,874,993	4,933,116	29,524,355	35,421	0	0	15,684	2,272,567	671,345	541,913,053	686,964	150,877	159,600	676,237,975
9	97,528,784	4,933,934	29,808,631	222,709	65,664	0	15,687	29,012,426	27,126,176	558,041,533	857,678	1,754,932	159,627	749,527,779
10	56,918,115	4,701,024	17,696,101	96,742	191,649	0	7,092	2,505,943	11,612,540	459,043,739	576,212	77,639	317,353	553,744,148
11	100,017,699	4,932,746	28,766,233	354,678	0	0	15,683	1,542,827	1,044,931	541,872,352	652,561	246,536	159,588	679,605,835
12	52,743,097	4,813,910	15,657,553	639,984	533,892	0	6,634	462,549	839,846	478,066,753	412,184	313,473	258,436	554,748,311

13	46,238,468	7,505,830	18,565,129	208,766	1,853,273	0	6,876	1,580,355	576,625	432,047,083	316,822	114,505	70,858	509,084,590
14	21,175,886	8,190,267	32,966,596	6,134,697	420,525	0	61	426,906	1,482,851	410,581,960	571,890	58,574	-763,261	481,246,951
15	25,232,368	4,416,372	13,660,563	0	18,486	0	642,088	1,831,211	3,096,653	552,235,121	33,917	28,174	40,203	601,235,156
16	24,984,980	2,035,943	13,327,896	83,746	184,000	0	1,316,635	3,419,598	405,210	560,449,924	-443	25,041	1,211,332	607,443,861
17	36,092,939	4,747,183	26,643,766	872,126	86,221	0	0	3,401,155	1,922,404	649,535,877	370,538	64,199	4,253,497	727,989,905
18	43,442,841	3,344,887	32,545,818	1,427,565	-12,341	0	1,848,283	3,231,168	1,771,183	607,158,799	161,600	27,810	1,194,869	696,142,482
19	76,895,076	4,001,399	23,992,921	1,870,275	0	0	1,825,716	3,071,617	1,488,216	587,661,410	0	486,951	767,244	702,060,825
20	2,142,134,067	3,280,695	25,764,616	2,780,586	94,799	0	1,683,510	17,183,812	440,828	846,393,232	226,693	505,835	3,357,133	3,043,845,806
21	58,758,185	15,215,145	12,090,465	1,479,197	1,304,123	0	0	5,810,288	915,414	521,467,658	352,035	278,618	2,488,911	620,160,038
22	50,041,289	2,503,391	11,075,951	1,981,835	262,438	0	0	5,437,285	259,788	647,003,861	62,409	148,400	271,488	719,048,134
TOTAL	3,515,346,420	121,125,194	585,406,688	111,430,357	7,343,157	0	53,062,066	176,932,227	149,085,287	12,013,926,285	18,018,294	8,893,237	18,842,175	16,779,411,387
INDIANA														
1	64,062,746	7,140,767	3,169,029	4,123,914	300,391	0	2,529,961	3,623,497	334,749	515,024,513	319,466	91,426	43,824	600,764,283
2	89,240,797	8,097,184	23,681,110	-990,426	-1,304	0	536,316	2,756,920	1,593,715	534,140,673	1,098,544	4,363	1,210,867	661,368,759
3	33,242,724	7,194,381	7,293,825	-268,800	2,930	0	4,334,573	2,791,554	7,647,327	572,214,452	87,940	44,171	1,387,850	635,972,927
4	39,858,297	4,250,414	13,698,447	-317,746	0	0	1,261,165	2,558,877	672,318	552,118,862	44,173	58,871	4,634,097	618,837,775
5	37,599,185	3,599,277	7,418,044	68,184	464,543	0	250,422	322,528	2,727,160	492,911,755	371,584	94,701	220,419	546,047,803
6	111,567,772	3,871,576	36,573,780	-1,433,913	332	0	458,071	7,532,869	1,557,170	539,576,847	1,693,640	85,213	-100,084	701,383,273
7	70,310,043	4,465,479	20,707,345	672,955	13,102	0	571,503	1,331,448	5,158,386	576,594,599	314,465	86,010	0	680,225,335
8	62,439,667	3,887,900	16,271,678	50,374	94,490	1,177,337	0	3,210,644	2,458,669	640,811,496	68,024	293,045	2,676,115	733,439,438
9	63,699,061	4,651,241	10,529,416	451,609	126,624	0	271,242	951,259	3,952,905	554,004,172	0	248,531	444,622	639,330,681
10	467,398,630	2,460,394	41,093,788	-7,038,324	-8,178	0	4,608,000	15,306,757	1,657,548	789,381,893	6,316,649	27,368	187,957	1,321,392,483
TOTAL	1,039,418,921	49,618,613	180,436,462	-4,682,172	992,930	1,177,337	14,821,253	40,386,352	27,759,947	5,766,779,262	10,314,485	1,033,700	10,705,667	7,138,762,757
IOWA														
1	29,788,016	4,230,354	34,984,632	1,258,622	-33,553	0	0	1,994,343	2,928,415	572,864,353	739,981	653,997	658,340	650,067,500
2	17,276,892	6,262,685	34,889,147	1,099,881	130,876	0	0	1,126,139	2,436,095	501,329,338	1,753,831	82,794	94,191	566,481,869
3	68,313,156	6,154,388	28,523,465	2,183,314	1,082,219	0	109,672	2,603,470	1,721,976	617,502,621	222,478	658,943	2,547,802	731,623,504
4	553,337,899	4,703,521	116,039,180	9,024,399	413,667	0	0	7,716,132	3,202,501	569,921,703	888,592	443,385	2,063,714	1,267,754,693
5	24,502,574	6,419,032	32,576,680	594,056	12,826	0	0	3,847,926	1,528,794	697,413,011	-25,065	228,782	325,950	767,424,566
6	19,877,180	7,235,061	43,951,471	779,307	26,279	0	0	1,645,789	3,098,700	728,916,760	228,831	325,149	505,951	806,590,478
TOTAL	713,095,717	35,005,041	290,964,575	14,939,579	1,632,314	0	109,672	18,933,799	14,916,481	3,687,947,786	3,808,648	2,393,050	6,195,948	4,789,942,610
KANSAS														
1	29,265,673	6,193,026	14,067,134	4,459,075	223,510	0	0	678,455	1,634,550	808,611,063	80,162	38,838	206,551	865,458,037
2	482,565,378	3,564,936	20,937,361	3,557,515	5,463,739	0	2,074,479	4,559,678	1,511,593	478,359,040	25,170	257,576	2,704,175	1,005,580,640
3	40,804,563	2,070,531	13,478,019	196,767	215,706	0	0	9,973,587	1,232,839	389,403,333	119,529	56,649	821,290	458,372,813
4	31,619,778	2,531,072	14,379,661	2,111,808	529,979	0	44,511	5,113,047	1,006,727	432,606,240	4,276,996	330,551	575,486	495,125,856
5	41,506,535	5,871,215	21,825,275	595,517	954,562	0	0	1,345,856	2,893,417	677,838,916	64,972	93,055	958,859	753,948,179
TOTAL	625,761,927	20,230,780	84,687,450	10,920,682	7,387,496	0	2,118,990	21,670,623	8,279,126	2,786,818,592	4,566,829	776,669	5,266,361	3,578,485,525
KENTUCKY														
1	48,845,192	4,746,443	6,971,693	1,727,899	-56,158	0	0	1,550,987	76,479	642,055,751	349,014	92,674	762,684	707,122,658
2	44,470,698	4,716,792	19,811,041	4,597,922	460,052	0	0	4,247,946	833,608	459,397,056	1,721,433	50,599	575,148	540,882,295
3	57,918,066	12,727,071	12,559,998	3,018,452	178,516	0	0	18,642,839	3,973,798	562,254,195	874,578	425,810	4,746,959	677,320,281
4	37,498,741	5,681,591	12,735,139	-2,452,270	14,463	0	1,329,633	2,474,522	3,081	411,613,737	167,819	38,271	37,800	469,142,528
5	83,378,188	8,052,595	9,228,694	3,184,873	21,439	0	0	3,663,739	2,451,272	620,156,932	46,845	43,738	61,032	730,289,347
6	968,829,847	5,975,301	25,238,661	13,362,978	18,372,986	166,840	0	6,451,963	2,632,459	535,171,672	22,403	45,318	2,459,260	1,578,729,688
7	67,868,711	6,047,397	16,046,685	1,957,498	296,529	0	0	14,497,294	1,458,498	583,846,757	0	0	6,734,294	698,753,663
TOTAL	1,308,809,443	47,947,190	102,591,911	25,397,352	19,287,827	166,840	1,329,633	51,529,290	11,429,195	3,814,496,100	3,182,092	696,410	15,377,177	5,402,240,460

See Appendix A for a listing of the congressional districts which represent the county in which the state capital is located and congressional districts which represent only portions of a county. See Appendix B for a listing of the programs included in each recipent category.

table continues

Table 3.1 **Federal Outlays to Categories of Recipients by Congressional District, 1983 *(continued)***

District	State Gov't.	Counties	Cities/ Towns	Special Districts	Schools	Interstate Agencies	Indian Tribes	Non-Profits	Private Universities	Individuals	For Profits	Small Businesses	All Others	Total
LOUISIANA														
1	83,104,770	5,379,001	36,209,192	5,413,912	160,041	4,592,669	0	6,376,088	10,873,487	518,093,152	269,227	205,433	1,018,010	671,694,983
2	64,864,965	9,099,392	39,011,066	0	201,998	0	5,262	2,738,842	16,910,194	442,468,226	2,859,931	169,412	190,323	578,519,612
3	34,582,147	11,324,919	7,508,361	2,758,041	232,255	0	420,864	1,186,314	0	363,597,175	1,790,551	57,791	2,603,563	426,061,981
4	56,079,039	3,526,784	18,349,533	2,061,246	2,362,180	0	0	2,875,636	397,109	495,124,101	1,069,794	162,473	748,247	582,756,142
5	93,160,101	8,748,222	10,241,118	2,346,148	58,597	250,000	0	2,998,667	867,012	590,246,147	226,433	90	2,298,564	711,441,100
6	1,109,244,363	1,671,896	30,290,994	31,107,721	12,020,914	0	89,383	4,828,400	-220,988	491,921,968	151,539	140,824	1,236,039	1,682,483,053
7	53,301,816	5,605,668	13,206,036	2,860,920	79,131	723,000	556,580	5,063,034	0	471,760,631	355,614	212,265	3,963,408	557,688,104
8	83,594,339	7,299,549	8,055,552	203,434	100,216	0	564,300	4,824,982	181,018	466,704,986	280,549	5,370	1,784,455	573,598,750
TOTAL	1,577,931,540	52,655,433	162,871,852	46,751,422	15,215,332	5,565,669	1,636,389	30,891,964	29,007,832	3,839,916,387	7,003,638	953,658	13,842,609	5,784,243,724
MAINE														
1	336,264,683	2,047,887	30,747,883	4,799,789	284,969	0	1,050,916	7,918,442	2,274,071	696,518,076	391,526	764,746	1,858,870	1,084,921,858
2	107,049,830	3,153,699	30,171,515	12,463,489	884,981	19,669	3,314,576	5,344,669	1,162,869	606,588,599	367,377	7,589,749	1,914,245	780,025,267
TOTAL	443,314,513	5,201,586	60,919,398	17,263,278	1,169,950	19,669	4,365,492	13,263,111	3,436,940	1,303,106,675	758,903	8,354,495	3,773,115	1,864,947,125
MARYLAND														
1	56,153,744	22,843,028	20,925,208	808,271	591,386	0	0	2,717,369	221,964	548,546,842	-5,008	7,051	300,290	653,110,145
2	355,737,734	19,553,157	-1,488,868	10,908,788	548,676	0	27,605,611	1,809,597	609,215	506,475,597	791,366	-465	115,663	922,666,071
3	140,264,763	4,082,049	32,407,406	1,879,978	-5,340	0	890	3,896,797	6,358,174	638,707,215	1,113,847	549,048	6,227,653	835,482,478
4	292,601,132	18,466,756	1,459,800	190,596	1,701,661	0	556,131	1,361,239	1,060,026	404,769,531	288,314	172,645	205	722,628,036
5	57,139,339	22,981,224	1,525,562	610,270	1,348,535	0	0	1,193,475	106,978,981	276,120,064	797,643	429,927	6,727,910	475,852,929
6	88,808,849	27,226,212	13,359,343	1,662,400	311,825	0	1,374,750	771,875	437,900	479,737,965	-31,785	639,533	19,349,920	633,648,787
7	285,741,030	-2,351,239	55,948,109	3,789,992	-53,366	0	0	10,381,179	9,662,268	724,595,301	1,451,142	797,104	10,444,173	1,100,405,694
8	16,332,836	13,008,886	5,792,387	-150,931	326,052	163,172	0	37,917,632	749,403	444,033,688	26,316,000	59,005,507	19,433,952	622,928,584
TOTAL	1,292,779,426	125,810,072	129,928,947	19,699,364	4,769,429	163,172	29,537,382	60,049,163	126,077,931	4,022,986,203	30,721,519	61,600,350	62,599,766	5,966,722,724
MASSACHUSETTS														
1	106,874,115	1,436,058	20,243,361	719,244	-20,476	0	265,734	2,948,345	3,598,983	611,445,090	227,880	683,217	2,334,565	750,756,117
2	92,458,385	1,705,681	25,359,687	20,524	88,520	0	4,974,416	3,738,709	1,991,390	667,759,780	1,439,731	570,742	2,006,816	802,114,381
3	86,319,174	571,389	40,969,914	2,603,942	53,753	0	149,787	9,455,455	3,630,122	608,852,672	41,676	449,914	4,721,798	757,819,596
4	81,357,583	430,430	33,665,834	352,761	0	0	2,328,355	37,393,108	7,087,084	541,601,764	496,015	590,490	1,086,509	706,389,933
5	60,491,884	2,345,484	38,180,320	586,360	2,873,289	0	2,781,365	4,948,644	142,280	533,930,185	-73,408	2,034,211	1,954,040	650,194,654
6	88,878,253	839,524	36,349,398	1,683,917	0	0	2,397,898	5,270,880	556,788	654,571,040	4,925,651	34,793	1,546,078	797,054,221
7	138,321,076	436,265	34,131,096	1,122,657	1,627	334,777	209,836	2,539,102	17,600,532	620,928,831	1,372,731	2,451,636	2,462,742	821,912,908
8	271,188,708	460,855	55,717,972	130,912,718	157,194	9,918	64,767,754	241,608,782	140,208,123	696,125,249	15,587,816	2,858,327	6,803,821	1,626,407,237
9	639,151,845	553,751	70,840,404	-1,006,149	4,801	5,536	619,052	142,572,615	16,643,523	757,676,646	331,163	464,487	6,053,681	1,633,911,355
10	76,944,970	619,095	33,509,165	561,947	5,000	0	69,680	4,684,334	17,075,755	619,282,787	305,993	70,213	1,932,887	755,061,826
11	306,208,944	286,669	42,880,976	1,450,138	2,314	2,669	2,507,448	5,083,978	2,153,802	625,871,685	85,188	193,127	1,910,118	988,637,056
TOTAL	1,948,194,938	9,685,202	431,848,125	139,008,060	3,166,022	352,900	81,071,325	460,243,952	210,688,381	6,938,045,729	24,740,437	10,401,157	32,813,056	10,290,259,284
MICHIGAN														
1	151,812,062	6,278,502	43,714,445	5,657,387	633,455	0	62,316,687	4,356,547	2,286,532	628,905,152	715,167	603,424	355,042	907,634,401
2	159,842,805	18,642,996	17,728,346	1,041,030	81,225	0	1,693,678	706,724	964,043	493,832,964	243,071	219,249	1,748,694	696,744,825
3	666,220,878	20,762,381	13,401,570	25,000	446,916	0	530,184	7,294,218	512,183	581,523,294	72,453	65,832	2,937,425	1,293,792,333
4	71,709,693	4,610,248	9,095,920	789,664	470,741	0	185,646	4,236,349	2,240,738	564,824,737	191,754	32,865	1,598,934	659,987,290
5	73,050,285	2,390,616	12,867,835	7,799,738	853,017	0	2,151,623	11,563,502	2,087,148	565,075,561	154,560	31,472	3,850,026	681,875,382
6	875,944,667	16,858,855	19,212,100	-4,962,059	1,077,701	0	101,160	873,879	977,515	504,931,494	630,063	111,699	6,749,107	1,422,506,181
7	79,720,176	6,238,078	28,112,213	37,020	1,175,606	0	2,228,126	9,093,264	1,780	480,310,264	1,213,887	255,651	4,233,182	612,619,247
8	74,447,723	16,169,491	22,288,168	158,706	725,120	0	469,430	2,165,163	376,563	584,001,058	6,230,015	1,122,392	251,137	708,404,966
9	65,477,007	9,776,061	14,926,471	104,800	136,084	0	1,307,899	6,331,586	967,782	636,090,470	153,156	0	2,083,013	737,354,329

10	293,765,651	5,626,631	11,798,682	-4,810,032	267,688	0	1,990,715	4,118,649	473,768	570,332,568	0	38,706	615,360	884,218,387
11	75,295,130	6,490,988	43,591,962	48,650	2,289,503	0	5,081,062	8,433,122	1,706,786	760,037,994	844,828	67,976	639,398	904,527,400
12	43,645,337	15,557,307	17,473,568	163,355	1,018,292	0	52,330	1,396,314	92,384	482,110,813	50,726	41,659	311,787	561,913,872
13	162,075,903	14,186,103	58,114,011	0	2,048,150	0	293,218	13,213,695	964,024	616,549,229	2,016,933	1,694,355	1,988,941	873,144,561
14	76,523,109	3,684,588	20,566,776	0	662,226	0	6,314	712,226	101,410	521,188,456	2,312,565	440,450	32,087	626,230,207
15	133,345,914	5,644,239	43,192,332	50,340	517,874	0	4,392,288	1,081,895	693,014	570,798,706	572,736	463,391	1,284,366	762,037,095
16	106,670,455	7,227,402	38,505,324	599,868	1,737,556	0	11,006	6,171,925	177,653	594,900,914	731,646	153,062	1,196,942	758,083,753
17	93,786,947	3,911,747	24,269,754	0	470,730	0	8,154	3,538,660	1,202,995	578,958,870	698,082	265,927	41,438	707,153,304
18	38,664,694	2,239,616	5,066,704	0	206,463	0	0	831,549	153,113	477,132,159	23,938	115,347	1,982,735	526,416,318
TOTAL	3,241,998,438	166,295,849	443,926,180	6,703,467	14,818,346	0	82,819,520	86,119,266	15,979,430	10,211,504,705	16,855,581	5,723,456	31,899,615	14,324,643,851
MINNESOTA														
1	57,954,612	6,268,166	13,692,427	32,246	438,890	0	20,613	29,112,704	1,330,437	531,276,442	286,053	13,883	170,764	640,597,237
2	63,531,595	14,090,203	12,452,695	702,593	414,322	0	443,224	1,616,284	706,635	693,514,280	155,280	0	413,437	788,040,548
3	60,397,715	5,214,830	10,175,008	443,103	113,497	0	56,455	764,062	635,132	362,051,225	1,733,805	13,974	1,813,259	443,412,065
4	749,700,390	2,578,985	40,294,380	-2,122,167	1,451,481	0	12,356,423	8,006,662	4,842,409	143,968,546	55,472	293,818	5,662,178	967,088,578
5	123,675,752	11,604,332	33,916,728	536,885	1,064,068	0	442,835	7,850,678	1,854,937	593,630,778	9,649,876	521,588	2,513,697	787,262,154
6	167,859,966	19,118,961	15,938,251	1,187,648	334,784	0	303,605	3,566,801	509,435	790,727,888	1,116,685	32,408	609,792	1,001,306,223
7	101,092,411	10,578,402	40,881,579	3,477,107	1,436,586	0	4,959,887	8,169,933	1,627,510	661,337,622	138,743	136,171	2,706,060	836,542,010
8	103,968,053	11,834,505	25,595,007	1,656,426	1,051,482	0	6,641,153	3,436,687	1,069,124	575,518,997	3,425,594	110	1,894,809	736,091,947
TOTAL	1,428,180,493	81,288,383	192,946,076	5,913,841	6,305,110	0	25,224,195	62,523,811	12,575,619	4,352,025,778	16,561,507	1,011,952	15,783,996	6,200,340,762
MISSISSIPPI														
1	54,309,237	8,118,349	5,412,858	769,345	712,512	0	0	8,602,049	1,412,538	553,048,123	1,592,753	28,477	0	634,006,242
2	83,377,156	19,468,057	15,854,469	1,436,684	2,001,420	0	0	15,656,915	236,871	618,886,404	474,115	1,195,488	1,019,620	759,607,199
3	62,202,236	7,882,421	3,549,949	646,254	198,641	214,300	5,783,384	4,453,542	1,647,058	533,437,682	0	50	258,852	620,274,370
4	794,248,768	8,496,380	16,099,495	12,028,049	13,032,354	70,625	890	32,091,720	3,027,231	606,704,785	774,752	2,048,474	2,089,006	1,490,712,528
5	34,562,186	11,556,266	15,078,551	4,557,905	3,742,792	153,500	150,000	5,110,452	1,005,027	478,157,488	269,049	86,315	429,898	554,859,429
TOTAL	1,028,699,583	55,521,473	55,995,322	19,438,237	19,687,719	438,425	5,934,274	65,914,678	7,328,725	2,790,234,483	3,110,669	3,358,804	3,797,376	4,059,459,768
MISSOURI														
1	53,772,312	45,025,660	9,398,804	2,828,964	620,121	716,800	14,100,000	13,941,194	128,185,258	915,791,607	1,310,025	100,069	450,400	1,186,241,213
2	59,312,751	8,091,054	15,037,326	175,968	1,170,487	0	0	3,646,094	701,591	680,864,414	1,443,445	481,480	122,063	771,046,672
3	24,392,981	4,399,454	13,176,569	1,778,032	665,782	0	0	4,790,972	5,581,107	228,981,210	1,235,197	1,268,386	1,073,936	287,343,626
4	701,123,925	9,883,342	23,629,594	25,630,376	8,277,826	0	0	3,014,997	508,859	668,927,979	458,820	212,460	994,334	1,442,662,513
5	46,695,820	2,684,534	30,839,358	460,972	472,037	0	89,686	14,515,470	221,836	623,651,659	1,269,742	250,872	5,220,095	726,372,084
6	29,726,166	2,686,989	20,359,151	10,847,905	408,357	0	1,400,182	7,115,516	4,791,154	689,517,379	1,383,334	848,909	97,069	769,182,111
7	41,426,503	2,389,898	21,451,972	784,826	-20,527	0	0	2,976,607	4,381,067	696,534,975	309,558	4,793	523,897	770,763,569
8	237,841,571	3,984,547	10,159,803	5,243,868	2,257,626	0	0	7,735,675	152,577	705,329,358	-32,977	97,494	142,656	972,912,198
9	164,843,461	4,519,431	35,577,726	3,384,310	1,232	0	0	5,470,398	2,216,177	572,788,613	481,876	64,576	344,503	789,692,303
TOTAL	1,359,135,491	83,664,909	179,630,304	51,135,221	13,852,941	716,800	15,589,868	63,206,924	146,739,626	5,782,387,193	7,859,019	3,329,039	8,968,954	7,716,216,289
MONTANA														
1	340,118,827	6,167,392	13,681,672	4,511,216	6,257,822	0	5,163,369	5,104,051	1,689,184	461,962,236	6,896	185,302	909,292	845,757,259
2	43,105,443	6,744,111	11,644,307	1,207,354	6,289,320	0	9,827,594	3,450,283	474,830	471,224,826	3,493,314	414,766	433,797	558,309,945
TOTAL	383,224,270	12,911,503	25,325,979	5,718,570	12,547,142	0	14,990,963	8,554,334	2,164,014	933,187,062	3,500,210	600,068	1,343,089	1,404,067,204
NEBRASKA														
1	378,058,587	4,912,767	9,986,926	5,184,566	1,671,592	0	5,532,580	4,932,274	1,932,060	707,270,831	372,628	204,078	567,597	1,120,626,487
2	76,773,304	3,125,172	27,543,001	623,244	6,210,234	0	322,144	6,620,951	4,048,016	461,225,269	1,214,550	252,119	531,114	588,489,117
3	46,359,868	7,453,589	9,969,098	97,649	323,841	0	0	2,552,265	350,846	894,667,860	47,733	199,664	293,960	962,316,373
TOTAL	501,191,759	15,491,528	47,499,025	5,905,459	8,205,667	0	5,854,724	14,105,490	6,330,922	2,063,163,960	1,634,911	655,861	1,392,671	2,671,431,977

See Appendix A for a listing of the congressional districts which represent the county in which the state capital is located and congressional districts which represent only portions of a county. See Appendix B for a listing of the programs included in each recipent category.

table continues

Table 3.1 **Federal Outlays to Categories of Recipients by Congressional District, 1983 *(continued)***

District	State Gov't.	Counties	Cities/ Towns	Special Districts	Schools	Interstate Agencies	Indian Tribes	Non-Profits	Private Universities	Individuals	For Profits	Small Businesses	All Others	Total
NEVADA														
1	1,562,083	6,935,584	3,720,414	914,697	825,947	0	77,541	3,965,063	569,795	103,870,637	126,637	234,763	1,272,761	124,075,921
2	181,172,832	3,933,370	12,621,832	665,893	751,661	0	5,129,467	2,809,339	387,233	121,047,374	427,719	65,040	709,999	329,721,760
TOTAL	182,734,915	10,868,954	16,342,246	1,580,590	1,577,608	0	5,207,008	6,774,402	957,028	224,918,011	554,356	299,803	1,982,760	453,797,681
NEW HAMPSHIRE														
1	51,374,176	2,155,445	28,855,146	68,603	936,517	0	962,112	785,072	2,213,367	472,518,060	143,618	115,545	2,116,807	562,244,468
2	200,199,141	1,261,697	38,547,371	3,199,568	-7,150	5,000	0	2,436,129	12,824,027	509,686,095	27,249	59,030	1,926,325	770,164,482
TOTAL	251,573,317	3,417,142	67,402,517	3,268,171	929,367	5,000	962,112	3,221,201	15,037,394	982,204,155	170,867	174,575	4,043,132	1,332,408,950
NEW JERSEY														
1	68,643,078	12,532,037	13,078,479	39,123,559	0	0	14,159,448	3,751,585	0	562,303,879	951,745	275,948	93,476	714,913,234
2	90,201,757	73,278,944	17,021,003	111,166,117	60,224	433,222	0	5,623,488	246,257	765,719,801	189,269	69,179	219,085	1,064,228,345
3	50,325,515	3,515,302	13,813,148	285,360	834,904	0	0	1,147,289	914,510	663,968,575	266,953	226,680	124,720	735,422,956
4	1,244,356,685	7,516,554	51,073,166	4,520,651	3,239,393	226,930	200,452	35,696,999	745,563	630,750,738	289,342	378,739	622,099	1,979,617,311
5	28,016,298	2,859,207	18,128,037	787,864	175,633	74,082	0	264,939	4,818,683	589,783,643	202,364	31,368	21,229	645,163,347
6	68,825,691	10,305,099	22,018,789	1,465,414	44,330	0	0	1,279,161	480,199	546,508,376	682,283	347,351	2,595,337	654,552,030
7	41,917,733	19,803,956	10,011,501	588,660	30,350	0	0	3,664,002	15,868,354	601,971,208	8,660,497	625,804	1,346,491	704,488,557
8	59,869,796	8,103,805	40,729,416	1,156,572	210,091	0	0	3,369,150	0	628,408,872	1,087,128	526,556	-101,808	743,359,578
9	16,974,885	22,010,775	14,323,304	14,262	-484	0	0	2,428,024	2,001,056	646,186,119	1,113,668	870,291	105,300	706,027,199
10	133,195,201	15,756,645	44,634,289	13,998,790	110,941	0	6,615,560	18,621,369	10,247,447	632,107,644	3,844,483	1,881,345	2,263,713	883,277,427
11	96,890,056	10,487,610	15,216,620	1,598,991	107,004	0	0	248,781	1,834,240	613,923,371	124,738	336,394	0	740,767,804
12	24,429,389	10,043,086	7,537,215	19,310	159,442	0	0	956,279	389,099	405,121,028	1,120,955	546,907	39,000	450,361,710
13	140,343,288	11,247,452	2,870,973	74,087	-75,712	0	16,687,500	240,914	0	750,838,054	63,638	298,017	0	922,588,211
14	97,514,780	20,763,525	44,179,688	324,833	409,598	0	0	609,565	2,899,134	666,911,190	737,526	678,525	1,822,822	836,851,186
TOTAL	2,161,504,153	228,223,996	314,635,626	175,124,470	5,305,714	734,234	37,662,960	77,901,545	40,444,542	8,704,502,498	19,334,589	7,093,103	9,151,464	11,781,618,894
NEW MEXICO														
1	151,983,730	7,338,369	37,800,246	7,719,423	4,815,968	0	20,253,353	6,362,873	1,352,357	435,952,321	211,087	621,186	4,979,485	679,390,398
2	53,601,417	7,151,193	27,247,789	517,380	8,999,358	0	2,577,726	1,991,068	193,526	508,081,372	894,754	310,685	1,051,664	612,617,932
3	279,365,054	4,362,165	10,143,822	2,881,120	9,180,260	0	9,289,488	4,682,682	884,894	202,087,936	20,588	55,204	467,323	523,420,536
TOTAL	484,950,201	18,851,727	75,191,857	11,117,923	22,995,586	0	32,120,567	13,036,623	2,430,777	1,146,121,629	1,126,429	987,075	6,498,472	1,815,428,866
NEW YORK														
1	74,546,620	8,810,118	7,743,450	3,475,088	244,904	0	101,398	15,570,024	2,532,006	398,799,184	201,269	419,651	650,651	513,094,363
2	50,050,528	7,667,914	8,998,075	11,750	129,731	0	1,396	944,202	940,846	398,177,294	101,628	121,099	48,420	467,192,882
3	71,907,126	13,722,512	13,159,614	2,808,992	93,564	0	2,288	6,278,978	409,612	687,210,277	820,133	90,587	2,017,965	798,521,649
4	44,015,783	11,237,659	5,088,928	5,162,596	196,536	0	0	3,844,929	3,467,881	562,073,619	436,196	259,522	76,820	635,860,470
5	45,870,914	13,743,670	11,738,012	5,129,752	248,062	105,929	0	1,488,340	5,780,761	621,229,197	325,051	143,350	1,140,693	706,943,731
6	43,578,013	702,226	-11,647,411	15,905,504	0	0	0	7,864,177	938,712	649,025,599	634,554	447,490	2,077,744	709,526,607
7	43,915,054	0	-2,195	0	0	0	0	2,550,029	1,190,079	651,672,565	637,142	347,310	0	700,309,984
8	57,206,962	516,996	28,135,946	237,509	0	0	0	4,931,978	829,251	655,180,485	761,398	1,152,902	95,000	749,048,428
9	43,518,017	0	203,512	0	0	0	0	1,559,175	964,051	648,145,176	633,693	175,293	0	695,198,918
10	75,757,520	91,800	18,628,064	199,000	656,484	0	0	48,666,969	3,134,932	652,932,006	1,026,702	1,424,368	2,477,420	804,995,266
11	76,209,255	0	450,252	834,000	657,295	0	0	3,992,127	664,281	659,174,420	1,036,756	114,794	0	743,133,180
12	79,779,488	143,350	460,032	210,108	655,795	0	0	5,935,469	821,969	657,685,824	1,034,391	50,000	976,416	747,752,842
13	76,717,672	288,324	-114	0	668,024	0	0	5,858,456	1,882,338	660,116,935	1,044,634	1,394,669	1,198,428	749,169,365
14	40,853,481	544,669	26,789,816	119,333	12,632,085	0	0	8,493,694	3,966,835	480,670,766	344,197	2,248,509	3,950,777	580,614,162
15	646,773,986	655,855	319,911,669	22,848	423,317	0	47,956	99,772,980	54,558,526	656,886,244	6,382,440	15,491,034	4,369,965	1,805,296,821
16	653,816,286	88,006	308,090,928	1,309,460	423,313	0	82,935	10,947,717	9,054,773	656,717,654	6,370,131	15,433,368	3,781,643	1,666,116,214
17	535,437,834	148,502	292,493,559	8,954,377	419,838	0	36,725	23,294,067	30,992,072	757,610,984	8,595,854	12,180,841	6,891,322	1,677,055,975

18	97,559,548	1,523,344	23,017,270	856,444	226,846	0	0	137,057,583	111,317,381	705,765,069	4,445,836	7,692,222	3,290,923	1,092,752,467
19	85,524,176	1,359,666	2,195,796	482,550	0	0	0	11,801,532	861,445	670,880,871	1,086,495	49,720	1,592,884	775,835,135
20	72,810,994	11,580,807	17,284,670	2,149,225	825,080	0	0	16,426,271	125,197,998	658,456,099	653,821	4,298,389	1,947,053	911,630,407
21	32,134,340	6,299,546	12,243,981	726,778	738,394	0	0	5,666,834	2,379,016	384,365,264	-25,769	134,798	2,313,312	446,976,494
22	41,971,995	10,439,686	57,115,874	41,185	298,235	59,170	0	15,121,111	13,875,252	359,474,326	1,029,340	343,854	1,866,161	501,636,189
23	2,698,496,447	7,213,342	54,440,695	15,737,956	70,149	355,091	0	44,488,227	21,040,136	752,108,050	6,680,688	146,342	1,090,975	3,601,868,098
24	24,559,040	4,663,359	36,526,493	60,261	26,171	0	0	3,883,633	535,171	352,030,725	116,572	20	-500,003,848	-77,602,403
25	55,667,144	10,166,455	16,209,212	2,072,766	613,607	111,963	0	1,779,995	1,643,072	546,718,639	169,414	286,097	752,122	636,190,486
26	74,773,949	8,145,621	26,151,787	2,808,856	699,476	19,900	1,646,626	3,688,141	3,189,516	582,085,281	1,315,431	81,993	342,605	704,949,182
27	71,653,745	11,831,183	20,401,296	3,640	546,610	1,500	6,957	4,185,192	21,158,817	543,847,105	1,382,070	230,284	283,868	675,532,268
28	734,894,037	8,752,659	39,346,719	5,413,712	22,537	0	0	22,392,178	69,985,384	472,442,240	208,571	268,591	1,426,022	1,355,152,650
29	71,265,856	9,792,186	25,688,740	32,601,229	153,576	156,403	0	4,322,549	909,152	663,048,903	579,472	7,491	77,960	808,603,519
30	83,342,290	10,129,871	25,521,824	34,496,079	825,526	0	490,306	5,912,614	23,501,529	694,718,267	1,786,373	147,283	795,033	881,666,994
31	108,260,158	10,973,601	23,675,150	0	136,850	0	6,000	4,829,758	1,039,755	811,667,369	1,241,302	0	604,365	962,434,307
32	67,697,395	10,200,844	42,474,874	10,351,988	-44,573	0	0	3,375,042	2,054,008	616,786,026	1,105,779	379,732	162,700	754,543,815
33	97,224,736	12,594,045	25,250,585	0	0	0	0	4,587,367	427,204	718,678,449	1,560,220	135,367	1,122,613	861,580,587
34	45,773,448	11,791,932	24,841,480	494,671	323,977	74,507	3,472,448	9,519,153	8,778,765	509,135,070	191,040	894,584	1,188,061	616,479,135
TOTAL	7,123,563,839	205,819,747	1,502,628,583	152,677,657	22,911,411	884,463	5,895,036	551,030,491	530,022,525	20,495,515,986	53,912,823	66,591,553	-451,393,927	30,260,060,187
NORTH CAROLINA														
1	60,297,445	11,279,558	22,323,689	723,401	554,779	0	0	2,824,611	1,979,438	536,647,319	269,967	300,000	335,192	637,535,399
2	73,753,397	10,147,436	12,920,203	480,744	-4,854	0	8,912	18,787,934	52,626,900	536,223,387	1,335,911	99,353	564,806	706,944,129
3	47,061,166	9,500,791	6,265,006	1,207,581	512,067	0	57,523	3,343,349	502,831	452,750,716	140,196	40	-1,536	521,339,731
4	1,216,019,615	7,071,074	15,792,596	19,141,604	35,214	79,625	106,147	12,883,998	11,903,883	494,060,286	37,100	293,165	424,410	1,777,848,717
5	37,901,771	7,907,303	11,103,137	1,067,620	0	0	0	12,494,793	1,091,988	544,961,660	937,033	16,145	135,360	617,616,810
6	44,389,402	6,352,439	28,813,955	353,360	-15,402	0	0	3,286,949	1,847,521	530,291,701	-41,921	35,583	2,157,631	617,471,218
7	57,271,602	14,403,361	9,133,688	838,204	880,985	0	1,001,465	4,554,374	793,831	446,326,571	310,920	77,736	445,024	536,037,761
8	34,049,485	7,730,031	7,155,333	375,484	-26,422	0	0	3,531,702	3,734,329	561,075,952	444,566	0	30,759	618,101,219
9	38,072,572	6,108,006	7,670,688	2,025,060	-3,587	0	0	3,839,160	2,174,279	482,110,630	259,347	184,182	946,470	543,386,808
10	30,945,982	8,265,136	4,851,668	978,653	0	0	0	1,549,302	964,827	515,863,545	0	0	229,631	563,648,744
11	36,936,225	9,685,780	6,632,443	679,090	100,459	0	4,355,366	4,398,369	1,159,153	680,810,030	0	0	394,126	745,151,041
TOTAL	1,676,698,662	98,450,916	132,662,406	27,870,801	2,033,239	79,625	5,529,413	71,494,541	78,778,980	5,781,121,798	3,693,119	1,006,204	5,661,873	7,885,081,576
NORTH DAKOTA														
TOTAL	275,962,839	7,805,338	19,648,169	2,633,270	5,430,197	0	11,914,843	4,775,690	1,455,852	962,082,027	371,533	107,451	376,072	1,292,563,281
OHIO														
1	93,155,379	6,022,926	38,831,363	3,281,710	213,182	625,000	5,133,758	5,885,917	5,096,580	605,659,474	3,632,861	263,049	1,256,498	769,057,696
2	55,400,977	5,208,348	22,520,762	-53,598	205,834	0	0	4,305,508	1,247,544	526,819,508	761,559	155,940	1,649,714	618,222,095
3	63,512,676	8,354,646	12,094,399	-885	851,342	0	3,516,805	5,300,097	1,227,846	547,743,671	1,362,778	0	835,707	644,799,083
4	29,314,455	5,785,065	3,016,768	130,356	0	0	568,707	2,327,976	2,129,493	549,097,174	725,492	0	8,891	593,104,377
5	25,687,352	2,633,735	15,026,984	142,128	0	0	0	4,821,612	718,088	447,156,847	-12,705	88,328	1,434,000	497,696,369
6	67,319,837	8,838,492	3,812,435	934,228	-6,571	0	0	1,494,690	1,304,817	526,479,778	13,372	0	776,398	610,967,476
7	44,601,778	6,738,646	10,941,941	90,192	1,380,528	0	35,164	3,216,472	3,286,652	462,177,928	433,705	2,557,537	1,092,347	536,552,889
8	34,532,689	3,792,821	7,265,691	-12,926	0	0	0	2,486,465	37,909	455,858,351	79,640	58,626	0	504,099,265
9	42,323,406	1,893,373	12,011,977	294,490	154,510	0	0	10,423,840	153,965	436,258,746	1,695,874	928,943	5,089,703	511,228,828
10	286,032,624	15,041,867	20,491,642	1,092,612	237,113	0	0	9,001,313	2,105,943	558,594,675	148,798	137,370	1,244,764	894,128,721
11	27,464,295	2,524,661	5,341,263	80,800	-76,078	0	1,272,044	971,890	1,381,792	395,701,301	0	0	-48,685	434,613,282
12	952,049,763	3,811,429	26,052,766	2,510,986	31,343	0	10,346,241	8,165,492	1,048,511	488,870,739	266,281	160,865	2,620,437	1,495,934,853
13	25,303,074	8,405,755	14,149,155	0	213,057	0	0	812,514	1,377,589	398,748,763	350,918	291,339	148,378	449,800,542
14	60,026,404	8,400,431	41,387,502	1,077,525	651,422	0	3,179,000	5,900,539	532,298	593,392,308	69,070	428,811	1,805,456	716,850,766
15	876,431,724	4,023,829	30,093,571	2,818,888	40,351	0	48,331	25,861,689	381,085	554,463,356	253,816	213,000	4,655,947	1,499,285,585

See Appendix A for a listing of the congressional districts which represent the county in which the state capital is located and congressional districts which represent only portions of a county. See Appendix B for a listing of the programs included in each recipent category.

table continues

Table 3.1 **Federal Outlays to Categories of Recipients by Congressional District, 1983 *(continued)***

District	State Gov't.	Counties	Cities/ Towns	Special Districts	Schools	Interstate Agencies	Indian Tribes	Non-Profits	Private Universities	Individuals	For Profits	Small Businesses	All Others	Total
OHIO *continued*														
16	42,275,275	5,491,148	16,279,578	247,538	10,066	0	2,953,660	4,432,219	974,062	554,583,175	80,189	66,698	2,300,622	629,694,230
17	57,361,929	26,608,300	44,718,401	446,319	144,422	0	1,081,804	5,129,815	614,194	706,289,406	149,651	208,350	1,739,651	844,492,242
18	40,531,505	6,070,078	11,573,842	-422,590	0	0	0	1,672,758	276,372	652,493,807	81,132	27,303	14,407	712,318,614
19	81,425,221	6,822,434	40,698,941	15,270,217	-120,190	0	0	1,861,902	339,369	725,145,433	1,000,404	37,321	663,857	873,144,908
20	74,058,354	5,324,055	31,026,977	19,156,381	247,694	0	10,824,298	14,490,144	2,165,636	648,524,906	189,475	702,619	138,599	806,849,139
21	72,490,102	5,583,057	46,426,093	16,698,369	-2,957	0	0	11,320,521	41,091,640	670,530,972	604,945	464,884	3,697,104	868,904,730
TOTAL	3,051,298,816	147,375,095	453,762,052	63,782,740	4,175,068	625,000	38,959,812	129,883,374	67,491,386	11,504,590,316	11,887,255	6,790,982	31,123,795	15,511,745,691
OKLAHOMA														
1	39,302,843	2,246,098	16,661,901	2,965,198	1,132,535	0	1,300,568	7,924,636	2,983,342	499,907,787	66,360	97,165	1,960,371	576,548,805
2	78,927,742	2,962,909	7,960,878	4,052,311	5,913,493	0	24,594,302	3,462,234	1,166,586	579,498,857	27,657	19,248	1,819,495	710,405,712
3	100,815,848	3,080,944	18,125,831	1,572,030	3,947,991	0	8,503,849	5,511,619	927,303	661,131,627	141,724	1,028	625,000	804,384,794
4	94,098,223	3,589,464	17,999,438	6,333,871	3,749,460	0	4,715,628	2,516,525	704,952	497,341,603	627,978	56,604	1,451,950	633,185,694
5	437,020,130	2,580,332	22,603,524	16,013,974	884,603	133,200	3,250,383	3,832,855	1,697,581	485,231,818	2,302,466	194,034	1,499,676	977,244,577
6	161,818,563	2,593,238	12,898,412	5,050,574	899,945	5,000	6,671,499	970,745	356,500	678,026,471	311,393	5,218	238,365	869,845,923
TOTAL	911,983,349	17,052,985	96,249,985	35,987,958	16,528,028	138,200	49,036,229	24,218,613	7,836,264	3,401,138,162	3,477,578	373,297	7,594,857	4,571,615,505
OREGON														
1	144,240,180	13,201,647	13,925,355	10,029,382	655,541	128,519	64,665,492	14,581,671	5,725,240	557,750,687	255,992	33,522	1,764,188	826,957,415
2	170,910,574	4,476,663	10,914,658	1,579,253	1,636,659	0	3,438,514	5,799,612	95,157	666,057,434	11,429	368,628	3,798,478	869,087,059
3	65,886,935	10,088,231	26,786,938	1,211,030	1,646,451	678,547	140,103	8,373,420	2,358,980	688,387,898	252,982	101,449	3,660,711	809,573,675
4	76,890,038	9,679,507	27,776,386	375,978	1,617,131	0	651,000	2,902,588	37,703	658,514,538	277,790	0	1,764,563	780,487,222
5	475,762,278	6,348,802	6,535,212	27,692,469	641,645	0	36,630	12,880,021	402,671	453,937,033	265,355	104,852	3,714,236	988,321,204
TOTAL	933,690,006	43,794,850	85,938,549	40,888,112	6,197,427	807,066	68,931,739	44,537,312	8,619,751	3,024,647,589	1,063,548	608,451	14,702,176	4,274,426,576
PENNSYLVANIA														
1	165,328,177	15,000	48,031,595	92,231,836	1,226,359	140,000	-4,404	30,599,484	173,965,052	747,001,865	1,369,452	323,099	3,663,228	1,263,890,744
2	169,712,327	0	39,748,022	171,000	2,367,603	50,000	-4,421	24,556,517	3,384,831	750,353,324	1,786,900	1,590,529	2,083,269	995,799,901
3	185,645,113	0	41,037,689	0	1,518,175	0	-4,412	20,714,936	10,206,213	748,177,497	1,811,183	1,153,094	1,432,996	1,011,692,484
4	24,481,955	7,146,750	5,072,849	806,154	-112,662	0	0	7,094,020	441,382	414,122,705	-155,165	210,868	5,123,849	464,232,705
5	37,445,453	8,583,898	18,457,677	-1,022,714	-2,216	0	0	846,615	3,305,802	561,128,648	81,043	32,557	513,108	629,369,873
6	36,608,598	12,832,622	10,707,774	394,223	261,257	0	0	143,097	235,989	736,507,817	-7,996	16,136	1,555,062	799,254,579
7	55,093,413	16,153,437	10,929,764	144,177	121,514	0	-425	1,927,032	7,522,333	637,573,466	491,390	1,425,123	24,415	731,405,637
8	28,427,133	12,670,166	14,757,439	408,585	142,028	0	0	443,997	291,645	448,541,071	838,348	401,772	1,734,654	508,656,837
9	49,143,373	5,130,664	9,709,601	220,001	-34,932	0	0	1,977,297	330,432	573,406,901	1,529,718	51,307	8,488,670	649,953,031
10	55,551,690	5,988,724	17,029,337	6,445,535	470,239	0	646,245	12,746,772	3,339,385	761,456,037	-5,036	15	9,534,758	873,203,701
11	47,458,228	20,045,640	16,024,068	743,976	345,669	0	1,443,837	6,191,509	2,910,625	870,974,702	374,715	414,340	1,402,558	968,329,867
12	40,839,418	9,143,274	9,893,012	-77,201	-75,609	0	2,808	2,226,647	2,305,458	666,585,639	191,325	148,386	12,694,068	743,877,226
13	46,025,144	12,861,208	14,001,299	-7,563	950,999	0	-769	1,816,176	1,851,068	635,355,832	356,137	575,057	11,376,555	725,161,142
14	127,302,392	17,131,457	71,256,616	54,076,458	2,129,336	0	10,882,802	17,467,830	34,551,244	846,814,838	2,936,919	1,884,193	944,854	1,187,378,938
15	33,255,446	3,859,876	16,476,039	2,474,714	384,102	0	0	3,455,292	7,488,365	663,952,904	279,309	231,152	6,789,027	738,646,225
16	30,696,381	9,421,122	6,862,789	47,366,341	-20,950	0	0	224,915	1,535,427	540,717,661	610,721	532,725	11,288,333	649,235,465
17	2,190,089,737	6,936,718	18,669,133	14,110,352	775,168	75,792	0	3,831,633	1,335,429	761,600,747	47,325	0	6,247,748	3,003,719,782
18	64,825,318	7,436,418	10,311,160	54,018	108,987	0	16,832	964,362	26,159	633,931,463	283,098	44,790	380,364	718,382,968
19	28,642,657	8,916,609	24,403,671	2,726,858	44,047	0	0	3,358,437	1,128,165	551,480,978	206,179	57,620	588,551	621,553,772
20	53,137,975	6,071,166	8,261,930	836,923	-113,902	0	12,746	1,014,667	19,809	587,183,078	462,710	95,232	701,174	657,683,508
21	50,523,805	7,210,989	13,203,928	911,593	66,113	0	1,052,269	4,940,669	3,135,735	656,722,918	1,369,920	77,656	14,485,565	753,701,160
22	64,388,647	13,121,616	7,232,569	2,086,799	61,370	0	869	1,511,760	978,307	715,915,057	362,862	127,663	10,427,076	816,214,594
23	105,323,887	5,143,461	8,374,777	521,461	0	0	0	2,891,109	83,934	620,963,019	232,809	160,904	6,237,702	749,933,062
TOTAL	3,689,946,262	195,820,813	440,452,739	225,623,527	10,612,696	265,792	14,043,976	150,944,773	260,372,789	15,130,468,167	15,453,866	9,554,217	117,717,583	20,261,277,201

RHODE ISLAND														
1	218,765,070	30,849	33,423,845	5,652,660	651,504	0	16,129	9,197,962	18,427,836	646,560,047	607,544	583,191	462,623	934,379,259
2	187,433,615	28,601	24,295,798	879,295	-15,874	0	151,056	7,657,000	2,448,705	585,721,620	624,902	442,045	1,568,251	811,235,015
TOTAL	406,198,685	59,450	57,719,643	6,531,955	635,630	0	167,185	16,854,962	20,876,541	1,232,281,667	1,232,446	1,025,236	2,030,874	1,745,614,274
SOUTH CAROLINA														
1	61,047,244	10,766,248	29,632,121	84,972	706,024	0	0	10,423,148	2,245,737	401,221,841	780,766	254,212	675,020	517,837,333
2	808,734,446	8,976,879	8,631,147	1,543,275	199,736	78,625	0	8,992,670	7,191,389	499,454,621	465,683	82,340	799,614	1,345,150,425
3	43,742,067	7,534,276	9,527,811	234,562	373,715	0	912,273	3,558,231	2,161,383	522,174,071	195,021	68,378	128,484	590,610,272
4	40,791,728	11,703,748	11,180,458	2,074,100	-8,300	0	0	-10,476,558	751,759	524,710,101	0	41,709	314,969	581,083,714
5	41,115,546	8,631,173	15,340,347	2,969,547	462,769	0	121,950	5,490,888	2,754,391	518,686,022	338,814	25,062	310,669	596,247,178
6	54,938,783	9,950,868	6,271,844	3,166,775	1,396,281	0	0	4,656,545	773,225	463,845,026	37,653	14,400	625,232	545,676,632
TOTAL	1,050,369,814	57,563,192	80,583,728	10,073,231	3,130,225	78,625	1,034,223	22,644,924	15,877,884	2,930,091,682	1,817,937	486,101	2,853,988	4,176,605,554
SOUTH DAKOTA														
TOTAL	230,229,009	6,298,610	27,476,610	941,870	7,378,322	0	13,015,588	9,204,902	3,219,930	634,876,807	2,067,429	183,251	399,030	935,291,358
TENNESSEE														
1	33,856,829	5,489,258	15,411,573	340,958	-2,781	0	0	1,529,746	1,045,487	560,987,348	185,961	182,849	205,800	619,233,028
2	55,584,471	7,117,384	11,507,059	2,186,756	0	0	0	4,472,704	1,832,034	579,374,456	1,299,050	277,920	2,437,983	666,089,817
3	34,209,386	4,672,603	23,093,755	1,940,018	68,628	0	0	9,944,776	4,489,415	552,927,919	35,482	33,694	1,534,403	632,950,079
4	36,080,214	5,015,008	13,628,688	1,412,040	-53,783	0	0	6,455,360	1,614,620	577,316,981	327,877	103,121	241,884	642,142,010
5	1,068,799,424	15,299,469	30,528,780	3,605,771	12,737,033	56,890	72,223	56,924,506	24,055,060	599,791,773	1,132,393	500,381	492,936	1,813,996,639
6	29,904,172	3,773,158	7,236,720	3,722,646	9,583	0	0	3,970,862	81,840	469,463,966	83,195	117,129	722,124	519,085,395
7	46,217,637	5,076,427	21,268,790	256,829	465,535	0	0	4,114,060	604,236	498,609,734	87,567	90	1,771,157	578,472,063
8	48,608,251	6,425,913	15,680,715	430,580	16,134	0	0	12,949,520	4,612,563	487,383,316	254,095	683,784	1,662,236	578,707,108
9	61,562,029	5,136,022	28,888,685	0	352,704	0	0	7,429,027	774,526	467,600,656	258,470	0	4,177,779	576,179,898
TOTAL	1,414,822,414	58,005,242	167,244,766	13,895,598	13,593,053	56,890	72,223	107,790,561	39,109,781	4,793,456,149	3,664,090	1,898,968	13,246,302	6,626,856,037
TEXAS														
1	62,744,494	6,539,051	34,005,241	236,536	-269,742	0	163,326	588,318	4,945,769	742,648,084	108,576	22,715	81,237	851,813,606
2	46,884,637	4,034,687	12,203,788	847,919	135,139	0	837,569	5,816,703	342,690	646,880,926	546,524	11,474	5,369,960	723,912,017
3	25,278,635	2,294,101	30,865,851	27,283	-9,346	0	34,171	1,546,192	1,546,043	398,567,073	673,169	175,848	1,370,337	462,369,358
4	36,116,385	2,538,123	21,915,766	66,957	131,338	0	0	1,082,880	2,525,426	650,410,741	50,847	71,424	5,782,451	720,692,338
5	85,996,393	4,321,506	24,689,185	28,594	515,725	0	35,813	683,475	7,904,431	402,193,838	517,864	11,828	3,433,149	530,331,801
6	72,041,618	2,465,828	54,235,004	46,606	-73,008	0	3,138	1,345,782	2,792,897	522,763,072	287,902	24,302	1,224,304	657,157,446
7	18,866,719	8,120,207	15,842,810	76,396,179	79,331	0	-3,285	1,476,740	291,534	311,670,334	397,576	21,715	-218,713	432,941,147
8	19,042,538	5,171,494	16,982,825	829,408	41,629	0	-3,268	105,356	347,321	320,489,447	396,575	0	156,237	363,559,562
9	40,005,040	7,004,116	24,213,732	677,662	-192,452	0	-380	-168,555	614,943	517,217,575	267,818	51,090	4,751,347	594,441,936
10	2,677,066,809	3,352,661	45,201,418	25,100,540	632,825	12,600	0	12,829,554	3,058,472	646,399,737	1,342,725	641,750	5,851,453	3,421,490,545
11	36,175,148	2,816,132	42,827,681	124,820	3,759,750	80,000	0	7,441,789	2,904,904	631,131,548	830,209	14,362	3,054,304	731,160,647
12	19,840,841	6,029,300	22,348,732	87,429	190,175	0	0	653,167	727,480	444,207,112	173,777	700,409	5,511,623	500,470,044
13	22,147,829	3,227,878	24,357,460	338,969	719,421	0	0	2,156,563	273,585	718,911,927	356,003	251,411	3,501,666	776,242,712
14	58,138,582	5,336,563	20,583,280	946,081	460,933	0	0	1,380,346	237,350	664,832,056	113,280	0	4,358,422	756,386,892
15	70,774,620	16,637,799	34,919,477	144,609	2,467,822	0	0	6,925,454	0	468,555,793	36,371	425,000	1,225,962	602,112,906
16	28,726,936	3,219,306	31,677,511	97,500	1,879,326	0	419,014	4,196,133	0	368,516,152	929,224	407,122	5,183,961	445,252,185
17	31,844,375	4,307,515	14,238,564	109,120	358,674	0	0	1,146,620	1,665,425	825,894,595	-1,043	5,025	2,090,003	881,658,874
18	41,455,160	5,184,048	16,174,406	445,710	79,270	0	-3,282	6,818,191	36,828,946	311,376,045	491,736	159,286	-40,265	418,969,252
19	28,845,457	5,908,162	16,346,396	256,844	555,351	0	0	3,067,255	967,789	645,154,209	286,605	15,130	1,640,594	703,043,792
20	40,083,272	3,167,721	13,590,063	7,430,297	2,244,472	0	0	12,805,692	1,619,237	437,850,509	227,035	288,549	628,514	519,935,359
21	40,372,625	4,950,618	17,039,692	98,346	671,233	0	0	1,942,530	2,580,187	581,278,874	170,058	46,166	13,401,759	662,552,088

See Appendix A for a listing of the congressional districts which represent the county in which the state capital is located and congressional districts which represent only portions of a county. See Appendix B for a listing of the programs included in each recipent category.

table continues

Table 3.1 **Federal Outlays to Categories of Recipients by Congressional District, 1983** ***(continued)***

District	State Gov't.	Counties	Cities/ Towns	Special Districts	Schools	Interstate Agencies	Indian Tribes	Non-Profits	Private Universities	Individuals	For Profits	Small Businesses	All Others	Total
TEXAS *continued*														
22	21,395,335	4,877,858	18,681,086	286,558	1,065,719	0	-1,507	1,693,537	2,024,592	302,130,370	-13,213,912	442,534	750,348	340,132,520
23	64,155,400	10,251,694	18,096,907	67,986	2,930,204	0	0	13,450,498	668,236	480,827,332	306,750	113,219	1,757,999	592,626,223
24	24,482,550	2,477,695	20,924,154	6,945,476	11,192	0	315,218	1,441,882	1,362,009	405,806,918	477,693	182,651	1,271,793	465,699,232
25	32,030,320	5,178,229	15,815,675	445,209	79,181	0	-3,278	97,474	930,399	311,018,792	395,724	0	-40,220	365,947,505
26	19,658,280	2,816,652	11,830,887	47,813	111,874	0	0	199,778	243,385	369,595,124	92,350	83,218	375,833	405,055,196
27	25,792,285	6,455,771	23,046,867	649,040	850,326	0	0	4,829,306	-103,302	284,995,687	23,528	0	303,142	346,842,650
TOTAL	3,689,962,285	138,684,717	642,654,460	122,779,493	19,426,361	92,600	1,793,250	95,552,660	77,299,747	13,411,323,870	-3,715,035	4,166,228	72,777,197	18,272,797,833
UTAH														
1	65,022,122	5,573,506	8,748,112	2,628,528	1,714,711	0	383,337	3,136,855	1,391,634	394,359,353	2,470,367	66,083	1,899,052	487,393,660
2	469,205,390	12,985,037	27,292,171	5,939,313	635,902	0	167,851	11,197,846	61,849	444,471,925	2,897,473	437,932	3,261,925	978,554,615
3	11,870,327	2,803,042	8,641,912	338,477	1,809,867	0	1,719,760	2,141,634	1,214,396	146,288,608	48,954	13,427	1,313,018	178,203,421
TOTAL	546,097,839	21,361,585	44,682,195	8,906,318	4,160,480	0	2,270,948	16,476,335	2,667,879	985,119,886	5,416,794	517,442	6,473,995	1,644,151,696
VERMONT														
TOTAL	260,324,159	359,092	32,252,456	2,814,465	352,394	0	259,288	4,871,340	2,791,587	552,194,627	1,626,608	1,035,576	928,066	859,809,658
VIRGINIA														
1	47,336,391	5,804,149	9,721,253	779,890	3,150,237	0	2,286	3,633,954	3,998,601	498,636,392	10,417	27,338	3,967,292	577,068,200
2	52,377,973	0	20,180,288	1,500,138	1,526,845	0	120,000	11,931,101	118,738	329,244,956	384,228	407,616	1,830,370	419,622,253
3	1,011,792,968	20,133,353	43,560,788	20,572,898	23,088	0	12,142	4,233,096	2,671,325	613,903,051	1,150,214	152,327	3,525,249	1,721,730,498
4	65,433,550	2,517,551	26,003,132	1,112,269	1,402,786	0	0	840,290	939,876	496,441,269	30	0	1,363,680	596,054,434
5	42,687,334	4,618,701	6,425,715	6,021,835	0	0	0	2,098,687	723,588	584,829,021	0	0	90,792	647,495,673
6	38,176,198	3,081,027	20,800,960	1,521,982	4,257	0	0	4,187,277	3,524,530	611,353,168	-21,762	284,096	2,397,100	685,308,833
7	68,477,658	5,666,034	7,024,825	2,421,380	73,710	0	0	3,058,092	1,869,909	508,845,559	489,070	21,816	648,227	598,596,280
8	19,628,098	8,936,487	5,488,451	86,326	168,806	0	0	4,972,208	0	250,924,654	360,557	2,124,296	132,786	292,822,670
9	74,506,510	8,616,437	5,249,787	18,505,341	15,979	0	78,944	2,934,482	904,094	655,792,494	0	28,970	2,456,300	769,089,338
10	16,850,232	104,304,422	1,815,971	-2,711	1,655,679	0	0	4,488,702	160,953	318,551,694	13,196,164	7,099,195	3,442,520	471,562,820
TOTAL	1,437,266,912	163,678,161	146,271,170	52,519,348	8,021,387	0	213,372	42,377,889	14,911,614	4,868,522,258	15,568,918	10,145,654	19,854,316	6,779,350,999
WASHINGTON														
1	62,736,109	14,539,435	12,241,923	18,072,490	2,789,233	0	728,529	11,968,783	1,079,122	478,814,647	1,574,673	225,925	2,495,258	607,266,125
2	34,377,926	5,056,979	5,834,991	53,625	4,656,000	0	5,586,889	1,933,811	392,682	477,200,695	246,770	3,467	1,149,707	536,493,542
3	853,940,163	14,444,386	16,209,234	4,795,876	1,130,526	0	2,245,195	2,411,375	706,742	637,699,121	52,224	15,753	4,598,186	1,538,248,781
4	134,999,019	9,265,728	9,475,135	1,295,292	2,105,225	0	5,394,840	11,842,678	44,590	494,874,433	705,153	17,291	560,833	670,580,217
5	74,451,511	5,705,342	12,723,407	1,601,950	1,759,455	0	3,080,057	7,817,979	2,718,849	652,981,675	630,605	126,700	8,905,683	772,503,213
6	57,590,331	10,598,205	58,242,713	1,662,713	3,085,984	0	2,029,437	5,295,727	1,408,329	499,600,502	728,814	127,591	4,210,528	644,580,873
7	48,859,109	7,289,406	17,859,070	1,747,181	259,736	0	223,913	40,012,341	253,405	515,102,984	3,144,991	315,435	3,736,426	638,803,995
8	46,086,621	6,965,296	19,113,431	860,180	183,817	0	1,928,231	6,198,283	-211,975	516,327,315	2,202,389	658,291	2,982,823	603,294,700
TOTAL	1,313,040,788	73,864,777	151,699,903	30,089,307	15,969,975	0	21,217,091	87,480,976	6,391,743	4,272,601,372	9,285,619	1,490,452	28,639,444	6,011,771,447
WEST VIRGINIA														
1	34,971,629	4,865,310	18,383,450	9,617,056	3,330	0	160,532	4,702,427	1,210,335	607,293,945	515,404	161,468	1,165,111	683,049,997
2	55,772,584	9,788,416	13,031,153	2,821,344	346,983	0	0	3,992,050	1,108,500	596,968,364	-7,593	11,628	126,942	683,960,371
3	713,921,983	8,653,966	11,863,666	17,047,276	-6,380	0	926,728	1,847,389	574,188	555,021,133	290,345	63,487	138,601	1,310,342,382
4	51,382,074	6,614,917	18,876,124	15,214,903	0	0	926,100	4,540,185	651,837	671,125,587	904,238	185,561	3,662,234	774,083,760
TOTAL	856,048,270	29,922,609	62,154,393	44,700,579	343,933	0	2,013,360	15,082,051	3,544,860	2,430,409,029	1,702,394	422,144	5,092,888	3,451,436,510

WISCONSIN															
1	79,338,569	5,942,154	15,981,791	-103,897	231,343	0	0	3,437,233	206,702	441,275,233	-25,234	32,760	1,025,118	547,341,772
2	896,511,222	5,208,771	10,824,742	1,616,241	-129,592	0	0	8,711,027	705,783	422,068,057	2,567,687	178,658	3,219,055	1,351,481,650
3	95,832,448	6,735,016	12,405,082	490,468	160,149	0	56,692	2,177,939	754,178	474,436,464	0	70	1,690,026	594,738,532
4	101,452,350	12,042,105	37,608,659	24,748,129	219,611	191,623	5,271	2,689,190	11,736,810	446,424,210	142,889	72,125	262,703	637,595,675
5	126,039,466	12,253,341	29,986,227	31,590,908	0	0	6,669	11,834,849	8,734,909	483,930,290	869,340	994,063	143,852	706,383,914
6	67,977,875	4,782,879	13,906,966	1,609,189	177,391	0	1,758	2,361,382	757,088	503,960,134	0	342,518	688,481	596,565,661
7	95,151,779	7,406,384	12,750,010	1,027,566	415,894	0	4,544,239	8,076,753	1,798,221	455,823,329	213,072	0	1,073,160	588,280,407
8	66,521,431	6,656,448	10,548,982	-37,812	1,618,010	0	6,989,470	2,110,369	400,229	435,812,076	0	0	301,216	530,920,417
9	35,998,251	5,044,879	8,898,807	2,157,142	178,452	0	49,600	3,479,921	744,558	338,084,792	377,139	0	1,236,809	396,250,350
TOTAL	1,564,823,389	66,071,976	152,911,265	63,097,935	2,871,258	191,623	11,653,699	44,878,663	25,838,478	4,001,814,584	4,144,893	1,620,194	9,640,420	5,949,558,377
WYOMING														
TOTAL	159,015,410	5,496,016	15,228,101	1,359,433	2,444,220	0	2,149,300	867,700	116,538	271,691,873	-9,463	18,586	-18,199	458,359,515
U.S. TOTAL	72,563.1 mil	3,687.0 mil	9,931.1 mil	2,049.4 mil	637.2 mil	17.6 mil	971.1 mil	3,778.1 mil	2,683.5 mil	246,989.7 mil	469.8 mil	271.9 mil	499.8 mil	344,549.3 mil

See Appendix A for a listing of the congressional districts which represent the county in which the state capital is located and congressional districts which represent only portions of a county. See Appendix B for a listing of the programs included in each recipent category.

Table 3.2 **Federal Outlays to Categories of Recipients by Congressional District, 1984**

District	State Gov't.	Counties	Cities/ Towns	Special Districts	Schools	Interstate Agencies	Indian Tribes	Non-Profits	Private Universities	Individuals	For Profits	Small Businesses	All Others	Total
ALABAMA														
1	68,982,191	5,401,256	18,556,790	2,372,711	344,405	0	840,011	9,510,814	1,346,218	596,746,969	891,956	424,314	1,278,498	706,696,133
2	1,243,316,865	4,943,866	18,116,956	1,954,274	620,831	0	0	9,137,788	2,811,780	611,445,428	529,185	78,214	1,739,445	1,894,694,632
3	81,537,970	4,035,587	12,201,874	31,400	583,760	23,586	0	8,227,343	18,046,702	598,782,335	733,177	367,715	613,363	725,184,812
4	69,859,279	4,748,932	22,917,183	243,708	327,832	0	14,997	8,694,290	288,515	687,484,516	199,058	1,469	196,092	794,975,870
5	57,472,516	6,768,959	13,128,440	6,264,149	148,758	0	0	10,398,207	2,056,973	513,724,688	267,814	123,223	189,386	610,543,113
6	100,921,608	15,289,213	23,169,425	3,539,965	228,169	-246,771	0	4,387,281	5,216,997	726,953,967	9,044,682	1,203,472	1,155,369	890,863,376
7	82,107,257	8,345,194	19,266,330	94,761	55,325	-49,300	0	11,251,540	3,979,130	614,102,356	8,064	0	667,095	739,827,753
TOTAL	1,704,197,686	49,533,007	127,356,997	14,500,968	2,309,080	-272,485	855,008	61,607,263	33,746,315	4,349,240,259	11,673,936	2,198,407	5,839,248	6,362,785,689
ALASKA														
TOTAL	430,777,606	23,126,180	69,561,323	0	3,684	530,000	29,091,116	23,779,092	501,804	174,985,532	2,066,436	134,817	13,846,261	768,403,851
ARIZONA														
1	301,368,826	5,811,507	38,637,301	943,769	879,520	0	6,305,567	5,968,147	3,895,023	852,974,160	5,311,267	1,093,756	108,111	1,223,296,955
2	169,498,160	13,236,884	39,947,764	3,347,303	3,909,812	0	15,022,241	9,888,413	413,732	729,580,474	4,896,311	2,228,613	1,753,220	993,722,927
3	15,293,060	2,909,589	24,762,990	6,752	5,784,904	0	4,182,033	4,347,101	115,224	318,677,707	1,311,839	441,392	1,576,536	379,409,127
4	391,027,878	5,694,480	46,221,208	0	5,529,728	0	61,084,328	4,671,575	2,291,269	749,092,360	1,648,571	96,836	632,158	1,267,990,392
5	32,699,423	11,319,798	11,136,081	9,209	566,448	0	74,756	3,844,356	664,463	677,339,386	220,979	203,136	533,130	738,611,165
TOTAL	909,887,347	38,972,258	160,705,344	4,307,033	16,670,412	0	86,668,926	28,719,592	7,379,711	3,327,664,087	13,388,968	4,063,733	4,603,155	4,603,030,566
ARKANSAS														
1	122,142,413	8,033,903	12,480,291	254,679	328,279	0	0	12,399,893	1,091,662	761,194,979	35,227	136,248	1,086,514	919,184,088
2	672,547,106	4,056,210	29,764,880	1,214,666	104,654	0	7,389,436	3,219,843	4,911,731	620,515,207	105,972	803,125	2,397,598	1,347,030,428
3	68,770,588	11,466,577	20,350,983	-866,700	870,949	0	0	903,001	3,212,077	769,189,376	2,253,877	23,430	1,213,414	877,387,572
4	105,278,920	6,697,846	17,410,792	227,610	268,872	0	0	11,121,639	1,275,995	763,924,595	273,277	47,777	3,286,821	909,814,144
TOTAL	968,739,027	30,254,536	80,006,946	830,255	1,572,754	0	7,389,436	27,644,376	10,491,465	2,914,824,157	2,668,353	1,010,580	7,984,347	4,053,416,232
CALIFORNIA														
1	116,372,978	13,457,215	17,873,052	-764,271	2,186,638	0	4,362,115	6,931,660	53,894	702,325,100	2,198,501	49,122	5,567,442	870,613,446
2	85,308,082	10,856,018	17,413,335	5,701,951	1,787,990	-231,673	2,447,002	6,896,274	1,386,847	803,354,967	714,463	1,624,408	910,330	938,169,994
3	3,843,742,705	9,153,227	17,035,712	30,345,814	2,060,414	0	2,624,949	145,522,658	847,914	472,872,353	8,288,525	834,281	843,264	4,534,171,816
4	643,825,940	11,813,321	15,720,474	244,055	3,890,769	0	855,960	69,210,904	2,668,905	474,256,662	-2,525	567,242	745,980	1,223,797,687
5	124,462,580	18,970,563	55,840,182	635,793	2,276,133	0	-31,098	14,401,743	2,107,359	837,846,771	450,647	251,918	3,899,952	1,061,112,543
6	65,212,735	23,452,418	14,569,299	7,640,315	470,835	0	35,044	15,624,095	1,052,875	605,553,208	211,911	1,119,614	3,751,528	738,693,878
7	60,723,894	9,310,947	4,752,304	6,539,513	1,207,410	0	0	4,040,539	380,386	533,292,113	146,493	210,140	788,834	621,392,573
8	162,500,910	8,336,508	107,603,693	78,717,005	1,904,975	0	231,643	33,579,854	2,956,834	592,168,260	10,676,581	1,908,824	1,597,767	1,002,182,853
9	81,256,948	6,841,992	15,066,779	-569,767	464,184	0	307,768	5,785,565	228,967	610,273,294	880,947	258,938	1,142,162	721,937,776
10	71,002,569	8,641,030	30,757,994	-137,491	2,072,001	0	450,524	6,072,653	843,645	479,043,763	384,543	213,080	577,914	599,922,224
11	40,388,377	7,551,154	11,849,806	438,070	140,539	0	18,238	13,147,174	114,513,523	563,033,613	1,701,748	954,938	2,608,828	756,346,009
12	64,111,833	39,062,160	28,197,920	734,036	1,896,002	0	99,865	16,632,922	2,433,689	469,814,464	6,252,335	422,405	4,192,606	633,850,238
13	54,310,750	8,152,442	10,013,579	12,896,752	872,794	0	145,624	8,315,269	1,961,752	416,420,767	-145,070	1,093,322	706,750	514,744,730
14	68,866,701	11,077,013	22,916,764	28,615,993	2,027,098	0	2,044,128	6,652,101	4,226,617	713,149,560	8,236	198,099	410,974	860,193,284
15	68,263,872	5,157,883	38,362,462	403,731	2,376,394	0	40,385	8,678,849	702,552	545,340,852	881,793	741,387	1,396,117	672,346,277
16	67,913,576	9,557,218	13,176,997	19,488,658	4,344,682	0	283,591	2,928,673	1,229,495	579,424,841	42,008	346,627	74,964	698,811,329
17	115,683,634	15,855,199	13,946,036	1,485,130	2,564,979	-247,577	2,438,138	10,281,468	94,099,837	629,831,698	1,191,321	701,945	4,955,523	892,787,332
18	260,171,461	51,524,030	12,639,279	6,557,986	1,308,776	-133,112	283,742	5,190,422	35,277	767,189,672	935,037	0	811,940	1,106,514,509
19	59,868,133	12,504,939	7,209,527	8,988,020	1,972,854	0	416,922	4,300,220	1,049,262	438,814,875	965,271	742,315	189,108	537,021,445
20	87,819,887	16,080,772	9,318,604	128,091,713	2,883,652	0	155,281	14,530,816	2,779,445	614,393,810	108,703,268	102,912	1,679,550	986,539,711
21	74,363,799	8,985,196	12,259,798	846,733	-204,794	0	346,022	4,433,435	1,180,148	576,917,254	779,508	396,519	256,423	680,560,041
22	86,169,422	8,405,236	17,312,994	1,643,146	852,239	0	119,873	11,278,884	10,776,945	587,352,645	1,350,998	337,161	633,596	726,233,137
23	165,999,366	8,598,342	10,661,826	2,201,464	10,100	0	119,746	20,495,117	9,804,961	547,562,822	855,928	112,086	931,443	767,353,200

24	83,777,684	8,665,344	11,489,656	4,284,890	10,098	0	183,257	20,552,276	485,946	535,361,253	3,678,111	666,587	1,602,279	670,757,380
25	90,718,337	12,328,064	12,705,445	6,091,737	1,178,489	0	279,610	10,734,125	14,653,067	535,682,209	1,962,378	1,301,532	1,396,322	689,031,316
26	72,994,796	7,370,412	9,495,602	1,603,264	86,651	0	105,115	6,233,756	349,625	469,868,581	242,528	146,893	55,967	568,553,189
27	84,283,199	8,392,339	50,832,921	5,864,435	241,107	0	119,689	9,549,830	3,230,347	567,067,488	9,698,121	646,868	2,589,376	742,515,720
28	83,797,668	8,509,683	12,041,861	1,737,633	492,848	0	119,672	13,246,266	64,903,051	542,228,796	1,603,123	834,322	636,668	730,151,590
29	84,671,957	45,316,686	15,652,631	1,738,007	311,556	0	119,698	6,023,611	509,111	564,402,509	581,520	406,719	2,246,447	721,980,451
30	85,647,973	8,378,371	20,736,387	3,241,392	2,000,878	0	106,108	5,993,957	815,995	565,184,139	4,071,799	1,558,815	3,233,337	700,969,151
31	90,036,136	8,398,260	20,927,395	1,901,470	1,388,752	0	406,852	5,187,567	4,899,176	577,584,528	2,775,230	104,135	178,061	713,787,560
32	83,827,230	8,425,157	12,751,197	1,744,681	464,195	0	120,157	7,076,870	699,200	548,630,971	1,247,717	496,053	1,209,496	666,692,922
33	88,074,016	11,065,476	14,900,214	1,083,085	1,299,474	0	119,812	7,669,536	4,226,567	550,046,100	847,592	350,272	328,418	680,010,563
34	89,167,889	8,401,325	17,552,346	4,257,446	2,426,568	0	119,817	4,814,374	368,869	560,272,272	459,706	400,384	786,616	689,027,612
35	72,997,349	13,541,030	7,537,765	24,458,482	3,421,481	0	1,743,093	3,261,600	4,882,089	604,466,824	8,431	335,394	1,057,950	737,711,487
36	307,504,717	23,686,629	9,506,763	1,621,151	281,404	0	278,051	26,480,152	189,533	1,075,699,308	1,118,543	220,121	1,114,126	1,447,700,498
37	232,621,527	15,511,188	17,278,757	10,769,842	1,549,657	0	1,378,018	23,673,933	785,283	517,729,994	0	448,893	587,639	822,334,731
38	30,690,529	23,456,874	7,206,014	551,807	351,965	0	87,919	2,183,929	232,535	436,383,425	141,500	161,654	-369	501,447,781
39	34,689,213	2,799,681	9,656,054	-456,403	91,374	0	87,993	3,126,375	2,233,603	457,206,185	9,033,826	134,418	413,391	519,015,710
40	40,774,150	6,091,484	8,036,745	-1,029,095	899,403	0	87,912	17,543,922	2,509,206	457,816,536	28,882	698,487	2,012,656	535,470,289
41	82,956,295	5,191,591	22,730,884	9,178,369	1,481,676	0	91,379	89,318,010	5,180,719	421,368,835	2,760,094	1,951,810	1,545,064	643,754,726
42	64,526,210	6,248,127	15,709,257	3,087,436	508,910	0	107,072	16,312,677	347,326	517,136,466	2,599,119	1,662,692	472,820	628,718,112
43	52,548,986	6,453,534	11,921,774	11,013,471	2,802,134	0	853,681	20,402,643	495,080	567,559,716	197,937	279,131	139,591	674,667,676
44	61,657,471	6,727,298	5,805,654	24,733	288,129	0	138,450	6,567,918	107,433	617,154,567	28,482	28,133	62,030	698,590,296
45	66,703,211	6,844,681	11,364,169	503,660	2,512,753	0	4,209,820	7,930,908	12,744,556	606,899,703	23,494	100,156	725,717	720,562,828
TOTAL	8,453,006,695	575,148,057	830,337,903	434,015,841	63,456,164	-612,362	28,658,637	748,815,529	382,169,445	25,855,983,770	190,580,599	26,120,751	61,066,594	37,648,747,623
COLORADO														
1	819,313,789	7,893,712	12,346,966	22,533,188	-299,818	96,960	1,957,881	30,640,809	8,330,478	638,764,844	2,323,494	883,392	3,259,474	1,548,045,169
2	55,152,676	3,489,510	16,875,150	0	587,090	0	0	10,547,287	1,550,174	321,523,469	443,054	2,594,006	3,451,103	416,213,520
3	67,982,102	10,002,569	19,747,320	2,654,588	739,377	0	1,749,134	5,099,120	532,805	524,576,486	264,472	302,512	1,159,843	634,810,328
4	74,675,724	10,239,961	8,329,192	9,412	989,357	0	0	6,928,669	251,757	523,041,004	174,154	554,198	1,301,160	626,494,588
5	26,774,621	3,882,041	12,723,165	70,144	3,731,558	0	0	3,001,786	2,142,381	350,571,677	643,289	470,469	908,631	404,919,762
6	22,800,404	7,067,199	7,026,046	0	419,162	0	66,489	3,721,590	659	267,807,846	189,487	617,953	709,925	310,426,760
TOTAL	1,066,699,316	42,574,992	77,047,840	25,267,332	6,166,726	96,960	3,773,504	59,939,262	12,808,254	2,626,285,326	4,037,950	5,422,530	10,790,135	3,940,910,127
CONNECTICUT														
1	794,715,623	1,813,686	18,602,338	26,642,291	0	0	0	6,696,503	2,250,942	639,082,884	2,164,692	1,197,090	3,453,595	1,496,619,643
2	53,308,543	145,000	14,775,397	66,050	0	0	616,563	5,140,951	3,906,619	485,191,175	67,678	14,970	1,501,930	564,734,877
3	79,370,293	58,275	48,301,713	502,865	10,500	0	0	7,660,073	98,088,193	668,482,759	365,606	956,924	782,813	904,580,015
4	79,152,638	0	23,686,863	1,599,915	0	0	0	4,570,573	2,237,211	648,322,958	225,619	173,515	1,401,149	761,370,441
5	78,305,994	148,904	20,384,597	0	3,750	0	186,792	2,852,198	181,349	634,323,929	0	35,801	548,317	736,971,631
6	85,284,687	0	15,940,829	0	0	0	0	2,633,014	62,460	627,706,984	8,014,919	82,406	162,386	739,887,684
TOTAL	1,170,137,778	2,165,865	141,691,736	28,811,121	14,250	0	803,355	29,553,312	106,726,774	3,703,110,688	10,838,514	2,460,706	7,850,190	5,204,164,289
DELAWARE														
TOTAL	244,239,100	22,040,447	32,737,024	2,328,584	8,639,299	1,104,700	32,479	6,871,377	1,088,109	669,544,718	1,874,367	116,102	2,657,294	993,273,600
DISTRICT OF COLUMBIA														
TOTAL	474,757,169	65,409	37,842,322	162,753,293	32,056,930	703,336	769,466	369,207,238	149,455,293	679,982,348	7,576,096	6,448,499	35,431,046	1,957,048,445
FLORIDA														
1	47,934,682	7,351,020	6,501,756	1,242,566	504,378	0	8,345	4,859,516	0	533,913,539	253,101	224,033	76,652	602,869,589
2	1,943,070,407	6,541,601	19,562,481	78,304	380,654	220,788	473,482	7,617,548	887,805	614,894,241	15,999	121,467	3,703,318	2,597,568,096
3	56,119,734	1,030,478	22,789,558	8,785,797	199,513	0	0	2,814,469	3,778,106	599,017,513	714,514	77,490	583,879	695,911,050
4	42,877,215	7,526,445	14,130,682	654,173	399,433	0	0	2,197,305	5,650,833	955,624,461	47,387	281,672	566,255	1,029,955,861
5	34,055,332	10,207,736	25,541,379	6,095,084	478,959	0	49,738	4,707,474	495,908	625,911,022	394,773	35,440	482,602	708,455,447
6	89,938,193	7,775,872	6,138,955	2,556,299	1,638,816	0	0	3,065,757	966,332	989,021,581	36,105	311,158	441,545	1,101,890,612

See Appendix A for a listing of the congressional districts which represent the county in which the state capital is located and congressional districts which represent only portions of a county. See Appendix B for a listing of the programs included in each recipent category.

table continues

Table 3.2 Federal Outlays to Categories of Recipients by Congressional District, 1984 *(continued)*

District	State Gov't.	Counties	Cities/ Towns	Special Districts	Schools	Interstate Agencies	Indian Tribes	Non-Profits	Private Universities	Individuals	For Profits	Small Businesses	All Others	Total
FLORIDA *continued*														
7	57,566,155	24,352,310	13,238,718	12,484,695	335,352	0	0	5,704,176	2,520,303	698,507,645	5,234,498	3,755,358	607,116	824,306,325
8	25,381,423	5,255,392	15,348,142	6,104,847	250,444	0	0	1,975,502	757,608	1,412,196,635	15,000	155,348	0	1,467,440,341
9	27,689,481	5,209,126	11,381,141	-2,472	-99,166	0	0	2,583,325	1,707,648	1,136,659,475	745,535	292,372	487,980	1,186,654,444
10	32,866,140	23,132,105	13,666,429	1,408,255	614,591	0	2,586	2,896,408	1,259,771	923,684,025	96,051	136,770	681,744	1,000,444,875
11	31,382,564	11,015,185	16,831,535	3,708,027	1,121,076	0	0	2,828,870	1,158,319	752,390,274	142,812	131,207	508,946	821,218,814
12	32,351,864	8,877,998	2,880,487	771,976	566,978	0	363,726	8,598,800	46,599	1,051,459,588	321,868	354,675	116,039	1,106,710,599
13	18,891,532	36,670,408	2,796,823	634,538	703,656	0	7,320	1,890,451	4,309,255	1,321,061,045	63,238	842,577	563,607	1,388,434,450
14	23,314,601	8,769,096	4,980,819	-458,065	754,482	0	664,514	1,902,735	967,952	1,048,552,320	2,993,839	2,052,511	30,964	1,094,525,769
15	40,544,532	28,555,088	23,452,619	10,676,636	1,287,450	0	227,454	9,014,126	2,732,646	983,853,865	2,066,524	1,769,514	156,656	1,104,337,111
16	31,398,968	11,448,306	6,992,814	568,860	0	0	2,851,454	3,509,597	36,116	832,776,788	38,006	0	39,060	889,659,968
17	68,611,209	12,998,724	13,671,489	659,624	0	0	53,317	8,071,172	3,571,608	667,026,778	14,413	1,135,497	133,789	775,947,619
18	74,785,385	20,745,621	18,296,765	127,674	150,000	0	53,338	10,609,485	731,292	679,291,508	4,153,397	0	224,342	809,168,807
19	63,730,213	13,630,020	14,134,821	175,076	395,576	0	46,733	7,944,741	5,574,754	641,514,256	50,752	0	394,071	747,591,012
TOTAL	2,742,509,630	251,092,530	252,337,412	56,271,893	9,682,192	220,788	4,802,007	92,791,456	37,152,855	16,467,356,559	17,397,813	11,677,089	9,798,565	19,953,090,789
GEORGIA														
1	92,283,521	9,083,375	23,184,478	918,851	1,177,991	0	0	8,559,360	610,485	565,016,891	178,704	636,044	1,235,099	702,884,799
2	146,165,059	10,368,306	5,200,002	211,490	275,633	0	0	8,209,659	493,087	567,166,423	98,926	45,322	1,323,651	739,557,558
3	73,352,110	5,296,995	8,345,744	230,321	513,398	0	0	10,343,225	1,577,342	507,279,807	153,491	757,082	551,343	608,400,858
4	384,312,041	10,430,851	16,540,915	1,410,837	150,497	2,000	-29,047	95,382,640	4,986,755	259,515,624	1,142,373	612,901	3,035,180	777,493,566
5	1,074,627,887	17,406,930	47,907,728	31,624	1,383,868	0	146,465	22,578,361	40,129,774	774,182,919	1,015,271	630,670	5,716,805	1,985,758,301
6	60,343,553	8,291,468	5,954,602	24,650,044	150,523	0	16,300	7,552,247	312,930	484,650,144	468,512	0	907,890	593,298,213
7	33,857,135	8,230,097	5,051,637	88,682	70,670	0	0	2,181,362	1,827,302	472,556,585	0	244,780	27,415	524,135,665
8	103,336,430	11,385,387	27,227,166	148,008	64,969	0	0	8,778,756	3,811,296	595,910,683	0	0	878,921	751,541,616
9	51,759,912	7,231,431	2,802,507	294,042	76,003	0	0	6,098,532	1,674,885	523,682,525	15,910	0	-264	593,635,483
10	92,772,929	7,676,480	19,640,957	285,898	564,164	0	0	14,859,510	3,342,382	491,901,933	0	0	18,350	631,062,603
TOTAL	2,112,810,577	95,401,319	161,855,736	28,269,797	4,427,716	2,000	133,718	184,543,652	58,766,238	5,241,863,535	3,073,187	2,926,799	13,694,389	7,907,768,662
HAWAII														
1	246,624,493	-492,648	39,405,170	124,492	0	576,600	1,261,682	10,555,926	2,480,173	371,566,191	2,266,945	1,352,289	1,336,984	677,058,298
2	120,502,234	13,407,180	14,423,573	-975,276	0	0	0	5,862,196	217,269	446,930,198	39,659	79,002	841,431	601,327,465
TOTAL	367,126,727	12,914,532	53,828,743	-850,784	0	576,600	1,261,682	16,418,122	2,697,442	818,496,389	2,306,604	1,431,291	2,178,415	1,278,385,763
IDAHO														
1	285,325,966	19,818,180	14,721,350	1,079,506	1,589,860	0	3,030,885	4,903,431	1,010,011	537,103,638	0	626	859,259	869,442,712
2	71,004,091	6,004,134	13,301,832	128,379	1,781,650	0	2,106,786	3,939,456	0	463,365,153	29,584	529,671	743,628	562,934,364
TOTAL	356,330,057	25,822,314	28,023,182	1,207,885	3,371,510	0	5,137,671	8,842,887	1,010,011	1,000,468,791	29,584	530,297	1,602,887	1,432,377,076
ILLINOIS														
1	114,439,364	3,849,662	83,489,609	154,527,681	0	303,181	711,175	11,814,116	72,412,744	573,283,106	6,396,085	1,868,968	2,002,635	1,025,098,326
2	101,916,748	3,562,042	27,110,470	-187,165	0	0	509,213	4,569,243	41,486	573,090,306	987,498	308,132	436,971	712,344,943
3	103,052,903	3,562,791	25,242,094	-111,019	5,649	0	509,320	3,459,613	651,180	596,523,697	442,201	454,766	1,431,513	735,224,707
4	62,697,513	2,554,794	17,071,048	1,580,750	127,400	0	220,186	3,950,642	469,213	500,956,578	52,682	307,491	708,141	590,696,436
5	102,393,830	3,562,317	25,031,519	-871,774	0	0	509,252	3,426,792	323,154	609,077,469	572,518	60,291	1,356,138	745,441,506
6	43,885,692	6,219,521	33,348,134	2,770,242	141,533	0	189,691	3,499,441	15,454	469,452,573	117,570	248,278	173,822	560,061,952
7	110,504,538	8,754,128	67,671,499	373,196	650,920	0	556,519	59,681,942	13,121,706	600,810,516	2,624,399	5,877,419	4,184,159	874,810,942
8	102,051,944	3,562,749	26,161,486	-117,748	1,161,426	0	509,314	4,286,456	152,494	573,212,360	73,945	139,634	495,181	711,689,242
9	102,483,355	3,563,340	27,573,645	156,951	0	0	509,399	10,841,966	42,790,855	590,766,276	207,704	2,612,856	3,211,458	784,717,803
10	63,106,949	3,957,171	22,805,324	-87,657	135,928	0	230,301	4,400,807	1,120,503	485,683,211	152,838	45,248	404,415	581,955,037
11	106,547,018	3,562,482	25,702,642	-189,158	5,353	0	562,282	3,584,578	1,244,357	573,161,032	109,867	494,375	466,672	715,251,500
12	56,202,048	4,099,533	20,505,449	1,482,926	120,017	0	215,424	1,617,957	178,261	503,854,865	26,398	133,508	429,422	588,865,807

13	51,155,179	3,639,749	20,415,376	2,061,961	1,751,032	0	223,281	2,595,364	611,449	479,511,205	20,681	862,814	1,436,378	564,284,470
14	29,423,361	19,411,808	17,448,580	876,731	4,857	0	1,975	1,234,561	1,975,262	543,066,930	155,890	208,259	10,310	613,818,524
15	42,175,477	3,142,581	26,356,380	950,902	1,032,285	0	0	2,457,421	2,987,844	575,852,503	2,511	53,937	0	655,011,841
16	32,459,404	1,648,160	12,984,073	3,304,741	636,841	0	0	4,131,317	401,298	601,259,885	46,241	36,707	0	656,908,667
17	35,240,024	5,118,579	13,545,227	1,905,432	3,954	0	0	3,304,761	3,334,542	661,589,487	137,300	0	550,502	724,729,807
18	47,384,550	2,711,323	22,306,055	7,170,714	70,666	0	0	3,553,667	4,181,287	638,239,005	299,919	-26,014	845,452	726,736,624
19	112,424,137	3,901,128	19,590,919	5,242,375	680,234	0	0	3,952,068	2,105,111	658,777,027	147,446	509,867	1,788,959	809,119,273
20	2,686,335,140	4,435,794	22,387,000	2,155,242	421,222	1,421,685	0	2,909,049	718,517	732,085,705	685,907	252,647	6,501	3,453,814,409
21	90,581,299	6,110,740	11,435,347	1,829,580	2,435,953	0	0	4,015,783	1,150,321	660,109,553	207,120	239,817	1,071,467	779,186,981
22	77,974,757	2,944,500	11,247,246	2,661,688	116,062	0	0	9,237,699	1,794,919	771,889,332	185,268	222,672	57,382	878,331,525
TOTAL	4,274,435,230	103,874,892	579,429,121	187,486,592	9,501,332	1,724,866	5,457,332	152,525,245	151,781,954	12,972,252,622	13,651,989	14,911,670	21,067,478	18,488,100,324
INDIANA														
1	72,055,230	6,247,598	37,236,846	13,458,308	476,343	0	0	3,123,826	611,438	572,032,229	0	717,985	923,204	706,883,006
2	120,514,763	4,301,026	10,888,847	3,314,189	53,504	0	0	2,319,215	561,085	615,631,476	0	165,806	250,563	758,000,474
3	40,682,547	2,246,380	20,339,581	16,104,100	311,256	0	0	1,256,679	9,346,970	646,148,793	41,382	140,153	13,579,830	750,197,671
4	46,325,229	4,534,834	8,574,798	7,124,566	57,425	0	14,868	2,896,134	943,999	612,828,809	14,333	109,031	1,416,192	684,840,218
5	38,757,277	4,010,850	19,280,251	2,034,000	1,290,597	0	0	1,886,597	3,464,832	597,196,233	9,800,226	140,324	305,266	678,166,452
6	161,312,385	2,316,494	13,949,458	5,561,257	42,128	0	0	2,910,350	1,554,993	618,527,616	258,300	47,180	1,491,521	807,971,681
7	67,375,909	4,097,038	13,248,346	921,566	31,269	0	0	10,971,048	8,603,784	641,523,259	28,567	141,453	207,250	747,149,489
8	60,122,801	4,100,398	11,967,734	658,210	239,714	0	0	2,938,419	2,584,617	675,318,908	1,019,860	389,139	156,779	759,496,578
9	95,587,990	5,543,779	14,641,389	973,592	732,189	0	0	2,399,172	5,925,297	548,894,087	0	248,546	54,642	675,000,683
10	903,034,021	70,151	24,880,465	30,190,001	0	0	0	7,733,853	117,786	611,244,202	0	0	1,257,239	1,578,527,719
TOTAL	1,605,768,152	37,468,549	175,007,714	80,339,789	3,234,425	0	14,868	38,435,293	33,714,801	6,139,345,610	11,162,668	2,099,617	19,642,486	8,146,233,972
IOWA														
1	21,647,111	4,661,969	57,182,063	110,000	960,092	0	0	3,374,362	3,480,620	587,101,848	0	1,344,358	2,703,180	682,565,603
2	15,404,914	4,547,305	42,262,750	1,463,297	633,298	0	0	1,991,832	4,113,877	542,367,005	1,332,834	244,201	496,780	614,858,093
3	76,292,775	4,053,194	37,070,467	1,266,774	1,212,107	0	216,219	4,666,401	2,101,712	554,897,364	91,557	894,950	2,402,647	685,166,167
4	663,059,189	4,770,878	105,588,959	1,225,011	627,032	507,500	6,893,857	4,309,429	4,254,721	526,587,595	1,214,629	764,057	3,494,678	1,323,297,535
5	18,129,105	6,533,328	50,476,198	209,345	79,103	0	0	5,604,937	2,246,882	653,999,906	0	260,417	749,873	738,289,094
6	15,559,381	5,369,561	46,127,153	110,470	526,338	0	0	2,221,542	5,433,294	664,820,748	606,695	643,911	1,438,037	742,857,130
TOTAL	810,092,475	29,936,235	338,707,590	4,384,897	4,037,970	507,500	7,110,076	22,168,503	21,631,106	3,529,774,466	3,245,715	4,151,894	11,285,195	4,787,033,622
KANSAS														
1	38,309,336	6,154,914	10,025,804	2,930,358	204,041	0	0	1,729,178	1,905,175	856,827,836	148,366	113,442	474,452	918,822,902
2	631,984,952	6,032,550	24,950,900	251,075	4,093,591	0	1,639,979	4,285,979	2,783,169	501,478,724	-55,354	382,015	600,880	1,178,428,460
3	48,274,309	3,812,377	26,752,507	2,305,143	95,140	0	0	9,295,138	2,325,836	480,261,008	213,557	11,558	240,186	573,586,759
4	46,805,736	2,523,650	7,955,976	5,492,987	459,766	0	270,110	6,397,988	1,038,911	545,685,891	4,668,509	133,798	1,486,284	622,919,606
5	49,661,684	5,819,048	6,217,511	1,574,935	103,383	0	0	6,268,225	3,886,535	748,631,463	0	177,008	75,027	822,414,819
TOTAL	815,036,017	24,342,539	75,902,698	12,554,498	4,955,921	0	1,910,089	27,976,508	11,939,626	3,132,884,922	4,975,078	817,821	2,876,829	4,116,172,546
KENTUCKY														
1	67,732,435	5,999,260	10,022,795	2,111,034	189,438	0	0	3,641,608	596,779	679,128,119	280,324	108,973	156,495	769,967,260
2	59,832,454	5,246,273	10,666,652	2,747,729	545,320	0	0	7,808,127	904,558	474,233,457	1,831,446	99,426	40,539	563,955,981
3	65,502,631	9,500,924	9,607,412	25,917,175	452,932	0	0	9,894,857	7,870,921	614,879,399	853,926	466,755	1,503,880	746,450,812
4	50,478,673	12,171,399	12,996,701	2,348,429	226,473	0	0	3,459,944	413,994	525,832,073	86,040	0	956,231	608,969,957
5	118,935,657	8,571,433	10,088,408	-2,944,715	108,148	0	0	9,978,516	3,507,610	623,237,164	0	356,413	918,909	772,757,543
6	1,284,461,619	6,873,997	30,762,586	5,825,489	108,151	0	0	48,096,303	4,141,995	480,074,478	192,729	139,432	3,269,811	1,863,946,590
7	91,625,416	10,639,175	3,881,627	165,547	145,335	0	0	15,723,268	2,140,800	606,578,905	36,198	0	7,908	730,944,179
TOTAL	1,738,568,885	59,002,461	88,026,181	36,170,688	1,775,797	0	0	98,602,623	19,576,657	4,003,963,595	3,280,663	1,170,999	6,853,773	6,056,992,322

See Appendix A for a listing of the congressional districts which represent the county in which the state capital is located and congressional districts which represent only portions of a county. See Appendix B for a listing of the programs included in each recipent category.

table continues

Table 3.2 **Federal Outlays to Categories of Recipients by Congressional District, 1984 *(continued)***

District	State Gov't.	Counties	Cities/ Towns	Special Districts	Schools	Interstate Agencies	Indian Tribes	Non-Profits	Private Universities	Individuals	For Profits	Small Businesses	All Others	Total
LOUISIANA														
1	84,287,000	2,813,023	36,935,661	7,284,545	334,002	0	0	10,881,513	16,606,390	534,485,792	1,178,327	69,777	1,338,305	696,214,334
2	79,694,730	10,169,162	34,184,729	1,738,048	478,925	0	33,907	4,242,097	6,632,886	461,827,429	12,638,741	145,983	330,697	612,117,333
3	47,826,633	10,005,723	5,964,084	1,719,699	33,373	0	724,287	2,779,118	48,164	387,189,962	873,323	119,652	160,123	457,444,142
4	76,993,201	4,091,854	17,905,678	2,861,914	4,306,400	0	0	6,591,081	234,317	528,200,978	739,293	192,011	495,494	642,612,221
5	123,512,235	7,942,993	9,112,115	71,941	69,718	0	0	10,038,657	36,057	547,491,297	241,677	0	866,363	699,383,053
6	1,394,554,341	5,314,446	20,476,944	291,500	190,707	0	563,974	10,100,223	956,830	428,121,221	385,986	930,883	183,576	1,862,070,630
7	70,088,365	7,094,917	14,416,449	1,132,357	392,501	0	414,787	10,659,132	500	449,648,395	376,008	179,617	1,206,240	555,609,269
8	143,952,595	7,179,938	10,650,777	45,258	561,753	0	298,818	13,530,813	344,374	478,856,233	755,350	20,550	178,773	656,375,232
TOTAL	2,020,909,100	54,612,055	149,646,436	15,145,262	6,367,379	0	2,035,773	68,822,635	24,859,518	3,815,821,307	17,188,705	1,658,473	4,759,571	6,181,826,213
MAINE														
1	428,317,761	2,608,458	22,358,664	6,654,673	83,225	0	0	9,207,050	2,476,985	714,920,583	1,171,454	1,023,301	1,956,256	1,190,778,410
2	126,618,500	4,494,693	31,061,466	9,262,203	12,559	0	5,010,078	5,478,949	1,380,114	655,377,184	937,563	7,490,214	2,273,962	849,397,485
TOTAL	554,936,261	7,103,151	53,420,130	15,916,876	95,784	0	5,010,078	14,685,999	3,857,099	1,370,297,767	2,109,017	8,513,515	4,230,218	2,040,175,895
MARYLAND														
1	61,721,826	14,253,968	17,329,459	2,687,645	50,000	-370	0	4,052,132	593,268	562,193,553	63,840	41,517	679,876	663,666,714
2	302,891,024	12,840,542	1,370,022	1,458,401	0	423,600	0	1,156,174	957,649	563,186,277	470,923	24,979	3,525,260	888,304,849
3	197,374,828	6,895,979	45,754,451	25,794,783	0	0	132,790	8,522,459	1,072,671	671,121,932	1,597,949	632,145	1,711,362	960,611,349
4	318,212,644	15,858,883	6,395,951	24,226,351	0	0	0	2,423,057	1,402,499	385,980,976	799,284	146,440	651,328	756,097,412
5	71,115,958	16,111,562	24,081,666	-591,461	445,000	0	0	3,144,210	105,350,533	294,304,103	1,143,828	318,273	2,816,849	518,240,520
6	98,617,125	14,357,467	33,098,037	5,011,651	0	0	-4,773	2,515,250	703,510	565,277,737	56,520	1,214,812	6,732,596	727,579,932
7	354,241,407	1,381,878	69,873,623	609,228	68,396	0	0	11,006,348	15,865,349	758,333,254	1,531,579	586,216	3,432,857	1,216,930,134
8	25,285,493	12,010,340	6,583,306	339,655	0	171,000	3,889,995	37,800,877	602,918	473,535,786	20,338,956	34,450,205	16,555,395	631,563,925
TOTAL	1,429,460,305	93,710,617	204,486,515	59,536,253	563,396	594,230	4,018,012	70,620,507	126,548,397	4,273,933,616	26,002,878	37,414,587	36,105,522	6,362,994,836
MASSACHUSETTS														
1	104,379,270	1,548,342	28,629,963	2,853,039	7,492	0	0	5,059,767	4,306,884	663,359,330	0	739,238	1,771,462	812,654,788
2	87,324,330	746,126	48,791,067	9,241,427	16,000	0	0	6,868,404	1,947,614	694,589,334	651,946	708,995	757,717	851,642,959
3	84,177,474	1,282,236	49,236,433	12,320,253	112,006	0	0	8,804,156	4,051,026	633,084,168	78,612	969,274	1,468,006	795,583,644
4	85,546,154	808,859	18,592,361	1,741,112	36,094	0	0	25,764,314	2,242,685	562,378,499	3,722	1,022,977	4,653,787	702,790,564
5	60,810,237	3,082,356	53,830,547	13,609,866	16,005	0	0	8,796,874	461,946	555,429,933	209,567	627,284	1,686,321	698,560,935
6	83,362,583	2,430,643	26,111,486	3,272,897	12,372	1,241,360	0	4,500,427	1,164,699	678,270,927	3,267,650	469,480	2,114,903	806,219,427
7	156,571,215	444,018	23,443,872	1,058,710	14,804	224,123	32,949	5,353,518	20,355,613	635,727,261	9,209,028	3,604,127	352,308	856,391,545
8	319,073,055	731,275	44,456,202	133,449,675	49,493	467,932	68,792	129,754,686	203,308,385	701,982,677	11,953,420	5,257,055	5,654,799	1,556,207,445
9	749,229,611	1,411,948	56,232,952	17,616,315	139,824	661,198	1,647,554	87,601,507	12,410,163	759,349,022	283,389	680,180	3,310,254	1,690,573,918
10	78,124,269	907,819	16,860,642	33,441,777	5,300	0	305,094	6,415,654	17,332,921	725,984,241	285,849	60,200	2,354,658	882,078,424
11	306,649,708	425,433	20,972,546	3,069,453	9,832	318,747	46,860	6,093,838	1,467,912	637,052,752	65,315	430,629	4,845,364	981,448,389
TOTAL	2,115,247,907	13,819,054	387,158,072	231,674,524	419,222	2,913,360	2,101,248	295,013,145	269,049,848	7,247,208,143	26,008,498	14,569,439	28,969,579	10,634,152,039
MICHIGAN														
1	165,223,303	12,059,513	27,340,732	83,018,952	2,074	0	90,984	6,255,590	3,146,758	646,621,608	603,899	1,405,279	23,412	945,792,104
2	182,191,545	9,793,712	20,089,347	3,094,653	950,147	0	19,594	4,045,909	2,115,063	556,965,625	65,266	809,156	497,747	780,637,764
3	904,886,705	10,592,833	37,910,829	2,746,610	503,007	0	126,485	6,742,878	1,544,549	539,016,357	122,211	225,126	2,534,418	1,506,952,008
4	90,707,668	4,464,595	15,619,926	608,387	524,875	-2,310	0	6,929,328	3,058,704	613,481,370	0	96,236	795,544	736,284,323
5	77,213,710	6,298,271	11,362,495	5,265,110	666,972	0	251,439	5,310,382	5,046,692	589,512,436	24,672	105,922	90,384	701,148,485
6	1,166,546,418	6,567,269	62,239,357	60,000	486,801	0	741,819	3,995,711	152,138	489,896,861	0	410,617	2,806	1,731,099,797
7	93,535,074	7,741,486	27,126,510	2,226,167	1,278,329	0	42,805	3,369,715	860,693	502,659,402	1,113,854	304,125	0	640,258,159
8	91,226,159	6,416,077	19,693,791	2,504,013	934,289	77,953	5,818	3,528,066	432,119	606,735,896	53,259	1,249,583	16,832	732,873,855
9	78,231,748	6,408,367	13,812,769	673,335	1,132,112	0	860,527	4,913,672	1,089,189	656,231,933	0	700,000	236,091	764,289,744

10	359,266,944	7,839,755	9,803,034	5,993,076	347,515	0	602,076	5,602,690	534,672	592,895,134	0	348,707	248,178	983,481,781
11	90,795,361	11,607,981	4,106,231	24,885,853	3,712,717	0	5,132,166	8,671,375	2,132,462	797,720,932	952,089	332,345	3,044	950,052,555
12	52,905,629	4,349,629	21,248,332	54,000	872,262	0	100,000	1,647,388	83,000	511,622,301	103,654	65,130	0	593,051,324
13	179,473,793	20,632,215	37,721,924	238,200	5,813,675	0	195,646	16,339,765	204,680	635,482,019	1,212,142	2,606,023	2,421,962	902,342,044
14	86,335,453	6,508,300	13,940,410	0	769,861	0	34,181	2,654,142	0	547,069,737	497,673	984,434	10,951	658,805,143
15	147,213,735	10,363,824	23,810,721	4,162	236,244	0	73,920	3,965,294	696,501	589,396,892	677,650	363,431	962,735	777,765,110
16	129,202,583	8,909,114	32,510,480	3,609,140	1,293,859	0	59,579	4,972,705	0	669,139,400	49,872	557,762	13,414	850,317,908
17	100,390,210	6,712,440	16,605,057	71,725	225,250	0	44,142	3,906,963	888,478	601,480,029	931,466	626,258	44,173	731,926,192
18	43,497,019	3,440,941	11,018,865	0	1,649,436	0	36,315	2,769,208	313,021	501,893,016	139,946	152,321	776,495	565,686,583
TOTAL	4,038,843,056	150,706,322	405,960,808	135,053,383	21,399,424	75,643	8,417,497	95,620,782	22,298,719	10,647,820,948	6,547,652	11,342,457	8,678,186	15,552,764,877
MINNESOTA														
1	78,967,300	6,314,965	26,794,158	7,278	786,023	0	154,241	32,793,750	2,237,258	588,666,115	362,683	57,408	2,738,660	739,879,840
2	80,277,171	11,772,377	13,405,826	-360,417	327,230	0	1,173,248	2,673,082	800,486	697,620,801	0	0	53,434	807,743,238
3	67,992,596	6,131,831	4,157,786	0	281,282	0	133,103	1,251,044	889,481	409,489,664	517,190	68,597	499,438	491,412,013
4	997,570,675	25,909	19,287,644	22,853,477	1,768,733	83,450	1,285,159	4,438,395	4,851,561	119,348,790	59,841	621,579	419,853	1,172,615,068
5	145,666,783	7,668,728	25,606,051	173,028	1,307,548	0	843,124	8,903,549	3,002,140	634,644,686	2,402,441	2,399,300	368,277	832,985,655
6	148,476,994	13,602,457	6,166,409	0	123,341	0	0	3,067,340	383,561	759,925,719	0	8,237	429,030	932,183,088
7	120,574,952	8,153,965	16,912,188	1,207,384	2,356,491	0	2,936,070	6,723,505	2,023,583	650,528,656	559,293	26,277	3,169,152	815,171,516
8	123,644,722	10,418,644	25,292,407	3,198,871	976,292	0	6,928,849	3,207,130	1,901,432	674,576,096	3,263,518	0	107,336	853,515,297
TOTAL	1,763,171,195	64,088,875	137,622,469	27,079,621	7,926,940	83,450	13,453,794	63,057,797	16,089,502	4,534,800,528	7,164,966	3,181,398	7,785,180	6,645,505,715
MISSISSIPPI														
1	77,124,373	8,324,349	12,925,758	7,739,351	114,868	0	0	8,790,128	1,615,573	545,162,606	919,655	125,522	352,294	663,194,477
2	118,641,350	19,657,659	10,421,238	410,946	1,951,675	0	0	26,907,324	319,683	553,844,377	70,211	201,648	3,396,831	735,822,942
3	83,914,464	7,910,483	13,950,611	2,979,361	435,033	0	8,090,428	11,025,511	2,479,397	526,226,489	-5,598	0	624,773	657,630,952
4	883,597,411	10,729,752	16,911,840	5,016,365	85,821,624	-7,552	175,000	29,493,786	3,962,215	561,932,252	432,186	1,986,640	447,070	1,600,498,589
5	42,650,005	12,537,924	26,218,513	1,432,358	887,297	511,500	150,000	7,258,046	1,222,707	483,150,828	118,362	168,545	1,325,870	577,631,955
TOTAL	1,205,927,603	59,160,167	80,427,960	17,578,381	89,210,497	503,948	8,415,428	83,474,795	9,599,575	2,670,316,552	1,534,816	2,482,355	6,146,838	4,234,778,915
MISSOURI														
1	64,024,956	17,019,078	21,860,554	14,741,515	27,917	0	0	14,596,559	85,440,850	964,532,010	1,633,531	143,634	3,350,953	1,187,371,557
2	76,455,971	2,918,126	28,762,799	390,546	11,801	0	0	2,365,566	1,033,750	742,610,054	791,014	1,252,355	0	856,591,981
3	30,608,528	1,223,530	9,608,873	-252,161	373,472	0	0	2,863,968	828,040	273,080,976	4,828	2,308,875	2,770,176	323,419,106
4	1,043,337,137	3,797,792	12,373,904	3,952,273	2,619,538	0	0	6,238,507	710,148	697,262,095	147,269	288,106	3,460,048	1,774,186,815
5	51,154,815	2,819,752	28,890,113	18,620	71,707	0	0	9,954,441	0	672,915,169	311,813	314,150	404,709	766,855,289
6	45,555,408	3,139,018	18,471,525	1,181,784	899,343	0	819,118	11,010,726	7,360,826	737,805,701	1,548,370	1,858,600	538,098	830,188,517
7	57,794,137	2,477,019	36,922,676	0	185,171	0	42,693	9,361,150	4,791,209	754,012,146	726,390	34,817	374,634	866,722,042
8	101,483,690	4,412,708	14,611,269	680,500	636,790	0	0	14,776,447	204,197	764,661,044	348,799	229,858	243,636	902,288,938
9	202,278,144	3,433,756	23,476,248	100,349	339,326	0	0	6,843,128	4,122,539	645,562,555	439,002	83,777	346,534	887,025,358
TOTAL	1,672,692,786	41,240,779	194,977,961	20,813,426	5,165,065	0	861,811	78,010,493	104,491,559	6,252,441,750	5,951,015	6,514,172	11,488,788	8,394,649,604
MONTANA														
1	320,631,578	15,305,288	15,742,340	7,853,796	8,975,207	90,000	6,696,583	4,589,989	3,081,130	495,400,406	8,214	25,186	690,927	879,090,644
2	42,389,777	9,946,869	14,018,747	1,497,940	11,938,835	0	11,623,928	3,018,204	1,303,689	506,167,349	2,096,996	487,135	283,108	604,772,577
TOTAL	363,021,355	25,252,157	29,761,087	9,351,736	20,914,042	90,000	18,320,511	7,608,193	4,384,819	1,001,567,755	2,105,210	512,321	974,035	1,483,863,221
NEBRASKA														
1	393,771,169	6,589,765	14,339,329	694,906	2,978,096	1,955	6,138,303	16,198,928	4,294,734	664,861,669	734,169	159,370	827,116	1,111,589,509
2	66,106,146	3,770,160	23,548,181	9,785,961	2,314,510	0	460,135	7,011,994	4,286,156	504,801,569	1,637,496	610,002	1,111,809	625,444,119
3	51,754,855	7,522,471	10,176,663	1,271,898	1,488,060	0	0	3,649,272	439,960	769,394,369	22,729	284,395	2,444,799	848,449,471
TOTAL	511,632,170	17,882,396	48,064,173	11,752,765	6,780,666	1,955	6,598,438	26,860,194	9,020,850	1,939,057,607	2,394,394	1,053,767	4,383,724	2,585,483,099

See Appendix A for a listing of the congressional districts which represent the county in which the state capital is located and congressional districts which represent only portions of a county. See Appendix B for a listing of the programs included in each recipient category.

table continues

Table 3.2 Federal Outlays to Categories of Recipients by Congressional District, 1984 *(continued)*

District	State Gov't.	Counties	Cities/ Towns	Special Districts	Schools	Interstate Agencies	Indian Tribes	Non-Profits	Private Universities	Individuals	For Profits	Small Businesses	All Others	Total
NEVADA														
1	28,165,042	21,034,476	4,653,813	-19,108	216,812	510,052	1,002,397	2,945,516	787,258	406,099,006	142,106	321,018	1,918,024	467,776,410
2	244,736,702	6,312,825	9,210,000	7,844,358	693,155	0	6,980,928	7,210,312	2,825,857	466,014,242	46,842	124,358	1,055,629	753,055,210
TOTAL	272,901,744	27,347,301	13,863,813	7,825,250	909,967	510,052	7,983,325	10,155,828	3,613,115	872,113,248	188,948	445,376	2,973,653	1,220,831,620
NEW HAMPSHIRE														
1	52,959,519	1,980,463	52,205,967	2,648,023	0	0	0	2,533,816	2,805,598	507,309,999	12,160	288,299	215,324	622,959,168
2	254,511,328	1,653,228	26,138,691	8,489,235	0	0	0	2,977,311	15,654,373	528,000,049	61,828	38,538	395,308	837,919,889
TOTAL	307,470,847	3,633,691	78,344,658	11,137,258	0	0	0	5,511,127	18,459,971	1,035,310,048	73,988	326,837	610,632	1,460,879,057
NEW JERSEY														
1	79,981,023	12,682,684	16,820,461	63,468,804	29,916	0	0	5,616,899	0	592,686,710	928,949	585,957	422,181	773,223,584
2	99,444,147	7,781,901	30,067,563	37,277,374	0	0	0	6,717,340	11,204	799,550,688	149,324	139,811	1,021,919	982,161,271
3	57,687,878	4,749,412	23,900,483	1,550,788	65,620	0	0	2,548,252	944,935	707,290,672	131,011	308,584	-1,788	799,175,847
4	1,495,639,003	8,713,627	12,382,113	6,720,088	18,903	240,000	-27,482	5,156,472	693,704	586,087,290	602,913	449,368	2,604,564	2,119,280,563
5	29,795,923	5,860,932	4,622,414	897,714	131,464	0	0	1,104,874	429,223	585,035,546	0	76,679	0	627,954,769
6	82,982,026	9,747,336	26,606,407	0	37,108	0	0	2,006,732	499,035	581,280,085	405,105	654,259	302,619	704,520,711
7	51,536,863	20,254,875	9,591,564	7,771	56,154	0	0	3,977,609	25,266,655	662,360,702	1,605,672	913,921	9,063,848	784,635,634
8	70,812,280	5,497,385	16,540,733	43,065	67,273	0	0	5,968,072	0	650,861,654	248,794	343,677	1,844,713	752,227,646
9	20,864,473	13,355,120	5,165,243	125,896	32,921	0	0	1,769,237	3,242,344	679,930,620	83,563	1,277,498	1,233,838	727,080,754
10	143,148,333	11,807,647	35,215,327	178,027,945	190,211	0	0	15,583,590	12,070,347	643,353,372	5,226,595	2,328,856	681,027	1,047,633,251
11	105,461,291	10,908,967	10,061,829	0	260,313	0	0	3,663,653	1,629,130	634,970,561	7,381	244,649	-24,461	767,183,313
12	35,572,891	6,362,375	8,021,804	193,622	76,240	0	0	2,078,931	447,051	524,154,547	993,163	1,005,816	1,072,786	579,979,226
13	55,675,248	9,694,421	6,003,735	1,581,257	321,644	0	641,771	3,066,853	4,249	712,806,822	341,012	178,880	1,031,180	791,347,072
14	114,234,777	7,595,049	73,364,689	0	105,122	0	0	4,751,432	2,644,370	693,552,740	321,956	662,854	1,711,541	898,944,529
TOTAL	2,442,836,156	135,011,730	278,364,366	289,894,324	1,392,889	240,000	614,289	64,009,945	47,882,247	9,053,922,010	11,045,437	9,170,809	20,963,968	12,355,348,171
NEW MEXICO														
1	76,460,812	5,676,107	30,161,157	129,889	2,489,561	0	6,921,273	8,605,119	1,265,876	394,855,165	245,620	1,306,911	2,618,661	530,736,151
2	55,256,225	9,159,626	19,322,604	250,200	4,834,823	0	1,460,835	4,953,728	139,808	490,524,782	394,010	422,300	584,485	587,303,426
3	512,131,154	9,516,539	10,435,503	22,207	26,294,712	0	20,816,394	6,790,991	2,082,264	360,730,292	47,278	226,044	597,156	949,690,534
TOTAL	643,848,191	24,352,272	59,919,264	402,296	33,619,096	0	29,198,502	20,349,838	3,487,948	1,246,110,239	686,908	1,955,255	3,800,302	2,067,730,111
NEW YORK														
1	92,985,906	9,930,126	8,265,289	8,762,668	0	0	3,137	8,217,067	7,154,570	418,211,905	203,699	424,939	226,796	554,386,102
2	68,236,313	5,347,512	11,589,570	-1,331,623	47,902	0	1,578	2,366,805	1,575,587	417,436,537	602,454	155,074	0	506,027,708
3	99,608,258	10,612,862	22,287,060	7,737,224	7,168	0	1,581	5,875,806	3,178,480	724,038,759	142,648	609,363	1,255,628	875,354,836
4	58,925,635	10,076,987	4,081,039	7,831,979	65,870	0	0	5,536,295	5,562,486	594,943,566	633,039	320,531	2,547	687,979,974
5	62,633,788	12,570,455	6,919,140	7,235,997	22,599	0	0	2,675,744	7,273,210	653,399,033	163,237	1,093,930	98,702	754,085,835
6	75,947,181	0	13,849	0	0	0	0	12,160,084	847,417	667,531,671	20,456	596,506	-14,436	757,102,727
7	76,256,921	0	1,780	0	0	0	0	9,483,153	1,505,793	670,438,719	396,163	756,960	0	758,839,488
8	102,387,387	463,598	19,568,773	358,015	0	0	0	11,348,627	10,464,007	661,592,268	433,782	1,650,972	756,537	809,023,966
9	75,844,156	0	316,441	0	0	0	0	7,270,122	915,597	666,616,791	20,428	104,529	0	751,088,065
10	147,632,438	136,045	1,280,993	55,303,502	0	0	0	17,729,369	2,721,692	650,377,431	87,848	1,960,991	63,473	877,293,783
11	131,554,734	0	4,400,123	0	0	0	0	10,781,655	816,753	655,969,927	161,405	5,412	140,616	803,830,626
12	140,684,303	247,702	134,355	0	150,762	0	0	16,224,530	23,878	654,426,897	0	50,000	556,956	812,499,383
13	131,744,595	0	169,621	0	37,804	0	0	11,756,821	3,340,391	656,872,759	971,964	2,365	2,127,997	807,024,316
14	79,933,427	218,040	4,149,329	0	0	0	0	13,024,454	4,426,588	590,833,215	3,354,671	2,608,797	47,971	698,596,492
15	734,747,459	2,435,748	278,812,086	386,134,179	0	45,000	300,913	140,541,287	77,619,708	679,974,566	2,202,065	1,399,580	2,086,159	2,306,298,750
16	732,818,405	1,060,220	233,667,896	17,281,317	0	0	1,114,100	17,924,006	23,851,478	679,612,804	1,208,790	299,390	4,970,855	1,713,809,261
17	613,399,265	291,728	179,489,059	17,857,144	0	0	230,442	75,994,354	74,435,012	679,627,656	2,367,088	885,907	2,502,519	1,647,080,175

18	172,829,130	235,339	88,017,484	0	144,007	0	0	34,119,743	13,595,811	683,038,125	7,076,253	10,548,692	4,399,752	1,014,004,337
19	150,086,834	1,324,432	1,326,626	31,764,617	0	0	0	22,956,806	1,224,917	659,828,774	27,122	12,121	2,905,077	871,457,327
20	95,378,556	6,019,038	12,481,445	5,544,331	834,651	0	0	14,106,205	93,944,279	688,951,100	5,823,963	2,656,191	1,523,658	927,263,416
21	84,987,639	4,898,070	27,012,154	966,587	65,812	-441,000	0	3,443,219	4,402,278	586,372,829	156,141	135,257	171,676	712,170,662
22	101,317,685	12,335,937	10,469,818	1,019,214	322,989	0	0	9,472,441	15,433,267	534,045,097	266,286	395,918	287,164	685,365,817
23	4,358,258,054	5,936,993	36,271,095	15,682,744	10,500	0	0	16,783,945	23,362,799	745,205,093	2,529,218	261,834	1,327,223	5,205,629,498
24	76,022,016	7,540,546	19,600,561	-262,553	30,659	0	0	4,597,627	943,699	617,864,633	276,482	0	0	726,613,670
25	104,844,336	10,160,196	45,182,417	1,497,055	81,894	0	0	5,197,470	2,376,686	681,814,308	0	272,344	135,018	851,561,724
26	113,077,170	13,725,612	40,336,347	839,560	29,003	0	33,765	7,917,168	4,316,708	664,497,352	1,231,291	272,313	397,236	846,673,525
27	93,737,634	8,557,847	21,208,898	6,734,177	36,731	0	456,723	5,965,974	15,241,029	608,636,770	1,688,641	229,723	741,720	763,235,866
28	114,622,114	8,915,366	49,356,034	636,290	40,037	0	0	1,284,524	53,342,911	654,246,315	-10,000	1,357,702	2,164,670	885,955,963
29	95,755,319	10,039,059	20,063,237	17,916,352	169,856	0	18,317	4,307,315	221,913	619,440,784	34,505	91,201	422,612	768,480,470
30	86,902,977	5,044,276	21,759,755	-12,234	0	0	102,480	4,816,027	49,775,087	617,732,220	-1,365	289,023	1,392,034	787,800,279
31	104,053,886	9,388,383	29,789,800	-88,426	13,176	0	82,821	3,006,192	1,543,089	670,497,988	28,087	81,641	2,087,967	820,484,605
32	113,101,098	5,871,380	35,961,927	10,950,051	23,156	0	42,285	5,738,692	1,402,313	674,394,746	454,929	472,769	284,342	848,697,689
33	117,728,404	12,772,675	24,663,100	-2,856,724	0	0	110,620	5,189,930	1,483,580	705,503,155	0	620,575	431,849	865,647,165
34	101,717,774	7,730,811	34,548,476	6,326,202	137,981	0	5,785,238	-7,722,678	8,224,242	718,877,163	349,665	2,289,975	1,288,602	879,553,451
TOTAL	9,509,760,799	183,886,984	1,293,195,577	603,827,645	2,272,557	-396,000	8,284,000	510,090,781	516,547,256	21,852,850,955	32,900,956	32,912,524	34,782,920	34,580,916,953
NORTH CAROLINA														
1	85,638,812	12,479,523	11,285,745	117,130	88,057	0	0	9,427,218	3,579,216	553,736,649	290,973	0	934,446	677,577,769
2	93,366,013	10,715,690	9,700,620	89,262	-5,031	0	106,586	26,993,626	61,309,312	569,034,204	2,245,777	211,374	1,393,736	775,161,169
3	69,160,614	12,878,919	8,900,595	626,936	51,380	0	113,862	8,376,237	934,386	464,429,640	0	0	1,027,384	566,499,953
4	1,309,410,944	11,424,660	15,053,057	1,323,572	281,396	0	399,016	8,230,089	6,860,719	446,768,948	140,265	789,143	56,788,148	1,857,469,957
5	56,634,081	7,559,076	8,890,267	-385,147	100,750	0	0	20,001,250	1,541,751	567,876,493	-77,187	37,483	332,324	662,511,141
6	53,641,522	4,551,691	7,822,798	4,548,520	80,860	0	135,844	4,752,879	2,659,040	554,956,512	0	28,854	920,928	634,099,448
7	76,284,026	11,981,157	11,247,494	513,095	143,376	0	2,222,988	10,650,148	754,465	460,842,587	0	118,066	361,416	575,118,818
8	49,642,041	7,445,103	7,210,906	64,388	18,838	0	0	6,837,514	6,429,616	598,894,489	155,969	0	1,315,899	678,014,762
9	48,926,337	6,378,266	19,951,416	277,427	11,211	0	46,593	7,461,411	3,780,894	507,146,173	506,715	235,916	227,885	594,950,244
10	43,303,989	6,388,172	4,075,393	587,569	-10,294	0	0	4,286,115	1,700,883	534,287,874	0	0	1,045,518	595,665,218
11	57,162,405	15,330,443	15,919,946	1,033,510	789	0	4,557,290	7,424,308	1,779,858	707,571,032	0	0	2,558,316	813,337,898
TOTAL	1,943,170,784	107,132,700	120,058,237	8,796,262	761,332	0	7,582,179	114,440,794	91,330,140	5,965,544,601	3,262,512	1,420,836	66,906,000	8,430,406,377
NORTH DAKOTA														
TOTAL	361,481,470	7,765,007	32,000,922	8,620,261	7,847,029	0	16,282,581	5,060,316	2,833,114	955,538,917	62,753	198,682	1,253,643	1,398,944,695
OHIO														
1	117,529,400	5,524,974	23,810,399	5,418,066	725,066	0	0	11,145,521	12,221,754	637,404,762	1,645,650	222,528	3,352,388	819,000,508
2	74,944,878	4,810,092	17,772,504	1,393,440	35,527	376,000	0	3,994,226	1,177,904	564,236,708	132,734	145,275	1,256,378	670,275,666
3	81,493,636	36,883,176	16,998,156	7,112,654	14,256	0	0	6,198,155	693,187	567,221,252	967,462	87,706	99,962	717,769,602
4	48,463,180	4,534,175	11,175,498	341,326	5,362	0	0	2,522,896	2,760,728	639,926,712	690,161	0	890,119	711,310,156
5	45,201,224	3,173,661	5,453,178	293,251	80,760	0	0	4,562,159	1,097,734	548,806,119	0	11,792	86,504	608,766,382
6	97,204,143	7,313,038	14,404,778	226,868	217,750	0	0	4,736,643	1,084,449	572,691,321	21,184	0	-40,820	697,859,353
7	64,986,278	4,036,110	15,405,344	1,198,060	1,931,389	24,900	0	2,614,873	10,065,871	524,657,737	2,850,926	1,832,823	1,511,112	631,115,423
8	50,687,175	2,078,545	19,496,073	-607,930	40,699	0	0	3,159,041	130,504	518,321,421	38,693	135,774	70,328	593,550,322
9	88,323,906	2,668,272	13,597,644	4,017,799	193,264	0	0	6,461,562	275,080	621,341,682	2,209,776	211,908	1,272,962	740,573,856
10	366,482,742	20,835,712	32,594,814	10,388,866	489,745	0	0	7,159,773	4,614,838	598,901,603	870,310	440,320	1,952,640	1,044,731,363
11	43,782,906	1,606,428	17,895,502	177,845	452,114	0	0	1,631,613	1,476,853	474,945,849	0	0	322,452	542,291,563
12	1,358,100,121	5,072,524	15,019,988	2,434,863	5,648	0	-37	7,806,641	1,191,319	468,569,741	42,426	383,709	204,721	1,858,831,664
13	38,907,167	6,777,681	22,112,611	859,464	447,381	0	0	2,065,626	2,256,240	507,667,572	786,131	32,335	1,588,910	583,501,118
14	78,556,534	5,654,769	16,639,095	5,808,608	588,295	0	0	2,428,075	201,837	619,049,169	225,042	608,178	1,355,460	731,115,064
15	935,362,356	5,685,172	10,494,562	778,000	7,474	0	-47	13,253,847	374,809	487,404,191	414,454	393,840	902,381	1,455,071,039

See Appendix A for a listing of the congressional districts which represent the county in which the state capital is located and congressional districts which represent only portions of a county. See Appendix B for a listing of the programs included in each recipent category.

table continues

Table 3.2 Federal Outlays to Categories of Recipients by Congressional District, 1984 *(continued)*

District	State Gov't.	Counties	Cities/ Towns	Special Districts	Schools	Interstate Agencies	Indian Tribes	Non-Profits	Private Universities	Individuals	For Profits	Small Businesses	All Others	Total
OHIO *continued*														
16	56,024,941	3,741,803	15,939,930	6,686,522	105,957	0	0	1,849,794	1,057,310	602,669,979	28,895	76,482	711,587	688,893,199
17	73,300,934	9,802,189	41,535,418	389,324	394,955	0	0	4,721,836	850,043	656,565,306	2,181,401	328,845	352,070	790,422,320
18	57,857,113	4,315,178	16,104,108	4,686,070	5,900	0	0	2,656,448	282,098	699,268,397	65,912	29,705	1,132,029	786,402,958
19	87,671,189	3,318,680	21,166,804	6,034,925	29,182	0	0	2,411,485	598,352	672,182,834	275,093	0	0	793,688,544
20	97,253,498	6,517,203	37,932,994	46,497,666	240,836	0	0	4,242,293	2,592,415	684,654,363	1,187,697	534,197	629,247	882,282,409
21	96,773,102	3,505,708	36,239,838	6,728,475	0	0	0	13,253,351	44,120,225	706,926,709	2,557,039	1,024,166	974,057	912,102,669
TOTAL	3,958,906,424	147,855,090	421,789,238	110,864,162	6,011,560	400,900	-84	108,875,859	89,123,550	12,373,413,425	17,190,986	6,499,583	18,624,487	17,259,555,181
OKLAHOMA														
1	42,544,949	2,284,661	29,407,533	2,359,044	1,416,427	0	2,609,161	6,103,624	3,005,020	510,900,033	478,933	307,816	-170,005	601,247,196
2	95,200,994	3,176,909	8,840,455	-309,366	8,475,008	0	25,979,913	7,072,799	1,688,342	633,696,340	4,070	43,139	441,182	784,309,784
3	119,583,656	2,870,487	17,512,306	1,124,856	5,993,856	0	12,093,601	9,019,994	2,448,777	685,263,512	0	311	471,221	856,382,577
4	112,195,238	4,756,770	19,684,427	3,337,549	3,276,091	0	3,261,589	6,641,573	877,695	483,906,689	115,149	81,476	2,228,411	640,362,658
5	557,653,024	2,340,724	31,574,155	-154,268	1,612,558	79,339	3,237,276	4,683,040	1,627,635	540,428,285	583,056	207,670	483,315	1,144,355,808
6	144,868,889	3,099,668	20,725,669	591,394	1,456,703	132,638	4,794,462	4,569,169	214,497	672,037,715	1,043,576	60,663	1,174,208	854,769,252
TOTAL	1,072,046,749	18,529,219	127,744,546	6,949,209	22,230,643	211,977	51,976,003	38,090,199	9,861,966	3,526,232,573	2,224,784	701,075	4,628,333	4,881,427,275
OREGON														
1	57,333,984	10,967,979	16,599,709	10,221,605	341,972	995,340	1,704,596	16,553,906	4,262,458	578,082,380	1,496,076	430,431	5,289,835	704,280,271
2	51,779,386	5,411,393	6,905,200	794,751	2,381,855	479,980	5,366,148	3,403,816	214,820	698,531,127	28,553	476,448	200,588	775,974,066
3	74,270,458	7,870,464	12,119,767	63,902,636	814,559	1,033,196	242,260	3,759,991	2,641,519	743,739,012	202,160	114,682	92,311	910,803,014
4	71,188,147	3,153,103	23,908,299	13,660,623	274,962	-1,437,244	60,153	7,086,875	400,193	598,078,610	227,140	0	199,528	716,800,389
5	833,879,498	7,628,833	12,398,392	4,583,912	529,468	0	2,565,613	8,083,061	1,536,920	578,057,901	339,634	287,067	908,348	1,450,798,646
TOTAL	1,088,451,473	35,031,772	71,931,367	93,163,527	4,342,816	1,071,272	9,938,769	38,887,650	9,055,910	3,196,489,029	2,293,563	1,308,628	6,690,610	4,558,656,386
PENNSYLVANIA														
1	178,333,635	0	45,134,679	148,187,397	167,310	15,257	91,247	37,652,007	106,307,398	766,090,244	711,706	472,928	5,401,222	1,288,565,030
2	197,484,828	0	36,381,805	-33,126	1,208,474	15,318	91,614	30,911,597	15,962,472	769,513,373	2,455,266	1,083,606	4,083,834	1,059,159,061
3	177,151,479	0	36,202,956	-33,058	367,185	15,287	91,426	21,879,312	2,140,285	767,132,370	733,024	1,775,856	2,145,681	1,009,601,804
4	56,712,642	4,007,886	4,903,732	10,891,500	20,978	0	-11	1,716,485	1,188,130	710,523,210	37,924	644,291	2,177,788	792,824,555
5	43,444,676	7,488,934	16,143,619	6,846,227	94,486	0	0	723,935	3,638,025	597,853,511	19,611	48,021	1,464,266	677,765,310
6	44,929,499	9,184,644	12,802,949	3,108,750	220,997	0	0	1,853,370	542,543	815,246,054	709,956	130,522	229,648	888,958,932
7	57,546,418	9,467,691	9,591,427	-3,182	853,557	1,471	8,800	4,581,295	7,032,743	674,876,254	2,252,756	865,329	277,903	767,352,463
8	29,735,273	6,663,220	15,664,416	3,107,288	-481,718	0	0	2,818,678	278,142	478,975,045	624,679	412,900	319,600	538,117,524
9	58,542,538	3,641,899	16,542,967	3,461,638	426,224	0	0	3,415,271	555,147	698,821,130	19,745	138,529	1,187,870	786,752,956
10	63,276,341	5,021,819	19,392,106	22,505,808	353,490	0	0	12,037,510	2,985,664	810,319,509	250,816	20,551	3,118,889	939,282,503
11	55,455,928	9,277,710	13,026,581	15,586,334	17,278	0	0	6,369,345	2,847,324	908,201,418	63,716	614,554	3,669,143	1,015,129,331
12	56,383,823	7,090,832	9,015,506	1,823,097	40,105	0	0	6,131,275	2,680,700	771,706,437	260,857	81,165	898,254	856,112,051
13	48,897,372	3,851,921	11,273,929	-223,657	554,533	2,666	15,944	4,747,993	2,510,410	670,489,261	396,737	602,492	494,761	743,614,364
14	126,711,352	42,357,240	91,972,231	32,577,654	714,672	0	484,765	24,436,469	26,249,000	898,792,742	3,725,900	2,323,821	1,310,616	1,251,656,461
15	38,042,461	4,491,023	14,000,803	8,724,400	321,068	0	-336	4,516,803	10,064,908	718,172,057	315,451	405,202	1,702,304	800,756,144
16	37,634,715	7,862,535	10,768,276	298,544	48,340	0	550,000	948,450	2,966,016	593,356,695	0	579,392	1,791,900	656,804,862
17	2,895,275,574	4,598,636	19,444,836	4,949,406	258,490	937,500	181,740	3,959,970	1,345,593	695,853,206	1,548,003	84,423	3,406,631	3,631,844,008
18	69,005,970	4,981,719	7,106,526	-200,816	0	0	0	2,557,771	0	684,466,955	0	0	138,996	768,057,122
19	33,139,204	5,606,434	113,412	-1,861,213	321,288	0	0	5,123,937	2,062,527	593,468,951	0	159,725	13,093,822	651,228,086
20	65,995,551	4,726,112	8,277,931	5,204	42,111	0	0	2,965,786	0	713,961,479	8,599,225	174,961	1,121,390	805,869,750
21	61,492,293	3,592,216	21,797,786	5,056,681	258,305	0	0	4,376,758	3,701,287	683,672,331	3,105,607	183,292	7,359,188	794,595,742
22	80,034,334	6,987,583	5,964,168	15,983,422	73,113	0	0	5,025,119	1,100,774	803,672,449	200,000	214,223	3,145,135	922,400,320
23	121,117,658	5,266,523	8,485,725	6,026,174	126,998	0	0	4,373,088	2,281,331	675,873,903	616,320	265,608	275,306	824,708,633
TOTAL	4,596,343,564	156,166,573	434,008,365	286,784,471	6,007,284	987,500	1,515,190	193,122,224	198,440,419	16,501,038,583	26,647,299	11,281,391	58,814,147	22,471,157,011

RHODE ISLAND														
1	317,119,733	89,005	34,022,253	1,064	0	0	90,378	10,367,484	13,573,336	660,174,135	804,883	592,877	1,828,340	1,038,663,487
2	222,347,813	257,899	22,076,895	4,871,487	0	0	183,818	8,904,317	11,248,691	608,651,613	706,562	175,021	4,426,812	883,850,929
TOTAL	539,467,546	346,904	56,099,148	4,872,551	0	0	274,196	19,271,801	24,822,027	1,268,825,748	1,511,445	767,898	6,255,152	1,922,514,416
SOUTH CAROLINA														
1	67,307,637	16,116,215	23,355,622	11,274,237	376,564	-15,441	0	13,789,554	696,701	407,798,426	19,700	1,480,044	278,131	542,477,390
2	917,803,883	10,177,600	11,310,119	620,253	27,494	0	0	13,561,649	8,921,251	453,184,948	170,828	111,774	75,837	1,415,965,636
3	56,334,832	7,856,943	13,121,545	1,325,277	221,384	-406	950,633	8,155,561	4,660,032	542,277,059	9,946	93,589	143,282	635,149,677
4	35,186,380	10,297,595	15,928,915	2,506,256	21,580	30,402	0	3,978,781	4,668,433	566,447,456	0	0	727,366	639,793,164
5	56,563,940	9,348,499	10,975,089	-252,389	-155,761	0	3,979	10,047,559	4,732,642	536,421,090	0	7,664	473,586	628,165,898
6	76,842,187	12,102,257	22,912,084	282,371	2,166,201	0	0	9,269,713	906,394	481,934,319	689,789	0	394,614	607,499,929
TOTAL	1,210,038,859	65,899,109	97,603,374	15,756,005	2,657,462	14,555	954,612	58,802,817	24,585,453	2,988,063,298	890,263	1,693,071	2,092,816	4,469,051,694
SOUTH DAKOTA														
TOTAL	317,315,537	7,824,637	34,684,672	918,613	11,355,047	0	40,049,690	6,786,356	8,023,025	877,710,453	0	435,676	68,621,817	1,373,725,523
TENNESSEE														
1	55,407,422	9,442,111	7,907,632	966,364	-34,109	0	0	6,041,516	2,888,564	568,768,893	114,858	326,987	1,345,135	653,175,373
2	70,788,023	6,080,921	19,205,257	685,822	0	0	0	6,388,481	3,860,067	586,462,787	112,348	562,155	273,624	694,419,485
3	52,647,063	4,170,947	18,120,150	3,959,160	137,991	0	0	11,084,654	4,556,223	582,784,684	136,305	23,505	2,763,483	680,384,165
4	68,085,216	5,550,888	6,914,975	1,756,042	0	0	0	13,561,396	3,008,771	592,565,364	0	220,407	238,392	691,901,451
5	1,247,751,491	556,995	19,642,219	7,894,219	0	0	367,041	46,141,412	20,271,205	543,007,749	976,996	480,212	2,006,578	1,889,096,117
6	51,084,419	4,171,344	11,224,078	-589,790	18,057	0	0	9,620,219	359,537	497,149,585	3,301,450	58,796	918,567	577,316,262
7	72,517,300	6,961,858	17,485,798	1,502,550	39,633	0	0	7,491,465	1,390,565	504,418,016	0	0	1,535,351	613,342,537
8	87,802,231	5,539,411	37,699,603	4,134,791	75,427	0	0	22,294,168	6,106,176	626,017,584	2,445,042	999,468	815,171	793,929,071
9	87,025,763	7,073,425	17,544,657	-8,727	0	0	0	9,007,691	99,781	488,082,679	0	158,950	390,702	609,374,921
TOTAL	1,793,108,929	49,547,900	155,744,369	20,300,431	236,999	0	367,041	131,631,002	42,540,889	4,989,257,341	7,086,999	2,830,480	10,287,003	7,202,939,383
TEXAS														
1	81,399,666	5,039,712	21,999,953	57,950	463,754	0	190,823	2,908,420	1,921,629	757,443,104	52,500	4,721	385,713	871,867,946
2	58,597,570	5,301,155	11,411,857	-82,246	258,768	0	1,075,572	8,685,963	305,366	638,327,432	0	59,380	4,658,524	728,599,342
3	30,472,832	2,555,113	37,823,635	2,561	41,607	0	161,537	3,674,981	1,992,194	416,974,848	1,623,484	916,831	2,107,775	498,347,398
4	50,074,008	4,383,556	20,709,361	-102,310	349,983	0	0	4,119,519	3,841,498	724,624,278	195,891	277,294	425,237	808,898,314
5	80,033,049	4,665,650	20,399,489	0	751,872	0	169,299	2,484,674	5,495,746	420,608,344	944,629	180,347	474,967	536,208,065
6	81,951,498	3,656,936	28,751,051	45,600	11,264	12,000	14,836	3,221,858	6,246,574	618,910,679	15,993	78,422	1,214,303	744,131,015
7	23,734,651	5,318,894	39,922,174	23,705,187	0	0	0	1,809,175	5,475	333,183,178	245,326	75,903	795,051	428,795,013
8	23,846,363	5,663,462	20,210,319	2,648,728	209,159	0	0	1,627,230	77,447	342,806,264	178,350	0	844,210	398,111,532
9	48,953,097	7,470,306	54,352,718	-1,269,837	138,790	0	0	3,456,249	919,962	537,147,061	43,452	195,143	733,927	652,140,868
10	3,208,907,764	2,777,637	31,932,889	-157,014	628,596	0	0	8,640,322	4,236,878	465,735,375	5,636,840	445,558	1,265,175	3,730,050,021
11	46,580,758	2,585,899	2,890,766	368,411	3,941,135	0	0	6,615,577	3,451,484	637,691,142	923,751	37,285	1,454,690	706,540,898
12	25,592,025	3,280,356	13,936,116	918,366	570,681	0	0	1,241,377	423,789	475,732,635	905,502	387,342	569,619	523,557,809
13	30,544,895	5,232,845	14,025,462	-734,501	190,352	0	0	3,334,612	152,658	713,809,204	15,000	544,791	675,700	767,791,018
14	63,940,331	6,466,071	10,802,194	-208,167	271,873	0	0	5,567,187	579,910	636,877,370	27,036	0	107,316	724,431,122
15	89,982,480	8,595,346	27,029,727	84,500	2,814,410	0	21,316	10,569,465	0	447,592,180	190,088	48,557	1,773,321	588,701,390
16	38,026,896	3,917,063	37,560,018	37,908	2,475,123	0	402,004	7,196,081	169,384	399,869,559	2,171,217	818,430	1,122,745	493,766,428
17	44,397,840	5,328,612	9,986,131	-560,176	229,422	0	0	3,367,874	1,872,522	785,815,342	186,364	3,676	642,026	851,269,633
18	31,435,341	5,673,960	16,753,727	25,247,993	0	0	0	9,073,005	39,600,723	332,881,014	560,899	346,790	2,127,321	463,700,774
19	36,301,731	5,373,325	14,953,352	-589,585	836,605	0	0	6,655,363	1,868,639	491,604,901	210,154	51,968	224,190	557,490,643
20	50,578,549	3,358,274	48,920,826	11,223,575	2,633,476	0	0	12,344,507	395,301	459,242,525	791,259	658,517	303,307	590,450,116
21	41,071,936	4,774,874	25,333,000	-508,293	3,332,155	0	0	4,477,519	5,094,490	614,689,089	317,137	369,677	304,452	699,256,037

See Appendix A for a listing of the congressional districts which represent the county in which the state capital is located and congressional districts which represent only portions of a county. See Appendix B for a listing of the programs included in each recipent category.

table continues

Table 3.2 Federal Outlays to Categories of Recipients by Congressional District, 1984 *(continued)*

District	State Gov't.	Counties	Cities/ Towns	Special Districts	Schools	Interstate Agencies	Indian Tribes	Non-Profits	Private Universities	Individuals	For Profits	Small Businesses	All Others	Total
TEXAS *continued*														
22	31,866,152	5,199,680	32,593,036	-3,193	808,936	0	0	3,764,699	4,857,921	311,355,124	45,844	1,092,956	537,076	392,118,229
23	84,493,184	8,797,092	19,540,446	85,527	1,822,499	0	0	17,022,903	75,485	463,181,043	420,698	112,467	1,117,587	596,668,932
24	29,959,587	2,713,175	15,479,753	3,572,000	117,473	0	11,391,617	2,163,066	2,200,720	425,333,904	15	400,769	121,908	493,453,987
25	42,300,227	5,839,378	18,221,256	-6,949	0	0	0	1,645,394	794,553	332,509,578	178,906	0	795,741	402,278,084
26	26,682,321	2,706,216	8,552,880	-55,852	186,364	0	0	1,459,674	187,160	421,742,849	0	61,023	27,340	461,549,975
27	66,489,740	7,437,287	17,173,131	0	1,822,321	0	0	11,052,435	752,540	433,238,193	1,052,166	0	1,030	539,018,843
TOTAL	4,468,214,492	134,111,874	621,265,268	63,720,183	24,906,618	12,000	13,427,004	148,179,129	87,520,048	13,638,926,217	16,932,502	7,167,847	24,810,251	19,249,193,432
UTAH														
1	55,796,794	6,633,358	13,123,534	516,105	1,867,437	0	958,726	2,129,170	849,948	380,827,084	5,013,621	14,984	482,748	468,213,509
2	521,448,908	11,951,120	27,953,381	174,490	866,913	2,000	8,000	3,194,973	1,239,582	404,504,474	346,172	1,834,299	294,058	973,818,370
3	53,336,537	7,016,327	12,416,617	9,473,734	2,086,847	45,000	3,895,546	2,596,368	1,651,391	349,697,723	323,871	42,581	259,081	442,841,623
TOTAL	630,582,239	25,600,805	53,493,532	10,164,329	4,821,197	47,000	4,862,272	7,920,511	3,740,921	1,135,029,281	5,683,664	1,891,864	1,035,887	1,884,873,502
VERMONT														
TOTAL	310,197,129	319,624	31,757,073	979,483	817,121	0	69,292	7,870,878	5,500,348	579,364,522	326,140	1,381,966	581,310	939,164,886
VIRGINIA														
1	57,475,819	7,510,162	12,813,328	3,421,561	0	0	-235,459	8,797,239	7,276,817	555,530,304	132,607	333,835	2,063,926	655,120,139
2	61,713,956	-76	15,118,355	6,108,779	14,400	0	0	13,147,688	355,158	385,115,627	1,326,395	490,419	462,900	483,853,601
3	1,182,381,782	15,344,573	30,631,811	5,549,242	52,461	134,304	-20,165	8,064,127	2,993,404	597,296,054	569,818	372,036	38,400,908	1,881,770,355
4	84,075,913	3,634,925	20,174,141	292,500	0	-6,039	0	2,921,977	1,187,736	554,385,222	0	0	371,568	667,037,943
5	58,894,560	5,189,173	6,995,109	3,201,360	0	0	0	6,878,990	1,682,838	628,349,055	1,172,208	0	1,156,831	713,520,124
6	48,998,908	2,810,272	10,872,265	566,725	96,356	0	0	3,372,928	5,631,120	683,751,305	797,252	223,114	2,044,668	759,164,913
7	71,506,246	7,972,162	2,935,416	6,192,578	31,228	0	0	5,057,406	2,295,056	509,689,470	329,402	97,534	694,587	606,801,085
8	20,282,080	8,362,561	8,335,363	0	0	0	433,050	7,935,256	50,000	273,141,913	1,364,374	2,102,077	275,597	322,282,270
9	102,032,781	9,119,044	20,679,118	9,028,301	75,404	11,320	0	6,708,725	3,230,625	682,553,635	63,000	99,503	604,150	834,205,606
10	18,259,684	13,841,599	7,145,189	0	129,940	0	0	95,568,252	233,490	338,703,919	6,531,048	6,826,533	277,472	487,517,126
TOTAL	1,705,621,729	73,784,395	135,700,094	34,361,046	399,789	139,585	177,426	158,452,588	24,936,244	5,208,516,504	12,286,104	10,545,051	46,352,607	7,411,273,162
WASHINGTON														
1	79,835,482	6,197,512	11,505,699	994,484	2,686,175	0	766,027	9,413,501	2,083,587	515,791,073	3,089,365	306,427	853,631	633,522,963
2	55,076,343	5,053,429	6,049,519	7,793,369	2,070,200	0	8,834,234	2,721,378	378,538	589,936,081	424,669	0	357,231	678,694,990
3	1,039,802,126	5,311,208	13,728,217	3,169,388	526,220	0	1,068,386	4,824,326	1,005,790	571,012,462	370,124	69,056	372,224	1,641,259,526
4	163,016,137	5,118,836	15,686,220	4,955,160	2,855,401	0	9,213,175	13,111,591	2,000	560,132,390	619,072	11,070	3,493,953	778,215,005
5	85,880,591	5,401,653	13,925,485	10,902,974	1,394,035	0	2,464,796	7,621,197	3,486,856	687,850,499	699,443	150,226	18,254,250	838,032,005
6	67,586,906	4,984,518	10,376,211	4,249,103	1,879,568	0	2,441,981	5,390,040	1,160,270	519,535,488	718,513	113,217	29,176	618,464,989
7	60,665,624	6,691,565	48,075,212	966,604	275,077	138,735	431,941	32,761,453	1,231,338	548,604,090	2,894,956	1,278,999	324,277	704,339,870
8	58,186,735	5,079,618	12,987,577	978,698	115,372	0	2,134,258	6,364,950	61,991	550,080,338	2,005,319	1,023,863	350,784	639,369,500
TOTAL	1,610,049,943	43,838,339	132,334,139	34,009,779	11,802,047	138,735	27,354,797	82,208,435	9,410,370	4,542,942,422	10,821,461	2,952,857	24,035,525	6,531,898,848
WEST VIRGINIA														
1	40,790,607	5,711,482	29,405,650	7,915,929	123,619	0	0	6,416,552	1,260,825	662,325,684	508,327	220,349	1,379,893	756,058,917
2	65,111,053	10,608,454	13,274,427	13,219,242	261,112	-1,970	0	7,305,962	2,274,110	627,123,612	-401,770	539,828	747,562	740,061,622
3	719,730,234	8,649,631	15,397,664	9,456,069	17,052	333,900	0	4,431,835	205,885	617,279,679	604,879	149,953	236,346	1,376,493,127
4	58,925,779	7,322,378	10,269,921	7,457,047	0	0	0	8,446,762	2,047,745	721,337,775	3,139,190	237,925	1,468,648	820,653,170
TOTAL	884,557,673	32,291,945	68,347,662	38,048,287	401,783	331,930	0	26,601,111	5,788,565	2,628,066,750	3,850,626	1,148,055	3,832,449	3,693,266,836

WISCONSIN														
1	101,041,405	8,405,241	20,232,817	525,409	44,387	0	0	1,843,395	709,142	597,936,557	1,591,300	93,789	920,542	733,343,985
2	1,144,115,731	8,918,673	14,556,108	150,389	406,818	0	603	6,413,746	924,981	538,239,152	1,901,104	653,767	659,458	1,716,940,531
3	127,834,744	6,518,126	13,817,699	536,918	177,615	0	114,797	3,993,891	1,245,091	648,505,039	0	0	256,427	803,000,346
4	126,098,370	40,815,163	18,766,831	29,806,256	119,433	0	0	5,202,404	3,606,130	623,719,232	-408,866	393,594	787,740	848,906,287
5	157,072,349	6,549,363	19,464,993	36,850,289	0	0	271,988	9,542,814	14,255,115	672,337,315	267,810	1,756,785	1,116,705	919,485,526
6	90,251,972	5,947,173	26,826,035	434,607	298,061	0	3,536	2,160,801	872,786	678,061,273	0	409,773	90,249	805,356,265
7	129,250,487	12,789,634	16,578,585	102,600	328,887	0	6,965,316	6,020,215	2,515,731	682,254,763	842,954	210,275	48,398	857,907,845
8	97,521,252	14,231,697	14,010,289	51,900	1,046,351	0	9,792,980	3,219,193	541,603	639,381,168	0	0	44,710	779,841,143
9	50,671,244	5,804,680	9,578,487	2,110,179	111,647	0	0	1,107,136	1,415,024	527,313,264	0	0	152,701	598,264,362
TOTAL	2,023,857,555	109,979,750	153,831,844	70,568,548	2,533,199	0	17,149,220	39,503,595	26,085,602	5,607,747,763	4,194,302	3,517,983	4,076,930	8,063,046,292
WYOMING														
TOTAL	265,110,536	13,215,468	17,044,467	6,518,500	5,816,358	0	1,662,970	3,172,296	404,241	414,302,616	329,473	51,584	1,177,388	728,805,897
U.S. TOTAL	87,876.3 mil	3,354.8 mil	9,491.1 mil	3,351.0 mil	481.9 mil	12.6 mil	492.8 mil	4,601.2 mil	2,886.8 mil	261,818.6 mil	561.3 mil	275.5 mil	765.8 mil	375,969.7 mil

See Appendix A for a listing of the congressional districts which represent the county in which the state capital is located and congressional districts which represent only portions of a county. See Appendix B for a listing of the programs included in each recipent category.

Table 3.3 Federal Outlays to Categories of Recipients by Congressional District, 1985

District	State Gov't.	Counties	Cities/ Towns	Special Districts	Schools	Interstate Agencies	Indian Tribes	Non-Profits	Private Universities	Individuals	For Profits	Small Businesses	All Others	Total
ALABAMA														
1	71,090,309	4,943,781	16,599,682	1,802,492	531,993	0	2,146,780	4,085,041	1,996,243	659,329,372	3,415,126	500,000	1,978,752	768,419,571
2	1,316,512,900	4,844,870	23,889,483	-67,257	1,795,789	0	0	4,201,023	2,000,521	678,537,812	922,501	0	1,690,779	2,034,328,421
3	80,367,218	5,371,737	16,400,750	202,770	389,693	0	0	5,023,595	21,283,539	660,276,861	950,005	49,113	741,181	791,056,462
4	65,660,230	6,863,584	11,803,816	1,714,197	70,855	0	0	3,322,724	372,226	767,990,487	369,877	0	412,072	858,580,069
5	59,446,104	5,607,767	14,151,444	4,324,199	332,326	0	0	2,701,853	2,866,190	602,381,162	843,470	13,332	800,093	693,467,940
6	111,541,941	16,142,621	16,990,649	6,154,518	591,348	0	0	4,879,278	8,429,500	788,775,705	11,768,681	494,889	2,177,452	967,946,582
7	87,918,767	7,817,712	14,420,693	507,681	153,217	0	0	5,717,809	6,515,919	683,928,960	130,030	49,580	382,544	807,542,913
TOTAL	1,792,537,469	51,592,072	114,256,518	14,638,600	3,865,221	0	2,146,780	29,931,323	43,464,138	4,841,220,359	18,399,690	1,106,914	8,182,873	6,921,341,957
ALASKA														
TOTAL	436,915,795	38,763,110	61,365,162	5,660,703	588,970	0	33,656,617	23,358,000	1,368,011	198,516,936	1,095,132	1,404,265	958,937	803,651,638
ARIZONA														
1	276,751,138	6,250,041	23,934,997	798,268	3,941,961	0	1,579,429	2,723,715	6,750,436	971,459,732	10,983,247	790,126	2,239,096	1,308,202,185
2	197,900,716	10,525,308	29,620,113	6,709,207	6,318,898	0	13,734,316	5,676,514	2,731,652	843,391,543	7,128,480	596,639	3,058,371	1,127,391,756
3	17,662,124	3,178,897	18,987,347	42,475	2,563,033	0	4,542,100	4,446,357	237,322	366,561,660	1,058,368	26,715	594,712	419,901,110
4	342,671,278	6,470,623	35,061,238	1,187,388	16,688,659	0	59,746,771	1,701,557	3,131,309	859,954,688	5,215,069	166,627	1,444,184	1,333,439,393
5	30,258,624	7,844,077	12,162,508	15,058	2,604,021	0	21,614	2,356,830	790,386	792,829,326	1,210,073	433,725	1,476,918	852,003,162
TOTAL	865,243,880	34,268,946	119,766,202	8,752,396	32,116,572	0	79,624,231	16,904,973	13,641,106	3,834,196,950	25,595,238	2,013,832	8,813,282	5,040,937,607
ARKANSAS														
1	124,807,765	7,767,600	12,751,182	869,509	1,888,899	0	453,697	4,967,780	1,985,161	1,025,816,204	124,313	30,518	2,317,754	1,183,780,382
2	673,031,123	4,006,683	31,513,741	1,990,702	1,106,600	0	295,989	2,885,315	6,793,376	704,964,628	893,085	718,567	2,550,395	1,430,750,204
3	72,465,306	5,645,628	16,130,482	804,558	955,698	0	0	2,195,137	5,108,387	848,267,556	6,763,332	28,116	1,720,390	960,084,590
4	109,146,691	6,292,695	8,446,704	278,319	251,627	0	0	4,141,041	2,239,113	912,585,233	248,082	10,000	4,996,273	1,048,635,778
TOTAL	979,450,885	23,712,606	68,842,109	3,943,088	4,202,824	0	749,686	14,189,273	16,126,037	3,491,633,621	8,028,812	787,201	11,584,812	4,623,250,954
CALIFORNIA														
1	139,885,552	13,738,878	8,982,561	4,149,867	2,505,803	0	3,465,530	4,759,489	143,001	801,779,075	2,591,790	24,582	7,015,606	989,041,734
2	119,456,303	13,106,923	8,828,421	622,179	3,796,569	0	1,076,287	2,512,825	2,301,073	958,927,761	615,294	108,097	1,018,914	1,112,370,647
3	3,552,229,608	8,036,360	27,714,363	40,352,808	2,074,718	0	3,115,796	10,545,699	1,573,839	526,282,187	1,936,171	342,800	877,618	4,175,081,966
4	839,911,356	10,817,792	13,851,100	198,590	7,635,649	0	1,084,097	2,246,624	2,063,340	535,491,333	357,389	865,490	1,128,365	1,415,651,124
5	161,103,630	8,863,448	61,019,053	9,850,020	3,560,402	0	26,077	9,261,631	5,158,043	1,011,773,900	1,491,487	178,535	6,127,118	1,278,413,344
6	82,353,025	16,032,164	16,223,156	616,656	4,887,810	0	-6,773	12,546,466	2,931,226	679,302,440	658,871	1,126,631	-265,515	816,406,158
7	82,449,742	9,969,907	6,980,561	7,458,119	1,912,178	0	0	1,891,695	198,132	594,021,814	266,322	207,185	1,576,327	706,931,982
8	202,445,968	23,341,270	16,797,326	38,837,079	3,207,331	0	607,344	30,231,371	8,031,503	656,569,380	676,696	1,961,350	1,358,795	984,065,413
9	109,239,451	6,722,183	18,279,090	-1,738,760	2,397,638	0	401,141	1,502,686	913,002	672,165,775	1,721,923	133,076	1,534,629	813,271,833
10	92,283,841	8,108,778	14,621,931	82,840,236	3,255,646	0	482,128	1,459,659	128,375	532,365,566	432,706	60,222	2,606,147	738,645,233
11	50,078,749	21,597,852	8,547,940	-180,390	1,331,861	0	11,808	3,477,588	27,547,108	603,792,694	676,131	1,407,646	1,635,416	719,924,404
12	68,505,326	4,760,963	13,028,158	134,096	3,385,864	0	64,655	23,331,933	118,438,282	460,505,593	5,582,427	1,816,583	2,661,819	702,215,700
13	70,409,727	6,081,274	9,217,747	-101,205	1,449,285	0	94,281	2,297,609	3,904,789	453,790,735	870,599	110,320	3,570,220	551,695,380
14	82,948,222	9,769,630	6,205,478	5,086,311	2,828,089	0	804,965	2,255,800	8,459,822	707,966,585	92,879	86,278	508,845	827,012,905
15	96,543,548	9,527,282	14,122,843	3,127,914	3,909,216	0	21,759	4,228,248	157,690	556,364,312	1,534,166	379,514	1,861,956	691,778,448
16	90,151,797	8,448,322	65,646,805	6,638,152	9,107,192	0	282,702	2,235,503	1,154,057	592,563,979	1,595,307	241,168	1,319,816	779,384,801
17	149,798,097	15,384,172	12,218,591	866,314	3,901,646	0	1,557,616	2,741,907	111,816,113	732,226,340	4,082,639	138,993	4,408,626	1,039,141,054
18	319,238,817	23,330,722	9,133,102	851,386	1,973,341	0	699,366	529,746	685,768	1,044,763,649	1,861,935	27,327	1,413,596	1,404,508,755
19	76,583,073	9,109,667	8,886,092	5,258,282	5,055,902	0	300,334	1,390,716	2,379,092	471,856,607	1,722,223	973,918	827,299	584,343,206
20	100,922,108	13,936,299	9,559,096	90,688,322	9,344,674	0	2,320,462	16,003,803	1,729,096	726,170,462	3,912,838	75,016	3,538,944	978,201,121
21	100,049,451	8,821,053	11,570,095	-621,474	846,706	0	423,382	2,745,690	1,134,892	660,395,966	1,632,730	338,322	2,982,103	790,318,916
22	114,033,387	8,226,271	18,162,576	3,088,892	2,992,535	0	118,493	8,636,712	9,235,633	612,979,007	1,877,860	593,712	3,049,319	782,994,397
23	223,693,079	8,272,838	11,832,495	3,194,818	491,704	0	118,367	4,794,474	19,226,051	612,452,393	3,189,007	18,142	1,205,802	888,489,170

24	113,944,974	8,271,297	12,910,327	8,567,789	515,729	0	133,345	11,225,455	1,823,898	611,718,339	3,451,112	733,410	3,575,784	776,871,458
25	122,277,240	11,746,420	13,999,026	3,191,198	840,083	0	517,191	7,799,074	23,828,824	611,769,800	2,939,907	645,089	1,908,579	801,462,431
26	99,872,615	7,262,024	10,717,803	2,804,460	704,643	0	103,905	4,280,690	710,795	537,077,062	1,209,031	56,907	1,070,318	665,870,254
27	113,714,524	13,933,038	37,140,676	3,193,306	1,601,822	-2,494	118,311	3,988,414	4,634,964	611,564,951	11,639,600	941,250	1,476,326	803,944,689
28	115,120,440	8,480,345	13,025,145	3,191,776	491,400	0	110,734	11,082,047	78,246,049	611,566,543	2,920,382	563,286	1,195,870	845,994,018
29	113,722,525	41,287,739	14,560,824	3,193,531	538,013	0	118,320	2,066,640	1,194,019	611,554,460	1,255,533	40,637	1,594,962	791,127,203
30	113,927,468	8,255,161	25,929,246	4,488,331	3,498,949	0	118,114	2,329,985	1,872,986	610,498,136	10,166,383	592,586	1,402,387	783,079,733
31	116,571,821	8,274,758	27,482,688	3,177,448	3,829,902	0	118,395	1,420,568	6,397,267	611,947,365	4,453,745	532,637	1,809,397	786,015,990
32	114,722,018	8,301,259	13,177,494	3,933,261	1,098,526	0	118,774	5,969,072	843,974	613,948,803	2,629,498	574,099	1,026,616	766,343,395
33	118,465,402	9,479,384	17,498,887	3,196,573	3,213,150	0	118,432	6,443,693	9,522,146	612,164,724	2,321,926	110,011	1,889,902	784,424,231
34	118,226,073	8,277,777	19,569,328	3,396,725	4,855,078	0	118,438	2,768,115	818,948	612,167,681	1,471,265	329,680	1,533,698	773,532,806
35	97,991,230	12,390,379	11,091,511	3,806,219	6,828,398	0	812,979	645,674	6,080,606	647,589,541	609,155	28,714	1,069,534	788,943,941
36	410,413,257	27,371,367	15,931,111	200,730	1,730,778	0	266,512	1,146,412	419,412	1,196,619,118	1,035,548	547,965	1,698,696	1,657,380,906
37	298,320,649	12,220,820	8,320,887	9,299,431	2,091,146	0	2,108,086	996,204	1,147,836	575,534,167	278,055	357,423	1,086,583	911,761,287
38	39,891,343	8,387,198	7,507,261	-76,636	956,799	0	78,100	134,619	702,900	494,694,121	1,939,210	129,767	1,603,383	555,948,066
39	44,203,675	4,236,294	12,586,555	-88,329	1,373,079	0	78,166	427,257	3,125,912	495,139,328	4,187,953	40,587	1,454,494	566,764,970
40	49,346,187	4,684,184	11,857,074	2,827,871	3,970,295	0	78,094	20,148,806	4,477,400	494,909,517	1,705,694	1,194,282	1,362,619	596,562,024
41	105,815,283	4,096,254	7,596,234	7,415,336	7,090,939	0	86,918	98,529,197	6,345,805	453,329,162	5,112,792	1,950,377	908,608	698,276,906
42	85,547,899	6,738,970	11,174,188	5,012,397	1,406,666	0	102,426	15,866,813	1,215,928	564,756,212	3,497,937	698,726	880,435	696,898,599
43	72,415,336	6,761,361	14,563,588	-644,176	8,461,574	0	921,213	18,353,280	1,323,905	633,402,483	1,581,759	210,632	1,032,116	758,383,071
44	85,118,790	6,547,143	12,523,733	-128,233	2,485,136	0	131,691	8,060,021	712,144	685,597,926	745,354	47,365	2,223,242	804,064,314
45	90,701,781	7,470,156	14,475,889	-113,697	5,779,506	0	2,981,340	2,853,892	1,174,823	677,724,544	6,163,209	61,487	2,601,934	811,874,865
TOTAL	9,564,644,391	500,477,375	725,068,056	371,063,523	145,213,375	-2,494	26,409,302	378,163,804	485,930,468	28,779,781,537	110,694,436	21,601,825	86,367,251	41,195,412,849
COLORADO														
1	793,944,586	6,728,438	24,130,852	19,311,116	1,620,055	45,598	1,124,625	25,115,195	11,786,578	694,589,587	3,801,713	482,473	2,093,371	1,584,774,187
2	63,469,032	3,243,817	10,924,994	0	386,480	0	0	8,358,056	4,009,702	353,066,338	981,746	5,100,140	1,731,259	451,271,564
3	69,841,690	7,736,548	25,601,365	1,375,084	935,792	0	1,890,730	4,416,382	515,327	580,385,672	968,207	175,136	12,580,847	706,422,780
4	81,095,915	8,347,495	8,028,830	50,922	1,931,318	0	0	4,630,757	3,440,584	643,290,370	167,213	724,311	990,754	752,698,470
5	27,504,748	3,276,318	6,527,799	59,000	6,226,717	0	0	4,176,057	3,486,112	387,345,200	896,347	183,916	1,212,342	440,894,556
6	23,982,565	2,856,309	5,834,916	188,962	497,977	0	0	2,954,309	121,572	292,437,101	683,677	536,228	1,769,933	331,863,551
TOTAL	1,059,838,536	32,188,926	81,048,757	20,985,084	11,598,339	45,598	3,015,355	49,650,755	23,359,875	2,951,114,268	7,498,903	7,202,204	20,378,507	4,267,925,107
CONNECTICUT														
1	793,307,309	15,436	26,020,045	12,698,007	3,375	0	0	5,730,674	5,197,444	690,265,550	1,303,174	1,033,655	2,327,216	1,537,901,885
2	58,009,008	18,745	17,162,508	262,848	0	0	508,158	2,947,685	8,049,752	521,878,986	582,115	0	1,334,997	610,754,803
3	84,856,592	2,687	51,538,221	749,776	0	0	0	6,248,010	120,473,101	734,178,130	1,640,237	1,312,483	1,829,258	1,002,828,495
4	81,518,376	0	15,375,673	19,653,005	0	69,547	0	3,754,642	4,670,295	679,847,455	1,936,301	234,062	1,741,621	808,800,977
5	82,193,632	103,491	16,035,829	369,395	41,250	0	185,363	2,242,868	626,362	714,956,814	14,701	50,762	2,168,650	818,989,117
6	97,370,960	0	30,151,649	1,555,632	0	0	91	1,148,912	92,829	699,331,672	84,137	54,196	2,123,760	831,913,838
TOTAL	1,197,255,877	140,359	156,283,924	35,288,663	44,625	69,547	693,612	22,072,791	139,109,783	4,040,458,608	5,560,665	2,685,158	11,525,502	5,611,189,114
DELAWARE														
TOTAL	246,273,713	12,975,317	18,657,760	2,477,252	526,588	71,798	190,065	5,261,569	3,708,964	733,838,300	369,489	409,646	2,915,717	1,027,676,178
DISTRICT OF COLUMBIA														
TOTAL	511,761,483	150,037	50,177,758	5,286,482	197,261	350,429	45,696,081	264,956,412	391,424,671	748,965,419	7,528,819	9,222,112	63,840,228	2,099,557,192
FLORIDA														
1	49,898,437	5,651,999	6,510,648	530,998	5,833,361	0	0	1,292,361	56,266	601,905,023	118,750	-62,582	1,414,041	673,149,302
2	1,932,901,619	6,602,891	8,123,815	2,057,375	2,243,048	322,338	720,388	6,366,682	1,395,183	685,946,754	158,536	82,062	3,964,388	2,650,885,080
3	57,256,760	1,232,006	12,281,525	25,457,345	1,903,394	0	0	286,299	4,573,480	658,956,823	763,260	20,930	489,577	763,221,399
4	43,303,574	9,282,900	10,210,531	83,727	866,708	0	0	1,162,618	11,824,837	1,059,328,764	591,896	447,732	136,926	1,137,240,214
5	34,946,888	10,114,004	30,879,337	5,612,941	569,901	0	0	601,718	875,780	687,380,457	1,658,282	97,782	752,167	773,489,257
6	103,048,522	7,201,977	7,046,689	1,793,306	3,472,649	0	0	1,595,921	2,170,747	1,118,423,539	141,656	405,448	835,510	1,246,135,964

See Appendix A for a listing of the congressional districts which represent the county in which the state capital is located and congressional districts which represent only portions of a county. See Appendix B for a listing of the programs included in each recipent category.

table continues

Table 3.3 **Federal Outlays to Categories of Recipients by Congressional District, 1985 *(continued)***

District	State Gov't.	Counties	Cities/ Towns	Special Districts	Schools	Interstate Agencies	Indian Tribes	Non-Profits	Private Universities	Individuals	For Profits	Small Businesses	All Others	Total
FLORIDA *continued*														
7	60,689,205	20,760,422	8,048,220	9,296,843	1,367,472	0	0	4,611,790	3,650,658	754,280,026	11,512,596	229,986	313,280	874,760,498
8	27,106,325	8,167,248	9,013,217	8,799,533	595,417	0	0	1,430,507	1,008,108	1,495,015,840	292,179	167,509	-11,464	1,551,584,418
9	31,986,449	6,638,726	9,560,285	3,894	786,255	0	0	126,011	2,154,393	1,299,394,047	977,331	41,895	123,648	1,351,792,934
10	31,857,721	31,771,653	14,145,720	3,037,832	614,898	0	0	1,540,990	2,400,643	1,033,795,070	277,570	31,747	790,452	1,120,264,297
11	33,404,622	10,132,397	17,911,426	5,366,893	236,354	0	0	2,270,288	1,373,395	832,803,983	1,185,491	186,158	459,789	905,330,796
12	32,707,018	7,674,290	6,144,863	3,834,841	648,507	0	589,343	7,490,379	282,693	1,179,849,564	573,374	93,320	166,045	1,240,054,238
13	17,910,373	7,963,035	2,899,671	614,405	622,803	0	125,920	243,745	2,897,245	1,474,603,513	240,111	302,076	113,328	1,508,536,225
14	24,788,864	8,049,509	6,989,229	1,526,340	527,576	0	1,069,436	293,495	370,449	1,166,398,738	2,305,527	668,651	793,255	1,213,781,068
15	43,690,797	34,785,991	18,625,796	928,124	575,280	0	147,685	2,279,704	3,747,686	1,027,710,103	4,087,944	736,086	199,674	1,137,514,870
16	30,916,109	6,948,477	4,429,417	3,633	130,493	0	2,644,742	23,352	305,943	948,231,033	567,195	0	2,023,878	996,224,272
17	65,633,717	7,972,384	6,787,060	25,858,929	446,968	0	111,259	955,985	4,813,577	752,834,285	1,957,226	884,419	2,282,381	870,538,189
18	69,733,930	16,159,473	9,800,423	12,448	447,144	0	111,303	2,028,547	1,783,571	753,306,881	3,620,677	0	1,777,535	858,781,929
19	61,272,549	9,020,375	3,277,038	10,907	1,287,326	0	97,521	462,242	7,526,471	736,172,655	1,227,961	0	1,566,571	821,921,618
TOTAL	2,753,053,480	216,129,757	192,684,910	94,830,313	23,175,552	322,338	5,617,596	35,062,634	53,211,126	18,266,337,100	32,257,561	4,333,219	18,190,981	21,695,206,566
GEORGIA														
1	93,366,993	10,832,812	13,793,481	69,850	1,340,362	0	0	4,579,213	1,112,301	635,848,594	1,059,423	1,028,621	158,562	763,190,212
2	150,228,760	8,951,130	14,564,015	120,165	611,585	0	0	4,014,871	742,904	654,639,025	493,992	0	282,161	834,648,608
3	71,538,243	6,204,918	10,448,648	1,771,090	1,273,017	0	0	4,144,534	2,347,418	577,919,918	434,398	546,094	1,051,611	677,679,889
4	313,786,708	6,116,920	5,453,255	125,731,195	-79,933	0	34,274	3,271,619	9,094,091	286,785,346	1,687,892	1,154,154	4,645,015	757,680,535
5	972,536,671	16,285,797	8,599,094	54,000	940,489	0	217,016	13,633,862	60,298,241	860,914,358	3,537,641	264,063	4,885,840	1,942,167,073
6	56,452,644	7,204,848	3,660,294	18,502	207,690	0	24,152	931,598	529,673	543,238,729	362,046	0	755,303	613,385,480
7	34,695,112	5,680,822	3,721,648	138,182	191,009	0	0	1,354,590	2,545,847	523,306,477	143,030	781,158	101,509	572,659,384
8	106,289,416	9,509,526	22,458,175	-66,851	130,912	0	0	2,072,278	4,567,470	676,686,805	0	0	765,891	822,413,622
9	53,449,784	5,921,930	24,414,341	673,792	118,451	0	0	3,059,206	2,820,887	588,616,959	50,337	0	6,080	679,131,768
10	97,059,235	8,030,043	9,541,289	212,874	1,772,007	0	0	11,202,031	6,950,653	554,785,599	435,946	44,400	1,939,702	691,973,778
TOTAL	1,949,403,566	84,738,746	116,654,241	128,722,799	6,505,589	0	275,443	48,263,802	91,009,486	5,902,741,810	8,204,705	3,818,490	14,591,674	8,354,930,350
HAWAII														
1	324,898,403	-230,007	26,632,318	100,979	0	100,000	3,664,770	7,962,979	4,137,737	413,291,393	951,156	1,594,151	2,107,947	785,211,826
2	140,626,048	10,923,235	7,301,765	2,430	0	0	0	4,461,258	959,037	496,882,164	241,095	126,791	538,669	662,062,492
TOTAL	465,524,451	10,693,228	33,934,083	103,409	0	100,000	3,664,770	12,424,237	5,096,774	910,173,557	1,192,251	1,720,942	2,646,616	1,447,274,318
IDAHO														
1	315,679,837	-19,142	15,309,486	272,622	3,054,835	0	2,918,268	4,812,678	2,687,612	611,171,715	98,717	267,628	1,149,047	957,403,302
2	76,830,756	5,577,385	8,710,870	255,148	4,724,546	55,000	1,703,558	2,322,989	220,390	560,152,574	211,247	437,855	489,138	661,691,457
TOTAL	392,510,593	5,558,243	24,020,356	527,770	7,779,381	55,000	4,621,826	7,135,667	2,908,002	1,171,324,289	309,964	705,483	1,638,185	1,619,094,759
ILLINOIS														
1	126,980,553	3,638,315	96,355,575	234,425,922	327,279	0	301,046	11,466,177	85,404,614	639,334,458	7,108,826	779,477	2,800,175	1,208,922,417
2	108,092,978	3,582,528	20,565,371	19,755	327,207	0	111,021	1,697,866	1,207,060	638,455,184	2,309,684	73,398	639,152	777,081,203
3	108,602,501	3,583,281	31,435,655	19,507	339,573	0	111,045	937,438	2,294,798	638,886,305	2,128,906	229,333	771,853	789,340,195
4	65,980,312	2,363,145	16,639,961	166,173	440,148	0	48,006	1,620,730	1,949,477	542,504,716	759,157	110,608	343,345	632,925,778
5	108,505,094	3,582,804	51,466,026	19,757	347,232	0	111,030	856,663	2,095,763	638,501,437	1,848,451	36,030	838,150	808,208,436
6	45,975,049	2,304,548	21,225,568	51,479	501,690	0	41,357	2,363,594	1,168,782	519,072,557	586,338	49,540	1,476,572	594,817,075
7	113,323,596	8,011,635	77,585,706	944,420	522,295	0	111,044	61,969,769	15,156,271	638,809,737	5,601,825	6,023,718	2,803,418	930,863,434
8	108,386,021	3,583,239	20,521,396	31,459	2,817,972	0	111,044	3,288,335	1,144,287	638,579,767	1,466,646	328,054	826,199	781,084,419
9	108,570,442	3,583,833	24,018,618	157,576	327,326	0	111,062	8,173,786	79,605,351	639,022,934	1,547,504	2,180,643	935,594	868,234,669
10	77,627,203	4,968,291	20,935,638	8,935	1,995,732	0	50,211	3,899,271	3,994,186	533,960,535	1,028,604	2,234	1,163,564	649,634,403
11	110,932,251	3,582,970	20,812,391	19,757	356,239	0	219,035	854,829	2,608,383	638,530,976	2,590,211	300,789	1,204,601	782,012,433
12	56,771,284	4,166,445	14,286,703	8,357	345,846	0	46,968	183,953	980,008	560,529,439	660,164	134,435	2,137,458	640,251,061

13	54,382,880	2,428,991	14,834,452	8,662	4,470,002	0	48,681	1,422,789	2,643,047	531,031,115	640,571	554,473	426,828	612,892,491
14	34,404,877	2,483,285	21,743,287	1,213,878	687,049	0	431	825,890	3,597,639	613,889,109	557,712	69,493	1,225,208	680,697,858
15	58,267,562	3,011,271	25,933,141	4,633,398	2,533,685	0	0	1,354,589	4,769,947	707,604,852	148,809	74,463	333,011	808,664,728
16	35,086,898	1,692,966	11,172,951	1,254,027	1,456,645	0	0	2,474,457	696,014	714,079,186	89,815	24,560	923,867	768,951,385
17	39,952,740	1,770,016	11,002,127	4,506,108	1,280,592	0	0	2,500,719	4,061,404	811,685,310	113,142	57,773	1,003,361	877,933,292
18	47,332,768	2,111,208	10,718,363	5,017,718	133,107	0	0	772,567	8,288,498	733,027,585	686,863	26,014	356,412	808,471,102
19	131,468,255	3,597,000	9,154,429	2,200,147	3,002,730	0	0	1,631,940	4,433,556	774,448,974	144,632	670,223	119,700	930,871,586
20	2,432,668,553	2,094,894	26,296,553	3,537,517	689,249	0	0	875,491	1,675,193	840,499,215	1,110,864	181,643	522,351	3,310,151,523
21	96,646,724	4,652,510	7,570,190	573,000	6,812,273	0	0	1,520,482	2,339,487	718,759,435	7,914,920	220,788	736,287	847,746,097
22	93,971,021	2,635,033	14,358,227	1,081,499	730,490	0	0	4,505,531	1,751,753	872,511,447	443,440	50,000	856,656	992,895,097
TOTAL	4,163,929,559	73,428,208	568,632,326	259,899,052	30,444,363	0	1,421,981	115,196,866	231,865,518	14,583,724,273	39,487,085	12,177,687	22,443,763	20,102,650,682
INDIANA														
1	83,991,237	10,141,004	27,479,974	6,729,117	588,745	0	0	2,250,896	801,465	605,114,128	738,268	183,559	2,139,695	740,158,086
2	140,656,904	4,640,398	12,225,061	6,768,685	203,127	0	0	271,339	3,187,424	672,998,064	395,020	1,126,685	642,271	843,114,979
3	47,506,335	3,688,441	13,867,667	8,509,053	261,629	0	0	1,197,575	15,759,559	699,952,541	150,514	6,113	407,783	791,307,211
4	41,273,850	3,202,818	6,451,936	5,200,587	104,021	0	15,868	1,710,928	2,823,615	666,238,477	149,477	38,182	-1,344	727,208,415
5	44,338,482	4,137,482	32,536,244	108,750	1,532,711	0	0	115,537	7,563,675	677,915,354	6,350,307	42,073	433,831	775,074,447
6	191,649,755	2,148,176	9,984,981	3,937,895	74,936	0	0	2,634,230	4,140,270	676,843,556	239,933	315,034	1,059,385	893,028,150
7	98,967,855	4,731,133	18,281,875	2,080,025	35,439	0	0	14,216,018	3,884,464	717,771,598	52,312	517,641	940,974	861,479,334
8	70,822,394	3,566,527	16,407,066	1,975,052	338,222	0	0	482,863	5,052,849	744,277,526	108,390	331,052	460,043	843,821,984
9	115,429,810	4,653,722	8,111,819	1,643,522	645,780	0	0	1,456,705	862,177	600,761,152	0	328,480	3,481,866	737,375,035
10	835,012,084	390,107	19,421,758	6,602,519	82,389	0	0	6,303,180	5,650,823	653,211,302	767,055	50,000	996,041	1,528,487,258
TOTAL	1,669,648,706	41,299,808	164,768,381	43,555,205	3,866,999	0	15,868	30,639,272	49,726,321	6,715,083,699	8,951,276	2,938,819	10,560,545	8,741,054,900
IOWA														
1	56,204,516	4,945,415	8,502,072	640,684	2,232,640	0	0	1,947,131	5,683,659	697,547,247	954,755	1,044,360	1,109,580	780,812,059
2	42,533,231	4,508,393	12,740,981	2,414,096	104,705	0	0	1,027,537	7,782,412	668,533,315	742,158	177,197	1,599,905	742,163,930
3	116,712,261	4,692,687	6,104,351	2,716,214	1,416,937	0	392,199	3,609,060	5,430,547	707,264,983	561,850	80,566	1,065,972	850,047,627
4	697,721,660	4,378,677	42,914,604	4,396,928	221,655	0	0	3,528,472	8,636,241	612,699,253	733,316	464,138	2,787,775	1,378,482,719
5	57,515,601	6,359,566	12,407,275	115,681	133,398	0	0	1,648,798	4,357,796	840,640,847	143,099	238,999	1,598,668	925,159,728
6	47,969,278	5,216,467	13,211,941	1,237,349	167,702	0	0	1,554,649	8,102,001	896,574,334	1,582,738	77,375	905,243	976,599,077
TOTAL	1,018,656,547	30,101,205	95,881,224	11,520,952	4,277,037	0	392,199	13,315,647	39,992,656	4,423,259,979	4,717,916	2,082,635	9,067,143	5,653,265,140
KANSAS														
1	37,629,830	6,064,074	8,851,318	1,953,885	172,711	0	0	841,427	2,656,702	1,110,027,607	850,884	26,431	52,113	1,169,126,982
2	576,716,684	5,356,351	10,833,178	2,623,121	9,741,473	0	1,435,892	2,555,362	5,688,443	554,492,259	765,932	124,065	1,010,457	1,171,343,217
3	48,205,924	1,620,086	28,151,214	9,802,463	172,022	0	0	8,112,566	2,578,066	519,946,094	1,044,652	219,014	743,188	620,595,289
4	46,546,550	2,344,218	8,555,288	6,606,900	522,098	0	167,126	4,337,409	1,204,015	616,991,619	4,443,694	31,352	1,609,992	693,360,261
5	50,052,693	6,654,327	10,907,053	444,305	367,083	0	0	1,881,913	7,604,408	824,598,161	118,590	88,026	349,481	903,066,040
TOTAL	759,151,681	22,039,056	67,298,051	21,430,674	10,975,387	0	1,603,018	17,728,677	19,731,634	3,626,055,740	7,223,752	488,888	3,765,231	4,557,491,789
KENTUCKY														
1	76,354,940	6,822,944	7,088,522	448,874	717,854	0	0	880,499	1,373,183	759,677,117	280,324	19,066	1,271,681	854,935,004
2	64,998,073	4,948,483	10,077,549	3,481,619	1,212,792	0	0	4,513,797	2,063,957	532,161,601	1,183,561	36,684	98,048	624,776,164
3	76,231,659	11,766,949	20,446,853	20,245,342	566,069	0	0	11,703,595	15,074,628	627,394,579	1,474,910	972,172	354,646	786,231,402
4	56,514,532	11,556,273	12,156,474	2,055,440	181,449	0	0	1,197,495	683,752	605,273,159	196,576	0	38,602	689,853,752
5	117,060,425	7,688,078	6,859,365	846,932	130,590	0	0	2,786,790	7,131,071	729,089,319	104,696	91,478	583,490	872,372,234
6	1,158,075,198	5,229,620	17,512,852	4,585,423	233,321	0	0	3,021,704	8,243,174	533,109,673	311,212	786,966	1,621,219	1,732,730,362
7	101,692,055	8,950,086	4,529,282	1,028,500	196,226	0	0	8,623,980	3,231,410	690,324,810	64,698	0	23,466	818,664,513
TOTAL	1,650,926,882	56,962,433	78,670,897	32,692,130	3,238,301	0	0	32,727,860	37,801,175	4,477,030,258	3,615,977	1,906,366	3,991,152	6,379,563,431

See Appendix A for a listing of the congressional districts which represent the county in which the state capital is located and congressional districts which represent only portions of a county. See Appendix B for a listing of the programs included in each recipent category.

table continues

Table 3.3 **Federal Outlays to Categories of Recipients by Congressional District, 1985 *(continued)***

District	State Gov't.	Counties	Cities/ Towns	Special Districts	Schools	Interstate Agencies	Indian Tribes	Non-Profits	Private Universities	Individuals	For Profits	Small Businesses	All Others	Total
LOUISIANA														
1	84,518,489	1,432,790	23,746,574	10,105,326	2,188,425	0	0	8,129,735	20,661,285	541,590,877	2,477,999	193,045	1,374,301	696,418,845
2	83,248,876	7,306,164	19,494,858	1,143,920	841,444	0	34,878	2,253,616	16,045,352	515,526,740	4,026,293	285,405	2,015,293	652,222,839
3	51,310,860	10,216,038	22,554,311	253,065	295,428	0	541,180	892,085	0	496,052,542	325,115	0	505,722	582,946,346
4	78,472,829	4,294,081	17,332,735	2,014,608	4,864,625	0	0	1,521,180	520,130	601,089,567	1,426,969	122,656	1,525,935	713,185,315
5	133,103,961	7,075,475	7,734,302	742,584	273,178	0	0	3,017,004	72,512	710,625,699	647,406	0	543,678	863,835,800
6	1,365,408,204	4,264,431	16,731,017	8,263,623	580,370	0	565,176	1,726,070	2,924,119	485,993,399	1,929,565	1,098,324	107,277	1,889,591,575
7	74,994,129	7,249,323	7,206,282	973,398	541,475	0	476,439	6,021,204	-3,386	567,335,646	1,806,952	25,445	3,051,428	669,678,336
8	162,872,894	9,238,575	7,274,893	54,450	393,440	0	55,064	3,479,100	821,720	572,860,322	934,369	17,487	342,275	758,344,589
TOTAL	2,033,930,242	51,076,877	122,074,973	23,550,974	9,978,385	0	1,672,737	27,039,994	41,041,733	4,491,074,792	13,574,668	1,742,362	9,465,908	6,826,223,645
MAINE														
1	436,981,630	2,228,652	24,841,848	7,549,396	117,207	0	13,098	8,379,678	8,633,669	761,402,536	601,814	1,286,024	6,881,209	1,258,916,760
2	156,478,915	3,538,058	30,546,199	811,169	97,294	0	5,879,740	5,076,828	5,342,787	729,909,658	757,415	7,745,786	2,364,171	948,548,021
TOTAL	593,460,545	5,766,710	55,388,047	8,360,565	214,501	0	5,892,838	13,456,506	13,976,456	1,491,312,194	1,359,229	9,031,810	9,245,380	2,207,464,781
MARYLAND														
1	67,241,178	16,531,909	11,797,614	-471,849	49,572	0	0	2,454,177	785,394	625,444,783	150,582	28,700	1,972,567	725,984,627
2	381,730,595	16,197,539	661,134	0	0	0	0	549,262	1,492,260	613,196,650	835,714	51,180	202,073	1,014,916,408
3	223,215,484	7,859,344	46,012,121	23,952,117	0	0	72,530	6,486,452	2,636,786	731,621,321	2,328,768	1,245,890	1,430,881	1,046,861,694
4	375,313,408	28,090,935	3,332,739	12,180,960	0	737,100	0	1,073,924	1,424,525	420,709,689	403,002	302,648	11,307	843,580,238
5	79,164,220	13,446,457	952,689	0	0	0	0	107,887,611	14,285,259	322,863,129	1,622,441	312,071	5,201,287	545,735,164
6	102,157,726	13,477,533	5,828,408	516,931	0	0	0	465,179	2,075,299	618,547,303	231,798	847,693	6,347,715	750,495,585
7	333,108,551	1,629,686	74,954,813	175,000	207,939	0	0	11,415,503	20,017,736	826,987,404	2,434,154	143,085	2,845,060	1,273,918,930
8	27,813,444	14,756,029	5,986,135	0	0	179,850	12,786,519	30,413,411	581,252	532,598,297	12,139,315	39,264,635	27,513,114	704,032,001
TOTAL	1,589,744,606	111,989,433	149,525,654	36,353,159	257,511	916,950	12,859,049	160,745,519	43,298,511	4,691,968,575	20,145,774	42,195,902	45,524,004	6,905,524,647
MASSACHUSETTS														
1	124,617,468	1,581,837	15,268,383	1,418,992	0	0	0	3,013,598	11,927,035	726,560,045	160,564	513,986	512,096	885,574,002
2	98,228,521	818,068	48,506,740	7,206,549	108,082	0	0	4,799,133	5,692,973	753,060,541	1,291,444	70,020	3,191,062	922,973,133
3	103,267,882	607,562	24,296,112	5,134,092	0	0	0	9,346,162	13,042,638	687,521,853	387,076	475,284	3,472,774	847,551,435
4	119,838,944	731,346	28,838,008	1,130,739	36,094	0	0	5,967,896	6,677,823	621,582,826	231,335	1,499,560	1,070,811	787,605,382
5	69,418,552	4,899,753	25,180,468	9,086,543	36,860	0	0	6,897,364	1,316,441	612,301,695	472,191	1,877,853	1,110,217	732,597,938
6	93,716,011	1,766,705	24,928,357	7,346,243	21,945	1,076,700	0	1,877,118	2,892,396	742,568,379	1,751,657	208,405	1,921,764	880,075,680
7	163,835,191	391,895	26,841,039	5,462,424	0	4,145	31,815	2,155,641	30,375,135	659,463,956	1,317,500	4,601,336	1,688,310	896,168,386
8	360,167,494	588,446	42,596,733	65,691,536	40,091	96,654	66,426	144,478,723	248,418,354	762,040,051	15,422,438	4,604,317	5,899,729	1,650,110,991
9	821,136,694	899,392	45,487,255	21,324,167	294,235	1,186,228	500,378	90,572,303	26,355,741	837,953,911	1,238,355	560,550	6,380,936	1,853,890,143
10	90,301,968	1,252,592	24,529,661	4,160,570	4,490	0	238,961	7,392,634	25,505,751	793,276,667	313,698	206,913	2,051,194	949,235,099
11	349,957,799	300,816	33,645,181	9,673,982	-3,250	5,895	45,248	3,917,483	4,571,877	670,184,911	572,156	154,578	3,720,267	1,076,746,943
TOTAL	2,394,486,525	13,838,410	340,117,937	137,635,838	538,547	2,369,621	882,828	280,418,055	376,776,164	7,866,514,834	23,158,412	14,772,802	31,019,160	11,482,529,133
MICHIGAN														
1	168,393,564	3,616,431	41,811,315	26,150,269	827,532	0	171,034	2,496,110	5,790,786	712,845,853	1,254,355	588,635	32,189	963,978,073
2	213,167,843	6,249,323	20,094,689	235,145	1,758,671	0	19,593	2,411,188	4,178,825	611,498,315	570,043	829,976	24,212	861,037,822
3	1,166,726,703	3,687,594	23,543,466	4,299,408	1,339,147	0	369	4,220,174	3,703,565	593,351,081	380,494	114,231	1,513,401	1,802,879,633
4	92,328,034	5,484,572	11,217,544	271,729	1,284,445	55,000	157,024	4,718,223	5,639,501	681,768,685	15,410	9,125	525,298	803,474,590
5	85,832,045	10,510,993	11,443,514	3,991,452	1,464,994	0	341,914	2,938,021	9,827,704	642,802,744	2,707,236	38,584	906,352	772,805,554
6	860,146,860	4,716,252	29,593,235	60,000	398,111	0	817,098	1,587,544	2,562,689	536,124,473	682,931	155,676	12,292	1,436,857,159
7	93,824,445	7,899,592	25,956,254	2,235,307	3,822,239	0	96,607	802,996	1,691,445	548,353,860	1,687,593	292,436	2,747	686,665,520
8	91,274,902	5,757,092	24,190,426	4,403,661	479,211	0	0	842,729	1,936,471	672,623,876	234,816	1,079,015	311,786	803,133,986
9	85,180,614	7,679,147	10,248,071	537,734	1,284,442	0	641,046	3,261,768	1,091,913	717,593,891	0	0	191,281	827,709,908

10	362,873,011	5,984,528	12,161,763	-324,663	310,076	0	773,804	5,035,286	1,381,632	661,845,068	319,072	74,214	180,601	1,050,614,391
11	98,516,230	9,121,403	20,212,301	1,044,008	7,148,549	0	5,464,930	7,870,220	2,957,595	862,076,865	1,034,002	4,894	166,802	1,015,617,799
12	50,572,483	5,713,207	13,693,118	54,000	1,307,103	0	0	470,292	0	550,195,389	373,380	51,605	101,031	622,531,608
13	187,208,990	8,154,793	51,503,032	-34,261	7,578,809	0	200,031	13,137,822	2,065,634	712,867,929	3,148,123	1,118,850	32,189	986,981,941
14	87,754,379	3,949,462	18,435,368	-100,330	1,848,090	0	34,180	1,041,941	176,847	597,586,552	1,697,977	539,070	1,774,369	714,737,904
15	153,996,215	3,589,755	41,347,560	1,732,487	1,217,368	0	73,918	1,152,268	861,164	659,994,110	1,593,030	52,993	262,768	865,873,635
16	130,294,295	4,604,829	59,459,283	1,911,568	3,219,518	0	59,577	4,569,412	552,318	661,054,354	1,094,568	191,636	21,079	867,032,438
17	102,294,614	3,869,903	25,027,757	-129,567	481,266	0	44,140	3,367,439	1,760,313	637,771,389	2,342,994	179,997	37,875	777,048,121
18	44,270,462	5,471,354	6,777,822	0	3,052,158	0	53,808	2,059,258	789,159	553,190,078	115,426	11,794	184,039	615,975,358
TOTAL	4,074,655,691	106,060,230	446,716,516	46,337,947	38,821,728	55,000	8,949,075	61,982,691	46,967,560	11,613,544,514	19,251,448	5,332,731	6,280,310	16,474,955,441
MINNESOTA														
1	83,868,847	6,542,800	24,938,400	7,278	447,629	0	349,820	35,859,231	2,931,346	695,647,860	388,338	35,878	407,469	851,424,897
2	85,738,845	10,518,993	12,023,973	228,302	1,099,151	0	564,887	1,238,897	2,312,711	879,699,308	0	47,435	289,656	993,762,158
3	71,216,186	6,120,841	4,556,340	0	217,191	0	160,205	394,969	3,740,800	475,784,711	577,437	598,823	1,332,836	564,700,338
4	954,154,830	84,546	31,055,601	38,172,918	2,938,900	0	1,175,112	4,110,668	15,660,092	28,155,443	782,312	203,691	711,350	1,077,205,463
5	150,155,835	6,402,821	12,671,108	10,785	1,159,096	0	1,412,259	9,801,140	8,275,467	612,992,945	1,804,040	1,228,662	289,353	806,203,511
6	159,150,366	11,376,010	3,824,082	0	193,289	0	0	1,361,694	852,449	935,755,039	6,023	49,700	265,184	1,112,833,835
7	129,490,983	8,965,967	14,497,433	2,647,610	4,292,406	0	5,458,923	5,329,313	6,675,072	778,035,601	697,491	95,910	3,990,670	960,177,378
8	131,663,554	11,064,725	12,825,574	2,215,631	1,363,515	0	7,672,786	3,022,527	2,077,542	718,842,600	966,520	50,000	522,927	892,287,901
TOTAL	1,765,439,447	61,076,701	116,392,511	43,282,524	11,711,177	0	16,793,992	61,118,439	42,525,479	5,124,913,506	5,222,162	2,310,099	7,809,445	7,258,595,482
MISSISSIPPI														
1	65,511,954	8,255,300	8,940,557	1,488,962	122,592	0	0	6,003,419	3,517,560	657,733,803	1,059,947	60,182	197,303	752,891,580
2	102,551,113	21,779,612	10,680,516	22,788	3,204,091	0	0	16,365,243	555,722	750,208,312	3,199,799	0	2,799,486	911,366,682
3	76,112,468	8,015,424	4,380,933	6,574,635	1,568,291	0	9,070,720	3,932,208	4,643,056	598,254,197	63,344	7,100	457,161	713,079,537
4	963,688,164	9,305,452	12,107,221	253,929	563,119	0	0	14,455,883	6,209,469	636,038,981	1,188,482	1,983,849	2,037,187	1,647,831,737
5	42,580,551	17,831,204	21,538,429	1,202,230	2,047,656	164,500	0	4,635,012	2,295,117	537,903,526	149,840	155,356	615,434	631,118,855
TOTAL	1,250,444,251	65,186,993	57,647,655	9,542,544	7,505,749	164,500	9,070,720	45,391,765	17,220,924	3,180,138,820	5,661,412	2,206,487	6,106,571	4,656,288,391
MISSOURI														
1	70,027,717	10,808,733	22,937,969	16,498,103	58,580	14,849,378	0	15,508,903	94,077,741	1,029,034,753	2,566,690	235,430	3,453,672	1,280,057,670
2	78,791,133	4,432,824	34,309,670	1,708,681	39,616	0	0	3,299,058	2,253,153	798,199,990	3,709,367	805,988	1,309,972	928,859,452
3	36,328,320	1,142,859	11,020,133	878,249	225,433	0	0	2,934,299	1,415,133	292,317,942	727,362	545,181	173,982	347,708,892
4	1,042,463,267	3,355,674	10,790,792	3,008,671	5,956,821	0	0	2,726,807	621,209	775,553,673	254,938	0	1,463,416	1,846,195,266
5	59,203,230	3,014,472	30,160,684	336,668	218,134	350,000	0	10,282,957	50,322	702,677,499	276,332	0	3,418,604	809,988,904
6	48,246,153	3,312,612	25,309,646	752,304	2,083,952	0	595,179	8,467,260	11,664,935	835,719,056	3,236,121	0	333,059	939,720,277
7	64,590,146	2,356,483	22,020,975	-28,768	356,133	0	42,112	2,835,245	7,331,677	820,968,949	703,596	10,000	210,780	921,397,328
8	108,408,178	4,050,966	14,417,658	681,263	852,169	0	0	5,983,377	702,188	876,231,272	638,010	262,467	933,239	1,013,160,787
9	206,301,260	3,316,485	12,568,449	580,247	331,788	0	25,000	4,940,863	9,089,009	721,650,028	518,897	194,434	2,082,133	961,598,594
TOTAL	1,714,359,403	35,791,109	183,535,978	24,415,417	10,122,625	15,199,378	662,291	56,978,769	127,205,367	6,852,353,161	12,631,314	2,053,501	13,378,857	9,048,687,170
MONTANA														
1	362,855,689	12,313,812	7,106,316	5,751,648	14,159,350	0	5,394,799	8,770,021	4,331,637	518,178,302	51,567	354,152	888,694	940,155,987
2	54,990,816	7,553,708	14,849,473	1,096,147	17,605,177	0	10,677,341	3,171,579	2,338,817	691,607,256	2,080,013	510,928	582,024	807,063,279
TOTAL	417,846,505	19,867,520	21,955,789	6,847,795	31,764,527	0	16,072,140	11,941,600	6,670,454	1,209,785,558	2,131,580	865,080	1,470,718	1,747,219,266
NEBRASKA														
1	414,658,445	5,374,934	10,675,002	802,906	5,300,947	0	5,674,293	4,843,909	7,515,353	826,439,891	1,087,490	211,342	1,456,499	1,284,041,011
2	70,103,504	3,499,610	12,124,282	4,619,739	7,205,249	0	375,444	6,750,592	8,039,598	554,467,135	1,319,965	7,168	1,773,448	670,285,734
3	74,585,526	8,341,302	8,157,942	1,735,797	2,180,711	0	0	1,779,268	614,276	1,096,028,762	102,196	0	1,580,099	1,195,105,879
TOTAL	559,347,475	17,215,846	30,957,226	7,158,442	14,686,907	0	6,049,737	13,373,769	16,169,227	2,476,935,788	2,509,651	218,510	4,810,046	3,149,432,624

See Appendix A for a listing of the congressional districts which represent the county in which the state capital is located and congressional districts which represent only portions of a county. See Appendix B for a listing of the programs included in each recipent category.

table continues

Table 3.3 Federal Outlays to Categories of Recipients by Congressional District, 1985 *(continued)*

District	State Gov't.	Counties	Cities/ Towns	Special Districts	Schools	Interstate Agencies	Indian Tribes	Non-Profits	Private Universities	Individuals	For Profits	Small Businesses	All Others	Total
NEVADA														
1	30,016,433	8,163,683	6,593,140	6,408,908	1,701,636	0	451,319	932,709	1,391,087	456,614,355	1,511,890	390,256	1,501,818	515,677,236
2	264,594,466	6,835,610	8,760,878	9,714,032	2,377,510	-5,732	6,073,342	4,371,534	1,322,808	516,423,248	269,363	259,184	292,342	821,288,583
TOTAL	294,610,899	14,999,293	15,354,018	16,122,940	4,079,146	-5,732	6,524,661	5,304,243	2,713,895	973,037,603	1,781,253	649,440	1,794,160	1,336,965,819
NEW HAMPSHIRE														
1	64,084,499	2,720,891	24,355,924	3,172,747	0	0	0	872,198	5,478,774	544,288,691	140,048	294,268	735,838	646,143,878
2	255,880,721	1,789,752	17,030,851	1,240,215	0	0	0	2,523,148	23,641,628	581,047,548	123,940	1,083,474	850,351	885,211,628
TOTAL	319,965,220	4,510,643	41,386,775	4,412,962	0	0	0	3,395,346	29,120,402	1,125,336,239	263,988	1,377,742	1,586,189	1,531,355,506
NEW JERSEY														
1	76,552,753	9,585,508	12,113,301	245,500	12,825	0	0	3,105,332	14,278	597,926,374	1,068,924	53,656	1,939,587	702,618,037
2	100,859,211	42,989,584	45,811,133	0	0	0	0	4,927,694	11,204	923,010,351	1,076,957	3,628	2,364,915	1,121,054,677
3	55,884,287	8,272,204	25,523,408	595,600	174,387	0	0	1,663,426	2,496,098	780,542,072	740,264	120,645	1,392,312	877,404,702
4	1,572,598,346	8,167,788	10,822,190	0	532,924	238,000	0	2,698,550	1,523,953	642,442,021	383,091	494,013	851,879	2,240,752,755
5	34,519,436	8,744,293	4,548,975	0	260,982	0	0	564,349	451,978	616,239,317	401,154	614,922	250,167	666,595,574
6	89,271,821	10,195,875	28,928,441	5,501,605	122,666	0	0	751,713	1,388,976	618,581,832	1,695,443	665,247	1,491,302	758,594,921
7	51,391,839	7,239,617	19,598,431	14,993	65,082	0	0	7,559,635	7,888,115	729,307,976	1,211,818	710,776	1,517,907	826,506,189
8	68,471,365	5,503,395	23,258,649	-305,043	2,728	0	0	3,342,411	1,287,694	701,863,574	1,112,061	276,916	1,182,465	805,996,215
9	19,781,220	9,577,802	5,279,612	0	138,992	0	0	421,957	6,872,504	739,257,008	730,077	629,396	906,306	783,594,875
10	147,013,572	11,950,163	40,986,283	189,964,016	78,229	0	0	14,106,762	6,246,526	723,316,008	8,283,120	2,004,078	3,617,136	1,147,565,894
11	108,118,398	11,386,193	1,791,229	0	72,518	0	0	96,008	4,244,535	700,693,790	135,514	180,791	109,848	826,828,824
12	49,359,214	6,788,236	3,832,607	841,943	163,501	0	0	16,992,190	28,253,063	646,752,519	2,380,426	670,884	1,857,993	757,892,576
13	55,771,126	12,364,608	1,730,968	0	3,400,835	0	438,012	1,088,964	1,263	794,989,745	1,249,158	213,355	1,792,663	873,040,696
14	111,880,921	13,203,829	46,164,913	681,808	326,993	0	0	837,410	5,403,119	774,817,878	1,337,474	352,717	3,160,576	958,167,638
TOTAL	2,541,473,509	165,969,094	270,390,140	197,540,422	5,352,662	238,000	438,012	58,156,401	66,083,306	9,989,740,464	21,805,481	6,991,024	22,435,056	13,346,613,572
NEW MEXICO														
1	92,784,006	5,353,907	29,313,408	99,000	2,524,404	0	3,678,794	5,558,057	1,778,363	439,401,850	1,465,674	853,864	2,230,990	585,042,317
2	69,486,682	7,741,929	16,504,700	780,387	5,635,932	0	1,855,570	1,596,245	902,598	569,754,545	430,792	332,125	928,779	675,950,284
3	494,483,682	10,850,403	9,762,937	1,781,373	59,089,005	0	20,564,427	5,409,814	2,446,772	410,966,735	575,177	425,545	1,039,952	1,017,395,822
TOTAL	656,754,370	23,946,239	55,581,045	2,660,760	67,249,341	0	26,098,791	12,564,116	5,127,733	1,420,123,130	2,471,643	1,611,534	4,199,721	2,278,388,423
NEW YORK														
1	100,157,701	10,670,184	6,668,607	9,312,429	90,808	0	69,740	9,957,727	174,130	451,995,933	490,767	207,519	1,642,579	591,438,124
2	70,277,839	6,748,518	8,490,873	0	67,985	0	68,073	1,266,775	1,258,709	451,142,053	1,491,981	128,113	112,252	541,053,171
3	109,781,685	12,551,021	16,126,329	20,798,001	14,047	0	68,208	2,471,845	6,016,261	797,318,791	629,994	700,187	-93,010	966,383,359
4	64,610,057	10,575,067	3,339,015	13,626,268	61,557	0	0	890,752	9,276,479	673,181,110	1,091,556	198,381	1,237,529	778,087,769
5	62,768,696	11,729,186	5,820,915	13,456,986	27,606	0	0	1,397,633	7,078,555	666,895,618	1,438,904	472,750	59,107	771,145,957
6	73,542,404	449,689	4,489	0	0	0	0	6,050,069	1,618,219	725,828,896	549,306	702,465	1,876,235	810,621,771
7	73,842,337	0	30,767	0	0	0	0	2,503,441	2,183,594	728,866,583	580,579	462,032	-61,300	808,408,032
8	95,628,676	1,121,920	585,762	624,585	4,979	0	0	2,840,390	31,780,715	731,343,781	1,211,001	691,689	1,362,705	867,196,203
9	73,517,919	0	1,045	0	0	0	0	1,223,839	1,767,562	724,868,791	541,220	106,796	2,295	802,029,467
10	109,143,389	407,250	822,121	12,831,228	0	0	0	4,755,595	1,330,918	712,650,710	1,278,917	1,808,037	51,294	845,079,459
11	127,596,860	7,195	1,084,860	0	0	0	0	4,235,305	2,139,210	719,629,392	1,475,286	32,631	1,259,487	857,460,227
12	137,716,740	7,179	828,278	0	0	0	0	5,837,678	930,279	717,987,896	1,194,493	310,389	1,196,917	866,009,849
13	127,784,469	136,505	831,359	0	72,956	0	0	6,676,734	5,232,616	720,658,348	1,219,730	22,569	2,258,868	864,894,155
14	77,216,881	121,342	18,427,793	0	137,565	0	0	9,237,682	6,433,502	636,548,859	2,401,175	1,886,385	45,082	752,456,266
15	780,535,796	1,218,525	294,782,695	534,519,062	0	36,156	175,605	139,462,597	127,453,579	730,479,998	12,691,054	1,875,475	4,880,539	2,628,111,081
16	774,478,328	2,297,390	243,379,015	0	0	36,156	810,590	23,499,448	33,900,555	730,671,101	10,948,758	-26,456	1,599,934	1,821,594,817
17	640,507,107	141,330	190,004,919	6,912,000	0	27,689	-8,106	37,890,143	79,780,783	740,508,506	8,254,375	1,093,766	1,199,247	1,706,311,759

18	155,203,865	0	55,592,256	752,000	23,222	0	0	15,940,592	18,409,807	777,146,994	8,065,745	5,173,687	6,910,683	1,043,218,852
19	137,944,841	1,660,775	280,111	12,590,833	0	0	0	12,375,479	2,720,341	752,128,745	1,147,051	95,229	2,678,742	923,622,147
20	110,483,990	6,861,362	11,010,172	17,505,215	85,565	0	0	14,346,402	93,539,353	719,911,758	12,344,332	1,344,171	2,146,653	989,578,973
21	86,797,876	5,267,288	6,677,262	0	47,767	0	-12,406	1,304,923	4,034,996	630,437,377	146,977	57,326	307,976	735,067,361
22	102,390,672	12,606,997	17,516,341	214,472	630,716	0	0	6,921,274	19,791,666	589,124,493	374,005	110,814	275,816	749,957,265
23	4,252,232,050	6,312,649	35,813,600	6,506,096	78,329	0	0	18,295,061	26,307,808	785,967,480	3,068,627	224,944	939,766	5,135,746,411
24	77,676,078	8,208,538	17,961,831	89,100	39,605	0	0	3,593,061	2,517,579	687,022,229	394,485	0	1,085,084	798,587,591
25	109,950,484	12,318,140	23,961,288	2,241,521	205,172	0	0	3,569,870	7,343,206	747,482,355	162,560	141,856	778,556	908,155,008
26	118,570,071	13,581,132	32,282,650	1,198,594	26,523	0	2,890,192	4,582,795	5,292,290	721,551,463	778,640	406,334	-14,669	901,146,015
27	97,968,237	9,337,447	28,851,347	5,050,293	41,525	0	303,356	4,819,598	35,971,349	658,159,571	1,451,243	332,677	991,027	843,277,671
28	113,214,480	9,423,462	22,344,866	4,536,276	210,596	0	0	2,038,034	75,976,046	701,997,750	124,447	971,664	621,996	931,459,616
29	99,517,220	8,369,458	16,836,765	19,655,910	165,839	0	0	3,759,369	10,901,200	677,055,581	418,869	0	654,468	837,334,680
30	89,759,007	5,122,357	18,002,515	786,992	34,666	0	44,344	1,916,492	63,136,667	669,876,015	919,076	250,000	2,035,786	851,883,916
31	105,051,622	6,235,547	21,454,080	-121	106,816	0	84,901	2,047,678	3,520,007	728,681,092	454,406	275,037	459,724	868,370,790
32	115,978,263	7,918,086	28,903,999	14,379,247	60,039	0	50,999	4,863,209	4,374,675	727,905,767	850,608	359,945	1,164,230	906,809,066
33	122,717,849	10,681,016	22,064,667	867,360	38,758	0	110,617	3,404,286	3,867,480	755,437,262	620,389	682,995	526,035	921,018,716
34	106,264,940	8,806,228	49,284,392	1,791,951	134,690	0	5,041,740	10,386,199	13,926,085	775,554,944	779,067	837,958	260,976	973,069,171
TOTAL	9,500,828,429	190,892,783	1,200,066,987	700,246,298	2,407,330	100,000	9,697,852	374,361,974	709,986,220	23,766,017,240	79,589,625	21,937,365	40,452,610	36,596,584,713
NORTH CAROLINA														
1	85,224,756	13,373,066	11,186,766	414,284	43,621	0	0	3,101,630	3,554,785	626,526,656	265,870	0	860,645	744,552,079
2	97,817,981	10,189,533	19,643,172	43,785	25,341	0	88,783	24,573,399	79,714,703	632,588,699	1,635,912	136,005	730,157	867,187,470
3	65,028,634	12,785,952	7,528,274	179,831	48,806	0	116,126	3,022,072	1,612,010	516,042,728	0	0	1,391,699	607,756,132
4	1,448,335,370	8,404,047	13,402,990	10,272,536	110,883	0	293,633	4,481,039	18,868,808	501,290,298	651,925	1,220,892	7,088,752	2,014,421,173
5	53,585,089	7,333,051	14,639,766	91,840	78,259	0	0	17,497,670	3,849,362	626,345,334	0	81,292	413,217	723,914,880
6	54,645,501	4,828,939	8,991,482	1,364,673	0	0	99,041	1,730,679	6,147,770	607,784,682	228,315	3,525,107	214,399	689,560,588
7	75,302,821	14,814,098	15,242,344	1,112,565	143,800	0	1,595,173	5,050,071	1,772,701	508,919,842	457,615	50,720	473,374	624,935,124
8	45,911,864	6,571,182	4,876,908	266,911	-29,281	0	0	5,081,833	5,872,030	660,460,390	26,490	0	532,709	729,571,035
9	48,801,566	6,856,175	16,439,281	15,750	11,211	0	101,225	3,016,307	8,218,445	558,521,945	535,602	37,549	810,235	643,365,290
10	42,913,391	6,740,400	4,053,164	706,892	-48,852	0	0	1,818,035	3,895,517	584,948,389	0	0	64,382	645,091,318
11	53,700,632	11,707,009	5,406,017	1,602,663	111,578	0	3,118,415	2,318,606	3,798,899	782,775,391	0	49,860	1,710,201	866,299,271
TOTAL	2,071,267,605	103,603,452	121,410,163	16,071,730	495,366	0	5,412,396	71,691,341	137,305,030	6,606,204,354	3,801,729	5,101,425	14,289,770	9,156,654,360
NORTH DAKOTA														
TOTAL	346,019,091	7,267,300	24,186,680	5,194,196	13,043,861	0	13,726,925	3,827,726	6,663,506	1,304,179,058	627,021	228,108	573,501	1,725,536,973
OHIO														
1	120,649,554	22,974,060	20,686,283	7,054,754	603,381	0	0	8,956,120	8,962,637	683,355,496	2,796,400	267,922	1,071,129	877,377,735
2	73,746,199	6,493,369	14,719,399	16,422	169,462	0	0	1,960,688	5,029,711	612,327,221	389,886	-2,689	644,491	715,499,537
3	78,908,910	5,835,158	33,760,282	9,097,620	79,513	0	0	4,006,926	394,147	606,228,578	1,588,212	351,931	524,258	740,775,535
4	46,590,764	4,485,465	6,704,332	615,994	11,984	0	0	850,035	4,603,543	702,675,288	2,394,242	0	360,875	769,292,521
5	41,508,892	3,493,508	11,805,638	-248,616	176,963	0	0	4,267,146	1,907,485	606,504,503	23,000	9,479	1,761,420	671,209,418
6	93,710,059	8,331,362	4,649,612	988,273	420,021	0	0	3,207,317	2,967,720	650,887,633	365,028	50,000	1,385,887	766,962,912
7	68,673,355	4,371,608	5,540,616	0	3,955,007	0	0	4,531,966	19,150,595	587,226,723	5,936,976	1,893,151	263,200	701,543,197
8	51,165,651	1,942,601	7,493,969	-750	4,248	0	0	2,174,553	194,824	568,219,805	123,582	85,421	371,834	631,775,738
9	89,235,556	3,163,587	43,734,224	5,731,887	254,795	0	0	3,886,515	694,263	668,558,107	2,613,467	157,262	312,365	818,342,029
10	386,201,741	7,067,654	24,303,425	939,934	1,203,819	0	0	4,891,033	10,316,123	654,463,754	1,747,964	286,607	1,306,397	1,092,728,452
11	47,759,012	4,626,090	9,438,720	442,463	607,941	0	0	735,937	2,707,597	516,357,804	3,867	39,732	285,762	583,004,926
12	1,495,853,276	2,660,307	8,186,432	5,677,700	42,124	0	-58,249	4,341,006	4,212,169	523,519,721	131,416	226,372	2,069,473	2,046,861,747
13	37,557,145	5,674,718	25,441,767	994,060	315,567	0	0	296,404	4,888,352	554,006,252	975,322	80,547	1,613,683	631,843,818
14	79,407,756	7,623,724	14,903,244	3,786,523	346,986	0	748,351	1,383,755	224,852	664,400,229	1,081,498	571,167	748,610	775,226,695
15	845,636,634	2,672,359	11,305,423	405,154	21,920	0	-74,916	12,240,941	769,100	531,359,436	243,878	94,217	2,832,361	1,407,506,508

See Appendix A for a listing of the congressional districts which represent the county in which the state capital is located and congressional districts which represent only portions of a county. See Appendix B for a listing of the programs included in each recipent category.

table continues

Table 3.3 **Federal Outlays to Categories of Recipients by Congressional District, 1985 *(continued)***

District	State Gov't.	Counties	Cities/ Towns	Special Districts	Schools	Interstate Agencies	Indian Tribes	Non-Profits	Private Universities	Individuals	For Profits	Small Businesses	All Others	Total
OHIO *continued*														
16	53,082,171	4,108,708	10,751,728	5,412,539	128,095	0	0	752,971	3,859,455	656,420,991	71,927	23,488	220,103	734,832,176
17	70,248,438	8,576,853	44,758,293	3,511,532	540,785	0	0	1,775,065	1,957,025	706,005,431	2,708,651	249,186	914,079	841,245,338
18	55,780,317	5,477,474	7,568,616	491,921	22,245	0	0	1,871,278	644,598	760,544,215	196,042	33,677	966,013	833,596,396
19	85,572,465	4,777,077	31,345,985	20,639,890	1,216,349	0	0	560,781	1,601,784	730,283,776	1,215,213	0	1,060,956	878,274,277
20	95,810,407	4,578,799	41,053,157	45,749,956	1,183,852	0	49,336	2,809,672	5,145,371	747,341,881	2,257,449	187,275	2,601,170	948,768,326
21	91,730,633	4,588,884	34,739,016	-59,103	2,766,690	0	0	18,274,538	54,920,567	749,004,769	4,271,601	1,087,480	7,018,645	968,343,720
TOTAL	4,008,828,937	123,523,366	412,890,161	111,248,154	14,071,747	0	664,522	83,774,648	135,151,918	13,479,691,614	31,135,621	5,697,603	28,332,711	18,435,011,002
OKLAHOMA														
1	48,911,719	2,004,583	15,326,079	5,069,478	1,695,502	0	2,175,920	3,688,646	7,739,332	565,142,086	1,937,995	380,902	2,455,480	656,527,722
2	102,703,122	2,723,982	11,384,857	1,101,114	10,996,132	0	22,142,623	3,609,126	1,703,476	694,539,452	81,315	28,405	713,507	851,727,110
3	134,091,857	2,486,948	12,914,917	2,171,751	8,492,943	0	10,942,193	4,771,325	3,206,307	751,502,197	483,474	-110	679,226	931,743,027
4	114,429,658	2,015,035	12,942,842	4,100,056	7,123,351	0	2,762,623	2,848,204	1,805,781	563,050,062	81,027	118,393	2,709,405	713,986,437
5	555,504,313	2,202,783	33,962,694	239,788	1,918,952	-5,721	2,949,923	2,059,222	4,306,379	600,992,388	1,112,960	43,384	1,036,408	1,206,323,473
6	184,651,867	2,312,282	13,210,571	495,847	2,789,798	0	5,037,952	1,178,859	1,257,744	831,666,592	1,620,332	48,033	518,950	1,044,788,827
TOTAL	1,140,292,535	13,745,614	99,741,960	13,178,034	33,016,678	-5,721	46,011,233	18,155,382	20,019,018	4,006,892,776	5,317,103	619,007	8,112,977	5,405,096,596
OREGON														
1	52,443,836	11,321,349	18,843,128	-406,170	389,470	810,488	1,086,890	16,410,111	9,817,939	629,451,910	2,066,788	43,129	737,443	743,016,310
2	55,492,162	6,372,424	10,005,552	62,086	4,623,867	400,000	4,963,494	4,029,396	471,223	788,474,090	187,514	371,264	692,698	876,145,771
3	89,057,658	35,633,321	17,197,393	5,213,296	2,496,438	51,286	396,371	3,909,461	4,145,713	805,165,164	687,653	359,991	2,464,949	966,778,694
4	82,958,713	3,030,594	15,165,660	1,149,522	3,319,888	0	129,570	6,002,915	3,373,407	654,746,242	466,556	232,567	672,256	771,247,891
5	848,945,989	7,741,803	12,519,922	6,810,888	616,493	0	154,900	5,892,196	6,206,783	639,038,348	2,052,992	287,323	1,210,727	1,531,478,365
TOTAL	1,128,898,359	64,099,492	73,731,654	12,829,622	11,446,156	1,261,774	6,731,225	36,244,080	24,015,065	3,516,875,754	5,461,503	1,294,274	5,778,072	4,888,667,030
PENNSYLVANIA														
1	183,614,110	124,382	81,969,451	104,623,642	478,668	0	57,785	37,957,033	116,881,486	841,888,425	4,738,829	198,954	3,289,938	1,375,822,702
2	198,299,594	-620	46,645,055	0	2,356,145	69,900	58,017	28,683,446	25,401,909	845,478,554	4,550,526	1,843,836	-145,067	1,153,241,296
3	186,965,040	-619	52,692,190	0	502,460	0	57,898	17,288,286	5,351,915	843,081,620	2,322,641	1,322,221	1,571,628	1,111,155,280
4	60,638,985	4,774,536	6,239,884	4,281,650	26,471	0	0	470,871	1,391,574	771,670,058	297,509	269,779	497,184	850,558,501
5	43,328,508	7,586,449	5,023,380	1,983,021	205,655	0	0	3,362,718	7,494,980	634,559,094	168,803	170,783	214,582	704,097,974
6	45,795,009	7,844,748	9,096,524	-642,726	181,188	0	0	90,416	1,080,328	902,154,178	165,784	86,114	238,688	966,090,250
7	59,659,431	8,042,337	10,221,157	-33,461	1,586,093	0	5,573	1,185,765	9,266,568	755,034,176	4,312,116	187,893	774,232	850,241,878
8	30,243,934	4,543,658	8,400,040	136,810	4,834,556	0	0	763,025	791,601	528,048,069	384,948	124,366	0	578,271,008
9	61,622,523	2,970,612	9,527,971	883,537	633,541	0	0	1,891,484	951,422	766,442,129	317,826	40,643	745,101	846,026,789
10	65,123,261	5,445,046	15,937,367	1,542,533	501,687	0	338,483	11,733,606	5,657,105	894,331,579	160,276	18,390	865,312	1,001,654,645
11	57,768,380	30,765,753	13,879,620	2,830,596	87,257	0	939,305	3,743,273	4,576,666	1,003,073,247	599,363	247,539	2,312,057	1,120,823,055
12	57,185,463	5,411,918	11,063,900	3,609,850	32,114	0	0	2,538,388	4,456,430	844,816,177	1,619,412	74,580	213,667	931,021,900
13	50,077,590	5,229,642	18,808,526	-120,090	866,219	0	10,097	840,568	4,910,762	732,421,538	926,550	980,288	16,240	814,967,930
14	143,462,792	25,089,933	36,436,790	86,659,571	1,069,614	67,500	831,926	17,684,925	39,941,118	837,081,989	6,778,926	1,694,461	2,490,846	1,199,290,391
15	38,425,801	3,541,002	13,825,844	4,470,311	366,803	0	0	1,513,479	13,835,086	786,990,324	352,285	80,799	985,734	864,387,469
16	39,282,907	6,937,279	7,823,908	1,885,428	107,544	0	0	609,233	3,837,929	649,544,356	26,559	0	378,686	710,433,829
17	2,890,098,713	4,523,470	20,078,914	4,137,165	601,254	104,000	0	3,313,456	2,983,890	765,787,700	1,901,662	137,685	2,077,933	3,695,745,842
18	72,562,816	10,100,132	5,060,699	-24,890	0	0	0	51,020	0	835,532,883	9,497	0	1,115,124	924,407,281
19	33,199,812	6,017,220	6,455,897	7,242,007	578,747	0	0	3,116,469	4,181,637	650,740,439	220,923	-8,406	1,333,034	713,077,779
20	67,171,688	8,452,902	7,587,454	-2,242	69,559	0	0	581,196	0	820,947,518	10,796,131	84,615	606,593	916,295,412
21	63,626,941	7,608,152	17,055,860	4,742,870	163,211	0	0	4,843,812	7,083,079	750,632,223	4,228,073	486,938	1,336,359	861,807,519
22	81,318,532	4,843,343	8,743,394	132,743	82,691	11,236,400	0	1,714,233	1,929,311	897,171,215	641,088	86,879	236,322	1,008,136,151
23	121,217,290	4,151,206	7,219,519	2,105,358	771,205	0	0	3,484,042	2,818,614	741,835,236	198,656	146,381	696,417	884,643,923
TOTAL	4,650,689,123	164,002,480	419,793,343	230,443,683	16,102,682	11,477,800	2,299,084	147,460,743	264,823,411	18,099,262,726	45,718,383	8,274,737	21,850,609	24,082,198,804

RHODE ISLAND														
1	310,891,710	93,878	35,912,323	2,134,650	0	0	90,377	9,881,360	22,043,661	688,017,522	1,345,851	205,002	2,311,468	1,072,927,801
2	211,949,556	156,311	21,722,702	2,830,688	652,285	0	352,242	9,401,319	18,988,884	656,271,823	547,810	103,594	1,575,248	924,552,463
TOTAL	522,841,266	250,189	57,635,025	4,965,338	652,285	0	442,619	19,282,679	41,032,545	1,344,289,345	1,893,661	308,596	3,886,716	1,997,480,264
SOUTH CAROLINA														
1	81,379,023	10,698,096	11,200,294	2,979,985	1,770,719	100,000	0	7,544,584	2,763,674	457,136,296	234,141	488,158	2,175,805	578,470,774
2	893,312,945	8,385,570	6,732,573	5,137,185	374,626	0	225,046	9,844,864	16,751,755	500,409,899	631,831	13,471	1,541,451	1,443,361,216
3	63,545,953	8,129,174	11,159,652	403,674	467,310	0	1,114,342	3,745,351	6,532,026	603,417,987	38,480	0	1,528,636	700,082,585
4	38,942,961	10,379,750	9,595,885	5,071,368	58,178	0	0	1,164,570	8,037,104	619,614,278	52,969	0	476,191	693,393,254
5	63,680,040	8,435,785	13,572,950	388,625	805,043	0	4,209	3,138,348	5,698,660	600,955,538	0	40,000	647,702	697,366,900
6	85,041,045	11,716,692	10,344,880	324,654	2,774,427	0	0	3,516,395	1,301,922	541,368,433	645,805	9,500	794,741	657,838,495
TOTAL	1,225,901,967	57,745,067	62,606,234	14,305,491	6,250,303	100,000	1,343,597	28,954,112	41,085,141	3,322,902,431	1,603,226	551,129	7,164,526	4,770,513,224
SOUTH DAKOTA														
TOTAL	349,553,437	7,366,214	23,657,601	783,448	21,997,014	0	19,883,755	5,989,957	11,965,047	1,071,561,893	308,228	318,727	265,681	1,513,651,002
TENNESSEE														
1	55,962,787	3,972,698	13,659,669	642,320	25,320	0	0	2,024,607	3,562,250	635,172,552	227,976	73,963	1,774,611	717,098,753
2	70,314,001	5,958,340	16,058,839	2,072,205	0	0	0	3,408,458	7,376,501	647,772,719	921,088	364,463	897,794	755,144,408
3	51,802,177	4,488,914	20,016,903	1,085,352	69,470	0	0	4,898,585	8,472,577	651,315,765	683,769	490,961	2,340,355	745,664,828
4	63,350,857	4,614,355	4,935,251	220,320	0	0	0	5,527,693	3,832,576	671,957,559	0	291,590	596,422	755,326,623
5	1,236,239,696	717,366	23,202,554	22,856,441	0	0	743,544	41,200,785	29,876,328	595,693,594	1,247,067	396,213	1,812,448	1,953,986,036
6	49,750,459	3,498,298	8,630,398	549,111	-16,523	0	0	7,118,412	628,386	557,186,317	2,631,372	11,048	482,107	630,469,385
7	71,646,061	6,119,238	13,154,113	9,702,250	105,831	0	-1	3,864,065	2,495,822	574,844,392	927,007	135,952	555,531	683,550,261
8	85,234,051	5,881,895	14,084,517	2,472,207	148,695	0	-1	13,924,425	8,369,334	720,120,648	1,926,405	307,765	655,388	853,125,329
9	92,234,432	7,292,634	16,515,249	0	0	0	-3	5,159,910	2,186,215	543,109,592	2,573,535	155,967	1,267,128	670,494,659
TOTAL	1,776,534,521	42,543,738	130,257,494	39,600,206	332,793	0	743,539	87,126,940	66,799,989	5,597,173,137	11,138,219	2,227,922	10,381,784	7,764,860,282
TEXAS														
1	82,525,642	5,993,139	9,282,894	57,950	1,227,642	0	89,000	0	3,018,212	846,351,812	0	0	911,806	949,458,096
2	60,953,912	5,572,495	11,346,420	49,500	301,998	0	775,687	848,090	43,607	717,250,634	71,360	3,583	4,868,001	802,085,286
3	31,209,110	2,440,920	27,064,765	0	69,715	0	89,638	2,092,704	4,908,133	461,080,681	1,933,501	262,262	543,695	531,695,125
4	52,386,029	3,420,108	8,805,769	92,000	1,146,343	0	0	1,104,447	6,929,710	805,076,936	711,677	121,389	664,175	880,458,583
5	90,821,471	5,325,401	22,640,704	0	1,523,313	0	93,945	1,387,663	5,090,285	465,375,296	1,030,694	60,322	1,392,134	594,741,228
6	90,766,477	3,091,393	7,949,383	45,600	338,387	0	8,233	2,781,115	6,033,439	701,140,360	110,536	34,195	3,756,412	816,055,530
7	25,155,015	5,083,955	27,144,128	80,728,255	7,037	0	0	371	2,513,948	376,865,718	13,301	224,797	1,007,770	518,744,296
8	23,601,080	5,070,987	18,086,218	0	361,728	0	0	21,789	2,585,491	376,960,627	13,235	50,000	1,198,105	427,949,259
9	55,961,254	4,609,914	21,788,304	608,604	259,077	0	0	282,604	1,365,181	610,337,545	369,150	821,467	1,927,061	698,330,161
10	3,501,867,196	2,674,871	25,613,934	13,301,088	1,767,154	0	0	5,911,134	9,440,105	520,363,284	10,182,253	199,633	447,286	4,091,767,938
11	46,008,970	2,680,907	14,296,797	-471,946	9,112,210	0	0	2,241,939	7,539,202	712,199,565	596,137	21,478	1,331,990	795,557,250
12	27,680,730	3,570,759	23,135,152	16,023,071	1,062,383	0	0	1,716,228	1,043,988	527,168,569	1,129,739	194,722	786,626	603,511,966
13	31,855,770	3,956,104	11,671,677	41,000	1,264,158	0	0	2,287,992	167,888	903,485,605	1,792,557	358,103	1,778,497	958,659,351
14	67,177,450	7,261,148	11,697,957	46,500	407,760	0	0	1,110,949	3,491,691	768,596,065	57,238	0	929,548	860,776,306
15	91,184,798	7,897,458	22,209,385	3,379,752	2,466,198	0	0	4,548,869	132,028	534,967,552	1,514,418	0	2,253,214	670,553,671
16	40,166,832	4,129,926	28,440,957	3,539,205	3,450,273	0	485,226	3,536,237	435,871	455,351,114	3,437,206	607,914	997,238	544,577,999
17	45,949,729	4,548,330	11,524,379	1,021,563	1,320,731	0	0	1,476,377	4,392,250	980,078,773	196,135	1,702,070	1,447,839	1,053,658,177
18	32,392,970	5,079,122	15,833,777	0	7,031	0	0	8,076,512	50,915,732	376,789,512	13,291	418,644	485,678	490,012,269
19	41,697,465	4,391,866	12,432,391	50,000	1,313,829	0	0	5,211,567	3,269,485	759,547,663	655,527	27,331	1,666,976	830,264,100
20	51,980,570	3,284,332	47,094,849	14,726,615	6,811,822	0	0	10,559,388	2,144,547	513,729,287	1,118,513	35,344	292,393	651,777,660
21	40,842,309	4,091,725	18,162,584	356,919	8,416,671	0	0	2,356,917	10,477,716	671,673,968	793,233	460,417	582,981	758,215,441

See Appendix A for a listing of the congressional districts which represent the county in which the state capital is located and congressional districts which represent only portions of a county. See Appendix B for a listing of the programs included in each recipent category.

table continues

Table 3.3 Federal Outlays to Categories of Recipients by Congressional District, 1985 *(continued)*

District	State Gov't.	Counties	Cities/ Towns	Special Districts	Schools	Interstate Agencies	Indian Tribes	Non-Profits	Private Universities	Individuals	For Profits	Small Businesses	All Others	Total
TEXAS *continued*														
22	36,237,612	4,472,494	46,890,703	0	425,358	0	0	2,899,019	8,227,911	360,455,521	4,083,359	901,070	1,750,368	466,343,415
23	91,613,802	10,239,683	27,322,705	148,506	4,645,268	0	0	14,277,584	560,052	554,790,509	885,670	124,821	983,766	705,592,367
24	34,165,059	2,587,454	14,798,498	2,715,236	275,743	0	593,276	341,603	2,330,895	470,456,177	62,966	881,633	1,220,438	530,428,976
25	44,617,371	5,073,421	15,356,615	0	7,023	0	0	21,857	4,421,697	376,159,685	13,276	0	222,852	445,893,797
26	31,307,298	2,906,698	7,562,922	0	1,325,970	0	0	240,982	1,086,034	468,314,194	1,560,712	211,451	352,328	514,868,589
27	69,352,295	6,867,137	30,821,223	422,199	1,880,613	0	0	6,049,945	0	516,533,228	664,990	0	1,227,167	633,818,797
TOTAL	4,839,478,214	126,321,750	538,975,089	136,881,617	51,195,435	0	2,135,005	81,383,880	142,565,099	15,831,099,881	33,010,673	7,722,646	35,026,345	21,825,795,634
UTAH														
1	70,262,118	7,171,586	8,768,201	264,140	3,914,459	0	974,286	1,343,040	2,317,028	422,538,125	15,825,739	0	1,435,710	534,814,432
2	560,451,935	9,642,769	37,667,384	9,845,553	1,280,367	0	432,202	3,616,217	1,414,275	424,102,098	602,145	2,931,236	3,623,300	1,055,609,480
3	60,050,952	9,811,414	12,126,286	197,616	3,663,305	-484	2,371,988	1,905,362	2,106,582	400,473,384	561,386	114,210	65,273	493,447,275
TOTAL	690,765,005	26,625,769	58,561,871	10,307,309	8,858,131	-484	3,778,476	6,864,619	5,837,885	1,247,113,607	16,989,270	3,045,446	5,124,283	2,083,871,187
VERMONT														
TOTAL	322,828,468	968,195	28,063,849	524,997	629,365	0	75,282	5,442,212	13,060,372	628,645,597	319,378	340,048	1,314,498	1,002,212,261
VIRGINIA														
1	59,215,091	9,721,963	17,707,974	1,867,954	0	0	2,460	3,431,024	10,065,399	614,286,622	230,760	45,756	734,975	717,309,978
2	63,021,941	-39,402	34,831,051	11,170,357	0	0	0	10,743,984	1,070,981	422,280,838	4,192,445	193,743	-42,725	547,423,213
3	1,200,733,855	34,399,161	15,584,526	8,422,056	0	50,000	-3,869	2,063,120	4,378,475	659,074,386	1,235,673	24,996	4,361,731	1,930,324,110
4	82,409,837	4,974,842	28,177,167	428,450	0	0	0	1,351,304	2,484,804	616,140,872	96,131	0	314,667	736,378,074
5	56,164,926	5,113,729	5,010,577	3,051,446	0	0	0	2,761,182	3,584,397	697,167,652	1,221,528	0	41,196	774,116,632
6	48,765,140	2,525,471	10,589,493	3,542,101	37,649	0	0	3,038,369	9,157,778	750,428,561	1,302,727	314,638	1,252,125	830,954,053
7	79,893,372	8,025,445	8,108,505	790,622	0	0	0	4,577,706	2,501,117	565,472,296	895,730	141,228	38,068	670,444,089
8	21,071,351	6,631,253	2,934,482	0	0	0	248,370	6,265,507	0	303,126,051	3,473,547	1,936,945	156,416	345,843,922
9	98,521,215	14,127,153	5,733,321	4,590,201	174,552	0	0	3,162,441	5,744,520	783,010,067	0	521,113	1,223,577	916,808,160
10	19,368,423	17,142,467	2,002,865	-28,151	0	0	0	94,935,880	375,718	376,284,565	7,061,779	5,424,125	2,749,999	525,317,670
TOTAL	1,729,165,152	102,622,082	130,679,961	33,835,036	212,201	50,000	246,961	132,330,516	39,363,189	5,787,271,910	19,710,320	8,602,544	10,830,029	7,994,919,901
WASHINGTON														
1	92,294,435	5,361,306	4,307,401	47,929,344	4,241,758	0	492,298	9,371,205	4,537,853	567,958,036	1,497,400	1,066,449	1,215,261	740,272,744
2	67,060,928	10,009,674	6,830,054	9,238,517	5,290,614	0	6,897,768	2,595,618	342,425	673,510,100	6,071,811	15,922	1,459,236	789,322,666
3	1,096,921,177	10,287,891	10,387,749	1,634,999	1,036,126	0	1,460,091	1,731,800	1,574,416	629,573,428	719,847	-933	1,103,759	1,756,430,350
4	191,196,810	6,262,282	6,490,136	740,275	7,114,073	0	8,123,779	14,810,721	44,299	638,237,663	997,165	333,488	497,838	874,848,529
5	108,332,234	4,772,511	9,934,489	5,011,445	3,668,295	0	1,843,408	4,650,378	9,880,670	819,480,692	1,679,024	44,918	1,553,836	970,851,900
6	77,760,810	7,385,690	29,079,973	6,793,165	7,446,904	0	2,171,493	2,902,135	5,305,618	556,562,837	1,536,552	275,700	1,214,567	698,435,443
7	75,538,767	4,808,561	9,033,992	2,764,071	586,128	144,979	1,911,858	34,541,471	4,638,854	606,787,571	695,594	1,668,992	1,409,925	744,530,762
8	71,121,552	3,287,985	7,455,561	1,041,164	754,760	0	1,994,744	5,280,078	1,218,530	608,590,039	632,946	1,514,180	1,502,174	704,393,713
TOTAL	1,780,226,713	52,175,900	83,519,354	75,152,980	30,138,657	144,979	24,895,439	75,883,405	27,542,665	5,100,700,365	13,830,339	4,918,716	9,956,596	7,279,086,108
WEST VIRGINIA														
1	49,440,148	5,728,153	14,021,230	3,394,122	188,147	0	0	3,790,675	4,014,883	726,286,708	2,165,980	170,017	682,182	809,882,245
2	75,089,285	9,201,513	17,523,545	-402,849	360,039	0	0	4,035,578	4,498,587	699,933,190	31,165	54,909	802,315	811,127,277
3	708,693,375	9,329,541	22,185,461	3,064,577	40,807	24,829	0	1,473,297	595,910	685,730,487	1,132,513	22,100	484,156	1,432,777,053
4	67,759,613	6,652,231	16,989,681	311,157	195,686	21,120	0	4,848,342	2,814,728	812,887,406	3,614,305	79,235	587,597	916,761,101
TOTAL	900,982,421	30,911,438	70,719,917	6,367,007	784,679	45,949	0	14,147,892	11,924,108	2,924,837,791	6,943,963	326,261	2,556,250	3,970,547,676

WISCONSIN														
1	107,350,597	6,398,990	14,244,818	475,884	693,041	0	0	811,994	1,932,962	662,925,958	1,997,462	189,273	605,753	797,626,732
2	1,115,777,528	7,065,840	21,605,549	243,342	530,841	30,000	0	7,330,167	5,017,066	612,949,451	3,001,045	490,802	946,008	1,774,987,639
3	138,251,230	6,589,568	11,689,584	136,368	75,521	0	172,069	3,054,001	1,122,478	729,260,379	0	0	204,538	890,555,735
4	130,856,541	14,385,604	19,413,347	36,034,439	109,924	0	0	5,106,942	8,408,197	674,931,619	600,302	418,534	1,649,420	891,914,868
5	166,827,872	7,837,551	18,493,198	23,871,612	0	0	614,931	6,310,912	17,134,024	730,228,536	1,403,792	657,937	2,530,612	975,910,975
6	97,618,582	5,225,651	7,226,691	439,761	861,495	0	0	1,888,620	2,432,620	751,385,562	0	540,323	238,427	867,857,731
7	143,342,876	7,688,458	12,496,671	407,657	1,287,531	0	5,889,876	6,753,347	2,958,723	746,828,580	32,260	326,523	136,913	928,149,416
8	99,403,737	6,368,130	12,034,645	-160,748	290,221	0	9,099,106	2,462,017	1,794,182	698,110,288	0	0	87,084	829,488,662
9	52,003,495	5,405,085	10,386,834	1,331,869	565,634	0	0	146,080	3,289,475	573,838,328	49,439	38,948	512,953	647,568,140
TOTAL	2,051,432,458	66,964,877	127,591,337	62,780,183	4,414,208	30,000	15,775,982	33,864,080	44,089,727	6,180,458,700	7,084,299	2,662,340	6,911,707	8,604,059,898
WYOMING														
TOTAL	275,677,521	19,244,727	22,629,306	353,145	6,919,171	0	1,741,521	2,760,462	834,696	453,025,728	570,008	149,062	661,750	784,567,097
U.S. TOTAL	90,995.5 mil	3,133.4 mil	8,331.8 mil	3,100.7 mil	713.9 mil	33.2 mil	477.4 mil	3,158.4 mil	4,228.4 mil	292,470.4 mil	707.8 mil	242.3 mil	680.1 mil	408,273.0 mil

See Appendix A for a listing of the congressional districts which represent the county in which the state capital is located and congressional districts which represent only portions of a county. See Appendix B for a listing of the programs included in each recipent category.

Table 3.4 **Federal Outlays to Categories of Recipients by Congressional District, 1986**

District	State Gov't.	Counties	Cities/ Towns	Special Districts	Schools	Public Universities	Indian Tribes	Non-Profits	Private Universities	Individuals	For Profits	Small Businesses	All Others	Total
ALABAMA														
1	65,431,631	6,640,550	15,909,418	3,144,595	262,461	377,641	1,504,791	4,589,682	1,418,264	708,704,114	4,476,807	0	1,435,706	813,895,660
2	1,235,712,663	4,859,364	15,323,622	1,943,734	2,255,281	912,047	35,000	4,869,553	2,858,208	700,228,841	847,552	0	1,399,906	1,971,245,771
3	62,398,905	5,056,844	16,475,549	8,956	382,646	11,625,091	0	5,105,543	21,279,510	687,967,640	1,028,851	0	91,193	811,420,728
4	61,450,636	8,167,118	10,029,282	-125,929	48,891	1,118,626	0	3,364,606	507,686	807,292,656	318,739	0	113,149	892,285,460
5	50,502,169	5,208,793	26,274,297	2,460,407	1,014,633	6,236,431	0	3,771,125	3,922,396	643,109,243	1,167,269	0	663,494	744,330,257
6	96,567,054	14,947,943	22,227,430	11,096,958	2,025,840	5,021,207	0	2,382,283	7,029,809	853,025,537	12,206,640	219,728	1,451,491	1,028,201,919
7	73,755,205	7,909,182	12,859,595	242,715	524,616	10,065,209	0	5,638,997	6,172,084	705,568,179	269,051	250,000	359,707	823,614,541
TOTAL	1,645,818,263	52,789,794	119,099,193	18,771,436	6,514,368	35,356,252	1,539,791	29,721,789	43,187,957	5,105,896,210	20,314,909	469,728	5,514,646	7,084,994,336
ALASKA														
TOTAL	445,607,160	40,744,599	57,589,737	1,908,030	-819	11,253,288	28,971,427	24,161,152	1,122,473	221,875,043	818,326	254,862	2,259,448	836,564,726
ARIZONA														
1	253,717,454	7,144,296	50,304,792	262,500	4,808,342	7,916,808	1,230,165	3,756,111	3,358,586	1,050,322,821	30,259,493	48,167	2,886,735	1,416,016,270
2	183,978,821	9,796,176	34,353,249	834,228	9,850,592	17,823,754	9,856,260	7,395,477	2,640,235	890,589,990	16,048,646	3,492,000	2,688,708	1,189,348,137
3	17,377,497	3,005,122	27,238,474	26,500	2,482,844	860,471	3,085,340	3,169,351	244,477	401,213,082	1,083,913	39,950	1,147,472	460,974,493
4	479,014,608	7,095,064	35,587,940	0	19,196,561	402,865	53,847,896	3,408,135	2,792,373	916,490,475	19,546,227	155,868	935,959	1,538,473,971
5	31,978,830	8,936,910	14,524,633	0	5,008,322	2,886,844	124,653	2,226,487	1,607,488	797,434,875	2,073,478	561,691	576,527	867,940,738
TOTAL	966,067,210	35,977,568	162,009,088	1,123,228	41,346,661	29,890,742	68,144,314	19,955,562	10,643,158	4,056,051,243	69,011,756	4,297,676	8,235,403	5,472,753,609
ARKANSAS														
1	135,561,715	7,967,755	11,206,120	409,327	1,391,978	171,027	0	5,577,323	1,514,976	999,171,857	259,587	72,072	997,630	1,164,301,367
2	674,490,720	4,501,016	33,094,471	3,394,360	6,274,161	593,554	449,778	3,758,984	6,126,268	764,398,992	2,468,213	340,920	3,675,194	1,503,566,631
3	67,884,621	7,532,612	18,461,101	158,952	410,199	5,970,760	0	2,819,758	9,318,985	886,697,462	8,836,579	42,750	620,837	1,008,754,616
4	110,005,486	6,405,698	12,582,085	754,520	130,679	2,718,207	0	5,876,953	1,967,730	906,360,783	285,038	0	2,985,641	1,050,072,820
TOTAL	987,942,542	26,407,081	75,343,777	4,717,159	8,207,017	9,453,548	449,778	18,033,018	18,927,959	3,556,629,094	11,849,417	455,742	8,279,302	4,726,695,434
CALIFORNIA														
1	126,488,258	15,867,163	12,257,007	2,958,777	2,672,013	838,935	3,908,804	5,721,417	902,434	837,754,211	1,943,604	215,000	5,920,551	1,017,448,173
2	143,594,244	18,445,265	13,777,682	3,491,954	2,874,451	528,763	3,146,881	4,314,849	1,502,918	954,543,843	813,583	21,622	2,600,350	1,149,656,406
3	3,901,725,897	8,590,229	23,996,352	6,170,506	1,788,741	454,755	2,856,184	13,393,807	650,125	563,448,213	4,331,921	99,147	3,997,218	4,531,503,095
4	901,484,636	13,174,347	11,015,617	3,253,767	8,804,746	8,959,177	765,460	2,700,661	5,627,832	574,163,872	910,734	906,707	2,751,795	1,534,519,351
5	173,542,932	26,380,144	60,334,556	6,089,126	6,951,323	2,786,942	0	9,428,675	4,013,321	948,375,557	1,217,807	533,387	3,307,237	1,242,961,009
6	81,941,745	12,061,874	13,615,740	2,675,645	4,025,100	100,486	0	11,631,353	1,913,581	667,637,242	1,733,102	1,244,461	3,738,196	802,318,525
7	78,715,987	11,141,255	7,990,679	4,600,868	2,666,557	0	0	2,171,939	739,804	651,957,083	777,378	0	582,924	761,344,475
8	162,220,428	7,915,534	15,240,920	80,081,829	2,245,900	41,295,313	221,677	33,681,698	9,299,963	668,862,987	2,346,993	2,214,841	1,658,532	1,027,286,615
9	120,777,736	6,346,837	16,232,799	140,844	6,915,058	745,268	294,526	1,823,194	1,265,445	668,638,863	71,817,460	409,525	2,035,288	897,442,843
10	86,304,869	25,948,341	15,328,095	62,120,169	3,838,798	1,728,252	587,536	2,213,954	494,496	544,797,725	807,851	0	1,408,736	745,578,822
11	50,070,097	6,898,863	8,172,455	3,068,067	2,215,125	17,392	11,636	9,337,650	1,081,100	644,813,873	600,215	1,773,624	1,221,848	729,281,944
12	56,701,701	4,872,181	11,461,858	373,929	5,746,191	6,186,941	63,712	22,549,279	137,274,750	452,653,552	5,503,685	4,117,331	1,995,917	709,501,027
13	66,880,264	6,336,628	9,785,421	179,066	2,039,121	138,865	92,906	2,191,912	3,167,168	474,967,746	1,732,014	247,267	2,472,252	570,230,631
14	89,086,874	16,285,085	15,454,642	3,313,610	4,424,112	131,713	891,397	2,427,709	3,502,829	718,234,483	127,912	151,000	151,873	854,183,241
15	112,205,866	11,110,726	19,382,468	158,752	5,399,860	0	1,278	4,194,015	0	548,259,203	1,242,390	55,007	1,590,344	703,599,909
16	74,347,840	9,811,547	35,193,272	-4,038,236	9,534,819	3,923,098	271,394	3,385,854	547,640	584,911,511	1,047,092	731,580	2,072,709	721,740,119
17	169,463,863	16,359,240	14,613,154	626,124	4,719,404	228,150	1,816,122	1,922,593	111,721,039	736,658,497	3,208,092	0	2,806,606	1,064,142,884
18	196,420,483	22,526,028	11,123,491	531,016	5,296,034	639,152	486,429	1,721,798	3,048,438	1,011,775,073	2,363,452	0	211,327	1,256,142,721
19	59,883,326	8,803,701	9,057,747	1,951,017	6,389,998	10,922,850	307,286	826,291	978,550	504,133,629	2,471,185	1,268,910	1,032,601	608,027,089
20	118,825,295	17,194,232	10,673,034	292,333,223	7,720,489	562,427	1,303,648	15,142,309	1,464,290	790,142,040	1,572,844	128,657	2,123,167	1,259,185,656
21	99,151,304	11,277,208	12,905,745	1,941,616	3,171,489	110,280	356,299	1,901,805	1,575,783	742,274,766	3,583,518	425,995	1,565,481	880,241,289
22	121,177,239	8,303,485	16,981,695	4,036,181	3,034,914	397,745	0	6,545,240	10,650,729	651,216,312	3,920,648	313,928	3,399,685	829,977,801
23	212,698,270	8,294,670	11,913,891	4,031,896	1,395,870	23,748,807	0	5,138,513	4,448,536	649,513,513	3,250,923	8,421	1,682,711	926,126,021

24	121,026,039	8,958,424	11,627,737	6,209,474	1,395,609	264,131	0	12,745,204	1,697,454	648,805,419	3,250,893	255,170	2,478,510	818,714,066
25	123,382,488	13,025,459	12,719,178	4,062,416	1,637,221	884,284	136,875	7,306,534	26,058,223	649,537,555	3,368,311	629,367	1,678,189	844,426,102
26	106,258,310	7,281,188	10,748,589	3,547,260	1,439,228	168,538	0	2,498,411	1,651,504	569,634,802	3,136,690	304,289	1,321,969	707,990,777
27	121,065,740	8,290,744	31,200,665	4,029,988	3,462,950	287,043	0	4,892,388	4,934,276	648,618,770	11,165,152	1,418,629	3,077,638	842,443,983
28	121,313,803	8,542,371	13,148,828	4,115,755	1,799,032	271,878	0	10,451,216	71,634,426	648,596,145	3,780,070	247,406	2,014,994	885,915,925
29	120,999,819	34,655,599	14,190,349	4,063,152	1,395,307	191,920	0	8,231,666	2,059,286	648,661,864	3,250,189	83,779	1,776,729	839,559,659
30	120,789,934	8,276,946	30,157,434	9,685,745	4,513,885	191,587	550,000	2,134,814	2,739,774	647,536,653	7,521,717	8,403	1,805,039	835,911,931
31	122,496,951	8,311,594	26,291,820	4,523,803	3,186,924	476,633	0	1,435,846	10,705,929	649,090,163	3,936,986	8,423	2,779,087	833,244,158
32	121,648,118	8,323,165	13,792,528	4,045,747	1,400,665	790,023	0	4,654,894	1,703,602	651,152,564	3,262,669	8,450	2,222,023	813,004,449
33	123,142,243	8,299,228	17,990,904	4,034,112	2,859,946	599,520	0	5,196,823	7,212,160	649,308,509	4,182,509	292,736	2,075,608	825,194,297
34	121,120,857	8,299,622	19,503,110	4,062,902	2,418,615	192,112	0	1,716,979	2,992,375	649,313,679	4,183,216	8,426	1,673,532	815,485,424
35	112,497,219	11,519,413	9,815,877	8,453,796	7,602,793	1,232	234,476	456,693	5,032,411	665,848,694	1,879,885	2,083,974	1,157,055	826,583,518
36	456,018,155	27,551,772	19,720,308	-593,524	2,076,164	1,095,029	269,296	1,071,650	328,328	1,303,759,944	1,404,494	130,129	1,378,074	1,814,209,818
37	326,715,322	12,075,068	12,277,753	131,846	3,287,303	2,388,586	1,282,528	1,492,222	1,697,821	645,577,098	585,855	125,000	1,200,690	1,008,837,094
38	44,808,213	8,830,689	7,908,359	16,769,016	1,088,415	24,557	523,304	121,900	1,787,695	586,633,747	7,292,822	0	2,485,916	678,274,634
39	46,458,129	4,506,561	11,497,140	211,956	2,364,141	847,613	523,746	235,719	2,551,304	587,158,580	7,363,982	0	2,485,675	666,204,546
40	47,214,994	6,249,054	11,032,307	264,124	5,136,877	8,797,345	523,265	20,884,816	2,320,488	586,970,317	7,373,320	1,011,210	2,375,831	700,153,948
41	73,398,843	4,196,407	54,774,735	616,184	3,570,755	30,447,299	99,568	110,433,688	1,015,317	500,660,651	5,301,868	2,200,311	553,906	787,269,533
42	91,200,382	6,864,707	11,573,841	3,625,104	2,147,779	472,748	202,816	13,166,352	1,968,113	623,157,882	6,962,065	94,118	2,687,849	764,123,756
43	79,516,703	6,978,674	13,419,829	5,755,686	10,817,237	1,050,388	1,460,139	20,630,944	2,049,504	711,531,915	3,778,940	673,428	1,569,111	859,232,498
44	93,059,746	6,291,194	12,577,841	64,513	8,841,309	1,123,053	150,857	8,179,486	1,405,909	757,631,471	1,221,266	280,243	1,459,662	892,286,550
45	101,466,952	7,935,747	14,686,416	628,216	10,049,579	1,071,414	2,633,046	3,100,179	1,786,270	752,558,084	12,816,694	157,910	824,320	909,714,826
TOTAL	9,999,308,115	519,208,210	757,163,870	568,397,019	186,361,847	156,082,243	25,973,094	405,404,940	461,202,940	30,371,478,298	224,343,999	24,887,810	91,408,753	43,791,221,137
COLORADO														
1	781,222,209	8,391,848	13,508,420	25,574,995	7,422,559	2,210,074	1,893,452	21,738,680	11,386,517	691,188,584	5,791,709	601,871	3,240,824	1,574,171,741
2	48,617,851	4,976,326	7,638,079	-28,863	506,342	21,710,323	0	5,868,897	434,626	377,495,470	1,589,664	2,111,732	594,012	471,514,460
3	71,015,416	12,114,462	13,055,587	1,612,863	2,420,019	824,269	2,757,868	4,821,552	36,447	600,944,069	1,334,535	0	1,587,294	712,524,381
4	62,443,980	9,881,013	8,682,396	977,622	1,434,399	16,555,745	0	4,618,853	3,606,172	658,509,424	106,742	296,403	2,099,666	769,212,415
5	30,769,227	4,541,718	9,841,376	-65,086	5,162,557	1,954,745	0	4,050,868	2,508,744	442,019,900	1,486,421	443,924	571,066	503,285,460
6	27,454,482	4,468,060	7,114,405	11,259	1,080,819	75,381	2,094	8,844,474	273,485	373,768,833	952,827	555,429	1,017,171	425,618,720
TOTAL	1,021,523,165	44,373,427	59,840,263	28,082,790	18,026,695	43,330,537	4,653,414	49,943,325	18,245,991	3,143,926,280	11,261,897	4,009,359	9,110,033	4,456,327,176
CONNECTICUT														
1	805,510,625	402,433	20,148,003	543,101	11,262	451,123	0	5,678,654	3,642,928	732,532,298	4,009,250	844,347	3,406,901	1,577,180,924
2	72,277,211	131,655	20,558,083	518,733	46,573	6,030,317	643,947	3,548,937	6,555,824	606,052,236	662,527	43,813	73,073	717,142,929
3	91,069,041	0	62,457,047	2,531,833	0	1,214,613	0	5,879,645	120,574,165	760,571,862	1,669,362	816,978	244,900	1,047,029,447
4	72,834,828	265,608	16,148,755	7,342,838	0	83,334	0	4,215,151	3,139,523	668,794,384	13,549,327	44,250	2,552,650	788,970,648
5	82,665,567	25,379	17,356,568	1,014,329	-2,375	11,928	185,646	1,894,448	404,663	727,640,748	63,429	25,761	591,285	831,877,375
6	102,082,128	0	18,029,397	43,745	0	353,502	126	1,002,002	59,373	733,352,302	304,441	189,836	106,219	855,523,073
TOTAL	1,226,439,401	825,075	154,697,853	11,994,579	55,460	8,144,817	829,719	22,218,837	134,376,476	4,228,943,831	20,258,336	1,964,984	6,975,028	5,817,724,396
DELAWARE														
TOTAL	238,424,805	9,828,145	12,707,055	285,943	185,118	11,339,512	38,343	9,767,391	2,487,669	777,006,144	1,475,500	73,687	2,215,147	1,065,834,459
DISTRICT OF COLUMBIA														
TOTAL	509,692,757	0	2,272,975	88,253,842	0	1,739,532	22,446,877	195,346,442	272,510,795	786,761,519	9,358,296	6,365,375	164,239,780	2,058,988,190
FLORIDA														
1	42,420,656	9,062,958	5,889,637	95,360	7,608,493	2,643,834	0	1,733,502	0	654,912,314	359,000	0	493,012	725,218,766
2	2,096,284,849	9,041,239	11,785,259	245,112	1,640,444	16,638,097	840,801	7,194,284	1,889,247	662,442,320	289,908	0	5,289,896	2,813,581,456
3	52,577,119	380,056	29,309,643	510,765	1,919,577	205,680	0	304,135	4,179,324	679,214,926	728,668	0	1,619,100	770,948,993
4	38,485,535	11,149,747	11,188,173	592,423	3,899,269	7,144	0	1,117,343	10,213,559	1,080,688,677	3,095,708	65,087	1,561,884	1,162,064,548
5	30,421,986	17,247,234	15,544,425	12,177,507	907,782	866,934	0	119,676	1,761,243	727,031,807	1,228,253	219,919	1,015,102	808,541,869
6	73,608,307	8,347,242	7,356,434	673,034	2,351,857	19,334,565	0	1,918,544	6,800,143	1,241,595,749	123,446	813,428	1,894,054	1,364,816,801

See Appendix A for a listing of the congressional districts which represent the county in which the state capital is located and congressional districts which represent only portions of a county. See Appendix B for a listing of the programs included in each recipent category.

table continues

Table 3.4 Federal Outlays to Categories of Recipients by Congressional District, 1986 *(continued)*

District	State Gov't.	Counties	Cities/ Towns	Special Districts	Schools	Public Universities	Indian Tribes	Non-Profits	Private Universities	Individuals	For Profits	Small Businesses	All Others	Total
FLORIDA *continued*														
7	50,483,155	13,288,929	10,936,925	24,496,404	1,189,219	2,289,182	0	3,491,410	3,630,198	742,921,626	16,499,104	19,681	1,313,231	870,559,064
8	31,110,828	10,315,122	15,246,156	8,734,140	2,565,508	884,547	0	1,520,466	913,541	1,348,967,854	286,648	50,000	184,100	1,420,778,910
9	26,064,653	6,778,688	8,544,238	377,205	639,583	543,200	0	295,597	721,403	1,316,262,237	580,358	0	416,337	1,361,223,498
10	31,806,337	17,381,710	4,945,089	750,120	422,087	0	0	1,700,603	2,528,844	1,006,441,290	210,826	0	2,104,300	1,068,291,207
11	27,202,307	17,036,701	14,539,137	2,924,518	2,290,107	1,349,095	0	575,062	1,150,707	921,150,958	1,258,045	133,768	603,977	990,214,382
12	28,738,966	14,262,032	8,200,298	2,136,723	974,191	0	293,894	7,053,748	347,937	1,331,820,225	211,770	0	429,397	1,394,469,179
13	19,460,853	11,590,504	4,506,441	1,522,234	1,162,143	-81,125	0	381,242	188,828	1,616,261,181	2,032,543	0	1,906,835	1,658,931,679
14	23,085,635	8,677,010	6,272,195	232,280	133,351	827,360	875,814	159,846	820,115	1,330,468,951	780,576	50,000	235,982	1,372,619,116
15	50,194,775	25,715,704	14,085,902	1,258,904	681,550	0	244,172	811,092	3,442,255	1,188,017,758	8,644,436	0	1,174,687	1,294,271,234
16	43,608,256	8,341,190	7,775,859	-118,839	149,361	87,019	2,654,203	27,173	1,638,041	1,080,317,490	1,074,002	21	197,255	1,145,751,031
17	100,987,035	52,754,497	17,153,399	-781,226	511,595	484,959	187,026	769,020	7,935,082	816,241,963	3,363,424	50,072	1,171,885	1,000,828,731
18	104,447,604	20,893,847	19,937,702	28,819	761,797	298,176	152,085	1,448,777	5,652,420	816,839,896	4,645,283	72	2,691,036	977,797,515
19	91,690,124	13,407,759	29,741,839	-684,762	1,061,679	357,978	133,254	802,358	10,288,323	796,469,401	2,452,543	63	889,142	946,609,701
TOTAL	2,962,678,980	275,672,169	242,958,751	55,170,722	30,869,592	46,736,644	5,381,249	31,423,878	64,101,211	19,358,066,621	47,864,540	1,402,111	25,191,212	23,147,517,680
GEORGIA														
1	99,061,369	13,173,178	9,983,842	353,942	1,714,134	1,035,129	0	4,688,077	1,110,975	686,200,455	1,771,161	162,852	499,417	819,754,531
2	129,948,305	9,752,741	8,405,338	38,115	726,507	400,011	0	3,968,138	713,078	664,958,144	818,844	0	369,087	820,098,308
3	88,316,648	6,442,693	12,991,220	586,493	1,324,707	2,681,012	0	3,759,254	2,981,116	626,539,291	559,860	500,730	501,541	747,184,565
4	328,392,536	10,237,124	6,528,257	87,818,462	1,444,171	339,073	41,925	6,066,120	12,980,546	285,878,485	2,044,852	571,410	3,818,889	746,161,850
5	1,143,664,971	23,995,490	41,482,610	0	291,871	7,711,247	265,461	14,066,790	57,449,467	885,127,519	3,983,238	234,000	2,197,204	2,180,469,868
6	63,159,838	9,289,217	9,643,362	61,052	269,574	1,086,235	29,544	623,570	0	613,063,461	314,941	0	382,583	697,923,376
7	38,170,819	5,591,077	4,078,139	92,026	241,704	142,136	0	1,141,013	1,951,509	571,370,452	419,916	0	731,356	623,930,147
8	117,065,969	9,941,072	9,846,965	289,823	1,520,524	96,341	0	2,273,510	4,303,977	693,255,514	2,939	0	1,010,964	839,607,598
9	59,942,821	8,687,924	12,442,434	238,460	113,299	-86,869	0	3,226,073	2,361,796	624,266,742	24,899	0	25,000	711,242,578
10	88,369,261	8,772,423	7,422,638	132,864	1,280,013	20,714,220	0	12,463,081	8,914,790	590,352,811	0	50,000	328,490	738,800,592
TOTAL	2,156,092,537	105,882,938	122,824,804	89,611,237	8,926,504	34,118,536	336,930	52,275,627	92,767,254	6,241,012,874	9,940,650	1,518,992	9,864,530	8,925,173,413
HAWAII														
1	295,336,355	1,394,995	61,539,110	20,912	0	14,881,976	4,193,184	11,264,601	3,181,610	455,484,124	822,069	1,036,376	4,307,473	853,462,785
2	129,878,799	11,050,819	14,858,085	2,228	0	1,486,129	0	3,591,845	2,762,014	525,843,940	817,449	48,485	2,460,425	692,800,218
TOTAL	425,215,154	12,445,814	76,397,195	23,140	0	16,368,105	4,193,184	14,856,446	5,943,624	981,328,064	1,639,518	1,084,861	6,767,898	1,546,263,003
IDAHO														
1	288,662,838	7,862,737	14,321,876	230,726	3,472,383	5,953,863	6,090,946	4,473,578	3,027,454	641,845,780	317,314	33,970	961,140	977,254,604
2	85,378,316	7,755,388	12,000,033	343,932	5,303,938	351,206	1,947,196	3,461,401	54,193	581,168,871	365,663	525,908	1,092,880	699,748,926
TOTAL	374,041,154	15,618,125	26,321,909	574,658	8,776,321	6,305,069	8,038,142	7,934,979	3,081,647	1,223,014,651	682,977	559,878	2,054,020	1,677,003,530
ILLINOIS														
1	109,600,648	3,539,708	217,148,421	208,301,564	1,366,870	780,235	199,173	14,602,070	82,373,811	696,774,330	8,164,152	1,412,315	2,229,016	1,346,492,313
2	99,526,014	3,483,942	21,503,225	129,606	1,366,570	75,889	115,473	2,213,276	3,255,954	695,666,947	3,245,673	3,884	1,871,647	832,458,100
3	99,546,921	3,484,674	24,651,228	129,633	1,341,391	75,905	115,497	830,998	5,344,532	696,314,772	3,593,128	95,823	1,872,040	837,396,543
4	60,073,784	2,601,063	31,294,178	56,042	724,070	32,815	49,931	1,040,337	3,172,244	600,253,235	1,846,644	1,679	879,868	702,025,891
5	99,640,451	3,484,211	26,893,957	-4,354,810	1,366,675	75,895	115,482	800,750	3,321,200	695,871,407	4,232,286	3,884	1,871,791	833,323,179
6	45,009,569	5,874,433	20,896,237	103,511	512,784	158,322	43,016	1,520,253	3,388,164	585,546,187	1,303,903	320,485	714,175	665,391,038
7	110,951,354	8,575,629	60,191,066	129,632	1,366,841	3,255,971	115,496	23,254,722	6,831,334	695,916,053	4,444,388	3,885	2,603,018	917,639,388
8	99,578,156	3,484,634	21,555,164	129,632	3,665,679	314,214	115,496	3,009,523	3,181,586	695,707,639	3,352,048	3,885	1,872,018	835,969,673
9	99,581,997	3,485,211	23,249,332	129,653	1,367,068	285,916	115,515	8,324,876	65,313,005	696,185,450	3,246,855	422,903	1,978,899	903,686,681
10	62,922,223	4,500,700	20,806,008	770,926	3,883,189	34,322	52,225	4,051,440	3,184,325	589,381,866	1,563,434	37,282	916,891	692,104,831
11	99,906,121	3,484,372	21,778,963	-711,366	1,366,522	224,690	115,487	1,303,215	3,181,347	695,653,588	5,732,560	192,519	1,871,878	834,099,897
12	53,257,913	4,246,208	15,296,615	1,611,945	1,789,731	32,105	48,851	344,166	1,397,621	611,226,686	1,478,443	1,643	1,142,800	691,874,728

13	52,072,623	5,201,270	14,021,930	8,102,398	677,282	33,276	50,633	1,555,662	4,073,285	596,434,057	1,593,759	257,331	967,754	685,041,261
14	31,614,600	3,437,675	3,234,579	178,646	73,226	1,311,252	448	496,522	1,605,045	646,921,040	523,369	274,119	121,130	689,791,654
15	38,370,632	3,000,297	12,989,235	924,808	1,989,134	566,068	0	1,379,369	5,148,976	751,439,949	202,017	0	1,150,016	817,160,500
16	36,938,578	2,605,888	8,109,274	4,259,968	1,679,529	187,310	0	2,606,619	396,864	714,329,299	382,623	0	1,117,737	772,613,689
17	38,709,055	3,396,964	13,927,814	4,063,468	2,359,514	174,567	0	3,038,917	2,777,353	824,839,018	194,265	25,773	973,304	894,480,011
18	51,107,770	2,547,216	48,570,474	4,945,686	43,905	0	0	1,343,980	7,518,352	759,618,509	876,098	0	321,036	876,893,025
19	86,637,045	3,753,455	9,384,876	7,367,084	3,761,794	48,016,632	0	1,886,966	10,257,857	772,808,583	233,828	798,752	95,390	945,002,262
20	2,466,288,228	2,579,875	12,968,514	2,891,000	1,005,132	0	0	962,806	1,951,981	842,230,036	2,156,250	49,658	2,699,987	3,335,783,467
21	87,142,171	4,758,598	10,594,584	578,455	8,579,441	182,988	0	1,621,581	1,204,966	765,800,223	22,112,977	0	1,052,013	903,627,996
22	82,055,686	3,212,533	12,527,825	1,691,728	1,883,915	4,051,848	0	4,856,022	603,083	857,081,533	309,683	16,207	151,637	968,441,700
TOTAL	4,010,531,538	84,738,558	651,593,498	241,429,209	42,170,261	59,870,220	1,252,724	81,044,071	219,482,885	15,486,000,408	70,788,381	3,922,026	28,474,046	20,981,297,826
INDIANA														
1	94,828,572	6,946,340	33,071,396	4,911,485	647,879	24,600	0	964,862	551,967	694,375,547	2,383,002	45,227	269,560	839,020,438
2	155,313,845	5,676,984	21,779,623	2,136,157	1,177,844	895,899	0	1,064,094	3,016,996	718,826,284	1,015,482	863,809	662,734	912,429,751
3	55,748,986	4,639,991	14,630,468	585,497	614,412	236,350	0	2,696,869	11,254,862	722,402,300	523,242	65,000	-14,535	813,383,441
4	50,533,664	5,549,527	8,442,549	3,178,721	0	0	55,000	1,068,787	2,188,435	685,442,908	2,789,600	0	494,076	759,743,267
5	57,979,164	4,629,403	12,107,207	758,251	1,460,285	0	0	200,341	4,368,400	734,000,405	498,644	0	377,821	816,379,921
6	199,505,605	2,661,594	10,014,873	4,414,717	1,514,565	288,723	0	2,211,162	4,340,419	742,756,891	1,415,156	638,921	849,979	970,612,605
7	74,821,147	4,616,924	11,373,574	1,162,582	28,512	26,869,366	0	14,826,324	6,383,827	739,147,108	276,408	1,004,210	390,446	880,900,428
8	75,503,837	4,437,057	16,150,664	922,677	243,483	383,516	0	1,205,457	4,269,954	772,749,844	394,717	282,468	318,424	876,862,098
9	109,369,606	5,266,199	8,929,347	257,465	113,835	7,795,407	0	1,636,506	272,065	640,432,058	146,519	288,313	70,455	774,577,775
10	1,037,214,947	351,316	39,677,021	559,712	5,967,478	1,936,509	0	7,225,037	12,503,510	715,230,021	2,351,402	0	2,473,291	1,825,490,244
TOTAL	1,910,819,374	44,775,334	176,176,722	18,887,264	11,768,292	38,430,370	55,000	33,099,439	49,150,435	7,165,363,367	11,794,173	3,187,948	5,892,251	9,469,399,969
IOWA														
1	65,877,874	5,645,250	9,703,770	166,998	2,663,837	190,751	0	2,189,049	4,502,557	743,805,678	2,030,502	613,699	422,350	837,812,315
2	52,498,905	5,491,429	13,897,343	1,103,005	2,103	0	0	988,412	5,982,419	818,303,336	699,935	0	393,488	899,360,375
3	111,056,023	5,539,587	7,732,286	799,517	1,338,611	7,276,551	688,161	4,859,697	3,560,565	764,446,875	1,278,637	45,276	107,344	908,729,130
4	741,707,184	4,829,985	40,632,915	3,070,296	755,995	9,200,426	0	2,605,956	15,868,992	678,656,192	1,381,221	102,377	2,993,653	1,501,805,192
5	62,334,076	7,470,744	7,024,966	1,755,133	2,478,909	14,981	0	1,550,765	5,458,175	923,890,705	329,081	166,547	302,397	1,012,776,479
6	54,011,794	6,888,018	12,166,997	25,501	141,020	0	0	2,534,478	7,643,543	981,142,937	2,226,730	0	417,442	1,067,198,460
TOTAL	1,087,485,856	35,865,013	91,158,277	6,920,450	7,380,475	16,682,709	688,161	14,728,357	43,016,251	4,910,245,723	7,946,106	927,899	4,636,674	6,227,681,951
KANSAS														
1	33,611,779	7,067,642	11,579,758	1,939,522	279,395	889,615	0	1,157,265	4,755,595	1,165,898,238	956,271	0	283,428	1,228,418,508
2	586,218,622	5,007,929	12,082,004	2,299,789	9,173,159	13,481,844	1,486,250	3,263,251	6,443,267	576,649,113	1,228,190	0	925,002	1,218,258,420
3	53,533,352	6,713,334	14,656,774	333,833	55,500	67,901	0	8,051,669	3,944,424	575,753,711	885,073	376,490	3,177,429	667,549,490
4	49,541,456	3,998,592	15,312,271	6,007,150	540,867	777,490	160,132	3,027,493	1,067,966	692,624,267	5,459,964	103,629	1,493,432	780,114,709
5	44,940,970	5,421,294	9,430,839	695,312	785,389	183,861	0	1,533,385	5,934,072	740,667,198	386,286	39,125	1,079,799	811,097,530
TOTAL	767,846,179	28,208,791	63,061,646	11,275,606	10,834,310	15,400,711	1,646,382	17,033,063	22,145,324	3,751,592,527	8,915,784	519,244	6,959,090	4,705,438,657
KENTUCKY														
1	64,180,347	6,526,748	6,095,210	476,716	371,910	363,885	0	1,426,414	2,271,048	801,050,191	15,000	7,422	360,706	883,145,597
2	62,478,664	5,471,391	6,918,849	1,627,996	579,969	373,488	0	4,534,091	3,298,485	564,830,942	586,279	0	154,902	650,855,056
3	58,908,327	12,114,005	17,182,060	25,123,985	511,250	864,000	0	13,538,912	15,398,203	689,330,220	2,703,767	112,767	2,483,920	838,271,416
4	48,514,491	9,486,224	24,686,080	1,069,711	31,390	0	0	1,107,372	567,236	641,662,236	210,633	0	916,871	728,252,244
5	133,211,175	8,819,985	6,746,247	1,501,794	76,506	0	0	2,482,795	5,965,976	746,512,424	403,283	0	299,772	906,019,957
6	1,141,214,363	6,270,109	28,342,157	76,981	300,910	19,188,402	0	3,935,237	11,355,326	553,794,106	767,161	445,000	3,497,339	1,769,187,091
7	108,352,571	7,019,973	8,519,057	1,259,419	177,118	0	0	7,847,242	2,820,866	722,285,603	79,858	0	268,812	858,630,519
TOTAL	1,616,859,938	55,708,435	98,489,660	31,136,602	2,049,053	20,789,775	0	34,872,063	41,677,140	4,719,465,722	4,765,981	565,189	7,982,322	6,634,361,880

See Appendix A for a listing of the congressional districts which represent the county in which the state capital is located and congressional districts which represent only portions of a county. See Appendix B for a listing of the programs included in each recipent category.

table continues

Table 3.4 Federal Outlays to Categories of Recipients by Congressional District, 1986 *(continued)*

District	State Gov't.	Counties	Cities/ Towns	Special Districts	Schools	Public Universities	Indian Tribes	Non-Profits	Private Universities	Individuals	For Profits	Small Businesses	All Others	Total
LOUISIANA														
1	81,856,901	-779,419	21,802,944	34,495,919	1,691,514	823,062	0	7,972,551	22,767,602	549,808,046	3,146,304	177,127	1,091,716	724,854,267
2	92,767,020	13,475,702	17,515,557	405,746	1,747,376	949,064	0	1,897,219	14,198,782	582,049,290	89,478,983	91,675	629,230	815,205,643
3	64,905,738	21,395,671	10,513,513	1,153,418	1,310,588	153,793	645,634	904,106	113,139	600,068,766	221,194	0	2,058,382	703,443,940
4	81,456,903	4,887,623	14,955,808	58,069	4,991,785	305,532	0	1,211,426	1,085,710	609,689,620	1,399,564	0	2,218,416	722,260,457
5	124,421,932	7,488,514	12,607,665	23,233	305,421	611,352	0	3,441,982	207,756	677,953,287	1,736,244	0	501,603	829,298,991
6	1,448,635,334	5,145,683	18,248,308	57,500	1,049,004	12,786,669	449,093	1,722,181	5,881,931	534,997,539	4,447,073	49,995	3,307,472	2,036,777,782
7	79,227,741	6,238,517	8,145,518	3,858,125	462,395	974,718	278,924	4,845,475	1,426,704	563,458,139	3,179,342	0	2,463,850	674,559,447
8	172,860,869	9,411,459	6,693,357	54,450	582,137	1,135,033	148,511	3,400,888	912,189	579,903,780	4,097,948	50,000	384,487	779,635,109
TOTAL	2,146,132,437	67,263,751	110,482,671	40,106,460	12,140,220	17,739,223	1,522,162	25,395,829	46,593,812	4,697,928,467	107,706,653	368,797	12,655,155	7,286,035,636
MAINE														
1	429,195,990	2,145,238	21,534,436	4,906,567	115,780	2,004,004	0	9,717,535	5,218,706	787,827,100	1,449,376	501,987	1,733,942	1,266,350,661
2	146,621,852	3,495,305	26,323,579	4,504,671	154,568	6,399,918	5,733,202	4,494,702	4,077,354	774,828,427	944,259	7,858,478	1,397,925	986,834,240
TOTAL	575,817,842	5,640,543	47,858,015	9,411,238	270,348	8,403,922	5,733,202	14,212,237	9,296,060	1,562,655,527	2,393,635	8,360,465	3,131,867	2,253,184,901
MARYLAND														
1	67,875,460	18,493,035	6,935,216	533,279	0	2,231,865	0	2,323,562	1,259,668	639,068,455	429,492	4,000	85,884	739,239,916
2	487,288,407	15,005,742	857,185	171,045	0	35,375	0	190,182	1,109,420	354,587,264	1,000,746	165,966	199,725	860,611,057
3	244,801,078	10,335,515	38,314,729	69,661	0	1,626,252	84,926	8,906,503	115,850,006	845,069,664	2,313,863	1,344,679	1,199,003	1,269,915,880
4	359,823,037	47,835,983	1,827,588	12,330	0	8,069	0	1,267,403	1,111,103	459,539,917	420,349	272,000	428,409	872,546,187
5	60,381,082	18,320,112	2,471,522	11,879,455	0	28,497,956	0	5,876,423	6,567,123	394,385,289	2,296,673	690,544	3,655,035	535,021,215
6	57,236,149	17,497,580	9,927,967	243,630	0	157,006	0	629,434	1,503,736	605,482,779	383,727	1,737,010	6,355,648	701,154,668
7	415,324,882	2,215,243	61,003,773	21,315	150,000	1,498,715	-66,236	10,958,751	27,741,568	1,099,015,718	3,122,873	0	355,536	1,621,342,138
8	45,525,455	18,795,156	1,756,205	0	0	0	0	28,510,874	857,887	587,105,433	25,222,236	39,766,064	33,010,973	780,550,283
TOTAL	1,738,255,551	148,498,368	123,094,185	12,930,715	150,000	34,055,238	18,690	58,663,131	156,000,511	4,984,254,520	35,189,959	43,980,264	45,290,213	7,380,381,345
MASSACHUSETTS														
1	120,722,011	949,860	24,563,134	1,704,543	-17,440	13,731,723	0	5,714,388	9,416,870	734,700,231	359,770	598,737	1,043,785	913,487,612
2	119,468,431	966,499	29,136,108	9,147,416	0	6,007	0	3,727,777	3,574,681	765,265,260	1,491,349	48,904	1,863,649	934,696,082
3	108,394,325	578,161	35,293,178	2,515,926	0	242,478	0	8,350,880	8,988,902	722,527,634	628,312	157,835	281,731	887,959,362
4	100,213,137	707,573	23,683,666	9,017,285	0	244,339	0	44,641,062	5,044,421	645,576,235	125,392	1,279,358	77,427	830,609,896
5	75,914,529	3,920,838	27,318,868	2,871,358	0	772,967	0	6,538,208	505,939	645,075,229	373,859	4,107,167	310,751	767,709,713
6	95,376,625	2,577,042	15,941,615	6,821,356	0	189,777	0	5,781,817	1,926,502	766,766,704	984,763	117,900	1,695,187	898,179,287
7	166,577,416	1,060,226	23,907,094	1,930,901	79,522	120,060	91,094	4,119,061	32,585,951	694,074,426	2,559,939	5,535,928	1,032,302	933,673,920
8	334,537,400	2,157,045	32,139,035	124,161,134	223,468	1,105,567	190,189	150,702,757	221,387,893	794,570,090	17,246,089	6,503,763	7,402,632	1,692,327,061
9	879,937,358	2,493,937	45,130,034	14,045,434	583,866	1,008,459	268,741	82,757,587	17,848,807	869,694,026	1,780,809	1,512,637	1,583,801	1,918,645,497
10	98,492,371	1,555,176	21,155,979	5,643,387	0	689,113	187,205	12,195,369	17,499,001	852,093,439	347,707	295,646	634,404	1,010,788,798
11	276,221,000	1,367,067	22,866,279	3,957,777	456,110	226,514	129,553	13,036,644	9,634,621	718,321,101	814,807	108,559	1,134,019	1,048,274,051
TOTAL	2,375,854,602	18,333,425	301,134,991	181,816,517	1,325,525	18,337,004	866,782	337,565,550	328,413,586	8,208,664,376	26,712,798	20,266,435	17,059,688	11,836,351,280
MICHIGAN														
1	173,475,269	3,723,952	33,345,707	59,206,945	2,174,596	1,248,463	87,070	3,440,626	1,866,531	742,747,948	1,769,816	71,030	1,395,815	1,024,553,768
2	182,381,234	7,014,543	18,249,425	0	2,718,595	26,434,178	18,751	2,721,667	3,104,076	630,356,268	1,025,889	918,570	260,016	875,203,212
3	1,132,525,534	4,300,218	8,107,836	1,632,852	1,904,508	39,800	64,454	4,346,892	2,233,131	608,260,484	331,057	0	1,016,990	1,764,763,757
4	100,831,493	6,354,925	8,950,017	620,232	1,416,978	82,048	150,273	4,764,198	2,778,111	677,996,202	8,065	0	932,364	804,884,905
5	84,089,660	6,511,319	13,546,652	3,929,189	1,244,416	0	215,432	2,189,379	10,536,879	613,404,213	1,600,356	86,132	206,400	737,560,027
6	786,764,281	6,884,429	2,052,062	249,538	470,330	17,099,961	785,186	2,015,726	7,837,735	588,149,009	2,197,446	456,689	106,892	1,415,069,284
7	114,944,171	4,424,707	15,631,017	492,803	3,276,187	222,082	111,447	948,402	1,903,569	622,725,647	2,937,326	310,283	-54,001	767,873,641
8	108,957,785	7,686,463	15,386,507	1,205,779	315,711	226,007	0	978,113	2,279,978	702,862,291	408,855	837,054	0	841,144,543
9	91,047,466	7,924,164	11,097,359	51,880	994,549	329,967	1,445,777	3,727,295	506,753	723,143,947	824,427	0	210,180	841,303,765

10	399,722,810	7,769,966	9,083,383	595,769	3,639,585	271,366	1,024,112	4,876,512	855,049	688,067,607	453,140	0	2,080,593	1,118,439,893
11	103,401,725	10,063,997	20,548,070	349,525	6,344,864	2,073,713	5,781,133	7,763,051	2,456,130	841,871,112	519,861	0	461,253	1,001,634,435
12	56,561,221	7,369,920	15,190,001	0	1,060,511	0	0	830,563	0	641,889,400	1,350,100	49,639	704,081	725,005,435
13	189,407,159	15,588,683	40,811,689	0	2,082,155	2,350,110	162,070	12,739,937	1,701,548	742,532,220	1,769,816	1,327,107	226,181	1,010,698,675
14	93,525,711	4,387,905	14,995,361	0	1,449,058	6,677	32,711	511,419	647,521	680,479,823	1,841,689	0	828,013	798,705,887
15	155,761,543	3,679,982	36,449,950	5,995	1,753,064	341,795	70,740	1,492,744	2,033,798	691,656,585	1,863,304	0	70,077	895,179,577
16	137,986,527	5,306,425	35,078,445	686,060	5,415,470	212,320	57,016	3,171,902	3,099,070	695,474,576	3,005,919	0	68,786	889,562,516
17	110,828,632	3,867,528	20,997,232	0	1,365,925	8,623	42,243	3,385,509	887,481	701,104,883	3,997,246	122,655	49,947	846,657,904
18	54,203,069	4,105,989	10,085,181	0	2,696,715	344,172	63,686	2,752,865	575,035	648,140,086	283,956	59,916	44,912	723,355,582
TOTAL	4,076,415,291	116,965,115	329,605,896	69,026,567	40,323,216	51,291,282	10,112,100	62,656,800	45,302,394	12,240,862,302	26,188,267	4,239,075	8,608,500	17,081,596,805
MINNESOTA														
1	80,322,776	7,335,861	10,793,217	7,550	209,920	420,249	257,819	35,817,413	2,721,295	739,276,106	496,233	0	593,927	878,252,365
2	78,167,756	10,513,939	15,501,320	464,099	2,969,124	628,133	566,544	1,188,529	1,627,111	925,225,238	17,275	0	187,360	1,037,056,427
3	88,504,016	7,205,503	6,845,886	132,960	244,734	0	222,825	508,139	2,252,546	526,577,238	1,294,772	459,650	1,185,993	635,434,261
4	944,428,311	634,667	16,772,698	11,715,523	7,569,006	15,333,321	933,639	6,233,128	14,548,632	42,519,185	1,180,861	31,000	2,740,231	1,064,640,203
5	163,974,051	6,404,179	23,964,259	12,505	1,670,724	13,077,292	1,008,720	10,776,993	4,248,214	623,474,274	2,867,357	83,500	217,512	851,779,580
6	189,676,473	12,936,957	5,048,309	-131	55,509	0	0	1,919,470	129,128	1,037,171,144	149,840	101,391	382,730	1,247,570,820
7	134,692,614	10,704,250	21,017,701	1,318,252	3,987,017	381,826	3,565,557	6,063,023	4,687,451	799,473,592	606,608	43,050	3,048,474	989,589,415
8	138,749,960	11,902,008	23,275,097	119,860	1,557,650	575,783	7,523,573	2,817,960	2,279,313	738,499,296	984,961	0	601,806	928,887,267
TOTAL	1,818,515,956	67,637,362	123,218,487	13,770,618	18,263,684	30,416,604	14,078,677	65,324,655	32,493,690	5,432,216,073	7,597,907	718,591	8,958,033	7,633,210,338
MISSISSIPPI														
1	72,254,948	8,542,605	8,565,629	1,815,204	1,594,681	644,856	0	6,220,389	4,796,270	678,319,223	1,144,678	45,325	24,170	783,967,978
2	107,569,893	22,229,520	9,438,080	678,930	6,301,651	3,190,803	0	17,090,743	1,158,862	678,969,073	554,989	0	2,289,983	849,472,528
3	71,106,136	7,982,301	4,323,401	355,146	3,208,969	9,166,612	9,697,670	3,903,712	7,776,966	640,810,389	144,558	0	448,264	758,924,124
4	965,866,455	10,325,011	14,635,867	2,523,816	84,533	2,823,946	0	19,950,084	5,719,954	655,754,374	1,161,695	2,093,063	2,163,080	1,683,101,878
5	39,601,981	15,648,241	19,748,701	15,079,553	8,811,692	3,098,050	0	9,209,201	2,093,418	609,308,638	462,409	484,068	1,369,514	724,915,467
TOTAL	1,256,399,413	64,727,679	56,711,678	20,452,649	20,001,526	18,924,267	9,697,670	56,374,129	21,545,470	3,263,161,697	3,468,329	2,622,456	6,295,011	4,800,381,974
MISSOURI														
1	62,804,457	8,913,363	27,354,569	20,307,319	2,501,271	274,488	0	15,352,534	92,131,149	1,111,513,429	4,414,764	234,615	2,491,136	1,348,293,093
2	70,663,891	4,383,429	38,546,236	11,092,861	4,042,858	0	0	3,817,400	4,177,090	869,598,856	7,697,347	0	1,476,458	1,015,496,426
3	30,412,934	1,796,045	13,344,059	3,378,707	1,803,756	0	0	3,487,590	1,924,854	327,812,541	3,074,888	234,876	502,747	387,772,996
4	1,005,310,034	3,955,336	11,991,875	5,611,748	6,180,051	2,740,772	0	2,378,703	844,167	798,831,739	424,158	0	4,190,867	1,842,459,451
5	51,524,706	2,893,387	33,377,112	9,740,563	414,923	153,000	70,000	11,205,854	0	793,807,344	218,316	324,380	1,798,717	905,528,302
6	41,557,525	3,353,151	15,223,585	303,270	3,229,334	488,430	569,648	10,934,258	16,134,092	780,475,105	3,452,897	170,640	739,349	876,631,284
7	64,110,907	2,664,179	16,471,880	30,672	281,733	108,050	3,277	2,340,498	7,523,930	828,277,210	1,009,345	50,000	363,690	923,235,371
8	110,590,644	6,956,257	10,490,681	1,447,240	1,627,246	806,152	0	6,314,205	147,000	908,529,815	1,828,115	95,604	726,069	1,049,559,028
9	173,579,684	3,708,831	15,130,136	3,952,008	166,594	13,612,793	25,000	5,793,278	12,222,381	762,674,934	1,078,674	43,795	1,084,704	993,072,811
TOTAL	1,610,554,782	38,623,978	181,930,132	55,864,388	20,247,767	18,183,685	667,925	61,624,319	135,104,663	7,181,520,973	23,198,505	1,153,910	13,373,736	9,342,048,762
MONTANA														
1	360,890,274	9,203,247	9,734,425	3,994,936	15,577,612	7,089,848	5,409,578	4,260,132	5,831,877	536,480,752	303,343	217,086	960,531	959,953,641
2	50,685,592	11,280,253	11,689,331	242,231	20,013,544	472,856	10,404,077	4,092,096	1,262,415	709,141,861	2,086,312	1,790,982	324,444	823,485,994
TOTAL	411,575,866	20,483,500	21,423,756	4,237,167	35,591,156	7,562,704	15,813,655	8,352,228	7,094,292	1,245,622,613	2,389,655	2,008,068	1,284,975	1,783,439,635
NEBRASKA														
1	409,726,539	5,888,011	15,344,812	1,863,846	5,038,517	10,439,824	6,141,743	5,923,795	14,988,335	882,887,143	1,731,920	0	365,312	1,360,339,798
2	75,956,628	3,394,065	21,295,651	12,924,412	8,831,026	677,829	427,371	8,697,349	5,762,748	646,043,438	2,684,885	213,936	1,274,600	788,183,937
3	56,503,620	9,246,062	5,087,978	2,354,149	2,611,617	212,589	0	2,541,892	474,302	1,197,628,210	943,157	0	1,795,687	1,279,399,263
TOTAL	542,186,787	18,528,138	41,728,441	17,142,407	16,481,160	11,330,242	6,569,114	17,163,036	21,225,385	2,726,558,791	5,359,962	213,936	3,435,599	3,427,922,998

See Appendix A for a listing of the congressional districts which represent the county in which the state capital is located and congressional districts which represent only portions of a county. See Appendix B for a listing of the programs included in each recipent category.

table continues

Table 3.4 **Federal Outlays to Categories of Recipients by Congressional District, 1986 *(continued)***

District	State Gov't.	Counties	Cities/ Towns	Special Districts	Schools	Public Universities	Indian Tribes	Non-Profits	Private Universities	Individuals	For Profits	Small Businesses	All Others	Total
NEVADA														
1	33,738,456	18,322,826	5,769,855	308,155	1,814,604	1,430,896	434,259	2,367,919	-86,807	544,615,848	3,857,371	67,703	1,032,885	613,673,969
2	247,251,591	8,620,172	11,361,977	5,115,000	2,417,928	6,412,623	7,019,507	7,430,432	1,121,483	503,076,231	713,810	373,188	3,179,147	804,093,090
TOTAL	280,990,047	26,942,998	17,131,832	5,423,155	4,232,532	7,843,519	7,453,766	9,798,351	1,034,676	1,047,692,079	4,571,181	440,891	4,212,032	1,417,767,059
NEW HAMPSHIRE														
1	48,470,756	3,028,704	18,262,836	1,381,136	51,081	9,270,984	0	883,993	5,104,346	573,604,289	334,156	312,913	1,943,900	662,649,093
2	260,353,169	1,759,443	19,991,111	428,610	10,054	102,745	0	4,055,434	22,998,729	605,134,404	382,993	1,621,990	789,801	917,628,484
TOTAL	308,823,925	4,788,147	38,253,947	1,809,746	61,135	9,373,729	0	4,939,427	28,103,075	1,178,738,693	717,149	1,934,903	2,733,701	1,580,277,577
NEW JERSEY														
1	76,407,965	12,087,219	8,957,672	4,331,082	49,164	168,298	0	3,294,683	0	632,823,486	2,621,897	0	456,518	741,197,985
2	99,939,581	11,291,506	21,741,094	430,691	60,618	231,972	0	7,068,823	0	968,251,464	286,640	-4,094	1,330,010	1,110,628,305
3	55,898,681	5,976,816	12,153,765	0	298,178	0	0	1,936,023	1,971,164	854,714,474	692,211	0	1,423,787	935,065,100
4	1,566,648,120	9,147,847	8,521,029	10,693,844	601,765	389,492	0	4,646,239	1,526,154	703,473,932	217,982	92,800	694,853	2,306,654,057
5	46,119,014	8,353,608	4,514,858	0	-3,936	222,195	0	611,656	151,181	637,607,114	1,054,229	297,970	61,636	698,989,525
6	65,979,829	10,277,913	13,200,924	590,898	-24,402	9,270,080	0	979,407	2,280,625	682,412,276	1,860,877	40,000	910,911	787,779,337
7	60,350,584	6,984,287	9,927,331	296,347	121,310	78,764	0	2,027,007	1,880,300	756,795,899	53,416,767	383,782	806,482	893,068,860
8	81,452,114	6,066,732	22,872,097	0	1,517,135	419,155	0	3,143,991	1,772,767	707,281,265	875,050	0	793,517	826,193,823
9	27,502,211	13,440,685	34,770,924	2,479,940	31,382	-2,054	0	931,277	5,464,053	792,641,426	828,598	47,000	1,864,681	880,000,122
10	337,204,791	14,387,835	23,550,859	637,821	-179,530	1,523,188	0	15,410,685	2,259,726	724,248,276	8,468,924	2,414,847	2,567,470	1,132,494,894
11	119,353,291	10,339,132	7,872,081	517,645	-63,070	147,626	0	238,933	4,678,200	703,112,352	258,479	180,573	190,146	846,825,388
12	54,010,092	6,678,092	5,488,730	833,524	-18,116	2,618,133	0	14,487,653	34,576,881	708,746,790	1,786,241	1,209,325	664,337	831,081,682
13	58,678,713	14,113,640	5,191,439	0	3,628,664	0	420,499	1,518,288	8,821	888,991,086	2,877,853	291,050	283,264	976,003,316
14	142,366,026	9,242,862	26,244,286	337,809	-16,640	72,970	0	1,077,924	4,327,514	710,147,731	1,707,907	0	1,389,285	896,897,674
TOTAL	2,791,911,013	138,388,173	205,007,089	21,149,601	6,002,522	15,139,819	420,499	57,372,590	60,897,386	10,471,247,571	76,953,654	4,953,253	13,436,897	13,862,880,067
NEW MEXICO														
1	92,446,597	5,376,486	15,077,968	35,000	2,011,512	5,033,877	3,878,217	5,636,612	264,230	485,974,690	1,774,805	1,933,649	1,855,212	621,298,855
2	60,488,035	8,680,077	13,234,015	3,692,089	8,213,672	4,957,003	872,455	2,054,932	3,005,671	594,110,403	675,343	178,441	690,538	700,852,674
3	506,020,350	8,676,852	7,578,924	60,500	46,436,492	2,049,368	15,808,152	7,302,279	2,690,198	436,376,396	1,090,370	232,194	555,805	1,034,877,880
TOTAL	658,954,982	22,733,415	35,890,907	3,787,589	56,661,676	12,040,248	20,558,824	14,993,823	5,960,099	1,516,461,489	3,540,518	2,344,284	3,101,555	2,357,029,409
NEW YORK														
1	89,925,436	11,343,614	20,741,812	-346,518	273,766	950,868	188,555	12,397,916	1,244,000	497,228,509	883,474	40,000	333,594	635,205,026
2	70,608,548	5,921,815	16,539,921	0	231,964	0	2,301	558,221	1,116,091	496,287,726	1,112,099	0	0	592,378,686
3	106,283,289	26,694,906	19,524,437	17,311,928	229,194	10,629,691	2,306	4,579,218	7,060,667	878,592,090	7,968,817	488,344	115,352	1,079,480,239
4	64,615,998	11,233,713	6,059,490	9,906,698	43,619	0	0	735,039	4,327,969	743,564,789	1,546,073	4,000	970,416	843,007,804
5	62,941,570	12,544,576	9,685,899	9,764,666	99,613	0	0	3,505,779	10,514,291	736,652,074	2,559,091	0	0	848,267,559
6	142,696,385	987,474	585,165	66,944	0	7,986	0	9,588,847	2,409,947	770,820,609	831,625	0	0	927,994,981
7	143,278,354	0	548,884	0	0	8,018	0	5,268,784	2,524,500	773,968,377	1,137,317	0	1,446,706	928,180,940
8	172,136,129	1,412,275	816,109	453,464	1,067	334,183	0	4,996,081	34,108,332	777,019,425	1,718,410	40,000	130,620	993,166,094
9	142,502,813	0	519,059	0	0	189,975	0	4,038,139	2,357,011	769,774,050	830,497	0	0	920,211,543
10	215,507,938	1,750,660	12,143,282	28,850	0	823,919	0	5,010,260	3,507,782	731,413,472	2,163,412	43,700	219,020	972,612,295
11	217,512,178	1,625,523	11,358,098	0	0	0	0	5,219,193	3,616,047	738,570,538	2,139,157	0	1,747,997	981,788,731
12	227,408,926	1,643,175	10,973,169	0	0	162,685	0	5,350,341	3,397,980	736,913,409	2,134,278	246,178	2,532,102	990,762,243
13	217,828,351	1,720,420	10,985,710	0	0	86,367	0	5,365,564	5,376,432	739,654,409	2,142,216	49,932	379,784	983,589,184
14	134,983,618	625,886	3,769,718	0	0	88,600	0	7,105,222	1,966,899	715,011,055	1,100,751	17,600	20,350	864,689,699
15	817,357,275	145,449	427,561,483	10,632,257	28,880	6,844,814	0	137,408,385	173,062,745	774,447,772	31,783,405	144,899	4,685,319	2,384,102,684
16	549,546,738	1,481,278	343,696,785	112,251	28,879	2,544,475	775,908	18,208,851	52,374,718	774,869,585	27,773,290	145,555	5,348,281	1,776,906,595
17	496,179,081	80,570	264,589,466	85,964	22,116	1,098,451	0	39,438,430	92,503,619	784,769,176	66,066,524	790,979	5,227,972	1,750,852,349

18	262,494,354	318,681	232,166	1,310,410	-2,000	534,685	0	12,065,575	4,986,083	821,972,773	3,907,080	0	3,483,147	1,111,302,953
19	217,590,451	1,583,741	1,119,837	32,150,444	0	118,363	0	13,169,846	4,280,370	800,353,269	1,788,896	46,481	1,426,151	1,073,627,849
20	97,942,825	13,812,224	18,244,967	2,416,382	-6,700	210,848	0	10,747,990	25,250,616	780,746,801	257,748	922,189	858,331	951,404,221
21	93,040,544	4,812,782	13,655,934	0	154,773	7,893	0	1,619,659	5,644,562	668,006,563	295,716	0	69,181	787,307,606
22	106,521,983	10,474,600	10,834,776	4,196,899	717,522	55,171	0	10,393,878	24,373,400	653,493,680	229,691	40,000	67,021	821,398,621
23	4,494,078,491	8,251,075	18,871,890	-281,390	32,863	19,255,934	0	16,942,033	20,614,947	786,820,363	4,421,758	52,550	4,885,696	5,373,946,209
24	85,910,772	7,367,297	13,313,979	32,522	129,484	104,280	0	4,175,438	3,958,895	700,672,218	552,293	54,122	365,526	816,636,825
25	111,380,765	12,998,026	25,975,907	-266,147	23,007	405,633	0	3,248,310	6,484,680	726,666,367	774,570	41,892	474,635	888,207,646
26	122,960,825	12,878,553	30,788,597	626,117	108,222	892,017	1,119,170	6,597,076	5,398,653	706,704,661	1,056,191	574,537	1,602,299	891,306,918
27	103,403,876	9,716,696	19,565,931	436,964	-1,294	2,748,431	349,241	4,859,998	25,577,694	653,613,049	1,541,767	302,870	474,193	822,589,415
28	116,381,356	11,278,833	25,966,649	175,665	10,061	20,410,248	0	1,937,356	79,302,450	714,556,856	551,446	863,820	439,708	971,874,449
29	110,807,951	8,876,906	16,785,309	6,954,068	607,791	236,750	0	2,322,496	27,917,808	670,476,265	780,828	389,890	668,568	846,824,629
30	99,936,661	5,142,343	19,228,264	6,721,374	39,250	251,424	0	1,454,498	69,310,250	670,167,427	1,727,626	621,862	1,427,019	876,027,999
31	107,449,155	9,558,448	16,888,001	-2,328	199,924	1,198,838	234,451	2,737,958	4,992,737	709,856,451	967,501	99,147	2,094,396	856,274,680
32	139,591,048	9,078,152	18,887,240	6,004,007	53,525	132,560	39,704	5,136,677	6,329,528	726,804,329	1,444,084	105,828	1,231,294	914,837,976
33	122,308,872	12,686,409	34,536,479	127,739	0	5,122,512	107,528	4,558,377	6,214,409	736,495,113	1,322,700	1,541,879	865,300	925,887,316
34	108,203,653	10,355,731	15,526,018	-3,534,896	114,922	72,802	5,216,952	2,835,492	6,374,037	760,358,025	611,683	401,950	214,826	906,751,194
TOTAL	10,371,316,209	228,401,830	1,460,520,429	105,084,333	3,140,448	75,528,420	8,036,116	373,576,927	728,480,149	24,727,321,274	176,122,015	8,070,204	43,804,805	38,309,403,159
NORTH CAROLINA														
1	93,549,875	18,538,763	5,476,099	3,169,665	0	783,459	0	2,512,334	3,063,134	679,454,263	385,005	34,500	1,034,085	808,001,182
2	102,629,862	13,468,023	12,458,071	1,231,743	0	3,426,638	88,525	26,330,380	73,817,474	664,235,359	2,418,173	1,214,221	699,516	902,017,985
3	79,352,404	17,372,890	6,208,170	161,282	-839	0	89,766	2,790,195	2,027,899	566,300,341	258,042	-9,223	5,779	674,556,705
4	1,459,963,910	9,314,605	13,320,415	4,191,481	-500	30,416,822	461,855	2,383,524	18,510,056	552,553,796	801,549	447,309	7,724,201	2,100,089,023
5	62,903,429	8,658,389	7,944,730	47,501	0	327,941	0	19,656,459	2,348,618	653,716,451	-17,061	93,200	867,626	756,547,283
6	45,408,905	5,621,673	6,020,514	1,602,150	675,000	5,371,516	94,783	2,133,299	5,442,489	646,893,273	593,039	0	1,174,101	721,030,742
7	85,869,927	15,108,858	8,865,409	269,768	0	994,318	1,989,991	4,280,797	1,225,236	561,108,158	2,107,791	50,000	316,256	682,186,509
8	54,078,296	7,714,607	5,026,511	56,370	0	0	0	4,928,790	6,229,918	686,680,046	134,732	0	334,474	765,183,744
9	46,962,605	10,405,577	10,664,494	-5,052	0	466,350	96,873	2,398,492	6,842,057	601,428,838	1,306,219	21,873	1,497,112	682,085,438
10	48,939,174	7,526,478	10,206,804	166,550	0	369,345	0	1,340,005	2,424,877	614,933,575	0	0	499,291	686,406,098
11	66,606,237	28,878,012	4,558,422	266,157	0	157,838	4,246,381	2,585,789	3,106,109	799,439,537	0	191,126	3,211,509	913,247,118
TOTAL	2,146,264,623	142,607,875	90,749,639	11,157,615	673,661	42,314,227	7,068,174	71,340,064	125,037,867	7,026,743,637	7,987,489	2,043,006	17,363,950	9,691,351,827
NORTH DAKOTA														
TOTAL	315,474,371	18,547,024	13,939,339	1,707,701	16,102,984	12,881,686	14,962,414	4,239,024	7,846,928	1,351,615,076	792,888	354,599	575,932	1,759,039,966
OHIO														
1	134,369,062	23,606,275	20,877,417	14,891,407	1,088,886	3,176,018	0	9,989,367	9,199,276	728,753,787	2,888,360	39,970	965,595	949,845,420
2	95,533,438	6,455,102	13,693,863	60,507	766,792	1,632,416	0	1,978,580	6,585,604	658,532,018	836,254	0	972,703	787,047,277
3	94,839,013	7,323,579	15,952,083	10,771,464	223,490	628,146	0	3,664,606	667,138	641,941,429	2,849,886	299,741	559,620	779,720,195
4	63,408,581	4,134,209	7,957,672	145,100	12,164	7,500	0	1,079,188	4,827,738	709,110,668	9,006,725	0	464,377	800,153,923
5	47,591,366	3,295,441	12,041,127	-65,025	47,947	1,003,752	0	3,659,523	1,687,410	639,716,480	45,148	0	1,019,708	710,042,877
6	135,798,922	9,593,483	7,882,324	250,599	547,542	0	0	3,970,691	2,207,406	666,063,866	885,390	0	1,244,196	828,444,418
7	81,226,952	7,357,873	8,599,448	168,550	3,604,825	163,989	0	4,901,953	15,375,582	617,027,746	8,471,686	49,590	664,032	747,612,227
8	62,558,387	6,552,787	12,445,152	165,591	110,964	1,079,344	0	2,678,254	184,016	601,011,071	215,046	0	166,404	687,167,016
9	105,251,423	4,017,074	18,478,240	11,799,933	363,914	1,677,737	0	4,734,038	644,471	716,789,538	5,908,695	58,822	732,285	870,456,169
10	430,538,824	8,236,570	25,211,051	475,984	8,595,052	1,192,856	0	5,722,341	9,998,912	647,243,763	2,774,148	270,102	305,221	1,140,564,824
11	45,630,017	4,705,091	11,224,037	1,206,778	462,018	1,932,224	0	1,416,495	1,927,311	575,333,572	0	184,322	1,608,600	645,630,465
12	1,445,387,977	3,418,464	18,446,880	13,344,243	191,079	3,319,176	0	6,092,052	5,350,171	550,618,873	74,619	103,100	4,002,554	2,050,349,187
13	54,452,208	6,911,823	15,811,785	804,904	344,341	-2,036	0	223,157	4,119,675	603,329,071	3,587,474	19,619	702,853	690,304,875
14	83,650,937	6,490,201	32,684,195	3,150,865	854,671	1,144,060	716,177	1,923,449	0	697,418,142	1,235,385	0	2,302,128	831,570,209
15	856,089,062	3,520,457	17,901,175	25,185	57,356	16,450,943	0	15,918,063	3,870,505	565,243,936	175,000	129,266	3,975,089	1,483,356,038

See Appendix A for a listing of the congressional districts which represent the county in which the state capital is located and congressional districts which represent only portions of a county. See Appendix B for a listing of the programs included in each recipent category.

table continues

Table 3.4 Federal Outlays to Categories of Recipients by Congressional District, 1986 *(continued)*

District	State Gov't.	Counties	Cities/ Towns	Special Districts	Schools	Public Universities	Indian Tribes	Non-Profits	Private Universities	Individuals	For Profits	Small Businesses	All Others	Total
OHIO *continued*														
16	64,525,508	4,405,579	13,792,406	3,583,262	185,215	3,351,535	0	766,460	2,492,595	673,350,539	199,571	0	1,121,535	767,774,205
17	90,398,406	2,123,097	15,100,798	2,099,874	332,166	0	0	1,561,252	1,417,198	774,712,432	2,799,171	0	1,012,669	891,557,063
18	84,715,457	6,065,172	6,565,306	1,156,257	18,297	0	0	1,759,977	595,250	766,677,152	638,249	40,510	500,879	868,732,506
19	100,009,997	3,823,742	29,417,042	16,349,144	4,124,191	108,835	0	886,648	2,936,531	800,380,005	2,094,614	140,000	175,050	960,445,798
20	105,899,035	3,842,505	42,357,638	30,474,500	4,372,237	1,458,874	0	2,811,360	4,654,267	816,187,089	1,717,762	50,000	2,649,044	1,016,474,311
21	106,575,518	3,722,792	40,122,001	2,996,259	4,531,425	157,403	0	10,137,943	49,779,348	818,009,393	4,662,972	156,578	1,158,806	1,042,010,439
TOTAL	4,288,450,088	129,601,317	386,561,640	113,855,381	30,834,573	38,482,772	716,177	85,875,397	128,520,404	14,267,450,571	51,066,156	1,541,620	26,303,348	19,549,259,443
OKLAHOMA														
1	47,783,601	2,280,668	23,592,499	1,794,500	876,579	10,315	2,082,646	3,694,963	5,929,994	632,179,046	2,360,132	28,113	869,830	723,482,886
2	110,135,559	2,929,493	7,916,103	308,530	9,182,444	1,141,370	23,948,104	3,918,068	1,791,428	720,727,844	109,416	0	1,276,231	883,384,591
3	130,820,026	2,575,586	23,296,046	4,035,163	6,564,855	10,829,275	9,819,172	6,051,607	9,726,262	756,777,928	755,564	2,981	541,737	961,796,202
4	115,858,510	2,133,842	25,558,090	2,262,352	5,088,078	4,085,654	3,062,275	4,370,756	388,200	589,711,945	449,412	31,636	1,409,154	754,409,903
5	582,142,924	2,346,598	25,666,814	3,119,073	1,575,075	2,321,695	2,388,900	5,070,967	2,964,628	647,964,807	3,574,586	0	2,988,027	1,282,124,093
6	220,151,260	2,664,217	14,539,516	340,251	3,233,908	179,111	4,432,013	1,073,675	1,832,051	854,352,885	3,147,202	25,844	4,140,959	1,110,112,892
TOTAL	1,206,891,880	14,930,404	120,569,068	11,859,869	26,520,939	18,567,420	45,733,110	24,180,036	22,632,563	4,201,714,455	10,396,312	88,574	11,225,938	5,715,310,567
OREGON														
1	58,819,143	10,534,787	19,399,145	1,274,306	153,821	37,613,222	1,428,917	13,953,675	5,305,326	669,396,757	1,038,889	199,180	978,603	820,095,772
2	58,865,192	6,527,471	10,605,087	2,402,544	4,744,438	760,203	6,343,286	3,900,155	0	831,628,940	555,127	356,996	538,848	927,228,286
3	111,165,041	8,490,349	16,677,536	29,228,033	2,991,636	441,596	924,307	4,600,908	2,309,552	828,256,839	849,402	325,668	945,507	1,007,206,375
4	90,647,487	3,354,925	14,022,740	9,730,999	4,039,164	14,873,236	54,904	6,633,121	399,687	701,897,472	829,684	121,531	453,730	847,058,680
5	855,411,296	5,833,353	14,683,374	7,308,249	7,156,106	22,189,270	184	7,423,817	12,186,347	670,126,081	4,177,326	259,678	1,510,874	1,608,265,955
TOTAL	1,174,908,159	34,740,885	75,387,883	49,944,131	19,085,165	75,877,527	8,751,598	36,511,676	20,200,912	3,701,306,088	7,450,428	1,263,053	4,427,563	5,209,855,068
PENNSYLVANIA														
1	143,108,426	0	58,187,495	121,402,092	826,041	2,043,138	59,663	37,011,287	106,785,648	691,093,517	1,820,729	20,750	398,645	1,162,757,433
2	162,707,464	0	48,194,418	0	749,225	395,312	59,903	17,588,626	26,564,178	694,006,910	13,291,379	2,852,352	724,048	967,133,814
3	147,154,654	300,000	47,392,496	0	767,670	348,890	59,780	19,725,762	5,769,772	692,195,353	1,824,295	12,230	644,049	916,194,951
4	55,862,785	5,136,668	6,521,648	2,548,309	143,295	728,200	0	957,453	842,963	600,680,733	131,889	161,935	104,027	673,819,905
5	31,477,719	6,157,764	8,317,964	1,035,581	259,484	455,096	0	1,455,130	3,503,291	516,430,448	962,250	410,638	451,082	570,916,446
6	39,897,787	7,781,016	23,685,242	-346,511	88,267	100,000	0	67,174	412,515	675,609,818	72,576	0	761,759	748,129,642
7	48,111,602	8,131,183	10,332,245	0	893,285	2,791,760	5,754	852,884	11,086,785	611,901,906	932,861	1,177	47,078	695,088,519
8	21,723,383	6,105,351	8,476,242	6,152,984	2,316,779	0	0	521,742	411,360	454,911,539	311,701	85,679	1,134,032	502,150,791
9	52,642,129	5,147,289	7,298,735	864,293	600,680	42,000	0	1,731,985	598,050	561,631,930	208,756	98,183	771,453	631,635,483
10	52,421,208	5,492,000	17,534,501	5,743,309	366,391	7,677	0	3,358,293	2,305,161	692,756,786	130,585	0	466,218	780,582,130
11	49,157,970	12,429,109	13,795,233	4,620,537	72,830	30,345	0	4,096,203	3,295,436	786,617,004	171,038	37,860	419,046	874,742,612
12	47,701,969	6,534,344	7,523,814	2,257,761	36,572	0	0	1,728,830	4,068,392	666,844,331	196,868	39,997	442,552	737,375,429
13	43,223,045	2,512,386	19,488,168	-9,655	1,347,518	92,713	10,426	10,895,344	2,725,188	593,740,740	768,389	1,090,825	96,863	675,981,950
14	115,377,622	20,564,638	31,843,125	23,079,060	10,428,932	5,616,608	579,640	21,457,408	41,202,848	667,686,479	8,424,985	768,982	2,501,727	949,532,053
15	36,864,065	4,738,545	3,583,697	3,656,149	1,147,693	0	0	1,656,547	10,778,150	597,719,869	113,181	0	440,704	660,698,600
16	33,625,919	6,478,687	6,781,282	846,333	163,143	270,398	0	1,401,476	2,037,036	479,408,013	2,507	50,000	142,070	531,206,864
17	2,770,925,832	5,491,907	24,076,119	2,273,023	464,669	385,163	0	3,338,805	1,565,733	567,588,260	2,913,446	144,000	5,843,139	3,385,010,096
18	59,116,057	5,025,542	5,532,943	158,766	0	0	0	92,800	0	666,488,115	0	40,000	0	736,454,223
19	30,891,697	5,540,589	6,845,493	19,974,883	613,403	0	0	2,198,836	2,150,288	473,838,434	379,419	0	220,740	542,653,783
20	55,689,479	4,915,063	6,249,232	-79,005	64,688	0	0	408,227	0	655,859,321	5,718,877	5,696	338,436	729,170,013
21	55,039,201	5,359,168	20,324,143	2,778,493	222,364	70,965	0	3,722,348	3,714,799	572,594,835	644,530	69,987	153,285	664,694,118
22	73,942,813	9,517,120	9,757,972	1,625,979	200,789	45,000	0	1,589,963	1,060,838	692,821,476	635,030	0	-11,045,805	780,151,175
23	69,438,982	5,402,224	7,966,205	4,555,154	135,981	23,722,540	0	2,760,437	7,248,823	556,867,976	138,617	85,000	571,238	678,893,177
TOTAL	4,196,101,807	138,760,594	399,708,411	203,137,535	21,909,699	37,145,805	775,166	138,617,559	238,127,254	14,169,293,793	39,793,908	5,975,291	5,626,385	19,594,973,206

RHODE ISLAND														
1	215,026,194	13,536	12,193,214	1,114,506	114,655	167,013	0	7,480,228	15,984,482	529,839,396	409,335	0	104,345	782,446,904
2	148,069,899	32,124	8,542,011	208,757	45,296	5,751,873	67,632	4,016,337	9,986,737	515,709,487	180,841	119,439	553,469	693,283,902
TOTAL	363,096,093	45,660	20,735,225	1,323,263	159,951	5,918,886	67,632	11,496,565	25,971,219	1,045,548,883	590,176	119,439	657,814	1,475,730,806
SOUTH CAROLINA														
1	61,803,174	4,794,722	5,147,769	270,336	1,490,897	406,638	0	4,525,293	496,273	384,654,154	282,866	0	531,381	464,403,503
2	565,229,630	4,212,271	5,082,257	2,107,976	320,199	5,328,156	9,174	4,706,651	7,098,992	399,354,763	564,199	0	359,754	994,374,022
3	45,553,033	4,777,762	4,115,159	393,515	322,751	7,172,688	1,060,462	1,458,140	3,956,090	468,636,141	93,080	0	586,094	538,124,915
4	35,871,653	4,783,449	4,716,252	591,752	55,042	0	0	1,194,228	2,171,330	477,811,875	56,319	0	804,615	528,056,515
5	55,325,870	5,751,716	3,629,473	285,531	841,675	187,612	3,066	2,638,898	1,964,431	454,125,706	21,545	0	74,088	524,849,611
6	74,274,751	8,757,608	7,950,386	62,667	2,160,405	0	0	3,488,110	642,132	444,908,970	274,923	0	138,800	542,658,752
TOTAL	838,058,111	33,077,528	30,641,296	3,711,777	5,190,969	13,095,094	1,072,702	18,011,320	16,329,248	2,629,491,609	1,292,932	0	2,494,732	3,592,467,318
SOUTH DAKOTA														
TOTAL	253,147,637	5,280,305	13,864,499	881,424	20,555,407	4,204,109	14,027,375	4,978,584	6,317,032	851,147,101	257,224	154,091	243,075	1,175,057,863
TENNESSEE														
1	53,303,325	4,761,562	4,148,844	2,633	-9,440	551,142	0	776,722	1,321,384	495,278,059	248,891	0	114,442	560,497,564
2	49,995,532	4,135,786	8,161,129	286,716	0	11,313,081	0	1,761,683	4,100,285	503,981,863	183,012	17,500	772,318	584,708,905
3	46,877,591	3,535,568	8,649,104	210,990	0	385,205	0	2,742,419	2,281,719	519,675,213	1,270,845	543,163	1,013,097	587,184,914
4	63,821,494	3,417,365	4,194,318	652,342	0	360,510	0	3,373,951	942,302	520,263,497	0	246,228	17,828	597,289,835
5	825,027,654	1,889,509	15,285,865	6,006,042	0	1,765,815	-140	38,819,881	16,632,171	479,583,082	389,931	0	566,882	1,385,966,692
6	45,684,877	2,836,562	6,105,095	55,000	0	244,021	0	4,266,159	85,003	445,319,267	28,975	0	282,939	504,907,898
7	62,488,944	4,986,287	11,607,533	205,091	0	153,851	0	1,353,796	813,847	443,825,432	1,026,085	13,560	107,319	526,581,745
8	65,006,760	4,802,348	8,776,981	3,078,976	89,644	29,105	0	8,580,760	1,586,704	532,859,002	307,908	0	214,361	625,332,549
9	72,779,225	6,761,015	11,506,609	0	0	84,982	0	1,727,093	1,065,004	439,646,844	2,831,121	0	608,601	537,010,495
TOTAL	1,284,985,402	37,126,002	78,435,478	10,497,790	80,204	14,887,712	-140	63,402,464	28,828,419	4,380,432,260	6,286,768	820,451	3,697,787	5,909,480,597
TEXAS														
1	48,658,220	4,311,698	3,694,326	57,950	809,781	0	146,452	75,818	675,308	614,380,952	0	0	153,761	672,964,266
2	39,433,486	2,929,580	3,588,855	170,986	97,553	248,087	110,567	328,293	79,279	582,441,310	74,106	0	935,888	630,437,990
3	20,400,641	1,708,133	5,048,825	248,851	175,854	2,075,051	0	195,114	1,053,923	383,677,756	301,889	167,379	0	415,053,416
4	31,095,040	2,057,325	5,917,089	88,720	994,475	22,500	0	56,711	1,319,365	612,319,396	540,594	0	234,181	654,645,396
5	51,617,939	4,368,063	4,508,000	260,808	313,566	200,366	0	85,000	3,014,518	387,073,882	558,625	10,194	422,640	452,433,600
6	39,234,909	2,503,528	4,139,663	87,424	39,627	22,380,429	0	949,462	4,773,221	532,159,300	68,602	0	1,366,517	607,702,681
7	36,238,143	2,576,590	5,833,956	28,098,117	296,085	212,507	0	958,777	67,021	333,472,677	0	43,298	0	407,797,171
8	21,985,338	2,574,140	5,838,390	849,723	837,850	211,444	0	15,436	101,686	333,697,206	311,640	0	67,608	366,490,461
9	40,150,678	2,983,976	6,543,672	353,143	289,907	3,271,115	0	132,151	652,831	536,005,291	711,000	99,934	54,372	591,248,069
10	2,474,930,613	2,073,106	10,982,734	5,051,635	2,072,246	9,539,169	0	4,138,496	1,844,705	408,269,681	2,374,763	0	214,508	2,921,491,656
11	30,243,322	2,007,972	7,750,592	1,639,382	10,902,080	27,029	0	1,840,560	1,851,189	496,243,002	578,098	281	193,381	553,276,889
12	19,335,560	2,869,684	10,112,858	2,289,902	615,351	0	0	1,707,698	590,554	420,472,492	696,368	8,503	288,224	458,987,194
13	18,906,936	3,717,969	5,139,054	108,335	660,684	159,925	0	1,034,996	72,737	631,604,164	1,372,884	0	551,040	663,328,724
14	39,271,806	4,317,492	4,871,553	104,725	315,565	1,965,109	0	321,540	1,068,523	552,061,788	113,380	0	413,021	604,824,503
15	73,175,484	6,882,722	11,412,097	60,500	1,042,431	0	0	3,918,247	0	420,570,739	149,589	12,948	180,221	517,404,979
16	38,902,393	3,294,454	14,391,070	343,240	1,560,060	391,527	-2,478	617,960	212,965	376,141,593	3,142,766	0	0	438,995,550
17	25,388,004	3,746,720	3,754,548	0	850,527	0	0	1,397,601	949,362	670,394,562	67,609	1,636,663	632,172	708,817,768
18	25,568,228	2,591,228	6,294,569	853,331	295,855	2,866,841	0	7,572,800	37,120,383	333,449,844	116,772	45,501	251,979	417,027,332
19	29,527,051	3,225,140	7,785,888	130,217	358,517	1,750,673	0	4,231,586	615,040	531,502,087	370,051	0	100,320	579,596,570
20	37,051,470	2,292,133	17,942,940	16,544,815	4,387,168	286,358	0	6,282,596	1,846,053	420,761,831	1,519,671	232,738	806,000	509,953,774
21	24,814,214	3,133,947	6,116,291	14,927	1,306,548	566,007	0	713,476	966,410	516,827,866	1,576,875	249,000	357,832	556,643,394

See Appendix A for a listing of the congressional districts which represent the county in which the state capital is located and congressional districts which represent only portions of a county. See Appendix B for a listing of the programs included in each recipent category.

table continues

Table 3.4 **Federal Outlays to Categories of Recipients by Congressional District, 1986 *(continued)***

District	State Gov't.	Counties	Cities/ Towns	Special Districts	Schools	Public Universities	Indian Tribes	Non-Profits	Private Universities	Individuals	For Profits	Small Businesses	All Others	Total
TEXAS *continued*														
22	23,598,638	2,751,805	18,961,380	1,400,137	704,970	97,468	0	320,099	1,441,346	314,635,648	1,928,006	0	165,230	366,004,727
23	71,471,778	6,145,535	9,348,116	310,642	6,101,429	33,724	0	12,605,795	793,335	452,143,144	1,056,836	50,000	83,750	560,144,083
24	19,612,724	1,823,573	7,115,999	11,620,306	137,130	105,198	317,100	0	319,314	389,784,616	68,867	743,663	243,807	431,892,296
25	35,071,199	2,571,698	6,282,881	886,502	295,523	361,030	0	15,484	924,140	332,841,337	0	50,000	0	379,299,794
26	19,612,372	2,250,603	5,213,182	108,338	977,418	730,377	0	520,081	881,658	380,614,371	1,463,115	297,770	94,704	412,763,991
27	55,305,644	4,525,155	9,440,428	118,415	758,062	122,627	0	4,619,595	34,553	411,585,482	1,328,732	0	431,524	488,270,217
TOTAL	3,390,601,831	86,233,969	208,028,958	71,801,071	37,196,263	47,624,558	571,641	54,655,373	63,269,421	12,375,132,018	20,490,837	3,647,872	8,242,680	16,367,496,492
UTAH														
1	47,495,988	5,279,915	5,005,911	477,848	4,002,547	4,201,468	1,115,889	1,297,837	892,966	333,942,051	3,005,605	0	147,618	406,865,643
2	398,822,226	5,737,695	11,982,302	15,451,062	360,557	6,102,595	0	2,636,829	515,474	335,166,679	603,290	2,271,803	281,597	779,932,109
3	44,598,858	6,047,572	6,006,637	91,880	2,872,320	0	1,698,676	1,519,872	1,699,695	319,126,129	285,809	46,127	66,799	384,060,374
TOTAL	490,917,072	17,065,182	22,994,850	16,020,790	7,235,424	10,304,063	2,814,565	5,454,538	3,108,135	988,234,859	3,894,704	2,317,930	496,014	1,570,858,126
VERMONT														
TOTAL	196,025,561	1,119,990	11,088,326	252,980	594,022	2,973,103	0	3,229,057	3,421,195	482,506,387	139,493	424,281	377,317	702,151,712
VIRGINIA														
1	36,021,102	7,550,032	11,576,933	737,875	0	2,825,825	1,628	4,611,584	4,474,235	471,724,322	130,007	0	259,249	539,912,792
2	38,740,926	-229	20,828,861	8,110,150	0	1,778,342	0	6,682,391	228,499	352,647,647	1,648,230	0	-225,789	430,439,028
3	972,093,361	2,922,206	8,952,065	1,713,025	0	500,968	0	2,927,455	1,081,081	522,525,387	577,294	43,013	179,808	1,513,515,663
4	57,637,662	4,227,369	11,648,877	-16,678	0	1,413,792	0	929,809	1,846,587	499,085,938	64,551	0	326,869	577,164,777
5	48,963,837	3,465,779	2,986,643	102,000	0	125,384	0	1,205,017	1,206,814	507,987,496	301,156	0	250,669	566,594,795
6	36,412,048	4,464,501	11,950,826	814,856	0	203,039	0	6,107,118	2,619,512	565,631,946	1,288,324	0	337,071	629,829,241
7	53,181,058	4,394,239	3,166,610	974,627	0	6,092,611	0	2,214,188	226,905	460,574,594	692,378	0	142,649	531,659,860
8	14,652,987	6,524,636	2,660,953	0	0	0	2,565	4,947,440	0	265,386,334	889,607	1,160,254	85,694	296,310,469
9	70,528,967	7,026,047	4,454,457	2,402,335	-2,683	9,733,682	0	1,410,665	5,907,885	602,227,275	0	470,511	6,571	704,165,712
10	15,145,708	12,061,089	1,648,720	0	0	217,268	0	9,260,088	75,106	322,754,373	7,042,971	6,718,521	1,031,391	375,955,235
TOTAL	1,343,377,656	52,635,669	79,874,945	14,838,190	-2,683	22,890,911	4,193	40,295,755	17,666,624	4,570,545,314	12,634,518	8,392,299	2,394,182	6,165,547,573
WASHINGTON														
1	56,422,406	2,716,249	5,763,009	31,977,078	1,565,609	7,301,588	364,805	4,068,520	936,622	453,471,119	305,159	553,512	102,992	565,548,670
2	51,744,484	6,206,284	5,726,765	2,053,115	3,498,246	207,919	4,812,897	2,382,899	0	547,750,454	2,922,916	0	219,750	627,525,729
3	695,498,350	5,043,505	7,916,720	855,553	857,606	246,516	881,450	2,562,919	51,415	498,789,152	639,865	0	220,672	1,213,563,722
4	90,686,597	4,180,881	4,944,896	517,954	5,470,837	281,841	7,442,384	10,251,435	-909	495,370,821	697,510	0	650,722	620,494,970
5	67,275,983	4,904,299	10,137,317	540,376	2,771,368	7,590,238	940,339	2,500,888	3,293,145	609,101,421	915,192	108,772	303,435	710,382,773
6	65,690,464	6,663,554	29,015,073	4,233,162	8,829,778	0	522,062	1,857,698	625,487	440,602,468	250,846	5,948	852,015	559,148,555
7	95,902,678	3,906,813	12,683,023	1,028,336	1,882,965	15,453,935	212,942	23,066,630	1,082,901	477,106,718	411,156	1,663,381	226,929	634,628,408
8	57,861,212	3,003,796	10,143,363	1,164,589	2,593,944	697,424	1,138,395	4,831,835	1,049,877	479,100,151	364,551	499,331	166,747	562,615,216
TOTAL	1,181,082,175	36,625,380	86,330,167	42,370,163	27,470,353	31,779,461	16,315,274	51,522,825	7,038,538	4,001,292,305	6,507,195	2,830,944	2,743,263	5,493,908,043
WEST VIRGINIA														
1	35,612,469	3,876,199	5,475,753	-4,140,166	85,554	72,656	0	2,089,750	414,247	571,655,926	1,422,997	34,261	31,380	616,631,026
2	51,136,708	9,083,434	14,424,820	4,266,655	2,983,631	6,343,468	0	2,921,476	1,799,012	550,712,447	260,233	0	-440	643,931,444
3	509,997,965	6,610,132	4,414,455	3,644,055	24,254	32,001	0	739,279	205,495	556,964,707	195,397	0	509,080	1,083,336,820
4	59,093,176	5,104,217	6,144,568	1,125,434	-42,508	23,600	0	3,438,666	1,168,180	639,814,675	784,694	0	0	716,654,702
TOTAL	655,840,318	24,673,982	30,459,596	4,895,978	3,050,931	6,471,725	0	9,189,171	3,586,934	2,319,147,755	2,663,321	34,261	540,020	3,060,553,992

WISCONSIN														
1	82,613,409	3,827,521	13,585,918	0	530,565	74,505	0	665,953	411,129	523,245,266	424,897	0	810	625,379,973
2	793,084,618	3,444,075	9,770,725	280,020	135,166	25,347,749	0	3,366,214	2,518,631	457,066,586	34,980	0	410,720	1,295,459,484
3	96,014,261	4,437,141	7,916,602	389,504	447,595	227,134	136,160	2,664,605	842,892	536,759,570	0	38,600	-720	649,873,344
4	111,513,742	7,089,358	14,432,205	22,798,143	121,625	0	0	4,436,715	1,158,886	558,583,453	494,933	108,800	141,195	720,879,057
5	134,195,467	7,350,931	15,102,472	11,524,922	103,830	602,218	0	3,991,755	14,247,285	601,812,323	983,266	100,000	529,523	790,543,992
6	70,782,152	3,785,974	7,049,731	400,400	470,654	0	6,775	952,714	387,434	565,845,392	0	371,665	0	650,052,892
7	95,153,711	5,966,745	7,423,782	242,532	1,096,858	1,023,791	3,596,616	2,622,499	1,148,599	565,631,781	8,205	71,244	321,348	684,307,711
8	74,440,362	6,708,452	11,995,579	41,377	144,799	-1,375	6,611,828	1,467,681	330,951	533,699,689	0	0	227,472	635,666,815
9	42,484,339	3,021,148	6,708,274	637,849	460,422	0	0	57,995	567,289	461,013,832	34,528	0	142,927	515,128,602
TOTAL	1,500,282,061	45,631,345	93,985,288	36,314,748	3,511,514	27,274,022	10,351,379	20,226,131	21,613,096	4,803,657,891	1,980,809	690,309	1,773,276	6,567,291,870
WYOMING														
TOTAL	161,933,914	11,789,484	8,456,035	86,152	13,803,351	3,608,616	1,321,153	1,647,653	690,451	359,193,742	425,152	38,102	144,274	563,138,079
U.S. TOTAL	88,303.5 mil	3,207.5 mil	7,815.5 mil	2,335.2 mil	852.3 mil	1,313.8 mil	400.7 mil	2,874.7 mil	3,871.8 mil	290,094.0 mil	1,209.8 mil	188.9 mil	672.8 mil	403,140.6 mil

See Appendix A for a listing of the congressional districts which represent the county in which the state capital is located and congressional districts which represent only portions of a county. See Appendix B for a listing of the programs included in each recipent category.

Table 3.5 **Federal Outlays to Categories of Recipients by Congressional District, 1987**

District	State Gov't.	Counties	Cities/ Towns	Special Districts	Schools	Public Universities	Indian Tribes	Non-Profits	Private Universities	Individuals	For Profits	Small Businesses	All Others	Total
ALABAMA														
1	56,269,585	1,509,643	2,938,554	7,176,979	352,925	12,371,539	2,161,046	4,482,309	862,735	751,910,506	6,495,651	0	531,307	847,062,779
2	1,290,504,220	1,897,013	5,995,285	8,066,740	2,437,964	12,946,095	0	5,175,711	2,918,557	754,250,374	2,602,975	0	2,109,228	2,088,904,162
3	54,462,113	2,041,815	6,853,458	3,725,758	580,196	21,365,533	0	6,014,756	19,372,411	725,104,114	985,253	134,400	856,971	841,496,778
4	57,590,284	2,741,607	9,522,749	3,577,855	52,722	5,779,786	0	3,316,813	418,884	849,222,433	340,466	0	487,138	933,050,737
5	45,062,788	2,650,751	2,665,059	5,905,545	2,965,228	17,115,015	0	3,009,827	2,226,608	686,155,000	861,153	39,984	1,003,879	769,660,837
6	64,301,151	7,103,457	1,767,972	15,517,892	314,971	69,264,465	0	2,934,837	10,578,756	889,316,072	12,133,063	0	1,471,901	1,074,704,538
7	64,958,276	3,796,814	1,281,054	3,662,667	145,868	19,014,519	68,592	6,293,927	8,653,335	755,085,344	928,274	296,403	1,613,567	865,798,641
TOTAL	1,633,148,416	21,741,101	31,024,131	47,633,437	6,849,874	157,856,952	2,229,638	31,228,180	45,031,286	5,411,043,844	24,346,835	470,787	8,073,991	7,420,678,472
ALASKA														
TOTAL	475,461,301	25,565,743	38,919,559	229,895	1,047,325	18,418,443	31,183,045	32,600,302	1,537,011	239,115,129	1,277,824	576,704	1,534,529	867,466,810
ARIZONA														
1	265,738,730	1,633,067	26,487,688	624,701	4,924,774	29,732,212	1,824,097	3,334,543	2,624,343	1,165,055,421	24,129,792	63,246	2,454,639	1,528,627,254
2	182,281,082	2,060,099	14,569,185	1,611,725	6,123,451	43,918,033	12,040,510	10,258,444	1,902,584	980,671,810	13,781,735	2,518,534	2,089,001	1,273,826,193
3	12,402,559	367,170	11,466,545	2,502,157	2,071,411	10,181,605	3,321,115	2,511,224	271,562	435,565,084	1,481,444	48,959	288,546	482,479,381
4	390,353,879	1,983,586	23,278,324	4,991,325	25,117,750	1,049,174	54,849,290	4,855,888	1,874,184	1,009,301,389	14,727,113	0	487,688	1,532,869,591
5	39,103,341	3,739,020	8,824,918	599,035	3,243,157	7,883,648	293,475	3,716,203	534,346	870,846,577	2,319,058	128,356	500,839	941,731,973
TOTAL	889,879,592	9,782,941	84,626,660	10,328,943	41,480,543	92,764,672	72,328,487	24,676,303	7,207,019	4,461,440,282	56,439,143	2,759,095	5,820,712	5,759,534,392
ARKANSAS														
1	135,616,903	2,173,385	3,239,752	3,721,698	1,805,801	5,762,982	0	5,558,639	1,641,263	1,135,215,205	472,472	0	534,021	1,295,742,121
2	698,159,675	121,763	4,184,393	3,369,900	1,095,243	10,524,807	464,237	3,888,663	7,721,105	812,924,453	2,475,454	507,728	3,422,978	1,548,860,399
3	69,049,488	1,067,349	14,738,544	2,863,668	227,663	8,456,279	0	4,223,594	3,108,858	941,986,025	12,956,893	0	291,174	1,058,969,535
4	104,568,025	89,533	2,136,566	1,975,170	165,163	13,502,998	0	6,971,802	1,244,782	979,345,848	355,878	0	1,579,914	1,111,935,679
TOTAL	1,007,394,091	3,452,030	24,299,255	11,930,436	3,293,870	38,247,066	464,237	20,642,698	13,716,008	3,869,471,531	16,260,697	507,728	5,828,087	5,015,507,734
CALIFORNIA														
1	109,956,108	7,498,908	3,741,540	140,302	3,143,223	6,489,618	3,123,192	5,026,973	459,835	887,063,792	2,446,822	0	6,171,250	1,035,261,562
2	145,647,376	6,922,900	4,178,265	1,555,680	3,119,829	6,134,091	1,702,021	2,934,192	1,367,790	1,055,463,806	636,101	0	3,029,218	1,232,691,269
3	4,122,120,987	383,417	9,174,702	17,888,227	3,516,753	3,063,545	1,532,995	14,289,330	1,622,649	597,770,796	9,732,807	291,797	3,461,430	4,784,849,436
4	912,356,062	4,922,438	3,916,223	783,055	9,591,584	44,803,964	44,994	3,024,950	3,573,646	614,145,228	3,378,894	461,400	2,926,987	1,603,929,423
5	188,639,750	1,110,131	86,652,760	19,540,698	9,298,164	8,257,469	398	13,078,957	5,185,662	999,267,345	2,493,173	817,355	5,055,576	1,339,397,438
6	89,676,185	671,590	5,730,550	2,870,640	4,817,155	134,397,390	0	15,212,541	2,270,494	705,046,318	1,874,264	1,946,934	1,462,470	965,976,530
7	85,776,165	11,932,214	354,076	4,219,043	2,772,704	0	0	3,947,142	326,456	687,602,678	832,176	307,216	7,081,194	805,151,063
8	134,300,867	3,579,921	7,789,911	57,207,564	2,051,665	89,883,127	228,803	41,583,327	5,354,437	702,365,631	3,486,879	2,614,931	7,430,426	1,057,877,488
9	130,337,483	1,635,921	7,594,310	2,911,245	7,257,238	2,900,469	303,993	1,168,797	1,171,947	701,436,602	60,932,119	879,548	7,796,957	926,326,630
10	93,345,054	10,682,268	6,209,815	30,091,364	3,898,599	5,342,083	392,305	1,859,801	514,850	580,044,742	1,296,246	16,634	3,734,748	737,428,507
11	54,587,294	1,748,301	929,846	3,167,446	2,392,971	367,084	11,926	9,853,270	1,008,431	675,556,552	2,052,971	1,563,652	536,684	753,776,428
12	60,599,791	514,316	225,810	-233,921	7,033,459	8,005,556	65,302	20,855,070	159,493,145	483,316,356	6,932,258	4,868,785	1,862,429	753,538,356
13	71,427,569	3,711,611	-2,280,884	-474,756	3,207,708	3,222,030	95,225	2,378,386	3,313,585	511,409,444	1,696,976	264,108	1,944,191	599,915,194
14	97,150,376	4,794,908	1,432,867	10,893,698	4,012,011	0	329,100	2,988,533	3,371,655	772,084,812	205,734	49,711	467,811	897,781,217
15	120,956,902	5,956,482	13,491,168	193,936	6,734,125	1,864,601	-600	3,845,207	0	633,011,555	1,349,019	45,274	1,431,885	788,879,554
16	74,253,345	4,321,689	643,984	6,144,753	9,884,125	18,855,143	0	2,760,645	359,472	618,354,938	574,229	193,632	6,478,986	742,824,941
17	181,711,338	4,339,874	9,877,914	1,368,934	4,543,891	-761,536	2,063,298	2,111,591	348,223	867,112,200	2,764,040	0	2,868,746	1,078,348,513
18	218,503,382	7,074,190	6,142,077	1,594,628	5,087,180	4,610,124	418,359	1,110,619	2,647,612	1,112,762,486	2,507,558	0	1,645,685	1,364,103,901
19	52,059,299	10,677,421	3,724,312	2,022,445	5,508,709	29,538,378	384,796	1,969,928	781,026	540,327,756	1,934,378	886,367	1,682,722	651,497,538
20	120,042,892	5,270,043	4,919,403	218,284,991	7,600,660	4,562,547	2,205,285	18,020,801	1,750,252	858,904,522	2,164,870	106,753	4,941,946	1,248,774,966
21	107,404,069	1,905,979	4,074,150	3,144,902	3,452,806	1,160,624	368,597	2,077,641	1,664,986	784,736,340	3,211,273	441,049	2,159,653	915,802,068
22	130,510,732	242,491	3,219,790	1,237,807	2,394,318	2,929,995	0	8,500,495	32,278,026	686,092,680	5,153,221	259,497	1,784,548	874,603,600
23	165,723,209	254,927	2,034,981	931,765	999,800	106,197,506	0	7,748,400	5,232,331	684,974,321	4,820,941	3,548	1,347,241	980,268,971

24	130,451,087	445,553	2,030,564	977,081	987,256	2,662,565	0	15,247,551	1,778,732	684,370,012	4,424,827	280,451	1,234,151	844,889,830
25	132,405,937	5,757,397	2,658,641	930,220	1,259,760	3,335,285	147,682	6,694,692	2,873,623	684,203,519	5,035,176	208,120	2,545,072	848,055,127
26	114,442,695	223,779	1,789,972	812,607	1,063,438	2,657,143	0	2,561,776	1,561,689	600,837,632	4,181,690	301,217	1,099,858	731,533,498
27	131,260,004	254,807	25,692,585	1,139,404	2,234,753	2,670,801	0	8,984,868	3,423,732	684,175,697	12,419,176	3,546	1,408,484	873,667,856
28	130,291,627	815,007	2,176,390	931,189	1,357,522	3,308,253	0	12,033,035	77,726,522	684,145,819	4,487,200	53,546	1,687,648	919,013,758
29	130,319,647	28,270,498	2,850,078	931,389	1,033,067	2,661,988	0	7,934,312	1,788,346	684,193,498	4,376,358	3,546	1,660,482	866,023,210
30	130,093,596	254,383	2,553,959	929,774	3,044,740	2,657,371	0	3,057,032	2,827,032	683,006,706	6,123,654	3,540	1,920,822	836,472,609
31	130,763,531	254,986	3,493,663	931,981	2,592,585	4,729,877	0	2,954,314	12,622,023	684,629,482	4,890,443	87,033	2,484,514	850,434,432
32	130,820,052	255,803	3,231,155	934,966	990,832	3,883,415	0	2,227,433	1,785,175	686,824,935	4,535,176	75,004	1,426,652	836,990,599
33	130,443,816	255,067	2,397,116	1,020,511	2,591,086	7,817,760	0	7,864,853	8,064,010	684,914,739	5,186,499	3,550	1,870,819	852,429,825
34	130,450,008	255,080	2,387,034	1,215,448	2,279,063	2,679,651	0	1,853,954	5,678,380	684,877,907	6,163,028	3,550	2,571,723	840,414,825
35	121,698,892	179,097	1,949,788	4,448,193	8,238,324	839,318	422,873	242,346	5,540,193	712,708,878	3,776,336	2,240,329	1,198,049	863,482,616
36	476,182,123	11,176,527	4,016,419	514,647	2,225,074	7,837,005	386,127	798,055	669,670	1,408,285,089	3,224,874	0	1,376,700	1,916,692,311
37	341,247,926	5,007,342	3,695,211	-4,330,785	4,005,288	5,187,050	400,627	1,816,880	543,592	700,967,556	677,262	0	801,010	1,060,018,959
38	48,784,425	4,808,449	605,014	26,492,359	994,817	125,480	540,126	93,117	1,989,010	624,418,155	7,537,737	128,846	766,935	717,284,468
39	49,023,678	191,325	1,279,358	477,000	2,047,680	4,372,643	540,583	398,707	3,138,626	624,959,042	7,479,748	248,107	767,583	694,924,079
40	48,953,479	5,058,785	778,794	-353,206	5,396,126	12,693,299	540,086	24,355,840	2,245,337	624,502,421	9,360,507	975,187	1,279,014	735,785,668
41	69,998,921	285,001	26,787,161	947,566	2,672,188	39,986,366	200,797	128,763,412	954,185	535,557,854	6,882,423	2,261,486	1,093,524	816,390,884
42	98,374,759	294,204	1,895,229	10,562,769	1,875,806	1,869,274	209,335	15,314,095	2,089,392	659,410,167	5,654,743	495,962	1,350,033	799,395,768
43	84,798,945	1,489,565	2,202,578	3,579,000	10,864,260	7,163,723	895,775	21,471,102	1,552,719	760,030,686	5,175,646	864,782	1,584,943	901,673,724
44	98,845,872	219,389	733,732	22,978	6,974,784	9,069,893	304,231	9,916,530	1,366,915	810,353,281	1,569,950	707,472	1,701,320	941,786,345
45	108,316,911	1,873,338	5,543,036	507,339	8,541,435	7,481,626	2,191,954	4,339,865	1,948,780	799,949,807	16,481,619	12,886	1,864,398	959,052,994
TOTAL	10,435,054,167	167,777,322	284,525,046	439,106,877	185,588,559	617,513,595	20,050,184	465,270,364	376,264,192	32,466,173,781	252,121,025	24,976,349	110,996,517	45,845,417,978
COLORADO														
1	848,128,303	8,436,804	14,425,782	35,892,223	1,342,989	32,042,857	1,816,231	21,763,586	11,245,302	728,317,730	3,831,860	656,712	3,561,382	1,711,461,762
2	42,520,952	468,509	12,254,497	37,914	290,901	39,370,319	-22,021	5,014,716	7,053,933	411,762,397	1,199,991	3,302,581	1,714,129	524,968,817
3	72,552,550	7,088,392	12,579,276	3,537,993	1,958,953	10,629,335	1,416,242	5,041,364	0	648,721,518	689,412	39,963	1,500,690	765,755,687
4	56,148,985	4,804,677	3,408,562	2,275,078	2,026,478	34,477,083	0	5,179,297	2,224,030	767,898,340	270,967	266,890	738,662	879,719,048
5	33,639,934	1,552,146	4,308,911	2,969,340	5,012,211	7,082,492	0	3,650,314	3,551,488	486,462,685	989,849	260,556	741,997	550,221,923
6	31,815,271	3,290,332	160,902	297,975	1,330,619	808,669	478	3,982,747	428,985	406,157,737	670,657	648,873	2,249,298	451,842,544
TOTAL	1,084,805,995	25,640,859	47,137,929	45,010,524	11,962,151	124,410,755	3,210,930	44,632,024	24,503,738	3,449,320,407	7,652,737	5,175,575	10,506,158	4,883,969,782
CONNECTICUT														
1	1,034,861,111	0	12,713,564	5,736,604	0	1,335,446	0	4,820,399	4,363,523	770,042,891	2,792,572	345,939	1,628,824	1,838,640,874
2	72,440,957	136,677	5,576,981	1,508,898	30,178	16,722,557	665,637	5,852,878	5,841,360	635,302,087	398,300	39,804	354,300	744,870,615
3	96,542,247	0	7,363,907	9,383,241	11,622	2,908,903	0	7,784,030	140,992,513	789,899,394	1,822,821	950,595	1,245,664	1,058,904,937
4	96,466,689	28,310	915,610	7,943,916	0	774,570	0	3,860,827	3,037,600	698,034,432	15,372,892	48,349	1,253,795	827,736,991
5	88,232,900	29,323	762,869	3,424,977	30,000	1,228,512	191,614	1,343,456	370,457	757,124,121	93,722	355,371	207,152	853,394,473
6	97,769,578	0	7,963,131	1,515,024	0	15,156,994	0	959,572	71,357	770,598,992	251,067	92,314	75,248	894,453,277
TOTAL	1,486,313,483	194,310	35,296,063	29,512,659	71,800	38,126,982	857,251	24,621,163	154,676,810	4,421,001,916	20,731,374	1,832,372	4,764,983	6,218,001,166
DELAWARE														
TOTAL	261,957,872	2,698,857	7,706,012	3,998,753	276,921	17,654,108	0	6,518,579	1,297,532	824,070,589	11,919,517	161,062	2,017,617	1,140,277,419
DISTRICT OF COLUMBIA														
TOTAL	511,019,012	605,029	3,958,404	85,924	0	3,653,605	36,564,090	189,576,982	198,191,973	827,578,620	19,169,348	7,304,390	177,925,996	1,975,633,373
FLORIDA														
1	46,905,699	2,460,289	2,362,339	1,452,072	7,699,104	4,112,691	0	1,687,369	0	694,972,512	711,415	38,700	949,382	763,351,572
2	2,084,414,617	2,115,685	7,621,648	1,312,882	1,473,435	33,375,344	867,831	13,474,783	865,996	712,974,556	331,083	0	4,022,702	2,862,850,562
3	55,622,902	53,709	13,950,186	970,826	3,716,885	637,632	0	292,281	4,049,391	716,269,586	2,054,327	0	577,996	798,195,723
4	42,357,915	1,845,415	1,388,282	2,552,383	4,105,086	1,101,228	0	1,715,087	10,408,813	1,149,007,205	4,501,647	0	1,736,335	1,220,719,395
5	33,079,538	5,147,523	15,446,625	7,664,790	1,088,120	3,211,617	0	1,144,683	1,365,208	782,606,783	1,458,170	89,058	764,629	853,066,745
6	58,366,573	2,174,674	5,914,746	1,256,361	2,597,964	52,612,292	0	1,799,907	2,004,459	1,364,893,094	233,001	1,007,867	1,624,819	1,494,485,756

See Appendix A for a listing of the congressional districts which represent the county in which the state capital is located and congressional districts which represent only portions of a county. See Appendix B for a listing of the programs included in each recipent category.

table continues

Table 3.5 Federal Outlays to Categories of Recipients by Congressional District, 1987 *(continued)*

District	State Gov't.	Counties	Cities/ Towns	Special Districts	Schools	Public Universities	Indian Tribes	Non-Profits	Private Universities	Individuals	For Profits	Small Businesses	All Others	Total
FLORIDA *continued*														
7	50,166,546	11,112,784	13,243,637	13,374,280	1,244,758	15,418,546	0	3,053,585	4,323,278	785,246,938	10,053,840	64,383	801,467	908,104,041
8	21,794,179	7,268,650	13,356,114	9,548,726	2,685,272	975,837	0	3,003,468	785,934	1,403,329,015	301,322	0	780,254	1,463,828,772
9	29,005,847	7,828,705	3,378,829	897,210	775,863	412,750	0	365,371	538,638	1,387,195,876	847,875	0	440,806	1,431,687,769
10	35,395,838	10,520,169	5,063,441	1,519,230	652,126	135,400	0	1,978,711	2,479,424	1,071,693,045	267,941	0	1,051,972	1,130,757,296
11	29,277,576	11,261,007	5,955,504	2,311,263	1,739,983	2,030,942	0	300,121	1,170,654	984,658,685	2,454,785	268,682	639,597	1,042,068,800
12	31,975,766	14,246,453	1,536,483	5,683,492	853,528	2,122	265,945	8,146,220	471,101	1,447,749,841	610,767	0	1,210,280	1,512,751,999
13	21,724,908	15,900,267	11,417,687	2,171,627	1,219,752	0	0	278,285	249,740	1,732,998,132	516,233	0	931,458	1,787,408,089
14	25,037,065	554,849	900,208	590,379	100,581	2,610,068	889,034	68,142	793,063	1,424,211,161	844,085	50,000	1,721,437	1,458,370,072
15	33,519,806	16,127,584	2,898,559	919,303	440,783	27,630,919	237,350	644,018	4,293,715	1,254,867,959	11,622,106	0	901,188	1,354,103,290
16	48,900,464	6,582,421	1,679,033	267,246	135,727	320,319	3,186,510	90,559	1,777,227	1,142,667,270	2,887,826	0	1,664,516	1,210,159,118
17	113,094,175	30,894,837	5,379,134	178,527	488,264	1,916,967	253,852	662,022	8,878,501	867,317,558	9,614,336	251,575	2,511,403	1,041,441,152
18	117,953,602	15,816,756	5,301,350	282,580	468,449	1,097,599	218,938	1,538,165	11,161,042	867,748,911	13,389,395	45,675	3,203,744	1,038,226,206
19	103,010,352	3,848,571	5,000,171	158,163	1,142,053	961,691	191,829	2,507,769	8,170,145	844,627,190	8,252,337	0	2,016,429	979,886,700
TOTAL	2,981,603,368	165,760,348	121,793,976	53,111,339	32,627,732	148,563,965	6,111,289	42,750,546	63,786,330	20,635,035,317	70,952,492	1,815,940	27,550,415	24,351,463,057
GEORGIA														
1	102,572,311	3,433,518	12,660,925	4,610,574	2,085,893	7,246,495	0	4,512,157	899,764	741,001,981	2,025,061	0	963,824	882,012,503
2	124,294,366	3,161,551	289,428	1,720,783	1,392,234	6,953,059	0	4,150,202	740,855	736,555,079	864,535	0	248,914	880,371,006
3	95,103,335	652,990	11,767,060	4,846,935	2,307,448	7,809,332	0	4,474,958	2,734,035	680,009,922	686,348	597,808	624,789	811,614,960
4	339,145,494	2,996,370	1,614,928	78,305,668	1,433,089	1,974,475	-50,281	6,364,156	15,555,333	305,602,794	1,639,469	582,046	4,519,541	759,683,082
5	1,397,541,273	2,940,833	26,882,551	17,909,312	1,171,305	13,325,178	-184,183	15,142,441	69,163,343	928,582,012	3,579,601	99,740	4,843,353	2,480,996,757
6	69,179,149	631,553	1,195,907	3,106,269	-59,857	2,704,746	-20,498	682,252	89,176	655,157,538	728,658	199,695	654,850	734,249,439
7	40,471,241	2,187,400	6,825,331	2,807,042	186,362	47,522	0	1,188,664	1,907,172	613,721,015	823,764	102,177	596,667	670,864,357
8	127,865,210	2,473,688	2,225,592	3,604,234	810,765	2,296,731	0	2,409,398	4,652,381	758,229,183	0	0	669,870	905,237,052
9	63,142,258	3,644,117	1,720,140	4,459,211	124,400	1,078,131	0	3,659,401	1,988,750	671,736,711	67,559	0	225,369	751,846,048
10	88,388,836	2,043,924	2,009,898	3,899,852	2,143,743	24,519,304	0	14,346,477	3,860,412	631,523,716	0	0	347,843	773,084,004
TOTAL	2,447,703,472	24,165,944	67,191,760	125,269,879	11,595,383	67,954,973	-254,962	56,930,106	101,591,221	6,722,119,951	10,414,995	1,581,466	13,695,020	9,649,959,208
HAWAII														
1	372,288,510	218,563	12,069,303	283,894	0	27,353,440	4,623,574	8,805,868	2,963,024	481,965,508	890,752	885,003	4,114,910	916,462,348
2	136,691,769	10,662,367	4,290,793	92,311	0	6,248,197	138,394	5,327,620	3,175,632	557,702,258	349,880	309,500	1,456,524	726,445,246
TOTAL	508,980,279	10,880,930	16,360,096	376,205	0	33,601,637	4,761,968	14,133,488	6,138,656	1,039,667,766	1,240,632	1,194,503	5,571,434	1,642,907,594
IDAHO														
1	306,346,410	1,647,138	11,318,936	1,211,151	3,150,159	14,420,859	4,359,513	5,054,146	2,631,294	660,526,394	619,715	201,042	1,506,755	1,012,993,511
2	89,323,397	1,530,365	4,477,535	414,415	4,426,735	6,821,212	3,471,312	3,147,320	1,855,955	678,200,265	381,257	704,190	249,307	795,003,266
TOTAL	395,669,807	3,177,503	15,796,471	1,625,566	7,576,894	21,242,071	7,830,825	8,201,466	4,487,249	1,338,726,659	1,000,972	905,232	1,756,062	1,807,996,777
ILLINOIS														
1	115,013,212	34,514	115,117,089	195,088,450	984,772	2,611,603	164,753	14,201,665	92,639,830	727,321,798	9,930,549	1,012,198	2,610,345	1,276,730,778
2	104,171,049	-10,483	2,717,355	6,617,730	984,555	1,410,072	109,490	3,951,520	3,606,756	725,992,780	3,356,160	0	645,883	853,552,867
3	104,117,917	-10,486	3,353,042	5,000,790	986,688	1,335,409	109,513	1,003,898	6,559,758	726,440,308	4,254,357	0	646,019	853,797,214
4	61,379,372	10,866	3,177,151	2,737,784	636,803	1,823,498	47,344	735,360	3,524,049	634,380,919	1,759,608	439,920	958,923	711,611,597
5	104,817,838	-10,484	4,510,122	5,000,626	984,631	1,606,754	109,498	1,123,901	3,285,010	726,021,323	3,356,419	0	895,753	851,701,391
6	46,597,550	18,771	2,963,479	9,757,380	526,831	917,599	40,787	1,387,587	3,033,758	618,341,292	1,579,170	182,213	1,540,139	686,886,555
7	117,684,866	5,306,235	56,349,780	5,377,770	986,151	10,280,535	109,511	23,409,992	6,310,889	726,529,662	4,736,089	37,436	1,217,219	958,336,135
8	104,149,099	-10,485	2,814,575	5,669,303	3,010,088	1,415,393	109,511	3,211,434	3,285,408	726,080,942	3,420,388	168,789	646,012	853,970,457
9	104,138,967	-10,487	3,581,721	5,486,251	992,418	1,428,159	109,529	8,701,906	69,341,895	726,546,236	3,395,383	541,453	931,937	925,185,367
10	65,700,851	1,141,660	10,370,591	2,969,618	4,516,737	1,622,677	49,519	4,538,291	3,303,752	617,673,007	1,550,240	0	830,855	714,267,797
11	104,108,896	-10,485	2,865,668	5,343,347	984,677	17,263,068	109,503	1,803,141	3,331,412	726,026,410	5,737,710	0	875,173	868,438,520
12	55,058,952	1,040,488	1,873,147	2,642,952	1,955,958	1,230,753	46,320	1,623,465	1,482,389	644,147,103	1,515,710	39,529	919,568	713,576,336

13	53,914,322	9,420	1,459,430	2,850,935	650,502	907,827	48,009	1,743,594	3,708,292	629,006,129	1,605,955	826,494	633,278	697,364,188
14	26,245,861	-1,607,394	3,143,548	3,586,607	39,143	10,706,485	425	953,991	1,077,410	705,647,571	698,715	232,465	1,437,586	752,162,413
15	35,018,842	822,159	24,138,463	2,270,026	2,022,387	9,490,288	0	890,330	4,701,121	845,065,418	253,665	0	311,410	924,984,110
16	36,473,519	30,464	2,006,183	5,208,230	2,004,412	756,549	0	2,668,802	384,254	798,878,904	-468,628	0	1,853,196	849,795,885
17	35,674,671	82,223	4,019,555	5,393,747	2,514,963	6,310,829	0	3,281,340	2,559,611	917,069,303	153,805	0	1,062,084	978,122,131
18	51,591,290	511,359	1,771,259	10,037,284	47,376	2,130,073	0	5,735,455	6,014,958	825,818,904	655,654	0	5,223,211	909,536,824
19	50,038,266	1,426,813	1,509,221	3,904,604	3,257,242	92,190,676	0	1,506,430	28,400,909	858,899,649	71,889	983,914	491,163	1,042,680,777
20	2,634,680,063	673,964	684,494	21,961,216	998,432	954,461	0	1,390,982	1,658,621	936,003,303	1,818,840	0	2,872,504	3,603,696,880
21	82,069,325	252,168	2,156,911	7,224,418	7,724,716	7,820,700	0	1,227,889	1,158,504	805,256,875	-3,415,730	0	286,257	911,762,032
22	72,445,033	523,455	7,084,565	3,806,135	2,114,592	21,389,484	0	5,193,707	972,633	914,826,981	661,549	0	376,400	1,029,394,534
TOTAL	4,165,089,759	10,214,255	257,667,348	317,935,203	38,924,073	195,602,894	1,163,711	90,284,680	250,341,220	16,561,974,820	46,627,497	4,464,411	27,264,915	21,967,554,788
INDIANA														
1	97,446,403	7,275,585	6,794,245	5,929,373	514,695	1,611,229	0	1,111,428	557,599	734,220,614	1,963,229	47,788	1,045,082	858,517,271
2	152,698,872	1,764,291	5,933,471	2,613,400	1,100,255	10,652,779	5,580	340,213	3,220,292	771,123,982	1,255,127	1,028,012	1,130,784	952,867,058
3	57,503,820	1,381,129	4,906,059	5,391,330	346,388	855,637	27,185	2,603,288	14,325,066	769,272,643	905,763	49,380	1,471,621	859,039,309
4	52,126,745	1,856,872	10,634,892	1,588,013	8,187	721	31,554	1,199,290	2,316,007	735,357,048	507,195	0	1,079,276	806,705,800
5	60,024,074	77,102	3,167,258	2,728,947	1,556,006	469,097	1,167	285,174	4,267,372	721,593,861	705,376	0	200,350	795,075,786
6	192,204,269	117,603	1,446,733	697,491	637,198	3,250,725	0	2,375,096	3,969,387	794,160,050	2,018,053	258,483	1,417,691	1,002,552,778
7	70,147,189	772,997	3,819,970	2,609,026	17,116	34,076,084	9,834	17,863,711	2,895,050	799,729,427	146,437	405,405	1,660,770	934,153,016
8	76,439,723	95,463	13,988,623	1,305,742	153,710	4,744,677	0	737,309	4,295,632	828,406,585	513,840	335,470	749,449	931,766,223
9	103,863,244	6,145,081	3,992,459	2,201,818	380,111	37,379,213	0	1,617,377	464,623	682,606,552	78,173	289,181	1,377,266	840,395,098
10	999,786,529	328,292	-3,168,590	497,022	2,415,181	13,500,741	0	6,264,015	11,780,221	749,125,123	3,788,803	375,000	2,224,332	1,786,916,671
TOTAL	1,862,240,868	19,814,416	51,515,120	25,562,162	7,128,848	106,540,903	75,320	34,396,901	48,091,250	7,585,595,886	11,881,997	2,788,719	12,356,620	9,767,989,010
IOWA														
1	69,959,123	80,672	2,423,064	186,597	2,378,277	2,138,218	0	2,159,253	5,453,799	817,402,613	2,776,773	714,997	399,700	906,073,086
2	56,524,547	143,170	7,818,495	593,496	93,224	0	0	1,209,339	6,738,672	722,058,059	576,458	0	259,329	796,014,789
3	79,408,413	-40,724	3,510,980	542,749	1,439,881	58,929,107	504,638	4,619,959	4,147,955	830,161,075	955,552	25,452	837,990	985,043,027
4	743,180,275	568,977	46,289,850	2,400,463	313,783	33,667,667	0	3,448,408	9,028,862	649,811,107	1,286,563	255,366	2,597,165	1,492,848,486
5	67,374,046	951,231	4,836,169	276,820	1,980,808	619,067	0	2,410,129	4,445,257	1,056,091,009	350,839	184,836	784,957	1,140,305,168
6	58,693,592	736,212	7,227,805	107,781	1,714,687	0	75,180	928,423	7,484,976	1,118,752,718	2,300,649	27,937	308,910	1,198,358,870
TOTAL	1,075,139,996	2,439,538	72,106,363	4,107,906	7,920,660	95,354,059	579,818	14,775,511	37,299,521	5,194,276,581	8,246,834	1,208,588	5,188,051	6,518,643,426
KANSAS														
1	49,593,446	686,242	8,347,083	1,521,758	1,309,462	4,371,423	13,743	1,490,362	7,166,195	1,286,251,848	1,209,335	0	287,544	1,362,248,441
2	600,630,043	1,067,553	3,611,225	1,899,542	10,024,632	39,790,278	1,606,569	4,871,074	3,374,309	622,611,363	2,362,062	244,642	125,480	1,292,218,772
3	52,781,114	1,049,398	2,700,685	3,632,064	207,103	7,558,755	0	8,136,161	2,394,280	610,748,001	1,025,540	204,033	70,442	690,507,576
4	51,623,836	290,420	11,608,519	1,458,382	566,777	11,191,160	164,892	5,677,505	1,238,039	763,295,184	4,757,174	95,249	700,357	852,667,494
5	46,467,253	528,565	7,621,938	2,472,442	2,150,393	6,111,239	0	1,950,444	4,358,045	962,922,498	253,525	0	839,885	1,035,676,227
TOTAL	801,095,692	3,622,178	33,889,450	10,984,188	14,258,367	69,022,855	1,785,204	22,125,546	18,530,868	4,245,828,894	9,607,636	543,924	2,023,708	5,233,318,510
KENTUCKY														
1	66,728,839	1,497,521	9,046,593	875,721	162,904	4,339,220	0	934,138	713,996	861,516,971	4,122,918	0	809,585	950,748,406
2	64,965,813	528,574	2,400,839	323,990	1,868,957	5,729,033	0	5,201,170	2,953,248	608,734,273	544,582	0	2,112,690	695,363,169
3	63,241,882	2,631,348	9,229,072	13,699,079	3,295,044	7,062,951	16,206	7,802,568	6,084,082	723,807,437	10,143,127	78,006	1,630,353	848,721,156
4	50,873,799	6,408,070	4,648,245	4,759,758	18,853	1,603,266	0	1,379,084	497,938	670,778,777	306,255	0	1,063,171	742,337,215
5	142,976,220	1,318,406	5,387,407	2,414,353	374,249	6,845	0	4,424,596	5,895,740	781,037,653	267,610	0	269,820	944,372,899
6	1,195,146,193	3,478,939	13,781,238	2,024,376	711,225	37,414,678	0	4,233,377	6,355,360	589,989,761	326,861	279,000	1,603,627	1,855,344,635
7	114,715,032	-89,691	6,625,471	1,454,981	115,648	4,575,570	0	8,417,513	3,721,825	743,532,160	85,599	0	779,689	883,933,797
TOTAL	1,698,647,778	15,773,167	51,118,865	25,552,258	6,546,880	60,731,563	16,206	32,392,446	26,222,189	4,979,397,032	15,796,952	357,006	8,268,935	6,920,821,277

See Appendix A for a listing of the congressional districts which represent the county in which the state capital is located and congressional districts which represent only portions of a county. See Appendix B for a listing of the programs included in each recipent category.

table continues

Table 3.5 **Federal Outlays to Categories of Recipients by Congressional District, 1987 *(continued)***

District	State Gov't.	Counties	Cities/ Towns	Special Districts	Schools	Public Universities	Indian Tribes	Non-Profits	Private Universities	Individuals	For Profits	Small Businesses	All Others	Total
LOUISIANA														
1	88,259,511	4,617,507	6,457,146	9,246,475	1,731,897	6,206,437	0	8,567,836	28,263,186	581,851,227	5,864,663	99,985	3,955,436	745,121,307
2	90,420,645	1,294,999	4,485,017	915,142	2,567,416	15,027,315	0	2,084,685	10,264,185	614,223,430	96,200,771	0	1,993,194	839,476,799
3	68,519,506	5,191,891	6,247,150	2,806,460	845,680	2,468,637	508,530	680,115	326,790	635,335,754	601,090	0	1,656,818	725,188,419
4	85,406,554	1,479,501	8,854,852	252,577	5,231,720	4,113,212	0	1,246,302	1,775,023	644,087,578	2,485,292	0	1,240,335	756,172,946
5	122,761,267	1,475,522	5,167,797	205,677	113,278	25,513,609	0	2,846,396	112,831	761,983,022	4,187,890	0	1,618,937	925,986,227
6	1,446,701,379	65,119	8,661,660	253,462	322,982	28,280,620	462,721	1,125,901	990,731	564,024,066	9,808,793	0	1,443,651	2,062,141,085
7	77,828,760	1,257,450	4,459,867	3,055,349	208,142	14,034,886	358,249	5,536,867	2,008,958	621,754,981	4,288,850	88,000	2,285,942	737,166,301
8	188,207,359	4,195,304	3,400,650	326,597	933,170	2,126,424	149,041	3,559,088	533,107	617,000,138	5,561,317	50,000	2,147,082	828,189,276
TOTAL	2,168,104,980	19,577,293	47,734,139	17,061,739	11,954,285	97,771,140	1,478,541	25,647,190	44,274,811	5,040,260,195	128,998,667	237,985	16,341,395	7,619,442,361
MAINE														
1	447,007,828	1,049,926	7,576,332	3,518,555	7,032	8,574,273	30,000	10,438,382	7,302,921	821,332,121	658,096	715,331	1,406,906	1,309,617,703
2	155,154,560	2,112,838	14,685,136	3,328,284	46,780	17,717,326	7,613,834	4,546,957	3,874,475	810,952,568	874,707	9,490,544	1,155,665	1,031,553,674
TOTAL	602,162,388	3,162,764	22,261,468	6,846,839	53,812	26,291,599	7,643,834	14,985,339	11,177,396	1,632,284,689	1,532,803	10,205,875	2,562,571	2,341,171,377
MARYLAND														
1	74,201,992	8,880,096	8,776,829	1,323,436	0	6,523,482	0	2,639,163	497,735	682,707,267	406,886	0	539,839	786,496,725
2	509,597,028	4,974,270	19,263,658	10,746	0	2,056,802	0	3,555	777,939	691,385,225	542,350	19,605	194,240	1,228,825,418
3	237,543,700	2,883,801	4,546,730	11,612,061	0	10,369,695	230,764	8,180,400	131,772,100	793,472,466	2,404,994	2,158,498	2,269,466	1,207,444,675
4	356,158,295	14,498,012	544,219	693,981	0	0	0	416,037	695,606	513,932,048	44,762,229	385,501	1,432,107	933,518,037
5	57,532,858	8,437,822	1,656,142	4,396,237	0	42,398,477	0	4,645,557	2,480,891	410,946,571	4,406,850	823,661	6,859,928	544,584,993
6	44,741,084	8,885,701	5,136,328	7,135,357	25,000	1,498,884	0	633,419	1,513,188	643,303,318	515,518	2,749,448	7,749,892	723,887,137
7	426,570,603	308,262	9,598,772	16,699,379	0	24,575,080	181,485	10,698,331	36,057,414	879,119,639	3,089,379	0	126,206	1,407,024,552
8	55,780,472	7,551,461	1,759,964	1,056,006	0	0	14,026	32,947,996	581,012	621,208,670	29,814,931	17,171,534	33,402,240	801,288,313
TOTAL	1,762,126,033	56,419,427	51,282,642	42,927,203	25,000	87,422,421	426,275	60,164,458	174,375,885	5,236,075,205	85,943,137	23,308,247	52,573,918	7,633,069,851
MASSACHUSETTS														
1	126,312,930	36,601	4,489,253	2,607,938	20,875	26,082,028	0	5,114,052	8,474,626	767,267,562	185,749	372,926	1,993,705	942,958,246
2	136,379,516	240,933	6,768,385	11,097,329	498,189	2,134,411	0	4,488,413	3,386,987	799,644,827	1,632,801	186,643	1,773,435	968,231,869
3	109,305,010	290,881	18,746,480	3,330,746	25,190	21,016,398	0	11,751,481	8,785,918	750,347,551	721,989	437,734	1,788,183	926,547,562
4	112,541,898	185,501	1,699,577	2,677,348	10,605	3,421,549	0	57,103,268	6,408,911	673,803,373	92,969	429,021	603,285	858,977,304
5	84,181,360	4,226,948	2,290,243	4,569,794	-20,610	5,107,422	0	6,560,054	444,953	667,820,539	1,156,211	4,521,825	710,388	781,569,128
6	107,823,325	1,346,639	25,447,588	1,772,619	20,000	4,174,276	0	6,659,180	1,797,331	800,145,540	1,184,789	382,592	3,175,196	953,929,077
7	175,403,147	89,842	6,642,148	3,176,807	32,787	1,079,143	77,273	4,884,159	44,143,311	715,896,448	2,208,007	4,124,124	2,585,323	960,342,519
8	305,889,231	334,660	1,753,854	76,399,325	167,132	35,132,910	161,333	176,799,583	250,468,278	819,886,773	10,984,305	9,740,002	13,476,349	1,701,193,734
9	899,478,106	131,612	18,659,786	7,483,745	101,267	5,768,343	227,968	97,153,110	16,948,844	901,740,657	1,391,646	440,250	2,650,389	1,952,175,723
10	111,676,034	37,045	12,338,105	5,094,490	48,353	1,902,585	105,651	8,436,378	25,474,818	891,173,584	688,531	513,425	2,424,045	1,059,913,043
11	383,788,246	69,598	741,782	6,112,134	359,298	2,713,978	109,898	21,713,300	8,935,556	745,602,217	832,368	71,240	2,880,959	1,173,930,573
TOTAL	2,552,778,806	6,990,262	99,577,199	124,322,276	1,263,086	108,533,043	682,122	400,662,979	375,269,533	8,533,329,071	21,079,365	21,219,782	34,061,256	12,279,768,779
MICHIGAN														
1	192,834,936	1,168,855	4,700,786	324,648	1,425,629	1,691,621	89,869	2,825,906	2,152,424	769,743,710	2,153,011	300,856	2,073,070	981,485,322
2	142,260,167	29,778,290	6,238,954	46,137	1,932,393	113,362,498	19,353	2,285,512	3,420,253	665,150,611	683,255	892,014	1,985,018	968,054,455
3	1,110,387,478	2,476,722	3,626,008	4,265,016	1,889,627	7,449,456	125,000	3,958,318	2,614,480	653,161,071	675,564	0	2,378,235	1,793,006,975
4	107,726,895	841,763	3,533,474	1,134,838	1,005,010	2,571,911	155,103	4,844,658	2,781,321	728,635,417	0	0	650,049	853,880,439
5	88,765,447	1,984,061	5,425,665	4,322,812	617,276	0	121,184	2,039,357	10,005,654	654,703,862	1,721,436	0	1,051,473	770,758,227
6	684,211,985	3,878,070	1,769,068	909,215	668,876	52,958,104	365,320	1,259,426	913,285	620,410,764	1,864,873	611,040	1,765,809	1,371,585,834
7	120,233,224	13,268,940	14,679,433	351,055	5,143,998	274,119	75,000	981,432	1,630,803	662,363,279	3,624,829	100,000	196,403	822,922,516
8	113,618,357	2,694,114	10,325,323	2,901,816	230,308	2,223,323	0	1,087,854	2,924,769	788,176,691	547,450	893,158	308,098	925,931,261
9	95,735,818	2,637,146	6,984,056	2,219,981	1,552,874	3,418,266	1,301,896	4,042,361	154,140	768,850,443	1,379,978	0	574,018	888,850,977

10	442,503,636	594,039	5,878,351	2,471,813	5,893,854	12,713,233	1,012,980	6,945,575	937,381	744,427,407	576,196	0	513,481	1,224,467,946
11	105,542,229	2,171,924	10,282,387	4,839,308	7,251,618	11,713,716	4,640,117	7,951,921	2,462,584	880,818,316	445,768	0	836,398	1,038,956,286
12	59,356,439	4,634,969	1,555,002	3,161,097	1,060,577	0	0	591,897	0	690,201,640	1,252,357	0	386,673	762,200,651
13	199,037,828	20,126,355	13,235,163	0	1,425,629	16,225,628	89,869	17,421,041	1,697,748	769,728,076	2,153,011	1,107,910	1,026,160	1,043,274,419
14	102,335,664	611,534	778,874	5,349	1,485,418	866	33,762	557,086	644,899	720,154,480	1,867,888	0	291,966	828,767,786
15	169,040,563	3,909,538	1,058,254	-3,505	1,301,354	7,517,734	73,014	1,452,721	2,292,163	718,227,694	2,077,487	42,013	1,439,850	908,428,881
16	151,925,136	2,003,238	3,851,735	24,974,267	4,305,542	334,781	58,849	2,175,013	3,825,894	727,151,237	3,142,848	0	489,647	924,238,187
17	121,849,126	72,193	1,344,048	97,994	803,017	1,119	43,601	3,538,136	874,747	732,166,780	5,168,115	293,024	574,597	866,826,496
18	54,453,938	993,888	450,631	0	2,088,667	4,407,981	65,733	3,208,980	495,280	684,449,482	239,236	0	316,974	751,170,792
TOTAL	4,061,818,867	93,845,638	95,717,213	52,021,841	40,081,667	236,864,357	8,270,649	67,167,194	39,827,824	12,978,520,960	29,573,302	4,240,015	16,857,920	17,724,807,448
MINNESOTA														
1	76,513,685	807,523	8,798,898	773,244	515,491	13,504,431	176,416	39,344,678	2,351,668	848,311,072	579,973	0	1,355,255	993,032,334
2	77,706,348	436,740	17,340,517	622,934	4,669,115	6,114,458	487,196	1,475,279	1,680,623	1,152,766,148	33,290	0	1,002,970	1,264,335,618
3	91,782,762	881,911	1,929,736	19,086	48,993	728,000	186,880	562,472	2,668,644	562,665,308	1,411,384	723,408	1,317,580	664,926,164
4	927,237,317	37,368	8,709,602	44,524,962	3,987,355	63,903,605	545,566	4,988,780	8,529,403	45,827,444	1,101,305	503,105	3,142,379	1,113,038,193
5	152,240,651	291,436	7,608,978	1,769,106	2,371,718	52,913,203	1,731,788	9,251,917	4,692,078	656,955,861	2,110,335	738,506	648,200	893,323,776
6	197,082,136	236,395	2,885,521	964,432	142,523	1,207,404	0	2,228,295	149,249	1,093,136,774	61,425	0	1,112,601	1,299,206,755
7	132,384,324	2,097,155	11,399,218	1,235,156	4,937,140	17,688,014	2,859,233	6,992,298	4,104,988	954,342,136	740,148	179	3,739,868	1,142,519,858
8	139,150,405	1,230,572	10,913,174	791,389	2,317,174	9,527,997	7,247,277	2,867,889	1,877,279	671,299,712	1,110,029	0	814,100	849,146,997
TOTAL	1,794,097,629	6,019,101	69,585,645	50,700,308	18,989,509	165,587,112	13,234,356	67,711,608	26,053,933	5,985,304,455	7,147,888	1,965,198	13,132,953	8,219,529,695
MISSISSIPPI														
1	78,308,229	1,657,471	8,098,859	1,550,447	3,893,440	13,334,435	0	6,823,981	3,658,461	740,904,878	1,433,974	123,810	292,597	860,080,581
2	116,815,678	12,734,337	771,285	519,431	8,195,841	15,686,291	0	18,120,354	402,847	824,664,085	403,578	0	2,633,993	1,000,947,720
3	76,338,742	367,165	1,268,887	2,094,493	4,297,687	15,427,543	9,645,118	5,638,508	3,355,657	674,879,886	140,828	0	507,098	793,961,612
4	1,039,028,204	3,193,066	5,212,819	1,877,320	1,602,196	21,828,428	0	17,389,994	5,687,019	691,459,717	2,269,330	2,157,293	1,989,116	1,793,694,502
5	43,578,266	9,143,560	7,541,455	8,423,750	6,937,719	21,375,188	0	6,166,643	1,884,984	639,013,853	547,644	0	1,337,852	745,950,912
TOTAL	1,354,069,119	27,095,598	22,893,306	14,465,440	24,926,883	87,651,885	9,645,118	54,139,480	14,988,968	3,570,922,418	4,795,354	2,281,103	6,760,656	5,194,635,328
MISSOURI														
1	68,019,251	1,198,160	8,711,156	18,210,082	1,342,992	1,493,429	0	20,775,587	113,251,077	1,188,727,250	2,831,963	100,000	1,462,684	1,426,123,631
2	76,763,110	479,867	16,006,992	15,733,274	2,159,510	1,620,999	0	8,287,066	4,171,468	894,096,845	5,491,206	0	870,042	1,025,680,379
3	32,908,090	839,283	1,299,649	4,127,346	899,670	700,727	0	5,725,001	1,913,394	326,209,203	2,081,650	279,387	791,487	377,774,887
4	1,075,603,041	2,377,690	5,492,710	890,417	6,281,682	5,894,812	0	2,754,016	115,330	849,535,626	577,612	0	3,103,108	1,952,626,044
5	54,847,049	40,715	10,922,625	16,282,709	493,081	862,940	70,395	10,850,665	0	827,126,153	406,381	458,229	1,941,359	924,302,299
6	42,917,632	45,041	8,516,075	456,409	6,623,488	8,076,443	603,359	11,079,609	15,167,573	842,649,389	7,909,502	153,527	828,567	945,026,614
7	68,685,921	88,368	9,577,660	1,073,845	347,273	5,825,291	3,300	3,279,994	6,605,785	881,451,912	1,086,448	0	555,649	978,581,446
8	118,045,106	1,072,416	6,055,738	1,506,596	1,715,042	6,545,000	0	6,263,493	142,000	972,639,560	1,249,063	304,252	1,518,965	1,117,057,231
9	213,492,369	774,662	5,722,771	1,968,775	800,544	29,315,041	0	6,344,563	6,579,524	821,744,368	1,032,202	50,000	819,246	1,088,644,066
TOTAL	1,751,281,567	6,916,201	72,305,376	60,249,453	20,663,281	60,334,681	677,054	75,359,994	147,946,152	7,604,180,307	22,666,028	1,345,395	11,891,108	9,835,816,597
MONTANA														
1	381,820,936	4,931,266	5,945,096	3,509,749	15,147,348	17,629,080	5,781,639	3,409,761	5,405,891	578,955,162	224,053	413,013	1,191,611	1,024,364,605
2	63,199,673	2,113,461	5,740,065	2,354,778	18,573,122	4,698,036	10,753,731	3,241,647	2,141,536	809,377,341	2,191,828	527,951	332,918	925,246,087
TOTAL	445,020,609	7,044,727	11,685,161	5,864,527	33,720,470	22,327,116	16,535,370	6,651,408	7,547,427	1,388,332,503	2,415,881	940,964	1,524,529	1,949,610,692
NEBRASKA														
1	458,266,707	665,180	4,795,905	1,128,455	4,571,403	25,509,603	5,008,000	2,752,163	4,456,954	997,036,598	2,115,356	49,982	1,602,981	1,507,959,288
2	80,968,971	501,531	7,068,047	11,709,659	9,724,350	9,892,971	133,112	8,276,419	7,441,738	688,794,965	2,658,806	225,197	3,776,466	831,172,231
3	60,535,592	2,302,172	3,189,046	1,895,771	2,974,386	6,621,863	0	1,755,850	562,899	1,329,137,357	2,144,989	0	1,747,957	1,412,867,882
TOTAL	599,771,270	3,468,883	15,052,998	14,733,885	17,270,139	42,024,437	5,141,112	12,784,432	12,461,591	3,014,968,920	6,919,151	275,179	7,127,404	3,751,999,401

See Appendix A for a listing of the congressional districts which represent the county in which the state capital is located and congressional districts which represent only portions of a county. See Appendix B for a listing of the programs included in each recipent category.

table continues

Table 3.5 **Federal Outlays to Categories of Recipients by Congressional District, 1987 *(continued)***

District	State Gov't.	Counties	Cities/ Towns	Special Districts	Schools	Public Universities	Indian Tribes	Non-Profits	Private Universities	Individuals	For Profits	Small Businesses	All Others	Total
NEVADA														
1	34,177,774	10,821,576	1,693,185	4,189,014	1,858,651	7,941,107	346,607	1,067,250	1,976,849	602,218,352	4,502,636	175,027	2,451,858	673,419,887
2	251,464,549	4,443,492	15,747,936	4,476,893	2,480,270	15,359,848	6,331,954	4,309,712	1,064,904	540,452,399	891,934	71,053	2,638,404	849,733,347
TOTAL	285,642,323	15,265,068	17,441,121	8,665,907	4,338,921	23,300,955	6,678,561	5,376,962	3,041,753	1,142,670,751	5,394,570	246,080	5,090,262	1,523,153,234
NEW HAMPSHIRE														
1	48,957,477	247,141	4,671,032	1,490,391	55,461	17,644,356	0	1,838,757	3,920,719	597,394,121	210,554	319,284	836,033	677,585,327
2	262,724,388	530,469	27,180,754	390,557	41,287	3,119,874	0	2,939,662	42,344,230	634,917,345	420,842	806,105	1,287,471	976,702,983
TOTAL	311,681,865	777,610	31,851,786	1,880,948	96,748	20,764,230	0	4,778,419	46,264,949	1,232,311,466	631,396	1,125,389	2,123,504	1,654,288,310
NEW JERSEY														
1	79,659,198	1,855,878	917,194	39,374,974	-25,425	3,767,965	0	2,790,479	40,000	662,241,284	1,465,251	0	1,539,453	793,626,252
2	113,295,377	2,592,323	7,225,756	4,410,099	42,436	3,675,101	0	5,557,063	0	1,009,071,156	662,436	2,389	3,899,465	1,150,433,601
3	60,530,893	638,741	10,034,190	1,910,490	2,747,161	609,002	0	1,870,675	1,677,950	894,279,826	971,795	45,644	938,056	976,254,423
4	1,638,182,745	3,819,232	8,838,349	2,197,016	394,241	2,808,664	177,899	6,168,207	1,197,955	736,989,182	262,147	339,978	2,217,798	2,403,593,411
5	36,989,757	1,692,158	3,468,130	187,275	-21,827	169,479	0	561,443	119,304	663,675,957	1,328,985	305,770	176,425	708,652,855
6	56,308,226	3,697,692	12,905,977	2,480,311	0	33,541,806	0	386,027	511,557	714,784,405	2,866,811	0	671,079	828,153,890
7	64,100,728	219,939	9,473,773	1,909,079	91,876	2,589,528	0	1,722,162	1,604,808	788,189,637	2,462,824	78,447	529,172	872,971,973
8	85,669,220	74,097	5,716,605	2,065,602	187,196	3,797,407	0	3,943,461	1,723,327	736,410,917	1,165,696	50,000	2,696,641	843,500,171
9	30,294,295	2,429,114	5,621,953	2,963,902	21,310	32,627	0	107,517	6,096,967	822,327,387	993,878	0	400,921	871,289,870
10	269,996,988	9,093,382	10,207,596	24,162,558	-214,206	12,061,040	0	19,392,345	1,445,851	747,880,639	5,934,019	2,520,607	591,802	1,103,072,620
11	126,587,298	509,026	7,528,209	7,332,593	10,388	1,187,580	0	170,153	5,208,481	727,172,446	250,341	111,394	191,018	876,258,927
12	51,421,171	1,080,681	3,388,941	1,385,510	25,404	12,532,556	0	21,141,021	41,159,326	737,386,473	1,691,086	1,068,044	460,968	872,741,181
13	62,888,328	4,210,622	4,685,967	379,025	4,004,473	571,542	303,972	1,383,481	8,388	929,726,918	1,985,991	213,223	486,173	1,010,848,103
14	152,414,928	55,377,108	15,819,122	9,451,496	-785,423	2,412,090	0	1,837,627	4,493,126	731,786,723	2,028,843	0	1,344,884	976,180,525
TOTAL	2,828,339,151	87,289,993	105,831,762	100,209,929	6,477,604	79,756,385	481,871	67,031,660	65,287,041	10,901,922,950	24,070,103	4,735,496	16,143,856	14,287,577,802
NEW MEXICO														
1	73,931,040	1,770,075	25,415,206	169,225	3,883,756	23,548,061	3,745,529	6,152,394	0	533,397,486	1,684,074	665,965	2,837,959	677,200,770
2	58,495,632	6,328,749	4,554,026	445,029	5,039,922	23,472,902	1,200,520	2,648,641	282,139	665,103,546	1,407,325	214,261	1,965,939	771,158,631
3	537,476,012	4,078,907	2,751,054	371,002	45,108,678	7,776,405	14,628,280	8,444,208	2,900,181	474,348,540	1,082,677	122,489	1,229,132	1,100,317,565
TOTAL	669,902,684	12,177,731	32,720,286	985,256	54,032,356	54,797,368	19,574,329	17,245,243	3,182,320	1,672,849,572	4,174,076	1,002,715	6,033,030	2,548,676,966
NEW YORK														
1	104,020,110	7,508,963	3,828,479	167	59,676	31,111,724	62,107	13,317,564	755,834	517,204,139	547,924	167,928	1,299,303	679,883,918
2	79,502,963	1,807,076	5,162,683	166	96,408	1,450,210	62,010	1,057,919	628,368	516,321,576	894,979	36,981	1,430,031	608,451,370
3	116,171,577	32,414,312	27,023,723	63,820	96,600	2,713,210	62,133	8,588,310	6,493,608	915,476,107	4,709,212	935,605	6,221,038	1,120,969,256
4	70,959,244	-1,005,370	991,434	191,740	-15,031	983,581	0	348,047	3,877,646	776,233,955	386,971	146	0	852,952,363
5	70,296,697	1,552,237	1,343,550	41,918	-18,480	2,511,203	0	4,733,147	10,256,955	768,953,806	6,503,243	0	1,007,373	867,181,650
6	164,421,123	257,638	171,642	0	0	137,785	0	4,785,721	2,499,028	803,708,516	839,359	0	0	976,820,812
7	165,091,693	0	199,342	0	5,416	25,134	0	5,044,512	2,535,014	806,988,137	1,104,783	0	54,488	981,048,519
8	198,365,787	-7,496	1,703,286	20,419	0	1,473,325	0	5,406,037	15,149,009	809,882,228	1,736,400	0	3,261,496	1,036,990,490
9	164,198,081	0	171,409	-50,839	0	24,998	0	3,783,241	2,495,638	802,619,012	838,221	0	0	974,079,760
10	248,260,004	677,011	104,539,496	6,624,544	35,614	1,117,015	0	8,148,211	4,233,420	754,105,231	2,324,894	0	1,321,868	1,131,387,308
11	250,691,108	683,641	34,243,514	6,689,415	0	0	0	8,915,674	4,274,876	761,514,575	2,347,660	0	1,975,212	1,071,335,675
12	255,874,702	698,776	34,172,806	6,674,157	0	5,389,681	0	8,591,271	4,265,125	759,885,852	2,342,305	31,783	0	1,077,926,458
13	251,049,557	860,882	34,217,660	6,698,980	0	0	0	8,321,029	7,079,308	762,630,130	2,351,017	251,984	1,114,776	1,074,575,324
14	155,578,956	271,033	39,641,389	2,113,879	0	122,700	0	8,658,937	2,217,773	741,234,170	1,263,178	0	647,600	951,749,615
15	1,042,300,921	170,000	435,962,000	0	126,207	3,025,959	0	172,040,622	190,440,077	803,865,419	29,689,028	265,041	4,156,838	2,682,042,113
16	598,618,754	81,595	145,507,740	0	0	4,591,202	798,816	18,656,839	53,588,452	804,114,653	27,201,357	263,858	4,686,808	1,658,110,073
17	544,346,679	43,577	111,354,440	5,682	0	1,172,951	0	51,960,425	103,802,348	815,559,057	56,133,154	1,757,069	5,534,612	1,691,669,996

18	302,653,160	162,584	178,267	137,287	0	346,504	0	12,342,094	7,610,348	855,993,758	3,646,788	308,000	12,859,252	1,196,238,041
19	250,275,810	163,522	1,634,447	15,489,469	10,000	475,237	0	15,890,296	4,649,598	832,947,074	2,020,697	0	7,489,171	1,131,045,322
20	110,641,951	22,072,574	14,636,479	259,019	317,813	440,558	0	9,798,073	22,940,793	810,958,818	1,892,659	1,060,229	1,187,151	996,206,117
21	104,027,376	1,717,287	11,420,033	91,345	320,262	1,394,501	0	951,692	5,514,518	698,175,622	253,056	0	246,860	824,112,554
22	120,673,000	3,040,425	12,780,978	3,895,327	677,733	5,453,248	0	10,201,620	22,343,904	689,494,034	224,217	234,961	549,350	869,568,796
23	4,346,533,613	4,779,296	14,795,471	1,002,826	67,961	29,733,925	0	21,850,640	21,019,693	819,063,226	5,854,374	149,707	5,997,135	5,270,847,867
24	96,721,395	10,134,174	8,640,167	-28,438	3,917	2,667,080	0	4,408,996	3,621,036	737,654,376	485,864	194,388	1,455,856	865,958,811
25	124,225,128	5,849,360	14,338,895	155,045	79,926	7,025,949	0	3,890,468	8,156,317	766,910,577	462,700	32,125	636,654	931,763,145
26	136,775,229	14,585,002	14,770,862	846,326	56,698	5,743,595	973,692	6,714,365	6,010,345	737,223,062	939,459	197,495	1,825,345	926,661,475
27	107,274,253	2,670,163	18,716,736	1,906,065	0	6,841,138	0	4,368,230	24,006,270	683,152,201	1,868,728	0	2,085,723	852,889,507
28	117,537,625	13,645,435	20,015,889	511,059	103,564	23,404,901	0	1,625,824	83,100,445	741,652,761	631,637	587,591	906,198	1,003,722,930
29	126,235,917	5,310,708	3,785,699	4,509,606	208,863	2,772,115	147,733	6,589,284	9,975,510	706,395,830	923,419	721,625	1,390,833	868,967,142
30	109,671,946	1,485,154	22,577,877	10,953,276	9,017	5,106,394	55,809	10,601,086	84,418,135	709,125,822	2,450,473	844,083	1,284,014	958,583,084
31	119,178,151	3,658,344	15,772,652	-155,148	-188,429	2,953,249	148,771	3,168,540	4,116,497	745,794,254	691,304	261,055	819,658	896,218,899
32	138,291,715	5,271,709	18,045,173	-767,415	-3,530	15,680,424	47,336	9,435,320	5,527,558	758,170,801	1,451,938	101,779	799,482	952,052,290
33	133,640,365	9,090,257	21,376,210	5,972,148	10,170	10,544,652	125,173	5,275,837	5,396,989	767,329,016	1,107,489	1,494,905	1,327,643	962,690,854
34	120,039,597	3,172,028	11,983,934	411,918	56,090	3,557,780	4,250,300	2,892,180	6,640,982	793,010,273	604,863	0	773,248	947,393,192
TOTAL	11,044,144,187	152,821,897	1,205,704,362	74,263,763	2,116,466	179,991,926	6,733,879	462,362,051	739,641,419	25,773,348,068	166,723,351	9,898,338	74,345,017	39,892,094,725
NORTH CAROLINA														
1	97,043,318	10,778,786	579,321	3,163,329	110,629	9,945,491	0	2,679,109	2,696,838	732,131,740	282,105	11,200	1,067,104	860,488,970
2	104,920,163	4,778,464	1,637,838	4,399,359	0	15,755,494	98,884	36,885,723	95,097,789	704,423,177	4,195,454	1,279,834	1,682,997	975,155,176
3	85,630,297	9,462,038	1,008,389	3,181,155	75,509	0	115,980	2,965,992	1,260,978	609,773,572	74,600	0	360,299	713,908,809
4	1,602,165,547	6,441,778	4,319,442	5,849,860	0	91,162,610	359,983	2,797,840	11,528,547	583,248,695	1,017,391	1,038,716	8,610,305	2,318,540,714
5	65,088,533	4,097,698	6,736,359	3,133,326	0	4,471,097	0	24,288,779	2,858,833	689,135,283	0	612,076	1,325,663	801,747,647
6	45,047,251	944,723	-816,755	3,898,814	0	12,202,826	97,830	2,230,885	4,768,733	688,416,663	571,988	0	1,271,544	758,634,502
7	88,471,813	5,540,284	2,040,913	4,406,011	-100	8,283,021	1,827,953	3,167,027	948,707	597,550,222	2,501,600	0	2,026,251	716,763,702
8	58,457,097	4,956,120	2,897,125	1,469,549	0	0	0	5,792,834	5,176,567	737,149,005	166,621	0	596,564	816,661,483
9	49,046,095	3,092,657	21,526,324	3,898,967	0	3,939,348	99,987	2,696,611	6,575,081	638,028,892	1,087,587	51,310	0	730,042,859
10	49,834,933	3,018,114	7,828,664	1,147,514	0	5,278,244	0	1,252,280	2,702,300	656,933,443	0	0	829,398	728,824,890
11	69,762,370	5,507,771	6,181,165	2,976,532	0	3,904,134	4,253,075	2,879,122	3,039,073	846,070,420	29,035	0	1,956,845	946,559,542
TOTAL	2,315,467,417	58,618,432	53,938,786	37,524,416	186,038	154,942,265	6,853,692	87,636,202	136,653,446	7,482,861,112	9,926,381	2,993,136	19,726,970	10,367,328,294
NORTH DAKOTA														
TOTAL	364,681,040	7,309,667	8,765,038	5,776,391	10,031,048	31,933,592	15,326,351	4,059,538	6,388,949	1,637,097,379	1,092,165	254,901	824,646	2,093,540,705
OHIO														
1	126,862,782	-437,218	3,054,527	15,829,986	1,375,578	33,286,400	0	14,520,613	7,636,744	797,781,425	4,715,921	114,795	740,440	1,005,481,992
2	91,924,082	2,908,841	236,409	2,549,908	968,819	6,071,178	0	1,850,267	5,545,630	645,721,081	1,315,446	0	674,600	759,766,261
3	99,800,200	1,763,623	23,744,635	13,939,552	470,047	1,449,800	0	4,126,975	362,112	678,899,911	2,299,765	1,000,637	350,638	828,207,895
4	66,335,194	1,594,676	7,767,159	244,152	621,750	850,644	0	1,419,879	4,756,995	755,426,689	3,556,056	0	381,455	842,954,650
5	46,246,198	20,838	4,354,969	1,949,063	185,052	7,063,871	0	4,296,367	1,441,044	693,491,773	60,305	348,010	1,473,736	760,931,225
6	143,667,705	3,300,868	5,056,534	1,671,010	972,501	771,851	0	5,711,650	2,733,542	705,789,265	845,927	0	826,732	871,347,585
7	82,422,770	3,479,195	1,715,862	594,321	4,522,974	8,740,654	0	4,359,480	13,778,775	658,973,199	17,295,778	0	602,954	796,485,963
8	63,754,152	33,917	6,499,965	1,551,259	566,793	5,405,668	0	2,791,254	0	640,938,383	200,165	35,700	750,303	722,527,559
9	106,158,824	46,563	7,363,770	9,136,050	165,013	12,700,648	4,135	4,757,103	608,301	760,142,283	9,665,343	271,531	958,172	911,977,737
10	452,967,200	1,969,148	1,109,995	1,823,387	7,338,759	27,879,391	0	39,470,218	10,732,663	677,154,192	1,661,451	0	757,124	1,222,863,528
11	43,618,695	759,872	4,411,364	1,683,303	791,834	11,575,009	0	1,348,692	1,896,792	607,343,264	30,430	0	723,297	674,182,553
12	1,523,639,511	142,781	11,191,227	10,842,426	225,261	2,981,120	0	6,632,768	3,071,399	584,192,620	85,701	50,000	504,839	2,143,559,653
13	57,970,601	2,179,900	3,669,419	2,539,523	4,074,680	142,787	0	383,845	4,105,640	639,350,701	5,430,706	50,028	1,670,384	721,568,214
14	85,654,226	2,318,310	354,447	8,022,925	1,259,975	10,494,621	739,199	2,090,797	156,411	727,854,203	1,220,585	50,000	564,255	840,779,957
15	936,248,058	87,719	8,417,680	4,191,311	51,047	19,505,099	0	12,972,234	787,261	599,424,066	0	0	329,531	1,582,014,005

See Appendix A for a listing of the congressional districts which represent the county in which the state capital is located and congressional districts which represent only portions of a county. See Appendix B for a listing of the programs included in each recipent category.

table continues

Table 3.5 **Federal Outlays to Categories of Recipients by Congressional District, 1987 *(continued)***

District	State Gov't.	Counties	Cities/ Towns	Special Districts	Schools	Public Universities	Indian Tribes	Non-Profits	Private Universities	Individuals	For Profits	Small Businesses	All Others	Total
OHIO *continued*														
16	66,459,499	2,079,139	758,233	6,189,392	948,271	3,724,019	0	1,008,377	1,942,538	709,768,143	2,824,966	0	1,376,563	797,079,140
17	93,163,085	3,404,516	3,349,997	9,833,686	336,522	5,317,285	0	2,266,110	1,399,465	814,729,144	3,109,907	0	301,435	937,211,152
18	89,258,744	1,596,832	374,786	1,995,992	264,832	0	0	3,214,125	545,880	796,967,465	13,814,112	0	1,131,451	909,164,219
19	105,480,212	48,415	676,599	31,168,958	2,209,283	1,452,446	0	1,227,668	3,417,560	836,193,030	1,705,203	49,386	2,331,672	985,960,432
20	111,830,738	31,782	15,422,136	48,707,951	2,242,655	3,469,379	0	2,894,459	4,634,303	852,024,769	1,672,724	47,035	3,224,038	1,046,201,969
21	112,220,638	49,517	9,727,072	10,142,422	1,953,444	2,085,340	0	13,996,116	60,319,046	853,671,530	3,104,795	433,780	3,041,321	1,070,745,021
TOTAL	4,505,683,115	27,379,235	119,256,786	184,606,577	31,545,091	164,967,211	743,334	131,338,998	129,872,102	15,035,837,135	74,615,285	2,450,902	22,714,939	20,431,010,710
OKLAHOMA														
1	51,375,387	392,001	8,244,962	3,569,654	1,096,962	2,604,927	1,322,660	4,837,821	8,394,847	681,983,764	2,263,638	204,656	2,156,813	768,448,092
2	107,356,426	1,803,124	4,889,466	1,228,729	10,407,395	13,165,964	20,706,754	4,304,294	2,011,222	754,753,768	134,866	0	1,057,325	921,819,333
3	137,557,249	829,791	9,268,230	2,137,575	8,458,900	22,743,601	7,568,530	8,249,139	1,456,350	776,724,380	1,849,944	967	1,107,585	977,952,240
4	116,319,091	1,806,166	14,367,946	792,213	9,547,888	29,145,522	3,171,056	5,378,185	865,194	645,997,530	954,038	197,579	6,538,999	835,081,407
5	581,520,785	1,865,617	7,298,199	1,683,417	1,903,751	8,127,285	2,285,348	9,792,936	2,097,421	693,160,557	4,368,740	28,238	1,171,697	1,315,303,992
6	239,874,288	4,659,371	4,018,672	2,030,063	4,214,674	4,197,312	3,582,772	1,774,352	1,606,218	901,078,763	5,837,169	16,945	756,670	1,173,647,268
TOTAL	1,234,003,226	11,356,071	48,087,476	11,441,651	35,629,570	79,984,611	38,637,120	34,336,727	16,431,252	4,453,698,761	15,408,395	448,385	12,789,088	5,992,252,332
OREGON														
1	59,437,876	1,695,390	16,253,470	1,026,308	127,269	5,436,864	1,688,845	17,802,407	5,199,227	698,854,149	681,328	119,555	1,127,686	809,450,373
2	55,428,337	2,455,799	6,110,991	2,011,353	4,173,487	7,489,827	6,820,442	2,974,743	100,000	858,131,991	702,766	1,085,511	841,898	948,327,146
3	107,195,354	3,895,654	7,813,694	19,326,032	3,237,493	15,869,607	1,237,780	5,150,142	2,422,545	871,325,555	615,527	186,547	741,828	1,039,017,757
4	68,040,670	685,890	10,462,260	11,568,355	5,592,251	52,160,113	325,200	5,641,297	479,254	740,775,643	645,887	188,536	125,926	896,691,282
5	867,961,660	765,338	4,667,104	1,498,616	9,293,394	49,119,160	0	5,761,769	11,646,243	702,818,934	2,959,365	164,945	3,207,588	1,659,864,117
TOTAL	1,158,063,897	9,498,072	45,307,519	35,430,664	22,423,893	130,075,571	10,072,267	37,330,358	19,847,269	3,871,906,271	5,604,873	1,745,094	6,044,927	5,353,350,675
PENNSYLVANIA														
1	205,816,390	7,121	16,191,390	144,038,828	1,516,710	7,088,701	131,546	57,685,283	120,757,804	967,124,121	5,750,764	392,386	2,296,797	1,528,797,841
2	216,517,875	7,149	1,273,883	18,617,924	1,622,805	19,203,760	132,075	17,052,387	36,934,749	971,320,045	17,272,488	2,272,242	183,983	1,302,411,365
3	210,132,888	7,134	1,280,661	18,579,731	1,519,681	6,635,443	131,804	22,879,747	9,573,916	968,813,404	5,762,028	0	272,706	1,245,589,142
4	79,521,676	2,652,138	3,747,087	2,931,432	46,608	7,034,465	0	679,575	865,585	840,472,174	679,004	29,155	1,983,884	940,642,783
5	43,618,160	931,759	602,756	5,566,534	-81,999	1,816,044	0	3,332,080	5,375,004	728,020,360	1,388,150	661,419	760,136	791,990,405
6	58,589,836	3,926,790	3,128,729	5,408,234	207,319	215,866	0	308,932	702,676	934,528,416	450,584	0	-9,288	1,007,458,094
7	70,522,122	228,109	480,183	2,765,042	1,172,357	809,459	12,686	713,518	14,055,908	858,283,028	3,018,539	48,944	73,107	952,183,001
8	32,274,777	1,411,306	3,765,788	4,643,348	1,961,635	0	0	515,747	806,675	647,858,438	318,433	199,080	125,499	693,880,728
9	77,882,470	1,677,996	1,718,405	3,594,047	582,555	310,320	0	1,592,800	803,247	781,202,227	312,965	650	587,864	870,265,545
10	77,937,315	1,049,212	701,936	20,489,960	51,386	215,424	0	2,272,566	3,283,326	966,400,805	212,661	0	94,284	1,072,708,875
11	74,041,879	3,107,635	2,063,440	5,780,062	99,019	96,531	0	4,279,679	3,080,990	1,080,640,664	791,477	0	177,142	1,174,158,518
12	71,769,611	3,042,921	606,342	4,024,004	94,928	459,617	0	2,241,839	3,530,700	922,891,109	370,456	240,000	590,333	1,009,861,860
13	63,962,406	1,220,569	2,358,528	4,060,115	469,026	1,155,180	22,986	12,374,595	3,766,094	835,031,014	2,859,797	1,830,445	28,858	929,139,613
14	116,528,936	10,706,149	4,501,714	61,359,445	8,749,559	47,240,162	1,551,209	21,554,698	50,103,931	927,514,171	7,869,727	1,702,761	3,025,623	1,262,408,087
15	55,072,449	957,007	-1,324,038	8,947,505	769,607	123,652	0	1,637,745	13,335,906	848,356,375	1,514,831	40,000	468,512	929,899,550
16	49,294,657	944,601	2,425,614	1,819,447	442,308	803,036	0	654,158	2,407,284	680,555,100	-58,950	0	0	739,287,254
17	3,070,232,658	1,764,974	3,480,197	9,907,992	744,414	5,940,404	0	8,022,010	2,818,871	788,855,176	4,922,829	197,344	5,426,319	3,902,313,188
18	86,743,926	444,886	84,987	1,430,323	1,371	0	0	70,786	0	925,917,863	0	0	479,883	1,015,174,026
19	46,537,223	1,667,817	146,529	22,058,744	711,474	0	0	2,720,737	3,211,392	670,406,525	881,995	0	755,880	749,098,316
20	81,699,497	399,509	1,361,276	2,076,712	230,893	322,150	0	1,028,611	0	913,130,671	2,513,855	50,000	765,502	1,003,578,676
21	79,981,896	1,177,346	6,422,964	5,631,290	224,219	20,799	0	4,372,137	5,918,959	808,127,517	1,776,748	0	939,412	914,593,286
22	110,665,219	3,755,838	1,717,278	3,260,378	236,350	92,966	0	2,118,637	1,703,058	949,968,989	707,134	0	1,409,761	1,075,635,608
23	70,796,329	997,546	1,883,315	4,264,923	117,222	61,677,083	0	3,350,777	1,260,729	774,373,833	449,647	0	704,092	919,875,497
TOTAL	5,050,140,199	42,085,511	58,618,964	361,256,020	21,489,446	161,261,063	1,982,306	171,459,044	284,296,803	19,789,792,027	59,765,162	7,664,426	21,140,288	26,030,951,259

RHODE ISLAND														
1	330,982,638	69,561	7,685,335	7,780,891	0	2,276,376	89,272	18,843,169	36,608,834	736,228,778	2,132,083	53,781	1,055,400	1,143,806,116
2	201,431,567	355,055	2,709,994	4,295,536	7,257	21,208,539	721,751	7,084,137	4,088,064	721,730,009	935,930	395,887	1,438,744	966,402,472
TOTAL	532,414,205	424,616	10,395,329	12,076,427	7,257	23,484,915	811,023	25,927,306	40,696,898	1,457,958,787	3,068,013	449,668	2,494,144	2,110,208,588
SOUTH CAROLINA														
1	79,687,605	1,166,056	1,102,484	1,586,395	2,237,927	13,293,368	0	7,667,491	1,660,378	550,777,497	1,121,952	333,003	2,398,029	663,032,185
2	980,499,941	4,239,044	11,763,340	3,190,319	477,315	45,695,775	280,129	8,043,242	14,263,825	577,304,168	1,725,111	428,358	4,674,843	1,652,585,410
3	61,507,087	3,802,385	2,260,659	1,061,378	860,521	11,031,883	1,361,946	3,378,083	4,049,961	674,396,982	445,733	0	452,342	764,608,960
4	50,767,215	2,317,967	233,698	11,328,820	67,406	34,200	0	1,196,171	6,991,883	676,632,941	939,905	0	2,057,842	752,568,048
5	76,367,608	4,018,016	8,669,472	357,034	1,808,978	179,120	4,210	3,754,075	5,342,335	648,400,583	124,435	0	763,728	749,789,594
6	101,993,446	3,380,130	4,213,008	6,295,200	3,375,905	1,481,259	0	6,868,441	1,492,864	649,896,738	1,197,067	0	656,148	780,850,206
TOTAL	1,350,822,902	18,923,598	28,242,661	23,819,146	8,828,052	71,715,605	1,646,285	30,907,503	33,801,246	3,777,408,909	5,554,203	761,361	11,002,932	5,363,434,403
SOUTH DAKOTA														
TOTAL	363,675,988	596,753	12,283,146	3,971,332	20,069,447	23,042,875	29,495,026	6,288,353	14,723,144	1,371,044,521	755,596	240,901	833,764	1,847,020,846
TENNESSEE														
1	79,310,665	378,818	3,508,869	2,928,226	2,506	5,578,093	0	2,755,765	3,128,562	707,213,287	221,162	0	317,336	805,343,289
2	68,556,348	1,601,834	7,587,668	10,034,592	2,000	24,786,811	0	3,389,964	6,406,035	714,431,498	813,442	100,000	890,094	838,600,286
3	73,670,878	1,170,807	10,741,064	5,196,483	0	2,704,324	0	4,241,333	6,785,143	728,827,298	1,979,036	1,055,465	1,960,833	838,332,664
4	99,319,370	1,398,783	12,284,134	2,476,834	27,011	2,195,214	0	5,538,741	3,845,762	740,238,914	76,600	309,559	431,306	868,142,228
5	1,284,917,387	2,307,499	11,472,475	16,584,476	14,918	10,446,347	653,008	53,155,650	31,367,261	676,997,575	2,808,582	0	4,182,345	2,094,907,523
6	67,246,057	557,934	3,690,394	1,850,360	14,941	4,923,588	0	7,003,102	444,918	633,710,550	260,240	190,000	199,979	720,092,063
7	95,468,134	2,646,499	9,351,564	2,677,355	0	5,009,134	0	1,700,145	2,810,061	634,832,165	2,902,166	200,500	649,402	758,247,125
8	98,812,833	829,460	2,529,804	9,017,345	2,286	5,688,473	0	13,803,265	4,852,386	755,002,523	2,148,009	0	895,544	893,581,929
9	101,958,869	3,565,183	1,057,200	5,140,020	0	17,317,724	0	4,650,932	4,562,616	617,878,260	8,040,962	263,476	1,764,101	766,199,344
TOTAL	1,969,260,541	14,456,817	62,223,173	55,905,691	63,662	78,649,708	653,008	96,238,897	64,202,744	6,209,132,070	19,250,200	2,119,000	11,290,940	8,583,446,451
TEXAS														
1	80,858,675	1,659,624	9,088,358	1,220,122	2,237,898	513,543	152,252	98,214	2,603,789	877,402,613	0	0	802,230	976,637,318
2	63,869,317	1,041,911	1,356,367	547,170	9,183	6,238,550	940,038	2,008,451	0	829,789,087	288,415	0	5,595,319	911,683,807
3	32,837,769	34,861	7,029,582	2,044,794	560,032	3,063,015	87,713	1,470,272	2,704,738	559,317,372	1,877,923	124,147	2,588,251	613,740,468
4	50,224,381	271,095	4,526,368	474,817	2,900,319	3,233,699	0	1,195,247	6,104,778	888,181,780	2,607,666	0	2,480,980	962,201,131
5	50,902,138	3,187,314	10,962,603	2,142,535	349,085	31,837,171	91,927	3,044,211	3,507,963	563,496,638	462,421	215,857	2,711,560	672,911,424
6	59,594,742	593,346	7,277,577	505,982	15,587	35,618,057	8,056	1,258,804	3,335,363	779,923,714	354,756	112,294	1,582,108	890,180,386
7	45,543,922	61,403	5,336,535	29,249,130	57,417	18,493,201	0	476,616	260,129	491,220,288	84,760	180,945	3,239,407	594,203,755
8	36,458,552	61,328	7,045,194	1,041,888	467,849	224,009	0	328,572	124,750	491,544,768	34,752	501,526	2,306,421	540,139,609
9	52,257,991	6,247,740	5,883,987	3,602,079	848,444	19,578,880	0	474,135	1,159,266	722,775,975	5,295,257	50,000	1,703,016	819,876,772
10	3,695,352,069	503,747	9,721,760	2,289,915	2,197,436	47,311,946	0	8,186,866	4,001,612	588,994,024	3,443,815	50,000	4,694,941	4,366,748,131
11	49,750,112	346,685	3,378,382	794,129	10,340,150	3,021,236	0	2,102,022	5,905,428	739,239,116	1,446,866	0	2,608,516	818,932,642
12	29,696,089	33,913	10,166,234	587,397	1,281,977	4,930,046	0	2,098,821	1,638,081	602,178,487	8,813,330	100,042	1,363,609	662,888,026
13	29,733,533	161,838	1,219,542	626,705	2,268,035	4,340,829	0	2,541,431	0	1,041,484,893	3,356,142	0	894,695	1,086,627,643
14	62,325,536	1,720,064	5,331,851	1,763,697	928,739	9,280,302	0	1,532,509	976,747	821,368,184	237,180	0	654,184	906,118,993
15	117,020,046	2,904,729	7,830,383	1,476,854	1,957,347	8,662,413	0	4,911,149	78,000	619,718,467	1,152,170	0	3,287,571	768,999,129
16	60,398,913	351,153	19,026,123	1,146,356	3,588,261	7,196,061	466,959	4,401,241	743,521	555,813,892	6,817,348	151,232	1,609,976	661,711,036
17	43,416,939	2,731,365	3,872,576	525,285	2,248,097	964,847	0	1,869,939	2,989,794	1,064,806,129	196,641	200,825	1,062,349	1,124,884,786
18	37,515,027	61,356	2,612,389	1,046,312	117,372	11,992,499	0	8,456,281	58,003,095	491,763,835	568,799	210,644	591,111	612,938,720
19	38,551,322	214,411	4,657,915	676,374	957,879	13,646,026	0	5,584,755	2,278,387	995,012,984	1,492,428	0	643,898	1,063,716,379
20	61,204,878	333,048	19,874,667	28,611,362	8,510,779	3,349,253	0	14,770,787	5,091,246	612,930,392	6,486,428	50,000	3,525,375	764,738,216
21	39,636,060	767,520	7,546,350	2,230,848	2,368,420	3,862,507	0	1,645,688	1,888,378	681,855,295	3,902,418	0	1,261,715	746,965,197

See Appendix A for a listing of the congressional districts which represent the county in which the state capital is located and congressional districts which represent only portions of a county. See Appendix B for a listing of the programs included in each recipent category.

table continues

Table 3.5 Federal Outlays to Categories of Recipients by Congressional District, 1987 *(continued)*

District	State Gov't.	Counties	Cities/ Towns	Special Districts	Schools	Public Universities	Indian Tribes	Non-Profits	Private Universities	Individuals	For Profits	Small Businesses	All Others	Total
TEXAS *continued*														
22	28,867,458	432,610	16,499,601	480,270	1,550,785	20,361,511	0	4,040,078	8,225,041	465,173,248	10,437,083	178,994	1,440,128	557,686,808
23	100,282,055	7,523,018	6,505,653	5,992,706	9,058,235	21,377,617	0	15,729,872	2,256,631	662,902,355	4,445,123	248,401	3,473,728	839,795,394
24	31,968,005	35,362	1,810,410	7,977,449	295,236	996,307	560,908	893,099	854,632	566,703,433	1,083,486	1,020,151	4,243,864	618,442,341
25	44,441,342	61,287	1,392,094	1,045,137	57,308	19,754,583	0	329,597	2,144,876	490,292,036	34,860	0	433,532	559,986,652
26	24,154,443	28,467	1,746,693	322,991	2,278,683	11,623,209	0	1,332,295	3,350,160	552,842,657	11,425,904	252,230	1,025,755	610,383,488
27	88,146,622	1,931,946	8,796,024	2,174,956	3,933,252	6,761,480	0	9,644,448	-10,000	615,818,445	2,230,928	0	1,609,803	741,037,903
TOTAL	5,055,007,936	33,301,139	190,495,220	100,597,261	61,383,805	318,232,797	2,307,853	100,425,402	120,216,405	18,372,550,108	78,576,900	3,647,288	57,434,041	24,494,176,156
UTAH														
1	65,713,520	1,016,676	4,576,659	1,104,037	5,122,644	28,221,147	846,618	1,478,345	1,747,630	492,243,014	1,312,849	78,400	944,171	604,405,710
2	635,040,266	601,364	14,220,386	19,635,597	731,231	48,430,801	419,015	6,068,906	741,519	478,096,113	3,946,285	2,731,111	1,879,103	1,212,541,696
3	75,014,007	675,106	2,200,161	807,914	4,056,838	5,039,070	2,167,172	2,123,373	10,913,923	453,510,686	406,551	974,868	441,161	558,330,831
TOTAL	775,767,793	2,293,146	20,997,206	21,547,548	9,910,713	81,691,018	3,432,805	9,670,624	13,403,072	1,423,849,813	5,665,685	3,784,379	3,264,435	2,375,278,237
VERMONT														
TOTAL	329,210,475	261,588	27,748,742	2,525,968	669,179	31,531,676	111,584	7,762,415	9,900,295	685,687,917	287,594	397,184	2,082,563	1,098,177,180
VIRGINIA														
1	51,860,065	6,681,502	7,830,767	3,830,970	0	5,406,083	276,333	6,689,703	9,011,010	687,444,614	1,500,944	0	829,891	781,361,882
2	48,492,378	500	19,384,568	26,425,049	0	13,516,395	0	9,751,990	2,356,636	509,454,750	4,357,437	0	1,678,259	635,417,962
3	1,148,249,667	15,826,429	16,252,204	2,058,906	0	30,222,212	0	4,547,133	3,266,432	742,251,737	1,297,120	65,138	2,185,940	1,966,222,917
4	77,724,946	2,453,270	7,576,011	1,323,393	0	8,271,020	0	2,041,504	1,616,211	696,440,727	284,240	0	1,036,026	798,767,349
5	69,984,694	958,871	3,611,898	104,000	0	998,596	0	3,125,121	2,930,010	721,300,050	342,641	0	0	803,355,882
6	49,646,367	-211,841	12,452,057	1,537,620	4,266	3,417,159	0	4,298,149	7,188,328	797,685,034	1,723,513	336,100	1,027,271	879,104,022
7	54,790,959	2,192,889	2,706,679	16,116,014	0	46,829,920	0	3,245,440	719,954	634,236,634	818,775	218,902	509,601	762,385,768
8	21,340,078	847,201	1,916,545	310,861	0	17,285	-32,739	11,527,576	10,680	381,702,050	1,829,238	2,111,319	2,352,309	423,932,403
9	85,800,277	8,268,452	1,451,170	1,730,962	0	28,506,992	0	3,540,819	3,394,994	834,358,465	50,000	612,589	742,300	968,457,020
10	20,197,668	7,326,450	1,037,639	1,243,404	0	4,067,378	0	19,548,770	241,464	453,240,019	7,898,585	11,056,232	90,250,380	616,107,989
TOTAL	1,628,087,099	44,343,723	74,219,538	54,681,179	4,266	141,253,040	243,594	68,316,205	30,735,719	6,458,114,081	20,102,493	14,400,280	100,611,977	8,635,113,194
WASHINGTON														
1	79,275,918	108,078	1,410,753	109,953,042	902,408	9,723,232	586,082	7,017,906	2,293,528	656,859,957	697,157	1,434,125	2,140,746	872,402,932
2	77,601,220	2,518,473	8,511,109	2,249,946	5,301,429	5,777,256	8,343,329	3,948,195	0	797,321,197	3,169,835	0	2,234,910	916,976,898
3	1,107,983,962	2,395,566	2,058,202	537,249	939,475	6,660,492	1,799,213	2,497,928	449,252	726,225,916	1,439,539	100,000	2,326,943	1,855,413,737
4	93,628,257	2,312,290	3,937,284	5,695,442	5,898,255	15,667,286	11,028,519	16,570,624	495,221	748,104,398	1,533,003	186,422	1,895,010	906,952,011
5	91,135,819	2,130,349	8,313,672	1,026,157	3,228,972	34,669,706	1,686,090	3,871,332	7,958,344	936,210,433	2,567,964	156,123	811,898	1,093,766,859
6	98,052,104	1,748,575	12,129,101	1,076,843	13,090,718	3,182,170	2,363,537	3,310,642	4,796,671	628,576,541	5,118,406	0	2,342,372	775,787,679
7	121,110,397	1,752,726	7,893,015	9,884,873	959,568	117,474,892	586,722	41,051,641	4,338,632	680,444,494	1,035,375	2,443,928	1,390,241	990,366,504
8	85,843,962	141,006	2,815,055	5,386,487	1,190,907	14,997,847	1,826,657	5,668,894	3,728,878	682,929,682	727,586	707,448	676,995	806,641,404
TOTAL	1,754,631,639	13,107,062	47,068,191	135,810,040	31,511,732	208,152,880	28,220,149	83,937,161	24,060,527	5,856,672,619	16,288,865	5,028,046	13,819,114	8,218,308,025
WEST VIRGINIA														
1	56,223,970	943,425	4,797,375	11,415,908	120,203	6,900,992	0	3,946,248	2,445,592	788,590,723	3,709,320	29,933	517,032	879,640,721
2	80,405,027	2,293,981	12,929,179	4,836,160	1,100,207	19,390,689	0	4,022,066	2,744,795	759,726,467	734,382	35,087	950,022	889,168,062
3	794,744,090	2,149,788	10,498,628	12,771,259	752,483	4,203,082	0	1,580,042	516,012	754,460,733	1,111,602	0	3,431,509	1,586,219,228
4	94,124,957	2,477,418	5,709,350	2,554,530	299,998	8,614,345	0	5,196,217	3,462,988	870,401,201	1,270,737	0	1,365,660	995,477,401
TOTAL	1,025,498,044	7,864,612	33,934,532	31,577,857	2,272,891	39,109,108	0	14,744,573	9,169,387	3,173,179,124	6,826,041	65,020	6,264,223	4,350,505,412

WISCONSIN														
1	112,222,853	3,149,056	5,067,233	1,032,218	773,555	5,997,556	0	857,217	1,625,489	760,465,018	2,259,679	0	368,635	893,818,509
2	1,159,967,903	1,305,296	5,857,610	317,139	2,540,536	127,030,875	659,494	5,806,926	3,170,472	690,240,391	60,199	201,840	3,940,752	2,001,099,433
3	126,652,797	422,357	4,567,257	484,056	1,246,579	21,101,851	128,904	2,782,435	1,028,876	784,707,566	62,405	0	1,008,481	944,193,564
4	152,523,015	6,440,141	9,022,045	44,151,814	223,995	3,994,035	0	6,227,452	4,112,558	790,042,722	1,328,705	75,000	2,543,944	1,020,685,427
5	183,103,338	4,437,418	11,297,794	36,344,087	282,664	6,935,853	231,788	7,062,920	23,251,807	848,565,943	2,388,251	325,365	1,985,600	1,126,212,829
6	96,983,617	304,967	1,446,096	62,926	1,329,157	5,327,390	224,705	1,671,529	1,996,382	808,727,211	183,946	560,687	382,356	919,200,969
7	126,608,091	1,777,628	3,696,117	107,633	2,349,423	18,520,283	3,708,071	6,292,724	2,155,544	726,618,926	55,766	382,859	733,957	893,007,022
8	103,696,122	3,951,949	8,912,662	189,315	220,103	2,154,729	6,737,366	2,436,405	1,230,735	757,994,537	56,810	0	813,369	888,394,102
9	59,839,838	1,474,534	2,104,255	2,307,384	780,951	273,208	0	261,073	2,393,964	662,370,042	92,694	283,624	422,825	732,604,391
TOTAL	2,121,597,575	23,263,346	51,971,070	84,996,571	9,746,963	191,335,780	11,690,328	33,398,680	40,965,827	6,829,732,355	6,488,455	1,829,375	12,199,919	9,419,216,244
WYOMING														
TOTAL	252,040,529	5,792,355	10,407,764	346,365	9,617,084	12,014,959	3,105,349	9,044,544	741,316	513,848,152	1,867,276	35,488	872,518	819,733,699
U.S. TOTAL	97,738.2 mil	1,333.1 mil	4,050.5 mil	2,891.5 mil	888.6 mil	5,144.1 mil	441.5 mil	3,450.6 mil	4,086.4 mil	328,379.5 mil	1,428.9 mil	190.0 mil	1,003.1 mil	451,025.8 mil

See Appendix A for a listing of the congressional districts which represent the county in which the state capital is located and congressional districts which represent only portions of a county. See Appendix B for a listing of the programs included in each recipent category.

Table 3.6 Federal Outlays to Categories of Recipients by Congressional District, 1988

District	State Gov't.	Counties	Cities/ Towns	Special Districts	Schools	Public Universities	Indian Tribes	Non-Profits	Private Universities	Individuals	For Profits	Small Businesses	All Others	Total
ALABAMA														
1	62,399,516	4,938,029	15,117,058	20,492,192	404,813	9,896,641	2,541,705	4,959,471	427,993	800,977,160	7,032,657	0	0	929,187,235
2	1,562,591,524	11,668,633	20,156,352	15,891,836	1,214,826	2,660,107	65,669	5,187,076	-516,058	797,670,400	12,752,473	38,209	1,397,302	2,430,778,349
3	66,927,427	9,189,571	15,252,617	10,333,493	225,212	19,019,822	0	5,015,187	4,780,675	764,565,950	6,074,633	86,227	250,000	901,720,814
4	67,533,989	5,343,782	8,883,715	10,251,400	10,689	1,536,463	0	4,606,048	182,400	897,791,109	7,120,806	0	0	1,003,260,401
5	49,438,712	9,029,806	7,241,673	11,872,032	1,910,767	23,046,450	0	3,387,930	248,683	718,327,116	10,619,005	0	25,000	835,147,174
6	47,607,818	11,909,808	20,024,815	24,496,580	123,589	69,661,478	0	4,052,163	2,880,074	936,447,512	29,376,050	0	127,737	1,146,707,624
7	74,554,640	10,938,007	6,536,790	12,302,194	60,081	5,338,951	114,698	7,148,627	2,247,754	796,367,409	7,438,495	250,000	106,112	923,403,758
TOTAL	1,931,053,626	63,017,636	93,213,020	105,639,727	3,949,977	131,159,912	2,722,072	34,356,502	10,251,521	5,712,146,656	80,414,119	374,436	1,906,151	8,170,205,355
ALASKA														
TOTAL	595,746,321	55,190,025	39,694,862	285,505	3,329	18,885,204	41,627,164	55,348,608	380,042	261,958,183	12,664,850	685,534	2,672,305	1,085,141,932
ARIZONA														
1	301,402,115	5,771,378	43,493,517	12,898,281	930,624	28,333,124	929,622	3,075,174	448,408	1,239,131,763	19,000,495	125,808	405,200	1,655,945,508
2	209,373,808	9,082,450	28,110,576	7,954,166	3,335,458	61,238,467	10,849,776	11,084,681	2,512,315	1,047,006,563	10,433,551	2,997,044	1,488,753	1,405,467,611
3	25,940,876	9,592,240	32,203,281	1,571,660	922,724	3,675,221	2,697,541	1,289,614	181,208	474,101,918	7,370,068	127,951	0	559,674,302
4	414,948,358	13,281,040	28,553,924	319,880	19,575,679	229,667	73,181,121	1,935,573	299,052	1,075,702,297	9,608,758	0	187,245	1,637,822,593
5	49,968,957	6,995,140	16,041,764	322,214	855,855	3,797,526	67,891	4,207,509	3,339,504	917,913,119	3,224,843	229,356	50,224	1,007,013,902
TOTAL	1,001,634,114	44,722,247	148,403,062	23,066,201	25,620,340	97,274,006	87,725,952	21,592,551	6,780,487	4,753,855,659	49,637,715	3,480,159	2,131,422	6,265,923,915
ARKANSAS														
1	142,636,607	4,608,416	5,275,722	16,974,983	1,370,023	2,406,468	109,080	5,306,299	357,004	1,136,382,307	6,572,779	0	0	1,321,999,688
2	767,805,818	12,341,685	12,544,504	15,968,313	796,546	10,147,458	450,865	5,060,316	1,532,498	859,555,629	10,170,910	701,944	3,191,885	1,700,268,371
3	61,758,268	9,775,143	6,002,916	10,948,708	-6,903	13,135,957	0	4,561,785	1,698,704	991,410,821	9,135,193	0	0	1,108,420,592
4	110,409,908	6,362,771	6,395,712	11,984,026	122,640	4,538,547	0	5,671,937	456,415	1,014,089,479	8,497,046	90,454	437,091	1,169,056,026
TOTAL	1,082,610,601	33,088,015	30,218,854	55,876,030	2,282,306	30,228,430	559,945	20,600,337	4,044,621	4,001,438,236	34,375,928	792,398	3,628,976	5,299,744,677
CALIFORNIA														
1	120,254,129	8,807,158	2,338,343	16,367,802	1,171,932	4,806,860	2,526,220	6,060,776	88,314	947,813,632	8,510,657	0	4,779,556	1,123,525,379
2	158,117,890	7,200,198	5,676,646	16,054,417	2,436,192	2,116,813	563,065	4,615,917	490,418	1,113,066,553	9,059,755	101,200	12,000	1,319,511,064
3	4,917,749,155	10,260,281	6,516,168	10,365,238	399,101	809,504	2,789,275	11,013,176	121,266	644,954,946	14,919,784	137,000	6,605,640	5,626,640,534
4	931,754,865	12,711,478	5,569,501	17,845,888	6,888,236	50,870,324	764,934	2,978,623	3,763,698	662,735,305	14,440,223	93,447	1,492,383	1,711,908,905
5	188,463,833	13,185,025	48,384,616	40,811,906	1,732,834	5,486,528	0	13,091,392	1,367,374	1,056,725,097	22,738,239	632,492	294,116	1,392,913,453
6	92,848,215	16,223,012	3,084,657	21,617,861	2,346,816	152,706,111	0	19,921,079	1,007,101	754,875,295	13,130,748	1,693,631	146,158	1,079,600,685
7	93,993,753	10,753,086	264,861	33,167,730	609,713	0	0	4,735,509	122,148	736,923,385	9,071,824	335,002	0	889,977,011
8	135,029,633	29,527,411	5,678,585	33,011,210	262,469	104,468,698	222,212	35,970,586	5,455,557	746,275,235	16,422,713	2,206,616	18,175,686	1,132,706,611
9	142,480,240	6,435,414	11,646,086	38,355,351	2,501,609	609,875	295,237	1,625,002	297,111	741,732,114	82,346,830	797,175	0	1,029,122,045
10	101,233,673	7,610,447	4,844,573	40,097,425	308,909	3,037,329	590,651	1,155,663	159,340	615,681,393	10,198,220	50,000	1,343,140	786,310,765
11	58,879,726	20,163,079	1,170,465	12,815,425	147,892	67,605	11,664	10,735,084	160,649	718,801,232	5,395,540	1,114,187	658,517	830,121,065
12	66,228,455	10,408,233	1,796,772	10,327,977	1,632,158	9,562,933	63,866	24,787,170	158,664,376	514,787,644	16,583,950	4,399,992	1,871,386	821,114,912
13	77,693,669	5,629,972	1,938,967	15,642,561	134,479	628,856	93,130	3,862,416	1,446,403	544,380,227	6,916,956	301,913	2,071,497	660,741,047
14	105,855,377	8,373,404	2,499,758	9,368,873	634,071	0	246,395	3,198,282	1,269,522	825,534,643	6,734,571	94,902	40,200	963,849,997
15	132,581,999	13,202,637	4,998,050	13,218,989	1,536,965	917,815	-250	4,775,108	0	644,256,613	9,107,221	71,273	899,127	825,565,547
16	88,614,147	4,872,128	855,249	30,809,199	8,768,353	10,507,197	-59,423	2,757,704	168,013	656,136,228	6,242,761	599,317	301,508	810,572,381
17	196,269,113	8,504,100	6,132,322	12,372,422	3,302,636	545,413	568,627	1,734,581	51,732	853,355,858	9,125,088	0	2,505,674	1,094,467,567
18	231,172,397	12,953,116	14,619,372	20,696,478	856,038	1,468,043	101,038	1,318,605	318,774	1,127,933,199	9,180,740	0	256,083	1,420,873,883
19	54,474,133	4,789,288	1,827,430	29,092,496	4,306,374	23,914,648	455,368	5,927,248	270,617	576,991,486	3,845,282	1,378,805	0	707,273,175
20	130,149,213	5,322,357	2,472,692	65,323,492	5,295,765	4,077,063	3,573,370	20,002,060	778,033	911,169,714	18,122,940	509	123,436,704	1,289,723,911
21	119,427,720	3,344,055	1,095,399	17,252,251	1,260,808	359,679	358,021	1,529,585	318,485	839,292,849	8,294,280	187,327	278,646	992,999,104
22	143,144,402	2,999,165	1,976,837	20,483,732	581,193	1,287,167	97	10,073,120	35,867,908	729,450,694	9,685,169	391,586	657,440	956,598,509
23	141,760,013	2,248,721	960,529	13,227,251	261,953	151,010,182	97	11,876,141	4,345,124	728,522,635	8,259,442	102,596	819,854	1,063,394,537

24	145,132,569	2,248,302	960,350	25,618,692	261,905	742,176	96	17,120,656	407,076	727,956,853	11,550,007	455,248	656,620	933,110,551
25	137,973,026	12,560,841	1,220,475	20,656,212	454,546	1,984,799	173,993	10,841,048	832,888	727,616,195	12,049,510	52,918	655,998	927,072,448
26	124,679,937	1,992,200	843,167	10,825,221	275,862	982,634	85	2,186,224	447,391	638,987,479	5,754,572	2,564	576,498	787,553,832
27	143,631,331	7,283,620	32,401,910	19,023,883	439,999	741,963	96	7,760,082	2,331,101	727,731,763	11,206,396	355,910	782,498	953,690,552
28	144,628,794	3,035,943	1,059,401	15,350,502	261,792	2,587,224	96	10,611,919	75,874,064	727,582,277	9,994,221	2,919	656,337	991,645,489
29	141,561,227	33,028,173	962,751	14,757,239	1,261,848	828,856	96	7,753,732	411,988	727,635,124	8,060,456	2,920	656,478	936,920,888
30	141,860,812	5,104,974	4,402,903	15,689,192	696,606	740,728	96	2,936,106	846,017	726,372,979	8,703,157	45,874	655,339	908,054,783
31	142,505,298	3,360,253	2,915,822	17,963,522	451,114	1,282,430	97	937,512	11,100,250	728,112,285	9,197,005	402,596	685,143	918,913,327
32	142,792,266	2,256,446	2,114,826	14,022,893	262,853	1,631,422	97	1,387,339	408,551	730,429,870	5,205,169	162,634	658,998	901,333,365
33	143,060,473	3,685,767	1,249,568	15,469,073	661,032	2,281,457	97	2,687,953	2,328,384	728,418,517	4,875,224	451,260	657,103	905,825,906
34	141,702,833	3,294,149	1,050,196	15,442,196	401,464	742,757	20,322	1,241,910	939,369	728,362,989	8,636,902	2,923	657,134	902,495,144
35	133,619,702	2,107,611	1,734,588	14,595,939	5,340,586	8,826,791	54,391	515,339	3,312,934	762,605,411	6,067,138	2,757,019	4,214	941,541,662
36	499,428,989	12,604,358	4,042,088	17,822,960	512,457	6,441,091	310,005	668,568	609,474	1,509,298,631	9,422,763	98,950	517,995	2,061,778,329
37	353,741,168	11,993,393	3,313,734	16,192,890	1,394,093	3,507,366	381,630	1,441,919	488,973	752,150,131	4,766,485	0	465,339	1,149,837,123
38	52,901,427	10,832,025	171,123	30,991,022	99,592	30,475	524,569	217,126	405,390	665,305,838	5,551,379	0	0	767,029,967
39	53,249,571	1,795,220	87,938	14,785,773	354,932	2,461,522	525,012	181,050	499,986	665,906,576	9,290,926	246,518	0	749,385,023
40	53,067,960	14,655,071	321,186	16,024,491	1,343,496	11,242,857	524,530	28,460,943	477,032	665,303,517	12,868,765	619,341	0	804,909,189
41	77,739,301	2,460,793	3,101,861	8,159,315	1,342,151	44,206,901	123,748	140,650,452	1,395,572	574,184,938	12,075,092	3,530,281	660,327	869,630,734
42	107,295,238	3,108,175	2,825,302	17,765,848	368,628	1,682,209	203,365	13,562,372	529,410	701,599,019	8,081,669	176,451	745,864	857,943,548
43	92,610,896	8,808,386	1,057,194	15,158,086	6,452,000	2,061,383	651,969	21,592,967	467,396	814,088,551	4,192,257	1,776,669	227,129	969,144,882
44	108,033,868	3,915,000	442,601	19,844,821	2,839,505	2,550,877	187,493	9,937,301	489,606	869,582,548	6,171,834	2,044,014	39,060	1,026,078,529
45	121,211,950	7,295,339	2,864,050	13,765,555	4,561,298	2,123,682	1,378,709	2,495,897	753,919	859,201,744	17,216,962	85,661	32,220	1,032,986,986
TOTAL	11,630,604,389	382,949,806	205,490,910	908,251,299	77,414,253	628,940,242	18,224,184	488,933,244	321,888,732	34,449,829,211	509,270,823	27,961,638	176,635,613	49,826,394,344
COLORADO														
1	853,434,224	19,162,289	9,008,423	48,521,170	579,524	49,541,631	1,180,986	24,852,543	4,709,098	765,953,848	18,125,135	331,678	2,651,876	1,798,052,423
2	39,623,199	5,845,067	3,784,554	11,168,751	115,283	49,086,181	0	5,419,137	14,395,671	443,377,223	6,845,909	2,140,699	79,604,834	661,406,508
3	92,971,194	12,409,310	6,310,781	12,751,033	1,969,006	2,766,196	1,175,105	4,300,190	0	690,175,123	8,875,940	262,552	71,558	834,037,988
4	66,054,114	10,155,638	4,666,969	17,296,198	4,277,322	30,779,681	0	4,756,180	3,055,292	875,101,966	8,717,037	319,769	0	1,025,180,165
5	45,058,216	5,568,845	29,999,569	5,330,250	7,581,965	4,642,729	0	3,074,960	1,602,947	526,663,640	3,937,446	0	34,600	633,495,166
6	42,605,535	2,596,331	3,118,785	14,816,978	368,219	633,337	1,490	1,982,661	303,583	444,708,990	4,111,371	643,635	45,655	515,936,570
TOTAL	1,139,746,481	55,737,480	56,889,080	109,884,381	14,891,319	137,449,755	2,357,581	44,385,671	24,066,590	3,745,980,789	50,612,838	3,698,333	82,408,523	5,468,108,821
CONNECTICUT														
1	1,049,713,765	6,366,664	49,264,846	27,088,084	0	5,831,885	0	7,467,891	875,657	814,619,175	16,617,487	332,528	1,180,276	1,979,358,259
2	81,287,795	4,260,356	17,090,359	6,830,216	10,174	15,636,783	380,549	6,320,619	2,955,634	670,585,884	10,784,610	0	41,350	816,184,329
3	113,217,704	3,742,852	26,295,994	26,059,732	1,738	1,327,792	0	8,121,105	137,146,698	831,542,159	10,747,688	1,189,661	84,120	1,159,477,242
4	97,407,282	1,123,005	14,948,144	23,970,768	0	81,810	0	4,953,747	3,970,199	737,419,572	18,891,991	107,301	53,192	902,927,011
5	113,962,146	817,339	6,749,365	17,245,590	4,843	312,968	186,095	2,054,193	57,462	797,585,117	4,841,731	45,464	33,440	943,895,753
6	104,117,190	1,551,812	6,638,479	9,414,315	0	22,998,635	0	1,115,374	39,308	813,676,958	3,836,287	50,000	76,952	963,515,310
TOTAL	1,559,705,883	17,862,028	120,987,187	110,608,705	16,755	46,189,873	566,644	30,032,929	145,044,958	4,665,428,866	65,719,793	1,724,954	1,469,330	6,765,357,904
DELAWARE														
TOTAL	277,070,845	5,035,562	18,057,673	16,265,023	75,662	16,480,482	-11,842	9,210,016	478,564	876,465,954	17,058,944	78,687	1,807,189	1,238,072,759
DISTRICT OF COLUMBIA														
TOTAL	597,648,458	70,601,991	90,448,436	58,864,249	0	3,745,214	16,513,518	168,979,583	231,363,363	870,364,502	58,319,240	22,507,980	175,737,292	2,365,093,826
FLORIDA														
1	58,443,379	5,741,716	7,027,454	14,047,321	5,116,463	348,341	0	1,519,140	271,232	746,616,356	9,006,882	200,254	868,000	849,206,538
2	2,276,265,788	9,696,680	11,645,302	30,224,584	1,076,724	29,187,965	842,833	5,934,470	214,000	758,335,369	10,159,545	0	5,402,057	3,138,985,317
3	64,290,752	2,435,661	16,696,915	27,162,506	1,599,442	298,607	0	598,396	1,121,845	769,749,865	18,345,002	0	99,200	902,398,192
4	58,737,435	10,237,148	6,705,592	8,686,649	1,777,802	1,085,431	0	1,838,592	3,046,668	1,240,105,934	9,544,714	0	21,600	1,341,787,564
5	39,708,242	8,156,257	6,911,657	14,242,567	708,252	2,193,802	0	996,800	282,143	843,126,030	8,801,114	411,276	336,050	925,874,190
6	58,631,618	4,283,790	10,998,292	14,043,142	565,381	52,574,955	0	2,367,912	2,247,088	1,486,654,000	8,204,502	994,319	39,594	1,641,604,592

See Appendix A for a listing of the congressional districts which represent the county in which the state capital is located and congressional districts which represent only portions of a county. See Appendix B for a listing of the programs included in each recipent category.

table continues

Table 3.6 **Federal Outlays to Categories of Recipients by Congressional District, 1988 *(continued)***

District	State Gov't.	Counties	Cities/ Towns	Special Districts	Schools	Public Universities	Indian Tribes	Non-Profits	Private Universities	Individuals	For Profits	Small Businesses	All Others	Total
FLORIDA *continued*														
7	57,778,073	21,714,281	7,096,488	31,948,245	875,440	11,381,366	0	3,561,246	612,419	849,968,296	13,083,993	23,182	78,100	998,121,130
8	26,885,883	5,411,837	7,501,168	15,316,187	1,028,868	1,033,703	0	2,042,179	139,755	1,466,306,271	5,035,914	0	186,000	1,530,887,765
9	35,455,251	4,139,555	20,867,270	5,122,067	151,447	100,000	0	113,738	292,225	1,470,934,907	2,147,519	0	0	1,539,323,978
10	44,477,153	8,790,717	6,308,792	16,723,056	341,166	0	0	3,476,656	515,877	1,147,077,418	5,897,844	0	102,500	1,233,711,178
11	33,791,867	9,857,354	8,765,533	13,564,828	960,783	1,844,043	0	1,044,257	1,782,052	1,072,663,861	5,500,309	346,193	3,109,028	1,153,230,108
12	38,889,566	13,438,712	4,857,946	11,926,627	443,960	2,122	269,601	5,825,882	58,438	1,572,243,870	3,685,588	0	1,046,474	1,652,688,787
13	27,172,609	10,295,864	11,395,875	30,246,658	98,684	0	0	142,576	104,088	1,876,105,950	11,409,519	0	114,721	1,967,086,543
14	30,597,755	6,427,191	2,859,993	12,475,732	375,817	1,010,080	885,240	95,017	107,433	1,526,890,691	2,263,288	235,492	0	1,584,223,728
15	27,452,771	24,865,463	9,194,055	11,780,410	520,724	46,389,670	276,998	681,363	1,844,910	1,329,221,362	20,003,949	0	16,346,634	1,488,578,309
16	59,741,817	6,154,198	21,915,847	11,191,264	122,264	82,206	3,337,400	261,284	729,978	1,212,120,687	3,020,156	0	0	1,318,677,101
17	138,112,885	8,306,613	11,527,032	27,158,852	571,501	1,442,156	189,194	2,537,520	2,484,402	924,684,216	7,955,874	498,294	1,152,000	1,126,620,539
18	145,198,099	15,903,090	14,322,620	23,408,206	418,947	381,685	154,255	3,600,808	11,049,129	925,164,446	12,184,200	50,000	0	1,151,835,485
19	126,077,764	7,857,026	10,419,045	12,710,266	961,802	246,806	135,154	5,629,634	2,144,835	900,532,959	6,164,042	0	1,729,519	1,074,608,852
TOTAL	3,347,708,710	183,713,151	197,016,875	331,979,167	17,715,467	149,602,939	6,090,675	42,267,470	29,048,515	22,118,502,486	162,413,953	2,759,010	30,631,477	26,619,449,895
GEORGIA														
1	122,236,381	2,950,727	20,154,712	13,479,247	5,879,328	2,127,180	0	6,084,182	513,329	784,179,825	10,428,669	36,000	0	968,069,580
2	147,795,804	4,048,605	10,437,435	6,398,097	772,579	2,565,299	0	5,505,156	149,913	758,676,541	8,162,585	0	0	944,512,014
3	108,916,952	2,416,942	15,391,351	11,749,122	2,884,140	5,314,871	0	4,896,686	757,360	730,202,034	6,116,878	626,249	1,230,477	890,503,062
4	369,840,872	11,661,513	5,775,399	190,559,356	489,475	941,172	-22,118	4,207,670	6,500,956	322,878,674	10,124,129	540,348	1,601,387	925,098,832
5	1,579,904,215	26,602,626	49,312,625	47,638,184	735,958	12,659,224	-140,043	9,436,238	52,619,202	981,786,429	18,639,707	296,037	1,582,323	2,781,072,724
6	81,561,903	1,751,541	8,227,222	7,982,919	207,982	1,346,952	-15,586	4,648,518	73,283	697,370,644	12,094,821	0	131,916	815,382,116
7	48,237,543	7,211,173	1,596,410	7,930,596	84,501	327,395	0	2,657,671	883,121	655,760,104	3,720,490	133,500	0	728,542,504
8	149,070,390	6,876,575	15,161,121	10,630,175	240,777	487,782	0	3,001,204	1,694,538	789,719,339	9,099,002	0	39,500	986,020,403
9	76,641,211	11,587,544	154,447	2,502,403	242,473	182,918	0	3,675,533	458,920	715,375,303	5,280,261	0	-36,165	816,064,848
10	105,520,663	5,420,303	14,454,034	17,154,243	2,052,575	27,155,196	0	14,008,825	3,259,491	669,505,942	6,125,741	138,419	56,880	864,852,312
TOTAL	2,789,725,933	80,527,549	140,664,756	316,024,342	13,589,788	53,107,989	-177,747	58,121,683	66,910,113	7,105,454,835	89,792,283	1,770,553	4,606,318	10,720,118,395
HAWAII														
1	399,147,106	6,684,510	10,428,936	2,034,274	0	31,222,971	5,904,882	10,564,695	1,418,940	517,254,471	6,062,128	881,992	1,539,396	993,144,302
2	159,451,794	8,927,479	21,186,877	1,174,532	0	8,737,318	702,893	7,607,426	983,615	600,017,129	7,452,797	0	270,706	816,512,565
TOTAL	558,598,900	15,611,989	31,615,813	3,208,806	0	39,960,289	6,607,775	18,172,121	2,402,555	1,117,271,600	13,514,925	881,992	1,810,102	1,809,656,867
IDAHO														
1	447,866,637	6,967,194	17,367,443	8,872,115	1,570,364	10,400,024	2,713,504	6,533,681	1,096,177	762,406,919	3,773,986	191,088	1,582,380	1,271,341,513
2	110,206,428	5,695,242	6,958,048	4,436,895	3,808,433	2,450,473	1,850,666	3,165,472	2,065,851	708,618,592	3,106,557	171,766	149,195	852,683,617
TOTAL	558,073,065	12,662,436	24,325,491	13,309,010	5,378,797	12,850,497	4,564,170	9,699,153	3,162,028	1,471,025,511	6,880,543	362,854	1,731,575	2,124,025,130
ILLINOIS														
1	124,386,101	4,474,755	97,078,391	311,004,664	984,887	558,056	146,448	16,066,362	93,842,047	764,907,463	20,489,180	1,088,020	5,042,494	1,440,068,868
2	113,384,981	4,469,773	36,935,752	27,149,010	984,671	574,982	105,896	4,273,616	1,119,743	763,830,901	6,470,917	0	244,276	959,544,518
3	113,266,908	4,470,712	42,232,630	17,710,098	984,878	402,910	105,918	853,059	1,195,158	764,001,160	3,446,404	99,465	244,327	949,013,627
4	65,980,765	3,453,338	19,611,195	11,567,946	390,530	437,617	45,790	1,082,381	1,297,998	691,117,043	6,553,780	343,040	105,626	801,987,049
5	118,532,339	4,517,252	38,824,681	18,438,345	984,747	580,698	105,904	605,164	812,806	763,886,626	6,425,280	0	546,095	954,259,937
6	53,087,953	3,642,057	14,546,859	8,759,776	417,358	258,145	39,448	1,968,341	671,184	657,729,412	4,037,845	372,997	99,367	745,630,742
7	124,036,630	5,374,952	105,531,259	23,595,542	984,866	14,603,779	105,917	32,850,861	4,514,099	764,425,418	26,757,743	941,903	488,727	1,104,211,696
8	113,932,424	5,324,535	37,050,319	20,166,320	1,508,243	589,288	105,917	3,121,320	812,904	764,030,495	4,873,160	50,000	244,324	951,809,249
9	123,194,510	10,023,522	41,539,704	23,272,370	990,029	572,080	105,934	12,120,800	55,355,891	764,568,054	14,509,387	491,354	244,365	1,046,988,000
10	72,131,411	5,393,002	21,417,402	19,359,217	3,540,074	1,195,242	47,893	3,381,102	747,795	654,178,302	6,019,208	96,500	110,478	787,617,627
11	116,542,805	4,470,325	36,959,552	19,142,597	995,792	23,127,851	105,909	1,505,734	827,843	763,921,966	4,350,819	96,710	244,306	972,292,208
12	66,105,034	3,418,375	15,777,991	15,199,620	1,618,414	407,158	44,799	1,824,960	428,355	684,972,119	10,219,144	210,821	103,342	800,330,132

13	62,498,684	3,693,201	17,262,325	14,053,845	561,365	259,552	46,433	984,547	924,473	671,520,553	3,905,656	365,222	107,111	776,182,967
14	31,535,352	5,893,362	2,024,548	6,918,508	1,177	4,482,700	411	1,758,232	374,399	763,243,793	10,449,057	0	32,348	826,713,887
15	40,487,763	1,138,240	5,087,028	10,761,007	1,637,184	3,077,657	0	1,501,747	715,622	936,501,676	5,965,350	0	515,760	1,007,389,035
16	44,014,873	1,247,732	6,515,555	14,204,305	690,092	140,481	218,160	2,971,134	59,613	871,035,815	7,251,949	0	140,520	948,490,229
17	44,550,880	751,440	4,555,438	16,649,294	349,903	773,310	0	2,584,390	732,459	1,001,569,524	11,562,919	0	742,888	1,084,822,445
18	59,026,731	671,000	5,683,653	19,052,442	23,147	370,773	0	3,928,544	2,010,009	899,682,978	13,024,504	0	143,472	1,003,617,254
19	54,758,793	8,474,177	2,883,527	10,299,845	860,048	91,167,692	0	4,380,025	4,542,958	934,981,978	9,084,306	1,255,425	0	1,122,688,774
20	2,608,172,209	9,755,478	8,494,048	13,849,888	313,238	130,391	0	1,436,997	495,468	1,002,054,435	3,678,722	99,250	2,583,305	3,651,063,429
21	93,610,668	11,515,855	7,511,520	20,315,078	4,983,180	3,278,683	173,093	1,477,301	322,434	847,532,343	6,633,672	0	0	997,353,827
22	80,512,438	5,924,432	1,868,835	7,880,642	538,416	10,472,716	0	5,373,700	362,554	971,908,806	4,237,602	0	12,356	1,089,092,496
TOTAL	4,323,750,252	108,097,517	569,392,212	649,350,358	24,342,238	157,461,762	1,503,868	106,050,318	172,165,811	17,701,600,860	189,946,604	5,510,707	11,995,487	24,021,167,995
INDIANA														
1	105,605,271	10,922,513	13,058,984	17,469,865	-86,133	559,043	571	847,779	138,292	778,139,397	11,358,278	35,645	1,356,134	939,405,639
2	163,221,571	2,309,535	8,998,571	22,077,904	190,798	3,190,296	33,259	2,276,114	786,428	853,188,718	8,434,414	1,150,920	295,431	1,066,153,960
3	63,756,040	1,461,865	18,193,518	24,505,378	137,136	379,211	79,565	3,177,401	10,140,392	820,847,657	9,612,644	99,850	52,000	952,442,656
4	56,139,860	1,000,009	5,646,532	15,859,451	88,479	2,426	49,200	2,508,707	578,184	785,700,307	6,429,468	63,485	0	874,066,108
5	66,856,179	677,492	12,471,765	7,429,545	1,438,447	343,530	0	55,517	1,022,578	854,019,482	10,941,633	0	0	955,256,168
6	204,212,955	1,224,258	6,717,443	21,781,914	94,305	513,992	0	2,555,083	1,276,820	858,567,107	12,436,543	97,565	446,250	1,109,924,235
7	69,914,504	2,852,803	9,407,908	13,976,333	56,941	35,530,383	106,483	18,420,021	3,261,426	860,294,865	9,891,687	491,915	0	1,024,205,269
8	84,538,510	1,687,294	6,403,680	10,500,564	200,545	1,027,604	0	1,730,869	384,763	884,557,590	9,760,683	312,655	0	1,001,104,757
9	115,044,900	6,208,089	17,374,311	9,688,351	233,456	21,026,265	0	2,158,771	137,160	730,994,066	11,797,552	363,718	-116,721	914,909,918
10	1,169,297,466	4,512,504	5,611,721	11,346,013	248,150	2,738,692	0	8,982,262	4,152,948	792,566,985	6,073,851	500,000	1,764,311	2,007,794,903
TOTAL	2,098,587,255	32,856,362	103,884,433	154,635,318	2,602,124	65,311,442	269,078	42,712,524	21,878,991	8,218,876,174	96,736,753	3,115,753	3,797,405	10,845,263,612
IOWA														
1	78,055,204	2,049,425	9,160,382	305,041	1,290,542	621,183	0	2,176,879	915,858	895,516,292	12,358,717	722,994	147,153	1,003,319,670
2	63,216,662	620,709	14,043,010	2,745,089	10,802	0	0	1,343,345	1,414,895	921,964,760	6,769,617	0	22,000	1,012,150,889
3	65,466,491	6,423,590	9,301,839	2,023,620	397,801	75,385,855	685,095	3,604,036	1,073,588	1,028,470,330	8,597,270	33,026	0	1,201,462,541
4	748,263,303	4,921,826	38,110,305	2,897,365	94,603	26,003,991	0	2,844,489	12,810,158	801,634,678	9,165,830	456,643	2,435,143	1,649,638,334
5	75,720,239	3,355,169	11,835,418	2,909,489	725,287	263,605	0	2,421,373	435,108	1,244,147,595	7,296,982	151,085	0	1,349,261,350
6	65,603,311	1,949,329	12,748,881	1,515,705	311,190	0	0	1,822,702	1,330,706	1,341,155,077	8,934,213	60,672	-1,000	1,435,430,786
TOTAL	1,096,325,210	19,320,048	95,199,835	12,396,309	2,830,225	102,274,634	685,095	14,212,824	17,980,313	6,232,888,732	53,122,629	1,424,420	2,603,296	7,651,263,570
KANSAS														
1	43,952,471	2,196,665	5,666,702	4,313,618	201,483	1,070,490	0	390,929	2,298,907	1,572,662,807	7,175,739	0	0	1,639,929,811
2	582,212,137	17,821,137	5,487,387	8,614,929	10,522,436	30,718,584	812,828	2,271,924	3,971,745	673,581,098	8,354,156	187,293	706,074	1,345,261,728
3	58,914,198	7,645,848	14,765,468	7,688,935	83,824	10,995,075	0	2,250,526	419,921	651,565,014	9,187,232	197,532	0	763,713,573
4	61,319,190	3,815,455	12,003,109	10,845,218	439,855	2,513,191	160,519	3,799,555	201,943	801,174,480	9,122,900	102,405	916,560	906,414,380
5	56,171,840	5,727,634	7,038,557	4,442,273	524,932	1,405,746	0	2,142,320	671,913	934,769,555	9,876,977	0	0	1,022,771,747
TOTAL	802,569,836	37,206,739	44,961,223	35,904,973	11,772,530	46,703,086	973,347	10,855,254	7,564,429	4,633,752,954	43,717,004	487,230	1,622,634	5,678,091,239
KENTUCKY														
1	84,015,541	2,373,558	15,232,746	533,245	302,337	216,955	0	529,973	105,524	922,672,171	7,339,649	0	31,684	1,033,353,383
2	80,485,855	2,822,796	8,404,433	924,041	833,394	2,670,702	0	4,458,522	176,634	645,804,448	4,618,664	0	2,023,934	753,223,423
3	77,715,304	12,057,668	35,356,932	22,241,564	370,167	1,895,930	42,885	5,291,996	1,830,074	761,480,065	11,931,486	456,137	318,805	930,989,013
4	64,548,826	21,018,890	30,860,317	1,708,338	-2,455	862,922	13,365	1,526,346	127,239	707,325,343	3,184,823	0	0	831,173,954
5	173,853,996	3,337,110	15,671,505	296,514	235,194	5,934	0	3,130,453	1,799,665	827,812,978	6,082,380	0	0	1,032,225,729
6	1,143,724,401	11,294,736	34,041,548	3,951,549	255,850	26,545,495	0	5,549,498	1,827,462	633,684,611	4,985,206	199,080	1,380,997	1,867,440,433
7	139,941,188	6,194,144	16,481,652	146,980	-1,204	1,613,119	0	9,942,507	1,024,658	779,829,531	3,685,122	42,200	84,545	958,984,442
TOTAL	1,764,285,111	59,098,902	156,049,133	29,802,231	1,993,283	33,811,057	56,250	30,429,295	6,891,256	5,278,609,147	41,827,330	697,417	3,839,965	7,407,390,377

See Appendix A for a listing of the congressional districts which represent the county in which the state capital is located and congressional districts which represent only portions of a county. See Appendix B for a listing of the programs included in each recipent category.

table continues

Table 3.6 **Federal Outlays to Categories of Recipients by Congressional District, 1988 *(continued)***

District	State Gov't.	Counties	Cities/ Towns	Special Districts	Schools	Public Universities	Indian Tribes	Non-Profits	Private Universities	Individuals	For Profits	Small Businesses	All Others	Total
LOUISIANA														
1	96,203,893	7,233,301	20,274,971	19,820,203	1,589,722	1,996,999	113,244	8,278,488	19,839,040	613,700,757	22,998,191	103,829	409,479	812,562,118
2	92,836,783	5,754,645	27,277,733	2,937,366	1,405,558	18,632,538	111,651	1,857,962	4,576,137	654,874,636	101,609,534	54,019	0	911,928,562
3	78,563,208	3,884,778	7,619,289	971,258	218,172	2,097,642	988,868	1,237,645	17,170	686,706,314	3,575,605	0	193,423	786,073,373
4	97,074,838	5,673,730	16,265,243	397,364	5,287,516	4,599,680	0	628,933	156,834	679,558,904	9,697,369	0	447,867	819,788,280
5	141,097,003	6,398,189	14,865,964	1,426,136	72,792	7,538,116	90,205	4,630,315	48,079	754,556,437	9,367,982	0	186,872	940,278,090
6	1,394,608,935	8,321,273	10,840,327	4,057,079	86,671	35,721,396	450,569	1,008,716	3,936,728	597,411,912	9,081,257	0	1,125,151	2,066,650,014
7	89,128,984	5,150,337	16,363,280	2,460,857	56,725	4,376,562	394,402	5,183,759	664,810	656,599,197	9,672,923	0	938,047	790,989,882
8	208,671,028	3,856,263	13,936,226	256,784	211,835	1,649,229	387,282	3,693,256	456,213	654,364,850	6,662,862	149,760	383,704	894,679,292
TOTAL	2,198,184,672	46,272,517	127,443,033	32,327,047	8,928,991	76,612,161	2,536,221	26,519,074	29,695,011	5,297,773,008	172,665,724	307,608	3,684,543	8,022,949,610
MAINE														
1	484,474,782	6,254,342	13,468,068	18,581,841	-5,544	1,886,945	5,000	10,234,524	1,963,036	866,460,100	6,415,254	696,056	516,025	1,410,950,430
2	177,143,432	6,233,075	38,202,195	17,962,466	24,371	8,832,678	6,648,953	5,455,348	924,131	860,750,773	6,944,748	9,452,409	411,240	1,138,985,818
TOTAL	661,618,214	12,487,417	51,670,263	36,544,307	18,827	10,719,623	6,653,953	15,689,872	2,887,167	1,727,210,873	13,360,002	10,148,465	927,265	2,549,936,248
MARYLAND														
1	89,993,016	20,357,875	8,626,648	12,984,465	0	4,102,080	0	4,707,783	74,109	731,447,086	10,746,520	0	3,075	883,042,657
2	532,183,662	4,065,182	30,423,771	6,944,504	23,608	476,579	0	27,011	365,083	732,904,133	10,802,593	173,505	600	1,318,390,230
3	259,981,548	10,643,432	22,675,733	49,824,712	500,000	4,804,939	125,142	11,770,042	143,883,302	832,160,725	9,425,531	3,007,566	2,163,010	1,350,965,681
4	348,737,320	12,091,950	9,053,371	14,980,853	0	0	0	899,177	384,750	547,260,877	49,270,677	534,521	1,000,950	984,214,446
5	55,437,574	19,792,477	29,509,957	13,281,649	0	48,903,529	0	3,012,517	1,672,163	434,205,560	9,907,414	889,247	8,680,973	625,293,061
6	64,346,841	5,650,541	15,763,082	15,762,345	195,601	486,494	0	1,086,822	421,522	676,370,652	8,484,342	2,936,481	7,464,412	798,969,134
7	486,461,605	9,723,273	25,296,973	44,553,972	0	34,059,894	188,065	11,841,211	42,554,642	918,135,511	18,818,275	0	99,069	1,591,732,490
8	79,245,617	6,138,981	10,143,947	14,284,698	0	0	79,047	34,272,108	487,399	666,482,543	44,231,918	17,118,765	46,290,482	918,775,505
TOTAL	1,916,387,183	88,463,711	151,493,482	172,617,197	719,209	92,833,515	392,254	67,616,671	189,842,969	5,538,967,086	161,687,270	24,660,085	65,702,571	8,471,383,204
MASSACHUSETTS														
1	131,840,904	3,467,750	9,211,038	19,686,562	23,190	26,096,904	33,333	5,809,688	6,038,297	807,102,624	7,522,720	139,820	177,694	1,017,150,522
2	168,626,393	1,015,247	32,470,523	22,980,050	-9,913	586,900	0	2,731,811	546,017	843,206,647	11,331,910	148,780	416,625	1,084,050,990
3	118,635,810	3,121,612	22,300,012	13,812,537	38,764	29,555,526	55	10,133,340	3,665,764	791,203,216	10,308,039	1,054,865	123,137	1,003,952,678
4	139,264,177	1,562,169	11,746,379	14,180,871	133,895	568,600	69	61,288,192	8,889,370	708,721,060	6,024,686	717,023	48,850	953,145,342
5	102,336,537	6,881,303	13,323,540	21,008,008	40,727	2,729,409	231	5,426,558	13,247	701,330,835	10,342,446	3,965,426	20,000	867,418,268
6	132,140,395	1,861,784	17,972,258	23,356,572	3,434	1,104,737	7	5,832,892	528,226	841,495,528	13,057,623	246,401	27,000	1,037,626,858
7	187,587,795	6,118,763	24,251,868	25,242,139	4,573	457,972	30,626	1,961,505	29,605,446	751,478,587	10,921,074	4,947,722	347,620	1,042,955,690
8	299,278,475	16,861,262	56,682,311	90,191,782	0	56,739,872	63,589	182,551,956	241,778,649	861,733,251	44,277,454	12,718,064	9,191,328	1,872,067,994
9	1,034,878,601	14,825,760	58,636,076	44,065,139	5,157	2,716,534	89,558	103,855,355	5,832,256	948,614,736	33,144,736	1,476,884	931,296	2,249,072,089
10	129,915,939	840,684	22,030,527	19,469,475	8,696	962,181	386,129	10,209,210	26,862,441	936,988,040	7,203,941	543,909	231,665	1,155,652,838
11	406,436,038	9,745,395	29,597,181	27,415,184	18,123	1,059,157	43,174	17,881,825	2,353,095	783,963,862	13,382,504	432,938	454,675	1,292,783,151
TOTAL	2,850,941,065	66,301,729	298,221,714	321,408,319	266,646	122,577,792	646,772	407,682,333	326,112,807	8,975,838,386	167,517,134	26,391,832	11,969,890	13,575,876,419
MICHIGAN														
1	213,865,420	3,466,292	126,814,402	45,143,276	356,444	37,962	87,280	2,125,192	678,322	809,652,701	6,633,636	303,182	1,436,455	1,210,600,564
2	115,437,822	17,033,936	24,516,991	590,044	406,523	149,937,591	18,796	3,296,231	860,644	715,402,298	4,819,316	2,646,112	10,697	1,034,977,002
3	1,181,135,698	3,843,623	12,004,620	3,421,064	350,865	2,293,391	100,000	5,023,140	563,105	689,968,611	8,085,982	0	2,228,202	1,909,018,301
4	119,122,000	3,423,655	4,880,696	848,249	155,728	409,109	236,126	6,290,186	1,085,088	770,601,452	6,118,444	0	0	913,170,734
5	98,831,797	4,076,555	14,727,367	2,778,431	-11,112	0	117,693	1,435,603	2,307,520	691,075,950	6,609,358	0	0	821,949,162
6	754,346,776	33,173,306	16,518,498	847,319	241,356	49,141,802	781,983	1,693,344	4,166,172	658,231,814	10,112,494	172,077	911,769	1,530,338,709
7	130,638,339	8,263,273	16,244,596	3,041,151	1,097,301	191,726	127,216	957,470	645,323	702,323,371	7,749,897	50,000	0	871,329,663
8	123,601,747	3,325,953	12,591,780	3,611,033	529,989	964,609	0	803,079	849,240	841,055,841	5,093,240	1,092,513	273,732	993,792,757
9	104,847,550	2,347,427	10,753,699	2,048,870	358,094	955,451	1,872,222	5,643,637	67,099	814,210,372	6,928,177	0	0	950,032,598

10	201,208,462	197,827,103	5,476,260	168,382	1,159,339	3,491,879	1,690,837	4,935,306	111,197	789,414,131	3,846,949	0	260,280	1,209,590,126
11	117,774,781	7,442,803	15,414,026	1,630,129	6,212,588	3,182,861	6,538,432	8,189,009	588,585	964,048,741	5,931,952	0	261,760	1,137,215,667
12	67,934,449	7,122,503	13,377,223	0	525,770	0	0	712,097	0	737,619,781	8,818,364	0	214,200	836,324,387
13	223,404,109	14,908,926	36,241,720	50,000	546,380	27,911,368	87,280	13,345,790	292,234	809,477,915	14,138,751	1,139,677	26,455	1,141,570,605
14	113,237,859	2,756,263	14,536,666	0	249,526	14,262	32,790	72,551	113,419	766,275,703	3,802,408	0	9,939	901,101,386
15	186,452,483	4,057,264	29,747,761	1,502,882	422,991	1,454,156	70,911	619,097	389,967	757,013,914	16,065,437	500,000	1,496,305	999,793,169
16	168,323,274	4,057,681	25,226,631	0	478,706	140,360	57,154	1,368,092	701,448	771,539,837	4,468,666	0	53,203	976,415,052
17	137,774,233	2,906,982	22,137,931	0	156,402	18,417	42,345	2,193,933	321,286	774,313,832	8,198,324	513,386	12,835	948,589,906
18	59,805,432	2,841,387	1,992,688	0	617,437	3,119,724	63,839	2,772,605	181,652	728,925,578	6,624,941	0	0	806,945,283
TOTAL	4,117,742,231	322,874,935	403,203,555	65,680,830	13,854,327	243,264,668	11,924,903	61,476,363	13,922,301	13,791,151,843	134,046,337	6,416,947	7,195,831	19,192,755,070
MINNESOTA														
1	89,346,332	1,852,276	15,184,329	7,187,601	70,122	3,560,212	208,550	40,237,058	1,383,904	963,495,363	7,199,793	0	62,820	1,129,788,359
2	87,767,942	1,344,482	22,221,453	6,685,977	1,378,973	1,608,435	52,511	2,210,128	330,208	1,262,038,048	5,654,965	49,560	0	1,391,342,683
3	103,048,104	2,678,962	359,268	7,131,249	535	227,784	171,100	617,257	438,228	601,741,739	12,111,337	373,587	0	728,899,150
4	977,001,833	8,382,681	24,172,851	53,586,621	1,808,646	77,092,442	0	7,680,319	4,030,287	49,876,020	8,364,463	223,561	1,953,680	1,214,173,405
5	160,368,502	16,638,541	24,183,781	26,211,759	416,818	54,664,346	828,739	8,942,236	977,606	694,692,066	9,088,281	864,927	136,800	998,014,402
6	210,968,519	2,373,170	3,749,121	4,292,976	16,974	346,888	0	1,397,643	167,893	1,155,743,648	6,202,173	107,791	0	1,385,366,795
7	148,683,854	3,698,555	15,720,648	10,223,344	3,603,912	4,203,400	3,079,986	5,817,856	1,221,810	935,902,215	6,127,130	0	2,919,495	1,141,202,204
8	156,269,281	4,773,316	10,454,123	7,892,939	1,683,553	3,037,504	7,583,611	2,305,376	156,113	816,289,881	6,995,767	50,000	173,662	1,017,665,126
TOTAL	1,933,454,367	41,741,983	116,045,574	123,212,466	8,979,533	144,741,010	11,924,497	69,207,873	8,706,049	6,479,778,979	61,743,910	1,669,426	5,246,457	9,006,452,124
MISSISSIPPI														
1	91,944,799	3,115,348	4,875,685	6,827,029	452,889	2,886,223	92,630	10,013,790	1,564,469	771,148,547	7,316,491	228,649	0	900,466,549
2	130,562,580	11,672,155	7,183,587	16,287,973	1,512,830	4,791,803	0	9,863,532	214,139	789,519,232	11,871,765	0	1,766,178	985,245,774
3	89,727,644	7,819,054	20,550,487	12,995,129	3,367,492	12,651,102	8,911,609	6,570,395	1,680,848	720,276,734	6,351,894	250,000	0	891,152,388
4	1,075,871,912	13,444,802	56,266	23,158,450	84,759	12,417,253	0	27,504,482	2,245,688	729,637,933	12,953,574	1,986,007	1,071,291	1,900,432,416
5	51,307,324	9,181,316	10,998,054	17,417,474	5,901,741	4,661,972	0	6,183,053	4,331,599	676,965,008	8,892,708	0	65,400	795,905,648
TOTAL	1,439,414,258	45,232,675	43,664,079	76,686,055	11,319,711	37,408,353	9,004,239	60,135,252	10,036,743	3,687,547,454	47,386,432	2,464,656	2,902,869	5,473,202,776
MISSOURI														
1	76,871,861	12,585,562	25,806,467	37,940,192	102,946	2,145,368	0	26,729,392	117,119,519	1,254,673,718	20,318,946	1,016,701	823,900	1,576,134,572
2	83,515,485	7,883,447	26,496,382	14,943,074	175,084	442,859	0	7,112,937	984,863	939,562,722	15,437,695	50,000	40,500	1,096,645,048
3	36,894,729	1,925,531	7,560,717	4,334,016	58,877	191,439	0	5,670,319	710,550	343,848,321	13,471,470	89,860	0	414,755,830
4	1,048,369,060	1,047,426	2,621,285	7,219,937	6,200,311	4,053,096	0	3,774,551	97,390	900,726,774	7,592,500	0	2,844,630	1,984,546,960
5	62,052,799	0	21,312,949	45,073,659	376,686	2,042,651	23,333	15,038,137	46,998	870,308,855	16,661,356	954,134	561,350	1,034,452,907
6	47,871,939	11,213,082	27,289,191	7,459,223	1,455,481	2,796,943	571,024	9,401,694	5,131,981	926,528,419	6,028,281	145,847	0	1,045,893,106
7	76,393,639	989,145	19,067,171	4,825,807	251,834	2,644,973	3,550	3,459,700	2,336,840	922,892,061	4,111,545	0	0	1,036,976,265
8	127,813,436	1,832,435	6,964,991	6,233,578	1,642,482	3,366,354	0	7,420,059	138,000	1,031,442,250	9,277,804	67,794	0	1,196,199,183
9	182,468,904	6,269,229	4,489,493	6,867,476	668,147	28,297,406	30,000	5,918,544	5,239,573	889,810,363	11,428,523	0	0	1,141,487,657
TOTAL	1,742,251,851	43,745,856	141,608,647	134,896,962	10,931,848	45,981,090	627,907	84,525,333	131,805,714	8,079,793,484	104,328,120	2,324,336	4,270,380	10,527,091,528
MONTANA														
1	460,802,480	13,317,725	6,261,726	13,003,867	7,328,006	13,123,552	4,581,244	3,900,148	1,141,660	597,164,876	6,957,878	117,398	1,162,383	1,128,862,943
2	74,720,104	10,104,937	9,523,849	6,044,832	15,479,903	689,235	6,506,170	2,214,742	1,100,727	837,719,923	9,159,817	483,923	0	973,748,162
TOTAL	535,522,584	23,422,662	15,785,575	19,048,699	22,807,909	13,812,787	11,087,414	6,114,890	2,242,387	1,434,884,799	16,117,695	601,321	1,162,383	2,102,611,105
NEBRASKA														
1	462,428,589	4,955,748	5,584,922	12,938,612	4,068,832	15,657,023	9,086,362	3,299,386	3,003,387	1,133,297,746	7,985,838	280,000	379,016	1,662,965,462
2	84,099,447	3,950,764	12,386,153	23,002,676	12,731,831	10,706,852	385,946	4,506,533	4,148,260	737,474,190	8,014,912	517,416	74,300	901,999,279
3	66,784,006	2,402,533	1,169,121	6,238,713	2,083,709	2,276,696	0	1,873,784	60,766	1,595,697,854	10,689,786	0	855,750	1,690,132,718
TOTAL	613,312,042	11,309,045	19,140,196	42,180,001	18,884,372	28,640,571	9,472,308	9,679,703	7,212,413	3,466,469,790	26,690,536	797,416	1,309,066	4,255,097,459

See Appendix A for a listing of the congressional districts which represent the county in which the state capital is located and congressional districts which represent only portions of a county. See Appendix B for a listing of the programs included in each recipent category.

table continues

Table 3.6 Federal Outlays to Categories of Recipients by Congressional District, 1988 *(continued)*

District	State Gov't.	Counties	Cities/ Towns	Special Districts	Schools	Public Universities	Indian Tribes	Non-Profits	Private Universities	Individuals	For Profits	Small Businesses	All Others	Total
NEVADA														
1	39,421,223	22,737,818	3,921,856	18,276,010	1,157,157	3,910,584	805,387	1,138,935	0	666,365,922	12,344,913	180,381	946,903	771,207,088
2	333,591,234	6,025,723	3,026,387	13,632,765	1,995,653	11,449,614	5,937,327	5,180,357	194,530	586,108,887	4,882,564	34,843	289,331	972,349,216
TOTAL	373,012,457	28,763,541	6,948,243	31,908,775	3,152,810	15,360,198	6,742,714	6,319,292	194,530	1,252,474,809	17,227,477	215,224	1,236,234	1,743,556,304
NEW HAMPSHIRE														
1	58,071,517	4,375,679	24,863,348	10,392,288	641	12,541,958	0	1,830,561	878,633	628,057,332	5,920,066	181,269	183,383	747,296,675
2	338,178,364	5,148,764	16,257,687	7,464,311	140	386,633	0	3,232,054	25,113,554	671,120,617	8,294,365	601,225	397,165	1,076,194,879
TOTAL	396,249,881	9,524,443	41,121,035	17,856,599	781	12,928,591	0	5,062,615	25,992,187	1,299,177,949	14,214,431	782,494	580,548	1,823,491,554
NEW JERSEY														
1	99,505,059	7,605,144	12,659,419	41,545,551	5,000	1,062,472	0	1,845,141	140,000	701,874,266	11,961,502	0	0	878,203,553
2	129,960,741	1,939,310	14,388,646	18,823,174	3,356	842,078	27,400	5,608,427	0	1,069,195,995	12,680,961	46	387,676	1,253,857,810
3	78,975,174	6,106,875	2,846,207	17,573,631	2,890,348	88,839	0	3,240,739	322,806	943,254,000	8,568,514	15,500	0	1,063,882,633
4	1,873,653,584	8,796,491	5,405,662	12,403,541	15,996	2,121,919	93,569	3,736,182	339,300	778,349,611	6,261,678	49,865	0	2,691,227,398
5	44,225,574	398,168	11,668,052	5,124,734	-29,438	21,044	0	787,330	27,068	699,598,469	5,277,184	398,084	1,400	767,497,669
6	64,503,975	8,051,775	8,947,030	16,154,214	0	32,581,057	0	926,639	1,072,042	755,072,950	4,633,341	99,711	0	892,042,734
7	82,178,205	1,462,798	21,154,309	11,188,814	34,986	845,179	0	1,316,522	468,944	830,695,079	4,782,304	100,000	0	954,227,141
8	105,651,983	1,936,352	7,331,745	20,066,474	696,574	881,203	0	4,439,761	346,580	774,455,008	10,177,211	100,000	0	926,082,892
9	37,393,140	441,880	8,813,997	16,619,631	0	0	0	121,847	1,141,483	866,334,531	7,425,473	167,932	0	938,459,915
10	207,682,639	8,854,352	37,503,090	183,276,835	100,000	14,675,713	0	24,061,777	187,579	784,819,615	30,667,092	2,866,523	0	1,294,695,215
11	156,203,314	6,488,687	1,818,569	5,400,230	13,275	319,443	0	58,930	1,270,419	763,295,047	5,206,870	357,323	0	940,432,108
12	56,941,075	8,087,349	1,780,185	8,489,574	-10,127	18,280,437	0	19,690,372	36,768,398	780,848,223	10,138,132	987,031	1,352,093	943,352,742
13	76,000,111	5,384,991	3,192,271	5,814,795	4,263,674	310,150	370,147	90,049	118,792	982,663,510	2,863,200	695,772	0	1,081,767,462
14	192,567,305	10,916,577	13,927,999	29,312,949	-30,478	734,452	0	4,930,753	1,073,306	763,518,206	23,173,678	0	0	1,040,124,746
TOTAL	3,205,441,879	76,470,750	151,437,182	391,794,148	7,953,166	72,763,986	491,116	70,854,469	43,276,718	11,493,974,510	143,817,140	5,837,787	1,741,169	15,665,854,020
NEW MEXICO														
1	82,567,592	9,832,319	29,421,728	35,000	1,333,063	20,104,648	3,375,347	5,294,586	287,002	568,383,393	6,454,214	2,068,332	2,099,675	731,256,899
2	70,031,265	6,989,962	13,482,773	652,000	4,399,856	13,246,620	870,786	2,199,505	401,515	691,313,385	6,791,786	169,293	174,538	810,723,284
3	546,508,157	19,653,847	13,467,544	1,560,540	33,674,021	8,892,944	11,859,580	10,174,887	276,839	507,916,890	5,772,385	193,131	607,801	1,160,558,566
TOTAL	699,107,014	36,476,128	56,372,045	2,247,540	39,406,940	42,244,212	16,105,713	17,668,978	965,356	1,767,613,668	19,018,385	2,430,756	2,882,014	2,702,538,749
NEW YORK														
1	83,173,102	10,318,556	22,254,728	-2,106,734	48,116	39,474,889	86,290	13,977,744	228,065	545,641,562	6,271,418	198,000	33,573	719,599,309
2	82,943,558	3,613,512	17,570,227	0	43,307	728,376	86,156	652,020	227,710	544,697,719	1,824,585	0	33,520	652,420,690
3	121,320,635	10,030,423	28,436,602	39,342,862	41,188	1,354,846	86,327	4,457,385	2,460,835	966,862,217	14,076,048	890,436	1,437,263	1,190,797,067
4	75,182,478	5,848,621	3,751,414	58,400	1,484	0	0	582,701	630,913	820,088,856	3,919,152	0	0	910,064,018
5	74,200,492	10,215,637	9,005,719	8,475,428	8,769	745,932	0	5,069,471	2,616,232	812,431,708	13,242,683	500,000	0	936,512,071
6	173,944,162	572,460	4,024,747	0	0	437,865	0	8,293,788	570,012	842,571,116	11,992,095	500,000	0	1,042,906,244
7	174,653,571	1,100,036	144,088	0	0	29,000	0	8,322,138	572,337	846,009,383	3,407,581	50,000	0	1,034,288,133
8	210,531,638	1,798,202	39,045,109	0	119	739,641	0	7,223,426	3,045,045	831,480,467	5,723,324	0	3,152	1,099,590,123
9	173,708,202	612,940	131,293	0	0	82,020	0	7,335,461	866,157	841,443,393	8,050,536	0	0	1,032,230,002
10	270,775,183	12,055,739	149,560,602	0	0	317,217	0	4,880,922	1,618,253	789,754,965	4,498,899	43,700	0	1,233,505,480
11	271,708,433	12,173,795	81,351,856	38,000	0	441	0	7,461,880	2,793,557	797,509,314	22,303,275	0	0	1,195,340,550
12	275,876,917	12,168,184	79,565,052	0	0	9,658,343	0	7,133,808	1,549,744	795,615,129	37,806,089	30,000	0	1,219,403,267
13	273,579,341	12,441,159	72,972,903	0	0	442	0	6,464,165	3,020,487	798,611,901	13,807,850	235,303	0	1,181,133,550
14	170,038,358	4,192,502	44,998,199	0	0	139	0	6,240,737	907,620	779,686,754	15,612,852	0	0	1,021,677,162
15	638,159,917	14,634,952	421,779,385	312,545,801	0	4,149,054	0	201,139,330	171,581,587	898,716,724	28,647,494	1,095,420	5,390,481	2,697,840,145
16	613,547,485	14,727,352	59,614,029	4,284,730	0	17,796,264	776,383	17,605,765	33,635,183	897,786,246	62,990,952	236,142	5,390,439	1,728,390,972
17	571,828,543	11,997,449	65,394,207	4,763,713	0	1,682,060	0	65,565,413	92,647,027	883,250,413	57,981,435	1,459,169	4,155,634	1,760,725,062

18	330,615,237	3,324,402	154,606,384	0	0	362,985	0	8,469,872	5,512,098	835,186,866	109,194,702	0	10,947	1,447,283,494
19	265,291,094	2,473,729	102,863,247	45,289,832	0	428,659	0	14,607,661	1,645,486	828,715,359	16,254,438	60,000	135,021	1,277,764,524
20	118,552,277	4,026,189	45,248,011	38,281	6,450	457,927	0	11,846,129	22,018,641	855,202,579	16,999,214	1,102,326	505,689	1,076,003,713
21	110,272,973	4,843,239	15,961,632	141,299	945,953	419,702	0	998,370	2,348,392	733,223,058	5,812,417	200,000	127,729	875,294,765
22	128,797,697	5,837,995	15,001,050	1,143,667	525,211	917,653	0	8,201,538	14,553,182	721,772,444	12,872,776	362,921	80,414	910,066,549
23	4,468,827,703	18,193,568	34,084,412	-224,828	78,456	24,896,080	0	21,130,001	16,965,881	858,989,917	15,623,870	614,173	4,474,384	5,463,653,617
24	101,767,977	7,754,990	16,730,479	137,705	427,389	886,963	0	3,533,628	882,099	774,808,415	6,382,282	0	26,822	913,338,747
25	133,357,198	7,461,496	23,720,672	1,155,672	55,107	4,407,366	0	5,732,896	3,184,807	802,344,102	4,740,552	103,500	29,240	986,292,609
26	145,884,671	22,293,316	40,750,257	1,787,632	287,194	1,317,372	1,134,415	8,287,163	3,664,661	764,027,338	10,082,559	112,868	30,000	999,659,446
27	105,432,083	20,369,342	27,989,725	3,269,359	-926	10,299,434	202,312	4,209,339	12,213,243	723,449,287	7,176,949	135,875	147,007	914,893,029
28	117,296,512	17,434,835	16,673,852	1,766,557	27,222	41,426,671	0	1,463,844	69,804,882	781,319,942	5,058,048	681,566	80,279	1,053,034,211
29	121,220,546	6,925,618	12,723,632	5,084,386	15,125	467,884	22,182	5,688,021	1,907,768	740,868,091	4,977,839	1,010,926	473,305	901,385,323
30	118,877,290	6,728,320	21,094,549	13,921,624	17,544	1,441,255	66,807	6,359,793	107,287,586	748,665,848	5,981,710	904,187	1,111,222	1,032,457,735
31	124,443,356	6,920,777	22,995,495	0	19,490	1,321,285	140,664	2,677,991	1,149,126	784,582,477	8,100,878	388,708	0	952,740,246
32	122,316,669	4,194,940	23,791,901	305,128	18	23,562,384	46,275	13,565,701	1,485,843	799,787,925	7,905,944	584,663	326,704	997,874,095
33	140,606,287	7,574,807	28,434,542	314,043	73	10,244,350	122,526	5,701,623	1,941,997	808,604,877	10,886,295	1,204,509	56,790	1,015,692,719
34	126,702,385	7,436,335	14,214,240	1,268,300	11,705	1,463,603	4,468,097	2,851,162	2,371,077	834,221,706	8,245,458	138,780	1,400	1,003,394,247
TOTAL	11,035,433,968	292,295,416	1,716,484,238	442,800,858	2,558,992	201,518,101	7,238,435	497,730,886	587,907,533	27,087,928,096	568,452,200	12,843,172	24,061,016	42,477,252,912
NORTH CAROLINA														
1	110,340,379	8,252,120	12,378,617	17,680,695	0	5,074,613	0	3,083,879	1,677,224	792,817,735	8,118,480	0	0	959,423,742
2	119,449,533	8,698,469	10,500,329	20,323,773	0	5,713,673	279,441	38,332,790	95,923,120	748,562,915	14,519,896	1,201,638	0	1,063,505,577
3	98,596,632	9,278,240	4,814,609	11,756,735	48,400	97,553	129,834	3,208,344	361,914	653,202,888	8,189,568	0	0	789,684,717
4	1,622,684,409	14,730,628	23,306,796	13,927,337	0	130,015,032	452,778	2,311,231	4,021,895	627,607,933	5,326,690	586,634	9,139,226	2,454,110,589
5	74,994,696	4,493,160	5,866,852	14,243,180	0	1,114,155	0	31,506,091	1,478,075	736,171,357	6,704,850	689,735	1,400	877,263,551
6	51,822,920	3,648,264	5,982,195	12,005,058	0	7,913,414	94,226	2,846,054	853,419	732,803,095	7,955,436	0	663,200	826,587,281
7	101,968,032	17,008,889	18,758,519	17,878,222	0	2,263,885	1,550,411	2,204,349	677,005	637,438,626	6,442,093	0	1,868,607	808,058,638
8	68,752,370	6,223,054	6,161,903	8,855,872	0	8,843	0	5,218,102	839,636	774,852,078	5,725,192	0	0	876,637,050
9	56,048,993	5,849,322	17,101,583	13,810,320	0	1,311,613	72,991	2,099,916	1,527,004	676,205,459	7,484,078	51,275	0	781,562,554
10	57,899,691	3,244,793	13,996,977	8,860,360	0	1,351,961	0	1,112,430	450,742	697,233,413	6,821,577	0	0	790,971,944
11	80,692,830	5,712,051	5,397,809	13,827,362	13,596	1,566,881	2,853,264	2,097,482	594,074	899,046,403	4,069,707	25,968	1,892,223	1,017,789,650
TOTAL	2,443,250,485	87,138,990	124,266,189	153,168,914	61,996	156,431,623	5,432,945	94,020,668	108,404,108	7,975,941,902	81,357,567	2,555,250	13,564,656	11,245,595,293
NORTH DAKOTA														
TOTAL	402,400,524	12,452,576	19,498,474	21,444,238	11,686,900	19,852,877	10,861,398	3,283,104	12,508,793	1,550,653,792	7,138,972	287,915	25,000	2,072,094,563
OHIO														
1	127,614,795	6,066,382	17,365,686	22,710,387	249,174	41,276,384	0	14,644,871	945,239	841,219,366	28,396,596	200,161	325,000	1,101,014,043
2	103,442,344	4,261,167	11,366,528	11,557,426	193,808	2,455,971	0	2,880,860	675,590	681,398,321	17,038,042	25,866	524,696	835,820,618
3	108,976,953	3,673,696	29,870,919	20,753,616	427,598	4,830,146	0	3,996,052	1,233,566	717,876,103	14,947,175	348,946	512,430	907,447,200
4	75,756,487	5,029,377	4,448,242	7,782,935	103,559	61,083	0	1,085,567	1,383,631	806,268,633	8,012,315	0	900	909,932,728
5	52,290,140	14,106,229	4,563,836	5,509,749	1,480,661	2,726,038	0	4,266,852	555,831	745,375,727	7,007,437	4,389,977	44,170	842,316,647
6	161,676,615	4,426,636	6,419,564	8,101,314	89,135	233,540	0	5,283,717	169,449	757,330,672	11,320,599	0	0	955,051,241
7	91,644,315	4,913,543	7,462,276	8,389,306	3,511,104	2,413,942	0	3,457,637	2,175,890	708,767,700	18,095,287	200,634	0	851,031,634
8	69,670,658	638,608	8,230,602	5,982,392	14,351	1,752,924	0	2,209,672	16,000	684,421,431	7,975,187	0	0	780,911,825
9	114,780,479	1,297,552	14,399,150	20,750,744	28,716	9,101,938	24,783	5,754,203	155,586	801,368,996	16,561,523	159,188	68,700	984,451,558
10	462,702,384	22,657,849	28,876,275	10,332,677	186,766	16,191,755	0	4,572,271	2,973,261	717,840,728	9,990,221	0	469,336	1,276,793,523
11	48,464,179	5,554,696	4,633,794	13,671,789	790,714	4,927,776	0	2,235,976	1,635,712	646,440,888	4,831,702	0	32,133	733,219,359
12	1,591,841,600	2,588,534	8,097,103	30,788,877	12,700	4,323,379	0	6,301,873	1,083,796	620,016,454	12,678,154	342,765	1,670,496	2,279,745,732
13	63,232,193	2,654,929	15,745,196	14,157,270	558,429	275,879	0	3,062,485	1,381,309	682,017,192	6,538,239	1,571	1,090,001	790,714,692
14	94,550,331	4,459,402	4,913,238	33,074,878	121,273	5,963,112	717,907	4,942,920	0	768,328,456	7,122,105	0	0	924,193,623
15	976,233,088	1,978,515	24,964,586	12,461,692	95,440	21,509,418	0	5,072,340	792,027	635,228,387	12,212,706	0	1,884,913	1,692,433,111

See Appendix A for a listing of the congressional districts which represent the county in which the state capital is located and congressional districts which represent only portions of a county. See Appendix B for a listing of the programs included in each recipent category.

table continues

Table 3.6 **Federal Outlays to Categories of Recipients by Congressional District, 1988 *(continued)***

District	State Gov't.	Counties	Cities/ Towns	Special Districts	Schools	Public Universities	Indian Tribes	Non-Profits	Private Universities	Individuals	For Profits	Small Businesses	All Others	Total
OHIO *continued*														
16	73,268,871	2,482,285	12,729,538	14,079,262	24,631	4,178,862	0	831,603	853,352	752,967,229	7,434,728	0	0	868,850,361
17	102,886,158	66,237	15,523,401	16,802,270	368,670	2,048,367	0	1,956,041	347,310	860,318,176	6,648,125	0	47,296	1,007,012,051
18	97,843,653	616,614	10,055,621	10,707,970	71,063	0	0	3,555,135	268,384	838,117,399	50,014,764	190,000	341,003	1,011,781,605
19	113,825,885	2,915,105	16,554,495	40,180,964	611,690	365,225	189,890	157,432	1,079,810	880,545,671	4,760,457	48,591	185,366	1,061,420,581
20	120,662,882	4,093,664	37,637,656	65,285,571	534,888	2,633,974	270,916	1,706,483	1,077,487	896,107,518	11,376,408	49,300	847,009	1,142,283,757
21	123,551,881	3,247,818	31,054,408	22,284,991	526,135	1,383,441	207,795	13,292,701	65,514,162	898,099,778	27,468,726	551,432	0	1,187,183,267
TOTAL	4,774,915,890	97,728,838	314,912,114	395,366,080	10,000,505	128,653,154	1,411,291	91,266,691	84,317,392	15,940,054,826	290,430,495	6,508,431	8,043,449	22,143,609,156
OKLAHOMA														
1	61,518,605	3,353,285	4,131,052	20,256,643	1,441,074	2,099,148	1,739,009	3,824,418	3,182,052	727,761,762	10,555,306	0	0	839,862,353
2	126,936,124	16,053,673	7,324,632	6,757,405	7,600,804	3,451,792	25,434,016	4,881,771	299,712	786,983,044	6,297,374	0	0	992,020,347
3	155,031,412	12,997,180	15,793,787	11,812,990	6,474,011	25,364,494	7,498,409	11,770,612	1,827,997	817,492,014	7,728,362	0	0	1,073,791,268
4	127,895,190	10,746,980	6,294,172	7,246,861	16,958,786	22,822,127	2,688,334	6,129,407	1,000,312	681,061,771	6,034,768	133,764	1,249,290	890,261,761
5	662,306,569	4,809,503	8,768,913	8,630,041	1,394,525	3,910,276	2,407,266	14,696,774	533,060	721,968,586	8,611,309	54,667	467,729	1,438,559,217
6	255,444,731	5,703,915	1,929,839	6,297,980	3,063,825	1,433,868	4,568,739	1,144,396	357,435	1,011,879,228	4,941,684	69,134	185,567	1,297,020,341
TOTAL	1,389,132,632	53,664,535	44,242,395	61,001,920	36,933,025	59,081,705	44,335,772	42,447,378	7,200,568	4,747,146,404	44,168,803	257,565	1,902,586	6,531,515,287
OREGON														
1	72,213,698	2,272,466	2,439,419	15,020,785	9,651	5,049,654	2,735,256	16,933,706	3,965,182	741,101,516	2,912,508	384,928	85,550	865,124,320
2	70,931,119	4,225,566	2,286,064	13,426,659	3,168,950	1,399,867	4,090,999	3,062,521	100,000	953,099,158	2,081,951	600,587	35,000	1,058,508,440
3	115,909,801	21,006,941	881,724	21,887,101	677,919	23,483,466	-22,464	4,533,974	1,147,996	916,800,768	7,049,664	0	525,473	1,113,882,362
4	81,736,042	14,245,841	10,266,648	13,267,528	946,180	14,712,115	109,215	7,011,540	267,828	787,300,280	3,206,434	586,916	27,500	933,684,067
5	874,796,525	22,211,369	6,923,033	15,110,203	1,832,073	35,673,335	9,480	3,709,387	11,670,861	745,836,859	3,505,060	323,240	1,228,101	1,722,829,525
TOTAL	1,215,587,184	63,962,183	22,796,888	78,712,275	6,634,772	80,318,437	6,922,486	35,251,128	17,151,868	4,144,138,582	18,755,617	1,895,671	1,901,624	5,694,028,715
PENNSYLVANIA														
1	206,172,018	5,680,942	44,665,818	118,666,380	340,509	4,809,267	59,808	43,957,200	128,381,428	1,013,218,399	11,359,310	1,724,882	2,529,468	1,581,565,429
2	211,717,898	5,703,771	30,218,652	29,911,453	539,368	21,565,109	60,048	17,713,320	32,274,453	1,017,584,242	23,278,429	2,251,606	232,004	1,393,050,353
3	205,993,247	5,692,070	25,181,263	31,745,223	353,521	1,233,680	59,925	22,356,063	2,951,914	1,014,972,559	9,763,424	124,472	231,528	1,320,658,890
4	79,211,918	2,620,666	6,338,864	9,299,468	182,774	2,708,229	0	2,306,029	425,324	885,216,534	7,352,762	96,544	391,680	996,150,790
5	49,476,378	4,778,633	8,444,257	14,994,324	456,856	509,835	0	3,121,274	1,287,028	772,483,838	7,534,261	405,480	75,000	863,567,164
6	60,540,863	2,159,655	12,297,432	8,351,158	62,840	557,828	0	1,484,640	165,676	978,662,382	3,773,551	661,334	0	1,068,717,360
7	70,402,215	2,093,706	9,155,583	9,395,548	293,870	118,742	5,768	409,007	11,228,646	904,645,826	2,342,767	639,773	32,285	1,010,763,737
8	34,172,129	2,677,719	10,086,103	6,408,250	1,849,964	0	0	433,872	242,495	690,645,302	5,538,949	0	0	752,054,782
9	81,061,402	810,592	6,490,153	64,290,257	701,313	296,019	0	2,257,711	320,566	824,083,559	4,541,151	92,493	256,148	985,201,363
10	79,489,444	860,319	8,806,971	16,162,331	781,918	188,004	0	2,229,875	750,323	1,015,443,835	9,173,343	47,129	25,750	1,133,959,241
11	74,241,125	4,655,695	7,526,821	15,966,486	80,157	15,888	0	5,771,529	813,613	1,130,018,963	13,341,245	0	25,750	1,252,457,271
12	74,999,608	3,559,359	9,822,022	14,049,176	311,744	253,860	0	1,890,376	917,015	967,762,015	7,476,067	526,696	160,950	1,081,728,888
13	66,336,846	2,456,082	18,734,476	9,138,572	-921,942	215,151	10,451	13,022,243	2,500,854	884,953,223	6,087,158	1,493,194	40,378	1,004,066,685
14	90,733,316	37,633,395	60,552,802	54,443,358	2,246,431	75,845,073	1,560,605	34,689,985	43,696,726	975,922,218	31,419,232	4,944,538	6,408,272	1,420,095,951
15	57,269,001	1,456,737	4,770,538	17,619,578	203,017	392,693	0	1,685,443	7,799,219	898,659,133	7,729,496	98,387	70,790	997,754,032
16	52,440,292	1,444,252	10,572,919	7,830,443	85,064	655,812	0	1,787,001	1,114,741	724,510,738	7,218,047	93,192	0	807,752,500
17	2,779,279,183	11,008,165	9,841,880	15,024,482	479,454	910,635	0	19,602,931	1,099,844	833,373,076	6,664,507	0	5,928,955	3,683,213,112
18	90,917,554	0	402,000	3,615,711	0	0	0	109,845	0	973,873,400	5,364,876	0	80,500	1,074,363,886
19	49,162,352	1,470,234	7,961,282	9,112,547	512,286	0	0	2,781,935	940,877	718,020,609	5,648,464	0	0	795,610,587
20	88,368,169	320,352	2,049,971	7,564,035	235,476	0	2,240	377,204	0	960,833,063	8,229,916	0	385,360	1,068,365,786
21	85,225,636	1,581,280	5,944,886	10,836,524	-68,029	0	0	4,286,557	1,341,120	852,283,765	8,004,516	0	75,740	969,511,995
22	114,254,064	4,310,821	8,701,274	13,304,338	83,675	53,908	0	1,881,176	555,520	998,894,311	8,295,935	0	183,219	1,150,518,240
23	67,414,334	5,172,416	965,657	21,289,737	151,912	57,522,954	0	3,670,103	2,158,911	814,212,986	8,330,787	50,547	1,122,166	982,062,509
TOTAL	4,768,878,991	108,146,861	309,531,624	509,019,376	8,962,179	167,852,687	1,758,844	187,825,321	240,966,292	20,850,273,973	208,468,193	13,250,267	18,255,943	27,393,190,551

RHODE ISLAND														
1	370,932,182	4,330,054	39,212,594	17,215,480	23,380	67,103	86,700	17,076,652	27,434,914	773,035,431	11,106,832	399,731	415,422	1,261,336,474
2	237,036,300	3,800,989	6,897,912	11,248,896	9,248	15,472,666	1,904,551	6,264,939	718,069	759,189,338	5,393,977	179,113	137,984	1,048,253,983
TOTAL	607,968,482	8,131,043	46,110,506	28,464,376	32,628	15,539,769	1,991,251	23,341,591	28,152,983	1,532,224,769	16,500,809	578,844	553,406	2,309,590,457
SOUTH CAROLINA														
1	80,076,382	5,581,805	4,933,007	19,676,705	1,630,918	20,894,601	0	9,574,449	507,796	592,203,871	11,440,287	967,433	41,200	747,528,455
2	1,013,507,055	10,123,762	5,629,554	17,098,047	307,425	20,966,148	249,497	12,671,668	3,313,349	610,622,687	10,926,710	426,787	942,849	1,706,785,538
3	68,642,803	3,122,859	1,479,034	6,733,668	277,511	13,083,242	0	5,904,841	988,254	714,782,837	11,828,444	0	1,100,000	827,943,493
4	55,832,840	5,875,024	11,065,492	14,855,032	38,341	231,420	0	2,073,024	1,509,631	716,275,780	13,009,243	0	410,000	821,175,827
5	85,992,924	5,791,629	13,633,663	8,220,679	1,593,901	140,177	4,088	3,757,387	1,575,565	685,440,255	7,447,649	0	0	813,597,917
6	113,451,283	7,865,047	3,064,260	7,488,500	2,150,968	271,928	0	8,348,078	619,152	695,226,718	7,791,269	0	0	846,277,202
TOTAL	1,417,503,287	38,360,126	39,805,010	74,072,631	5,999,064	55,587,516	253,585	42,329,447	8,513,747	4,014,552,148	62,443,602	1,394,220	2,494,049	5,763,308,432
SOUTH DAKOTA														
TOTAL	401,031,090	11,230,902	21,769,338	19,308,965	18,332,773	10,413,947	17,413,300	4,800,946	2,508,964	1,412,423,261	7,887,700	1,863,786	319,885	1,929,304,857
TENNESSEE														
1	93,011,662	4,421,015	9,165,307	9,308,880	0	3,421,200	0	2,586,399	943,075	749,818,541	8,894,749	0	0	881,570,828
2	78,817,754	7,669,052	9,956,155	16,889,410	0	24,525,262	101,226	2,372,564	2,134,038	754,592,265	14,491,917	417,258	-5,908	911,960,993
3	82,882,319	2,950,509	16,468,564	14,216,948	0	1,495,033	0	3,458,039	2,076,932	771,928,788	10,577,805	1,120,869	887,658	908,063,464
4	115,983,995	3,179,182	5,546,388	9,201,665	0	647,641	0	7,151,601	661,778	779,515,536	6,515,099	257,754	0	928,660,639
5	1,335,216,102	14,642,191	23,009,945	40,187,480	0	5,573,397	630,874	56,847,411	17,451,729	716,939,136	18,980,723	0	2,460,649	2,231,939,637
6	80,870,051	2,912,059	3,374,091	6,421,785	12,957	1,983,568	0	4,017,647	109,454	673,633,161	13,016,225	0	0	786,350,998
7	111,734,421	4,554,227	12,368,775	18,710,665	4,549	1,001,787	0	1,591,087	332,067	677,542,909	9,443,691	49,312	18,200	837,351,691
8	117,862,884	2,522,052	8,569,748	14,404,285	468,614	1,032,776	0	14,341,877	511,555	855,957,296	20,223,163	0	0	1,035,894,249
9	108,095,205	5,033,713	29,413,962	18,235,651	0	21,561,590	0	2,888,780	1,097,336	655,907,100	2,861,870	286,524	0	845,381,731
TOTAL	2,124,474,393	47,884,000	117,872,935	147,576,769	486,120	61,242,254	732,100	95,255,405	25,317,963	6,635,834,732	105,005,243	2,131,717	3,360,599	9,367,174,230
TEXAS														
1	90,836,955	4,729,799	4,526,356	8,055,691	1,285,025	139,276	208,909	110,854	504,717	913,227,280	6,630,478	0	64,560	1,030,319,900
2	70,993,982	3,322,578	3,062,392	9,494,322	39,425	2,029,678	1,527,208	2,036,506	0	870,189,069	11,967,351	0	6,778,005	981,440,516
3	35,386,608	912,580	1,953,601	9,722,657	58,418	4,589,194	85,963	503,681	2,052,545	598,378,208	11,259,792	99,600	150,986	665,153,834
4	56,148,412	4,829,177	5,910,696	11,015,496	910,049	2,235,995	0	779,426	1,152,769	944,140,567	9,459,106	0	318,376	1,036,900,070
5	35,999,686	1,926,454	526,463	10,220,527	156,026	51,293,964	90,093	4,696,348	3,841,374	602,609,883	6,693,972	72,091	158,241	718,285,121
6	66,569,072	2,085,547	2,663,132	7,892,696	-32,951	41,285,929	7,895	1,422,347	2,638,209	822,923,595	9,420,189	99,986	2,009,461	958,985,107
7	40,280,876	-154,101	1,886,636	100,631,189	23,124	27,936,544	0	434,083	327,789	528,250,117	7,885,946	131,709	1,757,074	709,390,986
8	40,069,897	162,989	344,886	9,377,615	23,009	-10,072	0	502,669	299,663	528,792,302	9,085,420	0	497,921	589,146,299
9	49,850,687	3,378,395	5,150,587	12,850,177	799,570	29,723,456	0	621,897	1,262,985	766,507,194	17,048,348	289,514	2,196,066	889,678,875
10	4,599,256,955	23,433,638	13,742,090	88,497,594	1,402,146	51,354,402	675	7,914,863	1,001,355	630,074,129	5,911,120	711,203	3,574,944	5,426,875,114
11	55,538,073	2,070,367	9,937,440	13,532,730	10,859,314	634,303	0	2,733,308	1,660,456	775,677,007	9,619,726	0	0	882,262,724
12	31,942,429	1,459,625	24,396,048	13,313,192	847,072	2,228,084	0	1,744,392	291,334	644,017,535	7,469,856	162,977	1,200,000	729,072,544
13	33,385,819	1,605,864	4,747,521	8,458,230	1,169,842	1,747,940	0	2,107,390	118,600	1,058,253,288	8,515,290	0	0	1,120,109,784
14	70,248,058	3,162,192	3,634,447	7,004,748	663,450	5,524,310	14,580	1,963,012	640,522	885,216,802	8,631,870	33,472	100,354	986,837,817
15	131,484,488	11,454,733	12,901,648	20,053,040	63,090	1,428,381	0	4,973,443	0	669,769,594	11,662,551	29,550	59,699	863,880,217
16	66,432,813	3,900,294	12,528,781	16,670,262	4,509,497	3,368,592	612,216	3,868,036	39,761	593,998,751	7,695,876	0	60,200	713,685,079
17	47,515,768	1,365,116	1,742,932	6,993,207	1,274,999	341,110	0	2,140,184	1,066,717	988,618,123	5,219,321	134,636	120,246	1,056,532,360
18	40,089,117	119,294	1,394,643	6,838,016	95,998	14,978,527	0	9,922,505	66,822,303	528,623,413	8,607,899	555,019	491,692	678,538,427
19	40,992,629	4,645,057	3,058,023	9,469,118	419,369	12,320,716	0	5,391,785	680,989	916,006,825	7,252,156	0	0	1,000,236,667
20	67,685,334	4,859,204	26,417,360	31,824,779	4,593,603	3,474,336	0	20,505,062	1,609,208	658,766,373	6,759,321	330,284	597,849	827,422,712
21	44,267,658	2,017,843	6,811,442	9,362,045	1,615,322	1,215,948	0	2,154,599	1,189,758	795,366,285	8,860,679	125,000	79,403	873,065,984

See Appendix A for a listing of the congressional districts which represent the county in which the state capital is located and congressional districts which represent only portions of a county. See Appendix B for a listing of the programs included in each recipent category.

table continues

Table 3.6 Federal Outlays to Categories of Recipients by Congressional District, 1988 *(continued)*

District	State Gov't.	Counties	Cities/ Towns	Special Districts	Schools	Public Universities	Indian Tribes	Non-Profits	Private Universities	Individuals	For Profits	Small Businesses	All Others	Total
TEXAS *continued*														
22	31,205,193	14,764,525	12,735,291	6,679,236	180,155	6,281,954	0	1,158,476	1,984,949	502,484,615	17,681,049	368,367	908,182	596,431,992
23	101,518,851	11,473,387	1,520,258	25,525,844	6,037,439	31,220,309	0	19,394,887	330,053	709,372,391	7,943,019	292,233	9,424	914,638,096
24	36,399,381	141,843	3,112,796	69,949,158	117,719	886,229	584,572	371,608	532,050	605,965,744	7,138,220	743,849	104,729	726,047,898
25	69,788,827	95,787	505,586	6,782,198	23,081	735,979	0	1,063,910	2,672,484	527,283,920	1,308,938	50,000	491,140	610,801,850
26	27,020,345	6,341,138	637,120	12,775,115	2,015,924	5,413,113	0	193,062	939,262	592,485,531	9,534,776	50,000	26,520	657,431,907
27	97,415,439	4,321,362	5,848,035	12,299,473	1,588,459	2,854,633	0	11,635,438	0	659,353,808	7,833,496	0	145,477	803,295,620
TOTAL	6,078,323,351	118,424,687	171,696,211	545,288,356	40,738,174	305,232,831	3,132,111	110,343,772	93,659,852	19,316,352,349	237,095,764	4,279,490	21,900,551	27,046,467,500
UTAH														
1	68,656,507	8,292,877	4,891,350	10,609,047	5,035,155	13,552,392	1,146,191	1,337,189	874,346	513,738,258	8,625,467	114,870	260,464	637,134,113
2	635,609,056	9,462,589	17,440,148	15,068,707	198,331	55,893,985	355,950	7,064,715	634,997	500,792,904	7,306,165	2,889,800	784,319	1,253,501,667
3	79,639,917	3,585,918	3,067,681	4,893,174	4,118,375	1,026,253	1,046,801	1,780,424	8,905,024	480,668,958	2,616,869	526,890	221,600	592,097,883
TOTAL	783,905,480	21,341,384	25,399,179	30,570,928	9,351,861	70,472,630	2,548,942	10,182,328	10,414,367	1,495,200,120	18,548,501	3,531,560	1,266,383	2,482,733,663
VERMONT														
TOTAL	337,827,387	13,205,874	14,003,659	7,261,773	94,139	31,647,591	161,618	7,885,589	11,235,004	715,509,935	5,658,910	292,803	699,233	1,145,483,515
VIRGINIA														
1	63,753,941	10,982,471	20,712,986	1,913,220	0	4,895,688	260,257	6,139,420	4,201,174	731,376,093	10,081,315	0	1,352,641	855,669,206
2	58,748,789	2,422,862	41,437,263	14,904,318	0	6,492,981	0	8,393,440	1,133,300	544,898,502	8,359,307	0	1,245,238	688,036,000
3	1,338,631,494	23,430,200	25,214,836	3,757,897	0	36,397,233	0	3,770,530	689,891	785,939,076	11,817,273	-1,667	2,861,068	2,232,507,832
4	95,996,765	5,705,135	10,427,079	1,110,193	0	4,564,713	0	2,254,357	241,928	741,412,624	7,287,538	0	84,265	869,084,597
5	86,609,461	3,035,882	7,572,847	2,004,870	0	236,861	0	3,128,088	461,395	761,086,437	3,958,172	0	63,751	868,157,764
6	60,878,282	3,461,123	15,448,263	2,686,066	0	1,028,963	0	3,654,267	2,442,800	844,452,643	9,034,172	0	544,840	943,631,419
7	54,629,656	8,947,950	6,542,464	3,282,243	0	50,509,681	0	3,833,869	193,756	676,462,678	5,714,522	353,377	127,404	810,597,600
8	27,548,634	2,487,742	10,627,056	629,232	5,000	20,119	-23,798	7,997,519	60,000	405,276,443	4,097,199	2,324,132	141,098	461,190,377
9	93,561,343	6,364,946	6,021,915	5,190,676	212	27,348,753	0	5,767,368	2,231,147	879,388,651	5,218,436	571,662	105,000	1,031,770,109
10	31,704,196	10,071,468	27,136,146	10,319,194	173,445	2,740,408	0	23,183,351	443,944	477,544,018	18,542,195	14,653,394	88,043,052	704,554,811
TOTAL	1,912,062,561	76,909,779	171,140,855	45,797,909	178,657	134,235,400	236,459	68,122,210	12,099,335	6,847,837,166	84,110,129	17,900,898	94,568,357	9,465,199,715
WASHINGTON														
1	90,637,970	5,609,878	27,806,482	94,018,374	930,714	3,370,991	673,437	6,190,994	596,718	701,226,972	8,633,030	2,231,284	525,907	942,452,752
2	89,187,441	4,538,698	9,549,912	14,960,855	5,030,942	2,209,458	9,704,464	4,395,131	0	844,896,696	8,394,970	0	253,619	993,122,187
3	1,418,287,630	7,467,877	2,400,478	15,071,469	602,834	1,321,120	1,282,823	2,962,538	84,218	772,406,272	6,424,609	173,565	1,005,561	2,229,490,995
4	105,738,138	6,512,158	2,454,697	8,604,480	7,718,412	1,772,227	9,819,167	21,881,705	82,509	776,602,583	7,265,913	40,000	1,219,003	949,710,992
5	102,365,399	5,666,463	2,717,101	8,734,123	3,130,146	23,888,313	1,371,520	4,091,074	15,715,104	916,462,162	6,906,226	803,883	32,800	1,091,884,315
6	110,071,877	5,434,258	21,068,407	15,625,680	9,922,359	662,082	1,938,642	3,585,959	757,067	670,974,227	10,992,833	0	0	851,033,390
7	94,303,512	11,741,789	6,826,355	34,297,228	197,089	173,839,092	461,928	51,283,596	1,441,677	724,517,875	6,136,410	2,613,258	112,245	1,107,772,053
8	97,922,065	9,165,043	3,912,923	10,504,436	319,321	3,768,682	1,107,990	4,892,741	1,015,508	727,371,578	4,534,003	1,261,457	233,901	866,009,647
TOTAL	2,108,514,033	56,136,164	76,736,354	201,816,645	27,851,817	210,831,965	26,359,971	99,283,738	19,692,801	6,134,458,367	59,287,994	7,123,447	3,383,036	9,031,476,331
WEST VIRGINIA														
1	63,930,807	1,848,377	7,965,054	21,591,260	22,584	1,658,717	0	4,752,025	848,448	825,163,841	9,522,810	195,297	52,000	937,551,220
2	90,110,057	7,968,500	6,720,139	6,880,584	4,771,704	22,498,272	0	4,798,143	1,275,411	795,468,375	5,190,530	56,045	21,469	945,759,229
3	690,413,949	6,880,316	10,903,903	27,054,492	318,900	1,115,793	0	1,785,502	540,077	793,850,701	6,076,339	29,000	1,175,573	1,540,144,545
4	107,243,098	3,795,648	7,966,899	16,423,398	30,369	4,023,266	0	6,125,458	1,118,629	908,725,945	4,035,026	0	55,400	1,059,543,136
TOTAL	951,697,911	20,492,841	33,555,995	71,949,734	5,143,557	29,296,048	0	17,461,128	3,782,565	3,323,208,862	24,824,705	280,342	1,304,442	4,482,998,130

WISCONSIN														
1	122,332,440	2,382,956	11,018,386	6,451,151	499,927	1,868,330	0	1,200,765	458,539	814,986,223	7,086,508	49,900	0	968,335,125
2	1,106,554,038	14,913,741	13,363,927	7,594,474	853,783	143,647,493	856,140	5,474,809	2,541,774	773,011,701	8,233,709	397,327	3,149,339	2,080,592,255
3	132,777,984	5,086,266	4,739,565	3,330,121	54,770	4,726,456	61,896	2,537,731	363,302	870,881,204	5,135,125	50,000	578,779	1,030,323,200
4	156,729,468	9,001,042	9,798,379	62,118,180	178,458	1,299,166	0	7,810,433	975,829	835,287,226	12,401,407	0	592,535	1,096,192,122
5	185,544,424	5,458,877	10,239,722	12,052,052	197,281	4,484,396	219,151	7,324,762	21,552,467	894,247,767	12,780,722	591,233	5,475	1,154,698,329
6	110,629,756	1,412,002	2,555,921	4,004,923	453,952	2,134,406	228,541	535,436	459,410	864,262,854	6,103,448	557,555	0	993,338,204
7	130,955,048	5,778,524	10,619,697	4,351,115	340,742	3,864,453	4,155,006	5,986,176	472,203	848,671,340	7,373,969	1,500	0	1,022,569,774
8	107,178,610	4,532,012	8,736,282	17,145,050	162,665	923,866	12,467,035	2,072,721	436,138	805,612,210	6,500,736	0	0	965,767,325
9	65,663,115	2,104,306	4,767,352	2,883,093	60,839	66,762	0	324,336	692,343	709,801,491	7,443,383	0	20,680	793,827,700
TOTAL	2,118,364,884	50,669,726	75,839,231	119,930,160	2,802,416	163,015,327	17,987,769	33,267,169	27,952,005	7,416,762,017	73,059,007	1,647,515	4,346,807	10,105,644,033
WYOMING														
TOTAL	345,514,229	8,308,784	13,705,043	2,972,075	9,121,656	10,952,051	1,914,476	9,289,161	511,254	549,168,394	9,657,463	15,767	512,006	961,642,359
U.S. TOTAL														
	105,054.8 mil	3,316.9 mil	7,150.0 mil	7,360.3 mil	548.7 mil	4,643.5 mil	429.2 mil	3,587.9 mil	3,167.5 mil	349,197.8 mil	4,598.7 mil	242.0 mil	824.3 mil	490,121.6 mil

See Appendix A for a listing of the congressional districts which represent the county in which the state capital is located and congressional districts which represent only portions of a county. See Appendix B for a listing of the programs included in each recipent category.

Table 3.7 Federal Outlays to Categories of Recipients by Congressional District, 1989

District	State Gov't.	Counties	Cities/ Towns	Special Districts	Schools	Public Universities	Indian Tribes	Non-Profits	Private Universities	Individuals	For Profits	Small Businesses	All Others	Total
ALABAMA														
1	69,112,354	1,926,197	6,370,313	26,863,855	296,408	19,425,260	3,496,074	5,195,815	1,488,758	861,610,777	9,924,005	0	0	1,005,709,816
2	1,233,254,541	26,227,576	5,061,018	27,401,672	1,651,622	19,035,613	0	8,170,907	2,987,015	848,441,615	24,869,705	38,208	1,283,291	2,198,422,783
3	69,525,150	4,590,796	6,795,993	18,342,067	308,435	33,724,778	0	5,448,117	11,560,986	817,948,278	7,479,071	86,226	-127,397	975,682,500
4	76,015,839	2,514,712	4,158,988	16,085,248	89,734	6,383,069	0	4,601,325	559,779	958,612,774	7,508,068	0	0	1,076,529,536
5	56,556,787	4,507,691	2,149,122	15,958,666	2,844,824	19,222,976	0	3,138,811	2,202,209	782,810,009	11,684,758	0	0	901,075,853
6	52,194,415	1,976,766	5,168,542	29,520,787	611,769	87,526,621	0	5,797,354	7,410,633	992,632,662	27,069,136	0	0	1,209,908,686
7	82,749,372	2,961,118	5,266,915	17,843,677	70,221	21,408,032	23,596	6,663,443	5,795,837	847,700,792	8,335,153	349,108	86,247	999,253,509
TOTAL	1,639,408,457	44,704,856	34,970,891	152,015,972	5,873,013	206,726,349	3,519,670	39,015,772	32,005,217	6,109,756,907	96,869,896	473,542	1,242,141	8,366,582,683
ALASKA														
TOTAL	521,728,219	61,765,890	60,394,534	12,046,514	180,953	17,814,606	53,227,037	74,008,076	1,041,369	285,035,370	20,041,914	140,745	1,485,751	1,108,910,978
ARIZONA														
1	312,670,410	4,503,754	41,367,735	22,174,274	7,724,329	41,750,757	1,416,980	4,170,894	3,432,419	1,347,903,135	26,806,293	96,318	594,476	1,814,611,774
2	329,769,147	24,448,048	24,512,606	26,947,173	7,239,759	74,518,476	14,738,559	12,735,949	1,782,859	1,132,579,483	16,050,665	1,269,220	1,382,067	1,667,974,013
3	26,794,415	3,216,399	24,284,480	6,050,583	5,088,150	11,070,453	4,486,393	-10,265,934	350,462	521,812,713	20,641,315	96,130	0	613,625,559
4	368,666,370	6,197,123	29,137,480	10,313,789	37,859,524	987,286	86,703,434	2,432,946	2,522,193	1,165,388,306	14,922,517	16,663	0	1,725,147,631
5	83,559,100	2,531,129	24,782,588	7,851,652	5,267,906	10,110,630	429,824	4,887,687	146,019	990,302,633	2,998,238	163,815	0	1,133,031,222
TOTAL	1,121,459,441	40,896,453	144,084,889	73,337,471	63,179,669	138,437,602	107,775,190	13,961,543	8,233,953	5,157,986,271	81,419,028	1,642,147	1,976,543	6,954,390,199
ARKANSAS														
1	171,267,424	6,150,901	4,283,822	24,728,666	2,602,973	10,234,082	0	6,309,841	1,742,123	1,239,934,427	6,952,278	0	0	1,474,206,537
2	741,205,471	15,647,350	19,096,150	20,436,943	1,117,034	17,379,580	445,452	5,952,519	9,566,128	926,775,434	12,901,930	589,337	4,344,680	1,775,458,008
3	74,886,685	6,103,236	6,790,481	14,702,122	145,937	29,196,079	0	5,318,880	1,687,586	1,087,395,710	17,765,136	0	0	1,243,991,852
4	132,227,506	1,238,152	14,531,433	14,546,839	496,376	14,897,270	0	4,501,811	1,758,163	1,096,829,748	9,191,402	87,630	0	1,290,306,330
TOTAL	1,119,587,086	29,139,639	44,701,886	74,414,570	4,362,320	71,707,011	445,452	22,083,051	14,754,000	4,350,935,319	46,810,746	676,967	4,344,680	5,783,962,727
CALIFORNIA														
1	102,938,063	5,898,652	10,623,728	28,560,143	3,376,772	9,567,959	4,318,928	7,522,859	219,562	1,020,456,523	11,079,293	138,887	4,743,297	1,209,444,666
2	114,036,984	4,852,111	9,486,537	17,798,579	7,373,753	8,407,209	720,011	5,085,573	3,129,932	1,217,789,637	9,508,187	0	131,000	1,398,319,514
3	4,846,860,937	166,089,547	19,791,395	10,254,799	2,319,837	4,108,335	3,594,494	11,308,632	1,137,265	686,793,993	17,029,216	90,680	3,210,994	5,772,590,124
4	754,392,285	42,542,507	8,004,407	26,623,784	12,297,520	69,636,956	826,541	2,809,862	535,629	703,644,354	10,340,395	161,020	1,471,145	1,633,286,405
5	169,028,385	-1,197,764	56,407,729	44,371,359	7,598,742	13,146,815	0	15,384,580	5,200,099	1,184,222,621	24,178,026	1,389,315	13,390,700	1,533,120,607
6	78,154,184	2,500,218	11,693,993	23,419,719	5,269,077	169,850,626	0	24,442,925	2,295,813	820,072,375	13,108,563	3,150,193	151,722	1,154,109,408
7	68,280,894	22,567,353	5,757,149	46,004,830	2,711,222	0	0	4,584,941	616,580	791,340,032	10,277,032	100,000	92,260	952,332,293
8	100,914,735	14,346,829	19,219,267	41,328,131	2,078,312	131,785,407	279,728	39,122,501	2,509,395	790,665,743	21,036,113	3,976,382	768,381	1,168,030,924
9	107,460,587	11,474,427	26,007,070	55,328,792	6,933,921	3,251,148	291,692	3,951,851	1,287,542	786,609,180	68,960,702	545,854	0	1,072,102,764
10	73,693,512	4,970,724	13,857,809	27,527,461	1,982,640	6,179,360	803,582	1,747,724	652,399	655,519,837	11,318,473	308,080	1,414,423	799,976,024
11	49,190,903	7,857,826	6,459,841	24,127,303	1,988,065	547,230	11,524	9,947,433	916,883	768,399,894	6,711,791	2,054,446	1,273,027	879,486,166
12	48,488,979	4,703,002	7,680,000	15,376,234	6,220,748	11,872,969	63,099	28,994,571	178,733,611	545,535,991	18,685,724	4,812,162	1,938,416	873,105,505
13	55,377,890	18,598,744	10,598,015	26,869,650	1,526,528	4,369,368	92,012	3,482,743	4,331,623	581,267,751	7,715,859	518,090	2,181,436	716,929,710
14	71,559,786	5,140,088	6,289,536	11,512,835	5,048,826	0	1,114,241	3,055,238	3,968,654	895,201,145	7,332,682	0	25,200	1,010,248,231
15	91,776,577	9,664,893	8,950,780	15,610,159	6,148,718	2,889,543	60,000	5,108,467	15,000	692,777,596	10,230,529	0	949,293	844,181,555
16	59,414,158	3,933,482	5,158,698	42,703,250	16,143,676	20,671,220	0	5,084,694	576,557	700,793,714	6,990,854	50,000	287,427	861,807,730
17	134,146,822	5,417,221	15,454,856	17,716,292	6,522,315	2,439,020	663,018	5,859,985	861,317	926,141,398	10,651,673	30,552	2,479,490	1,128,383,959
18	172,388,072	8,850,538	16,371,824	24,247,430	6,364,885	6,096,357	5,878,241	1,315,504	3,355,432	1,219,601,445	10,529,480	0	0	1,474,999,207
19	41,316,632	4,005,683	11,880,530	35,854,861	6,329,984	33,470,295	418,596	5,095,351	1,632,462	619,616,996	5,517,513	1,291,836	51,700	766,482,439
20	93,048,006	3,241,263	18,062,706	22,424,583	10,326,502	4,089,250	788,762	21,455,771	1,889,404	978,419,483	21,019,804	0	1,122,650	1,175,888,186
21	82,872,682	1,335,723	11,185,790	25,690,613	2,844,536	1,240,531	353,681	6,657,593	2,726,633	890,489,438	11,635,794	496,303	91,425,030	1,128,954,348
22	97,616,063	1,686,200	14,179,247	29,077,215	2,924,041	3,325,233	0	10,094,562	40,270,400	772,940,189	17,097,734	387,380	690,540	990,288,804
23	97,638,067	4,141,643	9,665,804	20,435,620	1,113,183	169,522,859	0	11,533,430	2,854,113	771,498,991	11,397,787	0	784,807	1,100,586,303

24	99,661,038	1,062,095	9,631,644	34,885,004	1,125,001	2,037,357	0	19,358,586	2,406,224	770,805,131	16,397,386	0	689,679	958,059,145
25	96,794,066	22,936,809	11,192,353	27,856,414	1,476,126	3,559,118	178,942	11,933,763	2,285,548	770,285,571	16,368,385	30,000	689,026	965,586,120
26	84,791,891	1,851,692	8,484,791	16,908,613	1,311,905	2,080,552	0	4,118,527	2,282,978	676,672,084	9,794,434	99,841	605,523	809,002,832
27	98,081,809	2,245,397	38,525,808	28,714,069	2,210,360	2,110,497	0	5,121,804	1,902,026	770,617,104	14,445,703	716,203	689,481	965,380,261
28	99,486,017	1,346,975	10,387,727	23,570,987	1,124,515	2,818,651	0	12,158,176	86,531,749	770,454,105	14,090,599	363,868	689,381	1,023,022,752
29	96,099,547	31,836,453	13,071,863	22,739,977	1,124,757	2,036,916	0	8,155,432	1,889,394	770,625,158	11,583,541	0	689,529	959,852,568
30	96,477,990	1,672,946	18,360,801	23,136,485	3,298,173	2,229,032	0	3,352,399	3,747,016	769,188,617	14,130,264	100,000	688,333	936,382,057
31	97,084,428	1,702,925	20,029,119	27,119,478	2,076,067	4,972,613	429,658	2,552,251	11,130,865	771,014,561	13,334,332	329,120	689,967	952,465,384
32	97,156,021	1,846,128	13,443,779	21,327,818	1,129,076	3,871,873	0	1,573,794	1,896,649	773,527,094	8,480,199	74,133	692,177	925,018,742
33	97,610,977	1,321,020	11,688,560	23,541,895	3,452,028	8,847,147	0	2,889,233	7,434,210	771,425,947	9,543,831	343,693	690,186	938,788,727
34	96,195,677	1,160,864	20,902,833	42,030,184	2,841,008	2,038,954	0	2,438,923	4,640,243	771,300,927	13,204,191	0	690,219	957,444,022
35	82,002,749	2,239,467	10,428,351	18,569,819	11,310,186	1,515,533	830,861	363,103	17,337,025	817,195,626	6,246,353	639,246	4,426	968,682,744
36	373,049,322	25,822,484	22,076,243	26,475,387	2,138,943	11,055,730	294,447	1,193,653	294,050	1,633,050,483	10,146,153	4,118	517,461	2,106,118,473
37	278,707,661	23,901,221	10,973,976	16,405,261	4,369,762	5,456,517	2,058,338	1,891,179	308,411	818,344,882	5,619,002	3,700	464,860	1,168,504,770
38	40,270,340	8,516,109	8,116,827	19,089,157	790,461	179,396	518,270	238,538	621,149	711,125,680	9,959,542	49,362	0	799,474,831
39	40,592,919	992,312	10,810,194	20,327,043	2,227,681	8,012,278	518,708	765,456	1,900,760	711,797,896	13,321,745	0	0	811,266,992
40	40,833,958	9,595,970	11,964,746	21,318,174	6,138,927	37,085,473	518,231	16,411,951	956,425	711,247,055	17,863,760	147,610	0	874,082,280
41	55,461,618	851,079	23,716,355	15,945,961	3,879,260	147,492,747	463,066	64,161,781	2,349,723	615,126,324	15,685,495	3,510,609	865,975	949,509,994
42	74,681,283	2,301,006	9,425,457	26,244,699	2,312,975	2,687,905	200,865	16,232,772	2,021,665	745,518,126	12,582,848	462,401	420,509	895,092,510
43	64,647,553	7,893,465	14,000,736	20,444,702	16,555,437	4,946,674	909,431	20,932,320	2,266,093	871,760,867	8,571,774	2,276,790	16,890	1,035,222,733
44	73,952,850	1,687,159	16,806,083	36,267,369	7,824,588	6,216,815	701,598	12,583,339	2,946,642	931,950,125	8,509,244	3,624,111	546	1,103,070,469
45	85,687,748	2,300,589	17,152,737	26,174,167	11,556,538	5,201,849	1,423,211	4,621,310	3,276,365	917,325,942	22,312,039	177,297	9,450	1,097,219,244
TOTAL	9,779,922,669	507,705,076	653,977,695	1,171,956,306	215,717,578	942,921,314	29,323,775	446,695,080	420,141,512	36,890,157,631	614,544,046	32,453,282	138,386,560	51,843,902,523
COLORADO														
1	934,429,616	98,995,599	15,152,909	47,647,063	1,545,943	64,013,848	1,925,096	26,260,984	12,082,355	824,319,768	23,755,932	632,854	4,079,258	2,054,841,225
2	40,616,493	3,042,751	6,926,479	12,550,332	514,411	64,820,558	0	39,032,146	10,312,127	475,782,586	8,100,733	2,217,118	28,958,814	692,874,548
3	99,431,051	12,176,756	7,562,327	15,090,493	5,817,861	12,856,030	2,426,112	4,043,982	0	738,021,553	29,110,323	328,234	0	926,864,723
4	71,429,909	7,804,602	8,336,580	11,226,143	2,323,759	51,567,274	0	6,036,493	3,052,957	781,396,850	8,963,510	199,183	0	952,337,261
5	47,405,153	2,575,420	5,962,261	6,441,443	13,262,661	5,783,353	0	5,441,934	4,765,076	564,875,204	5,189,805	100,115	44,600	661,847,023
6	42,274,503	1,841,661	613,471	18,109,955	1,107,330	1,587,393	398	2,288,212	1,649,618	486,215,117	4,579,498	946,664	104,020	561,317,840
TOTAL	1,235,586,725	126,436,789	44,554,027	111,065,429	24,571,965	200,628,456	4,351,606	83,103,751	31,862,134	3,870,611,079	79,699,801	4,424,168	33,186,692	5,850,082,621
CONNECTICUT														
1	915,296,665	8,491,176	-162,797	47,188,562	0	1,971,225	0	8,690,231	3,550,196	868,003,123	20,448,023	149,409	-498,749	1,873,127,064
2	102,979,861	1,898,813	12,007,823	10,374,323	30,000	23,651,135	1,095,793	7,098,374	5,233,729	715,161,624	10,914,793	0	54,000	890,500,268
3	142,294,502	3,205,187	16,228,651	37,191,054	10,000	3,628,536	0	9,327,027	155,007,574	883,526,415	9,656,607	1,214,100	-6,466	1,261,283,187
4	122,193,866	144,863	3,053,649	32,596,925	0	842,556	0	4,423,683	4,875,010	786,269,119	25,545,983	61,965	-835,420	979,172,200
5	141,316,314	458,231	-255,639	19,697,117	34,422	1,667,145	183,860	1,847,270	482,308	849,095,939	4,561,391	102,985	548,399	1,019,739,742
6	130,665,342	518,644	1,052,479	13,152,236	0	25,173,220	0	1,346,754	49,581	867,134,452	3,902,226	788,022	52,000	1,043,834,955
TOTAL	1,554,746,551	14,716,914	31,924,166	160,200,217	74,422	56,933,817	1,279,653	32,733,338	169,198,398	4,969,190,672	75,029,023	2,316,481	-686,236	7,067,657,416
DELAWARE														
TOTAL	299,780,091	5,188,107	20,131,128	24,943,868	507,967	24,310,207	37,974	10,244,665	1,838,140	933,948,550	29,042,204	307,380	1,806,517	1,352,086,798
DISTRICT OF COLUMBIA														
TOTAL	692,793,847	15,072,782	35,276,325	124,487,709	0	29,529,195	10,790	198,412,755	289,172,961	915,782,720	53,147,525	11,660,046	180,351,576	2,545,698,231
FLORIDA														
1	73,260,705	1,918,549	5,033,084	13,773,391	11,765,490	2,614,787	0	1,659,136	206,947	811,592,039	11,578,926	140,993	1,443,509	934,987,556
2	2,414,810,211	50,195,175	6,047,048	10,740,958	3,271,632	48,376,996	1,166,402	6,564,148	129,000	822,871,775	10,299,526	0	3,890,064	3,378,362,935
3	81,074,899	700,563	5,345,269	40,865,190	4,474,130	1,533,117	0	3,878,382	5,584,845	819,024,611	19,399,050	0	0	981,880,056
4	80,324,417	1,848,984	4,879,702	13,142,794	5,100,532	2,880,204	0	1,759,095	10,905,551	1,350,822,595	13,849,079	0	500	1,485,513,454
5	49,869,754	4,382,906	17,824,623	19,691,164	2,936,205	6,255,485	0	1,964,379	1,239,411	918,745,618	8,239,983	188,724	142,442	1,031,480,694
6	75,231,646	1,416,600	6,896,419	13,017,071	3,965,347	76,655,002	0	2,959,853	322,000	2,274,130,040	8,250,702	1,206,007	9,447	2,464,060,134

See Appendix A for a listing of the congressional districts which represent the county in which the state capital is located and congressional districts which represent only portions of a county. See Appendix B for a listing of the programs included in each recipent category.

table continues

Table 3.7 Federal Outlays to Categories of Recipients by Congressional District, 1989 *(continued)*

District	State Gov't.	Counties	Cities/ Towns	Special Districts	Schools	Public Universities	Indian Tribes	Non-Profits	Private Universities	Individuals	For Profits	Small Businesses	All Others	Total
FLORIDA *continued*														
7	73,563,597	7,940,831	6,245,167	37,311,446	1,724,678	20,230,716	0	3,615,690	1,823,870	900,352,625	19,306,488	0	133,100	1,072,248,208
8	33,420,129	274,580	6,422,908	20,554,910	2,924,613	1,446,986	0	5,852,084	1,001,538	1,613,823,473	5,149,955	146,178	186,000	1,691,203,355
9	44,674,088	545,780	16,281,877	7,951,231	1,032,263	223,599	0	451,384	1,055,877	1,548,634,518	3,418,761	0	0	1,624,269,378
10	56,225,222	21,443	6,750,521	19,895,524	2,013,815	1,000,002	0	2,428,351	2,035,939	1,247,606,146	6,353,024	0	37,276	1,344,367,263
11	44,709,944	2,507,629	6,744,465	15,276,067	5,541,848	3,738,508	0	3,599,122	1,329,237	1,170,621,425	8,133,023	290,871	7,431,433	1,269,923,573
12	48,975,427	3,955,726	5,439,986	15,442,487	2,633,264	0	274,308	8,493,474	558,968	1,723,297,187	3,555,192	27,851	3,910,517	1,816,564,388
13	33,509,165	12,411,449	3,581,400	32,287,695	1,588,912	0	0	251,736	295,472	2,051,942,124	12,629,025	0	99,140	2,148,596,117
14	38,554,968	142,689	2,066,398	15,676,628	3,284,054	3,208,383	1,147,347	500,149	951,817	1,648,415,946	3,252,875	582,251	3,490	1,717,786,995
15	35,388,414	22,533,248	6,391,217	13,800,703	2,798,566	16,907,691	549,607	1,717,981	6,106,217	1,418,752,930	31,557,080	0	3,672,910	1,560,176,564
16	75,871,015	367,988	7,812,506	13,292,469	784,672	342,478	3,659,633	433,003	2,301,676	1,292,970,457	7,346,670	0	0	1,405,182,568
17	175,723,923	4,193,916	16,475,273	17,478,097	3,020,208	2,280,566	285,136	3,429,055	9,256,526	984,326,285	17,746,170	326,633	0	1,234,541,789
18	181,436,656	11,373,690	18,143,698	29,968,464	2,991,251	1,173,529	250,235	3,559,207	48,178,244	984,726,878	29,280,422	126,674	0	1,311,208,947
19	160,986,384	3,103,810	14,310,914	132,587,099	3,659,542	1,028,219	219,250	2,546,140	7,703,893	957,286,671	16,420,433	0	545,691	1,300,398,046
TOTAL	3,777,610,563	129,835,555	162,692,476	482,753,388	65,511,023	189,896,268	7,551,918	55,662,370	100,987,029	24,539,943,344	235,766,383	3,036,182	21,505,519	29,772,752,017
GEORGIA														
1	140,214,023	3,738,193	1,325,292	18,793,448	7,189,712	8,942,876	0	7,416,603	1,807,150	836,541,687	11,616,077	0	0	1,037,585,061
2	171,704,283	2,831,109	2,616,890	15,044,124	1,642,497	8,315,424	0	5,865,800	432,717	820,243,033	8,628,068	0	-21,616	1,037,302,329
3	117,048,527	569,609	4,241,688	17,988,259	5,151,248	10,516,862	0	5,353,462	1,393,790	751,218,724	8,189,197	0	0	921,671,366
4	307,183,700	5,150,875	4,280,475	116,059,183	1,716,727	4,217,366	0	7,293,286	11,594,576	351,430,934	11,794,008	1,014,138	3,540,641	825,275,909
5	1,294,854,626	46,231,584	42,984,400	59,121,794	704,123	19,986,197	0	14,803,111	73,137,247	1,059,739,960	29,415,479	1,947,966	1,509,949	2,644,436,436
6	86,959,268	1,378,949	1,690,926	16,501,365	344,311	2,732,140	0	3,138,001	119,762	755,508,269	12,966,418	0	126,990	881,466,400
7	52,242,764	5,021,583	2,583,779	10,713,483	223,665	997,348	0	2,889,141	2,104,228	710,897,070	4,400,919	35,759	0	792,109,739
8	157,591,851	2,766,155	2,781,358	16,063,592	570,273	4,087,166	0	3,923,712	4,078,863	844,674,090	8,950,725	0	58,326	1,045,546,111
9	81,444,636	2,249,493	1,532,500	4,554,105	357,311	1,342,658	0	4,321,584	2,282,144	775,282,389	5,655,819	0	25,420	879,048,060
10	115,654,090	4,198,612	3,021,606	25,344,295	2,890,430	35,848,578	0	14,273,633	2,707,743	723,224,446	6,802,580	687,006	350,000	935,003,018
TOTAL	2,524,897,768	74,136,162	67,058,914	300,183,649	20,790,297	96,986,615	0	69,278,333	99,658,220	7,628,760,602	108,419,290	3,684,869	5,589,711	10,999,444,429
HAWAII														
1	508,655,283	14,920,101	-1,901,632	19,317,873	0	37,696,810	6,690,733	12,665,007	2,378,135	553,337,565	8,005,197	484,217	1,570,373	1,163,819,663
2	155,482,926	4,948,582	-377,113	13,247,470	0	12,814,438	0	3,747,113	2,214,132	645,341,429	8,939,021	0	278,876	846,636,873
TOTAL	664,138,209	19,868,683	-2,278,745	32,565,343	0	50,511,248	6,690,733	16,412,120	4,592,267	1,198,678,994	16,944,218	484,217	1,849,249	2,010,456,536
IDAHO														
1	382,146,230	8,592,294	13,865,599	10,098,539	4,474,649	22,460,307	2,551,577	6,087,234	2,741,261	737,415,001	4,166,062	645,142	1,259,499	1,196,503,394
2	110,013,391	6,221,557	4,910,790	5,791,205	5,527,430	12,327,175	1,760,277	2,500,426	4,587,186	661,413,152	3,084,978	148,649	94,049	818,380,265
TOTAL	492,159,621	14,813,851	18,776,389	15,889,744	10,002,079	34,787,482	4,311,854	8,587,660	7,328,447	1,398,828,153	7,251,040	793,791	1,353,548	2,014,883,659
ILLINOIS														
1	145,421,736	2,891,042	60,513,991	264,420,044	468,922	1,936,234	105,082	13,682,805	102,369,581	810,498,329	23,400,311	1,400,848	127,208	1,427,236,133
2	118,309,320	1,154,560	2,983,822	33,709,360	468,819	1,639,795	105,059	5,382,520	3,863,876	810,016,739	5,238,523	1,148,433	127,180	984,148,005
3	118,195,282	1,154,803	3,313,484	24,271,827	470,146	1,686,236	105,081	995,804	4,831,340	810,104,441	5,353,764	292,696	127,207	970,902,112
4	69,035,224	688,067	3,838,906	14,127,889	326,695	3,004,660	45,428	825,866	3,537,680	725,431,900	8,162,257	49,983	54,993	829,129,549
5	120,772,180	1,198,314	4,759,598	25,084,180	468,855	1,895,805	105,067	1,257,895	3,770,099	809,996,778	7,102,338	0	127,190	976,538,300
6	56,596,329	928,322	3,324,734	11,389,550	189,362	1,267,105	39,136	2,841,083	3,435,130	705,046,161	5,503,916	266,376	47,377	790,874,581
7	125,621,518	3,572,298	80,152,689	31,172,004	483,778	18,772,667	105,080	32,558,962	10,640,902	810,474,235	28,400,451	279,050	608,891	1,142,842,525
8	118,882,652	1,517,066	2,984,414	26,727,973	2,255,149	2,098,253	105,080	4,829,925	4,022,815	810,148,343	8,349,722	0	127,205	982,048,597
9	128,346,889	4,329,237	3,833,607	29,801,246	474,374	1,855,227	105,097	16,577,619	85,812,227	810,518,183	15,108,736	789,807	159,247	1,097,711,496
10	75,226,058	1,766,740	1,515,065	23,482,421	4,269,754	1,759,621	47,515	4,258,888	4,080,000	698,319,190	8,308,054	199,739	57,519	823,290,564
11	121,470,752	1,272,215	3,239,443	25,703,757	464,208	27,089,467	105,072	2,551,614	3,777,968	810,053,051	6,331,901	96,493	127,196	1,002,283,134
12	68,973,352	1,015,068	1,266,099	19,419,643	2,631,714	1,776,537	44,445	743,268	1,629,532	728,886,926	11,921,161	164,827	53,804	838,526,376

13	65,361,186	616,307	2,959,237	16,457,697	214,567	1,273,076	46,067	1,349,491	4,329,704	714,805,191	4,809,750	510,497	55,766	812,788,537
14	33,908,779	3,343,808	788,337	10,068,247	1,145,466	9,955,266	408	1,623,939	1,403,929	822,010,376	8,666,971	47,900	493	892,963,921
15	43,906,049	1,724,906	1,776,825	12,585,504	3,736,868	10,514,758	0	1,451,751	5,222,645	996,957,756	5,554,998	0	0	1,083,432,058
16	47,552,128	179,635	3,632,572	16,168,272	2,174,367	1,239,474	0	3,170,020	785,407	926,633,833	7,553,064	0	50,000	1,009,138,772
17	49,182,869	1,022,781	2,953,697	21,720,528	2,673,374	6,973,253	0	2,283,462	3,519,017	1,020,028,771	11,828,471	0	104,600	1,122,290,823
18	59,568,885	683,724	1,804,899	21,001,406	167,032	2,847,293	0	1,850,148	5,262,843	928,694,485	13,619,219	0	0	1,035,499,934
19	59,077,739	6,927,293	2,380,799	11,856,235	3,046,345	114,960,999	0	4,551,627	132,315	936,496,046	5,849,760	679,929	2,925	1,145,962,012
20	2,429,781,708	73,571,089	3,483,239	17,461,974	1,241,387	1,371,430	0	2,385,984	2,970,796	1,009,832,209	5,637,096	0	3,649,564	3,551,386,475
21	102,143,219	642,995	7,902,967	29,653,167	10,002,830	8,822,734	98,843	1,344,400	1,527,137	892,083,918	6,765,201	0	0	1,060,987,411
22	87,099,170	2,466,060	4,717,772	15,348,917	3,002,176	24,838,185	0	5,307,555	840,282	997,952,773	3,920,690	0	82,213	1,145,575,793
TOTAL	4,244,433,025	112,666,330	204,126,194	701,631,841	40,376,188	247,578,075	1,162,460	111,824,626	257,765,227	18,584,989,632	207,386,352	5,926,578	5,690,578	24,725,557,107
INDIANA														
1	130,950,443	5,063,474	3,449,232	26,308,181	214,443	3,058,773	0	1,145,878	993,094	827,278,659	9,553,370	0	1,231,066	1,009,246,614
2	162,985,036	1,106,269	4,330,538	19,393,391	239,820	10,611,306	24,033	2,367,582	3,972,538	860,235,057	10,683,338	1,742,963	208,331	1,077,900,202
3	78,871,915	832,229	7,164,574	31,746,257	126,992	1,629,195	53,748	3,535,615	15,612,984	861,634,573	8,988,270	49,950	533,557	1,010,779,859
4	71,509,747	785,497	6,503,683	15,375,585	38,075	959,327	0	2,957,698	2,774,560	822,170,062	6,279,280	0	32,500	929,386,014
5	81,943,429	106,990	6,216,998	8,859,151	2,299,298	1,193,978	50,000	5,517	5,201,762	899,243,415	11,369,305	0	0	1,016,489,844
6	192,636,049	918,527	3,868,796	25,392,582	104,795	3,570,284	0	3,213,636	5,359,535	889,784,476	11,715,279	226,022	1,003,744	1,137,793,726
7	92,884,190	2,645,244	6,328,587	13,942,333	18,015	50,598,353	19,254	19,899,948	2,700,271	905,678,331	9,776,716	87,343	0	1,104,578,585
8	106,266,643	551,293	16,783,322	12,258,480	237,202	6,459,672	0	2,610,000	3,003,295	910,434,347	10,715,788	-3,528	13,017	1,069,329,531
9	114,470,043	4,788,055	7,621,005	14,221,978	1,693,991	57,630,248	0	2,350,091	342,142	763,969,752	11,740,488	50,000	23,458	978,901,251
10	1,015,552,555	29,053,363	25,000	6,790,497	625,045	14,624,838	0	10,530,404	14,997,160	843,194,981	5,201,430	210,000	993,108	1,941,798,381
TOTAL	2,048,070,049	45,850,941	62,291,735	174,288,435	5,597,676	150,335,973	147,035	48,616,369	54,957,342	8,583,623,654	96,023,266	2,362,750	4,038,782	11,276,204,007
IOWA														
1	85,879,198	792,890	2,735,890	7,125,255	3,779,761	3,493,357	0	3,717,252	5,624,719	952,155,326	13,915,741	0	277,454	1,079,496,843
2	69,836,187	510,544	6,967,071	9,746,923	389,935	444,129	0	1,623,712	6,923,310	949,499,651	6,680,100	156,555	30,956	1,052,809,073
3	72,050,805	2,363,466	8,302,289	8,487,906	1,527,557	89,285,419	741,648	4,453,428	4,587,252	977,784,065	9,090,453	61,221	0	1,178,735,509
4	732,026,803	16,821,765	36,693,982	9,023,009	4,747,767	54,640,041	0	4,485,357	5,749,137	829,449,408	10,914,923	430,554	2,532,870	1,707,515,616
5	84,575,036	1,679,755	4,954,059	8,225,642	3,178,272	1,534,461	0	1,465,239	3,312,409	1,135,129,833	7,703,883	5,969	0	1,251,764,558
6	73,636,770	652,748	5,288,951	6,848,807	1,811,483	2,098,865	88,345	2,391,494	8,998,296	1,169,496,073	11,515,421	89,164	0	1,282,916,417
TOTAL	1,118,004,799	22,821,168	64,942,242	49,457,542	15,434,775	151,496,272	829,993	18,136,482	35,195,123	6,013,514,356	59,820,521	743,463	2,841,280	7,553,238,016
KANSAS														
1	47,634,897	2,206,369	4,010,581	4,882,080	2,702,996	6,186,722	0	1,510,672	11,518,986	1,276,983,361	7,965,052	0	10,000	1,365,611,716
2	566,742,329	23,230,547	666,848	12,604,863	18,507,741	51,221,289	1,009,880	1,522,494	2,804,969	706,208,510	8,678,323	176,028	708,385	1,394,082,206
3	67,828,071	718,297	12,017,255	9,066,977	460,880	12,576,718	0	12,199,076	2,390,674	698,140,134	9,656,180	396,385	0	825,450,647
4	69,707,201	2,386,804	-184,032	12,768,398	1,265,737	7,688,223	158,591	3,497,635	1,775,559	799,458,243	12,992,083	0	849,818	912,364,260
5	63,482,307	1,735,018	10,633,231	4,151,845	2,754,740	9,182,975	0	2,192,381	4,740,193	938,812,417	9,311,935	120,000	0	1,047,117,042
TOTAL	815,394,805	30,277,035	27,143,883	43,474,163	25,692,094	86,855,927	1,168,471	20,922,258	23,230,381	4,419,602,665	48,603,573	692,413	1,568,203	5,544,625,871
KENTUCKY														
1	98,220,530	1,539,543	7,372,962	9,881,840	391,378	5,501,687	0	691,114	206,156	959,495,423	9,932,818	0	0	1,093,233,451
2	94,634,925	886,133	4,290,842	8,131,352	1,286,853	9,278,873	0	6,094,422	1,593,296	687,632,844	5,594,023	0	1,657,344	821,080,907
3	89,840,436	8,096,883	20,354,959	21,214,861	411,116	7,759,729	15,248	7,297,192	3,271,949	810,707,059	19,158,325	529,554	293,136	988,950,448
4	74,972,913	7,991,509	4,796,137	15,689,018	36,991	3,366,825	4,752	1,242,616	565,255	755,006,698	3,365,236	0	51,825	867,089,774
5	208,397,250	2,704,074	3,074,526	7,945,610	477,038	468,060	0	4,975,391	10,133,436	880,427,459	6,995,159	0	1,350	1,125,599,354
6	1,209,151,664	25,390,664	47,296,713	21,180,841	300,515	62,617,677	0	6,862,357	6,728,840	681,577,521	5,278,002	49,998	1,272,013	2,067,706,805
7	162,430,542	1,036,681	6,187,569	9,023,123	478,065	6,870,027	0	10,831,576	3,641,676	829,434,413	4,425,928	299,767	40,569	1,034,699,935
TOTAL	1,937,648,260	47,645,487	93,373,708	93,066,645	3,381,956	95,862,878	20,000	37,994,668	26,140,608	5,604,281,417	54,749,491	879,319	3,316,237	7,998,360,674

See Appendix A for a listing of the congressional districts which represent the county in which the state capital is located and congressional districts which represent only portions of a county. See Appendix B for a listing of the programs included in each recipent category.

table continues

Table 3.7 **Federal Outlays to Categories of Recipients by Congressional District, 1989 *(continued)***

District	State Gov't.	Counties	Cities/ Towns	Special Districts	Schools	Public Universities	Indian Tribes	Non-Profits	Private Universities	Individuals	For Profits	Small Businesses	All Others	Total
LOUISIANA														
1	117,488,544	4,293,885	26,468,041	28,308,099	1,560,789	8,820,895	0	10,405,311	33,338,367	654,022,315	27,076,924	185,505	779,000	912,747,674
2	116,245,373	3,226,436	33,221,937	12,434,184	1,141,216	26,254,775	50,000	3,157,250	10,452,924	698,123,234	98,053,757	120,875	0	1,002,481,961
3	96,249,826	1,863,455	5,866,397	8,660,163	279,567	3,376,517	675,177	2,036,761	125,178	742,025,139	3,996,484	0	106,795	865,261,460
4	120,371,673	4,036,470	30,472,391	13,361,333	9,853,763	8,103,221	208,497	382,419	107,158	721,804,108	16,639,903	0	42,000	925,382,938
5	174,772,799	1,494,393	11,213,062	13,938,946	114,277	31,431,314	0	3,846,543	295,310	846,034,650	15,175,047	0	0	1,098,316,341
6	1,599,874,601	49,723,295	10,569,885	29,982,138	129,280	54,107,687	444,983	850,214	3,735,680	650,628,383	14,002,831	0	1,221,437	2,415,270,414
7	111,401,206	3,184,943	10,203,877	16,813,711	421,488	15,926,343	511,894	4,457,268	6,085,189	717,645,095	13,243,075	0	892,779	900,786,868
8	237,632,075	6,425,110	8,144,211	9,177,886	648,314	5,035,475	684,007	4,208,918	923,002	702,280,619	11,224,230	47,297	487,616	986,918,760
TOTAL	2,574,036,098	74,247,988	136,159,802	132,676,460	14,148,694	153,056,227	2,574,558	29,344,683	55,062,807	5,732,563,545	199,412,251	353,677	3,529,627	9,107,166,416
MAINE														
1	478,443,357	20,380,168	8,419,625	25,687,161	303,188	7,224,604	0	10,599,672	6,925,978	923,677,400	7,013,398	885,429	-108,737	1,489,451,242
2	201,519,009	2,366,467	11,897,278	14,025,930	37,339	24,100,622	7,200,110	6,481,103	3,365,682	914,187,577	8,047,024	10,797,299	380,445	1,204,405,886
TOTAL	679,962,366	22,746,635	20,316,903	39,713,091	340,527	31,325,226	7,200,110	17,080,775	10,291,660	1,837,864,977	15,060,422	11,682,728	271,708	2,693,857,128
MARYLAND														
1	88,035,198	8,276,415	13,699,738	41,709,311	29,971	7,192,708	50,000	4,561,877	441,897	774,889,947	9,667,055	0	9,458,703	958,012,820
2	376,422,380	-526,234	13,881,595	7,734,240	566,972	2,506,530	0	9,097	886,664	788,063,768	9,947,569	0	0	1,199,492,581
3	216,085,990	5,204,752	23,782,402	30,187,569	2,762	12,279,151	139,686	13,899,632	184,005,313	882,911,144	9,655,344	3,509,054	25,831,824	1,407,494,622
4	374,128,961	8,701,763	1,259,771	18,215,937	0	0	0	1,082,807	1,053,305	589,000,325	58,613,282	473,909	815,151	1,053,345,210
5	58,481,719	12,195,080	10,665,189	16,393,671	0	59,868,110	0	2,523,967	1,339,582	464,871,520	15,664,014	1,172,109	6,603,590	649,778,551
6	64,808,239	6,677,053	7,197,388	13,911,152	82,725	2,237,567	0	2,105,330	1,859,110	723,940,529	8,271,370	2,941,934	14,833,052	848,865,449
7	516,717,859	22,445,733	26,720,214	48,121,419	-9,227	44,095,733	209,922	15,781,742	37,796,543	968,559,130	19,956,931	143,269	36,579,280	1,737,118,549
8	100,324,422	8,036,291	981,722	20,378,383	0	0	74,268	44,128,318	401,094	718,711,915	55,023,498	21,774,308	34,496,168	1,004,330,386
TOTAL	1,795,004,768	71,010,853	98,188,019	196,651,681	673,203	128,179,798	473,876	84,092,770	227,783,508	5,910,948,279	186,799,063	30,014,583	128,617,768	8,858,438,169
MASSACHUSETTS														
1	171,555,667	1,315,006	5,117,805	25,481,041	112,255	35,435,159	16,530	5,958,158	10,033,568	856,993,609	8,443,825	441,740	1,807,046	1,122,711,409
2	194,959,321	995,023	10,621,587	99,970,155	0	2,777,436	0	3,040,644	3,660,560	892,266,216	11,896,190	168,466	367,621	1,220,723,219
3	141,384,042	1,265,414	15,467,470	18,222,011	29,390	35,227,194	0	8,776,313	9,762,162	839,118,783	10,210,762	1,090,243	12,286	1,080,566,069
4	164,000,072	1,072,034	3,539,082	17,561,667	176,891	3,958,564	0	69,861,886	7,395,213	756,124,661	4,939,147	1,144,891	94,523	1,029,868,630
5	124,648,086	9,317,615	5,829,902	26,521,276	140,128	6,305,599	0	5,143,928	702,082	748,053,106	10,566,994	4,164,154	62,928	941,455,798
6	155,675,736	2,184,475	2,867,063	29,501,537	29,821	4,278,135	0	6,522,681	2,327,399	894,892,628	11,309,312	389,065	15,883	1,109,993,735
7	217,111,667	2,453,608	5,979,604	33,588,759	58,054	1,958,699	14,858	2,693,167	34,240,834	799,563,699	10,444,711	4,946,019	162,069	1,113,215,748
8	351,582,032	13,587,170	11,772,932	41,241,197	9,510	64,634,216	31,020	207,539,032	273,933,162	907,807,429	35,155,920	14,362,309	9,195,284	1,930,851,213
9	888,475,727	7,907,685	23,488,967	53,722,411	31,360	9,131,952	43,832	114,773,200	11,972,006	1,003,754,007	26,141,520	1,784,866	451,153	2,141,678,688
10	154,587,521	849,583	15,906,600	17,995,565	47,536	5,942,582	583,424	10,329,292	27,165,741	999,124,374	7,546,221	486,652	161,084	1,240,726,174
11	419,975,906	34,479,502	8,142,693	30,725,124	83,711	4,102,241	21,130	23,751,861	6,832,851	833,553,074	14,071,365	302,705	351,754	1,376,393,920
TOTAL	2,983,955,778	75,427,114	108,733,704	394,530,744	718,656	173,751,777	710,794	458,390,161	388,025,578	9,531,251,587	150,725,967	29,281,110	12,681,631	14,308,184,603
MICHIGAN														
1	216,249,830	873,821	19,372,042	9,899,110	2,741,812	1,172,880	86,232	3,927,464	1,952,730	855,876,340	6,727,826	257,678	974,080	1,120,111,844
2	116,781,171	7,335,000	18,287,781	12,070,830	2,533,364	167,545,354	18,570	4,220,052	3,521,620	751,236,962	5,054,215	4,017,341	82,408	1,092,704,669
3	1,485,988,556	50,671,435	9,597,034	7,080,352	4,143,741	9,170,345	0	6,611,056	3,999,108	730,006,798	8,130,615	0	2,246,868	2,317,645,907
4	120,896,391	3,178,286	5,876,627	2,573,733	1,456,093	3,208,889	230,241	6,348,750	3,487,594	832,743,958	6,422,932	0	75,000	986,498,494
5	101,778,908	4,880,159	3,206,090	7,832,662	341,628	173,065	211,080	4,343,898	13,151,197	738,365,091	6,586,073	0	0	880,869,851
6	728,052,661	8,804,647	2,172,972	9,117,854	189,038	78,614,824	872,630	1,906,363	193,862	702,598,860	11,044,763	466,004	1,439,881	1,545,474,359
7	151,262,728	3,630,267	9,220,632	6,593,527	4,707,388	213,257	108,133	1,587,026	4,056,895	750,532,140	6,775,148	234,434	0	938,921,575
8	126,047,304	2,136,371	6,099,521	5,288,824	5,808,437	3,336,474	0	1,371,819	4,725,615	851,603,644	3,486,399	1,254,411	0	1,011,158,819
9	107,626,203	756,828	5,984,001	3,861,887	1,543,983	5,014,456	2,345,908	5,531,772	108,394	883,302,552	9,094,533	0	0	1,025,170,517

10	224,964,852	497,128	5,682,529	2,733,273	4,747,933	17,605,988	974,238	5,306,571	1,062,553	851,020,092	3,381,747	0	0	1,117,976,904
11	121,526,392	9,306,104	7,469,759	7,239,999	14,668,272	15,592,387	11,242,395	7,945,447	1,464,329	998,128,761	5,317,590	0	0	1,199,901,434
12	69,574,942	5,890,974	4,104,225	5,365,591	1,100,238	61,526	0	1,451,649	0	795,960,915	8,855,448	50,000	0	892,415,508
13	224,510,319	13,844,264	20,609,118	5,683,246	2,051,280	30,401,220	86,232	18,122,705	1,793,583	855,813,909	13,715,326	917,989	-52,920	1,187,496,270
14	114,320,181	1,663,273	6,980,025	2,120,363	799,646	481,564	32,396	357,328	651,884	820,690,461	5,087,572	0	-111,172	953,073,521
15	188,055,650	1,494,741	7,315,710	7,132,286	1,956,178	8,020,998	70,059	1,327,048	2,292,104	801,690,398	12,894,603	49,696	-240,420	1,032,059,051
16	169,616,803	1,297,670	10,594,066	6,865,903	4,536,024	1,425,142	56,467	3,252,578	5,477,391	817,206,300	5,917,159	0	-193,777	1,026,051,727
17	139,312,517	456,481	7,049,197	6,949,592	1,192,149	569,033	41,836	4,225,475	955,937	824,692,534	12,069,729	211,963	-143,568	997,582,875
18	61,151,680	340,395	1,746	2,059,447	1,328,221	8,150,916	63,073	692,772	657,848	782,504,898	5,812,949	45,733	0	862,809,676
TOTAL	4,467,717,085	117,057,845	149,623,075	110,468,479	55,845,424	350,758,318	16,439,491	78,529,773	49,552,644	14,643,974,612	136,374,625	7,505,249	4,076,380	20,187,922,999
MINNESOTA														
1	97,986,488	1,543,412	5,158,020	9,030,171	112,997	14,935,780	197,750	42,948,678	2,783,358	913,703,802	6,729,889	50,000	1,000	1,095,181,345
2	95,960,112	638,323	1,988,316	10,252,564	5,806,234	6,609,064	43,685	2,189,221	2,004,049	1,237,712,813	5,895,967	99,463	0	1,369,199,810
3	112,392,216	1,401,727	294,095	7,263,915	73,145	1,777,716	521,003	1,172,164	3,208,294	650,877,031	12,714,142	722,615	0	792,418,063
4	909,797,846	25,936,799	8,041,587	43,252,080	3,470,477	75,194,793	318,161	8,459,455	10,548,208	54,639,085	8,429,230	144,582	2,303,066	1,150,535,368
5	173,952,499	12,796,586	3,485,821	35,555,776	1,623,749	89,626,261	822,738	17,193,704	4,240,317	744,955,597	11,319,892	235,660	160,000	1,095,968,600
6	228,158,711	725,718	65,579	6,536,437	-4,782	1,895,522	0	4,669,107	986,025	1,236,997,414	6,585,128	49,562	0	1,486,664,422
7	165,379,908	4,295,188	14,415,014	12,120,534	6,352,946	21,008,458	7,396,782	7,773,623	5,543,369	971,968,454	6,634,011	0	2,798,187	1,225,686,474
8	172,375,460	3,357,931	9,261,203	13,539,170	3,039,989	11,851,163	7,795,556	4,105,835	2,105,727	871,020,406	7,137,450	0	0	1,105,589,890
TOTAL	1,956,003,240	50,695,685	42,709,635	137,550,647	20,474,754	222,898,756	17,095,675	88,511,787	31,419,348	6,681,874,601	65,445,708	1,301,882	5,262,253	9,321,243,972
MISSISSIPPI														
1	101,422,067	2,603,002	4,592,825	12,169,593	2,901,666	10,881,380	0	10,487,103	2,896,603	834,367,763	6,474,225	195,622	0	988,991,849
2	141,182,001	4,280,512	415,384	21,709,172	10,118,901	19,019,865	0	12,635,349	393,236	886,172,187	14,229,947	0	1,756,393	1,111,912,947
3	99,185,390	4,923,682	6,002,879	17,159,895	7,063,259	26,047,286	14,935,677	7,339,571	2,200,084	766,428,805	6,781,121	0	0	958,067,650
4	1,093,695,002	24,715,677	1,012,666	20,851,849	669,237	20,353,957	0	26,071,759	6,108,200	790,393,865	18,847,699	138,674	1,535,854	2,004,394,439
5	56,102,611	5,803,926	4,974,068	12,617,853	10,499,802	15,604,585	0	6,763,522	2,973,805	734,078,330	9,308,601	0	43,400	858,770,503
TOTAL	1,491,587,071	42,326,799	16,997,822	84,508,362	31,252,865	91,907,073	14,935,677	63,297,304	14,571,928	4,011,440,951	55,641,593	334,296	3,335,647	5,922,137,388
MISSOURI														
1	86,493,900	2,404,194	23,580,087	25,281,348	271,066	3,517,969	0	26,149,538	128,299,110	1,338,172,883	15,969,956	259,433	149,497,575	1,799,897,059
2	90,601,365	752,434	16,720,753	20,476,695	519,803	2,550,042	0	4,652,423	4,767,346	994,389,885	14,247,808	75,881	0	1,149,754,434
3	42,271,448	1,695,178	7,835,497	7,359,004	90,810	1,109,140	0	4,889,276	2,118,299	363,666,644	14,217,088	530,733	0	445,783,118
4	1,049,737,284	1,894,704	5,422,325	12,035,419	15,026,130	3,672,809	0	4,208,634	378,986	948,633,649	7,035,253	0	2,969,652	2,051,014,846
5	70,182,054	0	19,261,300	17,947,060	1,104,111	1,844,053	0	10,543,356	0	926,289,870	16,734,516	315,723	265,800	1,064,487,844
6	55,139,419	3,869,877	12,708,866	9,862,791	3,061,081	12,639,212	609,167	7,370,783	15,491,051	966,987,145	9,531,566	74,192	0	1,097,345,151
7	87,388,437	832,770	15,668,759	6,684,677	1,542,951	7,674,328	138,411	2,611,742	8,730,380	1,005,515,163	4,360,630	0	0	1,141,148,248
8	147,859,543	2,149,033	12,746,255	12,291,144	2,604,324	10,499,109	0	6,661,949	0	1,080,111,179	7,092,600	144,974	10,000	1,282,170,111
9	217,808,039	58,793,927	5,035,286	14,461,165	1,870,388	45,649,596	0	6,851,459	5,345,049	942,393,729	7,212,762	45,738	0	1,305,467,138
TOTAL	1,847,481,490	72,392,116	118,979,128	126,399,303	26,090,665	89,156,258	747,578	73,939,160	165,130,221	8,566,160,149	96,402,179	1,446,674	152,743,027	11,337,067,948
MONTANA														
1	353,390,851	15,236,293	6,010,978	23,267,782	11,477,319	27,065,831	10,494,146	5,080,644	2,339,373	642,882,600	7,193,541	147,096	1,462,134	1,106,048,588
2	69,041,395	8,407,279	5,614,823	9,287,456	28,370,861	4,823,492	16,618,995	3,642,328	2,647,737	930,923,121	9,548,150	43,780	-22,756	1,088,946,661
TOTAL	422,432,246	23,643,572	11,625,801	32,555,238	39,848,180	31,889,323	27,113,141	8,722,972	4,987,110	1,573,805,721	16,741,691	190,876	1,439,378	2,194,995,249
NEBRASKA														
1	386,524,179	10,943,279	3,337,495	14,167,994	7,958,469	31,771,141	7,555,152	3,471,150	4,853,883	1,073,704,194	8,495,757	16,358	281,104	1,553,080,155
2	86,434,462	2,035,186	4,558,951	26,409,268	17,817,168	18,465,500	278,140	5,035,381	8,651,992	772,244,625	9,707,269	400,526	74,300	952,112,768
3	69,288,891	2,608,257	4,953,071	7,554,341	3,296,221	8,787,021	0	2,019,252	816,202	1,358,822,932	11,130,030	0	865,467	1,470,141,685
TOTAL	542,247,532	15,586,722	12,849,517	48,131,603	29,071,858	59,023,662	7,833,292	10,525,783	14,322,077	3,204,771,751	29,333,056	416,884	1,220,871	3,975,334,608

See Appendix A for a listing of the congressional districts which represent the county in which the state capital is located and congressional districts which represent only portions of a county. See Appendix B for a listing of the programs included in each recipent category.

table continues

Table 3.7

Federal Outlays to Categories of Recipients by Congressional District, 1989 *(continued)*

District	State Gov't.	Counties	Cities/ Towns	Special Districts	Schools	Public Universities	Indian Tribes	Non-Profits	Private Universities	Individuals	For Profits	Small Businesses	All Others	Total
NEVADA														
1	50,533,124	30,408,387	12,205,584	23,857,861	2,760,706	5,903,643	708,396	1,404,199	0	741,555,386	17,956,364	126,000	3,613,194	891,032,844
2	273,319,186	10,616,653	7,117,104	18,957,743	3,356,546	17,554,772	9,066,684	4,633,598	105,030	645,507,726	6,233,734	29,388	436,332	996,934,496
TOTAL	323,852,310	41,025,040	19,322,688	42,815,604	6,117,252	23,458,415	9,775,080	6,037,797	105,030	1,387,063,112	24,190,098	155,388	4,049,526	1,887,967,340
NEW HAMPSHIRE														
1	65,549,340	1,455,585	15,367,053	15,120,072	83,664	18,822,352	0	2,252,682	3,336,383	675,835,247	6,231,805	812,247	42,000	804,908,430
2	270,292,379	7,576,335	9,067,567	9,065,460	194,749	4,044,635	0	4,116,113	28,507,106	716,176,411	8,674,724	879,018	-16,334	1,058,578,163
TOTAL	335,841,719	9,031,920	24,434,620	24,185,532	278,413	22,866,987	0	6,368,795	31,843,489	1,392,011,658	14,906,529	1,691,265	25,666	1,863,486,593
NEW JERSEY														
1	106,801,511	2,694,878	4,924,664	30,277,155	26,961	4,539,886	0	4,001,208	0	753,945,966	9,934,040	40,507	0	917,186,775
2	137,768,082	1,852,468	6,972,775	31,797,863	2,703	4,719,488	0	5,901,022	0	1,147,170,253	12,693,527	0	307,660	1,349,185,841
3	83,464,188	1,052,664	4,443,240	26,086,119	4,623,737	758,899	0	3,939,342	1,504,501	1,006,218,977	7,432,667	0	0	1,139,524,333
4	1,596,772,923	37,257,163	76,299,435	18,964,915	71,031	3,231,149	84,495	3,938,342	1,705,001	829,214,848	9,045,524	89,326	60,000	2,576,734,152
5	46,311,132	1,421,493	4,180,857	6,946,765	252	487,427	0	753,421	163,052	743,602,348	7,678,039	186,816	0	811,731,603
6	68,649,211	3,924,232	568,568	19,677,330	-3,754	37,207,259	0	2,897,646	57,675	804,649,151	6,218,788	98,624	0	943,944,731
7	86,230,431	756,197	8,174,585	13,582,664	30,789	2,547,031	0	2,057,208	1,548,106	881,769,605	6,852,859	0	15,000	1,003,564,474
8	113,846,900	2,199,167	3,204,841	33,662,509	28,919	4,176,618	0	4,353,427	1,574,526	819,845,420	11,814,544	12,388	0	994,719,259
9	39,943,875	1,425,441	141,482	18,166,146	19,979	749,083	0	1,279,274	6,399,757	920,900,366	8,401,707	235,561	0	997,662,670
10	224,992,707	5,180,027	2,976,662	169,816,182	0	25,252,474	0	18,132,035	1,437,515	826,132,413	32,352,866	2,883,928	50,000	1,309,206,810
11	164,014,383	1,631,166	673,203	7,985,095	2,633	1,903,548	0	277,227	4,414,432	805,694,806	5,177,512	406,063	0	992,180,067
12	61,017,163	10,069,859	3,167,032	14,592,164	17,584	39,257,579	0	16,619,332	41,335,842	830,710,627	8,547,408	1,731,638	889,489	1,027,955,717
13	79,691,377	5,056,929	3,799,777	6,812,982	7,013,023	691,606	291,671	218,871	46,076	1,049,950,613	5,112,338	239,241	0	1,158,924,503
14	208,190,390	3,547,307	10,151,470	44,229,407	-2,239	3,099,051	0	5,456,007	3,227,370	804,213,279	24,943,743	0	0	1,107,055,786
TOTAL	3,017,694,273	78,068,991	129,678,590	442,597,298	11,831,619	128,621,097	376,166	69,824,362	63,413,852	12,224,018,672	156,205,562	5,924,091	1,322,149	16,329,576,722
NEW MEXICO														
1	84,174,610	6,420,799	15,754,555	10,663,531	3,594,473	32,370,376	3,693,379	5,732,574	53,000	615,295,631	8,082,374	963,756	2,948,498	789,747,556
2	75,246,484	3,278,008	7,690,267	12,092,002	7,099,213	27,624,113	2,233,548	2,960,277	316,288	724,851,093	8,060,000	50,000	124,761	871,626,054
3	577,723,049	23,749,724	8,690,803	9,558,583	56,344,441	8,108,570	16,594,866	10,740,613	1,714,889	546,243,353	6,064,878	211,905	519,994	1,266,265,668
TOTAL	737,144,143	33,448,531	32,135,625	32,314,116	67,038,127	68,103,059	22,521,793	19,433,464	2,084,177	1,886,390,077	22,207,252	1,225,661	3,593,253	2,927,639,278
NEW YORK														
1	115,932,055	4,805,204	381,910	401,797,615	68,399	41,252,965	0	12,545,836	501,307	581,817,573	6,349,571	50,000	0	1,165,502,435
2	115,748,186	1,396,683	4,985,710	12,389,099	28,348	1,864,515	0	919,305	547,660	580,784,070	2,133,519	0	0	720,797,096
3	163,917,952	3,503,210	15,580,206	37,732,863	14,664	3,106,458	0	4,835,230	6,065,915	1,032,097,626	19,566,402	816,906	10,538,525	1,297,775,958
4	94,208,484	164,571	5,475,269	5,288,376	47,508	843,390	0	394,298	3,739,410	877,522,570	4,128,958	0	0	991,812,834
5	93,440,372	4,049,410	5,763,099	9,967,624	197,698	3,108,829	0	5,791,820	9,438,134	869,295,096	11,125,154	0	0	1,012,177,237
6	187,797,927	1,189,709	-1,036,194	4,546,140	12,580	622,543	0	5,915,289	2,653,328	886,803,595	16,978,978	0	0	1,105,483,896
7	188,563,837	1,566,606	56,572	162,591	0	164,092	0	5,602,024	2,913,194	890,439,590	8,087,293	0	0	1,097,555,799
8	227,215,237	1,719,802	516,850	13,448,514	-4,979	1,002,673	0	6,154,761	6,568,098	875,054,477	14,425,997	0	119,000	1,146,220,430
9	187,543,174	1,348,095	5,713	107,518	0	134,361	0	4,978,160	2,558,186	885,640,937	12,747,450	0	0	1,095,063,594
10	291,602,679	9,085,328	63,363,154	42,223,297	0	257,091	0	6,528,618	4,997,549	826,653,798	5,857,051	49,470	0	1,250,618,033
11	292,769,655	7,729,021	64,252,688	38,975,397	0	259,608	0	8,916,463	5,133,143	834,812,850	23,400,931	0	0	1,276,249,756
12	298,231,069	11,790,048	64,064,306	37,452,337	0	16,577,525	0	6,695,660	4,990,503	832,783,174	35,717,939	0	0	1,308,302,560
13	294,670,678	7,855,979	64,426,566	30,637,102	0	261,954	0	9,183,169	6,537,975	835,947,135	15,266,673	119,470	80,000	1,264,986,699
14	183,127,679	2,827,783	60,642,153	10,532,360	8,800	281,148	0	7,244,721	2,737,301	826,533,941	14,751,872	0	0	1,108,687,759
15	1,170,275,455	12,957,919	114,679,766	199,045,846	0	22,291,252	0	210,076,399	195,154,971	950,635,331	35,799,261	747,136	4,214,584	2,915,877,920
16	1,169,970,755	8,513,924	20,557,742	48,154,045	0	23,588,661	766,961	22,123,477	56,846,170	949,005,702	71,980,632	0	4,114,552	2,375,622,621
17	1,002,927,960	5,723,727	16,539,832	36,995,285	0	16,577,244	0	72,508,263	103,819,456	932,616,897	63,373,376	1,587,585	3,783,488	2,256,453,113

18	354,618,626	3,111,233	552,074	65,710,290	66,000	1,656,015	0	9,593,847	14,620,395	876,176,798	124,288,402	0	0	1,450,393,681
19	295,272,426	3,013,914	1,830,858	84,514,023	0	1,366,695	0	17,183,392	8,771,341	872,166,821	30,111,736	112,043	0	1,314,343,249
20	171,482,537	5,504,213	6,970,080	59,320,978	0	597,581	0	11,038,724	25,586,474	906,804,769	16,052,321	1,348,377	5,000	1,204,711,054
21	140,297,913	4,389,333	5,418,294	11,605,812	234,311	1,926,381	0	5,859,843	5,326,527	780,410,991	6,015,378	310,000	0	961,794,783
22	166,739,936	2,423,790	2,384,789	14,998,203	694,179	3,469,713	0	6,670,072	13,331,613	769,948,652	17,470,538	306,157	0	998,437,642
23	4,483,804,293	186,287,299	11,705,147	22,373,250	8,609	65,465,434	0	26,671,296	22,428,020	905,123,521	17,368,094	49,958	4,549,357	5,745,834,277
24	126,468,610	4,344,807	1,240,001	9,350,320	-2,350	4,119,052	0	6,360,878	3,561,548	821,484,182	6,579,581	0	24,300	983,530,929
25	171,564,040	7,028,957	6,396,824	13,889,569	67,899	12,459,585	50,000	7,316,909	7,136,106	846,211,190	5,552,974	142,996	0	1,077,817,048
26	187,658,158	11,978,654	19,201,537	12,479,162	2,400,406	6,847,296	2,579,061	7,298,617	6,788,058	811,591,437	10,606,937	111,294	0	1,079,540,617
27	146,788,610	4,702,359	11,927,632	22,995,109	0	14,077,851	0	6,339,311	23,432,557	768,590,115	8,486,395	199,200	172,946	1,007,712,085
28	150,917,154	15,510,346	4,801,077	13,981,893	108,473	45,995,396	0	2,445,334	79,941,958	828,819,498	6,270,443	528,151	182,940	1,149,502,664
29	165,476,293	4,927,473	4,528,113	14,129,064	116,048	3,118,996	71,271	9,190,192	5,881,320	787,248,050	5,433,519	1,415,672	485,347	1,002,021,358
30	170,916,831	6,181,069	17,585,500	8,224,145	0	7,467,232	390,893	19,451,033	107,942,276	792,223,446	6,548,600	298,241	1,139,494	1,138,368,758
31	177,549,185	5,055,110	6,569,080	11,880,092	8,974	8,535,632	590,244	2,575,417	4,512,976	829,249,960	8,931,973	358,653	0	1,055,817,296
32	180,349,586	7,688,191	6,796,314	20,748,936	-65,238	27,810,340	78,782	16,853,325	6,042,975	849,774,447	8,741,921	800,431	335,016	1,125,955,027
33	205,500,523	9,622,558	6,554,072	11,106,190	24,859	4,260,985	117,075	4,060,364	6,066,962	856,680,924	12,184,428	2,436,742	56,790	1,118,672,472
34	172,656,001	13,024,451	5,971,596	9,430,980	133,440	4,958,730	4,803,936	4,058,957	6,879,289	888,244,283	8,806,304	99,887	133,500	1,119,201,354
TOTAL	13,546,003,876	381,020,777	620,688,331	1,336,194,026	4,168,628	346,327,221	9,448,223	553,381,003	763,452,695	28,659,193,447	661,140,597	11,888,369	29,934,839	46,922,842,032
NORTH CAROLINA														
1	133,123,272	6,995,010	1,543,912	27,275,224	46,000	8,548,569	0	4,826,162	2,601,663	823,576,431	8,380,434	0	0	1,016,916,677
2	142,780,135	10,438,885	4,055,676	27,197,719	0	12,663,507	303,843	58,038,955	111,102,573	796,772,417	12,817,035	1,641,356	0	1,177,812,101
3	121,312,062	8,898,048	3,051,042	17,435,238	296,826	1,364,719	204,735	4,093,619	1,757,649	693,592,966	9,136,294	0	0	861,143,199
4	1,429,850,308	39,385,614	6,446,749	21,082,685	94,000	156,507,931	661,405	5,804,967	12,601,321	689,802,730	8,526,205	312,995	9,177,218	2,380,254,128
5	91,557,503	2,579,041	1,939,383	15,631,230	-10,283	4,470,114	0	32,249,450	3,580,541	785,108,739	6,655,637	721,490	0	944,482,845
6	63,041,007	3,366,577	2,177,215	16,370,841	0	19,077,487	92,977	2,941,457	3,900,129	784,191,947	9,358,952	49,863	3,101,240	907,669,692
7	122,296,887	10,600,225	4,389,430	23,055,998	0	9,661,408	1,770,936	3,553,468	2,059,853	681,435,107	8,055,503	0	442,795	867,321,610
8	83,581,429	1,921,608	2,081,459	13,437,853	0	1,843,390	0	5,643,027	4,403,147	823,682,199	6,442,142	0	0	943,036,253
9	66,988,829	3,313,099	21,738,375	17,693,123	0	5,493,846	110,941	2,241,077	5,438,090	727,588,265	7,729,044	53,454	0	858,388,143
10	69,593,729	3,268,639	3,463,779	12,360,262	0	5,009,273	0	2,298,954	2,869,851	747,309,115	7,389,784	0	0	853,563,385
11	99,435,418	5,494,087	1,213,705	17,680,301	3,000	4,979,743	4,377,828	3,945,045	2,844,986	969,421,278	4,266,882	4,621	3,122,230	1,116,789,125
TOTAL	2,423,560,580	96,260,833	52,100,725	209,220,473	429,543	229,619,987	7,522,665	125,636,181	153,159,803	8,522,481,194	88,757,912	2,783,779	15,843,483	11,927,377,158
NORTH DAKOTA														
TOTAL	379,095,663	12,366,416	14,886,861	35,927,571	11,633,332	50,770,283	20,914,184	3,906,129	5,335,494	1,623,105,405	7,775,797	217,098	-273,153	2,165,661,080
OHIO														
1	152,870,066	759,709	9,224,792	23,692,107	352,642	45,018,660	0	14,616,343	3,850,569	891,819,710	25,357,737	159,616	266,790	1,167,988,742
2	113,665,732	796,657	7,167,255	13,599,334	209,355	11,185,207	0	2,673,936	3,542,482	724,801,979	15,905,238	0	0	893,547,175
3	120,507,712	4,107,301	11,914,309	14,740,968	565,760	5,408,450	0	4,396,508	411,128	765,664,695	13,986,734	611,641	354,150	942,669,355
4	82,769,276	1,380,969	386,505	8,776,877	344,768	1,529,267	0	2,806,086	5,979,139	847,274,086	7,984,610	0	51,545	959,283,128
5	56,974,758	1,028,386	6,499,229	6,274,295	104,612	8,779,006	0	4,297,402	2,213,171	790,833,249	6,369,919	3,262,013	48,694	886,684,734
6	178,438,556	3,243,714	8,839,579	11,769,104	936,128	1,390,409	0	7,880,541	1,905,264	794,268,737	12,277,690	0	0	1,020,949,721
7	101,289,000	5,401,722	827,923	11,349,310	5,473,385	13,118,216	0	5,803,822	12,505,004	724,744,590	24,935,269	0	36,190	905,484,432
8	76,899,385	127,989	3,032,594	8,877,046	32,263	5,046,694	0	2,976,429	12,559	728,518,493	7,089,090	0	35,686	832,648,228
9	125,932,421	1,171,987	12,331,497	25,423,004	214,997	15,978,856	40,501	4,556,628	509,660	847,096,456	21,754,657	366,673	572,170	1,055,949,507
10	452,419,770	58,786,561	7,469,830	12,695,204	1,782,261	34,437,481	0	6,299,043	13,072,547	756,251,671	15,235,638	67,825	884,079	1,359,401,910
11	53,377,640	1,280,160	4,493,153	34,856,145	630,279	20,642,533	0	2,111,620	1,738,447	691,277,122	5,658,313	0	529,652	816,595,065
12	1,559,657,884	885,165	10,104,938	20,265,115	7,076	7,683,680	0	7,150,521	3,364,379	673,662,671	13,298,922	466,871	2,195,113	2,298,742,334
13	69,503,220	600,942	2,937,392	16,289,816	1,465,080	418,502	0	3,308,192	4,635,511	720,961,143	11,686,462	2,080	1,264,389	833,072,728
14	105,358,876	1,470,384	6,596,903	36,088,145	381,047	13,633,097	708,514	5,194,752	0	821,395,755	8,003,694	0	223,825	999,054,993
15	991,533,699	56,820	685,250	21,607,746	176,166	25,431,849	0	7,335,635	51,424	695,305,851	12,193,565	38,265	1,684,797	1,756,101,067

See Appendix A for a listing of the congressional districts which represent the county in which the state capital is located and congressional districts which represent only portions of a county. See Appendix B for a listing of the programs included in each recipent category.

table continues

Table 3.7 Federal Outlays to Categories of Recipients by Congressional District, 1989 *(continued)*

District	State Gov't.	Counties	Cities/ Towns	Special Districts	Schools	Public Universities	Indian Tribes	Non-Profits	Private Universities	Individuals	For Profits	Small Businesses	All Others	Total
OHIO *continued*														
16	81,132,735	-1,639,513	622,401	15,197,557	168,086	6,969,163	0	694,584	2,975,035	801,028,248	10,299,410	0	34,120	917,481,826
17	113,479,690	-2,176,149	5,884,759	21,027,521	478,358	6,053,493	0	2,169,182	1,761,546	915,813,839	8,928,654	0	69,400	1,073,490,292
18	107,899,696	2,152,173	4,309,464	12,491,174	389,538	50,750	0	3,527,210	1,318,070	889,263,330	9,772,645	0	27,915	1,031,201,965
19	124,996,934	715,039	9,306,789	22,493,603	2,717,353	1,635,380	23,719	646,670	3,368,280	934,874,889	7,148,912	367,983	213,270	1,108,508,823
20	132,504,049	2,166,607	28,909,978	25,833,270	2,831,938	6,642,415	25,899	3,338,254	4,446,843	950,887,812	14,867,728	89,580	305,390	1,172,849,762
21	135,529,842	3,900,687	27,102,749	26,311,648	2,851,708	2,744,520	25,956	14,744,374	73,974,416	952,909,831	29,022,413	362,624	1,500	1,269,482,267
TOTAL	4,936,740,942	86,217,311	168,647,289	389,658,988	22,112,800	233,797,628	824,589	106,527,732	141,635,474	16,918,654,156	281,777,300	5,795,171	8,798,675	23,301,188,055
OKLAHOMA														
1	71,429,755	1,912,155	12,975,814	23,557,783	1,866,287	4,775,670	4,018,335	5,102,177	10,655,573	779,963,449	15,335,654	153,331	60,000	931,805,983
2	148,963,360	10,485,056	4,206,523	13,625,041	11,608,457	16,481,947	34,417,417	6,496,208	1,361,566	845,330,166	6,193,642	0	0	1,099,169,383
3	168,775,432	21,772,865	16,794,725	13,054,542	11,744,164	34,779,759	18,981,332	8,554,681	1,777,558	880,250,051	4,619,530	49,960	0	1,181,154,599
4	138,341,191	6,946,303	3,879,129	5,893,057	15,221,987	33,310,678	5,461,296	7,523,821	999,176	706,228,619	7,448,904	123,825	1,302,809	932,680,796
5	619,613,846	3,885,500	11,997,924	17,656,870	2,171,205	12,756,529	4,874,077	8,565,990	2,566,779	753,961,528	11,821,798	1,372	394,423	1,450,267,841
6	267,259,107	4,771,379	8,206,865	6,126,241	5,469,403	7,904,435	6,181,287	1,065,002	2,372,969	884,590,256	6,668,689	132,306	189,020	1,200,936,958
TOTAL	1,414,382,690	49,773,258	58,060,980	79,913,534	48,081,504	110,009,018	73,933,744	37,307,879	19,733,621	4,850,324,070	52,088,217	460,794	1,946,252	6,796,015,559
OREGON														
1	88,510,255	12,354,961	15,181,284	15,653,040	463,061	5,824,387	2,463,620	21,526,494	7,744,068	799,263,605	3,217,843	682,263	5,890	972,890,771
2	88,035,558	3,691,625	8,361,993	15,008,246	10,689,845	6,575,487	6,029,912	3,700,674	98,624	982,724,695	2,453,430	573,166	26,000	1,127,969,255
3	134,106,343	7,877,739	3,874,315	25,514,664	3,103,563	55,582,086	0	5,903,003	3,058,882	974,888,320	7,760,705	0	31,097	1,221,700,719
4	97,157,439	11,460,362	9,854,856	15,272,930	6,532,272	25,916,559	235,038	7,357,698	337,331	844,905,413	3,790,061	1,239,395	27,500	1,024,086,855
5	864,883,104	41,213,768	9,141,541	19,031,624	8,553,839	61,868,769	15,880	2,858,665	8,582,527	792,541,368	6,603,456	333,543	1,002,583	1,816,630,669
TOTAL	1,272,692,699	76,598,455	46,413,989	90,480,505	29,342,581	155,767,289	8,744,450	41,346,534	19,821,432	4,394,323,401	23,825,496	2,828,367	1,093,070	6,163,278,268
PENNSYLVANIA														
1	234,754,486	3,399,942	30,631,008	132,429,390	793,474	8,154,200	52,013	51,590,753	143,685,291	1,071,356,821	10,456,152	1,993,464	2,258,654	1,691,555,648
2	240,851,409	3,972,657	15,448,661	35,324,587	696,261	27,586,443	52,222	21,373,595	39,198,973	1,075,491,300	26,668,613	2,299,503	142,817	1,489,107,040
3	234,421,355	2,178,831	8,948,566	37,127,252	694,833	6,631,090	52,115	25,864,442	7,338,796	1,072,991,056	12,688,751	233,592	439,507	1,409,610,186
4	98,320,533	2,759,716	874,807	14,475,786	73,335	9,592,356	0	2,319,596	831,182	943,485,371	7,750,329	49,750	-100,060	1,080,432,701
5	59,297,595	1,347,928	201,161	15,620,127	229,654	2,869,973	0	2,861,496	5,502,626	825,527,689	6,432,142	401,784	70,198	920,362,374
6	70,022,162	2,564,087	4,745,969	9,759,989	111,641	2,917,849	0	1,722,985	1,055,133	1,033,830,990	3,555,913	0	29,300	1,130,316,018
7	80,195,264	1,134,282	1,307,677	10,516,839	1,199,262	940,126	5,016	337,089	16,469,086	959,047,263	5,023,155	857,004	253,418	1,077,285,479
8	38,768,842	105,799	1,361,368	8,428,764	3,783,886	411,107	0	2,176,449	904,842	742,653,428	4,452,002	0	32,159	803,078,646
9	95,476,840	954,067	4,095,766	23,995,115	823,299	743,921	0	3,314,114	1,121,422	879,563,239	5,066,389	0	576,972	1,015,731,143
10	93,760,099	1,028,027	5,522,803	16,611,978	1,313,179	541,628	0	4,076,559	4,817,895	1,080,505,042	8,750,696	0	431,492	1,217,359,398
11	88,768,229	3,474,962	3,968,281	41,194,210	237,962	1,242,332	0	8,063,403	3,713,523	1,192,320,953	10,551,019	0	25,752	1,353,560,626
12	88,810,812	4,282,895	4,806,939	13,899,642	304,788	986,233	0	2,729,867	4,222,396	1,030,763,381	7,657,190	1,560	39,956	1,158,505,659
13	73,598,603	700,523	3,097,303	11,725,317	1,146,352	1,281,187	9,089	15,283,680	3,048,230	945,223,530	7,317,739	2,129,208	366,195	1,064,926,956
14	106,901,655	31,496,396	7,126,815	76,813,938	8,560,029	92,605,398	2,051,977	32,911,640	55,820,928	1,035,767,149	34,487,031	2,255,164	1,820,468	1,488,618,588
15	67,067,626	1,944,205	4,387,009	21,720,334	738,492	1,401,087	0	1,841,185	13,436,906	958,405,145	7,456,905	101,610	78,707	1,078,579,210
16	61,755,010	596,664	4,580,429	13,829,930	160,972	2,011,030	0	2,284,043	2,836,529	776,206,573	5,832,391	792,401	76,103	870,962,075
17	2,714,848,300	64,497,173	11,413,628	32,140,367	765,229	3,445,380	0	19,845,444	2,577,482	885,288,597	5,698,712	0	5,354,712	3,745,875,024
18	102,771,918	14,541	309,615	3,696,357	2,500	0	0	103,168	0	1,033,687,894	5,370,776	0	0	1,145,956,769
19	57,792,068	1,225,078	803,024	10,706,610	839,951	0	40,580	3,021,648	3,805,717	764,362,420	5,074,646	158,087	0	847,829,830
20	99,673,024	11,011	1,268,000	8,566,504	243,346	500,000	0	1,594,923	0	1,020,750,230	8,862,283	399,595	79,055	1,141,947,972
21	100,174,019	1,331,303	2,259,525	14,314,436	9,415	522,554	0	5,653,321	7,007,991	908,636,659	9,791,436	0	46,074	1,049,746,732
22	134,352,646	4,329,052	4,018,369	12,153,396	398,238	1,526,288	0	700,662	1,836,269	1,059,696,924	9,088,965	0	200,209	1,228,301,018
23	79,665,938	2,437,823	3,116,948	11,462,810	257,842	100,288,738	0	3,743,939	411,807	866,087,662	8,527,394	190,000	77,964	1,076,268,864
TOTAL	5,022,048,432	135,786,964	124,293,670	576,513,678	23,383,940	266,198,920	2,263,012	213,414,001	319,643,024	22,161,649,315	216,560,629	11,862,722	12,299,651	29,085,917,958

RHODE ISLAND														
1	385,524,021	6,831,232	2,224,079	29,333,210	73,337	2,187,522	226,784	19,793,666	34,248,342	821,488,167	11,867,310	311,653	405,097	1,314,514,421
2	257,332,555	5,361,197	2,456,023	15,740,440	0	23,850,133	1,267,469	8,391,698	4,711,332	809,476,482	5,925,387	0	141,026	1,134,653,741
TOTAL	642,856,576	12,192,429	4,680,102	45,073,650	73,337	26,037,655	1,494,253	28,185,364	38,959,674	1,630,964,649	17,792,697	311,653	546,123	2,449,168,162
SOUTH CAROLINA														
1	91,249,547	2,394,744	7,122,919	20,320,203	1,883,311	28,340,192	0	8,108,083	2,077,302	639,737,254	12,163,002	477,930	510	813,874,997
2	880,090,834	26,423,771	674,084	18,082,204	582,950	45,805,096	2,426	5,895,366	11,081,613	654,602,616	13,764,605	103,380	2,385,586	1,659,494,531
3	78,709,144	2,460,979	966,401	8,388,046	755,772	19,055,101	0	6,580,240	3,649,233	770,760,803	12,097,750	0	0	903,423,469
4	64,225,598	1,547,939	2,692,685	16,215,297	71,023	1,842,520	0	4,019,680	5,823,544	768,122,634	13,909,272	0	34,929	878,505,121
5	97,297,949	3,681,198	1,501,911	10,282,290	1,707,527	1,415,970	274,229	4,364,969	5,927,647	728,849,685	7,782,858	0	0	863,086,233
6	129,080,601	6,976,387	736,615	11,430,631	5,404,928	1,999,443	0	6,840,089	2,668,933	744,068,589	8,398,662	0	0	917,604,878
TOTAL	1,340,653,673	43,485,018	13,694,615	84,718,671	10,405,511	98,458,322	276,655	35,808,427	31,228,272	4,306,141,581	68,116,149	581,310	2,421,025	6,035,989,229
SOUTH DAKOTA														
TOTAL	365,557,649	12,537,593	18,874,576	22,611,184	29,406,571	31,499,338	38,969,959	6,317,864	9,787,283	1,493,327,585	9,292,210	997,163	375,152	2,039,554,127
TENNESSEE														
1	105,428,540	2,315,482	4,915,922	12,022,481	195,033	9,278,407	0	2,349,710	3,333,785	808,711,444	9,708,142	0	31,000	958,289,946
2	89,806,875	6,826,841	7,614,078	21,573,494	0	35,381,078	55,315	3,627,148	6,628,943	807,886,076	14,809,288	433,855	18,000	994,660,991
3	96,932,477	1,335,229	3,855,137	17,820,923	100,116	4,869,264	0	3,866,130	7,130,336	825,368,296	11,120,362	893,965	1,111,639	974,403,874
4	132,623,184	1,522,844	5,497,622	16,142,217	136,698	3,254,369	0	7,914,917	3,320,296	849,493,950	6,807,056	307,718	0	1,027,020,871
5	1,291,232,651	63,153,526	4,130,479	38,610,026	1,142	14,476,695	345,638	63,243,155	25,651,150	769,547,916	23,713,829	0	2,491,515	2,296,597,722
6	91,757,855	1,500,933	7,027,835	8,938,370	10,950	8,005,248	0	7,211,073	232,727	732,309,326	13,694,022	0	0	870,688,339
7	127,738,358	3,237,759	2,294,501	16,538,370	8,969	5,479,628	0	2,454,055	2,645,933	726,345,039	11,948,742	49,312	0	898,740,665
8	135,239,763	840,991	2,861,793	14,627,533	181,523	7,585,006	0	14,265,952	4,408,073	875,751,685	22,287,796	0	0	1,078,050,116
9	124,592,505	4,787,948	1,776,729	33,233,357	0	28,597,468	0	5,642,341	3,562,617	713,111,806	11,032,683	49,950	0	926,387,405
TOTAL	2,195,352,208	85,521,553	39,974,096	179,506,772	634,431	116,927,163	400,953	110,574,481	56,913,860	7,108,525,538	125,121,920	1,734,800	3,652,154	10,024,839,929
TEXAS														
1	103,602,458	1,878,220	6,391,101	13,563,512	3,957,538	1,693,211	354,005	850,212	2,384,824	988,909,471	6,196,064	0	0	1,129,780,617
2	80,758,127	1,119,354	2,348,089	13,443,851	348,928	8,593,711	1,998,517	1,630,976	38,474	940,532,684	11,571,632	0	5,895,244	1,068,279,587
3	40,736,527	470,042	13,881,590	10,256,105	486,759	3,643,212	84,960	684,605	4,006,972	645,474,405	13,762,971	221,915	-3,857	733,706,206
4	64,369,802	885,624	7,929,649	16,190,243	5,392,935	5,229,191	0	800,979	5,151,884	1,012,876,675	13,005,462	50,000	206,528	1,132,088,972
5	40,950,112	1,708,916	21,924,150	10,181,910	153,826	53,455,200	89,042	6,949,664	4,866,535	650,250,576	7,689,341	1,055,397	-4,042	799,270,626
6	75,356,674	1,545,400	11,280,054	12,038,794	58,248	60,389,548	34,343	1,404,394	2,477,175	893,844,888	9,326,709	344,090	522,937	1,068,623,253
7	46,413,664	1,474,304	979,207	33,398,177	302,633	30,382,160	0	1,389,497	87,156	569,291,242	6,447,237	1,988,379	970,000	693,123,656
8	46,349,857	-192	1,869,606	11,042,829	328,426	170,670	0	1,070,013	140,941	570,035,047	8,452,660	91,974	0	639,551,831
9	59,008,277	2,692,891	9,910,562	21,244,715	1,099,538	37,256,780	0	227,268	1,241,121	826,006,210	17,511,899	773,700	40,000	977,012,962
10	4,341,147,982	9,922,103	17,073,475	25,776,443	5,029,441	71,824,508	0	13,791,875	2,405,053	685,788,107	11,746,417	640,120	3,764,539	5,188,910,063
11	167,302,456	985,072	11,037,648	17,770,462	19,254,348	2,871,268	0	2,950,327	7,574,365	827,785,170	10,583,903	69,856	0	1,068,184,875
12	37,431,685	3,866,262	30,043,467	10,570,937	2,390,011	6,564,949	0	360,800	2,040,829	692,750,555	18,116,493	180,000	870,000	805,185,988
13	38,831,434	844,605	9,722,920	13,127,634	3,980,261	4,622,122	0	2,324,180	0	1,070,074,430	10,787,783	22,373	24,430	1,154,362,172
14	79,323,050	2,370,011	6,470,292	12,438,959	2,066,013	13,230,518	0	2,102,780	1,285,343	957,120,979	8,513,147	0	0	1,084,921,092
15	150,046,237	8,385,785	13,332,709	24,068,818	1,614,107	13,105,241	0	5,175,603	76,542	748,109,832	15,861,699	99,330	22,463	979,898,367
16	76,603,352	2,561,655	21,952,829	31,595,130	17,175,331	13,409,426	531,034	4,232,432	537,462	637,917,687	13,100,092	0	60,200	819,676,630
17	56,269,071	732,534	2,845,887	11,846,404	3,899,655	2,173,702	0	2,620,315	4,015,388	1,109,240,644	5,549,053	17,098	0	1,199,209,752
18	46,377,611	0	5,787,461	9,591,981	377,019	15,801,474	0	11,234,948	74,747,599	569,614,581	6,778,714	428,340	0	740,739,728
19	46,875,037	1,166,860	14,155,148	8,863,179	3,637,243	17,159,521	0	5,472,770	2,030,125	972,267,343	9,059,743	0	0	1,080,686,969
20	77,255,526	1,711,964	21,666,209	36,430,537	10,379,489	6,470,624	0	18,423,308	6,004,322	706,713,590	15,078,858	117,558	317,655	900,569,640
21	50,232,787	5,305,893	19,569,925	10,131,229	5,764,625	2,832,299	0	1,016,830	1,734,741	866,188,227	15,899,296	97,568	46,300	978,819,720

See Appendix A for a listing of the congressional districts which represent the county in which the state capital is located and congressional districts which represent only portions of a county. See Appendix B for a listing of the programs included in each recipent category.

table continues

Table 3.7 **Federal Outlays to Categories of Recipients by Congressional District, 1989 *(continued)***

District	State Gov't.	Counties	Cities/ Towns	Special Districts	Schools	Public Universities	Indian Tribes	Non-Profits	Private Universities	Individuals	For Profits	Small Businesses	All Others	Total
TEXAS *continued*														
22	36,398,178	6,215,108	66,023,698	9,000,224	1,332,339	27,248,090	0	626,440	4,774,737	547,044,671	26,932,932	348,641	0	725,945,058
23	115,730,619	8,944,129	22,682,992	27,814,719	11,772,184	39,160,174	38,411	18,080,361	2,764,892	766,982,858	13,417,086	50,000	0	1,027,438,427
24	40,644,566	109,582	15,246,052	34,629,371	428,288	1,191,009	591,756	534,453	1,968,641	653,684,394	8,530,301	150,000	221,307	757,929,721
25	74,873,097	0	801,605	8,353,597	550,388	1,353,479	0	1,968,579	1,918,043	568,208,160	643,132	138,252	0	658,808,332
26	32,525,198	2,368,688	5,650,092	18,184,134	2,117,481	14,446,538	0	266,443	5,396,775	637,804,118	14,114,417	971,752	0	733,845,655
27	111,012,369	2,641,314	21,420,436	16,233,408	5,892,141	11,214,196	0	10,330,057	0	713,431,387	9,680,722	-299	0	901,855,732
TOTAL	6,136,425,753	69,906,125	381,996,853	467,787,304	109,789,196	465,492,839	3,722,067	116,520,109	139,669,939	20,827,947,932	308,357,765	7,856,044	12,953,704	29,048,425,630
UTAH														
1	64,630,673	4,621,297	4,566,395	9,546,763	6,150,186	35,111,367	4,209,728	1,580,178	1,068,354	552,116,766	9,069,660	58,451	167,602	692,897,420
2	538,659,483	4,153,948	7,925,755	24,605,384	828,190	74,394,552	19,987	9,870,207	1,080,891	545,021,073	9,277,392	3,086,490	770,027	1,219,693,379
3	74,443,937	2,409,563	7,443,127	10,236,566	5,009,964	6,593,319	1,612,601	2,069,517	22,770,669	521,041,840	2,886,393	200,073	21,600	656,739,169
TOTAL	677,734,093	11,184,808	19,935,277	44,388,713	11,988,340	116,099,238	5,842,316	13,519,902	24,919,914	1,618,179,679	21,233,445	3,345,014	959,229	2,569,329,968
VERMONT														
TOTAL	320,818,240	14,816,820	8,467,407	8,940,640	322,855	44,473,204	107,069	8,565,792	9,528,497	760,457,834	5,955,232	633,451	513,269	1,183,600,310
VIRGINIA														
1	71,970,308	12,052,465	14,479,447	13,429,060	0	8,326,246	233,978	5,982,006	9,413,016	778,525,221	12,309,012	85,826	1,213,737	928,020,322
2	63,885,221	662,404	26,454,294	29,180,647	0	19,023,711	0	7,889,348	3,275,955	583,956,521	11,184,450	0	432,256	745,944,807
3	1,127,733,434	28,906,215	11,822,678	12,891,224	0	50,002,083	0	3,618,080	2,655,467	840,811,115	12,383,652	133,630	2,226,809	2,093,184,387
4	108,073,114	4,718,946	11,034,900	9,702,800	0	13,333,654	0	2,131,030	874,650	781,200,786	8,069,700	0	338,655	939,478,234
5	100,869,310	469,939	1,331,884	4,466,676	12,441	1,689,085	0	3,874,018	3,949,155	814,584,188	4,494,595	-125	53,434	935,794,600
6	69,865,137	2,452,391	6,887,617	8,412,266	0	4,603,901	0	4,766,614	10,173,456	895,343,618	9,361,040	52,911	246,840	1,012,165,791
7	61,560,968	5,996,972	2,285,388	4,736,217	0	58,901,634	0	4,593,734	1,282,834	723,544,440	5,794,799	76,210	80,740	868,853,936
8	33,998,973	2,145,239	1,805,604	8,959,737	2,500	591,576	0	12,153,183	0	436,297,542	7,031,061	2,895,506	140,072	506,020,993
9	114,248,233	4,856,763	3,077,935	7,726,218	358,616	50,555,876	0	5,226,211	1,616,895	931,493,127	5,541,608	662,425	118,108	1,125,482,015
10	32,928,488	18,273,871	2,512,618	21,955,458	109,828	4,777,968	0	37,392,327	890,423	510,949,988	20,481,212	14,785,512	91,199,426	756,257,118
TOTAL	1,785,133,186	80,535,205	81,692,365	121,460,303	483,385	211,805,734	233,978	87,626,551	34,131,851	7,296,706,545	96,651,129	18,691,895	96,050,077	9,911,202,203
WASHINGTON														
1	101,210,517	3,049,106	9,132,640	58,947,887	1,618,183	7,171,079	592,181	8,716,513	2,665,019	755,563,455	8,118,770	1,876,139	747,889	959,409,377
2	99,823,786	4,712,657	4,739,611	21,209,574	8,594,276	7,010,487	10,501,517	1,213,400	0	906,449,557	9,185,931	0	6,000	1,073,446,795
3	1,424,727,574	25,786,735	4,519,029	12,547,955	996,597	8,185,283	1,570,826	1,659,212	545,052	829,604,044	7,820,186	440,081	1,060,864	2,319,463,440
4	115,757,373	5,008,140	3,205,891	10,400,581	9,748,886	9,357,007	14,826,665	21,836,224	620,170	804,828,132	8,488,396	1,291,476	651,945	1,006,020,886
5	115,251,986	3,903,720	4,264,612	14,560,160	5,047,866	49,547,716	1,823,167	2,948,889	8,899,043	877,205,173	8,646,893	642,756	42,800	1,092,784,782
6	121,569,725	2,719,497	-5,256,930	28,269,026	19,649,734	3,871,306	2,588,715	2,675,336	5,923,136	718,717,972	10,758,898	15,000	23,794	911,525,209
7	107,664,868	935,551,060	31,458,638	41,929,463	632,993	198,778,326	224,107	57,326,640	5,220,303	780,744,379	6,346,767	2,171,586	628,050	2,168,677,180
8	109,216,134	3,964,970	12,899,684	13,293,559	929,558	11,482,740	1,633,988	1,190,786	4,545,166	783,490,144	5,164,690	496,214	370,577	948,678,209
TOTAL	2,195,221,963	984,695,885	64,963,174	201,158,204	47,218,094	295,403,943	33,761,166	97,567,002	28,417,889	6,456,602,857	64,530,531	6,933,252	3,531,918	10,480,005,878
WEST VIRGINIA														
1	72,567,279	716,108	8,714,000	18,819,519	209,393	7,431,971	0	4,426,794	4,579,143	877,399,620	12,808,834	57,799	257,274	1,007,987,734
2	105,428,966	2,788,097	1,721,244	11,508,592	1,053,702	42,261,643	0	35,891,275	3,818,997	842,132,916	4,902,299	59,568	88,017	1,051,655,316
3	767,383,130	15,086,500	2,209,863	24,768,530	656,556	4,115,645	0	2,222,006	908,045	855,165,454	7,345,131	0	1,107,571	1,680,968,431
4	119,454,365	1,575,101	2,408,068	17,675,381	531,176	6,327,213	1,115,147	8,156,058	2,136,959	951,742,505	4,824,723	0	23,400	1,115,970,096
TOTAL	1,064,833,740	20,165,806	15,053,175	72,772,022	2,450,827	60,136,472	1,115,147	50,696,133	11,443,144	3,526,440,495	29,880,987	117,367	1,476,262	4,856,581,577

WISCONSIN														
1	125,756,228	2,960,780	7,094,551	7,851,245	1,399,842	7,654,486	0	1,571,073	1,673,038	866,113,969	6,407,130	0	822,310	1,029,304,651
2	1,076,568,190	57,599,305	13,730,709	11,172,651	3,399,177	174,523,724	640,198	5,848,013	442,836	821,211,708	8,220,391	358,537	3,001,644	2,176,717,084
3	142,062,070	3,167,647	3,455,968	4,226,642	1,110,515	21,095,267	862,672	3,481,304	953,671	965,509,914	6,221,770	0	0	1,152,147,440
4	161,947,578	9,524,902	5,268,004	114,163,988	43,649	5,081,858	0	7,363,605	5,196,800	890,028,391	12,970,277	75,797	7,075	1,211,671,925
5	191,555,933	9,575,616	2,328,532	13,960,295	623,146	11,678,322	1,623,462	8,769,053	27,217,580	948,319,710	12,976,688	178,595	8,951	1,228,815,883
6	108,966,651	532,707	2,376,182	4,425,141	3,590,963	6,281,467	219,089	1,309,648	2,779,523	941,504,037	6,205,984	49,592	0	1,078,240,984
7	143,894,325	3,856,725	5,559,298	7,136,333	3,994,429	21,048,688	5,558,906	8,485,393	2,343,879	966,160,925	7,476,401	0	176,150	1,175,691,453
8	112,968,879	7,741,332	12,591,968	17,752,695	209,448	3,205,895	14,737,210	3,449,756	1,740,356	892,215,531	6,056,705	50,000	0	1,072,719,774
9	68,670,540	4,072,618	3,330,052	3,495,579	795,440	348,966	0	209,912	3,214,864	773,963,037	6,412,064	0	22,957	864,536,027
TOTAL	2,132,390,395	99,031,632	55,735,264	184,184,570	15,166,608	250,918,672	23,641,537	40,487,757	45,562,546	8,065,027,221	72,947,409	712,521	4,039,087	10,989,845,220
WYOMING														
TOTAL	272,867,312	15,747,007	12,403,926	11,045,459	10,863,528	16,943,383	1,853,106	9,736,219	1,235,179	585,041,011	10,799,295	23,660	549,498	949,108,583
U.S. TOTAL	106,886.7 mil	4,358.1 mil	4,492.5 mil	9,804.4 mil	1,182.9 mil	7,495.0 mil	584.7 mil	4,008.9 mil	4,491.3 mil	370,844.9 mil	5,263.6 mil	242.0 mil	928.7 mil	520,583.7 mil

See Appendix A for a listing of the congressional districts which represent the county in which the state capital is located and congressional districts which represent only portions of a county. See Appendix B for a listing of the programs included in each recipent category.

Table 3.8 Federal Outlays to Categories of Recipients by Congressional District, 1990 est.

District	State Gov't.	Counties	Cities/ Towns	Special Districts	Schools	Public Universities	Indian Tribes	Non-Profits	Private Universities	Individuals	For Profits	Small Businesses	All Others	Total
ALABAMA														
1	84,010,343	1,367,337	6,853,361	35,888,820	653,310	16,644,257	2,831,713	7,346,240	1,167,100	941,707,384	12,370,521	0	156,531	1,110,996,916
2	1,570,241,267	5,368,593	9,252,024	31,616,801	2,049,487	11,838,050	0	12,834,263	1,192,920	927,850,012	16,100,012	258,129	1,412,344	2,590,013,903
3	86,636,792	3,154,379	7,964,578	20,372,774	460,490	36,003,256	182,022	7,328,401	9,116,205	888,311,985	9,849,160	0	0	1,069,380,042
4	96,372,143	1,831,262	15,758,655	20,584,788	410,142	4,853,601	0	6,178,689	177,569	1,046,330,801	9,783,259	0	-11,395	1,202,269,514
5	71,062,533	4,304,457	8,522,262	20,125,602	2,619,591	17,591,405	0	5,027,464	1,722,681	828,152,170	14,545,839	133,905	0	973,807,910
6	64,893,386	1,922,613	15,643,111	39,952,103	602,463	91,554,462	32,942	6,835,288	4,700,325	1,091,472,308	49,205,472	141	0	1,366,814,615
7	103,601,718	961,814	5,246,377	20,603,083	1,254,240	15,993,669	0	10,274,063	3,079,092	933,742,747	10,738,692	0	154,523	1,105,650,017
TOTAL	2,076,818,181	18,910,454	69,240,368	189,143,971	8,049,723	194,478,701	3,046,677	55,824,409	21,155,893	6,657,567,407	122,592,954	392,175	1,712,002	9,418,932,916
ALASKA														
TOTAL	612,204,832	10,737,333	35,233,106	15,896,164	69,582,727	41,258,508	76,258,378	70,166,274	824,616	315,992,162	26,202,030	1,282,546	1,149,853	1,276,788,529
ARIZONA														
1	360,386,449	5,316,411	36,220,138	52,111,227	6,682,171	30,942,443	1,326,737	6,044,208	2,727,982	1,495,087,520	20,809,394	428,538	563,736	2,018,646,955
2	438,773,972	9,858,337	26,888,475	38,968,286	8,721,564	96,449,137	22,311,800	14,362,697	1,664,714	1,251,796,864	14,426,156	345,144	2,747,365	1,927,314,510
3	39,136,358	981,627	13,858,244	7,571,740	21,375,833	10,991,618	6,830,919	5,103,090	508,115	585,154,957	9,806,192	0	3,032,181	704,350,873
4	520,979,188	2,730,984	62,520,235	13,535,336	32,739,513	1,534,712	100,407,443	2,005,993	2,143,928	1,291,947,780	12,394,056	1,226,252	288,367	2,044,453,786
5	100,873,503	3,062,081	9,046,036	10,523,262	8,220,041	5,012,621	718,047	22,521,488	73,009	1,075,910,249	4,612,380	1,298,344	26,894,846	1,268,765,906
TOTAL	1,460,149,470	21,949,440	148,533,128	122,709,852	77,739,121	144,930,531	131,594,945	50,037,476	7,117,748	5,699,897,371	62,048,176	3,298,278	33,526,495	7,963,532,031
ARKANSAS														
1	188,442,039	2,765,918	10,488,940	33,867,296	1,555,283	7,840,072	0	7,036,978	1,288,407	1,179,698,591	9,578,326	387,824	0	1,442,949,673
2	943,709,731	3,495,487	3,933,962	25,684,639	1,868,818	17,451,236	533,043	7,981,814	4,704,550	998,873,416	14,868,896	0	2,721,726	2,025,827,317
3	84,220,446	3,596,352	6,287,792	17,911,675	474,881	31,736,939	0	7,043,905	1,581,512	1,165,733,506	10,128,876	518,613	861,830	1,330,096,327
4	145,412,556	144,495	2,539,517	18,415,016	347,628	11,487,781	0	4,470,920	1,351,868	1,141,213,424	12,149,586	0	0	1,337,532,790
TOTAL	1,361,784,772	10,002,252	23,250,211	95,878,625	4,246,610	68,516,028	533,043	26,533,617	8,926,336	4,485,518,937	46,725,684	906,437	3,583,555	6,136,406,106
CALIFORNIA														
1	142,994,714	4,168,503	6,897,752	36,748,591	5,910,501	6,030,524	4,126,423	12,279,581	71,041	1,132,172,373	10,049,819	429,761	8,292,612	1,370,172,195
2	181,015,727	5,230,631	8,504,702	21,039,291	5,670,157	5,722,338	2,205,387	5,992,933	1,414,985	1,267,536,229	11,673,837	0	34,473	1,516,040,690
3	6,220,345,987	4,054,068	16,604,717	12,674,374	2,655,361	5,646,491	3,748,583	12,945,693	989,797	765,909,501	23,286,801	0	17,338,739	7,086,200,112
4	1,128,983,152	4,139,139	12,373,781	31,151,652	7,200,553	79,928,635	1,063,133	6,570,110	381,885	773,992,717	13,765,458	793,061	146,085	2,060,489,361
5	239,245,733	7,938,241	70,297,356	60,349,427	5,944,453	14,223,460	0	30,375,258	5,270,422	1,241,177,325	30,010,476	2,910,625	3,621,745	1,711,364,522
6	112,656,925	3,372,423	10,267,334	28,157,844	2,917,982	195,859,472	0	31,288,528	1,900,254	889,743,033	14,985,890	3,923,650	311,028	1,295,384,362
7	110,587,115	23,990,215	2,774,258	56,452,340	2,940,706	0	0	6,094,397	492,306	880,865,714	12,205,564	660,820	185,078	1,097,248,515
8	157,911,170	12,582,223	14,809,759	48,651,176	2,898,993	148,465,165	262,715	38,664,095	1,608,621	880,269,451	21,960,772	2,304,796	1,036,104	1,331,425,040
9	165,252,567	3,309,539	23,325,221	82,542,901	3,619,979	2,921,042	349,050	4,136,764	459,801	868,853,050	95,807,081	927,128	23,356	1,251,527,478
10	116,957,965	2,766,131	11,788,127	43,172,191	1,378,379	12,480,870	473,355	2,530,204	281,716	725,653,236	10,805,549	430,697	2,511,588	931,230,009
11	219,157,928	19,085,578	6,685,446	29,339,048	1,592,585	0	13,790	8,638,414	796,515	851,836,895	6,535,099	4,331,404	1,683,849	1,149,696,550
12	76,933,350	4,226,148	6,075,794	17,399,270	6,162,604	21,002,247	75,507	20,601,621	181,213,097	607,869,563	19,030,740	7,396,159	2,963,313	970,949,413
13	89,549,252	969,015	7,269,392	47,107,982	663,859	117,486	110,105	1,513,466	3,820,193	644,593,322	6,990,892	1,843,647	3,873,571	808,422,182
14	122,372,868	7,549,754	4,128,194	13,423,877	2,706,935	0	1,451,427	4,283,654	3,668,119	995,787,332	8,870,521	39,529	37,231	1,164,319,442
15	153,467,148	16,117,373	10,301,900	15,210,797	2,797,765	2,061,549	0	3,431,694	0	763,221,299	11,182,304	59,087	1,600,259	979,451,175
16	95,787,137	6,838,037	7,722,637	45,542,101	10,810,917	18,659,038	0	5,915,637	378,953	767,718,373	8,071,421	289,880	358,233	968,092,365
17	226,219,822	8,310,180	10,923,882	20,309,637	5,033,482	471,389	353,179	9,240,271	706,673	964,295,141	11,074,159	42,270	4,382,387	1,261,362,472
18	267,360,144	10,711,165	16,513,495	25,624,612	3,869,920	4,724,325	552,890	22,001,526	2,022,817	1,324,670,060	12,305,416	0	42,528	1,690,398,899
19	65,767,397	3,392,538	6,690,346	43,998,023	3,531,694	35,469,897	406,175	8,508,333	2,291,845	690,622,716	9,782,253	1,743,290	68,946	872,273,454
20	150,277,384	2,832,951	13,581,740	29,657,831	6,240,885	3,732,480	488,455	27,167,119	1,171,863	1,070,815,402	24,513,856	0	1,862,167	1,332,342,134
21	137,949,046	891,604	8,742,763	29,425,625	1,485,866	639,888	423,229	2,077,587	2,626,060	990,971,231	11,077,059	266,093	138,658,616	1,325,234,665
22	164,793,313	1,492,747	13,515,795	34,002,753	2,921,051	1,070,385	0	12,650,490	45,620,131	860,620,345	13,101,925	736,482	23,022	1,150,548,439
23	164,188,780	4,487,115	10,513,980	24,479,571	1,149,708	197,030,519	0	10,910,382	2,195,354	859,826,334	11,087,069	533,203	203,982	1,286,605,996

24	167,421,496	1,759,906	11,824,818	41,781,333	1,190,338	430,912	0	19,604,621	1,768,116	859,687,461	23,235,097	329,409	22,994	1,129,056,501
25	163,539,091	19,131,402	12,961,390	33,662,944	1,752,018	9,202,011	228,446	10,089,698	3,872,609	858,908,408	15,813,903	0	22,972	1,129,184,892
26	143,449,294	1,378,902	9,229,333	20,213,918	827,828	916,452	0	6,483,448	10,996,593	754,705,395	8,199,467	241,508	20,188	956,662,325
27	164,042,475	7,985,164	49,860,877	34,320,378	2,167,304	430,789	0	7,898,380	873,373	859,481,250	15,823,709	938,435	22,987	1,143,845,121
28	166,980,899	1,406,845	11,167,439	29,038,704	925,779	1,261,925	0	11,465,702	106,169,598	859,345,866	13,157,433	124,036	22,984	1,201,067,211
29	162,828,576	49,304,174	12,113,375	28,150,765	682,195	430,819	0	9,289,634	806,888	859,669,064	11,006,456	0	22,989	1,134,304,934
30	163,325,968	2,397,840	17,947,651	27,673,905	1,974,151	825,236	0	4,095,794	2,157,468	857,862,281	12,290,841	0	22,949	1,090,574,085
31	164,029,518	940,348	22,524,210	32,774,937	2,456,251	2,940,836	0	2,617,517	12,812,698	859,885,179	11,630,631	0	23,003	1,112,635,130
32	164,316,382	2,199,519	16,019,167	25,742,119	8,239,018	7,912,283	0	2,087,577	809,986	862,643,813	6,424,557	0	23,077	1,096,417,496
33	164,612,489	1,133,122	12,792,626	29,057,532	1,897,510	5,467,565	0	3,758,792	9,386,662	861,205,701	5,869,372	377,598	23,011	1,095,581,980
34	162,991,456	1,690,709	15,650,883	54,131,364	1,514,952	733,935	0	2,839,044	2,216,107	860,198,977	11,796,325	0	23,012	1,113,786,763
35	151,522,049	4,337,285	8,468,889	21,964,916	6,483,117	1,091,222	921,700	52,161	6,294,661	920,679,589	5,735,787	3,135,978	148	1,130,687,501
36	593,563,923	15,786,226	13,502,087	33,537,492	1,736,870	13,085,722	332,997	1,947,908	199,619	1,841,544,637	14,092,245	0	276,306	2,529,606,031
37	425,095,325	12,951,476	8,924,811	18,010,849	3,309,555	5,009,151	1,479,825	3,101,058	160,182	923,230,142	8,296,973	0	226,540	1,409,795,885
38	61,444,043	4,913,742	6,119,478	24,263,828	888,633	139,645	619,378	460,541	348,813	797,871,205	7,012,256	0	0	904,081,564
39	61,769,679	1,131,219	10,749,801	25,757,852	2,522,778	6,470,160	619,901	899,146	2,004,625	798,703,315	11,548,496	0	0	922,176,973
40	62,098,279	9,309,741	8,667,436	27,998,502	4,834,902	57,584,535	619,332	1,613,396	673,130	798,039,549	22,789,584	1,140,909	0	995,369,295
41	91,076,442	2,074,023	23,295,498	17,620,482	2,550,871	166,933,365	212,348	59,132,159	2,880,632	681,391,176	14,884,966	4,049,664	1,899,483	1,068,001,109
42	123,528,379	2,923,430	8,772,578	29,824,768	2,066,544	2,489,081	240,051	15,096,323	834,237	833,296,844	10,184,210	2,352,500	14,020	1,031,622,964
43	106,761,749	9,862,755	9,096,399	29,645,849	7,690,614	3,394,271	1,482,339	20,626,089	1,269,085	969,174,006	6,068,232	4,380,783	417,241	1,169,869,413
44	124,403,430	2,982,533	10,187,902	39,373,547	8,272,389	2,946,295	321,732	18,869,698	1,633,289	1,032,387,414	8,963,764	3,113,105	445,973	1,253,901,070
45	140,922,370	3,271,762	10,216,918	33,437,359	8,331,127	3,328,441	797,019	4,282,593	1,977,197	1,012,781,845	26,926,787	818,124	367,877	1,247,459,419
TOTAL	14,239,497,939	317,327,440	610,401,938	1,454,444,253	162,419,081	1,049,281,853	23,978,470	494,129,037	429,528,017	40,781,713,759	669,925,053	50,663,631	193,156,662	60,476,467,132
COLORADO														
1	1,089,516,478	17,987,741	2,734,218	100,761,577	1,435,640	72,370,939	2,453,860	39,279,422	11,035,972	903,047,988	23,978,874	670,118	2,774,474	2,268,047,302
2	43,027,531	1,138,582	4,909,872	15,339,696	408,251	75,423,886	0	86,103,859	2,126,019	533,448,929	8,605,593	2,017,090	179,088	772,728,396
3	103,949,461	10,699,105	5,378,287	24,329,540	4,944,796	6,335,514	3,652,722	8,628,398	0	814,630,471	12,314,713	65,816	-3,320	994,925,503
4	75,798,573	12,122,341	11,061,114	13,790,457	2,116,027	62,154,079	0	3,484,900	1,211,251	845,575,674	12,315,497	808,471	0	1,040,438,385
5	52,404,858	2,475,162	21,109,172	10,881,697	9,647,274	4,795,546	0	5,027,240	3,138,241	629,932,705	5,522,540	453,956	49,814	745,438,204
6	46,244,092	1,794,767	-40,226	21,857,083	989,550	1,557,005	0	6,611,685	853,330	547,877,745	5,740,169	2,484,007	110,969	636,080,177
TOTAL	1,410,940,993	46,217,697	45,152,436	186,960,051	19,541,539	222,636,969	6,106,581	149,135,505	18,364,814	4,274,513,512	68,477,386	6,499,457	3,111,026	6,457,657,966
CONNECTICUT														
1	1,217,428,194	4,322,805	11,533,116	52,710,635	39,640	1,428,511	0	9,541,721	4,159,539	965,989,600	20,131,599	863,310	147,980	2,288,296,649
2	99,245,545	496,741	2,444,193	13,345,965	5,738,805	30,625,745	1,261,058	9,515,157	6,398,904	795,674,819	15,338,580	212,140	210,024	980,507,677
3	140,964,764	2,703,583	12,351,472	47,437,742	1,158,868	4,774,225	56,345	12,042,392	156,014,419	978,945,421	11,827,560	2,179,052	142,988	1,370,598,832
4	120,572,046	58,697	7,339,733	59,839,128	135,994	885,786	0	4,949,117	3,091,610	877,610,378	26,891,303	53,235	262,272	1,101,689,298
5	144,959,372	404,169	11,008,915	26,881,789	43,372	864,035	220,014	2,982,072	385,942	943,085,193	6,072,893	1,810,741	1,042,064	1,139,760,573
6	128,381,067	511,793	3,050,049	17,571,534	0	28,548,510	0	1,816,879	32,258	964,990,209	5,727,700	1,662,633	86,872	1,152,379,506
TOTAL	1,851,550,989	8,497,788	47,727,478	217,786,793	7,116,679	67,126,813	1,537,417	40,847,339	170,082,672	5,526,295,620	85,989,635	6,781,111	1,892,201	8,033,232,535
DELAWARE														
TOTAL	350,460,091	5,052,770	13,153,290	31,171,473	724,320	24,473,484	45,441	12,353,920	1,341,366	1,031,502,590	7,795,285	65,882	525,511	1,478,665,424
DISTRICT OF COLUMBIA														
TOTAL	704,423,068	58,184,373	99,301,876	213,297,485	3,019,976	13,886,040	303,287	325,411,620	293,256,372	1,014,542,563	70,007,886	13,662,967	132,925,164	2,942,222,676
FLORIDA														
1	85,352,878	2,694,607	7,741,744	20,998,776	10,298,445	2,711,704	0	2,032,586	163,761	899,647,482	12,428,929	0	1,621,907	1,045,692,819
2	2,970,882,775	11,239,794	8,875,838	14,003,645	2,527,021	53,243,701	1,395,760	7,285,447	227,143	916,146,942	13,135,472	0	7,614,972	4,006,578,511
3	93,803,115	1,081,770	8,659,868	42,907,156	2,445,915	866,187	0	5,890,585	2,503,020	910,581,631	24,450,108	0	136,714	1,093,326,068
4	75,523,207	4,789,627	8,103,027	14,997,953	3,458,330	421,128	0	3,044,230	7,165,660	1,508,819,560	10,466,839	0	91,903	1,636,881,465
5	57,523,428	4,901,940	720,794	27,715,142	3,708,849	8,271,830	0	1,854,410	1,889,818	1,034,074,714	9,770,444	65,314	252,706	1,150,749,387
6	83,151,887	2,756,808	5,289,643	18,336,430	3,026,919	78,660,339	0	4,032,135	7,394	1,810,769,573	12,138,517	816,328	68,946	2,019,054,920

See Appendix A for a listing of the congressional districts which represent the county in which the state capital is located and congressional districts which represent only portions of a county. See Appendix B for a listing of the programs included in each recipent category.

table continues

Table 3.8 **Federal Outlays to Categories of Recipients by Congressional District, 1990 est. *(continued)***

District	State Gov't.	Counties	Cities/ Towns	Special Districts	Schools	Public Universities	Indian Tribes	Non-Profits	Private Universities	Individuals	For Profits	Small Businesses	All Others	Total
FLORIDA *continued*														
7	85,199,198	16,161,496	10,407,426	41,401,272	1,638,523	19,417,722	0	6,882,572	1,757,709	1,002,882,659	13,761,961	81,476	112,555	1,199,704,571
8	38,226,884	1,416,366	8,038,393	27,446,176	2,907,825	1,659,806	0	7,161,223	1,269,888	1,802,015,283	6,496,267	211,947	188,580	1,897,038,637
9	51,735,428	1,052,360	20,682,702	9,607,685	979,734	392,209	0	200,144	1,173,716	1,712,218,183	3,538,710	329,025	79,277	1,801,989,173
10	64,844,782	2,644,026	6,938,241	22,644,517	599,257	152,127	0	3,629,416	1,579,988	1,390,605,554	7,910,019	0	68,946	1,501,616,875
11	50,776,734	2,280,638	6,858,951	20,657,216	6,534,639	1,903,825	0	4,119,500	2,573,467	1,325,251,782	7,533,187	92,003	12,241,367	1,440,823,310
12	56,570,080	7,299,722	12,449,215	15,739,649	908,125	152,127	279,480	9,981,629	637,590	1,951,132,354	3,817,362	102,822	243,985	2,059,314,141
13	38,928,014	12,055,220	4,286,204	43,181,697	494,713	0	0	277,926	0	2,313,376,189	14,650,496	0	162,993	2,427,413,452
14	44,933,933	0	12,301,263	20,854,148	815,412	3,361,917	1,308,038	1,225,024	453,579	1,857,173,280	4,278,418	172,672	63,099	1,946,940,784
15	40,643,505	22,181,834	11,956,491	17,123,186	1,768,897	858,660	-539,957	1,002,880	3,786,910	1,589,379,294	17,243,792	0	542,953	1,705,948,444
16	88,624,729	626,731	9,164,341	16,286,150	45,002	289,374	3,829,571	56,974	1,440,678	1,449,092,956	4,476,642	0	0	1,573,933,149
17	206,571,689	3,251,550	16,206,079	21,153,653	597,276	2,567,018	305,291	2,940,091	4,210,250	1,104,673,571	7,378,126	645,038	0	1,370,499,633
18	217,978,176	17,330,622	24,052,658	36,457,492	276,840	964,918	326,650	3,305,365	70,688,741	1,105,108,341	16,542,332	1,871,945	44,241,810	1,539,145,890
19	188,559,110	7,541,096	16,792,262	73,476,563	7,563,061	990,631	286,203	2,430,373	11,849,611	1,073,116,254	7,747,753	0	1,768,871	1,392,121,788
TOTAL	4,539,829,549	121,306,208	199,525,142	504,988,508	50,594,782	176,885,223	7,191,037	67,352,511	113,378,924	26,756,065,602	197,765,375	4,388,570	69,501,585	32,808,773,017
GEORGIA														
1	152,562,773	3,347,938	6,912,379	25,853,450	7,468,874	5,333,394	0	6,236,387	1,417,859	913,705,761	13,626,104	0	0	1,136,464,919
2	175,210,996	2,197,858	5,009,976	21,041,294	1,647,307	6,159,108	0	7,313,160	348,706	860,141,534	10,922,862	64,432	0	1,090,057,235
3	128,939,557	588,512	12,309,419	22,395,884	1,933,614	9,383,815	0	8,264,306	512,217	800,204,818	10,888,529	0	6,090,842	1,001,511,513
4	352,096,966	4,478,804	1,940,865	55,163,730	400,258	6,101,750	0	14,498,537	10,025,468	387,245,639	13,059,322	482,958	5,536,088	851,030,384
5	1,755,114,337	13,640,747	40,717,946	62,106,463	914,345	21,717,379	22,867	11,157,380	97,682,960	1,159,621,906	27,591,467	513,879	666,182	3,191,467,858
6	94,007,081	798,309	4,186,282	21,646,721	469,599	2,417,069	0	389,331	32,533	840,454,163	16,934,168	0	2,834	981,338,090
7	57,225,663	157,780	2,929,087	16,457,484	193,014	675,579	0	3,922,842	2,623,454	792,520,767	5,570,207	49,609	0	882,325,486
8	177,480,345	2,203,828	3,645,749	18,556,016	654,304	2,986,998	0	2,627,124	3,146,478	912,418,770	12,668,252	0	101,358	1,136,489,222
9	91,145,800	3,739,083	187,423	7,967,238	25,218	974,748	0	6,488,125	2,100,611	861,709,459	7,140,748	0	0	981,478,452
10	122,386,529	4,147,599	20,336,998	30,912,528	1,447,217	42,833,453	0	16,075,859	2,054,655	794,728,166	9,849,054	1,336,746	47,918	1,046,156,722
TOTAL	3,106,170,046	35,300,457	98,176,125	282,100,809	15,153,752	98,583,293	22,867	76,973,052	119,944,940	8,322,750,982	128,250,714	2,447,624	12,445,221	12,298,319,881
HAWAII														
1	601,884,498	10,398,132	8,557,181	25,422,179	24,206,970	42,201,168	6,361,772	17,163,619	1,542,559	611,880,123	8,898,785	402,176	193,683	1,359,112,845
2	166,521,199	16,526,909	21,465,489	19,400,543	-2,838	8,331,340	0	7,758,419	720,300	716,074,938	8,698,829	0	543,140	966,038,269
TOTAL	768,405,697	26,925,041	30,022,670	44,822,722	24,204,132	50,532,508	6,361,772	24,922,038	2,262,859	1,327,955,061	17,597,614	402,176	736,823	2,325,151,114
IDAHO														
1	359,362,813	2,618,069	10,357,210	12,696,087	2,910,546	15,818,011	4,194,553	8,008,557	1,478,656	801,630,790	5,026,123	888,633	1,840,509	1,226,830,555
2	133,218,369	3,371,711	4,342,283	6,060,814	4,159,119	9,238,693	3,145,964	3,824,733	2,952,993	701,631,290	3,963,619	14,454	21,879	875,945,923
TOTAL	492,581,182	5,989,780	14,699,493	18,756,901	7,069,665	25,056,704	7,340,516	11,833,290	4,431,649	1,503,262,080	8,989,742	903,088	1,862,388	2,102,776,479
ILLINOIS														
1	131,717,804	4,514,269	22,855,686	223,484,810	2,694,050	5,004,459	129,533	11,590,776	95,835,519	899,833,752	24,484,745	770,209	225,101	1,423,140,711
2	124,816,323	2,468,752	18,429,095	54,397,246	167,006	2,550,865	129,504	1,808,298	976,680	899,650,652	4,445,009	2,246,489	225,051	1,112,310,972
3	123,638,961	2,469,271	18,381,301	42,839,370	167,041	2,595,653	129,531	1,856,521	1,046,134	899,788,279	3,898,200	399,032	225,098	1,097,434,393
4	72,469,146	1,598,233	10,886,542	22,415,423	512,756	2,577,302	55,998	1,437,015	1,846,312	764,233,420	5,741,369	296,463	97,313	884,167,292
5	129,542,564	2,524,207	22,258,365	43,911,919	167,018	2,780,552	129,514	1,005,311	1,035,904	899,658,568	6,439,938	0	225,069	1,109,678,929
6	64,253,185	3,145,673	9,049,315	18,830,577	212,829	1,655,931	48,243	3,322,548	1,917,425	791,187,105	6,559,076	197,646	83,836	900,463,388
7	139,440,265	8,248,498	106,019,610	51,431,418	315,225	24,949,259	129,530	44,747,146	18,842,380	899,983,485	37,570,848	172,601	985,173	1,332,835,438
8	124,966,256	3,024,674	17,942,541	45,792,473	2,423,652	2,583,911	129,530	3,909,924	4,081,426	899,749,927	8,208,398	0	225,096	1,113,037,808
9	138,140,833	6,289,253	18,496,313	48,976,698	304,449	3,302,896	129,551	19,933,134	69,813,713	900,816,760	17,388,778	227,080	225,133	1,224,044,590
10	74,389,486	2,874,279	8,939,408	35,258,924	5,121,234	1,405,798	58,571	4,187,300	3,221,044	776,222,250	10,299,303	195,304	101,784	922,274,684
11	128,896,839	2,469,057	18,475,315	44,524,158	364,014	33,046,161	129,520	1,909,098	1,157,838	899,680,325	5,093,273	0	225,079	1,135,970,676
12	73,741,407	1,648,334	8,292,434	32,531,452	367,716	1,562,016	54,787	3,037,826	724,281	796,645,053	14,525,918	519,327	95,208	933,745,759

13	69,897,951	3,100,584	10,046,156	25,262,067	632,070	1,530,971	56,785	625,787	2,240,051	795,183,457	4,648,307	189,022	529,584	913,942,791
14	37,071,547	3,128,885	1,758,140	26,679,854	1,433,808	9,075,832	502	2,104,476	1,342,140	802,642,196	10,808,405	350,868	26,728	896,423,381
15	45,206,525	1,381,859	1,237,877	13,698,353	2,391,352	8,335,819	0	1,606,418	2,066,080	820,170,392	7,087,893	0	0	903,182,567
16	49,529,226	789,918	3,697,655	21,646,235	1,396,356	351,845	0	4,667,339	585,917	853,912,391	8,705,199	0	0	945,282,081
17	49,913,734	101,188	1,952,166	24,612,268	2,473,914	5,032,656	0	2,933,188	3,212,341	963,308,930	14,152,054	0	58,432	1,067,750,870
18	67,266,327	959,658	4,749,611	27,876,195	78,017	3,365,264	0	2,331,901	4,353,277	906,616,764	17,577,322	0	0	1,035,174,335
19	61,420,875	6,336,580	4,768,161	14,992,536	3,242,695	118,893,396	17,173	7,555,386	654,151	886,925,475	7,614,965	488,004	0	1,112,909,398
20	3,286,470,633	6,038,704	5,272,303	20,431,042	1,415,197	681,999	0	1,695,966	2,038,614	1,011,233,208	5,174,510	0	-102,070	4,340,350,107
21	104,331,829	474,188	12,023,875	36,594,414	6,608,935	9,842,538	0	2,680,213	1,316,205	964,792,792	8,565,347	0	0	1,147,230,337
22	92,209,190	1,837,863	6,667,859	15,235,821	2,036,972	18,791,191	0	5,121,632	529,251	1,044,097,019	4,595,633	8,078	0	1,191,130,510
TOTAL	5,189,330,907	65,423,929	332,199,728	891,423,255	34,526,303	259,916,311	1,328,272	130,067,203	218,836,681	19,376,332,201	233,584,488	6,060,125	3,451,614	26,742,481,018
INDIANA														
1	169,352,830	30,777,283	8,319,250	27,246,881	554,003	3,623,416	0	1,275,965	172,209	897,985,986	10,986,672	100,986	1,960,663	1,152,356,145
2	191,252,291	889,344	4,546,571	24,856,538	1,678,195	6,085,454	0	3,410,704	2,360,188	902,134,669	12,384,936	1,641,310	8,408	1,151,248,608
3	103,406,222	617,540	7,169,875	38,255,458	84,410	1,529,020	0	4,216,893	13,487,934	916,351,658	11,150,907	575,205	913,681	1,097,758,804
4	91,706,086	798,661	9,551,758	17,926,634	214,429	880,736	0	3,198,634	2,229,424	861,741,381	8,047,582	0	51,710	996,347,033
5	107,770,417	226,620	5,623,048	10,824,093	1,374,807	856,231	0	9,180	4,498,430	883,296,156	13,937,010	0	0	1,028,415,991
6	215,820,438	196,132	2,921,983	20,191,439	35,435	94,143	0	2,456,087	2,493,558	939,349,072	14,613,906	0	801,643	1,198,973,837
7	111,348,932	3,098,914	3,390,299	15,731,322	163,101	57,625,879	13,757	19,169,150	1,881,427	877,808,135	12,499,376	0	0	1,102,730,290
8	138,585,955	176,238	13,412,423	15,153,907	298,830	5,021,687	0	3,068,748	2,746,802	950,636,465	11,104,470	0	0	1,140,205,525
9	131,825,049	4,861,230	19,133,736	16,137,456	345,016	83,897,136	8	3,362,002	208,396	811,554,284	15,178,662	460,906	-736	1,086,963,145
10	1,328,915,949	3,351,976	338,082	8,082,426	30,977	13,054,175	0	11,903,918	6,544,495	926,397,465	5,313,707	658,203	52,739	2,304,644,113
TOTAL	2,589,984,168	44,993,939	74,407,026	194,406,154	4,779,202	172,667,877	13,766	52,071,281	36,622,863	8,967,255,270	115,217,228	3,436,611	3,788,107	12,259,643,491
IOWA														
1	90,505,600	918,147	5,467,422	9,186,135	1,318,245	2,516,419	0	5,275,604	4,555,165	886,089,525	15,339,949	65,724	28,044	1,021,265,980
2	73,693,233	0	4,155,364	13,030,491	923,623	251,695	0	2,447,381	5,257,626	825,680,169	8,356,102	406,158	0	934,201,842
3	77,582,719	1,966,883	4,843,796	11,971,323	1,970,968	102,854,014	149,240	5,179,031	3,498,784	841,839,505	11,059,670	12,581	0	1,062,928,516
4	952,176,829	3,694,378	21,434,992	15,523,642	2,720,918	54,135,130	0	2,970,071	6,051,545	817,784,541	12,168,872	493,366	2,736,959	1,891,891,243
5	89,809,264	1,155,254	7,036,871	10,800,867	2,022,138	474,543	0	2,074,551	2,913,752	999,154,239	9,583,082	-473	0	1,125,024,088
6	78,483,739	860,439	8,874,959	9,434,036	1,572,799	1,401,489	0	3,155,934	6,800,875	984,835,162	11,626,929	173,557	0	1,107,219,917
TOTAL	1,362,251,383	8,595,100	51,813,404	69,946,495	10,528,692	161,633,291	149,240	21,102,572	29,077,748	5,355,383,141	68,134,604	1,150,912	2,765,003	7,142,531,586
KANSAS														
1	53,916,753	24,451,907	6,204,382	7,208,028	2,475,756	3,691,049	0	876,064	1,310,116	1,317,542,640	9,804,019	0	0	1,427,480,713
2	672,706,457	11,501,061	6,342,421	12,282,543	15,668,502	55,096,741	2,371,595	2,501,190	2,606,502	738,870,517	9,263,524	362,304	63,474	1,529,636,830
3	79,065,730	1,861,846	5,008,925	17,589,327	764,217	16,391,387	0	831,157	1,110,861	771,170,043	11,986,183	0	0	905,779,677
4	81,396,663	2,718,584	191,675	13,203,641	1,230,621	4,826,394	189,777	1,515,093	1,234,246	889,954,395	13,330,580	285,593	1,607,867	1,011,685,129
5	76,237,063	1,435,970	8,311,745	6,554,132	3,263,597	5,058,322	0	3,176,307	4,106,052	1,000,881,757	11,735,316	0	0	1,120,760,262
TOTAL	963,322,667	41,969,368	26,059,148	56,837,671	23,402,693	85,063,893	2,561,371	8,899,811	10,367,777	4,718,419,352	56,119,621	647,897	1,671,341	5,995,342,612
KENTUCKY														
1	112,686,900	2,032,430	6,825,232	12,978,268	327,878	3,535,179	0	895,909	331,606	996,035,676	10,017,277	0	0	1,145,666,355
2	109,322,902	1,318,921	3,632,598	8,816,619	647,557	5,605,079	0	6,039,846	1,279,549	726,690,384	6,471,557	0	2,679,137	872,504,149
3	102,510,503	16,942,323	25,221,685	27,885,313	264,913	5,207,734	0	11,668,753	2,573,602	896,085,847	15,390,982	74,996	582,892	1,104,409,543
4	86,770,419	18,072,364	7,237,418	20,679,495	29,135	2,028,376	0	2,107,992	387,684	825,855,338	4,248,616	0	0	967,416,837
5	237,363,216	1,637,117	6,115,813	10,219,427	30,788	10,253	0	5,722,578	6,394,802	935,437,231	8,700,715	108,969	0	1,211,740,910
6	1,532,087,720	8,216,478	10,187,396	21,481,973	217,572	57,244,298	0	16,110,278	6,251,977	733,164,419	6,783,393	519,149	271,513	2,392,536,165
7	187,304,405	1,621,975	5,955,206	11,321,164	10,223	5,377,825	0	9,062,264	2,229,489	892,153,638	5,823,737	267,936	1,637	1,121,129,500
TOTAL	2,368,046,064	49,841,609	65,175,348	113,382,259	1,528,066	79,008,744	0	51,607,620	19,448,709	6,005,422,535	57,436,276	971,050	3,535,179	8,815,403,459

See Appendix A for a listing of the congressional districts which represent the county in which the state capital is located and congressional districts which represent only portions of a county. See Appendix B for a listing of the programs included in each recipent category.

table continues

Table 3.8 **Federal Outlays to Categories of Recipients by Congressional District, 1990 est. *(continued)***

District	State Gov't.	Counties	Cities/ Towns	Special Districts	Schools	Public Universities	Indian Tribes	Non-Profits	Private Universities	Individuals	For Profits	Small Businesses	All Others	Total
LOUISIANA														
1	191,479,691	1,904,962	19,175,304	27,872,886	587,452	2,083,235	0	13,947,656	28,970,336	722,064,954	27,941,208	411,721	448,151	1,036,887,557
2	171,863,909	3,788,508	29,877,834	18,393,491	460,438	24,818,089	0	6,015,120	11,477,698	772,779,083	133,453,423	93,843	0	1,173,021,434
3	153,624,962	8,706,918	3,356,217	9,699,008	673,131	3,727,052	1,368,162	452,017	65,127	826,360,782	4,216,243	0	0	1,012,249,621
4	189,432,375	4,050,503	17,934,518	20,000,251	4,345,354	6,759,244	0	14,456,080	215,448	783,760,615	15,363,996	0	55,157	1,056,373,542
5	274,612,294	2,345,054	9,270,171	19,334,347	105,884	22,101,402	116,801	3,504,109	232,246	829,490,670	9,959,365	0	0	1,171,072,342
6	1,897,736,063	8,212,720	10,429,055	15,103,597	46,611	37,502,895	574,191	1,260,042	513,629	703,064,297	10,293,784	0	92,142	2,684,829,027
7	173,773,283	3,302,936	21,060,855	18,400,019	240,100	16,540,966	692,394	3,395,197	428,717	759,362,505	13,571,233	359,648	1,459,769	1,012,587,620
8	338,940,775	8,418,251	13,221,303	12,582,654	289,013	4,010,052	700,047	1,893,770	1,028,269	758,174,155	6,525,821	0	246,909	1,146,031,020
TOTAL	3,391,463,351	40,729,851	124,325,257	141,386,254	6,747,983	117,542,935	3,451,595	44,923,992	42,931,470	6,155,057,061	221,325,073	865,212	2,302,128	10,293,052,163
MAINE														
1	556,818,473	5,640,548	8,279,483	29,241,113	355,235	8,483,456	4,973,785	13,828,158	7,923,906	1,020,285,769	10,397,991	1,622,659	7,238	1,667,857,814
2	220,318,992	2,700,945	22,345,268	22,615,468	1,874,620	25,935,600	10,246,239	6,245,750	2,855,959	1,011,725,476	10,420,591	20,818,186	896,048	1,358,999,142
TOTAL	777,137,465	8,341,493	30,624,752	51,856,581	2,229,855	34,419,056	15,220,024	20,073,908	10,779,866	2,032,011,245	20,818,582	22,440,845	903,285	3,026,856,957
MARYLAND														
1	106,849,468	20,385,893	4,432,174	114,567,310	1,076,733	9,548,945	60,657	2,662,034	325,675	843,914,029	12,119,489	0	585,003	1,116,527,411
2	543,805,366	2,571,863	2,458,785	9,149,536	1,698,767	1,951,501	0	75,503	1,131,652	880,681,674	11,797,171	369,297	0	1,455,691,115
3	330,272,672	3,359,917	29,504,951	44,558,188	105,786	11,657,749	167,154	20,092,171	183,309,269	970,176,829	12,688,342	2,579,790	1,035,149	1,609,507,967
4	406,141,123	2,255,242	3,331,133	24,538,690	2,937,393	783,874	0	1,657,171	1,393,058	654,044,925	66,260,112	136,103	1,417,882	1,164,896,707
5	62,667,448	8,731,384	89,389	21,310,047	262,226	66,257,203	0	12,799,949	1,321,513	511,922,716	19,137,598	2,216,185	7,600,268	714,315,926
6	76,206,210	12,302,989	2,304,091	22,353,842	685,078	1,065,611	0	2,812,514	1,918,789	795,572,231	8,368,593	6,206,602	11,355,469	941,152,018
7	630,032,271	1,307,739	20,216,828	79,552,581	223,211	54,933,106	251,201	14,783,324	53,001,143	1,058,049,685	21,883,972	173,269	328,012	1,934,736,343
8	81,891,743	6,125,991	4,382,244	25,028,309	125,648	190,924	0	32,642,048	287,308	803,979,056	60,201,383	24,971,929	100,278,387	1,140,104,968
TOTAL	2,237,866,303	57,041,018	66,719,594	341,058,503	7,114,843	146,388,912	479,012	87,524,715	242,688,407	6,518,341,144	212,456,660	36,653,174	122,600,170	10,076,932,455
MASSACHUSETTS														
1	172,752,004	58,008	5,966,339	26,488,028	498,699	40,574,572	0	8,482,064	11,337,161	946,351,756	11,992,178	65,803	650,135	1,225,216,747
2	211,035,637	242,867	10,659,715	97,233,700	470,612	2,986,706	0	4,618,466	3,987,095	990,510,262	18,321,006	526,027	742,871	1,341,334,965
3	153,507,301	775,896	16,559,036	23,737,485	81,337	40,312,971	0	10,596,001	9,914,837	936,920,955	13,347,918	2,278,853	75,669	1,208,108,257
4	177,998,179	0	8,474,303	20,487,445	86,316	1,667,053	0	65,965,535	9,456,783	845,047,578	6,871,114	1,393,577	25,855	1,137,473,737
5	135,130,722	63,029	7,075,737	38,480,561	3,871,670	6,979,539	0	7,707,507	523,339	839,114,841	16,172,166	8,114,707	60,328	1,063,294,145
6	169,342,007	0	6,261,622	34,251,461	568,484	3,270,929	0	10,222,018	2,315,121	996,470,960	13,341,219	555,836	39,989	1,236,639,645
7	245,282,985	867,561	8,904,355	54,085,307	134,751	1,457,700	131,687	3,373,442	36,346,480	894,932,437	10,596,513	1,217,853	340,818	1,257,671,890
8	407,106,582	8,436,720	26,333,469	72,673,255	564,796	74,364,439	0	200,320,724	306,050,326	1,018,278,187	41,621,324	20,005,193	6,982,934	2,182,737,951
9	1,396,182,776	2,015,969	29,388,009	85,203,423	96,404	5,588,353	212,990	115,634,522	11,957,834	1,110,679,695	30,889,584	1,708,394	1,005,469	2,790,563,422
10	167,099,334	542,202	2,200,268	31,402,772	1,082,885	6,002,156	590,762	10,190,446	35,181,785	1,111,938,765	9,441,914	555,197	229,248	1,376,457,735
11	566,797,801	2,001,581	127,826,964	57,918,599	183,416	2,914,659	0	24,182,557	5,417,313	928,057,879	18,265,091	129,687	690,706	1,734,386,253
TOTAL	3,802,235,327	15,003,834	249,649,817	541,962,035	7,639,369	186,119,077	935,440	461,293,283	432,488,074	10,618,303,314	190,860,026	36,551,127	10,844,023	16,553,884,747
MICHIGAN														
1	214,513,091	4,289,295	13,772,023	20,741,427	1,525,715	394,826	62,812	8,463,996	1,788,721	952,651,981	6,631,335	489,836	1,844,316	1,227,169,373
2	120,053,678	7,294,031	12,755,865	15,447,934	1,543,576	214,895,076	28,219	8,636,893	3,074,887	808,791,760	5,727,218	1,132,668	154,295	1,199,536,100
3	1,878,559,630	1,653,944	6,127,659	6,468,636	5,551,302	10,428,891	186,955	7,064,415	3,375,347	784,590,001	9,730,886	65,533	-90,118	2,713,713,082
4	127,157,252	3,111,638	3,285,482	2,992,151	1,742,000	1,354,302	238,749	5,436,190	2,827,525	859,603,913	8,329,178	0	0	1,016,078,380
5	107,715,788	5,484,825	33,645,310	13,555,410	878,224	0	139,145	5,474,570	9,418,672	803,001,954	7,812,654	0	0	987,126,551
6	897,556,619	7,245,416	-4,503	11,635,608	647,144	89,962,358	930,541	2,150,150	148,197	776,753,986	12,190,148	647,192	2,325,744	1,802,188,599
7	140,419,454	7,469,714	2,588,041	8,168,824	3,997,402	99,076	128,480	1,321,463	3,805,326	829,595,520	4,237,523	268,930	8,963	1,002,108,715
8	132,372,203	2,240,334	9,917,884	5,721,981	3,425,574	2,113,318	0	1,225,175	2,682,906	903,386,793	4,267,861	1,167,515	0	1,068,521,543
9	114,005,435	7,838,888	8,804,584	4,330,647	2,456,812	7,878,775	875,851	9,011,330	0	946,650,267	8,773,427	0	0	1,110,626,017

10	150,652,671	2,020,684	7,914,059	5,281,208	1,672,632	11,611,612	1,327,272	8,004,169	725,963	901,159,424	4,318,216	0	117,797	1,094,805,709
11	178,798,801	7,140,758	19,351,032	8,874,316	11,820,617	11,449,969	9,266,548	11,500,180	1,541,100	1,092,272,245	6,352,050	114,998	0	1,358,482,613
12	73,301,513	4,975,107	8,009,295	6,356,195	1,443,083	0	0	907,534	0	888,853,012	10,032,256	65,881	0	993,943,877
13	222,486,871	23,664,291	39,615,536	6,998,022	1,582,414	32,571,607	62,812	16,376,246	1,617,566	952,702,737	16,403,042	1,945,499	210,976	1,316,237,618
14	116,655,272	2,062,170	10,399,086	2,503,919	346,683	119,815	23,597	217,774	607,691	917,062,061	5,036,191	0	0	1,055,034,259
15	187,649,445	3,504,731	21,393,025	13,376,492	609,161	7,761,865	51,032	180,497	1,801,234	889,354,781	16,875,237	365,971	0	1,142,923,472
16	170,197,721	3,808,108	20,182,001	7,546,353	2,368,473	302,401	41,131	2,093,974	4,659,516	898,251,998	6,779,902	0	0	1,116,231,577
17	140,968,580	2,209,178	14,172,322	7,425,801	191,579	154,729	30,474	2,704,288	795,292	919,554,119	8,848,654	120,378	0	1,097,175,395
18	64,815,211	0	555,287	1,701,618	221,313	6,093,073	75,475	1,339,264	1,003,926	873,005,594	7,021,402	560,717	0	956,392,880
TOTAL	5,037,879,236	96,013,112	232,483,990	149,126,541	42,023,703	397,191,692	13,469,094	92,108,109	39,873,869	15,997,242,145	149,367,181	6,945,116	4,571,972	22,258,295,761
MINNESOTA														
1	99,392,566	198,858	11,161,997	10,927,744	14,991	11,161,246	285,120	38,440,100	2,764,478	870,408,988	8,724,915	0	0	1,053,481,005
2	97,641,345	113,402	5,248,904	12,864,686	4,559,620	4,414,289	50,638	2,514,098	1,533,208	945,641,655	7,367,325	1,211	0	1,081,950,380
3	113,477,534	609,269	1,346,196	10,277,179	323,533	942,128	388,553	1,860,720	3,606,059	701,707,018	18,848,452	616,478	0	854,003,119
4	1,007,955,325	2,665,974	10,872,289	64,105,191	1,876,146	85,471,140	0	6,963,329	9,826,862	58,239,616	10,505,383	673,305	892,201	1,260,046,762
5	177,451,285	6,828,498	29,627,809	50,200,691	2,326,915	104,716,688	1,342,186	14,262,477	4,038,889	824,526,717	12,984,870	419,189	4,127,216	1,232,853,430
6	230,668,794	-62,492	3,161,537	15,530,167	203,363	1,050,366	12,742	3,054,972	774,441	1,356,986,838	8,921,758	408,001	0	1,620,710,488
7	172,389,182	937,814	8,620,489	14,002,053	5,511,621	15,413,600	7,638,140	8,601,043	5,536,516	914,521,272	8,025,740	0	4,792,957	1,165,990,426
8	173,128,749	1,296,317	9,700,586	17,266,773	2,962,891	10,557,242	5,894,651	4,327,020	1,528,181	934,193,642	7,802,562	0	489,423	1,169,148,037
TOTAL	2,072,104,780	12,587,639	79,739,807	195,174,483	17,779,079	233,726,700	15,612,030	80,023,759	29,608,634	6,606,225,747	83,181,007	2,118,184	10,301,797	9,438,183,647
MISSISSIPPI														
1	115,418,964	914,206	2,091,053	13,197,116	2,915,725	6,876,071	0	14,856,024	3,166,911	884,586,029	8,490,167	0	0	1,052,512,265
2	159,434,125	4,329,862	2,481,970	27,672,501	8,636,426	16,046,855	0	12,492,308	414,111	808,855,845	16,747,973	0	3,040,253	1,060,152,229
3	112,959,805	616,377	5,692,100	21,355,200	5,555,172	25,653,703	15,667,854	9,447,903	2,470,279	838,396,122	8,622,552	658,819	0	1,047,095,885
4	1,359,138,842	8,980,941	282,749	29,857,076	876,187	30,180,413	0	37,636,214	4,233,776	851,788,093	17,306,383	466,066	466,524	2,341,213,263
5	61,906,160	5,480,381	1,379,856	17,575,304	6,640,438	13,580,626	0	10,814,918	2,352,464	810,253,821	12,182,380	0	234,969	942,401,316
TOTAL	1,808,857,895	20,321,767	11,927,729	109,657,196	24,623,947	92,337,668	15,667,854	85,247,367	12,637,540	4,193,879,909	63,349,454	1,124,884	3,741,746	6,443,374,957
MISSOURI														
1	115,195,814	834,662	12,658,009	26,769,108	1,252,550	6,151,764	0	25,093,790	162,746,186	1,489,367,589	19,707,471	926,390	551,488	1,861,254,823
2	134,399,899	370,693	32,473,849	24,437,757	1,590,789	374,759	0	2,161,033	1,918,388	1,101,270,637	9,658,767	130,293	418,033	1,309,204,899
3	61,190,329	798,232	11,411,200	9,525,981	164,158	354,776	0	5,671,307	1,536,794	401,795,733	16,522,924	210,821	180,708	509,362,963
4	1,237,628,595	1,567,606	2,249,889	11,514,566	11,166,989	5,372,019	0	5,258,957	210,990	1,019,781,641	8,957,912	0	2,341,793	2,306,050,956
5	73,973,570	0	9,889,018	32,721,047	1,412,336	3,875,959	0	16,310,240	14,787	1,024,693,723	22,352,006	321,394	1,585,362	1,187,149,444
6	58,052,423	825,694	14,059,892	13,027,896	4,232,068	7,467,913	674,142	8,953,914	8,890,079	977,864,042	9,594,120	167,572	0	1,103,809,757
7	91,968,637	652,945	7,003,019	9,592,446	1,505,552	8,234,657	382,129	5,040,254	6,727,140	1,083,259,082	4,803,146	0	0	1,219,169,008
8	151,845,254	1,740,851	2,684,583	17,280,006	1,617,891	8,266,881	0	6,814,650	118,228	1,104,943,784	7,316,689	371,908	25,855	1,303,026,580
9	333,523,110	1,343,704	16,772,893	19,651,543	1,392,803	45,050,654	0	9,388,710	5,371,980	976,986,615	7,490,176	0	0	1,416,972,188
TOTAL	2,257,777,632	8,134,387	109,202,355	164,520,351	24,335,136	85,149,383	1,056,271	84,692,855	187,534,573	9,179,962,846	106,403,212	2,128,379	5,103,239	12,216,000,617
MONTANA														
1	483,564,044	7,071,749	1,978,289	16,594,458	9,865,701	31,322,845	9,561,195	5,700,528	8,071,745	694,393,539	9,071,381	474,190	1,599,435	1,279,269,100
2	76,277,117	1,913,496	11,259,046	9,342,662	19,347,998	3,769,572	22,846,608	1,791,453	2,613,387	818,967,113	13,087,806	721,075	148,521	982,085,854
TOTAL	559,841,161	8,985,245	13,237,335	25,937,121	29,213,699	35,092,417	32,407,804	7,491,981	10,685,131	1,513,360,651	22,159,187	1,195,265	1,747,956	2,261,354,954
NEBRASKA														
1	535,579,826	747,100	7,147,153	25,018,959	6,991,097	35,839,635	7,692,723	5,895,492	4,146,470	957,287,986	10,218,852	-4,191	38,312	1,596,599,415
2	130,946,145	1,089,871	6,481,714	39,861,920	17,719,683	17,312,321	6,574	8,541,503	8,487,999	833,857,892	10,645,232	593,247	107,039	1,075,651,140
3	100,973,696	632,133	2,625,091	8,404,930	3,270,802	4,988,306	0	3,565,199	483,194	1,095,975,817	13,505,781	-2,755	1,491,846	1,235,914,041
TOTAL	767,499,668	2,469,104	16,253,959	73,285,810	27,981,581	58,140,263	7,699,297	18,002,194	13,117,663	2,887,121,695	34,369,865	586,300	1,637,197	3,908,164,595

See Appendix A for a listing of the congressional districts which represent the county in which the state capital is located and congressional districts which represent only portions of a county. See Appendix B for a listing of the programs included in each recipent category.

table continues

Table 3.8 Federal Outlays to Categories of Recipients by Congressional District, 1990 est. *(continued)*

District	State Gov't.	Counties	Cities/ Towns	Special Districts	Schools	Public Universities	Indian Tribes	Non-Profits	Private Universities	Individuals	For Profits	Small Businesses	All Others	Total
NEVADA														
1	58,250,689	6,456,325	8,301,701	32,382,322	1,572,866	6,073,030	1,347,495	732,468	0	866,122,764	15,373,694	514,843	2,876,012	1,000,004,209
2	349,045,489	5,915,098	9,192,557	29,812,315	2,671,338	21,227,692	8,549,229	5,889,929	273,871	729,838,344	4,537,591	159,963	1,491,157	1,168,604,572
TOTAL	407,296,178	12,371,423	17,494,259	62,194,637	4,244,205	27,300,721	9,896,723	6,622,397	273,871	1,595,961,108	19,911,285	674,806	4,367,169	2,168,608,782
NEW HAMPSHIRE														
1	74,238,573	772,871	18,782,120	20,409,863	3,546,992	27,554,469	0	2,067,445	3,245,517	745,344,530	7,727,394	48,956	1,057,608	904,796,337
2	349,249,263	275,189	18,884,237	13,839,359	359,797	3,768,712	0	4,989,856	36,445,880	794,432,598	11,288,188	1,017,713	51,744	1,234,602,538
TOTAL	423,487,836	1,048,060	37,666,358	34,249,221	3,906,789	31,323,181	0	7,057,301	39,691,397	1,539,777,128	19,015,582	1,066,669	1,109,352	2,139,398,875
NEW JERSEY														
1	115,728,005	7,043,319	4,687,700	40,697,009	42,776	3,442,097	0	6,228,312	344,697	836,818,414	10,982,732	7,906	0	1,026,022,966
2	150,643,466	2,219,718	12,689,728	39,099,207	137,879	2,491,471	0	8,369,960	0	1,267,433,651	16,043,463	0	576,586	1,499,705,150
3	92,341,684	789,108	5,310,294	31,844,879	2,975,497	775,554	0	4,576,518	1,443,471	1,115,137,868	9,012,528	0	0	1,264,207,400
4	2,198,299,318	3,223,897	6,919,602	26,368,483	1,099,292	2,175,240	103,221	5,040,617	1,181,069	920,933,890	12,701,476	131,441	0	3,178,177,547
5	52,672,830	1,167,065	4,465,241	8,532,031	458,660	135,997	0	946,540	0	827,961,421	7,977,130	367,035	0	904,683,951
6	75,008,107	3,995,289	4,098,970	26,930,260	45,150	33,147,317	0	1,974,908	594,972	900,487,025	7,056,163	65,882	0	1,053,404,042
7	97,124,956	592,352	16,820,467	19,375,981	50,832	1,780,275	0	1,961,531	1,235,761	982,922,539	6,354,020	334,626	0	1,128,553,342
8	123,007,248	145,469	13,802,249	37,976,920	97,117	4,235,328	0	5,622,657	1,730,058	909,795,725	13,078,056	65,882	0	1,109,556,708
9	44,597,832	88,596	104,328	22,856,409	0	0	0	1,367,768	3,053,877	1,027,322,312	12,824,307	64,693	0	1,112,280,122
10	239,027,892	1,449,312	12,948,798	219,234,483	43,094	29,841,572	0	25,705,878	3,803,593	918,953,199	42,531,304	1,095,173	86,183	1,494,720,483
11	179,431,024	871,698	46,973,879	9,288,327	338,458	663,232	0	245,199	3,372,188	896,775,603	7,264,095	435,074	25,855	1,145,684,633
12	67,077,134	1,289,449	23,097,565	14,669,772	27,472	54,933,962	0	15,220,806	48,454,935	925,489,745	10,213,043	2,236,754	0	1,162,710,636
13	87,908,334	-85,134	-21,352	9,412,309	8,102,261	622,518	349,024	575,223	-1,770	1,162,075,391	3,473,946	266,299	0	1,272,677,049
14	226,538,719	8,579,960	27,039,030	57,644,155	681,424	2,130,777	0	4,894,622	4,708,540	891,205,514	31,248,759	0	0	1,254,671,499
TOTAL	3,749,406,551	31,370,098	178,936,498	563,930,226	14,099,913	136,375,340	452,245	82,730,558	69,921,393	13,583,312,296	190,761,022	5,070,764	688,624	18,607,055,529
NEW MEXICO														
1	85,632,015	3,830,787	26,890,304	13,383,551	3,051,511	39,670,942	3,818,035	7,685,997	248,322	665,873,339	8,750,349	1,302,038	1,524,834	861,662,023
2	73,092,296	2,982,918	6,708,875	13,770,407	4,473,080	41,937,549	1,476,377	2,884,840	308,438	787,228,945	9,863,863	0	238,806	944,966,395
3	679,285,672	8,280,574	6,689,055	12,892,074	47,097,340	8,524,923	28,224,177	12,382,324	1,627,954	579,133,611	7,398,870	607,741	475,423	1,392,619,739
TOTAL	838,009,984	15,094,279	40,288,235	40,046,032	54,621,931	90,133,414	33,518,588	22,953,161	2,184,713	2,032,235,896	26,013,082	1,909,779	2,239,063	3,199,248,157
NEW YORK														
1	90,942,040	748,622	3,366,098	649,155,531	321,032	52,990,980	0	14,836,879	592,953	646,561,421	7,444,350	598,970	422,814	1,467,981,690
2	90,979,894	83,115	10,156,578	19,489,697	349,343	126,337	0	5,073,536	976,382	645,284,560	2,246,537	0	0	774,765,980
3	132,642,802	5,973,530	18,463,449	11,904,472	39,355	1,034,219	0	7,345,407	7,818,531	1,148,103,523	16,831,437	794,608	15,909,494	1,366,860,828
4	81,271,579	9,127,486	2,791,333	6,936,689	117,604	1,672,685	0	826,348	639,335	977,964,377	5,004,378	131,038	0	1,086,482,853
5	81,612,614	13,112,180	16,182,780	12,583,798	106,222	2,219,571	0	4,267,887	6,834,998	968,877,444	12,222,392	283,947	0	1,118,303,834
6	219,002,894	89,303	0	5,749,114	352,589	789,347	0	2,807,527	1,183,051	979,099,908	21,184,450	0	0	1,230,258,182
7	194,401,229	1,196,161	0	201,190	59,937	173,261	0	2,807,057	4,547,834	983,074,046	3,779,404	0	0	1,190,240,120
8	235,714,146	2,157,077	702,503	16,645,297	212,194	1,105,751	0	4,649,611	7,621,511	969,584,944	15,535,997	0	0	1,253,929,031
9	193,348,969	929,292	0	133,043	59,613	4,982	0	2,736,789	387,293	977,794,118	10,048,942	0	0	1,185,443,041
10	294,353,563	3,637,085	85,174,973	59,746,308	4,609,533	273,112	0	6,125,132	5,817,843	917,192,013	6,051,540	0	0	1,382,981,100
11	295,076,524	3,148,061	87,003,472	55,744,755	4,654,672	106,808	0	6,266,977	4,702,297	926,304,073	29,421,252	0	25,855	1,412,454,746
12	298,317,444	3,541,637	86,691,412	54,115,452	10,803,835	18,833,303	0	6,043,304	4,584,194	923,998,429	44,713,391	0	0	1,451,642,403
13	297,664,166	3,814,022	87,524,907	45,493,867	4,690,566	106,961	0	9,820,992	4,150,202	927,567,865	17,594,636	0	0	1,398,428,183
14	187,446,501	994,799	27,269,516	15,425,736	1,470,893	173,607	0	8,970,314	1,443,730	924,325,681	18,687,541	64,762	0	1,186,273,079
15	642,244,289	33,300,155	165,601,312	52,108,104	1,034,147	2,605,998	0	221,932,906	189,836,037	1,054,975,981	43,436,848	761,961	367,734	2,408,205,469
16	642,095,392	7,630,317	50,204,325	63,502,556	430,074	3,263,610	914,030	28,025,650	50,737,962	1,054,840,743	90,220,577	60,966	367,731	1,992,293,932
17	606,895,814	3,399,955	37,982,725	48,786,319	901,401	667,714	0	90,689,405	87,124,442	1,036,826,377	74,862,932	645,384	1,633,208	1,990,415,675

18	375,534,056	4,214,387	515,261	82,443,390	944,909	2,570,350	0	12,796,387	23,651,470	978,020,307	142,536,797	0	0	1,623,227,313
19	299,153,399	4,365,748	2,542,916	99,169,050	471,236	1,966,353	0	20,767,573	14,491,199	973,163,674	27,523,858	143,621	0	1,443,758,627
20	132,612,276	31,337,639	11,718,524	41,437,722	621,778	646,834	0	14,856,332	26,095,539	1,011,951,377	20,212,533	553,898	0	1,292,044,453
21	121,211,400	11,172,463	7,604,298	17,179,272	2,228,102	1,088,625	0	3,281,796	4,320,240	867,151,644	8,046,086	65,882	0	1,043,349,808
22	145,954,845	3,393,527	5,651,602	19,933,559	520,390	2,226,440	0	4,980,558	13,126,858	858,603,956	15,806,195	194,839	0	1,070,392,769
23	5,582,812,127	13,115,079	24,911,012	31,392,705	677,120	30,557,037	0	26,972,782	22,585,576	997,468,898	20,146,374	657,771	38,376	6,751,334,856
24	112,367,520	7,388,083	4,774,747	12,279,364	1,519,351	2,640,076	0	5,047,617	4,203,334	906,210,479	8,650,374	0	39,320	1,065,120,265
25	147,374,280	6,269,534	13,337,425	18,150,961	2,717,236	12,417,599	112,725	5,794,194	7,163,125	926,401,963	5,813,761	281,184	0	1,145,833,986
26	160,059,023	15,972,474	18,096,067	16,769,142	5,295,993	5,256,296	3,964,273	5,804,985	8,017,461	887,276,485	13,349,056	0	0	1,139,861,254
27	115,338,447	1,790,728	22,969,417	27,979,919	727,894	12,231,695	0	6,437,964	20,619,989	842,340,711	10,998,403	359,018	152,821	1,061,947,007
28	130,264,638	19,305,573	9,807,362	16,501,772	79,856	45,897,308	0	3,168,820	86,036,087	916,180,451	7,481,470	800,381	0	1,235,523,716
29	131,678,864	6,458,202	11,052,509	17,447,506	1,325,684	1,717,558	83,123	5,330,124	4,785,624	856,469,036	7,636,080	892,311	885,369	1,045,761,991
30	128,949,541	26,365,108	19,218,590	16,597,743	229,166	4,640,265	241,302	2,019,304	128,412,197	871,517,059	9,596,129	363,553	2,017,962	1,210,167,921
31	135,688,847	3,085,093	7,218,978	20,110,536	436,851	15,983,696	289,236	2,823,267	1,600,550	905,546,453	10,385,580	114,459	135,242	1,103,418,787
32	132,348,190	2,968,294	17,891,071	24,799,307	329,915	26,665,948	92,359	16,477,932	2,855,303	931,924,120	10,737,188	803,167	593,290	1,168,486,085
33	152,576,317	7,901,286	19,506,349	21,710,553	944,258	4,100,529	138,430	3,465,144	7,071,228	939,733,917	15,127,998	1,398,238	103,170	1,173,777,416
34	138,848,095	4,598,571	7,523,889	12,453,176	223,547	4,292,648	4,195,344	3,396,566	4,884,778	968,787,229	11,036,745	58,577	0	1,160,299,163
TOTAL	12,726,781,724	262,584,584	883,455,399	1,614,077,607	49,506,294	261,047,505	10,030,822	566,647,064	758,919,151	31,701,123,264	764,371,230	10,028,535	22,692,384	49,631,265,562
NORTH CAROLINA														
1	144,335,131	4,613,389	1,635,248	32,182,057	270,410	10,497,364	60,657	4,376,271	3,196,436	880,096,204	11,230,085	0	0	1,092,493,253
2	154,404,684	2,060,502	4,246,864	31,945,246	136,200	14,016,583	88,647	41,206,958	118,369,368	870,542,872	16,762,330	1,324,205	0	1,255,104,458
3	129,691,883	8,070,290	2,706,653	21,428,261	1,811,380	1,095,771	249,780	4,185,363	1,321,344	755,824,349	10,813,489	0	0	937,198,562
4	1,965,518,306	6,065,568	8,532,495	26,878,972	63,229	166,145,549	1,542,405	7,307,465	8,006,245	759,067,116	9,329,590	1,098,276	12,439,900	2,971,995,116
5	98,853,675	2,344,411	4,629,251	20,852,802	23,110	4,959,347	0	32,969,031	4,010,716	873,874,019	8,875,078	365,232	0	1,051,756,671
6	67,474,068	1,458,829	3,245,989	20,779,302	346,383	19,841,497	112,329	4,734,187	3,443,158	875,745,637	11,417,901	0	761,964	1,009,361,244
7	132,372,628	562,618	5,000,321	29,799,984	4,313,534	7,748,776	1,808,455	3,577,917	696,507	747,233,969	11,342,887	0	776,536	945,234,132
8	90,113,479	930,405	2,663,788	20,020,906	655,237	247,763	0	8,190,653	3,012,692	895,607,140	8,544,031	-15,715	0	1,029,970,379
9	72,432,018	1,513,626	17,298,318	24,344,993	82,332	5,140,486	114,806	4,029,172	3,975,430	811,192,716	10,445,206	106,430	0	950,675,533
10	75,480,212	1,268,839	-262,515	15,867,443	7,194	3,876,117	0	2,921,077	2,379,363	829,243,468	8,737,238	0	0	939,518,436
11	107,870,122	6,901,155	3,380,077	23,065,926	1,156,554	3,982,146	6,023,262	4,234,791	2,651,536	1,066,847,012	6,227,160	721,048	3,181,041	1,236,241,831
TOTAL	3,038,546,206	35,789,630	53,076,489	267,165,890	8,865,563	237,551,401	10,000,342	117,732,884	151,062,795	9,365,274,503	113,724,995	3,599,475	17,159,442	13,419,549,615
NORTH DAKOTA														
TOTAL	436,809,013	3,982,195	15,079,915	35,790,980	7,839,613	59,590,943	17,851,616	9,947,167	4,566,497	1,427,744,248	9,889,837	129,179	34,473	2,029,255,675
OHIO														
1	154,007,975	510,945	11,894,106	29,101,000	565,503	45,432,411	0	16,955,585	1,721,962	980,325,516	30,894,018	581,995	291,626	1,272,282,641
2	123,789,490	15,507,329	8,831,482	16,442,740	393,488	15,334,216	0	2,469,975	2,297,661	798,086,613	20,634,291	0	188,544	1,003,975,827
3	129,457,143	3,130,384	11,504,566	30,345,242	66,991	8,001,757	0	6,657,197	852,276	842,766,273	19,669,717	334,053	162,805	1,052,948,404
4	90,067,249	1,355,953	2,849,187	12,631,727	497,770	240,453	0	3,703,063	5,370,594	883,062,003	9,651,078	0	0	1,009,429,077
5	61,861,145	537,101	2,544,525	9,155,273	22,186	6,675,107	0	5,631,900	1,392,009	806,010,252	8,113,031	4,674,978	87,241	906,704,749
6	193,851,578	4,039,544	5,259,177	13,673,496	402,138	994,066	0	8,183,544	2,413,739	847,497,829	15,054,418	0	1,724	1,091,371,251
7	109,297,168	5,528,150	3,143,812	13,862,070	5,195,361	9,858,347	0	5,106,401	13,204,773	762,095,716	20,013,705	131,513	0	947,437,017
8	82,891,269	55,688	1,279,167	11,053,121	46,287	4,670,936	0	2,940,924	73,936	762,510,324	11,501,082	65,882	0	877,088,617
9	187,240,259	989,593	15,307,879	54,824,680	672,976	8,952,923	0	7,259,763	594,119	932,344,433	23,269,067	750,640	112,171	1,232,318,502
10	676,740,935	3,530,405	9,692,560	20,604,653	1,339,624	25,132,340	0	7,302,819	9,884,599	819,711,048	14,897,714	0	49,776	1,588,886,473
11	57,662,578	344,255	21,277,431	79,674,844	422,502	15,443,751	0	3,155,973	1,710,951	765,735,850	7,350,438	0	0	952,778,574
12	1,996,068,922	302,279	3,497,254	39,431,308	85,999	7,094,246	0	8,898,098	3,446,844	719,076,847	15,882,755	564,431	1,093,666	2,795,442,650
13	74,686,442	432,397	2,101,671	19,492,863	445,570	109,142	0	4,531,595	4,680,361	788,201,220	9,474,787	65,882	1,761,529	905,983,459
14	113,188,513	255,660	21,365,723	41,712,092	807,099	10,892,019	848,759	7,095,048	359,382	906,956,016	9,936,491	0	233,416	1,113,650,218
15	1,067,632,941	16,384	713,751	27,385,309	626,508	26,851,655	0	10,984,706	-5,143	738,550,310	16,275,208	355,762	-34,403	1,889,352,988

See Appendix A for a listing of the congressional districts which represent the county in which the state capital is located and congressional districts which represent only portions of a county. See Appendix B for a listing of the programs included in each recipent category.

table continues

Table 3.8 Federal Outlays to Categories of Recipients by Congressional District, 1990 est. *(continued)*

District	State Gov't.	Counties	Cities/ Towns	Special Districts	Schools	Public Universities	Indian Tribes	Non-Profits	Private Universities	Individuals	For Profits	Small Businesses	All Others	Total
OHIO *continued*														
16	87,310,488	320,586	6,129,798	22,595,262	161,937	6,833,088	0	1,198,098	2,255,288	878,033,819	13,498,140	0	0	1,018,336,503
17	121,835,796	130,050	7,469,006	27,009,910	746,762	4,597,714	0	3,520,448	1,119,182	1,008,827,852	10,248,621	0	0	1,185,505,340
18	116,204,431	1,706,318	1,626,121	16,174,484	17,673	0	0	4,709,015	731,427	965,885,260	11,900,219	0	2,129	1,118,957,076
19	135,232,053	198,615	6,950,993	30,486,300	38,825	12,365	0	866,265	3,238,121	1,030,197,154	6,075,629	344,355	563,525	1,214,204,201
20	143,362,849	1,142,432	19,396,073	38,645,479	53,764	5,722,852	0	5,447,180	4,029,180	1,047,172,025	13,019,460	140,572	359,093	1,278,490,959
21	147,817,624	828,160	15,389,494	38,155,617	10,798,756	6,807,564	0	19,440,161	84,422,914	1,049,822,990	33,621,255	684,244	359,599	1,408,148,377
TOTAL	5,870,206,847	40,862,227	178,223,778	592,457,469	23,407,721	209,656,951	848,759	136,057,756	143,794,177	18,332,869,348	320,981,125	8,694,308	5,232,439	25,863,292,904
OKLAHOMA														
1	70,552,647	380,943	15,820,824	36,692,096	2,676,227	2,286,295	2,076,354	3,948,886	7,984,210	864,384,836	13,615,761	0	84,115	1,020,503,196
2	150,590,827	4,711,927	5,542,692	11,624,721	15,046,262	13,081,491	29,535,600	3,912,011	977,655	913,365,151	8,226,993	0	0	1,156,615,329
3	184,774,837	2,056,425	11,478,771	15,937,972	12,474,361	36,526,093	14,883,382	8,161,046	1,028,291	944,306,788	6,741,538	188,633	0	1,238,558,137
4	153,976,435	1,225,457	7,042,611	7,338,684	6,033,450	33,397,010	5,637,010	6,244,138	928,671	760,342,988	9,216,101	172,935	355,827	991,911,318
5	725,291,093	836,608	7,375,470	21,456,345	2,610,277	9,307,246	3,618,003	9,946,712	1,779,534	829,224,157	12,851,425	185,953	679,851	1,625,162,673
6	325,351,193	1,495,807	6,446,857	7,131,767	5,222,671	4,985,224	6,609,885	6,772,067	2,112,920	975,382,957	7,632,281	59,820	325,806	1,349,529,255
TOTAL	1,610,537,032	10,707,168	53,707,225	100,181,585	44,063,247	99,583,359	62,360,236	38,984,859	14,811,281	5,287,006,876	58,284,099	607,341	1,445,599	7,382,279,908
OREGON														
1	94,768,647	23,679,120	13,777,528	19,771,943	7,504,513	11,124,288	4,250,516	22,720,737	9,418,172	874,970,535	5,574,457	1,297,893	25,855	1,088,884,204
2	92,632,986	3,342,282	3,985,451	19,142,941	6,155,611	6,650,814	6,591,500	4,542,541	0	1,075,422,469	2,862,672	942,538	34,473	1,222,306,278
3	142,218,962	8,752,391	3,293,632	33,966,363	2,236,477	48,054,098	0	7,757,995	3,853,890	1,082,561,445	9,996,912	0	0	1,342,692,165
4	101,472,780	6,937,349	7,550,262	19,610,139	5,332,813	29,285,054	579,569	12,259,466	255,933	939,678,455	4,213,228	1,617,270	43,091	1,128,835,408
5	1,057,306,605	7,012,789	6,994,063	25,064,397	6,700,192	57,788,880	30,012	4,456,286	3,944,376	874,431,742	4,055,932	2,076,227	108,777	2,049,970,278
TOTAL	1,488,399,980	49,723,932	35,600,936	117,555,784	27,929,607	152,903,133	11,451,597	51,737,024	17,472,370	4,847,064,645	26,703,201	5,933,927	212,196	6,832,688,333
PENNSYLVANIA														
1	230,483,047	4,594,153	63,290,822	178,967,307	408,716	15,200,906	62,497	34,808,189	159,020,246	1,187,896,328	6,218,390	2,605,121	1,658,944	1,885,214,666
2	237,124,255	2,344,728	25,560,179	39,869,430	410,358	25,386,575	62,748	19,856,421	26,581,813	1,192,564,251	32,889,988	3,362,428	706,935	1,606,720,108
3	229,836,962	2,043,953	22,354,838	41,204,330	409,517	6,357,874	62,619	28,089,185	2,630,001	1,190,039,793	11,266,451	131,764	731,340	1,535,158,625
4	88,684,327	4,282,173	6,584,849	17,709,068	833,644	10,112,279	0	2,775,370	864,287	1,035,746,271	10,032,263	693,610	0	1,178,318,140
5	57,248,350	5,346,440	2,891,406	19,606,444	58,119	1,236,434	0	4,139,576	2,607,465	924,272,789	9,040,005	589,689	0	1,027,036,715
6	68,438,929	1,850,998	8,997,734	13,306,879	813,346	1,625,979	0	1,971,089	914,125	1,126,178,115	4,500,548	0	0	1,228,597,743
7	78,200,993	728,271	11,250,804	12,136,491	903,485	966,841	6,027	475,869	22,894,535	1,067,865,089	5,534,294	665,877	67,903	1,201,696,478
8	38,135,909	93,061	1,337,852	9,326,594	2,046,929	0	0	2,468,211	553,482	835,509,064	5,140,456	65,882	0	894,677,441
9	91,945,113	1,137,221	9,100,118	16,525,951	362,235	1,990,642	0	3,703,178	1,258,510	952,564,632	5,954,411	194,906	2,368	1,084,739,286
10	90,461,307	938,844	8,476,456	22,739,962	856,698	521,444	0	4,515,765	3,193,273	1,187,475,220	11,514,510	161,139	48,393	1,330,903,013
11	84,344,386	3,467,324	6,628,553	31,495,583	1,614,955	1,351,056	0	6,909,393	2,524,882	1,290,245,181	12,871,481	0	37,145	1,441,489,939
12	83,937,964	3,993,235	1,972,071	19,707,772	517,148	1,593,226	0	1,243,637	3,941,738	1,122,330,841	10,044,515	24,242	0	1,249,306,390
13	72,553,606	797,763	13,261,729	12,798,349	107,000	1,784,241	10,921	15,018,613	2,710,468	1,056,590,775	8,007,317	2,863,079	121,535	1,186,625,396
14	102,245,689	14,637,164	19,336,617	90,508,799	5,739,767	112,856,839	2,666,892	42,775,197	50,824,695	1,146,858,240	40,915,026	2,614,671	1,157,794	1,633,137,390
15	64,333,003	896,197	8,552,121	25,160,888	990,271	365,512	0	763,260	10,488,223	1,061,493,992	40,254,070	197,646	67,223	1,213,562,405
16	59,154,348	538,567	5,928,040	12,625,005	124,192	3,492,222	84,920	1,423,043	2,570,477	861,891,308	7,055,371	985,685	0	955,873,177
17	3,217,443,880	6,146,753	54,095,144	36,289,744	641,390	4,050,880	0	24,286,305	2,559,036	969,236,310	7,032,880	0	2,405,134	4,324,187,457
18	101,204,138	0	543,041	5,825,807	0	0	0	56,488	0	1,144,230,507	6,307,790	65,882	0	1,258,233,654
19	55,743,573	204,918	5,983,451	13,645,028	481,890	211,525	0	1,968,442	3,129,229	837,824,607	5,894,239	201,433	0	925,288,334
20	98,845,859	0	1,596,049	12,059,070	39,823	0	0	974,317	0	1,128,141,843	11,609,551	395,622	0	1,253,662,135
21	94,246,897	1,947,816	6,051,650	17,723,560	48,145	2,136,796	0	6,793,865	6,029,317	999,568,862	10,871,785	0	0	1,145,418,695
22	127,787,892	3,311,799	8,180,361	22,169,756	482,448	228,816	0	751,572	1,043,820	1,153,602,200	11,797,572	329,408	179,174	1,329,864,818
23	76,849,430	530,848	2,479,019	16,405,300	153,029	93,257,176	0	5,157,148	262,199	945,540,004	10,826,192	212,590	1,034	1,151,673,968
TOTAL	5,449,249,858	59,832,224	294,452,902	687,807,118	18,043,105	284,727,262	2,956,624	210,924,133	306,601,825	24,417,666,222	285,579,105	16,360,674	7,184,923	32,041,385,974

RHODE ISLAND														
1	449,671,662	2,723,008	11,721,989	48,768,173	3,149,636	2,378,915	271,379	21,862,911	40,846,067	901,036,475	17,844,330	180,092	146,955	1,500,601,593
2	279,580,845	2,478,644	5,318,774	26,799,408	192,492	23,587,525	1,895,075	10,676,102	3,471,283	892,569,673	6,238,489	0	109,143	1,252,917,455
TOTAL	729,252,508	5,201,652	17,040,763	75,567,581	3,342,129	25,966,441	2,166,454	32,539,013	44,317,350	1,793,606,148	24,082,820	180,092	256,098	2,753,519,047
SOUTH CAROLINA														
1	114,680,769	2,448,021	11,331,892	27,277,054	2,312,213	22,646,345	0	2,435,707	2,134,275	701,243,283	15,622,831	452,818	1,005,238	903,590,448
2	1,532,219,586	3,907,531	4,824,519	21,718,537	118,151	39,809,136	21,842	10,480,561	14,332,933	712,384,810	16,154,360	258,011	4,688,276	2,360,918,252
3	100,904,886	2,168,263	1,926,910	10,275,639	252,566	22,172,970	0	8,722,325	2,160,308	847,163,910	15,724,054	0	-462	1,011,471,369
4	81,473,468	1,330,725	5,524,408	21,066,527	53,433	2,599,292	0	2,891,648	2,751,255	849,151,135	17,956,640	0	0	984,798,533
5	123,322,414	2,539,315	5,419,602	12,371,459	1,907,171	870,134	314,431	6,365,021	4,028,661	792,595,641	9,815,978	0	0	959,549,826
6	164,622,199	4,113,813	5,854,034	11,920,515	2,470,871	3,827,182	0	9,306,248	1,348,925	807,265,316	10,975,329	0	0	1,021,704,432
TOTAL	2,117,223,322	16,507,669	34,881,366	104,629,730	7,114,405	91,925,058	336,273	40,201,511	26,756,357	4,709,804,095	86,249,193	710,829	5,693,052	7,242,032,859
SOUTH DAKOTA														
TOTAL	453,718,624	3,281,064	19,869,376	25,547,091	21,314,172	24,844,126	33,145,284	8,557,130	8,986,066	1,315,118,337	11,895,309	90,775	266,242	1,926,633,596
TENNESSEE														
1	151,490,394	480,961	9,673,264	14,379,356	77,787	5,837,109	0	1,498,645	2,719,734	885,095,939	11,153,240	0	0	1,082,406,428
2	128,271,429	4,488,119	5,786,264	28,328,829	295,488	37,479,315	0	2,311,023	7,214,106	889,534,316	18,700,372	887,375	0	1,123,296,635
3	134,893,143	2,377,279	7,172,332	26,459,496	1,052,540	4,008,309	0	3,411,642	6,798,811	908,646,625	13,366,580	2,877,208	2,484,243	1,113,548,208
4	189,266,715	1,703,615	2,855,029	20,961,998	150,075	3,901,732	0	8,988,121	2,936,254	916,225,739	8,669,982	405,113	0	1,156,064,373
5	1,702,728,863	4,989,167	34,071,812	54,403,964	99,927	13,504,477	394,756	63,434,614	33,670,712	851,225,805	27,664,374	0	1,879,097	2,788,067,569
6	131,324,381	0	817,407	12,482,776	471,879	5,882,529	0	5,787,792	358,245	804,627,273	17,596,706	0	0	979,348,988
7	180,932,535	1,082,478	5,566,537	28,804,527	350,042	3,761,818	12,270	5,978,007	1,497,194	782,772,168	10,566,959	71,636	0	1,021,396,170
8	191,770,155	1,382,886	3,984,055	44,948,515	174,976	4,314,064	0	16,451,932	3,352,212	915,585,823	26,727,975	0	762	1,208,693,354
9	175,687,108	6,704,069	8,390,496	23,828,410	123,814	26,132,497	0	19,245,381	3,526,380	773,664,699	3,443,093	64,886	0	1,040,810,834
TOTAL	2,986,364,721	23,208,575	78,317,198	254,597,871	2,796,527	104,821,850	407,026	127,107,158	62,073,648	7,727,378,386	137,889,280	4,306,218	4,364,102	11,513,632,561
TEXAS														
1	131,502,600	1,734,807	2,979,681	18,455,761	2,555,144	3,020,441	73,092	2,078,747	2,322,846	1,068,031,557	13,276,909	0	0	1,246,031,586
2	102,706,602	1,042,131	2,349,464	20,586,656	73,365	5,142,474	2,659,235	3,694,291	20,820	1,046,996,795	13,042,152	36,749	9,939,172	1,208,289,907
3	51,515,247	294,902	7,974,304	12,348,796	352,714	3,951,283	93,909	1,922,667	2,494,431	722,808,735	16,127,851	851,438	-870	820,735,406
4	81,524,567	862,303	4,725,729	24,827,628	2,513,748	2,040,049	1,201	396,669	5,088,400	1,119,092,697	11,617,142	0	378,897	1,253,069,030
5	52,787,130	2,941,427	11,986,808	12,590,816	430,406	52,268,755	113,808	9,242,574	3,514,043	727,832,358	12,654,997	846,514	-912	887,208,722
6	95,520,684	1,689,308	5,398,280	14,586,803	362,457	71,704,731	8,538	2,427,359	1,697,730	969,681,586	11,647,709	774,928	1,347,122	1,176,847,234
7	57,993,969	2,088,996	319,102	41,982,781	0	34,934,728	0	4,423,062	468,556	638,410,871	15,638,972	723,407	1,386,452	798,370,895
8	57,898,651	0	1,201,365	16,604,582	0	380,225	0	3,686,380	208,730	638,483,340	17,031,174	103,435	34,927	735,632,810
9	71,957,416	1,435,802	10,602,948	29,570,267	1,137,466	38,490,246	0	2,385,397	4,070,599	911,881,774	21,775,256	0	73,005	1,093,380,175
10	5,065,993,142	16,286,287	13,453,809	55,765,797	1,029,540	78,671,949	0	10,260,672	2,904,630	760,577,995	8,548,387	65,346	208,108	6,013,765,660
11	136,240,774	98,333	11,289,977	24,195,476	14,955,023	1,641,426	0	4,494,124	5,944,450	871,891,147	11,747,506	0	0	1,082,498,237
12	46,459,712	4,768,245	4,002,046	21,565,917	2,887,556	3,041,318	0	2,715,174	539,643	773,933,482	9,135,342	296,201	2,378,650	871,723,286
13	49,099,910	1,957,419	9,305,336	16,769,223	2,333,998	3,263,662	0	2,126,764	147,872	1,103,122,571	8,350,418	118,902	0	1,196,596,074
14	100,736,539	3,151,522	8,652,258	19,151,125	2,038,157	13,935,168	0	3,310,762	1,274,022	971,506,880	12,068,260	113,652	0	1,135,938,344
15	190,305,338	10,722,281	27,427,008	32,439,237	100,608	6,950,903	0	8,358,993	0	807,089,717	13,512,147	50,070	40,246	1,096,996,548
16	96,137,419	3,693,854	10,508,939	34,603,420	9,660,868	15,650,163	1,051,998	6,852,548	1,988,207	696,528,199	10,703,795	28,162	89,630	887,497,201
17	68,492,227	792,969	6,031,391	14,819,190	2,998,062	2,604,905	0	2,259,612	2,967,070	1,117,140,211	6,858,176	-1,183	0	1,224,962,631
18	57,928,291	0	7,876,841	11,110,635	105,771	20,780,560	0	8,876,833	87,891,084	638,522,999	15,375,852	185,610	35,075	848,689,551
19	58,957,731	2,828,641	4,079,431	11,141,912	861,980	14,213,702	0	5,741,806	1,453,163	881,429,061	10,332,722	0	0	991,040,149
20	98,877,028	3,034,729	21,348,548	47,287,724	6,971,632	7,226,066	0	17,499,110	8,526,876	787,232,247	14,575,166	189,857	638,454	1,013,407,436
21	64,295,565	1,833,910	9,931,546	14,872,167	3,743,856	608,861	0	664,640	791,213	923,756,515	12,056,605	176,291	68,946	1,032,800,115

See Appendix A for a listing of the congressional districts which represent the county in which the state capital is located and congressional districts which represent only portions of a county. See Appendix B for a listing of the programs included in each recipient category.

table continues

Table 3.8 Federal Outlays to Categories of Recipients by Congressional District, 1990 est. *(continued)*

District	State Gov't.	Counties	Cities/ Towns	Special Districts	Schools	Public Universities	Indian Tribes	Non-Profits	Private Universities	Individuals	For Profits	Small Businesses	All Others	Total
TEXAS *continued*														
22	50,547,614	17,644,710	45,555,613	10,788,704	1,272,241	16,267,809	0	2,067,681	4,578,743	603,698,946	24,116,059	249,354	16,100	776,803,573
23	147,043,088	4,858,901	18,757,044	37,440,572	9,742,731	38,596,517	102,039	22,546,337	931,021	832,596,923	11,043,142	906,259	0	1,124,564,575
24	51,818,354	135,100	9,113,477	36,037,911	415,638	261,897	240,019	861,692	3,858,931	731,940,123	10,977,923	2	-833	845,660,233
25	85,491,236	321,366	428,524	9,579,115	578,469	934,745	0	3,692,572	2,596,345	636,706,282	8,007,449	130,588	35,036	748,501,727
26	39,246,399	1,994,900	2,896,448	22,957,793	1,714,784	14,510,480	3,442	384,262	7,148,288	711,408,233	6,687,242	1,379,226	0	810,331,498
27	140,772,403	532,761	13,795,085	24,943,332	5,511,383	7,618,333	0	16,073,553	0	767,929,841	11,523,851	0	0	988,700,541
TOTAL	7,251,849,637	86,745,603	271,991,003	637,023,336	74,347,595	458,711,395	4,347,282	149,044,281	153,427,713	22,460,231,084	338,432,205	7,224,806	16,667,204	31,910,043,145
UTAH														
1	81,567,656	5,785,529	2,354,972	12,212,587	2,838,050	35,233,675	1,177,201	1,875,868	2,097,519	604,707,164	11,099,202	240,261	597,937	761,787,620
2	629,017,094	5,598,835	19,557,503	28,377,143	581,116	77,136,333	0	10,718,900	1,632,310	595,963,645	9,791,823	3,797,017	149,057	1,382,320,777
3	94,926,747	2,551,436	4,438,420	9,099,107	3,814,478	5,833,235	3,061,755	2,470,964	7,889,970	573,853,287	3,453,587	472,526	34,473	711,899,986
TOTAL	805,511,497	13,935,800	26,350,895	49,688,837	7,233,644	118,203,243	4,238,956	15,065,732	11,619,799	1,774,524,096	24,344,613	4,509,803	781,468	2,856,008,382
VERMONT														
TOTAL	364,683,329	6,594,931	16,437,173	12,692,344	325,399	44,570,899	128,122	10,549,817	9,531,483	841,204,345	7,620,386	822,487	525,589	1,315,686,302
VIRGINIA														
1	88,033,237	1,627,391	16,412,588	20,815,409	7,657,384	9,847,796	278,059	4,731,836	11,769,062	854,819,928	11,314,915	257,419	2,511,613	1,030,076,638
2	78,937,834	2,835,565	24,601,127	18,433,435	11,460,381	11,536,941	0	8,009,654	4,195,729	643,931,116	11,464,433	200,991	448,455	816,055,660
3	1,397,198,486	3,466,181	18,695,549	19,833,835	280,687	54,979,613	0	5,037,493	3,237,623	931,975,792	14,625,517	131,764	135,773	2,449,598,313
4	130,437,814	2,095,399	14,354,355	9,902,554	4,597,897	11,287,363	0	1,915,498	879,208	855,861,701	9,121,828	0	53,156	1,040,506,773
5	120,597,388	106,551	1,377,920	5,548,622	1,117	1,378,930	0	4,157,810	2,974,155	896,055,334	5,580,612	0	34,473	1,037,812,912
6	84,170,013	2,388,846	12,033,752	11,586,233	14,926	3,916,361	0	3,881,794	7,591,365	987,071,903	13,331,160	65,866	87,645	1,126,139,863
7	81,103,341	8,397,266	5,609,570	3,591,934	2,665,741	68,846,752	0	5,455,436	897,551	799,395,834	5,532,127	97,667	34,473	981,627,693
8	41,014,110	1,178,076	3,916,060	13,173,974	498,705	1,175,392	0	26,560,905	0	483,729,591	6,793,681	2,378,652	320,982	580,740,128
9	132,551,994	6,240,251	11,926,177	8,278,320	146,832	59,492,544	0	9,599,037	1,228,970	1,006,747,515	7,099,653	197,646	10,707	1,243,519,646
10	41,013,529	10,195,118	8,606,142	39,996,673	3,204,246	7,206,160	0	58,265,856	670,069	561,429,510	22,572,360	9,190,488	4,602,036	766,952,187
TOTAL	2,195,057,747	38,530,644	117,533,240	151,160,989	30,527,917	229,667,852	278,059	127,615,319	33,443,732	8,021,018,225	107,436,285	12,520,493	8,239,313	11,073,029,813
WASHINGTON														
1	146,884,178	535,699	5,745,288	39,032,212	2,494,202	5,202,963	1,369,021	5,873,865	511,801	832,209,390	9,217,328	2,277,027	172,591	1,051,525,564
2	139,108,055	2,216,153	6,132,392	27,277,852	6,301,195	6,319,950	15,971,116	2,073,673	257,420	1,008,368,557	9,704,488	0	23,075	1,223,753,927
3	1,436,514,589	2,107,792	14,286,691	16,912,677	905,390	6,695,165	1,967,387	9,243,178	575,024	925,087,718	8,326,862	314,340	106,414	2,423,043,227
4	165,153,425	4,194,672	8,115,496	15,180,937	8,360,020	5,909,933	10,863,214	33,940,889	1,087,622	874,251,164	8,981,557	1,797,065	1,629,003	1,139,464,997
5	160,488,629	1,361,606	12,448,803	13,870,201	11,818,833	53,305,944	1,406,007	4,491,236	7,247,137	943,849,436	10,124,651	544,584	59,122	1,221,016,187
6	174,895,745	3,004,464	14,790,565	35,256,581	14,020,872	2,446,603	2,921,347	1,967,055	5,062,810	790,954,841	11,878,340	0	243,191	1,057,442,414
7	158,056,913	13,990,865	16,330,946	40,007,487	7,828,204	239,552,055	1,033,084	66,536,947	7,314,025	852,642,302	8,155,344	2,423,406	481,633	1,414,353,211
8	157,723,710	615,184	24,063,915	17,771,488	893,282	7,698,992	1,495,082	2,999,941	975,833	855,010,681	6,395,149	1,562,672	279,429	1,077,485,358
TOTAL	2,538,825,244	28,026,435	101,914,096	205,309,435	52,621,997	327,131,606	37,026,257	127,126,785	23,031,673	7,082,374,088	72,783,718	8,919,093	2,994,457	10,608,084,885
WEST VIRGINIA														
1	70,677,744	1,303,946	16,681,663	22,018,115	243,724	6,594,014	0	6,413,285	5,387,691	956,877,520	13,054,057	62,206	84,513	1,099,398,478
2	107,368,389	2,108,339	1,885,937	10,924,754	267,018	36,689,547	0	17,357,863	3,164,311	906,179,960	6,560,361	180,437	28,310,462	1,120,997,379
3	881,646,759	3,770,606	1,170,350	29,901,255	425,881	3,034,816	0	2,252,785	530,703	910,058,839	8,000,392	0	255,564	1,841,047,949
4	117,695,353	1,113,095	7,253,410	24,180,706	18,021	8,675,512	1,306,007	5,860,742	1,614,360	1,013,284,491	3,806,582	0	38,093	1,184,846,372
TOTAL	1,177,388,246	8,295,986	26,991,361	87,024,830	954,644	54,993,889	1,306,007	31,884,676	10,697,065	3,786,400,810	31,421,391	242,643	28,688,631	5,246,290,178

WISCONSIN														
1	189,951,673	2,338,143	14,448,283	11,190,921	167,137	6,172,842	0	4,086,751	1,400,692	903,164,994	8,338,533	18,150	1,036,498	1,142,314,618
2	1,398,779,327	9,135,075	6,520,907	14,073,063	2,525,415	189,479,601	1,070,909	7,992,382	369,229	795,536,435	13,040,788	825,973	2,554,413	2,441,903,518
3	205,661,090	2,126,866	4,785,707	5,198,454	1,047,009	13,496,962	1,692,998	5,160,707	1,124,196	906,693,468	6,056,434	0	818,740	1,153,862,631
4	247,925,785	2,752,510	14,221,710	27,608,993	2,034,661	3,608,739	0	10,511,046	5,740,465	983,241,485	14,982,401	45,557	395,345	1,313,068,698
5	294,163,297	7,570,247	15,714,341	17,449,337	2,017,915	10,487,923	266,142	10,082,670	32,907,447	1,049,484,082	14,139,930	243,871	-435	1,454,526,765
6	159,132,386	81,001	805,237	5,765,935	2,188,241	4,035,587	711,770	1,525,055	2,536,025	965,297,878	8,103,334	296,468	0	1,150,478,919
7	201,890,868	2,149,900	9,840,779	10,413,576	3,967,406	13,993,982	5,514,157	3,540,168	1,497,307	967,073,911	9,538,412	36,516	0	1,229,456,983
8	166,861,673	475,024	3,658,125	21,982,638	5,105,852	1,297,578	13,709,675	2,062,943	1,666,816	920,538,132	7,337,394	0	0	1,144,695,851
9	101,200,591	6,417,742	2,201,618	5,997,027	832,217	251,754	0	198,300	2,737,784	821,446,596	8,744,652	0	460,180	950,488,461
TOTAL	2,965,566,690	33,046,507	72,196,707	119,679,945	19,885,853	242,824,969	22,965,651	45,160,023	49,979,962	8,312,476,980	90,281,877	1,466,536	5,264,742	11,980,796,444
WYOMING														
TOTAL	322,197,712	20,565,181	11,969,830	11,772,340	10,269,784	15,139,213	4,767,284	11,255,129	1,153,561	630,699,808	12,148,744	128,841	408,394	1,052,475,819
U.S. TOTAL														
	128,106.8 mil.	1,974.2 mil.	5,501.7 mil.	12,348.1 mil.	1,201.2 mil.	7,651.0 mil.	644.9 mil.	4,628.2 mil.	4,471.6 mil.	400,406.8 mil.	5,927.0 mil.	309.8 mil.	771.6 mil.	573,942.7 mil.

See Appendix A for a listing of the congressional districts which represent the county in which the state capital is located and congressional districts which represent only portions of a county. See Appendix B for a listing of the programs included in each recipent category.

Chapter 4

Trends in Federal Outlays for Functional Policy Categories for the United States and Major Regions, 1983-1990

Figure 4.1

Outlays for Agriculture Programs for the United States and Regions, 1983-1990

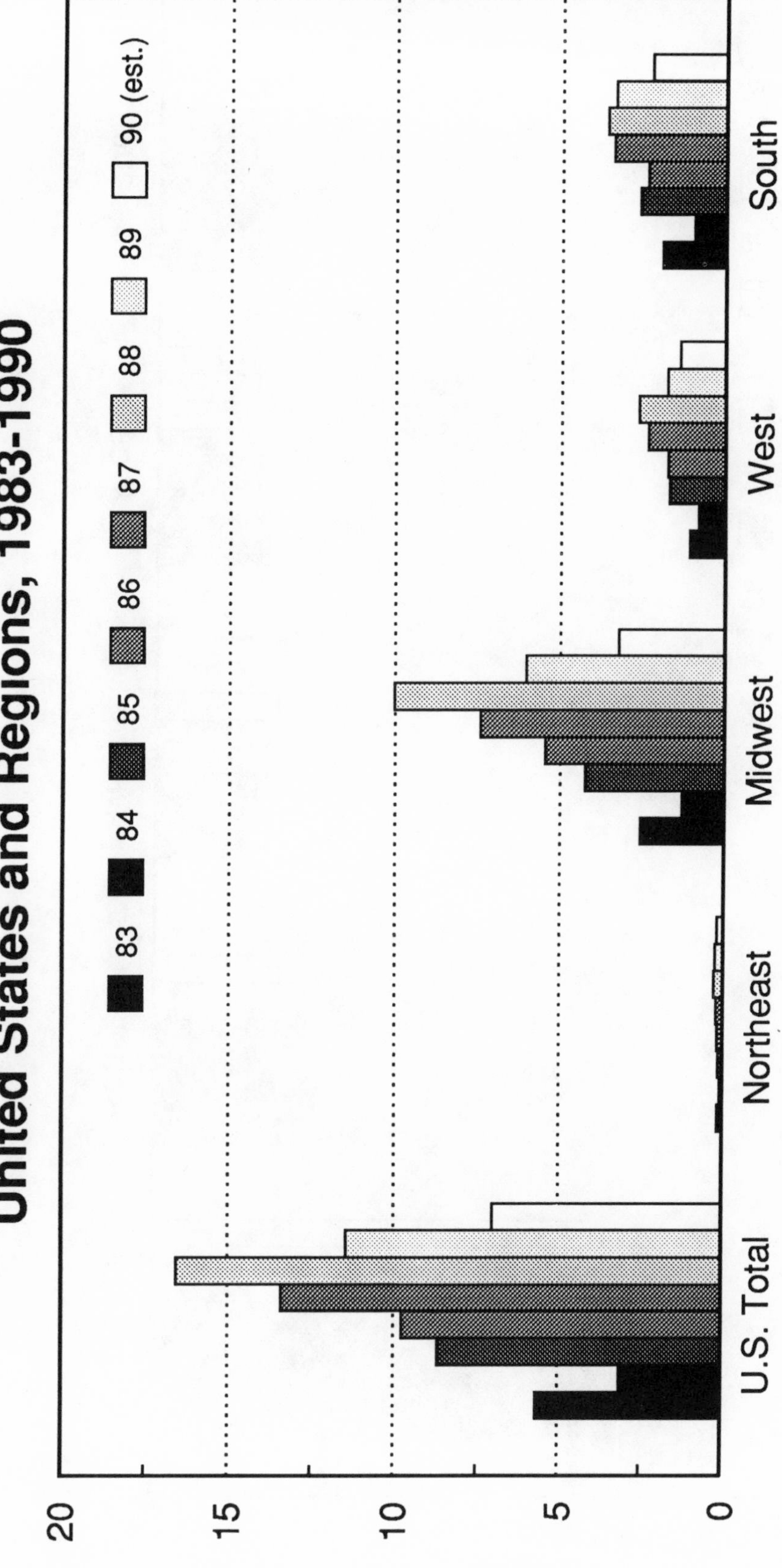

In billions of nominal dollars.
See Appendix C for programs in policy groups.
See Appendix D for states in each region.

Figure 4.2

Outlays for Business and Commerce Programs for the United States and Regions, 1983-1990

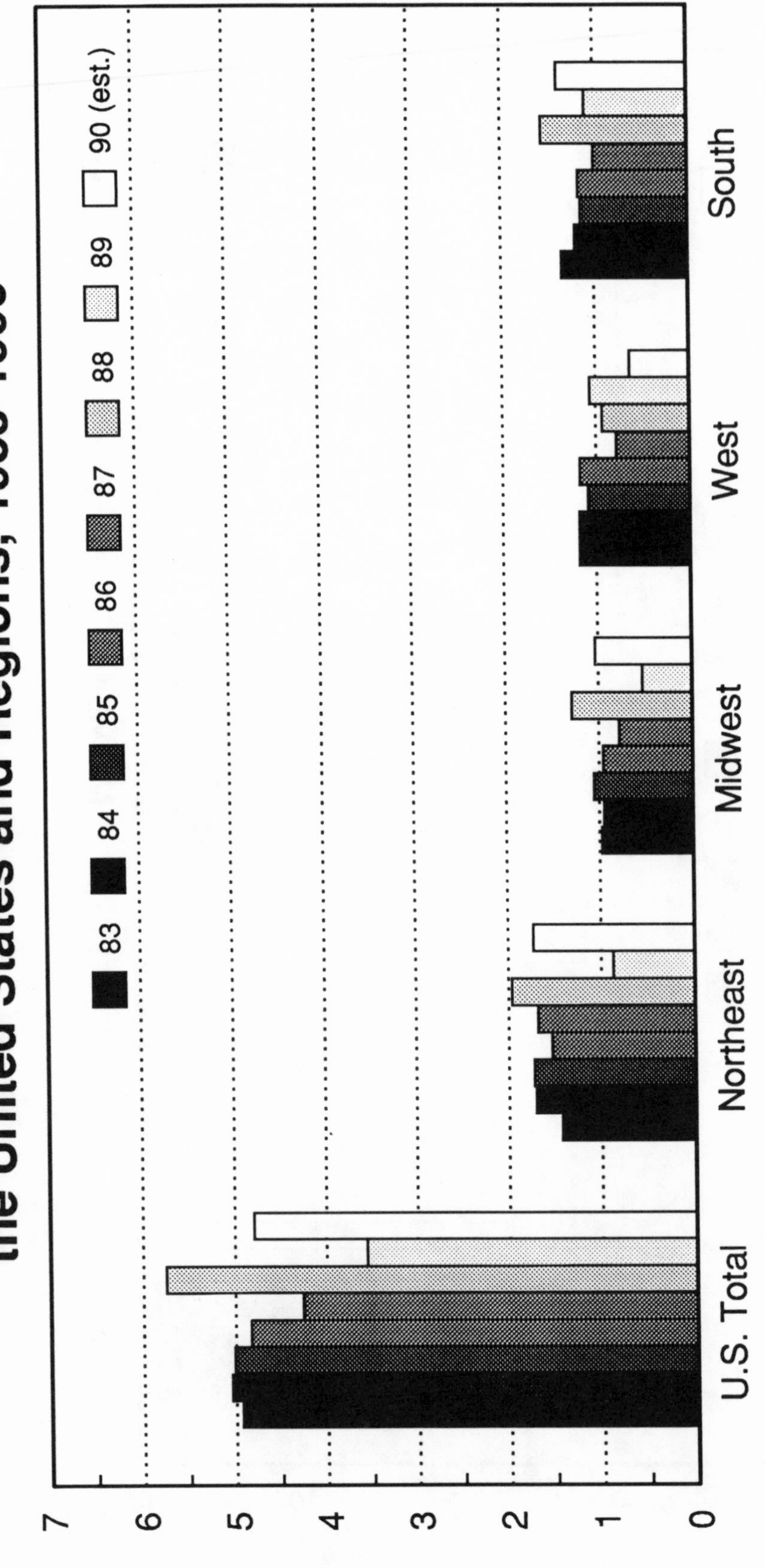

In billions of nominal dollars.
See Appendix C for programs in policy groups.
See Appendix D for states in each region.

Figure 4.3

Outlays for Community Development Programs for the United States and Regions, 1983-1990

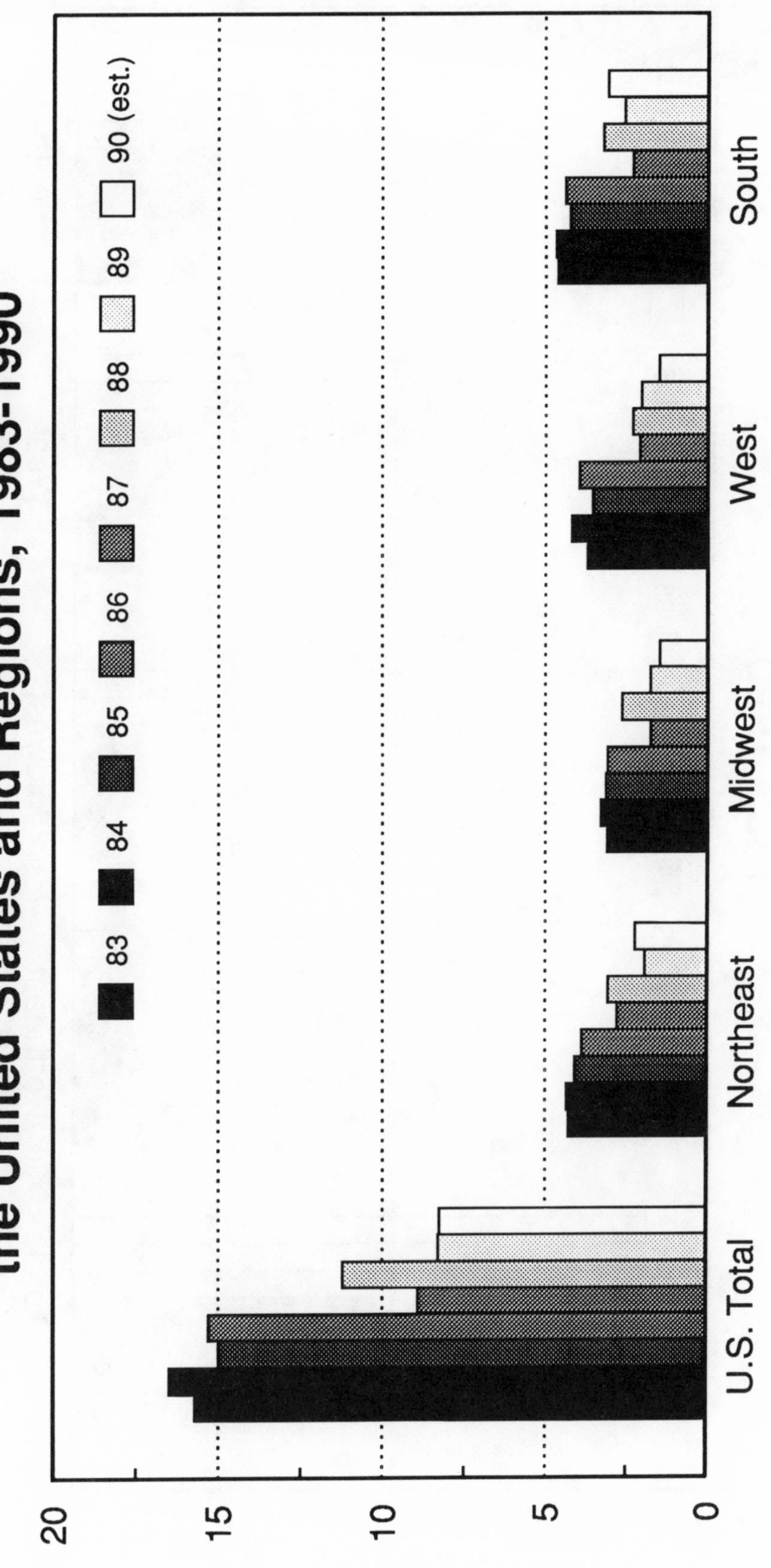

In billions of nominal dollars.
See Appendix C for programs in policy groups.
See Appendix D for states in each region.

Figure 4.4

Outlays for Disaster Prevention and Relief Programs for the United States and Regions, 1983-1990

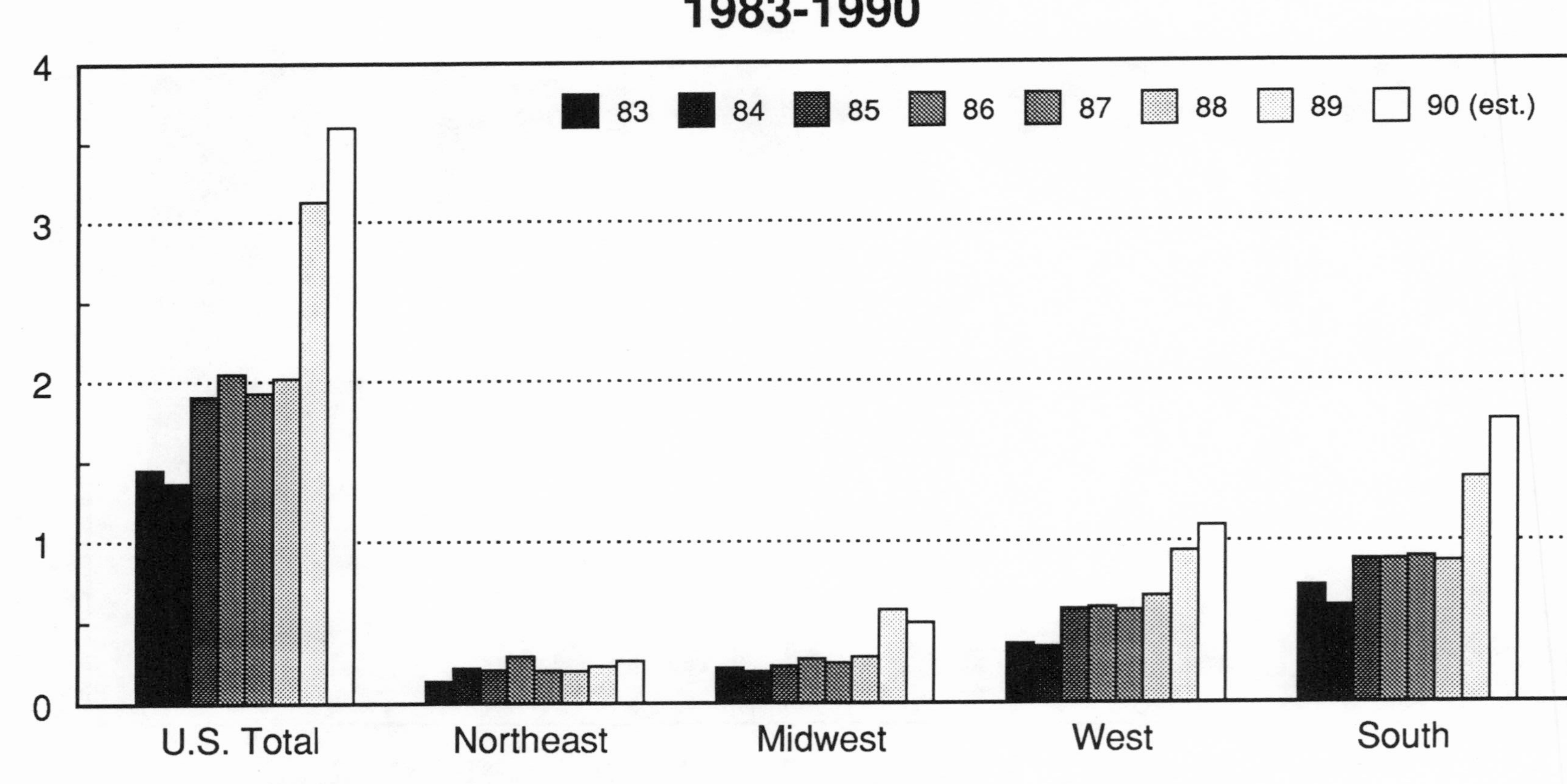

In billions of nominal dollars.
See Appendix C for programs in policy groups.
See Appendix D for states in each region.

Figure 4.5
Outlays for Education Programs for the United States and Regions, 1983-1990

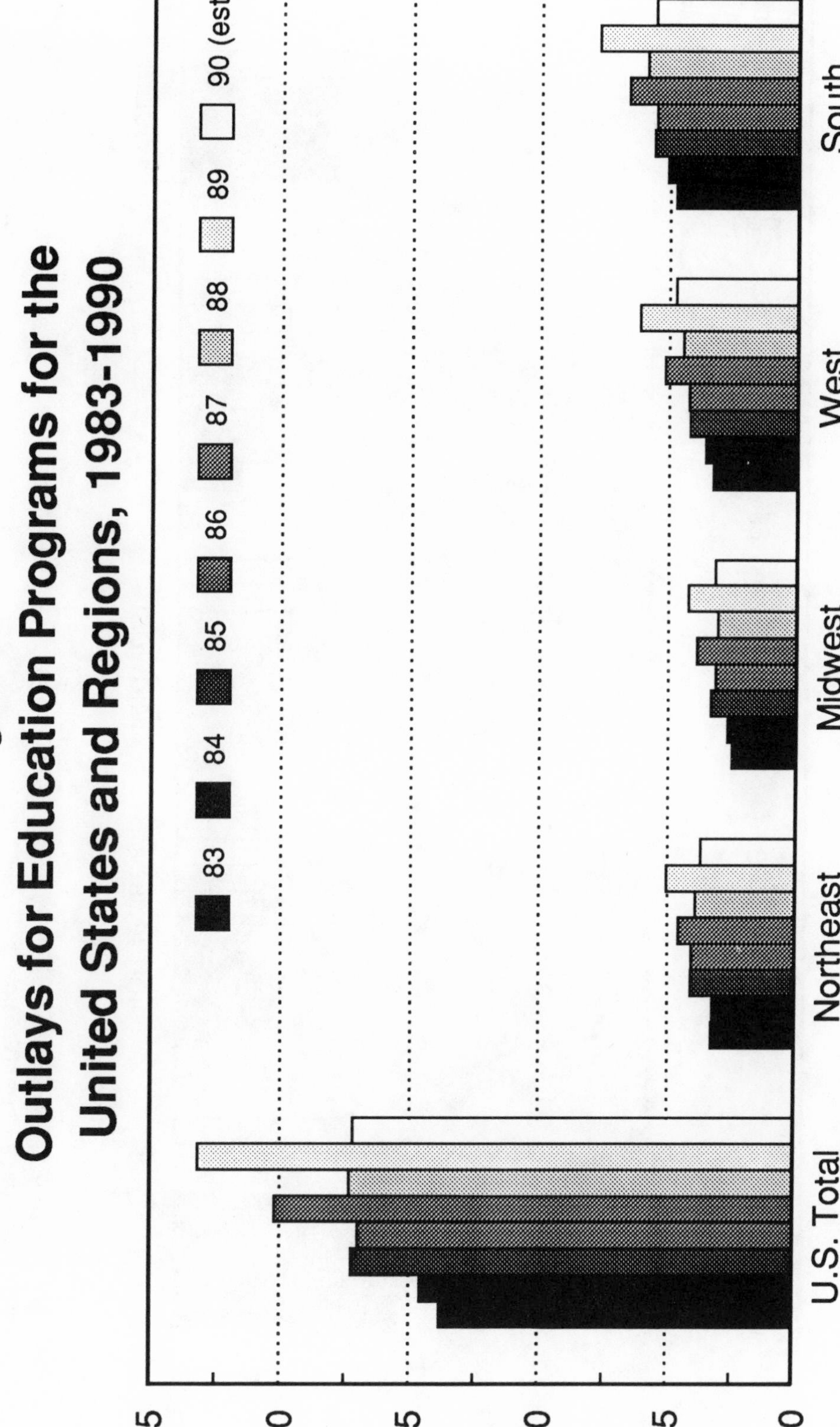

In billions of nominal dollars.
See Appendix C for programs in policy groups.
See Appendix D for states in each region.

Figure 4.6

Outlays for Employment, Labor, and Training Programs for the United States and Regions, 1983-1990

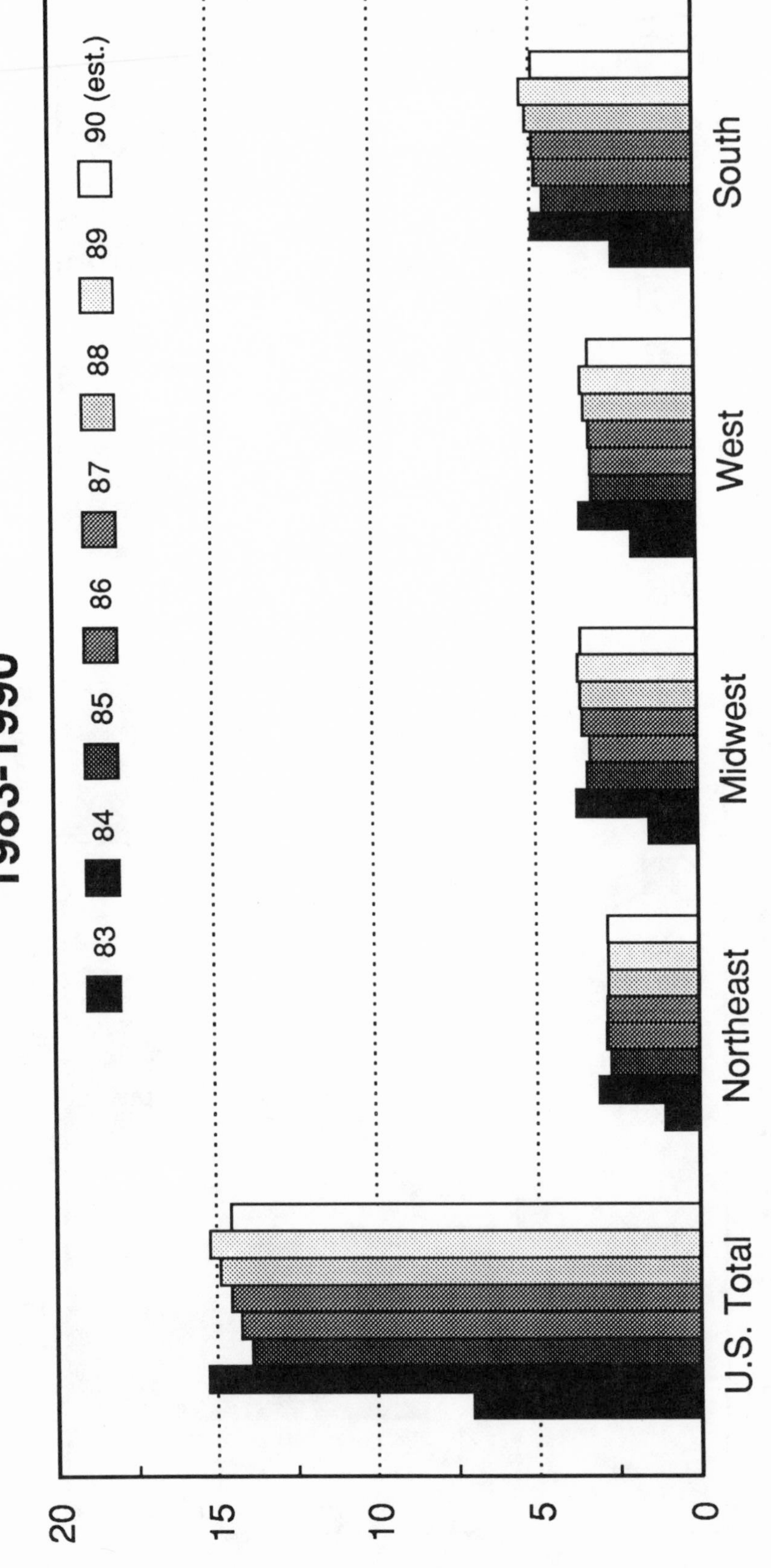

In billions of nominal dollars.
See Appendix C for programs in policy groups.
See Appendix D for states in each region.

Figure 4.7

Outlays for Environmental Quality Programs for the United States and Regions, 1983-1990

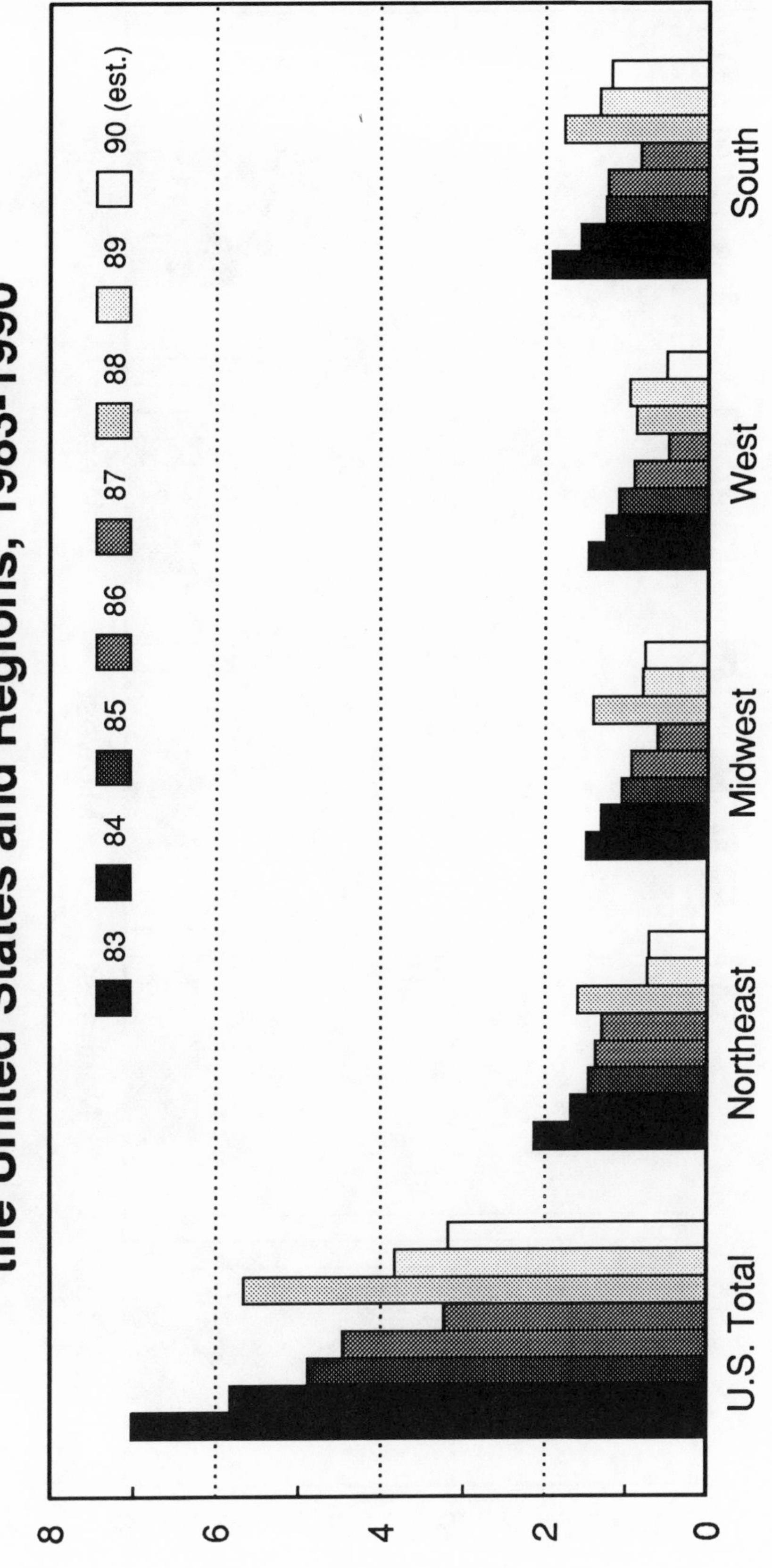

In billions of nominal dollars.
See Appendix C for programs in policy groups.
See Appendix D for states in each region.

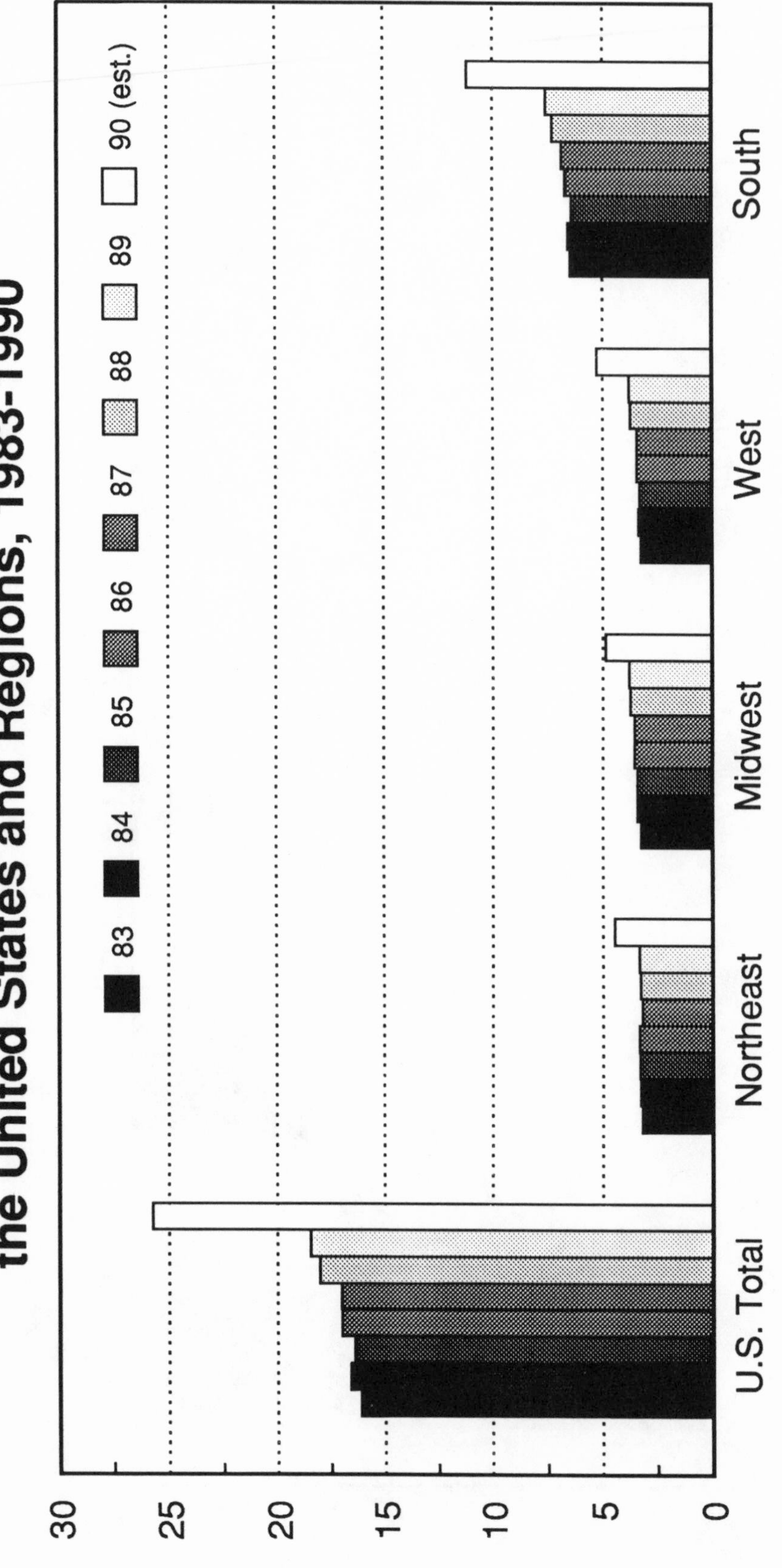

Figure 4.8

Outlays for Food and Nutrition Programs for the United States and Regions, 1983-1990

In billions of nominal dollars.
See Appendix C for programs in policy groups.
See Appendix D for states in each region.

Figure 4.9
Outlays for Health Programs for the United States and Regions, 1983-1990

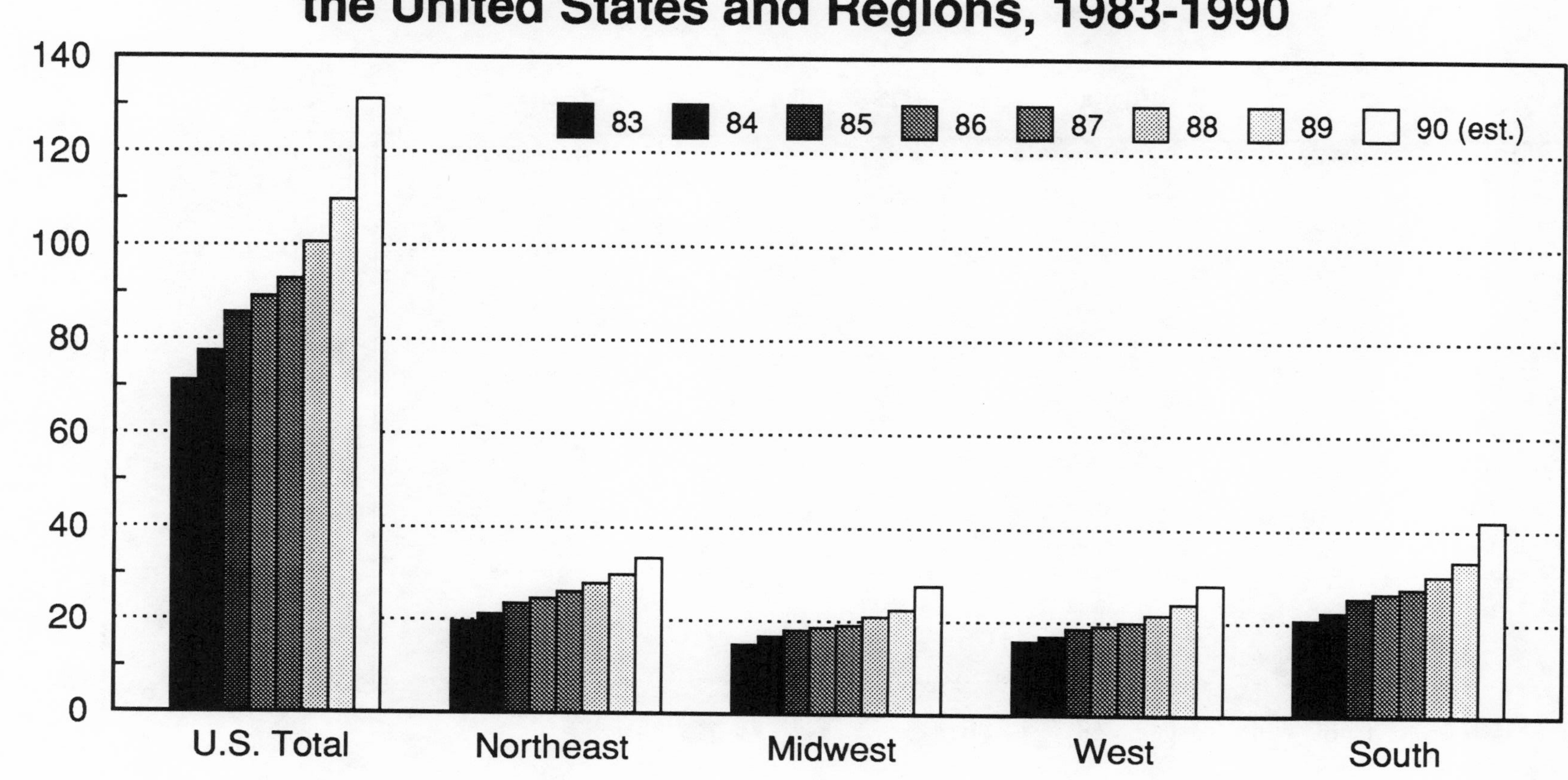

In billions of nominal dollars.
See Appendix C for programs in policy groups.
See Appendix D for states in each region.

Figure 4.10

Outlays for Housing Programs for the United States and Regions, 1983-1990

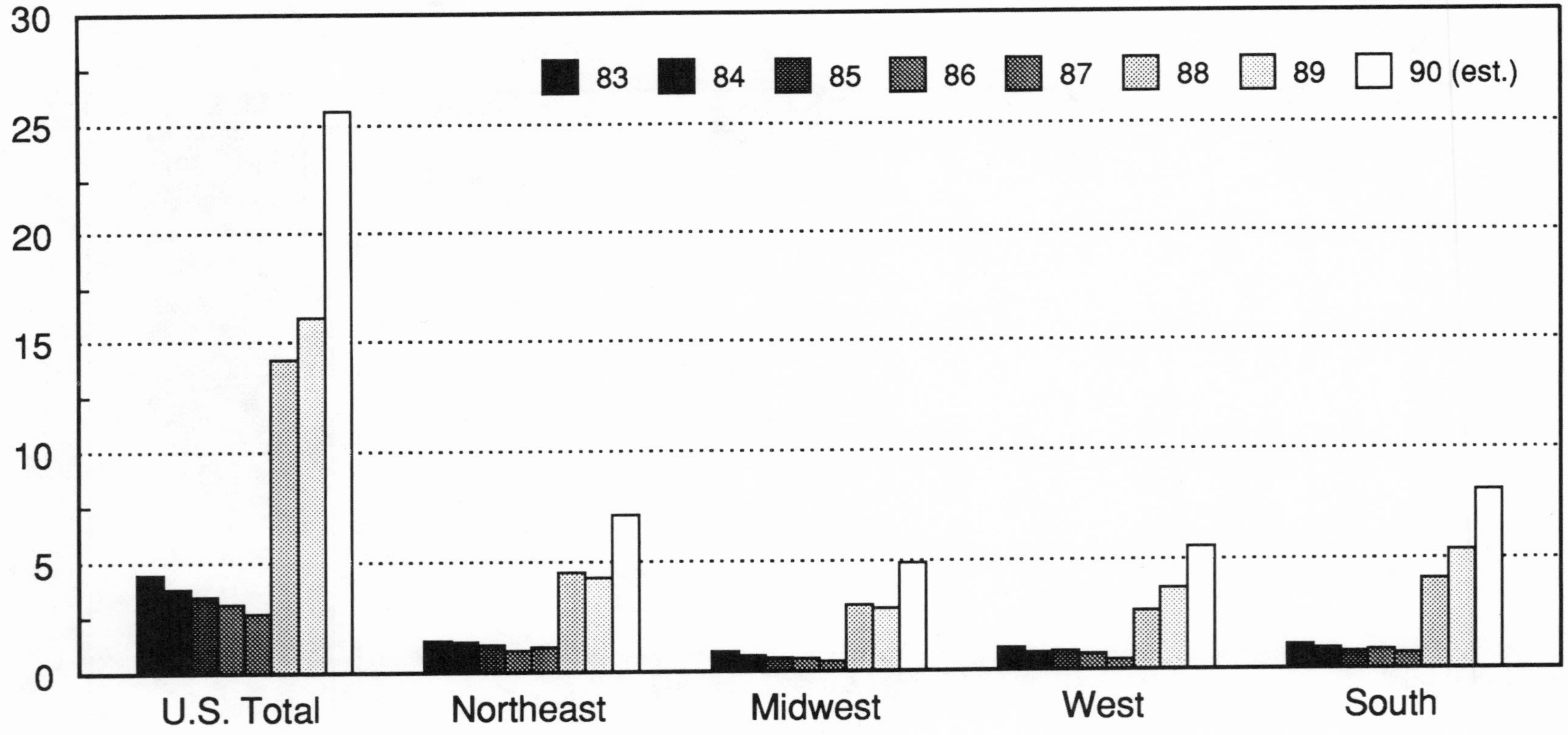

In billions of nominal dollars.
See Appendix C for programs in policy groups.
See Appendix D for states in each region.

Figure 4.11

Outlays for Income Security and Social Service Programs for the United States and Regions, 1983-1990

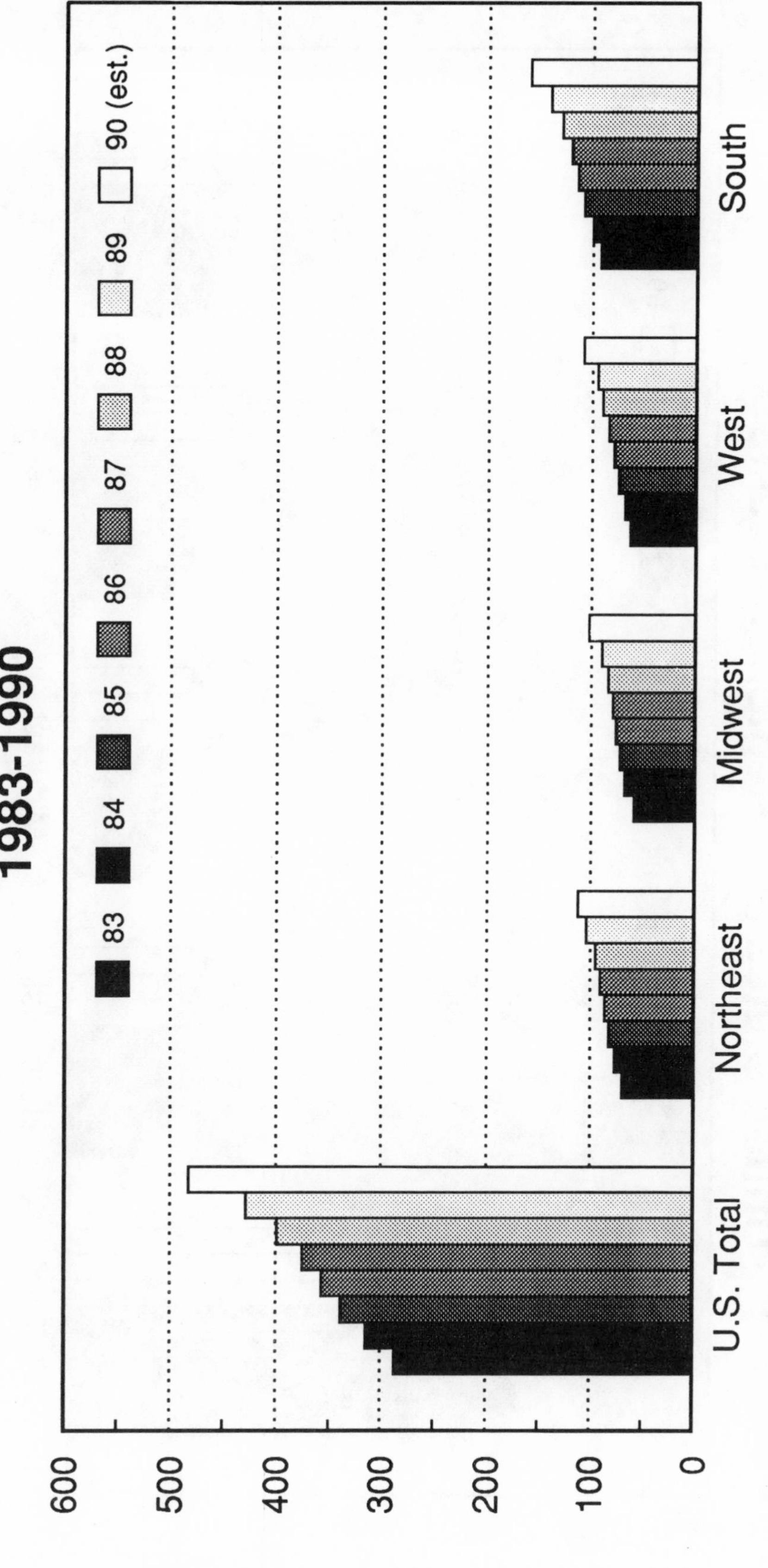

In billions of nominal dollars.
See Appendix C for programs in policy groups.
See Appendix D for states in each region.

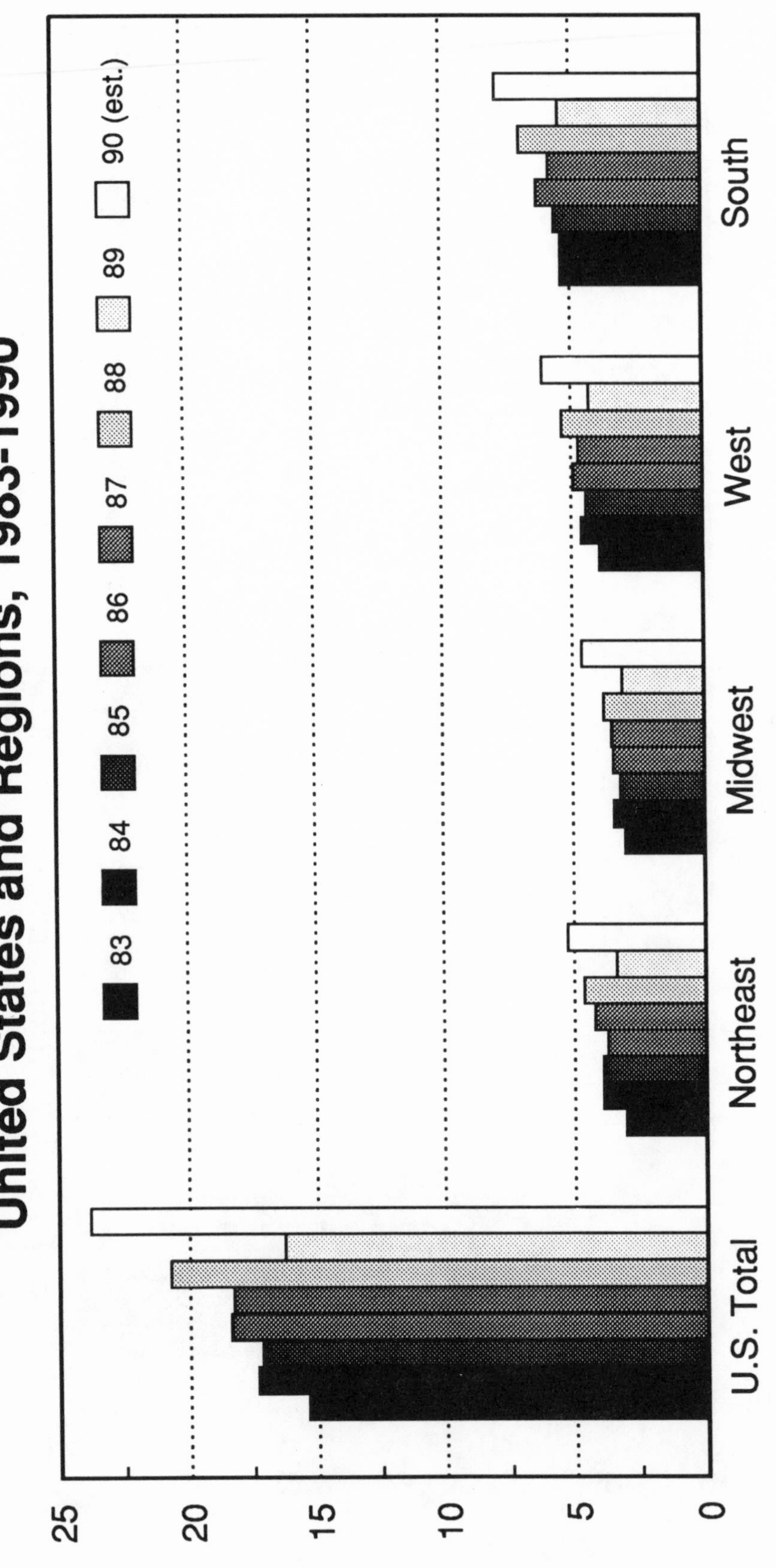

Figure 4.12

Outlays for Transportation Programs for the United States and Regions, 1983-1990

In billions of nominal dollars.
See Appendix C for programs in policy groups.
See Appendix D for states in each region.

CHAPTER 5

Trends in Federal Outlays for Functional Policy Categories by Congressional District, 1983-1990

Table 5.1 **Outlays for Agriculture Programs by Congressional District, 1983-1990**

Congressional District	1983	1984	1985	1986	1987	1988	1989	1990 (est.)
ALABAMA								
1	2,991,888	1,197,752	3,595,155	4,088,695	8,175,211	9,626,060	8,593,561	7,843,827
2	6,564,279	6,994,585	8,662,756	13,099,195	24,787,641	23,473,275	24,231,977	32,109,488
3	18,854,103	15,807,589	20,450,826	22,655,818	26,572,778	21,727,850	27,748,807	32,480,886
4	4,110,337	1,976,950	4,892,375	4,981,596	10,828,193	11,271,685	11,227,832	11,565,055
5	20,668,088	7,841,473	33,389,329	24,283,158	38,558,945	31,163,185	32,082,127	21,009,069
6	31,327	120,983	24,583	72,248	103,876	943,280	153,243	18,369
7	6,700,873	2,746,603	10,128,462	8,393,540	19,125,307	19,370,415	18,048,875	19,085,134
TOTAL	59,920,895	36,685,935	81,143,486	77,574,250	128,151,951	117,575,750	122,086,422	124,111,828
ALASKA								
TOTAL	8,281,666	3,912,893	4,724,468	5,691,927	6,803,386	8,086,531	5,766,078	2,922,113
ARIZONA								
1	13,820,400	3,535,687	19,395,770	13,398,180	24,260,264	18,438,124	19,707,371	7,848,896
2	21,158,851	4,776,586	19,959,750	14,713,866	22,841,897	20,047,054	21,304,793	7,861,513
3	6,723,300	1,598,953	6,689,195	5,686,601	8,528,218	7,634,820	6,845,615	3,641,542
4	11,479,974	3,226,493	15,033,290	10,791,888	18,857,164	15,007,610	15,858,830	6,605,010
5	24,936,727	6,564,046	39,884,052	32,357,259	46,060,868	36,706,472	38,776,133	16,303,119
TOTAL	78,119,252	19,701,764	100,962,057	76,947,794	120,548,411	97,834,080	102,492,742	42,260,079
ARKANSAS								
1	153,840,539	51,797,941	236,969,764	178,516,405	264,141,368	236,810,580	272,915,890	174,704,874
2	37,224,608	13,429,436	37,108,944	31,487,239	37,441,600	35,757,212	40,080,006	28,160,007
3	12,565,545	10,248,714	9,208,776	11,652,574	9,624,600	16,733,741	36,704,440	20,756,054
4	57,254,158	15,492,727	84,473,269	58,065,034	89,483,512	78,234,788	102,640,306	41,235,416
TOTAL	260,884,850	90,968,818	367,760,753	279,721,252	400,691,080	367,536,321	452,340,642	264,856,350
CALIFORNIA								
1	21,193,704	5,900,146	1,405,700	902,282	2,521,438	3,540,760	3,938,908	388,014
2	35,455,943	16,936,591	114,991,804	61,118,677	105,971,665	92,679,235	116,901,356	59,511,130
3	19,243,639	26,630,785	30,530,692	45,437,269	34,679,695	38,346,042	17,688,897	5,681,912
4	26,294,210	19,789,394	30,869,148	40,108,236	40,321,735	42,609,097	24,878,136	11,216,126
5	6,559	38,069	2,494,711	1,989,929	1,946,344	1,539,407	1,101,453	30,050
6	493,350	820,259	1,969,913	2,283,007	2,931,999	2,723,860	1,744,829	343,939
7	83,559	133,661	286,854	343,999	559,168	899,622	788,472	334,715
8	14,274,666	15,169,260	17,066,880	17,210,994	9,942,037	13,320,914	18,103,021	18,179,032
9	68,273	69,850	119,626	75,658	216,311	322,854	735,625	133,952
10	36,343	44,936	73,941	84,342	520,279	377,780	336,433	110,163
11	116,906	115,563	63,744	21,589	79,777	230,870	135,522	41,142
12	351,981	3,657,902	674,815	423,873	455,372	592,770	925,048	75,132
13	23,518	34,421	48,682	88,745	144,441	189,290	234,441	96,720
14	4,408,709	5,205,831	7,187,803	5,754,197	10,485,041	9,555,095	9,888,170	3,551,990
15	14,791,285	4,382,348	13,051,640	10,516,118	20,137,047	16,103,682	17,704,798	7,341,866
16	1,388,274	659,676	1,444,428	2,000,532	3,170,562	5,026,185	5,909,520	6,045,864
17	35,666,725	13,946,550	43,201,778	47,689,881	100,027,296	63,423,820	78,617,820	21,268,303
18	27,660,823	5,174,059	26,610,583	27,139,801	48,981,958	46,448,749	54,658,074	11,680,720
19	197,331	115,348	74,826	146,237	284,600	1,014,038	540,304	1,175,539
20	17,833,919	9,072,736	27,619,055	24,940,475	45,190,377	39,149,083	38,508,877	22,310,817
21	54,372	51,242	24,500	49,551	25,360	41,567	206,472	13,101
22	19,240	-111,144	55,622	32,052	37,790	25,028	8,906	3,827
23	19,219	34,256	55,563	18,351	37,750	25,002	8,897	3,823
24	19,216	34,250	55,552	32,012	37,743	24,997	8,895	3,823
25	19,198	34,218	55,500	31,981	537,707	1,524,973	508,887	3,819
26	16,871	30,071	48,774	28,105	33,138	21,947	7,810	3,356
27	19,210	34,240	428,333	32,002	58,732	24,990	8,893	3,821
28	19,208	34,235	55,528	31,998	37,727	24,986	508,891	3,821
29	19,212	34,243	55,540	32,005	37,735	24,992	8,893	3,822
30	19,178	34,183	55,444	31,949	37,670	24,948	8,878	3,815
31	19,224	34,264	55,576	32,025	359,759	25,008	8,899	3,824
32	19,285	34,374	55,754	32,127	37,880	25,088	8,928	3,836
33	52,230	34,275	55,593	32,035	43,951	53,016	8,902	3,825
34	23,316	34,277	55,596	32,037	37,773	25,017	8,902	3,826
35	141,504	167,877	135,496	184,752	153,407	132,341	72,903	35,205
36	5,046,674	5,401,573	7,142,071	9,296,363	9,249,892	12,735,906	5,233,854	1,786,031
37	4,594,449	5,166,540	6,981,139	9,440,303	7,895,973	10,758,825	4,444,461	1,504,424
38	15,979	23,081	6,835	7,586	9,060	0	124,108	5,505
39	19,934	45,704	18,143	7,318	9,068	0	124,213	5,510

table continues

Appendix A lists the congressional districts which represent the county in which the state capital is located, and those congressional districts which represent only portions of a county. Appendix C lists the programs included in each functional policy category.

Table 5.1 Outlays for Agriculture Programs by Congressional District, 1983-1990 *(continued)*

Congressional District	1983	1984	1985	1986	1987	1988	1989	1990 (est.)
CALIFORNIA *continued*								
40	15,978	-6,921	-3,152	7,585	9,060	404,000	420,209	5,505
41	99,252	84,105	138,325	215,017	216,308	115,984	333,111	3,492
42	18,061,050	523,328	802,418	22,458	26,524	15,241	53,524	4,464
43	2,889,258	97,820	151,882	235,212	237,037	125,695	275,948	5,376
44	112,739	127,429	209,579	325,776	327,732	175,730	625,923	5,291
45	7,222,273	3,018,388	9,431,939	10,194,977	14,300,178	10,317,618	7,405,758	2,741,768
TOTAL	258,147,786	142,893,296	345,914,174	318,661,420	462,362,098	414,766,052	413,774,770	175,682,035
COLORADO								
1	1,778,699	2,112,678	2,898,547	4,289,833	2,973,128	3,643,742	1,347,568	113,505
2	1,828,088	3,515,451	6,699,325	3,980,159	7,228,760	6,155,298	2,901,047	2,968,325
3	20,690,194	9,514,739	14,933,705	15,632,551	26,859,453	26,474,205	18,204,502	25,271,778
4	56,405,574	55,319,358	131,896,582	149,945,190	224,588,532	306,462,205	168,437,966	214,740,859
5	9,294,015	1,202,666	2,684,945	2,373,863	4,400,952	6,162,211	4,355,610	7,346,754
6	1,022,455	744,616	2,111,189	2,093,331	3,864,124	3,861,203	2,406,021	3,747,655
TOTAL	91,019,025	72,409,508	161,224,293	178,314,926	269,914,948	352,758,863	197,652,715	254,188,877
CONNECTICUT								
1	261,958	467,865	364,667	916,732	1,786,254	1,157,593	960,652	68,262
2	3,552,451	3,042,557	3,193,495	3,957,872	2,964,472	4,070,804	5,749,450	4,233,926
3	1,160,668	907,109	1,301,276	882,878	1,098,254	805,908	892,778	1,047,742
4	9,729	4,818	54,429	11,314	8,384	12,334	141,728	13,533
5	16,577	12,947	15,117	14,490	25,921	26,150	22,218	28,054
6	2,054,516	107,808	118,630	211,736	1,090,230	503,101	449,177	123,790
TOTAL	7,055,898	4,543,104	5,047,614	5,995,022	6,973,515	6,575,890	8,216,003	5,515,306
DELAWARE								
TOTAL	5,305,652	4,334,515	7,176,970	9,685,402	10,747,051	15,632,493	10,706,430	4,781,636
DISTRICT OF COLUMBIA								
TOTAL	10,053,063	12,056,454	15,171,958	13,839,301	13,913,688	15,137,255	32,469,243	29,498,423
FLORIDA								
1	1,651,305	599,053	2,890,633	3,157,001	4,479,191	4,909,347	5,513,275	7,501,022
2	14,029,222	8,817,006	16,533,759	14,853,397	20,773,936	25,891,847	21,653,637	24,628,669
3	48,205	109,297	56,828	34,303	74,645	100,837	62,908	41,654
4	279,901	243,894	223,972	245,397	356,373	1,706,112	428,571	2,597,804
5	142,024	72,695	114,464	930,810	96,504	161,388	141,653	128,845
6	8,682,647	10,501,918	11,566,192	14,468,150	9,068,617	11,796,287	15,754,060	16,170,493
7	59,762	138,321	86,397	59,125	179,564	217,056	121,258	99,664
8	603,639	-1,294	0	0	0	0	220,000	0
9	76,322	35,726	1,100,306	469,188	369,415	141,808	329,094	564,770
10	446,383	190,625	292,440	264,069	853,023	300,129	495,678	428,186
11	113,749	214,540	340,992	538,787	122,585	598,145	212,674	177,769
12	1,773,203	629,306	904,724	639,119	811,725	1,082,921	3,062,465	4,092,226
13	309,474	105,593	81,432	82,524	92,454	132,585	2,206,245	121,988
14	264,142	60,468	125,343	152,912	99,374	189,025	1,485,243	81,696
15	109,928	3,861	23,973	28	655	18	1,767	0
16	11,050	7,214	8,056	12,398	5,760	3,808	4,118	3,528
17	13,746	11,940	20,879	42,399	153,141	662,999	1,509,816	12,084
18	13,752	11,944	20,887	42,416	18,148	448,004	9,820	12,089
19	12,049	55,465	231,301	67,164	690,179	348,894	108,604	10,592
TOTAL	28,640,504	21,807,573	34,622,577	36,059,189	38,245,289	48,691,208	53,320,886	56,673,078
GEORGIA								
1	5,532,299	4,049,975	8,542,414	10,386,473	20,460,120	25,704,884	18,083,192	18,643,663
2	14,104,306	8,147,064	27,041,069	37,480,190	61,958,130	65,592,592	54,439,978	34,799,570
3	11,105,952	7,803,038	18,055,039	18,816,188	28,572,404	58,620,098	20,971,456	17,479,280
4	261,192	302,813	361,814	360,745	1,083,547	953,089	458,845	283,800
5	1,021,797	1,291,097	1,131,473	1,655,365	1,240,857	1,016,849	684,547	797,690
6	961,465	485,106	1,241,485	1,001,402	2,719,088	1,878,751	1,896,496	1,763,023
7	1,462,508	311,880	474,927	481,910	1,741,654	1,867,728	1,715,806	1,041,778
8	6,269,624	6,207,724	10,313,265	13,512,015	30,291,227	31,451,054	22,983,339	23,239,357
9	2,696,182	1,017,386	1,515,399	1,738,491	5,612,872	4,776,811	4,874,874	1,896,790
10	15,038,265	14,436,862	15,142,732	18,390,553	15,867,277	20,841,417	24,755,146	25,598,115
TOTAL	58,453,591	44,052,945	83,819,617	103,823,332	169,547,176	212,703,272	150,863,678	125,543,067

Appendix A lists the congressional districts which represent the county in which the state capital is located, and those congressional districts which represent only portions of a county. Appendix C lists the programs included in each functional policy category.

table continues

Table 5.1 Outlays for Agriculture Programs by Congressional District, 1983-1990 *(continued)*

Congressional District	1983	1984	1985	1986	1987	1988	1989	1990 (est.)
HAWAII								
1	7,695,716	4,546,358	4,017,181	3,529,675	2,754,945	3,190,096	4,213,183	3,140,908
2	2,776,211	2,941,458	3,468,687	3,257,499	5,571,481	12,636,461	5,405,142	7,824,215
TOTAL	10,471,927	7,487,816	7,485,868	6,787,174	8,326,426	15,826,557	9,618,325	10,965,123
IDAHO								
1	36,483,034	29,776,754	54,592,514	58,865,567	34,934,849	109,673,633	29,533,138	29,718,633
2	45,050,078	36,328,151	90,387,193	95,062,890	134,806,427	165,388,652	57,268,945	66,665,548
TOTAL	81,533,112	66,104,905	144,979,707	153,928,457	169,741,276	275,062,285	86,802,083	96,384,181
ILLINOIS								
1	37,281	35,564	155,463	108,577	160,015	199,102	700,158	5,466
2	37,273	35,557	155,429	108,553	159,980	199,058	125,130	5,465
3	37,281	35,564	155,462	108,576	160,013	209,100	125,156	5,466
4	1,865,637	1,106,040	5,751,453	8,227,200	13,200,801	35,708,266	10,058,831	862,482
5	37,276	35,559	155,441	108,561	159,992	199,074	125,140	5,466
6	131,961	64,945	372,170	395,207	567,838	694,665	336,084	29,394
7	92,280	35,564	155,460	108,574	160,011	1,114,088	125,155	5,466
8	37,280	32,816	155,460	108,574	160,011	199,098	125,155	5,466
9	37,286	35,569	155,486	308,592	219,038	254,131	620,176	5,467
10	394,283	134,650	796,178	1,054,052	1,460,833	1,775,805	1,099,256	107,404
11	37,277	35,561	155,448	108,566	159,999	199,083	125,146	5,466
12	4,241,740	793,125	5,127,926	7,108,491	12,815,446	15,288,474	10,547,225	1,709,694
13	376,442	222,149	1,013,557	1,366,317	2,196,449	6,301,035	1,572,865	149,064
14	9,702,134	3,339,590	30,940,768	45,164,302	71,573,473	92,038,981	56,334,996	10,088,106
15	31,134,434	10,819,130	89,741,869	126,955,831	188,874,915	241,746,201	146,119,727	18,517,833
16	31,725,336	2,076,701	59,866,356	81,681,428	129,443,443	164,313,585	107,036,755	40,814,158
17	40,924,341	1,234,996	82,288,703	117,622,657	179,441,446	227,067,430	142,803,035	66,862,404
18	20,687,573	7,486,316	51,945,631	74,986,470	111,814,207	146,613,330	90,000,214	27,385,929
19	52,658,318	25,052,835	87,346,759	125,224,521	198,627,184	217,260,136	140,832,437	62,643,475
20	20,404,940	9,579,136	58,534,073	74,085,102	130,218,391	161,905,141	95,475,275	31,090,049
21	10,281,236	2,964,979	8,805,580	13,813,533	26,213,888	28,576,134	14,894,798	3,897,621
22	18,633,798	12,842,106	31,332,376	39,384,489	73,573,707	90,293,695	53,275,309	44,628,569
TOTAL	243,515,407	77,998,455	515,107,049	718,138,173	1,141,361,080	1,432,155,612	872,458,023	308,829,910
INDIANA								
1	3,784,097	1,151,940	5,465,629	8,395,735	10,905,582	15,512,970	9,521,020	2,163,042
2	20,284,937	3,968,761	23,244,300	37,813,817	55,228,578	98,393,740	43,923,811	15,199,669
3	7,597,917	3,298,284	15,416,052	23,982,366	36,353,441	47,646,225	29,817,648	8,524,524
4	12,638,696	5,172,031	20,854,629	33,445,025	52,981,987	67,003,563	39,972,728	23,863,031
5	14,070,985	8,042,964	42,017,533	62,253,720	17,626,555	110,037,345	77,566,739	19,481,870
6	6,224,710	3,942,079	18,737,325	32,636,463	47,277,798	69,673,044	38,733,285	8,588,658
7	27,857,185	19,601,050	55,743,909	73,534,826	102,098,843	130,737,212	87,398,969	40,574,131
8	15,414,792	6,776,798	30,414,740	43,974,736	66,614,396	83,243,987	48,065,786	21,759,343
9	9,004,539	4,281,034	17,797,859	27,296,277	40,899,381	54,748,235	33,096,583	15,919,497
10	3,727,372	281,274	589,072	822,922	2,000,299	2,065,116	1,308,110	47,943
TOTAL	120,605,231	56,516,215	230,281,048	344,155,886	431,986,861	679,061,435	409,404,679	156,121,708
IOWA								
1	48,746,887	5,040,475	72,169,205	101,501,626	146,964,407	191,107,225	128,697,946	73,592,986
2	43,584,384	7,128,503	88,542,984	219,010,770	83,535,122	255,848,938	161,221,562	82,309,894
3	99,179,174	13,893,510	123,472,604	170,009,119	203,232,080	374,126,081	211,108,774	112,795,910
4	46,040,787	15,627,969	60,761,244	73,900,016	11,991,404	138,230,765	102,243,275	37,806,391
5	112,779,511	10,951,579	149,955,055	206,530,372	311,751,900	464,801,514	269,174,312	125,698,588
6	130,171,035	22,009,289	207,214,172	280,153,558	386,410,378	576,779,435	332,968,845	131,120,728
TOTAL	480,501,778	74,651,325	702,115,264	1,051,105,461	1,143,885,291	2,000,893,958	1,205,414,714	563,324,498
KANSAS								
1	201,929,186	193,344,282	403,013,742	449,628,575	537,333,614	788,353,655	404,974,754	293,177,430
2	26,567,868	20,479,910	34,933,115	49,676,390	57,890,486	83,088,780	59,637,624	33,745,226
3	2,032,549	1,205,276	2,994,841	4,002,355	11,694,458	15,475,090	15,757,570	5,667,125
4	21,878,448	25,277,966	54,411,961	56,358,733	90,322,790	85,017,904	29,266,644	21,325,921
5	28,908,650	28,608,436	56,768,508	-18,761,079	173,447,617	115,256,788	62,293,975	40,417,158
TOTAL	281,316,701	268,915,870	552,122,167	540,904,974	870,688,965	1,087,192,217	571,930,567	394,332,860

Appendix A lists the congressional districts which represent the county in which the state capital is located, and those congressional districts which represent only portions of a county. Appendix C lists the programs included in each functional policy category.

table continues

Table 5.1 Outlays for Agriculture Programs by Congressional District, 1983-1990 *(continued)*

Congressional District	1983	1984	1985	1986	1987	1988	1989	1990 (est.)
KENTUCKY								
1	11,284,949	8,207,281	20,483,277	37,025,496	71,985,206	97,908,929	61,534,394	49,822,236
2	7,210,395	3,094,146	8,688,904	15,139,450	29,214,609	35,929,170	26,123,964	12,664,039
3	39,697	68,983	25,096	77,820	155,699	230,059	247,415	15,899
4	2,129,198	398,828	929,387	1,591,893	2,548,674	3,519,176	3,403,797	835,932
5	5,708,187	1,408,933	2,031,969	3,576,703	8,980,405	12,187,133	14,185,531	7,509,291
6	18,658,074	17,312,283	17,827,522	22,380,628	16,727,552	24,492,904	29,287,164	24,516,436
7	4,249,661	419,069	740,499	1,290,185	4,029,876	3,519,655	4,521,198	4,521,060
TOTAL	49,280,161	30,909,523	50,726,654	81,082,175	133,642,021	177,787,026	139,303,463	99,884,892
LOUISIANA								
1	164,709	49,112	71,992	301,237	149,112	60,096	153,438	9,227
2	0	20,947	21,191	204,528	82,573	0	63,048	0
3	450,487	229,512	469,284	321,128	410,400	589,432	1,199,509	520,500
4	5,499,183	1,926,172	8,468,419	6,768,078	9,898,700	11,077,819	11,905,070	5,084,016
5	64,467,821	11,385,111	96,519,294	75,599,920	120,638,808	91,688,897	113,081,835	56,489,354
6	15,125,280	15,513,345	17,067,620	17,247,775	17,473,330	18,144,089	21,000,930	17,843,952
7	49,333,311	13,692,002	69,895,184	36,017,077	51,094,501	47,826,256	66,778,272	49,061,313
8	14,935,080	4,969,757	26,623,754	14,543,477	25,595,242	24,440,837	31,137,094	24,914,448
TOTAL	149,975,871	47,785,958	219,136,737	151,003,220	225,342,665	193,827,426	245,319,197	153,922,810
MAINE								
1	6,615,608	1,291,376	3,335,537	2,363,421	3,824,169	3,821,887	3,704,797	4,394,484
2	8,511,202	5,276,461	5,669,126	6,582,110	8,542,126	12,816,133	13,496,393	19,010,549
TOTAL	15,126,810	6,567,837	9,004,663	8,945,531	12,366,295	16,638,020	17,201,190	23,405,034
MARYLAND								
1	5,559,160	4,415,430	10,870,571	15,977,518	24,332,246	32,647,059	16,474,087	7,396,253
2	161,380	199,021	581,485	660,945	1,404,701	1,760,648	961,530	142,908
3	147,477	265,036	451,206	535,747	614,578	1,161,594	461,685	95,996
4	1,939,058	1,614,320	3,191,108	2,175,733	3,870,154	2,137,333	4,301,220	862,789
5	6,463,686	9,351,697	8,130,138	9,146,568	4,545,807	6,975,168	10,223,044	10,430,553
6	1,458,403	738,295	1,953,106	3,122,264	6,076,413	6,070,810	4,443,448	1,510,209
7	55,724	112,395	160,220	163,715	112,692	189,132	154,100	876
8	1,259,413	306,220	1,026,761	1,359,470	12,695,899	2,825,251	1,223,358	224,974
TOTAL	17,044,301	17,002,415	26,364,596	33,141,960	53,652,491	53,766,994	38,242,472	20,664,558
MASSACHUSETTS								
1	6,936,902	5,541,050	5,251,776	6,247,016	5,381,131	6,040,355	9,643,768	9,007,704
2	90,641	69,933	75,677	71,462	168,288	73,540	75,478	889,795
3	76,883	71,183	77,317	105,405	176,625	79,892	80,399	71,252
4	57,566	171,544	108,409	55,592	678,467	675,329	443,554	49,527
5	22,029	32,764	249,494	22,148	27,970	36,306	40,294	40,211
6	257,500	19,142	20,404	27,448	22,736	1,473,926	33,479	41,817
7	157,003	154,601	374,713	388,603	436,214	267,335	256,586	38,708
8	989,766	1,711,127	2,423,621	847,333	1,540,331	1,564,612	1,494,451	19,710
9	400,052	274,159	304,719	663,572	1,577,662	1,333,962	1,341,745	474,185
10	48,973	128,964	111,733	100,731	534,836	586,837	1,358,147	2,078,304
11	179,214	127,692	154,993	354,161	337,617	370,374	360,239	1,518,878
TOTAL	9,216,530	8,302,159	9,152,855	8,883,470	10,881,875	12,502,468	15,128,139	14,230,089
MICHIGAN								
1	11,548	12,404	27,192	54,770	54,859	553,943	547,839	775
2	5,567,084	3,668,138	12,185,088	17,805,451	25,733,182	36,139,907	23,218,494	10,350,633
3	5,159,453	2,475,271	11,075,825	14,845,131	23,075,402	32,897,666	18,628,914	7,950,017
4	11,908,246	3,122,913	18,702,022	24,951,076	36,005,423	51,964,399	37,013,244	12,963,362
5	4,024,437	932,375	5,694,756	7,716,799	11,764,588	15,433,779	10,709,486	5,263,241
6	17,837,211	15,137,968	21,590,416	25,663,046	21,530,520	26,643,205	31,198,811	28,987,920
7	2,017,596	952,338	4,664,744	6,296,675	8,538,342	12,745,940	6,981,832	5,286,279
8	12,072,458	4,579,854	21,445,695	28,198,062	52,796,224	89,160,347	36,571,084	21,937,908
9	6,737,481	1,783,058	7,488,598	11,027,642	15,896,870	21,698,124	16,160,721	7,412,274
10	8,308,812	3,355,097	13,842,003	19,746,137	28,303,436	38,687,037	28,560,403	13,873,441
11	5,039,369	1,161,672	2,879,097	3,985,835	5,288,016	43,417,931	7,227,795	4,064,014
12	1,207,835	388,471	1,597,713	2,371,353	3,587,105	4,634,842	2,642,315	498,549

Appendix A lists the congressional districts which represent the county in which the state capital is located, and those congressional districts which represent only portions of a county. Appendix C lists the programs included in each functional policy category.

table continues

Table 5.1 Outlays for Agriculture Programs by Congressional District, 1983-1990 *(continued)*

Congressional District	1983	1984	1985	1986	1987	1988	1989	1990 (est.)
MICHIGAN *continued*								
13	110,548	12,404	27,192	54,770	54,859	80,981	52,839	775
14	202,439	48,224	279,734	387,233	706,777	855,463	503,239	1,011
15	449,474	489,120	863,737	1,376,380	2,000,445	3,194,522	1,530,349	274,472
16	2,097,545	1,290,845	5,349,297	8,268,154	11,019,127	15,835,387	9,090,004	4,282,740
17	95,909	18,804	176,533	248,110	306,625	410,676	281,433	41,560
18	455,319	105,187	753,061	853,743	1,638,249	1,985,462	1,287,000	301,869
TOTAL	83,302,764	39,534,143	128,642,703	173,850,369	248,300,048	396,339,612	232,205,801	123,490,842
MINNESOTA								
1	50,477,410	15,610,546	81,790,063	116,306,862	184,302,274	276,031,530	157,033,647	99,320,451
2	110,043,000	47,075,072	186,317,654	258,723,697	444,574,958	536,520,481	344,003,437	161,216,795
3	3,629,810	1,176,329	5,634,580	8,944,375	14,543,668	19,854,705	13,078,816	5,978,999
4	17,705,686	14,600,319	17,608,409	20,064,182	15,123,366	16,220,190	18,488,100	25,909,646
5	156,254	584,587	955,895	879,964	1,041,423	1,262,522	808,734	115,251
6	27,330,128	840,741	4,134,340	6,308,259	10,225,108	13,578,698	9,789,330	3,508,799
7	102,323,145	64,106,378	151,747,898	162,502,442	278,636,904	238,452,545	121,599,633	114,639,871
8	6,129,148	1,791,686	5,855,898	8,635,548	-91,406,497	18,601,791	16,716,019	7,381,775
TOTAL	317,794,581	145,785,658	454,044,736	582,365,328	857,041,204	1,120,522,461	681,517,716	418,071,586
MISSISSIPPI								
1	33,577,043	6,687,020	40,590,563	35,680,307	64,084,733	49,393,440	57,667,426	33,626,297
2	100,474,676	21,053,663	163,786,906	110,327,328	200,110,372	158,022,272	194,961,476	89,390,530
3	21,259,085	12,817,027	21,531,270	21,958,090	18,178,314	27,799,634	32,543,973	34,646,817
4	13,656,081	12,075,513	11,833,454	14,824,404	15,118,439	16,472,540	12,085,847	14,394,197
5	730,984	589,957	1,846,004	2,001,333	12,014,826	6,334,365	8,084,280	5,994,933
TOTAL	169,697,869	53,223,180	239,588,198	184,791,462	309,506,684	258,022,252	305,343,001	178,052,775
MISSOURI								
1	597,440	203,451	458,344	399,109	803,751	642,824	314,655	143,781
2	401,787	433,077	1,397,614	1,535,778	1,828,588	2,829,950	1,395,775	281,444
3	39,503	109,661	255,461	175,831	175,757	293,376	1,713,037	98,032
4	20,024,542	14,877,734	28,703,503	36,442,679	46,469,893	61,803,216	54,777,047	47,482,199
5	455,293	367,103	603,877	779,080	1,424,449	2,349,283	1,270,654	196,897
6	30,479,203	18,452,971	54,173,133	68,588,270	105,765,290	155,523,316	117,934,378	114,152,641
7	3,786,935	2,442,927	4,622,431	5,420,533	7,972,304	13,486,483	32,343,675	13,936,783
8	30,548,150	14,290,635	63,113,645	71,245,236	99,398,515	110,555,626	96,105,693	47,865,507
9	31,847,185	26,952,962	50,674,312	65,922,429	83,520,280	118,693,525	86,861,609	82,730,529
TOTAL	118,180,037	78,130,522	204,002,320	250,508,945	347,358,828	466,177,599	392,716,524	306,887,814
MONTANA								
1	43,789,408	37,624,024	38,703,205	38,946,370	50,363,769	40,678,452	30,470,133	25,717,739
2	106,820,662	96,571,476	228,356,281	215,276,398	289,731,453	289,799,815	175,344,879	234,517,652
TOTAL	150,610,070	134,195,500	267,059,486	254,222,768	340,095,222	330,478,267	205,815,012	260,235,390
NEBRASKA								
1	122,142,152	45,186,876	152,643,906	218,932,702	284,232,820	394,645,561	274,993,721	97,737,736
2	10,339,116	3,582,434	14,971,903	22,223,455	30,557,980	41,323,455	27,847,966	8,399,440
3	276,598,556	90,402,761	361,320,564	468,751,721	566,752,170	802,965,151	505,600,132	191,530,031
TOTAL	409,079,824	139,172,071	528,936,373	709,907,878	881,542,970	1,238,934,167	808,441,819	297,667,207
NEVADA								
1	25,998	19,056	41,741	19,103	46,663	35,529	37,748	15,294
2	3,301,468	5,134,979	5,722,083	6,656,825	6,757,711	5,784,738	9,554,414	6,701,822
TOTAL	3,327,466	5,154,035	5,763,824	6,675,928	6,804,374	5,820,267	9,592,162	6,717,117
NEW HAMPSHIRE								
1	3,445,835	2,887,651	2,675,555	3,465,689	1,906,106	3,274,365	3,650,423	4,155,790
2	4,082,401	655,230	1,969,299	1,706,805	3,246,554	2,060,646	3,354,630	1,632,425
TOTAL	7,528,236	3,542,881	4,644,854	5,172,494	5,152,660	5,335,011	7,005,053	5,788,216

table continues

Appendix A lists the congressional districts which represent the county in which the state capital is located, and those congressional districts which represent only portions of a county. Appendix C lists the programs included in each functional policy category.

Table 5.1 Outlays for Agriculture Programs by Congressional District, 1983-1990 *(continued)*

Congressional District	1983	1984	1985	1986	1987	1988	1989	1990 (est.)
NEW JERSEY								
1	56,255	62,153	192,513	140,205	170,619	366,499	218,298	122,782
2	395,229	231,783	682,479	892,849	2,367,614	3,682,417	2,491,729	4,550,032
3	76,844	130,033	177,382	228,561	682,876	564,179	229,874	138,033
4	1,813,445	314,993	5,852,739	2,714,047	4,549,158	3,434,027	830,844	1,787,527
5	272,770	277,054	430,022	973,213	1,109,211	1,465,156	1,149,366	-64,240
6	4,114,190	5,624,068	5,650,068	6,528,492	4,140,304	5,834,126	7,383,339	8,051,211
7	6,272,450	195,668	120,598	335,341	289,125	423,884	193,746	74,013
8	15,741	3,649	70,751	35,573	29,484	54,189	27,727	1,604
9	75	-1,740	62	47,077	77	0	58	-65
10	51,946	5,877	81,303	0	0	10,000	500,000	0
11	8,663	-709	19,118	25,365	35,948	55,647	20,728	1,276
12	160,808	205,831	723,827	1,248,917	1,123,083	2,384,021	1,900,015	396,579
13	358,654	89,879	217,894	348,766	967,555	755,749	371,679	110,005
14	5	6	4	5	5	0	4	-4
TOTAL	13,597,074	7,138,546	14,218,761	13,518,411	15,465,057	19,029,895	15,317,405	15,168,753
NEW MEXICO								
1	5,365,083	1,295,065	1,448,013	1,425,824	2,132,742	3,528,715	2,177,421	4,144,560
2	30,580,715	19,771,439	45,143,454	54,587,859	68,507,625	67,659,925	56,055,399	79,249,505
3	1,931,767	3,386,536	5,229,879	6,580,096	8,478,973	5,428,478	5,109,406	4,539,629
TOTAL	37,877,565	24,453,040	51,821,346	62,593,779	79,119,340	76,617,118	63,342,226	87,933,694
NEW YORK								
1	82,990	40,042	107,106	75,251	69,797	40,540	148,701	22,559
2	18,977	-70,487	106,939	43,676	69,688	40,477	148,469	22,524
3	14,626	149,611	231,151	216,463	69,826	192,945	148,764	22,569
4	245	-85	-3,548	0	0	0	0	0
5	243	-18,000	0	0	0	500,000	0	0
6	40,000	0	0	0	0	500,000	0	0
7	0	0	0	0	0	0	0	0
8	-964	180,000	10,478	7,656	51,041	13,398	1,069	0
9	0	0	0	0	0	0	0	0
10	25,000	25,000	100,000	0	0	0	4,600	0
11	0	0	0	0	0	0	4,645	0
12	0	0	0	0	267,591	500,000	629,635	0
13	0	0	0	0	0	0	4,652	0
14	-1,567	0	0	0	0	0	1,468	0
15	10,870	-1,214	183,400	80,049	31,636	526,296	840,427	0
16	10,870	-1,214	183,398	80,047	381,636	176,295	840,424	0
17	248,325	-930	148,932	67,501	65,552	145,857	261,567	0
18	-64	9,500	36,153	26,593	485,286	46,538	3,712	0
19	537	340	27,283	20,563	131,629	34,837	6,772	0
20	2,140	1,356	2,307	4,025	5,098	5,471	16,102	0
21	212,869	215,826	283,377	346,152	711,737	771,922	464,921	145,674
22	333,628	148,898	322,599	349,316	452,099	440,072	440,698	130,711
23	5,468,245	1,198,659	5,179,318	3,373,871	7,377,178	4,672,069	4,693,246	2,181,183
24	1,375,909	402,696	1,187,727	1,791,639	2,935,679	4,156,670	2,623,439	3,071,715
25	1,620,752	1,109,552	2,297,468	3,173,040	7,592,066	12,769,864	11,334,499	7,797,021
26	4,643,287	571,358	1,773,038	2,833,904	9,268,835	7,712,479	7,199,993	5,360,417
27	4,167,101	677,675	1,945,115	2,396,964	3,212,813	4,439,384	2,178,090	516,802
28	12,058,275	15,146,542	14,986,082	20,599,095	8,372,369	12,700,964	15,199,295	12,582,408
29	3,172,355	1,042,025	5,005,666	7,340,761	13,005,262	15,666,775	9,823,382	2,763,193
30	2,740,617	1,076,982	4,354,751	4,986,142	9,909,202	11,169,601	6,913,724	2,834,977
31	3,297,284	1,695,438	5,330,222	6,238,092	10,412,581	11,666,857	8,101,179	4,382,315
32	1,770,999	829,466	4,169,608	5,173,735	7,971,023	9,308,806	5,688,137	2,399,990
33	1,690,296	55,781	380,676	349,830	648,051	808,457	649,220	474,221
34	2,477,329	994,787	3,119,357	4,354,097	8,305,126	10,474,734	9,866,056	6,671,677
TOTAL	45,481,174	25,479,606	51,468,603	63,928,462	91,802,804	109,481,305	88,236,884	51,379,955
NORTH CAROLINA								
1	11,667,336	4,988,543	16,769,782	29,396,710	49,740,936	60,625,761	35,567,019	11,842,631
2	7,055,267	2,353,594	7,147,440	9,955,891	17,232,385	19,319,482	15,046,764	8,686,658
3	5,012,442	2,338,909	4,037,465	9,548,229	21,702,151	31,387,007	19,259,374	10,699,090
4	20,988,772	20,499,837	24,501,071	25,038,699	22,465,681	30,823,684	27,908,102	33,500,550
5	1,303,958	412,979	479,700	337,327	3,392,274	1,962,791	2,103,226	922,614
6	5,303,746	4,370,480	4,263,016	4,369,414	5,258,783	5,313,121	5,922,644	5,977,221
7	3,496,983	1,450,457	2,791,775	5,263,733	10,130,570	11,626,160	9,181,570	3,522,602
8	4,937,328	1,923,930	4,378,245	5,756,204	14,110,159	16,452,980	9,728,309	6,409,312
9	422,900	249,425	335,293	448,791	3,041,596	1,909,040	1,392,867	914,109
10	913,352	609,136	1,087,555	1,245,728	4,601,902	3,103,678	2,198,192	2,372,152
11	2,161,375	657,763	1,169,812	734,726	2,424,054	1,522,112	1,913,752	886,018
TOTAL	63,263,459	39,855,052	66,961,154	92,095,452	154,100,491	184,045,816	130,221,819	85,732,956

Appendix A lists the congressional districts which represent the county in which the state capital is located, and those congressional districts which represent only portions of a county. Appendix C lists the programs included in each functional policy category.

table continues

Table 5.1 Outlays for Agriculture Programs by Congressional District, 1983-1990 *(continued)*

Congressional District	1983	1984	1985	1986	1987	1988	1989	1990 (est.)
NORTH DAKOTA								
TOTAL	298,369,790	261,908,154	535,024,989	540,211,144	771,557,791	649,355,500	262,138,292	298,492,016
OHIO								
1	73,743	28,157	179,283	147,975	3,572,848	4,247,517	2,741,620	1,113,705
2	1,268,544	465,413	1,885,329	2,586,892	1,597,761	1,705,259	1,587,444	91,074
3	379,024	240,421	1,021,232	1,555,430	2,650,425	3,216,582	1,748,261	223,263
4	9,195,226	6,219,931	20,473,594	31,659,676	48,192,108	60,851,979	34,106,537	14,400,623
5	11,553,580	8,107,829	23,545,875	36,374,099	58,621,116	71,623,685	39,370,660	6,188,833
6	11,642,061	4,006,162	18,498,684	26,312,492	39,473,003	53,073,524	30,376,551	21,700,804
7	10,429,321	5,638,004	28,226,297	37,908,764	55,356,926	74,039,541	43,613,849	17,681,865
8	4,596,623	3,764,222	12,939,882	21,419,872	36,976,054	46,975,915	29,316,978	7,597,420
9	1,384,274	874,721	2,907,913	4,845,095	8,217,796	10,157,336	5,714,861	983,307
10	8,452,378	1,452,789	7,461,519	9,648,260	14,281,685	18,868,199	13,451,908	9,526,109
11	1,207,448	371,228	1,753,439	2,650,032	3,334,566	5,005,232	3,144,472	1,469,720
12	13,027,062	6,877,492	9,512,958	13,839,103	16,604,053	21,051,882	15,778,432	9,476,369
13	1,834,579	1,726,636	5,258,368	8,293,230	12,787,834	20,436,482	9,796,663	5,099,506
14	60,717	45,920	112,854	158,742	380,559	289,512	139,921	29,485
15	2,442,433	4,272,365	7,676,972	11,690,621	11,747,247	15,785,288	13,188,512	9,176,676
16	6,886,691	6,251,095	8,612,817	10,045,489	10,000,997	13,797,262	12,135,064	9,775,855
17	3,443,357	182,387	1,226,642	1,630,697	2,755,277	3,472,224	2,072,870	1,146,561
18	3,854,673	1,062,436	3,888,995	5,330,635	8,568,627	10,365,844	7,745,023	4,481,646
19	166,868	13,244	28,977	219,485	106,451	176,218	62,205	34,996
20	77,166	4,781	-9,452	189,669	38,748	6,094	4,852	4,042
21	966	4,791	2,305	190,086	38,833	229,261	254,863	4,050
TOTAL	91,976,733	51,610,026	155,204,483	226,696,344	335,302,915	435,374,836	266,351,545	120,205,908
OKLAHOMA								
1	706,860	501,145	1,133,757	1,336,164	1,774,243	1,736,121	1,739,136	484,815
2	6,226,153	3,545,024	6,719,009	7,199,473	12,862,023	12,732,997	15,751,380	7,191,187
3	13,086,958	11,048,371	12,031,689	20,404,524	13,389,616	20,180,842	30,583,231	20,792,972
4	30,038,946	16,229,614	45,704,499	41,347,391	53,997,603	59,073,108	33,015,924	29,457,227
5	8,217,938	21,046,320	27,119,211	37,443,900	45,732,071	43,238,949	15,176,789	14,027,625
6	97,231,744	91,564,388	200,031,444	205,856,511	215,183,177	297,160,267	113,202,941	120,558,208
TOTAL	155,508,598	143,934,862	292,739,610	313,587,963	342,938,734	434,122,283	209,469,401	192,512,035
OREGON								
1	56,034,582	4,197,106	8,415,838	8,474,788	10,094,780	9,568,708	2,734,694	2,475,988
2	27,213,789	26,029,157	57,046,386	58,653,306	48,520,469	90,416,183	53,809,980	67,975,390
3	139,761	193,943	299,325	243,942	287,646	233,070	364,086	35,380
4	3,047,886	2,879,515	4,355,480	4,068,043	4,956,593	4,620,988	2,449,510	929,673
5	12,985,279	84,363,600	113,496,449	139,985,711	141,832,870	169,215,501	156,371,714	10,819,546
TOTAL	99,421,296	117,663,321	183,613,478	211,425,790	205,692,357	274,054,451	215,729,984	82,235,977
PENNSYLVANIA								
1	30,585	79,871	120,346	215,360	219,307	307,476	1,091,142	68,843
2	395,627	41,203	120,829	216,225	220,189	308,712	469,019	69,119
3	6,135	80,028	120,582	215,782	219,737	308,078	468,057	68,978
4	1,243,537	360,273	1,167,619	1,523,815	3,235,701	3,080,032	2,564,471	970,666
5	175,995	126,480	528,326	877,659	1,325,110	1,381,870	769,065	242,936
6	646,412	527,283	1,413,818	1,843,292	3,272,597	4,316,456	2,495,988	798,254
7	4,711	19,455	231,305	267,417	1,020,841	135,891	218,180	36,891
8	149,171	139,683	190,664	289,155	513,625	605,348	285,587	280,059
9	2,178,353	873,957	2,080,072	3,662,341	5,188,650	10,085,777	9,507,176	2,766,611
10	1,869,543	716,070	1,257,113	1,751,962	2,875,202	3,400,082	7,626,047	7,517,939
11	882,203	589,497	1,399,434	2,328,547	3,550,810	5,424,559	3,794,042	8,493,265
12	1,649,570	332,708	547,961	1,036,716	1,526,235	3,475,054	3,293,254	1,125,152
13	69,036	68,176	162,158	251,073	382,105	527,275	305,797	105,332
14	7,863	30,147	22,883	11,195	22,738	508,801	73,141	13,821
15	806,202	526,170	1,625,683	2,206,543	3,316,923	4,250,097	2,561,938	15,296
16	440,876	350,628	726,576	1,213,220	1,687,629	2,230,896	1,290,753	239,558
17	8,234,857	2,960,846	6,078,901	8,026,193	13,288,626	11,224,239	7,020,693	9,171,484
18	7,854	100,841	7,874	-658	22,712	30,267	23,115	13,806
19	4,043,121	647,829	1,490,251	2,949,937	4,514,279	8,272,170	4,554,349	878,629
20	69,731	44,602	98,836	157,102	238,461	371,464	352,657	170,194
21	778,369	546,273	1,508,895	2,102,109	3,322,624	4,232,900	3,268,015	1,999,517
22	717,728	531,260	611,347	844,973	1,075,671	1,350,593	2,717,439	907,392
23	15,254,269	15,181,361	14,918,959	19,963,975	14,956,899	19,084,732	24,010,015	22,082,116
TOTAL	39,661,749	24,874,644	36,430,433	51,953,931	65,996,671	84,912,769	78,759,937	58,035,857

table continues

Appendix A lists the congressional districts which represent the county in which the state capital is located, and those congressional districts which represent only portions of a county. Appendix C lists the programs included in each functional policy category.

Table 5.1 Outlays for Agriculture Programs by Congressional District, 1983-1990 *(continued)*

Congressional District	1983	1984	1985	1986	1987	1988	1989	1990 (est.)
RHODE ISLAND								
1	376,209	140,107	185,323	447,784	921,005	698,008	667,179	810,099
2	3,059,858	2,595,514	2,470,785	2,899,306	2,110,252	2,189,641	2,689,860	3,146,075
TOTAL	3,436,067	2,735,621	2,656,108	3,347,090	3,031,257	2,887,649	3,357,039	3,956,174
SOUTH CAROLINA								
1	1,262,833	1,026,088	3,262,787	4,372,158	7,334,077	6,272,829	4,291,447	4,925,144
2	10,942,035	8,759,418	11,590,300	15,279,153	18,882,492	21,762,723	19,157,888	15,400,569
3	11,644,872	10,711,260	12,360,426	15,225,137	16,896,911	18,047,915	21,124,514	24,974,058
4	337,907	271,251	242,223	264,863	1,100,043	684,976	736,138	854,325
5	6,111,089	2,522,856	9,363,599	8,701,738	17,311,762	17,614,240	13,759,166	18,168,086
6	7,952,672	5,226,546	11,043,721	15,774,643	24,924,974	32,110,811	23,998,227	13,501,602
TOTAL	38,251,408	28,517,419	47,863,056	59,617,692	86,450,259	96,493,494	83,067,380	77,823,784
SOUTH DAKOTA								
TOTAL	80,232,269	96,383,042	231,448,330	291,930,124	447,234,174	457,626,784	283,040,458	199,383,825
TENNESSEE								
1	419,371	308,085	433,505	623,666	4,976,790	3,251,003	7,207,840	3,036,762
2	11,621,812	12,184,672	10,476,546	14,233,181	11,167,798	13,754,592	17,774,714	18,143,226
3	491,391	284,903	221,686	420,113	3,515,360	1,266,953	2,565,735	1,074,676
4	4,595,250	1,651,332	2,699,439	4,372,779	14,358,207	13,434,320	17,647,324	12,344,196
5	5,557,373	5,151,309	5,932,008	6,626,666	6,737,598	7,509,095	6,008,982	6,574,726
6	4,061,257	935,277	1,358,965	2,505,001	9,312,016	7,856,822	12,947,137	5,657,107
7	11,043,074	3,798,576	11,968,395	12,833,895	23,707,984	25,860,868	23,534,011	22,907,604
8	14,391,605	10,064,261	36,857,166	40,848,871	39,764,142	99,421,149	60,966,486	38,276,027
9	1,134,856	352,060	1,756,654	1,284,085	1,973,981	1,652,758	2,107,011	1,183,095
TOTAL	53,315,989	34,730,475	71,704,364	83,748,257	115,513,876	174,007,561	150,759,240	109,197,419
TEXAS								
1	12,144,877	5,406,400	8,160,214	8,784,386	13,124,147	16,069,200	24,910,081	9,004,741
2	6,603,031	2,007,294	7,992,849	559,436	13,914,809	5,591,054	11,986,369	5,922,486
3	302,644	397,617	403,405	508,641	1,021,774	1,110,059	628,701	146,800
4	4,524,103	4,949,257	6,565,960	8,910,539	15,066,935	15,400,271	10,914,896	5,100,966
5	111,190	97,702	224,465	174,799	320,393	357,894	179,059	41,931
6	32,865,390	28,351,883	33,880,474	41,230,632	41,400,148	46,241,616	55,545,430	40,523,454
7	659,205	163,446	3,109,018	603,661	709,413	600,446	832,917	726,931
8	656,403	163,140	3,094,170	601,094	707,227	599,803	830,008	724,516
9	13,234,391	3,273,840	18,112,980	8,554,127	13,575,364	12,702,125	18,002,868	9,371,942
10	14,234,330	8,738,748	9,734,206	8,400,636	13,160,962	12,006,254	10,875,944	11,883,856
11	15,610,755	7,179,339	11,867,989	16,818,490	34,783,778	33,098,199	29,627,083	8,158,299
12	130,052	94,645	161,667	208,483	382,931	465,367	267,891	55,623
13	141,959,350	79,628,983	202,780,121	189,129,750	281,253,444	276,655,852	204,637,323	156,407,731
14	54,524,763	23,593,545	81,406,512	70,339,833	98,813,252	108,384,093	120,535,154	48,643,038
15	25,638,111	8,699,192	26,613,858	28,998,629	43,751,559	49,496,546	58,198,128	32,324,135
16	3,250,319	1,301,127	5,559,136	5,320,898	7,138,205	6,930,274	5,460,327	5,225,087
17	133,011,992	33,657,247	147,157,450	102,431,533	169,482,939	126,315,529	147,616,398	89,446,221
18	658,693	163,319	3,106,603	603,192	708,862	599,979	1,007,270	726,366
19	237,120,870	60,351,668	280,198,961	216,674,721	319,183,426	308,814,188	300,402,276	150,009,059
20	159,378	55,195	93,982	175,978	786,029	1,012,068	497,210	345,311
21	37,758,144	24,263,746	34,033,673	33,236,711	-21,375,001	46,292,708	54,024,007	26,265,643
22	11,359,137	3,153,112	16,533,359	10,540,802	14,839,307	14,400,515	17,131,428	9,134,089
23	8,045,177	3,586,139	11,695,611	12,962,904	23,593,000	22,433,706	26,245,759	9,521,746
24	142,821	97,439	219,039	177,713	325,802	367,188	416,082	43,115
25	657,953	163,136	3,103,116	602,515	708,066	599,306	831,336	725,551
26	1,285,987	2,022,629	1,821,225	3,111,476	6,653,877	6,620,566	3,734,099	824,768
27	17,241,152	7,156,249	34,160,527	32,818,749	47,204,157	44,495,969	50,980,590	9,946,366
TOTAL	773,890,219	308,716,038	951,790,570	802,480,328	1,141,234,804	1,157,660,775	1,156,318,637	631,249,770
UTAH								
1	10,561,806	10,266,568	15,370,737	17,373,235	25,638,903	24,207,803	20,183,177	24,987,167
2	1,720,372	1,350,131	3,530,568	2,062,052	2,507,798	2,117,676	569,042	120,432
3	4,975,543	6,670,572	7,929,980	8,585,861	11,196,630	10,651,260	10,592,941	12,936,038
TOTAL	17,257,721	18,287,271	26,831,285	28,021,148	39,343,331	36,976,739	31,345,160	38,043,636
VERMONT								
TOTAL	5,341,703	4,556,520	5,018,713	5,698,285	5,906,729	15,543,176	10,885,733	10,601,505

Appendix A lists the congressional districts which represent the county in which the state capital is located, and those congressional districts which represent only portions of a county. Appendix C lists the programs included in each functional policy category.

table continues

Table 5.1 **Outlays for Agriculture Programs by Congressional District, 1983-1990 *(continued)***

Congressional District	1983	1984	1985	1986	1987	1988	1989	1990 (est.)
VIRGINIA								
1	2,239,193	1,381,169	4,208,279	7,492,960	13,738,078	15,369,123	6,482,266	6,175,228
2	189,178	81,459	310,073	827,701	1,067,974	1,443,445	580,988	193,297
3	847,605	833,607	870,630	2,323,690	3,366,916	4,171,641	2,313,972	2,186,048
4	7,807,590	4,281,994	8,287,026	10,609,934	16,023,231	22,318,534	13,341,056	10,543,010
5	1,570,106	1,465,395	1,899,520	2,502,250	7,354,939	9,021,722	5,229,330	4,951,583
6	607,974	714,303	883,207	1,596,366	4,682,620	4,351,627	2,446,522	688,927
7	3,382,470	2,093,904	3,017,481	5,356,968	9,497,480	11,240,565	7,282,062	5,928,854
8	72,572	68,618	113,712	148,672	299,709	611,212	382,557	139,879
9	13,351,860	16,563,147	16,353,863	15,114,387	12,436,000	15,945,034	19,772,885	28,805,001
10	651,526	289,566	1,265,052	1,364,210	2,081,269	2,783,712	2,435,801	3,493,662
TOTAL	30,720,074	27,773,163	37,208,842	47,337,138	70,548,216	87,256,615	60,267,439	63,105,490
WASHINGTON								
1	745,174	279,602	627,459	626,580	781,075	901,334	727,514	733,165
2	761,195	675,005	1,140,549	1,318,370	2,608,125	3,034,593	1,032,604	1,525,028
3	19,962,553	22,375,745	29,435,087	42,742,121	31,661,509	42,823,059	23,602,727	10,963,518
4	13,895,459	17,918,120	39,065,229	43,875,234	85,890,221	74,967,880	42,767,378	53,102,739
5	80,560,082	71,066,401	145,190,164	143,876,530	219,750,945	177,933,453	80,974,789	89,230,969
6	57,299	58,220	174,187	148,749	219,576	48,077	298,747	108,126
7	558,022	361,733	858,487	793,478	1,011,269	1,042,469	914,711	1,004,213
8	249,721	331,548	1,034,936	744,454	913,441	1,091,188	835,075	2,658,339
TOTAL	116,789,506	113,066,374	217,526,099	234,125,516	342,836,161	301,842,052	151,153,545	159,326,096
WEST VIRGINIA								
1	647,140	244,731	314,193	342,676	913,140	1,001,517	1,639,404	5,468,885
2	8,138,009	7,782,220	7,439,745	9,911,082	10,730,657	13,340,406	17,161,335	16,225,685
3	3,545,727	798,759	1,048,152	1,596,853	2,229,875	2,146,958	3,334,681	7,426,788
4	119,528	80,257	117,935	107,391	168,549	222,092	363,048	1,065,064
TOTAL	12,450,404	8,905,967	8,920,025	11,958,002	14,042,221	16,710,973	22,498,468	30,186,422
WISCONSIN								
1	13,638,027	2,320,949	18,122,423	25,848,730	39,447,457	57,867,248	31,479,829	18,980,387
2	36,423,007	18,427,870	44,209,056	62,059,036	78,125,424	136,074,190	84,217,818	53,809,985
3	17,432,263	4,494,354	23,881,209	43,436,785	61,703,637	117,897,368	73,269,087	42,411,750
4	626,306	194,241	961,059	1,184,435	2,076,646	2,855,827	2,047,166	596,969
5	37,020	80,419	134,007	107,538	138,598	438,423	254,786	20,146
6	13,229,043	3,055,398	15,436,249	26,165,630	38,084,273	52,939,245	35,695,424	16,019,429
7	5,648,520	1,763,480	7,202,350	12,973,670	-56,988,412	28,952,200	29,479,499	5,655,326
8	5,130,183	1,457,039	8,269,631	14,082,529	20,020,077	27,537,482	23,572,578	6,525,302
9	6,576,860	1,673,407	8,394,854	13,056,222	20,027,829	26,522,245	18,131,540	8,068,922
TOTAL	98,741,229	33,467,158	126,610,837	198,914,575	202,635,529	451,084,227	298,147,727	152,088,215
WYOMING								
TOTAL	17,233,359	31,491,115	36,800,590	36,305,276	37,210,692	40,143,563	33,362,035	35,764,565
U.S. TOTAL	5,676.8 mil.	3,119.9 mil.	8,658.6 mil.	9,751.4 mil.	13,393.5 mil.	16,528.9 mil.	11,416.9 mil.	7,027.4 mil.

Appendix A lists the congressional districts which represent the county in which the state capital is located, and those congressional districts which represent only portions of a county. Appendix C lists the programs included in each functional policy category.

Table 5.2 Outlays for Business and Commerce Programs by Congressional District, 1983-1990

Congressional District	1983	1984	1985	1986	1987	1988	1989	1990 (est.)
ALABAMA								
1	7,153,455	8,035,296	6,610,488	5,580,495	1,756,590	9,018,443	1,469,995	79,787
2	7,536,347	34,629,390	30,247,335	8,106,056	31,482,980	32,699,274	2,598,103	8,790,011
3	1,577,130	227,000	1,718,630	1,433,117	1,763,986	1,931,884	921,256	1,820,931
4	3,294,600	1,398,570	2,078,750	2,455,883	3,257,051	4,327,390	1,277,200	120,817
5	3,756,486	4,830,734	4,694,075	4,011,380	574,561	3,922,642	2,009,775	0
6	18,480,966	12,813,990	15,990,159	20,705,171	6,500,305	22,893,364	5,152,059	13,677,945
7	7,429,495	4,218,457	4,826,805	4,028,620	1,986,782	6,731,240	2,469,283	2,461,988
TOTAL	49,228,479	66,153,437	66,166,242	46,320,722	47,322,255	81,524,237	15,897,671	26,951,479
ALASKA								
TOTAL	12,579,786	7,817,589	12,347,227	11,844,730	6,582,287	8,980,919	11,707,603	5,278,446
ARIZONA								
1	27,187,014	6,258,332	14,579,566	25,204,326	12,913,511	14,519,623	12,433,694	2,440,522
2	11,670,032	7,327,719	17,306,682	18,516,597	4,555,119	9,442,415	13,391,775	18,999,360
3	47,800	526,880	208,000	568,425	513,400	388,954	263,098	0
4	11,206,135	13,720,168	9,077,847	7,637,560	3,336,263	4,210,859	6,444,076	1,758,865
5	0	0	715,896	668,150	67,729	1,220,455	11,428,782	4,907,882
TOTAL	50,110,981	27,833,099	41,887,991	52,595,058	21,386,022	29,782,305	43,961,425	28,106,628
ARKANSAS								
1	6,823,226	1,820,900	2,928,300	1,201,700	1,132,900	1,915,297	950,525	5,645,750
2	11,581,424	28,517,272	29,185,036	26,841,784	24,891,863	30,492,899	11,191,096	8,805,642
3	13,922,102	1,865,500	1,891,500	1,779,144	419,740	2,376,961	5,025,973	1,813,332
4	8,459,915	3,657,643	2,224,922	3,799,063	953,230	2,388,733	5,646,009	0
TOTAL	40,786,667	35,861,315	36,229,758	33,621,691	27,397,733	37,173,890	22,813,603	16,264,724
CALIFORNIA								
1	35,149,449	40,792,145	33,530,975	26,183,887	4,382,036	2,253,747	14,329,146	25,344,943
2	4,552,408	2,945,564	3,050,241	4,257,054	3,600,172	2,164,236	4,808,576	677,152
3	24,613,360	26,904,122	19,298,921	21,053,328	17,434,282	19,532,054	13,065,698	43,312,407
4	12,340,249	12,836,637	7,254,360	7,897,845	10,873,194	12,888,432	9,158,848	12,411,993
5	37,018,797	17,281,921	49,425,226	40,105,094	58,542,368	32,970,417	30,512,853	120,611,916
6	9,704,946	8,666,754	6,924,071	6,074,233	836,893	752,796	9,404,246	9,978,884
7	7,472,911	6,774,316	8,195,817	9,189,163	8,134,510	6,569,568	23,816,811	4,266,954
8	13,675,271	132,364,210	36,049,016	57,453,629	30,533,724	17,957,262	11,152,420	1,110,387
9	5,396,797	7,177,510	7,191,681	76,866,833	60,171,192	74,627,089	71,584,672	540,582
10	21,081,611	6,202,066	24,288,540	22,429,729	18,264,011	21,664,970	8,486,877	25,135,549
11	10,367,650	6,997,401	20,638,004	7,550,633	3,789,031	18,013,533	6,395,605	3,805,186
12	6,644,081	6,537,349	5,613,716	4,816,288	198,721	530,205	6,695,449	330,848
13	14,594,415	18,422,532	5,510,374	5,211,742	323,100	1,569,400	10,687,698	3,376
14	7,709,326	5,798,590	4,069,913	7,913,263	5,398,747	1,202,911	3,598,707	613,485
15	7,924,281	4,450,387	7,764,429	8,682,193	5,681,966	6,709,587	6,187,663	3,874,714
16	8,548,493	8,038,699	7,381,890	4,830,577	3,891,271	4,751,905	9,219,525	1,392,244
17	7,418,845	4,277,816	5,397,282	4,388,468	584,353	1,428,110	6,493,711	782,206
18	19,228,061	15,067,264	11,154,440	8,877,906	2,088,624	2,817,829	10,786,625	225,137
19	7,629,546	8,741,670	6,189,264	7,590,109	4,364,414	6,314,003	11,326,855	1,004,303
20	69,367,651	121,984,685	91,372,247	64,820,309	108,616,475	73,466,906	16,607,432	193,569
21	6,428,829	6,753,243	6,385,326	8,757,047	4,012,432	1,007,626	96,368,182	1,730,662
22	13,961,805	11,746,596	11,562,303	9,854,302	337,932	231,716	9,314,148	1,345,655
23	9,363,853	8,107,523	7,973,348	6,352,738	144,867	70,918	6,814,291	1,916,412
24	9,450,209	8,156,012	8,130,813	6,351,555	340,259	283,881	6,562,068	1,111,275
25	9,551,205	13,910,032	8,603,146	6,507,004	644,703	1,521,219	7,305,855	1,110,223
26	8,219,734	7,116,908	6,999,127	5,680,478	217,154	108,635	5,761,357	975,676
27	15,566,422	18,615,762	17,672,575	13,761,670	741,878	4,656,348	9,684,032	15,602,502
28	12,216,861	11,214,018	11,288,716	8,035,756	1,683,913	1,309,230	8,970,607	2,482,921
29	11,882,681	12,203,256	9,564,136	7,480,179	944,809	1,021,235	8,642,365	1,111,034
30	15,364,845	14,319,599	14,036,311	11,581,164	478,558	1,353,661	13,995,501	1,109,107
31	15,922,026	14,507,404	15,487,698	12,279,212	1,536,901	457,448	15,961,909	11,082,212
32	12,736,446	9,370,375	8,701,740	7,033,277	145,365	31,316	9,511,137	1,115,300
33	11,632,199	10,020,978	9,895,730	7,981,229	144,947	209,005	8,625,891	1,112,093
34	13,648,284	14,391,263	11,299,708	9,283,531	409,954	21,256	26,084,883	1,112,145
35	3,916,787	12,624,409	11,121,976	13,034,691	4,990,229	5,148,373	18,249,412	8,762,734
36	6,398,522	14,145,538	12,923,804	12,409,022	4,605,852	4,992,878	23,133,532	13,290,098
37	15,968,038	9,304,271	6,328,179	4,461,515	3,833,759	2,817,514	9,594,031	10,049,879
38	4,946,120	20,482,059	4,773,989	20,414,437	26,275,373	17,228,814	8,145,265	2,404,731
39	6,653,898	3,851,319	6,814,022	5,436,201	81,906	16,789	9,212,298	4,918,673

Appendix A lists the congressional districts which represent the county in which the state capital is located, and those congressional districts which represent only portions of a county. Appendix C lists the programs included in each functional policy category.

table continues

Table 5.2 Outlays for Business and Commerce Programs by Congressional District, 1983-1990 *(continued)*

Congressional District	1983	1984	1985	1986	1987	1988	1989	1990 (est.)
CALIFORNIA *continued*								
40	8,215,353	2,681,861	7,744,634	5,867,652	628,165	944,656	11,925,769	5,588,632
41	12,183,758	19,509,593	13,349,702	33,906,472	21,133,513	4,573,437	24,183,263	1,148,421
42	9,840,154	10,053,820	8,714,828	5,919,417	170,403	700,851	7,025,161	1,608,251
43	11,826,459	7,295,868	8,140,240	12,064,225	4,070,898	3,428,255	18,835,056	1,550,419
44	7,686,047	2,513,305	8,263,950	6,877,750	479,918	273,916	17,153,662	0
45	7,608,711	2,731,997	6,520,951	6,324,220	1,245,592	594,713	12,865,484	0
TOTAL	591,627,393	727,888,651	602,597,358	643,847,027	427,008,360	361,188,649	678,244,576	347,854,891
COLORADO								
1	33,066,483	11,413,175	38,231,819	25,310,171	26,677,617	37,759,656	25,392,594	34,843,649
2	7,229,729	3,411,601	1,744,088	3,871,596	2,059,972	3,682,607	2,419,900	4,823,281
3	5,864,178	2,039,182	1,016,222	3,433,432	2,379,491	3,400,309	2,399,933	2,390,686
4	4,082,365	2,367,482	1,643,115	1,091,060	1,250,117	3,368,243	3,948,759	3,735,703
5	5,030,598	1,699,543	2,001,486	3,911,453	2,521,784	4,276,044	2,115,656	5,632,775
6	2,491,746	2,340,176	650,910	1,902,078	369,374	3,391,949	476,865	-1,928
TOTAL	57,765,099	23,271,159	45,287,640	39,519,790	35,258,355	55,878,808	36,753,707	51,424,166
CONNECTICUT								
1	38,748,662	47,553,527	16,846,361	37,532,047	24,337,265	40,123,341	18,556,619	45,434,049
2	3,379,456	2,300,000	2,378,925	2,143,300	1,042,961	4,613,397	647,869	4,891,441
3	9,477,496	6,968,800	7,241,016	6,223,504	2,101,225	15,859,825	1,630,012	12,175,033
4	10,637,677	8,777,416	24,831,861	22,570,117	11,401,909	26,583,466	10,468,069	2,947,315
5	4,979,600	3,856,000	4,190,287	4,208,273	219,888	7,049,156	803,913	7,856,268
6	3,325,446	10,522,000	6,737,420	2,184,599	84,350	6,410,763	25,385	4,395,755
TOTAL	70,548,337	79,977,743	62,225,870	74,861,839	39,187,598	100,639,948	32,131,867	77,699,862
DELAWARE								
TOTAL	13,336,626	11,088,252	10,021,706	12,876,082	13,251,894	11,623,478	5,744,127	5,800,115
DISTRICT OF COLUMBIA								
TOTAL	63,086,322	58,245,291	13,563,301	8,765,382	6,866,737	63,864,159	42,365,140	84,757,576
FLORIDA								
1	5,052,134	3,803,431	4,111,775	6,827,660	2,572,181	7,113,328	1,834,893	4,103,682
2	41,389,702	7,588,493	6,743,027	9,648,159	33,488,127	30,441,982	23,635,212	57,960,028
3	13,276,521	13,772,608	7,823,067	18,207,436	3,512,665	15,017,686	10,777,581	28,881,618
4	10,564,752	5,227,256	4,548,465	6,658,397	129,643	5,951,653	5,604,187	13,079,321
5	10,332,555	8,098,651	10,711,647	15,434,360	4,356,295	6,502,203	6,976,522	14,921,200
6	6,754,376	4,838,494	5,152,966	5,013,562	1,164,857	5,536,725	3,037,830	7,619,525
7	13,607,070	16,797,276	16,205,710	10,837,737	4,877,354	15,074,748	7,629,391	25,835,138
8	10,157,387	8,591,607	13,466,540	13,284,348	12,837,814	10,001,645	11,001,220	18,377,387
9	1,692,896	1,385,363	2,082,537	1,052,377	1,601,426	4,362,734	3,430,753	9,463,225
10	10,002,067	2,267,840	11,862,788	5,398,223	1,049,694	9,116,963	5,986,028	12,044,323
11	6,207,848	5,944,642	4,220,113	8,404,647	1,338,674	7,679,712	2,154,567	10,714,748
12	3,096,981	3,457,663	6,726,704	6,829,105	5,662,708	6,516,939	4,730,099	7,456,594
13	20,831,347	26,898,915	2,727,976	3,730,667	758,462	6,273,401	1,529,445	6,712,913
14	5,970,805	5,177,714	6,906,052	5,429,197	82,909	8,640,108	2,191,318	14,253,510
15	18,840,254	17,950,278	10,057,898	21,860,091	12,629,050	24,283,386	21,632,046	33,377,291
16	3,774,166	6,323,923	3,309,308	4,864,125	158,857	8,240,091	4,771,228	10,343,501
17	10,790,658	11,483,600	26,527,720	41,781,076	20,942,280	23,886,585	9,720,263	11,753,871
18	11,331,905	18,273,075	4,302,003	10,146,848	303,182	12,920,439	10,000,485	16,781,074
19	9,458,252	10,065,630	1,248,592	7,207,886	551,919	9,645,572	7,289,355	55,186,260
TOTAL	213,131,675	177,946,459	148,734,887	202,615,901	108,018,097	217,205,901	143,932,423	358,865,211
GEORGIA								
1	5,992,508	3,748,850	2,838,436	5,855,155	3,839,987	11,902,047	6,790,491	1,026,108
2	4,418,549	2,376,490	356,850	1,817,430	177,650	6,266,976	955,900	213,488
3	5,011,782	4,129,005	2,089,252	5,233,488	7,584,568	9,544,076	1,328,400	7,787,313
4	22,946,458	12,453,213	35,052,452	37,475,043	28,715,527	43,254,673	21,186,122	51,641,806
5	45,389,989	42,312,496	2,404,047	12,872,244	26,964,416	54,673,199	9,651,946	22,504,954
6	4,986,920	29,110,206	65,787	1,318,107	2,940,265	3,207,500	1,371,272	2,413,628
7	3,609,621	2,968,100	439,500	2,293,688	5,021,459	4,351,565	5,293,048	5,961,113
8	3,855,700	2,588,500	267,500	2,261,275	881,056	8,736,178	3,255,515	199,554
9	106,700	106,700	109,500	855,540	3,113,812	2,263,747	1,490,280	0
10	7,544,939	4,054,720	3,972,229	3,886,745	1,056,420	11,580,221	2,558,425	4,513,117
TOTAL	103,863,166	103,848,280	47,595,553	73,868,714	80,295,160	155,780,182	53,881,399	96,261,081

table continues

Appendix A lists the congressional districts which represent the county in which the state capital is located, and those congressional districts which represent only portions of a county. Appendix C lists the programs included in each functional policy category.

Table 5.2 Outlays for Business and Commerce Programs by Congressional District, 1983-1990 *(continued)*

Congressional District	1983	1984	1985	1986	1987	1988	1989	1990 (est.)
HAWAII								
1	9,427,387	22,122,555	21,174,458	36,760,834	29,569,296	9,574,565	13,748,076	706,887
2	1,916,858	4,968,515	2,462,476	2,437,458	9,939,053	7,616,063	614,920	3,033,725
TOTAL	11,344,245	27,091,070	23,636,934	39,198,292	39,508,349	17,190,628	14,362,996	3,740,612
IDAHO								
1	8,758,272	3,566,602	8,355,400	7,406,655	10,207,086	11,652,114	7,109,227	7,998,983
2	3,508,052	772,713	2,994,419	4,674,932	4,423,548	5,697,864	2,329,963	2,201,970
TOTAL	12,266,324	4,339,315	11,349,819	12,081,587	14,630,634	17,349,978	9,439,190	10,200,953
ILLINOIS								
1	22,093,577	129,740,475	192,228,173	172,306,708	158,230,744	163,758,967	129,364,429	210,995,813
2	15,919,822	11,348,945	10,938,401	10,630,393	1,357,426	17,141,780	1,709,528	27,109,297
3	15,873,156	11,351,330	10,940,698	10,632,626	1,357,711	17,491,381	2,037,133	27,052,743
4	7,261,781	5,155,496	4,976,994	4,596,628	1,105,726	11,112,481	740,607	11,303,180
5	15,871,046	11,349,821	10,939,244	14,310,213	3,036,531	18,856,307	3,318,352	30,601,456
6	19,947,070	6,251,229	4,074,749	7,667,519	512,535	8,647,693	2,224,446	13,723,913
7	20,762,602	11,741,764	14,033,784	12,458,503	2,946,790	21,324,750	4,235,261	26,145,491
8	15,872,972	11,351,199	10,940,572	10,632,503	1,526,485	17,145,183	1,709,867	26,145,491
9	16,899,682	13,194,079	12,901,888	10,684,265	1,407,001	21,214,472	2,437,724	26,153,199
10	9,146,375	6,000,354	7,138,608	6,339,019	773,580	10,572,394	865,613	11,822,428
11	15,871,780	11,350,346	10,939,751	10,631,705	1,357,594	17,240,605	1,806,232	26,143,527
12	7,574,888	5,846,451	6,212,000	5,611,728	616,871	8,806,840	770,532	11,058,718
13	9,403,236	7,818,714	5,686,294	8,128,112	688,922	9,998,189	2,091,381	14,520,159
14	1,554,223	1,586,282	1,755,249	1,080,424	144,567	2,310,445	850,662	1,719,602
15	3,163,028	2,102,023	1,719,460	1,599,336	518,472	4,861,183	3,122,098	1,670,404
16	4,124,533	3,068,489	3,032,689	4,473,583	2,170,409	4,671,463	3,132,943	6,886,407
17	3,558,658	8,263,436	3,508,305	5,377,031	1,788,876	4,388,846	1,139,247	4,376,659
18	2,689,700	11,644,522	2,939,498	10,604,857	2,954,087	6,584,098	1,708,658	7,482,364
19	2,665,887	5,876,350	3,050,541	2,197,308	3,123,082	4,894,258	2,630,728	2,592,605
20	10,870,190	62,809,730	36,793,616	1,954,966	35,155,289	34,585,885	2,266,894	1,878,841
21	14,422,411	7,194,417	3,325,000	6,356,000	78,500	16,096,826	7,143,587	17,943,337
22	845,346	150,946	178,500	1,495,500	2,317,400	2,029,380	2,051,370	897,232
TOTAL	236,391,965	345,196,397	358,254,014	319,768,925	223,168,597	423,733,424	177,357,291	508,222,867
INDIANA								
1	20,734,175	15,655,008	18,641,501	17,003,703	10,351,308	18,100,945	9,200,460	3,624,201
2	7,358,509	8,802,288	15,636,122	15,246,961	12,927,494	13,087,723	7,344,537	13,037,396
3	10,554,889	7,501,449	8,058,809	7,488,643	1,609,183	9,365,886	4,555,064	8,612,275
4	6,644,765	4,455,191	4,547,664	2,964,480	3,031,681	6,228,238	3,151,585	9,526,523
5	7,708,308	1,183,080	1,352,614	1,135,042	50,000	3,109,160	251,522	680,481
6	11,786,945	8,613,077	9,522,494	7,238,620	7,390,726	7,657,351	2,001,938	3,184,920
7	5,905,349	4,765,057	4,426,096	3,081,592	1,603,987	5,244,577	291,437	3,069,654
8	5,702,326	5,877,561	3,790,753	7,005,347	2,494,634	5,177,590	4,267,637	6,545,620
9	1,701,417	2,282,146	2,543,369	2,197,960	1,938,916	5,771,669	1,236,101	1,117,466
10	40,301,157	38,479,549	37,185,072	22,526,515	27,818,009	27,057,798	2,105,589	1,170,128
TOTAL	118,397,841	97,614,406	105,704,494	85,888,862	69,215,938	100,800,937	34,405,871	50,568,664
IOWA								
1	2,545,000	2,718,109	2,950,879	2,929,778	975,923	2,874,797	645,975	2,015,135
2	4,528,615	3,959,763	5,033,522	4,250,177	1,411,916	5,417,033	2,211,243	3,544,779
3	2,663,079	3,428,394	3,422,931	2,613,171	1,490,860	3,173,422	868,081	4,453,869
4	39,175,835	31,300,547	35,069,638	26,881,802	32,559,600	33,361,837	34,029,207	52,779,394
5	1,539,782	1,617,500	1,118,500	857,246	1,478,340	2,076,964	793,127	827,684
6	1,320,773	4,785,290	3,340,666	1,976,768	621,468	3,521,202	538,928	233,705
TOTAL	51,773,084	47,809,603	50,936,136	39,508,942	38,538,107	50,425,255	39,086,561	63,854,566
KANSAS								
1	4,953,959	190,414	368,000	648,000	987,995	653,100	1,223,968	2,032,992
2	7,106,253	20,598,304	22,621,803	19,633,273	19,297,607	20,995,462	2,963,086	2,007,559
3	5,490,120	5,275,384	13,560,485	2,938,640	7,293,433	12,860,071	13,202,383	7,795,826
4	7,688,444	6,055,667	5,108,035	7,346,858	2,799,462	9,463,462	2,492,406	5,246,925
5	12,636,009	74,500	509,500	156,421	1,392,912	683,618	748,604	0
TOTAL	37,874,785	32,194,269	42,167,823	30,723,192	31,771,409	44,655,713	20,630,447	17,083,302

Appendix A lists the congressional districts which represent the county in which the state capital is located, and those congressional districts which represent only portions of a county. Appendix C lists the programs included in each functional policy category.

table continues

Table 5.2 **Outlays for Business and Commerce Programs by Congressional District, 1983-1990 *(continued)***

Congressional District	1983	1984	1985	1986	1987	1988	1989	1990 (est.)
KENTUCKY								
1	733,573	103,289	582,153	611,768	1,497,867	856,976	2,942,575	1,018,919
2	1,395,400	252,902	1,741,690	685,000	970,112	1,334,865	1,894,211	0
3	14,495,408	8,162,580	17,852,560	24,124,404	9,720,249	23,512,377	8,071,024	34,889,085
4	5,672,633	4,604,555	2,402,320	3,348,474	4,842,931	3,700,459	1,588,000	2,493,596
5	517,300	0	528,000	1,997,000	800,000	706,750	3,230,000	0
6	8,173,107	8,692,112	1,169,347	9,047,688	39,655,779	9,579,101	33,903,315	7,070,873
7	1,146,000	1,084,932	1,490,838	1,570,500	545,414	1,057,097	1,917,095	0
TOTAL	32,133,421	22,900,370	25,766,908	41,384,834	58,032,352	40,747,625	53,546,220	45,472,472
LOUISIANA								
1	23,244,463	21,928,819	17,696,270	24,021,661	6,020,383	17,329,451	22,854,489	3,405,143
2	17,990,035	25,844,390	11,737,549	95,753,697	93,457,580	95,250,414	99,501,906	797,995
3	3,448,877	3,166,358	3,606,454	3,028,422	2,843,709	3,283,572	6,373,829	2,245,251
4	6,449,471	7,361,745	7,853,190	5,023,355	1,609,100	2,407,006	7,662,407	115,399
5	4,388,525	2,146,200	1,886,613	1,508,145	841,318	1,522,694	3,106,728	121,367
6	17,866,319	36,830,508	35,451,541	12,483,488	36,227,589	5,492,879	30,954,480	11,690,472
7	4,594,005	3,047,551	3,765,314	3,396,161	218,659	2,804,501	4,634,656	5,931,659
8	2,639,947	3,017,449	3,344,788	1,574,589	3,527,390	1,110,425	5,233,272	565,723
TOTAL	80,621,641	103,343,020	85,341,721	146,789,517	144,745,726	129,200,941	180,321,767	24,873,009
MAINE								
1	16,047,109	16,491,710	16,701,694	16,432,669	15,988,418	18,885,018	3,435,020	5,725,338
2	4,417,755	2,076,618	3,327,670	4,890,382	1,978,047	10,537,766	3,005,946	2,307,339
TOTAL	20,464,864	18,568,328	20,029,364	21,323,051	17,966,465	29,422,784	6,440,966	8,032,677
MARYLAND								
1	11,220,628	3,975,572	6,415,000	5,014,611	132,320	3,904,526	20,577,224	43,600,706
2	24,289,355	4,840,229	3,179,910	2,449,917	202,312	5,659,124	424,321	0
3	17,300,920	40,236,105	36,014,264	32,792,213	25,329,124	44,910,444	13,964,684	1,344,031
4	6,361,314	17,131,607	16,416,835	15,755,863	11,191,768	17,529,363	7,687,049	380,499
5	7,912,475	5,359,128	65,000	4,627,293	1,067,280	10,296,266	522,741	461,144
6	9,107,833	3,918,928	4,419,500	5,042,283	2,596,100	5,941,185	2,652,177	1,550,514
7	23,418,616	18,153,116	17,266,560	14,152,486	1,976,795	33,555,796	17,325,844	1,636,161
8	1,170,397	81,763	0	3,192,599	10,602,992	8,810,629	1,872,433	0
TOTAL	100,781,538	93,696,448	83,777,069	83,027,264	53,098,691	130,607,332	65,026,473	48,973,055
MASSACHUSETTS								
1	6,076,119	2,847,641	4,815,554	4,516,668	2,865,778	7,111,695	1,462,225	1,183,715
2	14,457,016	9,581,773	13,923,852	11,845,341	8,889,832	10,651,592	53,237,987	126,258,279
3	7,066,452	17,804,709	2,704,868	6,511,866	2,077,740	8,748,945	287,620	4,177,118
4	10,550,464	5,298,999	9,419,050	11,120,398	1,713,483	11,607,658	2,019,909	4,504,442
5	9,205,075	18,566,455	3,932,420	4,671,327	207,676	9,467,682	169,908	2,581,121
6	11,243,414	6,239,505	12,341,794	5,157,425	1,155,010	12,842,593	3,667,629	5,522,627
7	18,342,615	10,557,696	8,415,528	8,902,519	5,244,975	12,486,697	4,923,286	14,458,949
8	75,407,137	67,839,871	44,048,004	84,572,285	67,869,883	32,156,591	12,011,047	37,538,445
9	42,978,811	23,693,647	21,987,327	19,593,063	15,846,101	21,951,905	13,305,475	42,770,192
10	3,946,325	5,072,463	5,738,106	4,431,055	3,678,890	7,486,254	849,435	7,640,960
11	27,698,437	14,339,627	15,900,484	12,314,355	8,612,297	18,803,224	6,754,355	28,494,136
TOTAL	226,971,865	181,842,386	143,226,987	173,636,303	118,161,665	153,314,836	98,688,876	275,129,984
MICHIGAN								
1	54,146,988	45,477,886	38,837,048	71,581,476	4,411,325	73,468,217	16,027,263	16,516,499
2	7,657,073	8,069,009	8,018,397	5,532,238	29,188,083	14,350,938	3,686,872	2,864,445
3	7,377,729	17,393,638	7,700,956	6,748,419	6,146,530	16,824,908	3,644,086	1,119,995
4	2,243,323	1,422,379	2,190,966	2,169,087	1,154,179	3,243,276	270,220	1,422,363
5	9,442,594	3,927,419	9,846,357	8,637,785	4,007,399	12,425,803	90,997	5,967,886
6	13,437,332	23,782,313	5,610,515	4,146,168	989,642	31,879,594	2,098,696	1,111,152
7	3,491,336	10,455,642	9,686,800	8,423,370	5,734,175	13,734,841	1,989,698	-51,007
8	11,219,478	6,511,879	6,039,238	4,763,989	2,148,099	7,263,072	2,400,125	1,275,181
9	2,569,747	2,629,822	3,325,373	2,563,137	779,899	6,225,920	2,357,585	96,166
10	2,673,359	251,879	1,483,770	175,098	5,011,581	1,154,578	318,769	85,445
11	2,558,964	1,177,250	243,750	1,642,750	2,024,532	1,938,600	2,392,584	531,626
12	7,471,094	5,164,206	5,010,301	3,942,051	-23,486	8,599,732	1,398,124	1,098,939

Appendix A lists the congressional districts which represent the county in which the state capital is located, and those congressional districts which represent only portions of a county. Appendix C lists the programs included in each functional policy category.

table continues

Table 5.2 Outlays for Business and Commerce Programs by Congressional District, 1983-1990 *(continued)*

Congressional District	1983	1984	1985	1986	1987	1988	1989	1990 (est.)
MICHIGAN *continued*								
13	19,798,297	7,223,476	12,396,513	11,064,501	1,876,149	27,782,042	12,915,369	5,783,460
14	9,978,507	3,953,334	6,006,760	5,168,603	682,454	11,329,229	4,758,153	2,172,743
15	18,576,452	6,977,685	15,958,660	13,543,817	1,524,279	28,341,458	10,289,995	6,464,550
16	17,957,543	5,540,052	11,326,511	9,669,694	1,373,561	26,428,677	9,003,729	5,747,676
17	10,730,308	4,898,038	9,807,396	8,490,480	1,315,237	20,762,838	6,467,209	3,360,081
18	357,265	630,904	2,419,639	1,720,813	33,014	2,083,856	1,400	50,679
TOTAL	201,687,389	155,486,811	155,908,950	169,983,477	68,376,652	307,837,579	80,110,874	55,617,877
MINNESOTA								
1	3,102,539	493,000	1,799,530	970,239	1,451,016	2,492,595	1,286,000	0
2	2,668,680	50,000	50,000	710,000	166,000	2,168,723	158,038	968,413
3	1,595,576	1,862,000	1,443,607	1,773,248	160,355	2,225,711	866,928	176,044
4	31,964,469	40,569,806	39,263,858	36,391,446	58,748,915	52,396,594	15,524,026	38,413,126
5	24,299,328	18,050,311	1,876,996	11,799,807	1,460,238	23,295,694	504,091	318,170
6	28,261,987	1,450,000	1,904,084	2,442,220	27,772	5,455,694	56,896	0
7	10,023,618	2,694,927	2,567,726	3,295,110	3,337,985	5,525,817	2,759,875	2,757,898
8	7,663,544	3,776,494	2,630,576	4,581,526	2,938,180	6,703,920	4,224,716	1,470,994
TOTAL	109,579,740	68,946,538	51,536,377	61,963,595	68,290,461	100,264,748	25,380,570	44,104,644
MISSISSIPPI								
1	250,000	880,200	2,242,100	599,775	618,128	805,960	2,341,157	96,166
2	874,086	485,175	1,628,275	3,561,182	4,962,756	587,000	914,340	72,631
3	347,614	1,109,025	157,825	145,300	580,000	5,043,401	4,245,737	9,009,382
4	13,930,570	5,440,733	6,009,115	7,339,577	33,876,512	36,626,854	4,557,330	3,918,002
5	4,168,497	3,992,209	3,753,327	3,759,742	3,585,105	5,244,330	1,812,389	1,758,483
TOTAL	19,570,767	11,907,342	13,790,642	15,405,576	43,622,501	48,307,545	13,870,953	14,854,664
MISSOURI								
1	7,715,478	21,512,257	33,866,164	25,535,102	15,155,067	42,889,604	7,264,468	16,177,030
2	2,613,826	0	1,835,608	10,201,539	-78,151	16,132,143	10,419,946	26,943,859
3	314,933	283,621	0	4,118,685	-50,202	5,242,225	4,504,343	11,909,871
4	32,115,859	25,713,721	25,366,920	26,902,728	25,024,152	24,248,184	7,133,915	10,298,330
5	14,312,975	11,249,375	11,363,317	18,640,877	14,672,547	10,727,291	1,168,723	17,072,692
6	11,491,943	4,732,281	3,963,430	3,237,862	2,704,708	18,191,032	2,077,255	1,532,623
7	3,390,520	3,192,179	2,691,136	2,508,954	1,076,560	4,240,482	1,784,929	1,935,934
8	600,500	840,500	1,789,625	2,038,870	1,418,000	1,097,600	1,168,500	438,516
9	2,758,842	2,200,590	2,603,110	1,344,919	1,058,290	2,523,141	286,200	2,611,410
TOTAL	75,314,876	69,724,524	83,479,310	94,529,537	60,980,971	125,291,704	35,808,279	88,920,265
MONTANA								
1	8,026,026	7,025,922	1,961,234	6,345,619	9,578,630	7,595,942	2,687,497	13,539,444
2	3,442,706	2,847,268	3,263,161	1,605,011	2,784,484	2,810,400	3,232,577	812,957
TOTAL	11,468,732	9,873,190	5,224,395	7,950,630	12,363,114	10,406,342	5,920,074	14,352,402
NEBRASKA								
1	17,642,785	16,433,301	17,250,025	12,157,391	13,876,432	14,862,545	2,612,198	4,644,117
2	8,793,124	12,556,590	10,142,299	9,046,942	4,829,665	9,489,732	8,649,175	18,149,105
3	340,600	100,000	215,000	194,000	170,800	394,630	1,014,047	3,376
TOTAL	26,776,509	29,089,891	27,607,324	21,398,333	18,876,897	24,746,907	12,275,420	22,796,598
NEVADA								
1	7,141,917	6,489,150	6,596,770	6,014,667	4,778,579	1,079,024	11,284,459	0
2	5,238,702	8,852,912	4,923,145	8,197,937	4,550,705	3,312,767	3,763,441	4,804,742
TOTAL	12,380,619	15,342,062	11,519,915	14,212,604	9,329,284	4,391,791	15,047,900	4,804,742
NEW HAMPSHIRE								
1	5,357,358	3,672,448	5,234,500	4,268,932	2,767,544	8,162,769	939,540	2,067,039
2	4,843,206	2,977,347	9,110,321	7,107,165	22,301,751	8,427,577	1,311,191	1,324,820
TOTAL	10,200,564	6,649,795	14,344,821	11,376,097	25,069,295	16,590,346	2,250,731	3,391,859

Appendix A lists the congressional districts which represent the county in which the state capital is located, and those congressional districts which represent only portions of a county. Appendix C lists the programs included in each functional policy category.

table continues

Table 5.2 Outlays for Business and Commerce Programs by Congressional District, 1983-1990 *(continued)*

Congressional District	1983	1984	1985	1986	1987	1988	1989	1990 (est.)
NEW JERSEY								
1	7,073,968	12,876,160	5,649,984	8,955,455	4,372,547	16,706,596	7,528,971	9,922,812
2	50,210,567	39,336,388	4,223,173	4,143,141	10,791,635	9,119,565	2,953,314	2,549,989
3	3,031,425	2,434,529	5,058,001	2,469,276	6,383,069	4,676,632	3,102,917	7,168,545
4	24,758,897	9,146,617	14,614,906	10,545,665	17,187,808	10,937,731	16,437,806	12,110,015
5	600	2,282,331	4,403,706	3,127,098	2,247,936	6,400	18,216	0
6	6,525,759	5,164,837	4,776,617	3,997,087	7,463,888	5,290,368	628,265	432,107
7	8,141,221	10,082,691	6,917,003	56,392,664	8,772,262	7,871,589	-108,559	12,013,640
8	9,343,624	7,698,927	8,230,298	7,562,030	4,984,764	5,298,087	2,886,397	3,528,874
9	11,666,000	9,549,000	6,136,919	4,892,229	6,754,540	9,834,060	1,321,560	283,538
10	38,451,698	123,825,014	179,295,331	142,211,540	53,583,818	139,280,027	59,824,901	84,788,439
11	4,855,803	3,019,571	3,973,390	2,692,670	4,324,887	153,492	336,415	629,489
12	3,316,070	3,035,033	2,241,328	1,911,670	2,465,799	1,373,139	160,968	32,357
13	644,108	3,979,459	3,610,723	3,137,527	3,526,711	4,343,590	2,646,173	861,547
14	20,760,448	12,686,600	16,469,770	10,578,677	10,114,827	16,500,847	6,639,325	29,806,032
TOTAL	188,780,187	245,117,155	265,601,146	262,616,729	142,974,490	231,392,124	104,376,668	164,127,384
NEW MEXICO								
1	11,717,807	9,834,557	8,446,560	2,834,538	11,351,597	3,399,262	9,460,267	3,918,401
2	6,503,079	1,262,984	2,139,249	1,945,510	1,332,930	645,379	2,825,305	385,896
3	12,972,465	10,359,571	10,934,464	8,091,794	10,983,022	10,251,007	1,281,340	544,694
TOTAL	31,193,351	21,457,112	21,520,273	12,871,842	23,667,549	14,295,648	13,566,912	4,848,991
NEW YORK								
1	3,075,971	13,368,194	6,945,406	6,790,056	8,354,911	16,867,345	142,344,025	710,286,403
2	8,011,658	5,138,591	6,102,377	3,594,836	4,987,138	5,598,167	3,325,993	10,178,494
3	8,527,884	8,372,943	5,590,327	26,544,487	15,107,064	16,188,566	15,191,217	22,130,201
4	5,731,342	5,187,835	5,416,562	6,621,353	1,283,426	5,636,822	4,465,356	0
5	5,627,701	5,463,837	5,316,454	4,749,760	280,114	4,999,019	4,938,861	32,056,366
6	0	0	0	13,503	7,996	554,641	3,205	923
7	0	298,452	0	345,508	270,029	238,734	168,218	926
8	261,946	280,208	246,892	528,641	982,916	25,985,216	780,242	43,038
9	0	0	26,000	13,485	7,985	5,803	3,201	921
10	20,588,345	234,700	6,116,080	806,203	479,122	717,421	472,333	0
11	0	0	0	51,545	40,762	158,022	34,874	0
12	0	0	0	0	308,260	657,661	659,795	0
13	360,000	170,000	340,000	340,000	355,321	464,248	34,924	0
14	101,200	50,000	0	17,600	12,881	76,335	87,420	0
15	115,071,878	398,113,633	456,066,010	287,267,583	608,537,670	551,545,238	160,850,055	190,272
16	113,321,001	77,436,015	76,532,728	53,364,552	100,387,630	73,426	558,336	0
17	109,641,566	61,340,256	59,894,952	85,161,843	111,295,601	51,852,932	31,624,926	34,355
18	2,419,514	5,624,130	1,858,950	683,404	849,719	87,188,839	540,470	147,386
19	769,739	697,238	734,674	1,384,601	1,785,447	64,612,373	781,855	1,412,225
20	13,447,114	7,987,916	21,533,100	15,124,081	14,934,381	13,092,759	7,375,879	12,133,965
21	6,218,488	4,011,688	2,199,797	3,203,299	7,084,660	5,821,610	1,108,026	2,029,986
22	4,362,036	6,147,407	3,086,021	7,368,323	7,484,361	5,663,211	3,192,579	825,764
23	31,449,893	24,681,859	20,155,643	24,408,108	33,460,776	31,904,147	17,006,440	32,612,892
24	796,191	9,767,844	6,215,096	4,867,730	11,918,339	6,122,385	2,644,537	5,021,385
25	9,626,937	17,554,201	11,400,718	8,906,412	9,533,077	8,046,734	3,274,410	8,269,326
26	7,300,784	22,058,835	13,776,326	13,644,122	13,444,103	10,939,044	5,234,875	11,160,696
27	14,778,680	16,544,113	18,350,916	14,994,639	15,037,493	12,745,059	6,224,960	5,200,250
28	10,835,762	17,189,850	10,303,893	7,431,481	13,319,471	8,512,904	7,162,122	13,143,291
29	8,991,656	11,663,061	17,000,364	16,853,146	14,306,412	12,246,019	4,270,076	20,983,388
30	13,429,583	10,128,856	8,366,838	7,242,315	2,918,735	5,638,494	7,320,350	17,290,189
31	13,820,730	12,221,587	9,327,119	6,307,773	12,800,613	8,336,987	1,223,651	2,429,803
32	16,070,070	22,687,695	22,367,470	29,961,728	24,840,350	8,745,859	2,717,563	24,878,244
33	16,734,717	10,748,135	12,730,634	9,445,540	14,909,082	11,765,652	1,467,330	3,266,619
34	5,011,324	17,152,833	5,070,825	7,575,472	8,273,368	8,306,698	3,835,323	9,529,134
TOTAL	566,383,712	792,321,913	813,072,171	655,613,129	1,059,599,214	991,308,371	440,923,428	945,256,441
NORTH CAROLINA								
1	431,298	734,738	715,065	336,342	1,377,672	1,030,871	354,734	89,089
2	717,400	641,608	1,499,353	314,091	1,227,279	5,258,971	1,785,282	3,969,611
3	153,626	343,025	383,525	1,284,000	867,000	872,000	1,579,772	0
4	3,806,006	6,684,240	51,340,752	7,199,312	49,969,742	14,004,861	47,562,602	87,685,240
5	1,307,983	4,063,050	3,071,110	1,741,756	5,040,793	4,374,416	1,813,018	0
6	1,869,005	653,864	7,219,368	1,220,628	1,328,492	5,567,141	3,529,702	0
7	2,368,108	1,731,011	3,003,761	1,473,087	496,260	9,217,474	1,594,931	86,361
8	1,165,600	360,000	694,000	872,450	1,404,600	1,644,669	750,000	0
9	3,393,057	2,666,071	6,634,343	3,544,310	311,710	9,022,275	3,249,264	4,298,411
10	1,112,339	477,963	1,319,570	1,115,880	759,404	3,816,844	1,054,609	280,403
11	1,976,978	807,921	3,548,596	2,554,295	5,518,338	4,238,758	3,847,095	0
TOTAL	18,301,400	19,163,491	79,429,443	21,656,151	68,301,290	59,048,280	67,121,009	96,409,115

Appendix A lists the congressional districts which represent the county in which the state capital is located, and those congressional districts which represent only portions of a county. Appendix C lists the programs included in each functional policy category.

table continues

Table 5.2 Outlays for Business and Commerce Programs by Congressional District, 1983-1990 *(continued)*

Congressional District	1983	1984	1985	1986	1987	1988	1989	1990 (est.)
NORTH DAKOTA								
TOTAL	10,415,823	8,486,330	9,127,588	3,474,936	8,186,383	10,979,770	5,291,215	6,995,352
OHIO								
1	27,894,624	16,163,920	17,832,404	24,252,095	10,044,491	24,034,651	21,184,812	22,211,119
2	11,268,854	9,727,490	7,726,405	5,451,135	236,896	10,825,623	6,632,081	3,006,192
3	19,206,338	19,614,349	19,145,822	18,535,991	10,816,764	24,601,130	2,410,217	28,320,498
4	1,101,707	1,531,000	2,217,683	1,127,000	514,396	4,212,302	185,900	0
5	795,800	0	40,000	848,400	1,590,360	609,000	1,315,000	0
6	109,517	54,450	307,541	754,507	107,000	1,740,261	1,870,707	105,782
7	3,909,793	2,784,906	3,238,360	1,700,460	152,222	5,098,235	949,942	3,376
8	4,177,806	3,015,425	3,011,554	1,742,600	2,854	5,822,470	41,849	0
9	9,004,620	3,641,276	10,001,866	17,147,706	4,108,384	7,088,052	9,965,798	22,060,866
10	5,137,600	9,469,532	1,467,126	1,427,571	1,638,344	12,902,853	1,680,853	2,139,196
11	1,582,416	366,000	2,277,951	1,479,132	1,614,655	4,448,800	17,868,976	4,621,866
12	17,809,131	6,877,888	31,275,999	44,031,747	45,867,957	45,015,118	4,781,990	14,863,707
13	3,301,060	3,554,401	3,009,905	3,372,200	2,144,364	2,774,869	2,524,456	0
14	17,679,009	13,631,324	12,878,955	8,742,200	3,926,887	13,038,100	11,501,344	8,634,900
15	13,502,045	6,374,798	33,373,608	27,993,637	40,523,127	35,396,326	5,828,703	5,507,374
16	11,383,180	6,579,764	6,925,982	6,036,806	3,727,440	12,329,969	1,709,485	2,869,339
17	11,461,804	7,738,922	9,302,841	8,289,774	6,152,316	11,233,345	3,839,180	3,083,430
18	2,104,500	1,142,396	2,849,300	1,372,810	627,567	3,168,710	3,810,397	2,144,329
19	5,883,191	9,145,433	10,594,578	6,712,343	288,577	16,496,990	1,403,178	1,777,310
20	19,782,281	41,652,875	36,697,632	25,132,828	25,623,135	36,573,856	3,317,622	6,238,042
21	8,605,934	11,576,781	12,907,254	8,088,465	32,098	21,362,456	3,030,734	5,436,429
TOTAL	195,701,210	174,642,929	227,082,767	214,239,407	159,739,833	298,773,116	105,853,224	133,023,755
OKLAHOMA								
1	4,627,917	12,127,939	5,276,921	6,690,093	2,053,962	2,884,913	6,590,137	16,653,569
2	244,030	1,208,416	157,200	807,399	1,212,421	4,720,750	1,948,448	654,785
3	385,950	1,904,100	701,100	3,172,100	3,136,024	4,598,800	1,551,630	0
4	5,537,123	8,752,609	4,011,790	10,206,905	9,648,285	5,569,572	3,589,073	3,851,884
5	16,843,953	12,946,702	489,861	3,694,214	21,278,439	12,146,624	13,879,525	20,406,816
6	13,590,662	7,116,499	862,806	2,661,337	11,401,478	6,215,212	7,881,208	10,261,251
TOTAL	41,229,635	44,056,265	11,499,678	27,232,048	48,730,609	36,135,870	35,440,020	51,828,306
OREGON								
1	14,516,441	9,771,955	5,030,721	4,011,349	948,301	207,872	20,729,592	1,349,157
2	13,870,913	1,682,165	2,147,076	3,212,643	4,317,407	2,041,345	1,820,648	1,492,991
3	13,841,646	10,746,671	23,613,215	15,309,658	12,170,283	13,441,581	3,403,337	6,752
4	9,232,871	4,143,634	3,502,267	12,905,577	4,206,389	1,936,771	4,741,326	3,613,527
5	9,977,417	6,570,607	16,395,762	16,048,439	3,779,251	11,974,024	6,872,360	5,121,927
TOTAL	61,439,288	32,915,032	50,689,040	51,487,666	25,421,631	29,601,593	37,567,263	11,584,354
PENNSYLVANIA								
1	26,121,247	95,528,166	118,311,623	95,440,619	75,014,857	65,046,571	41,434,766	68,036,272
2	26,301,448	19,933,765	20,171,197	27,441,697	11,770,970	33,232,623	19,202,159	3,376
3	26,738,474	19,107,787	18,932,363	16,810,585	45,861	22,896,114	7,209,062	0
4	4,805,600	1,376,000	900,762	874,723	602,441	7,468,756	2,845,162	4,261,300
5	4,776,834	4,358,946	4,172,662	5,831,867	136,395	8,606,297	598,548	132,052
6	8,072,789	8,066,742	7,936,838	6,640,599	3,512,120	13,662,082	1,243,173	9,609,560
7	12,802,445	9,206,558	9,182,123	10,639,648	158,778	9,045,304	1,383,603	16,798,321
8	5,793,720	3,925,253	1,292,923	2,708,888	105,853	5,108,760	332,543	1,274,982
9	4,332,309	3,086,065	3,009,224	1,197,811	1,747,427	3,506,959	2,816,502	1,047,165
10	6,185,378	1,689,320	9,611,022	6,085,079	4,411,607	6,587,247	5,645,093	3,532,417
11	13,373,770	12,273,878	11,915,178	5,153,491	1,269,601	7,759,062	4,158,921	7,164,779
12	8,656,200	2,717,850	2,815,972	2,647,901	1,500,031	8,690,694	5,165,491	6,069,054
13	11,769,904	7,652,205	8,406,128	4,034,031	1,211,843	8,538,300	2,486,297	9,290,153
14	44,373,966	67,676,262	58,403,434	28,833,136	43,842,583	74,088,435	26,139,533	50,795,152
15	9,925,057	7,095,862	5,306,330	7,371,970	6,239,045	8,337,554	6,449,266	5,502,695
16	5,573,150	7,995,669	7,425,168	5,599,001	1,584,996	10,012,011	7,450,942	9,090,250
17	63,350,429	64,721,769	61,532,574	63,506,991	90,011,800	82,857,954	28,640,395	34,949,804
18	718,000	402,000	5,671,704	359,000	0	477,000	309,615	0
19	6,231,014	5,329,303	6,055,892	4,720,457	140,121	8,587,082	2,751,625	0
20	0	1,800,000	5,775,478	0	1,282,400	1,220,000	1,268,000	3,232,800
21	8,307,869	2,475,903	7,865,248	5,404,519	6,069,245	7,538,305	4,573,086	1,479,658
22	6,352,100	5,013,532	391,812	5,068,607	499,652	7,754,726	759,734	675,213
23	1,039,130	2,731,388	878,734	3,213,498	4,397,918	3,081,596	3,755,643	2,817,145
TOTAL	305,600,834	354,164,223	375,964,391	309,584,118	255,555,545	404,103,433	176,619,159	235,762,151

Appendix A lists the congressional districts which represent the county in which the state capital is located, and those congressional districts which represent only portions of a county. Appendix C lists the programs included in each functional policy category.

table continues

Table 5.2 Outlays for Business and Commerce Programs by Congressional District, 1983-1990 *(continued)*

Congressional District	1983	1984	1985	1986	1987	1988	1989	1990 (est.)
RHODE ISLAND								
1	15,971,514	13,330,846	19,891,416	15,385,663	14,700,280	21,474,698	6,569,661	12,690,655
2	8,791,483	4,480,132	6,459,411	724,992	2,497,711	7,667,113	857,381	3,537,874
TOTAL	24,762,997	17,810,978	26,350,827	16,110,655	17,197,991	29,141,811	7,427,042	16,228,529
SOUTH CAROLINA								
1	3,351,398	6,841,442	2,997,550	5,686,914	348,752	4,813,801	7,233,921	1,480,401
2	42,010,743	28,883,277	32,423,176	25,494,006	42,247,356	29,008,434	6,032,257	25,013,698
3	2,802,846	1,300,747	1,148,900	1,906,800	1,544,280	3,058,164	1,368,478	2,275,605
4	9,137,455	6,956,192	7,130,140	4,093,566	1,215,205	11,752,521	2,486,402	8,733,100
5	2,117,850	684,000	1,594,319	1,978,500	2,755,000	2,097,224	690,400	1,413,658
6	1,420,858	1,265,446	916,250	969,400	2,101,676	1,774,331	1,744,702	1,375,972
TOTAL	60,841,150	45,931,104	46,210,335	40,129,186	50,212,269	52,504,475	19,556,160	40,292,434
SOUTH DAKOTA								
TOTAL	10,011,356	9,489,362	8,604,489	8,316,743	8,276,028	8,964,746	4,244,975	8,738,655
TENNESSEE								
1	2,683,658	2,450,233	2,067,110	1,626,010	675,860	5,175,603	3,319,954	381,909
2	7,304,548	6,289,032	4,666,732	3,878,933	4,951,324	4,376,111	2,918,758	6,585,584
3	6,036,424	7,193,402	3,881,523	3,433,894	3,362,184	6,586,059	2,176,365	3,839,517
4	1,334,127	951,000	0	0	501,682	1,262,463	372,716	0
5	51,487,723	37,066,734	44,453,194	32,432,601	38,072,300	38,807,684	7,533,675	11,413,890
6	4,775,492	1,257,260	1,935,440	1,499,960	614,655	2,040,875	706,349	161,020
7	5,783,360	6,582,856	9,479,827	8,130,697	11,116,483	18,067,956	5,776,224	12,899,020
8	3,330,032	16,150,596	2,945,123	2,428,705	2,082,875	7,261,882	1,592,061	1,050,128
9	13,611,328	8,496,426	8,370,576	6,689,497	520,171	29,198,109	984,260	184,471
TOTAL	96,346,692	86,437,539	77,799,525	60,120,296	61,897,534	112,776,741	25,380,362	36,515,539
TEXAS								
1	6,126,150	2,489,450	1,557,750	5,552,576	3,226,664	2,562,968	2,885,246	1,401,050
2	4,903,733	466,500	451,500	394,500	478,318	1,559,330	1,896,249	901,556
3	20,048,427	10,722,843	6,527,931	12,933,503	5,986,690	1,202,296	13,865,705	13,903,858
4	5,886,586	2,512,000	2,616,838	2,095,847	512,738	457,180	3,157,126	4,856,112
5	7,787,583	6,849,567	6,453,672	5,872,304	554,088	157,786	14,123,090	14,538,299
6	8,086,287	16,891,585	3,896,807	2,085,022	734,063	1,197,551	4,503,603	5,173,527
7	59,121,772	15,875,578	38,418,749	35,588,517	10,378,655	42,674,261	21,490,109	53,360,644
8	9,129,542	7,908,005	7,399,402	6,477,111	190,477	0	866,929	2,432,375
9	6,852,563	16,916,067	9,558,782	7,794,133	4,038,063	4,067,522	7,964,263	5,879,588
10	83,990,250	71,909,438	79,750,908	73,653,974	27,440,795	120,183,626	18,745,214	48,774,143
11	4,140,403	4,299,214	4,347,827	3,577,218	1,628,589	7,297,366	6,645,101	9,523,860
12	3,297,111	5,906,629	20,790,518	10,760,513	3,303,564	5,414,300	7,667,383	12,233,330
13	7,553,134	4,472,473	4,016,970	3,641,564	648,955	1,063,660	6,567,547	7,345,818
14	3,510,705	884,500	889,500	991,070	268,577	504,323	1,157,948	1,913,712
15	12,840,284	3,069,166	11,698,448	11,062,740	3,432,604	10,148,198	8,739,978	7,964,500
16	13,467,298	10,154,007	14,005,973	11,776,825	2,253,205	7,761,285	32,465,043	32,287,834
17	8,387,816	0	3,548,563	1,515,081	494,425	488,908	2,668,289	2,888,715
18	8,434,646	21,032,981	7,505,822	6,394,986	617,673	238,068	1,585,109	672,811
19	7,821,355	3,984,835	4,072,624	2,924,424	1,321,274	3,219,048	7,568,098	0
20	5,583,341	20,908,481	23,722,049	16,155,310	21,620,365	10,297,674	30,474,763	52,716,770
21	4,842,103	5,878,208	5,289,266	5,548,974	1,217,793	2,657,702	7,910,601	7,993,786
22	3,963,765	3,286,198	4,059,674	3,530,257	91,902	657,015	54,461,058	58,605,263
23	9,629,477	9,820,341	11,493,804	10,769,651	1,105,619	1,422,057	16,875,871	23,056,819
24	7,159,203	7,199,990	6,234,179	6,274,503	405,410	16,825,208	14,297,855	15,591,500
25	8,288,913	7,151,241	7,422,481	6,327,875	33,735	0	869,633	668,684
26	2,261,235	3,680,698	3,781,109	2,900,373	598,703	310,234	4,690,582	0
27	14,075,084	500,000	15,258,042	10,205,672	1,165,550	2,151,956	16,168,716	11,307,768
TOTAL	337,188,766	264,769,996	304,769,187	266,804,523	93,748,493	244,519,522	310,311,107	395,992,323
UTAH								
1	2,004,300	50,000	429,500	219,736	1,255,562	103,744	1,964,856	0
2	24,383,464	13,076,534	19,155,690	22,090,775	24,722,386	22,790,436	12,670,444	29,828,748
3	2,914,273	11,480,385	160,200	1,484,162	625,717	2,091,765	4,974,867	248,552
TOTAL	29,302,037	24,606,919	19,745,390	23,794,673	26,603,665	24,985,945	19,610,167	30,077,301
VERMONT								
TOTAL	9,061,938	7,218,722	7,163,906	6,709,464	7,109,056	7,833,797	1,385,711	2,124,866

Appendix A lists the congressional districts which represent the county in which the state capital is located, and those congressional districts which represent only portions of a county. Appendix C lists the programs included in each functional policy category.

table continues

Table 5.2 Outlays for Business and Commerce Programs by Congressional District, 1983-1990 *(continued)*

Congressional District	1983	1984	1985	1986	1987	1988	1989	1990 (est.)
VIRGINIA								
1	1,420,390	3,741,120	5,098,200	8,836,456	4,663,393	6,191,102	4,221,464	3,657,483
2	8,282,069	7,011,613	17,415,123	13,284,164	12,092,581	15,962,054	6,632,906	11,038,796
3	31,299,688	3,809,273	33,172,711	29,740,462	35,063,879	34,878,691	6,909,780	13,144,682
4	4,500,000	4,459,173	5,493,128	7,030,581	589,467	7,330,452	1,932,627	4,249,760
5	32,552	2,817,098	2,755,461	2,399,586	1,962,185	7,358,822	1,246,591	3,376
6	892,490	518,322	6,003,498	4,023,012	4,960,326	5,090,651	1,410,763	80,779
7	774,200	231,086	1,262,845	1,542,544	1,209,050	2,263,477	964,014	1,394,589
8	4,365,416	3,219,575	100,000	2,606,707	474,515	1,852,825	1,255,892	0
9	487,983	727,688	1,429,300	1,233,572	1,615,476	1,049,260	963,131	3,746,827
10	6,810,209	4,713,938	3,916,288	5,116,796	1,303,709	12,419,539	1,875,500	449,735
TOTAL	58,864,997	31,248,886	76,646,554	75,813,880	63,934,581	94,396,873	27,412,668	37,766,028
WASHINGTON								
1	21,156,355	8,164,563	30,194,370	33,906,117	27,198,644	18,845,138	30,627,746	11,306,765
2	1,702,321	5,743,167	5,818,889	6,061,050	1,343,951	1,117,885	5,235,147	3,495,445
3	23,762,076	16,760,149	11,095,833	17,712,547	20,581,314	20,220,242	8,944,845	3,796,109
4	3,833,128	4,963,186	3,063,131	2,476,031	4,762,957	1,822,050	3,364,522	4,471,945
5	8,744,850	8,801,088	9,791,064	6,641,295	6,750,722	4,630,344	9,411,707	150,019
6	9,906,360	8,436,063	12,715,552	12,829,573	2,798,530	1,123,368	18,099,856	7,140,636
7	12,559,479	38,522,363	7,784,709	6,511,352	643,335	612,347	8,386,322	15,951,221
8	12,210,885	8,268,604	1,862,306	6,796,852	1,419,040	1,326,267	8,732,553	16,657,885
TOTAL	93,875,453	99,659,183	82,325,856	92,934,817	65,498,493	49,697,641	92,802,698	62,970,024
WEST VIRGINIA								
1	4,168,818	3,838,350	3,894,397	3,875,685	2,818,091	8,901,994	3,783,751	5,788,355
2	150,425	1,111,331	2,252,500	2,043,730	216,350	2,113,995	596,568	270,892
3	13,180,144	22,882,248	5,505,434	5,020,419	28,320,929	29,642,429	6,676,152	6,327,869
4	6,955,469	3,147,450	3,114,900	2,899,000	1,638,344	4,207,132	2,308,095	0
TOTAL	24,454,856	30,979,379	14,767,231	13,838,834	32,993,714	44,865,550	13,364,566	12,387,117
WISCONSIN								
1	8,141,515	6,912,410	7,909,356	7,179,816	3,011,926	9,774,170	5,663,506	10,885,499
2	35,664,071	6,981,255	36,354,923	28,374,207	52,231,799	34,164,064	31,827,079	15,133,319
3	2,826,654	4,344,163	3,504,140	4,004,729	2,283,358	2,913,778	2,478,124	4,580,736
4	23,086,456	26,433,272	26,525,316	20,554,701	21,878,370	27,289,777	13,990,459	23,809,346
5	17,000,280	11,590,910	10,339,898	7,950,568	9,953,939	11,233,381	199,237	21,314,759
6	3,862,022	2,124,540	1,804,761	1,898,520	1,514,174	3,630,581	2,724,377	1,288,802
7	4,210,144	3,189,792	2,960,778	1,907,778	2,752,131	6,521,987	2,822,047	4,345,575
8	3,686,320	4,303,856	2,306,500	3,485,861	2,727,282	3,483,790	4,617,177	4,982,599
9	3,425,497	2,480,200	2,199,518	2,570,697	1,366,167	2,711,343	868,968	1,170,038
TOTAL	101,902,959	68,360,399	93,905,191	77,926,877	97,719,147	101,722,872	65,190,974	87,510,671
WYOMING								
TOTAL	3,045,086	4,711,708	4,147,829	3,711,477	7,043,581	3,952,061	2,876,735	2,627,820
U.S. TOTAL	4,930.8 mil.	5,045.1 mil.	5,016.7 mil.	4,835.9 mil.	4,252.7 mil.	5,749.9 mil.	3,553.7 mil.	4,787.3 mil.

Appendix A lists the congressional districts which represent the county in which the state capital is located, and those congressional districts which represent only portions of a county. Appendix C lists the programs included in each functional policy category.

Table 5.3

Outlays for Community Development Programs by Congressional District, 1983-1990

Congressional District	1983	1984	1985	1986	1987	1988	1989	1990 (est.)
ALABAMA								
1	21,641,515	25,096,620	23,200,963	23,454,156	5,631,585	18,345,389	6,184,165	6,015,349
2	34,297,607	67,563,427	75,130,439	44,097,584	55,188,692	68,176,501	23,897,360	40,976,222
3	28,550,602	19,780,218	24,801,089	25,769,692	11,808,932	16,660,483	15,360,510	21,476,984
4	22,283,392	25,521,539	18,322,748	15,791,552	10,196,988	8,970,887	4,747,790	6,649,301
5	13,853,282	22,961,978	20,019,614	24,951,376	5,691,729	9,345,685	5,354,930	5,683,272
6	31,462,922	35,881,946	36,792,691	44,367,129	11,920,255	27,683,552	8,549,500	13,485,971
7	23,500,228	24,093,246	19,374,785	18,381,425	5,676,462	9,769,631	6,478,517	2,820,348
TOTAL	175,589,549	220,898,974	217,642,328	196,812,914	106,114,644	158,952,128	70,572,772	97,107,447
ALASKA								
TOTAL	83,334,877	141,966,113	77,557,466	86,601,805	73,918,453	62,346,558	78,796,244	9,825,720
ARIZONA								
1	48,811,410	47,167,344	41,519,354	67,531,948	36,840,007	47,411,239	44,157,201	6,492,031
2	37,036,899	44,929,353	43,060,204	43,844,103	13,732,409	20,207,044	23,968,607	19,909,052
3	7,453,189	18,818,949	14,741,624	15,613,999	7,273,993	17,747,713	14,880,993	1,405,497
4	50,266,885	46,248,398	35,206,941	32,838,051	16,210,343	16,718,504	15,364,916	3,201,759
5	13,145,487	21,850,482	15,519,176	19,447,587	4,698,234	4,888,709	15,207,647	6,680,461
TOTAL	156,713,870	179,014,526	150,047,299	179,275,687	78,754,985	106,973,209	113,579,364	37,688,799
ARKANSAS								
1	25,692,623	15,778,696	17,320,120	15,812,670	3,674,435	6,832,780	4,530,249	20,494,083
2	56,991,076	62,213,785	74,439,897	66,572,358	40,787,015	54,872,615	34,061,306	15,617,890
3	31,568,283	29,828,492	25,280,657	32,163,788	21,750,965	15,334,527	19,885,388	14,741,648
4	23,492,913	21,573,563	16,030,221	21,341,163	2,231,420	10,159,610	16,714,769	785,395
TOTAL	137,744,895	129,394,536	133,070,895	135,889,979	68,443,835	87,199,532	75,191,712	51,639,017
CALIFORNIA								
1	52,725,301	62,319,137	51,658,520	50,126,168	8,645,216	9,386,236	39,008,244	38,470,183
2	18,089,003	31,764,900	15,645,114	31,564,031	5,993,688	6,658,500	10,804,981	885,875
3	93,602,057	108,293,576	126,647,243	142,350,141	119,559,878	124,801,386	69,975,810	258,763,718
4	26,308,263	43,506,998	37,285,258	53,301,840	30,527,152	38,589,570	16,502,601	92,971,196
5	154,847,406	64,560,231	77,031,031	89,766,521	93,085,306	49,156,888	51,688,513	124,480,328
6	25,819,028	41,663,565	31,470,327	28,005,650	5,882,990	17,971,801	9,756,081	10,082,261
7	16,373,889	19,000,771	21,928,954	21,054,388	12,457,029	9,855,038	26,228,861	3,280,787
8	34,690,184	191,838,997	76,747,432	106,298,864	59,314,608	41,420,147	21,791,020	13,512,721
9	18,591,151	19,155,825	21,020,048	20,876,615	3,576,853	10,812,972	17,113,343	19,843,258
10	45,306,453	35,798,097	103,499,620	101,413,099	41,134,201	26,257,546	12,510,976	25,135,549
11	50,342,809	16,135,460	28,275,449	17,142,804	4,693,328	18,354,467	6,670,695	3,573,689
12	17,268,814	67,165,600	15,670,269	15,397,159	-356,934	934,866	7,434,300	67,514
13	25,129,580	29,473,147	15,204,767	15,304,457	-807,400	4,150,270	10,591,583	3,376
14	25,242,081	61,593,473	20,957,418	32,536,804	13,812,956	4,193,237	7,039,236	1,842,860
15	25,734,077	42,753,511	18,576,872	22,973,729	11,654,811	9,101,360	7,985,836	8,619,165
16	25,160,769	38,668,803	79,225,732	38,317,637	7,656,471	6,782,586	11,948,093	-2,216,539
17	28,793,253	28,344,260	23,793,711	26,837,010	5,940,789	4,548,863	11,477,683	4,384,924
18	75,136,596	91,008,326	58,255,862	29,268,539	3,275,281	7,337,313	12,415,231	3,663,981
19	19,573,986	26,887,185	20,319,526	16,520,883	9,409,459	12,613,660	13,452,500	1,138,286
20	177,281,075	252,281,269	112,521,110	315,253,066	222,198,963	176,548,244	21,665,699	4,868,976
21	21,836,134	20,739,821	19,772,908	25,826,040	8,023,661	1,722,235	99,127,156	1,594,969
22	29,579,554	25,435,572	28,799,164	29,025,626	2,236,008	3,599,912	9,847,595	1,258,438
23	24,544,168	21,115,295	23,035,114	24,917,113	3,273,802	3,356,279	11,846,028	1,585,336
24	25,578,714	23,951,150	28,364,904	26,837,745	2,367,241	10,132,628	18,995,804	2,728,604
25	25,914,401	27,108,184	23,919,532	24,633,770	3,397,948	3,486,452	8,661,429	1,145,338
26	21,515,311	18,344,185	20,430,834	21,207,747	1,393,890	852,827	6,074,365	893,594
27	52,011,196	62,740,553	53,996,719	47,163,939	27,039,117	38,426,636	36,388,846	37,465,437
28	25,398,591	22,019,212	24,122,381	25,122,208	2,678,597	1,579,880	8,268,664	2,277,506
29	26,963,229	25,509,683	25,620,060	26,091,418	2,479,797	2,011,515	9,168,583	1,017,565
30	142,773,698	30,113,541	36,212,418	37,390,301	1,704,593	2,035,909	14,061,180	1,822,489
31	31,501,365	30,732,273	37,243,986	37,933,813	3,833,546	1,596,771	16,298,924	11,247,383
32	35,500,984	22,978,383	24,545,705	25,361,730	1,814,940	1,024,226	9,746,956	1,021,472
33	26,405,746	27,614,879	29,355,672	30,658,354	1,925,320	1,189,145	8,985,638	930,989
34	28,828,967	29,360,962	30,464,806	31,395,225	1,870,907	919,718	31,726,676	1,647,261
35	20,623,296	45,272,771	27,890,373	29,609,027	6,140,950	7,670,035	18,171,283	8,566,143
36	28,916,662	32,706,607	38,874,840	46,721,328	14,477,602	17,211,049	28,534,713	41,276,017
37	26,161,215	39,261,805	30,868,858	29,400,598	6,917,207	18,080,395	13,985,671	37,134,697
38	12,131,094	27,475,851	11,812,239	29,081,961	26,436,129	17,696,731	7,891,297	2,404,731
39	15,143,307	12,097,448	16,716,982	16,121,175	858,266	125,906	10,794,849	4,923,337

Appendix A lists the congressional districts which represent the county in which the state capital is located, and those congressional districts which represent only portions of a county. Appendix C lists the programs included in each functional policy category.

table continues

Table 5.3 Outlays for Community Development Programs by Congressional District, 1983-1990 *(continued)*

Congressional District	1983	1984	1985	1986	1987	1988	1989	1990 (est.)
CALIFORNIA *continued*								
40	17,169,307	12,206,323	19,281,129	17,293,863	4,215,519	11,482,602	19,044,614	14,132,612
41	20,055,073	35,195,025	19,033,063	58,909,163	27,852,997	4,337,432	24,482,196	4,916,780
42	40,606,996	26,864,220	23,465,718	22,933,038	11,106,661	7,828,014	13,685,637	6,299,039
43	25,714,662	28,612,836	18,950,938	24,577,313	4,754,723	4,437,127	13,975,976	2,025,351
44	21,593,577	11,794,789	18,273,993	18,247,064	453,067	432,683	17,587,987	957,525
45	21,436,589	19,519,751	19,406,014	20,607,605	2,761,887	2,131,625	14,234,311	436,175
TOTAL	1,723,919,611	1,950,984,250	1,606,192,613	1,901,376,573	827,669,023	742,842,683	857,647,664	803,080,901
COLORADO								
1	60,661,133	91,141,600	61,375,724	58,852,310	64,605,792	47,815,425	94,663,811	119,474,669
2	17,502,872	23,083,208	19,239,569	13,719,444	13,870,781	5,296,903	7,222,652	6,435,774
3	20,186,088	29,380,891	33,552,835	24,859,674	10,539,501	13,705,448	16,560,744	6,835,385
4	23,990,181	19,936,235	18,011,715	21,089,608	8,759,969	11,355,137	16,602,317	11,864,386
5	18,802,957	16,689,111	10,089,937	14,445,868	9,611,400	33,914,151	7,832,775	6,606,788
6	9,713,857	15,421,401	8,949,833	12,017,554	3,747,893	3,772,035	564,091	-58,282
TOTAL	150,857,087	195,652,446	151,219,614	144,984,457	111,135,335	115,859,099	143,446,389	151,158,719
CONNECTICUT								
1	72,162,799	82,062,876	68,805,958	68,642,449	56,929,846	79,681,523	47,226,134	54,323,298
2	14,038,271	13,651,530	13,479,724	17,090,966	1,975,621	14,104,829	5,008,399	7,653,282
3	47,108,014	35,221,741	20,900,893	36,938,971	4,302,068	17,776,596	2,781,366	12,472,401
4	41,809,949	18,614,029	34,926,804	24,288,300	20,952,723	18,088,662	4,101,643	2,834,115
5	14,819,869	21,016,494	13,294,388	14,655,165	-141,686	8,472,114	42,144	7,507,593
6	19,816,747	23,970,851	34,446,527	18,104,118	8,608,295	6,601,871	1,467,784	4,847,808
TOTAL	209,755,649	194,537,520	185,854,294	179,719,969	92,626,867	144,725,595	60,627,470	89,638,497
DELAWARE								
TOTAL	41,400,539	50,274,194	40,912,832	32,268,889	25,461,790	22,877,549	29,696,125	13,238,220
DISTRICT OF COLUMBIA								
TOTAL	353,830,276	226,797,500	77,771,186	130,053,540	30,006,261	133,152,715	150,202,780	92,019,754
FLORIDA								
1	13,630,846	12,540,354	11,181,948	13,675,984	3,708,867	12,956,662	7,186,703	10,764,827
2	86,274,236	49,401,125	82,453,907	54,138,926	63,684,324	59,028,801	50,679,901	78,830,372
3	20,322,478	24,482,145	31,476,580	28,735,357	10,956,807	20,630,656	19,164,879	29,740,411
4	20,501,566	20,499,041	16,220,443	21,657,220	2,149,190	10,234,570	7,218,573	18,088,204
5	43,713,181	38,922,827	41,546,724	39,775,875	21,952,927	11,386,869	21,623,247	12,685,691
6	25,074,365	18,410,737	17,152,856	20,118,615	9,450,256	19,727,759	13,263,472	17,236,553
7	32,483,331	45,648,844	33,795,923	43,766,496	25,487,389	34,434,399	24,046,542	28,170,538
8	20,469,646	24,513,329	23,426,087	27,100,415	25,876,042	13,702,292	10,292,705	18,886,305
9	9,510,830	15,766,661	15,824,710	15,859,480	11,265,893	24,391,319	16,710,344	15,598,349
10	18,179,555	35,710,156	46,520,592	19,933,224	12,577,698	13,292,632	7,806,536	15,578,969
11	25,975,731	28,663,190	28,486,090	29,684,820	13,082,184	19,686,653	15,058,240	29,416,449
12	10,800,706	14,860,780	20,214,780	23,315,738	21,934,974	22,156,275	14,057,674	15,257,591
13	85,457,556	37,688,214	9,101,010	16,705,634	25,766,314	20,984,402	10,475,167	8,845,115
14	13,394,511	12,294,050	15,825,387	14,074,910	290,295	8,123,262	2,746,952	14,214,097
15	35,745,826	56,310,692	39,263,537	35,708,044	15,158,104	47,332,197	30,383,060	47,122,215
16	12,588,411	15,487,176	10,513,394	14,402,587	7,433,360	26,808,688	6,077,817	10,343,517
17	23,953,865	26,297,426	36,157,470	63,197,957	32,440,151	26,671,011	9,988,632	11,753,926
18	25,431,775	31,954,360	14,075,143	25,743,888	7,410,057	13,884,661	11,119,397	16,817,010
19	21,984,851	26,112,773	7,464,287	36,019,943	3,523,246	12,699,971	123,475,209	56,352,829
TOTAL	545,493,264	535,563,880	500,700,868	543,615,113	314,148,077	418,133,079	401,375,050	455,702,968
GEORGIA								
1	35,422,100	28,171,685	20,212,107	21,922,567	16,119,937	25,081,287	10,372,817	1,328,774
2	16,102,401	13,520,354	21,443,647	15,163,923	1,932,640	12,765,112	3,967,152	2,288,980
3	30,313,626	13,449,972	17,189,220	20,235,897	11,891,908	14,490,668	4,636,315	13,277,114
4	76,936,384	127,610,009	149,169,514	118,475,792	85,694,257	197,150,590	92,031,798	53,018,067
5	85,654,965	95,294,772	32,377,542	75,966,498	64,857,276	88,233,486	52,355,662	105,495,834
6	15,657,292	40,565,066	10,752,733	19,508,127	5,134,878	11,094,893	3,231,189	12,011,420
7	20,365,317	11,901,691	8,662,392	8,622,549	8,832,390	8,730,722	7,476,633	5,890,385
8	23,560,876	29,885,310	27,360,139	16,818,295	4,026,946	15,029,623	3,823,684	1,176,319
9	23,213,876	10,300,105	30,965,710	20,715,494	9,802,384	11,399,200	4,098,116	5,130,574
10	24,439,362	33,128,259	17,198,382	23,908,889	7,526,134	22,418,570	12,492,852	19,145,353
TOTAL	351,666,199	403,827,223	335,331,386	341,338,031	215,818,749	406,394,150	194,486,217	218,762,820

Appendix A lists the congressional districts which represent the county in which the state capital is located, and those congressional districts which represent only portions of a county. Appendix C lists the programs included in each functional policy category.

table continues

Table 5.3 Outlays for Community Development Programs by Congressional District, 1983-1990 *(continued)*

Congressional District	1983	1984	1985	1986	1987	1988	1989	1990 (est.)
HAWAII								
1	31,525,734	41,524,398	75,268,725	85,273,425	53,648,849	44,172,698	37,479,692	20,781,017
2	24,124,572	24,591,096	18,315,047	26,198,196	14,036,260	28,184,107	1,604,828	35,551,296
TOTAL	55,650,306	66,115,494	93,583,772	111,471,621	67,685,109	72,356,805	39,084,520	56,332,313
IDAHO								
1	43,650,650	31,992,755	40,264,505	44,244,314	31,150,728	39,276,951	26,226,251	23,206,949
2	18,911,532	22,636,903	18,853,965	26,933,967	11,338,121	14,107,438	8,191,183	6,380,305
TOTAL	62,562,182	54,629,658	59,118,470	71,178,281	42,488,849	53,384,389	34,417,434	29,587,254
ILLINOIS								
1	162,157,120	248,758,652	349,979,211	437,010,520	311,804,005	388,665,076	314,730,436	190,428,990
2	27,438,237	26,572,450	20,652,101	22,145,260	859,928	35,793,800	3,152,394	26,177,365
3	28,877,747	27,596,791	32,107,368	25,383,518	1,436,315	41,098,150	3,427,801	26,120,614
4	18,391,640	20,461,448	17,448,349	32,336,711	2,072,511	21,520,982	3,560,086	10,826,392
5	35,896,890	26,289,526	51,081,288	22,842,738	2,472,492	37,475,547	4,742,900	29,669,452
6	110,848,909	41,392,745	22,170,303	25,596,327	9,857,356	15,792,969	4,367,712	13,908,149
7	34,348,986	54,304,753	33,023,704	29,396,900	18,976,602	71,063,302	42,838,246	27,570,819
8	27,535,776	26,484,367	20,755,663	22,404,725	912,086	35,887,166	3,259,555	25,285,644
9	28,870,269	29,783,203	23,962,597	24,875,565	1,496,998	40,536,084	4,510,997	25,940,214
10	19,328,522	25,389,405	23,722,236	23,199,727	9,691,027	23,015,355	1,776,238	11,427,596
11	28,657,787	26,675,572	21,411,441	21,870,592	978,932	36,397,237	3,083,736	25,223,440
12	16,657,780	23,201,137	15,688,111	18,141,630	1,120,008	16,536,697	1,366,033	10,715,247
13	19,580,659	25,816,224	16,065,534	25,778,731	1,036,199	19,605,608	3,251,283	14,083,454
14	41,611,303	38,518,373	24,563,809	5,788,011	2,535,690	3,897,516	767,078	1,585,494
15	16,526,525	29,706,815	33,092,425	13,128,614	26,108,969	7,331,975	4,491,146	1,560,677
16	15,665,113	15,357,887	13,353,114	14,173,516	3,663,884	8,792,527	4,243,627	6,870,224
17	29,336,481	16,917,402	14,855,756	19,722,901	5,727,797	6,909,693	4,965,434	4,400,934
18	33,372,412	34,663,077	16,902,087	55,207,870	11,694,051	9,116,835	3,369,116	7,117,403
19	35,169,251	35,178,832	19,918,639	29,647,323	11,193,827	18,802,780	18,014,392	20,482,395
20	65,087,002	106,960,507	101,791,317	46,602,900	94,034,384	65,529,802	32,106,028	80,939,453
21	26,405,769	18,386,053	13,635,661	15,299,173	3,545,080	21,682,950	10,639,161	17,928,028
22	15,338,387	18,152,054	17,625,935	17,297,601	7,320,305	3,454,172	7,068,595	8,776,089
TOTAL	837,102,563	916,567,273	903,806,649	947,850,852	528,538,445	928,906,224	479,731,993	587,038,074
INDIANA								
1	10,853,008	55,855,953	43,322,467	43,648,452	13,592,940	22,134,477	11,741,040	11,403,640
2	33,345,796	20,467,739	28,786,464	33,783,307	14,722,103	26,791,736	13,621,755	12,893,995
3	14,093,043	35,573,417	23,450,771	20,393,060	9,812,550	23,490,258	14,628,269	8,011,821
4	18,526,166	19,057,878	15,102,749	15,746,931	12,128,647	13,264,171	12,116,182	11,752,545
5	19,723,622	21,591,191	36,675,742	17,445,117	5,077,080	13,759,000	7,389,721	-643,094
6	45,835,048	26,208,111	22,473,049	22,401,304	8,166,892	27,631,828	23,250,868	14,226,183
7	29,119,314	23,591,433	28,836,728	24,197,364	9,407,678	21,677,887	18,242,253	12,922,665
8	26,445,496	15,905,051	19,231,182	20,871,317	15,402,663	9,337,704	18,337,037	10,954,440
9	13,527,452	16,703,933	15,579,938	12,697,519	8,838,286	17,750,111	10,875,610	5,669,696
10	81,907,996	88,164,726	57,500,141	67,960,286	28,381,463	39,716,779	12,480,620	1,505,078
TOTAL	293,376,942	323,119,432	290,959,232	279,144,657	125,530,302	215,553,950	142,683,355	88,696,968
IOWA								
1	17,392,370	20,513,610	12,738,622	13,743,573	2,791,776	3,818,928	3,201,735	767,754
2	19,200,715	18,890,774	16,754,540	16,328,566	4,819,832	8,817,359	4,160,455	3,508,379
3	15,559,306	16,951,935	13,400,838	13,883,734	3,106,452	5,036,675	8,450,296	6,209,691
4	92,141,558	72,158,393	82,138,324	82,772,743	86,073,555	72,730,361	91,213,322	82,806,784
5	15,660,648	19,596,577	18,057,982	15,379,023	5,593,372	8,991,482	6,142,285	3,156,395
6	27,104,352	19,413,353	16,739,310	14,744,493	3,529,082	7,529,010	4,376,589	1,627,377
TOTAL	187,058,949	167,524,642	159,829,616	156,852,132	105,914,069	106,923,815	117,544,682	98,076,380
KANSAS								
1	24,818,892	19,458,243	15,406,664	17,885,100	9,185,766	9,235,420	6,701,261	5,064,344
2	37,979,216	48,269,507	45,939,472	43,606,756	32,043,689	34,438,400	27,407,686	12,144,816
3	20,505,801	37,148,606	44,484,481	25,377,518	8,758,075	20,448,104	18,151,254	3,055,443
4	16,919,818	16,551,584	17,112,322	23,056,981	10,016,000	15,904,517	4,576,150	2,720,099
5	27,527,709	11,048,229	15,003,927	11,105,345	9,826,342	9,144,033	8,098,742	988,290
TOTAL	127,751,436	132,476,169	137,946,866	121,031,700	69,829,872	89,170,474	64,935,093	23,972,992

Appendix A lists the congressional districts which represent the county in which the state capital is located, and those congressional districts which represent only portions of a county. Appendix C lists the programs included in each functional policy category.

table continues

Table 5.3 Outlays for Community Development Programs by Congressional District, 1983-1990 *(continued)*

Congressional District	1983	1984	1985	1986	1987	1988	1989	1990 (est.)
KENTUCKY								
1	12,397,928	16,459,387	13,347,709	12,283,502	8,227,022	5,883,077	4,717,017	3,138,107
2	28,843,291	18,396,352	18,421,299	13,497,670	2,466,858	1,327,116	3,240,656	-69,663
3	29,320,738	41,429,896	49,182,683	52,311,399	14,569,114	37,294,876	14,122,408	34,692,040
4	17,512,135	27,839,168	17,839,294	17,187,270	12,018,959	23,634,633	8,762,394	32,659,556
5	20,262,109	13,464,179	13,910,495	13,812,587	6,559,547	5,247,166	5,345,372	3,256,977
6	52,372,827	95,791,142	50,831,757	59,154,047	67,491,707	47,698,602	112,895,032	42,698,309
7	23,117,054	13,747,446	12,903,401	13,145,350	5,888,204	5,215,498	4,640,668	1,333,205
TOTAL	183,826,082	227,127,570	176,436,638	181,391,825	117,221,411	126,300,968	153,723,547	117,708,530
LOUISIANA								
1	64,907,721	43,192,439	33,274,046	54,393,095	12,284,446	19,636,729	22,058,019	1,598,143
2	38,928,838	43,042,236	26,503,017	30,902,061	920,788	14,236,884	21,296,728	1,414,261
3	20,526,722	18,567,991	32,493,622	32,190,368	12,289,785	4,096,392	6,930,936	-1,890,685
4	21,343,244	22,412,002	22,613,459	18,417,856	7,990,504	5,365,157	29,441,185	-847,725
5	20,952,465	14,300,662	14,951,549	19,593,811	6,608,494	6,635,091	9,203,493	5,732,961
6	64,542,239	73,849,971	80,670,424	68,415,580	60,845,708	32,105,018	91,527,713	34,775,193
7	22,282,576	23,464,174	15,914,587	18,498,577	6,689,176	7,273,069	10,007,283	10,970,020
8	16,161,571	19,933,217	17,159,907	16,143,468	9,418,818	5,981,975	11,540,562	7,243,569
TOTAL	269,645,377	258,762,693	243,580,613	258,554,817	117,047,719	95,330,314	202,005,920	58,995,738
MAINE								
1	50,774,438	50,880,178	53,161,928	43,842,120	31,092,104	35,300,811	21,950,074	8,545,924
2	44,762,467	34,603,578	32,444,876	33,555,895	20,618,715	44,404,348	14,030,255	20,705,771
TOTAL	95,536,905	85,483,756	85,606,804	77,398,015	51,710,819	79,705,159	35,980,329	29,251,695
MARYLAND								
1	41,458,373	31,116,701	22,217,416	20,147,373	14,586,505	30,555,943	48,337,775	159,070,414
2	55,764,511	18,572,756	17,309,935	16,913,904	24,078,758	32,945,162	9,158,817	-1,523,119
3	30,590,318	87,022,044	57,794,522	62,476,381	26,553,257	48,116,801	15,707,566	526,788
4	57,039,004	51,635,652	98,734,762	70,342,005	49,295,234	35,371,038	35,334,139	21,146,785
5	23,098,255	42,025,527	12,642,374	32,733,816	8,672,911	33,698,935	15,449,467	5,881,180
6	37,160,012	46,234,822	13,846,067	22,065,081	14,714,931	23,153,389	8,089,569	3,079,114
7	42,385,233	58,184,961	45,417,204	49,142,423	1,055,400	34,926,712	19,663,939	-307,694
8	11,425,958	14,766,895	22,595,496	22,740,339	14,203,661	28,166,268	15,313,225	166,744
TOTAL	298,921,665	349,559,357	290,557,777	296,561,322	153,160,657	266,934,248	167,054,497	188,040,213
MASSACHUSETTS								
1	23,132,602	30,257,945	18,842,134	28,379,886	7,120,688	12,474,612	8,276,720	7,163,165
2	30,004,605	52,247,428	32,573,176	32,987,504	14,681,054	28,740,904	77,438,970	126,542,915
3	33,482,321	52,671,191	19,916,362	23,650,883	10,892,849	13,152,076	1,758,660	1,197,074
4	31,196,970	17,676,779	19,692,448	29,193,876	3,340,067	10,901,187	4,713,191	4,474,216
5	32,694,192	52,897,463	18,293,121	17,203,769	3,588,694	11,813,117	-633,794	2,748,937
6	31,967,243	23,082,997	31,747,541	20,843,729	25,852,874	21,348,984	3,235,980	5,219,416
7	34,603,112	25,926,692	29,150,109	30,050,802	11,752,114	22,677,292	7,586,898	15,955,025
8	256,133,345	178,596,756	106,767,941	167,083,945	83,013,844	116,798,737	21,349,871	40,281,304
9	85,548,352	82,726,601	72,594,203	77,096,006	38,111,092	71,369,266	49,385,998	75,280,901
10	31,413,577	51,730,352	27,875,456	27,272,381	15,116,242	27,190,700	16,965,252	9,902,129
11	48,125,218	28,965,442	42,621,116	35,182,240	8,647,120	32,713,715	12,091,334	31,398,560
TOTAL	638,301,536	596,779,647	420,073,607	488,945,021	222,116,639	369,180,591	202,169,079	320,163,642
MICHIGAN								
1	105,368,646	118,991,823	57,797,357	83,262,293	145,577	160,722,300	13,936,304	-6,571,060
2	29,699,809	28,573,858	20,790,961	19,374,054	31,869,741	20,746,128	12,379,506	3,269,103
3	25,253,783	58,240,938	27,569,290	20,684,269	11,144,918	29,469,252	8,591,204	4,849,268
4	13,440,833	13,475,165	13,269,832	15,800,499	5,192,572	4,807,480	6,418,308	1,685,111
5	24,398,186	21,693,508	25,158,636	21,652,248	10,384,360	13,651,104	2,261,490	54,218,792
6	55,514,288	107,798,845	73,581,050	46,227,883	34,756,718	75,261,726	36,066,307	28,758,056
7	20,882,227	25,478,355	33,147,457	18,445,200	23,578,773	12,646,773	9,306,928	-610,195
8	38,976,333	25,878,278	30,529,379	19,049,003	12,172,687	13,768,135	6,983,723	4,066,386
9	17,066,168	16,675,778	15,557,371	17,976,634	8,144,419	12,626,484	5,586,713	11,383,325
10	14,247,531	22,889,482	12,302,032	15,200,685	14,437,421	5,782,720	4,528,717	2,797,155
11	47,514,605	38,678,998	25,092,359	23,837,265	13,356,930	17,244,003	15,004,719	3,270,301
12	18,113,429	24,892,763	16,421,512	18,951,455	4,992,791	11,218,972	2,908,035	1,035,275

Appendix A lists the congressional districts which represent the county in which the state capital is located, and those congressional districts which represent only portions of a county. Appendix C lists the programs included in each functional policy category.

table continues

Table 5.3 Outlays for Community Development Programs by Congressional District, 1983-1990 *(continued)*

Congressional District	1983	1984	1985	1986	1987	1988	1989	1990 (est.)
MICHIGAN *continued*								
13	45,347,151	39,034,360	32,320,823	30,653,439	14,421,665	23,804,520	12,661,033	3,271,694
14	20,880,841	19,645,918	18,699,120	14,820,609	-315,074	10,599,813	3,987,585	735,316
15	42,035,267	31,818,690	35,981,417	30,423,812	2,525,473	20,289,554	1,034,018	2,922,717
16	33,176,778	41,569,368	33,351,596	30,539,479	28,642,470	16,885,915	4,862,384	3,457,627
17	21,512,713	21,870,999	23,600,134	19,290,895	-775,733	14,736,086	1,954,286	877,035
18	6,841,632	13,396,001	11,261,335	14,228,600	1,201,044	2,545,458	382,245	77,009
TOTAL	580,270,219	670,603,127	506,431,662	460,418,324	215,876,751	466,806,424	148,853,506	119,492,915
MINNESOTA								
1	19,593,080	30,934,919	29,871,225	15,313,666	7,888,328	15,347,162	4,846,229	-486,179
2	24,715,226	22,321,342	19,039,488	24,043,956	17,370,749	23,057,259	2,177,544	5,596,765
3	15,024,500	10,176,361	10,071,374	13,287,793	1,502,244	2,488,500	756,778	176,044
4	60,412,706	78,172,303	95,337,113	72,138,883	89,492,314	101,658,323	68,403,073	75,777,105
5	35,216,121	30,625,671	14,611,377	28,031,914	4,176,987	28,195,769	7,992,872	7,950,459
6	57,113,523	19,301,659	14,937,460	17,797,309	5,451,702	7,421,405	1,269,666	28,409
7	54,083,971	23,411,784	24,459,756	26,688,867	10,201,735	16,118,732	13,430,085	5,886,002
8	32,370,381	29,825,005	24,780,809	28,972,081	9,318,538	12,109,658	11,315,923	5,711,805
TOTAL	298,529,508	244,769,043	233,108,603	226,274,469	145,402,596	206,396,808	110,192,170	100,640,408
MISSISSIPPI								
1	13,510,507	25,364,292	16,550,978	15,987,702	8,638,944	6,624,946	6,533,108	2,707,694
2	25,738,353	19,814,317	20,629,274	23,324,813	8,215,047	4,128,176	2,776,045	4,388,137
3	16,342,768	29,055,998	22,830,976	21,071,237	7,923,093	25,931,896	17,671,281	21,115,130
4	57,090,380	42,845,303	41,992,458	51,166,106	57,823,900	53,583,859	16,094,929	17,849,989
5	27,788,073	34,230,261	33,693,669	48,472,361	19,852,596	14,134,949	5,643,191	1,830,735
TOTAL	140,470,081	151,310,171	135,697,355	160,022,219	102,453,580	104,403,826	48,718,554	47,891,685
MISSOURI								
1	36,320,007	44,155,749	53,609,827	40,630,540	15,453,848	58,455,542	174,957,798	15,992,439
2	15,693,169	35,108,012	31,451,792	40,181,903	22,277,763	34,000,028	12,900,286	36,919,836
3	8,615,893	9,447,811	8,315,924	11,552,666	1,501,225	6,431,672	7,024,060	11,679,194
4	85,409,730	62,221,796	62,836,894	59,601,000	54,837,249	40,520,223	25,696,726	22,784,182
5	25,220,554	20,672,012	34,568,035	46,104,866	23,774,962	52,502,959	19,204,956	15,481,678
6	31,724,910	16,841,121	22,174,869	14,288,341	3,514,185	25,349,800	7,839,720	9,948,984
7	21,823,960	37,997,682	22,067,854	15,653,962	7,222,342	18,883,642	12,441,281	4,202,154
8	20,170,818	19,390,524	18,094,526	17,088,177	6,859,906	7,990,709	12,632,748	778,564
9	46,723,268	33,459,526	22,863,971	26,429,697	12,018,818	13,401,885	13,901,013	36,817,336
TOTAL	291,702,308	279,294,233	275,983,693	271,531,153	147,460,298	257,536,461	286,598,588	154,604,368
MONTANA								
1	40,158,119	41,527,486	39,020,245	44,749,961	31,748,065	29,503,438	31,501,802	21,298,865
2	21,926,798	27,897,820	25,516,129	26,366,804	10,520,880	14,128,038	12,263,501	4,888,946
TOTAL	62,084,917	69,425,306	64,536,374	71,116,765	42,268,945	43,631,476	43,765,303	26,187,811
NEBRASKA								
1	39,971,833	47,552,585	38,006,443	39,061,588	28,188,716	27,934,049	23,478,936	18,847,714
2	25,133,685	36,919,537	20,286,637	38,313,140	16,002,555	19,943,368	10,379,720	23,111,675
3	17,450,373	19,357,667	18,401,890	16,361,642	6,703,103	5,079,955	8,356,513	2,833,038
TOTAL	82,555,891	103,829,789	76,694,970	93,736,370	50,894,374	52,957,372	42,215,169	44,792,428
NEVADA								
1	11,196,170	25,146,226	19,623,766	23,749,137	12,564,011	26,081,859	41,496,068	12,216,867
2	21,836,223	33,218,189	34,210,644	38,658,473	30,678,636	12,375,437	14,093,643	18,331,218
TOTAL	33,032,393	58,364,415	53,834,410	62,407,610	43,242,647	38,457,296	55,589,711	30,548,085
NEW HAMPSHIRE								
1	26,238,912	33,680,638	23,984,100	19,490,471	3,945,130	24,893,287	9,359,315	31,006,926
2	43,272,576	40,714,195	35,331,397	33,720,134	56,206,841	25,756,947	14,100,990	11,217,814
TOTAL	69,511,488	74,394,833	59,315,497	53,210,605	60,151,971	50,650,234	23,460,305	42,224,740

Appendix A lists the congressional districts which represent the county in which the state capital is located, and those congressional districts which represent only portions of a county. Appendix C lists the programs included in each functional policy category.

table continues

Table 5.3 Outlays for Community Development Programs by Congressional District, 1983-1990 *(continued)*

Congressional District	1983	1984	1985	1986	1987	1988	1989	1990 (est.)
NEW JERSEY								
1	70,564,761	83,076,381	17,687,123	22,860,198	34,591,193	41,652,730	8,612,842	9,922,812
2	192,676,530	75,430,666	57,582,721	26,158,626	17,974,307	15,109,261	7,413,056	6,449,473
3	18,352,038	20,185,661	28,859,163	16,511,464	10,675,071	8,690,974	3,008,535	7,156,320
4	168,012,723	32,397,129	39,141,844	42,880,951	32,231,432	24,581,169	100,268,037	19,804,666
5	21,655,016	10,613,276	12,372,758	11,402,502	3,637,595	11,314,787	3,954,859	5,722,492
6	18,219,932	21,660,141	40,160,391	17,225,698	15,044,672	9,041,527	4,071,712	4,753,362
7	23,755,612	25,132,377	19,194,274	14,954,758	8,288,959	17,741,835	14,801	14,633,057
8	40,422,817	21,282,032	22,691,357	21,897,895	5,191,990	6,618,753	2,588,994	7,862,330
9	18,393,879	17,207,218	14,293,656	47,191,242	9,047,789	9,844,578	-161,208	-242,495
10	64,184,377	215,098,838	221,295,368	214,198,379	123,667,153	154,840,784	101,656,132	86,373,688
11	18,055,485	19,305,029	12,408,242	18,055,967	7,621,964	5,921,492	1,132,352	89,481,843
12	11,295,099	12,951,505	10,159,383	12,145,491	3,476,191	1,698,066	3,343,848	40,723,756
13	28,082,316	16,294,462	10,289,154	15,320,690	5,450,259	4,653,631	2,679,268	-53,929
14	36,914,157	29,988,124	53,244,808	27,589,802	63,310,545	20,131,508	8,051,077	29,806,032
TOTAL	730,584,742	600,622,839	559,380,242	508,393,664	340,209,121	331,841,095	246,634,304	322,393,406
NEW MEXICO								
1	43,171,696	35,996,224	31,441,310	17,867,279	24,361,564	19,370,568	12,614,724	343,497
2	30,001,898	26,015,122	26,788,876	26,909,151	10,278,853	9,224,196	9,535,216	3,020,703
3	28,666,478	44,194,026	47,820,901	36,861,313	24,202,680	23,893,846	15,058,082	8,427,500
TOTAL	101,840,072	106,205,372	106,051,087	81,637,743	58,843,097	52,488,610	37,208,022	11,791,700
NEW YORK								
1	16,280,266	23,213,953	23,764,404	32,103,243	11,235,932	19,047,578	390,358,028	783,229,203
2	16,813,313	15,314,322	15,413,556	22,016,993	6,538,020	8,750,988	5,719,285	12,624,630
3	25,356,215	32,827,945	38,678,850	54,443,164	52,503,157	52,403,951	47,761,303	21,905,754
4	21,603,304	22,041,120	29,412,502	27,738,229	-1,154,416	5,672,119	4,597,374	0
5	21,638,620	26,159,573	29,165,192	28,514,453	197,697	5,022,581	5,076,935	31,562,709
6	3,712,491	6,424	320,393	1,698,183	29,927	210,381	-678,790	923
7	0	0	-332	244,323	55,096	34,834	-129,463	75,288
8	1,066,617	1,236,185	1,805,035	1,342,200	1,996,252	26,577,429	557,151	-96,664
9	14,503	39,728	97,524	217,488	-48,550	70,103	323,201	921
10	58,676,163	61,081,571	12,970,997	1,189,061	71,489,393	65,754,515	72,932	-559,499
11	22,792	0	61,408	211,977	55,411	1,213,395	819,874	95,682
12	1,080,818	455,000	885,052	447,169	306,748	1,854,414	1,017,577	0
13	421,384	41,722	376,327	55,751	159,221	189,387	138,244	0
14	23,371,933	-15,157,346	-3,242,340	80,213	28,135,924	21,078,336	40,277,119	0
15	258,917,357	611,483,817	748,139,082	594,086,668	769,066,747	628,913,390	167,878,031	4,173,687
16	260,600,700	226,489,655	208,876,740	286,494,656	107,048,698	2,006,920	1,634,745	1,391,605
17	240,891,871	221,186,449	166,756,695	219,648,269	80,335,061	23,112,752	6,418,951	1,039,145
18	2,734,992	694,143	491,840	254,405	888,171	89,255,246	159,563	750,069
19	2,768,994	34,037,342	14,379,064	34,510,573	16,894,030	110,812,950	48,678,492	2,037,982
20	23,967,790	19,544,739	46,313,558	27,893,161	34,989,481	16,371,831	32,517,196	12,018,757
21	14,982,288	27,213,643	7,020,036	16,353,864	10,090,724	7,838,435	1,661,467	2,180,220
22	63,012,317	20,433,665	32,529,855	22,573,747	16,727,935	5,568,878	5,705,085	1,103,019
23	107,042,833	91,525,337	81,585,839	68,967,635	78,066,684	65,589,536	64,393,885	70,660,255
24	27,746,371	16,869,588	23,798,764	16,596,645	15,740,152	10,469,561	2,098,867	6,566,078
25	17,364,290	50,068,104	30,269,992	31,217,424	14,998,844	15,690,600	10,125,801	10,910,243
26	32,420,034	47,089,906	30,461,525	33,329,735	25,714,218	45,389,368	15,523,766	11,641,969
27	23,625,304	31,917,428	39,333,550	33,067,613	17,550,052	26,264,020	11,844,595	7,555,727
28	58,992,200	60,804,798	31,597,365	35,262,140	32,564,862	22,104,427	19,843,728	34,990,437
29	56,542,218	40,816,521	38,669,286	34,728,024	21,151,030	12,607,465	11,368,155	21,832,516
30	59,001,817	19,359,810	21,139,423	23,030,968	30,307,096	20,465,081	10,962,822	17,264,897
31	26,891,505	28,434,189	23,954,530	18,274,949	11,915,352	6,704,478	829,036	-12,804,038
32	46,948,831	38,569,341	41,261,819	44,299,800	25,628,967	8,387,291	15,286,483	23,852,421
33	28,052,444	18,758,459	22,886,552	21,696,336	20,553,484	11,862,538	1,455,896	3,315,267
34	30,214,774	40,543,212	46,039,559	19,437,845	10,070,964	11,082,798	14,687,039	6,481,626
TOTAL	1,572,777,349	1,813,100,341	1,805,213,643	1,752,026,905	1,511,802,365	1,348,377,578	938,984,373	1,075,800,828
NORTH CAROLINA								
1	32,095,963	20,893,915	17,690,575	20,043,823	8,266,979	16,575,322	5,212,430	2,469,257
2	22,247,983	17,926,223	24,226,653	18,728,510	3,145,887	13,605,229	7,001,166	3,154,878
3	14,233,658	18,639,342	15,677,785	17,436,400	3,788,990	8,045,548	6,566,448	3,362,748
4	46,626,975	53,229,108	102,478,345	59,612,087	87,065,146	57,001,617	83,462,358	247,079,130
5	15,983,564	13,413,607	20,762,596	14,355,479	10,023,964	8,338,443	3,020,746	415,760
6	35,189,334	17,184,336	16,536,633	14,968,745	3,850,515	10,322,406	11,248,427	5,148,190
7	19,006,044	21,891,030	21,643,561	19,562,138	3,344,258	27,860,509	7,455,516	1,334,910
8	11,382,256	13,071,300	11,292,606	12,472,213	8,333,888	10,470,213	2,634,699	95,489
9	13,061,441	25,991,109	21,626,716	17,850,208	21,623,333	15,763,026	21,640,072	3,752,883
10	11,404,679	9,945,313	10,507,680	16,340,315	9,102,184	15,466,550	5,290,888	-3,268,509
11	15,361,028	25,491,876	16,622,760	31,681,720	10,207,663	7,327,276	4,580,700	1,737,763
TOTAL	236,592,926	237,677,159	279,065,910	243,051,639	168,752,807	190,776,139	158,113,450	265,282,497

table continues

Appendix A lists the congressional districts which represent the county in which the state capital is located, and those congressional districts which represent only portions of a county. Appendix C lists the programs included in each functional policy category.

Table 5.3 Outlays for Community Development Programs by Congressional District, 1983-1990 *(continued)*

Congressional District	1983	1984	1985	1986	1987	1988	1989	1990 (est.)
NORTH DAKOTA								
TOTAL	51,521,666	89,219,542	71,628,552	44,787,732	33,107,942	34,318,153	33,170,519	14,857,112
OHIO								
1	38,891,929	27,396,515	47,299,908	55,484,650	14,733,729	24,847,851	26,585,462	21,133,609
2	18,292,744	18,630,830	18,570,225	17,072,545	2,721,733	12,951,870	6,871,408	3,006,192
3	20,110,353	57,735,359	36,257,009	32,291,012	32,454,032	39,721,950	8,239,280	28,322,899
4	5,903,638	14,377,560	10,645,214	10,704,002	8,474,481	8,017,784	647,485	-7,224
5	15,377,754	9,306,806	11,821,164	13,969,561	7,397,689	18,280,516	7,516,737	1,290,290
6	7,724,920	15,717,311	8,275,309	12,927,729	5,982,943	9,792,453	9,205,982	2,921,616
7	7,540,577	18,226,546	7,712,888	13,268,262	4,860,539	7,131,364	1,676,432	156,909
8	9,115,376	20,816,046	9,706,245	19,047,961	7,858,790	8,450,244	3,528,457	415,554
9	13,322,587	11,864,402	52,746,628	31,787,096	12,059,135	18,054,052	17,431,270	25,236,954
10	35,459,798	65,060,720	27,049,738	31,816,091	3,604,300	20,933,857	9,748,359	4,406,573
11	3,690,112	18,025,184	12,611,325	13,346,629	3,233,854	8,930,114	23,142,795	9,001,190
12	62,993,582	43,630,534	82,540,297	96,438,217	76,395,387	69,483,890	38,826,423	45,441,036
13	12,569,141	26,468,725	29,161,680	18,069,488	4,762,683	17,314,544	3,633,655	86,606
14	41,660,019	22,999,254	21,969,186	39,670,346	4,379,882	14,645,169	11,485,972	41,649,165
15	47,671,520	18,341,352	44,912,763	50,775,382	41,764,957	54,149,991	17,768,644	9,476,213
16	13,623,505	25,228,860	19,123,996	20,632,981	6,213,588	17,163,528	1,289,302	9,336,282
17	61,973,226	50,485,481	44,524,625	15,990,020	12,761,355	16,272,074	5,003,498	2,169,708
18	13,375,197	22,308,406	10,465,837	10,061,324	2,819,113	12,412,764	5,145,639	3,156,883
19	48,751,915	25,648,802	47,081,871	35,859,828	21,104,655	39,537,377	3,731,581	1,777,310
20	58,137,486	78,974,082	74,235,653	54,574,678	44,919,644	72,647,440	13,174,842	4,905,467
21	36,221,564	29,351,407	24,019,710	23,954,967	-1,184,038	22,468,437	3,859,884	6,348,003
TOTAL	572,406,941	620,594,182	640,731,271	617,742,769	317,318,453	513,207,269	218,513,106	220,231,237
OKLAHOMA								
1	20,788,117	34,430,075	22,920,287	27,421,789	10,130,617	5,553,813	13,599,990	24,909,378
2	26,541,371	18,559,702	17,365,393	13,601,193	8,143,026	10,535,154	13,041,750	9,197,727
3	28,065,588	29,900,985	19,554,541	28,002,806	7,758,922	23,359,192	21,074,237	17,131,346
4	32,374,738	31,850,988	19,571,965	32,202,046	25,667,582	17,271,941	9,128,750	14,690,512
5	43,517,127	40,561,928	36,242,558	36,548,072	40,141,567	30,760,081	32,006,197	30,104,708
6	33,827,130	34,382,812	22,418,790	24,413,238	26,741,838	15,281,999	18,212,653	19,670,442
TOTAL	185,114,070	189,686,490	138,073,534	162,189,145	118,583,552	102,762,179	107,063,577	115,704,112
OREGON								
1	140,766,849	36,701,659	22,935,052	28,354,536	17,520,988	5,559,447	26,079,667	-647,131
2	28,290,610	12,213,177	14,625,770	19,164,896	9,570,614	6,467,401	10,915,054	5,747,205
3	27,966,332	81,811,789	56,913,294	55,447,882	24,384,843	19,068,928	8,256,760	6,433,555
4	32,623,475	34,511,600	16,535,583	35,010,499	22,070,133	16,764,748	14,153,946	9,297,393
5	52,112,316	101,597,307	133,455,324	158,320,051	132,341,732	168,001,720	154,704,643	16,722,512
TOTAL	281,759,582	266,835,532	244,465,024	296,297,864	205,888,309	215,862,244	214,110,070	37,553,533
PENNSYLVANIA								
1	127,326,032	185,016,435	180,611,870	168,896,649	140,830,239	131,560,100	124,621,307	75,317,036
2	30,591,024	36,056,985	43,534,957	39,299,377	1,461,201	25,116,221	9,357,276	3,721,935
3	30,230,570	36,352,993	49,634,616	38,840,735	1,015,993	23,955,240	7,144,634	2,221,184
4	15,213,593	17,767,859	12,248,846	12,837,714	3,709,418	10,250,831	4,185,680	5,991,181
5	11,832,674	30,410,023	14,153,610	15,873,566	1,540,760	14,840,140	2,151,698	4,686,813
6	17,997,431	19,946,634	14,097,531	21,264,484	6,876,363	12,855,994	4,479,257	9,609,560
7	21,359,797	18,525,099	18,657,546	17,584,238	1,377,448	9,140,366	1,257,624	17,012,111
8	23,043,847	20,518,974	11,952,096	16,143,810	4,700,047	11,887,395	2,317,623	871,333
9	15,088,468	23,974,071	13,317,740	11,308,253	3,582,778	63,896,015	18,127,878	1,426,132
10	33,872,299	43,264,565	21,531,988	22,653,678	20,819,350	12,806,391	8,193,942	6,614,494
11	25,289,317	35,297,514	41,985,412	24,949,082	4,190,643	12,209,613	28,913,121	34,010,142
12	30,124,986	12,651,181	15,155,349	13,979,642	2,347,031	15,628,374	6,047,446	6,323,109
13	29,777,528	15,206,743	18,562,128	12,572,329	2,418,942	16,593,815	3,068,161	8,317,805
14	110,100,566	103,748,866	134,925,885	69,735,603	55,753,855	107,886,979	58,593,072	55,558,516
15	21,309,262	25,008,081	18,120,377	12,426,080	5,119,703	9,472,801	8,686,755	5,609,744
16	68,785,295	19,252,123	15,881,968	13,800,884	4,024,723	12,650,965	9,451,164	9,305,739
17	113,421,283	92,632,843	113,097,288	94,097,015	90,447,174	84,301,986	45,663,148	33,363,849
18	13,877,348	11,886,449	15,135,941	10,689,726	173,687	499,570	319,615	0
19	32,339,003	14,645,576	18,781,987	31,485,295	22,338,906	10,084,728	3,037,517	364,560
20	11,164,057	13,090,439	15,428,330	11,071,710	1,636,042	1,199,971	1,447,055	3,010,534
21	31,352,126	28,487,417	25,147,651	22,566,502	10,489,766	8,922,434	6,820,676	986,409
22	25,624,780	31,104,522	19,619,898	6,131,472	3,041,745	13,611,346	5,398,876	755,117
23	24,472,428	25,896,439	18,695,948	28,700,956	12,870,935	26,826,701	19,737,107	15,969,378
TOTAL	864,193,714	860,741,832	850,278,962	716,908,801	400,766,747	636,197,978	379,020,633	301,046,680

Appendix A lists the congressional districts which represent the county in which the state capital is located, and those congressional districts which represent only portions of a county. Appendix C lists the programs included in each functional policy category.

table continues

Table 5.3 Outlays for Community Development Programs by Congressional District, 1983-1990 *(continued)*

Congressional District	1983	1984	1985	1986	1987	1988	1989	1990 (est.)
RHODE ISLAND								
1	40,429,925	38,646,711	41,538,222	49,128,302	30,406,761	46,255,229	8,902,999	16,779,605
2	28,959,143	37,487,179	32,167,555	23,823,735	18,608,284	14,855,922	10,035,998	10,740,370
TOTAL	69,389,068	76,133,890	73,705,777	72,952,037	49,015,045	61,111,151	18,938,997	27,519,976
SOUTH CAROLINA								
1	21,600,622	33,272,420	23,998,046	20,992,108	4,544,333	13,387,375	9,274,820	8,774,848
2	70,028,224	66,375,395	67,378,912	53,735,082	58,748,482	58,284,752	26,685,539	601,747,294
3	21,177,223	23,604,082	21,928,892	23,368,170	8,323,987	9,185,155	8,462,232	10,714,228
4	22,431,697	26,970,149	23,171,446	22,901,692	10,090,813	19,420,324	6,007,104	9,222,078
5	24,775,262	16,426,734	20,023,989	13,090,176	11,400,958	16,539,815	3,010,247	8,796,992
6	16,154,098	29,483,519	18,687,458	24,979,333	11,962,091	12,880,003	7,203,530	4,566,783
TOTAL	176,167,126	196,132,299	175,188,743	159,066,561	105,070,664	129,697,424	60,643,472	643,822,224
SOUTH DAKOTA								
TOTAL	54,781,876	73,959,291	47,856,164	58,315,117	36,633,836	36,898,842	36,082,651	18,421,758
TENNESSEE								
1	18,552,851	16,956,174	17,224,953	12,502,588	4,084,747	10,564,129	4,356,427	2,969,287
2	24,769,473	31,673,552	27,686,346	23,584,149	13,493,218	18,853,668	20,686,819	18,565,079
3	17,385,629	16,930,243	21,051,295	21,907,222	7,495,533	10,781,255	2,224,588	3,212,209
4	17,361,389	10,833,787	7,406,146	16,446,190	13,222,747	4,959,224	6,122,602	4,109,451
5	84,363,203	70,414,047	82,508,338	71,715,487	60,187,742	76,252,217	28,144,121	42,331,976
6	12,618,262	14,641,774	11,253,178	13,754,463	5,061,213	4,400,780	8,211,422	720,305
7	22,580,898	25,626,127	28,428,604	23,203,551	10,515,294	26,677,362	8,201,924	13,726,093
8	18,588,513	47,302,650	21,494,771	23,666,958	9,349,676	13,602,614	3,127,206	32,788,921
9	29,339,713	22,430,550	21,749,567	20,429,321	471,416	37,483,845	16,320,476	614,411
TOTAL	245,559,931	256,808,904	238,803,198	227,209,929	123,881,586	203,575,093	97,395,585	119,037,732
TEXAS								
1	38,911,315	24,327,761	12,574,369	12,061,452	7,882,960	4,992,204	5,465,288	1,346,463
2	17,279,277	16,308,561	16,789,632	15,442,428	3,469,122	3,220,776	2,385,003	1,310,559
3	34,056,141	40,192,121	29,676,856	23,473,731	6,384,233	1,578,832	13,542,456	13,603,434
4	23,194,796	23,486,291	10,553,025	13,786,831	3,435,576	5,736,014	7,436,181	4,840,339
5	19,228,757	22,732,505	25,517,195	15,085,229	10,728,813	1,169,598	21,316,244	14,340,487
6	66,751,438	42,060,026	20,957,329	27,675,619	15,487,191	17,860,456	27,782,113	26,513,773
7	94,230,059	69,851,676	113,046,681	125,337,659	33,647,594	91,116,369	21,956,082	52,903,594
8	19,497,750	29,124,280	23,403,454	22,790,790	6,881,465	249,633	2,138,309	2,305,774
9	17,840,706	49,542,473	22,961,994	21,557,147	8,312,030	4,419,155	8,087,152	7,342,336
10	140,646,539	141,039,935	181,540,608	148,934,436	56,102,637	163,772,806	88,316,785	67,299,760
11	50,108,427	4,265,332	14,503,412	15,836,232	5,826,665	10,715,342	9,189,183	11,630,988
12	22,632,133	17,851,296	41,911,653	22,472,215	9,770,149	29,249,424	30,195,261	12,283,226
13	28,673,392	19,833,611	17,091,574	18,728,890	1,802,113	5,797,692	8,509,046	8,776,680
14	27,717,965	15,241,757	18,479,028	16,442,597	5,718,743	5,490,086	6,978,859	8,694,330
15	43,388,860	28,715,876	30,628,236	28,179,422	6,706,133	15,015,075	15,103,632	11,820,016
16	28,826,569	30,583,390	28,760,574	28,010,197	5,229,632	16,856,346	33,855,236	35,831,810
17	18,820,051	16,381,955	17,379,994	14,322,104	7,041,943	3,090,697	4,756,719	5,429,834
18	18,692,921	48,129,805	20,548,101	19,255,838	1,592,616	631,750	1,462,281	995,399
19	21,401,907	21,264,450	18,361,347	19,180,479	5,862,269	7,830,158	15,992,325	1,888,651
20	17,444,775	57,362,963	61,267,581	78,144,016	35,826,008	33,497,504	25,966,456	49,042,569
21	17,630,212	25,218,167	18,551,115	17,817,431	7,058,284	7,758,647	23,314,167	10,504,948
22	22,330,294	37,181,906	51,112,980	28,591,676	15,494,091	12,601,063	65,204,511	55,552,218
23	22,794,207	23,274,326	28,721,693	24,464,187	3,433,367	4,971,147	19,583,529	24,304,463
24	28,244,672	18,949,022	18,796,695	28,214,782	6,492,263	54,867,701	30,750,049	15,415,236
25	18,884,901	24,458,349	20,310,727	18,521,660	1,931,872	1,033,941	1,546,802	846,063
26	12,543,261	11,392,109	10,341,312	12,053,652	558,538	466,793	5,095,638	61,921
27	25,462,232	17,642,118	31,930,951	27,558,011	9,454,233	6,618,109	19,697,232	11,249,053
TOTAL	897,233,555	876,412,059	905,718,116	843,938,714	282,130,539	510,607,319	515,626,539	456,133,924
UTAH								
1	18,239,687	18,217,339	16,597,549	17,517,914	7,016,557	9,068,375	8,499,816	2,752,256
2	59,235,801	45,377,703	64,674,727	51,020,362	43,792,490	46,083,829	29,697,669	37,928,391
3	12,644,160	27,044,095	20,918,866	21,370,840	3,430,995	4,352,908	8,715,705	350,125
TOTAL	90,119,648	90,639,137	102,191,142	89,909,116	54,240,042	59,505,112	46,913,190	41,030,772
VERMONT								
TOTAL	40,737,660	42,388,696	40,597,065	31,445,243	36,468,191	25,724,369	11,458,129	11,982,959

Appendix A lists the congressional districts which represent the county in which the state capital is located, and those congressional districts which represent only portions of a county. Appendix C lists the programs included in each functional policy category.

table continues

Table 5.3 **Outlays for Community Development Programs by Congressional District, 1983-1990 *(continued)***

Congressional District	1983	1984	1985	1986	1987	1988	1989	1990 (est.)
VIRGINIA								
1	14,510,220	20,199,985	16,633,726	23,498,597	3,964,480	7,690,497	3,336,018	5,806,053
2	21,713,790	20,049,306	33,828,047	31,487,153	29,726,556	31,330,044	21,285,478	15,388,266
3	71,508,714	41,790,736	87,386,299	84,311,905	62,310,380	56,467,400	21,086,345	24,297,058
4	29,184,703	22,813,932	19,323,945	31,081,046	2,451,918	867,517	2,803,669	5,899,304
5	16,294,817	14,690,546	12,930,518	13,052,593	4,238,874	8,933,057	1,652,697	-1,165,776
6	22,155,509	9,854,597	16,880,575	27,495,085	11,310,095	11,268,835	6,479,145	1,368,744
7	14,948,578	17,670,008	16,053,329	16,357,471	19,450,973	8,795,018	6,076,561	5,195,993
8	12,555,973	11,759,601	9,028,677	11,956,223	888,382	2,786,383	799,852	-873,254
9	36,088,987	38,626,598	27,158,501	28,969,306	15,448,832	14,790,026	17,552,930	27,234,316
10	14,127,593	19,762,602	12,356,191	14,859,663	3,127,609	25,389,628	7,028,918	15,296,153
TOTAL	253,088,884	217,217,911	251,579,808	283,069,042	152,918,098	168,318,405	88,101,613	98,446,859
WASHINGTON								
1	37,674,338	19,166,607	60,196,244	74,130,669	109,711,841	112,648,603	57,616,225	10,808,793
2	12,003,660	22,724,618	27,398,615	24,057,576	15,184,587	17,321,674	12,917,914	8,618,028
3	68,918,431	61,727,935	62,709,519	83,519,259	60,447,498	67,888,943	38,690,335	27,544,258
4	17,385,125	28,871,101	16,098,505	18,151,649	10,422,381	7,618,607	14,144,677	12,965,371
5	32,110,512	51,068,873	23,729,793	26,688,483	16,250,877	10,838,124	17,683,659	9,648,252
6	64,094,903	17,623,910	41,925,731	66,914,823	14,338,424	21,728,369	2,599,143	11,216,142
7	22,959,969	49,559,051	13,267,200	19,695,667	8,796,404	20,330,066	50,006,118	20,445,695
8	27,071,658	19,070,529	12,478,755	20,525,255	7,127,962	3,952,418	14,099,687	18,518,324
TOTAL	282,218,596	269,812,623	257,804,362	333,683,381	242,279,973	262,326,804	207,757,758	119,764,863
WEST VIRGINIA								
1	30,277,108	33,753,872	21,208,799	16,888,739	15,993,410	19,181,558	13,474,866	13,191,933
2	28,728,095	39,824,457	28,579,395	48,351,381	23,996,124	15,962,836	10,870,589	9,638,614
3	30,842,240	61,765,795	39,604,455	101,185,196	51,264,622	47,736,281	15,748,486	10,923,126
4	41,337,739	21,571,637	22,755,461	20,760,213	7,485,515	11,463,943	2,359,447	481,518
TOTAL	131,185,182	156,915,761	112,148,110	187,185,529	98,739,671	94,344,618	42,453,388	34,235,191
WISCONSIN								
1	18,340,221	27,306,007	20,643,615	22,127,771	5,712,466	11,618,560	7,881,802	10,872,451
2	64,315,646	44,980,851	73,509,228	66,311,216	57,950,921	54,675,341	56,364,391	25,670,246
3	18,120,762	19,403,195	18,192,518	19,209,153	6,089,831	5,147,924	5,686,782	5,828,007
4	63,516,951	83,870,617	64,522,515	48,220,802	53,748,494	67,451,237	106,257,874	22,170,126
5	59,312,063	59,999,262	47,751,449	36,448,800	44,734,820	12,625,431	1,121,967	21,221,099
6	17,002,995	31,980,354	13,255,489	16,546,023	2,345,506	4,924,258	3,609,277	1,409,982
7	19,321,268	23,697,703	19,642,811	19,855,781	4,372,066	11,545,314	5,935,236	6,429,187
8	15,157,493	19,204,358	15,923,179	21,297,910	7,577,883	10,020,160	13,094,342	5,660,609
9	13,431,041	14,800,621	15,788,104	15,420,685	4,297,126	4,776,169	5,638,838	7,335,372
TOTAL	288,518,440	325,242,966	289,228,909	265,438,141	186,829,111	182,784,394	205,590,509	106,597,079
WYOMING								
TOTAL	32,909,471	52,471,182	61,078,159	49,925,927	26,571,311	20,834,959	28,173,413	19,948,933
U.S. TOTAL	15,696.9 mil.	16,477.9 mil.	14,994.2 mil.	15,286.2 mil.	8,903.1 mil.	11,205.6 mil.	8,266.3 mil.	8,245.7 mil.

Appendix A lists the congressional districts which represent the county in which the state capital is located, and those congressional districts which represent only portions of a county. Appendix C lists the programs included in each functional policy category.

Table 5.4 Outlays for Disaster Prevention and Relief Programs by Congressional District, 1983-1990

Congressional District	1983	1984	1985	1986	1987	1988	1989	1990 (est.)
ALABAMA								
1	-45,443	29,851	325,777	3,112,313	1,319,480	540,666	690,084	108,728
2	6,181,562	8,321,492	10,820,597	12,285,278	13,393,543	7,304,197	19,864,474	34,242,727
3	6,640,869	7,256,423	9,447,082	10,632,461	9,658,360	10,409,832	13,702,626	12,084,192
4	-2,262	51,510	99,088	116,135	2,697,922	901,358	2,167,501	414,302
5	1,428,409	2,109,666	2,590,177	2,463,655	3,258,369	2,457,203	4,679,589	3,574,013
6	60,366	0	232,581	243,544	299,056	162,915	363,025	392,480
7	376,482	401,179	162,052	617,006	3,839,164	2,739,299	2,992,674	282,970
TOTAL	14,639,983	18,170,121	23,677,354	29,470,392	34,465,894	24,515,470	44,459,973	51,099,413
ALASKA								
TOTAL	10,591,053	35,289,243	76,042,029	55,590,443	73,560,607	100,911,742	141,176,358	98,280,137
ARIZONA								
1	1,896,666	1,442,238	5,439,524	4,383,978	4,280,995	2,793,892	3,857,537	6,725,707
2	3,851,791	9,801,294	6,835,457	9,886,228	7,100,493	5,180,425	7,250,015	8,424,180
3	831,214	9,000,086	8,053,381	15,200,522	7,187,927	11,390,853	12,793,014	21,762,555
4	20,117,157	9,560,176	31,368,831	32,200,104	35,114,059	31,505,680	48,914,552	36,811,924
5	704,969	10,117,218	5,095,682	5,824,904	7,572,871	4,368,838	8,639,080	9,562,778
TOTAL	27,401,797	39,921,012	56,792,874	67,495,736	61,256,344	55,239,689	81,454,198	83,287,144
ARKANSAS								
1	121,148,937	35,847,295	190,856,280	114,112,491	167,845,586	142,229,369	208,445,054	134,571,401
2	34,764,187	8,997,519	28,901,323	21,209,062	23,410,348	33,685,203	35,730,280	25,659,555
3	10,806,617	4,114,234	3,607,838	6,580,434	3,588,735	6,442,166	22,082,578	9,469,487
4	34,805,086	7,616,138	42,524,107	26,541,781	39,236,572	34,068,554	49,426,825	23,368,969
TOTAL	201,524,827	56,575,186	265,889,548	168,443,768	234,081,241	216,425,292	315,684,737	193,069,411
CALIFORNIA								
1	22,563,527	6,369,507	1,762,736	5,016,782	2,156,813	3,667,448	2,750,395	1,971,927
2	34,917,029	14,938,427	109,218,377	57,148,062	90,164,298	78,778,490	113,177,683	57,344,318
3	13,403,903	9,971,293	16,927,201	35,445,191	15,212,330	26,046,569	18,428,510	192,539,413
4	21,966,823	9,303,923	19,785,575	27,808,889	17,632,177	24,888,993	25,619,953	105,894,389
5	464,376	657,755	796,007	982,871	947,944	1,125,504	1,588,729	1,392,507
6	1,066,694	613,780	1,586,266	3,026,517	1,986,278	2,003,169	3,382,295	2,148,140
7	409,471	585,307	997,130	1,898,501	262,669	388,731	969,340	399,909
8	6,895,448	7,498,404	5,941,664	10,171,419	3,872,243	5,026,267	9,903,071	11,646,409
9	514,334	748,526	771,970	1,794,283	2,279,126	2,391,735	3,416,174	1,960,782
10	-16,270	390,479	212,278	635,522	251,966	195,943	348,543	98,369
11	693,433	1,909,154	625,562	544,852	-174,061	-313,556	395,371	25,769
12	704,511	783,952	1,206,820	1,676,701	1,092,455	1,266,232	1,957,978	1,445,248
13	680,398	592,987	245,150	514,287	293,199	155,886	186,616	79,104
14	4,722,930	1,645,263	5,150,116	6,766,863	5,402,999	3,866,050	7,202,266	3,416,584
15	8,711,205	1,083,065	5,204,549	2,908,412	7,490,713	3,877,994	6,411,312	3,743,460
16	6,644,805	4,421,386	10,462,706	9,401,959	7,871,041	17,642,967	16,833,058	13,007,838
17	3,541,703	3,435,478	3,049,262	2,459,528	2,414,518	3,045,040	5,190,854	4,741,473
18	3,310,460	1,382,448	1,928,241	1,608,358	1,326,860	1,900,204	3,620,948	2,103,459
19	2,592,404	3,791,465	5,715,909	2,401,392	5,866,425	5,797,317	4,814,174	3,246,129
20	5,631,490	13,241,847	8,256,860	6,098,718	6,977,119	5,065,432	8,959,325	8,551,685
21	795,914	-138,865	637,087	1,421,196	1,632,496	1,411,911	2,329,042	1,498,520
22	1,349,731	134,484	-74,930	31,940	202,532	653,997	225,563	100,223
23	1,333,489	43,291	-75,390	31,906	202,317	636,676	215,035	76,960
24	1,333,241	43,283	-51,260	31,900	202,279	636,557	214,994	76,945
25	1,331,978	43,242	-3,155	31,870	202,088	635,954	573,848	206,749
26	1,170,557	38,001	-62,210	28,008	177,597	558,884	188,761	67,556
27	1,332,858	3,532,295	598,291	-718,516	245,604	2,400,262	223,655	74,149
28	1,332,665	53,686	-75,343	31,887	202,192	636,282	214,902	76,912
29	1,338,720	42,667	-76,831	31,946	202,235	639,028	214,948	76,929
30	1,433,688	43,198	-75,229	31,838	201,885	1,359,812	348,041	181,545
31	1,456,338	43,301	-75,407	66,351	185,088	689,467	451,813	76,977
32	1,338,070	195,555	301,038	32,016	203,012	638,863	215,773	77,224
33	1,334,222	66,737	-63,098	60,155	219,022	668,434	254,470	80,715
34	1,373,957	-11,782	-54,956	31,925	246,602	670,150	246,887	77,005
35	3,012,751	3,651,736	4,721,128	5,072,779	5,562,127	5,065,224	8,745,032	5,828,916
36	2,551,588	2,563,359	3,237,743	6,203,220	2,529,229	4,616,410	3,512,426	33,480,071
37	2,593,576	2,637,030	4,490,083	7,018,002	3,975,302	4,915,294	4,545,810	31,733,159
38	0	-215,275	19,377	20,202	-10,259	113,789	90,561	14,483
39	70,151	-56,320	14,707	20,220	-10,267	113,885	77,197	14,348

Appendix A lists the congressional districts which represent the county in which the state capital is located, and those congressional districts which represent only portions of a county. Appendix C lists the programs included in each functional policy category.

table continues

Table 5.4

Outlays for Disaster Prevention and Relief Programs by Congressional District, 1983-1990 *(continued)*

Congressional District	1983	1984	1985	1986	1987	1988	1989	1990 (est.)
CALIFORNIA *continued*								
40	475,573	105,264	846,797	1,114,170	1,212,539	1,041,063	1,904,239	1,168,358
41	689,104	-387,760	4,883,091	1,295,226	1,663,616	1,278,100	1,855,084	1,622,405
42	1,902,148	216,285	312,835	27,280	241,574	479,668	349,978	385,295
43	3,960,451	1,532,269	5,594,281	4,909,399	7,396,627	6,198,143	12,408,645	5,659,665
44	1,044,072	27,742	620,504	2,814,868	3,017,606	2,225,709	3,085,879	2,936,119
45	1,412,728	1,307,916	2,924,081	4,367,218	5,000,596	4,266,211	6,347,539	5,517,831
TOTAL	175,386,243	98,875,785	228,357,613	212,316,114	208,230,751	229,366,189	283,996,717	506,865,974
COLORADO								
1	3,078,343	37,624,486	3,005,737	3,186,953	2,345,540	2,245,687	3,115,454	4,991,544
2	406,131	36,968	83,587	84,583	84,701	55,005	8,650	229,862
3	5,653,923	2,570,420	2,110,351	2,439,765	1,607,283	1,046,740	2,913,946	5,900,742
4	3,192,557	3,125,440	2,642,562	3,943,853	2,551,214	6,563,881	4,684,606	7,706,543
5	3,689,247	3,418,323	6,061,327	5,024,793	5,137,109	10,207,934	11,043,996	9,843,921
6	204,654	1,483,827	485,027	553,157	536,393	368,542	416,718	446,640
TOTAL	16,224,855	48,259,464	14,388,591	15,233,104	12,262,240	20,487,789	22,183,370	29,119,252
CONNECTICUT								
1	3,851,404	3,594,105	3,491,389	6,461,892	1,637,284	2,328,009	17,234,847	12,843,677
2	3,999,987	4,165,009	7,060,337	11,357,941	6,531,430	7,451,765	11,788,240	9,800,861
3	-35,450	637,059	1,012,318	6,606,608	1,700,523	1,345,169	1,845,117	1,144,996
4	957	44,027	101,858	1,740,533	182,814	63,419	149,209	119,066
5	36,769	34,309	125,791	1,432,108	79,496	63,669	158,924	47,859
6	17,449	297,529	61,849	1,176,836	17,631	30,625	389,921	143,263
TOTAL	7,871,117	8,772,038	11,853,542	28,775,918	10,149,178	11,282,656	31,566,258	24,099,722
DELAWARE								
TOTAL	2,480,620	2,397,082	2,142,823	2,783,944	1,829,243	3,414,131	3,081,970	3,568,973
DISTRICT OF COLUMBIA								
TOTAL	3,838,927	158,631,559	6,502,504	7,431,901	5,626,168	7,791,478	5,522,380	7,770,285
FLORIDA								
1	1,841,103	293,326	3,931,896	4,483,938	4,926,349	4,267,318	6,460,798	7,837,242
2	19,461,668	7,092,678	9,468,052	20,662,758	11,176,613	9,892,846	13,397,626	19,755,309
3	1,988,646	-76,633	1,451,573	1,529,538	1,781,494	1,146,273	2,038,123	180,511
4	4,774,084	1,914,412	2,327,215	3,427,403	3,537,851	9,918,895	19,205,517	5,992,485
5	224,878	707	86,160	443,652	564,214	405,351	785,840	111,710
6	4,957,315	4,618,580	3,196,725	5,856,745	3,001,464	4,703,380	6,285,487	7,394,641
7	443,142	-40,016	775,915	1,901,032	1,058,207	795,864	1,728,111	1,261,078
8	-23,423	0	11,002	2,398,133	129,678	46,525	95,325	104,802
9	782,885	-104,248	430,959	348,578	33,231	-349	37,425	44,058
10	1,018,105	0	6,654	279,211	16,513	0	0	0
11	120,141	550,718	2,063,680	2,253,501	1,471,067	900,446	4,419,902	4,292,303
12	603,806	648,145	781,710	289,420	200,275	302,553	337,429	306,272
13	-5,929	13,313	52,765	54,392	51,515	40,987	53,275	62,606
14	226,616	-192,926	106,713	152,136	64,232	172,086	31,170	38,939
15	-24,610	-22,841	79,194	155,274	128,866	0	18,196	359,732
16	98,266	31	84,522	112,520	89,341	101,059	105,633	16
17	225,866	105	280,711	345,181	306,013	346,151	361,819	55
18	225,206	199,835	280,880	345,317	306,133	346,287	664,472	142,450
19	516,812	-26,543	721,720	918,017	999,836	866,498	1,451,233	1,403,518
TOTAL	37,454,577	14,868,643	26,138,046	45,956,746	29,842,892	34,252,170	57,477,381	49,287,726
GEORGIA								
1	310,225	1,146,849	1,576,859	1,571,901	4,023,063	1,927,978	7,900,912	2,336,012
2	-69,311	528,927	1,091,484	815,307	1,772,509	773,167	1,871,893	465,633
3	1,791,178	1,929,873	3,107,191	3,170,622	4,214,499	4,165,859	6,854,569	3,521,933
4	6,179,110	1,844,874	2,625,137	1,911,258	1,361,742	1,806,709	2,119,118	6,193,781
5	342,087	3,490,847	6,408,914	4,502,852	2,535,443	3,873,876	4,503,049	13,918,506
6	35,366	447,124	434,600	647,084	1,281,021	916,225	1,400,233	395,562
7	60,780	93,258	193,597	186,177	993,875	795,078	820,485	54,741
8	-12,498	139,451	290,856	359,186	4,043,737	3,261,597	3,133,403	612,564
9	132,522	-234,415	-2,997	34,691	2,830,909	2,705,375	2,761,252	196,968
10	7,821,183	7,601,312	6,782,969	10,425,676	9,727,762	11,207,290	14,830,365	12,914,800
TOTAL	16,590,642	16,988,100	22,508,610	23,624,754	32,784,559	31,433,154	46,195,279	40,610,500

Appendix A lists the congressional districts which represent the county in which the state capital is located, and those congressional districts which represent only portions of a county. Appendix C lists the programs included in each functional policy category.

table continues

Table 5.4 Outlays for Disaster Prevention and Relief Programs by Congressional District, 1983-1990 *(continued)*

Congressional District	1983	1984	1985	1986	1987	1988	1989	1990 (est.)
HAWAII								
1	12,464,899	5,210,442	9,831,196	11,192,206	9,420,236	26,054,210	21,633,037	32,558,813
2	3,276,667	4,090,590	5,401,041	8,716,481	10,493,188	17,532,105	10,369,607	4,394,233
TOTAL	15,741,566	9,301,032	15,232,237	19,908,687	19,913,424	43,586,315	32,002,644	36,953,045
IDAHO								
1	3,502,949	3,661,872	3,824,744	4,902,321	6,020,993	14,331,437	17,718,167	8,607,390
2	341,938	2,799,952	5,277,981	4,662,103	5,124,444	7,866,629	14,255,909	7,353,746
TOTAL	3,844,887	6,461,824	9,102,725	9,564,424	11,145,437	22,198,066	31,974,076	15,961,136
ILLINOIS								
1	4,626,041	1,073,350	788,872	525,048	682,721	799,163	383,323	221,504
2	154,410	1,073,115	788,699	524,932	682,572	798,988	383,239	221,456
3	154,443	1,073,340	788,865	525,043	682,715	799,156	383,320	221,502
4	-1,785	556,168	639,699	360,142	398,822	272,360	307,127	226,884
5	154,422	1,073,198	788,760	524,973	682,624	799,050	383,269	221,473
6	544,938	399,754	293,804	195,547	424,173	1,206,096	739,364	85,991
7	690,167	1,590,951	904,941	525,036	823,130	853,502	363,199	221,500
8	154,441	1,073,328	788,856	525,036	778,733	906,381	383,315	221,500
9	154,467	1,073,506	788,986	525,123	682,820	873,614	383,379	221,536
10	275,636	561,425	2,128,490	3,381,943	4,661,802	3,620,578	4,305,617	5,815,292
11	220,729	1,073,247	788,797	524,997	843,359	818,328	384,597	221,483
12	576,853	469,852	401,629	1,286,102	2,197,689	1,518,954	1,802,438	125,177
13	1,151,074	1,674,513	3,920,842	271,428	594,371	866,352	466,714	88,665
14	421,124	2,683	885,801	46,965	65,228	138,159	226,715	27,634
15	-55,514	962,207	2,410,795	1,897,870	1,945,466	1,639,048	5,440,534	3,091,060
16	0	19,561	286,688	88,013	44,777	98,295	1,568,265	251,648
17	253,939	99,192	616,823	177,015	172,690	125,452	2,820,336	846,460
18	5,543	293,266	1,234,351	268,513	3,491,069	825,870	2,142,004	750,752
19	6,252,823	7,722,001	5,770,699	10,255,558	5,286,852	7,934,531	11,565,115	13,083,180
20	9,621,836	7,694,185	11,306,602	9,541,672	19,543,051	13,970,521	14,897,061	22,830,920
21	2,834,336	1,367,976	3,322,120	3,053,360	5,100,965	3,861,403	5,872,093	4,277,157
22	-2,617	178,170	951,654	528,239	264,616	150,274	580,439	258,494
TOTAL	28,187,305	31,104,987	40,596,774	35,552,555	50,050,244	42,876,074	55,781,465	53,531,268
INDIANA								
1	45,711	48,959	105,016	104,835	97,820	76,822	239,667	52,508
2	2,316,998	965,358	456,542	1,702,811	1,094,925	1,674,697	1,388,484	1,173,293
3	0	69,236	-29,499	-4,415	54,070	-4,222	271,689	74,826
4	1,202	0	0	0	0	38,413	1,355,231	189,280
5	464,543	1,223,890	1,320,571	1,277,293	1,174,066	1,972,293	3,218,548	1,591,424
6	925,599	1,295,082	751,255	2,723,021	831,529	1,478,586	1,952,212	1,959,524
7	4,299,707	6,548,431	4,650,339	9,079,138	4,160,804	6,517,240	8,658,319	10,460,529
8	70,178	305,220	222,493	174,206	129,503	244,965	713,014	143,837
9	-106,372	393,429	2,345,366	82,868	140,783	122,522	2,175,242	317,791
10	3,672,019	5,120,292	2,963,890	10,755,703	3,277,133	5,828,289	6,664,831	7,601,602
TOTAL	11,689,585	15,969,898	12,785,972	25,895,460	10,960,632	17,949,604	26,637,238	23,564,614
IOWA								
1	337,711	412,001	191,508	66,911	45,853	104,845	4,198,181	1,853,437
2	160	24,969	17,466	27,731	1,528	5,417	9,689,045	2,606,229
3	421,709	110,809	287,567	232,619	198,470	172,441	3,308,640	2,012,148
4	8,957,984	10,561,059	7,885,834	15,165,176	10,067,352	9,171,985	18,794,973	18,702,620
5	5,123,300	3,148,060	3,964,242	486,904	2,539,189	4,567,052	4,046,682	1,951,825
6	1,765,696	1,048,685	1,084,914	559,065	799,162	461,519	1,148,548	692,616
TOTAL	16,606,560	15,305,583	13,431,531	16,538,406	13,651,554	14,483,259	41,186,069	27,818,875
KANSAS								
1	8,079,580	2,835,626	2,187,453	1,151,057	1,240,002	1,185,757	4,191,897	2,182,874
2	13,756,259	14,772,931	15,253,929	17,552,318	16,384,367	24,154,913	30,829,234	29,537,955
3	1,402,199	75,311	212,645	61,323	47,782	24,348	81,957	82,015
4	1,426,010	358,341	438,100	542,902	566,777	400,686	1,074,127	655,378
5	12,264,472	698,391	428,302	-45,655	2,673,153	1,674,190	2,072,692	316,142
TOTAL	36,928,520	18,740,600	18,520,429	19,261,945	20,912,081	27,439,894	38,249,907	32,774,363

Appendix A lists the congressional districts which represent the county in which the state capital is located, and those congressional districts which represent only portions of a county. Appendix C lists the programs included in each functional policy category.

table continues

Table 5.4 **Outlays for Disaster Prevention and Relief Programs by Congressional District, 1983-1990 *(continued)***

Congressional District	1983	1984	1985	1986	1987	1988	1989	1990 (est.)
KENTUCKY								
1	-64,875	2,237,147	1,199,004	648,595	383,523	1,075,347	2,722,249	437,379
2	82,872	310,888	1,654,368	195,816	1,759,272	1,007,685	6,536,567	780,781
3	46,412	16,413	207,691	-356,357	252,788	77,979	481,429	275,797
4	14,463	6,660	26,227	26,390	31,500	86,893	1,466,115	39,484
5	21,439	1,114,416	281,967	189,629	707,031	188,592	6,098,644	-27,264
6	12,620,828	40,460,731	9,983,339	11,779,298	8,585,484	12,062,067	34,220,189	39,303,413
7	0	1,224,358	3,344,623	-62,749	908,697	35,207	1,352,447	79,005
TOTAL	12,721,139	45,370,613	16,697,219	12,420,622	12,628,295	14,533,770	52,877,640	40,888,596
LOUISIANA								
1	1,057,995	129,728	3,062,408	2,269,101	2,800,313	2,820,579	2,314,508	4,979,644
2	701,067	113,383	670,047	2,138,368	2,007,253	2,669,678	1,684,862	3,597,976
3	346,809	-70,814	405,806	4,612,888	431,624	771,571	514,691	383,316
4	3,269,376	4,381,353	5,720,142	5,448,563	5,361,772	6,111,083	11,049,844	5,000,720
5	11,315,962	3,510,283	16,243,438	9,485,360	18,739,841	16,176,339	21,995,125	12,562,184
6	19,004,159	10,611,887	8,667,061	31,325,792	5,716,493	12,691,009	19,164,146	21,250,840
7	45,647,130	13,622,840	69,300,386	37,383,597	51,384,555	44,101,686	64,766,582	41,919,396
8	13,651,621	3,317,518	23,000,440	11,315,814	16,908,443	14,909,491	21,559,940	12,434,553
TOTAL	94,994,119	35,616,178	127,069,729	103,979,483	103,350,295	100,251,434	143,049,697	102,128,630
MAINE								
1	1,465,584	2,325,947	2,587,214	3,104,922	8,042,246	2,520,100	4,503,082	3,239,014
2	2,892,126	3,100,172	3,750,649	4,733,700	8,100,747	5,813,770	5,402,220	5,763,472
TOTAL	4,357,710	5,426,119	6,337,863	7,838,622	16,142,993	8,333,870	9,905,302	9,002,486
MARYLAND								
1	12,957,080	4,163,892	9,132,928	6,314,822	9,127,575	5,294,703	3,863,188	1,607,189
2	595,457	12,177	1,653,395	1,730,073	1,850,496	1,344,501	2,819,652	1,848,218
3	73,323	24,750	63,316	369,563	283,249	339,642	173,218	67,766
4	5,559,882	2,922,319	6,593,941	7,665,764	5,941,352	5,811,440	9,000,272	18,239,707
5	4,594,359	2,389,027	4,117,043	5,989,466	3,864,460	5,267,984	8,206,504	7,703,179
6	6,195,456	1,640,546	2,455,423	3,897,198	2,158,613	1,532,281	2,736,482	1,125,842
7	67,555	0	38,416	379,951	343,238	270,502	576,012	180,547
8	522,114	140,649	1,090,070	819,773	756,911	644,959	1,022,262	-72,884
TOTAL	30,565,226	11,293,360	25,144,531	27,166,610	24,325,892	20,506,012	28,397,590	30,699,564
MASSACHUSETTS								
1	2,474,772	2,560,377	2,429,532	5,492,400	3,793,488	3,467,461	4,735,041	4,659,039
2	197,704	1,009,077	1,288,083	1,087,507	280,345	1,241,530	1,173,670	824,447
3	153,947	716,760	1,222,314	2,528,068	201,625	129,445	2,326,444	99,664
4	221,566	2,535,404	1,629,413	3,197,249	-123,717	1,412,906	486,098	306,446
5	3,997,484	3,089,421	4,213,714	4,476,532	4,353,800	3,459,963	5,756,053	4,775,473
6	24,454	77,014	538,018	1,509,103	417,313	377,429	606,714	255,932
7	711,459	886,326	920,948	3,571,651	1,100,316	793,084	1,791,458	1,476,994
8	1,561,527	2,024,939	1,368,508	5,260,819	1,694,484	1,561,240	2,852,830	3,431,053
9	2,448,719	2,488,381	1,925,929	6,527,249	2,521,333	2,254,603	3,835,481	3,984,014
10	16,331	-313,911	657,507	2,473,835	1,023,555	965,172	1,917,850	1,304,776
11	1,385,379	1,870,388	1,252,816	4,753,469	1,734,276	1,375,797	2,488,521	2,090,501
TOTAL	13,193,342	16,944,177	17,446,780	40,877,883	16,996,818	17,038,631	27,970,160	23,208,340
MICHIGAN								
1	0	0	13,511	54,913	31,505	27,678	43,492	9,957
2	0	15,197	159,841	260,035	105,031	263,763	1,353,647	199,592
3	9,848,633	8,338,478	6,338,643	16,976,015	7,548,842	7,980,183	11,830,532	22,126,795
4	3,757	28	-13	0	17,321	43,483	4,255,946	1,259,727
5	0	16,258	39,722	45,916	194,357	57,252	1,439,699	404,272
6	8,444,477	8,220,627	7,348,515	22,547,258	7,756,085	8,236,854	13,066,852	19,854,621
7	322,070	11,070	53,765	1,690,939	320,416	89,522	176,358	22,676
8	7,162	6,517	22,486	263,212	3,646,340	375,422	3,860,800	8,440
9	10,027	1,186,201	-13,311	30,612	3,098,091	824,192	4,062,540	101,227
10	1,245	14,878	40,478	143,347	4,161,628	1,089,985	4,344,256	272,115
11	2,369,190	3,067,716	6,495,975	5,562,205	6,561,605	6,083,729	10,819,895	8,602,325
12	506,402	501,880	747,882	809,610	931,046	476,156	1,075,909	100,420

Appendix A lists the congressional districts which represent the county in which the state capital is located, and those congressional districts which represent only portions of a county. Appendix C lists the programs included in each functional policy category.

table continues

Table 5.4 Outlays for Disaster Prevention and Relief Programs by Congressional District, 1983-1990 *(continued)*

Congressional District	1983	1984	1985	1986	1987	1988	1989	1990 (est.)
MICHIGAN *continued*								
13	44,803	15,480	164,773	54,913	31,505	27,678	43,492	9,957
14	0	9,845	15,363	56,394	48,613	25,917	32,771	13,779
15	0	0	18,116	32,676	28,093	24,059	64,304	8,089
16	0	0	30,498	55,194	43,188	38,868	333,555	38,424
17	0	12,512	26,647	49,955	36,347	24,244	47,867	9,187
18	0	47,691	61,703	5,231	5,770	2,220	10,333	378
TOTAL	21,557,766	21,464,378	21,564,593	48,638,425	34,565,783	25,691,206	56,862,247	53,041,981
MINNESOTA								
1	2,088,715	318,311	333,951	120,912	310	9,829	1,072,857	221,957
2	2,692,472	-317,574	289,518	415,593	367,121	299,685	5,432,455	1,347,714
3	749,619	7,128	34,914	15,582	1,406,764	154,874	716,142	11,099
4	10,703,662	9,532,502	7,639,216	15,479,827	8,885,830	13,016,944	16,441,215	18,613,854
5	46,676	22,938	172,379	208,028	1,157,656	228,292	485,323	162,402
6	3,713,213	9,641	14,951	75,826	3,025,093	795,703	379,912	127,423
7	8,999,404	6,227,304	5,612,445	5,390,185	6,962,958	9,625,202	30,948,681	30,407,850
8	1,735,443	406,640	634,110	1,491,350	2,321,265	2,644,575	9,085,085	3,544,780
TOTAL	30,729,203	16,206,889	14,731,484	23,197,303	24,126,998	26,775,103	64,561,671	54,437,080
MISSISSIPPI								
1	3,735,458	8,250,017	2,029,190	1,931,344	2,970,022	2,145,823	4,176,165	1,870,817
2	26,968,788	6,807,439	39,598,589	24,716,299	39,710,973	36,312,166	51,075,764	24,513,959
3	6,227,291	8,301,783	11,572,851	9,181,869	5,562,320	8,785,317	11,942,379	11,339,652
4	17,763,036	11,471,826	21,090,024	10,469,796	11,798,713	18,591,837	16,040,106	37,577,823
5	2,800,595	1,359,805	4,431,010	12,754,307	2,338,617	4,999,547	5,614,103	3,633,068
TOTAL	57,495,168	36,190,870	78,721,664	59,053,615	62,380,646	70,834,690	88,848,517	78,935,319
MISSOURI								
1	33,700	-2,143	58,580	106,009	115,094	28,903	114,967	143,852
2	281,520	194,096	49,863	74,033	361,778	112,771	120,014	72,655
3	37,199	43,591	38,168	55,972	37,008	19,186	179,387	57,282
4	6,828,352	11,159,989	12,511,917	18,148,326	17,313,862	14,187,742	29,827,920	27,253,687
5	11,093	97,075	193,810	116,133	80,980	63,589	155,588	117,004
6	-137,604	526,673	2,415,777	659,169	-1,164,508	1,493,946	8,246,732	7,432,546
7	-28,283	110,576	289,645	132,613	101,415	77,512	25,456,066	21,284
8	10,554,575	3,497,780	17,152,274	11,474,395	15,764,761	14,637,959	25,320,973	15,925,761
9	4,557,053	6,838,658	4,745,682	8,466,892	5,316,335	7,393,052	15,054,446	11,424,522
TOTAL	22,137,604	22,466,295	37,455,715	39,233,543	37,926,724	38,014,660	104,476,091	62,448,592
MONTANA								
1	9,506,495	8,852,761	11,697,040	11,568,022	10,108,785	12,241,226	21,412,321	20,453,812
2	4,693,843	8,387,018	15,398,950	17,939,296	17,457,649	15,921,699	62,980,043	23,540,452
TOTAL	14,200,338	17,239,779	27,095,990	29,507,318	27,566,434	28,162,925	84,392,364	43,994,265
NEBRASKA								
1	10,085,501	13,751,979	9,820,227	10,523,162	8,480,696	10,344,117	14,865,466	26,618,053
2	6,361,149	2,728,766	7,271,957	7,580,322	9,474,613	12,477,820	16,547,178	18,591,515
3	498,069	583,867	846,194	399,065	188,060	713,079	1,467,519	28,139,949
TOTAL	16,944,719	17,064,612	17,938,378	18,502,549	18,143,369	23,535,016	32,880,163	73,349,518
NEVADA								
1	639,835	56,314	4,768,316	1,462,628	1,717,848	1,147,150	2,137,698	1,876,852
2	5,465,030	2,373,828	7,179,567	7,068,003	4,442,634	3,697,466	10,623,673	8,944,563
TOTAL	6,104,865	2,430,142	11,947,883	8,530,631	6,160,482	4,844,616	12,761,371	10,821,414
NEW HAMPSHIRE								
1	2,382,446	2,020,600	2,911,322	3,904,623	4,150,579	3,655,745	5,784,680	6,283,198
2	4,585,339	1,376,338	925,350	2,735,353	5,280,064	5,179,194	-235,365	1,408,299
TOTAL	6,967,785	3,396,938	3,836,672	6,639,976	9,430,643	8,834,939	5,549,315	7,691,498

Appendix A lists the congressional districts which represent the county in which the state capital is located, and those congressional districts which represent only portions of a county. Appendix C lists the programs included in each functional policy category.

table continues

Table 5.4 Outlays for Disaster Prevention and Relief Programs by Congressional District, 1983-1990 *(continued)*

Congressional District	1983	1984	1985	1986	1987	1988	1989	1990 (est.)
NEW JERSEY								
1	0	19,296	41,151	42,190	38,327	39,627	34,068	52,415
2	95,005	2,559,184	1,223,287	2,257,160	629,179	911,422	545,077	155,470
3	783,837	2,916,293	2,369,622	2,800,150	2,980,842	3,016,909	4,775,767	3,431,502
4	8,997,650	8,750,332	8,007,985	13,614,858	5,362,698	10,922,007	11,680,346	18,467,850
5	0	267,434	362,810	64,556	119,041	338,724	325,594	250,221
6	1,886,833	2,654,791	1,886,553	3,506,250	1,779,037	2,683,637	3,583,828	4,376,579
7	0	160,265	399,180	377,227	444,015	101,809	103,259	62,287
8	211,782	1,802,566	193,702	127,112	99,614	76,119	121,893	119,000
9	0	141,918	0	0	856	0	0	0
10	0	130,971	304,698	255,199	226,390	320,033	327,293	52,805
11	0	469,717	437,660	229,868	-3,297	100,611	360,940	311,542
12	126,993	513,409	156,688	284,241	-10,552	199,542	113,661	29,595
13	-25,605	2,034,189	7,285,659	7,199,706	7,365,745	7,993,335	12,975,633	9,609,630
14	173,556	271,380	555,474	180,602	848,427	352,988	497,436	271,151
TOTAL	12,250,051	22,691,745	23,224,468	30,939,119	19,880,321	27,056,762	35,444,794	37,190,045
NEW MEXICO								
1	6,077,198	896,886	1,269,947	719,575	1,964,526	1,117,346	2,581,088	4,481,463
2	14,512,366	6,093,027	7,799,491	7,749,872	5,811,351	6,091,597	10,582,956	12,464,076
3	3,890,501	15,741,884	39,824,373	31,663,811	32,797,536	41,531,154	62,908,096	64,286,523
TOTAL	24,480,065	22,731,797	48,893,811	40,133,258	40,573,413	48,740,097	76,072,140	81,232,062
NEW YORK								
1	1,094,666	2,823,022	1,530,835	15,540,711	1,202,576	778,364	269,724	482,895
2	10,548	98,741	501,051	9,095,028	1,193,470	772,416	177,972	221,300
3	47,048	1,136,773	459,998	4,259,636	1,211,268	802,318	212,745	230,291
4	196,536	470,348	156,136	2,609,766	-29,107	9,194	58,559	0
5	122,395	538,172	831,364	3,785,524	576,678	398,358	769,275	65,803
6	0	6,424	315,514	969,809	0	0	0	0
7	0	0	0	0	0	0	0	0
8	0	20,656	28,168	155,163	461	423	590	0
9	0	0	0	0	0	0	0	0
10	591,332	18,000	249,994	2,161,534	1,956,826	1,843,083	646,454	4,311,858
11	597,123	0	262,442	2,202,701	2,126,316	2,139,663	802,572	4,354,083
12	595,761	0	251,866	2,177,722	1,958,787	1,856,886	651,295	4,344,151
13	597,977	60,001	298,797	2,223,622	1,981,072	1,893,793	733,717	4,360,308
14	188,693	481,825	7,067,486	689,741	620,399	588,124	206,282	1,375,906
15	0	0	416,489	-159,424	0	0	283,759	0
16	0	20,000	416,486	-159,423	13,500	0	283,756	0
17	0	0	318,952	-122,088	0	15,000	217,305	0
18	0	10,000	0	0	0	0	0	0
19	0	324	6,491	32,783	41,966	8,558	374	40,275
20	95,000	214,838	380,830	112,258	230,134	49,748	47,146	196,219
21	395,215	334,600	1,368,644	510,736	1,838,616	4,115,190	1,181,932	1,023,011
22	0	3,252,635	980,569	623,643	3,060,417	1,709,508	1,357,177	29,398
23	20,938,944	35,153,683	21,573,662	30,063,270	20,340,798	30,667,420	20,574,790	36,602,648
24	171,700	9,699,924	5,364,769	3,963,989	9,023,525	6,930,963	1,173,096	3,345,614
25	4,334,484	10,133,550	4,767,560	4,627,617	6,339,264	6,969,985	7,480,936	10,181,121
26	6,579,465	20,711,398	13,582,445	13,137,584	18,050,655	13,054,547	11,324,538	16,829,431
27	4,408,331	934,994	4,215,219	1,663,450	502,334	1,577,464	348,403	268,784
28	10,457,784	19,408,061	9,811,537	14,443,498	10,727,437	9,282,782	8,385,589	8,300,065
29	4,318,911	8,229,583	3,627,522	4,950,326	4,858,164	4,104,471	946,703	2,763,530
30	3,326,866	1,603,669	731,784	177,884	535,291	370,804	649,781	29,255
31	1,146,491	4,136,847	662,739	60,391	1,319,174	691,158	419,554	215,882
32	3,975,266	1,992,451	2,792,450	2,784,866	3,475,607	562,577	930,250	209,296
33	1,345,000	0	1,159,376	1,176,145	49,682	50,651	153,703	120,313
34	2,840,418	11,823,993	5,557,070	4,194,005	7,360,511	3,146,608	3,100,256	6,075,859
TOTAL	68,375,955	133,314,511	89,688,245	127,952,467	100,565,821	94,390,054	63,388,233	105,977,296
NORTH CAROLINA								
1	1,252,616	912,922	2,090,231	2,214,426	2,616,781	1,980,646	1,856,588	596,672
2	-4,854	97,993	210,322	146,661	881,689	870,642	578,302	283,201
3	1,004,343	1,093,101	2,131,683	2,384,198	3,286,785	2,918,922	3,630,728	2,003,918
4	15,093,519	16,864,880	12,594,846	20,908,836	17,711,362	17,924,694	23,918,296	131,142,634
5	4,169	18,817	89,346	51,807	2,484,684	872,173	1,510,401	356,702
6	1,515,666	1,254,307	944,499	1,356,559	2,701,512	2,929,942	3,157,886	2,664,880
7	1,454,611	2,584,709	4,784,350	2,915,332	3,148,555	3,142,215	5,260,521	2,725,459
8	-31,174	127,906	352,426	124,124	3,582,608	1,080,712	462,979	234,169
9	38,310	313,364	186,470	150,787	2,017,568	637,516	687,856	13,875
10	124,470	178,897	199,045	142,916	1,018,673	293,915	378,330	-101,682
11	254,368	861,514	483,354	1,304,505	3,213,469	1,023,864	2,375,269	1,730,737
TOTAL	20,706,044	24,308,410	24,066,572	31,700,151	42,663,686	33,675,241	43,817,156	141,650,563

Appendix A lists the congressional districts which represent the county in which the state capital is located, and those congressional districts which represent only portions of a county. Appendix C lists the programs included in each functional policy category.

table continues

Table 5.4 Outlays for Disaster Prevention and Relief Programs by Congressional District, 1983-1990 *(continued)*

Congressional District	1983	1984	1985	1986	1987	1988	1989	1990 (est.)
NORTH DAKOTA								
TOTAL	10,504,944	13,576,674	12,318,743	16,115,981	14,036,266	15,874,767	47,872,741	37,179,458
OHIO								
1	0	91,513	61,289	206,635	125,647	109,025	405,661	37,586
2	0	0	18,153	143,142	87,040	54,132	164,349	22,090
3	851,342	9,256	55,205	97,115	439,809	354,163	558,995	63,105
4	10,248	50	1,679	10,464	16,601	29,194	828,374	465,436
5	0	-91,749	-248,616	-99,287	2,228	737,488	1,948,029	485,470
6	-6,571	27,288	102,074	170,681	107,199	165,475	1,250,438	226,914
7	565,418	1,465,486	3,324,839	2,973,239	3,942,299	3,340,141	5,445,119	4,885,613
8	0	1,878,573	1,297,307	4,476,078	1,404,479	489,914	3,552,069	1,363,511
9	0	42,485	66,654	90,078	73,995	0	167,568	96,814
10	24,741	465,386	912,252	425,593	853,626	186,624	1,722,446	576,100
11	-77,623	442,914	449,362	367,861	358,076	421,838	563,915	568,793
12	11,428,722	7,633,804	5,464,849	8,340,799	6,461,563	9,987,573	11,143,453	18,178,622
13	0	9,025	38,412	49,552	44,059	9,790	492,889	266,538
14	-3,697	51,169	82,673	108,860	81,963	50,142	111,577	112,645
15	5,222,678	6,869,600	7,461,001	11,021,786	8,287,613	12,845,262	14,180,686	23,376,733
16	10,066	16,792	35,455	40,163	42,374	-7,082	702,159	785,473
17	0	243,780	1,299,660	327,705	52,415	0	354,355	161,949
18	0	11,329	14,274	104,271	8,189	-2,982	1,056,926	246,379
19	0	0	16,655	68,386	69,295	5,951	38,608	8,884
20	0	103,291	162,318	73,488	83,497	15,273	35,845	-113
21	0	0	10,217	73,650	65,929	273	252,660	41,413
TOTAL	18,025,324	19,269,992	20,625,711	29,070,259	22,607,897	28,792,194	44,976,121	51,969,955
OKLAHOMA								
1	200,295	923,198	1,514,534	813,445	2,355,965	767,642	2,615,715	1,342,457
2	1,810,537	4,409,263	6,778,507	6,755,667	9,958,671	7,139,748	20,079,147	12,043,010
3	4,939,813	9,699,770	8,707,972	11,634,552	11,035,616	12,032,662	30,619,186	17,415,329
4	5,383,968	6,972,863	6,661,342	6,344,779	13,059,608	18,948,830	18,774,315	8,889,047
5	5,103,879	5,246,044	3,608,966	7,256,922	11,420,612	8,518,709	12,315,247	18,390,268
6	4,289,915	4,715,295	3,853,464	5,943,970	11,958,175	7,163,518	9,755,154	12,678,255
TOTAL	21,728,406	31,966,432	31,124,786	38,749,336	59,788,647	54,571,109	94,158,763	70,758,367
OREGON								
1	2,389,996	-12,021	59,915	190,243	154,127	122,998	138,787	153,258
2	2,770,020	1,615,390	2,994,186	2,735,304	3,128,249	4,040,912	10,068,650	6,765,043
3	1,600	39,478	50,471	40,519	26,297	18,486	24,638	41,410
4	2,555,100	113,856	377,745	214,976	244,831	4,813,729	2,293,616	1,603,831
5	6,238,934	7,044,922	4,193,988	10,640,086	7,219,314	9,059,010	9,142,501	13,356,392
TOTAL	13,955,650	8,801,625	7,676,305	13,821,128	10,772,817	18,055,135	21,668,192	21,919,933
PENNSYLVANIA								
1	132,310	0	43,071	395,575	376,648	299,430	620,748	425,685
2	132,842	-26,535	875,170	397,164	378,161	300,633	623,242	427,396
3	132,570	20,000	43,155	410,850	377,385	315,016	636,963	426,519
4	80	6,547	391,861	111,523	209,253	2,798	724,174	88,415
5	204,429	34,667	77,417	84,609	76,049	307,679	131,307	43,558
6	0	11,797	50,970	62,972	58,063	65,946	214,135	99,086
7	12,760	3,655	20,735	40,155	53,136	53,749	73,651	55,661
8	-105,004	-1,132,327	1,823,585	896,608	567,453	1,669,943	2,297,324	539,176
9	-27,857	1,232,787	809,857	687,086	871,941	694,248	3,948,300	418,488
10	172,405	325,514	484,278	2,098,431	306,582	800,290	3,767,005	2,576,131
11	1,170	-1,465,325	73,299	1,763,279	190,740	86,566	295,853	97,037
12	5,588	518,756	89,324	50,432	154,258	148,356	1,185,352	71,832
13	419,796	517,283	820,094	1,139,239	87,174	-948,429	1,000,795	124,646
14	151,830	118,535	754,589	414,937	484,839	438,811	627,241	372,542
15	-1,188	59,800	92,061	104,823	109,545	90,135	90,527	234,773
16	-16,450	1,085,332	3,236,852	1,128,793	700,543	2,257,343	1,953,771	3,824,168
17	12,437,427	10,566,663	15,201,284	24,752,883	10,022,045	9,594,713	10,526,019	17,146,733
18	40,693	0	0	187,476	5,200	0	9,687	0
19	47,737	276,266	554,009	683,371	748,310	659,149	1,695,178	572,295
20	5,743	42,111	69,559	153,268	81,725	64,116	149,055	51,092
21	-2,558	2,753	1,733,308	575,813	158,890	-125,430	462,345	130,972
22	1,125	5,333	11,297,786	-9,591,744	100,545	35,306	1,343,479	138,947
23	7,821,672	8,316,174	7,707,482	12,065,668	5,390,233	8,509,826	11,702,423	13,590,427
TOTAL	21,567,120	20,519,786	46,249,746	38,613,211	21,508,717	25,320,193	44,078,573	41,455,579

Appendix A lists the congressional districts which represent the county in which the state capital is located, and those congressional districts which represent only portions of a county. Appendix C lists the programs included in each functional policy category.

table continues

Table 5.4 Outlays for Disaster Prevention and Relief Programs by Congressional District, 1983-1990 *(continued)*

Congressional District	1983	1984	1985	1986	1987	1988	1989	1990 (est.)
RHODE ISLAND								
1	2,271,690	2,340,880	3,040,623	5,993,335	5,067,239	4,142,160	1,857,017	4,793,817
2	1,460,043	1,623,965	1,035,954	4,023,377	2,146,977	1,922,877	1,691,443	2,105,489
TOTAL	3,731,733	3,964,845	4,076,577	10,016,712	7,214,216	6,065,037	3,548,460	6,899,306
SOUTH CAROLINA								
1	765,672	374,867	1,767,705	2,018,827	2,347,001	1,628,514	2,033,895	2,805,865
2	5,372,267	6,657,222	3,380,607	6,718,234	4,473,235	8,562,642	6,289,978	577,566,009
3	4,746,082	5,002,781	3,707,436	6,910,956	5,948,910	6,515,878	9,150,066	8,483,180
4	1,598	24,781	174,366	201,214	641,044	83,668	223,893	54,351
5	450,614	152,119	1,357,746	1,726,103	3,403,365	1,917,809	2,451,436	2,483,954
6	1,069,483	2,574,654	2,558,357	2,872,216	3,743,846	2,157,229	5,752,588	3,004,151
TOTAL	12,405,716	14,786,424	12,946,217	20,447,550	20,557,401	20,865,740	25,901,856	594,397,509
SOUTH DAKOTA								
TOTAL	12,391,829	14,532,451	25,089,721	29,066,611	19,700,155	23,947,450	53,374,895	48,320,117
TENNESSEE								
1	-2,781	572,806	146,740	138,896	3,816,912	1,813,817	5,677,171	170,260
2	6,954,284	7,080,117	4,997,557	9,501,805	8,374,603	7,562,116	12,158,640	12,044,033
3	80,282	589,247	836,932	883,360	2,645,644	1,270,049	2,696,046	1,289,666
4	-12,365	653,331	215,609	206,877	4,575,104	683,295	10,479,755	184,289
5	8,774,061	12,173,682	4,261,621	9,089,752	5,624,634	11,045,306	8,749,092	15,581,029
6	28,945	180,577	154,795	368,292	3,635,337	2,010,079	8,230,587	329,125
7	563,901	2,013,296	751,321	862,875	2,112,158	1,390,896	2,715,944	86,862
8	796,170	594,222	2,322,697	454,990	836,253	1,654,448	2,025,540	331,817
9	352,704	55,000	74,192	664,353	726,571	541,979	1,183,910	151,714
TOTAL	17,535,201	23,912,278	13,761,464	22,171,200	32,347,217	27,971,984	53,916,685	30,168,794
TEXAS								
1	6,036,255	376,903	1,280,192	765,292	810,758	1,192,500	15,154,591	2,071,717
2	9,045,149	1,493,086	6,468,986	-918,501	10,552,739	3,157,586	9,542,208	4,205,228
3	-110	46,887	60,787	59,385	41,332	45,197	35,060	-712
4	2,540,065	151,488	255,485	167,927	100,144	312,638	3,146,706	191,675
5	-115	62,494	147,552	5,920	4,344	10,155	125,868	36,243
6	13,961,688	12,820,041	10,081,818	15,947,742	7,577,649	12,350,597	24,035,674	19,013,762
7	642,933	897,859	487,739	64,777	670,644	480,902	684,365	587,515
8	639,717	2,105,948	607,245	64,450	667,289	478,497	682,028	584,920
9	13,096,372	8,500,036	18,119,247	8,261,418	13,382,294	12,137,401	17,369,089	9,100,751
10	19,986,432	15,042,208	23,578,132	20,156,177	12,239,332	16,964,784	55,485,238	43,416,418
11	4,823,017	4,405,227	8,477,741	12,966,720	9,893,137	11,069,049	21,756,482	19,409,061
12	5,827	565,217	697,995	607,890	648,921	503,943	1,005,433	1,077,532
13	3,793,034	467,046	956,279	1,023,215	1,501,364	1,010,067	4,052,879	2,734,083
14	35,243,848	12,698,446	52,093,165	31,030,196	43,207,634	39,366,319	63,566,631	33,645,050
15	8,039,184	73,738	197,824	201,763	78,919	598,216	7,877,391	13,328,132
16	1,183,141	1,813,003	2,137,853	2,441,752	3,157,796	2,359,265	3,740,731	3,593,827
17	8,337,849	477,884	643,766	913,824	1,026,183	926,496	12,710,116	6,014,248
18	642,433	760,836	487,360	64,726	670,123	480,528	683,833	587,058
19	3,740,419	201,667	274,425	216,060	281,580	221,248	390,002	622,228
20	1,431,984	2,542,113	6,724,471	3,209,363	3,433,217	3,699,876	5,310,386	4,390,096
21	2,364,668	334,147	2,963,408	1,016,800	1,076,160	1,353,365	10,511,996	17,661,582
22	7,765,264	3,342,887	10,491,600	4,831,477	9,004,917	6,526,574	9,708,881	7,330,098
23	5,643,495	1,105,668	4,422,441	5,487,259	5,581,740	5,725,070	12,288,973	13,157,707
24	76,309	133,847	146,181	131,036	127,187	99,591	112,016	99,345
25	641,712	2,010,841	486,813	64,654	669,371	479,989	683,065	589,776
26	534,235	173,055	1,067,015	577,570	341,333	1,766,173	685,309	1,457,303
27	8,203	68,045	1,203,682	862,109	890,114	623,555	1,071,792	1,328,453
TOTAL	150,223,007	72,670,617	154,559,203	110,221,000	127,636,222	123,939,581	282,416,746	206,233,096
UTAH								
1	2,917,460	7,376,301	8,380,469	7,717,147	5,873,571	8,126,774	8,985,940	10,952,669
2	7,934,381	5,125,100	7,065,819	2,391,977	7,759,249	5,350,226	3,186,232	7,071,693
3	992,780	3,641,350	8,624,067	3,913,572	4,201,323	4,044,111	5,302,420	9,910,218
TOTAL	11,844,621	16,142,751	24,070,355	14,022,696	17,834,143	17,521,111	17,474,592	27,934,579
VERMONT								
TOTAL	3,876,328	4,906,289	8,012,511	3,598,462	3,953,466	4,275,470	8,685,507	7,181,164

Appendix A lists the congressional districts which represent the county in which the state capital is located, and those congressional districts which represent only portions of a county. Appendix C lists the programs included in each functional policy category.

table continues

Table 5.4 Outlays for Disaster Prevention and Relief Programs by Congressional District, 1983-1990 *(continued)*

Congressional District	1983	1984	1985	1986	1987	1988	1989	1990 (est.)
VIRGINIA								
1	3,186,117	3,088,779	10,333,097	9,025,285	10,803,648	11,124,742	18,252,631	9,615,634
2	1,526,845	1,446,380	12,728,755	11,318,198	14,720,821	12,969,979	19,438,362	17,984,453
3	3,771,285	7,834,395	6,596,922	24,651,605	4,786,580	19,316,265	13,363,479	21,272,346
4	2,809,345	3,013,518	6,027,174	5,700,816	6,369,238	8,693,114	11,114,002	9,746,425
5	0	286	9,115	736,008	3,148,103	1,671,852	344,269	-18,695
6	4,257	47,612	143,299	12,924,059	2,904,928	1,126,952	926,332	312,640
7	433,791	752,588	2,688,386	1,884,589	4,126,049	3,772,976	1,905,084	3,147,782
8	407,733	-101,493	143,662	266,174	406,887	342,834	469,681	609,908
9	5,860,189	7,568,232	5,119,226	9,679,162	5,515,937	7,074,544	10,483,198	10,333,798
10	1,655,679	-731,167	5,578,787	4,912,011	4,487,043	2,169,199	6,430,425	4,006,242
TOTAL	19,655,241	22,919,130	49,368,423	81,097,907	57,269,234	68,262,457	82,727,463	77,010,533
WASHINGTON								
1	2,024,663	1,626,745	3,054,718	1,279,849	1,125,753	988,665	1,500,378	2,531,675
2	4,478,579	1,840,776	4,657,463	5,574,143	4,939,229	4,977,330	8,357,676	6,538,080
3	6,027,102	3,259,260	5,440,041	6,378,185	4,237,881	3,684,787	7,959,843	23,482,773
4	1,114,153	1,065,514	5,437,653	6,316,077	5,146,316	7,688,098	10,061,439	10,209,352
5	4,479,974	3,986,977	5,066,794	7,606,971	8,343,928	7,035,801	10,346,419	9,471,427
6	2,027,451	1,052,163	5,867,268	12,075,081	11,824,647	9,428,749	18,057,352	18,504,102
7	50,860	3,369	77,216	1,422,478	1,312,055	309,236	411,371	822,453
8	27,978	-6,076	547,359	2,584,060	1,771,792	677,426	772,331	388,857
TOTAL	20,230,759	12,828,727	30,148,513	43,236,844	38,701,601	34,790,091	57,466,811	71,948,719
WEST VIRGINIA								
1	8,448	297,735	3,108	909,438	34,199	49,906	977,689	202,970
2	3,597,822	7,258,724	2,466,242	28,882,470	10,488,056	12,520,547	16,037,832	21,359,012
3	2,527,435	4,613,438	1,499,835	70,471,360	8,426,369	6,116,933	2,071,159	4,889,470
4	43,209	419,823	53,446	94,585	33,579	70,510	325,308	-1,414
TOTAL	6,176,914	12,589,720	4,022,631	100,357,853	18,982,203	18,757,896	19,411,988	26,450,038
WISCONSIN								
1	0	0	-1,865	1,463	153	2,173	1,543,720	-7,746
2	12,495,285	11,977,262	9,719,129	15,982,283	9,081,929	10,565,127	18,607,651	20,310,367
3	960,286	361,831	159,326	462,370	754,185	550,949	15,369,554	579,445
4	0	41,523	108,971	542,429	271,937	111,742	179,353	-5,648
5	0	0	10,147	684,256	343,930	151,688	176,016	156,528
6	773,830	1,441,072	2,371,852	251,642	748,161	8,080,856	4,031,195	3,277,732
7	1,064,965	32,461	958,367	970,868	1,104,593	1,708,670	13,181,023	1,738,229
8	1,235,752	1,388,160	2,542,960	3,468,681	4,160,192	4,347,196	11,884,361	5,659,095
9	0	0	560	36,205	19,225	10,095	1,220,423	70,790
TOTAL	16,530,118	15,242,309	15,869,446	22,400,198	16,484,306	25,528,494	66,193,295	31,778,791
WYOMING								
TOTAL	3,546,463	7,588,215	9,443,279	14,184,960	9,811,679	10,525,631	16,649,672	13,651,195
U.S. TOTAL	1,448.7 mil.	1,366.0 mil.	1,905.2 mil.	2,047.3 mil.	1,927.4 mil.	2,019.9 mil.	3,130.4 mil.	3,599.6 mil.

Appendix A lists the congressional districts which represent the county in which the state capital is located, and those congressional districts which represent only portions of a county. Appendix C lists the programs included in each functional policy category.

Table 5.5 Outlays for Education Programs by Congressional District, 1983-1990

Congressional District	1983	1984	1985	1986	1987	1988	1989	1990 (est.)
ALABAMA								
1	16,723,514	17,966,655	22,186,790	20,885,131	25,714,975	13,769,884	23,157,279	18,367,540
2	145,460,742	143,672,369	153,840,440	157,154,046	193,665,564	201,529,224	237,301,479	82,225,182
3	33,961,012	32,385,251	43,353,393	38,907,855	41,460,752	28,656,604	41,431,411	37,424,985
4	13,527,979	13,782,682	11,874,812	12,306,218	13,415,549	11,101,877	13,089,677	12,889,221
5	23,370,938	23,599,499	26,326,225	23,895,008	27,876,751	33,401,803	29,344,997	25,431,646
6	46,982,609	41,597,239	50,076,626	43,690,148	65,145,089	38,726,489	50,876,677	49,650,922
7	22,736,117	20,926,276	28,072,043	30,196,010	34,263,892	21,273,525	34,404,911	26,920,362
TOTAL	302,762,910	293,929,971	335,730,329	327,034,417	401,542,572	348,459,406	429,606,431	252,909,859
ALASKA								
TOTAL	47,304,998	72,493,462	107,738,797	94,959,877	122,297,289	155,321,270	195,045,488	132,549,042
ARIZONA								
1	98,799,541	106,833,901	83,014,984	92,868,011	110,743,939	88,327,571	78,893,588	58,128,525
2	49,658,546	52,870,146	69,534,075	82,116,203	90,383,884	82,562,473	183,084,579	103,862,023
3	14,740,313	24,369,872	24,493,857	27,143,889	24,211,661	26,682,102	33,350,331	46,965,218
4	37,606,466	33,855,921	77,868,030	100,819,335	106,612,059	93,934,880	89,270,719	74,777,394
5	9,781,396	16,634,150	17,132,297	23,608,377	28,223,979	20,855,389	31,748,427	71,761,669
TOTAL	210,586,262	234,563,991	272,043,244	326,555,816	360,175,523	312,362,415	416,347,644	355,494,828
ARKANSAS								
1	17,032,136	16,458,355	19,768,944	15,828,039	18,506,483	13,272,774	22,911,685	19,889,522
2	97,952,639	96,516,436	101,308,568	108,127,398	125,418,232	125,320,116	140,826,083	51,957,948
3	17,763,415	19,141,758	29,271,245	30,306,267	37,038,381	20,492,783	34,243,937	33,100,766
4	12,809,935	14,328,151	16,678,507	15,094,965	19,889,621	12,163,172	21,719,165	18,905,361
TOTAL	145,558,125	146,444,700	167,027,264	169,356,669	200,852,717	171,248,845	219,700,870	123,853,597
CALIFORNIA								
1	22,635,499	19,108,915	21,839,779	21,995,233	21,696,961	16,638,263	25,767,377	28,953,336
2	17,303,554	17,652,533	25,124,859	22,386,780	22,370,770	15,597,395	28,651,666	26,241,109
3	548,722,181	696,622,770	374,094,313	408,188,206	624,068,250	568,513,524	1,135,189,851	661,491,543
4	46,362,789	25,594,198	189,592,904	218,384,430	254,451,382	221,722,719	108,505,820	126,227,474
5	16,681,457	11,225,485	20,535,471	21,591,022	37,717,117	27,403,756	34,712,333	41,500,629
6	22,910,226	18,386,648	27,094,648	14,752,559	50,374,981	52,167,934	53,976,820	46,856,244
7	8,016,546	8,166,644	9,441,623	10,326,627	10,023,101	10,026,905	12,532,587	11,747,505
8	58,382,258	58,889,467	80,622,022	73,198,431	93,923,639	87,735,177	102,355,150	108,959,821
9	6,717,071	7,792,390	12,729,174	17,861,966	17,621,940	12,363,113	20,594,620	19,279,587
10	12,482,451	14,723,568	16,916,705	12,896,857	16,196,682	13,286,273	16,373,510	19,802,969
11	33,048,804	56,954,521	20,043,940	15,426,145	14,458,486	12,757,220	14,057,272	10,904,178
12	27,261,965	19,410,809	73,786,623	75,519,065	86,099,472	82,292,600	88,778,736	94,188,814
13	16,546,830	7,777,107	9,294,518	10,652,453	15,005,102	9,622,936	15,423,818	10,760,927
14	14,600,725	11,877,046	16,813,484	17,441,703	14,430,770	11,466,605	16,256,611	19,395,143
15	20,690,918	16,494,133	23,637,947	20,328,856	22,096,020	20,015,147	25,361,801	31,962,935
16	19,626,763	20,127,817	29,099,852	25,093,791	32,075,676	21,603,821	39,936,603	31,077,047
17	43,775,327	43,695,197	53,398,715	48,837,051	19,051,581	16,494,270	23,171,628	24,420,012
18	12,185,416	17,296,970	15,952,338	22,253,256	24,052,123	18,609,693	28,688,862	42,156,140
19	23,662,776	27,107,522	36,652,724	29,811,791	37,130,858	29,438,711	42,166,079	47,383,817
20	17,866,786	22,096,751	28,429,195	20,302,493	24,439,351	18,929,038	26,639,658	25,883,682
21	9,046,280	8,460,791	10,635,482	12,707,753	14,294,403	10,254,593	15,133,178	8,920,556
22	20,081,863	10,877,611	16,314,898	19,230,611	37,124,605	38,001,541	48,869,032	57,836,825
23	50,064,916	41,847,360	61,267,084	50,501,449	66,362,372	70,014,058	84,029,547	114,595,479
24	15,409,475	11,840,549	13,199,857	12,691,528	18,031,686	11,570,444	19,060,244	26,499,950
25	16,671,757	25,010,355	31,119,529	26,631,545	16,887,218	6,459,806	24,508,882	22,620,988
26	8,856,799	3,146,303	7,311,815	9,402,541	12,012,015	6,466,199	14,325,148	25,205,387
27	15,934,650	13,072,733	16,898,511	15,569,506	18,190,617	16,608,487	17,789,175	10,885,552
28	45,485,135	33,463,436	48,137,172	40,949,335	46,723,752	38,295,195	46,367,782	46,867,733
29	32,185,243	33,095,748	33,316,123	36,195,974	40,760,191	37,860,304	44,017,088	7,517,401
30	12,416,447	10,534,898	15,496,044	20,887,177	19,630,481	13,100,573	21,771,015	18,924,398
31	16,982,996	13,487,838	19,598,203	19,640,567	24,379,474	16,204,868	25,756,439	11,464,004
32	9,235,363	7,090,169	12,782,094	13,148,390	13,753,810	8,006,789	15,323,238	17,420,861
33	15,456,337	13,540,930	26,340,448	22,418,174	29,778,195	13,275,790	29,863,393	25,837,306
34	12,068,024	11,259,197	16,166,818	13,582,902	19,831,969	8,824,917	19,127,028	12,820,755
35	17,093,323	15,085,620	18,125,184	18,929,635	20,438,755	12,584,439	21,835,276	16,051,816
36	24,100,796	16,251,903	73,799,534	85,937,948	98,090,257	83,258,026	44,799,004	44,551,293
37	19,252,531	14,762,565	58,963,364	67,331,769	76,929,967	66,068,911	29,922,645	35,720,169
38	9,625,308	7,106,621	9,902,449	16,492,581	17,401,398	16,784,652	19,196,345	9,774,426
39	13,441,023	16,363,387	14,777,263	16,112,667	19,047,853	10,026,460	21,723,136	19,564,503

Appendix A lists the congressional districts which represent the county in which the state capital is located, and those congressional districts which represent only portions of a county. Appendix C lists the programs included in each functional policy category.

table continues

Table 5.5 Outlays for Education Programs by Congressional District, 1983-1990 *(continued)*

Congressional District	1983	1984	1985	1986	1987	1988	1989	1990 (est.)
CALIFORNIA *continued*								
40	21,782,593	15,180,792	22,162,040	27,159,118	30,241,721	22,128,390	37,352,834	37,526,749
41	37,230,224	47,651,832	58,605,322	47,702,249	57,511,981	54,926,248	65,865,768	76,730,250
42	16,367,573	10,171,716	10,033,853	14,898,202	16,931,037	11,632,970	18,921,579	13,927,087
43	43,570,328	20,756,882	26,841,680	32,452,863	37,054,804	30,129,061	45,316,599	33,609,089
44	20,446,850	14,786,936	22,856,329	29,044,057	32,818,853	26,420,109	38,724,574	48,774,458
45	21,767,946	18,903,628	28,019,700	38,056,417	44,482,017	35,399,197	49,841,600	67,455,858
TOTAL	1,514,054,121	1,554,750,293	1,757,771,632	1,814,923,677	2,265,993,690	1,930,987,125	2,678,581,351	2,240,295,805
COLORADO								
1	90,378,740	137,512,136	100,672,644	108,214,630	126,362,515	121,330,792	157,188,171	75,180,313
2	21,765,003	22,891,582	31,233,614	31,408,109	37,706,783	36,951,509	47,831,784	36,605,011
3	17,378,001	18,368,224	22,401,085	16,879,411	22,153,773	14,575,967	28,059,179	25,384,007
4	19,561,513	21,599,415	32,582,947	27,878,971	34,842,447	29,455,896	40,357,175	46,311,240
5	17,328,942	19,594,114	26,203,286	24,578,250	29,062,995	27,096,212	37,107,176	31,912,321
6	7,182,731	9,390,406	9,825,458	10,427,260	13,245,027	11,577,101	11,489,779	9,225,441
TOTAL	173,594,931	229,355,876	222,919,034	219,386,631	263,373,541	240,987,476	322,033,264	224,618,334
CONNECTICUT								
1	76,386,824	84,623,128	90,112,677	98,626,355	111,934,408	118,165,447	126,301,661	85,740,401
2	26,020,258	19,899,881	30,057,370	28,606,024	28,183,124	21,435,096	32,073,597	36,287,399
3	32,835,697	38,395,050	53,640,067	57,051,605	62,392,069	53,197,354	69,651,788	62,856,413
4	7,102,094	7,737,310	10,326,140	13,249,160	13,717,561	7,226,598	17,259,193	11,351,372
5	4,529,315	4,872,397	5,256,185	5,323,930	4,511,967	3,939,635	5,535,419	5,355,184
6	7,194,218	7,739,101	8,056,339	6,644,048	7,719,020	6,752,822	7,379,980	8,683,662
TOTAL	154,068,406	163,266,867	197,448,778	209,501,122	228,458,149	210,716,953	258,201,638	210,274,429
DELAWARE								
TOTAL	36,779,886	41,213,263	44,973,758	44,670,821	59,324,295	67,179,352	81,639,533	31,240,298
DISTRICT OF COLUMBIA								
TOTAL	147,078,470	279,345,121	244,304,005	156,471,564	211,719,145	222,699,927	232,361,477	188,930,588
FLORIDA								
1	25,146,843	20,390,819	22,558,945	23,498,576	24,270,347	20,752,936	29,185,003	27,573,641
2	244,795,167	274,093,440	292,775,699	329,791,383	376,713,039	401,615,409	459,458,940	130,509,092
3	18,186,460	18,190,809	17,564,898	17,175,899	16,311,702	12,205,241	19,680,495	20,335,911
4	18,664,199	15,249,102	22,461,130	22,938,596	23,673,248	12,275,552	29,137,918	19,968,622
5	10,709,780	8,235,787	9,936,991	11,910,408	14,554,234	11,211,781	18,796,877	27,616,914
6	25,207,816	29,211,423	39,427,814	28,772,838	38,529,596	23,667,633	40,213,307	40,018,503
7	34,376,006	30,207,964	38,010,759	36,468,509	35,966,531	24,900,258	38,172,497	38,055,074
8	8,470,521	7,556,459	9,580,491	11,733,299	10,130,000	6,518,051	10,884,964	14,102,917
9	12,535,818	9,286,866	11,157,535	5,282,137	5,262,055	3,755,556	5,599,511	5,443,397
10	6,077,286	6,736,501	7,776,071	8,713,767	8,597,951	5,548,238	9,489,228	8,825,405
11	12,711,261	11,875,696	15,784,137	16,085,857	17,030,903	12,496,433	21,609,867	21,541,798
12	3,787,231	3,834,159	4,362,928	4,101,560	4,112,557	3,925,028	8,509,514	8,093,508
13	5,959,549	8,777,795	6,870,414	4,349,249	4,235,583	2,967,967	4,474,739	4,380,696
14	8,577,061	8,793,369	7,879,798	4,700,164	5,807,282	3,011,460	8,978,431	6,759,011
15	22,382,045	28,393,738	33,982,173	19,561,833	24,151,100	18,552,550	25,382,538	12,299,234
16	3,327,395	1,907,609	3,542,149	5,311,024	7,351,145	3,563,549	9,522,537	2,312,089
17	7,853,531	7,600,400	15,466,381	18,762,148	26,493,957	13,682,582	38,036,605	14,213,618
18	11,256,049	11,015,108	16,905,271	21,705,373	32,130,710	20,957,875	54,486,853	30,472,826
19	5,635,284	3,787,929	10,402,084	14,729,093	21,615,591	11,146,433	30,695,011	29,904,529
TOTAL	485,659,302	505,144,973	586,445,670	605,591,714	696,937,531	612,754,532	862,314,837	462,426,787
GEORGIA								
1	15,416,404	16,107,579	18,369,724	15,427,460	18,675,002	13,180,132	27,623,565	25,829,082
2	15,897,570	14,577,374	16,736,689	13,078,702	16,556,035	11,357,403	17,760,536	22,837,703
3	21,998,701	21,448,698	25,128,807	23,431,911	25,163,289	21,011,766	26,562,649	28,493,459
4	15,396,869	12,941,050	64,462,378	73,132,281	85,417,913	81,040,835	29,248,288	25,017,361
5	192,693,262	201,131,967	167,919,764	163,812,535	204,742,147	192,179,501	293,183,071	112,648,287
6	7,329,779	7,245,029	5,950,858	4,919,644	5,701,226	8,267,549	9,958,760	8,301,512
7	7,478,806	6,866,138	8,723,199	7,740,990	8,548,950	5,978,198	8,570,090	9,662,296
8	11,155,532	11,654,030	13,048,367	12,805,794	13,442,305	10,288,597	14,511,433	15,192,859
9	7,536,257	7,009,188	8,944,648	7,648,154	8,343,638	6,175,200	9,377,972	16,052,986
10	25,788,357	23,681,767	27,433,839	27,030,562	30,274,670	27,895,088	32,789,092	30,765,055
TOTAL	320,691,537	322,662,820	356,718,274	349,028,034	416,865,175	377,374,269	469,585,456	294,800,600

Appendix A lists the congressional districts which represent the county in which the state capital is located, and those congressional districts which represent only portions of a county. Appendix C lists the programs included in each functional policy category.

table continues

Table 5.5 Outlays for Education Programs by Congressional District, 1983-1990 *(continued)*

Congressional District	1983	1984	1985	1986	1987	1988	1989	1990 (est.)
HAWAII								
1	47,628,220	60,391,045	55,382,499	53,015,090	59,465,218	71,371,387	82,110,256	80,449,615
2	8,812,327	7,967,228	19,097,884	29,322,805	29,843,240	33,738,115	36,466,297	15,397,197
TOTAL	56,440,547	68,358,273	74,480,383	82,337,895	89,308,458	105,109,502	118,576,553	95,846,813
IDAHO								
1	36,324,070	39,005,021	42,217,534	39,995,407	49,839,635	42,153,632	60,052,242	27,131,892
2	11,500,877	13,979,936	23,250,208	24,029,006	30,631,065	24,975,043	40,898,427	27,141,905
TOTAL	47,824,947	52,984,957	65,467,742	64,024,413	80,470,700	67,128,675	100,950,669	54,273,798
ILLINOIS								
1	36,977,773	37,143,737	45,738,558	54,210,687	58,872,398	52,750,923	57,596,335	55,956,995
2	7,166,274	3,283,725	7,147,197	13,589,381	13,860,157	7,523,800	13,666,509	5,196,728
3	7,911,293	4,438,510	8,694,656	15,979,878	17,592,374	7,878,753	14,766,822	7,246,123
4	7,404,391	6,321,409	8,999,958	10,182,943	11,057,682	6,362,445	11,867,654	9,333,239
5	11,435,169	3,665,599	8,387,563	14,803,447	13,940,043	7,294,965	13,017,661	5,949,589
6	6,093,647	3,589,022	5,524,453	8,962,613	9,107,696	5,775,823	11,797,737	7,969,922
7	56,176,970	84,709,648	125,981,813	65,696,310	71,080,457	67,113,744	77,287,294	132,075,984
8	7,766,037	4,653,026	9,452,481	16,162,736	15,736,944	8,934,376	15,390,665	12,496,431
9	46,715,021	32,292,887	65,938,699	51,950,586	48,318,168	34,566,315	64,254,605	45,319,340
10	12,413,323	8,374,475	26,138,317	18,715,254	21,672,380	14,985,072	20,591,311	13,143,515
11	8,920,282	7,056,361	11,974,408	16,530,418	21,573,407	15,327,924	23,379,541	15,244,871
12	7,753,125	5,202,564	6,811,731	9,306,597	10,429,152	6,304,182	10,579,774	4,063,452
13	7,163,228	5,294,687	11,418,737	10,681,122	11,637,925	5,918,209	11,210,751	7,209,676
14	11,789,642	12,547,306	19,185,809	11,626,083	16,229,898	11,943,213	18,811,468	14,931,491
15	10,594,141	13,569,513	19,979,336	14,966,684	18,625,109	8,559,942	23,355,281	18,862,755
16	6,203,560	6,678,448	7,128,218	6,483,640	6,785,442	5,309,869	7,632,151	8,279,387
17	11,405,165	14,333,749	17,498,881	12,908,578	15,764,705	6,263,272	18,173,064	14,987,321
18	7,595,795	9,080,388	15,076,849	12,903,484	17,198,691	7,352,417	12,498,787	12,944,046
19	33,141,532	44,596,367	59,679,486	64,666,178	72,410,124	65,735,074	83,301,246	85,144,968
20	303,272,390	305,448,217	310,713,452	329,473,399	415,350,850	403,160,781	360,348,110	284,271,524
21	24,361,581	18,121,593	24,432,561	20,117,892	22,391,460	14,832,570	24,425,391	26,290,142
22	18,120,205	15,925,051	27,931,531	17,432,874	27,650,592	15,409,863	34,235,195	30,582,790
TOTAL	650,380,544	646,326,281	843,834,696	797,350,785	937,285,653	779,303,530	928,187,353	817,500,288
INDIANA								
1	7,417,232	9,051,330	11,464,886	11,713,208	11,426,484	7,950,325	14,013,277	14,327,698
2	15,240,307	10,899,430	28,236,622	25,952,629	32,375,494	26,494,763	22,147,177	18,331,245
3	10,491,362	11,618,864	16,468,808	13,017,127	16,267,377	11,778,970	19,173,453	23,249,087
4	19,058,741	19,840,602	10,721,137	11,888,728	8,779,497	5,685,761	10,405,916	11,961,107
5	7,185,633	17,824,504	17,896,790	8,599,559	8,482,653	4,869,050	10,348,241	10,045,173
6	8,566,875	6,267,943	28,144,152	33,696,847	31,303,834	33,177,718	15,391,338	6,539,980
7	27,870,950	23,597,499	46,603,078	41,446,846	42,973,252	34,137,906	50,241,167	44,794,874
8	10,873,696	10,767,840	14,285,017	11,684,721	13,746,858	7,042,953	16,230,038	15,090,540
9	24,456,801	42,711,261	48,305,643	31,618,874	42,293,193	32,850,984	46,234,369	57,468,639
10	20,945,024	7,474,891	90,189,001	116,953,965	118,598,014	125,901,629	187,322,464	123,032,590
TOTAL	152,106,621	160,054,165	312,315,136	306,572,503	326,246,657	289,890,059	391,507,439	324,840,935
IOWA								
1	8,939,322	10,056,276	13,829,286	13,659,890	17,340,813	9,327,386	20,367,446	17,310,933
2	8,475,220	10,175,633	13,695,015	12,779,511	12,924,788	5,282,364	15,134,943	16,550,758
3	25,205,901	26,931,328	37,190,757	31,835,461	40,206,300	26,816,595	44,642,152	41,894,689
4	64,625,254	98,048,930	88,177,450	93,945,536	120,254,791	107,876,691	107,191,290	129,549,737
5	7,438,167	7,571,707	12,475,174	13,225,339	12,373,601	8,584,994	12,443,826	13,144,369
6	11,003,856	13,006,040	16,687,876	18,216,336	18,037,253	7,855,862	20,604,428	18,748,989
TOTAL	125,687,720	165,789,914	182,055,558	183,662,073	221,137,546	165,743,892	220,384,085	237,199,474
KANSAS								
1	7,402,518	8,826,346	12,388,094	15,233,457	20,218,288	8,522,289	28,501,627	14,588,888
2	78,433,490	90,342,107	103,356,980	96,500,577	115,215,156	119,197,572	141,776,653	77,887,751
3	11,050,014	9,732,449	11,770,159	13,349,754	12,236,746	8,362,237	13,619,533	10,522,855
4	13,721,863	14,514,765	17,431,923	14,963,440	20,053,143	13,316,772	22,229,242	16,273,549
5	13,142,312	16,401,387	22,076,955	18,645,779	21,748,138	12,053,279	24,788,286	24,603,835
TOTAL	123,750,197	139,817,054	167,024,111	158,693,007	189,471,471	161,452,149	230,915,341	143,876,878

Appendix A lists the congressional districts which represent the county in which the state capital is located, and those congressional districts which represent only portions of a county. Appendix C lists the programs included in each functional policy category.

table continues

Table 5.5 Outlays for Education Programs by Congressional District, 1983-1990 *(continued)*

Congressional District	1983	1984	1985	1986	1987	1988	1989	1990 (est.)
KENTUCKY								
1	8,730,381	9,177,461	12,441,742	9,190,536	13,320,130	6,052,149	13,291,750	10,202,697
2	17,788,565	17,890,532	20,253,305	16,906,006	21,135,042	13,688,107	22,676,382	21,309,220
3	19,521,813	22,694,138	30,037,848	29,800,322	32,055,562	22,675,524	34,828,768	33,930,945
4	6,530,231	6,333,935	6,068,725	4,589,848	4,944,838	4,183,615	6,885,922	5,286,040
5	13,890,253	12,646,001	14,892,950	13,402,429	12,242,179	6,831,369	19,322,451	16,643,760
6	117,411,442	179,148,916	150,732,450	145,137,314	194,301,236	166,474,698	231,226,706	90,727,076
7	12,026,993	15,891,252	20,515,691	12,872,666	16,799,042	13,754,446	20,399,893	19,358,989
TOTAL	195,899,678	263,782,235	254,942,711	231,899,121	294,798,029	233,659,908	348,631,872	197,458,728
LOUISIANA								
1	15,400,861	19,487,432	29,510,165	31,506,146	40,725,066	29,041,385	46,301,319	33,410,285
2	15,008,588	16,670,233	30,633,614	27,683,384	29,760,723	20,231,371	35,212,969	39,287,807
3	4,084,385	4,779,976	4,803,654	9,013,023	6,771,425	7,678,694	7,556,262	5,518,636
4	12,705,847	13,956,858	16,616,662	16,099,241	20,422,263	16,511,308	27,897,643	18,920,701
5	16,564,811	17,690,455	27,786,413	17,487,584	34,270,189	18,098,035	44,300,066	38,689,366
6	151,866,368	196,137,410	167,259,258	182,795,968	202,422,728	189,184,132	270,643,276	62,656,939
7	11,799,834	13,862,026	20,909,641	18,774,043	27,139,411	13,792,087	32,606,436	23,953,656
8	10,052,645	9,995,624	20,027,428	25,151,609	28,819,318	22,766,986	21,911,602	11,049,050
TOTAL	237,483,340	292,580,015	317,546,837	328,511,000	390,331,123	317,303,999	486,429,573	233,486,439
MAINE								
1	40,457,118	54,376,488	61,864,214	54,378,014	65,205,386	61,294,498	88,648,685	42,961,029
2	22,887,745	22,757,378	39,999,919	24,170,880	37,272,154	22,649,855	37,102,186	38,380,190
TOTAL	63,344,863	77,133,866	101,864,133	78,548,894	102,477,540	83,944,353	125,750,871	81,341,218
MARYLAND								
1	12,627,598	11,735,404	14,169,544	13,225,975	15,574,406	10,910,349	15,855,774	10,959,976
2	16,114,203	14,544,051	9,919,885	7,967,588	13,314,278	6,268,118	9,690,692	9,232,810
3	24,210,275	15,795,295	60,865,572	92,985,240	94,258,129	108,735,398	85,482,222	71,331,008
4	10,811,856	9,446,798	11,172,960	9,376,045	48,941,261	44,889,740	69,483,214	115,212,543
5	51,294,357	55,616,827	71,505,015	45,157,648	56,507,188	53,642,763	54,171,188	47,044,525
6	26,119,997	14,768,856	18,361,490	16,680,590	18,524,616	16,407,159	21,962,211	27,411,816
7	112,929,471	117,787,853	98,724,516	108,168,082	109,581,117	126,967,611	186,912,508	54,141,499
8	111,567,069	88,475,717	85,580,656	82,910,714	74,562,912	85,163,708	101,197,115	144,615,930
TOTAL	365,674,826	328,170,801	370,299,639	376,471,882	431,263,907	452,984,846	544,754,925	479,950,107
MASSACHUSETTS								
1	32,412,205	29,199,818	49,509,784	37,289,694	41,963,781	27,093,486	46,944,855	49,947,718
2	9,702,405	12,970,449	16,864,111	12,131,722	13,782,454	8,184,897	15,037,554	17,309,266
3	21,465,452	19,882,502	33,985,672	25,643,993	25,915,817	20,732,346	28,706,221	23,521,671
4	21,178,368	15,488,936	21,411,518	19,467,326	23,015,994	23,211,163	25,835,968	22,292,751
5	14,812,883	12,826,445	17,569,301	15,805,120	17,493,768	14,378,486	21,075,368	22,058,937
6	10,126,772	11,201,346	11,826,226	10,931,536	11,763,485	7,317,985	13,139,714	10,399,236
7	14,625,705	14,063,377	20,300,400	30,805,961	38,998,215	22,734,604	27,861,343	20,898,133
8	162,062,879	150,222,524	222,595,869	201,171,606	227,057,433	228,490,956	252,159,417	293,378,024
9	63,213,900	48,101,844	69,298,099	132,858,154	97,231,845	79,934,900	97,186,529	93,137,360
10	7,556,420	6,990,262	9,661,759	10,507,480	9,731,082	8,529,701	14,024,438	12,737,810
11	141,693,901	121,386,686	158,074,049	99,313,162	198,662,706	201,473,364	219,288,149	26,717,320
TOTAL	498,850,891	442,334,189	631,096,788	595,925,755	705,616,579	642,081,888	761,259,553	592,398,224
MICHIGAN								
1	10,836,738	9,876,874	14,854,440	13,669,280	12,724,308	7,116,510	13,719,976	7,168,071
2	38,826,251	40,614,145	66,088,144	50,728,433	66,845,305	62,542,688	79,960,687	85,121,454
3	14,876,042	16,701,544	24,794,708	19,145,216	27,929,112	19,507,202	327,838,816	43,107,227
4	9,286,672	10,787,512	13,443,951	9,982,341	11,514,216	9,811,080	15,590,508	18,225,668
5	18,662,628	17,939,814	20,831,439	17,343,543	15,421,025	6,687,530	22,421,072	23,833,736
6	32,757,306	31,022,671	43,292,575	38,844,827	61,107,735	48,940,438	63,349,833	98,068,748
7	10,012,455	10,649,454	11,185,900	13,318,282	14,592,975	11,979,164	17,969,633	12,696,240
8	7,796,824	9,287,105	10,892,247	10,057,094	14,577,541	6,643,043	17,422,481	11,807,651
9	11,664,021	10,183,197	17,781,318	10,884,650	16,512,647	9,456,413	17,652,812	24,299,978
10	225,713,634	246,272,945	261,745,093	271,059,040	321,936,468	260,186,270	106,472,999	40,571,401
11	22,991,519	26,600,553	35,626,719	27,997,481	33,268,083	24,782,018	42,731,413	47,516,370
12	6,380,817	6,087,129	6,536,666	7,432,538	7,786,403	5,392,126	9,906,528	7,779,352

Appendix A lists the congressional districts which represent the county in which the state capital is located, and those congressional districts which represent only portions of a county. Appendix C lists the programs included in each functional policy category.

table continues

Table 5.5 Outlays for Education Programs by Congressional District, 1983-1990 *(continued)*

Congressional District	1983	1984	1985	1986	1987	1988	1989	1990 (est.)
MICHIGAN *continued*								
13	36,148,502	42,012,638	48,130,165	41,293,043	43,690,526	38,067,916	44,156,832	53,191,626
14	5,224,147	4,861,472	6,588,615	7,042,399	7,010,965	4,228,453	6,938,271	4,245,948
15	10,694,430	9,907,191	14,419,966	13,857,676	17,161,591	7,473,330	17,523,581	14,203,746
16	9,509,238	8,154,048	12,448,634	18,122,574	16,163,296	6,800,472	17,132,041	13,665,611
17	8,216,746	6,321,103	9,070,460	11,090,360	11,418,144	7,701,734	14,392,981	8,680,038
18	6,273,941	8,395,536	9,262,109	6,163,730	6,872,498	4,322,980	9,913,892	8,668,593
TOTAL	485,871,910	515,674,931	626,993,150	588,032,507	706,532,838	541,639,366	845,094,361	522,851,457
MINNESOTA								
1	20,679,690	25,967,058	30,339,764	26,191,792	33,281,665	21,320,773	34,967,700	34,869,017
2	10,652,167	10,730,457	16,044,792	14,007,662	17,858,428	7,886,462	18,203,464	18,173,094
3	6,336,780	6,072,573	8,408,672	6,660,274	8,786,820	4,510,427	9,845,920	12,613,109
4	91,297,460	121,253,245	119,507,874	133,387,167	165,357,951	161,497,990	184,962,682	61,514,451
5	37,401,887	45,587,922	57,712,727	46,523,521	65,897,998	51,883,200	81,677,164	77,657,875
6	13,970,335	10,278,689	9,576,640	8,030,551	11,484,992	6,643,766	10,116,399	9,182,643
7	21,292,565	24,990,251	39,577,861	29,908,310	39,948,819	20,408,699	47,366,290	46,068,003
8	15,752,747	18,210,938	21,928,265	18,082,167	23,881,236	15,479,406	26,659,418	26,652,637
TOTAL	217,383,631	263,091,134	303,096,596	282,791,444	366,497,910	289,630,723	413,799,036	286,730,829
MISSISSIPPI								
1	19,255,497	17,240,016	20,732,207	20,600,355	20,381,531	17,574,388	28,235,454	38,157,463
2	36,010,446	34,317,404	46,039,312	41,843,372	49,817,650	20,988,612	37,322,182	33,610,282
3	15,493,400	19,871,133	22,430,338	16,093,441	23,310,131	18,749,310	29,105,596	34,590,069
4	160,174,043	142,255,665	147,371,753	142,313,360	169,548,058	182,411,325	193,817,152	126,196,391
5	24,046,473	21,537,387	32,571,435	32,938,318	31,397,882	27,666,815	39,675,420	36,124,721
TOTAL	254,979,859	235,221,605	269,145,045	253,788,845	294,455,252	267,390,450	328,155,805	268,678,926
MISSOURI								
1	29,676,300	33,304,599	42,248,733	39,385,154	40,557,835	37,967,049	48,355,430	68,971,234
2	11,414,020	9,197,876	13,468,183	22,567,015	20,064,115	11,754,776	22,171,764	11,976,428
3	12,843,891	7,021,682	9,705,349	11,231,832	9,719,609	5,703,197	11,743,527	6,365,674
4	23,625,158	18,984,258	19,371,163	19,560,605	38,244,957	28,685,083	36,410,295	41,211,066
5	12,924,507	7,822,629	8,743,020	7,394,114	7,338,844	7,511,877	8,294,917	5,807,747
6	21,209,215	25,621,672	33,965,253	33,578,857	45,611,564	25,457,081	43,332,223	39,413,059
7	16,819,932	16,639,400	22,337,015	20,167,314	23,381,060	11,657,010	27,808,104	26,289,428
8	20,647,662	17,487,553	18,440,690	15,740,135	18,122,269	13,526,191	22,245,760	21,772,451
9	122,485,969	125,805,673	131,524,266	106,869,867	158,654,977	119,692,636	209,130,320	39,288,738
TOTAL	271,646,655	261,885,344	299,803,672	276,494,892	361,695,231	261,954,900	429,492,340	261,095,824
MONTANA								
1	47,168,995	48,412,161	57,580,729	62,405,517	72,260,250	62,139,677	71,645,185	83,250,799
2	18,478,123	24,576,501	31,618,498	33,861,682	35,930,327	32,537,098	48,706,675	40,326,095
TOTAL	65,647,118	72,988,662	89,199,227	96,267,199	108,190,577	94,676,775	120,351,860	123,576,894
NEBRASKA								
1	58,226,497	60,874,279	69,538,981	66,153,421	83,049,092	69,134,115	89,076,804	45,664,410
2	30,056,162	26,781,436	34,049,778	35,065,828	40,068,458	34,193,812	49,139,539	53,317,816
3	8,931,969	10,282,762	12,719,354	11,576,945	15,136,286	9,141,868	17,667,576	14,827,138
TOTAL	97,214,628	97,938,477	116,308,113	112,796,194	138,253,836	112,469,795	155,883,919	113,809,364
NEVADA								
1	4,599,705	7,640,164	15,079,640	11,914,626	14,170,521	10,175,301	18,083,441	16,542,132
2	19,786,030	27,500,554	32,461,296	35,181,186	36,116,270	40,650,493	47,013,924	26,654,815
TOTAL	24,385,735	35,140,718	47,540,936	47,095,812	50,286,791	50,825,794	65,097,365	43,196,947
NEW HAMPSHIRE								
1	17,522,388	17,106,651	28,775,459	19,218,601	21,230,426	14,118,810	21,395,303	21,746,029
2	30,478,819	37,505,667	37,554,147	49,699,904	57,046,400	50,840,602	58,582,497	35,885,046
TOTAL	48,001,207	54,612,318	66,329,606	68,918,505	78,276,826	64,959,412	79,977,800	57,631,075

Appendix A lists the congressional districts which represent the county in which the state capital is located, and those congressional districts which represent only portions of a county. Appendix C lists the programs included in each functional policy category.

table continues

Table 5.5 Outlays for Education Programs by Congressional District, 1983-1990 *(continued)*

Congressional District	1983	1984	1985	1986	1987	1988	1989	1990 (est.)
NEW JERSEY								
1	9,920,784	10,137,512	10,587,436	7,147,461	8,559,608	5,442,507	9,849,170	11,922,721
2	10,267,802	12,289,749	11,701,754	10,463,230	10,704,821	7,609,749	11,915,384	10,406,679
3	6,884,623	10,048,476	9,869,526	9,953,935	10,603,130	9,015,077	13,435,849	14,527,519
4	191,177,518	163,564,464	247,213,942	217,505,744	265,086,211	271,925,300	307,273,262	48,835,172
5	4,880,707	3,009,674	3,972,758	4,616,829	4,312,509	2,693,495	5,493,716	4,811,625
6	24,078,740	25,071,167	37,561,996	22,979,965	34,135,278	27,140,141	36,031,749	37,722,754
7	17,221,199	20,774,323	18,871,133	8,938,912	9,734,407	5,311,064	9,466,392	9,516,780
8	9,615,826	9,430,235	9,455,407	10,832,290	10,509,558	7,788,754	12,582,611	14,822,622
9	9,209,760	7,447,520	9,080,429	8,994,417	6,641,129	3,467,223	10,651,064	8,108,916
10	32,586,078	31,002,559	36,984,511	31,568,032	39,229,628	29,588,618	35,456,909	46,100,497
11	6,694,434	6,821,719	9,715,697	7,114,285	8,127,593	4,904,297	8,831,223	7,553,248
12	8,426,108	7,797,861	43,714,908	43,576,043	53,918,477	52,247,085	58,644,771	61,875,041
13	5,312,861	6,838,045	12,366,774	13,777,909	13,502,457	10,801,113	17,748,480	12,187,707
14	13,247,842	13,105,645	18,461,773	15,739,986	17,400,454	9,342,257	15,795,606	15,062,368
TOTAL	349,524,281	327,338,949	479,558,043	413,209,039	492,465,260	447,276,679	553,176,187	303,453,649
NEW MEXICO								
1	25,754,807	22,751,599	31,403,337	24,733,151	34,179,549	29,418,537	39,427,719	38,156,162
2	27,107,430	20,511,636	35,710,420	21,861,144	34,152,527	22,767,968	36,456,392	42,878,962
3	56,179,122	92,976,690	112,358,500	102,971,752	118,766,402	125,263,006	158,394,815	96,958,768
TOTAL	109,041,359	136,239,925	179,472,257	149,566,047	187,098,478	177,449,511	234,278,926	177,993,893
NEW YORK								
1	20,956,529	22,872,167	23,836,001	28,811,625	25,033,978	26,260,123	27,013,451	41,379,399
2	3,983,808	3,915,496	4,104,396	12,258,411	3,783,014	4,341,682	5,175,079	2,856,053
3	11,840,937	15,925,969	23,700,354	32,948,588	25,238,466	22,418,300	24,493,869	28,078,665
4	9,855,414	9,610,489	13,754,369	9,767,603	6,105,865	1,941,675	5,707,810	3,592,422
5	15,430,000	14,769,920	15,893,724	21,895,266	22,682,612	13,300,814	21,085,696	13,221,283
6	3,948,999	2,702,995	5,110,547	6,209,966	4,608,509	2,755,963	10,475,801	12,414,280
7	4,055,286	5,028,097	5,396,504	6,176,377	5,733,446	3,640,517	11,744,325	10,013,415
8	13,886,309	12,133,560	12,792,755	15,367,067	10,726,334	6,259,846	20,595,816	19,876,746
9	3,232,908	2,336,632	3,524,950	5,259,379	4,463,809	2,400,474	9,805,156	4,035,719
10	9,672,563	25,684,272	-9,881,737	21,771,318	21,061,160	17,927,706	19,679,014	23,277,286
11	5,141,502	2,711,752	6,008,287	20,616,740	20,404,856	17,478,569	18,308,972	21,139,516
12	6,394,484	5,088,072	8,490,121	23,740,989	23,179,182	19,551,964	25,199,673	24,133,086
13	8,316,351	6,443,260	10,540,880	22,345,443	23,128,128	19,571,565	22,393,521	21,584,984
14	31,426,014	41,494,771	37,348,208	9,308,658	9,160,902	6,816,173	8,604,542	7,595,180
15	117,084,006	117,313,281	176,773,522	242,909,395	258,106,921	199,127,260	234,192,139	355,275,030
16	64,842,489	23,671,922	65,940,506	124,065,371	118,974,243	68,619,898	88,775,924	33,017,161
17	89,164,551	40,501,694	69,174,877	110,125,221	118,041,328	67,625,043	93,863,958	49,819,182
18	134,722,382	127,633,300	91,491,376	10,289,429	12,629,133	10,889,075	43,024,813	58,185,017
19	10,051,398	4,966,312	7,129,484	9,016,797	11,860,159	9,705,304	33,130,965	46,043,474
20	52,546,805	53,425,148	81,397,553	23,909,256	19,563,135	19,061,547	24,448,913	24,762,422
21	5,891,069	8,298,155	8,595,253	10,803,796	9,816,984	8,562,897	13,240,969	13,056,499
22	19,406,666	23,822,879	21,099,823	19,854,538	22,864,203	8,197,446	19,678,746	14,981,910
23	544,544,403	610,054,701	633,078,681	671,322,789	789,121,431	707,228,169	912,748,223	472,560,532
24	7,785,296	8,848,582	10,447,939	11,760,441	13,333,323	10,920,382	14,759,626	16,064,697
25	12,336,384	14,779,484	23,573,507	18,332,768	21,572,899	13,090,569	24,678,138	28,781,733
26	12,665,061	18,980,712	24,515,866	19,632,796	21,037,900	16,800,711	29,497,677	28,324,460
27	27,221,871	22,605,578	43,715,906	29,914,682	28,967,696	17,388,413	32,358,707	29,075,881
28	73,987,486	43,634,416	66,704,134	76,516,516	81,022,466	77,242,605	86,699,800	89,780,859
29	9,073,572	6,025,972	21,418,192	35,751,569	19,123,444	10,586,830	16,630,841	13,526,949
30	14,801,650	23,437,121	32,581,095	42,021,062	48,275,218	64,675,324	67,846,387	89,816,077
31	15,821,198	9,541,295	10,722,947	17,872,727	16,863,088	12,266,005	20,734,504	27,668,960
32	9,444,259	13,647,187	17,080,175	22,511,474	21,768,994	21,121,083	30,558,273	36,029,797
33	10,778,375	11,423,973	18,464,712	29,270,471	29,951,171	21,041,372	24,749,601	28,638,097
34	19,832,400	27,185,881	32,140,238	17,667,529	17,305,924	10,421,061	19,141,918	15,277,702
TOTAL	1,400,142,423	1,380,515,044	1,616,665,143	1,780,026,057	1,885,509,922	1,539,236,367	2,061,042,847	1,703,884,472
NORTH CAROLINA								
1	18,852,506	20,231,928	23,437,209	19,698,782	22,618,607	14,526,122	18,182,310	19,637,907
2	37,805,036	44,200,905	58,432,309	50,814,349	71,534,927	60,548,436	73,007,526	52,866,325
3	16,499,850	16,782,669	15,673,823	18,176,410	16,721,254	13,089,040	16,065,307	14,747,238
4	201,846,645	189,875,432	197,084,482	205,056,367	253,623,350	254,900,623	245,229,022	310,022,511
5	14,846,017	15,180,793	17,691,788	14,398,802	17,245,858	12,325,103	17,436,466	17,668,134
6	16,350,448	14,849,573	20,941,549	15,245,880	19,085,040	11,345,903	24,280,600	19,944,458
7	28,623,817	30,239,412	33,314,513	30,824,332	30,243,023	23,849,779	33,195,551	25,392,376
8	13,608,962	15,844,571	14,274,026	14,359,097	13,358,261	10,221,997	13,882,094	10,930,323
9	14,827,105	14,055,309	18,192,010	17,013,295	17,154,475	11,298,295	16,436,135	15,776,446
10	10,626,745	11,197,139	13,548,470	10,166,734	12,252,673	8,787,001	14,895,681	14,336,867
11	14,292,128	14,184,835	16,686,837	14,795,964	16,280,198	10,972,854	17,884,235	16,755,557
TOTAL	388,179,260	386,642,566	429,277,016	410,550,012	490,117,665	431,865,153	490,494,928	518,078,143

Appendix A lists the congressional districts which represent the county in which the state capital is located, and those congressional districts which represent only portions of a county. Appendix C lists the programs included in each functional policy category.

table continues

Table 5.5 Outlays for Education Programs by Congressional District, 1983-1990 *(continued)*

Congressional District	1983	1984	1985	1986	1987	1988	1989	1990 (est.)
NORTH DAKOTA								
TOTAL	49,577,302	55,036,268	69,943,586	64,070,273	83,663,083	68,111,797	94,339,454	76,260,711
OHIO								
1	32,094,293	37,548,973	37,066,190	32,275,026	32,869,156	22,136,151	25,907,240	25,582,324
2	12,746,853	6,728,221	11,183,932	14,195,531	15,960,856	8,524,037	17,894,332	19,698,085
3	14,587,663	9,305,913	10,455,388	11,015,741	12,547,657	11,805,098	12,475,343	16,285,711
4	8,226,956	7,829,458	10,986,293	17,883,966	12,723,142	6,533,803	13,407,379	14,227,118
5	9,985,690	9,471,182	12,712,331	9,938,024	12,400,817	7,892,524	15,677,321	16,628,612
6	10,263,304	9,208,870	11,017,224	13,290,876	14,016,276	7,130,587	16,052,661	15,961,253
7	21,693,302	28,692,119	50,775,458	41,243,233	51,975,002	25,255,075	57,915,043	55,327,624
8	8,579,121	7,746,623	8,697,457	6,633,146	8,301,713	4,983,423	8,452,709	13,183,038
9	14,184,676	15,153,297	17,691,041	15,965,535	26,705,000	11,028,762	24,149,781	22,677,671
10	218,286,854	239,230,067	269,605,150	276,058,778	354,848,279	315,436,075	358,081,995	82,037,415
11	10,469,512	14,224,503	20,911,788	12,621,826	18,077,321	12,573,604	27,933,021	26,942,223
12	17,357,288	13,184,476	15,163,991	22,685,632	42,740,283	39,481,859	43,880,122	50,895,481
13	7,887,472	8,875,527	11,254,571	13,046,454	13,517,026	8,011,568	11,291,605	7,260,040
14	14,821,821	12,665,606	15,960,693	10,059,762	15,419,350	10,030,920	18,596,830	19,768,658
15	62,409,857	44,283,069	23,897,483	37,092,914	40,500,616	36,161,981	34,895,775	21,828,356
16	4,747,879	3,748,109	5,048,113	4,451,728	8,428,625	5,081,866	9,591,753	8,512,105
17	9,151,083	11,702,460	14,331,413	9,911,929	13,053,624	5,988,365	12,998,054	11,514,013
18	5,128,735	5,221,916	5,566,136	6,189,166	5,970,939	4,684,975	8,031,392	6,071,522
19	6,228,616	2,615,464	6,586,256	11,561,535	10,999,361	5,310,213	13,146,988	7,115,502
20	15,413,726	15,398,675	21,709,122	19,480,907	19,080,111	13,312,848	24,070,327	26,929,188
21	24,781,143	25,391,939	36,096,571	23,673,694	27,453,810	21,105,078	34,498,558	42,399,377
TOTAL	529,045,842	528,226,467	616,716,602	609,275,402	757,588,964	582,468,811	788,948,229	510,845,319
OKLAHOMA								
1	10,655,674	11,215,742	17,561,784	13,748,510	20,810,615	15,992,237	30,539,069	24,481,759
2	25,427,488	28,943,167	34,607,648	27,187,220	37,497,314	35,284,022	47,698,045	47,332,367
3	33,063,204	35,657,215	44,853,782	38,961,832	49,018,073	54,186,378	66,028,543	46,429,733
4	21,631,876	26,810,836	31,182,693	23,253,621	43,415,823	51,874,335	55,072,897	36,186,628
5	75,153,832	81,380,781	50,375,553	47,998,232	66,129,374	52,384,845	65,588,815	24,731,136
6	10,912,577	11,114,082	48,293,391	55,942,304	78,578,599	66,779,488	78,767,722	34,346,174
TOTAL	176,844,649	195,121,823	226,874,852	207,091,719	295,449,798	276,501,306	343,695,091	213,507,797
OREGON								
1	23,732,014	20,067,628	26,861,030	11,844,910	15,367,733	12,310,808	17,907,650	37,234,718
2	15,010,098	16,558,543	20,848,352	19,233,564	23,683,000	15,410,524	27,633,826	27,390,011
3	24,712,795	17,258,658	22,561,292	19,437,927	21,255,552	20,815,268	52,190,375	26,361,647
4	25,870,822	25,946,398	40,272,434	42,612,470	64,731,996	33,556,731	44,070,345	35,564,404
5	81,213,286	87,336,365	110,893,754	120,912,281	152,189,097	112,751,135	171,156,716	82,965,669
TOTAL	170,539,016	167,167,591	221,436,862	214,041,151	277,227,378	194,844,466	312,958,912	209,516,449
PENNSYLVANIA								
1	70,693,145	56,632,361	74,034,684	55,726,373	83,206,878	60,162,035	80,442,720	90,146,940
2	29,048,350	38,334,702	49,417,828	45,744,758	57,843,383	53,633,044	65,927,630	40,728,304
3	38,202,011	25,656,088	37,708,857	37,744,711	46,716,884	29,325,149	42,635,012	27,769,795
4	14,162,781	13,948,888	17,446,032	12,659,942	15,564,114	8,290,723	22,402,039	20,033,725
5	12,034,662	12,312,701	21,005,070	14,654,294	15,314,724	10,038,318	16,979,364	15,934,488
6	6,406,714	8,191,889	6,585,123	7,465,637	7,769,751	5,430,623	9,447,917	8,776,364
7	9,743,888	11,220,871	12,336,413	12,961,344	12,931,037	6,316,120	13,631,435	18,867,052
8	6,729,312	4,582,521	9,377,193	7,055,379	6,088,553	4,935,077	8,560,521	7,687,660
9	6,975,672	7,114,390	8,250,404	7,503,993	7,075,878	5,637,238	9,399,463	9,332,533
10	16,405,874	13,146,787	16,404,415	13,452,157	9,956,050	6,584,624	13,616,399	15,384,817
11	12,033,012	12,274,605	15,445,601	17,026,602	14,025,128	8,289,722	16,591,242	16,167,365
12	8,730,119	11,408,160	13,154,340	13,067,217	11,232,367	7,967,836	14,327,514	12,148,845
13	8,927,256	7,775,224	9,371,217	12,825,517	12,926,196	9,074,085	14,619,135	13,725,255
14	77,394,885	63,547,202	96,048,934	92,271,699	103,866,038	85,816,813	125,037,052	125,820,084
15	12,320,719	13,113,596	15,998,290	14,943,596	15,014,485	10,380,099	18,313,891	11,955,088
16	7,115,148	8,309,017	8,677,023	8,997,265	7,662,434	5,656,705	11,430,356	9,510,814
17	231,827,119	278,151,840	345,525,152	335,836,508	408,108,251	420,897,744	444,411,037	89,363,281
18	6,167,834	4,225,727	2,746,259	2,478,424	1,626,111	1,504,524	1,457,963	1,593,046
19	5,428,877	6,185,193	7,879,795	7,192,264	7,794,427	4,858,298	8,580,108	6,773,207
20	5,372,518	4,628,020	3,160,431	3,523,847	3,098,213	2,280,010	3,283,808	1,962,016
21	8,007,876	11,575,518	17,074,000	15,658,456	14,378,712	8,371,509	18,522,276	16,014,231
22	7,924,095	9,426,938	9,956,301	11,601,420	10,376,502	6,661,746	13,186,505	7,717,244
23	39,325,469	44,276,986	52,551,681	32,006,650	46,146,678	34,132,806	62,542,136	53,654,743
TOTAL	640,977,336	666,039,223	850,155,043	782,398,053	918,722,794	796,244,847	1,035,345,523	621,066,898

Appendix A lists the congressional districts which represent the county in which the state capital is located, and those congressional districts which represent only portions of a county. Appendix C lists the programs included in each functional policy category.

table continues

Table 5.5 Outlays for Education Programs by Congressional District, 1983-1990 *(continued)*

Congressional District	1983	1984	1985	1986	1987	1988	1989	1990 (est.)
RHODE ISLAND								
1	24,452,076	19,323,289	39,008,848	54,724,201	62,100,358	49,790,651	56,487,999	45,316,849
2	42,651,818	49,298,598	50,105,370	38,071,679	43,824,910	32,410,714	45,607,510	32,337,008
TOTAL	67,103,894	68,621,887	89,114,218	92,795,880	105,925,268	82,201,365	102,095,509	77,653,857
SOUTH CAROLINA								
1	22,878,878	19,550,811	22,225,080	19,350,150	21,200,701	15,595,334	20,868,782	21,221,690
2	132,642,514	136,125,360	143,813,620	142,209,666	191,780,049	165,336,908	207,384,897	646,956,116
3	12,663,167	12,942,327	15,171,265	13,274,863	14,606,960	12,704,022	19,267,048	25,611,106
4	12,587,634	12,936,260	14,211,337	15,073,647	14,742,629	7,764,997	14,549,732	12,149,449
5	16,615,495	15,500,183	15,774,013	16,404,890	15,609,961	12,843,821	17,461,572	20,793,779
6	12,756,779	13,891,579	12,980,460	14,403,619	15,398,074	11,875,252	18,818,355	28,372,019
TOTAL	210,144,467	210,946,520	224,175,775	220,716,835	273,338,374	226,120,334	298,350,386	755,104,158
SOUTH DAKOTA								
TOTAL	51,504,605	71,040,074	90,742,270	90,316,453	100,999,780	76,746,914	111,482,127	106,909,323
TENNESSEE								
1	11,090,313	11,508,212	14,842,808	11,870,443	12,939,145	9,776,667	15,852,244	15,971,596
2	21,534,821	18,010,153	24,488,431	21,201,529	25,607,826	19,445,109	30,693,937	34,845,598
3	20,495,526	18,415,604	24,346,223	20,026,613	21,496,742	13,208,029	23,024,645	21,919,033
4	14,412,609	14,715,005	13,436,303	12,653,978	13,443,415	10,010,233	15,008,489	13,092,653
5	164,913,282	163,710,704	165,679,672	168,392,416	205,756,931	176,600,923	269,888,720	89,504,850
6	10,382,156	16,057,407	16,656,800	12,551,747	14,822,610	9,371,427	17,633,108	17,407,608
7	12,257,167	10,498,370	14,479,903	14,541,654	17,003,053	11,662,648	19,648,593	11,380,538
8	27,536,861	32,561,989	33,638,204	23,109,340	25,285,418	17,108,567	26,812,944	25,569,772
9	15,081,666	10,534,982	16,644,425	24,130,175	26,628,824	13,948,727	30,820,296	28,260,942
TOTAL	297,704,400	296,012,426	324,212,769	308,477,895	362,983,964	281,132,330	449,382,976	257,952,590
TEXAS								
1	10,738,216	10,704,686	12,083,976	9,707,215	10,674,155	8,137,607	13,270,018	13,810,276
2	7,450,883	8,229,176	9,469,407	6,910,432	9,702,074	6,875,699	14,084,524	12,581,210
3	7,721,794	8,848,075	10,250,043	7,243,609	8,512,151	5,435,871	9,336,361	7,925,847
4	9,728,505	9,938,242	15,142,690	16,138,485	17,916,187	12,596,442	24,019,155	15,776,947
5	18,445,041	18,277,896	20,579,883	14,604,898	15,751,983	13,807,510	17,602,102	26,259,159
6	16,723,106	15,550,530	23,157,350	18,405,413	25,981,030	24,196,673	37,009,732	39,268,920
7	3,400,859	2,990,447	3,478,449	9,348,781	8,420,947	9,726,797	10,368,011	7,740,650
8	3,485,445	4,002,891	1,811,851	1,538,287	2,434,219	2,887,705	3,166,462	1,287,192
9	11,304,197	15,607,283	14,427,838	13,049,540	18,669,944	13,054,416	19,518,186	17,954,109
10	436,197,405	456,261,581	503,114,415	504,457,142	610,481,749	636,954,409	727,581,854	162,484,027
11	20,651,235	19,397,387	29,939,267	31,314,534	34,666,188	27,166,321	45,666,308	41,031,939
12	9,964,891	8,527,245	10,511,280	13,399,046	22,317,619	11,849,768	25,791,719	18,312,796
13	9,229,219	8,669,170	11,428,309	10,909,655	16,292,241	10,771,337	19,661,281	12,986,871
14	9,486,189	11,539,471	18,267,133	12,382,608	16,179,807	10,483,953	20,300,967	19,910,303
15	15,905,944	17,673,871	18,804,387	13,987,151	18,623,404	17,598,878	29,852,888	27,465,153
16	20,479,457	25,139,079	31,987,203	32,134,090	42,032,440	23,889,895	50,435,944	36,441,137
17	8,933,828	8,958,408	12,559,606	11,518,244	12,277,688	8,876,461	17,104,802	14,010,242
18	35,668,631	22,925,609	26,219,420	26,752,672	27,988,113	31,347,743	35,822,608	33,860,412
19	11,827,693	13,551,488	19,648,703	15,979,837	19,709,307	16,694,753	27,044,823	30,276,021
20	21,536,333	18,817,361	24,270,317	31,374,860	37,628,499	30,944,726	45,653,209	58,575,121
21	19,566,264	22,597,348	32,672,074	12,340,012	17,076,112	12,719,876	29,633,168	18,020,713
22	14,213,707	25,017,525	32,080,920	22,911,477	48,183,708	30,529,843	59,537,190	44,143,465
23	30,485,146	28,166,968	38,717,229	45,492,968	52,062,809	47,163,868	62,410,023	68,119,981
24	9,361,297	19,545,285	12,244,087	4,295,742	6,076,969	4,143,129	7,012,833	10,198,092
25	15,095,887	20,313,079	20,777,826	19,600,358	26,754,666	28,216,376	26,092,357	28,710,643
26	9,951,809	8,463,023	16,147,248	23,318,763	33,412,828	22,383,173	38,251,686	31,050,371
27	10,613,533	19,554,003	20,291,827	20,953,091	22,581,842	15,341,076	28,957,266	19,873,583
TOTAL	798,166,515	849,267,126	990,082,738	950,068,910	1,182,408,679	1,083,794,302	1,445,185,479	818,075,179
UTAH								
1	22,292,768	22,948,036	34,950,823	26,830,480	34,041,027	24,279,465	40,517,387	38,692,833
2	71,413,704	78,697,453	88,086,334	89,900,486	104,967,999	87,243,430	109,677,402	77,589,971
3	6,901,643	14,266,701	21,438,611	15,263,122	26,716,481	21,513,096	41,924,084	31,163,465
TOTAL	100,608,115	115,912,190	144,475,768	131,994,088	165,725,507	133,035,991	192,118,873	147,446,268
VERMONT								
TOTAL	37,201,049	44,399,850	58,001,110	42,388,866	66,008,419	51,999,564	72,380,015	63,223,036

Appendix A lists the congressional districts which represent the county in which the state capital is located, and those congressional districts which represent only portions of a county. Appendix C lists the programs included in each functional policy category.

table continues

Table 5.5 **Outlays for Education Programs by Congressional District, 1983-1990 *(continued)***

Congressional District	1983	1984	1985	1986	1987	1988	1989	1990 (est.)
VIRGINIA								
1	20,442,123	22,204,955	29,892,389	29,481,601	30,959,281	28,091,491	43,348,734	31,689,143
2	28,452,248	29,141,073	42,331,890	38,333,573	49,209,248	36,398,595	56,340,731	43,526,912
3	143,168,063	146,223,264	147,586,268	174,523,718	176,435,673	202,213,995	226,726,475	60,347,632
4	18,423,373	22,174,905	24,237,025	21,571,187	20,026,824	14,725,754	24,067,041	21,986,489
5	6,241,620	7,462,526	8,296,169	8,016,004	6,809,816	3,396,164	7,894,472	7,601,560
6	13,941,570	14,886,460	18,790,426	29,293,901	20,174,318	11,670,304	23,283,414	23,662,396
7	17,349,157	18,814,208	25,336,402	21,352,129	34,247,168	29,929,398	29,811,260	27,068,218
8	11,481,099	11,989,275	12,772,978	12,868,198	13,163,441	9,466,869	12,382,934	9,250,603
9	18,885,994	25,068,449	28,947,926	23,062,405	29,484,585	21,771,323	39,867,073	41,804,527
10	25,652,798	19,847,335	27,884,692	38,715,394	37,321,143	44,590,044	54,165,655	67,211,134
TOTAL	304,038,045	317,812,450	366,076,165	397,218,111	417,831,498	402,253,937	517,887,789	334,148,615
WASHINGTON								
1	26,610,985	26,335,521	31,046,941	20,458,416	19,008,487	15,016,721	18,767,324	12,603,932
2	17,718,327	16,363,293	21,068,676	20,035,022	20,733,993	17,153,248	25,534,694	19,135,225
3	88,560,220	112,725,263	106,010,554	120,778,508	165,188,606	161,075,344	175,845,687	56,732,416
4	38,694,536	45,506,563	58,251,409	30,188,632	27,406,019	24,678,330	33,982,647	38,888,393
5	28,754,204	26,131,397	45,460,003	33,704,750	47,588,352	26,195,078	51,568,595	49,460,826
6	21,494,103	17,992,088	28,916,922	30,385,266	37,027,431	27,146,962	42,654,812	34,683,067
7	42,811,053	35,971,769	40,278,646	73,703,872	90,057,658	98,565,251	123,710,476	149,610,110
8	12,357,329	8,456,688	13,415,546	24,490,484	26,002,541	17,694,378	24,342,862	12,538,565
TOTAL	277,000,757	289,482,581	344,448,697	353,744,949	433,013,088	387,525,311	496,407,097	373,652,534
WEST VIRGINIA								
1	10,984,556	13,398,500	18,786,482	13,942,087	16,928,549	8,442,199	20,877,956	19,211,536
2	12,703,657	16,483,133	23,407,511	35,051,027	22,460,181	17,781,040	57,361,547	79,122,809
3	52,759,019	68,653,544	64,262,500	136,676,857	108,816,202	89,930,215	90,236,581	26,456,246
4	14,460,064	17,919,784	19,638,228	16,301,157	18,868,817	12,229,582	17,424,703	18,763,126
TOTAL	90,907,296	116,454,961	126,094,721	201,971,128	167,073,749	128,383,036	185,900,787	143,553,717
WISCONSIN								
1	7,668,629	9,950,476	15,216,807	10,448,237	13,650,368	7,538,499	16,595,341	14,267,262
2	127,902,787	177,629,902	183,850,260	155,574,827	249,146,998	185,186,100	274,503,631	125,029,937
3	19,152,634	20,063,567	27,209,906	18,625,687	30,229,599	15,347,418	32,858,183	29,899,824
4	13,048,262	11,239,520	21,956,045	21,137,270	20,062,897	12,907,551	24,690,113	30,699,733
5	21,841,789	18,628,273	25,089,026	25,882,507	26,643,877	17,631,939	35,998,504	37,525,483
6	8,609,249	7,422,954	13,669,331	9,792,714	12,372,991	6,077,823	15,390,786	13,403,779
7	17,208,674	20,527,285	34,204,320	23,332,695	33,633,126	15,240,795	42,049,155	35,170,221
8	8,878,415	10,671,136	11,229,775	11,970,614	13,212,180	11,327,649	18,756,055	13,223,534
9	5,539,252	5,636,301	7,295,523	6,538,978	6,649,796	4,055,001	7,592,573	7,122,758
TOTAL	229,849,691	281,769,415	339,720,993	283,303,528	405,601,833	275,312,775	468,434,339	306,342,530
WYOMING								
TOTAL	9,337,211	39,477,240	33,895,475	38,899,910	41,761,857	49,167,881	52,087,414	33,081,181
U.S. TOTAL	13,808.2 mil.	14,560.6 mil.	17,253.6 mil.	16,989.8 mil.	20,210.7 mil.	17,323.9 mil.	23,166.6 mil.	17,204.9 mil.

Appendix A lists the congressional districts which represent the county in which the state capital is located, and those congressional districts which represent only portions of a county. Appendix C lists the programs included in each functional policy category.

Table 5.6 Outlays for Employment, Labor, and Training Programs by Congressional District, 1983-1990

Congressional District	1983	1984	1985	1986	1987	1988	1989	1990 (est.)
ALABAMA								
1	6,627,186	19,510,563	20,821,400	20,247,332	20,890,001	21,352,042	21,884,335	23,298,950
2	119,891,466	185,968,078	152,088,518	156,841,051	153,066,019	162,190,616	161,583,713	130,215,676
3	751,792	8,623,057	9,670,989	9,186,602	9,240,403	9,746,390	8,682,043	8,848,136
4	2,401,199	9,009,069	10,264,643	9,844,683	10,195,965	10,339,049	11,126,900	12,752,572
5	3,267,251	8,444,840	8,814,889	9,188,069	9,029,929	8,275,999	8,614,010	8,983,004
6	10,197,680	25,555,229	26,442,016	26,860,169	27,910,879	28,083,011	28,755,373	29,925,590
7	2,220,043	16,204,881	16,298,831	16,723,997	17,626,305	18,301,921	18,900,688	20,888,028
TOTAL	145,356,617	273,315,717	244,401,286	248,891,903	247,959,501	258,289,028	259,547,062	234,911,956
ALASKA								
TOTAL	42,217,297	49,574,323	49,491,540	46,747,691	52,338,595	51,535,865	53,547,093	42,955,824
ARIZONA								
1	40,745,826	70,803,456	62,662,182	56,580,373	60,572,218	64,626,468	63,699,169	49,567,960
2	22,441,783	46,320,931	42,515,621	44,755,117	46,239,534	49,048,623	55,677,502	80,179,062
3	605,834	9,696,462	9,314,184	10,077,326	10,965,318	11,840,955	12,614,945	13,826,533
4	38,857,836	66,473,701	55,160,754	61,394,854	65,653,475	68,737,536	67,571,765	45,987,228
5	324,089	21,121,223	21,637,403	22,485,987	23,601,755	25,525,604	25,508,483	27,343,231
TOTAL	102,975,368	214,415,773	191,290,144	195,293,657	207,032,300	219,779,187	225,071,864	216,904,014
ARKANSAS								
1	443,289	13,256,696	13,412,273	13,692,316	14,676,139	14,106,826	14,185,915	18,909,429
2	86,273,956	121,287,174	111,545,872	130,741,873	118,077,708	124,297,891	126,867,696	123,183,980
3	927,453	18,176,989	18,848,522	19,528,124	19,518,432	20,570,781	20,568,526	21,765,078
4	2,013,764	29,463,253	30,359,264	32,120,509	30,917,328	30,661,839	32,573,516	32,795,851
TOTAL	89,658,462	182,184,112	174,165,931	196,082,822	183,189,607	189,637,337	194,195,653	196,654,338
CALIFORNIA								
1	10,011,001	17,630,888	16,509,943	17,296,833	15,505,954	16,829,810	17,802,391	12,646,437
2	5,991,943	12,981,204	16,393,647	17,596,600	19,342,304	18,771,114	19,178,525	20,146,496
3	325,299,795	563,954,855	476,427,897	487,789,084	463,883,935	465,881,226	499,684,655	585,300,304
4	125,582,070	230,354,421	182,716,425	206,538,664	205,868,287	209,405,923	210,448,558	136,727,434
5	6,164,123	10,101,184	11,689,085	12,517,050	12,357,109	13,468,616	13,434,480	12,393,501
6	2,732,112	8,106,402	8,383,631	8,640,003	8,766,249	9,249,453	8,845,922	9,437,048
7	2,950,773	11,293,321	11,309,430	11,877,476	12,769,967	12,833,015	12,520,743	12,491,947
8	5,070,796	13,468,177	13,626,928	14,396,890	14,170,807	14,421,158	14,456,444	13,678,225
9	5,094,650	14,283,764	14,558,512	14,503,285	14,387,607	14,029,355	14,116,556	14,030,885
10	6,176,735	10,896,118	10,193,705	10,766,234	10,268,050	10,687,588	10,664,478	9,781,271
11	3,357,720	8,679,438	8,508,675	9,551,476	9,131,385	9,565,904	10,264,684	12,968,379
12	4,763,787	8,907,964	7,386,637	7,752,809	7,315,308	8,162,077	8,267,537	6,995,648
13	7,205,214	9,013,279	7,780,971	8,281,184	7,632,578	8,802,543	8,832,287	6,683,827
14	4,467,435	30,851,691	28,154,141	28,485,999	27,996,998	28,857,858	30,876,981	32,712,352
15	10,683,412	3,034,678	5,301,473	5,839,912	6,395,688	6,893,847	6,831,918	5,996,779
16	15,898,967	6,389,172	5,847,009	7,301,774	6,652,260	6,969,731	6,888,018	7,053,019
17	9,108,210	14,239,829	12,740,093	12,184,994	12,463,128	13,136,884	13,339,378	11,551,637
18	37,869,987	45,306,703	48,227,951	17,714,071	18,175,985	18,976,743	19,609,785	20,625,070
19	7,815,440	2,940,168	4,749,470	4,320,944	4,387,993	4,272,499	4,374,129	4,455,814
20	2,909,560	15,248,766	16,569,808	17,352,650	17,428,877	17,922,420	18,638,561	18,220,276
21	2,395,777	7,154,668	6,919,606	7,060,324	7,173,762	6,914,881	6,734,296	6,266,888
22	6,289,579	7,419,044	7,372,787	7,092,829	7,457,459	7,323,400	7,389,942	6,923,096
23	5,535,219	7,714,179	7,385,548	7,119,811	7,581,896	7,313,590	7,576,165	6,614,814
24	5,403,480	7,411,980	7,386,638	7,123,533	7,478,698	8,082,138	7,671,064	6,663,815
25	5,950,167	9,232,926	8,476,070	7,595,118	7,938,148	8,822,807	8,080,507	6,607,320
26	4,807,661	6,552,211	6,498,577	6,270,551	6,549,574	6,492,787	6,692,673	5,806,585
27	5,401,929	7,409,852	7,368,736	7,081,458	7,475,045	7,646,354	7,371,967	6,611,683
28	5,428,351	7,408,781	7,386,887	7,080,434	7,441,984	7,306,573	7,750,201	6,619,924
29	5,599,898	7,904,838	7,368,827	7,131,312	7,492,940	8,308,145	7,259,260	6,612,149
30	5,392,938	7,381,532	7,356,045	7,069,672	7,430,673	7,295,468	7,239,181	6,600,679
31	5,565,240	8,364,180	7,553,508	7,281,454	7,770,312	7,882,527	7,506,811	6,616,348
32	5,467,477	7,488,427	7,474,622	7,149,150	7,472,167	7,346,207	8,307,105	6,637,538
33	4,437,640	6,763,955	7,375,848	7,088,704	7,460,971	7,455,408	7,333,269	6,720,390
34	5,407,713	7,417,386	7,376,199	7,089,041	7,451,030	7,315,455	7,259,014	6,618,763
35	169,466	22,816,161	23,088,046	23,952,692	24,833,810	25,357,006	26,282,790	27,571,711
36	59,592,710	105,684,955	87,342,624	96,908,030	98,289,403	100,095,035	101,028,591	77,441,186
37	38,773,516	77,751,403	62,776,354	70,496,971	70,705,866	71,993,860	72,466,382	49,627,293
38	5,056,129	4,790,064	4,640,007	5,262,450	5,292,380	5,315,326	5,151,751	4,697,534
39	2,491,459	4,794,110	4,671,262	5,294,395	5,296,850	5,236,486	5,402,587	4,751,357

Appendix A lists the congressional districts which represent the county in which the state capital is located, and those congressional districts which represent only portions of a county. Appendix C lists the programs included in each functional policy category.

table continues

Table 5.6 **Outlays for Employment, Labor, and Training Programs by Congressional District, 1983-1990 *(continued)***

Congressional District	1983	1984	1985	1986	1987	1988	1989	1990 (est.)
CALIFORNIA *continued*								
40	2,559,552	4,789,708	4,710,043	5,262,059	5,291,987	5,693,563	5,207,269	4,697,186
41	4,063,296	4,442,743	4,743,702	4,770,930	4,971,805	5,053,199	5,173,084	4,924,401
42	5,270,090	6,499,330	6,450,306	6,408,484	6,590,623	6,484,649	6,419,135	6,454,016
43	6,123,636	6,425,831	6,727,009	7,194,913	7,285,238	7,259,957	7,035,112	6,692,303
44	6,081,579	6,490,613	7,146,504	7,238,342	7,626,346	7,812,029	7,852,565	7,385,598
45	8,838,774	6,340,599	7,124,238	8,065,063	7,726,023	8,101,492	7,987,351	8,111,780
TOTAL	811,257,006	1,394,131,496	1,229,795,423	1,260,795,652	1,242,985,459	1,263,046,107	1,303,254,100	1,248,170,704
COLORADO								
1	70,835,558	127,732,592	111,745,018	115,765,588	125,287,996	137,527,585	138,309,848	119,556,592
2	4,252,980	11,368,003	8,718,070	9,989,736	9,972,708	9,551,267	10,116,370	12,024,568
3	4,872,201	23,454,101	22,095,741	23,511,703	25,830,766	25,004,359	25,078,614	26,706,234
4	6,169,833	15,427,826	16,220,590	17,170,226	17,210,571	17,630,421	18,041,584	18,358,280
5	4,309,858	7,315,110	7,522,732	7,689,623	7,637,575	7,807,924	8,273,401	8,866,703
6	804,817	7,342,957	7,546,903	8,237,683	8,913,712	8,667,622	8,513,741	8,479,639
TOTAL	91,245,247	192,640,591	173,849,054	182,364,559	194,853,329	206,189,178	208,333,558	193,992,017
CONNECTICUT								
1	83,319,248	99,648,510	85,152,853	88,155,424	84,672,676	84,023,817	98,576,231	86,438,114
2	321,897	4,708,151	4,547,578	4,652,858	4,529,512	4,569,059	4,481,063	4,685,272
3	3,021,822	13,731,129	14,045,737	14,342,567	15,011,773	15,410,822	14,262,090	15,002,283
4	5,715,359	5,188,989	5,510,496	5,394,353	5,010,364	4,951,941	4,310,115	5,206,114
5	1,708,616	10,604,317	10,613,021	10,878,489	10,893,095	11,260,886	11,227,923	11,580,603
6	139,179	3,072,632	3,038,738	3,097,949	3,036,208	3,037,391	3,162,389	3,256,608
TOTAL	94,226,121	136,953,728	122,908,422	126,521,639	123,153,628	123,253,915	136,019,810	126,168,994
DELAWARE								
TOTAL	26,150,734	46,915,518	43,755,778	45,609,594	45,561,347	45,921,630	46,360,440	47,772,994
DISTRICT OF COLUMBIA								
TOTAL	221,318,794	232,514,376	229,908,355	219,495,002	239,719,642	249,252,120	249,198,065	175,301,801
FLORIDA								
1	3,535,891	7,804,316	8,581,051	9,240,468	9,501,378	9,929,518	10,777,857	11,518,373
2	173,635,723	313,539,240	255,007,066	248,070,356	247,874,209	260,295,991	280,938,010	246,953,093
3	6,588,814	31,143,640	33,597,749	34,761,275	35,904,957	37,552,296	39,936,724	43,267,374
4	2,424,915	25,512,975	26,447,972	27,441,340	29,220,147	30,749,105	31,733,120	33,384,642
5	6,378,951	8,652,154	10,346,876	10,774,611	11,112,067	11,888,884	14,504,472	16,638,805
6	3,335,710	22,486,445	24,444,189	27,034,877	31,324,245	32,222,004	30,075,906	30,714,152
7	6,672,945	14,716,185	14,900,102	16,302,417	18,404,998	18,659,952	19,314,235	20,659,090
8	8,601,109	25,749,636	26,424,846	26,100,310	24,693,767	25,356,427	26,238,863	27,872,952
9	3,205,868	26,763,176	27,721,513	28,562,962	27,821,070	29,162,916	30,766,211	32,366,177
10	7,196,340	18,978,159	20,544,121	21,795,491	23,604,434	23,826,389	24,938,202	28,066,429
11	2,833,131	11,100,733	12,023,596	13,130,061	13,144,892	14,101,319	14,570,616	15,679,932
12	474,433	15,394,500	16,622,147	17,252,319	17,934,676	19,072,592	20,396,408	22,026,784
13	1,512,400	27,642,468	29,458,112	30,879,074	31,368,628	33,698,565	36,217,037	39,246,520
14	812,027	9,786,285	9,902,669	10,034,811	10,523,583	10,365,564	10,612,948	11,118,525
15	7,817,070	8,935,606	8,820,403	8,586,690	8,473,654	8,337,282	8,444,276	8,866,104
16	1,825,907	7,170,368	7,125,786	7,059,331	7,514,151	7,560,311	7,431,925	7,293,710
17	5,978,987	3,715,071	3,575,731	3,610,693	3,958,620	4,507,832	4,971,433	3,924,210
18	6,198,573	3,806,133	3,576,739	3,612,114	3,825,124	4,271,791	3,450,376	3,925,754
19	5,252,915	3,954,888	3,876,840	4,232,895	4,534,089	4,650,047	3,838,534	4,189,193
TOTAL	254,281,708	586,851,979	542,997,510	548,482,096	560,738,689	586,208,785	619,157,154	607,711,817
GEORGIA								
1	1,988,931	19,917,974	20,362,484	21,207,703	22,122,941	23,471,670	23,802,793	25,279,644
2	16,547	49,819,183	52,375,320	23,088,461	12,372,928	11,850,790	24,334,464	12,931,675
3	3,051,366	10,661,872	11,724,751	11,564,787	15,818,878	10,846,873	11,179,783	11,723,465
4	39,587,144	93,949,736	63,782,912	72,438,490	79,964,464	82,468,247	86,519,472	14,078,671
5	98,397,464	71,253,414	73,093,319	95,112,762	104,506,650	101,803,904	103,523,888	169,998,365
6	8,045,479	11,655,026	12,290,753	15,627,035	16,911,241	17,896,198	17,789,175	19,587,159
7	194,696	11,867,521	12,172,682	12,664,471	13,410,476	14,068,883	15,090,278	16,321,407
8	2,777,898	24,965,383	25,030,615	26,117,975	26,956,930	28,024,840	30,707,598	31,934,825
9	1,015,693	6,642,372	6,942,786	7,276,268	8,798,752	8,196,543	8,533,278	9,207,743
10	4,786,758	9,855,866	10,361,754	10,672,758	10,963,820	12,020,442	11,930,275	12,180,242
TOTAL	159,861,976	310,588,347	288,137,376	295,770,710	311,827,081	310,648,390	333,411,004	323,243,195

Appendix A lists the congressional districts which represent the county in which the state capital is located, and those congressional districts which represent only portions of a county. Appendix C lists the programs included in each functional policy category.

table continues

Table 5.6 Outlays for Employment, Labor, and Training Programs by Congressional District, 1983-1990 *(continued)*

Congressional District	1983	1984	1985	1986	1987	1988	1989	1990 (est.)
HAWAII								
1	28,735,283	39,675,492	33,667,337	34,533,686	33,569,958	38,239,510	34,912,978	22,054,623
2	359,833	2,891,155	3,117,415	4,415,729	4,869,157	7,761,722	8,222,076	11,109,695
TOTAL	29,095,116	42,566,647	36,784,752	38,949,415	38,439,115	46,001,232	43,135,054	33,164,317
IDAHO								
1	33,114,562	53,114,266	49,840,656	48,409,864	52,681,356	52,701,915	55,197,358	51,934,953
2	9,412,510	38,657,002	38,408,431	41,244,661	43,160,903	43,055,269	44,592,430	44,476,240
TOTAL	42,527,072	91,771,268	88,249,087	89,654,525	95,842,259	95,757,184	99,789,788	96,411,193
ILLINOIS								
1	22,664,044	31,389,691	29,592,383	26,477,880	32,589,090	34,273,076	33,026,273	35,852,699
2	22,636,071	31,234,329	29,274,166	25,245,518	31,323,716	33,264,824	31,395,758	34,203,199
3	23,047,826	31,240,890	29,280,315	25,250,821	31,330,296	33,271,812	31,402,353	34,210,384
4	9,832,726	24,727,967	24,090,280	22,555,853	25,909,628	26,282,243	25,926,468	27,784,621
5	22,637,817	31,236,738	29,276,424	25,247,465	31,326,132	33,267,390	31,398,180	34,205,837
6	8,538,129	20,110,865	19,567,119	18,296,230	20,807,601	21,826,812	21,699,708	23,304,875
7	23,453,373	31,902,086	30,256,130	25,435,788	31,438,004	34,380,376	31,655,591	34,652,328
8	22,640,565	31,240,530	29,279,977	25,250,530	31,329,934	33,583,905	31,401,991	34,209,989
9	22,974,316	32,165,938	30,031,677	25,959,412	31,982,988	33,632,812	32,214,250	34,215,658
10	10,270,922	17,995,902	17,133,526	15,434,294	18,336,706	19,112,192	18,372,567	19,896,276
11	22,638,864	31,238,183	29,277,778	25,248,633	31,327,581	33,268,929	31,399,632	34,207,420
12	10,115,227	18,246,077	16,801,716	15,534,527	18,299,105	19,094,026	18,326,037	19,986,791
13	13,013,795	21,401,433	21,111,195	19,516,024	22,405,200	23,565,942	23,142,896	24,973,921
14	5,213,341	12,853,073	15,279,467	15,535,818	15,777,400	16,396,115	17,091,903	17,368,534
15	1,602,426	19,197,119	18,758,385	19,406,438	20,267,969	20,530,686	21,334,815	22,354,271
16	2,618,115	10,978,373	11,110,384	11,567,629	11,662,789	11,626,692	11,961,649	12,884,035
17	5,592,006	23,176,504	22,913,195	24,591,892	24,156,022	25,078,115	24,697,627	26,118,993
18	3,725,973	18,171,314	17,584,769	19,669,479	18,068,912	18,741,651	19,080,954	20,089,207
19	1,488,664	24,854,638	24,108,735	24,763,465	25,267,197	26,215,417	26,969,479	28,565,742
20	122,963,652	362,020,046	271,269,483	260,098,047	258,312,358	251,673,074	272,762,623	181,694,112
21	7,889,547	32,647,837	32,536,518	34,277,770	34,961,929	36,141,036	38,021,869	40,728,548
22	1,066,091	36,867,244	36,213,987	38,406,781	39,770,175	40,547,876	41,466,461	41,812,985
TOTAL	386,623,490	894,896,776	784,747,607	743,770,293	806,650,734	825,775,002	834,749,084	783,320,424
INDIANA								
1	4,756,491	18,514,776	18,796,116	19,555,706	20,829,634	19,790,293	20,869,136	22,434,084
2	14,089,739	31,717,322	27,201,928	27,108,024	29,527,893	30,072,925	27,235,353	19,749,201
3	6,939,788	13,563,790	15,022,344	15,397,631	16,007,273	15,830,027	16,671,019	17,816,498
4	6,882,610	22,988,680	21,864,145	23,876,109	23,874,903	23,858,522	24,698,784	25,352,710
5	267,297	21,994,484	22,131,255	22,885,285	23,705,364	24,122,630	25,298,781	26,953,634
6	15,749,461	44,895,368	37,168,712	37,652,110	40,733,228	41,451,919	36,552,795	23,570,270
7	850,339	20,736,268	20,484,769	21,339,424	21,903,308	21,860,152	22,540,815	23,875,830
8	9,425,938	20,502,395	20,089,588	21,951,565	21,532,540	22,137,375	22,470,624	23,842,399
9	299,264	13,525,014	13,800,023	14,035,646	14,142,361	14,553,821	14,966,610	15,685,052
10	56,653,328	147,768,569	117,562,208	119,451,235	131,408,404	133,668,532	123,182,703	137,136,633
TOTAL	115,914,255	356,206,665	314,121,089	323,252,736	343,664,909	347,346,195	334,486,620	336,416,310
IOWA								
1	-416,158	20,188,141	20,461,172	20,710,650	21,141,109	21,113,538	21,697,461	23,093,311
2	1,884,799	16,376,958	16,284,401	16,557,500	16,658,370	16,748,658	17,115,668	18,133,406
3	1,735,291	11,257,273	11,725,165	12,029,685	11,763,800	12,113,313	12,289,752	12,693,245
4	79,546,051	106,843,597	94,450,854	99,579,890	99,931,760	100,097,825	111,077,664	92,075,128
5	113,321	27,369,174	28,314,806	28,933,031	29,803,136	29,738,247	31,232,290	33,594,334
6	1,294,746	13,582,946	13,659,908	14,453,198	14,706,184	14,974,335	15,349,723	16,207,546
TOTAL	84,158,050	195,618,089	184,896,306	192,263,954	194,004,359	194,785,916	208,762,558	195,796,970
KANSAS								
1	123,349	21,628,941	21,570,154	22,498,735	22,585,829	22,399,960	23,453,677	26,486,195
2	53,108,396	96,264,077	89,169,606	91,456,799	93,651,218	96,965,629	106,591,966	103,074,318
3	8,453,506	42,821,572	43,318,507	44,762,709	46,493,966	48,377,509	53,870,782	46,528,910
4	4,140,434	17,379,561	16,662,689	16,573,999	16,973,629	17,156,665	17,071,331	16,926,243
5	269,971	39,613,024	40,576,722	41,228,160	42,146,068	42,417,057	43,084,917	45,384,058
TOTAL	66,095,656	217,707,175	211,297,678	216,520,402	221,850,710	227,316,820	244,072,673	238,399,724

Appendix A lists the congressional districts which represent the county in which the state capital is located, and those congressional districts which represent only portions of a county. Appendix C lists the programs included in each functional policy category.

table continues

Table 5.6 **Outlays for Employment, Labor, and Training Programs by Congressional District, 1983-1990 *(continued)***

Congressional District	1983	1984	1985	1986	1987	1988	1989	1990 (est.)
KENTUCKY								
1	159,956	22,868,966	22,288,273	23,154,723	23,697,633	23,843,971	24,801,338	25,460,062
2	269,093	7,296,374	7,500,567	7,947,949	9,758,335	10,410,462	10,319,736	9,082,100
3	9,316,460	28,628,060	29,328,686	29,718,988	30,359,569	30,745,388	31,492,410	33,103,988
4	156,816	29,455,233	30,039,011	30,578,628	31,188,480	31,782,115	32,930,308	34,651,294
5	466,705	18,784,994	19,376,923	19,846,694	20,284,794	20,022,627	21,247,990	21,450,285
6	106,668,019	160,835,560	129,273,729	135,898,710	145,613,210	145,291,475	154,562,629	118,664,924
7	14,013,734	30,193,255	31,890,082	33,241,521	33,694,291	34,298,788	37,552,686	39,985,171
TOTAL	131,050,783	298,062,442	269,697,271	280,387,213	294,596,312	296,394,826	312,907,097	282,397,825
LOUISIANA								
1	181,376	12,011,954	10,673,653	10,138,867	10,296,603	10,491,929	10,269,579	12,061,097
2	7,329,708	13,865,682	14,177,003	14,809,786	15,196,373	15,827,768	16,461,903	17,796,466
3	3,693,785	6,417,292	8,607,288	9,842,709	10,413,313	11,078,248	11,632,366	12,704,343
4	2,267,563	16,208,124	16,758,258	17,424,628	17,640,146	18,676,813	18,326,532	19,481,419
5	1,850,429	10,802,502	10,920,324	11,915,785	11,853,980	12,390,392	11,990,438	12,779,159
6	108,798,765	165,764,403	149,064,897	184,144,014	180,511,415	198,358,234	201,985,889	155,635,128
7	5,530,695	11,358,343	11,787,235	12,311,424	13,164,109	14,950,287	14,284,612	14,269,159
8	2,361,541	9,620,582	9,799,511	11,303,989	13,459,434	12,402,485	14,905,840	13,072,531
TOTAL	132,013,862	246,048,881	231,788,168	271,891,203	272,535,372	294,176,155	299,857,160	257,799,302
MAINE								
1	35,161,035	60,085,063	59,471,221	62,218,244	60,944,414	56,643,653	56,847,548	64,952,728
2	4,964,910	20,845,739	21,328,441	24,180,922	23,330,198	25,479,710	24,304,182	25,469,572
TOTAL	40,125,945	80,930,802	80,799,662	86,399,166	84,274,612	82,123,363	81,151,730	90,422,299
MARYLAND								
1	155,732	8,202,897	8,714,300	9,167,160	9,410,917	9,619,310	10,211,004	10,780,458
2	10,640,928	10,754,299	11,427,971	11,857,867	12,229,724	8,865,504	8,312,482	8,906,367
3	36,101,089	78,328,774	68,649,128	61,555,689	60,538,122	62,833,236	61,823,313	47,377,226
4	887,391	10,072,623	9,980,230	12,292,234	10,726,734	11,150,880	16,195,167	22,753,538
5	3,769,106	7,494,721	7,476,906	8,410,332	9,076,205	9,845,621	9,849,724	8,816,195
6	9,266,807	43,629,210	44,482,176	41,279,474	44,731,841	44,280,634	45,966,195	50,145,071
7	47,461,205	92,996,473	80,388,109	92,312,302	88,196,487	91,280,998	93,988,501	110,323,591
8	2,622,437	9,531,877	6,343,416	9,827,529	19,242,561	9,848,320	7,407,275	8,944,434
TOTAL	110,904,694	261,010,874	237,462,236	246,702,588	254,152,591	247,724,503	253,753,660	268,046,881
MASSACHUSETTS								
1	1,767,752	8,909,938	8,856,530	9,644,531	9,044,794	8,837,359	9,099,408	9,202,757
2	4,011,134	7,910,126	7,500,489	7,474,303	6,853,888	7,274,903	7,314,062	7,212,695
3	3,236,858	5,420,199	5,687,286	6,055,021	5,912,865	6,238,234	5,694,449	5,676,998
4	1,638,353	5,231,368	6,949,688	5,521,384	6,215,492	5,332,610	5,244,241	5,597,392
5	2,350,704	6,823,593	6,949,984	6,876,109	6,929,868	6,873,751	7,039,960	7,106,159
6	4,238,412	4,705,335	4,733,355	5,054,196	4,992,362	5,156,811	5,116,850	5,591,469
7	13,900,337	29,074,579	25,640,968	27,368,170	27,438,532	27,260,830	25,550,880	26,165,400
8	42,570,896	78,032,284	67,309,013	52,940,795	54,304,057	53,666,198	51,867,577	46,738,954
9	68,221,354	79,692,959	69,947,872	80,785,045	79,462,336	77,628,877	73,269,125	88,906,005
10	2,838,519	6,677,573	6,771,909	8,211,851	7,482,249	7,362,299	7,225,485	7,340,872
11	24,054,473	38,633,415	31,535,643	34,017,807	38,152,877	36,596,564	34,364,258	34,478,777
TOTAL	168,828,790	271,111,369	241,882,738	243,949,211	246,789,319	242,228,437	231,786,295	244,017,477
MICHIGAN								
1	36,680,163	30,031,197	29,193,674	21,502,037	32,297,355	44,238,764	41,393,862	39,410,035
2	14,999,680	13,912,169	13,732,910	11,711,611	14,658,380	15,614,057	16,320,687	16,509,807
3	8,383,534	14,350,804	30,687,707	26,783,576	22,828,279	21,242,951	49,139,775	124,416,358
4	135,818	10,149,463	10,808,721	10,633,958	10,992,029	10,559,445	10,622,976	10,646,969
5	9,194,143	11,224,084	11,369,357	11,573,453	11,629,149	11,990,636	12,415,579	12,801,883
6	119,264,759	290,437,356	173,880,643	158,462,408	147,517,208	151,266,733	172,733,019	33,897,226
7	10,580,937	4,129,392	4,121,321	4,447,498	5,220,278	5,068,248	4,826,522	4,991,373
8	5,727,737	8,276,666	7,509,696	8,271,710	8,617,967	9,005,558	9,731,277	10,681,119
9	5,943,374	13,448,621	13,658,263	13,692,819	13,672,676	14,484,430	15,537,861	15,902,808
10	16,993,770	50,601,401	47,312,997	55,796,135	59,507,886	54,029,878	39,369,230	11,914,861
11	3,295,394	21,107,936	20,219,642	22,351,486	22,547,873	23,090,234	23,736,377	26,543,774
12	13,048,815	6,278,953	8,182,008	8,851,961	9,374,402	9,732,200	10,286,665	11,056,145

Appendix A lists the congressional districts which represent the county in which the state capital is located, and those congressional districts which represent only portions of a county. Appendix C lists the programs included in each functional policy category.

table continues

Table 5.6 Outlays for Employment, Labor, and Training Programs by Congressional District, 1983-1990 *(continued)*

Congressional District	1983	1984	1985	1986	1987	1988	1989	1990 (est.)
MICHIGAN *continued*								
13	35,699,418	29,341,771	29,127,882	20,445,717	32,377,793	43,847,308	40,800,862	39,410,035
14	13,356,268	12,842,854	13,034,950	9,854,420	14,463,841	18,916,051	18,038,347	17,757,223
15	28,800,265	23,962,538	24,183,516	17,105,577	26,742,857	36,547,229	33,655,105	32,594,024
16	29,033,153	21,136,640	22,229,515	16,854,361	24,705,341	32,095,121	30,391,952	29,789,248
17	17,214,544	15,915,936	16,069,630	11,906,637	17,718,828	23,408,447	22,122,820	21,556,496
18	58,767	3,740,523	3,808,763	3,959,612	4,050,005	4,244,303	4,525,735	4,659,978
TOTAL	368,410,538	580,888,302	479,131,195	434,204,975	478,922,145	529,381,593	555,648,653	464,539,361
MINNESOTA								
1	658,820	9,903,438	10,403,102	10,385,911	10,502,206	10,655,832	10,660,786	10,818,339
2	94,831	13,962,882	14,036,610	14,038,244	14,600,270	15,370,024	15,643,347	17,764,026
3	48,406	15,816,703	16,013,093	16,321,869	16,746,318	17,054,495	17,914,347	19,160,322
4	91,883,417	132,074,511	116,096,901	99,850,286	120,206,128	120,079,103	119,184,244	113,144,501
5	6,474,196	22,423,884	21,780,802	21,804,714	23,360,290	23,752,836	23,578,654	23,259,551
6	503,206	49,488,101	50,318,503	51,325,511	52,757,927	53,725,945	54,969,914	58,082,035
7	8,282,579	30,655,057	31,529,907	31,018,474	31,708,168	33,210,763	34,333,973	32,174,533
8	5,114,476	45,480,893	47,707,886	48,490,577	49,422,736	50,442,107	50,234,224	52,943,594
TOTAL	113,059,932	319,805,469	307,886,804	293,235,586	319,304,042	324,291,105	326,519,488	327,346,900
MISSISSIPPI								
1	315,393	11,962,167	12,687,521	12,671,675	13,270,579	13,612,475	15,390,944	15,370,666
2	2,255,446	11,341,151	10,027,660	10,765,524	10,510,116	10,713,433	11,229,413	9,473,018
3	1,163,150	15,684,525	15,154,934	15,395,724	15,573,186	18,078,308	17,141,443	20,358,818
4	79,500,361	123,576,807	108,259,683	118,506,545	123,773,774	129,494,513	129,064,014	104,939,275
5	2,058,486	7,745,099	7,924,481	8,177,264	8,295,272	8,647,484	8,890,518	9,286,157
TOTAL	85,292,836	170,309,749	154,054,280	165,516,732	171,422,927	180,546,213	181,716,332	159,427,934
MISSOURI								
1	2,504,859	23,252,678	24,049,706	24,357,666	25,795,435	25,853,982	26,730,454	27,042,441
2	3,685,118	26,402,640	27,587,823	28,194,962	28,525,134	28,965,738	29,085,727	29,936,033
3	4,098,065	14,622,690	15,595,279	16,122,573	16,145,903	16,387,938	16,781,613	17,530,952
4	89,604,196	165,183,224	146,346,865	138,348,988	132,814,547	146,040,141	155,614,593	105,925,445
5	8,372,212	27,198,343	27,743,176	29,318,147	29,491,737	30,270,498	30,711,701	31,850,448
6	144,756	27,169,391	28,085,934	29,026,103	29,400,812	30,516,065	31,672,636	32,232,037
7	1,621,682	31,663,521	32,204,730	33,253,508	34,024,624	34,712,798	35,844,759	37,983,537
8	27,921,602	21,048,104	21,350,024	22,736,060	22,434,263	22,765,536	23,167,394	24,452,997
9	13,028,583	45,359,708	45,046,933	49,405,988	53,143,819	49,882,525	57,850,626	93,452,695
TOTAL	150,981,072	381,900,299	368,010,470	370,763,996	371,776,275	385,395,222	407,459,502	400,406,584
MONTANA								
1	33,999,488	69,065,339	63,468,245	65,946,757	68,171,973	68,450,022	72,097,695	67,675,521
2	3,436,679	32,747,963	33,345,815	34,742,881	37,438,533	37,085,869	38,467,239	40,778,968
TOTAL	37,436,167	101,813,302	96,814,060	100,689,638	105,610,506	105,535,891	110,564,934	108,454,489
NEBRASKA								
1	35,560,495	69,741,990	66,604,203	69,460,790	68,653,034	71,177,135	74,425,406	75,714,728
2	4,518,847	39,743,739	40,375,506	41,694,224	43,057,070	43,227,481	45,702,949	48,034,535
3	1,128,920	37,462,491	36,797,089	37,691,787	38,432,677	37,770,457	39,011,298	40,447,756
TOTAL	41,208,262	146,948,220	143,776,798	148,846,801	150,142,781	152,175,073	159,139,653	164,197,019
NEVADA								
1	4,030,614	9,387,360	9,577,978	11,469,452	12,328,987	13,188,214	14,136,109	16,648,949
2	24,524,572	56,636,751	50,917,202	52,804,224	53,474,926	53,791,383	54,990,327	60,418,983
TOTAL	28,555,186	66,024,111	60,495,180	64,273,676	65,803,913	66,979,597	69,126,436	77,067,932
NEW HAMPSHIRE								
1	1,001,871	6,111,188	5,951,636	5,964,150	6,056,490	6,242,491	6,778,777	6,598,343
2	21,724,100	34,841,751	32,470,446	32,015,025	30,505,262	32,891,682	35,096,678	35,004,080
TOTAL	22,725,971	40,952,939	38,422,082	37,979,175	36,561,752	39,134,173	41,875,455	41,602,423

Appendix A lists the congressional districts which represent the county in which the state capital is located, and those congressional districts which represent only portions of a county. Appendix C lists the programs included in each functional policy category.

table continues

Table 5.6 Outlays for Employment, Labor, and Training Programs by Congressional District, 1983-1990 *(continued)*

Congressional District	1983	1984	1985	1986	1987	1988	1989	1990 (est.)
NEW JERSEY								
1	5,810,017	11,197,823	10,550,216	11,311,755	11,574,108	11,619,480	12,768,471	13,067,822
2	5,926,506	9,954,813	10,925,560	11,397,157	12,026,614	11,723,353	12,309,060	12,639,727
3	-896,205	13,958,676	14,122,856	14,431,480	14,551,073	14,236,774	14,843,124	15,295,439
4	147,163,929	269,484,322	192,742,385	213,840,594	211,978,158	193,841,723	195,612,630	193,777,338
5	-629,399	9,004,696	8,331,696	8,056,390	7,993,226	7,905,095	8,053,267	8,210,407
6	3,990,929	10,702,762	10,814,501	10,846,258	11,058,416	11,093,429	10,807,668	12,516,710
7	9,199,963	11,097,830	10,115,742	10,217,882	10,107,164	10,001,098	9,914,151	10,400,904
8	5,878,370	6,903,584	6,396,904	6,949,179	7,140,905	6,909,947	6,847,799	6,710,047
9	6,213,850	9,207,838	8,594,944	9,371,202	8,785,086	8,588,909	8,793,756	9,013,617
10	8,802,811	6,028,099	5,656,870	5,948,060	5,722,275	5,266,645	5,668,364	5,754,518
11	5,218,746	7,278,433	7,078,510	6,889,899	6,798,369	6,595,339	6,462,278	6,875,972
12	3,415,165	7,446,420	8,126,289	8,263,097	8,281,867	9,559,708	9,171,603	8,679,615
13	11,658,599	14,826,706	14,956,295	15,497,608	15,842,875	16,175,087	16,511,182	16,882,154
14	8,815,975	21,194,689	21,309,576	20,412,235	20,359,005	19,412,578	18,925,145	19,311,266
TOTAL	220,569,255	408,286,690	329,722,344	353,432,796	352,219,141	332,929,165	336,688,498	339,135,536
NEW MEXICO								
1	36,305,203	32,918,661	35,785,727	47,825,836	33,598,029	37,078,676	36,316,250	40,708,656
2	1,344,127	18,111,389	18,731,735	18,943,036	19,613,071	20,443,146	21,465,976	22,868,481
3	16,289,510	54,043,333	49,377,514	49,986,662	56,148,921	58,119,557	63,985,946	55,877,793
TOTAL	53,938,840	105,073,383	103,894,976	116,755,534	109,360,021	115,641,379	121,768,172	119,454,930
NEW YORK								
1	7,651,680	6,350,152	5,774,493	7,304,976	6,878,342	7,091,022	7,268,741	7,620,622
2	103,925	6,476,924	6,661,253	6,780,976	6,867,616	6,980,120	7,234,074	7,608,738
3	263,287	10,608,319	10,522,962	11,033,723	12,127,828	12,381,281	11,677,083	12,549,503
4	66,078	7,392,245	7,358,313	7,412,375	7,522,460	7,478,530	7,480,074	7,739,499
5	6,975,686	5,469,692	6,254,590	7,502,737	7,508,377	8,281,468	7,793,489	7,723,567
6	675,866	7,361,923	7,260,418	7,119,175	6,936,201	7,230,590	6,705,171	6,822,744
7	62,967	7,384,492	7,290,029	7,148,210	6,964,489	6,758,040	6,760,017	6,850,569
8	282,998	7,204,747	7,233,817	7,067,820	7,013,689	6,877,892	6,778,962	7,117,633
9	62,626	7,344,521	7,278,069	7,109,518	6,926,792	6,721,460	6,723,576	6,813,488
10	609,777	4,089,052	3,794,950	4,217,018	6,913,513	6,104,135	4,966,031	6,416,243
11	65,979	3,684,382	3,647,944	3,556,060	6,590,907	5,662,453	4,576,777	6,479,075
12	1,250,928	4,205,416	4,289,623	4,077,820	6,841,027	6,124,593	5,238,078	6,464,296
13	66,073	3,689,650	4,863,206	3,561,144	6,600,292	5,649,633	4,606,365	6,488,851
14	3,546,902	9,968,631	6,032,965	5,884,421	6,745,230	6,338,910	5,955,061	6,804,219
15	26,998,594	11,414,783	8,833,143	10,256,749	9,879,308	13,024,624	10,279,102	4,879,539
16	27,214,279	12,399,122	10,590,159	10,609,876	10,641,940	12,800,869	9,854,937	4,562,302
17	20,931,879	10,957,445	8,856,330	9,685,048	9,455,779	11,132,559	8,327,244	5,361,557
18	1,907,720	8,172,047	8,052,175	7,050,432	7,651,569	7,255,358	6,966,454	7,532,987
19	146,833	7,933,840	8,257,820	8,116,774	8,320,674	8,293,829	8,136,433	8,723,268
20	3,986,191	11,779,771	11,919,621	11,789,293	11,634,834	11,770,174	12,030,347	12,739,907
21	1,665,967	13,306,155	13,139,533	12,976,461	12,954,864	13,123,252	14,666,564	14,069,624
22	4,835,022	9,265,525	8,324,079	9,009,051	8,962,388	8,924,671	8,924,072	9,170,746
23	329,293,231	658,054,122	507,993,228	563,455,537	544,325,803	524,729,198	530,462,481	498,449,572
24	-498,608,236	16,673,830	16,884,622	17,790,407	17,986,977	17,888,394	18,249,730	19,172,491
25	5,107,952	13,433,071	12,537,725	13,265,262	13,338,666	13,158,555	12,905,411	16,230,773
26	2,609,816	9,924,867	9,304,683	9,871,587	10,038,813	9,967,192	9,727,788	10,302,761
27	4,141,434	16,928,553	16,856,963	17,102,036	17,979,667	17,635,453	17,628,045	18,446,113
28	88,158,125	10,194,024	10,031,834	10,044,896	10,065,154	9,952,895	10,054,649	9,745,449
29	3,332,309	9,382,302	8,880,951	8,996,994	8,847,265	8,789,472	8,666,750	8,168,728
30	7,306,722	9,543,623	8,401,410	9,697,684	9,015,050	8,809,276	9,176,739	7,739,936
31	3,889,750	22,464,364	22,150,829	22,953,091	23,056,691	23,057,713	23,548,118	24,594,838
32	5,303,836	13,099,317	13,085,589	14,417,762	14,258,560	14,189,856	14,130,181	14,153,978
33	7,297,835	25,581,345	25,166,216	26,145,740	26,372,877	26,521,025	27,123,254	28,286,652
34	5,129,920	27,073,623	25,597,977	26,719,825	26,067,412	26,237,881	26,380,953	28,641,576
TOTAL	72,333,949	1,008,811,875	843,127,515	909,730,477	903,291,053	886,942,375	881,002,749	854,471,843
NORTH CAROLINA								
1	584,333	5,030,401	5,180,203	5,626,773	5,692,476	6,352,179	6,380,514	6,916,236
2	904,338	13,396,187	13,809,724	14,324,783	16,192,206	16,039,600	16,452,920	16,990,937
3	121,238	3,959,916	4,166,574	4,919,081	4,389,947	4,380,107	4,935,654	5,518,267
4	157,960,041	222,056,860	175,106,991	179,008,967	176,478,202	170,743,293	178,430,383	178,775,318
5	2,805,955	4,332,029	4,612,949	4,792,195	4,822,886	5,005,652	5,432,274	5,737,187
6	3,813,659	5,984,825	7,599,235	7,567,064	8,158,231	7,306,261	7,329,063	7,652,989
7	5,625,659	12,949,585	11,550,360	11,840,820	12,131,341	12,534,486	13,406,461	13,278,179
8	206,451	22,566,270	23,199,483	24,702,099	24,881,520	25,314,395	26,665,466	28,481,385
9	2,367,147	7,306,233	7,668,500	8,016,597	8,280,376	8,550,427	8,775,808	9,175,918
10	1,714,558	2,938,219	3,161,276	3,125,057	3,220,274	3,498,954	3,725,541	3,810,359
11	3,957,773	13,737,319	13,463,761	13,455,044	13,729,613	13,991,312	14,472,511	13,057,870
TOTAL	180,061,152	314,257,844	269,519,056	277,378,480	277,977,072	273,716,665	286,006,595	289,394,646

Appendix A lists the congressional districts which represent the county in which the state capital is located, and those congressional districts which represent only portions of a county. Appendix C lists the programs included in each functional policy category.

table continues

Table 5.6 Outlays for Employment, Labor, and Training Programs by Congressional District, 1983-1990 *(continued)*

Congressional District	1983	1984	1985	1986	1987	1988	1989	1990 (est.)
NORTH DAKOTA								
TOTAL	30,441,208	64,506,353	59,141,815	63,793,843	64,635,102	67,033,872	65,941,943	71,084,455
OHIO								
1	5,411,962	17,130,096	16,660,720	17,427,844	17,625,549	17,714,663	18,061,704	18,895,375
2	5,910,524	13,243,188	13,545,621	14,040,642	13,820,137	14,020,653	14,325,198	14,928,344
3	5,459,293	4,731,572	3,048,088	4,414,803	4,569,941	4,880,124	5,246,635	5,339,226
4	1,519,187	17,162,712	16,988,454	17,675,220	17,734,908	17,580,857	17,912,326	18,701,861
5	1,859,158	21,184,788	21,585,911	22,258,390	23,907,351	23,713,222	24,773,325	25,901,768
6	2,030,174	23,609,605	23,684,075	25,076,444	25,033,775	24,915,175	26,045,824	27,849,673
7	3,029,191	18,251,061	18,456,142	19,119,687	19,440,741	19,859,429	20,465,403	21,388,881
8	1,981,303	7,971,086	7,666,159	8,428,720	8,495,898	8,443,414	9,049,841	9,674,621
9	9,113,643	28,297,314	28,632,737	29,518,211	30,593,645	30,154,496	30,911,913	90,956,718
10	25,789,625	73,938,656	73,723,062	81,526,241	85,846,057	79,232,215	97,038,752	172,402,025
11	4,791,743	25,424,692	25,895,423	26,877,976	27,770,237	28,504,148	29,272,050	30,426,601
12	94,392,236	172,715,943	150,777,852	118,754,880	142,027,230	148,831,710	139,264,480	70,341,353
13	4,425,173	19,492,697	20,215,081	20,666,463	22,203,974	22,568,306	23,554,450	23,812,658
14	6,276,783	6,039,742	8,671,596	8,875,265	9,049,535	9,094,958	9,248,057	9,224,767
15	130,759,412	191,949,678	162,451,030	122,891,408	156,394,264	165,220,374	152,813,799	46,145,221
16	5,705,401	17,352,245	17,633,293	18,028,159	18,484,994	18,983,835	19,981,941	21,314,506
17	9,307,866	19,024,199	19,785,115	20,688,884	21,128,083	21,114,308	21,380,371	22,088,130
18	1,080,459	19,866,443	20,494,779	21,203,744	21,452,673	21,813,612	22,497,868	23,957,390
19	7,584,461	16,184,773	16,081,233	16,642,245	17,249,400	17,372,206	17,593,667	17,988,888
20	6,431,067	15,808,523	16,316,124	16,813,185	17,415,243	17,641,978	17,589,022	18,405,764
21	6,878,052	16,700,063	16,227,451	16,785,073	17,378,436	17,744,500	17,902,763	17,978,510
TOTAL	339,736,712	746,079,077	698,539,946	647,713,483	717,622,071	729,404,184	734,929,387	707,722,281
OKLAHOMA								
1	4,691,020	10,026,848	9,600,782	9,934,655	10,499,932	10,779,196	11,309,413	10,566,371
2	10,603,730	18,561,884	15,347,468	15,817,218	15,402,573	16,954,680	15,959,840	13,032,844
3	5,347,593	15,474,221	14,105,164	14,093,307	13,905,291	14,568,451	14,732,420	12,412,179
4	12,029,466	14,966,579	15,109,490	20,118,394	17,753,439	17,468,533	18,969,311	12,807,782
5	57,414,646	71,246,689	70,672,483	81,741,397	65,813,543	64,051,241	70,004,408	39,034,712
6	24,716,264	38,511,898	41,270,571	58,558,108	53,183,984	50,903,592	58,146,687	81,536,866
TOTAL	114,802,719	168,788,119	166,105,958	200,263,079	176,558,762	174,725,693	189,122,079	169,390,755
OREGON								
1	22,372,927	13,976,537	14,105,918	15,212,186	14,858,129	15,325,108	16,173,368	16,875,360
2	8,762,725	24,610,162	25,120,927	27,464,476	27,165,628	27,563,969	28,611,901	30,478,061
3	10,966,652	30,806,298	30,363,396	32,954,880	30,935,497	32,969,918	32,076,091	36,146,267
4	5,358,423	18,739,637	19,322,937	20,149,446	21,402,921	21,141,178	22,152,757	23,408,549
5	68,849,948	132,775,931	112,211,915	114,171,285	111,121,369	111,235,022	108,621,322	93,272,846
TOTAL	116,310,676	220,908,565	201,125,093	209,952,273	205,483,544	208,235,196	207,635,439	200,181,083
PENNSYLVANIA								
1	6,398,622	14,457,964	15,339,246	14,988,395	14,602,820	14,298,766	14,825,449	14,176,653
2	6,413,398	13,277,308	14,394,388	14,201,880	13,987,302	14,352,605	14,062,507	14,234,769
3	6,919,288	13,540,672	14,321,679	14,281,780	13,958,608	14,301,725	13,952,026	14,149,351
4	1,482,487	25,279,527	25,751,380	26,503,379	27,015,496	27,147,525	28,382,335	33,016,933
5	2,105,593	13,133,694	14,064,743	14,453,113	14,939,734	15,762,457	16,409,748	17,384,460
6	4,739,722	27,898,598	28,137,804	28,229,029	28,537,174	28,444,468	29,037,993	30,231,436
7	4,746,415	18,933,020	19,054,786	20,172,211	20,694,205	21,655,375	22,823,385	24,291,148
8	3,632,895	10,108,651	11,332,102	11,855,274	12,061,477	12,485,367	13,237,053	14,225,748
9	7,269,335	84,075,355	82,595,989	85,001,801	84,979,906	85,184,660	86,225,336	90,676,839
10	2,893,551	30,819,273	30,534,483	30,061,888	29,974,220	29,788,872	29,975,904	30,812,871
11	5,374,735	21,108,692	21,887,230	21,969,934	22,437,737	22,012,652	21,950,091	22,758,368
12	-393,465	29,688,607	28,899,896	31,129,543	31,836,401	32,267,607	34,005,497	35,195,657
13	6,218,894	9,772,859	12,481,829	12,679,664	13,039,032	13,367,209	13,587,439	14,249,894
14	6,534,373	29,291,525	30,499,888	31,858,177	32,159,991	33,941,618	33,354,350	33,233,563
15	5,801,134	18,351,950	17,115,118	19,608,099	19,294,825	19,677,590	20,466,183	21,428,680
16	3,574,011	9,296,108	8,895,692	9,849,994	9,267,697	10,312,515	10,793,100	11,426,353
17	287,855,261	510,584,428	440,752,902	450,057,132	439,943,654	422,002,467	417,591,409	411,687,882
18	4,252,878	29,199,523	29,437,487	30,083,325	30,783,267	31,010,186	31,729,513	33,095,884
19	2,901,704	18,275,505	19,518,102	19,425,274	19,952,045	20,559,449	21,594,709	22,705,071
20	3,252,412	27,812,136	28,098,670	28,762,402	29,442,061	29,648,779	30,472,518	31,769,887
21	4,426,341	27,616,694	27,484,072	28,989,061	29,997,843	29,512,089	29,556,353	31,134,585
22	4,606,475	22,800,050	25,584,666	26,393,775	27,609,630	27,917,134	29,295,759	31,167,655
23	1,344,501	23,273,959	23,585,922	24,138,777	24,716,029	27,089,876	25,819,577	26,896,351
TOTAL	382,350,560	1,028,596,098	969,768,076	994,693,906	991,231,154	982,740,992	989,148,234	1,009,950,036

Appendix A lists the congressional districts which represent the county in which the state capital is located, and those congressional districts which represent only portions of a county. Appendix C lists the programs included in each functional policy category.

table continues

Table 5.6 Outlays for Employment, Labor, and Training Programs by Congressional District, 1983-1990 *(continued)*

Congressional District	1983	1984	1985	1986	1987	1988	1989	1990 (est.)
RHODE ISLAND								
1	19,978,958	24,461,898	21,945,706	24,075,440	22,498,282	22,759,170	24,512,578	23,890,085
2	18,348,750	26,013,471	23,154,064	20,680,484	19,482,185	19,928,846	20,836,737	22,170,693
TOTAL	38,327,708	50,475,369	45,099,770	44,755,924	41,980,467	42,688,016	45,349,315	46,060,777
SOUTH CAROLINA								
1	1,441,268	7,488,829	7,159,804	7,346,910	7,601,791	7,998,633	8,170,694	9,725,964
2	101,224,127	129,259,770	104,179,917	104,100,285	109,457,714	105,739,164	115,852,940	135,695,032
3	129,792	7,589,572	7,743,603	8,204,866	9,890,192	10,417,224	9,446,451	10,127,835
4	160,894	11,346,709	11,563,686	11,863,393	12,205,614	12,745,504	13,498,495	14,426,271
5	200,304	5,551,474	5,721,097	6,362,286	5,993,900	6,749,650	6,896,778	6,987,112
6	166,845	12,869,979	13,175,653	14,206,518	14,661,975	15,166,450	16,320,191	17,363,307
TOTAL	103,323,230	174,106,333	149,543,760	152,084,258	159,811,186	158,816,625	170,185,549	194,325,521
SOUTH DAKOTA								
TOTAL	19,475,585	49,918,225	41,596,602	45,052,517	44,319,542	44,058,898	45,997,399	47,465,939
TENNESSEE								
1	1,609,641	12,274,158	12,596,224	13,327,989	13,850,802	14,335,287	14,983,148	15,913,140
2	4,006,521	19,849,570	20,895,796	20,891,874	21,274,217	22,974,602	22,702,488	23,391,300
3	3,736,618	14,661,465	15,258,188	15,631,438	16,445,119	16,728,904	17,749,378	18,393,106
4	222,243	9,007,687	8,948,160	9,183,250	9,496,978	9,368,283	9,805,653	10,763,108
5	90,605,470	182,961,876	161,740,204	162,707,217	150,844,736	165,376,749	168,405,635	150,996,344
6	200,795	6,211,396	6,256,565	7,186,017	7,338,967	7,942,260	7,432,753	8,029,262
7	2,319,636	11,207,505	11,317,401	11,568,451	11,755,532	12,792,024	12,694,849	13,470,957
8	1,623,110	16,908,399	17,491,605	17,463,048	18,540,525	18,067,879	19,073,317	20,063,003
9	6,383,524	16,976,016	17,313,974	17,832,765	17,558,834	18,164,219	18,577,093	19,276,024
TOTAL	110,707,559	290,058,071	271,818,117	275,792,049	267,105,710	285,750,207	291,424,314	280,296,243
TEXAS								
1	196,044	16,741,053	16,776,616	17,519,522	17,706,636	17,658,342	18,333,176	19,662,928
2	11,182,190	26,293,002	23,614,847	24,570,143	25,485,562	27,446,980	28,625,055	23,922,594
3	92,396	5,963,102	5,841,317	6,165,101	5,965,759	5,970,648	6,156,724	6,471,817
4	5,678,140	23,170,168	23,468,908	24,087,829	24,627,517	24,871,485	26,655,094	28,567,980
5	10,523,300	4,162,461	5,914,823	5,892,450	6,004,348	5,946,168	6,543,430	6,449,720
6	214,431	26,354,523	27,020,268	27,649,885	28,392,441	29,764,041	31,180,582	33,184,805
7	5,425,149	8,252,801	9,734,668	10,169,335	10,552,485	10,862,099	11,264,382	11,942,688
8	2,673,253	8,612,698	9,732,357	10,089,113	10,555,112	10,769,173	11,258,057	11,954,380
9	6,408,153	9,706,151	12,491,834	12,279,270	12,518,454	13,722,906	13,258,042	14,047,763
10	280,096,019	449,726,092	388,766,565	486,758,952	459,123,940	547,185,935	556,149,930	455,123,607
11	3,696,894	17,305,070	17,698,578	18,232,728	19,088,822	25,264,609	20,393,009	23,538,666
12	7,212,815	13,210,726	15,484,447	16,549,508	16,305,795	16,515,070	17,019,354	17,981,553
13	3,446,556	19,198,009	20,342,226	21,210,405	22,070,279	22,890,774	23,914,512	25,237,528
14	4,083,875	12,917,118	15,012,994	15,636,909	14,191,848	14,970,733	15,563,761	16,320,295
15	8,076,969	6,587,936	6,974,744	8,583,815	8,511,714	8,442,194	8,390,740	9,121,536
16	8,281,440	22,713,401	23,353,771	23,782,847	24,006,401	24,204,810	25,316,095	26,988,719
17	2,522,042	12,097,115	12,580,107	12,784,447	13,110,782	13,348,387	13,782,034	14,530,641
18	2,721,370	8,680,587	9,883,471	10,158,138	10,649,288	10,855,389	11,467,956	11,933,411
19	2,005,304	5,044,229	5,999,730	6,250,013	6,666,959	8,090,325	7,020,723	7,575,899
20	714,946	10,690,859	11,459,641	11,333,346	11,343,038	12,546,955	11,440,073	11,987,969
21	12,723,174	11,289,292	10,873,109	10,653,356	11,040,700	11,358,260	11,755,443	12,582,099
22	1,286,535	7,276,857	8,118,924	8,413,160	8,567,365	9,103,504	8,982,907	9,752,637
23	2,297,292	11,527,873	12,934,363	13,800,439	14,881,778	14,558,539	14,736,913	15,810,088
24	74,935	17,797,329	6,677,011	6,910,810	6,894,866	6,884,805	7,474,542	7,446,597
25	2,681,337	8,595,928	9,716,188	10,070,182	10,532,453	10,741,669	11,337,022	11,920,017
26	692,659	10,882,626	11,282,607	11,699,958	11,974,323	12,684,805	12,853,152	12,977,073
27	905,276	8,288,014	8,380,131	8,672,896	9,348,565	9,175,936	9,383,409	10,040,989
TOTAL	385,912,494	783,085,022	730,134,247	839,924,560	820,117,227	925,834,543	940,256,116	857,074,001
UTAH								
1	3,994,026	37,153,211	50,815,419	38,540,386	37,709,101	37,545,720	39,924,036	41,217,152
2	57,376,602	86,424,412	87,015,547	92,158,250	86,952,705	93,442,583	82,915,825	83,651,320
3	2,723,131	13,986,825	13,486,678	15,288,262	13,718,708	14,235,883	14,892,695	16,034,901
TOTAL	64,093,759	137,564,448	151,317,644	145,986,898	138,380,514	145,224,186	137,732,556	140,903,373
VERMONT								
TOTAL	21,752,426	39,359,382	34,647,508	39,345,543	38,976,616	36,756,050	38,091,531	39,489,268

Appendix A lists the congressional districts which represent the county in which the state capital is located, and those congressional districts which represent only portions of a county. Appendix C lists the programs included in each functional policy category.

table continues

Table 5.6 Outlays for Employment, Labor, and Training Programs by Congressional District, 1983-1990 *(continued)*

Congressional District	1983	1984	1985	1986	1987	1988	1989	1990 (est.)
VIRGINIA								
1	4,575,719	15,214,491	15,742,529	16,255,493	16,797,667	17,351,741	18,305,179	19,148,792
2	448,889	10,994,204	10,874,597	13,344,144	12,322,281	13,024,228	13,868,870	14,724,215
3	101,272,658	170,972,176	149,644,038	147,541,464	157,672,456	161,216,465	162,595,913	165,866,248
4	1,421,797	16,911,866	16,923,752	18,165,840	18,009,410	18,106,691	19,270,041	20,550,001
5	284,335	18,301,423	18,566,010	19,901,025	20,686,626	20,442,790	21,675,491	23,057,794
6	2,438,998	57,254,350	58,680,741	60,285,210	63,219,154	66,377,321	68,310,595	71,651,695
7	-131,617	14,579,729	15,916,772	14,045,690	14,764,712	14,861,038	15,246,656	16,379,391
8	1,510,251	9,838,397	9,952,484	10,940,623	9,660,636	10,132,472	9,922,269	10,046,178
9	395,648	16,737,682	17,907,463	17,963,107	18,000,477	17,992,968	18,934,663	22,675,684
10	91,570,457	93,131,302	93,861,558	90,340,222	94,919,553	94,358,352	98,312,090	7,506,206
TOTAL	203,787,136	423,935,620	408,069,944	408,782,817	426,052,972	433,864,066	446,441,768	371,606,205
WASHINGTON								
1	8,244,372	11,026,122	10,520,532	12,395,739	13,009,807	13,722,441	13,790,249	13,761,800
2	2,888,516	11,965,553	12,591,234	13,362,948	13,601,642	14,255,130	14,054,496	14,600,264
3	111,779,166	187,909,158	162,606,387	158,056,139	153,712,656	169,470,862	172,162,297	133,473,665
4	8,539,570	14,491,928	15,727,936	15,708,994	17,328,518	17,904,628	17,155,010	18,591,198
5	6,150,530	33,265,932	32,923,466	32,890,369	34,119,448	33,923,136	34,555,249	35,601,955
6	7,910,829	16,095,639	15,458,287	16,176,781	16,489,041	16,218,528	16,908,295	16,062,142
7	8,186,183	12,730,290	13,705,923	13,366,080	14,424,164	15,164,595	17,159,988	20,416,371
8	7,618,907	12,768,958	12,521,500	14,214,577	15,023,270	15,237,284	15,035,049	13,647,660
TOTAL	161,318,074	300,253,580	276,055,265	276,171,626	277,708,546	295,896,604	300,820,633	266,155,055
WEST VIRGINIA								
1	140,619	19,304,675	20,180,089	21,931,731	21,559,435	24,449,958	22,703,922	28,996,875
2	246,036	35,437,621	37,250,251	37,815,580	38,940,968	40,002,374	41,536,079	44,348,706
3	65,480,538	103,337,140	95,959,290	97,917,661	100,063,830	100,476,160	99,005,812	81,322,351
4	579,606	41,994,063	42,746,929	43,685,363	45,639,119	47,236,003	49,278,039	52,759,256
TOTAL	66,446,799	200,073,499	196,136,559	201,350,335	206,203,352	212,164,495	212,523,852	207,427,188
WISCONSIN								
1	5,293,337	7,505,313	5,389,340	6,467,299	7,040,632	6,658,870	6,915,902	7,203,736
2	114,157,927	202,041,969	159,614,720	132,316,620	168,144,101	161,382,060	161,955,545	148,851,377
3	2,248,952	13,882,874	14,203,112	14,939,581	15,557,696	15,743,453	16,412,897	20,042,611
4	5,285,417	13,034,813	11,727,147	12,215,752	11,697,703	12,387,146	12,176,131	12,528,647
5	6,645,911	14,907,696	12,845,722	13,382,076	12,966,696	13,417,416	13,329,697	13,526,670
6	2,128,384	15,273,104	15,692,135	16,458,426	16,954,172	17,491,687	18,059,211	18,865,577
7	6,092,228	30,937,793	32,076,058	31,923,338	33,837,200	33,337,541	34,730,466	35,579,903
8	2,178,168	16,722,903	16,328,736	17,489,541	17,788,319	18,062,187	18,602,071	18,544,393
9	3,471,585	6,385,918	6,514,971	6,948,923	7,134,383	7,392,597	7,738,558	8,221,815
TOTAL	147,501,908	320,692,382	274,391,941	252,141,556	291,120,901	285,872,957	289,920,478	283,364,728
WYOMING								
TOTAL	17,218,162	60,140,596	56,476,878	58,339,664	60,583,697	59,871,990	61,664,668	63,207,567
U.S. TOTAL	7,044.0 mil.	15,279.6 mil.	13,897.2 mil.	14,228.7 mil.	14,532.4 mil.	14,885.0 mil.	15,217.2 mil.	14,541.2 mil.

Appendix A lists the congressional districts which represent the county in which the state capital is located, and those congressional districts which represent only portions of a county. Appendix C lists the programs included in each functional policy category.

Table 5.7 Outlays for Environmental Quality Programs by Congressional District, 1983-1990

Congressional District	1983	1984	1985	1986	1987	1988	1989	1990 (est.)
ALABAMA								
1	7,150,020	2,123,216	6,313,500	2,864,057	127,430	12,329,210	2,726,958	2,887,020
2	12,387,950	9,633,669	20,324,250	8,377,766	11,463,938	27,179,727	15,641,966	12,660,965
3	19,218,615	9,280,394	8,935,426	13,879,015	9,639,567	14,703,066	14,347,921	20,139,987
4	10,512,321	16,480,957	6,212,299	1,703,854	5,719,964	7,424,376	2,690,676	4,201,032
5	5,467,005	7,158,209	6,629,548	11,239,183	3,119,794	7,173,026	1,211,041	2,364,524
6	19,933,775	17,919,034	21,868,773	13,777,868	8,499,972	27,366,213	8,168,332	5,587,800
7	9,296,781	9,722,108	7,286,168	3,911,888	3,693,822	7,450,579	3,140,543	1,958,551
TOTAL	83,966,467	72,317,587	77,569,964	55,753,631	42,264,487	103,626,197	47,927,437	49,799,878
ALASKA								
TOTAL	23,381,731	25,261,278	14,391,369	15,903,739	12,450,340	16,478,065	20,558,619	2,076,107
ARIZONA								
1	19,937,534	11,230,208	13,506,438	10,593,200	682,200	3,428,842	13,785,366	1,100,816
2	13,771,562	12,371,870	17,549,883	14,057,340	5,702,933	4,635,088	14,264,049	10,473,529
3	1,147,203	2,257,980	3,237,775	6,429,430	4,031,011	11,696,788	4,927,893	0
4	16,608,732	7,542,690	11,017,266	6,405,609	4,367,486	4,591,067	14,249,650	993,311
5	1,690,348	1,142,680	986,785	2,059,370	3,718,349	2,246,083	13,564,154	6,783,252
TOTAL	53,155,380	34,545,427	46,298,147	39,544,949	18,501,980	26,597,869	60,791,111	19,350,908
ARKANSAS								
1	13,119,369	1,291,202	1,290,287	1,139,442	1,660,659	1,995,846	2,942,335	14,974,499
2	26,627,850	7,715,974	12,230,826	6,019,094	4,073,619	4,706,584	26,465,363	5,000,236
3	15,060,356	15,781,342	13,446,042	17,484,381	18,955,026	10,427,208	16,002,552	14,477,558
4	11,877,811	8,269,591	5,902,849	4,750,035	1,666,933	7,209,860	10,621,568	0
TOTAL	66,685,386	33,058,109	32,870,004	29,392,952	26,356,237	24,339,498	56,031,818	34,452,293
CALIFORNIA								
1	10,954,509	6,987,887	5,453,601	6,153,092	4,643,546	5,311,251	3,984,619	-1,443,393
2	4,886,620	12,268,462	1,002,414	6,195,765	286,401	1,262,475	5,707,241	553,245
3	25,662,905	15,808,461	20,845,826	25,428,414	1,194,261	6,809,431	24,656,934	24,567,538
4	10,713,815	7,834,957	8,936,461	9,810,218	4,763,606	4,863,770	13,278,943	8,812,470
5	31,879,300	36,859,902	25,006,727	37,629,812	23,747,598	642,214	16,905,035	33,960,948
6	10,611,856	16,426,690	10,585,996	14,592,385	2,537,169	4,067,450	9,288,793	9,883,866
7	8,116,671	8,108,469	9,537,955	2,700,903	5,765,532	3,481,064	4,448,758	1,427
8	25,046,657	23,033,530	16,673,505	18,508,394	18,794,047	11,272,619	23,419,433	14,916,760
9	7,733,774	6,375,032	5,775,853	6,067,182	52,068	2,821,462	11,271,904	540,582
10	7,729,159	5,524,216	5,992,699	4,382,128	-1,688,555	109,362	7,688,936	191,493
11	15,711,575	5,457,524	5,745,155	4,749,707	828,900	1,750,831	6,663,635	291,382
12	10,513,709	24,215,893	8,955,462	8,975,319	1,021,261	2,289,853	11,068,662	431,516
13	7,178,185	4,471,528	5,449,132	4,389,279	-2,501,526	0	10,573,974	0
14	7,463,634	40,886,541	-221,643	8,456,131	5,878,282	1,658,441	3,269,708	613,485
15	10,222,864	27,653,406	724,821	2,337,875	5,418,924	1,252,667	2,283,004	413,312
16	12,981,546	23,860,273	60,584,354	20,819,332	240,709	470,024	4,292,587	584,403
17	11,537,925	3,661,830	2,509,367	3,146,561	416,792	1,025,356	4,649,196	1,236,662
18	20,655,145	39,230,257	8,843,041	8,749,285	2,104,086	4,304,214	10,713,556	2,227,978
19	4,601,669	6,477,620	5,610,948	3,744,146	4,219,398	3,525,291	8,287,394	6,606
20	5,696,984	4,784,349	4,786,298	2,964,577	457,178	266,844	13,651,085	2,688,920
21	6,226,130	5,963,594	6,479,188	9,156,418	5,283,125	550,057	9,876,911	325,532
22	14,441,028	11,789,289	15,848,225	14,045,214	1,360,472	2,319,342	9,398,136	994,615
23	10,310,887	9,019,961	12,469,193	12,413,562	2,520,106	1,542,087	7,908,048	993,559
24	9,605,535	8,379,820	12,111,012	11,475,026	1,345,142	331,354	6,503,296	993,374
25	9,596,440	8,371,885	11,242,164	11,815,049	1,522,455	-3,966,624	6,569,948	1,195,385
26	8,490,357	7,434,305	10,613,919	10,082,831	1,175,696	290,922	5,709,757	872,161
27	33,181,927	10,349,340	14,125,413	13,031,870	1,484,756	419,805	8,969,276	2,405,684
28	10,607,688	9,384,389	13,252,034	12,760,843	2,573,822	1,300,786	7,001,390	1,396,777
29	12,125,454	11,007,359	13,847,901	12,764,268	1,626,915	454,813	8,711,469	993,158
30	128,965,762	14,328,522	18,720,997	22,444,983	3,153,567	1,828,122	14,655,225	1,693,375
31	16,165,554	13,327,153	18,093,983	16,160,735	1,415,705	331,492	15,492,313	9,684,578
32	17,178,531	9,071,175	12,823,827	12,066,593	1,358,593	332,554	8,452,152	996,972
33	11,713,416	10,278,603	13,990,936	13,118,471	1,345,686	331,598	8,490,676	994,105
34	12,890,332	11,642,385	15,228,507	13,661,016	1,346,196	331,613	10,390,275	994,152
35	8,738,523	23,561,444	8,947,556	5,895,516	68,891	1,661,154	9,494,646	1,387,135
36	7,284,637	7,050,106	14,542,163	9,501,724	1,196,419	1,114,221	20,635,678	12,240,509
37	13,844,510	16,716,840	11,636,359	5,020,759	-5,122,670	6,275,558	9,784,863	8,380,309
38	4,282,570	1,209,431	4,632,370	4,075,676	40,721	14,898	7,802,906	2,401,355
39	6,653,298	3,300,738	6,718,508	5,695,701	40,756	223,954	9,343,186	4,918,673

Appendix A lists the congressional districts which represent the county in which the state capital is located, and those congressional districts which represent only portions of a county. Appendix C lists the programs included in each functional policy category.

table continues

Table 5.7 Outlays for Environmental Quality Programs by Congressional District, 1983-1990 *(continued)*

Congressional District	1983	1984	1985	1986	1987	1988	1989	1990 (est.)
CALIFORNIA *continued*								
40	8,316,931	1,332,405	11,323,561	6,651,622	409,291	1,617,970	13,443,485	8,283,674
41	6,854,458	1,651,862	4,415,754	3,392,345	7,550,103	470,349	9,132,485	0
42	9,488,013	6,200,519	9,279,018	8,668,221	682,958	2,018,087	7,239,369	1,536,365
43	11,999,576	11,674,002	7,331,839	5,629,358	-364,428	429,198	8,520,996	1,589,749
44	11,688,452	2,366,403	8,516,702	6,403,904	537,534	451,727	17,393,005	877,267
45	10,900,759	3,282,379	6,395,309	5,092,398	32,739	388,158	12,763,880	0
TOTAL	651,449,273	538,620,737	495,384,409	450,824,610	110,764,223	78,247,813	449,786,763	166,627,663
COLORADO								
1	16,147,923	5,595,391	16,798,483	3,062,921	9,712,684	20,061,404	17,756,703	8,750,065
2	4,973,315	13,103,155	6,985,326	3,554,044	11,704,843	2,853,461	5,775,888	4,364,378
3	6,688,767	8,482,767	15,134,438	2,300,250	-666,236	1,831,964	2,543,528	928,986
4	10,839,589	5,600,172	3,164,361	5,881,033	4,359,863	11,825,034	6,084,203	8,049,185
5	10,827,434	5,628,988	45,766	1,894,542	2,796,570	24,193,888	4,290,416	108,757
6	2,252,849	2,085,916	451,869	1,505,276	942,242	3,868,111	1,036,198	25,653
TOTAL	51,729,877	40,496,389	42,580,243	18,198,066	28,849,966	64,633,862	37,486,936	22,227,025
CONNECTICUT								
1	11,745,555	11,181,868	15,575,160	12,555,453	20,902,949	53,003,234	21,596,566	18,410,115
2	5,000,944	5,045,570	4,423,498	4,957,864	3,709,759	15,892,134	7,131,629	5,598,766
3	35,256,833	23,518,210	8,519,699	17,961,813	1,451,974	17,709,178	2,181,371	13,526,119
4	10,283,198	7,269,660	6,666,018	4,900,346	156,609	14,769,534	2,762,120	1,154,705
5	5,165,252	10,653,842	3,074,787	2,009,746	-1,052,500	5,677,659	-561,758	6,580,447
6	10,902,375	7,789,533	22,617,538	8,574,318	8,769,643	6,776,186	1,145,953	4,389,194
TOTAL	78,354,157	65,458,683	60,876,700	50,959,540	33,938,434	113,827,925	34,255,881	49,659,346
DELAWARE								
TOTAL	17,265,182	28,718,286	20,559,033	11,310,203	13,326,876	20,113,731	25,972,809	5,235,631
DISTRICT OF COLUMBIA								
TOTAL	59,818,744	12,435,053	38,144,667	16,939,369	13,529,674	57,050,904	34,942,054	42,396,967
FLORIDA								
1	5,515,991	36,908	2,639,202	2,139,236	737,797	8,514,388	2,165,348	7,273,299
2	21,911,664	16,950,447	7,720,662	7,802,829	9,651,558	16,389,053	7,311,497	22,251,156
3	6,966,435	7,717,176	-4,801,498	13,661,268	1,182,089	12,379,287	4,941,215	16,914,236
4	10,053,126	9,573,882	3,372,270	7,259,839	-14,758	7,915,056	4,171,345	13,303,820
5	29,156,390	24,424,889	26,462,870	12,238,013	3,399,508	10,286,805	4,969,991	1,101,424
6	18,258,320	7,520,199	7,565,603	8,854,568	6,367,426	15,701,358	11,849,770	13,588,869
7	19,691,284	20,344,299	11,982,667	5,046,131	15,552,406	18,708,973	6,666,325	19,655,968
8	8,077,185	10,336,276	6,124,395	6,681,144	12,170,884	8,488,351	5,696,974	16,531,230
9	425,561	1,937,320	2,103,415	6,005,646	10,826,203	18,971,499	3,363,879	9,568,111
10	6,726,486	24,928,191	33,184,749	7,233,937	9,781,085	10,517,963	3,125,400	9,964,092
11	16,459,656	14,159,421	14,473,555	13,320,746	3,970,627	8,426,131	3,638,489	11,334,255
12	2,998,949	1,788,656	4,069,694	3,249,667	10,622,985	15,107,139	2,475,052	10,757,735
13	23,069,714	207,055	132,620	1,761,173	21,687,692	11,997,482	618,435	3,592,899
14	6,768,058	3,426,551	6,794,576	5,068,759	139,726	8,172,760	2,053,041	14,253,510
15	20,397,539	12,643,739	4,545,678	3,736,618	238,147	15,648,777	6,248,863	17,363,746
16	3,839,715	6,880,399	2,452,779	5,180,598	6,742,385	25,964,806	5,393,555	10,343,501
17	11,221,643	13,779,380	-1,509,324	9,530,109	2,770,919	10,598,258	8,157,226	11,753,871
18	12,036,001	18,201,755	877,613	11,529,780	7,338,544	13,528,209	10,152,165	16,781,074
19	9,810,941	14,285,398	-3,922,052	23,193,311	2,433,525	9,604,954	7,159,990	10,302,529
TOTAL	233,384,659	209,141,940	124,269,476	153,493,372	125,598,749	246,921,250	100,158,559	236,635,326
GEORGIA								
1	20,282,664	11,797,051	-305,135	1,924,196	8,468,135	16,948,607	49,814	0
2	1,218,853	-852,620	9,106,318	1,193,797	224,121	9,418,245	1,838,975	461,949
3	19,961,275	3,727,282	2,553,034	3,719,143	8,157,144	10,140,639	1,415,685	11,092,333
4	8,939,660	17,062,849	1,613,129	5,737,617	-718,369	11,102,270	4,627,675	4,462,809
5	26,540,868	17,395,444	1,408,763	27,938,701	6,622,293	55,415,014	34,897,178	28,007,532
6	2,543,543	1,347,727	-313,655	7,227,843	807,952	9,976,661	3,742,383	4,021,248
7	11,241,876	2,992,787	318,181	406,948	5,446,623	3,372,729	2,577,458	5,857,450
8	9,446,519	14,297,207	13,550,060	1,606,253	1,818,278	12,236,165	93,389	526,291
9	13,991,400	-572,436	20,795,912	8,582,700	2,328,975	1,549,854	1,532,500	0
10	11,544,605	20,257,461	6,051,708	12,967,281	5,790,132	19,492,526	12,564,310	20,730,918
TOTAL	125,711,263	87,452,752	54,778,314	71,304,480	38,945,284	149,652,710	63,339,367	75,160,530

Appendix A lists the congressional districts which represent the county in which the state capital is located, and those congressional districts which represent only portions of a county. Appendix C lists the programs included in each functional policy category.

table continues

Table 5.7 Outlays for Environmental Quality Programs by Congressional District, 1983-1990 *(continued)*

Congressional District	1983	1984	1985	1986	1987	1988	1989	1990 (est.)
HAWAII								
1	12,561,810	6,396,432	17,949,121	27,476,746	11,960,502	12,335,715	421,384	3,170,625
2	11,930,879	14,551,698	4,214,909	11,116,188	12,274,542	24,101,382	8,680	35,428,232
TOTAL	24,492,689	20,948,130	22,164,030	38,592,934	24,235,044	36,437,097	430,064	38,598,856
IDAHO								
1	22,194,753	10,077,937	13,948,338	10,156,109	9,723,722	19,588,811	15,619,593	12,342,127
2	3,288,678	6,538,954	3,115,022	4,467,608	2,424,489	5,932,492	4,828,055	3,955,383
TOTAL	25,483,431	16,616,891	17,063,360	14,623,717	12,148,211	25,521,303	20,447,648	16,297,510
ILLINOIS								
1	17,152,242	14,701,638	10,719,911	11,318,518	1,863,554	37,091,540	7,743,454	6,159,222
2	15,769,481	14,486,914	9,382,348	9,878,537	-12,766	35,055,957	2,904,893	24,988,609
3	16,729,419	14,371,552	9,940,011	10,276,692	-142,229	35,409,321	3,232,749	25,900,809
4	9,603,932	7,960,731	5,990,173	19,436,654	313,833	18,815,759	1,170,315	10,741,643
5	25,415,209	13,928,865	38,495,513	7,040,537	1,655,241	36,771,866	4,524,689	29,449,676
6	7,892,961	29,879,785	13,659,618	16,247,782	9,215,945	14,539,126	2,564,704	13,088,344
7	18,240,432	15,298,880	11,610,229	11,365,526	520,878	37,662,131	5,061,761	25,434,050
8	15,786,862	14,302,612	9,286,617	9,880,498	-12,768	35,106,807	2,927,381	24,993,570
9	16,414,672	16,427,007	11,487,148	10,180,959	544,399	39,304,719	3,240,755	24,997,712
10	9,249,257	9,662,313	6,823,348	5,985,542	369,430	18,630,361	1,427,274	11,301,555
11	15,771,364	14,301,538	9,285,239	9,071,256	144,174	35,375,629	3,220,334	24,991,693
12	7,577,779	12,042,761	6,074,551	6,483,761	243,532	16,049,523	1,206,047	10,607,743
13	10,525,569	14,527,203	6,630,925	15,556,091	389,872	17,795,051	2,714,654	14,134,550
14	33,542,447	29,229,740	12,909,403	-5,248,242	907,491	2,825,810	-127,741	1,715,114
15	7,025,845	18,811,738	19,055,726	2,611,173	24,205,877	2,572,520	179,890	-101,186
16	6,057,880	3,689,820	4,298,693	-78,666	-14,670	4,663,852	1,990,615	4,699,765
17	17,913,936	6,247,588	1,518,813	6,724,106	1,825,810	2,254,074	1,500,277	1,080,669
18	22,295,593	14,188,431	2,452,684	35,928,606	-852,844	3,130,570	213,909	4,398,725
19	21,683,687	19,536,138	8,238,097	12,283,428	6,001,009	11,860,455	12,114,661	16,633,990
20	31,990,793	33,070,056	42,116,851	33,434,342	70,327,986	28,369,595	23,616,257	47,808,932
21	15,226,394	7,541,849	3,728,263	6,634,669	1,827,611	14,432,742	7,311,046	17,992,458
22	5,798,841	3,639,334	7,265,939	4,104,945	2,965,729	1,357,862	1,300,057	8,258,281
TOTAL	347,664,595	327,846,493	250,970,100	239,116,712	122,287,094	449,075,269	90,037,981	349,275,925
INDIANA								
1	-5,863,516	38,622,077	22,162,306	19,988,040	1,787,740	14,459,348	5,298,507	6,586,213
2	20,410,368	4,447,008	4,194,077	2,150,299	-1,979,668	10,697,197	5,032,915	346,024
3	201,991	21,645,733	7,766,380	3,777,728	6,640,735	16,449,240	7,351,654	4,780,960
4	8,400,078	4,259,355	1,893,388	2,179,525	5,343,329	5,197,950	5,849,967	6,253,789
5	3,801,925	11,606,144	28,842,204	7,660,171	4,423,957	11,354,852	6,098,536	-672,052
6	30,793,884	14,325,476	13,705,314	11,999,869	4,843,810	9,635,974	10,128,622	11,625,484
7	20,684,695	14,804,120	18,247,634	12,679,807	5,976,429	16,716,947	15,470,215	7,548,805
8	22,159,247	3,042,423	8,807,679	5,408,733	9,585,849	3,735,710	15,239,359	10,346,597
9	5,948,932	7,380,127	3,237,864	3,434,072	2,528,590	13,609,092	7,013,532	4,553,294
10	29,534,537	13,509,201	11,961,258	26,817,495	-835,736	12,356,964	5,900,538	397,354
TOTAL	136,072,141	133,641,665	120,818,104	96,095,739	38,315,035	114,213,273	83,383,845	51,766,467
IOWA								
1	7,653,168	8,916,827	1,340,754	1,038,060	1,072,373	1,512,912	215,194	-1,645,534
2	9,020,000	3,947,389	3,370,597	2,357,802	1,708,037	3,543,099	1,165,175	2,599,527
3	5,005,801	6,455,652	2,905,618	2,148,448	328,736	3,804,536	6,780,705	2,644,407
4	46,277,563	30,957,621	40,348,412	42,797,516	46,965,673	42,941,935	60,837,644	32,867,874
5	2,351,045	4,083,204	4,606,270	2,780,500	479,894	4,552,115	3,204,566	2,302,666
6	14,273,293	6,485,738	3,679,788	1,150,575	596,885	4,375,289	66,989	-75,008
TOTAL	84,580,870	60,846,431	56,251,439	52,272,901	51,151,598	60,729,886	72,270,273	38,693,932
KANSAS								
1	10,920,188	641,519	462,077	1,364,884	76,447	969,294	123,406	446,211
2	22,934,685	15,412,773	10,654,992	13,067,654	8,811,217	15,335,177	23,244,195	9,452,514
3	9,281,101	20,743,005	21,873,003	11,692,557	3,068,820	14,439,254	8,466,642	2,725,996
4	8,423,881	3,043,116	3,306,013	6,324,691	16,485	10,725,302	-1,160,090	-1,942,537
5	18,444,874	-1,146,236	2,152,958	688,443	4,778,430	4,367,801	5,316,695	-102,532
TOTAL	70,004,729	38,694,177	38,449,043	33,138,229	16,751,399	45,836,828	35,990,848	10,579,651

Appendix A lists the congressional districts which represent the county in which the state capital is located, and those congressional districts which represent only portions of a county. Appendix C lists the programs included in each functional policy category.

table continues

Table 5.7 **Outlays for Environmental Quality Programs by Congressional District, 1983-1990 *(continued)***

Congressional District	1983	1984	1985	1986	1987	1988	1989	1990 (est.)
KENTUCKY								
1	3,155,965	3,939,520	1,502,536	809,868	5,823,382	4,443,347	965,048	2,852,366
2	18,510,229	6,955,539	4,820,557	1,688,714	1,055,441	-238,842	1,287,346	20,770
3	8,717,245	10,871,626	17,195,544	16,059,651	784,987	23,438,478	8,770,501	19,082,214
4	4,757,369	7,235,479	1,174,337	2,944,141	1,186,228	2,474,385	1,667,219	-769,401
5	8,039,304	2,340,495	4,067,662	1,129,452	5,184,010	7,844,061	2,512,455	5,240,040
6	51,994,014	64,778,082	42,663,342	48,927,280	18,966,206	53,125,564	108,403,945	25,331,862
7	14,408,490	-93,039	296,649	2,490,260	4,057,974	3,977,127	2,665,777	1,400,517
TOTAL	109,582,616	96,027,702	71,720,627	74,049,366	37,058,228	95,064,120	126,272,291	53,158,369
LOUISIANA								
1	20,908,445	16,401,595	11,333,169	6,363,831	3,695,221	-464,661	9,359,419	372,388
2	25,661,986	22,736,706	10,666,630	11,032,384	-308,131	-387,261	13,687,057	2,139,378
3	8,689,382	4,469,214	20,048,946	13,273,102	10,525,615	1,511,162	3,698,695	-3,129,333
4	10,433,188	5,904,867	8,286,272	2,784,811	5,227,447	1,260,201	23,250,766	-258,655
5	4,574,347	661,978	2,784,234	6,459,912	2,222,618	2,276,661	3,514,211	3,741,299
6	24,357,964	19,445,327	14,750,231	21,050,197	9,103,541	20,440,243	30,063,242	12,603,807
7	9,603,009	7,347,933	1,738,066	858,389	1,418,885	2,108,516	5,900,778	7,593,676
8	1,858,311	4,660,050	1,811,547	895,092	3,310,558	4,638,194	5,849,013	6,325,016
TOTAL	106,086,632	81,627,670	71,419,096	62,717,717	35,195,755	31,383,055	95,323,181	29,387,578
MAINE								
1	16,797,350	9,289,413	15,959,090	8,715,537	4,927,449	13,777,539	10,948,448	6,073,710
2	27,282,915	14,918,000	12,436,971	11,503,014	9,669,038	34,209,660	6,786,234	18,653,050
TOTAL	44,080,265	24,207,413	28,396,061	20,218,551	14,596,487	47,987,199	17,734,682	24,726,759
MARYLAND								
1	29,739,018	15,649,949	10,549,511	4,999,359	12,900,302	23,226,449	14,563,071	2,535,058
2	2,585,974	2,826,254	3,024,277	3,112,443	18,607,448	31,476,960	9,140,263	-1,523,119
3	17,798,871	31,551,394	23,310,454	27,659,161	6,299,982	24,710,151	19,978,819	2,493,566
4	11,126,263	11,429,051	17,029,895	33,946,491	10,610,852	18,611,323	1,948,910	1,519,854
5	14,473,836	34,045,229	3,767,959	19,252,247	6,519,797	33,294,642	16,934,360	5,690,204
6	26,938,406	33,343,418	5,551,500	12,293,597	12,200,190	20,132,342	6,766,155	3,532,504
7	28,784,016	45,727,926	32,868,039	35,577,800	5,531,683	30,739,147	27,364,593	513,026
8	18,718,390	9,424,614	8,447,477	8,096,415	5,854,285	13,091,224	4,396,561	2,827,621
TOTAL	150,164,775	183,997,836	104,549,112	144,937,512	78,524,539	195,282,237	101,092,732	17,588,712
MASSACHUSETTS								
1	10,314,858	15,521,870	4,619,380	11,784,861	3,333,153	10,947,081	5,612,025	5,688,029
2	12,626,940	31,750,641	13,702,545	10,650,403	5,454,036	23,688,719	782,338	3,689
3	22,764,089	30,299,089	9,594,981	10,331,136	11,539,828	9,810,978	4,130,888	216,964
4	16,001,736	3,620,716	8,134,454	6,833,650	1,095,812	8,981,599	1,810,089	1,711,032
5	17,477,783	26,478,974	4,674,641	1,275,551	3,073,984	11,840,803	-69,979	0
6	13,690,991	7,762,578	13,199,156	4,389,405	23,278,337	16,899,452	-726,705	1,780,572
7	17,691,061	13,012,057	13,533,716	12,512,133	11,166,546	26,252,670	8,792,465	7,116,410
8	44,418,832	28,064,926	35,083,849	31,179,053	15,500,861	62,075,370	21,271,408	24,128,544
9	36,717,435	14,890,550	30,119,640	31,290,723	7,321,135	50,875,581	14,361,127	19,799,741
10	18,469,554	4,500,405	9,539,668	3,010,066	9,125,641	20,768,198	14,341,782	2,063,752
11	25,598,873	9,296,651	23,692,380	13,998,977	1,789,807	29,761,538	7,097,102	15,168,359
TOTAL	235,772,152	185,198,457	165,894,410	137,255,957	92,679,138	271,901,988	77,402,540	77,677,091
MICHIGAN								
1	23,092,480	23,061,837	19,908,032	10,313,469	448,210	114,852,360	10,823,031	-16,869,596
2	19,125,563	15,387,014	10,804,776	8,222,530	4,799,116	19,956,302	14,072,675	2,479,400
3	12,757,334	31,519,431	10,103,117	-1,216,992	3,848,770	8,201,356	4,264,768	35,817
4	4,416,399	2,821,528	1,133,485	650,062	2,402,425	4,853,702	3,008,815	915,439
5	13,154,358	4,542,002	5,240,884	3,936,452	3,983,259	9,079,222	44,168	47,336,826
6	27,371,970	62,636,073	28,049,117	9,120,751	18,873,179	63,101,631	17,870,413	10,984,123
7	10,198,820	13,582,783	22,016,704	2,344,168	15,725,826	8,765,413	23,201,658	-610,195
8	20,663,565	9,430,330	12,321,595	2,415,052	4,824,566	6,706,669	1,931,364	2,786,580
9	5,250,288	2,908,533	2,538,531	1,680,756	3,419,861	6,197,053	256,198	8,453,400
10	-699,378	4,071,732	-846,957	218,688	4,860,743	1,243,530	4,150,374	2,600,801
11	30,399,864	15,565,071	9,819,137	3,341,502	9,654,858	10,496,567	8,103,559	2,549,522
12	9,206,662	15,233,874	4,886,240	4,670,490	5,007,936	9,686,180	2,304,053	1,035,275

Appendix A lists the congressional districts which represent the county in which the state capital is located, and those congressional districts which represent only portions of a county. Appendix C lists the programs included in each functional policy category.

table continues

Table 5.7 Outlays for Environmental Quality Programs by Congressional District, 1983-1990 *(continued)*

Congressional District	1983	1984	1985	1986	1987	1988	1989	1990 (est.)
MICHIGAN *continued*								
13	28,366,705	23,427,007	21,378,921	10,462,865	-1,970,387	17,431,437	4,411,911	3,013,443
14	9,786,723	9,924,810	8,855,808	4,869,475	-602,609	7,662,269	1,621,198	735,316
15	25,963,225	20,055,312	19,343,177	12,417,840	2,198,625	18,452,663	1,169,734	3,174,152
16	22,339,913	28,831,108	18,356,814	12,074,357	27,462,675	15,603,440	4,790,573	3,235,248
17	12,328,508	12,609,641	13,488,059	7,709,963	-1,099,032	14,798,003	2,093,626	949,592
18	872,327	7,787,048	5,320,223	7,423,162	1,393,934	2,309,194	0	69,007
TOTAL	274,595,326	303,395,135	212,717,663	100,654,591	105,231,955	339,396,990	104,118,119	72,874,151
MINNESOTA								
1	9,542,103	16,533,022	15,341,910	1,880,444	5,828,596	14,627,592	2,266,805	-477,862
2	11,548,514	9,186,158	5,128,457	5,976,235	15,560,497	18,551,564	1,941,869	4,380,660
3	6,325,131	1,965,415	2,477,972	4,660,504	-71,616	2,111,636	277,383	176,044
4	32,743,395	24,949,026	31,902,007	21,300,275	21,447,487	34,028,393	49,977,053	13,314,890
5	25,366,687	18,621,754	2,511,619	14,025,531	1,851,002	26,578,753	2,066,150	232,706
6	14,654,724	4,625,236	2,517,656	3,709,752	2,066,299	5,776,651	558,725	0
7	37,558,295	7,528,173	8,337,674	6,055,202	5,468,423	9,706,246	6,959,235	742,794
8	14,829,969	7,033,326	3,615,341	7,315,057	3,474,136	6,194,585	5,240,155	1,313,038
TOTAL	152,568,817	90,442,110	71,832,636	64,922,999	55,624,824	117,575,420	69,287,375	19,682,269
MISSISSIPPI								
1	2,051,340	4,205,436	2,742,664	526,604	7,334,462	2,789,427	1,417,868	-87,206
2	8,378,550	2,330,437	3,117,180	1,299,797	2,284,044	1,363,625	2,213,106	2,885,361
3	4,192,063	12,921,145	4,497,900	8,473,643	5,379,366	23,052,796	14,729,006	19,062,221
4	10,911,013	6,424,423	6,316,849	5,592,236	4,891,244	4,691,989	2,360,455	7,673,845
5	13,015,804	17,370,852	9,996,152	23,602,210	14,633,640	9,451,718	2,091,144	476,461
TOTAL	38,548,770	43,252,293	26,670,745	39,494,490	34,522,756	41,349,555	22,811,579	30,010,681
MISSOURI								
1	8,039,337	14,647,441	9,842,791	12,898,607	1,965,030	30,155,167	24,562,430	15,797,811
2	5,918,663	14,203,438	10,494,860	21,196,135	8,783,767	16,132,143	10,175,070	26,637,545
3	5,127,838	5,757,576	4,505,663	7,321,558	1,373,642	6,301,198	6,138,132	11,679,194
4	44,419,838	29,881,889	24,329,193	19,627,847	12,992,157	15,128,090	16,129,557	677,370
5	10,446,893	-120,895	16,932,243	14,039,191	6,186,563	8,034,792	3,487,945	-914,683
6	15,050,307	6,407,447	14,074,620	7,047,753	3,565,649	22,352,944	8,225,908	5,535,677
7	13,316,832	29,351,078	11,979,661	5,232,330	3,995,936	14,729,762	6,866,551	2,143,574
8	23,714,185	5,428,940	5,805,423	2,706,334	4,613,766	6,270,196	9,156,208	139,958
9	38,552,161	22,857,396	10,157,045	15,563,531	7,632,062	11,341,678	13,457,492	12,224,539
TOTAL	164,586,054	128,414,309	108,121,499	105,633,286	51,108,572	130,445,971	98,199,293	73,920,984
MONTANA								
1	18,772,252	21,264,478	14,980,811	14,319,244	15,683,592	28,278,843	26,507,519	6,052,333
2	7,834,198	7,066,342	7,504,065	3,198,366	2,198,740	4,960,009	2,425,143	5,208,360
TOTAL	26,606,450	28,330,820	22,484,876	17,517,610	17,882,332	33,238,852	28,932,662	11,260,693
NEBRASKA								
1	8,557,335	10,027,447	6,853,728	11,007,407	9,139,861	11,717,365	17,048,806	8,345,907
2	14,511,038	16,071,443	5,397,313	14,623,233	6,678,910	12,668,714	3,811,170	9,230,153
3	5,977,020	4,605,025	3,789,510	736,919	2,246,480	1,226,558	3,613,181	2,190,402
TOTAL	29,045,393	30,703,915	16,040,551	26,367,559	18,065,251	25,612,637	24,473,157	19,766,462
NEVADA								
1	7,740,256	6,269,906	3,772,669	5,180,139	1,816,028	2,238,158	9,123,374	288,735
2	14,588,602	5,858,663	11,102,093	10,982,064	2,924,931	3,857,111	9,854,802	11,342,698
TOTAL	22,328,858	12,128,569	14,874,762	16,162,203	4,740,959	6,095,269	18,978,176	11,631,433
NEW HAMPSHIRE								
1	17,216,751	22,021,090	12,631,348	8,523,074	298,218	22,028,980	8,310,160	27,767,429
2	31,081,832	25,351,291	13,570,754	15,786,262	29,427,382	17,802,752	10,731,596	18,752,625
TOTAL	48,298,583	47,372,381	26,202,102	24,309,336	29,725,600	39,831,732	19,041,756	46,520,054

Appendix A lists the congressional districts which represent the county in which the state capital is located, and those congressional districts which represent only portions of a county. Appendix C lists the programs included in each functional policy category.

table continues

Table 5.7 Outlays for Environmental Quality Programs by Congressional District, 1983-1990 *(continued)*

Congressional District	1983	1984	1985	1986	1987	1988	1989	1990 (est.)
NEW JERSEY								
1	45,068,559	66,297,790	5,569,984	5,523,930	30,516,869	16,888,412	5,464,994	4,257,054
2	64,239,985	17,935,852	42,753,030	6,949,197	4,651,339	11,019,112	3,307,453	3,677,499
3	9,013,380	8,766,885	17,960,867	3,930,295	10,257,235	8,428,054	3,030,000	7,168,545
4	50,023,928	2,689,078	4,485,610	24,334,815	49,479,663	8,917,050	104,940,097	308,360
5	13,426,542	2,713,027	4,654,572	3,127,098	3,666,911	11,238,865	4,021,724	5,722,492
6	6,587,675	13,951,599	31,812,880	8,331,464	14,776,714	9,919,544	4,504,179	4,780,246
7	7,911,000	9,112,347	10,678,812	5,591,097	8,148,960	17,973,462	-142,269	14,419,557
8	28,598,906	9,045,718	10,638,514	7,768,517	5,834,596	6,998,245	2,400,286	7,862,330
9	11,454,680	9,549,000	6,099,419	36,312,781	6,753,140	7,925,182	0	0
10	25,706,527	19,108,309	19,670,528	14,078,361	11,933,614	31,097,771	3,954,981	1,454,234
11	4,724,995	3,405,164	-464,798	5,218,499	7,456,128	1,744,838	423,779	89,496,492
12	3,998,520	3,843,638	2,359,475	2,689,685	3,984,506	3,150,346	4,797,270	44,470,858
13	-2,057,140	5,560,054	727,395	4,699,593	5,285,271	4,483,084	2,666,090	-53,929
14	20,431,000	14,340,160	36,991,672	10,549,461	63,089,951	20,166,153	8,255,115	27,256,043
TOTAL	289,128,556	186,318,621	193,937,957	139,104,793	225,834,898	159,950,118	147,623,699	210,819,781
NEW MEXICO								
1	21,956,224	9,458,772	11,634,256	1,542,333	12,372,035	6,851,243	9,171,329	895,184
2	15,535,656	9,376,013	10,179,391	5,873,097	2,063,820	2,237,225	4,543,313	2,709,318
3	8,544,554	3,922,153	6,102,521	5,758,746	3,769,387	14,449,843	5,125,338	3,701,288
TOTAL	46,036,434	22,756,938	27,916,168	13,174,176	18,205,242	23,538,311	18,839,980	7,305,791
NEW YORK								
1	7,395,244	6,563,118	10,739,187	3,675,944	7,552,079	3,627,862	643,281	2,035,060
2	8,159,787	3,371,368	5,165,777	3,026,535	4,443,832	4,460,397	2,403,000	9,731,708
3	8,204,113	14,109,671	12,365,508	20,329,519	45,755,114	49,517,254	36,130,497	-12,062
4	11,856,945	12,919,814	18,942,830	14,274,050	-1,263,850	4,078,600	4,529,229	0
5	11,746,236	14,530,500	18,815,685	14,184,902	-1,333,875	4,602,577	4,537,948	31,872,091
6	-11,291,818	0	0	0	0	-415,930	-1,036,194	0
7	0	0	0	0	0	0	0	0
8	857,703	1,324,174	1,012,329	722,351	1,341,055	24,553,231	-1,004	-195,083
9	0	0	0	0	0	0	0	0
10	0	0	0	0	70,732,733	65,705,238	-14,329	-559,499
11	0	0	0	0	0	116,132	11,613	0
12	40,500	40,500	0	0	0	177,807	11,587	0
13	0	0	0	0	0	116,298	11,630	0
14	22,999,921	-15,355,305	-3,491,642	0	29,053,367	21,038,318	40,195,619	0
15	163,440,151	131,338,588	113,837,372	182,998,265	113,388,964	12,056,416	7,634,114	10,645,558
16	161,844,724	128,295,806	108,204,880	177,840,708	104,817,360	348,852	144,841	1,200,513
17	138,136,621	98,365,255	83,106,325	136,591,822	79,653,941	20,370,044	296,153	0
18	3,089,105	643,893	1,016,043	357,291	780,505	84,847,740	307,125	0
19	710,868	858,203	1,399,438	2,227,078	2,120,502	63,251,663	1,297,957	1,794,489
20	15,806,819	9,831,048	23,642,460	11,095,141	32,415,279	12,730,185	29,318,282	12,080,323
21	9,004,284	17,406,049	-1,557,019	6,053,459	8,758,776	5,125,262	117,564	1,090,552
22	56,202,910	9,789,014	21,323,569	9,025,651	15,134,111	2,268,071	1,172,043	1,098,342
23	46,209,047	26,980,071	20,740,751	20,883,233	28,701,342	11,422,379	18,690,643	4,721,095
24	21,420,850	7,842,722	13,120,028	5,529,522	12,305,453	6,394,444	-1,887,415	5,980,851
25	7,233,255	37,738,492	16,342,717	15,221,354	8,993,718	12,410,811	5,482,072	6,999,765
26	22,731,845	34,268,353	14,059,246	16,691,810	21,731,401	39,084,092	7,567,630	11,083,680
27	13,023,849	9,429,590	14,116,876	13,181,846	12,817,173	21,548,333	1,685,998	5,068,955
28	45,594,324	50,236,967	18,697,344	23,688,347	26,341,018	12,409,037	12,068,337	21,478,866
29	45,834,974	28,824,504	14,348,980	14,615,086	8,985,341	5,232,122	1,335,756	9,198,832
30	50,139,470	13,496,192	14,694,009	16,273,841	32,833,761	23,160,773	11,249,085	19,268,734
31	15,370,914	17,814,580	12,979,260	7,214,420	10,884,410	6,168,114	814,312	-12,813,250
32	37,593,359	18,063,235	16,088,365	10,777,671	19,657,926	7,066,588	2,769,220	5,302,899
33	16,963,397	9,338,528	12,884,597	10,608,349	19,719,381	9,267,374	639,987	3,319,162
34	20,234,818	17,594,898	28,696,419	2,126,272	7,906,892	5,899,678	1,313,706	4,742,012
TOTAL	950,554,215	705,659,828	611,291,334	739,214,470	724,227,707	538,639,761	189,440,287	155,133,594
NORTH CAROLINA								
1	19,189,591	6,104,353	4,575,925	3,665,069	3,597,939	13,845,598	1,543,912	1,446,729
2	16,097,941	8,599,174	19,592,790	10,587,028	9,235,134	22,562,081	17,664,344	7,486,992
3	1,876,876	3,728,179	2,704,065	1,732,660	1,160,100	6,323,371	3,226,895	3,134,847
4	20,540,487	22,741,197	21,978,676	22,743,036	18,402,943	40,488,044	47,055,038	36,047,216
5	4,907,887	-1,434,557	9,030,987	1,346,263	1,853,048	4,403,238	-8,549	528,949
6	23,689,239	1,594,401	4,791,429	1,261,887	-222,098	7,086,937	4,382,646	2,542,430
7	3,387,099	1,430,471	2,514,357	1,211,092	-301,576	18,300,393	3,249,553	317,208
8	1,138,305	2,856,222	1,719,728	273,619	6,446,000	7,745,601	1,914,875	-3,963
9	-1,324,306	2,406,907	3,184,250	36,648	14,870,322	8,267,400	475,315	507,957
10	605,977	-163,585	278,077	4,477,307	9,192,803	14,342,137	3,210,212	-3,874,884
11	1,722,167	11,359,718	1,738,198	14,140,405	1,256,391	4,247,763	16,316	349,674
TOTAL	91,831,263	59,222,480	72,108,482	61,475,014	65,491,006	147,612,563	82,730,557	48,483,156

Appendix A lists the congressional districts which represent the county in which the state capital is located, and those congressional districts which represent only portions of a county. Appendix C lists the programs included in each functional policy category.

table continues

Table 5.7 **Outlays for Environmental Quality Programs by Congressional District, 1983-1990 *(continued)***

Congressional District	1983	1984	1985	1986	1987	1988	1989	1990 (est.)
NORTH DAKOTA								
TOTAL	17,356,948	29,765,442	16,688,074	11,424,035	14,496,096	20,841,816	25,846,015	7,655,214
OHIO								
1	19,096,719	13,100,057	31,474,275	27,911,261	4,896,495	21,451,934	16,357,028	9,716,931
2	10,848,821	7,426,014	8,694,657	6,016,966	2,626,883	12,817,376	6,484,435	3,993,105
3	7,361,506	34,784,934	10,278,800	7,961,310	19,414,953	26,095,216	4,175,583	6,388,289
4	-1,457,117	5,888,733	1,574,395	1,859,648	8,246,691	7,588,579	-52,985	-35,533
5	7,907,228	875,414	2,905,532	3,448,428	3,696,498	17,821,708	3,983,476	1,150,810
6	138,620	8,264,991	-659,065	3,199,483	5,962,181	7,088,258	7,140,307	2,922,878
7	-756,442	7,144,038	-1,836,396	4,409,564	4,488,732	7,081,328	-172,604	0
8	1,858,841	10,237,193	110,797	4,940,292	6,672,204	6,439,884	2,644,784	161,635
9	6,369,913	-1,497,443	36,824,121	6,949,724	7,247,831	13,017,354	12,893,637	-1,189,622
10	25,089,985	42,740,963	17,305,379	22,074,284	1,746,083	18,820,620	7,747,233	5,378,940
11	-4,005,082	11,659,810	192,749	1,741,613	192,836	5,481,323	1,275,489	7,396,279
12	46,358,520	16,781,732	15,377,061	19,924,022	16,130,508	8,081,030	77,891,334	12,921,692
13	5,720,841	16,935,210	20,318,311	7,567,186	637,514	14,904,780	1,437,255	0
14	29,151,189	5,686,195	8,516,156	24,551,406	967,333	8,959,467	7,221,697	36,579,548
15	39,623,939	15,169,369	18,649,536	31,346,172	23,813,639	34,544,126	23,521,840	12,967,820
16	3,401,793	10,191,489	6,085,494	8,203,928	2,709,852	12,247,960	-1,973,102	260,431
17	53,501,508	40,186,957	32,304,767	5,667,614	6,352,949	13,652,040	2,382,123	2,130,174
18	6,435,797	14,832,513	1,463,459	957,806	2,375,512	11,727,290	1,378,115	4,769,715
19	37,910,577	15,261,343	35,459,870	22,627,676	20,853,404	39,302,667	3,472,966	1,777,310
20	23,087,651	17,281,666	10,987,206	8,408,689	-1,103,499	16,902,114	1,398,565	2,191,481
21	25,832,781	19,390,552	13,632,990	11,750,045	-557,270	21,868,615	3,333,125	5,812,697
TOTAL	343,477,588	312,341,729	269,660,095	231,517,117	137,371,329	325,893,669	182,540,301	115,294,583
OKLAHOMA								
1	3,324,036	12,941,724	4,482,721	7,428,364	3,156,916	1,419,073	8,849,891	16,337,991
2	7,681,970	12,350	4,299,798	496,179	4,886,307	4,072,154	6,723,890	7,446,999
3	12,896,362	8,747,160	5,821,295	11,119,393	3,250,305	13,641,817	9,930,386	13,502,645
4	17,618,347	8,290,614	4,291,093	10,217,803	8,935,792	5,866,008	4,836,176	6,453,365
5	16,379,987	7,841,608	5,711,508	6,759,774	3,286,419	6,649,465	14,438,485	6,499,517
6	10,478,496	9,842,298	5,012,546	6,589,680	4,303,965	4,899,184	10,455,661	405,069
TOTAL	68,379,197	47,675,754	29,618,961	42,611,193	27,819,705	36,547,701	55,234,489	50,645,586
OREGON								
1	9,497,828	16,274,317	12,389,055	15,852,562	17,475,742	3,673,870	15,814,166	-1,947,064
2	3,738,270	-1,436,832	1,529,327	2,427,255	504,119	41,756	6,496,198	67,557
3	12,623,479	3,775,757	12,739,619	13,328,510	11,164,952	5,615,387	7,833,471	1,512,937
4	20,398,665	22,230,373	4,536,398	10,118,171	6,665,795	7,980,841	10,412,047	5,368,560
5	34,876,488	10,114,950	12,324,417	9,804,518	6,077,143	12,739,882	13,504,452	6,620,493
TOTAL	81,134,730	50,958,565	43,518,816	51,531,017	41,887,750	30,051,736	54,060,334	11,622,483
PENNSYLVANIA								
1	19,215,204	22,442,034	58,676,600	26,779,580	6,767,366	24,400,309	8,915,818	-2,099,003
2	14,879,482	22,115,662	29,149,616	23,857,451	1,287,071	24,696,781	8,887,675	1,204,362
3	14,963,274	21,893,072	35,928,827	22,262,942	1,000,316	24,306,995	7,622,463	1,028,536
4	9,441,713	8,772,798	2,878,532	2,245,843	1,755,221	7,344,779	345,453	2,800,314
5	3,985,578	22,615,683	4,966,895	6,085,165	499,929	12,036,698	169,275	4,682,590
6	9,276,460	9,070,023	3,769,396	9,747,858	2,776,267	11,659,644	3,205,706	7,652,548
7	11,638,156	9,463,522	10,118,028	8,258,370	1,075,551	9,071,435	1,225,343	16,897,318
8	15,577,425	13,012,326	4,983,719	8,743,904	4,499,238	10,164,928	1,976,108	871,333
9	4,752,580	11,488,332	3,016,139	-369,714	203,290	61,300,955	13,807,723	707,444
10	21,521,814	30,728,765	8,251,155	6,668,598	15,483,204	12,678,326	4,369,822	4,698,743
11	9,978,504	22,379,771	8,410,047	3,949,725	2,179,194	8,573,396	26,176,065	31,527,276
12	20,631,504	190,079	1,994,821	1,040,692	14,148	14,085,991	4,104,964	3,901,296
13	21,758,946	7,463,175	11,567,177	4,897,408	2,591,622	16,262,250	3,157,485	8,232,057
14	33,550,307	37,985,999	27,907,989	18,866,608	1,596,537	60,340,267	6,195,565	1,191,843
15	7,931,425	9,431,685	3,541,927	-3,623,578	-1,436,053	4,762,928	3,692,172	5,502,695
16	62,431,443	10,740,373	8,651,738	4,731,624	1,595,161	10,332,079	4,368,775	9,337,238
17	69,759,619	103,483,522	71,886,760	53,496,541	56,859,559	8,386,783	111,792,360	13,654,913
18	932,409	336,659	5,646,814	495,042	-55,199	427,370	345,598	13,100
19	25,078,886	7,391,026	10,607,369	23,423,013	21,307,189	9,328,149	953,234	362,833
20	200,223	-10,503	5,472,449	-91,705	1,432,726	1,199,971	1,268,000	3,232,800
21	20,254,309	14,064,665	6,175,227	4,105,080	5,281,089	3,528,809	845,107	0
22	16,446,563	21,846,095	15,272	4,991,751	833,214	10,584,997	2,871,273	314,622
23	14,491,146	12,547,131	7,817,848	11,974,458	7,183,882	20,691,048	14,199,598	15,766,672
TOTAL	428,696,970	419,451,895	331,434,344	242,536,654	134,730,523	366,164,888	230,495,582	131,481,529

Appendix A lists the congressional districts which represent the county in which the state capital is located, and those congressional districts which represent only portions of a county. Appendix C lists the programs included in each functional policy category.

table continues

Table 5.7 Outlays for Environmental Quality Programs by Congressional District, 1983-1990 *(continued)*

Congressional District	1983	1984	1985	1986	1987	1988	1989	1990 (est.)
RHODE ISLAND								
1	23,833,292	18,913,961	16,409,590	11,489,372	11,733,203	38,344,532	4,768,185	6,104,692
2	15,154,298	17,434,796	17,283,507	6,921,884	7,158,344	8,681,744	5,680,975	6,927,814
TOTAL	38,987,590	36,348,757	33,693,097	18,411,256	18,891,547	47,026,276	10,449,160	13,032,506
SOUTH CAROLINA								
1	6,859,750	5,953,712	3,627,580	121,971	-14,218	5,597,326	1,026,995	3,105,500
2	6,802,065	4,329,508	2,948,407	3,945,156	5,262,513	7,532,385	22,459,836	13,909,805
3	9,798,448	12,235,421	10,886,956	9,795,039	5,971,128	6,711,058	7,610,972	10,592,358
4	10,522,701	12,848,466	7,561,994	9,427,719	6,128,568	12,785,982	2,016,850	6,017,490
5	12,388,096	3,779,035	8,200,244	-300,824	6,106,566	12,684,221	373,637	7,502,018
6	3,707,481	15,757,325	3,917,833	8,910,257	8,110,060	10,972,701	2,424,354	785,867
TOTAL	50,078,541	54,903,467	37,143,014	31,899,318	31,564,617	56,283,673	35,912,644	41,913,038
SOUTH DAKOTA								
TOTAL	26,121,671	20,000,530	13,365,940	9,855,228	12,552,372	17,327,465	16,218,282	13,651,586
TENNESSEE								
1	9,733,976	2,599,459	8,321,301	1,437,090	1,763,523	6,593,187	1,719,165	2,456,609
2	12,723,279	17,526,087	11,565,078	9,228,849	6,441,506	11,920,533	11,539,802	15,355,024
3	8,183,059	7,588,109	11,152,645	7,219,034	5,407,254	8,799,428	3,095,079	143,532
4	8,270,175	-4,950	156,023	8,261,703	15,387,679	3,287,974	4,825,251	4,177,423
5	21,210,726	12,218,313	10,538,576	18,686,919	6,818,259	56,672,359	6,345,978	10,725,244
6	1,318,317	7,085,208	2,861,052	4,288,600	4,515,002	2,815,464	6,400,763	1,021,354
7	12,723,073	10,190,133	7,544,731	5,336,779	-316,128	11,674,410	1,901,190	1,682,821
8	9,051,320	20,649,156	7,774,208	7,519,669	1,978,931	8,811,366	1,617,689	1,328,204
9	15,448,294	9,030,733	8,396,639	5,919,868	57,617	28,999,272	1,337,940	0
TOTAL	98,662,219	86,882,247	68,310,253	67,898,511	42,053,643	139,573,993	38,782,857	36,890,212
TEXAS								
1	31,248,179	13,509,450	3,251,028	525,693	3,514,527	1,803,249	1,681,800	1,084,724
2	8,629,387	5,853,646	6,177,726	3,238,325	818,255	504,326	582,768	1,081,558
3	7,416,580	5,205,434	5,501,352	4,381,869	278,710	278,515	13,483,879	13,595,466
4	15,564,035	1,892,250	1,733,004	4,061,882	612,552	193,315	2,947,051	4,763,309
5	9,374,319	6,139,802	15,675,980	5,057,418	1,036,163	157,786	14,123,090	14,248,685
6	31,409,298	17,492,366	11,344,675	18,738,072	11,239,989	14,356,175	23,207,911	26,959,867
7	8,845,841	34,990,521	22,970,353	22,533,807	3,753,774	1,170,094	226,933	669,956
8	10,042,353	14,232,235	12,633,387	12,538,277	1,523,769	-306,252	1,871,414	2,304,973
9	7,720,286	22,637,092	11,961,747	10,351,339	54,210	637,577	7,890,652	6,276,618
10	42,902,714	41,670,743	27,488,207	29,990,175	23,383,753	141,839,881	80,800,825	62,495,379
11	40,566,945	-8,970,241	5,046,085	2,708,369	2,494,067	2,204,818	5,656,587	8,607,386
12	11,261,649	2,335,564	7,507,005	3,560,846	4,614,240	13,929,448	5,231,675	0
13	16,981,227	2,905,844	3,791,972	2,197,600	-1,811,991	107,852	5,680,406	7,345,818
14	18,098,765	2,535,247	2,849,393	3,943,079	1,296,712	1,884,185	4,705,044	6,429,769
15	27,134,314	10,209,293	11,472,247	2,629,201	432,122	7,212,478	7,170,742	8,547,930
16	13,986,017	12,847,907	9,544,531	7,848,922	721,723	6,723,387	21,356,886	22,110,224
17	9,579,469	2,914,216	2,775,847	970,299	1,270,131	-7,508	1,836,507	2,952,126
18	9,328,125	13,054,903	11,953,194	9,285,349	1,840,375	319,014	1,178,685	1,431,522
19	10,236,361	3,800,817	4,164,706	3,950,375	181,267	26,815	10,612,733	-135,832
20	-376,842	37,632,219	35,208,983	39,335,025	15,471,558	21,470,411	13,195,258	19,015,863
21	8,420,920	4,082,168	4,393,106	4,246,191	168,916	359,119	8,565,718	7,953,067
22	14,058,216	3,800,824	4,399,560	3,893,088	6,325,918	957,705	54,093,915	57,644,574
23	7,095,097	9,023,218	12,672,780	8,014,741	280,497	644,971	15,281,496	14,668,629
24	11,554,133	5,403,525	6,236,133	6,021,264	11,937	144,148	14,024,424	15,293,095
25	9,451,236	12,579,441	11,260,860	9,023,243	1,566,407	814,237	1,298,748	1,323,128
26	5,862,232	4,097,136	3,334,494	3,522,287	516,075	420,608	4,906,563	115,888
27	10,800,427	-2,038,660	15,088,930	7,839,880	3,852,735	267,960	12,237,845	10,888,028
TOTAL	397,191,282	279,836,962	270,437,285	230,406,614	85,448,389	218,114,314	333,849,555	317,671,749
UTAH								
1	6,440,623	2,890,773	1,312,888	2,281,653	4,617,080	4,205,314	5,782,610	3,917,940
2	25,775,344	20,267,675	19,084,275	11,535,426	14,098,837	24,307,346	10,670,104	13,958,294
3	6,480,476	1,414,466	2,455,159	1,678,507	1,504,980	1,134,668	7,202,025	1,248,649
TOTAL	38,696,443	24,572,914	22,852,322	15,495,586	20,220,897	29,647,328	23,654,739	19,124,882
VERMONT								
TOTAL	16,031,991	13,943,655	14,027,793	8,014,798	24,451,017	16,821,079	10,019,702	6,883,979

Appendix A lists the congressional districts which represent the county in which the state capital is located, and those congressional districts which represent only portions of a county. Appendix C lists the programs included in each functional policy category.

table continues

Table 5.7 Outlays for Environmental Quality Programs by Congressional District, 1983-1990 *(continued)*

Congressional District	1983	1984	1985	1986	1987	1988	1989	1990 (est.)
VIRGINIA								
1	2,143,465	3,797,551	3,819,671	2,933,574	-3,280	5,721,851	287,255	2,158,344
2	9,608,347	-705,090	8,253,923	6,785,342	15,141,473	27,642,900	11,778,240	0
3	27,874,013	21,474,912	42,153,556	26,198,031	24,817,720	59,232,219	11,519,946	7,402,453
4	16,732,777	9,382,118	6,764,781	15,937,158	1,353,103	-1,750,947	-32,261	5,872,813
5	8,337,943	2,951,700	2,115,597	2,328,854	796,616	3,100,600	-62,750	-943,466
6	10,935,385	-1,008,754	1,227,526	2,240,000	-624,444	3,566,474	-59,916	-150,551
7	5,979,926	6,723,994	4,336,999	4,019,357	15,998,288	4,455,117	1,399,152	2,500,724
8	4,209,318	3,219,575	0	2,290,167	155,000	1,074,013	360,299	-963,026
9	29,989,928	31,354,679	12,991,138	28,463,419	16,568,685	9,708,331	19,513,205	29,233,861
10	6,778,745	13,219,806	4,460,988	6,127,745	3,360,383	15,716,716	4,588,284	20,313
TOTAL	122,589,847	90,410,491	86,124,179	97,323,647	77,563,544	128,467,274	49,291,454	45,131,466
WASHINGTON								
1	11,401,801	6,486,567	3,774,454	5,443,247	288,185	26,874,215	9,222,613	8,060,307
2	1,044,171	880,362	3,854,909	2,465,436	7,491,753	10,535,586	3,148,977	2,557,663
3	17,204,221	11,926,430	14,732,007	12,178,810	9,045,420	10,529,821	14,961,896	3,351,361
4	6,164,503	13,941,134	5,880,680	4,848,414	6,352,517	9,980,529	13,385,692	12,266,684
5	17,489,923	27,018,598	7,865,822	9,016,014	5,337,945	4,889,879	8,480,524	10,813,618
6	51,797,055	3,025,934	25,764,970	42,328,962	8,172,899	18,894,319	-7,496,313	9,893,366
7	11,894,509	9,858,730	620,790	7,282,126	2,908,194	3,485,427	30,408,201	16,844,868
8	17,653,884	7,949,993	2,170,612	6,730,732	4,039,298	1,837,940	12,454,634	18,096,094
TOTAL	134,650,067	81,087,748	64,664,246	90,293,742	43,636,211	87,027,716	84,566,225	81,883,962
WEST VIRGINIA								
1	17,222,890	17,855,019	4,434,701	-318,416	12,927,662	12,429,272	10,032,129	9,418,255
2	16,449,075	21,452,185	12,746,291	13,881,410	15,697,556	11,944,127	7,676,543	10,665,336
3	35,323,080	44,862,702	45,307,083	24,866,783	27,186,743	45,303,286	50,891,832	58,202,156
4	28,890,752	11,778,624	11,467,556	5,653,541	5,107,777	9,284,292	1,334,092	358,999
TOTAL	97,885,797	95,948,530	73,955,631	44,083,318	60,919,738	78,960,977	69,934,596	78,644,746
WISCONSIN								
1	5,138,507	9,859,675	3,782,589	2,394,399	241,830	6,467,483	2,826,628	9,148,942
2	15,314,912	17,904,364	13,501,954	17,896,907	15,370,099	23,649,095	17,731,024	15,837,432
3	3,932,710	2,104,613	3,231,902	1,381,497	2,203,767	1,924,453	711,103	480,641
4	44,580,920	39,092,476	28,755,990	16,927,618	36,349,895	45,669,916	64,658,322	16,053,986
5	48,391,006	48,191,664	34,947,433	20,804,774	44,687,196	12,293,740	1,065,110	21,795,445
6	3,026,075	18,076,053	911,769	2,995,560	272,203	2,429,396	1,335,940	158,546
7	4,595,338	3,791,966	2,729,692	3,888,171	767,376	8,278,030	2,925,533	2,629,884
8	1,883,227	707,854	1,427,740	1,177,362	116,165	2,925,320	2,004,438	147,664
9	3,685,037	4,621,171	5,541,712	1,595,095	2,419,501	2,124,565	-49,680	1,453,622
TOTAL	130,547,733	144,349,836	94,830,781	69,061,383	102,428,031	105,761,998	93,208,418	67,706,161
WYOMING								
TOTAL	14,382,175	58,049,720	54,518,023	26,027,339	24,531,187	80,544,857	42,132,683	21,667,477
U.S. TOTAL	7,017.9 mil.	5,821.7 mil.	4,884.5 mil.	4,463.1 mil.	3,238.7 mil.	5,663.3 mil.	3,832.3 mil.	3,179.7 mil.

Appendix A lists the congressional districts which represent the county in which the state capital is located, and those congressional districts which represent only portions of a county. Appendix C lists the programs included in each functional policy category.

Table 5.8 Outlays for Food and Nutrition Programs by Congressional District, 1983-1990

Congressional District	1983	1984	1985	1986	1987	1988	1989	1990 (est.)
ALABAMA								
1	240,070	396,677	405,448	299,571	39,469	165,367	149,231	71,198
2	450,954,792	456,705,405	464,712,467	454,037,641	412,512,930	420,086,488	424,746,365	638,457,687
3	6,944,300	8,484,332	6,425,458	10,262,258	5,913,030	7,588,156	9,930,681	11,525,090
4	42,351	35,168	29,302	0	0	0	0	0
5	895,202	1,526,942	1,303,721	1,447,893	1,204,561	478,896	962,862	1,419,008
6	1,253,159	404,734	834,769	516,315	785,045	845,563	1,025,090	1,033,901
7	80,197	63,581	167,073	50,000	0	0	0	0
TOTAL	460,410,071	467,616,839	473,878,238	466,613,678	420,455,035	429,164,470	436,814,229	652,506,885
ALASKA								
TOTAL	33,447,085	34,321,400	42,226,788	47,265,705	45,944,845	48,695,586	43,762,782	57,055,983
ARIZONA								
1	95,023,846	91,486,212	91,237,823	89,598,268	93,140,885	108,781,456	122,716,642	178,932,232
2	42,900,087	47,852,958	46,839,638	47,501,142	48,831,467	56,094,641	63,493,974	94,498,548
3	15,484	52,746	0	1,300	5,687	72,133	10,034	18,719
4	71,474,138	63,896,019	64,731,868	63,363,488	65,214,325	76,407,307	86,447,191	125,999,890
5	15,365	999,533	814,656	1,576,713	866,016	1,221,328	1,756,343	1,967,238
TOTAL	209,428,920	204,287,469	203,623,986	202,040,911	208,058,379	242,576,865	274,424,184	401,416,626
ARKANSAS								
1	5,152	0	0	0	0	0	0	0
2	209,405,174	206,081,391	186,628,949	188,964,202	192,324,440	205,882,981	213,913,351	295,823,436
3	5,112,458	5,125,907	3,646,139	6,579,641	3,305,625	5,298,743	7,998,100	9,353,632
4	584,320	1,047,759	858,108	1,210,256	399,136	427,116	0	0
TOTAL	215,107,104	212,255,057	191,133,196	196,754,099	196,029,201	211,608,840	221,911,451	305,177,068
CALIFORNIA								
1	747,391	89,493	493,009	433,388	39,169	2,352,728	138,141	22,916
2	710,930	337,761	546,549	709,488	207,064	360,806	417,749	0
3	611,575,146	686,187,739	651,288,899	730,198,423	729,809,524	791,881,207	786,620,219	1,199,755,134
4	297,357,925	316,338,458	315,638,208	327,483,199	325,332,802	356,409,459	351,902,186	523,249,215
5	800,295	627,738	698,173	934,384	892,512	681,303	941,108	0
6	145,922	307,096	416,628	827,253	6,709,965	7,064,952	6,288,509	2,127,227
7	424,006	356,580	251,394	297,169	284,456	261,988	317,279	0
8	8,587,272	8,273,549	6,361,891	11,698,384	4,928,472	6,325,425	10,532,589	12,930,357
9	201,136	135,917	170,168	203,877	127,128	158,667	211,426	24,399
10	118,419	94,527	93,408	525,912	66,555	82,286	120,204	0
11	727,383	1,012,420	236,872	20,647	150,305	23,915	63,481	0
12	484,841	212,440	1,514,532	2,248,969	3,463,905	3,849,236	4,567,533	2,161,355
13	102,661	71,532	69,771	46,704	68,416	60,312	122,415	0
14	50,363	76,249	4,110	1,712	1,217	0	1,010	0
15	309,487	33,711	256,541	184,738	230,659	174,723	196,052	0
16	265,786	433,107	329,589	829,345	520,947	327,935	717,400	0
17	4,125,402	5,914,049	6,452,256	6,003,873	343,450	447,433	544,316	5,211
18	32,328,024	29,478,077	31,196,408	199,937	63,109	234,972	319,217	9,504
19	259,809	166,714	919,547	175,838	149,644	197,614	244,796	0
20	418,623	157,903	91,008	123,705	92,106	80,067	49,264	17,224
21	174,600	191,988	197,753	208,319	187,883	182,673	4,064,157	53,212
22	353,099	457,230	492,899	595,066	535,515	408,078	188,665	0
23	4,737,869	4,173,835	4,934,494	5,239,691	5,709,996	5,575,457	5,354,786	3,186,972
24	371,158	351,455	377,640	479,817	429,775	309,750	82,309	0
25	364,634	2,005,687	1,377,283	994,625	445,348	309,457	2,819,969	0
26	434,918	308,570	336,575	421,269	377,333	271,954	72,265	0
27	372,545	351,354	377,532	479,679	429,652	334,674	82,285	0
28	892,254	566,129	622,153	857,758	1,087,455	948,607	453,320	877,678
29	359,802	356,050	388,921	487,350	429,682	309,683	82,291	0
30	634,503	808,029	674,865	840,514	661,904	638,554	524,188	0
31	386,261	974,011	377,998	497,936	446,426	326,010	705,679	0
32	576,256	352,728	391,343	508,350	458,199	332,508	131,660	0
33	447,397	459,388	465,610	590,670	564,378	440,459	327,457	0
34	406,505	426,678	469,945	622,242	521,989	410,169	176,996	0
35	119,204	123,156	109,734	108,633	119,108	104,687	141,794	0
36	103,733,306	110,222,746	110,337,167	114,520,315	113,851,241	124,484,516	123,037,472	182,592,316
37	93,644,797	99,542,569	98,739,080	102,387,084	101,660,880	111,215,216	109,823,364	163,332,898
38	1,187	0	0	0	0	0	0	0
39	15,375	0	0	0	0	0	10,094	0

Appendix A lists the congressional districts which represent the county in which the state capital is located, and those congressional districts which represent only portions of a county. Appendix C lists the programs included in each functional policy category.

table continues

Table 5.8 Outlays for Food and Nutrition Programs by Congressional District, 1983-1990 *(continued)*

Congressional District	1983	1984	1985	1986	1987	1988	1989	1990 (est.)
CALIFORNIA *continued*								
40	46,699	92,100	96,281	196,543	100,899	184,824	365,158	332,889
41	453,926	1,234,858	2,576,152	2,602,035	3,123,500	3,108,980	3,456,747	1,624,575
42	477,173	977,139	1,831,874	1,748,843	1,634,821	1,969,738	1,306,209	3,059,748
43	1,629,123	102,362	149,548	108,367	131,110	79,162	122,113	11,662
44	188,034	143,110	192,164	213,750	247,861	150,561	215,900	0
45	218,866	180,832	203,933	526,904	284,577	176,283	340,609	0
TOTAL	1,170,780,312	1,274,707,063	1,242,749,908	1,318,382,706	1,306,920,937	1,423,247,032	1,418,200,380	2,095,374,492
COLORADO								
1	144,637,329	149,609,335	142,626,391	155,774,290	184,595,172	190,048,662	197,235,421	253,618,934
2	-458,018	736,685	755,620	636,733	180,719	122,201	121,390	94,226
3	3,483,206	494,928	439,503	462,662	118,320	102,156	52,410	204,970
4	5,084,954	3,496,024	2,512,219	4,205,756	2,129,257	2,914,117	3,900,631	4,718,206
5	-959,402	1,137,808	1,238,974	1,386,228	244,086	111,419	67,617	229,844
6	496,807	4,226,269	5,440,669	12,824,453	6,827,329	6,410,097	6,628,543	8,508,543
TOTAL	152,284,876	159,701,049	153,013,376	175,290,122	194,094,883	199,708,652	208,006,012	267,374,723
CONNECTICUT								
1	118,318,655	119,141,344	114,633,140	114,056,128	99,350,173	107,505,286	109,590,751	121,710,323
2	1,830,527	1,766,386	1,379,659	2,336,825	1,113,356	1,695,206	2,288,724	2,785,305
3	1,781,514	2,961,121	3,965,355	3,748,805	3,856,977	4,188,995	4,680,823	3,222,758
4	492,800	0	465,364	280,206	0	0	0	0
5	0	0	4,000	0	4,000	6,000	6,000	0
6	0	0	0	0	106,384	98,740	102,076	346,512
TOTAL	122,423,496	123,868,851	120,447,518	120,421,964	104,430,890	113,494,227	116,668,374	128,064,898
DELAWARE								
TOTAL	42,892,704	41,745,803	39,592,433	35,625,642	34,092,146	36,808,557	39,827,761	55,800,191
DISTRICT OF COLUMBIA								
TOTAL	88,702,759	96,537,293	76,339,935	70,597,186	65,704,035	65,956,418	68,725,249	93,433,029
FLORIDA								
1	0	0	0	0	0	0	0	0
2	672,946,379	620,617,716	604,812,808	613,991,173	649,937,782	695,326,331	742,349,074	1,228,259,613
3	0	0	0	0	0	0	0	0
4	0	0	0	0	0	0	0	0
5	0	0	0	36,500	0	0	0	0
6	4,052,544	5,471,722	3,963,014	6,928,713	3,915,467	5,691,040	7,608,632	8,312,663
7	0	0	83,853	0	0	25,591	0	0
8	0	0	0	0	0	0	0	0
9	0	0	0	0	0	0	0	0
10	0	0	0	0	0	0	0	0
11	0	0	0	0	0	0	0	0
12	0	0	0	0	0	0	4,600	0
13	0	0	0	0	0	0	0	0
14	12,595	0	1,001	4,576	0	0	0	0
15	147,054	159,836	164,116	139,920	287,020	392,074	229,484	0
16	32,783	1,197	3,262	11,804	427	251	59	0
17	1,571	4,101	2,377	206	1,464	859	201	0
18	236,572	94,103	2,378	206	1,465	859	149,799	503,502
19	1,377	3,595	77,010	125,181	1,283	753	176	0
TOTAL	677,430,876	626,352,271	609,109,819	621,238,279	654,144,909	701,437,758	750,342,026	1,237,075,778
GEORGIA								
1	1,135,399	840,206	884,138	925,712	951,672	1,080,567	1,789,732	89,186
2	473,332	475,022	261,826	292,838	388,545	420,340	774,227	37,479
3	1,507,629	926,530	1,484,263	1,703,160	1,345,781	1,027,165	1,646,728	1,710,289
4	466,239,188	233,709,408	144,153,476	139,433,524	139,246,066	144,542,145	152,907,249	246,375,083
5	15,665,061	244,664,853	328,860,182	316,541,208	319,079,902	323,631,325	349,378,680	565,828,120
6	670,120	494,765	497,093	409,240	469,847	451,011	443,365	486,095
7	170,096	98,229	93,458	77,311	90,609	89,603	116,539	174,294
8	1,070,556	452,792	635,696	524,362	586,696	749,439	1,395,626	90,795
9	413,410	11,781	17,296	19,870	13,252	31,031	36,595	23,770
10	8,251,701	8,134,690	5,647,875	9,717,567	5,287,726	7,824,909	10,086,102	11,919,124
TOTAL	495,596,492	489,808,276	482,535,303	469,644,792	467,460,096	479,847,536	518,574,843	826,734,235

Appendix A lists the congressional districts which represent the county in which the state capital is located, and those congressional districts which represent only portions of a county. Appendix C lists the programs included in each functional policy category.

table continues

Table 5.8 Outlays for Food and Nutrition Programs by Congressional District, 1983-1990 *(continued)*

Congressional District	1983	1984	1985	1986	1987	1988	1989	1990 (est.)
HAWAII								
1	105,773,275	80,776,440	76,693,459	78,744,624	75,954,910	73,330,636	70,075,272	92,117,011
2	992,348	29,260,063	43,462,838	44,386,890	41,921,687	40,438,269	38,384,690	49,299,832
TOTAL	106,765,623	110,036,503	120,156,297	123,131,514	117,876,597	113,768,905	108,459,962	141,416,843
IDAHO								
1	43,750,604	40,828,384	42,052,333	44,022,354	44,224,140	47,530,285	44,778,140	64,395,535
2	14,873,720	14,668,112	15,698,496	16,144,711	16,657,683	17,790,021	16,303,102	22,713,500
TOTAL	58,624,324	55,496,496	57,750,829	60,167,065	60,881,823	65,320,306	61,081,242	87,109,036
ILLINOIS								
1	1,645,184	1,451,964	1,624,027	2,508,137	1,974,613	1,754,217	2,110,108	4,828,027
2	52,659	4,364	8,021	10,812	6,488	4,428	8,211	0
3	459,670	4,365	8,022	10,814	6,489	4,429	8,213	0
4	22,770	1,887	3,468	4,675	2,805	1,915	3,551	0
5	52,663	4,364	8,021	10,813	6,488	4,429	8,212	0
6	19,616	1,626	2,988	4,028	35,255	1,650	3,059	0
7	91,619	76,370	260,664	892,880	718,199	1,400,030	1,843,159	888,495
8	52,669	4,364	8,022	10,814	6,489	4,429	8,213	0
9	174,477	215,511	315,355	203,746	402,532	382,904	341,705	0
10	90,519	1,974	3,627	29,390	156,934	2,003	103,676	0
11	52,665	4,364	8,022	10,813	257,960	327,962	212,840	0
12	41,277	1,846	3,393	4,574	5,245	1,873	5,974	0
13	23,090	9,413	11,017	9,741	2,845	1,942	8,600	0
14	286,623	17	31	42	25	17	32	0
15	0	5,644	63,166	57,861	54,258	0	0	0
16	0	0	0	0	0	0	0	0
17	0	0	0	0	0	0	50,000	0
18	0	0	208,771	0	0	0	0	0
19	5,826,637	8,044,076	5,845,844	10,640,861	5,380,526	8,110,282	10,697,417	12,933,704
20	851,667,640	927,693,596	936,071,774	936,990,751	976,300,964	999,033,229	966,968,420	1,246,902,858
21	2,145,474	15,213	2,132	1,009	1,347	1,117	790	0
22	70,782	364,302	87,682	108,240	102,991	100,960	110,403	265,207
TOTAL	862,776,036	937,905,259	944,544,048	951,510,000	985,422,453	1,011,137,816	982,492,581	1,265,818,291
INDIANA								
1	0	0	0	0	0	0	0	0
2	39,416,119	37,070,173	36,808,305	38,407,789	33,386,179	34,120,260	35,942,049	40,592,542
3	0	0	0	0	0	0	0	0
4	0	0	0	0	0	0	0	0
5	0	0	0	0	0	0	0	0
6	59,797,245	58,810,748	58,395,302	60,932,837	52,966,198	54,119,693	57,021,013	64,398,884
7	4,485,159	6,449,191	4,803,892	9,036,218	4,382,882	6,891,898	8,778,498	10,401,419
8	5,410,130	344,580	0	484,800	0	0	0	0
9	97,653	113,067	214,684	110,150	190,172	189,864	197,666	550,859
10	236,980,724	246,940,754	244,617,726	255,278,573	223,603,792	227,994,900	240,485,879	277,576,039
TOTAL	346,187,030	349,728,513	344,839,909	364,250,368	314,529,223	323,316,615	342,425,105	393,519,744
IOWA								
1	102,846	0	0	0	0	0	0	0
2	0	0	0	0	0	0	0	0
3	608,614	1,523,930	1,501,007	1,302,480	1,413,278	1,244,867	719,268	1,645,792
4	159,337,496	169,866,197	169,988,741	198,018,687	177,736,761	176,839,890	173,449,484	229,427,068
5	1,816,860	412	171	168	12	0	0	0
6	0	45,178	43,179	0	444	0	0	0
TOTAL	161,865,816	171,435,717	171,533,098	199,321,335	179,150,495	178,084,757	174,168,752	231,072,861
KANSAS								
1	2,479	1,693	683	161,146	0	0	0	0
2	113,769,849	114,066,342	110,487,587	115,653,560	116,287,799	132,099,679	142,235,400	204,989,756
3	5,847,696	5,812,819	6,221,406	6,043,081	700,050	661,910	478,022	900,526
4	333,173	605,994	467,014	336,873	77,530	0	0	0
5	11,697	14,305	408,095	15,844	0	0	0	0
TOTAL	119,964,894	120,501,153	117,584,785	122,210,504	117,065,379	132,761,589	142,713,422	205,890,282

Appendix A lists the congressional districts which represent the county in which the state capital is located, and those congressional districts which represent only portions of a county. Appendix C lists the programs included in each functional policy category.

table continues

Table 5.8 Outlays for Food and Nutrition Programs by Congressional District, 1983-1990 *(continued)*

Congressional District	1983	1984	1985	1986	1987	1988	1989	1990 (est.)
KENTUCKY								
1	0	0	0	0	0	0	0	0
2	0	0	0	0	0	0	0	0
3	0	0	105,807	101,069	107,870	0	0	0
4	0	0	0	0	0	0	0	0
5	310,000	237,836	320,000	300,000	0	0	0	24,399
6	431,700,926	457,133,515	452,936,846	453,233,745	431,910,560	436,980,609	404,954,556	611,434,763
7	263,114	225,000	0	0	0	0	0	0
TOTAL	432,274,040	457,596,351	453,362,653	453,634,814	432,018,430	436,980,609	404,954,556	611,459,162
LOUISIANA								
1	62,281	65,812	67,632	0	141,635	121,600	93,027	0
2	84,962	93,235	161,430	236,043	248,277	360,777	440,343	469,386
3	17,305	0	0	0	0	0	0	0
4	0	0	67,035	75,422	248,193	534,712	654,230	1,036,187
5	0	0	0	600,000	0	0	0	0
6	446,153,280	477,562,181	476,462,137	526,432,877	570,707,474	633,940,271	644,140,396	832,063,743
7	0	0	0	0	0	0	0	0
8	0	26,422,391	34,061,548	37,783,184	40,969,940	45,647,897	46,341,240	59,278,428
TOTAL	446,317,828	504,143,619	510,819,782	565,127,525	612,315,519	680,605,257	691,669,235	892,847,744
MAINE								
1	93,428,634	91,241,989	87,857,892	87,392,569	77,998,712	75,495,798	82,207,335	108,812,987
2	2,547,147	1,719,764	1,166,201	2,209,605	1,102,724	1,731,594	2,332,843	2,843,660
TOTAL	95,975,781	92,961,753	89,024,093	89,602,174	79,101,436	77,227,392	84,540,178	111,656,647
MARYLAND								
1	407,280	432,675	528,800	786,577	503,828	304,893	0	0
2	4,820,097	4,515,979	4,777,228	4,572,327	4,777,838	1,180,351	0	0
3	529,182	1,325	0	1,423,418	1,658,067	2,755,665	3,082,211	2,835,503
4	240,207,293	243,670,871	245,186,504	249,426,051	239,899,201	247,761,605	257,236,911	346,148,033
5	5,604,328	5,947,924	4,803,374	4,963,784	3,029,127	5,117,329	6,576,108	7,163,538
6	4,000	0	0	0	0	0	0	0
7	6,926,866	7,335,692	7,203,107	7,608,905	7,793,640	7,727,788	8,457,980	15,888,570
8	716,431	66,682	172,344	66,003	421,672	337,819	343,590	124,371
TOTAL	259,215,477	261,971,148	262,671,357	268,847,065	258,083,373	265,185,450	275,696,800	372,160,015
MASSACHUSETTS								
1	2,773,604	3,000,448	2,201,140	3,480,545	1,638,545	2,574,307	3,490,034	4,275,769
2	0	0	0	0	0	0	0	0
3	238,083	323,825	994,244	223,702	151,624	394,269	308,197	0
4	1,100,790	1,126,976	1,231,099	2,168,896	2,187,207	2,346,121	2,637,178	507,223
5	0	0	0	0	0	0	0	0
6	0	0	0	0	0	0	0	0
7	37,612,718	37,700,119	37,246,177	36,699,699	33,868,074	34,859,425	35,660,225	51,109,245
8	93,716,597	83,916,500	84,017,296	82,452,932	74,563,098	76,900,806	79,622,425	111,138,874
9	130,746,076	131,433,832	129,453,766	127,164,304	118,355,170	121,227,298	124,394,232	189,231,577
10	4,380	2,527	2,674	0	0	0	0	0
11	53,716,524	52,976,984	51,480,025	52,560,733	48,213,228	49,398,722	51,510,015	71,933,220
TOTAL	319,908,772	310,481,211	306,626,422	304,750,812	278,976,946	287,700,948	297,622,307	428,195,907
MICHIGAN								
1	1,945,919	1,774,550	473,158	1,333,435	429,274	236,686	652,892	0
2	1,089,345	2,255,593	1,925,074	2,730,715	3,397,606	3,756,506	5,578,582	2,857,388
3	706,336,335	737,752,150	708,356,263	668,027,508	639,838,819	695,183,727	715,969,050	926,622,157
4	320,057	363,682	298,975	339,039	295,132	313,392	545,764	0
5	370,533	111,276	142,586	147,323	148,397	221,380	334,696	0
6	63,026,915	33,200,804	32,026,226	35,357,055	32,711,959	34,422,781	37,219,186	65,102,015
7	502,692	298,416	368,377	344,093	502,970	437,867	709,492	0
8	231,586	247,345	223,317	364,343	317,436	212,952	394,013	0
9	168,288	935,960	171,118	315,824	296,208	268,542	311,112	7,951
10	1,346,837	1,306,837	238,464	1,283,970	1,315,948	1,302,835	32,750	0
11	707,379	1,006,781	72,748	95,574	56,389	102,641	116,361	36,895
12	26,365	10,686	14,113	10,518	10,166	9,773	37,957	0

Appendix A lists the congressional districts which represent the county in which the state capital is located, and those congressional districts which represent only portions of a county. Appendix C lists the programs included in each functional policy category.

table continues

Table 5.8 Outlays for Food and Nutrition Programs by Congressional District, 1983-1990 *(continued)*

Congressional District	1983	1984	1985	1986	1987	1988	1989	1990 (est.)
MICHIGAN *continued*								
13	647,351	809,694	797,249	543,201	736,612	384,460	1,019,055	0
14	211,199	196,661	147,109	139,067	135,487	54,514	221,659	0
15	493,159	444,026	352,418	731,828	709,729	571,097	854,347	0
16	484,297	418,167	331,225	265,451	267,431	113,545	447,746	0
17	331,012	310,736	239,238	251,088	205,582	95,512	310,892	0
18	23,091	57,983	35,905	60,666	83,244	105,221	137,425	0
TOTAL	778,262,360	781,501,347	746,213,563	712,340,698	681,458,388	737,793,431	764,892,979	994,626,406
MINNESOTA								
1	1,077,303	2,057,431	1,676,132	2,428,504	2,224,662	2,196,790	2,869,768	1,817,898
2	1,363,221	178,686	193,466	209,692	6,349	6,471	5,274	6,007
3	20,940	5,642	14,623	11,254	0	0	0	0
4	181,876,176	193,299,794	192,320,158	201,417,603	216,928,955	233,275,370	239,336,174	342,202,117
5	965,084	727,223	960,569	1,424,149	281,309	561,706	761,581	493,290
6	1,989,561	1,051,077	213	0	0	0	0	22,947
7	1,319,786	141,665	281,416	107,023	104,177	110,152	111,210	118,425
8	1,021,809	157,837	934,639	514,870	24,040	30,587	32,064	31,428
TOTAL	189,633,880	197,619,355	196,381,216	206,113,095	219,569,492	236,181,076	243,116,071	344,692,110
MISSISSIPPI								
1	0	0	0	0	0	0	0	0
2	2,878,672	918,820	613,260	1,276,007	811,019	726,701	1,437,730	1,416,469
3	4,775,623	6,759,455	4,797,707	8,703,156	4,196,668	6,796,251	8,787,876	10,027,004
4	368,635,039	373,475,954	380,553,470	393,824,227	419,300,496	446,467,973	501,712,526	664,650,021
5	4,750	0	0	0	0	0	0	0
TOTAL	376,294,084	381,154,229	385,964,437	403,803,390	424,308,183	453,990,925	511,938,132	676,093,494
MISSOURI								
1	4,062,217	2,772,047	3,296,849	2,556,339	4,024,853	4,111,448	2,762,409	3,921,717
2	2,269,969	1,927,153	2,071,499	1,992,629	2,445,646	2,614,942	761,661	497,338
3	1,174,212	880,502	951,913	903,935	1,099,411	1,176,140	338,470	235,761
4	233,089,234	309,444,762	313,490,510	318,852,816	308,483,602	342,966,225	369,438,291	503,773,145
5	3,862,670	2,927,072	2,491,351	2,777,106	2,697,576	2,973,801	1,047,141	677,572
6	199,181	201,763	239,571	339,596	703,413	1,006,225	276,499	126,569
7	433,473	593,116	639,562	669,498	838,148	993,243	161,578	163,041
8	77,903,169	866,258	939,824	908,670	1,058,191	2,512,262	713,458	191,982
9	6,136,614	8,005,920	5,526,076	10,294,770	5,889,071	8,621,630	11,062,607	11,897,146
TOTAL	329,130,739	327,618,592	329,647,155	339,295,358	327,239,911	366,975,915	386,562,114	521,484,270
MONTANA								
1	47,912,405	49,911,698	51,056,187	55,161,921	55,148,767	59,738,316	60,478,288	80,902,775
2	61,344	105,424	144,089	106,787	460,544	785,148	844,609	1,899,289
TOTAL	47,973,749	50,017,122	51,200,276	55,268,708	55,609,311	60,523,464	61,322,897	82,802,065
NEBRASKA								
1	69,590,427	73,934,359	77,507,272	83,958,230	95,451,555	94,839,119	97,296,143	132,560,858
2	1,677,732	2,483,332	2,922,285	3,351,626	896,322	517,185	633,972	1,225,688
3	469,658	541,079	579,238	744,779	53,128	0	0	0
TOTAL	71,737,817	76,958,770	81,008,795	88,054,635	96,401,005	95,356,304	97,930,115	133,786,546
NEVADA								
1	0	0	0	141,128	0	0	0	0
2	27,019,245	35,812,139	36,230,065	39,478,700	40,155,169	45,117,583	49,896,709	72,728,929
TOTAL	27,019,245	35,812,139	36,230,065	39,619,828	40,155,169	45,117,583	49,896,709	72,728,929
NEW HAMPSHIRE								
1	1,210,219	1,193,031	808,388	1,505,906	741,827	1,052,800	1,589,222	1,935,240
2	39,743,214	34,440,961	30,732,497	28,886,612	24,920,295	25,599,235	27,861,012	44,905,218
TOTAL	40,953,433	35,633,992	31,540,885	30,392,518	25,662,122	26,652,035	29,450,234	46,840,458

Appendix A lists the congressional districts which represent the county in which the state capital is located, and those congressional districts which represent only portions of a county. Appendix C lists the programs included in each functional policy category.

table continues

Table 5.8 **Outlays for Food and Nutrition Programs by Congressional District, 1983-1990 *(continued)***

Congressional District	1983	1984	1985	1986	1987	1988	1989	1990 (est.)
NEW JERSEY								
1	1,863	33,600	4,150	0	0	0	0	0
2	0	0	0	0	0	0	0	0
3	0	0	0	0	0	0	0	0
4	396,297,759	407,508,637	428,518,460	393,992,033	368,580,482	385,591,946	400,248,690	530,770,551
5	28,167	0	0	0	0	0	0	0
6	1,977,457	2,859,740	2,005,714	3,532,186	1,989,161	2,846,490	3,556,787	4,348,139
7	33,779	98,945	0	51,276	58,195	4,000	0	0
8	0	0	0	0	0	0	0	0
9	17,361	12,320	10,236	9,154	5,214	0	0	0
10	440,226	400,453	571,754	696,380	852,070	771,568	883,147	927,831
11	32,708	5,208	4,815	3,229	5,052	0	0	0
12	49,027	300	113,377	109,370	82,588	26,515	333,773	1,452,994
13	11,933,261	0	0	0	0	0	0	0
14	0	0	0	0	0	0	0	0
TOTAL	410,811,608	410,919,203	431,228,506	398,393,628	371,572,761	389,240,519	405,022,397	537,499,516
NEW MEXICO								
1	39,394,150	311,216	418,056	315,131	601,855	463,266	561,681	542,966
2	2,005,841	1,796,898	1,401,259	2,363,180	1,271,888	1,762,822	2,713,601	2,911,465
3	96,977,750	134,349,179	131,616,911	140,556,536	146,767,562	159,211,480	160,458,790	218,101,051
TOTAL	138,377,741	136,457,293	133,436,226	143,234,847	148,641,305	161,437,568	163,734,072	221,555,482
NEW YORK								
1	512,595	297,923	514,802	504,568	356,409	289,683	358,248	415,257
2	131,395	196,711	225,266	182,416	300,735	289,231	347,705	414,609
3	193,842	212,538	164,127	351,171	498,743	601,964	805,237	588,145
4	205,904	124,507	80,963	127,089	144,724	154,841	195,188	50,598
5	668,465	636,266	855,802	977,259	1,048,952	1,373,299	1,452,253	1,405,033
6	1,657,748	3,788,580	1,081,115	3,931,821	3,421,217	6,817,485	4,140,614	1,243,300
7	1,365,423	3,509,272	813,444	3,329,156	3,435,170	6,900,153	4,211,835	1,248,371
8	2,346,900	3,569,791	2,036,442	3,954,154	3,265,148	5,295,543	3,663,911	1,816,218
9	1,358,032	3,490,277	809,041	3,311,136	3,416,576	6,808,237	4,134,997	1,241,613
10	2,844,594	3,332,928	3,274,111	3,241,328	3,232,129	3,305,216	3,867,685	3,283,456
11	3,402,450	3,365,566	3,306,173	3,273,069	3,263,780	3,337,582	3,905,560	3,315,610
12	3,934,898	3,867,699	3,884,988	3,762,254	3,256,335	3,484,710	4,056,640	3,308,047
13	2,876,557	3,398,378	3,334,900	3,277,749	3,268,447	3,342,354	3,911,144	3,320,350
14	970,352	1,430,077	1,415,753	1,418,008	1,433,965	1,450,449	1,661,261	1,514,489
15	3,935,321	8,976,406	12,647,212	12,000,239	9,109,286	10,234,013	10,284,185	10,217,523
16	3,607,537	7,258,955	11,235,481	9,224,404	5,881,134	5,671,869	5,763,184	7,432,965
17	3,182,676	9,471,672	10,175,909	9,723,372	9,074,218	8,719,748	9,224,320	9,064,622
18	7,165,698	2,400,312	2,577,061	2,772,729	2,749,004	2,819,425	3,251,103	3,464,657
19	2,785,691	1,836,748	1,879,899	2,069,776	2,046,200	2,136,496	2,465,772	2,621,342
20	2,794,565	3,412,964	1,683,583	1,413,578	1,193,317	1,356,842	1,217,786	1,300,408
21	224,051	312,757	286,762	399,557	469,534	619,982	649,998	534,631
22	291,127	413,331	393,915	443,382	460,007	829,858	765,439	671,576
23	966,580,525	1,338,256,973	1,364,408,520	1,408,008,495	1,393,836,722	1,388,424,850	1,388,766,645	1,904,286,168
24	399,066	210,480	266,803	259,852	302,146	305,096	400,860	471,975
25	664,415	820,170	902,577	1,000,844	2,426,570	3,436,509	4,459,438	5,295,885
26	468,560	164,592	224,037	234,876	185,882	330,327	425,949	834,510
27	3,656,654	863,195	778,908	1,017,471	887,969	754,969	1,172,104	731,481
28	322,210,908	10,023,359	7,355,612	12,430,207	5,018,670	7,259,208	9,210,598	10,626,537
29	820,287	969,133	921,211	683,258	781,173	916,688	1,063,869	867,781
30	592,681	1,030,268	735,908	1,129,608	1,511,569	1,529,193	1,939,630	2,739,395
31	550,749	536,795	450,384	881,867	644,645	759,464	766,421	679,013
32	599,629	921,603	949,192	941,448	927,637	1,185,990	1,308,037	1,789,617
33	664,949	793,157	486,450	1,116,460	841,196	998,901	986,786	876,528
34	174,255	280,434	306,265	330,727	834,940	1,227,527	1,554,549	1,822,485
TOTAL	1,343,838,500	1,420,173,817	1,440,462,618	1,497,723,327	1,469,524,150	1,482,967,703	1,482,388,951	1,989,494,195
NORTH CAROLINA								
1	341,226	55,419	39,375	188,055	0	0	87,975	0
2	846,339	724,897	1,109,165	978,464	1,328,152	1,689,831	1,717,156	639,465
3	4,995	4,706	4,979	4,766	4,980	4,834	4,735	10,974
4	430,174,805	425,375,747	413,303,425	420,634,781	411,159,755	417,577,455	421,457,660	675,481,122
5	0	0	156,105	227,842	331,838	138,333	221,063	0
6	1,539,068	1,180,219	1,617,700	2,000,049	1,564,549	1,754,781	2,183,274	2,542,430
7	157,370	140,534	132,155	120,770	126,195	122,605	222,746	278,093
8	0	0	0	0	0	0	0	0
9	6,654	10,659	53,805	1,708	5,702	3,967	0	0
10	20,669	0	1,745	1,550	2,306	2,194	0	0
11	887,595	121,964	125,654	28,947	73,344	30,148	9,389	10,655
TOTAL	433,978,721	427,614,145	416,544,108	424,186,932	414,596,821	421,324,148	425,903,998	678,962,739

Appendix A lists the congressional districts which represent the county in which the state capital is located, and those congressional districts which represent only portions of a county. Appendix C lists the programs included in each functional policy category.

table continues

Table 5.8 Outlays for Food and Nutrition Programs by Congressional District, 1983-1990 *(continued)*

Congressional District	1983	1984	1985	1986	1987	1988	1989	1990 (est.)
NORTH DAKOTA								
TOTAL	34,753,225	33,980,216	34,715,713	39,626,071	41,575,572	43,419,452	47,484,871	63,416,557
OHIO								
1	329,241	439,911	624,752	492,922	1,136,068	1,268,867	1,114,425	347,017
2	4,130	0	0	0	0	0	0	0
3	107,029	128,829	121,176	0	0	32,000	0	0
4	0	0	0	0	0	0	0	0
5	247,475	433,175	676,817	250,000	0	0	0	0
6	0	0	0	0	0	0	0	0
7	44,684	47,860	0	0	0	0	0	0
8	0	0	0	0	0	0	0	0
9	133,604	138,319	90,706	12,963	6,376	11,644	11,644	0
10	1,510,223	1,559,259	163,080	1,486,684	1,546,734	1,581,684	1,540,734	74,509
11	0	0	0	0	0	0	0	0
12	371,377,032	412,346,236	409,691,595	428,583,051	435,372,245	457,482,524	469,178,695	591,752,006
13	0	271	0	0	0	0	0	0
14	0	14,229	0	0	0	0	0	0
15	491,549,415	488,535,077	486,959,358	513,022,967	518,940,156	548,288,287	563,042,740	680,125,875
16	46,463	64,873	70,715	69,994	0	0	82,324	101,785
17	29,269	0	0	0	0	0	0	0
18	0	0	0	4,000	0	0	0	0
19	0	0	0	6,277	0	0	471	0
20	36,810	0	0	6,854	0	5,440	50,494	0
21	1,310,154	948,221	1,101,525	1,961,485	1,756,764	1,163,600	1,127,698	1,083,570
TOTAL	866,725,529	904,656,260	899,499,724	945,897,197	958,758,343	1,009,834,046	1,036,149,225	1,273,484,761
OKLAHOMA								
1	54,766	29,816	30,881	29,540	29,662	145,958	148,837	53,677
2	55,349	433,016	52,088	85,102	991,725	146,873	148,617	200,037
3	4,133,292	5,028,156	3,475,125	6,282,456	3,844,772	5,558,006	7,692,272	7,235,899
4	19,669,286	22,579,705	22,024,027	24,548,978	27,927,122	30,033,006	28,540,565	38,264,930
5	103,756,194	120,324,499	117,305,909	130,434,336	146,867,118	158,793,188	151,558,638	208,032,692
6	55,410,229	59,136,749	57,878,975	63,774,632	71,885,659	77,287,421	73,519,280	100,314,757
TOTAL	183,079,116	207,531,940	200,767,005	225,155,044	251,546,057	271,964,452	261,608,209	354,101,994
OREGON								
1	5,620,909	544,986	370,618	394,573	128,674	21,399	50,000	0
2	50,138,660	1,292,485	1,495,038	1,194,341	167,082	6,179	5,615	6,082
3	974,992	914,092	948,223	1,056,894	698,500	643,202	6,011,410	1,004,111
4	981,683	772,677	700,816	829,715	158,220	79,023	0	0
5	153,013,286	186,695,074	190,153,357	198,563,068	194,796,184	207,483,861	209,124,349	290,849,512
TOTAL	210,729,529	190,219,314	193,668,052	202,038,591	195,948,661	208,233,664	215,191,374	291,859,705
PENNSYLVANIA								
1	2,510,391	1,360,952	1,659,233	1,735,980	1,274,368	1,501,046	2,281,711	3,019,194
2	1,214,339	1,041,867	1,181,873	1,002,483	989,179	877,002	659,468	289,170
3	1,341,240	42,616	40,934	29,197	160,902	329,471	24,199	29,918
4	0	0	0	0	0	0	0	0
5	77,151	0	0	0	0	0	0	0
6	0	0	0	0	0	0	0	0
7	316,410	254,207	176,470	147,250	1,985	19,847	168,481	446,270
8	0	0	0	0	0	0	0	0
9	27,920	0	0	0	0	0	0	0
10	145,348	41,784	30,996	0	0	0	0	0
11	0	0	0	0	0	0	0	0
12	0	0	0	0	0	0	0	44,566
13	39,620	7,432	7,139	68,812	402,925	256,109	205,439	526,317
14	2,062,198	1,662,257	1,852,383	2,926,140	2,014,365	2,963,881	2,569,395	4,501,537
15	0	0	0	0	0	0	0	0
16	0	0	0	0	0	0	0	0
17	749,810,837	783,519,165	772,260,791	790,995,882	769,304,535	790,008,403	791,791,450	1,088,450,802
18	0	0	0	0	0	0	0	0
19	0	0	0	0	0	0	0	0
20	0	0	0	0	0	0	4,000	0
21	0	0	0	0	0	0	20,741	0
22	0	0	0	0	0	0	0	0
23	8,419,540	8,771,992	6,198,166	11,185,827	5,366,424	8,646,732	11,208,352	13,395,293
TOTAL	765,964,993	796,702,272	783,407,985	808,091,572	779,514,682	804,602,490	808,933,236	1,110,703,069

Appendix A lists the congressional districts which represent the county in which the state capital is located, and those congressional districts which represent only portions of a county. Appendix C lists the programs included in each functional policy category.

table continues

Table 5.8 **Outlays for Food and Nutrition Programs by Congressional District, 1983-1990 *(continued)***

Congressional District	1983	1984	1985	1986	1987	1988	1989	1990 (est.)
RHODE ISLAND								
1	32,310,225	30,822,310	30,811,823	29,923,263	28,543,356	29,161,836	29,847,358	25,749,718
2	25,896,844	24,842,187	24,758,945	24,278,041	23,021,037	23,889,224	24,852,381	26,344,117
TOTAL	58,207,069	55,664,497	55,570,768	54,201,304	51,564,393	53,051,060	54,699,739	52,093,835
SOUTH CAROLINA								
1	2,125,452	2,380,997	1,196,134	1,051,060	1,159,246	1,331,852	715,951	268,734
2	310,302,060	304,152,635	292,218,047	294,347,133	269,098,027	269,249,300	268,394,169	507,865,376
3	5,849,374	5,763,019	3,864,717	6,992,010	3,778,928	5,488,087	6,903,671	8,360,800
4	974,539	965,174	396,028	311,568	368,996	377,192	175,386	368,671
5	1,822,205	1,671,316	1,165,882	1,191,679	1,352,135	1,463,987	1,353,426	1,636,597
6	2,369,835	2,114,563	938,653	820,949	1,199,536	1,002,175	397,051	140,954
TOTAL	323,443,465	317,047,704	299,779,461	304,714,399	276,956,868	278,912,593	277,939,654	518,641,132
SOUTH DAKOTA								
TOTAL	39,852,349	48,633,048	48,951,581	55,905,367	57,668,572	59,173,927	60,709,389	75,697,605
TENNESSEE								
1	407,680	313,358	342,765	194,952	100,374	112,124	27,692	180,536
2	8,378,907	8,163,616	6,097,156	9,996,672	5,158,755	7,583,642	10,026,505	11,991,340
3	1,328,041	1,056,131	1,133,184	783,452	308,727	323,574	176,814	391,112
4	763,901	616,294	571,930	393,756	107,892	108,633	57,015	100,714
5	433,310,880	417,007,286	409,026,888	415,796,924	425,750,791	425,193,440	438,509,381	695,311,988
6	419,737	400,743	418,663	249,018	72,406	63,895	37,639	134,381
7	1,017,602	871,712	673,588	440,869	229,940	221,680	155,865	203,506
8	651,884	709,603	714,505	441,271	163,759	262,637	172,152	105,047
9	1,772,805	2,131,967	1,872,075	1,386,072	609,449	597,257	448,379	304,803
TOTAL	448,051,437	431,270,710	420,850,754	429,682,986	432,502,093	434,466,882	449,611,442	708,723,427
TEXAS								
1	3,145	9	0	0	0	0	0	0
2	426,892	501,081	476,290	300,000	0	0	0	0
3	93,863	2,016	0	250,000	0	0	0	0
4	-11,782	1,748	0	0	0	0	0	0
5	3,811,628	3,135,211	3,092,589	1,562,183	1,731,062	1,881,796	1,420,426	1,417,635
6	12,108,217	13,174,606	9,715,635	16,642,138	8,070,283	12,952,765	17,077,776	19,898,911
7	66,699	833	0	2,432,086	2,574,051	2,501,850	2,488,271	733,664
8	63,593	829	0	0	0	0	0	0
9	340,722	258,854	1,769,699	1,604,680	1,882,105	2,082,891	2,170,239	692,774
10	1,022,878,796	1,078,294,297	1,040,950,640	1,225,386,849	1,391,742,446	1,544,739,506	1,623,073,017	2,391,582,807
11	637,405	686	0	376,000	0	0	0	0
12	115,537	1,283	0	0	0	0	0	0
13	402,779	310	0	0	0	0	0	0
14	1,599,678	1,232,960	2,215,480	3,032,422	771,640	1,928,236	2,249,929	2,562,777
15	451,906	187	0	0	0	0	0	0
16	254,178	0	0	500,000	0	0	0	0
17	100,218	1,081	0	0	0	0	0	0
18	584,897	754,115	944,761	899,560	1,430,116	1,779,326	1,505,498	198,364
19	175,503	22,439	0	181,985	204,128	151,768	0	0
20	598,736	1,638	1,113,821	0	0	0	0	0
21	245,672	762	0	0	0	0	0	0
22	95,138	382	0	5,735	0	0	0	0
23	444,029	456,401	59,828	136,672	96,933	176,357	309,971	0
24	106,704	2,041	0	150,000	0	0	0	0
25	54,981	832	0	0	0	0	90,905	0
26	115,934	701	0	0	0	0	0	0
27	38,378	98,589	0	0	0	0	0	0
TOTAL	1,045,803,447	1,097,943,892	1,060,338,743	1,253,460,310	1,408,502,764	1,568,194,495	1,650,386,032	2,417,086,933
UTAH								
1	1,376,747	1,438,139	2,186,411	1,833,851	939,636	1,446,680	2,017,231	2,295,101
2	72,608,149	74,876,035	74,463,780	80,430,586	89,493,464	98,599,736	107,592,775	143,949,794
3	0	0	0	160,000	0	4,297	3,709	6,112
TOTAL	73,984,896	76,314,174	76,650,191	82,424,437	90,433,100	100,050,713	109,613,715	146,251,008
VERMONT								
TOTAL	39,146,940	37,553,224	33,305,481	34,962,309	32,763,548	34,876,094	35,052,773	51,484,712

Appendix A lists the congressional districts which represent the county in which the state capital is located, and those congressional districts which represent only portions of a county. Appendix C lists the programs included in each functional policy category.

table continues

Table 5.8 Outlays for Food and Nutrition Programs by Congressional District, 1983-1990 *(continued)*

Congressional District	1983	1984	1985	1986	1987	1988	1989	1990 (est.)
VIRGINIA								
1	587,449	615,397	641,844	595,702	716,698	765,755	987,748	942,624
2	1,816,024	2,089,670	1,836,240	2,540,665	2,333,052	2,184,145	2,133,748	3,300,471
3	308,360,004	306,148,372	293,172,558	282,908,926	280,792,476	308,341,238	331,438,312	444,549,242
4	1,426,671	1,841,085	1,655,647	1,936,126	1,753,221	2,580,381	3,050,916	2,804,593
5	137,849	182,207	170,040	176,809	191,914	238,017	214,536	403,673
6	785,673	734,027	788,526	784,655	523,236	888,467	960,691	1,892,467
7	870,673	1,698,628	2,381,818	910,114	1,264,483	1,745,158	1,814,557	2,622,176
8	384,003	616,588	670,429	773,370	1,078,186	1,238,398	1,340,685	1,798,800
9	6,373,557	6,828,349	5,212,366	9,602,775	4,778,124	6,684,753	8,772,724	10,749,523
10	1,087,113	1,124,167	1,092,615	1,171,350	1,351,111	1,661,930	1,704,756	1,775,734
TOTAL	321,829,016	321,878,490	307,622,082	301,400,491	294,782,501	326,328,242	352,418,673	470,839,302
WASHINGTON								
1	2,725,042	3,441,791	2,233,220	1,255,769	1,104,814	1,229,768	194,844	6,512
2	1,591,371	565,341	1,965,815	2,689,221	3,245,527	3,469,251	593,051	67,866
3	201,538,486	197,803,488	200,525,802	221,155,336	233,050,424	254,741,482	264,181,146	339,147,642
4	2,710,217	3,228,106	4,526,323	3,989,026	3,272,682	3,388,444	715,292	45,458
5	5,126,689	4,829,794	4,196,002	6,067,721	4,200,251	5,493,158	5,106,780	5,369,388
6	1,981,453	1,685,559	2,181,651	1,677,932	1,915,631	2,122,446	359,551	107,713
7	1,732,735	1,364,479	1,428,407	2,150,990	3,741,708	3,998,641	3,210,689	5,967,256
8	1,753,191	3,408,442	3,541,917	3,396,977	3,704,591	4,022,127	506,786	24,751
TOTAL	219,159,184	216,327,001	220,599,136	242,382,974	254,235,628	278,465,317	274,868,138	350,736,587
WEST VIRGINIA								
1	0	0	0	0	0	0	0	0
2	3,288,981	3,365,461	2,348,734	4,340,202	2,210,519	3,376,948	4,765,260	5,447,576
3	197,027,937	207,540,107	213,503,076	198,844,751	217,718,231	224,423,678	227,054,640	299,363,280
4	124,700	0	0	0	5,540	12,345	0	0
TOTAL	200,441,618	210,905,568	215,851,810	203,184,953	219,934,290	227,812,971	231,819,900	304,810,856
WISCONSIN								
1	0	0	0	0	0	0	0	0
2	211,310,945	253,396,529	232,784,850	240,089,039	249,947,003	275,199,814	267,227,577	348,061,141
3	0	0	80,642	482,593	6,560	6,741	7,093	6,965
4	636,451	175,000	257,419	160,000	0	0	0	0
5	113,521	777,759	868,392	1,027,743	1,273,393	1,103,807	1,198,835	1,012,222
6	0	75,000	120,000	100,000	0	0	0	0
7	931,533	0	0	4,335	7,847	17,169	20,345	22,655
8	147,894	3,630	9,574	13,495	22,610	32,778	32,840	42,897
9	0	4,000	0	0	0	0	0	0
TOTAL	213,140,344	254,431,918	234,120,877	241,877,205	251,257,413	276,360,309	268,486,690	349,145,879
WYOMING								
TOTAL	17,902,114	25,714,775	26,169,113	29,812,508	30,859,113	32,239,532	32,406,718	44,021,072
U.S. TOTAL	16,128.6 mil.	16,611.7 mil.	16,405.3 mil.	17,019.7 mil.	17,036.3 mil.	18,010.2 mil.	18,452.6 mil.	25,744.8 mil.

Appendix A lists the congressional districts which represent the county in which the state capital is located, and those congressional districts which represent only portions of a county. Appendix C lists the programs included in each functional policy category.

Table 5.9

Outlays for Health Programs by Congressional District, 1983-1990

Congressional District	1983	1984	1985	1986	1987	1988	1989	1990 (est.)
ALABAMA								
1	126,743,152	138,590,589	160,387,745	167,051,540	164,167,846	189,875,063	197,531,906	231,750,502
2	219,353,476	233,144,115	271,658,129	250,121,400	257,228,513	283,352,396	295,801,643	430,655,501
3	133,689,520	144,778,156	164,894,511	156,074,895	157,925,398	178,763,307	186,486,520	231,297,490
4	151,603,085	174,261,412	185,579,585	179,819,856	184,449,349	200,173,028	214,895,070	268,070,934
5	101,200,695	115,849,193	130,544,857	140,027,084	132,603,067	147,700,094	154,838,832	197,325,977
6	210,567,710	213,028,809	241,237,409	248,316,766	263,925,050	297,701,005	304,185,393	327,972,466
7	147,193,319	170,440,369	191,630,855	173,532,398	173,783,400	194,004,588	208,727,770	261,791,988
TOTAL	1,090,350,956	1,190,092,643	1,345,933,091	1,314,943,939	1,334,082,623	1,491,569,480	1,562,467,134	1,948,864,858
ALASKA								
TOTAL	124,205,565	131,440,282	134,566,527	145,193,975	175,999,939	208,419,829	247,513,373	328,967,394
ARIZONA								
1	177,911,591	149,849,060	189,548,518	203,884,061	204,674,347	224,531,146	286,791,669	339,695,791
2	191,309,517	195,398,233	230,538,883	238,677,766	253,513,039	270,894,328	340,775,491	466,479,375
3	43,993,471	41,638,028	52,434,678	59,434,085	61,659,171	74,946,623	82,504,881	105,361,283
4	166,310,455	148,093,117	181,965,572	190,505,038	205,551,386	231,300,447	295,071,098	415,423,626
5	62,362,024	110,764,934	135,944,927	120,131,177	133,497,089	144,969,685	198,678,559	259,199,000
TOTAL	641,887,058	645,743,372	790,432,579	812,632,127	858,895,033	946,642,230	1,203,821,697	1,586,159,075
ARKANSAS								
1	179,723,314	202,256,214	238,010,938	245,870,403	249,642,742	258,822,243	301,692,831	351,882,803
2	189,214,154	179,999,166	211,706,670	227,901,308	236,041,172	244,438,876	279,387,981	341,681,374
3	135,444,759	152,191,409	177,631,393	187,870,213	196,170,801	190,524,062	226,775,496	248,444,602
4	170,639,142	195,496,700	227,466,481	218,134,827	219,854,731	230,373,764	260,149,549	298,944,897
TOTAL	675,021,369	729,943,489	854,815,482	879,776,751	901,709,446	924,158,945	1,068,005,857	1,240,953,676
CALIFORNIA								
1	193,398,948	187,634,922	221,641,911	212,509,591	213,061,218	222,131,363	240,529,576	256,333,908
2	176,048,272	194,564,523	208,569,889	234,874,963	230,329,469	232,076,700	257,152,554	279,051,667
3	583,885,389	552,779,444	531,947,682	561,952,483	569,010,453	591,362,643	708,121,887	1,196,900,622
4	159,752,391	141,485,560	163,780,073	197,749,502	203,039,421	215,913,187	235,207,561	302,639,793
5	315,441,094	331,900,722	375,415,523	372,078,346	382,578,450	382,007,263	502,086,703	508,596,343
6	166,106,505	186,321,795	199,649,369	201,057,363	329,161,300	368,947,315	429,772,041	419,362,894
7	113,587,214	123,931,696	139,740,959	160,020,752	170,496,789	178,614,584	196,061,233	213,888,984
8	239,962,506	245,680,340	263,280,824	271,299,183	294,947,157	297,721,226	331,211,510	339,312,746
9	166,397,896	182,713,788	203,767,950	202,138,936	205,738,210	219,537,124	250,670,157	271,817,289
10	131,112,830	138,731,026	154,449,914	151,085,667	151,363,069	161,475,511	185,325,011	192,885,256
11	198,281,841	226,060,647	158,809,252	159,700,345	159,776,338	167,895,031	188,881,840	199,057,303
12	145,301,303	158,878,806	225,954,497	229,977,708	244,301,739	261,498,985	288,201,054	265,615,064
13	120,155,158	112,242,762	123,121,631	120,998,982	117,930,290	128,665,903	150,968,719	154,427,742
14	187,473,532	191,232,777	149,079,436	157,552,978	159,245,976	162,612,410	180,414,033	201,434,332
15	123,284,250	147,175,664	148,496,006	151,671,585	161,587,174	167,508,651	184,663,571	209,530,260
16	155,483,786	176,982,338	222,742,378	144,099,364	127,371,673	133,901,197	150,528,454	162,483,332
17	239,706,692	288,877,454	321,617,902	301,794,585	200,120,763	212,890,544	235,665,878	263,035,031
18	250,876,253	302,868,412	318,048,222	238,753,327	247,238,890	271,289,203	298,409,010	322,030,573
19	103,200,960	116,229,326	127,440,772	123,042,654	129,508,749	136,423,340	152,865,527	165,261,107
20	121,536,995	175,396,618	201,918,730	212,255,457	223,517,415	235,338,143	266,537,093	289,103,252
21	141,146,043	152,781,240	171,831,731	195,594,351	199,519,251	205,215,665	236,206,018	248,635,297
22	179,320,662	192,861,110	218,870,166	223,119,770	223,032,019	237,420,693	269,811,003	281,841,007
23	303,149,348	268,226,067	302,921,309	310,892,812	330,970,356	351,373,655	388,308,348	384,671,142
24	189,839,558	196,685,433	216,255,196	223,230,400	225,035,044	237,000,695	264,986,539	288,570,955
25	184,533,115	195,167,492	221,863,125	228,884,943	224,454,635	239,685,784	273,204,926	301,514,781
26	155,634,293	161,831,988	182,954,866	189,157,621	188,261,831	197,341,270	223,162,933	246,563,887
27	196,072,679	189,998,573	215,654,034	219,849,055	220,390,194	232,226,737	260,102,097	282,555,651
28	240,563,781	238,020,129	269,803,083	279,390,543	283,238,585	292,027,060	326,618,105	365,781,044
29	214,615,574	222,133,455	241,621,202	247,489,650	246,698,921	260,716,706	289,614,955	286,566,999
30	287,709,577	186,243,419	212,578,746	216,924,356	213,481,254	224,650,191	258,185,698	276,676,569
31	182,813,351	193,403,098	220,649,293	228,704,582	224,316,231	236,328,262	271,463,652	284,938,950
32	184,003,876	185,302,415	213,208,785	218,637,103	214,821,782	225,545,746	254,932,820	275,975,264
33	175,020,348	187,367,414	214,871,008	219,449,922	219,288,993	225,258,123	253,662,748	273,688,101
34	173,528,717	185,092,743	210,112,206	215,616,481	212,788,921	223,551,633	255,007,636	273,337,779
35	144,244,950	173,227,154	169,312,875	164,300,360	165,737,460	175,974,159	198,288,017	217,286,673
36	237,609,487	251,270,516	296,547,300	323,095,056	326,704,141	343,658,015	392,943,373	438,241,558
37	131,011,708	138,713,323	143,652,359	163,566,279	158,993,100	183,646,326	201,737,000	244,913,649
38	84,003,379	89,933,538	104,468,106	145,157,768	146,343,809	158,577,738	179,126,062	183,832,858
39	86,093,967	89,205,632	102,746,910	142,899,327	142,396,069	149,615,855	173,479,580	186,185,588

Appendix A lists the congressional districts which represent the county in which the state capital is located, and those congressional districts which represent only portions of a county. Appendix C lists the programs included in each functional policy category.

table continues

Table 5.9 Outlays for Health Programs by Congressional District, 1983-1990 *(continued)*

Congressional District	1983	1984	1985	1986	1987	1988	1989	1990 (est.)
CALIFORNIA *continued*								
40	106,654,845	105,895,534	131,053,461	167,890,119	169,372,436	178,959,212	211,107,767	229,778,871
41	130,471,997	183,966,345	212,218,514	231,892,318	259,203,440	270,766,561	314,197,232	310,507,938
42	152,148,767	157,558,169	179,823,128	197,661,756	198,614,744	209,751,730	236,063,265	255,447,004
43	213,751,922	147,167,122	159,087,588	184,871,260	186,432,321	196,161,679	219,635,902	234,162,391
44	130,549,690	132,680,682	159,947,145	176,165,321	178,689,716	189,646,896	226,588,196	245,416,947
45	126,811,440	138,841,314	157,352,405	176,947,919	179,348,537	188,945,612	220,057,730	228,344,214
TOTAL	8,242,296,889	8,545,262,525	9,388,877,458	9,696,002,840	9,858,458,335	10,381,856,326	11,831,765,014	13,058,202,616
COLORADO								
1	281,335,759	311,769,561	319,369,365	301,864,225	324,986,111	362,670,993	415,015,632	469,122,173
2	73,028,647	79,052,864	82,215,391	97,372,238	112,353,755	113,756,830	124,156,579	138,654,352
3	128,296,284	140,124,239	162,015,948	143,756,111	149,976,938	170,746,641	185,034,854	210,610,805
4	117,545,975	124,749,162	141,939,638	129,022,651	137,214,097	153,165,731	170,648,247	196,387,467
5	53,602,661	64,489,409	68,099,258	90,138,924	94,453,699	126,876,492	116,879,983	128,546,004
6	31,116,804	42,144,736	44,452,374	65,310,346	69,143,284	78,223,186	81,766,589	89,663,417
TOTAL	684,926,130	762,329,971	818,091,974	827,464,494	888,127,884	1,005,439,874	1,093,501,883	1,232,984,218
CONNECTICUT								
1	202,315,215	209,725,541	240,509,022	257,606,466	276,025,842	326,124,041	350,101,235	414,293,650
2	91,013,354	75,007,311	86,079,910	150,065,853	154,084,371	178,409,521	193,947,695	206,611,884
3	245,473,810	275,794,842	299,203,269	321,168,275	327,240,415	363,219,501	397,617,728	416,678,721
4	167,433,668	178,026,884	205,399,412	173,103,677	175,582,742	205,782,855	225,696,558	241,296,170
5	153,285,793	173,572,443	192,643,399	182,999,896	188,817,340	210,790,471	240,382,331	266,296,179
6	153,964,938	167,681,106	208,610,136	208,920,504	219,560,672	232,707,317	263,312,102	288,726,926
TOTAL	1,013,486,777	1,079,808,128	1,232,445,148	1,293,864,670	1,341,311,381	1,517,033,707	1,671,057,649	1,833,903,531
DELAWARE								
TOTAL	150,951,954	171,153,905	186,200,295	184,201,410	196,456,844	215,753,525	242,334,350	267,741,760
DISTRICT OF COLUMBIA								
TOTAL	489,374,486	438,574,258	557,209,017	520,638,359	562,196,863	650,660,071	672,709,469	712,411,292
FLORIDA								
1	98,858,229	103,300,964	122,476,877	131,242,704	135,266,610	156,102,244	171,544,489	202,654,192
2	358,546,533	366,172,936	380,217,120	329,165,283	352,106,900	391,956,123	461,540,517	650,462,574
3	134,277,747	151,289,559	158,170,988	166,406,737	160,477,541	186,390,201	204,460,862	252,168,781
4	183,787,229	195,440,653	218,921,289	201,329,356	201,692,802	223,619,697	247,778,340	288,686,535
5	155,438,545	141,986,084	161,983,954	148,870,482	144,992,479	163,506,919	178,559,534	208,196,895
6	135,663,108	161,055,879	191,679,889	215,058,567	226,658,203	248,112,342	274,272,096	306,508,847
7	164,075,365	176,120,936	193,591,602	156,341,205	175,569,968	192,421,796	204,958,786	254,438,389
8	365,957,018	328,315,534	375,069,057	265,946,986	276,931,082	286,655,200	316,153,130	364,299,839
9	192,293,179	211,743,486	245,521,622	232,163,608	243,031,781	265,915,350	279,677,985	318,565,877
10	153,705,130	208,791,585	246,288,702	168,508,229	176,087,214	190,159,290	204,921,601	242,319,471
11	100,908,287	124,409,017	142,075,590	159,943,077	155,406,673	169,091,174	183,950,202	216,804,728
12	121,204,685	153,686,911	178,057,182	207,078,054	219,723,535	238,955,058	254,914,628	302,492,623
13	157,934,017	183,448,142	212,976,863	243,315,080	269,178,927	272,542,028	290,610,394	328,954,931
14	151,188,994	156,195,203	184,070,799	231,855,491	233,386,599	255,136,971	278,399,288	323,090,604
15	187,906,702	184,859,896	204,121,044	276,448,103	287,140,360	324,462,513	317,811,449	346,822,416
16	154,283,909	170,631,979	191,943,378	256,990,025	267,551,957	306,415,479	322,501,882	373,623,026
17	180,941,721	203,129,212	218,590,265	277,253,400	284,661,066	326,401,921	377,205,640	447,338,232
18	193,926,237	222,011,039	235,705,201	293,809,831	308,381,064	349,075,026	428,910,464	527,272,672
19	170,189,503	196,620,302	207,036,233	276,703,708	269,041,677	306,949,814	353,549,662	423,577,336
TOTAL	3,361,086,136	3,639,209,317	4,068,497,656	4,238,429,926	4,387,286,437	4,853,869,148	5,351,720,949	6,378,277,968
GEORGIA								
1	136,882,638	147,022,870	158,358,129	178,582,738	190,470,295	220,779,737	220,364,095	255,298,546
2	135,395,695	156,708,466	194,849,110	176,582,992	181,658,253	217,200,024	223,217,456	264,403,764
3	125,735,097	99,015,026	115,010,662	147,833,008	156,825,289	179,296,202	181,747,978	221,170,717
4	121,333,812	73,658,909	69,567,805	90,286,448	87,444,978	100,564,677	106,601,588	108,886,961
5	252,649,823	332,510,243	362,850,646	356,780,423	365,705,191	403,966,013	458,569,572	572,350,855
6	82,103,781	95,255,155	109,937,998	139,663,939	137,523,307	163,001,998	167,176,845	189,832,693
7	82,900,664	79,596,027	89,990,131	105,684,130	113,988,672	123,118,847	131,974,547	153,504,139
8	145,412,141	176,061,544	203,747,696	192,664,602	201,840,339	236,942,946	241,258,796	279,414,024
9	107,572,346	108,279,660	148,570,614	145,053,895	142,395,602	159,888,256	171,698,872	202,056,190
10	119,260,702	137,357,831	145,054,170	162,228,290	165,711,031	196,533,617	201,827,861	227,407,931
TOTAL	1,309,246,699	1,405,465,731	1,597,936,961	1,695,360,465	1,743,562,957	2,001,292,317	2,104,437,610	2,474,325,819

Appendix A lists the congressional districts which represent the county in which the state capital is located, and those congressional districts which represent only portions of a county. Appendix C lists the programs included in each functional policy category.

table continues

Table 5.9

Outlays for Health Programs by Congressional District, 1983-1990 *(continued)*

Congressional District	1983	1984	1985	1986	1987	1988	1989	1990 (est.)
HAWAII								
1	120,896,895	120,560,083	144,190,436	161,339,601	159,852,124	169,942,804	169,441,467	189,446,153
2	99,447,812	111,461,109	114,288,791	118,247,867	132,335,636	148,730,056	135,029,120	189,840,727
TOTAL	220,344,707	232,021,192	258,479,227	279,587,468	292,187,760	318,672,860	304,470,587	379,286,880
IDAHO								
1	116,681,898	122,191,989	141,477,562	144,098,801	150,938,691	176,513,672	184,682,228	231,903,783
2	73,796,819	87,039,531	92,419,914	97,988,272	100,687,395	117,433,872	121,880,641	153,429,711
TOTAL	190,478,717	209,231,520	233,897,476	242,087,073	251,626,086	293,947,544	306,562,869	385,333,494
ILLINOIS								
1	239,637,448	242,790,327	269,676,995	287,842,036	293,819,895	346,166,464	341,517,800	366,161,844
2	161,722,752	179,602,011	199,649,484	220,230,020	215,515,696	264,491,935	256,791,188	303,266,171
3	162,319,045	178,391,069	199,272,021	219,865,974	212,839,641	261,550,795	251,982,283	303,850,475
4	101,773,575	128,194,414	142,778,306	165,112,747	148,462,033	175,808,497	184,633,556	202,726,908
5	175,639,389	177,822,341	228,053,569	216,433,331	215,171,886	269,958,886	257,887,161	310,924,429
6	94,137,457	124,819,877	122,065,089	159,150,694	154,557,522	169,029,518	171,706,494	199,390,718
7	224,448,329	244,615,420	264,840,699	283,144,228	280,791,057	336,658,432	336,689,372	402,363,463
8	161,093,628	178,897,986	200,414,822	220,513,139	214,702,107	263,000,098	254,342,692	302,015,136
9	201,748,360	212,317,431	237,272,992	256,233,841	263,229,809	317,074,279	307,607,813	362,812,424
10	123,760,069	128,349,603	143,231,037	161,347,873	159,380,818	186,205,249	185,744,082	213,266,933
11	161,059,179	179,044,617	198,586,849	218,649,826	228,244,457	282,628,965	277,413,386	324,791,428
12	113,407,553	128,503,383	139,550,975	155,072,954	152,314,634	176,260,533	177,252,526	205,848,481
13	101,576,066	118,649,601	125,763,656	164,485,635	152,714,220	178,774,385	179,734,157	209,283,621
14	112,750,344	136,042,743	135,883,015	112,471,353	121,527,474	130,524,936	172,254,705	154,402,107
15	125,530,621	151,668,987	182,737,045	130,286,094	153,600,475	140,880,315	152,164,407	167,538,928
16	121,273,400	135,886,610	154,798,070	110,470,583	112,766,400	124,421,156	133,689,223	155,259,182
17	159,484,953	161,362,584	179,098,752	147,643,118	145,672,896	152,590,189	166,515,832	182,592,945
18	165,117,003	162,965,582	171,829,684	174,512,575	142,824,106	153,430,478	164,596,226	187,645,940
19	160,343,060	194,628,130	212,709,636	162,548,277	164,286,098	178,804,549	187,610,711	202,819,536
20	383,405,160	384,715,546	433,478,302	389,929,203	418,846,708	393,166,047	432,167,475	584,845,615
21	136,614,384	169,641,997	188,802,870	195,999,246	195,772,550	219,558,456	231,867,551	273,280,831
22	171,236,082	209,784,150	243,093,223	196,882,593	199,907,880	210,382,603	230,089,434	256,561,711
TOTAL	3,558,077,856	3,928,694,412	4,373,587,091	4,348,825,341	4,346,948,362	4,931,366,765	5,054,258,072	5,871,648,826
INDIANA								
1	96,939,254	161,360,557	158,637,103	202,971,554	190,524,008	214,908,232	239,539,684	382,345,815
2	122,869,113	138,209,470	152,932,059	171,640,474	172,502,707	195,531,512	219,473,196	345,301,280
3	114,432,347	156,179,487	152,219,605	143,695,185	151,752,863	169,940,730	184,055,671	283,194,463
4	116,800,212	126,978,620	133,828,808	128,582,498	135,493,688	142,769,869	166,065,804	255,555,973
5	99,822,662	130,841,253	158,016,434	151,612,367	152,688,436	168,474,044	188,442,585	281,433,734
6	145,741,427	137,628,039	162,806,795	184,868,131	182,892,835	201,343,054	221,745,582	329,533,522
7	156,450,394	163,542,427	182,245,939	164,040,109	170,309,119	186,853,900	239,536,134	305,986,789
8	157,818,086	165,976,176	186,579,535	181,067,868	187,751,566	195,288,196	239,471,881	365,174,201
9	134,212,455	153,574,485	163,831,562	183,869,209	191,342,226	218,157,159	245,345,016	373,054,677
10	203,524,598	210,516,184	225,223,070	302,349,159	288,359,576	314,773,857	356,014,809	585,089,285
TOTAL	1,348,610,549	1,544,806,698	1,676,320,911	1,814,696,554	1,823,617,024	2,008,040,553	2,299,690,362	3,506,669,739
IOWA								
1	124,106,971	138,074,579	142,706,644	144,924,329	151,395,682	163,974,220	181,361,755	208,691,804
2	100,109,859	111,018,557	120,770,873	131,838,257	137,372,437	149,678,629	163,823,822	188,852,885
3	144,829,681	164,194,161	178,235,648	174,101,815	186,712,035	209,792,277	226,797,820	252,007,665
4	189,845,364	179,554,418	202,432,134	234,060,700	250,976,489	244,287,253	299,845,032	328,782,593
5	133,323,058	150,394,803	167,256,500	172,873,433	180,839,397	197,446,771	215,505,322	245,965,237
6	139,955,080	144,873,488	154,976,489	148,770,086	155,948,803	171,012,599	185,573,230	212,912,168
TOTAL	832,170,013	888,110,006	966,378,288	1,006,568,620	1,063,244,843	1,136,191,749	1,272,906,981	1,437,212,352
KANSAS								
1	149,944,308	152,708,769	166,754,550	149,586,948	152,329,875	164,735,805	182,225,256	207,097,759
2	173,087,501	178,287,685	179,173,598	173,573,497	184,766,413	197,696,986	227,041,988	255,312,224
3	95,993,339	126,266,463	137,121,466	165,486,692	156,958,722	181,983,258	192,616,029	214,743,412
4	97,028,135	118,098,463	126,945,693	161,690,974	163,297,954	187,670,366	193,029,592	219,641,824
5	181,761,052	177,880,306	197,630,734	167,737,181	176,982,534	190,555,246	212,289,518	241,643,737
TOTAL	697,814,335	753,241,686	807,626,041	818,075,292	834,335,498	922,641,661	1,007,202,383	1,138,438,957

Appendix A lists the congressional districts which represent the county in which the state capital is located, and those congressional districts which represent only portions of a county. Appendix C lists the programs included in each functional policy category.

table continues

Table 5.9 Outlays for Health Programs by Congressional District, 1983-1990 *(continued)*

Congressional District	1983	1984	1985	1986	1987	1988	1989	1990 (est.)
KENTUCKY								
1	134,656,754	154,977,628	187,258,138	169,810,187	181,848,081	195,264,624	215,656,961	241,797,117
2	112,308,154	115,898,032	138,313,230	138,628,244	146,521,835	159,625,409	181,654,263	203,760,181
3	122,248,384	137,820,256	169,067,193	180,876,975	171,219,813	213,231,110	216,194,204	252,729,514
4	91,621,412	119,109,346	138,150,488	141,102,556	144,771,687	158,016,915	174,968,225	193,990,247
5	145,994,505	169,143,435	208,581,333	211,171,172	225,963,515	250,759,454	285,069,374	327,215,409
6	185,263,252	221,216,368	232,544,807	239,350,675	241,826,158	261,948,008	327,789,148	348,733,875
7	137,686,580	148,258,578	183,669,510	185,801,012	197,019,740	221,421,030	247,331,345	277,980,189
TOTAL	929,779,041	1,066,423,643	1,257,584,699	1,266,740,821	1,309,170,829	1,460,266,550	1,648,663,520	1,846,206,532
LOUISIANA								
1	157,192,982	171,647,107	188,994,663	185,526,183	193,978,858	203,843,945	251,762,740	392,362,807
2	148,545,965	147,015,744	157,338,060	195,769,960	193,876,104	209,589,043	255,610,454	363,609,879
3	80,626,403	85,527,841	125,397,381	166,474,100	165,928,764	170,986,029	199,573,406	322,024,798
4	138,013,529	151,062,528	181,328,148	164,668,691	173,944,272	186,763,898	241,102,918	384,854,676
5	164,612,230	183,357,316	219,720,064	200,195,908	203,397,695	225,094,950	268,285,947	503,463,435
6	183,379,437	173,054,798	191,503,224	236,524,250	225,471,788	239,908,366	312,059,530	495,466,869
7	114,839,954	125,921,294	141,880,654	147,226,877	155,208,474	169,986,378	201,965,066	342,912,865
8	146,494,111	170,837,604	198,049,668	195,476,845	204,426,913	228,427,165	271,595,821	496,411,369
TOTAL	1,133,704,612	1,208,424,233	1,404,211,863	1,491,862,813	1,516,232,868	1,634,599,774	2,001,955,881	3,301,106,699
MAINE								
1	204,913,954	223,404,767	261,293,766	252,721,444	268,630,801	279,709,250	311,877,567	354,261,461
2	197,670,147	221,053,886	257,827,399	267,363,847	288,010,539	318,824,680	323,096,824	370,562,872
TOTAL	402,584,101	444,458,653	519,121,165	520,085,291	556,641,340	598,533,930	634,974,391	724,824,333
MARYLAND								
1	165,306,249	159,949,670	174,739,603	157,275,694	168,396,298	198,015,097	203,605,288	213,437,039
2	100,343,912	114,788,374	129,857,068	150,710,422	167,559,218	188,512,142	179,257,321	190,358,100
3	219,394,128	254,364,254	274,814,358	389,651,360	390,067,628	457,573,232	515,371,020	505,936,874
4	74,021,239	82,185,627	97,992,230	146,914,661	170,674,905	191,584,955	200,801,504	263,352,199
5	176,203,501	197,970,211	192,646,626	131,668,569	127,048,182	166,763,243	156,087,857	161,008,030
6	159,589,183	168,433,685	157,175,739	144,390,126	147,610,887	170,018,809	170,174,686	190,974,770
7	294,668,392	344,586,902	382,874,810	425,269,333	423,143,440	490,523,788	527,426,206	617,867,131
8	231,363,300	209,274,618	238,550,155	251,803,916	238,403,077	301,696,730	333,691,367	367,311,842
TOTAL	1,420,889,902	1,531,553,340	1,648,650,590	1,797,684,082	1,832,903,635	2,164,687,996	2,286,415,248	2,510,245,985
MASSACHUSETTS								
1	175,032,452	191,366,827	211,526,069	216,828,278	221,140,526	243,316,920	267,010,124	298,322,318
2	189,789,612	216,495,118	230,584,990	230,447,288	236,166,571	271,716,474	286,147,830	321,235,645
3	210,641,975	223,953,964	239,615,892	260,847,935	283,386,424	300,744,682	331,670,213	348,755,255
4	226,326,797	208,297,825	244,320,139	268,544,271	282,888,869	311,773,513	350,348,256	386,129,077
5	174,773,321	189,459,668	194,761,626	212,942,963	226,102,073	248,184,321	266,799,551	296,917,952
6	194,011,177	196,171,509	231,456,252	230,459,685	260,355,762	269,908,085	288,645,751	324,206,801
7	217,195,814	228,438,035	259,990,972	273,348,103	278,447,367	310,741,224	328,943,923	365,479,729
8	593,894,870	539,178,563	633,814,739	617,843,663	650,085,673	733,680,400	772,020,940	802,782,410
9	543,713,771	422,398,556	478,673,212	489,592,759	507,642,874	580,601,177	623,653,162	735,722,618
10	164,341,072	168,457,726	202,298,254	222,743,596	239,857,688	267,979,635	297,078,736	320,197,479
11	219,720,227	199,568,913	259,060,871	269,665,979	277,818,874	321,438,098	341,012,753	381,726,282
TOTAL	2,909,441,090	2,783,786,706	3,186,103,016	3,293,264,519	3,463,892,699	3,860,084,530	4,153,331,238	4,581,475,566
MICHIGAN								
1	204,308,860	228,396,312	248,693,968	247,817,632	247,108,648	372,747,362	290,720,076	292,089,340
2	203,542,063	230,410,209	252,145,570	252,753,717	282,994,042	313,777,668	330,363,846	351,432,274
3	116,939,797	171,932,820	171,753,563	170,762,084	178,042,594	191,421,515	242,933,281	354,511,184
4	140,326,110	163,697,819	181,623,030	170,599,539	177,975,709	188,595,968	203,126,668	225,146,144
5	157,373,976	152,328,140	180,632,804	147,234,640	153,128,753	164,797,591	170,103,802	235,159,729
6	296,630,472	285,866,171	251,055,559	264,207,933	273,115,769	310,202,304	301,625,041	386,740,728
7	120,133,807	140,049,597	163,441,891	180,732,457	200,049,386	200,891,225	214,060,353	228,323,833
8	152,945,275	158,895,247	179,361,439	182,364,961	192,987,109	201,774,494	213,836,688	233,054,106
9	149,914,730	163,125,337	181,320,251	167,868,664	180,200,348	188,959,029	197,693,419	232,246,619
10	143,946,204	178,191,096	200,182,794	213,776,240	233,133,026	228,660,432	225,605,091	221,480,568
11	211,897,629	217,250,356	238,610,536	209,540,204	223,374,318	231,601,189	252,709,676	279,462,901
12	92,567,820	106,381,401	107,140,815	146,338,485	151,636,832	162,385,566	168,364,144	182,913,674

Appendix A lists the congressional districts which represent the county in which the state capital is located, and those congressional districts which represent only portions of a county. Appendix C lists the programs included in each functional policy category.

table continues

Table 5.9 Outlays for Health Programs by Congressional District, 1983-1990 *(continued)*

Congressional District	1983	1984	1985	1986	1987	1988	1989	1990 (est.)
MICHIGAN *continued*								
13	240,113,751	266,263,900	292,305,358	288,791,718	297,887,571	327,215,521	341,435,933	374,013,679
14	118,762,299	132,155,386	146,242,231	179,512,371	180,729,840	196,339,273	207,018,527	227,268,867
15	187,051,546	201,862,068	223,594,521	228,010,070	227,300,763	252,446,707	255,710,206	284,244,720
16	163,589,040	200,428,714	211,053,760	212,847,118	236,802,756	233,549,272	242,885,449	266,287,669
17	142,252,393	157,773,824	177,207,523	198,566,314	197,649,259	222,053,859	227,235,808	249,354,445
18	80,764,878	96,468,939	106,218,378	154,437,240	153,012,896	159,818,755	168,737,089	184,233,726
TOTAL	2,923,060,649	3,251,477,336	3,512,583,994	3,616,161,387	3,787,129,620	4,147,237,729	4,254,165,097	4,807,964,207
MINNESOTA								
1	157,063,190	200,504,329	210,753,102	172,811,046	181,743,407	198,984,574	203,051,246	212,385,672
2	160,459,325	190,450,181	195,728,924	167,812,284	179,969,222	191,378,144	192,242,774	210,249,439
3	100,314,948	112,916,590	120,357,522	148,535,744	149,190,700	156,235,367	169,675,591	184,375,804
4	149,390,256	136,470,300	174,070,651	153,630,819	167,731,021	174,740,791	168,319,115	186,806,137
5	183,989,882	200,546,154	190,226,590	243,461,381	246,989,399	296,732,111	308,743,878	337,255,310
6	233,200,830	225,854,668	236,422,875	299,069,250	306,856,502	323,887,690	349,053,464	380,279,640
7	213,696,468	204,395,009	215,747,688	224,880,501	228,117,834	245,185,289	264,235,788	277,899,682
8	178,396,507	203,168,407	211,054,062	221,800,335	221,440,029	235,991,046	257,356,468	272,752,622
TOTAL	1,376,511,408	1,474,305,638	1,554,361,414	1,632,001,359	1,682,038,114	1,823,135,011	1,912,678,324	2,062,004,305
MISSISSIPPI								
1	131,918,826	148,626,757	165,008,270	169,752,146	187,100,881	203,447,602	222,599,222	272,568,322
2	173,043,458	200,319,103	209,635,209	191,554,144	204,643,220	208,208,496	230,869,294	268,340,667
3	122,988,105	140,265,923	149,323,592	161,726,413	177,274,064	208,489,134	220,601,788	269,981,456
4	218,172,785	217,484,552	226,341,907	234,657,423	249,546,090	265,686,955	302,329,979	414,562,977
5	94,850,552	107,307,274	111,244,069	167,105,307	157,577,679	163,008,619	168,794,262	193,593,504
TOTAL	740,973,726	814,003,610	861,553,047	924,795,432	976,141,935	1,048,840,807	1,145,194,545	1,419,046,925
MISSOURI								
1	316,566,550	300,491,454	328,187,582	377,966,731	397,804,259	449,132,451	483,400,674	544,343,455
2	166,868,796	195,074,043	218,921,701	240,315,913	238,152,348	256,144,283	277,723,987	325,948,126
3	75,380,565	75,870,863	85,870,832	92,809,318	90,465,650	99,909,143	108,937,138	130,953,333
4	236,183,190	225,297,772	238,974,337	236,971,386	250,948,383	258,554,346	285,810,737	348,078,741
5	163,029,483	167,563,190	207,202,116	214,852,086	214,243,947	225,784,523	246,484,910	263,979,188
6	172,616,551	187,106,498	218,965,309	189,102,040	192,795,387	222,949,396	229,467,920	253,043,630
7	167,375,660	201,595,178	210,368,632	183,804,020	192,941,777	209,287,529	229,140,867	250,004,118
8	180,533,288	207,323,608	240,759,837	229,090,839	244,262,949	258,598,628	294,143,183	327,018,878
9	182,702,555	205,310,399	218,325,256	224,500,795	232,386,000	239,384,864	268,968,110	334,277,738
TOTAL	1,661,256,639	1,765,633,005	1,967,575,602	1,989,413,128	2,054,000,700	2,219,745,164	2,424,077,527	2,777,647,207
MONTANA								
1	117,206,455	127,109,577	142,681,026	141,401,643	160,040,467	171,370,410	186,585,987	204,416,537
2	95,504,333	98,583,963	128,067,283	127,192,779	138,849,780	153,505,219	153,291,380	178,012,117
TOTAL	212,710,788	225,693,540	270,748,309	268,594,422	298,890,247	324,875,629	339,877,367	382,428,653
NEBRASKA								
1	161,949,895	171,985,794	185,866,693	176,192,174	190,091,073	203,365,737	222,477,600	329,233,383
2	113,330,045	126,693,621	128,516,116	192,643,913	202,443,495	219,990,836	229,768,017	358,405,226
3	145,696,046	156,653,689	193,982,351	151,169,712	160,661,219	170,035,196	186,662,051	280,235,378
TOTAL	420,975,986	455,333,104	508,365,160	520,005,799	553,195,787	593,391,769	638,907,668	967,873,987
NEVADA								
1	22,327,971	78,956,768	87,127,249	116,971,541	116,758,732	124,665,637	145,167,590	154,810,754
2	47,902,781	133,011,620	150,446,018	125,465,036	122,100,580	128,111,730	147,801,013	178,711,643
TOTAL	70,230,752	211,968,388	237,573,267	242,436,577	238,859,312	252,777,367	292,968,603	333,522,397
NEW HAMPSHIRE								
1	105,796,081	124,897,596	132,876,228	131,300,149	131,110,754	155,887,911	162,759,580	185,353,249
2	161,854,195	174,565,990	180,777,856	195,814,830	216,611,668	211,032,871	221,134,084	250,144,892
TOTAL	267,650,276	299,463,586	313,654,084	327,114,979	347,722,422	366,920,782	383,893,664	435,498,141

Appendix A lists the congressional districts which represent the county in which the state capital is located, and those congressional districts which represent only portions of a county. Appendix C lists the programs included in each functional policy category.

table continues

Table 5.9 Outlays for Health Programs by Congressional District, 1983-1990 *(continued)*

Congressional District	1983	1984	1985	1986	1987	1988	1989	1990 (est.)
NEW JERSEY								
1	164,500,152	199,364,831	152,914,514	169,668,046	201,405,976	202,308,572	207,841,045	244,467,460
2	240,553,900	215,331,818	280,988,076	245,374,667	250,835,718	280,215,185	294,596,650	340,363,697
3	125,299,859	139,025,530	171,175,354	180,678,685	193,456,034	208,341,383	219,762,666	259,659,294
4	231,519,883	236,976,518	257,421,472	320,310,398	329,878,830	333,835,762	458,921,819	452,096,374
5	131,061,892	118,678,261	141,466,075	146,098,160	139,888,266	158,399,794	163,671,824	186,847,356
6	110,676,657	132,415,707	165,646,986	171,256,955	187,589,138	195,830,528	193,725,474	215,805,653
7	129,824,994	150,318,205	171,360,357	181,563,635	191,488,816	216,872,013	215,710,421	263,618,017
8	168,700,682	164,875,869	194,003,663	186,868,684	193,419,699	214,708,161	225,987,690	270,754,301
9	129,601,277	133,190,831	156,666,213	184,207,005	159,733,675	171,468,234	179,102,611	204,038,539
10	245,474,764	251,501,162	289,673,139	279,253,749	289,134,866	339,271,331	337,148,521	409,831,178
11	170,805,766	190,103,313	218,788,147	222,436,005	235,830,224	253,891,477	273,646,977	408,058,597
12	89,590,529	114,131,203	163,864,831	179,593,458	193,307,629	208,942,468	242,959,581	304,313,690
13	159,340,195	123,040,171	139,021,316	178,925,658	186,336,273	200,268,077	214,555,146	242,328,682
14	203,871,561	219,697,252	278,514,046	264,538,875	332,625,413	320,282,388	331,021,662	407,969,556
TOTAL	2,300,822,110	2,388,650,670	2,781,504,188	2,910,773,981	3,084,930,555	3,304,635,371	3,558,652,087	4,210,152,394
NEW MEXICO								
1	133,141,280	104,607,589	120,182,134	121,331,514	138,448,553	146,479,719	163,299,319	168,736,710
2	111,567,208	108,456,738	127,942,146	122,313,057	126,818,544	140,510,417	156,513,088	163,823,730
3	74,157,520	137,437,602	151,881,185	159,669,542	172,653,340	192,766,527	213,527,847	248,214,268
TOTAL	318,866,008	350,501,929	400,005,465	403,314,113	437,920,437	479,756,663	533,340,254	580,774,709
NEW YORK								
1	116,714,471	136,661,803	151,995,502	171,318,289	193,630,160	181,982,879	191,289,443	220,540,504
2	89,047,047	104,740,363	115,879,030	135,121,500	137,654,229	144,498,037	154,689,825	179,398,944
3	154,964,938	195,196,088	211,237,375	248,790,637	291,530,346	307,290,898	313,539,769	310,955,494
4	124,315,134	146,083,185	163,244,861	185,742,691	177,964,760	191,527,646	209,296,845	226,730,359
5	124,028,202	145,886,931	163,436,397	189,751,728	182,903,238	197,552,826	215,343,252	257,348,979
6	147,991,050	187,126,924	205,778,185	290,356,182	310,940,339	326,322,137	354,813,479	396,472,001
7	154,369,492	184,812,428	202,926,987	287,890,149	312,624,300	328,892,483	357,394,834	398,784,318
8	199,329,182	237,696,908	259,114,016	355,523,663	366,530,638	397,782,574	405,045,724	449,643,000
9	153,028,041	182,307,392	200,460,166	285,282,473	309,698,154	325,447,159	354,429,141	396,057,185
10	204,081,450	251,813,667	272,430,196	362,901,053	472,183,062	486,630,799	456,734,488	510,269,862
11	202,380,702	251,746,642	275,056,499	366,857,401	406,766,082	426,804,410	462,647,524	518,422,371
12	207,252,707	261,548,777	284,652,676	375,548,028	415,408,936	435,730,189	479,100,053	525,944,844
13	202,458,213	252,098,817	276,665,405	367,400,646	406,971,160	427,562,250	465,852,599	520,849,107
14	147,589,623	155,901,222	179,184,667	280,518,089	334,200,614	339,504,565	387,070,460	392,402,925
15	755,601,277	962,083,141	1,033,992,876	908,119,157	946,948,822	902,524,653	972,508,369	1,116,633,068
16	615,183,554	737,670,409	766,532,636	603,872,223	573,545,714	491,794,555	535,645,019	599,986,404
17	605,613,630	701,494,151	732,980,483	644,991,494	648,314,071	617,712,529	648,053,720	683,894,738
18	470,560,827	294,014,862	318,807,615	448,259,128	492,314,228	600,517,415	557,802,091	624,401,937
19	211,134,466	261,566,259	285,920,947	388,121,322	426,903,966	508,511,396	485,231,726	540,600,266
20	281,781,674	266,390,616	266,818,166	235,133,986	273,177,385	270,192,517	307,123,177	306,337,977
21	96,079,315	172,014,904	166,978,949	187,886,237	204,444,803	212,878,523	226,212,531	250,696,426
22	146,973,336	166,475,744	191,705,441	213,387,182	236,472,417	231,166,348	251,019,710	280,336,622
23	515,672,806	546,104,538	588,034,639	622,889,151	623,866,507	639,533,133	728,964,773	953,726,891
24	97,141,689	165,494,015	185,314,000	180,453,096	201,454,735	207,513,521	214,244,092	247,341,967
25	139,470,581	235,771,133	233,453,533	213,093,386	222,396,279	234,112,192	247,335,327	276,066,616
26	167,369,879	238,484,106	239,106,060	222,309,858	242,011,034	273,382,447	262,700,834	296,795,869
27	160,689,769	182,090,697	203,297,258	186,177,525	199,618,923	216,613,954	214,420,846	238,292,563
28	251,095,606	236,557,746	227,031,684	234,402,587	260,113,020	261,034,312	276,723,256	310,675,474
29	203,650,306	205,371,804	207,197,984	185,482,877	192,954,484	198,737,704	212,319,286	243,004,356
30	240,892,116	218,958,944	243,088,231	230,650,374	274,029,700	278,719,856	284,920,759	324,322,078
31	219,278,102	197,306,915	211,533,301	174,315,403	192,002,190	196,853,353	207,804,167	217,774,291
32	178,382,103	207,645,324	224,645,681	197,397,724	220,282,790	229,680,743	244,263,377	279,915,433
33	195,826,742	209,630,904	233,205,846	196,628,167	221,972,754	216,882,212	224,980,077	251,661,303
34	152,029,461	221,117,831	251,312,262	196,035,945	215,819,787	223,949,920	238,044,899	263,525,970
TOTAL	7,931,977,490	9,119,865,188	9,773,019,554	10,372,609,349	11,187,649,622	11,529,840,136	12,147,565,472	13,609,810,142
NORTH CAROLINA								
1	131,394,855	144,862,574	156,791,847	168,015,196	172,901,243	201,493,383	219,721,646	249,441,472
2	195,632,199	221,230,759	252,734,752	261,405,253	297,460,204	332,465,250	386,421,725	371,259,445
3	94,503,433	117,725,307	127,202,026	146,867,533	154,033,597	172,845,239	195,124,370	226,858,348
4	253,270,843	252,689,595	274,029,370	308,982,424	332,748,289	362,874,891	401,070,666	593,652,038
5	117,019,628	131,933,764	155,125,110	153,383,763	163,633,243	186,445,580	205,981,040	233,727,835
6	111,584,473	101,600,799	115,528,150	115,133,887	118,955,928	134,998,349	149,299,082	168,163,185
7	85,175,776	101,393,662	113,566,482	130,006,588	134,141,320	165,915,656	176,195,267	198,522,142
8	100,514,680	119,219,041	130,455,974	130,530,576	143,198,127	152,286,916	171,343,808	188,207,875
9	81,440,470	97,756,729	108,060,556	110,029,297	129,625,880	130,839,566	140,457,355	158,827,051
10	85,814,708	97,710,289	108,496,703	120,840,282	129,035,002	145,019,872	152,617,086	164,176,659
11	129,324,393	158,816,534	161,143,816	175,040,440	170,045,442	186,461,146	209,512,066	236,355,982
TOTAL	1,385,675,458	1,544,939,053	1,703,134,786	1,820,235,238	1,945,778,275	2,171,645,848	2,407,744,111	2,789,192,034

Appendix A lists the congressional districts which represent the county in which the state capital is located, and those congressional districts which represent only portions of a county. Appendix C lists the programs included in each functional policy category.

table continues

Table 5.9

Outlays for Health Programs by Congressional District, 1983-1990 *(continued)*

Congressional District	1983	1984	1985	1986	1987	1988	1989	1990 (est.)
NORTH DAKOTA								
TOTAL	210,527,527	244,344,595	270,752,792	272,645,313	301,707,218	330,323,391	360,370,084	396,015,627
OHIO								
1	195,646,865	213,768,291	245,729,759	266,294,594	268,978,625	305,406,147	326,329,238	366,332,722
2	136,643,375	156,351,990	166,554,352	188,025,744	177,704,342	201,304,480	213,865,091	242,484,249
3	123,477,152	172,710,095	157,234,847	191,610,497	209,828,656	230,109,669	230,559,126	274,747,144
4	109,136,526	142,238,916	147,249,846	139,031,206	149,853,379	159,234,663	166,596,612	192,973,244
5	106,603,806	128,948,752	135,882,812	137,278,968	140,978,617	163,159,594	162,538,002	184,161,064
6	136,357,475	175,740,076	177,223,290	202,399,281	213,578,185	229,003,264	255,142,194	295,923,510
7	100,279,768	133,120,546	132,145,394	148,004,620	152,684,137	166,335,869	174,487,822	203,046,507
8	96,847,092	126,423,173	124,601,808	141,422,313	147,863,655	156,027,164	167,903,351	191,746,089
9	117,329,199	165,095,385	213,699,683	215,636,587	224,874,978	245,093,972	267,516,877	295,237,757
10	185,157,762	262,405,392	254,926,660	271,719,146	251,201,778	273,671,810	289,459,485	395,105,188
11	67,676,050	99,605,643	94,664,359	118,125,055	120,219,486	132,881,734	141,413,223	166,704,121
12	154,658,569	207,837,027	212,448,577	228,523,280	236,923,057	245,902,802	290,166,140	371,333,609
13	82,159,339	117,676,970	127,289,310	134,173,265	132,646,214	155,183,104	156,315,846	172,010,050
14	157,758,639	153,991,552	166,829,282	194,243,326	176,146,488	196,435,801	213,671,979	276,372,097
15	307,703,700	192,063,583	193,227,125	236,759,632	243,615,668	272,338,185	307,915,342	341,401,582
16	116,899,820	139,061,015	144,377,680	145,765,683	144,779,521	163,609,276	164,958,515	192,740,626
17	198,333,822	185,133,868	187,659,372	194,320,290	201,743,368	221,388,280	231,574,632	264,384,934
18	149,886,669	179,372,023	177,179,144	182,346,535	188,699,041	212,063,574	221,418,963	255,332,892
19	202,880,398	183,394,855	214,693,528	243,403,690	249,147,996	282,619,618	271,697,114	308,975,877
20	183,515,258	201,769,427	207,886,543	247,221,629	245,930,887	281,437,091	291,286,347	344,200,949
21	236,237,299	249,528,927	261,727,112	300,437,072	310,348,609	351,988,583	369,677,014	418,286,376
TOTAL	3,165,188,582	3,586,237,505	3,743,230,482	4,126,742,413	4,187,746,687	4,645,194,681	4,914,492,912	5,753,500,585
OKLAHOMA								
1	109,753,962	117,122,659	126,059,574	150,430,056	153,193,950	161,147,006	188,119,039	213,219,130
2	167,834,079	182,313,608	209,231,012	220,954,123	226,162,849	251,115,083	284,463,845	311,508,567
3	191,985,775	199,917,769	236,240,667	226,538,354	230,881,591	265,188,763	297,531,206	330,810,753
4	129,497,439	127,382,146	139,202,696	151,605,703	161,926,280	168,164,226	187,734,995	202,887,051
5	133,134,862	158,620,518	175,297,542	170,265,398	184,861,420	187,799,572	221,230,244	236,898,216
6	161,640,874	158,181,251	181,991,757	195,546,869	207,992,462	214,919,612	246,824,115	300,642,581
TOTAL	893,846,991	943,537,951	1,068,023,249	1,115,340,503	1,165,018,553	1,248,334,262	1,425,903,445	1,595,966,297
OREGON								
1	163,065,154	165,002,847	165,686,293	190,844,706	193,456,304	195,649,210	248,799,265	244,717,109
2	132,897,115	125,966,138	146,031,478	152,071,025	153,344,529	168,163,058	198,233,119	219,474,695
3	186,700,619	193,237,720	234,949,314	245,890,297	253,505,520	275,698,663	321,852,074	354,508,156
4	140,882,395	140,767,224	141,858,425	151,853,924	154,600,851	173,819,636	193,609,511	212,604,659
5	137,923,049	170,736,225	195,865,657	190,350,143	192,408,414	208,781,242	232,236,860	294,829,820
TOTAL	761,468,331	795,710,153	884,391,167	931,010,094	947,315,617	1,022,111,810	1,194,730,829	1,326,134,440
PENNSYLVANIA								
1	438,034,765	407,002,402	474,344,768	492,217,396	510,413,443	552,510,149	603,114,645	633,580,298
2	264,171,656	322,185,905	366,714,379	405,406,036	411,787,272	447,897,882	486,216,032	484,431,293
3	286,605,812	290,050,307	343,591,139	381,068,778	387,789,685	417,193,327	450,935,169	467,430,611
4	97,723,069	152,362,223	169,092,588	180,615,600	188,627,419	201,524,288	219,480,339	236,300,312
5	106,588,458	132,856,168	135,717,148	153,242,001	156,404,977	173,262,386	179,146,972	201,801,059
6	155,265,198	171,729,433	192,739,640	174,875,902	176,766,440	191,253,578	204,390,994	225,135,430
7	156,909,144	165,498,874	189,177,122	215,594,458	218,727,767	235,971,276	256,556,670	295,270,052
8	87,399,920	89,895,550	94,037,398	129,783,366	130,980,899	140,873,760	147,821,759	160,092,445
9	143,810,800	168,075,017	183,699,180	159,770,246	171,485,126	234,192,482	210,273,184	214,250,818
10	189,690,193	211,377,905	216,776,244	209,678,983	228,739,882	231,834,139	248,964,916	269,180,892
11	179,410,143	200,952,969	215,393,150	218,314,603	226,369,084	240,700,210	286,757,322	303,988,392
12	157,911,570	160,650,747	185,298,545	202,066,105	212,298,907	231,024,074	248,952,897	265,946,850
13	154,080,139	149,006,210	175,768,007	201,324,540	211,371,047	231,539,710	244,506,913	269,696,707
14	285,014,041	284,336,250	308,183,941	329,364,565	340,849,001	417,203,601	404,225,180	433,754,852
15	136,666,256	148,704,618	165,408,745	158,354,864	169,838,329	181,034,056	201,582,529	217,198,762
16	168,022,471	127,227,240	143,939,089	122,922,911	126,668,691	139,474,766	149,337,200	165,979,967
17	363,330,034	360,018,758	408,433,749	397,227,790	414,502,839	418,109,386	466,290,151	652,090,242
18	166,142,748	180,439,664	213,935,505	232,830,697	244,263,773	252,166,505	282,803,686	304,959,309
19	133,171,212	126,905,444	148,156,107	135,579,118	141,028,475	132,378,455	139,339,030	146,450,281
20	141,144,896	169,813,372	202,168,836	220,335,695	233,688,997	240,110,536	269,682,812	292,456,988
21	159,021,642	165,855,032	184,126,178	181,547,989	192,509,020	196,328,199	217,713,457	233,076,246
22	177,419,776	208,023,699	214,511,188	232,834,723	242,036,723	257,268,280	280,836,318	299,322,250
23	162,965,822	178,224,453	193,515,811	177,729,090	186,920,516	205,424,064	218,251,088	230,867,038
TOTAL	4,310,499,764	4,571,192,240	5,124,728,458	5,312,685,455	5,524,068,310	5,969,275,110	6,417,179,264	7,003,261,093

Appendix A lists the congressional districts which represent the county in which the state capital is located, and those congressional districts which represent only portions of a county. Appendix C lists the programs included in each functional policy category.

table continues

Table 5.9 Outlays for Health Programs by Congressional District, 1983-1990 *(continued)*

Congressional District	1983	1984	1985	1986	1987	1988	1989	1990 (est.)
RHODE ISLAND								
1	205,467,840	227,165,194	232,736,041	249,362,622	257,309,892	303,041,188	313,031,179	334,749,288
2	180,316,289	200,278,724	205,854,577	205,011,218	207,291,614	222,161,523	253,700,100	285,756,155
TOTAL	385,784,129	427,443,918	438,590,618	454,373,840	464,601,506	525,202,711	566,731,279	620,505,443
SOUTH CAROLINA								
1	98,893,050	107,175,919	125,570,064	146,922,808	151,944,358	167,548,469	183,203,458	217,192,318
2	153,275,760	160,357,627	176,786,711	190,616,152	203,893,993	214,330,898	235,905,113	891,928,826
3	103,124,210	117,847,150	141,642,333	132,910,508	137,365,203	147,127,219	164,376,646	203,616,424
4	99,036,341	111,633,329	125,743,982	126,978,982	127,800,693	143,341,750	148,572,163	178,438,616
5	115,010,895	120,629,437	149,319,621	132,968,476	143,483,258	161,659,646	169,515,384	212,377,907
6	103,300,120	130,947,553	145,102,922	174,545,949	180,975,090	196,432,062	210,915,471	267,820,473
TOTAL	672,640,376	748,591,015	864,165,633	904,942,875	945,462,595	1,030,440,044	1,112,488,235	1,971,374,563
SOUTH DAKOTA								
TOTAL	173,780,911	246,503,484	257,942,685	276,008,291	279,041,603	300,707,731	339,285,223	370,627,822
TENNESSEE								
1	110,366,582	121,268,948	144,781,319	152,804,058	163,952,319	185,192,061	199,435,413	358,337,927
2	119,250,119	135,829,378	152,001,169	152,162,267	163,566,711	181,617,077	197,285,984	331,593,462
3	113,357,006	128,097,929	150,200,513	167,356,120	173,334,732	190,818,812	203,466,417	335,563,725
4	124,757,358	143,988,260	164,664,314	192,949,854	208,453,182	220,005,574	246,124,661	434,625,369
5	252,317,438	246,444,563	270,581,599	311,167,619	328,399,415	361,293,283	380,012,701	558,742,640
6	97,048,135	124,951,088	137,120,691	162,742,076	171,275,967	184,809,210	208,188,795	342,309,348
7	122,019,023	144,237,836	161,207,255	168,591,756	173,725,645	203,572,823	220,128,907	390,452,425
8	138,997,747	198,748,645	211,787,844	204,109,224	210,765,596	238,456,113	258,830,437	449,248,998
9	127,767,085	153,033,066	173,180,066	195,366,280	203,982,381	251,058,314	259,174,738	411,945,632
TOTAL	1,205,880,493	1,396,599,713	1,565,524,769	1,707,249,254	1,797,455,948	2,016,823,267	2,172,648,054	3,612,819,527
TEXAS								
1	225,648,233	221,262,073	246,406,854	196,210,615	216,070,797	228,160,166	253,625,671	298,105,399
2	152,577,720	155,959,692	176,767,573	185,616,525	196,519,212	213,188,846	233,873,907	266,861,893
3	87,063,023	91,394,605	106,590,887	120,805,282	124,035,535	131,971,357	158,055,112	178,968,808
4	160,881,327	165,842,633	194,768,615	176,315,473	184,852,186	195,730,883	218,718,120	251,899,870
5	159,183,244	150,639,391	183,572,476	172,496,925	181,292,011	189,772,700	222,114,347	248,554,397
6	150,808,908	157,546,019	181,529,482	163,477,113	177,233,271	187,039,552	210,227,169	246,444,289
7	67,429,056	99,057,250	97,272,372	152,727,729	146,616,290	150,989,527	166,613,773	184,293,966
8	68,657,649	79,447,292	86,865,785	121,278,727	117,631,145	123,758,867	139,159,717	158,565,239
9	121,855,363	149,354,326	156,482,489	184,963,278	186,467,210	199,225,862	225,064,932	248,225,969
10	349,538,369	325,697,435	340,122,552	342,563,341	377,720,646	388,260,566	478,549,647	704,854,706
11	181,573,923	144,106,063	184,925,180	124,585,909	132,607,228	143,901,298	163,000,780	191,360,136
12	93,796,114	91,478,072	113,135,955	110,384,706	118,726,370	134,771,383	139,354,695	156,741,459
13	146,060,196	144,437,324	170,815,094	138,322,848	141,290,886	152,066,703	173,168,883	197,767,792
14	174,184,658	167,644,691	196,281,781	163,439,038	173,773,056	186,101,631	207,478,524	243,612,779
15	154,676,809	152,062,522	175,904,637	176,918,355	196,287,410	220,455,422	242,046,112	306,497,053
16	83,019,925	89,263,537	98,474,928	125,221,684	129,480,062	145,132,223	174,792,983	202,165,508
17	180,601,413	191,698,523	225,190,218	164,267,461	174,821,712	184,432,234	205,612,476	235,550,674
18	127,312,212	124,365,346	140,243,943	175,163,987	183,785,592	198,405,284	220,687,761	245,634,352
19	99,061,799	98,967,815	116,467,005	132,592,795	137,496,134	145,097,505	168,558,573	178,761,285
20	110,268,834	155,768,097	172,339,841	183,727,195	176,242,243	195,723,987	204,496,050	249,938,918
21	132,741,387	129,710,491	145,875,393	127,570,040	131,902,373	140,207,245	162,164,625	186,061,352
22	66,965,180	62,396,549	70,762,109	95,357,334	110,149,538	109,415,711	170,096,468	190,412,082
23	150,989,898	165,037,505	202,128,374	205,827,716	221,350,852	240,641,813	280,095,292	328,192,926
24	92,020,962	103,251,162	107,693,643	121,896,947	122,857,798	130,962,591	158,003,544	179,584,609
25	80,436,522	96,417,390	106,388,262	139,939,129	144,052,448	153,555,677	166,217,120	187,263,306
26	75,637,833	83,323,032	97,130,590	100,862,599	103,583,479	110,096,622	127,824,593	136,391,914
27	83,172,898	119,152,613	155,483,223	158,236,361	170,680,252	181,674,629	211,836,753	239,008,824
TOTAL	3,576,163,457	3,715,281,448	4,249,619,262	4,260,769,110	4,477,525,736	4,780,740,286	5,481,437,627	6,441,719,501
UTAH								
1	85,288,061	79,982,241	86,755,701	92,461,694	106,807,840	112,697,022	115,028,362	130,925,633
2	177,972,907	171,875,378	180,007,779	185,921,646	202,441,233	217,696,893	222,097,091	278,680,112
3	35,577,859	84,184,009	96,889,410	94,794,052	110,190,318	115,776,466	122,927,399	139,570,435
TOTAL	298,838,827	336,041,628	363,652,890	373,177,392	419,439,391	446,170,381	460,052,852	549,176,180
VERMONT								
TOTAL	183,269,790	210,247,888	225,654,719	225,839,781	245,853,758	261,984,314	272,834,062	314,076,279

Appendix A lists the congressional districts which represent the county in which the state capital is located, and those congressional districts which represent only portions of a county. Appendix C lists the programs included in each functional policy category.

table continues

Table 5.9 Outlays for Health Programs by Congressional District, 1983-1990 *(continued)*

Congressional District	1983	1984	1985	1986	1987	1988	1989	1990 (est.)
VIRGINIA								
1	95,653,106	115,279,721	133,788,781	122,496,153	123,989,610	137,316,734	150,550,007	211,666,197
2	84,863,068	87,604,417	110,450,701	119,126,993	132,684,902	152,280,463	153,365,119	196,724,420
3	268,037,045	244,141,018	291,922,579	292,222,837	302,512,880	315,882,341	333,617,358	482,359,497
4	116,380,297	133,522,493	150,035,037	169,026,686	161,390,901	167,612,426	193,734,697	299,458,660
5	131,632,581	142,494,461	163,422,427	142,457,878	147,165,112	158,784,660	181,027,842	280,688,924
6	132,078,299	131,141,781	154,765,033	147,777,218	141,930,247	153,425,614	170,816,577	240,747,380
7	132,176,012	134,518,601	154,486,538	156,885,870	184,499,685	179,566,724	197,266,154	260,295,056
8	48,085,895	55,143,876	54,484,684	75,141,082	74,510,818	79,244,407	91,193,973	112,340,745
9	147,274,929	164,870,677	176,503,785	170,232,620	178,068,412	184,872,775	210,680,033	319,225,597
10	76,818,026	81,002,548	80,269,879	109,925,748	112,449,094	143,882,159	147,509,742	189,116,749
TOTAL	1,232,999,258	1,289,719,592	1,470,129,445	1,505,293,085	1,559,201,661	1,672,868,303	1,829,761,502	2,592,623,225
WASHINGTON								
1	104,663,188	109,168,729	130,072,675	142,473,960	149,711,669	190,803,796	196,284,990	303,408,173
2	77,959,423	105,480,364	131,694,509	141,306,398	156,804,014	174,256,193	184,820,983	294,262,991
3	194,872,486	179,503,004	204,021,205	219,281,779	235,447,713	242,378,136	259,923,124	420,890,136
4	186,613,783	216,641,960	244,620,829	172,094,891	161,936,937	179,002,429	206,844,398	346,090,651
5	130,528,650	156,482,538	162,915,163	150,337,069	163,384,458	175,855,518	196,560,501	328,450,938
6	141,178,908	102,626,597	143,313,558	166,051,413	146,177,448	169,813,940	161,646,119	313,256,515
7	142,922,001	152,854,051	164,853,906	260,190,044	315,805,988	358,360,592	437,338,523	546,886,594
8	109,726,316	116,848,393	134,079,143	148,359,061	160,940,365	173,381,322	208,696,791	332,908,433
TOTAL	1,088,464,754	1,139,605,638	1,315,570,987	1,400,094,614	1,490,208,593	1,663,851,927	1,852,115,429	2,886,154,431
WEST VIRGINIA								
1	131,028,276	139,173,505	149,376,710	153,041,809	176,866,123	184,831,605	201,753,610	208,465,749
2	130,096,320	137,478,027	154,541,720	177,165,148	183,045,644	181,609,573	198,466,312	203,826,424
3	132,939,953	170,457,710	180,192,629	264,645,290	235,449,756	240,190,685	254,675,750	280,071,802
4	144,068,661	129,177,964	153,394,386	156,922,945	174,432,055	186,248,823	200,880,907	209,242,306
TOTAL	538,133,210	576,287,206	637,505,445	751,775,192	769,793,578	792,880,686	855,776,579	901,606,282
WISCONSIN								
1	108,769,460	159,403,360	165,043,051	168,795,447	175,873,448	188,320,290	203,484,872	317,215,629
2	252,015,498	282,784,335	309,689,962	300,182,083	333,686,392	338,092,490	369,498,006	531,731,409
3	141,623,204	202,414,782	218,301,675	189,298,854	201,865,287	209,084,984	227,138,261	369,798,689
4	172,372,138	212,004,503	216,063,390	245,651,667	276,270,384	295,282,963	339,157,003	441,770,016
5	204,047,451	264,240,040	266,358,453	299,773,995	338,312,563	317,381,539	339,480,493	537,241,250
6	122,432,690	189,924,889	187,026,761	173,115,579	178,475,357	187,393,238	206,145,252	311,434,826
7	138,037,976	201,576,741	217,157,338	202,717,003	208,879,809	223,227,212	243,201,693	377,906,282
8	113,547,720	167,712,202	181,104,613	173,055,495	180,766,273	193,083,480	209,635,245	318,878,652
9	69,352,906	111,044,737	120,566,155	130,781,008	137,385,165	141,954,279	154,342,943	223,364,338
TOTAL	1,322,199,042	1,791,105,589	1,881,311,398	1,883,371,131	2,031,514,677	2,093,820,475	2,292,083,769	3,429,341,091
WYOMING								
TOTAL	70,316,017	99,148,917	102,821,935	107,815,297	115,989,453	120,846,790	147,141,761	154,896,540
U.S. TOTAL	71,127.4 mil.	77,349.2 mil.	85,654.7 mil.	89,124.6 mil.	92,855.1 mil.	100,710.1 mil.	109,753.9 mil.	131,041.0 mil.

Appendix A lists the congressional districts which represent the county in which the state capital is located, and those congressional districts which represent only portions of a county. Appendix C lists the programs included in each functional policy category.

Table 5.10 Outlays for Housing Programs by Congressional District, 1983-1990

Congressional District	1983	1984	1985	1986	1987	1988	1989	1990 (est.)
ALABAMA								
1	6,417,805	4,837,672	5,992,860	8,046,487	6,653,110	34,759,730	38,539,521	58,308,207
2	7,532,428	2,808,351	7,071,036	4,556,490	8,628,658	29,091,798	35,699,444	72,337,698
3	1,682,582	3,409,485	3,030,252	3,864,132	4,169,279	22,067,850	29,076,194	36,403,260
4	4,132,320	1,940,926	1,706,631	1,024,149	4,737,299	21,918,836	28,905,768	40,086,221
5	5,172,805	4,016,386	3,268,368	8,742,867	5,039,892	23,820,575	25,926,303	42,997,602
6	18,034,600	14,881,441	12,814,559	11,903,970	11,879,969	51,760,509	41,584,784	71,693,341
7	8,402,937	7,187,006	6,523,519	4,630,235	5,537,333	27,476,141	29,226,730	46,018,081
TOTAL	51,375,477	39,081,267	40,407,225	42,768,330	46,645,541	210,895,438	228,958,743	367,844,409
ALASKA								
TOTAL	9,823,745	7,207,828	8,859,537	6,990,921	20,651,631	31,176,673	59,892,213	73,966,286
ARIZONA								
1	15,343,124	8,889,810	11,602,681	11,289,373	5,632,695	32,924,834	51,193,285	67,232,247
2	11,994,900	22,673,974	19,435,830	11,395,886	4,274,176	26,565,669	44,159,548	62,316,899
3	1,883,413	7,646,626	3,368,257	1,655,228	1,519,416	13,244,018	16,622,517	25,605,930
4	10,676,179	10,498,261	17,460,994	10,050,520	12,809,128	25,718,638	40,088,348	71,832,235
5	1,700,761	6,857,497	2,299,080	606,607	2,473,836	10,829,851	25,850,394	28,631,509
TOTAL	41,598,377	56,566,169	54,166,841	34,997,614	26,709,251	109,283,010	177,914,093	255,618,820
ARKANSAS								
1	12,029,193	2,672,164	3,002,989	1,632,165	4,047,307	26,642,168	38,394,526	60,300,994
2	6,331,646	4,423,137	4,767,713	3,732,940	4,356,039	30,032,918	40,505,599	58,305,743
3	8,863,064	3,138,834	3,445,083	1,931,757	2,192,951	20,370,027	26,242,015	39,706,718
4	10,059,351	3,139,776	3,690,994	2,326,379	3,900,887	21,770,461	28,438,099	46,204,896
TOTAL	37,283,254	13,373,911	14,906,779	9,623,241	14,497,184	98,815,574	133,580,239	204,518,352
CALIFORNIA								
1	9,860,595	14,435,288	6,540,189	8,764,904	7,712,310	28,453,573	37,108,782	55,399,757
2	6,300,559	5,676,530	2,706,825	9,237,185	3,009,208	27,635,933	33,577,966	49,930,258
3	7,779,375	5,917,221	9,661,169	21,081,426	5,231,339	40,286,726	37,078,565	230,660,390
4	8,362,892	6,729,656	8,504,808	13,769,614	5,429,928	36,208,852	45,408,393	149,589,740
5	26,396,126	26,302,178	23,126,403	15,709,543	16,694,088	60,137,580	87,802,414	141,911,549
6	10,418,059	13,050,033	7,216,872	10,627,313	5,864,241	31,113,282	46,789,771	71,915,353
7	8,109,898	7,200,322	7,294,052	5,248,958	14,398,418	42,774,519	60,320,332	99,028,422
8	13,805,034	15,480,841	10,502,954	8,540,148	14,264,724	49,664,188	78,730,424	104,312,134
9	6,657,465	9,669,352	8,656,180	8,787,911	14,696,644	49,833,441	94,379,470	112,575,441
10	7,777,582	8,147,712	7,437,594	5,655,973	6,004,190	28,942,537	47,298,808	55,589,363
11	8,189,238	10,157,648	7,776,117	5,651,314	1,397,705	18,200,499	42,211,030	49,920,749
12	7,690,260	7,135,722	6,883,110	5,345,573	621,955	19,927,441	31,339,517	40,172,735
13	7,416,341	7,276,421	7,094,717	6,062,703	2,547,270	21,681,605	60,605,906	74,952,492
14	7,935,305	4,459,328	508,845	6,831,696	3,221,563	18,414,257	22,665,034	35,057,130
15	6,285,040	2,136,737	2,962,721	1,930,578	1,862,743	21,796,570	28,507,750	44,055,804
16	9,610,852	5,747,895	4,035,342	5,413,537	6,755,330	33,175,134	50,619,192	74,434,611
17	10,287,286	9,048,839	5,985,021	4,978,633	5,140,555	22,399,037	39,861,693	45,015,743
18	18,505,776	14,079,169	13,285,997	9,653,988	5,154,488	30,208,312	49,978,450	54,529,824
19	5,739,611	4,469,012	5,411,053	1,881,151	8,786,511	24,779,773	47,438,388	61,733,924
20	5,242,020	6,796,124	7,351,216	4,827,524	7,124,119	33,172,931	53,016,070	69,572,178
21	8,776,298	8,133,254	9,387,339	8,323,029	4,898,710	26,948,138	45,828,402	60,216,396
22	15,914,721	13,530,384	14,599,443	11,635,924	3,810,792	28,675,317	51,106,173	66,655,967
23	12,228,932	10,216,711	9,255,640	7,395,624	1,983,005	20,455,221	36,621,659	47,862,003
24	12,501,995	10,173,326	11,706,592	8,641,201	2,175,341	31,461,073	47,991,276	67,681,766
25	15,463,574	9,755,022	9,777,362	7,589,599	3,265,020	32,880,050	48,796,957	68,671,106
26	10,794,361	7,421,391	8,277,992	6,486,145	1,732,556	16,416,591	30,404,796	38,368,868
27	14,173,059	24,236,843	12,458,572	9,472,841	2,443,912	25,908,043	44,446,380	57,190,828
28	11,829,545	9,128,438	9,396,134	7,894,960	2,486,207	27,821,059	45,139,677	63,919,572
29	14,394,768	13,215,693	11,392,058	8,820,226	2,380,956	22,289,327	42,699,888	53,077,777
30	21,952,199	14,659,159	15,460,254	15,234,456	2,759,046	25,038,360	47,545,043	51,973,576
31	18,124,524	14,644,430	16,035,703	12,994,124	3,458,170	27,487,690	55,163,476	72,165,379
32	12,530,003	10,891,131	10,599,678	8,796,893	2,141,315	19,240,805	37,412,720	46,374,813
33	13,948,431	11,144,282	11,961,813	9,556,828	2,978,715	20,924,085	40,153,330	50,503,602
34	15,307,682	12,767,090	12,932,724	9,737,032	3,626,044	23,532,427	49,114,314	57,015,410
35	4,672,673	9,368,518	8,504,868	6,374,792	2,007,951	16,405,724	32,196,321	36,357,676
36	4,009,367	11,260,267	16,330,805	14,760,045	3,262,051	33,366,277	56,158,706	104,836,894
37	14,465,228	7,904,928	8,793,946	7,142,403	2,244,425	26,421,769	37,225,221	80,624,084
38	5,237,488	1,690,247	6,415,944	6,535,493	1,712,043	15,864,038	28,841,786	40,104,474
39	6,952,859	4,587,042	8,279,620	8,109,673	1,845,287	20,806,602	35,158,436	52,171,501

Appendix A lists the congressional districts which represent the county in which the state capital is located, and those congressional districts which represent only portions of a county. Appendix C lists the programs included in each functional policy category.

table continues

Table 5.10

Outlays for Housing Programs by Congressional District, 1983-1990 *(continued)*

Congressional District	1983	1984	1985	1986	1987	1988	1989	1990 (est.)
CALIFORNIA *continued*								
40	9,255,595	5,071,853	8,989,886	8,310,276	2,242,267	25,639,590	42,114,776	60,813,927
41	8,027,469	3,199,043	4,784,415	3,871,886	1,458,101	16,644,298	32,831,560	39,360,913
42	11,429,613	6,462,935	7,893,158	7,571,939	2,440,874	19,871,789	35,813,527	47,167,098
43	11,774,421	4,888,898	9,325,475	8,232,409	2,434,858	18,887,998	42,712,768	48,637,283
44	9,486,938	2,827,602	10,670,236	8,364,590	2,572,751	26,478,183	58,979,402	65,479,945
45	9,706,579	7,058,217	10,648,271	6,638,057	5,861,598	23,696,519	48,451,830	62,360,849
TOTAL	485,327,635	418,152,732	416,819,113	378,490,118	204,139,325	1,231,967,162	2,067,646,381	3,059,949,302
COLORADO								
1	15,289,798	38,293,550	9,992,212	2,323,680	8,067,946	56,593,252	67,878,526	94,772,083
2	3,404,690	3,851,482	2,665,604	3,528,215	1,553,363	22,148,639	23,251,353	41,062,298
3	9,050,237	3,911,838	3,152,117	3,629,884	10,036,235	29,215,927	32,885,300	58,324,113
4	5,888,303	3,009,556	1,201,904	3,344,000	1,414,657	23,349,361	27,978,482	46,435,560
5	5,063,628	1,289,181	1,284,070	2,528,378	1,532,515	14,491,208	14,114,673	29,308,611
6	4,779,022	4,681,768	2,072,465	2,709,442	2,697,780	28,583,550	29,381,605	49,855,028
TOTAL	43,475,679	55,037,374	20,368,372	18,063,600	25,302,496	174,381,937	195,489,938	319,757,693
CONNECTICUT								
1	10,778,901	10,497,374	17,318,914	10,287,159	5,347,883	74,420,721	83,618,350	133,567,661
2	6,100,987	5,260,391	4,004,094	5,595,065	1,824,202	30,618,023	30,199,246	52,060,538
3	15,757,865	17,273,824	36,050,464	35,839,177	11,625,677	63,886,130	60,986,389	98,731,181
4	14,793,556	15,949,414	8,493,545	9,639,786	8,092,950	58,974,792	55,191,498	96,194,024
5	13,558,175	5,276,132	9,578,919	8,630,201	3,806,733	40,072,576	39,211,178	89,935,095
6	3,513,503	4,308,830	6,123,872	3,456,287	2,457,294	26,833,109	25,932,766	45,941,201
TOTAL	64,502,987	58,565,965	81,569,808	73,447,675	33,154,739	294,805,351	295,139,428	516,429,701
DELAWARE								
TOTAL	9,745,999	27,330,352	9,531,271	7,048,587	5,537,436	49,621,448	53,413,821	77,140,355
DISTRICT OF COLUMBIA								
TOTAL	49,789,235	7,225,968	21,916,415	3,504,192	31,338,881	135,688,894	136,605,860	207,793,273
FLORIDA								
1	3,887,580	2,062,259	4,164,262	2,586,477	3,049,660	27,628,695	26,798,228	47,629,555
2	11,742,654	4,298,697	2,683,416	11,093,339	2,511,825	26,282,865	27,232,900	43,519,684
3	14,559,367	8,316,532	525,668	14,902,237	5,617,229	49,475,029	51,769,412	96,838,714
4	10,704,305	5,422,457	3,672,387	7,579,429	5,341,373	24,704,109	25,396,024	45,201,619
5	8,062,403	5,503,841	6,305,490	8,069,748	2,423,991	27,781,751	25,760,874	44,594,710
6	5,960,649	3,182,348	4,459,666	3,736,041	3,473,600	24,218,691	686,014,007	49,179,405
7	13,515,103	9,605,366	8,824,435	6,608,517	7,568,838	33,603,718	37,675,128	69,359,319
8	9,121,922	3,470,764	6,171,766	11,776,411	3,853,446	22,365,268	28,024,105	50,178,437
9	2,254,791	1,631,240	2,430,658	2,258,156	3,448,235	12,899,520	14,646,150	28,404,637
10	7,587,952	2,484,288	10,183,382	6,288,510	2,902,374	31,515,839	31,160,629	52,395,695
11	5,568,976	3,464,313	4,291,222	5,100,657	2,342,269	24,574,032	22,763,986	42,797,855
12	3,452,318	2,837,510	3,599,718	5,564,367	1,805,588	17,328,591	21,262,452	46,952,082
13	2,359,888	5,053,178	2,298,405	3,706,482	2,516,855	41,080,047	49,237,400	81,803,703
14	7,135,954	5,853,052	7,528,116	5,743,057	2,689,094	23,539,928	20,509,374	55,371,209
15	12,627,166	10,941,762	5,191,269	8,851,600	2,344,163	35,033,222	33,234,998	63,412,225
16	4,139,735	10,424,098	6,024,315	5,591,468	2,872,066	22,651,133	23,015,687	39,660,839
17	11,728,482	12,222,769	6,007,484	10,244,720	4,242,406	32,387,608	33,851,309	48,420,523
18	12,270,098	16,452,580	7,669,853	15,089,030	5,685,603	47,656,737	51,298,154	80,816,657
19	10,280,275	10,631,365	4,764,381	9,349,825	4,299,595	28,578,776	32,833,087	55,396,668
TOTAL	156,959,618	123,858,421	96,795,891	144,140,074	68,988,211	553,305,560	1,242,483,904	1,041,933,537
GEORGIA								
1	7,285,524	7,891,612	3,083,459	2,559,909	4,843,013	30,761,415	30,270,250	51,248,275
2	3,545,174	3,695,005	219,626	2,823,832	2,751,240	20,274,315	27,037,117	40,570,080
3	8,262,949	4,389,746	1,303,111	3,124,934	7,534,241	30,623,433	27,184,005	45,942,179
4	9,143,072	7,425,246	3,242,681	7,320,429	8,939,458	39,648,990	44,612,543	66,064,707
5	15,492,031	25,014,239	6,343,748	10,877,728	24,647,925	98,096,097	95,200,458	146,818,763
6	2,414,273	3,755,684	1,577,674	1,420,610	3,930,834	21,484,776	29,084,535	48,452,923
7	2,971,942	2,883,516	402,000	2,876,356	5,893,570	14,308,753	17,534,721	34,990,548
8	4,377,818	9,130,139	3,065,206	3,824,620	4,225,973	30,692,376	27,870,876	40,918,587
9	1,242,220	14,231	83,875	996,500	2,239,528	9,681,450	11,756,099	19,391,970
10	9,387,190	3,557,849	6,426,392	2,982,420	4,392,166	31,902,402	37,595,024	75,557,091
TOTAL	64,122,193	67,757,268	25,747,772	38,807,338	69,397,948	327,474,007	348,145,627	569,955,121

Appendix A lists the congressional districts which represent the county in which the state capital is located, and those congressional districts which represent only portions of a county. Appendix C lists the programs included in each functional policy category.

table continues

Table 5.10 Outlays for Housing Programs by Congressional District, 1983-1990 *(continued)*

Congressional District	1983	1984	1985	1986	1987	1988	1989	1990 (est.)
HAWAII								
1	2,522,664	617,230	15,021,189	9,912,501	12,567,918	39,933,183	32,499,795	52,524,109
2	1,933,672	6,901,853	2,634,358	3,624,701	12,027,938	31,021,359	25,178,884	44,271,403
TOTAL	4,456,336	7,519,083	17,655,547	13,537,202	24,595,856	70,954,542	57,678,679	96,795,512
IDAHO								
1	2,596,867	1,082,599	1,591,627	2,609,834	1,006,548	17,125,997	25,194,880	35,327,353
2	1,293,962	1,785,211	811,939	1,226,732	568,213	12,341,932	17,061,234	24,333,694
TOTAL	3,890,829	2,867,810	2,403,566	3,836,566	1,574,761	29,467,929	42,256,114	59,661,047
ILLINOIS								
1	18,652,641	16,312,856	16,229,474	12,793,986	8,399,888	66,821,980	51,076,998	110,085,633
2	17,216,560	15,791,888	14,146,838	12,434,296	7,719,998	54,013,007	39,325,384	86,177,868
3	17,346,311	14,325,586	14,223,768	12,436,908	6,103,290	41,320,389	29,124,650	67,045,949
4	7,560,638	6,545,647	6,439,272	5,447,204	3,846,941	28,615,696	21,291,896	39,115,167
5	17,632,912	13,972,066	14,346,878	14,114,255	8,031,298	45,282,240	31,970,080	74,720,304
6	8,346,869	7,109,141	6,543,525	8,194,736	3,749,042	25,134,975	19,400,956	45,118,628
7	19,611,978	18,999,396	18,086,328	14,364,825	6,946,609	78,897,587	67,132,298	134,340,719
8	17,250,275	14,199,012	14,323,078	12,436,765	6,867,815	46,038,976	35,923,178	79,200,352
9	19,908,506	17,834,021	16,361,075	12,545,395	6,874,738	71,981,641	55,195,656	114,057,449
10	9,609,072	8,109,112	9,369,178	7,937,581	4,688,951	38,927,579	33,279,734	65,891,623
11	19,153,151	15,856,828	14,713,954	12,401,474	7,339,872	47,021,846	34,993,586	77,314,185
12	11,721,733	9,721,030	9,434,669	7,427,498	4,246,684	42,530,698	37,743,433	75,380,501
13	11,085,802	9,946,358	7,265,811	9,115,205	3,420,076	31,930,157	25,350,892	53,168,028
14	1,827,466	1,647,633	2,639,889	1,196,804	2,303,530	22,989,041	23,068,082	40,730,750
15	3,667,426	3,877,030	956,994	5,178,369	1,786,936	22,335,087	20,203,416	28,619,492
16	3,334,210	3,440,000	2,863,590	1,117,737	4,762,732	27,133,180	29,454,194	47,683,217
17	4,225,102	7,696,552	3,706,729	4,712,968	3,786,031	35,810,001	39,494,310	57,397,138
18	6,458,351	6,238,763	3,682,918	4,159,098	11,609,696	39,878,609	35,811,136	66,118,831
19	4,022,011	5,545,244	1,506,193	335,307	2,352,583	24,245,761	24,014,825	40,355,559
20	2,224,728	1,505,713	3,541,210	2,047,219	13,355,094	29,371,757	26,175,014	36,603,527
21	14,336,112	10,190,861	3,976,602	7,821,537	7,913,711	43,765,182	49,065,273	86,631,907
22	2,108,304	914,730	1,321,659	248,188	3,190,724	17,632,403	20,275,920	31,615,161
TOTAL	237,300,160	209,779,468	185,679,630	168,467,353	129,296,239	881,677,793	749,370,910	1,457,371,988
INDIANA								
1	19,025,919	10,337,666	12,532,809	7,694,376	6,785,437	38,329,951	29,143,308	46,103,416
2	3,854,341	2,780,071	2,914,000	3,859,065	2,793,442	19,012,917	21,246,511	33,986,051
3	6,422,448	20,200,882	6,863,019	3,638,376	3,626,622	35,066,376	37,251,229	65,698,059
4	4,467,536	4,155,692	2,924,656	2,616,476	1,960,840	21,410,780	20,263,066	38,033,154
5	2,036,637	5,269,580	1,483,076	1,646,946	1,312,490	20,252,027	19,381,306	33,885,220
6	5,682,259	4,796,227	3,512,285	2,152,348	2,723,647	20,814,105	19,738,619	35,770,491
7	6,160,577	4,232,179	4,389,029	2,769,600	3,085,846	22,834,724	22,001,672	38,312,758
8	5,558,788	4,721,954	5,194,997	2,510,844	2,334,646	21,037,978	23,813,260	38,406,099
9	2,909,412	4,765,620	2,452,032	1,225,479	3,250,501	25,560,222	24,389,334	37,250,365
10	12,895,106	10,804,589	7,158,422	5,183,434	2,844,490	16,050,634	9,631,538	15,799,103
TOTAL	69,013,023	72,064,460	49,424,326	33,296,943	30,717,961	240,369,715	226,859,843	383,244,715
IOWA								
1	4,093,737	12,435,096	3,493,516	2,329,124	508,344	19,393,710	19,701,894	34,319,927
2	6,775,929	3,495,848	3,738,950	2,063,109	1,340,423	18,316,321	16,848,864	30,751,360
3	4,567,645	5,605,688	3,190,853	1,783,664	1,996,558	19,578,127	19,335,790	32,793,189
4	15,606,826	12,039,602	5,283,936	4,253,629	1,612,366	21,448,251	22,422,037	35,710,756
5	2,424,699	3,303,476	4,919,382	1,042,446	1,564,374	17,542,467	16,958,359	29,523,780
6	2,992,271	6,372,900	3,330,629	1,890,924	879,907	17,736,742	17,029,336	26,384,048
TOTAL	36,461,107	43,252,610	23,957,266	13,362,896	7,901,972	114,015,618	112,296,280	189,483,061
KANSAS								
1	5,367,835	471,959	106,237	283,428	590,786	10,064,992	12,614,712	20,194,143
2	9,122,128	16,591,456	4,848,161	3,733,767	2,993,367	18,941,448	18,364,690	28,302,987
3	6,557,822	3,333,067	3,541,615	6,323,629	4,274,625	23,499,886	23,258,978	39,233,523
4	6,971,653	3,282,665	3,408,735	6,198,203	2,019,502	19,082,435	14,727,698	26,787,342
5	13,506,052	1,062,014	176,957	1,164,842	2,075,298	13,513,485	14,280,821	25,429,380
TOTAL	41,525,490	24,741,161	12,081,705	17,703,869	11,953,578	85,102,246	83,246,899	139,947,376

Appendix A lists the congressional districts which represent the county in which the state capital is located, and those congressional districts which represent only portions of a county. Appendix C lists the programs included in each functional policy category.

table continues

Table 5.10 Outlays for Housing Programs by Congressional District, 1983-1990 *(continued)*

Congressional District	1983	1984	1985	1986	1987	1988	1989	1990 (est.)
KENTUCKY								
1	2,422,464	1,058,463	2,044,374	1,589,926	3,282,792	23,798,354	29,192,147	47,939,316
2	2,370,360	893,368	63,961	578,474	1,925,107	19,568,145	23,989,675	36,903,131
3	10,068,294	4,513,306	13,838,446	11,415,408	12,219,773	50,212,684	52,404,881	85,416,844
4	6,207,094	2,909,824	8,469,115	21,216,170	4,648,276	40,218,869	32,105,815	52,100,530
5	2,765,802	4,771,432	838,784	2,392,699	4,701,713	27,665,929	30,244,663	52,132,046
6	10,235,811	35,250,800	3,456,108	619,161	5,391,276	34,031,491	53,039,287	74,897,813
7	3,348,477	1,332,230	3,744,475	3,285,045	3,759,157	25,537,774	24,499,749	40,897,073
TOTAL	37,418,302	50,729,423	32,455,263	41,096,883	35,928,094	221,033,246	245,476,217	390,286,752
LOUISIANA								
1	19,541,839	15,902,486	13,693,233	9,215,352	11,020,176	40,703,018	65,294,176	83,330,779
2	17,631,436	14,311,684	13,078,263	8,485,986	7,472,241	24,818,738	45,059,881	49,546,391
3	1,849,563	2,933,981	3,634,971	8,203,546	4,000,012	12,746,322	16,679,440	22,255,472
4	7,270,516	6,400,619	5,622,295	5,357,091	2,970,676	23,486,853	31,805,889	49,063,915
5	3,561,787	4,562,250	1,862,122	1,961,563	3,119,255	22,248,295	28,197,563	41,459,703
6	19,763,254	7,364,667	6,404,428	25,175,528	1,437,076	20,048,061	32,462,996	35,878,469
7	4,457,910	2,971,699	4,821,458	3,655,301	3,350,025	24,955,051	33,770,227	48,867,032
8	3,574,889	2,380,317	1,302,528	3,460,490	3,056,272	17,639,751	24,364,324	33,369,943
TOTAL	77,651,194	56,827,703	50,419,299	65,514,857	36,425,734	186,646,088	277,634,496	363,771,705
MAINE								
1	8,173,382	3,210,569	11,066,988	4,414,963	10,770,121	48,029,854	52,803,956	91,034,101
2	8,790,443	12,787,761	4,577,148	3,380,631	8,670,399	56,763,638	49,270,311	84,178,560
TOTAL	16,963,825	15,998,330	15,644,136	7,795,594	19,440,520	104,793,492	102,074,267	175,212,661
MARYLAND								
1	13,273,004	4,534,760	8,965,630	5,742,528	865,832	31,503,137	30,998,003	51,713,140
2	5,963,677	6,898,033	3,446,643	2,650,161	2,167,542	24,820,714	19,583,252	31,916,642
3	19,868,673	18,806,649	28,598,594	15,114,815	12,472,258	53,351,964	56,264,884	66,988,248
4	5,373,931	4,762,329	4,218,951	3,933,929	1,599,165	22,570,205	17,987,170	38,146,274
5	12,693,740	8,924,187	1,751,994	3,865,005	1,547,346	34,926,247	27,969,122	50,875,829
6	10,651,576	6,766,581	5,138,700	5,678,755	1,444,414	32,071,773	35,054,509	58,886,146
7	33,871,068	29,040,159	42,400,994	21,695,720	18,422,233	90,236,249	97,589,856	135,230,890
8	968,749	1,093,025	900,100	3,977,457	4,491,767	38,466,483	38,670,471	59,264,152
TOTAL	102,664,418	80,825,722	95,421,606	62,658,369	43,010,556	327,946,773	324,117,266	493,021,321
MASSACHUSETTS								
1	5,625,109	11,539,364	3,196,020	8,362,236	7,005,189	40,192,381	49,696,282	72,698,335
2	12,688,064	7,906,296	32,417,704	13,097,083	3,686,789	60,222,661	57,356,628	93,633,421
3	11,032,376	8,010,277	3,480,555	11,790,269	3,085,076	40,755,508	38,116,788	60,501,604
4	11,862,778	11,237,126	18,638,019	10,335,132	1,880,359	42,042,655	36,494,315	58,264,306
5	14,882,572	22,056,736	19,182,621	16,373,053	3,490,852	50,728,078	53,163,806	87,510,442
6	19,336,858	13,402,366	7,902,923	7,395,350	4,587,434	53,787,238	51,779,974	79,818,331
7	21,656,889	10,955,474	12,837,225	10,272,658	5,808,383	56,546,560	49,913,995	95,257,103
8	38,709,836	32,240,922	29,172,150	17,800,278	10,847,228	102,612,321	84,538,599	164,781,585
9	35,704,544	11,942,236	24,137,750	11,165,273	10,342,533	111,676,861	86,984,564	169,452,559
10	5,235,690	4,194,933	5,540,606	2,397,822	4,120,162	31,116,822	29,775,625	52,016,845
11	23,838,096	12,364,405	16,420,208	8,750,213	7,561,022	63,686,387	53,122,480	107,495,418
TOTAL	200,572,814	145,850,135	172,925,780	117,739,367	62,415,027	653,367,473	590,943,056	1,041,429,950
MICHIGAN								
1	26,041,220	13,975,174	22,403,635	21,072,758	2,271,788	40,675,520	27,651,281	40,786,346
2	7,418,905	3,570,521	7,787,968	6,937,140	3,128,771	29,146,563	22,071,908	37,248,455
3	16,504,129	6,370,446	12,112,780	6,180,499	2,874,863	29,241,852	30,519,636	47,273,474
4	3,814,349	7,522,540	4,442,298	1,680,616	1,412,173	18,119,590	19,549,493	30,473,231
5	10,042,750	897,544	6,856,000	4,680,479	2,022,484	28,006,118	19,650,384	34,462,037
6	11,291,092	3,574,256	8,212,930	10,584,327	5,557,005	39,506,786	27,517,492	50,954,906
7	14,559,798	13,302,101	8,050,322	6,715,337	3,155,369	30,159,133	15,282,941	27,556,207
8	4,788,233	3,666,021	5,051,710	5,320,688	4,378,280	20,316,332	15,212,983	23,860,784
9	7,092,870	5,188,368	2,665,770	2,361,155	3,840,322	20,288,909	17,147,061	30,263,732
10	694,541	697,879	1,664,694	218,057	6,755,564	16,355,229	16,145,075	27,158,612
11	3,744,173	1,505,297	2,839,436	4,960,722	2,559,034	18,405,620	23,149,106	34,373,251
12	8,606,466	8,025,099	5,144,691	4,589,555	798,792	29,625,735	20,781,586	33,445,529

Appendix A lists the congressional districts which represent the county in which the state capital is located, and those congressional districts which represent only portions of a county. Appendix C lists the programs included in each functional policy category.

table continues

Table 5.10 Outlays for Housing Programs by Congressional District, 1983-1990 *(continued)*

Congressional District	1983	1984	1985	1986	1987	1988	1989	1990 (est.)
MICHIGAN *continued*								
13	30,680,000	16,333,724	22,403,635	21,119,240	2,653,841	55,139,487	41,918,200	60,113,719
14	10,640,491	6,530,411	11,549,913	9,797,895	1,018,330	18,864,665	13,448,510	22,045,216
15	24,871,908	13,448,961	23,672,501	19,830,741	3,189,847	51,306,573	32,395,128	53,352,873
16	22,071,650	11,476,911	42,414,099	18,914,770	2,162,905	37,853,587	25,158,870	38,280,993
17	17,972,489	8,239,212	14,751,183	12,982,356	2,449,330	35,979,593	26,202,762	38,361,125
18	3,955,830	1,277,897	2,647,794	1,912,258	595,395	14,020,721	11,902,573	18,660,390
TOTAL	224,790,893	125,602,364	204,671,358	159,858,593	50,824,093	533,012,012	405,704,989	648,670,879
MINNESOTA								
1	3,307,820	4,403,783	1,164,507	1,047,062	1,424,742	25,865,685	26,318,722	46,100,346
2	4,119,606	562,327	332,553	126,631	1,299,235	20,214,296	24,754,270	37,469,315
3	4,971,800	2,366,490	2,779,443	3,046,113	3,387,073	28,772,015	28,199,758	52,981,848
4	22,714,527	8,865,051	8,611,940	8,117,077	5,963,867	47,669,070	43,788,662	59,718,137
5	31,946,166	20,976,545	5,251,856	12,681,120	6,638,443	66,548,720	53,224,950	105,968,439
6	8,205,364	2,320,875	2,169,268	2,998,010	6,586,218	23,504,862	19,405,577	43,867,782
7	8,898,037	1,814,612	1,757,391	2,979,071	2,300,227	24,970,583	30,281,724	46,933,492
8	10,782,691	10,709,824	1,906,917	7,692,645	3,404,345	30,146,748	36,938,849	50,627,020
TOTAL	94,946,011	52,019,507	23,973,875	38,687,728	31,004,150	267,691,979	262,912,511	443,666,379
MISSISSIPPI								
1	1,140,612	2,255,250	241,385	56,830	1,592,960	14,030,300	18,440,057	27,054,010
2	4,858,545	2,799,381	2,478,319	1,368,424	2,083,087	36,625,147	36,451,402	60,710,374
3	395,215	1,587,654	796,172	769,447	2,746,501	30,315,370	31,427,525	49,726,682
4	18,387,408	5,995,731	14,790,046	11,053,419	5,531,300	27,404,783	30,430,402	67,862,031
5	4,663,812	3,434,480	6,292,304	8,831,928	3,353,895	27,689,450	23,271,822	35,214,117
TOTAL	29,445,592	16,072,496	24,598,226	22,080,048	15,307,743	136,065,051	140,021,208	240,567,214
MISSOURI								
1	43,116,162	11,504,232	10,767,700	18,753,473	6,591,421	54,644,838	46,022,307	82,174,744
2	4,344,196	1,633,971	8,790,082	23,303,872	8,561,158	42,782,681	38,606,656	68,641,647
3	3,087,580	3,273,551	2,614,088	9,395,651	3,727,846	25,705,993	27,083,256	47,409,434
4	4,329,438	6,426,722	-151,934	1,362,326	7,990,817	19,682,701	20,217,687	34,461,149
5	25,818,728	22,611,484	14,068,626	10,312,182	5,141,850	37,064,629	39,721,790	72,188,517
6	2,966,181	2,619,954	3,609,025	2,415,175	1,702,352	34,493,700	22,530,007	41,777,193
7	3,939,147	3,225,377	1,964,146	2,921,862	1,233,223	18,003,588	15,036,003	25,627,535
8	1,092,578	2,416,593	1,050,392	835,155	1,766,886	18,622,778	23,421,829	40,131,155
9	3,239,939	3,452,478	3,559,133	6,464,769	2,115,269	23,297,662	25,662,370	39,646,310
TOTAL	91,933,948	57,164,362	46,271,258	75,764,463	38,830,822	274,298,570	258,301,905	452,057,684
MONTANA								
1	1,720,869	4,125,869	1,983,570	2,477,204	3,731,907	22,425,179	35,299,115	50,171,297
2	5,815,933	2,934,949	1,666,167	3,402,377	3,787,829	15,285,201	28,632,509	40,728,594
TOTAL	7,536,802	7,060,818	3,649,737	5,879,581	7,519,736	37,710,380	63,931,624	90,899,891
NEBRASKA								
1	4,014,631	7,120,310	4,923,952	8,650,724	2,716,248	24,602,077	24,269,672	37,838,736
2	10,147,818	6,975,369	6,862,931	1,758,816	6,869,348	28,448,022	32,554,316	58,459,481
3	295,505	1,412,468	304,428	671,794	1,195,096	14,402,353	16,783,872	26,368,736
TOTAL	14,457,954	15,508,147	12,091,311	11,081,334	10,780,692	67,452,452	73,607,860	122,666,953
NEVADA								
1	7,532,609	8,598,270	7,077,126	4,957,460	6,405,503	29,108,499	44,723,037	63,334,650
2	5,006,807	4,121,654	2,098,451	6,146,588	6,086,635	19,540,554	31,708,642	40,457,995
TOTAL	12,539,416	12,719,924	9,175,577	11,104,048	12,492,138	48,649,053	76,431,679	103,792,645
NEW HAMPSHIRE								
1	12,945,357	25,204,958	5,585,481	4,084,454	2,577,188	29,723,154	34,243,262	48,648,536
2	8,664,965	2,536,414	1,520,648	3,168,115	4,106,586	33,929,918	31,615,478	86,973,053
TOTAL	21,610,322	27,741,372	7,106,129	7,252,569	6,683,774	63,653,072	65,858,740	135,621,589

Appendix A lists the congressional districts which represent the county in which the state capital is located, and those congressional districts which represent only portions of a county. Appendix C lists the programs included in each functional policy category.

table continues

Table 5.10 **Outlays for Housing Programs by Congressional District, 1983-1990 *(continued)***

Congressional District	1983	1984	1985	1986	1987	1988	1989	1990 (est.)
NEW JERSEY								
1	7,582,947	16,948,865	10,605,497	7,011,764	7,831,114	50,997,965	50,065,021	86,534,539
2	10,226,724	6,407,905	35,691,691	12,045,492	8,341,004	48,696,216	54,405,661	80,639,109
3	5,824,538	12,839,223	9,947,352	4,829,291	9,512,434	39,189,917	47,342,122	76,953,566
4	6,870,436	7,418,806	6,790,531	10,355,633	15,863,982	32,478,068	39,988,136	63,665,334
5	64,270	2,549,141	4,678,415	3,188,734	2,834,651	10,703,345	13,445,121	23,919,126
6	17,745,320	19,771,078	9,302,383	11,120,137	10,162,694	33,275,652	30,327,038	52,874,432
7	11,398,786	20,779,420	15,191,307	7,730,667	11,619,381	33,518,479	33,357,104	55,874,886
8	12,193,848	12,069,360	15,123,557	13,312,131	10,234,832	40,762,716	56,244,539	82,702,538
9	21,449,074	10,924,756	6,962,699	6,694,348	8,492,481	32,240,763	27,994,800	45,276,844
10	40,161,288	30,221,066	42,940,978	18,587,503	38,636,096	163,592,789	138,120,178	218,098,597
11	11,420,485	4,690,837	4,119,804	2,805,363	11,941,607	20,517,397	22,181,800	37,162,508
12	4,807,243	3,486,809	3,140,236	3,444,789	3,495,216	15,323,098	20,811,879	31,888,062
13	784,115	5,685,638	5,392,202	3,417,351	4,731,964	15,816,579	15,005,313	24,063,256
14	39,250,010	59,471,949	20,117,814	13,557,726	21,331,835	85,532,403	97,367,894	166,314,981
TOTAL	189,779,083	213,264,852	190,004,466	118,100,928	165,029,291	622,645,388	646,656,606	1,045,967,775
NEW MEXICO								
1	13,209,658	7,626,925	6,281,539	557,839	1,561,070	17,285,613	25,531,648	59,048,145
2	12,083,362	6,302,247	4,161,574	2,132,294	3,728,230	18,818,448	23,480,499	34,050,207
3	4,890,972	8,416,290	9,603,029	3,315,191	4,932,102	15,693,118	24,726,189	39,992,886
TOTAL	30,183,992	22,345,462	20,046,142	6,005,324	10,221,402	51,797,179	73,738,336	133,091,238
NEW YORK								
1	2,890,845	9,876,210	4,036,694	18,058,266	6,232,885	21,723,168	21,899,616	37,524,139
2	8,021,350	5,019,274	5,678,446	12,022,117	6,355,919	16,539,523	17,092,460	37,753,064
3	5,944,398	3,644,781	5,651,750	7,556,326	5,617,711	19,295,549	17,386,784	27,199,982
4	5,733,609	5,173,292	6,757,271	7,974,351	609,566	12,460,059	15,582,138	18,533,923
5	6,717,690	5,105,952	5,599,171	7,551,215	1,549,446	32,553,377	23,472,632	65,452,522
6	2,599,487	-13,567	2,187,915	969,809	0	16,001,695	16,109,359	28,375,559
7	0	8,918	0	1,417,056	54,488	2,798,544	2,906,647	5,119,865
8	2,140,218	979,228	1,614,993	462,940	3,311,528	43,906,344	18,812,016	32,865,225
9	0	8,869	0	0	0	7,597,242	7,704,760	13,571,420
10	5,119,139	416,934	-287	219,020	33,709,192	93,637,850	116,079,070	162,544,533
11	882,689	3,821,051	1,249,487	1,825,061	34,679,691	107,422,510	129,863,909	188,199,230
12	1,646,556	3,510,611	1,160,932	2,532,102	32,629,879	123,993,769	143,146,584	211,536,169
13	2,604,954	2,106,277	765,616	387,684	33,866,017	92,182,541	114,961,331	160,140,813
14	1,039,613	75,017	38,360	20,350	10,982,333	44,112,721	49,787,048	75,213,848
15	112,318,862	93,178,920	94,269,303	64,243,972	99,845,583	72,020,957	73,335,869	136,626,042
16	112,563,269	101,875,034	90,428,414	65,671,862	100,384,612	116,414,555	121,016,814	221,680,090
17	90,276,681	71,579,435	69,237,813	50,846,066	78,821,477	98,877,354	75,734,347	139,206,547
18	1,176,310	5,302,336	7,583,191	4,793,557	12,972,162	269,068,485	177,891,684	315,116,794
19	1,833,134	4,956,702	3,375,967	2,742,545	9,173,153	117,207,783	52,712,830	94,554,525
20	17,395,881	9,755,850	12,498,767	14,673,818	15,533,106	61,957,277	60,417,345	102,922,405
21	9,864,809	7,737,307	5,071,984	2,146,950	7,810,199	25,490,959	25,511,897	41,763,608
22	7,418,954	9,820,997	3,323,164	3,938,061	7,794,152	28,997,448	28,161,459	49,711,966
23	22,285,399	21,329,247	22,053,151	12,246,610	17,793,420	47,943,276	41,226,753	68,032,600
24	12,295,055	18,198,109	7,878,949	7,543,447	14,333,173	26,701,132	20,045,125	36,358,732
25	11,960,892	19,290,400	13,781,998	9,837,097	10,143,445	28,345,672	28,129,364	47,522,340
26	7,771,869	25,551,866	25,721,015	20,586,175	15,070,773	32 680,901	31,691,944	63,859,536
27	17,495,476	13,540,390	15,905,921	8,902,935	18,787,732	37,646,315	34,601,961	59,006,908
28	12,133,907	21,165,767	13,982,648	16,147,315	12,909,332	25,090,143	28,647,033	51,568,854
29	15,015,786	15,913,370	12,087,752	9,437,916	7,730,268	21,038,241	19,412,159	38,747,549
30	19,187,335	18,350,406	13,090,797	9,394,935	5,632,693	31,719,210	36,116,161	62,799,568
31	18,687,277	23,790,462	13,215,359	11,744,016	16,091,373	34,967,510	31,114,245	49,835,299
32	27,747,356	25,441,317	19,613,266	10,991,482	18,155,271	31,274,709	28,057,129	46,526,654
33	22,500,382	24,011,557	18,069,998	24,000,579	20,987,048	40,473,376	31,520,716	58,021,603
34	6,479,868	21,332,813	19,282,224	6,518,013	10,685,887	23,735,118	21,778,283	43,645,514
TOTAL	591,749,049	591,855,132	515,212,028	417,403,649	670,253,514	1,805,875,314	1,661,927,472	2,791,537,424
NORTH CAROLINA								
1	1,660,884	1,937,398	2,849,429	1,728,844	4,058,651	26,969,797	38,542,338	61,319,701
2	3,389,855	2,892,188	5,402,207	6,306,408	5,629,608	35,332,063	41,659,690	65,259,710
3	1,067,032	1,960,419	1,753,036	447,425	3,699,942	22,884,079	32,106,740	45,985,902
4	2,411,799	-954,243	3,526,727	650,652	6,632,442	24,413,556	28,779,011	151,402,468
5	1,356,996	2,795,432	2,397,217	1,361,429	4,479,302	27,531,750	26,002,702	45,049,940
6	2,727,679	2,019,820	3,485,898	1,242,969	3,342,111	23,817,417	23,115,743	41,856,672
7	2,593,264	2,887,947	9,769,806	694,680	6,662,003	30,374,262	30,933,254	50,474,246
8	4,315,296	4,287,869	1,310,130	378,276	1,529,833	18,245,510	24,636,215	42,033,215
9	2,434,056	864,793	5,027,064	1,800,266	4,260,049	31,521,025	25,657,799	44,224,241
10	1,417,454	2,145,985	999,297	1,258,399	2,653,680	17,934,195	20,589,447	34,867,402
11	2,937,810	7,561,466	1,736,018	1,941,105	2,703,320	22,096,986	25,477,311	40,544,668
TOTAL	26,312,125	28,399,074	38,256,829	17,810,453	45,650,942	281,120,640	317,500,250	623,018,166

Appendix A lists the congressional districts which represent the county in which the state capital is located, and those congressional districts which represent only portions of a county. Appendix C lists the programs included in each functional policy category.

table continues

Table 5.10 Outlays for Housing Programs by Congressional District, 1983-1990 *(continued)*

Congressional District	1983	1984	1985	1986	1987	1988	1989	1990 (est.)
NORTH DAKOTA								
TOTAL	5,362,712	4,575,188	2,621,250	3,568,637	6,294,362	29,325,293	54,820,558	76,470,027
OHIO								
1	19,841,726	16,740,427	11,826,531	8,770,878	4,940,409	59,810,543	46,912,346	65,902,012
2	16,066,730	10,435,540	8,033,261	6,420,048	3,434,409	42,764,877	37,567,701	56,490,257
3	16,552,039	8,464,291	22,704,059	8,524,244	6,097,409	45,794,587	40,165,412	59,518,478
4	2,024,510	2,294,059	1,660,875	2,019,366	770,752	22,701,198	20,011,150	36,304,259
5	4,303,561	0	5,305,958	3,222,171	1,968,205	16,449,886	15,905,358	27,866,365
6	1,090,177	2,239,223	3,283,230	1,223,718	2,551,990	25,230,697	28,886,407	45,169,811
7	9,937,012	4,787,691	3,681,500	3,275,554	1,849,131	27,234,815	26,541,891	43,833,651
8	3,561,574	2,438,328	2,703,284	696,404	1,057,396	17,889,182	15,923,260	28,903,947
9	10,837,338	9,899,835	7,541,371	10,440,446	6,334,096	39,834,010	42,970,679	66,498,819
10	3,373,845	2,596,278	5,423,483	1,819,747	2,450,781	46,531,012	26,203,347	52,842,309
11	302,022	747,631	2,227,106	4,763,491	2,561,777	21,995,858	23,756,916	43,003,121
12	8,641,569	5,086,592	6,007,899	4,690,877	6,091,045	33,698,519	36,615,074	59,815,954
13	6,945,518	3,246,250	3,499,689	4,022,882	2,517,256	21,916,483	24,618,243	40,064,700
14	24,775,103	13,249,636	12,350,301	8,371,029	6,691,085	43,345,041	48,506,591	71,462,173
15	10,858,955	8,683,483	7,699,060	5,089,930	7,797,084	29,931,935	35,082,353	53,951,386
16	19,469,880	5,004,716	6,645,103	5,748,069	5,965,994	28,975,528	22,317,088	35,893,032
17	15,210,763	9,055,758	19,822,598	9,534,013	4,108,873	33,059,393	31,365,881	50,543,628
18	2,701,446	2,403,739	1,862,592	1,672,219	2,309,992	22,817,105	26,834,805	40,087,754
19	14,305,827	14,048,071	21,642,928	20,914,426	13,875,698	39,363,611	33,488,427	43,565,988
20	14,306,863	15,904,818	24,806,062	23,946,171	15,200,235	51,912,950	45,403,816	64,081,368
21	19,553,597	20,148,550	30,832,919	25,004,974	15,630,185	73,986,887	69,149,195	98,204,992
TOTAL	224,660,053	157,474,917	209,559,810	160,170,657	114,203,802	745,244,118	698,225,941	1,084,004,004
OKLAHOMA								
1	2,150,570	9,135,120	3,686,064	4,581,432	6,532,697	29,294,377	43,998,056	69,303,070
2	9,544,336	6,639,882	5,383,171	4,687,907	4,463,960	17,869,378	29,096,358	43,742,683
3	6,564,867	5,098,409	2,372,272	6,204,506	3,855,950	18,532,053	30,047,840	41,087,658
4	4,700,305	8,397,820	1,313,390	4,482,114	10,106,791	17,819,906	26,635,829	39,268,650
5	9,663,275	10,694,050	5,161,544	6,016,720	10,219,765	20,457,093	28,568,655	41,373,331
6	5,680,933	7,172,185	2,898,123	6,596,551	9,857,762	16,475,516	27,010,601	32,863,933
TOTAL	38,304,286	47,137,465	20,814,563	32,569,230	45,036,926	120,448,324	185,357,339	267,639,326
OREGON								
1	9,157,083	2,938,956	4,655,247	3,320,458	3,038,363	20,999,977	32,918,352	38,919,220
2	3,840,068	1,134,926	2,067,017	1,113,371	2,030,581	23,504,590	27,227,545	39,437,841
3	15,867,436	3,283,218	12,114,511	7,676,863	3,375,939	27,406,666	34,496,842	54,339,997
4	6,836,113	2,853,026	2,340,419	1,856,149	1,339,052	22,807,797	26,948,622	37,537,315
5	4,093,866	7,029,238	3,738,177	2,478,686	4,474,516	19,455,589	26,108,267	41,112,086
TOTAL	39,794,566	17,239,364	24,915,372	16,445,527	14,258,451	114,174,618	147,699,627	211,346,458
PENNSYLVANIA								
1	30,069,105	23,239,380	22,262,829	25,207,841	20,056,162	66,551,016	54,543,487	69,464,545
2	30,447,989	22,131,990	21,558,511	25,632,938	20,155,915	70,084,019	60,413,166	82,915,899
3	29,985,525	21,466,432	23,173,074	25,486,840	20,203,666	65,371,053	56,824,232	75,041,426
4	5,245,776	2,309,481	1,658,310	314,442	7,187,004	24,124,346	25,297,964	38,178,884
5	18,101,283	7,761,862	4,387,244	6,249,760	5,878,532	33,753,480	28,518,615	47,390,977
6	8,815,634	7,724,960	6,410,688	12,360,759	2,177,970	27,779,628	18,784,250	32,533,715
7	13,388,270	9,888,231	10,218,800	8,966,350	3,521,239	20,405,978	13,848,895	36,868,382
8	7,589,262	8,942,143	1,292,923	7,466,908	4,157,636	18,366,849	13,884,029	23,430,016
9	4,504,949	2,753,413	3,073,983	1,527,330	2,003,362	17,778,847	21,833,357	33,614,878
10	9,241,422	7,116,999	9,948,312	11,804,724	2,244,658	31,341,755	32,455,736	50,540,708
11	18,323,078	13,579,628	13,240,707	7,513,993	4,172,229	35,714,465	35,114,103	53,607,133
12	7,897,141	7,746,149	6,085,353	1,782,740	3,361,246	27,398,714	31,281,005	43,824,909
13	12,959,451	8,622,737	12,596,386	12,372,002	5,703,025	27,204,896	21,278,899	37,115,218
14	58,860,706	96,433,208	28,588,432	19,970,246	19,210,387	114,828,510	85,619,718	115,232,042
15	10,857,637	9,136,767	7,369,734	4,681,252	4,151,066	28,066,602	31,873,158	47,447,828
16	7,751,323	8,473,468	7,385,854	4,946,571	574,605	24,924,541	21,526,600	37,680,411
17	11,052,526	11,633,672	11,552,390	23,068,445	9,232,606	36,315,490	46,013,149	51,881,793
18	1,079,883	1,064,124	6,786,828	546,476	2,269,055	13,648,029	13,598,801	24,388,242
19	7,455,088	6,629,418	6,148,034	4,304,740	1,777,210	24,337,582	17,489,636	27,528,579
20	2,623,002	4,291,418	6,689,095	432,716	4,273,583	25,048,991	26,011,851	46,818,568
21	9,835,240	10,160,524	12,694,191	9,412,921	6,936,242	26,017,801	28,393,691	46,095,427
22	6,835,062	6,057,975	2,823,723	5,835,204	3,984,668	30,984,421	26,256,765	45,867,494
23	3,347,933	3,931,845	2,875,790	2,544,984	1,750,181	17,350,651	20,844,767	37,471,145
TOTAL	316,267,285	301,095,824	228,821,192	222,430,182	154,982,246	807,397,664	731,705,876	1,104,938,220

Appendix A lists the congressional districts which represent the county in which the state capital is located, and those congressional districts which represent only portions of a county. Appendix C lists the programs included in each functional policy category.

table continues

Table 5.10

Outlays for Housing Programs by Congressional District, 1983-1990 *(continued)*

Congressional District	1983	1984	1985	1986	1987	1988	1989	1990 (est.)
RHODE ISLAND								
1	16,488,132	16,401,496	19,091,704	5,212,400	7,241,781	70,772,777	72,199,642	129,100,935
2	9,929,175	11,915,820	7,225,221	3,183,692	3,561,962	51,097,772	50,498,255	93,117,491
TOTAL	26,417,307	28,317,316	26,316,925	8,396,092	10,803,743	121,870,549	122,697,897	222,218,426
SOUTH CAROLINA								
1	24,253,505	15,042,509	3,538,546	9,559,188	4,554,457	32,781,060	35,144,297	57,917,841
2	3,737,246	7,393,783	1,731,961	1,716,203	7,594,178	25,479,487	27,191,867	613,434,661
3	2,319,352	2,803,776	2,474,534	2,147,518	1,408,311	19,886,200	24,050,165	37,904,249
4	9,243,440	5,683,850	4,473,191	5,050,808	3,724,972	33,174,131	32,615,270	56,012,314
5	2,771,654	2,516,651	1,271,291	1,085,727	960,430	19,555,612	23,106,186	34,324,360
6	1,720,102	5,189,812	2,395,767	875,128	1,392,561	13,726,017	22,127,323	31,786,156
TOTAL	44,045,299	38,630,381	15,885,290	20,434,572	19,634,909	144,602,507	164,235,108	831,379,582
SOUTH DAKOTA								
TOTAL	5,090,731	4,484,227	3,372,880	6,117,553	8,245,357	44,939,363	60,874,793	92,664,868
TENNESSEE								
1	2,729,355	3,254,236	3,067,434	1,476,824	1,896,180	22,005,766	24,973,025	34,927,999
2	6,118,380	3,573,332	3,581,714	3,165,037	10,336,712	34,819,497	38,267,388	63,475,739
3	11,935,642	10,396,637	3,330,838	2,593,979	6,503,725	29,907,796	27,539,083	47,313,688
4	2,554,022	2,296,525	1,258,142	175,527	2,656,268	18,661,462	25,736,663	40,829,987
5	10,919,723	7,535,070	7,386,688	4,683,109	13,374,691	53,823,509	48,004,023	76,197,406
6	2,952,077	1,851,989	2,328,689	3,980,271	1,477,103	24,161,925	26,485,559	47,076,251
7	10,502,294	5,225,118	4,012,679	4,967,726	3,152,697	27,970,256	24,016,009	38,108,835
8	5,446,577	2,880,464	2,085,404	4,077,926	3,730,556	41,459,524	41,856,538	66,192,383
9	17,663,543	8,643,091	9,418,664	12,739,092	7,541,126	39,068,532	20,718,627	28,213,036
TOTAL	70,821,613	45,656,462	36,470,252	37,859,492	50,669,058	291,878,267	277,596,915	442,335,324
TEXAS								
1	6,718,254	1,761,001	911,806	1,243,459	1,841,614	16,685,150	23,721,396	35,476,328
2	7,187,875	1,834,558	891,918	1,686,134	1,244,226	23,988,454	26,722,008	47,031,881
3	8,196,318	8,150,186	5,759,141	5,335,150	5,344,600	19,916,698	34,753,539	50,777,037
4	6,458,653	3,207,085	3,185,107	2,561,164	3,108,519	19,366,311	28,507,174	53,188,309
5	8,215,842	7,600,321	7,352,777	6,055,921	5,421,219	17,210,971	31,477,262	45,729,601
6	7,027,068	3,690,813	3,734,845	2,438,585	1,638,006	18,796,800	24,613,291	39,832,945
7	8,853,986	9,214,681	8,257,359	7,290,154	3,132,298	19,089,669	20,229,978	32,258,109
8	10,182,568	11,393,768	8,534,129	8,192,353	3,400,811	18,576,608	19,429,791	37,595,169
9	14,610,586	22,520,548	8,308,873	6,596,043	4,902,545	29,764,084	42,487,407	62,707,325
10	10,663,278	7,291,991	11,088,427	6,971,416	5,711,874	25,085,353	62,006,600	62,389,549
11	4,575,214	8,054,697	4,721,172	3,364,504	3,389,599	24,005,644	31,167,617	54,216,275
12	7,654,659	6,226,416	6,013,203	4,334,692	1,393,432	13,072,599	23,072,774	27,590,687
13	7,001,275	4,738,076	5,042,997	3,693,035	1,727,961	15,571,236	25,441,879	41,475,175
14	3,935,827	1,707,903	1,739,409	1,592,104	1,257,482	17,787,705	23,426,925	42,491,611
15	14,629,202	8,173,953	9,344,315	3,865,753	4,686,436	34,081,903	41,113,089	68,224,549
16	14,862,980	16,709,504	10,604,238	8,934,150	2,804,962	17,269,897	46,034,384	66,386,543
17	8,441,540	714,511	4,010,339	1,853,364	1,815,417	13,593,735	20,287,909	32,398,841
18	8,766,219	10,564,310	7,464,056	7,085,317	1,690,148	16,248,901	16,980,711	26,338,719
19	8,110,856	3,184,418	4,828,976	2,704,969	1,561,312	14,379,005	22,000,162	29,025,956
20	4,083,940	10,020,878	9,167,860	9,309,689	12,435,227	30,429,344	49,635,518	71,130,546
21	5,772,713	4,875,087	6,305,029	4,234,082	4,250,641	15,699,938	23,633,562	38,248,774
22	4,148,277	5,769,831	5,144,748	4,876,895	2,051,099	18,220,300	72,499,226	88,903,854
23	10,899,787	11,519,814	10,514,828	8,427,374	11,174,788	33,127,657	51,169,954	73,665,768
24	8,997,899	19,374,898	7,431,898	7,174,956	6,784,269	24,905,443	39,624,675	61,255,151
25	8,756,380	10,311,875	7,455,678	6,976,656	1,531,335	9,014,152	10,056,107	14,042,109
26	4,699,977	3,702,462	4,148,016	3,645,744	2,386,922	18,004,161	29,739,055	36,374,670
27	11,097,978	989,270	15,591,712	9,342,099	4,313,676	19,833,728	36,174,193	53,275,798
TOTAL	224,549,150	203,302,854	177,552,856	139,785,761	101,000,417	543,725,445	876,006,188	1,292,031,280
UTAH								
1	3,318,624	6,867,086	3,517,378	2,929,196	1,361,266	16,926,410	22,965,658	31,001,513
2	20,500,798	8,729,051	9,535,625	1,582,946	3,587,874	25,982,921	22,649,964	44,562,919
3	4,266,132	5,505,759	5,885,167	1,607,887	1,032,679	7,997,901	17,228,569	16,151,069
TOTAL	28,085,554	21,101,896	18,938,170	6,120,029	5,981,819	50,907,232	62,844,191	91,715,501
VERMONT								
TOTAL	10,049,217	10,324,592	5,460,486	1,862,703	8,689,561	32,632,958	36,730,709	64,643,742

Appendix A lists the congressional districts which represent the county in which the state capital is located, and those congressional districts which represent only portions of a county. Appendix C lists the programs included in each functional policy category.

table continues

Table 5.10 Outlays for Housing Programs by Congressional District, 1983-1990 *(continued)*

Congressional District	1983	1984	1985	1986	1987	1988	1989	1990 (est.)
VIRGINIA								
1	1,004,372	2,127,026	5,189,071	6,059,421	4,284,623	34,314,033	37,324,257	60,323,905
2	10,089,052	558,718	8,704,260	8,556,246	4,010,546	42,149,603	28,670,797	47,053,216
3	10,342,442	10,445,011	9,087,325	22,751,549	9,092,189	51,647,924	45,699,127	77,254,066
4	6,961,971	5,746,011	15,309,642	7,336,004	5,125,305	33,299,618	36,418,554	57,153,605
5	870,495	3,544,317	942,126	2,496,690	424,450	20,069,971	19,384,773	29,612,494
6	4,662,430	7,046,523	3,883,125	13,806,464	4,829,696	25,997,369	26,502,934	45,436,701
7	1,925,845	692,087	719,568	1,801,205	813,725	17,109,616	15,549,042	25,223,631
8	4,356,717	4,057,899	173,696	3,496,380	3,244,835	18,179,824	24,885,808	40,603,506
9	3,109,342	6,933,676	1,984,429	3,502,300	1,207,764	19,798,142	21,637,663	34,373,187
10	8,189,356	5,197,888	4,068,186	3,506,146	1,430,672	45,097,591	37,328,232	64,229,749
TOTAL	51,512,022	46,349,156	50,061,428	73,312,405	34,463,806	307,663,691	293,401,187	481,264,060
WASHINGTON								
1	13,803,360	6,100,739	4,614,403	6,217,633	4,239,761	18,946,018	25,792,905	39,736,474
2	4,491,598	1,921,028	5,339,232	3,190,991	3,888,572	25,330,567	34,196,135	47,853,355
3	3,361,574	2,007,477	7,286,560	6,402,540	3,679,204	16,123,805	23,198,772	46,836,658
4	3,410,588	4,181,259	2,183,406	2,519,882	2,693,948	17,304,587	23,183,746	37,081,113
5	8,598,183	7,328,120	5,716,439	4,038,988	5,032,274	15,295,355	19,690,636	29,046,729
6	13,871,350	4,300,284	7,286,265	6,812,311	3,605,190	25,373,501	38,187,585	58,988,643
7	12,704,098	8,407,375	1,454,019	8,300,189	7,330,908	23,676,474	37,913,402	58,582,727
8	13,448,850	8,608,519	2,655,288	8,695,777	3,933,203	15,945,146	27,166,531	48,175,649
TOTAL	73,689,601	42,854,801	36,535,612	46,178,312	34,403,059	157,995,454	229,329,713	366,301,348
WEST VIRGINIA								
1	7,705,759	12,674,693	3,519,090	3,570,669	2,455,699	30,381,532	32,529,466	52,552,360
2	1,932,857	1,001,454	1,536,915	18,878,742	5,387,923	21,286,257	21,835,264	35,419,480
3	8,292,816	4,972,429	398,056	70,385,910	13,404,645	35,883,781	30,806,986	52,803,908
4	6,394,915	6,016,965	3,053,043	2,609,419	3,165,653	29,599,397	31,333,741	49,235,082
TOTAL	24,326,347	24,665,541	8,507,104	95,444,740	24,413,920	117,150,967	116,505,457	190,010,831
WISCONSIN								
1	7,652,927	4,955,047	5,592,753	3,665,304	2,494,906	29,743,253	27,042,607	64,388,092
2	4,027,015	3,022,717	5,156,346	6,139,220	4,318,843	25,177,071	29,336,704	50,038,466
3	4,935,854	3,923,451	3,368,691	1,642,362	1,286,602	18,214,844	17,886,115	28,057,190
4	20,533,034	10,328,734	10,241,847	8,770,456	12,468,750	38,207,224	35,340,260	73,771,754
5	22,213,680	11,619,174	11,751,564	9,995,034	15,125,141	37,928,608	32,211,627	73,323,347
6	6,429,649	2,736,656	1,347,427	1,133,373	485,912	17,827,675	17,603,311	28,478,867
7	3,195,972	8,559,010	2,343,371	2,467,950	1,942,730	22,762,551	24,742,620	38,888,027
8	4,629,155	11,547,744	2,045,271	2,061,896	1,524,842	28,749,065	32,766,624	53,020,292
9	4,602,838	3,040,914	2,342,358	1,634,902	1,619,270	19,999,479	16,358,029	31,810,794
TOTAL	78,220,124	59,733,448	44,189,628	37,510,498	41,266,998	238,609,769	233,287,898	441,776,830
WYOMING								
TOTAL	1,651,149	1,155,376	2,582,263	1,745,986	1,779,205	20,477,335	20,806,028	36,757,580
U.S. TOTAL	4,440.1 mil.	3,808.5 mil.	3,456.8 mil.	3,103.9 mil.	2,690.3 mil.	14,211.8 mil.	16,109.9 mil.	25,614.2 mil.

Appendix A lists the congressional districts which represent the county in which the state capital is located, and those congressional districts which represent only portions of a county. Appendix C lists the programs included in each functional policy category.

Table 5.11 Outlays for Income Security and Social Service Programs by Congressional District, 1983-1990

Congressional District	1983	1984	1985	1986	1987	1988	1989	1990 (est.)
ALABAMA								
1	611,834,394	662,643,339	716,197,274	760,568,568	797,340,314	852,640,978	914,852,942	1,013,602,719
2	1,155,749,443	1,173,468,437	1,254,340,492	1,245,289,426	1,241,944,921	1,307,422,146	1,376,010,527	1,688,527,603
3	606,662,946	673,230,490	718,872,877	747,266,704	768,806,353	825,375,006	877,786,558	981,120,325
4	715,623,837	754,598,840	814,025,334	847,416,769	883,739,011	943,280,446	1,005,818,068	1,120,498,914
5	527,752,788	564,008,465	608,601,093	646,804,744	676,160,481	724,160,801	778,815,072	871,546,366
6	734,961,708	780,876,122	832,818,198	885,197,869	927,506,881	980,574,585	1,040,096,646	1,151,000,614
7	629,697,591	693,508,207	745,324,373	758,047,802	792,206,512	848,644,121	903,102,091	1,009,731,944
TOTAL	4,982,282,707	5,302,333,901	5,690,179,641	5,890,591,882	6,087,704,473	6,482,098,084	6,896,481,904	7,836,028,484
ALASKA								
TOTAL	274,449,494	298,885,964	331,677,092	361,084,476	408,934,411	437,856,503	466,893,548	538,125,295
ARIZONA								
1	953,239,546	1,005,711,151	1,096,175,861	1,176,144,523	1,290,788,698	1,401,410,258	1,554,876,433	1,780,659,920
2	953,655,542	836,201,112	923,782,547	979,695,865	1,071,900,907	1,179,902,638	1,318,728,274	1,517,511,712
3	330,570,658	330,560,838	370,326,321	403,656,967	440,523,457	483,346,015	539,598,263	612,858,666
4	844,871,468	887,600,573	971,251,611	1,040,161,120	1,132,906,554	1,233,337,542	1,380,253,469	1,595,400,346
5	407,695,722	705,752,886	778,553,574	793,449,474	859,496,699	931,091,517	1,033,087,270	1,179,386,772
TOTAL	3,490,032,935	3,765,826,561	4,140,089,914	4,393,107,949	4,795,616,315	5,229,087,970	5,826,543,710	6,685,817,416
ARKANSAS								
1	760,780,820	837,849,752	910,434,199	954,914,433	988,603,517	1,041,404,594	1,122,469,790	1,243,056,106
2	898,660,762	925,787,126	976,625,370	1,037,658,264	1,072,342,134	1,139,824,799	1,214,461,740	1,412,652,798
3	767,197,850	829,002,026	896,485,768	942,621,865	992,660,951	1,049,679,731	1,144,756,245	1,240,126,859
4	765,393,311	859,776,057	928,681,213	953,136,173	987,248,763	1,047,375,417	1,120,201,609	1,236,428,268
TOTAL	3,192,032,743	3,452,414,961	3,712,226,550	3,888,330,735	4,040,855,365	4,278,284,541	4,601,889,384	5,132,264,032
CALIFORNIA								
1	854,377,335	782,108,358	910,976,772	945,960,937	997,165,642	1,069,391,880	1,102,789,177	1,248,242,045
2	829,876,536	869,446,388	940,972,277	1,013,189,520	1,074,221,381	1,157,139,354	1,186,921,974	1,366,668,983
3	1,838,339,564	1,938,636,507	1,939,739,820	2,051,940,796	2,114,316,180	2,808,113,422	2,980,607,438	3,323,414,735
4	860,263,328	795,599,225	890,104,357	958,463,863	988,516,909	1,091,251,170	1,103,973,179	1,421,205,296
5	996,495,737	959,822,215	1,151,714,520	1,100,359,149	1,171,925,743	1,242,888,609	1,345,310,969	1,448,148,108
6	557,894,470	666,959,196	746,376,801	738,178,751	785,072,392	843,949,208	898,077,820	986,682,652
7	575,183,569	598,202,260	674,262,851	725,763,361	771,065,634	826,255,724	852,764,137	975,848,679
8	673,407,026	690,977,093	769,374,345	787,570,623	827,809,091	880,147,993	896,527,168	1,027,647,004
9	679,061,361	698,309,577	777,587,885	783,618,211	828,149,399	879,235,895	885,340,518	1,025,032,985
10	537,782,530	551,216,991	617,571,303	630,005,214	671,816,453	716,279,961	728,355,351	829,685,627
11	581,352,213	612,358,672	653,753,144	692,294,106	727,881,856	774,934,470	815,172,371	902,983,784
12	518,602,894	537,336,369	523,264,814	510,066,464	542,787,984	581,727,339	596,608,551	673,075,480
13	464,870,097	476,468,558	523,475,596	540,431,912	579,964,222	621,586,385	635,917,599	724,630,198
14	809,495,577	782,844,508	779,816,445	799,950,676	848,923,517	917,245,252	951,210,193	1,097,141,578
15	587,690,885	605,404,215	630,332,483	653,168,656	697,705,248	752,666,575	763,997,627	902,067,918
16	632,412,833	637,787,620	664,085,327	652,229,942	687,702,362	730,822,471	751,462,242	844,192,154
17	577,233,244	741,463,494	834,673,939	861,071,926	921,034,821	984,368,328	976,877,795	1,168,034,444
18	892,902,816	983,593,208	1,278,984,061	1,178,810,554	1,259,604,910	1,307,832,540	1,315,702,080	1,561,322,981
19	471,954,581	484,411,044	522,448,803	545,949,194	587,523,738	631,035,972	659,096,069	746,175,948
20	477,062,405	683,073,863	794,773,627	872,096,561	931,390,868	997,866,471	1,027,833,114	1,180,272,944
21	635,109,562	654,036,777	756,998,264	834,986,685	887,431,220	950,873,485	969,046,037	1,104,373,218
22	674,077,670	678,515,119	726,385,681	767,635,703	817,571,592	871,684,634	866,964,955	1,010,417,080
23	646,880,718	641,314,045	729,516,294	772,155,837	821,071,840	874,948,500	871,341,143	1,018,688,138
24	632,524,562	634,156,846	729,007,371	771,927,794	820,225,433	875,156,351	870,342,057	1,017,059,386
25	619,225,681	623,128,176	724,195,280	765,501,588	813,523,777	869,004,650	868,232,434	1,008,741,740
26	542,919,672	546,302,108	635,042,903	672,348,108	714,403,519	762,736,688	759,658,992	890,809,882
27	651,303,364	663,471,749	727,815,712	773,784,522	820,115,094	875,361,039	866,735,852	1,008,205,050
28	629,943,559	638,563,957	732,496,284	776,155,838	824,039,916	878,598,342	874,661,156	1,019,006,095
29	672,849,013	681,672,286	751,600,449	792,394,715	841,838,027	899,302,869	894,665,624	1,008,779,456
30	651,358,032	656,033,801	723,462,722	765,812,256	813,869,056	870,306,932	864,779,433	1,010,781,584
31	668,646,471	672,769,126	727,532,259	769,856,997	818,135,236	874,242,798	870,020,142	1,009,387,064
32	634,279,202	638,442,523	730,640,840	771,489,345	816,814,375	871,811,549	867,832,206	1,015,692,184
33	633,940,288	638,282,901	725,113,307	766,842,424	814,836,269	870,258,692	865,268,420	1,010,357,662
34	644,610,661	648,820,017	723,963,752	766,452,352	814,455,697	869,552,338	864,610,009	1,009,346,686
35	634,971,343	679,225,727	737,209,575	772,162,790	816,345,382	884,398,821	892,833,768	1,051,811,213
36	1,248,521,316	1,288,175,598	1,444,854,356	1,585,991,418	1,679,093,745	1,825,941,518	1,882,210,663	2,227,976,937
37	631,236,887	654,326,439	728,243,422	815,416,959	861,252,360	938,956,689	978,948,644	1,173,718,935
38	451,093,033	472,610,820	536,408,770	631,658,438	674,755,899	724,934,060	755,708,162	835,927,841
39	469,398,064	490,663,795	532,819,328	628,023,298	670,772,935	715,748,661	748,993,602	836,865,596

Appendix A lists the congressional districts which represent the county in which the state capital is located, and those congressional districts which represent only portions of a county. Appendix C lists the programs included in each functional policy category.

table continues

Table 5.11 Outlays for Income Security and Social Service Programs by Congressional District, 1983-1990 *(continued)*

Congressional District	1983	1984	1985	1986	1987	1988	1989	1990 (est.)
CALIFORNIA *continued*								
40	474,309,940	492,541,584	534,101,659	628,593,519	671,680,666	716,749,840	750,431,529	840,340,621
41	454,238,926	466,127,983	506,103,749	557,790,127	597,927,922	644,177,779	662,665,670	751,911,982
42	581,298,530	586,267,794	650,145,105	712,040,985	758,209,630	809,267,613	819,079,223	943,872,907
43	637,188,390	625,161,904	699,693,390	783,655,984	838,607,610	901,718,032	929,874,668	1,055,483,926
44	663,804,782	681,790,630	768,366,524	847,776,209	907,323,074	977,588,016	1,005,615,337	1,157,369,290
45	629,936,967	676,315,689	753,552,757	837,032,536	888,410,313	962,123,314	986,964,812	1,131,074,561
TOTAL	30,229,925,637	31,224,736,759	34,659,558,924	36,608,606,843	38,817,288,940	42,130,182,232	43,062,029,912	49,600,472,578
COLORADO								
1	889,626,562	1,004,059,811	1,008,219,454	1,006,044,519	1,078,683,183	1,156,891,170	1,233,506,990	1,406,867,642
2	383,463,014	350,700,768	373,699,258	400,318,261	435,637,739	471,268,252	509,068,728	561,564,493
3	541,129,503	581,842,374	620,696,682	643,462,869	687,248,686	745,175,266	800,265,910	880,971,850
4	495,111,679	524,983,945	562,255,188	564,186,842	594,098,973	640,061,456	684,558,386	753,311,950
5	263,576,982	374,156,498	405,359,301	463,159,024	507,979,232	552,042,632	594,791,983	652,474,925
6	218,977,178	290,090,735	309,078,110	398,857,182	427,941,157	469,742,345	513,053,841	566,091,774
TOTAL	2,791,884,918	3,125,834,131	3,279,307,993	3,476,028,697	3,731,588,970	4,035,181,121	4,335,245,838	4,821,282,633
CONNECTICUT								
1	882,293,071	942,862,191	994,963,058	1,042,892,125	1,071,254,003	1,131,718,422	1,227,494,778	1,382,328,612
2	500,721,563	526,345,352	560,347,109	671,676,539	698,792,543	744,596,113	809,014,201	879,159,490
3	710,732,522	752,373,343	820,141,584	858,807,437	893,320,028	943,480,301	1,025,106,217	1,114,395,066
4	697,309,105	728,998,379	761,906,554	742,381,052	776,057,342	826,289,285	896,723,993	974,972,090
5	673,076,585	712,674,598	795,828,175	810,710,335	845,484,295	896,942,234	974,774,278	1,056,570,858
6	660,519,364	694,187,009	768,837,927	814,145,788	855,089,583	911,146,285	989,074,165	1,073,461,310
TOTAL	4,124,652,210	4,357,440,873	4,702,024,408	4,940,613,277	5,139,997,792	5,454,172,641	5,922,187,633	6,480,887,427
DELAWARE								
TOTAL	736,390,139	789,507,458	845,007,369	886,600,109	935,179,859	998,662,251	1,072,186,370	1,193,320,109
DISTRICT OF COLUMBIA								
TOTAL	1,124,149,973	1,170,959,452	1,268,295,469	1,270,704,217	1,363,177,574	1,408,823,840	1,512,966,915	1,455,265,993
FLORIDA								
1	559,590,824	583,485,473	640,616,396	682,462,409	727,627,451	789,267,646	865,409,868	956,414,715
2	1,492,356,707	1,480,070,507	1,522,464,696	1,490,453,409	1,557,123,255	1,768,640,611	1,929,985,973	2,347,078,788
3	602,326,171	661,927,891	715,516,606	722,686,481	762,939,358	825,020,826	894,450,741	991,842,253
4	924,122,193	996,560,764	1,094,958,082	1,108,207,834	1,181,326,630	1,281,170,542	1,402,895,597	1,539,442,786
5	873,794,824	662,316,055	721,362,513	752,937,959	812,735,905	880,418,558	965,909,769	1,070,179,478
6	740,971,753	1,036,979,949	1,158,277,563	1,282,205,773	1,405,962,487	1,538,731,887	2,337,439,447	1,851,601,967
7	706,540,435	751,867,463	800,061,128	786,375,142	833,951,772	909,431,077	971,870,824	1,081,176,130
8	1,683,553,000	1,438,810,139	1,517,319,773	1,366,337,829	1,422,495,552	1,489,418,403	1,643,792,596	1,802,635,616
9	984,377,094	1,163,463,165	1,321,337,417	1,335,867,656	1,408,596,610	1,499,124,995	1,586,662,260	1,727,145,632
10	869,974,936	957,005,314	1,061,222,043	1,035,211,910	1,102,507,486	1,187,559,651	1,294,988,140	1,432,699,648
11	565,090,280	785,255,560	860,646,820	939,532,561	1,007,730,534	1,100,865,233	1,206,116,527	1,338,178,194
12	821,683,240	1,080,588,302	1,199,479,872	1,354,491,330	1,466,626,637	1,604,268,792	1,764,999,602	1,962,788,025
13	910,684,921	1,340,876,992	1,488,979,108	1,629,427,644	1,749,528,053	1,895,558,669	2,079,050,422	2,296,851,881
14	1,000,338,076	1,072,468,784	1,185,670,385	1,348,015,160	1,444,803,395	1,553,232,650	1,680,454,151	1,851,193,114
15	980,256,107	1,005,463,548	1,042,881,342	1,204,115,891	1,275,758,710	1,355,523,354	1,449,801,928	1,587,999,729
16	826,303,257	867,518,689	974,941,425	1,118,468,458	1,187,199,776	1,268,069,926	1,363,908,269	1,500,004,970
17	711,102,743	742,110,829	812,818,191	913,080,169	976,048,713	1,061,803,404	1,157,162,716	1,296,846,446
18	730,144,888	763,687,015	820,227,393	920,385,838	984,793,939	1,069,823,281	1,167,710,014	1,302,047,491
19	663,383,972	711,069,309	791,102,788	882,980,679	943,943,739	1,027,626,922	1,113,947,497	1,249,940,893
TOTAL	16,646,595,420	18,101,525,748	19,729,883,542	20,873,244,131	22,251,700,003	24,105,556,427	26,876,556,337	29,186,067,758
GEORGIA								
1	599,169,390	653,509,936	713,822,340	770,348,412	811,751,947	878,853,536	940,106,286	1,041,725,903
2	615,070,881	667,996,431	731,031,941	743,274,503	775,499,022	840,821,117	893,432,203	998,507,458
3	569,642,430	577,754,679	625,749,883	692,617,915	722,565,927	778,376,984	832,954,082	916,912,649
4	845,358,169	467,481,997	435,607,743	436,997,761	455,210,333	485,935,327	525,751,215	603,728,615
5	824,942,970	1,241,025,262	1,397,929,821	1,388,153,842	1,436,002,472	1,516,795,941	1,644,769,580	1,968,081,809
6	497,295,484	542,761,303	591,741,889	664,547,405	705,997,272	767,471,914	827,982,599	912,917,554
7	485,642,748	508,592,632	556,744,271	606,466,239	649,673,611	700,340,656	757,366,944	831,569,152
8	627,022,940	698,912,367	765,926,270	792,896,261	833,204,724	904,095,504	963,862,411	1,061,695,355
9	543,770,145	578,517,823	639,336,717	680,572,514	723,669,187	785,285,288	848,394,428	940,388,465
10	534,300,704	567,147,915	620,938,892	672,346,730	704,589,440	767,447,885	826,130,417	908,769,412
TOTAL	6,142,215,861	6,503,700,345	7,078,829,766	7,448,221,582	7,818,163,936	8,425,424,151	9,060,750,165	10,184,296,371

Appendix A lists the congressional districts which represent the county in which the state capital is located, and those congressional districts which represent only portions of a county. Appendix C lists the programs included in each functional policy category.

table continues

Table 5.11 Outlays for Income Security and Social Service Programs by Congressional District, 1983-1990 *(continued)*

Congressional District	1983	1984	1985	1986	1987	1988	1989	1990 (est.)
HAWAII								
1	509,121,526	515,004,841	544,107,449	599,701,653	636,466,015	679,223,276	719,506,998	799,316,738
2	503,460,493	558,249,914	612,891,206	619,698,287	661,589,378	708,172,748	759,212,515	843,995,506
TOTAL	1,012,582,019	1,073,254,755	1,156,998,655	1,219,399,940	1,298,055,393	1,387,396,024	1,478,719,513	1,643,312,244
IDAHO								
1	594,594,505	636,428,573	685,978,547	713,707,018	744,686,906	801,231,251	852,596,794	967,137,342
2	425,233,854	474,626,093	510,711,569	542,979,765	568,626,290	609,887,385	647,292,921	724,636,268
TOTAL	1,019,828,359	1,111,054,666	1,196,690,116	1,256,686,783	1,313,313,196	1,411,118,636	1,499,889,715	1,691,773,610
ILLINOIS								
1	627,840,229	673,436,392	741,051,337	791,707,678	823,012,058	867,464,002	919,737,514	999,472,210
2	623,927,828	667,015,435	734,653,224	785,475,736	816,262,840	861,046,933	910,827,055	991,901,316
3	646,442,292	690,314,786	734,807,555	785,641,649	816,416,662	861,227,815	911,018,395	992,109,688
4	431,549,019	558,221,318	596,100,263	647,015,705	676,070,459	714,563,103	770,623,222	826,916,993
5	658,709,451	703,002,665	734,847,616	785,869,113	816,440,313	861,147,358	910,897,320	991,977,836
6	470,830,133	510,471,737	560,488,829	626,579,516	659,551,969	703,648,862	751,608,087	821,645,163
7	668,255,630	728,442,866	773,069,441	821,096,203	857,067,894	902,683,073	955,484,895	1,060,821,203
8	624,551,584	667,176,770	735,351,895	786,012,224	816,973,150	861,819,995	912,563,699	994,141,397
9	661,067,006	686,165,932	737,873,400	788,865,497	823,544,652	868,884,136	915,448,030	998,869,490
10	508,254,837	542,466,105	591,357,023	641,500,121	670,700,260	710,023,928	756,365,651	823,245,117
11	623,906,728	666,772,570	734,743,889	785,749,234	817,325,880	862,087,013	912,819,176	993,981,906
12	517,316,296	552,997,019	605,156,789	652,095,895	680,679,574	721,199,599	767,059,050	836,406,048
13	474,950,874	526,651,821	578,490,242	641,972,083	674,104,259	716,419,267	765,076,328	835,658,772
14	420,892,247	560,692,274	605,995,114	627,279,872	659,551,932	698,404,396	777,318,478	809,594,300
15	544,497,025	600,726,454	654,021,784	658,362,697	688,820,141	728,873,591	778,007,297	845,111,829
16	556,187,769	630,847,128	684,204,963	669,472,121	702,909,856	744,596,728	792,714,269	865,677,548
17	647,775,586	695,287,250	763,023,391	740,668,137	770,568,241	808,963,208	858,862,349	929,392,135
18	632,078,929	673,981,461	726,868,733	733,497,520	766,072,493	807,488,944	858,095,718	935,777,508
19	582,787,248	702,813,137	753,299,801	724,648,936	747,122,986	790,650,549	845,074,476	913,170,015
20	1,750,911,025	1,993,572,260	2,061,178,749	2,028,776,060	2,074,238,969	2,180,199,947	2,261,106,550	2,764,114,843
21	564,421,978	741,948,106	794,344,053	832,652,464	860,151,013	905,220,401	961,172,053	1,051,811,016
22	667,590,791	833,728,679	902,515,350	874,879,301	900,052,971	947,044,746	1,002,979,669	1,086,192,208
TOTAL	13,904,744,505	15,606,732,163	16,803,443,441	17,429,817,762	18,117,638,570	19,123,657,593	20,294,859,281	22,367,988,539
INDIANA								
1	579,429,798	643,785,159	680,224,270	777,235,688	817,556,903	868,414,324	939,325,584	1,160,912,834
2	584,544,467	698,501,103	740,483,645	789,648,749	824,000,517	870,587,002	937,804,880	1,143,101,759
3	605,470,756	685,309,527	731,306,549	754,158,117	789,899,553	837,898,790	904,052,437	1,071,550,829
4	572,761,266	642,409,359	680,996,133	699,949,964	729,421,803	771,597,431	830,429,224	980,135,242
5	507,373,325	628,409,544	677,459,845	726,597,895	760,615,673	806,282,960	868,481,592	1,033,276,644
6	625,261,164	720,199,878	777,841,823	835,950,720	869,649,169	918,999,852	980,210,535	1,173,813,142
7	590,870,426	680,440,381	722,657,455	739,025,866	763,820,900	807,790,984	897,708,846	1,031,390,602
8	679,838,240	728,102,297	774,899,317	794,091,859	831,839,095	879,329,914	950,018,012	1,150,578,741
9	587,666,317	595,016,344	635,812,230	681,850,163	714,049,923	757,035,536	821,332,982	1,006,375,321
10	1,078,868,552	1,040,302,402	1,091,428,041	1,171,613,799	1,190,276,832	1,237,009,338	1,312,118,331	1,730,078,972
TOTAL	6,412,084,310	7,062,475,995	7,513,109,309	7,970,122,821	8,291,130,367	8,754,946,132	9,441,482,423	11,481,214,086
IOWA								
1	569,899,556	637,752,541	677,961,681	704,931,689	736,588,185	779,053,766	829,949,150	913,236,910
2	492,410,799	573,766,808	612,327,289	651,972,276	684,630,570	723,889,795	773,133,542	843,251,072
3	564,690,919	583,274,916	624,083,904	650,142,742	680,467,976	719,834,453	764,774,156	832,990,255
4	787,500,493	827,490,127	875,190,319	948,132,124	970,820,195	997,257,746	1,066,120,145	1,231,847,682
5	637,545,350	699,995,190	746,670,488	777,999,122	809,313,584	853,624,268	907,063,906	992,488,909
6	639,447,826	687,154,452	731,908,545	754,829,860	786,317,331	828,609,278	882,685,663	963,433,264
TOTAL	3,691,494,943	4,009,434,034	4,268,142,226	4,488,007,813	4,668,137,841	4,902,269,306	5,223,726,562	5,777,248,091
KANSAS								
1	633,428,597	694,558,346	734,387,874	744,213,707	775,319,091	818,370,747	873,088,606	952,704,833
2	655,795,231	715,231,185	740,221,225	757,895,727	802,413,647	840,211,441	919,999,155	1,063,376,665
3	422,401,438	524,239,358	557,292,885	615,859,919	653,166,844	700,755,099	756,678,818	831,731,957
4	442,930,087	568,295,200	605,487,303	684,793,520	727,982,389	781,250,556	838,989,035	923,073,077
5	688,856,520	770,714,373	807,499,853	800,036,358	829,412,519	874,035,331	929,112,950	1,019,786,797
TOTAL	2,843,411,873	3,273,038,462	3,444,889,140	3,602,799,231	3,788,294,490	4,014,623,174	4,317,868,564	4,790,673,329

Appendix A lists the congressional districts which represent the county in which the state capital is located, and those congressional districts which represent only portions of a county. Appendix C lists the programs included in each functional policy category.

table continues

Table 5.11 Outlays for Income Security and Social Service Programs by Congressional District, 1983-1990 *(continued)*

Congressional District	1983	1984	1985	1986	1987	1988	1989	1990 (est.)
KENTUCKY								
1	680,382,162	738,718,265	798,100,999	808,226,619	839,308,411	888,540,557	952,967,491	1,039,215,531
2	498,995,990	530,075,778	576,314,694	607,698,225	638,729,362	684,699,826	740,441,962	812,191,668
3	625,776,191	676,853,161	698,591,441	742,800,980	780,093,613	832,402,611	886,974,610	968,452,333
4	445,318,066	576,246,820	656,682,087	684,729,683	715,772,581	759,415,106	811,813,440	886,112,766
5	700,162,063	747,827,174	821,923,331	851,929,609	892,859,310	958,153,714	1,034,536,161	1,144,053,703
6	1,005,391,083	1,092,117,590	1,112,992,689	1,130,717,430	1,144,810,727	1,194,934,248	1,252,906,553	1,528,688,655
7	667,012,043	708,936,967	766,190,044	796,911,473	831,018,781	886,816,651	953,804,128	1,051,752,151
TOTAL	4,623,037,598	5,070,775,755	5,430,795,285	5,623,014,019	5,842,592,785	6,204,962,713	6,633,444,345	7,430,466,808
LOUISIANA								
1	584,942,248	622,860,700	622,525,012	630,659,164	669,830,679	713,687,731	773,417,884	1,005,022,292
2	501,924,017	528,685,304	579,017,557	653,451,757	691,822,558	744,303,577	803,050,266	1,026,005,264
3	401,380,697	435,430,127	545,304,461	665,572,984	701,769,692	762,905,277	835,245,807	1,048,346,315
4	546,996,663	605,625,159	664,998,126	677,156,925	713,910,081	762,236,159	822,031,611	1,065,603,721
5	615,427,871	656,768,617	726,289,672	717,329,141	754,241,310	806,296,130	878,325,158	1,201,844,352
6	984,261,428	1,030,542,941	1,109,388,258	1,222,495,492	1,244,855,289	1,361,576,787	1,478,959,287	1,960,485,154
7	483,269,637	510,235,369	565,266,919	602,986,985	649,526,432	699,839,910	763,029,288	981,162,809
8	537,762,550	617,131,228	691,118,492	722,428,358	751,163,600	815,226,998	891,071,148	1,222,043,834
TOTAL	4,655,965,112	5,007,279,444	5,503,908,497	5,892,080,807	6,177,119,640	6,666,072,568	7,245,130,449	9,510,513,739
MAINE								
1	894,949,839	960,400,971	1,015,419,098	1,035,123,183	1,073,562,895	1,112,502,428	1,198,638,349	1,359,860,094
2	704,652,786	776,031,689	863,079,881	918,609,413	963,772,825	1,011,257,513	1,087,646,292	1,195,354,827
TOTAL	1,599,602,625	1,736,432,660	1,878,498,979	1,953,732,596	2,037,335,720	2,123,759,941	2,286,284,641	2,555,214,921
MARYLAND								
1	593,000,087	620,027,664	674,625,776	684,323,830	717,353,542	775,592,737	830,716,642	910,769,465
2	525,182,072	620,650,102	670,927,970	417,333,219	748,546,843	793,121,594	826,159,807	906,256,895
3	745,683,752	803,998,825	865,756,807	977,968,996	932,750,749	999,517,163	1,083,420,434	1,199,556,656
4	602,256,678	631,080,791	663,910,590	707,553,926	750,526,803	804,992,304	861,150,455	998,393,022
5	315,464,998	334,476,150	357,282,647	424,947,752	443,637,691	477,704,665	511,917,682	559,868,009
6	571,820,575	663,611,762	712,294,178	653,609,981	671,321,997	717,575,719	769,486,093	838,368,263
7	885,810,848	936,744,265	1,010,283,606	1,348,912,898	1,163,697,380	1,226,339,192	1,297,575,620	1,454,440,956
8	468,661,588	509,077,329	560,827,541	619,350,022	654,466,021	709,990,121	766,442,364	830,421,988
TOTAL	4,707,880,596	5,119,666,887	5,515,909,115	5,834,000,623	6,082,301,025	6,504,833,496	6,946,869,097	7,698,075,254
MASSACHUSETTS								
1	687,258,184	737,824,473	807,432,376	835,712,985	879,331,038	931,717,065	1,003,546,785	1,100,961,467
2	762,019,629	784,473,809	850,001,472	884,317,820	935,205,885	993,637,315	1,070,509,103	1,177,822,478
3	682,584,984	702,670,358	763,881,234	810,248,756	849,595,842	901,337,370	970,758,384	1,063,773,323
4	623,348,103	639,407,338	707,765,828	746,017,075	785,587,683	835,315,206	906,888,077	995,747,872
5	596,055,533	616,591,917	677,688,918	720,333,153	754,063,183	795,513,668	860,300,616	945,657,056
6	742,945,645	759,674,253	832,145,668	861,004,044	907,456,699	960,480,384	1,036,296,805	1,134,154,393
7	731,860,222	753,587,745	784,420,504	822,241,564	855,026,028	902,981,071	973,053,419	1,081,591,896
8	915,659,672	939,276,156	1,008,483,673	1,014,389,940	1,049,053,345	1,109,299,005	1,183,847,414	1,325,916,285
9	1,126,609,206	1,211,515,662	1,314,269,044	1,340,775,476	1,393,404,620	1,448,522,968	1,548,599,338	1,872,145,158
10	698,383,956	805,886,668	881,126,772	949,016,398	998,269,976	1,059,096,236	1,143,948,088	1,256,198,482
11	778,856,891	792,477,312	837,676,641	877,841,402	916,532,425	967,221,829	1,041,942,892	1,158,680,264
TOTAL	8,345,582,026	8,743,385,690	9,464,892,129	9,861,898,613	10,323,526,723	10,905,122,116	11,739,690,922	13,112,648,674
MICHIGAN								
1	756,143,323	794,063,978	857,175,971	899,114,943	935,546,350	980,021,188	1,031,512,054	1,124,976,947
2	564,022,851	640,995,279	682,458,755	712,288,856	744,507,574	784,076,914	830,565,043	902,442,811
3	1,143,837,068	1,304,097,481	1,613,207,782	1,585,317,446	1,596,436,408	1,665,959,043	1,790,786,907	2,301,706,249
4	625,834,017	704,067,754	755,057,764	754,819,612	790,396,030	829,421,971	879,158,697	958,349,859
5	628,669,058	658,312,354	704,830,891	685,658,759	721,847,487	761,933,510	810,228,480	883,176,323
6	922,308,863	944,778,245	697,068,851	752,873,803	765,814,638	809,732,335	849,009,675	981,577,105
7	570,457,803	599,381,195	639,112,295	734,016,359	771,964,309	815,805,692	868,014,002	946,550,306
8	651,014,656	692,334,998	738,137,972	783,298,679	824,804,464	866,942,380	919,759,716	1,002,884,625
9	702,429,428	735,885,865	789,328,524	803,820,488	843,934,577	891,379,818	948,333,661	1,037,970,518
10	648,450,938	716,238,164	771,025,071	816,961,834	863,238,966	903,308,519	939,309,105	995,942,831
11	832,644,250	887,226,156	947,894,332	942,934,659	983,613,420	1,037,584,793	1,101,012,922	1,202,168,625
12	538,446,794	561,980,217	599,063,803	695,256,366	742,524,718	793,797,986	853,732,937	932,798,488

Appendix A lists the congressional districts which represent the county in which the state capital is located, and those congressional districts which represent only portions of a county. Appendix C lists the programs included in each functional policy category.

table continues

Table 5.11 Outlays for Income Security and Social Service Programs by Congressional District, 1983-1990 *(continued)*

Congressional District	1983	1984	1985	1986	1987	1988	1989	1990 (est.)
MICHIGAN *continued*								
13	756,653,737	796,188,842	871,722,974	913,556,524	951,347,597	996,296,401	1,045,187,819	1,150,907,224
14	588,669,244	627,065,628	674,559,958	765,392,761	809,343,289	858,820,610	915,243,732	1,000,572,664
15	681,778,110	718,008,301	785,529,571	829,146,831	863,115,649	906,121,740	954,387,802	1,041,246,475
16	691,145,303	784,066,720	769,393,032	813,645,273	849,677,706	894,141,523	942,989,625	1,030,940,292
17	657,638,059	694,175,679	728,174,595	803,360,860	840,200,097	885,645,179	939,214,838	1,026,045,213
18	509,676,270	542,212,301	591,425,639	696,511,233	734,465,239	781,077,828	835,952,256	914,184,158
TOTAL	12,469,819,773	13,401,079,155	14,215,167,780	14,987,975,286	15,632,778,520	16,462,067,431	17,454,399,268	19,434,440,714
MINNESOTA								
1	532,787,550	638,646,827	674,437,691	694,030,725	722,224,793	760,685,904	811,505,678	878,217,122
2	647,284,696	723,434,415	759,977,110	741,389,325	765,264,686	801,691,039	853,711,710	920,010,791
3	416,593,533	475,679,952	537,630,234	603,327,686	635,457,323	673,041,815	727,055,990	787,192,778
4	414,941,060	492,790,202	401,822,745	415,948,393	423,311,005	432,968,354	451,665,724	643,904,960
5	683,367,043	734,903,967	713,349,501	750,867,932	791,629,330	835,722,245	896,976,271	963,508,236
6	909,874,049	907,811,221	1,085,986,247	1,215,648,843	1,272,276,381	1,340,212,996	1,431,989,864	1,556,387,600
7	663,838,914	693,948,666	727,225,004	765,913,018	790,853,119	830,001,657	887,797,624	955,289,221
8	673,284,601	794,438,453	834,249,262	865,945,022	897,067,694	942,091,109	1,002,364,132	1,080,085,364
TOTAL	4,941,971,447	5,461,653,704	5,734,677,795	6,053,070,945	6,298,084,331	6,616,415,119	7,063,066,993	7,784,596,072
MISSISSIPPI								
1	576,806,807	616,497,974	675,863,525	713,343,395	757,064,570	818,782,166	871,762,018	972,293,559
2	619,102,868	681,303,830	703,418,108	695,519,256	740,602,932	773,730,969	825,335,323	904,086,053
3	580,245,671	606,728,271	651,012,642	710,789,647	742,924,186	803,640,149	856,526,984	945,666,633
4	1,040,798,057	1,061,367,802	1,117,345,293	1,153,557,390	1,210,926,051	1,290,046,795	1,419,858,599	1,658,677,869
5	511,678,753	529,634,178	571,801,086	649,877,979	675,502,785	727,270,053	776,917,112	850,813,154
TOTAL	3,328,632,156	3,495,532,055	3,719,440,654	3,923,087,667	4,127,020,524	4,413,470,131	4,750,400,036	5,331,537,267
MISSOURI								
1	973,573,246	1,035,481,610	1,103,466,765	1,178,919,028	1,263,209,335	1,331,936,626	1,422,976,144	1,555,559,837
2	745,299,090	813,818,585	876,976,380	938,068,702	968,934,491	1,017,686,166	1,081,185,077	1,175,480,712
3	262,116,296	303,723,955	326,935,745	357,975,178	359,859,231	379,060,075	402,351,141	439,227,987
4	933,428,292	1,127,378,523	1,194,173,945	1,211,242,848	1,260,004,285	1,318,086,209	1,411,777,960	1,688,070,083
5	679,087,754	728,017,056	764,070,004	845,991,767	883,907,875	932,542,718	991,370,418	1,079,461,420
6	691,231,216	767,169,236	821,959,243	750,441,122	779,138,668	815,868,496	864,981,244	941,094,800
7	733,802,097	806,792,210	863,208,137	881,902,767	924,535,169	979,022,571	1,044,614,108	1,144,126,702
8	826,604,018	854,667,519	914,314,561	945,217,748	987,842,007	1,046,981,005	1,116,919,469	1,227,558,789
9	600,246,062	709,166,871	755,591,368	795,852,397	828,786,467	872,114,943	946,449,953	1,070,605,920
TOTAL	6,445,388,071	7,146,215,564	7,620,696,149	7,905,611,557	8,256,217,530	8,693,298,809	9,282,625,514	10,321,186,251
MONTANA								
1	541,795,470	600,954,326	634,315,027	658,619,235	696,334,542	741,522,962	783,184,957	885,598,388
2	410,074,074	457,346,012	520,774,038	548,145,988	586,970,546	626,077,966	654,868,096	724,425,074
TOTAL	951,869,544	1,058,300,338	1,155,089,065	1,206,765,223	1,283,305,088	1,367,600,928	1,438,053,053	1,610,023,463
NEBRASKA								
1	724,393,476	786,013,373	839,233,026	856,152,248	904,111,965	944,029,934	999,083,606	1,212,595,960
2	523,594,795	559,802,488	599,155,858	689,813,665	735,661,309	778,783,252	827,516,288	1,021,258,305
3	661,086,333	726,018,765	783,677,954	780,116,114	812,408,907	851,669,921	899,624,597	1,061,212,563
TOTAL	1,909,074,604	2,071,834,626	2,222,066,838	2,326,082,027	2,452,182,181	2,574,483,107	2,726,224,491	3,295,066,829
NEVADA								
1	108,598,704	434,542,861	484,495,218	574,408,236	633,975,423	702,261,020	785,935,231	882,865,703
2	151,337,470	545,422,184	594,604,758	588,315,243	623,905,259	677,249,724	750,795,367	847,044,943
TOTAL	259,936,174	979,965,045	1,079,099,976	1,162,723,479	1,257,880,682	1,379,510,744	1,536,730,598	1,729,910,647
NEW HAMPSHIRE								
1	512,227,057	552,449,678	587,580,716	616,279,563	642,264,027	676,606,830	731,574,560	793,546,456
2	602,410,062	643,724,886	700,105,954	722,450,981	753,169,341	787,469,364	842,495,331	955,647,113
TOTAL	1,114,637,119	1,196,174,564	1,287,686,670	1,338,730,544	1,395,433,368	1,464,076,194	1,574,069,891	1,749,193,569

Appendix A lists the congressional districts which represent the county in which the state capital is located, and those congressional districts which represent only portions of a county. Appendix C lists the programs included in each functional policy category.

table continues

Table 5.11 Outlays for Income Security and Social Service Programs by Congressional District, 1983-1990 *(continued)*

Congressional District	1983	1984	1985	1986	1987	1988	1989	1990 (est.)
NEW JERSEY								
1	635,416,516	672,683,743	666,593,893	703,362,877	738,464,712	790,341,540	844,204,386	928,519,650
2	854,830,289	899,761,150	1,019,711,391	1,067,069,526	1,110,651,167	1,190,056,560	1,263,556,333	1,385,566,646
3	710,671,781	767,160,327	834,400,806	906,787,714	950,465,256	1,011,143,141	1,076,998,547	1,180,673,920
4	1,082,208,389	1,244,613,097	1,302,240,711	1,354,081,625	1,380,782,390	1,412,353,701	1,495,333,156	1,816,758,873
5	617,229,757	616,154,975	642,975,823	668,021,242	697,033,974	738,637,915	784,803,186	857,381,350
6	592,035,985	630,714,043	663,951,102	729,974,031	764,995,449	815,129,717	867,448,469	949,797,182
7	653,964,057	715,172,364	777,165,166	813,483,338	849,946,001	903,334,320	957,627,218	1,052,181,434
8	692,258,579	723,740,681	766,478,790	786,309,676	823,030,654	876,127,859	925,837,398	1,019,166,133
9	670,874,108	701,947,149	758,030,743	818,049,200	851,215,480	900,177,557	956,715,730	1,042,779,252
10	776,841,734	794,291,254	863,766,717	876,500,863	909,315,244	970,839,350	1,020,094,577	1,140,481,591
11	711,194,542	742,498,320	804,972,809	820,144,026	852,360,881	908,850,547	958,205,426	1,055,367,923
12	431,875,003	559,484,046	681,399,859	748,364,263	782,491,715	835,492,381	890,969,186	971,256,883
13	873,481,544	771,840,748	848,419,287	942,638,826	987,730,808	1,049,995,004	1,119,620,048	1,220,759,580
14	771,239,108	812,945,084	884,535,871	852,360,330	886,213,798	944,168,592	992,027,759	1,096,545,266
TOTAL	10,074,121,390	10,653,006,982	11,514,642,968	12,087,147,537	12,584,697,531	13,346,648,185	14,153,441,419	15,717,235,684
NEW MEXICO								
1	547,218,794	446,920,580	486,733,073	526,328,732	581,763,011	626,559,510	677,868,849	730,684,681
2	530,571,004	524,059,264	575,331,491	601,432,711	639,725,788	691,174,717	740,113,085	796,075,620
3	310,298,384	590,214,355	642,142,391	670,989,085	720,943,050	797,539,410	848,582,591	956,939,609
TOTAL	1,388,088,182	1,561,194,199	1,704,206,955	1,798,750,528	1,942,431,849	2,115,273,637	2,266,564,525	2,483,699,910
NEW YORK								
1	460,480,587	492,652,142	524,173,253	582,123,488	598,325,712	630,712,301	698,368,022	737,362,275
2	448,317,263	487,906,892	520,308,959	571,992,359	593,449,043	625,146,780	692,638,741	725,610,656
3	759,405,315	827,585,017	896,667,002	981,366,835	1,031,698,481	1,087,586,887	1,192,311,369	1,259,344,468
4	603,843,003	655,543,793	732,489,348	805,243,098	844,720,125	891,951,322	968,181,361	1,035,042,799
5	672,860,522	716,975,817	727,864,913	801,725,189	840,618,293	888,259,121	963,760,976	1,027,371,187
6	694,813,248	750,776,040	798,915,311	915,720,137	969,337,152	1,021,355,782	1,076,187,190	1,165,071,973
7	696,695,134	753,638,452	801,643,103	917,345,765	972,887,381	1,025,284,046	1,080,383,842	1,169,823,569
8	714,694,387	774,257,438	827,692,007	950,366,398	1,009,747,789	1,045,215,431	1,103,908,853	1,199,753,704
9	692,924,046	749,558,241	797,303,950	912,374,118	967,615,926	1,019,729,590	1,074,535,914	1,165,092,645
10	731,412,855	791,490,952	840,875,378	947,500,366	1,006,680,440	1,061,990,484	1,113,426,791	1,205,937,330
11	738,041,511	797,659,101	849,016,135	956,875,042	1,016,526,347	1,072,509,609	1,123,397,101	1,218,014,360
12	735,945,326	796,147,010	847,298,813	954,952,698	1,014,423,256	1,070,336,552	1,121,953,237	1,215,983,852
13	738,626,297	799,362,198	851,624,563	958,509,854	1,018,249,700	1,074,488,927	1,125,552,575	1,221,234,910
14	526,096,486	675,418,499	714,486,457	847,019,719	895,734,064	944,862,493	1,002,136,655	1,094,426,349
15	1,315,943,120	1,465,745,574	1,563,694,742	1,386,846,053	1,472,239,642	1,580,863,783	2,186,551,200	1,867,606,825
16	1,309,401,212	1,427,318,392	1,516,691,853	1,336,862,220	1,417,270,034	1,523,565,060	2,128,492,010	1,741,267,074
17	1,328,247,468	1,316,322,857	1,400,066,180	1,297,673,166	1,376,942,986	1,460,087,168	1,937,723,719	1,668,265,521
18	808,804,102	876,235,171	937,473,992	1,086,483,796	1,163,187,982	1,159,115,125	1,224,729,635	1,342,674,136
19	757,732,120	822,761,401	890,905,135	1,018,012,625	1,085,012,062	1,095,153,328	1,169,170,295	1,266,882,728
20	745,006,951	791,033,794	820,048,245	878,907,488	921,943,928	974,568,418	1,075,618,003	1,119,186,100
21	418,416,812	673,642,726	714,630,884	757,707,938	798,624,802	842,751,447	918,872,425	972,543,235
22	411,241,386	637,552,743	689,434,793	763,495,055	813,196,448	848,946,565	929,194,459	988,126,920
23	1,868,199,310	2,767,079,860	2,867,633,568	2,915,156,762	2,897,530,718	2,972,874,134	3,145,323,115	3,990,981,915
24	-122,981,722	694,273,996	760,610,117	784,182,356	827,325,938	874,383,154	944,305,456	1,010,134,056
25	605,536,102	785,531,088	845,189,039	833,890,117	884,133,928	928,671,435	1,011,392,426	1,068,875,869
26	656,855,345	776,737,657	830,546,441	825,309,790	858,810,541	904,314,171	991,529,847	1,043,315,304
27	608,569,115	697,658,977	745,915,752	743,509,265	782,803,485	826,921,910	912,667,071	952,537,928
28	923,800,601	748,868,157	795,065,934	825,669,944	857,009,390	904,997,775	988,676,351	1,050,105,806
29	734,279,529	716,560,628	768,517,057	766,329,867	804,424,720	847,601,870	938,501,827	979,059,668
30	782,928,418	706,947,040	753,506,221	764,101,894	809,738,358	852,335,650	951,086,505	983,965,859
31	914,442,986	771,483,340	823,242,164	807,400,931	849,266,652	895,038,653	991,611,202	1,029,999,853
32	686,141,525	774,729,001	823,984,917	827,321,740	868,532,731	919,651,671	1,025,758,320	1,072,727,949
33	814,827,916	826,314,644	875,352,428	859,196,426	904,530,942	947,807,785	1,056,215,840	1,090,071,477
34	559,453,528	821,561,412	874,125,195	863,888,983	904,978,239	952,376,760	1,049,944,040	1,093,971,413
TOTAL	25,341,001,805	29,167,330,052	31,026,993,851	32,445,061,483	34,077,517,234	35,771,455,190	39,914,106,373	41,772,369,713
NORTH CAROLINA								
1	581,060,216	635,372,558	683,111,890	733,781,198	772,353,262	836,291,809	912,165,257	1,002,232,065
2	591,968,734	660,749,748	708,828,854	751,654,860	793,181,355	849,246,267	924,043,858	1,013,186,648
3	498,791,071	538,250,685	578,036,464	634,906,921	667,959,661	719,196,783	786,430,508	868,712,240
4	1,000,789,921	1,008,650,745	1,057,587,919	1,120,441,928	1,134,303,239	1,201,518,549	1,297,624,220	1,681,372,098
5	582,087,967	623,534,520	674,153,689	713,167,734	748,645,822	806,212,524	869,307,562	961,819,890
6	567,680,710	600,727,756	648,583,892	688,713,811	730,489,525	783,962,814	844,636,284	928,579,180
7	501,516,114	539,563,781	576,410,046	637,569,838	673,309,744	726,295,964	790,360,044	873,863,468
8	593,548,917	651,330,936	704,536,917	736,312,734	775,298,067	828,661,017	893,073,658	972,284,391
9	519,655,345	557,733,586	602,627,083	645,915,339	681,311,229	729,358,909	790,311,964	868,978,288
10	545,343,293	576,431,000	623,023,375	660,096,365	700,118,942	750,916,424	810,069,846	887,213,069
11	720,354,850	770,952,013	834,291,163	866,195,774	915,803,928	980,428,756	1,062,036,838	1,161,573,207
TOTAL	6,702,797,137	7,163,297,329	7,691,191,291	8,188,756,502	8,592,774,774	9,212,089,817	9,980,060,039	11,219,814,544

Appendix A lists the congressional districts which represent the county in which the state capital is located, and those congressional districts which represent only portions of a county. Appendix C lists the programs included in each functional policy category.

table continues

Table 5.11 **Outlays for Income Security and Social Service Programs by Congressional District, 1983-1990 *(continued)***

Congressional District	1983	1984	1985	1986	1987	1988	1989	1990 (est.)
NORTH DAKOTA								
TOTAL	804,184,274	883,611,631	951,492,054	996,066,834	1,061,024,147	1,125,216,573	1,201,443,976	1,318,476,707
OHIO								
1	675,329,275	730,267,187	768,513,340	835,625,677	914,569,914	968,379,087	1,033,610,126	1,142,245,233
2	586,319,168	639,645,235	679,187,479	746,763,150	733,976,314	778,660,618	831,211,121	914,834,345
3	613,521,570	653,754,978	681,601,045	731,170,257	773,792,388	821,372,449	879,205,321	976,875,489
4	572,198,717	683,467,014	725,486,042	739,779,446	771,133,727	815,503,759	869,860,899	951,912,215
5	459,418,851	576,510,166	614,333,730	644,403,113	677,081,731	719,284,019	767,804,264	841,604,010
6	585,353,386	668,469,040	723,691,916	770,589,392	804,771,246	859,177,899	924,295,370	1,028,786,364
7	497,327,033	580,335,658	614,094,453	653,530,098	681,341,679	719,786,291	767,059,301	845,543,410
8	487,383,314	563,717,973	597,983,219	637,910,981	664,696,407	704,315,343	755,368,725	832,921,025
9	479,736,385	702,164,766	741,952,253	809,880,000	855,296,737	902,803,832	961,289,211	1,061,712,218
10	643,276,431	741,989,971	780,826,709	817,893,307	842,332,805	882,032,607	944,090,321	1,109,670,305
11	421,407,443	510,614,608	546,161,760	611,478,071	644,123,777	685,939,987	734,685,188	807,022,377
12	884,134,499	1,126,503,128	1,234,846,531	1,282,635,679	1,328,020,038	1,374,327,945	1,455,605,592	1,780,111,795
13	426,608,718	548,054,541	583,874,231	646,681,558	681,357,139	722,535,475	773,236,308	843,464,785
14	654,388,526	693,430,754	735,146,174	777,951,064	813,565,395	860,424,694	923,074,868	1,014,496,193
15	1,151,589,512	1,088,109,623	1,067,020,624	1,129,803,810	1,163,033,975	1,233,372,563	1,328,513,793	1,534,481,946
16	595,428,849	652,295,502	697,849,414	728,322,408	764,691,788	811,633,649	868,052,620	952,210,976
17	768,525,583	728,076,745	770,830,405	858,634,712	901,820,159	954,820,937	1,020,693,569	1,118,910,876
18	694,164,590	758,121,352	803,852,322	834,107,366	866,948,981	914,612,494	972,836,400	1,065,275,866
19	812,265,369	762,067,617	812,024,674	894,133,447	937,065,428	989,942,123	1,055,013,427	1,154,878,914
20	732,329,037	786,962,974	842,477,726	923,633,142	967,233,561	1,021,139,921	1,086,825,299	1,202,154,829
21	749,939,044	807,594,605	840,748,709	921,454,552	964,988,295	1,019,071,770	1,085,248,866	1,190,482,253
TOTAL	13,490,645,300	15,002,153,434	15,862,502,755	16,996,381,231	17,751,841,484	18,759,137,461	20,037,580,588	22,369,595,424
OKLAHOMA								
1	543,731,694	555,638,553	611,891,068	677,377,739	732,332,104	784,811,137	845,940,941	919,961,364
2	652,896,333	731,288,352	785,369,215	820,008,356	853,676,242	907,374,089	974,557,559	1,068,167,522
3	740,917,810	791,962,128	854,104,597	866,165,803	888,929,526	954,888,558	1,019,482,290	1,117,182,420
4	535,986,908	551,725,538	594,332,771	627,573,441	675,224,850	721,704,918	769,608,557	847,209,904
5	624,794,052	757,111,352	811,067,132	847,893,394	902,445,601	953,701,683	1,009,957,585	1,128,056,238
6	706,282,196	675,356,666	731,278,703	756,083,013	804,372,632	846,978,939	903,427,257	1,025,824,456
TOTAL	3,804,608,994	4,063,082,589	4,388,043,485	4,595,101,747	4,856,980,954	5,169,459,324	5,522,974,189	6,106,401,905
OREGON								
1	612,891,995	616,335,066	663,264,890	708,322,847	735,867,694	788,573,226	867,935,935	930,797,272
2	757,942,394	723,739,363	781,711,013	825,203,410	856,566,891	922,454,723	1,001,839,544	1,097,508,696
3	756,344,787	810,723,250	875,617,808	909,111,824	951,960,995	1,016,374,859	1,095,138,493	1,207,108,290
4	717,709,037	648,581,187	703,666,935	759,340,445	799,382,542	861,664,834	933,318,609	1,021,771,239
5	633,618,054	908,485,406	958,165,811	996,070,879	1,019,470,585	1,094,517,031	1,185,314,788	1,373,148,378
TOTAL	3,478,506,267	3,707,864,272	3,982,426,457	4,198,049,405	4,363,248,707	4,683,584,672	5,083,547,368	5,630,333,875
PENNSYLVANIA								
1	924,812,518	956,686,145	1,019,673,083	1,118,439,437	1,177,235,166	1,223,746,633	1,306,318,095	1,406,511,984
2	917,286,838	948,824,010	1,022,233,196	1,122,375,055	1,180,185,759	1,232,125,954	1,315,223,774	1,405,176,005
3	915,332,848	944,263,040	1,018,099,868	1,119,327,525	1,176,267,689	1,217,783,402	1,300,136,011	1,401,906,163
4	435,679,679	762,963,576	815,220,683	861,895,457	902,907,208	948,565,073	1,016,307,837	1,097,763,299
5	594,392,555	634,096,245	670,806,209	729,824,489	764,837,567	810,394,183	869,471,069	948,170,557
6	777,033,479	861,956,399	928,219,397	928,824,575	967,446,950	1,009,477,269	1,074,710,708	1,158,342,044
7	696,094,349	735,721,952	811,798,986	881,826,726	924,271,160	971,341,307	1,034,774,075	1,120,253,654
8	480,859,846	511,011,498	556,985,743	641,116,396	676,129,971	719,388,686	775,463,216	846,644,578
9	627,837,747	756,186,197	813,841,148	809,016,807	841,365,456	883,650,605	945,092,909	1,018,972,597
10	817,002,630	872,161,327	939,367,626	977,019,723	1,017,760,496	1,069,213,023	1,142,986,647	1,234,244,825
11	923,416,238	965,288,372	1,029,049,779	1,075,339,423	1,116,332,175	1,163,545,392	1,233,371,727	1,325,548,628
12	708,985,553	832,446,009	886,355,359	935,429,845	974,837,508	1,020,200,515	1,089,600,782	1,172,071,986
13	686,603,807	719,810,317	781,204,049	857,771,696	897,132,001	946,988,688	1,015,534,921	1,102,662,256
14	932,148,570	986,612,650	918,538,177	980,754,268	1,023,719,625	1,074,673,394	1,146,063,665	1,228,760,716
15	702,734,925	759,307,228	822,343,551	851,827,648	899,060,180	948,340,363	1,017,435,885	1,100,126,715
16	573,166,028	627,369,289	680,092,679	686,041,373	722,629,852	767,907,287	826,754,258	896,438,579
17	1,689,952,156	1,893,929,832	1,995,216,414	1,957,760,580	1,992,962,013	1,977,179,460	2,125,879,701	2,677,774,882
18	700,711,630	754,903,005	905,091,827	968,464,492	1,007,655,943	1,055,060,138	1,126,462,378	1,216,126,798
19	582,732,134	629,290,642	683,071,597	677,228,088	711,545,363	754,795,844	809,840,569	873,756,578
20	640,876,071	780,772,414	883,366,936	947,320,396	987,729,470	1,034,681,548	1,105,745,118	1,193,880,276
21	710,255,118	745,827,212	810,613,527	838,322,266	880,824,860	924,735,974	990,790,421	1,069,089,961
22	783,958,819	883,637,649	960,337,782	1,000,044,012	1,037,584,782	1,084,862,124	1,160,437,525	1,247,612,997
23	676,164,704	738,657,144	794,514,790	804,078,077	832,253,505	875,527,292	937,373,576	1,009,914,183
TOTAL	17,498,038,242	19,301,722,153	20,746,042,405	21,770,048,357	22,712,674,700	23,714,184,153	25,365,774,866	27,751,750,262

Appendix A lists the congressional districts which represent the county in which the state capital is located, and those congressional districts which represent only portions of a county. Appendix C lists the programs included in each functional policy category.

table continues

Table 5.11 Outlays for Income Security and Social Service Programs by Congressional District, 1983-1990 *(continued)*

Congressional District	1983	1984	1985	1986	1987	1988	1989	1990 (est.)
RHODE ISLAND								
1	767,755,182	803,603,253	827,844,727	865,476,270	892,531,837	941,726,203	1,017,357,624	1,094,821,055
2	713,730,156	759,791,196	805,354,174	844,532,192	873,865,155	923,089,266	994,203,760	1,092,042,621
TOTAL	1,481,485,338	1,563,394,449	1,633,198,901	1,710,008,462	1,766,396,992	1,864,815,469	2,011,561,384	2,186,863,676
SOUTH CAROLINA								
1	446,652,931	469,598,415	516,855,798	577,977,054	609,393,284	658,877,257	713,923,656	803,396,316
2	859,922,788	847,353,891	887,659,763	918,052,524	933,481,237	980,747,010	1,041,558,679	1,913,044,978
3	560,345,522	599,118,617	657,598,518	684,818,771	724,550,907	780,406,625	841,575,110	944,186,117
4	550,173,317	604,146,403	657,699,207	689,564,963	723,562,920	770,249,897	827,279,056	912,995,841
5	556,449,052	599,344,849	655,652,440	675,741,006	700,205,423	751,598,102	806,836,031	905,392,010
6	515,748,809	561,311,388	617,439,485	684,903,489	721,908,344	780,886,033	846,570,537	962,175,706
TOTAL	3,489,292,419	3,680,873,563	3,992,905,211	4,231,057,807	4,413,102,115	4,722,764,924	5,077,743,069	6,441,190,967
SOUTH DAKOTA								
TOTAL	670,403,789	950,122,531	1,004,584,944	1,057,042,244	1,094,141,233	1,157,228,247	1,231,721,489	1,374,247,803
TENNESSEE								
1	593,895,258	627,783,648	680,041,398	728,992,384	772,718,539	831,063,235	896,292,154	1,125,026,535
2	624,825,069	646,407,029	695,254,607	739,100,394	777,615,364	835,555,816	896,733,865	1,100,360,435
3	589,817,610	636,551,023	690,161,978	746,719,870	785,611,391	841,468,662	903,119,832	1,108,800,496
4	614,019,429	668,353,919	719,111,154	768,724,395	809,012,882	872,793,409	943,875,372	1,205,847,249
5	1,076,559,603	1,077,036,608	1,130,311,649	1,185,298,368	1,217,281,511	1,280,211,581	1,381,870,385	1,840,905,450
6	494,106,012	548,913,382	597,458,423	646,956,655	685,776,016	739,954,426	799,463,944	996,041,273
7	532,558,572	576,763,372	629,743,238	663,697,882	701,221,735	756,057,325	818,866,837	1,057,639,195
8	512,269,406	702,669,212	759,018,489	768,293,990	808,846,742	867,458,442	931,699,589	1,189,584,073
9	523,206,888	570,694,463	618,770,518	668,504,695	711,860,842	763,615,753	834,190,061	1,065,823,243
TOTAL	5,561,257,847	6,055,172,656	6,519,871,454	6,916,288,633	7,269,945,022	7,788,178,649	8,406,112,039	10,690,027,950
TEXAS								
1	795,458,503	830,331,496	908,714,565	879,199,270	929,804,929	982,991,978	1,053,543,055	1,166,819,771
2	694,399,270	703,946,696	767,853,719	830,538,531	879,482,419	939,592,402	1,010,491,727	1,115,114,582
3	418,565,905	445,434,310	486,598,907	540,162,043	588,268,627	630,176,675	682,057,322	751,924,621
4	686,483,403	771,591,822	846,548,456	857,426,123	916,627,039	980,599,150	1,056,391,250	1,160,026,055
5	442,141,262	453,547,035	498,370,926	551,147,812	600,208,775	642,619,338	695,380,628	770,912,478
6	557,136,336	677,753,861	743,075,443	764,097,399	804,581,403	864,803,782	938,278,103	1,036,626,427
7	334,813,397	357,633,817	398,710,720	481,019,278	525,941,939	567,516,096	614,028,775	681,811,273
8	340,526,315	368,721,505	398,648,642	479,869,093	525,051,458	566,309,342	612,581,048	678,304,068
9	537,049,699	573,621,601	625,975,270	703,165,557	751,900,535	803,799,970	864,138,520	951,885,572
10	1,713,459,520	1,759,411,512	1,858,800,547	2,003,733,429	2,136,077,653	2,434,585,303	2,566,708,520	3,351,043,622
11	659,831,305	678,915,262	741,974,984	687,923,197	745,316,865	793,437,703	951,453,107	927,902,811
12	470,053,098	500,744,518	550,739,402	585,881,075	626,715,486	671,939,291	725,639,425	800,766,882
13	599,598,022	663,085,300	728,524,299	720,652,666	769,674,370	814,322,746	868,011,426	946,855,060
14	670,207,307	680,350,150	748,609,322	739,744,664	785,540,984	849,425,730	912,737,367	1,011,985,868
15	523,326,787	533,261,405	593,857,247	639,251,873	696,010,716	752,109,108	813,469,352	933,689,130
16	399,083,641	439,070,756	481,770,028	544,721,535	603,952,702	650,694,443	703,871,137	775,463,349
17	725,391,282	793,987,491	869,663,576	814,872,055	854,517,268	904,401,311	964,838,540	1,052,660,779
18	339,182,712	366,171,124	407,740,237	489,329,448	535,730,875	578,936,943	626,457,042	688,326,697
19	433,978,614	463,671,971	509,657,324	558,098,096	610,705,843	651,761,007	702,337,259	774,890,115
20	478,840,448	515,143,910	564,252,681	615,159,510	672,094,058	725,286,140	783,176,944	876,035,973
21	587,307,180	632,395,925	673,255,614	686,555,280	736,503,754	789,975,301	852,212,686	938,416,385
22	309,385,623	333,660,877	366,698,649	441,409,072	484,889,049	525,459,200	568,008,950	629,529,950
23	537,943,647	539,665,763	619,415,938	675,894,788	736,856,818	796,984,206	859,473,938	972,282,531
24	426,363,125	464,586,217	496,016,113	548,041,146	596,006,103	639,069,997	690,423,561	760,807,983
25	331,362,057	358,282,934	397,940,774	479,290,804	524,332,570	565,524,224	611,454,766	676,536,811
26	383,645,851	442,638,643	486,732,385	526,571,669	567,264,294	610,207,899	658,490,084	725,339,224
27	295,172,408	496,659,959	545,775,127	600,649,881	655,435,088	712,714,222	767,446,979	865,083,505
TOTAL	14,690,706,717	15,844,285,859	17,315,920,896	18,444,405,296	19,859,491,621	21,445,243,509	23,153,101,512	26,021,041,520
UTAH								
1	443,970,405	419,281,335	452,822,122	483,535,552	519,202,341	554,519,934	588,189,313	651,449,523
2	602,750,515	575,503,466	600,291,995	628,393,065	679,500,021	725,136,607	775,491,640	903,601,809
3	155,099,457	397,236,736	450,429,822	472,385,794	511,905,394	545,212,479	578,131,888	642,674,889
TOTAL	1,201,820,377	1,392,021,537	1,503,543,939	1,584,314,411	1,710,607,756	1,824,869,020	1,941,812,841	2,197,726,221
VERMONT								
TOTAL	692,296,157	745,275,644	789,692,453	818,925,522	839,111,526	892,128,283	943,438,417	1,067,657,286

Appendix A lists the congressional districts which represent the county in which the state capital is located, and those congressional districts which represent only portions of a county. Appendix C lists the programs included in each functional policy category.

table continues

Table 5.11 Outlays for Income Security and Social Service Programs by Congressional District, 1983-1990 *(continued)*

Congressional District	1983	1984	1985	1986	1987	1988	1989	1990 (est.)
VIRGINIA								
1	545,467,536	612,604,527	663,131,304	669,025,282	715,812,833	767,774,681	825,397,105	959,728,208
2	373,894,785	443,516,748	474,913,478	518,688,898	556,215,300	595,045,748	638,107,223	751,140,729
3	1,036,653,806	1,094,828,983	1,136,211,316	1,170,205,594	1,201,967,971	1,270,997,468	1,348,668,272	1,758,910,863
4	551,347,986	628,838,815	680,808,774	728,806,717	750,127,651	801,543,012	858,910,994	1,033,727,970
5	624,899,143	687,770,021	747,940,413	742,920,760	777,711,567	826,319,500	893,972,424	1,066,059,855
6	650,715,284	731,396,912	794,688,629	808,747,630	841,462,420	893,439,467	953,325,654	1,101,954,195
7	540,550,004	548,989,688	598,518,216	649,094,359	666,925,990	713,002,987	767,077,607	893,909,770
8	272,731,731	301,494,065	320,974,030	367,201,141	396,204,452	422,347,054	452,999,197	517,706,247
9	706,615,650	755,458,275	809,862,652	835,372,139	862,967,838	922,144,916	987,568,675	1,174,534,705
10	426,753,896	447,014,091	477,864,969	526,632,186	556,091,826	591,532,589	635,807,149	626,951,923
TOTAL	5,729,629,820	6,251,912,125	6,704,913,782	7,016,694,706	7,325,487,849	7,804,147,422	8,361,834,300	9,884,624,465
WASHINGTON								
1	532,212,184	574,849,366	628,637,521	677,787,601	731,048,121	789,083,501	853,930,046	1,054,615,831
2	511,490,419	644,955,426	733,148,541	796,343,968	847,689,982	919,940,861	991,512,885	1,208,397,257
3	977,493,675	963,448,608	1,037,457,175	1,095,795,320	1,160,959,652	1,253,879,203	1,344,550,897	1,757,737,405
4	543,606,146	618,239,500	681,545,685	713,527,494	756,309,914	811,954,763	866,139,063	1,104,723,361
5	640,065,993	695,896,874	758,951,859	769,847,171	811,001,199	860,959,789	920,494,214	1,146,208,671
6	565,346,935	592,314,840	630,974,485	662,963,479	714,552,753	771,513,503	829,368,678	1,059,558,117
7	568,326,757	611,772,204	676,650,303	718,995,736	772,392,598	829,409,898	900,995,944	1,117,304,773
8	565,650,213	610,822,132	675,049,093	716,540,934	769,035,138	826,640,345	889,535,574	1,098,106,358
TOTAL	4,904,192,321	5,312,298,951	5,822,414,661	6,151,801,704	6,562,989,358	7,063,381,865	7,596,527,300	9,546,651,773
WEST VIRGINIA								
1	639,806,268	703,709,848	759,575,860	797,404,204	831,187,309	871,898,438	929,286,251	996,691,934
2	639,010,759	679,307,595	728,225,138	783,485,411	807,306,391	845,303,006	901,077,714	968,039,041
3	792,296,994	921,390,468	984,304,758	1,092,748,553	1,092,504,204	1,136,340,006	1,209,869,814	1,372,587,596
4	722,607,423	782,926,334	835,044,563	877,409,029	918,287,916	961,017,056	1,018,795,924	1,088,594,673
TOTAL	2,793,721,444	3,087,334,245	3,307,150,319	3,551,047,197	3,649,285,820	3,814,558,506	4,059,029,703	4,425,913,244
WISCONSIN								
1	510,091,184	695,033,465	742,056,597	789,845,405	828,476,548	867,626,314	920,355,988	1,163,583,184
2	771,306,220	1,019,386,333	1,074,483,764	1,080,527,054	1,114,606,298	1,152,423,290	1,201,595,085	1,646,429,833
3	544,450,001	751,877,543	802,921,522	798,802,924	834,060,842	874,412,102	926,392,049	1,184,555,730
4	553,049,309	754,853,279	807,059,793	901,257,970	943,727,948	987,748,631	1,043,353,809	1,368,503,023
5	617,578,407	832,104,510	886,711,569	988,280,252	1,033,293,426	1,077,797,147	1,135,424,342	1,509,226,000
6	556,488,624	755,214,231	812,574,352	821,099,387	856,205,949	899,469,152	957,198,552	1,173,079,905
7	544,940,825	798,371,823	853,430,333	866,507,651	902,860,597	945,005,046	1,003,025,440	1,265,505,517
8	498,786,093	732,908,712	781,103,337	803,435,921	837,432,342	881,345,347	936,786,110	1,163,250,229
9	370,555,675	575,955,459	613,767,795	665,795,598	698,068,216	740,208,181	792,226,358	949,165,852
TOTAL	4,967,246,338	6,915,705,353	7,374,109,061	7,715,552,162	8,048,732,166	8,426,035,210	8,916,357,732	11,423,299,272
WYOMING								
TOTAL	309,286,857	465,541,402	500,503,190	529,504,398	561,965,279	598,979,689	649,985,954	723,457,134
U.S. TOTAL	287,045.5 mil.	314,484.7 mil.	338,984.6 mil.	356,874.7 mil.	375,077.0 mil.	399,254.4 mil.	428,442.0 mil.	482,781.3 mil.

Appendix A lists the congressional districts which represent the county in which the state capital is located, and those congressional districts which represent only portions of a county. Appendix C lists the programs included in each functional policy category.

Table 5.12 Outlays for Transportation Programs by Congressional District, 1983-1990

Congressional District	1983	1984	1985	1986	1987	1988	1989	1990 (est.)
ALABAMA								
1	1,039,167	9,895,488	3,199,933	6,713,778	4,594,777	4,898,191	2,980,344	6,044,741
2	270,850,655	240,386,206	318,218,576	270,861,692	316,741,661	557,732,480	237,154,929	380,847,756
3	-94	734,650	2,911,401	281,778	256,073	883,684	579,865	575,377
4	0	-10,239	1,267,129	630,249	1,005,825	531,043	676,797	1,535,566
5	348,210	4,434,740	3,119,161	3,318,927	2,040,482	1,986,992	1,969,431	3,315,118
6	2,349,220	6,658,674	5,980,651	16,002,069	6,716,905	7,239,990	4,935,298	8,272,050
7	231,176	2,204,045	388,440	382,089	221,859	962,813	1,158,920	898,814
TOTAL	274,818,334	264,303,564	335,085,291	298,190,582	331,577,582	574,235,193	249,455,584	401,489,421
ALASKA								
TOTAL	162,884,562	234,286,922	203,466,651	207,989,151	193,670,097	266,804,459	208,878,497	264,187,530
ARIZONA								
1	9,978,236	18,501,992	5,607,370	31,595,770	25,985,890	34,934,168	26,276,330	50,471,538
2	3,532,173	15,947,294	11,166,007	12,355,021	5,181,932	11,003,193	10,695,430	24,229,676
3	455,433	9,930,723	5,001,371	1,843,849	2,075,112	5,926,284	8,980,793	4,687,660
4	215,787,410	272,900,905	189,109,102	318,337,670	209,769,935	201,245,041	125,470,065	245,476,916
5	0	6,976,091	838,901	978,166	423,242	892,428	1,232,829	1,816,323
TOTAL	229,753,253	324,257,007	211,722,751	365,110,476	243,436,111	254,001,114	172,655,447	326,682,113
ARKANSAS								
1	78,602	1,582,731	2,262,698	1,222,663	821,781	2,635,170	1,278,531	2,138,416
2	137,354,416	141,203,195	152,059,952	136,013,688	149,947,737	192,612,675	160,678,418	225,860,277
3	230,333	4,846,826	2,307,616	2,759,899	1,830,338	3,017,371	2,606,965	1,552,128
4	417,255	3,000,704	254,500	3,675,361	1,286,436	1,137,472	1,807,272	1,410,951
TOTAL	138,080,606	150,633,456	156,884,766	143,671,611	153,886,292	199,402,688	166,371,186	230,961,771
CALIFORNIA								
1	757,338	4,099,589	5,264,829	6,640,526	1,887,970	1,143,632	30,287,718	18,817,857
2	720,981	5,701,247	2,533,946	6,684,361	4,074,464	4,243,255	2,829,252	2,400,824
3	1,045,838,280	1,136,080,385	1,196,636,947	1,312,527,934	1,408,309,438	1,606,396,949	1,041,655,123	2,061,815,440
4	193,845	9,250,661	8,094,133	14,400,243	8,013,261	16,259,024	3,469,160	61,562,810
5	106,154,145	11,398,758	33,102,291	31,144,094	67,247,944	45,465,709	36,014,627	52,235,943
6	5,834,234	15,028,540	10,377,314	2,257,908	2,414,708	12,947,918	16,448	395,648
7	0	3,251,707	4,467,179	7,496,284	6,086,972	6,277,955	21,535,570	21,278,744
8	6,433,964	159,982,612	54,359,685	80,473,766	43,662,011	34,530,141	839,286	1,834,895
9	3,672	1,623,524	4,412,338	2,162,582	3,303,417	6,471,653	5,773,089	26,248,133
10	26,683,790	19,785,244	86,423,774	84,989,531	42,239,723	25,735,150	4,490,062	20,160,787
11	28,710,616	2,825,361	15,136,030	4,133,026	3,659,012	16,492,163	124,826	18,317,617
12	0	31,014,420	283,671	542,553	11,632	198,963	-63,061	8,840
13	7,306,349	15,011,118	64,819	538,807	1,388,279	2,365,197	-33,904	67,585
14	3,004,364	6,710,009	8,674,458	8,141,765	6,671,897	2,033,024	3,412,489	2,238,616
15	2,858,928	4,410,407	5,453,405	7,367,283	5,005,611	5,238,397	4,182,122	3,182,564
16	1,840,635	3,892,491	9,257,457	5,891,897	6,607,066	5,865,038	7,189,265	7,183,395
17	1,776,980	6,852,687	3,349,698	2,477,593	3,727,765	1,585,757	3,683,660	3,874,619
18	2,852,726	5,938,028	1,577,500	1,140,357	356,072	1,148,506	830,955	384,247
19	6,980,312	11,938,794	5,631,218	4,033,027	3,066,270	7,761,036	5,430,757	5,774,063
20	160,997,314	233,572,606	90,813,714	296,453,229	220,488,773	177,808,299	6,538,737	6,108,468
21	884,159	89,280	-5,425	2,158,569	1,533,168	899,561	91,193,164	106,644,455
22	1,448,114	225,810	46,511	164,016	520,818	1,027,157	351,775	159,279
23	1,362,665	113,034	-100,582	-155,766	44,022	502,255	2,505,822	60,063
24	1,449,003	2,659,519	5,352,419	2,687,892	-83,295	9,219,361	10,645,270	13,322,334
25	1,361,122	4,701,906	-100,468	73,911	398,037	848,186	143,159	198,372
26	1,196,169	99,223	-84,324	-136,734	38,643	440,887	160,810	52,725
27	4,889,020	37,211,404	26,807,921	16,333,321	23,609,583	35,462,814	27,195,986	43,953,574
28	2,055,215	1,784,723	307,480	226,530	43,995	501,945	783,233	686,069
29	1,362,116	112,989	-100,541	-155,703	44,004	504,662	143,264	60,039
30	2,083,419	1,264,193	640,633	1,413,567	43,928	1,769,679	369,281	2,344,449
31	1,362,981	1,102,060	1,613,039	1,971,425	817,786	1,116,216	609,824	2,228,433
32	3,671,347	637,423	-348,427	-156,301	44,173	503,981	1,143,814	60,270
33	1,423,614	2,849,615	433,363	122,099	44,046	687,042	124,838	97,737
34	2,409,319	3,655,502	1,647,617	1,242,276	300,122	535,649	21,219,571	27,166,697
35	8,743	9,250,232	6,126,870	8,704,896	5,644,767	6,060,319	8,655,606	7,514,404
36	67,736	5,618,792	5,644,655	12,235,192	5,823,611	9,299,699	6,126,525	22,362,563
37	1,632,431	9,504,926	4,176,074	4,096,779	2,932,455	4,227,099	2,643,052	20,274,341
38	0	18,813,796	11,577	16,617,969	26,191,312	17,579,144	2,980	0
39	0	417,548	1,869,686	1,250,280	665,910	107,661	1,502,982	2,253,562

Appendix A lists the congressional districts which represent the county in which the state capital is located, and those congressional districts which represent only portions of a county. Appendix C lists the programs included in each functional policy category.

table continues

Table 5.12 Outlays for Transportation Programs by Congressional District, 1983-1990 *(continued)*

Congressional District	1983	1984	1985	1986	1987	1988	1989	1990 (est.)
CALIFORNIA *continued*								
40	1,418,415	3,005,118	396,917	1,934,182	4,594,992	10,663,396	7,216,858	7,919,141
41	6,900,489	27,650,540	8,751,570	50,196,629	20,105,799	3,889,750	15,561,208	21,170,776
42	1,262,686	8,628,854	4,135,259	3,820,962	10,110,843	5,779,767	6,340,505	6,248,655
43	2,468,000	5,562,046	293,673	5,879,824	3,864,109	3,174,751	4,862,442	7,158,705
44	0	27,742	53,895	1,042	-22,362	111,986	-29,692	2,316,283
45	0	2,442,720	801,487	710,150	1,092,904	435,237	704,234	949,500
TOTAL	1,449,665,238	1,835,797,183	1,614,285,283	2,010,733,771	1,946,625,654	2,095,315,968	1,388,382,693	2,609,093,521
COLORADO								
1	276,269,035	288,058,611	275,144,219	254,439,342	273,310,859	231,000,560	364,386,242	379,821,307
2	3,883,344	975	0	290,646	162,377	1,038,742	848,945	439,841
3	761,376	8,830,717	5,794,848	7,410,827	9,968,248	9,410,251	11,773,081	12,860,250
4	1,765,130	3,706,753	1,686,793	2,403,629	3,442,668	4,557,601	7,317,693	9,976,000
5	1,319,866	4,037,189	2,983,791	4,737,270	5,317,092	9,425,561	3,578,673	22,006,934
6	453	6,151,377	758,553	1,752,042	3,002,219	76,490	264	878,969
TOTAL	283,999,204	310,785,622	286,368,204	271,033,756	295,203,463	255,509,205	387,904,898	425,983,301
CONNECTICUT								
1	284,829,114	299,888,539	294,209,877	283,825,836	505,794,622	490,942,643	309,174,918	545,691,812
2	450,070	88,050	675,997	3,810,974	498,636	375,609	340,678	1,560,464
3	22,769	1,409,300	946,718	6,465,201	3,259,576	162,381	1,917,204	2,719,264
4	22,896,656	1,562,997	19,248,821	9,518,746	21,056,741	659,723	819,779	17,738,552
5	0	1,076,209	970,793	3,161,454	1,018,162	2,788,498	921,851	1,531,710
6	29,000	246,738	73,610	1,224,516	39,258	79,806	411,920	108,115
TOTAL	308,227,609	304,271,833	316,125,816	308,006,727	531,666,995	495,008,660	313,586,350	569,349,916
DELAWARE								
TOTAL	58,205,212	55,238,487	60,446,758	57,070,965	75,203,429	55,192,439	68,888,414	76,276,734
DISTRICT OF COLUMBIA								
TOTAL	365,113,223	235,802,333	72,354,235	166,568,115	43,607,449	167,505,073	193,934,178	315,308,434
FLORIDA								
1	15,934	5,059,558	1,392,923	3,951,372	2,751,548	4,381,940	5,141,217	5,763,762
2	354,216,247	358,156,465	397,229,218	560,179,696	438,442,239	451,094,924	460,412,916	504,442,255
3	2,407,246	9,142,337	25,458,820	5,646,230	9,645,684	7,737,329	14,460,189	8,309,130
4	916,663	1,973,885	3,148,037	3,546,184	1,793,674	2,139,047	2,908,457	4,736,217
5	5,479,052	5,748,862	6,551,493	17,685,587	17,656,196	593,122	15,704,593	7,581,723
6	1,477,172	4,032,555	1,739,806	2,743,409	2,847,167	4,273,806	1,821,978	2,345,019
7	586,070	12,923,215	9,296,843	25,503,464	9,040,329	15,252,624	15,807,017	14,835,284
8	2,392,874	6,172,347	8,799,533	10,932,848	13,844,742	5,639,904	5,022,393	8,491,813
9	150,214	6,648,939	6,127,435	1,915,284	34,305	5,483,571	12,921,597	16,071,744
10	3,241,515	4,174,290	5,740,491	3,467,513	2,596,337	2,540,890	3,816,172	4,565,322
11	1,159,101	5,991,230	5,613,249	6,719,534	8,756,525	11,301,606	11,836,867	13,758,670
12	-8,847	1,444,032	3,971,159	7,792,127	9,522,566	4,648,807	7,613,942	2,644,383
13	54,547,482	29,229,458	740,525	4,525,386	2,868,314	8,390,805	8,362,810	7,596,975
14	0	788,000	1,531,608	-35,057	0	0	660,800	1,966,933
15	8,480,265	36,005,807	26,945,225	21,767,753	14,927,545	31,779,749	23,831,118	18,052,211
16	0	0	0	0	0	0	0	0
17	0	532,000	25,846,486	41,130,459	29,999,462	15,856,096	211,880	0
18	0	0	0	0	0	0	992,000	32,922,946
19	-107,332	103,211	0	4,683	172,468	1,666,065	115,988,900	57,387,860
TOTAL	434,953,656	488,126,191	530,132,851	717,476,472	564,899,101	572,780,285	707,514,846	711,472,247
GEORGIA								
1	2,012,648	2,539,536	4,612,966	2,041,913	3,342,572	1,978,781	7,560,880	8,629,086
2	497,811	1,411,094	-79,404	561,037	1,399,745	989,516	1,256,690	1,501,474
3	1,002,518	789,393	3,103,320	2,968,812	3,092,608	2,943,330	1,812,809	5,937,230
4	54,235,233	96,017,411	141,431,909	103,410,415	83,117,405	175,100,643	91,100,578	32,712,188
5	361,096,152	341,308,944	181,155,473	367,348,628	550,163,218	689,025,167	324,411,488	573,736,906
6	557,395	26,006,806	406,018	328,419	1,027,087	4,018,630	2,514,742	4,932,695
7	697,121	645,458	-122,286	144,173	1,885,872	5,207,371	4,745,971	13,218
8	-14,189	1,297,154	-16,458	115,364	759,735	905,115	1,438,849	201,096
9	0	1,807,922	97,184	1,338,689	6,513,766	6,993,500	1,931,287	3,274,219
10	1,202,755	3,271,446	1,064,219	1,158,020	1,559,919	1,829,114	550,901	5,622,445
TOTAL	421,287,444	475,095,164	331,652,941	479,415,470	652,861,927	888,991,167	437,324,195	636,560,556

Appendix A lists the congressional districts which represent the county in which the state capital is located, and those congressional districts which represent only portions of a county. Appendix C lists the programs included in each functional policy category.

table continues

Table 5.12 Outlays for Transportation Programs by Congressional District, 1983-1990 *(continued)*

Congressional District	1983	1984	1985	1986	1987	1988	1989	1990 (est.)
HAWAII								
1	112,544,524	23,161,978	91,664,533	87,226,077	134,365,131	135,942,285	250,488,307	344,294,271
2	0	-1,012,287	15,659	3,887	52,313	2,387,081	-80,338	173,180
TOTAL	112,544,524	22,149,691	91,680,192	87,229,964	134,417,444	138,329,366	250,407,969	344,467,451
IDAHO								
1	82,918,215	102,490,013	104,773,052	93,604,374	105,768,986	212,522,246	152,912,707	97,895,905
2	923,824	3,721,622	1,447,988	2,744,546	3,159,725	2,326,708	2,994,254	3,508,509
TOTAL	83,842,039	106,211,635	106,221,040	96,348,920	108,928,711	214,848,954	155,906,961	101,404,415
ILLINOIS								
1	131,708,019	219,657,173	326,541,223	413,817,741	311,074,479	350,134,344	309,837,821	201,178,051
2	154,410	18,349	0	0	257,076	268,529	54,270	8,992,402
3	154,443	18,353	8,880,765	1,031,800	996,055	5,186,698	54,282	8,994,291
4	66,768	2,085,134	370,800	0	1,336,311	2,476,986	2,328,736	3,943,733
5	154,422	18,350	0	0	257,096	243,547	54,275	8,993,096
6	94,289,038	2,806,840	0	0	262,148	955,674	1,287,617	8,483,367
7	-122,147	25,622,624	7,964,745	2,567,827	17,020,108	29,707,857	35,927,673	52,137,042
8	154,441	18,353	0	0	353,153	350,811	54,281	8,994,187
9	154,467	189,620	0	19,730	357,158	317,952	139,245	8,995,677
10	69,835	6,130,342	7,290,000	7,040,495	9,272,459	4,279,623	245,612	4,320,382
11	154,429	18,351	0	0	417,811	262,800	55,588	8,993,512
12	65,324	1,667,839	0	932,550	562,740	277,515	61,517	3,813,005
13	67,706	2,168,846	0	0	243,963	1,593,154	463,101	3,944,029
14	599	877,571	2,567,837	918,764	1,308,988	915,695	420,222	15,945,441
15	636,205	2,064,447	4,993,204	978,831	1,894,040	4,653,609	3,690,972	2,455,320
16	1,739,635	3,996,768	1,254,812	5,177,807	3,570,057	4,771,343	3,182,781	3,684,036
17	1,413,202	1,903,837	5,122,335	3,915,978	3,014,399	3,203,588	4,039,250	6,116,153
18	1,928,700	5,354,416	6,540,189	6,825,508	11,801,326	5,798,002	3,248,599	9,353,540
19	1,824,826	7,355,384	3,006,254	2,711,378	4,029,954	6,262,574	3,629,722	4,033,663
20	692,835,399	549,185,196	396,513,736	454,981,795	494,713,419	440,846,963	362,158,738	693,270,659
21	578,546	2,325,589	1,154,700	-5,069	1,562,995	5,407,673	3,341,864	767,268
22	-1	3,102,699	677,069	1,482,849	1,627,170	300,942	4,013,310	223,940
TOTAL	928,028,265	836,586,081	772,877,669	902,397,984	865,932,905	868,215,879	738,289,477	1,067,632,793
INDIANA								
1	5,427,000	6,535,754	9,218,987	8,261,598	10,706,520	8,104,142	9,231,385	34,235,716
2	721,268	3,252,189	9,116,221	14,037,476	10,549,456	13,360,995	8,607,456	11,946,759
3	4,799,748	4,725,083	6,280,980	5,313,976	2,584,017	4,913,510	6,864,373	5,566,971
4	2,290,165	7,028,918	5,173,495	3,266,108	5,846,659	7,253,055	5,673,964	5,258,357
5	8,926,886	2,827,712	296,149	980,147	799,461	789,337	1,546,851	643,082
6	516,234	7,711,780	4,029,836	4,183,638	3,780,700	16,026,125	19,519,041	13,699,417
7	1,307,582	1,842,243	3,447,877	2,215,101	3,567,252	5,809,389	3,320,033	2,893,382
8	971,606	2,274,371	2,552,701	5,625,724	4,220,687	4,543,971	2,573,404	2,238,304
9	234,487	1,211,967	1,684,001	415,933	4,513,290	1,347,287	2,982,722	3,709,302
10	86,573,198	276,677,296	137,795,413	298,509,779	270,823,611	408,982,822	227,068,123	404,026,409
TOTAL	111,768,174	314,087,313	179,595,660	342,809,480	317,391,653	471,130,632	287,387,352	484,217,698
IOWA								
1	540,000	2,033,087	1,340,779	859,102	1,095,535	1,286,372	1,582,039	1,326,135
2	2,789,369	7,264,305	4,111,712	3,216,182	2,809,389	4,986,436	2,853,426	1,811,606
3	2,062,372	2,355,047	2,641,250	1,977,571	2,564,687	1,193,454	797,787	1,733,490
4	201,409,843	190,841,015	170,569,495	182,797,613	190,231,943	205,792,526	195,079,170	290,959,287
5	0	2,139,877	2,347,620	580,348	1,897,920	1,659,686	653,010	1,093,623
6	538,375	1,780,786	2,179,045	1,900,711	2,397,584	3,372,099	4,399,573	7,058,664
TOTAL	207,339,959	206,414,117	183,189,901	191,331,527	200,997,058	218,290,573	205,365,005	303,982,806
KANSAS								
1	-1,920	4,651,871	1,787,959	1,802,474	4,397,617	4,553,540	2,292,690	4,378,080
2	161,522,473	228,122,285	182,019,640	201,814,815	219,688,215	178,229,931	141,935,708	209,460,387
3	0	4,702,204	9,721,510	669,664	313,981	93,892	-236,753	6,699,428
4	5,020,771	8,761,464	8,918,475	11,783,330	11,457,093	6,509,784	7,852,474	5,535,480
5	0	2,934,239	2,986,918	639,688	1,644,067	2,816,988	1,351,650	2,208,355
TOTAL	166,541,324	249,172,063	205,434,502	216,709,971	237,500,973	192,204,135	153,195,769	228,281,731

Appendix A lists the congressional districts which represent the county in which the state capital is located, and those congressional districts which represent only portions of a county. Appendix C lists the programs included in each functional policy category.

table continues

Table 5.12 **Outlays for Transportation Programs by Congressional District, 1983-1990 *(continued)***

Congressional District	1983	1984	1985	1986	1987	1988	1989	1990 (est.)
KENTUCKY								
1	-24,768	843,342	1,749,231	996,645	902,489	1,179,254	1,418,479	882,248
2	776,005	1,646,480	1,411,623	685,853	516,745	1,402,688	932,190	1,024,715
3	4,084,631	15,128,054	15,769,090	18,523,077	13,634,600	13,715,369	4,602,279	9,596,895
4	1,329,633	8,131,361	5,823,353	3,481,040	9,906,789	21,241,921	7,189,760	19,311,777
5	149,915	1,499,815	143,096	612,289	871,753	1,099,482	606,098	-260,739
6	243,295,691	313,839,404	170,754,420	121,655,362	213,333,306	143,581,298	163,185,094	280,308,516
7	0	5,161,222	3,840,611	30,830	659,120	328,543	595,918	302,790
TOTAL	249,611,107	346,249,678	199,491,424	145,985,096	239,824,802	182,548,555	178,529,818	311,166,203
LOUISIANA								
1	29,171,996	13,145,202	10,555,322	36,581,720	8,744,947	19,962,512	13,006,616	10,260,286
2	0	6,969,912	4,060,283	6,010,537	1,520,410	14,665,764	8,108,611	18,294,074
3	-5,928	1,716,454	388,717	4,142,342	322,908	627,624	2,470,492	611,367
4	756,877	6,593,650	4,565,672	4,552,397	2,652,106	3,898,075	5,512,083	4,306,452
5	2,394,767	1,424,393	967,291	361,435	4,087,856	3,037,953	4,314,207	2,836,171
6	333,547,091	310,171,134	325,026,474	350,854,478	260,907,381	147,877,911	299,971,124	340,805,361
7	906,505	4,002,012	3,233,262	3,740,037	1,932,387	4,014,875	2,405,698	5,948,680
8	905,115	1,605,670	1,458,835	3,360,941	1,379,148	1,484,401	2,287,867	4,701,801
TOTAL	367,676,423	345,628,427	350,255,856	409,603,887	281,547,143	195,569,115	338,076,699	387,764,192
MAINE								
1	64,290,813	74,969,160	67,326,745	64,385,974	89,644,058	103,765,039	76,969,466	95,051,306
2	326,005	3,573,506	2,228,840	4,028,196	7,739,674	6,153,139	3,340,519	5,117,269
TOTAL	64,616,818	78,542,666	69,555,585	68,414,170	97,383,732	109,918,178	80,309,985	100,168,575
MARYLAND								
1	0	4,073,471	1,317,544	1,424,989	984,206	6,478,349	32,931,482	105,901,645
2	366,497,880	234,244,361	315,143,224	411,199,701	438,760,398	461,816,244	328,536,117	515,156,889
3	355,770	42,370,049	23,970,077	24,900,410	25,253,037	23,032,651	2,284,549	8,679,680
4	33,098,792	27,881,261	66,413,136	22,127,688	34,684,693	16,220,041	24,576,048	26,374,708
5	0	39,939	1,032,384	28,800	2,099,044	419,297	-61,044	43,072
6	215,103	5,487,040	295,256	54,604	4,573,141	4,283,793	1,873,050	3,720,118
7	36,308	638,809	232,967	125,630	36,778	294,438	36,095	81,545
8	303,345	1,080,906	0	123,100	2,406,315	519,867	2,041	525,906
TOTAL	400,507,198	315,815,836	408,404,588	459,984,922	508,797,612	513,064,680	390,178,338	660,483,563
MASSACHUSETTS								
1	411,106	2,920,318	1,498,756	2,669,202	3,224,375	616,935	2,915,195	917,618
2	4,974,416	8,848,559	6,390,252	10,044,259	10,150,505	4,509,281	76,408,498	70,465,278
3	527,076	13,017,959	3,137,618	3,812,738	3,938,745	2,284,345	776,920	4,980,827
4	2,704,355	1,912,019	1,130,739	10,858,389	1,671,816	1,540,330	2,144,762	1,640,631
5	2,781,365	13,548,455	2,054,867	4,480,120	826,359	86,038	20,073	1,421,828
6	2,453,898	3,217,514	7,170,478	3,855,685	1,948,222	3,931,051	3,366,858	3,103,544
7	965,941	576,022	208,416	1,817,073	550,375	187,985	129,607	10,220,959
8	194,410,819	138,332,524	56,540,421	123,784,749	71,430,050	61,543,265	1,606,047	24,705,792
9	136,756,800	193,420,576	227,980,457	211,280,290	270,478,886	401,947,487	197,565,098	603,320,948
10	326,596	33,804,046	4,644,441	7,897,007	5,715,211	6,301,669	2,436,305	10,783,367
11	3,250,231	1,799,648	2,151,724	3,877,211	2,157,232	3,876,131	1,363,853	21,174,879
TOTAL	349,562,604	411,397,639	312,908,169	384,376,723	372,091,777	486,824,517	288,733,216	752,735,671
MICHIGAN								
1	69,279,266	83,018,952	26,428,505	60,553,105	1,819,648	46,527,126	5,557,314	14,349,604
2	1,690,058	5,147,509	932,545	717,523	27,096,913	1,112,852	1,229,702	3,387,500
3	1,203,590	9,057,657	5,350,590	8,720,662	9,891,498	10,208,476	5,276,350	5,099,409
4	293,870	1,104,858	669,919	2,078,578	2,676,780	863,999	2,834,926	538,911
5	2,162,895	8,121,809	12,541,498	7,337,057	6,967,627	4,942,449	2,537,562	8,331,958
6	334,404,921	352,927,819	436,391,980	387,555,121	307,477,288	331,993,145	328,802,385	475,535,742
7	2,185,976	2,576,276	2,135,307	5,354,773	6,853,098	3,430,404	4,088,945	3,034,598
8	1,155,550	4,197,420	6,107,872	1,735,038	5,557,503	6,226,642	4,256,069	2,854,536
9	567,930	1,926,808	1,330,072	2,502,303	4,167,910	3,301,756	1,885,015	1,661,053
10	2,583,699	5,320,974	318,229	1,147,333	4,969,596	2,170,735	-105,131	1,881,048
11	829,868	7,017,770	1,234,943	1,242,902	515,234	3,771,411	3,848,094	1,121,021
12	0	197,010	0	375,000	0	1,411,092	1,365,356	615,095

Appendix A lists the congressional districts which represent the county in which the state capital is located, and those congressional districts which represent only portions of a county. Appendix C lists the programs included in each functional policy category.

table continues

Table 5.12 Outlays for Transportation Programs by Congressional District, 1983-1990 *(continued)*

Congressional District	1983	1984	1985	1986	1987	1988	1989	1990 (est.)
MICHIGAN *continued*								
13	4,553,256	5,665,616	0	7,548,099	15,774,912	6,641,098	7,547,101	12,144,638
14	0	1,098,000	1,319,864	316,611	319,859	2,989,102	2,613,113	296,385
15	4,378,633	4,162	1,937,956	2,419,489	0	1,502,882	100,000	4,317,005
16	0	449,390	0	1,335,000	45,000	1,080,000	-109,030	-124,648
17	0	0	0	0	0	0	0	0
18	0	0	0	0	0	0	0	39,942
TOTAL	425,289,512	487,832,030	496,699,280	490,938,594	394,132,866	428,173,169	371,727,771	535,083,798
MINNESOTA								
1	319,864	2,620,429	2,011,405	377,522	1,935,574	657,757	2,250,848	4,866,773
2	903,500	110,484	0	1,189,369	945,113	2,723,927	-143,255	519,087
3	1,398,527	0	0	0	1,391,650	151,244	149,825	0
4	267,386,481	288,795,761	301,193,753	281,611,592	261,161,775	336,373,856	239,122,045	266,916,063
5	8,885,702	976,141	10,785	12,505	1,034,859	184,390	1,721,417	0
6	675,184	0	0	0	2,994,879	691,101	-342,031	17,097
7	1,731,036	1,342,726	915,588	3,507,287	2,830,270	3,255,924	3,632,011	1,470,879
8	3,914,118	10,807,773	3,968,656	2,704,187	2,714,317	2,474,140	4,087,216	2,607,318
TOTAL	285,214,412	304,653,314	308,100,187	289,402,462	275,008,437	346,512,339	250,478,076	276,397,217
MISSISSIPPI								
1	0	1,884,269	300,266	2,054,174	961,865	1,914,682	2,585,213	922,967
2	0	531,472	779,371	1,829,467	492,278	1,131,962	92,518	1,618,879
3	0	1,939,415	-226,701	384,689	1,424,409	1,716,643	618,681	2,619,232
4	165,112,200	180,894,504	184,590,193	164,094,941	144,717,960	131,996,037	129,662,933	244,611,711
5	40,325	3,468,334	9,824,017	8,958,686	3,422,619	3,101,581	2,083,902	2,893,239
TOTAL	165,152,525	188,717,994	195,267,146	177,321,957	151,019,131	139,862,905	135,043,247	252,666,027
MISSOURI								
1	15,878,817	16,858,250	30,910,448	15,799,244	12,938,382	27,558,590	149,655,038	25,409,248
2	-36,112	11,209,754	11,100,471	8,142,241	13,224,857	17,579,837	2,521,741	53,225,041
3	-15,610	620,162	0	0	58,500	0	0	18,355,894
4	273,055,396	319,858,898	329,510,226	295,049,264	365,600,846	292,075,469	265,268,380	395,561,121
5	17,606	6,125,025	1,627,298	14,872,439	16,675,219	43,024,992	15,162,661	13,056,184
6	9,303,206	3,683,215	2,314,981	2,869,590	3,422,899	4,768,406	616,239	508,270
7	1,097,796	927,879	1,942,006	1,741,297	2,944,091	3,643,517	5,416,729	2,749,770
8	36,300,267	4,439,429	1,499,206	2,600,351	491,536	680,948	1,680,837	1,799,207
9	706,485	3,225,543	4,550,711	1,995,987	4,360,103	896,187	545,578	14,428,143
TOTAL	336,307,851	366,948,155	383,455,347	343,070,413	419,716,433	390,227,946	440,867,203	525,092,877
MONTANA								
1	145,902,718	106,596,452	138,661,577	121,434,639	122,000,813	175,375,205	99,193,722	155,143,034
2	4,277,429	9,618,033	6,732,164	8,648,643	6,163,170	6,826,475	7,963,670	10,593,215
TOTAL	150,180,147	116,214,485	145,393,741	130,083,282	128,163,983	182,201,680	107,157,392	165,736,249
NEBRASKA								
1	143,796,222	124,976,044	127,499,436	120,394,134	138,483,374	138,699,269	74,080,596	161,632,457
2	2,026,423	11,560,557	5,574,893	13,801,865	9,752,338	7,100,171	6,297,588	12,979,048
3	-64,528	3,112,388	2,431,584	2,783,705	4,436,379	4,318,316	4,428,610	3,190,576
TOTAL	145,758,117	139,648,989	135,505,913	136,979,704	152,672,091	150,117,756	84,806,794	177,802,081
NEVADA								
1	251,926	11,023,935	8,695,468	8,927,303	9,823,412	23,552,314	32,724,964	9,122,670
2	104,073,063	101,301,540	121,101,765	92,832,983	112,588,479	159,633,670	87,219,216	135,145,861
TOTAL	104,324,989	112,325,475	129,797,233	101,760,286	122,411,891	183,185,984	119,944,180	144,268,531
NEW HAMPSHIRE								
1	1,211,730	3,556,199	3,328,141	3,024,777	2,738,073	2,354,474	588,654	4,867,902
2	57,080,689	75,415,749	77,367,714	69,301,043	72,257,879	128,303,770	61,766,690	87,535,979
TOTAL	58,292,419	78,971,948	80,695,855	72,325,820	74,995,952	130,658,244	62,355,344	92,403,880

Appendix A lists the congressional districts which represent the county in which the state capital is located, and those congressional districts which represent only portions of a county. Appendix C lists the programs included in each functional policy category.

table continues

Table 5.12

Outlays for Transportation Programs by Congressional District, 1983-1990 *(continued)*

Congressional District	1983	1984	1985	1986	1987	1988	1989	1990 (est.)
NEW JERSEY								
1	14,159,448	5,162,133	245,500	4,024,776	3,006,821	24,604,616	2,783,084	3,080,376
2	117,636,356	42,579,989	2,533,945	4,042,247	3,041,639	3,499,164	2,958,186	4,767,639
3	0	1,624,117	620,597	938,403	79,314	236,387	12,513	243,477
4	436,751,209	325,887,742	362,774,963	376,181,223	406,498,792	645,988,532	291,836,187	580,817,918
5	0	247,674	24,430	0	0	0	34	0
6	0	-27,525	0	61,241	63,000	0	0	0
7	0	7,754,470	26,932	0	0	0	0	0
8	0	1,525,307	78,491	2,556	0	1,030	3,676	0
9	0	235,593	93,750	1,899,340	2,166,127	1,944,550	-160,485	223,383
10	23,438,215	179,024,985	185,109,858	181,773,439	109,856,980	122,070,272	98,631,177	139,904,079
11	0	2,420,532	1,419,177	1,319,814	0	4,174,897	814,952	137,212
12	0	1,324,275	137,745	888,416	788,079	155,362	1,904,908	979,078
13	16,687,500	662,477	55,641	0	0	50,809	9,686	0
14	0	0	0	0	0	95,000	39,000	648,859
TOTAL	608,672,728	568,421,769	553,121,030	571,131,455	525,500,752	802,820,619	398,832,918	730,802,021
NEW MEXICO								
1	20,010,646	11,957,601	9,112,411	3,703,293	12,634,319	10,760,168	5,327,115	649,823
2	544,201	4,264,037	4,365,228	7,197,588	6,830,848	5,426,153	3,070,169	2,250,852
3	96,244,926	143,991,756	140,343,674	127,601,253	133,662,492	86,520,321	115,967,052	161,919,521
TOTAL	116,799,773	160,213,394	153,821,313	138,502,134	153,127,659	102,706,642	124,364,336	164,820,196
NEW YORK								
1	0	8,329,594	5,904,055	19,113,248	4,154,765	7,428,549	390,211,016	662,995,977
2	0	3,133,249	1,533,998	10,081,562	1,652,964	4,004,435	2,284,253	2,387,057
3	2,846,252	6,473,642	14,038,979	19,623,672	6,427,216	2,712,436	10,629,578	12,185,666
4	0	23,646	1,970,280	3,912,012	-16,471	1,181,610	43,083	50,823
5	0	1,396,251	229,289	3,487,571	131,299	23,562	528,601	50,348
6	15,000,000	6,424	312,072	969,809	0	0	0	26,435,853
7	0	0	0	0	0	0	0	0
8	0	105	28,168	154,096	1,042	334,792	590	2,338
9	0	0	0	0	-50,839	0	0	0
10	58,487,146	61,035,324	12,831,228	1,057,121	0	10,000	59,951	0
11	0	0	0	0	0	0	0	0
12	0	0	0	0	0	0	0	0
13	0	0	0	0	0	0	0	0
14	0	0	0	0	0	0	0	0
15	0	383,749,494	542,550,224	305,392,607	657,099,569	613,108,867	160,438,455	101,882
16	0	0	416,486	-47,099	0	500,000	724,281	1,516,705
17	26,704,349	47,722,843	6,360,572	-36,069	150,000	360,000	171,758	346,424
18	0	0	0	0	0	0	0	0
19	0	31,764,941	12,601,313	32,150,444	15,420,314	45,211,552	47,786,892	55,487,617
20	0	2,310,103	14,263,109	8,332,857	2,442,141	3,322,193	3,068,877	3,969,394
21	397,471	2,242,475	1,121,960	1,030,072	1,203,042	2,527,305	1,545,662	9,174,905
22	0	2,194,907	2,614,476	4,373,400	1,364,372	2,420,625	4,154,252	4,743,368
23	563,075,588	762,177,794	763,232,058	816,006,121	627,162,616	831,980,730	706,585,021	1,036,219,602
24	0	587,013	1,499,970	515,005	3,339,291	4,315,791	4,165,116	1,289,957
25	1,466,269	1,737,990	2,218,756	4,229,239	3,557,547	2,732,705	3,901,847	3,524,925
26	1,268,911	1,942,279	3,835,841	2,651,248	3,231,497	4,860,044	6,432,552	6,495,852
27	1,031,435	11,791,054	14,946,263	9,559,501	4,462,005	4,408,518	10,083,489	11,903,727
28	116,066,887	2,574,385	4,287,751	1,281,173	5,130,634	9,090,416	7,418,098	9,753,674
29	0	1,719,624	13,456,916	8,481,724	11,385,847	5,794,274	8,240,840	6,160,525
30	494,715	0	27,137	251,083	355,500	247,140	2,241,000	-13,232
31	0	71,789	487,527	147,076	-5,776	478,583	113,400	5,980,912
32	0	10,999,061	15,335,991	22,578,277	10,162,029	300,916	12,631,143	14,492,018
33	0	180,000	453,529	667,142	647,793	768,146	515,009	7,244,134
34	0	10,327,896	4,370,008	2,759,607	1,046,098	3,080,273	10,199,035	1,405,684
TOTAL	786,839,023	1,354,491,883	1,440,927,956	1,278,722,498	1,360,454,495	1,551,203,461	1,394,173,799	1,883,906,135
NORTH CAROLINA								
1	0	1,583,080	287,479	2,234,032	2,897,805	1,517,555	1,236,847	1,344,302
2	19,000	416,439	539,839	1,580,285	939,193	780,703	967,091	443,830
3	0	2,623,030	549,764	741,838	836,804	323,505	1,094,620	996,684
4	288,595,272	250,785,402	342,946,567	378,518,105	482,123,472	571,366,095	374,916,669	515,584,321
5	877,169	4,544,208	1,292,110	1,803,552	7,739,702	3,478,176	2,601,692	1,873,813
6	620,805	5,061,331	1,350,421	3,319,957	3,340,899	2,352,344	6,856,976	4,719,533
7	536,882	4,187,646	6,006,111	3,546,915	2,782,676	8,090,417	3,507,450	1,784,423
8	442,100	1,137,923	139,987	1,852,993	1,224,527	1,822,940	62,256	273,730
9	1,807,116	10,075,942	5,935,296	3,951,185	7,086,431	8,128,615	21,769,411	14,552,914
10	268,839	407,385	360,431	1,322,040	642,625	448,819	939,337	1,798,486
11	454,678	1,385,554	2,506,318	2,846,203	5,405,930	951,324	1,048,226	3,740,102
TOTAL	293,621,861	282,207,940	361,914,323	401,717,105	515,020,064	599,260,493	415,000,575	547,112,138

Appendix A lists the congressional districts which represent the county in which the state capital is located, and those congressional districts which represent only portions of a county. Appendix C lists the programs included in each functional policy category.

table continues

Table 5.12 Outlays for Transportation Programs by Congressional District, 1983-1990 *(continued)*

Congressional District	1983	1984	1985	1986	1987	1988	1989	1990 (est.)
NORTH DAKOTA								
TOTAL	81,256,878	105,844,104	96,076,496	90,340,918	93,587,919	127,642,355	76,567,078	113,104,900
OHIO								
1	12,219,486	6,319,498	7,089,956	16,921,060	14,535,258	9,063,040	14,320,310	11,251,062
2	0	2,276,440	0	0	0	0	0	187,758
3	3,704,180	14,416,485	16,080,369	13,120,501	13,467,147	14,501,386	4,667,324	12,293,177
4	568,707	915,535	1,370,683	0	0	452,284	663,313	157,732
5	0	570,362	40,000	0	2,570,613	58,085	376,500	789,720
6	268,198	216,000	-157,543	587,046	0	1,200,000	-1,104	2,155,982
7	250,564	2,875,523	779,550	0	5,948	418,089	518,215	453,710
8	640,206	1,494,656	680,554	53,370	0	454,600	817,526	0
9	68,000	4,092,799	5,731,887	11,731,972	4,563,910	4,371,347	5,265,487	25,336,137
10	0	12,546,978	138,698	-79,075	4,046,533	1,244,490	1,569,058	76,286
11	1,272,044	1,057	4,323,337	2,670,301	2,586,867	3,221,800	21,938,146	62,459,806
12	426,145,155	460,198,589	505,259,888	492,615,447	492,969,857	551,243,974	437,040,474	837,845,649
13	0	2,146,110	783,660	1,077,760	2,342,656	2,043,411	417,903	575,773
14	3,256,000	7,871,182	2,911,200	2,879,800	4,125,746	6,507,410	5,114,800	3,607,405
15	54,008	2,450,757	988,514	821,815	798,717	2,049,635	6,514,227	22,967,298
16	2,982,660	6,642,622	5,412,539	3,473,416	3,183,719	4,206,899	3,247,253	5,781,848
17	1,124,441	3,524,699	4,540,312	2,281,241	6,651,335	3,168,341	2,668,610	2,524,119
18	88,000	1,139,745	1,854,853	54,600	10,967	0	819,004	389,315
19	-15,991	0	0	0	0	0	0	298,123
20	23,929,456	50,658,435	52,168,480	35,019,009	46,501,689	56,200,796	11,887,006	2,803,685
21	0	0	0	0	0	0	0	326,234
TOTAL	476,555,114	580,357,472	609,996,937	583,228,263	598,360,962	660,405,587	517,844,052	992,280,819
OKLAHOMA								
1	5,198,136	8,642,185	7,338,320	7,747,421	6,185,901	5,241,679	3,443,293	15,056,402
2	109,400	1,933,608	515,257	1,034,547	1,673,741	2,462,456	760,748	1,137,589
3	20,146	2,759,672	2,501,781	1,100,330	2,790,185	5,139,979	1,534,452	65,759
4	-239	8,345,247	3,790,836	8,928,178	11,219,805	7,451,669	1,385,872	4,030,021
5	158,430,943	165,821,209	215,667,858	214,200,001	188,622,883	245,989,668	212,527,683	279,865,125
6	5,193,249	2,711,465	431,527	470,050	10,037,091	1,032,867	1,344,992	2,866,697
TOTAL	168,951,635	190,213,386	230,245,579	233,480,527	220,529,605	267,318,318	220,997,040	303,021,593
OREGON								
1	74,187,596	8,729,081	106,433	2,019,038	212,560	2,003,583	9,593,781	23,463,627
2	33,338,812	2,876,840	1,493,133	3,348,458	3,964,017	3,448,550	6,248,337	4,763,519
3	15,883	64,348,528	32,588,630	29,696,542	17,712,227	17,969,528	4,122,791	7,230,220
4	3,685,134	5,069,159	867,354	3,786,775	14,293,230	7,938,577	4,498,806	7,646,019
5	152,015,001	196,753,228	181,009,112	180,723,189	207,143,342	174,523,536	143,317,340	182,839,858
TOTAL	263,242,426	277,776,836	216,064,662	219,574,002	243,325,376	205,883,774	167,781,055	225,943,243
PENNSYLVANIA								
1	95,761,636	149,798,838	111,069,520	128,061,937	136,763,860	107,441,328	115,642,810	178,047,354
2	-5,206	0	0	0	0	0	0	641,342
3	0	0	0	0	0	0	0	640,027
4	0	1,669,667	2,075,488	716,137	2,455,848	2,282,200	3,704,905	4,631,065
5	424,268	417,225	1,572,809	1,569,088	1,180,000	2,318,350	1,964,098	4,073,305
6	0	3,184,820	1,832,338	2,413,998	3,782,450	1,241,500	1,118,500	1,742,916
7	0	0	533	740	0	0	82,500	163,245
8	0	219,960	0	9,698	0	1,508,579	0	1,023,234
9	0	3,565,101	1,180,797	937,528	2,448,355	1,428,002	3,227,682	3,329,507
10	1,203,234	1,168,020	1,009,103	4,062,276	4,084,334	327,585	1,432,446	1,223,618
11	1,913,434	2,741,069	21,319,036	9,171,052	1,381,562	2,768,082	1,261,334	4,191,298
12	2,808	3,592,923	4,321,437	1,850,679	2,014,563	1,651,550	1,280,497	3,585,807
13	0	1,632,000	0	0	0	0	0	111,619
14	64,090,449	50,826,661	91,949,959	34,777,095	54,374,902	45,057,790	50,868,844	46,199,154
15	1,978,689	4,806,512	4,435,021	3,715,916	5,473,950	4,397,625	4,661,627	4,867,327
16	0	1,960,454	687,000	1,047,599	2,528,692	2,254,459	4,946,603	1,345,611
17	574,874,344	674,183,755	692,209,416	656,319,218	814,553,319	662,641,654	472,271,853	607,190,744
18	0	0	0	187,476	3,341	0	0	0
19	501,414	473,402	1,241,630	636,457	84,829	569,834	2,056,384	912,231
20	0	0	0	88,280	4,882	0	0	0
21	1,046,072	3,739,000	6,294,440	5,189,095	4,296,222	4,082,295	4,725,721	4,036,938
22	599,303	1,483,092	959,783	3,452,651	2,498,144	1,603,495	1,460,124	2,078,476
23	78,007	5,783,392	1,504,067	3,884,643	2,974,416	6,000,348	3,509,148	2,620,164
TOTAL	742,468,452	911,245,891	943,662,377	858,091,563	1,040,903,669	847,574,676	674,215,076	872,654,981

Appendix A lists the congressional districts which represent the county in which the state capital is located, and those congressional districts which represent only portions of a county. Appendix C lists the programs included in each functional policy category.

table continues

Table 5.12 **Outlays for Transportation Programs by Congressional District, 1983-1990 *(continued)***

Congressional District	1983	1984	1985	1986	1987	1988	1989	1990 (est.)
RHODE ISLAND								
1	70,271,363	140,361,330	126,136,466	134,619,666	120,256,717	122,563,048	111,374,055	175,855,050
2	890,742	9,598,696	2,839,076	5,197,732	6,817,175	2,336,004	3,322,783	8,478,343
TOTAL	71,162,105	149,960,026	128,975,542	139,817,398	127,073,892	124,899,052	114,696,838	184,333,394
SOUTH CAROLINA								
1	53,200	11,503,498	5,576,542	2,919,568	295,702	6,256,771	6,871,277	11,136,690
2	156,424,401	168,721,006	174,088,532	213,393,011	256,868,776	284,826,632	143,065,988	614,301,241
3	0	591,707	0	319,603	1,970,004	1,311,333	8,597	214,124
4	1,050,902	2,850,451	5,007,735	1,693,851	3,477,677	5,785,903	2,620,440	4,403,698
5	0	1,772,978	156,483	1,035,837	1,815,031	3,137,138	1,957,367	2,684,963
6	32,653	2,454,307	2,881,932	1,756,479	2,054,105	1,416,291	3,522,438	6,344,007
TOTAL	157,561,156	187,893,947	187,711,224	221,118,349	266,481,295	302,734,068	158,046,107	639,084,722
SOUTH DAKOTA								
TOTAL	69,125,928	88,750,051	103,996,623	95,514,199	104,173,470	119,649,951	86,939,184	117,367,214
TENNESSEE								
1	578,032	6,435,838	806,207	1,943,483	2,146,285	2,848,130	827,431	1,089,887
2	1,910,833	4,360,456	6,074,685	4,925,774	6,428,482	6,718,617	6,373,127	2,586,600
3	1,594,771	4,376,821	911,163	2,214,750	3,067,285	3,708,259	1,566,888	2,427,810
4	0	2,086,320	183,600	218,743	407,354	702,000	518,400	554,759
5	331,105,824	292,743,132	331,403,058	279,339,501	316,278,374	341,769,640	295,707,460	443,134,368
6	4,210,692	261,843	163,810	649,086	300,000	180,000	968,400	0
7	126,000	3,937,618	10,415,094	7,045,630	11,090,687	14,352,781	6,473,409	14,084,690
8	208,736	14,998,038	1,906,754	4,375,903	6,361,724	3,701,172	654,402	28,228,126
9	0	-8,727	0	0	0	8,316,565	14,197,146	0
TOTAL	339,734,888	329,191,339	351,864,371	300,712,870	346,080,191	382,297,164	327,286,663	492,106,240
TEXAS								
1	0	1,643,418	253,656	2,089,500	736,340	774,723	1,992,500	468,955
2	0	2,225,003	3,169,064	3,273,936	1,720,349	1,012,841	-56,370	699,045
3	16,133,900	24,826,886	14,737,392	8,456,000	5,824,921	1,461,449	13,000	539,462
4	132,475	13,527,048	1,333,161	972,928	2,537,963	5,627,023	3,828,341	1,246,972
5	433,000	6,804,127	133,200	0	9,383,272	303,561	6,697,834	2,817,814
6	30,504,833	17,729,618	665,000	1,601,879	3,934,293	3,684,276	6,085,126	4,144,476
7	77,239,919	25,580,922	82,043,006	93,847,960	30,765,233	91,187,832	22,602,837	29,618,509
8	233,700	4,772,780	936,840	-148,412	5,657,332	254,500	0	0
9	337,841	17,251,410	1,821,868	2,340,837	6,255,310	3,138,180	2,574,818	8,040,921
10	713,664,089	686,661,503	1,033,141,255	1,050,322,205	763,110,520	1,120,106,132	909,165,701	1,085,101,522
11	1,133,701	4,093,794	1,608,128	2,896,422	1,264,701	6,754,509	1,027,085	4,636,192
12	3,000,000	7,989,011	27,170,946	9,915,467	6,007,455	16,647,712	29,101,777	12,395,219
13	1,450,695	5,509,568	2,163,519	4,836,237	1,978,089	4,825,428	1,851,254	6,638,176
14	125,360	3,287,092	7,024,476	2,249,647	3,943,963	2,838,424	2,052,198	6,900,392
15	852,131	4,193,068	5,084,153	7,591,931	1,913,422	3,754,137	2,971,146	932,423
16	1,922,540	3,947,558	5,376,002	5,676,271	4,438,468	10,127,859	12,253,859	3,094,777
17	117,896	2,275,461	4,374,499	2,053,404	3,973,756	1,724,485	1,402,077	4,534,526
18	250,553	26,031,365	-185,989	-249,466	0	0	0	0
19	776,855	5,724,854	3,116,404	3,445,343	3,998,782	6,594,764	3,787,998	3,358,585
20	7,591,539	11,195,573	14,677,115	28,784,176	20,465,300	7,605,046	11,894,912	16,703,091
21	220,255	11,627,485	5,446,190	5,031,954	6,278,062	6,260,323	8,507,992	4,929,622
22	115,007	25,713,593	38,486,039	15,684,409	8,965,000	11,453,398	10,872,974	23,898,452
23	919,320	1,305,562	1,505,115	499,096	627,372	1,243	600,000	4,876,251
24	7,635,356	3,642,200	2,715,236	11,412,342	6,193,265	54,498,188	16,480,314	13,616,692
25	250,272	2,659,397	374,619	210,814	0	40,000	-66,830	92,380
26	0	468,500	0	198,205	0	0	276,780	34,180
27	2,543,984	3,816,410	1,104,503	3,615,195	1,960,959	2,988,803	1,980,062	5,649,735
TOTAL	867,585,222	924,503,206	1,258,275,397	1,266,608,279	901,934,127	1,363,664,836	1,057,897,385	1,244,968,370
UTAH								
1	1,311,992	6,600,043	4,059,326	2,938,657	2,650,735	3,543,237	3,715,853	2,680,318
2	175,164,427	169,625,827	203,939,877	163,948,310	247,183,976	258,809,493	124,256,405	160,314,645
3	48,914	12,865,248	6,853,818	3,503,936	1,196,323	1,466,821	2,389,046	1,409,942
TOTAL	176,525,333	189,091,118	214,853,021	170,390,903	251,031,034	263,819,551	130,361,304	164,404,905
VERMONT								
TOTAL	56,141,116	59,753,813	72,762,276	56,378,545	90,391,962	82,442,016	53,444,906	56,802,314

Appendix A lists the congressional districts which represent the county in which the state capital is located, and those congressional districts which represent only portions of a county. Appendix C lists the programs included in each functional policy category.

table continues

Table 5.12 Outlays for Transportation Programs by Congressional District, 1983-1990 *(continued)*

Congressional District	1983	1984	1985	1986	1987	1988	1989	1990 (est.)
VIRGINIA								
1	0	4,927,191	1,874,616	8,375,596	3,388,452	1,432,518	2,424,712	8,068,015
2	250,412	7,140,633	11,170,356	9,080,690	14,781,369	3,638,242	9,662,738	9,270,569
3	320,030,421	358,520,675	351,347,484	486,198,434	309,262,958	378,134,419	187,848,926	347,256,998
4	-50	1,002,367	572,578	1,327,196	996,729	1,669,286	1,645,310	388,822
5	0	4,293,444	3,178,966	2,064,228	2,850,970	2,629,450	1,020,511	1,318,712
6	467,129	491,583	5,238,935	12,986,138	9,390,840	6,649,954	5,100,490	4,266,504
7	166,249	2,030,766	2,712,089	4,123,739	3,641,586	3,400,413	5,553,496	11,273,348
8	50,420	160,000	40,000	0	126,286	114,395	0	-41,834
9	164,339	4,512,705	3,238,514	2,520,136	1,955,086	5,316,127	4,906,453	4,370,165
10	0	66,823	382,500	1,817,116	2,637,322	11,792,449	4,966,400	19,001,245
TOTAL	321,128,920	383,146,187	379,756,038	528,493,273	349,031,598	414,777,253	223,129,036	405,172,542
WASHINGTON								
1	19,308,015	5,968,751	47,718,940	60,853,052	108,598,097	85,020,753	48,257,867	26,634,055
2	268,345	8,325,808	17,300,701	8,996,483	6,275,237	5,556,949	7,158,137	7,227,445
3	279,124,984	287,711,070	366,809,746	458,564,389	279,194,115	529,937,805	543,914,248	408,771,133
4	1,214,012	5,488,084	362,620	2,306,088	5,804,711	2,066,555	980,557	7,040,143
5	3,372,148	12,124,650	4,472,492	4,784,864	8,590,273	2,930,147	8,038,562	4,253,149
6	1,833,385	4,166,640	6,887,378	12,258,728	5,119,614	2,225,869	8,906,912	10,983,209
7	1,786,579	33,906,581	4,404,628	2,386,199	4,967,130	18,318,887	22,624,203	16,984,090
8	1,630,641	3,336,398	0	1,300,046	358,828	841,703	898,912	1,744,131
TOTAL	308,538,108	361,027,982	447,956,505	551,449,849	418,908,005	646,898,669	640,779,398	483,637,354
WEST VIRGINIA								
1	1,035,859	2,625,086	2,980,979	2,823,196	2,171,179	5,448,092	2,557,062	4,334,480
2	1,146,089	3,398,800	1,791,058	19,595,947	5,507,102	2,158,312	1,115,198	733,845
3	331,960,242	188,587,494	189,294,711	237,017,255	194,175,068	83,598,505	143,698,817	214,317,146
4	2,932,647	1,174,629	1,136,846	2,603,003	1,123,387	1,789,914	1,614,498	4,634,584
TOTAL	337,074,837	195,786,009	195,203,594	262,039,401	202,976,736	92,994,823	148,985,575	224,020,055
WISCONSIN								
1	2,744,315	6,811,320	6,433,826	7,855,157	6,286,677	5,179,610	5,522,566	6,910,296
2	197,291,937	180,649,469	179,296,944	234,169,925	231,171,079	252,215,631	213,946,786	324,606,547
3	622,239	4,226,907	1,419,065	2,678,979	2,248,304	2,530,700	1,438,105	4,110,698
4	7,922,138	33,693,334	22,671,881	16,479,906	17,555,902	21,491,322	41,146,057	14,638,754
5	0	0	0	601,634	248,469	106,756	34,780	-3,693
6	1,318,650	2,122,842	679,864	434,007	662,994	2,048,781	864,804	592,760
7	852,294	6,792,153	1,820,127	465,460	2,191,600	1,054,380	1,337,807	3,401,859
8	950,062	4,007,666	957,346	4,821,868	5,826,205	4,425,359	9,356,669	2,592,370
9	2,166,563	1,506,187	1,035,986	3,670,852	1,505,468	2,473,907	5,614,586	6,434,768
TOTAL	213,868,198	239,809,878	214,315,039	271,177,788	267,696,698	291,526,446	279,262,160	363,284,358
WYOMING								
TOTAL	78,718,437	84,187,882	112,692,123	92,426,907	96,349,811	118,871,447	88,507,328	125,039,306
U.S. TOTAL	15,375.1 mil.	17,330.0 mil.	17,147.2 mil.	18,403.3 mil.	18,288.5 mil.	20,736.0 mil.	16,232.8 mil.	23,813.0 mil.

Appendix A lists the congressional districts which represent the county in which the state capital is located, and those congressional districts which represent only portions of a county. Appendix C lists the programs included in each functional policy category.

APPENDICES

Appendix A
Congressional districts representing county of state capital city and portions of counties

Congressional District	District representing all or part of the county of the state capital[1]	District representing part of one or of one or more counties[2]
ALABAMA		
1st		
2nd	✓	
3rd		
4th		✓
5th		
6th		✓
7th		✓
ALASKA		
At Large	✓	
ARIZONA		
1st	✓	✓
2nd	✓	✓
3rd	✓	✓
4th	✓	✓
5th		✓
ARKANSAS		
1st		
2nd	✓	
3rd		
4th		
CALIFORNIA		
1st		✓
2nd		✓
3rd	✓	✓
4th	✓	✓
5th		✓
6th		✓
7th		✓
8th		✓
9th		✓
10th		✓
11th		✓
12th		✓
13th		✓
14th		✓
15th		✓
16th		✓
17th		✓
18th		✓
19th		✓
20th		✓
21st		✓
22nd		✓
23rd		✓
24th		✓
25th		✓
26th		✓
27th		✓
28th		✓
29th		✓
30th		✓
31st		✓
32nd		✓

appendix continues

Appendix A *(continued)*
Congressional districts representing county of state capital city and portions of counties

Congressional District	District representing all or part of the county of the state capital[1]	District representing part of one or of one or more counties[2]
CALIFORNIA *continued*		
33rd		✓
34th		✓
35th		✓
36th		✓
37th		✓
38th		✓
39th		✓
40th		✓
41st		✓
42nd		✓
43rd		✓
44th		✓
45th		✓
COLORADO		
1st	✓	✓
2nd		✓
3rd		✓
4th		✓
5th		✓
6th	✓	✓
CONNECTICUT		
1st	✓	✓
2nd		✓
3rd		✓
4th		✓
5th		✓
6th	✓	✓
DELAWARE		
At Large	✓	
FLORIDA		
1st		✓
2nd	✓	✓
3rd		✓
4th		✓
5th		✓
6th		✓
7th		✓
8th		✓
9th		✓
10th		✓
11th		✓
12th		✓
13th		✓
14th		✓
15th		✓
16th		✓
17th		✓
18th		✓
19th		✓

appendix continues

Appendix A *(continued)*
Congressional districts representing county of state capital city and portions of counties

Congressional District	District representing all or part of the county of the state capital[1]	District representing part of one or of one or more counties[2]
GEORGIA		
1st		
2nd		
3rd		
4th	✓	✓
5th	✓	✓
6th	✓	✓
7th		
8th		
9th		✓
10th		✓
HAWAII		
1st	✓	✓
2nd	✓	✓
IDAHO		
1st	✓	✓
2nd	✓	✓
ILLINOIS		
1st		✓
2nd		✓
3rd		✓
4th		✓
5th		✓
6th		✓
7th		✓
8th		✓
9th		✓
10th		✓
11th		✓
12th		✓
13th		✓
14th		✓
15th		✓
16th		✓
17th		✓
18th	✓	✓
19th		✓
20th	✓	✓
21st		✓
22nd		✓
INDIANA		
1st		✓
2nd	✓	✓
3rd		✓
4th		
5th		✓
6th	✓	✓
7th		
8th		✓
9th		✓
10th	✓	✓

appendix continues

Appendix A *(continued)*
Congressional districts representing county of state capital city and portions of counties

Congressional District	District representing all or part of the county of the state capital[1]	District representing part of one or of one or more counties[2]
IOWA		
1st		
2nd		
3rd		
4th	✓	
5th		
6th		
KANSAS		
1st		
2nd	✓	
3rd		
4th		
5th		
KENTUCKY		
1st		
2nd		
3rd		✓
4th		✓
5th		✓
6th	✓	
7th		✓
LOUISIANA		
1st		✓
2nd		✓
3rd		✓
4th		✓
5th		✓
6th	✓	✓
7th		✓
8th	✓	✓
MAINE		
1st	✓	
2nd		
MARYLAND		
1st		✓
2nd		✓
3rd		✓
4th	✓	✓
5th		✓
6th		✓
7th		✓
8th		✓
MASSACHUSETTS		
1st		✓
2nd		✓
3rd		✓
4th		✓
5th		✓
6th		✓

appendix continues

Appendix A *(continued)*
Congressional districts representing county of state capital city and portions of counties

Congressional District	District representing all or part of the county of the state capital[1]	District representing part of one or of one or more counties[2]
MASSACHUSETTS *continued*		
7th	✓	✓
8th	✓	✓
9th	✓	✓
10th		✓
11th	✓	✓
MICHIGAN		
1st		✓
2nd		✓
3rd	✓	✓
4th		✓
5th		✓
6th	✓	✓
7th		✓
8th		✓
9th		✓
10th		✓
11th		✓
12th		✓
13th		✓
14th		✓
15th		✓
16th		✓
17th		✓
18th		✓
MINNESOTA		
1st		✓
2nd		✓
3rd		✓
4th	✓	✓
5th		✓
6th	✓	✓
7th		✓
8th		✓
MISSISSIPPI		
1st		✓
2nd		✓
3rd		✓
4th	✓	✓
5th		✓
MISSOURI		
1st		✓
2nd		✓
3rd		✓
4th	✓	✓
5th		✓
6th		✓
7th		
8th		✓
9th		✓
MONTANA		
1st	✓	
2nd		

appendix continues

Appendix A *(continued)*
Congressional districts representing county of state capital city and portions of counties

Congressional District	District representing all or part of the county of the state capital[1]	District representing part of one or of one or more counties[2]
NEBRASKA		
1st	✓	✓
2nd		✓
3rd		
NEVADA		
1st		✓
2nd	✓	✓
NEW HAMPSHIRE		
1st	✓	✓
2nd	✓	✓
NEW JERSEY		
1st		✓
2nd		✓
3rd		✓
4th	✓	✓
5th	✓	✓
6th		✓
7th	✓	✓
8th		✓
9th		✓
10th		✓
11th		✓
12th		✓
13th		✓
14th		✓
NEW MEXICO		
1st		
2nd		
3rd	✓	
NEW YORK		
1st		✓
2nd		✓
3rd		✓
4th		✓
5th		✓
6th		✓
7th		✓
8th		✓
9th		
10th		✓
11th		✓
12th		✓
13th		✓
14th		✓
15th		✓
16th		✓
17th		✓
18th		✓
19th		✓
20th		✓
21st		✓
22nd		✓
23rd	✓	✓

appendix continues

Appendix A *(continued)*
Congressional districts representing county of state capital city and portions of counties

Congressional District	District representing all or part of the county of the state capital[1]	District representing part of one or of one or more counties[2]
NEW YORK *continued*		
24th		✓
25th		✓
26th		
27th		✓
28th		✓
29th		✓
30th		✓
31st		✓
32nd		✓
33rd		✓
34th		✓
NORTH CAROLINA		
1st		
2nd		✓
3rd		✓
4th	✓	
5th		
6th		
7th		
8th		✓
9th		✓
10th		✓
11th		✓
NORTH DAKOTA		
At Large	✓	
OHIO		
1st		✓
2nd		✓
3rd		✓
4th		✓
5th		✓
6th		✓
7th		✓
8th		✓
9th		✓
10th		✓
11th		✓
12th	✓	✓
13th		✓
14th		✓
15th	✓	✓
16th		✓
17th		✓
18th		✓
19th		✓
20th		✓
21st		✓
OKLAHOMA		
1st		✓
2nd		✓
3rd		✓
4th	✓	✓
5th	✓	✓
6th	✓	✓

appendix continues

Appendix A *(continued)*
Congressional districts representing county of state capital city and portions of counties

Congressional District	District representing all or part of the county of the state capital[1]	District representing part of one or of one or more counties[2]
OREGON		
1st		✓
2nd		✓
3rd		✓
4th	✓	✓
5th	✓	✓
PENNSYLVANIA		
1st		✓
2nd		✓
3rd		✓
4th		✓
5th		✓
6th		✓
7th		✓
8th		✓
9th		✓
10th		✓
11th		✓
12th		✓
13th		✓
14th		✓
15th		✓
16th		✓
17th	✓	✓
18th		✓
19th		✓
20th		✓
21st		✓
22nd		✓
23rd		✓
RHODE ISLAND		
1st	✓	✓
2nd	✓	✓
SOUTH CAROLINA		
1st		✓
2nd	✓	
3rd		
4th		
5th		
6th		✓
SOUTH DAKOTA		
At Large	✓	
TENNESSEE		
1st		
2nd		
3rd		
4th		
5th	✓	
6th		
7th		✓
8th		✓
9th		✓

appendix continues

Appendix A *(continued)*
Congressional districts representing county of state capital city and portions of counties

Congressional District	District representing all or part of the county of the state capital[1]	District representing part of one or of one or more counties[2]
TEXAS		
1st		✓
2nd		✓
3rd		✓
4th		✓
5th		✓
6th		✓
7th		✓
8th		✓
9th		✓
10th	✓	✓
11th		✓
12th		✓
13th		
14th		✓
15th		✓
16th		
17th		✓
18th		✓
19th		
20th		✓
21st		✓
22nd		✓
23rd		✓
24th		✓
25th		✓
26th		✓
27th		✓
UTAH		
1st		
2nd	✓	✓
3rd	✓	✓
VERMONT		
At Large	✓	
VIRGINIA		
1st		
2nd		✓
3rd	✓	✓
4th		✓
5th		✓
6th		✓
7th		✓
8th		✓
9th		
10th		✓
WASHINGTON		
1st		✓
2nd		✓
3rd	✓	✓
4th		✓
5th		
6th		✓
7th		✓
8th		✓

appendix continues

Appendix A *(continued)*

Congressional districts representing county of state capital city and portions of counties

Congressional District	District representing all or part of the county of the state capital[1]	District representing part of one or of one or more counties[2]
WEST VIRGINIA		
1st		
2nd		
3rd	✓	
4th		
WISCONSIN		
1st		✓
2nd	✓	✓
3rd		✓
4th		✓
5th		✓
6th		✓
7th		✓
8th		✓
9th		✓
WYOMING		
At large	✓	

[1]Some federal monies are allocated to the states to be reallocated to substate recipients. Such programs, known as pass-through programs, are reported in FAADS as if the money were entirely allocated to the county in which the state capital is located. This poses a difficult problem in determining where the monies are ultimately allocated, since states employ different criteria for distributing funds. No satisfactory means of prorating such monies to outlying congressional districts exists. In this volume, we follow the convention adopted in FAADS, which is to report pass-through monies as being spent in the congressional district or districts which encompass the county containing the state capital. For this reason, the districts that represent the county in which the state capital is located in column one.

[2]In most cases, FAADS reports action-by-action outlays, but in a few instances, reports only county aggregates. These county aggregate records pose a coding problem in those situations where counties are represented by more than one member of Congress. The solution adopted here is to apportion outlays to each of these districts based on the proportion of the county's (1980) population that resides in the district. For example, during the 1980s, four congressional districts have encompassed portions of Harris county, Texas. In FAADS, expenditures for Social Security, Medicaid, and other high volume programs are not allocated to these four districts, but instead are reported as quarterly aggregates going to the county as a whole. In this volume, such expenditures have been divided among these four districts based on the proportion of the population of Harris county that lives in each of the districts. Consequently, in order to arrive at the total outlays to each district, these expenditures are summed with the outlays going to all of the other counties that are represented, either in whole or in part, by each Congressperson. The districts that are effected by this coding rule are identified in column two of this appendix.

Appendix B
Programs providing outlays to each recipient category

Catalog Number	Program Title	State Gov't.	Interstate Agencies	Counties	Cities/Towns	Special Districts	Schools	State Higher Education	Private Higher Education	Indian Tribes	Nonprofits	For Profits	Small Businesses	Individuals	All Others
10.001	Agricultural Research- Basic and Applied Research	✓	✓	✓				✓	✓		✓	✓	✓		✓
10.003	Morrill-Nelson Funds for Food and Agriculture Higher Education	✓	✓						✓						
10.025	Plant and Animal, Pest Control, and Animal Care	✓	✓	✓		✓	✓	✓	✓	✓	✓			✓	
10.028	Animal Damage Control	✓						✓	✓		✓				
10.052	Cotton Production Stabilization													✓	
10.053	Dairy Indemnity Program													✓	
10.054	Emergency Conservation Program	✓	✓											✓	
10.055	Feed Grain Production Stabilization													✓	
10.058	Wheat Production Stabilization													✓	
10.059	National Wool Act Payments													✓	
10.062	Water Bank Program													✓	
10.063	Agricultural Conservation Program	✓	✓			✓		✓			✓			✓	
10.064	Forestry Incentives Program	✓	✓					✓						✓	
10.065	Rice Production Stabilization													✓	
10.066	Emergency Livestock Assistance													✓	
10.067	Grain Reserve Program													✓	
10.068	Rural Clean Water Program	✓	✓											✓	
10.069	Conservation Reserve Program	✓			✓			✓				✓		✓	
10.070	Colorado River Salinity Control													✓	
10.071	Federal-State Cooperation in Warehouse Examination	✓				✓		✓							
10.153	Market News	✓	✓	✓		✓									
10.156	Federal-State Marketing Improvement Program	✓						✓			✓				
10.164	Wholesale Market Development	✓									✓				
10.200	Grants for Agricultural Research, Special Research	✓	✓					✓	✓		✓	✓	✓		✓
10.202	Cooperative Forestry Research	✓	✓					✓	✓					✓	
10.203	Payments to Agricultural Experiment Stations	✓	✓	✓				✓	✓						
10.205	Payments to 1890 Land-Grant Colleges and Tuskegee Institute	✓	✓					✓	✓		✓				
10.206	Grants for Agricultural Research- Competitive Research	✓	✓					✓	✓		✓	✓	✓	✓	✓
10.207	Animal Health and Disease Research	✓	✓					✓	✓						
10.208	Alcohol Fuels Research	✓	✓						✓		✓				
10.209	1890 Research Facilities	✓	✓					✓	✓						
10.210	Food and Agricultural Sciences National Needs							✓	✓						
10.211	Higher Education Strengthening Grants							✓	✓						
10.212	Small Business Innovation Research												✓		
10.213	Competitive Research Grants for Forest and Rangeland	✓						✓	✓		✓		✓		
10.214	Morrill-Nelson Funds for Food and Agricultural Higher Education	✓													
10.215	Low Input Farming Systems- Research and Education							✓	✓						
10.250	Agricultural and Rural Economic Research	✓	✓			✓		✓	✓		✓	✓			✓
10.350	Technical Assistance to Cooperatives	✓	✓					✓			✓				
10.375	Human Nutrition Information Service	✓	✓				✓	✓	✓		✓	✓	✓		
10.405	Farm Labor Housing Loans and Grants		✓	✓	✓			✓			✓	✓		✓	✓
10.411	Rural Housing Site Loans										✓			✓	
10.415	Rural Rental Housing Loans	✓	✓	✓	✓	✓				✓	✓	✓	✓	✓	✓
10.417	Very Low-Income Housing Repair Loans and Grants													✓	
10.418	Water and Waste Disposal Systems for Rural Communities	✓	✓	✓	✓	✓		✓		✓	✓	✓	✓	✓	✓
10.420	Rural Self-Help Housing Technical Assistance			✓	✓						✓			✓	✓
10.423	Community Facilities Loans	✓	✓	✓	✓	✓	✓	✓	✓	✓	✓	✓	✓	✓	✓
10.424	Industrial Development Grants							✓			✓			✓	
10.427	Rural Rental Assistance Payments													✓	
10.433	Rural Housing Preservation Grants	✓		✓	✓	✓		✓		✓	✓				
10.435	Agricultural Loan Mediation Program	✓													
10.475	Cooperative Agreements for Intrastate Meat and Poultry Inspection	✓	✓				✓	✓	✓						
10.500	Cooperative Extension Service	✓	✓					✓	✓		✓	✓			
10.550	Food Distribution	✓	✓	✓				✓		✓					
10.551	Food Stamps	✓	✓											✓	
10.553	School Breakfast Program	✓	✓					✓			✓				
10.555	National School Lunch Program	✓	✓					✓			✓				

appendix continues

Appendix B *(continued)*
Programs providing outlays to each recipient category

Catalog Number	Program Title	State Gov't.	Interstate Agencies	Counties	Cities/Towns	Special Districts	Ind. School Districts	State Higher Education	Private Higher Education	Indian Tribes	Nonprofits	For Profits	Small Businesses	Individuals	All Others
10.556	Special Milk Program for Children	✓	✓					✓			✓				
10.557	Special Supplemental Food Program for Women, Infants & Children	✓	✓					✓		✓					
10.558	Child and Adult Care Food Program	✓	✓					✓			✓				✓
10.559	Summer Food Service Program for Children	✓	✓					✓			✓				
10.560	State Administrative Expenses for Child Nutrition	✓													
10.561	State Administrative Matching Grants for Food Stamps	✓													
10.562	Nutritional Training and Education	✓													
10.564	Nutrition Training and Education	✓													
10.565	Commodity Supplemental Food Program	✓	✓					✓		✓					
10.567	Food Distribution Program on Indian Reservations	✓	✓					✓		✓					
10.568	Temporary Emergency Food Assistance (Administrative)	✓													
10.652	Forestry Research	✓	✓	✓	✓	✓	✓	✓	✓	✓	✓	✓	✓	✓	✓
10.663	Young Adult Conservation Corps- Grants to States	✓													
10.664	Cooperative Forestry Assistance	✓	✓	✓	✓	✓		✓	✓		✓			✓	✓
10.665	Schools and Roads-Grants to States	✓													
10.666	Schools and Roads-Grants to Counties	✓		✓											
10.667	School Funds-Grants to Arizona (Arizona School Fund)	✓													
10.668	Additional Loans-Grants to Minnesota	✓													
10.669	Accelerated Cooperative Assistance for Forest Programs	✓													
10.700	National Agricultural Library	✓	✓					✓	✓		✓	✓	✓		
10.800	Livestock, Meat and Poultry Market Supervision	✓													
10.900	Great Plains Conservation		✓								✓			✓	
10.901	Resource Conservation and Development	✓	✓	✓	✓	✓	✓	✓		✓	✓	✓	✓	✓	✓
10.904	Watershed Protection and Flood Prevention	✓	✓	✓	✓	✓	✓	✓	✓	✓	✓	✓	✓	✓	✓
10.909	Resource Appraisal and Program Development		✓	✓	✓	✓			✓						
10.910	Rural Abandoned Mine Program	✓	✓	✓	✓	✓	✓	✓	✓		✓	✓	✓	✓	✓
10.950	Agricultural Statistics Reports	✓	✓	✓				✓	✓		✓	✓			
10.960	Technical Agricultural Assistance							✓			✓				
10.961	International Agricultural Research-Collaborative Program							✓			✓				
10.962	International Training-Foreign Participant										✓				
10.999	Not in CFDA-Administered by Secretary of Agriculture	✓	✓					✓	✓		✓	✓		✓	✓
11.000	Secretary, Department of Commerce										✓				
11.108	Export Promotion Services	✓	✓					✓			✓		✓		✓
11.109	Trade Adjustment Assistance	✓	✓	✓	✓	✓		✓	✓		✓	✓	✓		✓
11.110	Trade Development							✓				✓			
11.300	Economic Development-Grants for Public Works and Development	✓	✓	✓	✓	✓	✓	✓	✓	✓	✓	✓			✓
11.301	Economic Development-Business Development Assistance											✓			
11.302	Economic Development-Support for Planning Organization	✓	✓	✓		✓		✓		✓	✓	✓			✓
11.303	Economic Development-Technical Assistance	✓	✓	✓	✓	✓	✓	✓	✓	✓	✓	✓			✓
11.304	Economic Development-Public Works Impact Projects	✓	✓	✓	✓	✓	✓	✓	✓	✓	✓				✓
11.305	Economic Development-State and Local Economic Development	✓	✓	✓	✓	✓		✓							
11.306	Economic Development-District Operational Assistance					✓									
11.307	Special Economic Development and Adjustment Assist./Long-Term	✓	✓	✓	✓	✓		✓	✓	✓	✓	✓			✓
11.311	Special Economic Development and Adjustment Assistance/Sudden	✓		✓	✓	✓					✓				
11.312	Research and Evaluation Program		✓					✓	✓		✓	✓		✓	✓
11.400	Geodetic Surveys and Services	✓						✓							
11.401	Nautical Charts and Related Data								✓						
11.405	Anadromous and Great Lakes Fisheries Conservation	✓	✓			✓		✓	✓		✓				
11.406	Commercial Fisheries Disaster Assistance	✓													
11.407	Interjurisdictional Fisheries Act of 1986	✓	✓					✓			✓				
11.408	Fishermen's Contingency Fund													✓	
11.409	Fishing Vessel and Gear Damage Compensation Fund													✓	
11.417	Sea Grant Support	✓	✓					✓	✓		✓				✓
11.419	Coastal Zone Management Program Administration	✓						✓			✓				
11.420	Coastal Zone Management Estuarine Research Reserve	✓	✓			✓		✓	✓		✓				
11.421	Energy Impact-Formula Grants	✓													
11.422	Coastal Energy Impact Grants	✓													

appendix continues

Appendix B *(continued)*
Programs providing outlays to each recipient category

Catalog Number	Program Title	State Gov't.	Interstate Agencies	Counties	Cities/Towns	Special Districts	Schools	State Higher Education	Private Higher Education	Indian Tribes	Nonprofits	For Profits	Small Businesses	Individuals	All Others
11.424	Coastal Energy Impact Program - Environmental Grants	✓													
11.426	Financial Assistance for Marine Pollution Research	✓	✓			✓		✓	✓		✓	✓			✓
11.427	Fisheries Development and Utilization Research	✓	✓	✓	✓		✓	✓	✓		✓	✓	✓	✓	✓
11.428	Intergovernmental Climate-Programs	✓	✓					✓	✓		✓	✓			
11.429	Marine Sanctuary Program	✓						✓	✓		✓				
11.430	Undersea Research	✓						✓	✓		✓	✓			
11.431	Climate and Atmospheric Research	✓						✓	✓		✓	✓			
11.432	Environmental Research Laboratories-Joint Institutes	✓						✓			✓				
11.550	Public Telecommunications Facilities-Construction	✓	✓	✓	✓	✓	✓	✓	✓	✓	✓	✓			✓
11.603	National Standard Reference Data System							✓	✓		✓	✓			
11.606	Weights and Measures Service										✓				
11.609	Measurement and Engineering Research and Standards	✓	✓	✓				✓	✓		✓	✓	✓		✓
11.800	Minority Business Development Centers	✓	✓	✓	✓			✓	✓	✓	✓	✓	✓	✓	✓
11.801	American Indian Program							✓		✓	✓				
11.999	Not in CFDA-Administered by Secretary of Commerce		✓	✓	✓	✓		✓	✓	✓	✓	✓	✓		✓
12.000	Administered by Secretary of Army	✓	✓		✓			✓	✓		✓	✓			✓
12.112	Payments to States in Lieu of Real Estate Taxes	✓													
12.400	Military Construction, Army National Guard	✓	✓					✓	✓						
12.607	Military Base Reuse Studies and Community Planning	✓		✓	✓	✓		✓							✓
12.608	Impact Assistance for Areas Affected by East Coast Trident Program	✓	✓	✓	✓	✓	✓	✓							
12.999	Not in CFDA-Administered by Secretary of Army				✓	✓					✓				
13.103	Food and Drug Administration-Research	✓	✓		✓			✓	✓		✓	✓	✓		
13.110	Maternal and Child Health Federal Consolidated Program	✓		✓	✓			✓	✓	✓	✓	✓	✓		✓
13.112	Characterization of Environmental Health Hazards	✓	✓	✓	✓			✓	✓		✓	✓	✓	✓	✓
13.113	Biological Response to Environmental Health Hazards	✓	✓	✓	✓			✓	✓		✓	✓	✓		✓
13.114	Applied Toxicological Research and Testing	✓	✓	✓	✓			✓	✓		✓	✓	✓	✓	✓
13.115	Biometry & Risk Estimation-Health Risks from Environ. Exposures	✓	✓	✓				✓	✓		✓	✓	✓		✓
13.116	Tuberculosis Control Programs	✓	✓	✓	✓	✓		✓			✓				
13.117	Grants for Preventive Medicine Residency Training	✓						✓	✓		✓				
13.118	Acquired Immunodeficiency Syndrome (AIDS) Activity	✓	✓	✓	✓			✓	✓	✓	✓	✓	✓		✓
13.119	Grants for Podiatric Medicine Training	✓		✓	✓			✓	✓		✓				
13.120	Mental Health Services for Cuban Entrants	✓						✓			✓		✓		
13.121	Diseases of the Teeth and Supporting Tissues	✓	✓		✓			✓	✓		✓	✓	✓	✓	✓
13.122	Disorders of Craniofacial Structure and Function	✓	✓		✓			✓	✓		✓	✓	✓	✓	✓
13.124	Nurse Anesthetist Traineeships	✓		✓	✓	✓		✓	✓		✓	✓	✓		
13.125	Mental Health Planning and Demonstration Projects	✓	✓					✓	✓		✓		✓		
13.126	Small Business Innovation Research	✓						✓			✓	✓	✓		✓
13.128	Refugee Assistance-Mental Health	✓													
13.131	Shared Research Facilities for Heart, Lung, and Blood Diseases	✓						✓	✓		✓		✓		
13.132	Acquired Immunodeficiency Syndrome (AIDS) Research	✓			✓			✓	✓		✓	✓	✓		✓
13.133	Health Services Delivery to AIDS Victims-Demonstration Grants	✓		✓	✓	✓		✓			✓		✓		
13.135	Centers for Research and Demonstration for Health Promotion							✓	✓		✓				
13.136	Injury Prevention and Control Research Projects	✓		✓	✓			✓	✓		✓		✓		
13.138	Protection and Advocacy for Mentally Ill Individuals	✓						✓			✓	✓			
13.141	Alcohol, Drug Abuse Treatment and Rehabilitation	✓						✓		✓					
13.142	NIEHS Hazardous Waste Worker Health and Safety				✓			✓			✓				
13.143	NIEHS Superfund Hazardous Substances-Basic Research	✓						✓	✓						
13.144	Drug and Alcohol Abuse Prevention- High-Risk Youth	✓		✓	✓	✓	✓	✓	✓	✓	✓	✓			✓
13.146	Temporary AIDS Drug Reimbursements	✓						✓			✓				
13.150	Mental Health Services for the Homeless Block Grant	✓													
13.151	Project Grants for Health Services to the Homeless	✓		✓	✓	✓		✓	✓	✓	✓	✓	✓		
13.152	Community Demonstration Grant Projects for Alcohol, Drug Abuse	✓		✓				✓			✓	✓	✓		
13.153	Pediatric AIDS Health Care Demonstration Program	✓		✓	✓	✓		✓	✓		✓	✓			
13.161	Health Program for Toxic Substances and Disease Research	✓													
13.162	National Health Service Corps Loan Repayment	✓			✓			✓			✓	✓			
13.166	Indian Health Service Health Promotion and Disease Prevention							✓		✓					
13.167	Research Facilities Improvement	✓		✓	✓			✓	✓		✓	✓			

appendix continues

Appendix B *(continued)*
Programs providing outlays to each recipient category

Catalog Number	Program Title	State Gov't.	Interstate Agencies	Counties	Cities/Towns	Special Districts	Ind. School Districts	State Higher Education	Private Higher Education	Indian Tribes	Nonprofits	For Profits	Small Businesses	Individuals	All Others
13.169	Model Projects for Pregnant and Postpartum Women	✓		✓	✓	✓		✓	✓		✓				
13.170	Community Youth Activity Demonstration Grants	✓		✓				✓							
13.171	Community Youth Activity Program Block Grants	✓													
13.172	Human Genome Research	✓		✓	✓			✓	✓		✓	✓	✓	✓	✓
13.173	Biological Research Related to Deafness	✓			✓			✓	✓		✓		✓	✓	✓
13.174	Conference Grant (Substance Abuse)	✓		✓				✓	✓		✓				
13.175	Drug Abuse Treatment Waiting List Reduction Grants	✓		✓	✓			✓			✓				
13.176	ADAMHA Small Instrumentation Program Grants	✓						✓	✓		✓	✓			
13.179	State Data Collection-Uniform Alcohol and Drug Abuse Data	✓		✓				✓	✓		✓		✓		
13.180	Medical Treatment Effectiveness Research							✓	✓		✓				
13.217	Family Planning-Services	✓	✓	✓	✓			✓			✓				
13.224	Community Health Centers	✓	✓	✓	✓	✓		✓		✓	✓	✓	✓		
13.226	Health Services Research and Development Grants	✓	✓	✓	✓			✓	✓		✓	✓	✓		
13.228	Indian Health Service-Health Management Development	✓	✓	✓	✓	✓	✓	✓	✓	✓	✓	✓	✓	✓	✓
13.229	Indian Health Services-Sanitation Management Development	✓		✓	✓			✓		✓	✓	✓	✓		✓
13.242	Mental Health Research Grants	✓	✓	✓	✓			✓	✓	✓	✓	✓	✓	✓	✓
13.244	Mental Health Clinical or Service Related Training Grants	✓	✓	✓	✓			✓	✓	✓	✓	✓	✓		✓
13.246	Migrant Health Centers Grants	✓	✓	✓	✓	✓		✓		✓	✓	✓	✓		
13.252	Alcoholism Treatment and Rehabilitation/Occupational Services											✓			
13.260	Family Planning-Personnel Training	✓	✓	✓				✓	✓		✓	✓	✓		
13.262	Occupational Safety and Health Research Grants	✓	✓	✓	✓			✓	✓		✓	✓	✓	✓	
13.263	Occupational Safety and Health-Training Grants	✓	✓		✓			✓	✓		✓		✓	✓	
13.268	Childhood Immunization Grants	✓	✓	✓	✓			✓	✓		✓				
13.271	Alcohol Scientist Development Award and Research	✓	✓		✓			✓	✓		✓				
13.272	Alcohol National Research Service Awards for Research	✓	✓		✓			✓	✓		✓			✓	
13.273	Alcohol Research Programs	✓	✓		✓			✓	✓		✓	✓	✓	✓	✓
13.274	Alcohol and Drug Abuse Clinical or Service-Related Training													✓	
13.277	Drug Abuse Scientist Development Award for Clinical Research	✓	✓		✓			✓	✓		✓				
13.278	Drug Abuse National Research Service Awards	✓	✓	✓	✓			✓	✓		✓	✓			✓
13.279	Drug Abuse Research Programs	✓	✓	✓	✓			✓	✓		✓	✓	✓	✓	✓
13.281	Mental Research Scientist Development Award	✓	✓		✓			✓	✓		✓				
13.282	Mental Health National Research Service Awards	✓	✓		✓			✓	✓		✓			✓	
13.288	National Health Service Corps Scholarship Program	✓	✓		✓			✓	✓		✓	✓			✓
13.293	State Health Planning and Development Agencies	✓	✓								✓				
13.294	Health Planning-Health Systems Agencies	✓	✓	✓	✓	✓		✓	✓		✓	✓			✓
13.297	National Research Service Awards	✓	✓					✓	✓		✓				✓
13.298	Nurse Practitioner and Nurse Midwife Education	✓	✓	✓	✓			✓	✓		✓		✓		
13.299	Advanced Nurse Education	✓	✓		✓			✓	✓		✓				
13.306	Laboratory Animal Sciences and Primate Research	✓	✓		✓			✓	✓		✓	✓	✓	✓	✓
13.333	General Clinical Research Centers	✓	✓		✓			✓	✓		✓	✓	✓	✓	✓
13.337	Biomedical Research Support	✓	✓	✓	✓			✓	✓	✓	✓	✓	✓		✓
13.339	Capitation Grants for Schools of Public Health	✓	✓					✓	✓		✓				
13.340	Health Professions Facilities										✓				
13.342	Health Professions Student Loans	✓	✓		✓			✓	✓		✓				
13.358	Professional Nurse Traineeships	✓	✓	✓	✓			✓	✓		✓				
13.359	Nurse Training Improvement-Special Projects	✓	✓	✓	✓			✓	✓		✓	✓	✓		
13.361	Nursing Research	✓	✓		✓			✓	✓		✓	✓	✓	✓	✓
13.363	Nursing Scholarships	✓		✓	✓	✓		✓	✓		✓		✓		
13.364	Nursing Student Loans	✓	✓	✓	✓			✓	✓		✓				
13.371	Biomedical Research Technology	✓	✓		✓			✓	✓		✓	✓	✓	✓	✓
13.375	Minority Biomedical Research Support	✓	✓		✓			✓	✓	✓	✓	✓		✓	✓
13.379	Grants for Graduate Training in Family Medicine	✓	✓	✓	✓			✓	✓		✓	✓	✓		
13.381	Health Professions-Advanced Financial Distress								✓						
13.389	Research Centers in Minority Institutions	✓			✓			✓	✓						
13.390	Academic Research Enhancement Award	✓	✓					✓	✓		✓				✓
13.391	Cancer Task Forces														

appendix continues

Appendix B *(continued)*
Programs providing outlays to each recipient category

Catalog Number	Program Title	State Gov't.	Interstate Agencies	Counties	Cities/Towns	Special Districts	Schools	State Higher Education	Private Higher Education	Indian Tribes	Nonprofits	For Profits	Small Businesses	Individuals	All Others
13.392	Cancer-Construction	✓	✓					✓	✓		✓	✓	✓		✓
13.393	Cancer Cause and Prevention Research	✓	✓	✓	✓	✓		✓	✓		✓	✓	✓	✓	✓
13.394	Cancer Detection and Diagnosis Research	✓	✓		✓			✓	✓		✓	✓	✓		✓
13.395	Cancer Treatment Research	✓	✓	✓	✓			✓	✓		✓	✓	✓		✓
13.396	Cancer Biology Research	✓	✓	✓	✓			✓	✓		✓	✓	✓	✓	✓
13.397	Cancer Centers Support	✓	✓		✓			✓	✓		✓		✓		
13.398	Cancer Research Manpower	✓	✓		✓			✓	✓		✓	✓	✓	✓	✓
13.399	Cancer Control	✓	✓	✓	✓			✓	✓		✓	✓	✓		✓
13.600	Administration for Children, Youth and Families-Head Start	✓	✓	✓	✓	✓	✓	✓	✓	✓	✓	✓	✓	✓	✓
13.608	Admin. for Children, Youth and Families-Child Welfare Research	✓	✓	✓	✓			✓	✓	✓	✓	✓	✓	✓	✓
13.612	Native American Programs	✓	✓		✓	✓		✓	✓	✓	✓	✓	✓	✓	✓
13.614	Child Development Associate Scholarships	✓		✓			✓	✓	✓		✓				
13.623	Administration for Children, Youth and Familites-Runaway Youth	✓	✓	✓	✓			✓	✓	✓	✓	✓	✓	✓	✓
13.628	Child Abuse and Neglect Prevention and Treatment	✓	✓	✓	✓	✓		✓	✓	✓	✓	✓	✓	✓	✓
13.630	Administration on Developmental Disabilities-Basic Support	✓	✓	✓	✓	✓		✓			✓	✓			✓
13.631	Administration on Developmental Disabilities-Special Projects	✓	✓	✓	✓			✓	✓	✓	✓		✓	✓	✓
13.632	Admin. on Developmental Disabilities-University Affiliated Programs	✓	✓	✓	✓		✓	✓	✓	✓	✓		✓	✓	✓
13.633	Special Programs for the Aging-Title III Part B	✓	✓		✓	✓		✓					✓		
13.634	Special Programs for the Aging-Title IV Part C	✓													
13.635	Special Programs for the Aging-Title III Part C	✓	✓		✓	✓		✓							
13.641	Special Programs for the Aging-Title III, Part D	✓													
13.642	Social Services for Low Income and Public Assistance Recipients	✓													
13.644	Public Assistance Training Grants-Title XX	✓	✓		✓										
13.645	Child Welfare Services-State Grants	✓	✓		✓			✓		✓	✓				
13.646	Work Incentive Program	✓	✓		✓										
13.647	Social Services Research and Demonstration Grants	✓		✓	✓		✓	✓	✓	✓	✓	✓	✓	✓	✓
13.648	Child Welfare Services Training Grants	✓	✓		✓			✓	✓		✓		✓	✓	✓
13.652	Admin. for Children, Youth and Families-Adoption Opportunities	✓	✓	✓	✓			✓	✓	✓	✓	✓	✓	✓	✓
13.655	Special Programs for the Aging-Title VI, Part A	✓	✓	✓	✓			✓		✓	✓	✓			
13.656	Temporary Child Care and Crisis Nurseries	✓						✓			✓			✓	
13.657	Drug Abuse Prevention and Education for Runaways			✓	✓			✓		✓	✓	✓	✓		
13.658	Foster Care- Title IV-E	✓	✓		✓										
13.659	Adoption Assistance	✓	✓		✓									✓	
13.660	Drug Abuse Prevention and Education Relating to Youth Gangs	✓		✓	✓			✓		✓	✓		✓		
13.661	Native American Programs-Research, Demonstration and Evaluation	✓	✓		✓		✓	✓		✓	✓	✓	✓		
13.662	Native American Programs-Training and Technical Assistance	✓	✓		✓			✓		✓	✓		✓	✓	✓
13.665	Community Services Block Grant	✓	✓	✓	✓			✓		✓	✓		✓		✓
13.666	Comprehensive Child Development Centers			✓	✓			✓	✓		✓				
13.667	Social Services Block Grant	✓	✓		✓										
13.668	Special Programs for the Aging-Title IV-Training	✓	✓	✓	✓	✓		✓	✓	✓	✓	✓	✓	✓	✓
13.670	Administration for Children, Youth and Families-Child Abuse	✓		✓	✓			✓	✓	✓	✓	✓	✓	✓	✓
13.671	Family Violence Prevention and Services	✓				✓									
13.672	Child Abuse Challenge Grants	✓			✓	✓		✓		✓	✓		✓		✓
13.673	Grants to States for Planning and Develop. of Dependent Care Pgms	✓		✓			✓	✓							
13.679	Child Support Enforcement	✓													
13.714	Medical Assistance Program	✓	✓		✓			✓							✓
13.766	Health Care Financing-Research, Demonstration and Evaluation	✓	✓	✓	✓	✓		✓	✓	✓	✓	✓	✓	✓	✓
13.773	Medicare-Hospital Insurance													✓	
13.774	Medicare-Supplementary Medical Insurance													✓	
13.775	State Medicaid Fraud Control Units	✓													
13.776	Professional Standards Review Organizations	✓	✓	✓	✓		✓	✓			✓	✓	✓		✓
13.777	State Survey and Certification of Health Care Provision	✓	✓	✓	✓			✓	✓		✓	✓	✓	✓	✓
13.780	Family Support Payments to States-Assistance Payments	✓						✓			✓				
13.783	Child Support Enforcement	✓													
13.786	State Legalization Impact Assistance Grants	✓													
13.787	Refugee and Entrant Assistance-State Administered Programs	✓		✓				✓			✓	✓			

appendix continues

Appendix B *(continued)*
Programs providing outlays to each recipient category

Catalog Number	Program Title	State Gov't.	Interstate Agencies	Counties	Cities/Towns	Special Districts	Ind. School Districts	State Higher Education	Private Higher Education	Indian Tribes	Nonprofits	For Profits	Small Businesses	Individuals	All Others
13.789	Low-Income Home Energy Assistance	✓		✓	✓			✓		✓	✓	✓			✓
13.790	Work Incentive Program/WIN Demonstration Program	✓													
13.792	Community Services Block Grant	✓		✓	✓			✓		✓	✓				
13.793	Community Services Block Grant-Discretionary Award	✓		✓	✓		✓	✓		✓	✓	✓	✓		
13.795	Comm. Services Block Grant-Discretionary Award/Food & Nutrition	✓		✓	✓			✓		✓	✓	✓	✓		
13.796	Emergency Community Services for the Homeless	✓		✓	✓			✓		✓	✓				
13.802	Social Security-Disability Insurance		✓						✓					✓	
13.803	Social Security-Retirement Insurance													✓	
13.805	Social Security-Survivors Insurance		✓					✓	✓	✓				✓	
13.806	Special Benefits for Disabled Coal Miners													✓	
13.807	Supplemental Security Income	✓	✓					✓			✓			✓	
13.808	Assistance Payments-Maintenance Assistance	✓													
13.810	Assistance Payments-State and Local Training	✓													
13.811	Child Support Enforcement Interstate Grants	✓													
13.812	Social Security-Research and Demonstration	✓	✓	✓	✓	✓		✓	✓		✓	✓	✓		
13.814	Refugee Assistance-State-Administered Programs	✓	✓	✓	✓			✓	✓	✓	✓				✓
13.815	Refugee Assistance-Voluntary Agency Programs										✓				
13.817	Refugee Assistance-Cuban and Haitian Entrants	✓	✓								✓	✓			
13.818	Low-Income Home Energy Assistance	✓	✓	✓	✓			✓		✓	✓				
13.819	Name unknown, administered by Sec. Veteran's Employment	✓									✓	✓	✓		
13.820	Scholarships for Students of Exceptional Financial Need	✓	✓	✓	✓			✓	✓		✓				
13.821	Biophysics and Physiological Sciences	✓	✓		✓			✓	✓	✓	✓	✓	✓	✓	✓
13.822	Health Careers Opportunity Program	✓	✓	✓	✓			✓	✓	✓	✓		✓		
13.824	Area Health Education Centers	✓	✓					✓	✓		✓				
13.837	Heart and Vascular Diseases Research	✓	✓	✓	✓			✓	✓	✓	✓	✓	✓	✓	✓
13.838	Lung Diseases Research	✓	✓		✓			✓	✓		✓	✓	✓	✓	✓
13.839	Blood Diseases and Resources Research	✓	✓	✓	✓			✓	✓		✓	✓	✓	✓	✓
13.840	Caries Research	✓	✓						✓		✓	✓	✓	✓	✓
13.841	Periodontal Diseases Research	✓	✓		✓				✓		✓	✓		✓	✓
13.842	Craniofacial Anomalies Research	✓	✓						✓		✓			✓	✓
13.843	Restorative Materials Research	✓	✓		✓				✓		✓		✓		✓
13.844	Pain Control and Behavioral Studies	✓	✓		✓				✓		✓				✓
13.845	Dental Research Institutes-Research Centers in Oral Biology	✓	✓					✓	✓						
13.846	Arthritis, Musculoskeletal, and Skin Diseases Research	✓	✓		✓			✓	✓	✓	✓	✓	✓	✓	✓
13.847	Diabetes, Endocrinology and Metabolism Research	✓	✓	✓	✓			✓	✓	✓	✓	✓	✓	✓	✓
13.848	Digestive Diseases and Nutrition Research	✓	✓		✓			✓	✓		✓	✓	✓	✓	✓
13.849	Kidney Diseases, Urology, and Hematology Research	✓	✓		✓			✓	✓		✓	✓	✓	✓	✓
13.852	Neurological Disorders Research				✓										
13.853	Clinical Research Related to Neurological Disorder	✓	✓	✓	✓			✓	✓		✓	✓	✓	✓	✓
13.854	Biological Basis Research in the Neurosciences	✓	✓	✓	✓			✓	✓	✓	✓	✓	✓	✓	✓
13.855	Allergy, Immunology and Transplantation Research	✓	✓	✓	✓			✓	✓		✓	✓	✓	✓	✓
13.856	Microbiology and Infectious Diseases Research	✓	✓	✓	✓			✓	✓		✓	✓	✓	✓	✓
13.859	Pharmacological Sciences	✓	✓		✓			✓	✓		✓	✓	✓		✓
13.862	Genetics Research	✓	✓		✓			✓	✓		✓	✓	✓	✓	✓
13.863	Cellular and Molecular Basis of Disease Research	✓	✓	✓	✓			✓	✓		✓	✓	✓	✓	✓
13.864	Population Research	✓	✓	✓	✓	✓		✓	✓		✓	✓	✓	✓	✓
13.865	Research for Mothers and Children	✓	✓		✓	✓		✓	✓		✓	✓	✓	✓	✓
13.866	Aging Research	✓	✓	✓	✓			✓	✓	✓	✓	✓	✓	✓	✓
13.867	Retinal and Choroidal Diseases Research	✓	✓		✓			✓	✓		✓		✓	✓	✓
13.868	Anterior Segment Diseases Research	✓	✓		✓			✓	✓	✓	✓	✓	✓		✓
13.869	Cataract Research	✓	✓		✓			✓	✓		✓	✓	✓		✓
13.870	Glaucoma Research	✓	✓		✓			✓	✓		✓		✓		
13.871	Strabismus, Amblyopia and Visual Processing	✓	✓	✓	✓			✓	✓		✓		✓		✓
13.878	Soft Tissue Stomatology and Nutrition Research	✓	✓						✓		✓	✓	✓		✓
13.879	Medical Library Assistance	✓	✓	✓	✓	✓		✓	✓		✓	✓	✓	✓	✓
13.880	Minority Access to Research Careers	✓	✓		✓			✓	✓		✓			✓	✓

appendix continues

Appendix B *(continued)*
Programs providing outlays to each recipient category

Catalog Number	Program Title	State Gov't.	Interstate Agencies	Counties	Cities/Towns	Special Districts	Schools	State Higher Education	Private Higher Education	Indian Tribes	Nonprofits	For Profits	Small Businesses	Individuals	All Others
13.884	Grants for Residency Training in General Internal Medicine	✓	✓		✓			✓	✓		✓				
13.886	Grants for Physician Assistant Training Program	✓	✓		✓			✓	✓		✓	✓			
13.888	Home Health Services and Training	✓	✓	✓	✓	✓		✓		✓	✓	✓	✓		
13.891	Alcohol Research Center Grants	✓	✓		✓			✓	✓		✓				
13.894	Resource and Manpower Development in the Environment	✓	✓		✓			✓	✓		✓	✓		✓	✓
13.895	Grants for Faculty Developmentin Family Medicine	✓		✓	✓			✓	✓		✓	✓	✓		
13.897	Residency Training and Advanced Education	✓	✓	✓	✓			✓	✓		✓				
13.900	Grants for Faculty Developmentin General Internal Medicine	✓		✓	✓			✓	✓		✓				
13.960	Social Security Payments to States for Determination of Disability	✓													
13.962	Health Administration Graduate Traineeships	✓	✓		✓			✓	✓		✓				✓
13.963	Graduate Programs in Health Administration	✓	✓		✓			✓	✓		✓				
13.964	Traineeships for Students in Schools of Public Health	✓	✓					✓	✓		✓				
13.965	Coal Miners Respiratory Impairment Treatment Clinic	✓	✓	✓	✓			✓			✓				
13.969	Grants for the Training of Health Professions in Government	✓						✓	✓		✓				
13.970	Health Professions Recruitment Program for Indians	✓	✓	✓				✓					✓		
13.971	Health Professions Preparatory Scholarship Programs	✓	✓					✓			✓				✓
13.972	Health Professions Scholarship Program	✓		✓	✓		✓	✓	✓	✓	✓				✓
13.973	Special Loans for National Health Service Corps										✓				✓
13.974	Family Planning- Services Delivery Improvement	✓	✓		✓			✓	✓		✓	✓	✓		
13.977	Preventive Health Service-Sexually Trans. Diseases Control Grants	✓	✓	✓	✓			✓							
13.978	Preventive Health Service-Sexually Transmitted Diseases Research	✓	✓	✓	✓	✓		✓	✓		✓				
13.982	Mental Health Disaster Assistance and Emergency Medicine	✓									✓				
13.984	Grants for Establishment of Departments of Family	✓						✓	✓		✓				✓
13.985	Eye Research-Facility Construction	✓	✓					✓	✓		✓				✓
13.987	Health Programs for Refugees	✓	✓	✓	✓			✓			✓				
13.988	Cooperative Agreements for State-Based Diabetes Control Pgms.	✓						✓			✓				
13.989	Senior International Fellowships	✓	✓		✓			✓	✓		✓	✓	✓	✓	✓
13.990	National Health Promotion	✓			✓			✓	✓		✓	✓	✓		
13.991	Preventive Health and Health Services Block Grant	✓	✓	✓	✓			✓		✓					
13.992	Alcohol and Drug Abuse and Mental Health Services	✓	✓		✓			✓		✓	✓		✓		
13.994	Maternal and Child Health Services Block Grant	✓	✓	✓	✓	✓		✓	✓		✓	✓	✓		✓
13.995	Adolescent Family Life- Demonstration Projects	✓		✓	✓	✓		✓	✓	✓	✓		✓		
13.996	Policy Research Program	✓	✓	✓	✓			✓	✓		✓	✓	✓	✓	✓
14.103	Interest Reduction Payments-Rental and Cooperative Housing											✓			
14.146	Public Housing	✓	✓	✓	✓	✓				✓					✓
14.149	Rent Supplements-Rental Housing for Lower Income Financing											✓			✓
14.156	Lower-Income Housing Assistance Program	✓	✓	✓	✓	✓		✓	✓	✓	✓	✓	✓	✓	✓
14.157	Housing for the Elderly or Handicapped		✓	✓	✓	✓		✓		✓	✓	✓		✓	✓
14.167	Mortgage Insurance-Two Year Operating Loss Loans		✓					✓			✓	✓		✓	✓
14.169	Housing Counseling Assistance Program				✓						✓				
14.174	Housing Development Grants			✓	✓										
14.178	Supportive Housing Demonstration Program	✓				✓		✓							
14.218	Community Development Block Grants/Entitlement	✓	✓	✓	✓			✓							
14.219	Community Development Block Grants/Small Cities		✓	✓	✓	✓		✓							✓
14.221	Urban Development Action Grants		✓	✓	✓	✓		✓		✓					
14.223	Indian Community Development Block Grant Program									✓					
14.225	Community Development Block Grants/Special Purpose Insular Area	✓								✓					
14.227	Comm. Development Block Grants/Special Purpose Tech. Assist.	✓	✓	✓	✓										
14.228	Community Development Block Grants/State's Program	✓				✓		✓							
14.229	Community Development Block Grants/Sec. Discretionary Fund	✓	✓	✓	✓					✓					
14.230	Rental Housing Rehabilitation	✓		✓	✓	✓		✓		✓					
14.231	Emergency Shelter Grants Program	✓			✓	✓		✓							
14.232	Comm. Develop. Block Grant/Sec. Discretionary Fund Sp. Projects	✓		✓				✓				✓			
14.400	Equal Opportunity in Housing									✓					
14.506	General Research and Technology Activity	✓		✓	✓			✓							✓
14.510	Supplemental Assistance for Facilities to Assist the Homeless				✓			✓			✓				

appendix continues

Appendix B *(continued)*
Programs providing outlays to each recipient category

Catalog Number	Program Title	State Gov't.	Interstate Agencies	Counties	Cities/Towns	Special Districts	Ind. School Districts	State Higher Education	Private Higher Education	Indian Tribes	Nonprofits	For Profits	Small Businesses	Individuals	All Others
14.850	Public and Indian Housing	✓	✓	✓	✓	✓		✓		✓	✓				✓
14.851	Low Income Housing-Homeownership Opportunities	✓		✓	✓	✓		✓		✓					
14.852	Public and Indian Housing-Comprehensive Improvement	✓		✓	✓	✓		✓		✓					
14.999	Public and Indian Housing-Comprehensive Improvement Assistance		✓	✓	✓	✓						✓		✓	✓
15.142	Self Determination Grants-Indian Tribal Government									✓					
15.143	Training and Technical Assistance-Indian Tribal Government									✓					
15.144	Indian Child Welfare Act-Title II Grants									✓					
15.145	Indian Grants-Economic Development									✓					
15.215	Sale of Mineral Material	✓													
15.219	Wildlife Habitat Management Technical Assistance	✓													
15.221	Cooperative Agreements for Research in Public Land	✓						✓			✓				✓
15.250	Regulation of Surface Coal Mining and Surface Effects	✓	✓					✓		✓	✓				
15.252	Abandoned Mine Land Reclamation (AMLR) Program	✓	✓			✓		✓		✓					
15.308	Grants for Mining and Mineral Resources and Research	✓	✓					✓	✓		✓				
15.419	HCRS/NPRA Park Practice Program				✓										
15.505	National Water Research Program	✓			✓	✓		✓	✓				✓		✓
15.600	Anadromous Fish Conservation	✓				✓		✓							
15.605	Sport Fish Restoration	✓									✓				
15.606	Migratory Bird Banding and Data Analysis	✓													
15.611	Wildlife Restoration	✓						✓	✓						
15.612	Endangered Species Conservation	✓						✓							
15.613	Marine Mammal Grant Program	✓													
15.800	Geologic and Mineral Resource Surveys and Mapping	✓	✓		✓		✓	✓	✓		✓	✓	✓		✓
15.801	Cartographic Information, Geologic Information, Hydrologic Info.										✓				
15.803	National Mapping, Geography and Surveys	✓									✓				
15.804	Water Resources Investigations	✓	✓			✓		✓	✓		✓				
15.805	Assistance to State Water Resources Research Institutes	✓						✓	✓						
15.806	National Water Resources Research Program	✓		✓				✓	✓		✓	✓	✓		
15.807	Earthquake Hazards Reduction Program	✓			✓			✓	✓		✓	✓	✓	✓	
15.808	Geological Survey-Research and Data Acquisition	✓			✓	✓		✓	✓		✓	✓			
15.904	Historic Preservation Fund Grants-In-Aid	✓		✓				✓							
15.914	National Register of Historic Places	✓													
15.915	Technical Preservation Services	✓													
15.916	Outdoor Recreation-Acquisition, Development and Planning	✓	✓	✓	✓	✓	✓	✓		✓					
15.919	Urban Park and Recreation Recovery Program	✓	✓	✓	✓	✓		✓							
15.951	Water Research Assistance to State Institutes	✓													
15.999	Not in CFDA-Administered by Secretary of Interior	✓	✓	✓	✓	✓		✓	✓	✓	✓	✓		✓	✓
16.000	Secretary of Immigration and Naturalization Service										✓				
16.200	Community Relations Service										✓				
16.201	Cuban and Haitian Entrant Resettlement Program		✓					✓			✓	✓		✓	
16.530	Criminal Justice-Part D Formula Grants	✓													
16.531	Part F-Discretionary Grants	✓	✓	✓	✓			✓	✓	✓	✓	✓			
16.532	Part E-National Priority Program Grants	✓	✓		✓						✓				
16.533	Law Enforcement Assistance-Educational Development	✓													
16.534	Law Enforcement Assistance-Training	✓									✓				
16.535	Law Enforcement Assistance Administration										✓				
16.536	Crime Prevention-Mobilization of Public & Non-Public Resources										✓				
16.540	Juvenile Justice and Delinquency Prevention-State Allocation	✓													
16.541	Juvenile Justice and Delinquency Prevention-Special Emphasis	✓	✓	✓	✓		✓	✓	✓		✓	✓			
16.542	National Institute for Juvenile Justice and Delinquency	✓	✓		✓			✓	✓		✓	✓			
16.543	Missing Children's Assistance	✓		✓	✓			✓	✓		✓	✓			
16.550	Criminal Justice Statistcs Development	✓	✓	✓	✓			✓	✓		✓	✓		✓	
16.551	Statistics on Crime and Criminal Justice	✓										✓			
16.560	Justice Research and Development Project Grants	✓	✓	✓	✓	✓		✓	✓		✓	✓		✓	
16.561	National Institute of Justice Visiting Fellowships	✓		✓	✓			✓			✓			✓	
16.562	Criminal Justice Research and Development-Graduate Research							✓	✓					✓	

appendix continues

Appendix B *(continued)*
Programs providing outlays to each recipient category

Catalog Number	Program Title	State Gov't.	Interstate Agencies	Counties	Cities/Towns	Special Districts	Schools	State Higher Education	Private Higher Education	Indian Tribes	Nonprofits	For Profits	Small Businesses	Individuals	All Others
16.571	Public Safety Officers' Death Benefits Program										✓			✓	
16.572	Mariel-Cubans	✓													
16.573	Criminal Justice Block Grants	✓		✓	✓			✓							
16.574	Criminal Justice Discretionary Grant Program	✓		✓	✓			✓			✓				
16.575	Crime Victim Assistance	✓													
16.576	Crime Victim Compensation	✓													
16.577	Emergency Federal Law Enforcement Assistance	✓													
16.579	Drug Control and System Improvement-Formula Grant	✓		✓				✓							
16.580	Drug Control and System Improvement-Discretionary Grants	✓		✓	✓			✓	✓		✓	✓			
16.581	Drug Law Enforcement Programs-Prison Capacity	✓													
16.582	Crime Victim Assistance/Discretionary Grants	✓			✓			✓			✓				
16.583	Children's Justice Act Discretionary Grants									✓					
16.601	Corrections-Training and Staff Development	✓	✓	✓	✓			✓	✓		✓	✓		✓	✓
16.602	Corrections-Research and Evaluation and Policy	✓	✓		✓			✓	✓		✓	✓		✓	
16.603	Corrections-Technical Assistance/Clearinghouse	✓	✓	✓	✓	✓		✓	✓	✓	✓	✓		✓	✓
16.604	Corrections-Policy Formulation	✓	✓						✓		✓	✓		✓	
16.605	Corrections-Clearinghouse										✓				
16.999	Not in CFDA-Administered by Attorney General of United States	✓		✓	✓			✓	✓		✓	✓			
17.002	Labor Force Statistics	✓		✓	✓			✓	✓		✓				
17.100	Labor-Management Relations Services	✓	✓					✓			✓				
17.130	Labor-Management Relations and Cooperative Programs	✓						✓	✓		✓				✓
17.207	Employment Service	✓	✓	✓	✓					✓	✓				✓
17.225	Unemployment Insurance	✓	✓	✓	✓										
17.230	Migrant and Seasonal Farmworkers	✓	✓	✓	✓	✓	✓	✓		✓	✓	✓	✓		✓
17.232	Comprehensive Employment and Training Programs	✓	✓	✓	✓	✓		✓		✓	✓	✓			✓
17.233	Employment and Training Research and Development	✓	✓	✓				✓	✓		✓	✓	✓		✓
17.234	Employment and Training-Indians and Native America	✓	✓	✓	✓	✓				✓	✓				✓
17.235	Senior Community Service Employment Program	✓	✓	✓	✓	✓		✓		✓	✓	✓			✓
17.245	Trade Adjustment Assistance-Workers	✓													
17.246	Employment and Training Assistance-Dislocated Workers	✓	✓							✓	✓				✓
17.247	Migrant and Seasonal Farmworkers	✓	✓	✓		✓		✓		✓	✓				✓
17.248	Employment and Training Research and Development	✓	✓					✓			✓	✓		✓	✓
17.249	Employment Services and Job Training-Demonstration Programs											✓			
17.250	Job Training Partnership Act	✓	✓	✓						✓	✓				✓
17.251	Native American Employment and Training Programs	✓	✓		✓					✓	✓	✓			✓
17.301	Non-Discrimination and Affirmative Action by Federal Contractors							✓							
17.302	Longshore and Harbor Workers' Compensation													✓	
17.307	Coal Mine Workers' Compensation													✓	
17.400	Trade Adjustment Assistance-Workers	✓													
17.500	Occupational Safety and Health	✓	✓		✓			✓	✓	✓	✓				✓
17.501	Employee Assistance Programs-Drug, Alcohol Abuse				✓	✓	✓	✓			✓				✓
17.600	Mine Health and Safety Grants	✓	✓								✓				
17.602	Mine Health and Safety Education and Training	✓													
17.700	Women's Special Employment Assistance	✓			✓			✓		✓	✓				
17.801	Disabled Veterans Outreach Program	✓													
17.802	Veterans Employment Program	✓	✓	✓	✓	✓		✓	✓	✓	✓	✓			✓
17.805	Homeless Verterans Employment and Training	✓		✓	✓			✓							✓
17.999	Not in CFDA-Administered by Department of Labor	✓	✓		✓			✓			✓			✓	✓
20.004	Administered by Secretary of Transportation	✓													
20.005	Boating Safety Financial Assistance	✓						✓			✓				
20.102	Airport Development Aid Program	✓	✓	✓	✓	✓					✓				
20.103	Airport Planning Grant Program	✓	✓	✓	✓	✓									
20.106	Airport Improvement Program	✓	✓	✓	✓	✓	✓	✓		✓	✓	✓	✓	✓	✓
20.107	Airway Science							✓	✓						
20.205	Highway Planning and Construction	✓						✓							
20.214	Highway Beautification-Control of Outdoor Advertising	✓													

appendix continues

Appendix B *(continued)*
Programs providing outlays to each recipient category

Catalog Number	Program Title	State Gov't.	Interstate Agencies	Counties	Cities/Towns	Special Districts	Ind. School Districts	State Higher Education	Private Higher Education	Indian Tribes	Nonprofits	For Profits	Small Businesses	Individuals	All Others
20.218	Motor Carrier Safety Assistance Program	✓													
20.303	Grants-in-Aid for Railroad Safety-State Participation	✓													
20.308	Local Rail Service Assistance	✓													
20.500	Urban Mass Transportation-Capital Improvement Grant	✓	✓	✓	✓	✓		✓		✓	✓	✓			✓
20.502	Urban Mass Transportation-Grants for University Research	✓				✓		✓	✓						
20.503	Urban Mass Transportation-Managerial Training Grant	✓	✓	✓	✓	✓		✓			✓	✓			✓
20.504	Mass Transportation Technology	✓	✓	✓		✓				✓	✓	✓			
20.505	Urban Mass Transportation-Technical Studies Grants	✓	✓	✓	✓	✓		✓		✓	✓	✓			✓
20.507	Urban Mass Transportation-Capital and Operating Asst.	✓	✓	✓	✓	✓		✓		✓	✓	✓			✓
20.509	Public Transportation for Non-urbanized Areas	✓	✓		✓	✓		✓				✓			
20.511	Human Resource Programs	✓	✓	✓	✓	✓		✓	✓		✓	✓			
20.512	Urban Mass Transportation Technical Assistance	✓	✓	✓	✓	✓		✓	✓		✓	✓			✓
20.513	Capital Assistance Program for Elderly and Handicapped	✓			✓			✓			✓				
20.600	State and Community Highway Safety	✓	✓	✓	✓			✓	✓		✓				✓
20.700	Pipeline Safety	✓													
20.804	Operating-Differential Subsidies											✓			
20.806	State Marine Schools	✓						✓							
20.811	Research and Development Assistance	✓	✓					✓			✓	✓			
20.901	Payments for Essential Air Services											✓			
20.902	University Transportation Centers Program							✓	✓						
20.999	Not in CFDA-Administered by Department of Transportation	✓									✓				
21.006	Tax Counseling for the Elderly										✓				
21.300	State and Local Government Fiscal Assistance-Revenue Sharing	✓	✓	✓	✓			✓		✓	✓				
23.001	Appalachian Regional Development	✓	✓	✓		✓					✓				
23.004	Appalachian Health Programs	✓	✓	✓	✓	✓		✓	✓		✓		✓		
23.005	Appalachian Housing Project Planning Loan	✓	✓		✓						✓				
23.009,	Appalachian Local Development District Assistance	✓	✓			✓		✓			✓	✓			
23.011	Appalachian State Research, Technical Assistance	✓	✓	✓	✓	✓	✓	✓	✓	✓	✓	✓	✓	✓	✓
23.012	Appalachian Vocational and Other Education Facility	✓		✓				✓			✓				
23.017	Appalachian Special Transportation Related Planning	✓	✓	✓	✓	✓					✓				✓
26.001	Air Carrier Payments											✓			
26.003	Payments for Essential Air Services											✓			
30.001	Employment Discrimination-Title VII of the Civil Rights Act				✓										
30.002	Employ. Discrimination-State and Local Anti-Discrimination	✓	✓	✓	✓			✓							
30.009	Employment Discrimination Project Contracts-Indian Tribes									✓					
39.006	National Historical Publications and Records Grant	✓	✓	✓	✓				✓	✓	✓				✓
43.999	Research Grants-Administered by NASA	✓		✓	✓			✓	✓		✓	✓			✓
45.001	Promotion of the Arts-Design Arts	✓		✓	✓			✓	✓		✓			✓	
45.002	Promotion of the Arts-Dance	✓			✓			✓	✓		✓			✓	
45.003	Promotion of the Arts-Arts in Education	✓		✓	✓	✓		✓	✓		✓				
45.004	Promotion of the Arts-Literature	✓		✓	✓			✓	✓		✓			✓	
45.005	Promotion of the Arts-Music	✓		✓	✓			✓	✓		✓			✓	
45.006	Promotion of the Arts-Media Arts: Film/Radio/Television	✓			✓			✓	✓		✓			✓	
45.007	Promotion of the Arts-State Program	✓						✓			✓				
45.008	Promotion of the Arts-Theater	✓			✓			✓	✓		✓			✓	
45.009	Promotion of the Arts-Visual Arts	✓		✓	✓			✓	✓		✓			✓	
45.010	Promotion of the Arts-Expansion Arts	✓		✓	✓			✓	✓	✓	✓	✓			
45.011	Promotion of the Arts-Inter-Arts	✓		✓	✓			✓	✓		✓				✓
45.012	Promotion of the Arts-Museums	✓		✓	✓			✓	✓		✓			✓	
45.013	Promotion of the Arts-Challenge Grants	✓			✓		✓	✓	✓		✓				
45.014	Promotion of the Arts-Opera-Musical Theater	✓						✓	✓		✓			✓	
45.015	Promotion of the Arts-Folk Arts	✓		✓	✓			✓	✓	✓	✓			✓	
45.021	Promotion of the Arts-Arts Administration Fellows							✓			✓			✓	
45.022	Promotion of the Arts-Advancement Grants										✓				
45.023	Promotion of the Arts-Local Program	✓		✓	✓			✓	✓		✓				

appendix continues

Appendix B *(continued)*
Programs providing outlays to each recipient category

Catalog Number	Program Title	State Gov't.	Interstate Agencies	Counties	Cities/Towns	Special Districts	Schools	State Higher Education	Private Higher Education	Indian Tribes	Nonprofits	For Profits	Small Businesses	Individuals	All Others
45.104	Promotion of the Humanities-Humanities Projects	✓	✓		✓		✓	✓	✓		✓				✓
45.111	Promotion of the Humanities-Exemplary Projects	✓	✓	✓			✓	✓	✓		✓				
45.113	Promotion of the Humanities-Public Humanities Projects	✓	✓		✓		✓	✓	✓	✓	✓			✓	
45.115	Promotion of the Humanities-Younger Scholars	✓	✓						✓					✓	
45.116	Promotion of the Humanities-Summer Seminars	✓	✓					✓	✓		✓				
45.121	Promotion of the Humanities-Summer Stipends													✓	
45.122	Promotion of the Humanities-Centers for Advanced Study	✓	✓					✓	✓		✓				
45.124	Promotion of the Humanities-Reference Materials	✓	✓	✓	✓			✓	✓		✓	✓		✓	
45.125	Promotion of the Humanities-Humanities Projects	✓	✓	✓	✓			✓	✓	✓	✓				
45.127	Promotion of the Humanities-Elementary and Secondary Schools	✓	✓	✓	✓		✓	✓	✓		✓		✓		
45.128	Promotion of the Humanities-Humanities Studies Programs	✓	✓					✓	✓		✓				
45.129	Promotion of the Humanities-State Programs	✓						✓			✓			✓	
45.130	Promotion of the Humanities-Challenge Grants	✓	✓	✓	✓		✓	✓	✓	✓	✓				
45.132	Promotion of the Humanities-Texts/Publication	✓	✓					✓	✓		✓				
45.133	Promotion of the Humanities-Interpretive Research	✓	✓				✓	✓	✓		✓			✓	
45.134	Promotion of the Humanities-Conferences	✓	✓		✓			✓	✓		✓			✓	
45.135	Promotion of the Humanities-Special Projects: Humanities	✓	✓		✓		✓	✓	✓	✓	✓				
45.137	Promotion of the Humanities-Humanities Projects	✓	✓	✓	✓	✓	✓	✓	✓		✓				
45.140	Promotion of the Humanities-Interpretive Research	✓	✓		✓			✓	✓		✓			✓	
45.141	Promotion of the Humanities-Regional Studies	✓	✓					✓	✓		✓				
45.142	Promotion of the Humanities-Fellowships for Universities							✓			✓			✓	
45.143	Promotion of the Humanities-Fellowships for Colleges	✓						✓	✓		✓			✓	
45.145	Promotion of the Humanities-Reference Materials	✓	✓					✓	✓		✓			✓	
45.146	Promotion of the Humanities-Texts/Editions	✓	✓					✓	✓		✓			✓	
45.147	Promotion of the Humanities-Texts/Translations	✓	✓					✓	✓		✓			✓	
45.148	Promotion of the Humanities-International Research							✓			✓				
45.149	Promotion of the Humanities-Office of Preservation	✓	✓	✓	✓			✓	✓		✓			✓	
45.150	Promotion of the Humanities-Higher Education	✓	✓	✓	✓		✓	✓	✓		✓				
45.151	Promotion of the Humanities-Summer Seminars	✓	✓				✓	✓	✓		✓				
45.152	Promotion of the Humanities-Travel to Collections													✓	
45.155	National Capital Arts and Cultural Affairs										✓				
45.301	Institute of Museum Services	✓	✓	✓	✓	✓		✓	✓	✓	✓	✓			✓
47.009	Graduate Research Fellowships	✓	✓	✓				✓	✓		✓			✓	✓
47.036	Intergovernmental Science and Technology Programs	✓	✓						✓		✓			✓	✓
47.041	Engineering Grants	✓	✓	✓	✓			✓	✓		✓	✓	✓	✓	✓
47.049	Mathematical and Physical Sciences	✓	✓	✓	✓		✓	✓	✓		✓	✓	✓	✓	✓
47.050	Geosciences	✓	✓	✓	✓			✓	✓		✓	✓	✓	✓	✓
47.051	Biological, Behavioral, and Social Sciences	✓	✓	✓	✓			✓	✓	✓	✓	✓	✓	✓	✓
47.053	Scientific, Technological, and International Affairs	✓	✓	✓	✓			✓	✓		✓	✓	✓	✓	✓
47.055	Two-Year and Four-Year College Research Instrumentation	✓	✓						✓						
47.057	Minority Research Initiation	✓	✓						✓						
47.059	Visiting Professorships for Women	✓	✓	✓					✓		✓				✓
47.060	Research Improvement in Minority Institutions	✓	✓	✓					✓						
47.063	Precollege Science and Mathematics Education	✓	✓	✓					✓		✓	✓		✓	✓
47.064	College Science Instrumentation			✓				✓	✓		✓	✓			✓
47.065	Advanced Scientific Computing	✓			✓			✓	✓		✓	✓	✓		✓
47.066	Teacher Preparation and Enhancement	✓		✓	✓		✓	✓	✓		✓	✓	✓		✓
47.067	Materials Development, Research, and Informal Science	✓		✓	✓		✓	✓	✓		✓	✓	✓		✓
47.068	Studies and Program Assessment	✓						✓	✓		✓	✓			
47.069	Research Initiation and Improvement	✓						✓	✓		✓				✓
47.070	Computer and Information Science and Engineering			✓				✓	✓		✓	✓	✓		✓
47.071	Undergraduate Science, Engineering and Mathematics				✓			✓	✓		✓	✓			
47.072	Young Scholars	✓		✓				✓	✓		✓				✓
47.073	Science and Technology Centers							✓	✓						
53.001	Employment Promotion of People with Disabilities							✓	✓		✓				
57.001	Social Insurance for Railroad Workers													✓	

appendix continues

Appendix B *(continued)*
Programs providing outlays to each recipient category

Catalog Number	Program Title	State Gov't.	Interstate Agencies	Counties	Cities/Towns	Special Districts	Ind. School Districts	State Higher Education	Private Higher Education	Indian Tribes	Nonprofits	For Profits	Small Businesses	Individuals	All Others
57.002	Benefits for Milwaukee Railroad Workers													✓	
57.003	Benefits for Conrail Employees													✓	
57.004	Benefits for Rock Island Railroad Emloyees													✓	
57.999	Not in CFDA-Administered by Conrail													✓	
59.007	Management and Technical Assistance	✓	✓					✓		✓	✓	✓	✓		
59.011	Small Business Investment Companies												✓		
59.026	Service Corps of Retired Executives Association	✓									✓				
59.032	Office of Women's Business Ownership										✓				
59.034	Small Business Economic Research	✓													
59.037	Small Business Development Center	✓						✓	✓		✓	✓			
60.001	Smithsonian Institution Programs in Basic Research													✓	
60.007	Museums-Assistance and Advice	✓	✓	✓	✓	✓		✓	✓	✓	✓				✓
63.007	Upper Great Lakes Health and Nutrition Demonstration										✓				
64.005	Grants to States for Construction of State Home Farms	✓													
64.014	Veterans State Domiciliary Care	✓													
64.015	Veterans State Nursing Home Care	✓													
64.016	Veterans State Hospital Care	✓													
64.023	Health Professional Scholarships-Nursing													✓	
64.100	Automobiles and Adaptive Equipment for Certain Disabilities													✓	
64.101	Burial Expenses Allowance for Veterans													✓	
64.102	Compensation for Service-Connected Deaths													✓	
64.104	Pension for Non-Service-Connected Disability for Veterans													✓	
64.105	Pension to Veterans Surviving Spouses, and Children													✓	
64.106	Specially Adapted Housing for Disabled Veterans													✓	
64.109	Veterans Compensation for Service-Connected Disabilities													✓	
64.110	Veterans Dependency and Indemnity Compensation													✓	
64.111	Veterans Educational Assistance													✓	
64.116	Vocational Rehabilitation for Disabled Veterans													✓	
64.117	Survivors and Dependents Educational Assistance													✓	
64.120	Post-Vietnam Era Veterans' Educational Assistance													✓	
64.121	Veterans' Job Training Act													✓	
64.124	All-Volunteer Force Educational Assistance													✓	
64.203	State Cemetery Grants	✓													
66.001	Air Pollution Control Program Support	✓	✓	✓	✓	✓		✓		✓	✓				
66.002	Air Pollution Fellowships							✓							
66.003	Air Pollution Control ManpowerTraining	✓	✓					✓	✓		✓				
66.027	Name unknown, Administered by Director of EPA	✓													
66.030	Noise Pollution Control-Technical Assistance	✓	✓						✓						✓
66.418	Construction Grants for Wastewater Treatment Works	✓	✓	✓	✓	✓		✓	✓	✓	✓	✓			✓
66.419	Water Pollution Control-State and Interstate Program	✓	✓	✓	✓	✓		✓		✓	✓				✓
66.425	Drinking Water Supply-Technical Assistance	✓	✓			✓		✓	✓		✓				✓
66.426	Water Pollution Control-State and Areawide Water Quality	✓	✓	✓		✓		✓		✓	✓				
66.428	Water Pollution Control-Professional Training Grants	✓	✓		✓		✓	✓	✓		✓			✓	✓
66.429	Water Pollution Control-Technical Training Grants	✓	✓					✓	✓		✓			✓	
66.430	Water Pollution Control Fellowships													✓	
66.432	State Public Water System Supervision	✓	✓	✓	✓	✓		✓	✓	✓	✓				✓
66.433	State Underground Water Source Protection	✓	✓		✓	✓		✓	✓	✓	✓				
66.434	Safe Drinking Water										✓				
66.435	Water Pollution Control-Lake Restoration Cooperative Agreements	✓			✓			✓		✓					
66.438	Construction Management Assistance	✓	✓		✓	✓		✓							
66.451	Hazardous Waste Management Financial Assistance	✓	✓	✓											
66.452	Solid Waste Management Demonstration Grants														✓
66.453	Solid Waste Management Training Grants	✓													
66.454	Water Quality Management Planning	✓													
66.455	Construction Grants for Abatement of Combined Sewer Overflow	✓			✓	✓		✓							
66.456	National Estuary Program	✓				✓		✓		✓	✓				

appendix continues

Appendix B *(continued)*
Programs providing outlays to each recipient category

Catalog Number	Program Title	State Gov't.	Interstate Agencies	Counties	Cities/Towns	Special Districts	Schools	State Higher Education	Private Higher Education	Indian Tribes	Nonprofits	For Profits	Small Businesses	Individuals	All Others
66.458	Capitalization Grants for State Revolving Funds	✓			✓			✓							
66.459	Nonpoint Source Reservation	✓													
66.500	Environmental Protection-Consolidated Research	✓	✓		✓	✓		✓	✓		✓	✓			✓
66.501	Air Pollution Control Research	✓	✓	✓	✓	✓	✓	✓	✓		✓	✓			✓
66.502	Pesticides Control Research	✓	✓					✓	✓		✓				
66.504	Solid Waste Disposal Research	✓	✓		✓	✓		✓	✓		✓				✓
66.505	Water Pollution Control-Research, Development & Demonstration	✓	✓	✓	✓	✓	✓	✓	✓	✓	✓	✓		✓	✓
66.506	Safe Drinking Water Research and Demonstration	✓	✓	✓	✓	✓		✓	✓		✓	✓		✓	✓
66.507	Toxic Substances Research	✓	✓	✓		✓		✓	✓		✓	✓			✓
66.508	Senior Environmental Employment Program							✓			✓				
66.600	Environmental Protection Consolidated Grants-Program Support	✓	✓			✓		✓		✓					
66.602	Environmental Protection Consolidated Grants-Special Purpose										✓				
66.700	Consolidated Pesticide Compliance Monitoring	✓	✓					✓		✓	✓				
66.701	Toxic Substances Compliance Monitoring Program	✓													
66.702	Asbestos Hazard Abatement (Schools) Assistance	✓		✓	✓		✓	✓			✓				✓
66.703	Asbestos Inspection and Management Plan Assistance	✓													
66.801	Hazardous Waste Management State Program Support	✓			✓			✓			✓				
66.802	Hazardous Substance Response Trust Fund	✓			✓	✓		✓		✓	✓				✓
66.804	State Underground Storage Tanks Program	✓				✓		✓			✓				
66.805	Underground Storage Tank Trust Fund Program Groups	✓													
66.806	Superfund Technical Assistance Grants for Citizen Grants										✓				
66.999	Not in CFDA-Administered by EPA	✓	✓	✓	✓	✓	✓	✓	✓	✓	✓	✓		✓	✓
72.001	Foster Grandparent Program	✓	✓	✓	✓	✓	✓	✓	✓	✓	✓		✓	✓	✓
72.002	Retired Senior Volunteer Program	✓	✓	✓	✓	✓	✓	✓	✓	✓	✓				✓
72.003	Volunteers in Service to America	✓	✓	✓	✓	✓	✓	✓	✓	✓	✓	✓			✓
72.004	University Year for Action	✓									✓				
72.005	Student Community Service Program	✓	✓	✓	✓	✓	✓	✓	✓	✓	✓				✓
72.008	Senior Companion Program	✓	✓	✓	✓	✓	✓	✓	✓	✓	✓				✓
72.010	Minigrant Program	✓	✓	✓	✓	✓	✓	✓		✓	✓				
72.011	State Office of Voluntarism	✓	✓	✓							✓				
72.012	Volunteer Demonstration Program	✓	✓	✓	✓	✓	✓	✓	✓	✓	✓				
72.013	Technical Assistance Program	✓	✓	✓	✓		✓		✓		✓				
72.014	Drug Alliance	✓	✓		✓		✓	✓			✓				✓
72.015	Literacy Corps										✓				
77.001	Radiation Control-Training Assistance and Advisory Counseling	✓	✓								✓				
77.003	Enhance Technology Transfer and Dissemination	✓	✓					✓	✓		✓				
77.999	Research Grants-Administered by the NRC	✓		✓	✓			✓	✓		✓				
81.004	University-Laboratory Cooperative Program	✓	✓	✓				✓	✓		✓				
81.007	Teacher Development Projects in Energy	✓	✓			✓		✓	✓			✓			
81.011	University Reactor Sharing and Fuel Assistance	✓	✓					✓	✓		✓				✓
81.023	Information Services-Exhibits, Public Speakers and Publications	✓	✓		✓				✓		✓		✓		
81.035	Research and Development in Energy Conservation	✓	✓					✓	✓			✓		✓	✓
81.036	Energy-Related Inventions	✓	✓	✓				✓	✓		✓	✓	✓	✓	✓
81.037	Research and Develop.-Fission, Fossil, Solar, Geothermal, Electric	✓	✓	✓	✓		✓	✓	✓			✓	✓	✓	✓
81.040	Grants for Offices of Consumer Services	✓													
81.041	State Energy Conservation	✓	✓				✓	✓			✓		✓		✓
81.042	Weatherization Assistance for Low-Income Persons	✓	✓	✓	✓		✓	✓	✓	✓	✓	✓	✓		✓
81.043	Supplemental State Energy Conservation	✓													
81.044	Public Education in Energy										✓				
81.045	Special Studies and Project in Energy Education														✓
81.046	Research and Development in Biomedical and Environmental Sci.			✓											
81.047	Pre-Freshman Enrichment	✓	✓					✓	✓		✓				✓
81.049	Basic Energy Sciences, High Energy and Nuclear Physics	✓	✓		✓		✓	✓	✓		✓	✓	✓	✓	✓
81.050	Energy Extension Service	✓	✓							✓	✓	✓			✓
81.051	Appropriate Energy Technology	✓	✓	✓	✓	✓	✓	✓	✓	✓	✓	✓	✓	✓	✓
81.052	Energy Conservation for Institutional Buildings	✓	✓	✓	✓	✓	✓	✓	✓	✓	✓	✓	✓	✓	✓

appendix continues

Appendix B *(continued)*
Programs providing outlays to each recipient category

Catalog Number	Program Title	State Gov't.	Interstate Agencies	Counties	Cities/Towns	Special Districts	Ind. School Districts	State Higher Education	Private Higher Education	Indian Tribes	Nonprofits	For Profits	Small Businesses	Individuals	All Others
81.053	Public Utility Regulatory Innovative Rates Support	✓	✓		✓				✓						
81.054	Public Utility Regulatory Support	✓	✓	✓				✓	✓			✓			✓
81.055	Small Hydroelectric Power Project Feasibility Study	✓	✓		✓						✓	✓			✓
81.056	Coal Loan Guarantees								✓			✓			
81.057	University Coal Research	✓	✓			✓		✓	✓		✓	✓	✓		✓
81.058	Geothermal Loan Guarantees				✓						✓				
81.061	Oil Shale State Grants	✓		✓				✓							
81.063	Office of Minority Economic Impact Loans							✓					✓		
81.065	Nuclear Waste Disposal Siting	✓	✓	✓				✓	✓	✓	✓	✓	✓		✓
81.071	Emergency Energy Conservation Act Plans	✓													
81.073	Emergency Energy Conservation Education Programs	✓	✓	✓								✓			✓
81.074	Alcohol Fuels Loan Guarantees									✓		✓			
81.075	Energy Graduate Traineeship Program	✓	✓					✓	✓						
81.076	Indian Energy Resources (CERT)	✓								✓					
81.077	University Research Instrumentation	✓	✓					✓	✓		✓				
81.078	Industrial Energy Conservation	✓	✓			✓	✓	✓	✓		✓	✓	✓		✓
81.079	Biofuels and Municipal Waste Technology	✓	✓								✓				
81.080	Energy Policy, Planning and Development	✓	✓					✓	✓		✓				
81.081	Energy Task Force for the Urban Consortium	✓	✓	✓	✓	✓		✓			✓	✓			
81.083	Minority Educational Institution Research Travel Fund							✓							
81.084	Minority Honors Training and Industrial Assistance	✓		✓	✓		✓	✓	✓		✓			✓	
81.086	Conservation Research and Development	✓	✓		✓	✓		✓	✓		✓	✓	✓	✓	
81.087	Renewable Energy Research and Development	✓	✓		✓		✓	✓	✓		✓	✓	✓		✓
81.088	International Affairs and Energy Emergencies							✓	✓		✓	✓			
81.089	Fossil Energy Research and Development	✓	✓					✓	✓	✓	✓	✓	✓		
81.090	State Heating Oil Grants	✓													
81.091	Socioeconomic and Demographic Research and Data	✓													
81.092	Environmental Restoration	✓		✓		✓		✓		✓	✓				✓
81.093	Nuclear Energy Policy, Planning and Development							✓			✓				
81.094	Minority Educational Institution Assistance							✓	✓						
81.095	Nuclear Energy, Reactor Systems, Development				✓				✓						
81.096	Clean Coal Technology Program										✓				
81.999	Not in CFDA-Administered by Department of Energy	✓	✓	✓	✓		✓	✓	✓	✓	✓	✓	✓	✓	✓
83.002	State Fire Incident Reporting Assistance	✓	✓		✓										
83.003	Public Education Assistance Program	✓	✓								✓				
83.004	Technical Support Services								✓						
83.005	Arson Task Force Assistance Program										✓				
83.008	Community-Based Anti-Arson Program	✓			✓	✓		✓				✓		✓	✓
83.103	State Assistance-National Flood Insurance Program	✓													
83.203	State Disaster Preparedness Grants	✓													
83.205	Industrial Preparedness Training										✓				
83.400	Emergency Management Institute-Training Assistance	✓			✓			✓			✓				✓
83.402	Emergency Management Institute-Radiological Emergency								✓						✓
83.403	Emergency Management Institute-Field Training Program	✓									✓				
83.405	National Fire Academy-Training Assistance	✓			✓			✓	✓		✓				
83.406	National Emergency Training Center-Training Program	✓		✓					✓		✓				✓
83.407	State Fire Incident Reporting Assistance	✓		✓	✓		✓	✓	✓						
83.409	Reimbursement for Firefighting on Federal Property														
83.410	Community-Based Anti-Arson Program	✓	✓	✓	✓			✓	✓		✓				✓
83.500	General Research, Development,and Demonstration Activity	✓	✓		✓			✓	✓	✓	✓			✓	✓
83.501	State Assistance Program	✓	✓					✓	✓		✓				
83.503	Civil Defense-State and Local Emergency Management										✓				✓
83.504	Other State and Local Direction, Control and Warning				✓						✓				
83.505	State Disaster Preparedness Grants	✓	✓	✓	✓		✓	✓	✓		✓				
83.506	Earthquake and Hurricane Preparedness Grants	✓	✓	✓				✓	✓		✓				✓
83.512	State and Local Emergency Operating Centers	✓	✓	✓	✓			✓			✓				

appendix continues

Appendix B *(continued)*
Programs providing outlays to each recipient category

Catalog Number	Program Title	State Gov't.	Interstate Agencies	Counties	Cities/Towns	Special Districts	Schools	State Higher Education	Private Higher Education	Indian Tribes	Nonprofits	For Profits	Small Businesses	Individuals	All Others
83.513	State and Local Warning and Communication Systems	✓	✓	✓	✓	✓		✓	✓		✓				
83.514	Population Protection Planning				✓										
83.515	Emergency Broadcast System Guidance and Assistance	✓			✓			✓			✓	✓			✓
83.516	Disaster Assistance	✓	✓	✓	✓	✓		✓			✓			✓	
83.519	Hazard Mitigation Assistance			✓				✓	✓	✓					
83.521	Earthquake Hazards Reduction Grants	✓													
83.999	Not in CFDA-Administered by FEMA	✓	✓	✓				✓				✓			
84.001	Academic Facilities Reconstruction and Renovation	✓	✓	✓	✓	✓	✓	✓	✓		✓	✓	✓		✓
84.002	Adult Education-State-Administered Basic Grant Program	✓	✓				✓								
84.003	Bilingual Education	✓	✓	✓	✓	✓	✓	✓	✓	✓	✓	✓	✓	✓	✓
84.004	Desegregation Assistance, Civil Rights Training	✓	✓	✓	✓		✓	✓	✓		✓	✓			
84.005	College Library Resources	✓	✓	✓	✓	✓	✓		✓	✓	✓		✓		✓
84.007	Supplemental Educational Opportunity Grants	✓	✓	✓	✓		✓	✓	✓	✓	✓	✓	✓		
84.008	Alcohol and Drug Abuse Education	✓									✓				
84.009	Education of Handicapped Children in State Operated Institutions	✓	✓	✓			✓	✓							
84.010	Educationally Deprived Children-Local Educational Agencies	✓	✓	✓			✓	✓							
84.011	Migrant Education-Basic State Formula Grant Program	✓	✓	✓			✓	✓							
84.012	Educationally Deprived Children-State Administration	✓	✓	✓			✓	✓							
84.013	Neglected and Delinquent Children	✓	✓	✓			✓	✓						✓	
84.014	Follow Through	✓	✓	✓	✓		✓	✓	✓	✓	✓	✓			✓
84.015	National Resource Centers and Fellowships Program	✓	✓	✓			✓	✓	✓		✓				
84.016	Undergraduate International Studies and Foreign Language	✓	✓	✓	✓		✓	✓	✓		✓				✓
84.017	International Research and Studies	✓	✓	✓				✓	✓		✓	✓		✓	
84.019	Fulbright-Hays Training Grants-Faculty Research Abroad	✓	✓	✓	✓			✓	✓						
84.020	Fulbright-Hays Training Grants-Foreign Curriculum	✓	✓	✓				✓	✓						
84.021	Fulbright-Hays Training Grants-Group Projects Abroad	✓	✓	✓	✓			✓	✓	✓	✓				✓
84.022	Fulbright-Hays Training Grants-Doctoral Dissertation Abroad	✓	✓	✓	✓			✓	✓	✓	✓				
84.023	Handicapped-Innovation and Development	✓	✓	✓	✓		✓	✓	✓		✓		✓		✓
84.024	Handicapped Early Childhood Education	✓	✓	✓	✓	✓	✓	✓	✓	✓	✓	✓	✓		✓
84.025	Handicapped Education-Deaf-Blind Centers	✓	✓	✓	✓			✓	✓		✓				
84.026	Handicapped Media Services and Captioned Films	✓	✓	✓	✓		✓	✓	✓		✓	✓	✓	✓	✓
84.027	Handicapped-State Grants	✓	✓	✓			✓	✓		✓					
84.028	Handicapped Regional Resource and Federal Centers										✓				
84.029	Handicapped Education-Special Education Personnel	✓	✓	✓	✓	✓	✓	✓	✓	✓	✓	✓	✓		✓
84.030	Clearinghouses for the Handicapped Program			✓							✓				
84.031	Higher Education-Institutional Aid	✓	✓	✓	✓		✓	✓	✓	✓	✓		✓	✓	
84.033	College Work-Study Program	✓	✓	✓	✓		✓	✓	✓	✓	✓	✓	✓		
84.034	Library Services	✓	✓	✓			✓	✓			✓				
84.035	Interlibrary Cooperation and Resource Sharing	✓	✓	✓			✓	✓			✓				✓
84.036	Library Career Training	✓	✓	✓	✓			✓	✓						
84.037	National Defense/Direct Student Loan Cancellations	✓	✓	✓	✓		✓	✓	✓		✓	✓	✓		
84.038	Perkins Loan Program	✓	✓	✓	✓		✓	✓	✓		✓	✓	✓		
84.039	Library Research and Demonstration			✓	✓			✓	✓						
84.040	Impact Aid-Construction			✓	✓		✓								
84.041	Impact Aid-Maintenance and Operation	✓	✓	✓	✓		✓	✓	✓	✓	✓	✓			✓
84.042	Student Support Services	✓	✓	✓	✓		✓	✓	✓	✓	✓	✓	✓		
84.044	Talent Search	✓	✓	✓	✓		✓	✓	✓	✓	✓	✓	✓		✓
84.047	Upward Bound	✓	✓	✓	✓		✓	✓	✓	✓	✓	✓	✓		✓
84.048	Vocational Education-Basic Grants to States	✓	✓	✓			✓	✓							
84.049	Vocational Education-Consumer and Homemaking Education	✓	✓	✓			✓	✓							
84.050	Vocational Education-Program Improvement and Support	✓	✓				✓	✓	✓	✓	✓				
84.051	National Vocational Education Research	✓	✓	✓	✓		✓	✓			✓	✓			
84.052	Vocational Education-Special Programs for the Disadvantaged	✓	✓				✓								
84.053	Vocational Education-State Councils	✓	✓	✓			✓								
84.055	Higher Education-Cooperative Education	✓	✓	✓	✓		✓	✓	✓		✓	✓			✓
84.060	Indian Education-Formula Grants to Local Educational Agencies	✓	✓	✓	✓	✓	✓	✓		✓	✓	✓	✓		✓

appendix continues

Appendix B *(continued)*
Programs providing outlays to each recipient category

Catalog Number	Program Title	State Gov't.	Interstate Agencies	Counties	Cities/Towns	Special Districts	Ind. School Districts	State Higher Education	Private Higher Education	Indian Tribes	Nonprofits	For Profits	Small Businesses	Individuals	All Others
84.061	Indian Education-Special Programs and Projects	✓	✓	✓	✓		✓	✓	✓	✓	✓		✓		✓
84.062	Indian Education-Adult Indian Education	✓	✓	✓				✓	✓	✓	✓	✓	✓		✓
84.063	Pell Grant Program	✓	✓	✓	✓	✓	✓	✓	✓	✓	✓	✓	✓	✓	✓
84.064	Higher Education-Veterans Education Outreach Program	✓	✓	✓	✓		✓	✓	✓		✓		✓		
84.065	Educational Television and Radio Programming											✓			
84.066	Educational Opportunity Centers	✓	✓	✓	✓			✓	✓		✓				✓
84.067	Use of Technology in Basic Skills Instruction											✓			
84.069	Grants to States for State Student Incentives	✓						✓	✓						
84.072	Indian Education-Grants to Indian Controlled Schools		✓	✓	✓		✓	✓		✓	✓	✓	✓		✓
84.073	National Diffusion Network	✓	✓	✓	✓	✓	✓	✓	✓		✓	✓	✓		✓
84.075	Public Service Education	✓	✓	✓	✓			✓	✓		✓				
84.077	Bilingual Vocational Training	✓	✓	✓	✓		✓	✓	✓		✓		✓	✓	✓
84.078	Postsecondary Education Programs for Handicapped Persons	✓	✓	✓	✓		✓	✓	✓		✓	✓			
84.083	Women's Educational Equity	✓	✓	✓	✓	✓	✓	✓	✓	✓	✓	✓	✓	✓	✓
84.084	Elementary and Secondary Education in the Arts										✓				
84.086	Handicapped Education-Severely Handicapped Program	✓	✓	✓	✓		✓	✓	✓		✓	✓			✓
84.087	Indian Education-Fellowships for Indian Students	✓	✓	✓	✓		✓	✓	✓	✓	✓				✓
84.091	Strengthening Research Library Resources	✓	✓	✓	✓			✓	✓		✓				✓
84.094	Patricia Roberts Harris Fellowships	✓	✓	✓	✓		✓	✓	✓		✓	✓			✓
84.097	Law School Clinical Experience Program	✓	✓	✓	✓		✓	✓	✓		✓		✓		✓
84.099	Bilingual Vocational Instructor Training	✓	✓	✓	✓		✓	✓	✓		✓				✓
84.100	Bilingual Vocational Materials, Methods, and Technology						✓				✓	✓			
84.101	Vocational Education-Indian and Hawaiian Natives	✓	✓	✓	✓		✓	✓	✓	✓	✓	✓	✓		✓
84.103	Training for Special Programs Staff and Leadership Personnel	✓	✓	✓				✓	✓		✓	✓	✓		✓
84.114	Capacity Building for Statistical Activities	✓	✓				✓				✓	✓		✓	
84.116	Fund for the Improvement of Postsecondary Education	✓	✓	✓	✓		✓	✓	✓	✓	✓	✓	✓	✓	✓
84.117	Educational Research and Development	✓	✓	✓	✓		✓	✓	✓		✓	✓	✓		
84.120	Minority Science Improvement	✓	✓	✓	✓		✓	✓	✓		✓			✓	✓
84.121	Vocational Education-State Planning and Evaluation	✓	✓				✓								
84.122	Secretary's Discretionary	✓	✓	✓	✓		✓	✓	✓	✓	✓	✓			
84.123	Law-Related Education	✓	✓	✓	✓		✓	✓	✓		✓	✓	✓		✓
84.126	Rehabilitation Services-Basic Support	✓	✓	✓			✓	✓			✓			✓	
84.128	Rehabilitation Services-Service Projects	✓	✓	✓	✓	✓	✓	✓	✓	✓	✓	✓	✓		✓
84.129	Rehabilitation Training	✓	✓	✓	✓		✓	✓	✓		✓	✓	✓		✓
84.132	Centers for Independent Living	✓	✓	✓				✓			✓	✓	✓		✓
84.133	National Institute on Disability and Rehabilitation Research	✓	✓	✓	✓		✓	✓	✓		✓	✓	✓	✓	✓
84.136	Legal Training for the Disadvantaged										✓	✓			
84.137	Not in CFDA-Administered by the Department of Education										✓				
84.138	Educational Services to Cuban and Haitian Entrants	✓													
84.141	Migrant Education-High School Equivalency Program	✓	✓	✓			✓	✓	✓		✓	✓			✓
84.142	College Facilities Loans	✓	✓	✓	✓		✓	✓	✓		✓	✓	✓		
84.144	Migrant Education-Coordination Program	✓	✓				✓								
84.146	Transition Program for Refugee Children	✓	✓	✓			✓	✓							
84.148	Allen J. Ellender Fellowship Program										✓				
84.149	Migrant Education-College Assistance Migrant Program	✓	✓	✓				✓	✓		✓				✓
84.151	Federal, State, and Local Partnerships for Education	✓	✓	✓			✓	✓			✓	✓	✓		
84.153	Business and International Education	✓	✓	✓	✓		✓	✓	✓		✓				
84.154	Public Library Construction	✓	✓				✓								
84.155	Removal of Architectural Barriers to the Handicapped	✓						✓							
84.157	Secretary's Initiative to Improve Quality of Ch. 1 ECIA Projects	✓													
84.158	Secondary Education and Transitional Services	✓	✓	✓	✓		✓	✓	✓		✓	✓			✓
84.159	Handicapped-Special Studies	✓		✓				✓							
84.160	Training Interpreters for Deaf Individuals	✓		✓	✓		✓	✓	✓						
84.161	Client Assistance for Handicapped Individuals	✓	✓					✓			✓	✓			
84.162	Emergency Immigrant Education	✓		✓				✓							
84.163	Library Services for Indian Tribes and Hawaiian Natives			✓	✓			✓		✓	✓	✓		✓	✓

appendix continues

Appendix B *(continued)*
Programs providing outlays to each recipient category

Catalog Number	Program Title	State Gov't.	Interstate Agencies	Counties	Cities/Towns	Special Districts	Schools	State Higher Education	Private Higher Education	Indian Tribes	Nonprofits	For Profits	Small Businesses	Individuals	All Others
84.164	Mathematics and Science Education	✓		✓				✓							
84.165	Magnet Schools Assistance	✓		✓	✓		✓	✓			✓				
84.167	Library Literacy	✓		✓	✓	✓	✓	✓	✓	✓	✓				✓
84.168	National Program for Mathematics and Science Education	✓		✓	✓		✓	✓	✓		✓				
84.169	Comprehensive Services for Independent Living	✓						✓							
84.170	Jacob K. Javits Fellowships	✓		✓	✓		✓	✓	✓		✓				
84.171	Excellence in Education	✓		✓	✓		✓	✓			✓				
84.172	Construction, Reconstruction, and Renovation of Academic Facilities			✓				✓	✓						
84.173	Handicapped-Preschool Grants	✓						✓							
84.174	Vocational Education-Community Based Organizations	✓		✓				✓							
84.176	Paul Douglas Teacher Scholarships	✓		✓			✓	✓	✓						
84.177	Rehabilitation Services-Independent Living Services	✓		✓	✓			✓							
84.178	Leadership in Educational Administration Development	✓		✓			✓	✓			✓				
84.180	Technology, Educational Media and Materials for the Handicapped			✓				✓			✓	✓			
84.181	Handicapped Infants and Toddlers	✓		✓				✓			✓				
84.183	Drug Prevention Programs	✓		✓	✓		✓	✓	✓	✓	✓				
84.184	National Program for Drug-FreeSchools and Communities	✓		✓	✓		✓	✓	✓	✓	✓				
84.185	Robert C. Byrd Honors Scholarships	✓													
84.186	Drug-Free Schools and Communities-State Grants	✓		✓				✓							
84.187	Supported Employment Services for Severely Handicapped	✓					✓	✓							
84.188	Drug-Free Schools and Communities-Regional Centers			✓				✓			✓				
84.189	Drug Abuse Education and Prevention Audio Visual Grant	✓		✓				✓			✓	✓			
84.190	Christa McAuliffe Fellowships	✓		✓				✓		✓				✓	
84.191	National Adult Education Research			✓											
84.192	Adult Education for the Homeless	✓		✓				✓							
84.193	Demonstration Centers-Retraining of Dislocated Workers			✓	✓		✓								
84.195	Bilingual Education Training Grants	✓					✓	✓				✓			
84.196	State Activities-Education of Homeless Children	✓													
84.197	College Library Technology and Cooperation Grants			✓				✓	✓						
84.198	Workplace Literacy	✓		✓			✓	✓							
84.199	Vocational Education-Cooperative Demonstration	✓		✓	✓		✓	✓	✓		✓	✓			
84.200	Graduate Assistance in Areas of National Need	✓		✓				✓	✓						
84.201	School Dropout Demonstration Assistance	✓		✓	✓		✓	✓			✓				
84.202	Grants to Institutions to Encourage Minority Participation	✓		✓	✓			✓	✓		✓				
84.203	Star Schools Program			✓				✓			✓	✓			
84.204	School, College, and University Partnership			✓			✓	✓							
84.206	Jacob K. Javits Gifted and Talented Students	✓		✓	✓		✓	✓	✓		✓				
84.207	Educational Personnel Training	✓		✓	✓		✓	✓	✓						
84.208	Native Hawaiian Model Curriculum Development	✓													
84.209	Native Hawaiian Family Based Education Centers							✓			✓	✓			
84.210	Native Hawaiian Gifted and Talented							✓							
84.211	FIRST Schools and Teachers	✓		✓	✓		✓	✓			✓	✓			
84.212	FIRST Family School Partnership	✓		✓			✓	✓							
84.213	Even Start-Local Education Agencies	✓		✓	✓		✓	✓			✓				
84.214	Even Start-Migrant Education	✓		✓				✓							
84.215	The Secretary's Fund for Innovation in Education	✓		✓	✓		✓	✓	✓		✓	✓			
84.216	Capital Expenses	✓													
84.217	Ronald E. McNair Post-Baccalaureate Achievement			✓				✓							
84.218	State Program Improvement Grants	✓													
84.219	Student Literacy Corps	✓		✓			✓	✓	✓						
84.220	Center for International Business Education			✓				✓	✓						
84.221	Native Hawaiian Special Education	✓													
84.222	National School Volunteer Program			✓				✓	✓		✓				
84.223	English Literacy Program	✓					✓	✓							
84.224	State Grants for Technology-Related Assistance	✓		✓				✓							
84.225	Education for Homeless Children and Youth	✓													

appendix continues

Appendix B *(continued)*
Programs providing outlays to each recipient category

Catalog Number	Program Title	State Gov't.	Interstate Agencies	Counties	Cities/Towns	Special Districts	Ind. School Districts	State Higher Education	Private Higher Education	Indian Tribes	Nonprofits	For Profits	Small Businesses	Individuals	All Others
84.995	Grants for Gallaudet College/Vocational & Adult Reimbursable Acts	✓			✓			✓	✓						
84.998	Helen Keller Center										✓				
84.999	Not in CFDA-Administered by Department of Education	✓	✓	✓	✓		✓	✓	✓	✓	✓	✓	✓		
89.003	National Historical Publications and Records Grant	✓	✓	✓	✓	✓		✓	✓	✓	✓				✓
90.001	Bicentennial Educational Grant Program	✓		✓	✓		✓	✓	✓		✓				

Notes: Some programs listed in this appendix exist for only a portion of the period 1983-90. For most programs, more than one category of recipients is eligible to receive assistance. However, since FAADS reports awards to specific recipients, the recipient categories reported in FAADS and this volume are mutually exclusive. This means that a dollar reported to one reicipient is not reported to any other recipient. Therefore it is valid to sum across recipient categories (e.g., cities and counties) to arrive at total outlays for congressional districts, states, or other levels of aggregation.

FAADS reported outlays for interstate agencies until 1985, by which time most of these agencies had been eliminated. Outlays are reported for state universities since 1985. Prior to 1985, outlays to state universities were reported under the category of state government. In many states, mainly in the Northeast, primary and secondary education is the responsibility of city or county government. In FAADS, outlays for primary and secondary education are reported separately only for independent school districts. Consequently, in this volume, monies received by cities or counties to fund primary and secondary education are reported to the city and county responsible for primary and secondary education.

Appendix C
Programs providing outlays in each functional policy category

Catalog Number	Program Title	Agriculture	Business and Commerce	Community Development	Disaster Prevention and Relief	Education	Employment, Labor and Training	Environmental Quality	Food and Nutrition	Health	Housing	Income Security and Social Service	Transportation
10.001	Agricultural Research- Basic and Applied Research	✓											
10.025	Plant and Animal, Pest Control, and Animal Care	✓											
10.028	Animal Damage Control	✓											
10.052	Cotton Production Stabilization	✓											
10.053	Dairy Indemnity Program	✓						✓					
10.054	Emergency Conservation Program				✓								
10.055	Feed Grain Production Stabilization	✓											
10.058	Wheat Production Stabilization	✓											
10.059	National Wool Act Payments	✓											
10.062	Water Bank Program	✓											
10.063	Agricultural Conservation Program	✓											
10.064	Forestry Incentives Program	✓											
10.065	Rice Production Stabilization	✓			✓								
10.066	Emergency Livestock Assistance	✓			✓								
10.067	Grain Reserve Program	✓											
10.068	Rural Clean Water Program	✓						✓					
10.069	Conservation Reserve Program	✓											
10.070	Colorado River Salinity Control	✓				✓		✓					
10.071	Federal-State Cooperation-Warehouse Examination	✓											
10.153	Market News	✓							✓				
10.156	Federal-State Marketing Improvement Program	✓											
10.164	Wholesale Market Development	✓											
10.200	Grants for Agricultural Research, Special Research	✓											
10.202	Cooperative Forestry Research	✓											
10.203	Payments to Agricultural Experiment Stations	✓											
10.205	Payments to 1890 Land-Grant Colleges and Tuskegee Institute	✓											
10.206	Grants for Agricultural Research-Competitive Research	✓										✓	
10.207	Animal Health and Disease Research	✓				✓		✓	✓	✓			
10.208	Alcohol Fuels Research	✓											
10.209	1890 Research Facilities	✓		✓		✓	✓	✓	✓	✓			
10.210	Food and Agricultural Sciences National Needs					✓							
10.211	Higher Education Strengthening Grants					✓							
10.212	Small Business Innovation Research	✓	✓										
10.213	Competitive Research Grants for Forest and Rangeland	✓											
10.214	Morrill-Nelson Funds for Food & Agricultural Higher Education					✓							
10.215	Low Input Farming Systems- Research and Education	✓											
10.250	Agricultural and Rural Economic Research	✓		✓					✓				
10.350	Technical Assistance to Cooperatives	✓		✓									
10.375	Human Nutrition Information Service	✓											
10.405	Farm Labor Housing Loans and Grants	✓									✓		
10.411	Rural Housing Site Loans										✓		
10.415	Rural Rental Housing Loans										✓		
10.417	Very Low-Income Housing Repair Loans and Grants										✓		
10.418	Water and Waste Disposal Systems for Rural Communities	✓		✓				✓					
10.420	Rural Self-Help Housing Technical Assistance										✓		
10.423	Community Facilities Loans		✓	✓	✓	✓							✓
10.424	Industrial Development Grants		✓	✓				✓					
10.427	Rural Rental Assistance Payments										✓		
10.433	Rural Housing Preservation Grants			✓									
10.435	Agricultural Loan Mediation Program	✓											
10.475	Cooperative Agreements for Intrastate Meat and Poultry Inspection								✓				
10.500	Cooperative Extension Service	✓		✓	✓			✓	✓			✓	

appendix continues

Appendix C *(continued)*
Programs providing outlays in each functional policy category

Catalog Number	Program Title	Agriculture	Business and Commerce	Community Development	Disaster Prevention and Relief	Education	Employment, Labor and Training	Environmental Quality	Food and Nutrition	Health	Housing	Income Security and Social Service	Transportation
10.550	Food Distribution				✓				✓			✓	
10.551	Food Stamps								✓			✓	
10.553	School Breakfast Program								✓				
10.555	National School Lunch Program								✓				
10.556	Special Milk Program for Children								✓				
10.557	Special Supplemental Food Program for Women, Infants, and Children											✓	
10.558	Child and Adult Care Food Program								✓			✓	
10.559	Summer Food Service Program for Children								✓			✓	
10.560	State Administrative Expenses for Child Nutrition								✓				
10.561	State Administrative Matching Grants for Food Stamps								✓				
10.562	Nutritional Training and Education								✓				
10.564	Nutrition Education and Training Program					✓			✓				
10.565	Commodity Supplemental Food Program								✓			✓	
10.567	Food Distribution Program on Indian Reservations									✓		✓	
10.568	Temporary Emergency Food Assistance (Administrative)								✓				
10.652	Forestry Research	✓											
10.663	Young Adult Conservation Corps- Grants to States	✓					✓						
10.664	Cooperative Forestry Assistance	✓											
10.665	Schools and Roads-Grants to States	✓		✓									
10.666	Schools and Roads-Grants to Counties	✓		✓									
10.667	School Funds-Grants to Arizona (Arizona School Fund)	✓		✓									
10.668	Additional Loans-Grants to Minnesota	✓											
10.669	Accelerated Cooperative Assistance for Forest Programs	✓											
10.700	National Agricultural Library	✓											
10.800	Livestock, Meat and Poultry Market Supervision	✓							✓				
10.900	Great Plains Conservation	✓		✓									
10.901	Resource Conservation and Development	✓		✓									
10.904	Watershed Protection and Flood Prevention			✓	✓								
10.909	Resource Appraisal and Program Development	✓											
10.910	Rural Abandoned Mine Program							✓					
10.950	Agricultural Statistics Reports	✓											
10.960	Technical Agricultural Assistance	✓				✓							
10.961	International Agricultural Research-Collaborative Program	✓	✓			✓							
10.962	International Training-Foreign Participant	✓											
11.000	Secretary, Department of Commerce		✓										
11.108	Export Promotion Services		✓										
11.109	Trade Adjustment Assistance		✓										
11.110	Trade Development		✓										
11.300	Economic Development-Grants for Public Works & Development Facilities		✓	✓									
11.301	Economic Development-Business Development Assistance		✓	✓									
11.302	Economic Development-Support for Planning Organizations		✓	✓									
11.303	Economic Development-Technical Assistance		✓	✓									
11.304	Economic Development-Public Works Impact Projects		✓	✓			✓						
11.305	Economic Development-State andLocal Economic Development Planning		✓				✓						
11.306	Economic Development - District Operational Assistance		✓	✓			✓						
11.307	Special Economic Development and Adjustment Assistance/Long-Term		✓	✓			✓						✓
11.311	Special Economic Development and Adjustment Assistance/Sudden		✓	✓									
11.312	Research and Evaluation Program						✓						
11.400	Geodetic Surveys and Services		✓										✓
11.401	Nautical Charts and Related Data		✓										✓
11.405	Anadromous and Great Lakes Fisheries Conservation		✓										
11.406	Commercial Fisheries Disaster Assistance		✓		✓								

appendix continues

Appendix C *(continued)*
Programs providing outlays in each functional policy category

Catalog Number	Program Title	Agriculture	Business and Commerce	Community Development	Disaster Prevention and Relief	Education	Employment, Labor and Training	Environmental Quality	Food and Nutrition	Health	Housing	Income Security and Social Service	Transportation
11.407	Interjurisdictional Fisheries Act of 1986		✓										
11.408	Fishermen's Contingency Fund		✓										
11.409	Fishing Vessel and Gear Damage Compensation Fund		✓										
11.417	Sea Grant Support					✓							
11.419	Coastal Zone Management Program Administration Grants	✓		✓									
11.420	Coastal Zone Management Estuarine Research Reserves			✓									
11.421	Energy Impact - Formula Grants		✓	✓	✓			✓		✓			✓
11.422	Coastal Energy Impact Grants		✓	✓		✓				✓	✓		
11.424	Coastal Energy Impact Program-Environmental Grants		✓	✓				✓					
11.426	Financial Assistance for Marine Pollution Research							✓					
11.427	Fisheries Development and Utilization Research		✓										
11.428	Intergovernmental Climate-Programs	✓	✓	✓				✓					
11.429	Marine Sanctuary Program							✓					
11.430	Undersea Research					✓							
11.431	Climate and Atmospheric Research					✓							
11.432	Environmental Research Laboratories Joint Institutes					✓		✓					
11.550	Public Telecommunications Facilities-Construction			✓		✓							
11.603	National Standard Reference Data System		✓										
11.606	Weights and Measures Service		✓										
11.609	Measurement and Engineering Research and Standards		✓										
11.800	Minority Business Development Centers		✓										
11.801	American Indian Program		✓									✓	
12.112	Payments to States in Lieu of Real Estate Taxes				✓								
12.400	Military Construction, Army National Guard				✓								
12.607	Military Base Reuse Studies and Community Planning Assistance		✓	✓									
12.608	Impact Assistance for Areas Affected by the East Coast Trident Program		✓	✓									
13.103	Food and Drug Administration-Research								✓	✓			
13.110	Maternal and Child Health Federal Consolidated Program									✓			
13.112	Characterization of Environmental Health Hazards							✓		✓			
13.113	Biological Response to Environmental Health Hazards							✓		✓			
13.114	Applied Toxicological Researchand Testing							✓		✓			
13.115	Biometry and Risk Estimation-Health Risks from Environmental Exposures							✓		✓			
13.116	Tuberculosis Control Programs									✓			
13.117	Grants for Preventive Medicine Residency Training									✓			
13.118	Acquired Immunodeficiency Syndrome (AIDS) Activity									✓			
13.119	Grants for Podiatric Medicine Training					✓				✓			
13.120	Mental Health Services for Cuban Entrants									✓			
13.121	Diseases of the Teeth and Supporting Tissues									✓			
13.122	Disorders of Craniofacial Structure and Function									✓			
13.124	Nurse Anesthetist Traineeships					✓				✓			
13.125	Mental Health Planning and Demonstration Projects									✓			
13.126	Small Business Innovation Research		✓							✓			
13.128	Refugee Assistance-Mental Health									✓		✓	
13.131	Shared Research Facilities for Heart, Lung, and Blood Diseases									✓			
13.132	Acquired Immunodeficiency Syndrome (AIDS) Research									✓			
13.133	Health Services Delivery to AIDS victims-Demonstration Grants									✓			
13.135	Centers for Research and Demonstration for Health Promotion									✓			
13.136	Injury Prevention and Research Projects									✓			
13.138	Protection and Advocacy for Mentally Ill Individuals									✓		✓	
13.141	Alcohol, Drug Abuse Treatment and Rehabilitation									✓			
13.142	NIEHS Hazardous Waste Worker Health and Safety Training							✓		✓			
13.143	NIEHS Superfund Hazardous Substances-Basic Research					✓		✓		✓			

appendix continues

Appendix C *(continued)*
Programs providing outlays in each functional policy category

Catalog Number	Program Title	Agriculture	Business and Commerce	Community Development	Disaster Prevention and Relief	Education	Employment, Labor and Training	Environmental Quality	Food and Nutrition	Health	Housing	Income Security and Social Service	Transportation
13.144	Drug and Alcohol Abuse Prevention- High-Risk Youth									✓			
13.146	Temporary AIDS Drug Reimbursements									✓			
13.150	Mental Health Services for the Homeless Block Grant									✓		✓	
13.151	Project Grants for Health Services to the Homeless									✓		✓	
13.152	Community Demonstration Grant Projects for Alcohol and Drug Abuse									✓		✓	
13.153	Pediatric AIDS Health Care Demonstration Program									✓			
13.161	Health Program for Toxic Substances and Disease Registry												
13.162	National Health Service Corps Loan Repayment									✓			
13.166	Indian Health Promotion and Disease Prevention Demonstration									✓			
13.167	Research Facilities Improvement									✓			
13.169	Model Projects for Pregnant and Postpartum Women									✓			
13.170	Community Youth Activity Demonstration Grants									✓		✓	
13.171	Community Youth Activity Program Block Grants									✓		✓	
13.172	Human Genome Research									✓			
13.173	Biological Research Related to Deafness									✓			
13.174	Conference Grant (Substance Abuse)									✓			
13.175	Drug Abuse Treatment Waiting List Reduction Grants									✓			
13.176	ADAMHA Small Instrumentation Program Grants					✓				✓			
13.179	State Data Collection-Uniform Alcohol and Drug Abuse Data									✓			
13.180	Medical Treatment Effectiveness Research												
13.217	Family Planning-Services									✓		✓	
13.224	Community Health Centers									✓			
13.226	Health Services Research and Development Grants									✓			
13.228	Indian Health Service-Health Management Development									✓			
13.229	Indian Health Services-Sanitation Management Development			✓						✓			
13.242	Mental Health Research Grants									✓			
13.244	Mental Health Clinical or Service Related Training Grants					✓				✓			
13.246	Migrant Health Centers Grants			✓						✓			
13.252	Alcoholism Treatment and Rehabilitation/Occupational Services									✓			
13.260	Family Planning-Personnel Training					✓				✓		✓	
13.262	Occupational Safety and Health Research Grants									✓			
13.263	Occupational Safety and Health-Training Grants					✓							
13.268	Childhood Immunization Grants									✓		✓	
13.271	Alcohol Scientist Development Award and Research					✓							
13.272	Alcohol National Research Service Awards for Research									✓			
13.273	Alcohol Research Programs									✓			
13.274	Alcohol and Drug Abuse Clinical or Service-Related Training					✓	✓			✓		✓	
13.277	Drug Abuse Scientist Development Award for Clinical Research									✓			
13.278	Drug Abuse National Research Service Awards									✓			
13.279	Drug Abuse Research Programs					✓				✓			
13.281	Mental Research Scientist Development Award					✓				✓			
13.282	Mental Health National Research Service Awards for Research Training									✓			
13.288	National Health Service Corps Scholarship Program					✓				✓			
13.293	State Health Planning and Development Agencies									✓			
13.294	Health Planning-Health Systems Agencies									✓			
13.297	National Research Service Awards					✓							
13.298	Nurse Practitioner and Nurse Midwife Education and Traineeships					✓							
13.299	Advanced Nurse Education					✓							
13.306	Laboratory Animal Sciences and Primate Research									✓			
13.333	General Clinical Research Centers									✓			
13.337	Biomedical Research Support					✓				✓			
13.339	Capitation Grants for Schools of Public Health					✓				✓			

appendix continues

Appendix C *(continued)*
Programs providing outlays in each functional policy category

Catalog Number	Program Title	Agriculture	Business and Commerce	Community Development	Disaster Prevention and Relief	Education	Employment, Labor and Training	Environmental Quality	Food and Nutrition	Health	Housing	Income Security and Social Service	Transportation
13.340	Health Professions Facilities									✓			
13.342	Health Professions Student Loans					✓							
13.358	Professional Nurse Traineeships					✓							
13.359	Nurse Training Improvement-Special Projects					✓							
13.361	Nursing Research					✓				✓			
13.363	Nursing Scholarships					✓							
13.364	Nursing Student Loans					✓							
13.371	Biomedical Research Technology					✓				✓			
13.375	Minority Biomedical Research Support					✓				✓			
13.379	Grants for Graduate Training in Family Medicine					✓				✓			
13.381	Health Professions-Advanced Financial Distress					✓							
13.389	Research Centers in Minority Institutions									✓			
13.390	Academic Research Enhancement Award									✓			
13.391	Cancer Task Forces					✓				✓			
13.392	Cancer-Construction					✓				✓			
13.393	Cancer Cause and Prevention Research					✓				✓			
13.394	Cancer Detection and Diagnosis Research					✓				✓			
13.395	Cancer Treatment Research					✓				✓			
13.396	Cancer Biology Research					✓				✓			
13.397	Cancer Centers Support					✓				✓			
13.398	Cancer Research Manpower					✓				✓			
13.399	Cancer Control					✓				✓			
13.600	Administration for Children, Youth and Families-Head Start					✓				✓		✓	
13.608	Administration for Children, Youth and Families-Child Welfare Research											✓	
13.612	Native American Programs			✓			✓			✓		✓	
13.614	Child Development Associate Scholarships					✓							
13.623	Administration for Children, Youth and Families-Runaway Youth											✓	
13.628	Child Abuse and Neglect Prevention and Treatment					✓				✓		✓	
13.630	Administration on Developmental Disabilities-Basic Support					✓	✓			✓		✓	
13.631	Administration on Developmental Disabilities-Special Projects			✓		✓	✓			✓		✓	
13.632	Administration on Developmental Disabilities-University Affiliated Programs					✓				✓		✓	
13.633	Special Programs for the Aging-Title III Part B									✓		✓	
13.634	Special Programs for the Aging-Title IV Part C									✓		✓	
13.635	Special Programs for the Aging-Title III Part C								✓	✓		✓	
13.641	Special Programs for the Aging-Title III, Part D											✓	
13.642	Social Services for Low Income and Public Assistance Recipients											✓	
13.644	Public Assistance Training Grants-Title XX					✓	✓					✓	
13.645	Child Welfare Services-State Grants											✓	
13.646	Work Incentive Program						✓					✓	
13.647	Social Services Research and Demonstration Grants											✓	
13.648	Child Welfare Services Training Grants					✓	✓					✓	
13.652	Administration for Children, Youth and Families-Adoption Opportunities											✓	
13.655	Special Programs for the Aging-Title VI, Part A			✓						✓	✓	✓	
13.656	Temporary Child Care and Crisis Nurseries											✓	
13.657	Drug Abuse Prevention and Education for Runaways									✓		✓	
13.658	Foster Care- Title IV-E											✓	
13.659	Adoption Assistance											✓	
13.660	Drug Abuse Prevention and Education Relating to Youth Gangs									✓		✓	
13.661	Native American Programs-Research, Demonstration, and Evaluation			✓						✓		✓	
13.662	Native American Programs-Training and Technical Assistance					✓	✓					✓	
13.665	Community Services Block Grant			✓			✓		✓	✓			
13.666	Comprehensive Child Development Centers											✓	

appendix continues

Appendix C *(continued)*
Programs providing outlays in each functional policy category

Catalog Number	Program Title	Agriculture	Business and Commerce	Community Development	Disaster Prevention and Relief	Education	Employment, Labor and Training	Environmental Quality	Food and Nutrition	Health	Housing	Income Security and Social Service	Transportation
13.667	Social Services Block Grant											✓	
13.668	Special Programs for the Aging-Title IV-Training											✓	
13.670	Administration for Children, Youth and Families-Child Abuse											✓	
13.671	Family Violence Prevention and Services											✓	
13.672	Child Abuse Challenge Grants											✓	
13.673	Grants to States for Planning and Development of Dependent Care Programs											✓	
13.679	Child Support Enforcement											✓	
13.714	Medical Assistance Program									✓		✓	
13.766	Health Care Financing Research, Demonstrations and Evaluations									✓		✓	
13.773	Medicare-Hospital Insurance									✓		✓	
13.774	Medicare-Supplementary Medical Insurance											✓	
13.775	State Medicaid Fraud Control Units											✓	
13.776	Professional Standards Review Organizations									✓			
13.777	State Survey and Certification of Health Care Provision									✓			
13.780	Family Support Payments to States-Assistance Payments											✓	
13.783	Child Support Enforcement											✓	
13.786	State Legalization Impact Assistance Grants											✓	
13.787	Refugee and Entrant Assistance-State Administered Programs					✓				✓		✓	
13.789	Low-Income Home Energy Assistance											✓	
13.790	Work Incentive Program/WIN Demonstration Program						✓					✓	
13.792	Community Services Block Grant			✓		✓	✓		✓	✓			
13.793	Community Services Block Grant-Discretionary Awards	✓	✓	✓			✓						
13.795	Community Services Block Grant-Discretionary Awards-Food and Nutrition								✓			✓	
13.796	Emergency Community Services for the Homeless											✓	
13.802	Social Security-Disability Insurance											✓	
13.803	Social Security-Retirement Insurance											✓	
13.805	Social Security-Survivors Insurance											✓	
13.806	Special Benefits for Disabled Coal Miners											✓	
13.807	Supplemental Security Income											✓	
13.808	Assistance Payments-Maintenance Assistance											✓	
13.810	Assistance Payments-State and Local Training					✓				✓		✓	
13.811	Child Support Enforcement Interstate Grants											✓	
13.812	Social Security-Research and Demonstration									✓		✓	
13.814	Refugee Assistance-State-Administered Programs									✓		✓	
13.815	Refugee Assistance-Voluntary Agency Programs											✓	
13.817	Refugee Assistance-Cuban and Haitian Entrants			✓			✓		✓	✓	✓	✓	
13.818	Low-Income Home Energy Assistance											✓	
13.819	Name not given, administered by Sec. Veterans' Employment											✓	
13.820	Scholarships for Students of Exceptional Financial Need					✓				✓			
13.821	Biophysics and Physiological Sciences					✓				✓			
13.822	Health Careers Opportunity Program					✓							
13.824	Area Health Education Centers					✓							
13.837	Heart and Vascular Diseases Research									✓			
13.838	Lung Diseases Research									✓			
13.839	Blood Diseases and Resources Research									✓			
13.840	Caries Research									✓			
13.841	Periodontal Diseases Research									✓			
13.842	Craniofacial Anomalies Research									✓			
13.843	Restorative Materials Research									✓			
13.844	Pain Control and Behavioral Studies									✓			
13.845	Dental Research Institutes-Research Centers in Oral Biology									✓			
13.846	Arthritis, Musculoskeletal, and Skin Diseases Research									✓			

appendix continues

Appendix C *(continued)*
Programs providing outlays in each functional policy category

Catalog Number	Program Title	Agriculture	Business and Commerce	Community Development	Disaster Prevention and Relief	Education	Employment, Labor and Training	Environmental Quality	Food and Nutrition	Health	Housing	Income Security and Social Service	Transportation
13.847	Diabetes, Endocrinology and Metabolism Research									✓			
13.848	Digestive Diseases and Nutrition Research								✓	✓			
13.849	Kidney Diseases, Urology, and Hematology Research									✓			
13.852	Neurological Disorders Research									✓			
13.853	Clinical Research Related to Neurological Disorders									✓			
13.854	Biological Basis Research in the Neurosciences									✓			
13.855	Allergy, Immunology and Transplantation Research									✓			
13.856	Microbiology and Infectious Diseases Research									✓			
13.859	Pharmacological Sciences									✓			
13.862	Genetics Research									✓			
13.863	Cellular and Molecular Basis of Disease Research									✓			
13.864	Population Research									✓			
13.865	Research for Mothers and Children									✓		✓	
13.866	Aging Research									✓			
13.867	Retinal and Choroidal Diseases Research									✓			
13.868	Anterior Segment Diseases Research									✓			
13.869	Cataract Research									✓			
13.870	Glaucoma Research									✓			
13.871	Strabismus, Amblyopia and Visual Processing									✓			
13.878	Soft Tissue Stomatology and Nutrition Research					✓				✓			
13.879	Medical Library Assistance					✓			✓	✓			
13.880	Minority Access to Research Careers					✓				✓			
13.884	Grants for Residency Training in General Internal Medicine					✓				✓			
13.886	Grants for Physician Assistant Training Program					✓				✓			
13.888	Home Health Services and Training					✓				✓			
13.891	Alcohol Research Center Grants									✓			
13.894	Resource and Manpower Development in the Environment					✓				✓			
13.895	Grants for Faculty Development in Family Medicine					✓				✓			
13.897	Residency Training and Advanced Education					✓				✓			
13.900	Grants for Faculty Developmentin General Internal Medicine									✓			
13.960	Social Security Payments to States for Determination of Disability											✓	
13.962	Health Administration Graduate Traineeships					✓							
13.963	Graduate Programs in Health Administration					✓							
13.964	Traineeships for Students in Schools of Public Health					✓				✓			
13.965	Coal Miners Respiratory Impairment Treatment Clinics									✓			
13.969	Grants for the Training of Health Professions in Geriatrics					✓							
13.970	Health Professions Recruitment Program for Indians					✓				✓			
13.971	Health Professions Preparatory Scholarship Programs for Indians									✓			
13.972	Health Professions Scholarship Program									✓			
13.973	Special Loans for National Health Service Corps Members									✓			
13.974	Family Planning- Services Delivery Improvement Research Grants									✓		✓	
13.977	Preventive Health Service-Sexually Transmitted Diseases Control Grants									✓			
13.978	Preventive Health Service-Sexually Transmitted Diseases Research					✓				✓			
13.982	Mental Health Disaster Assistance and Emergency Mental Health					✓				✓		✓	
13.984	Grants for Establishment of Departments of Family Medicine					✓				✓		✓	
13.985	Eye Research-Facility Construction									✓			
13.987	Health Programs for Refugees									✓		✓	
13.988	Cooperative Agreements for State-Based Diabetes Control Programs									✓			
13.989	Senior International Fellowships									✓			
13.990	National Health Promotion									✓			
13.991	Preventive Health and Health Services Block Grant									✓			
13.992	Alcohol and Drug Abuse and Mental Health Services Block Grant									✓			

appendix continues

Appendix C *(continued)*
Programs providing outlays in each functional policy category

Catalog Number	Program Title	Agriculture	Business and Commerce	Community Development	Disaster Prevention and Relief	Education	Employment, Labor and Training	Environmental Quality	Food and Nutrition	Health	Housing	Income Security and Social Service	Transportation
13.994	Maternal and Child Health Services Block Grant									✓			
13.995	Adolescent Family Life- Demonstration Projects									✓		✓	
13.996	Policy Research Program					✓							
14.103	Interest Reduction Payments-Rental and Cooperative Housing										✓		
14.146	Public Housing										✓		
14.149	Rent Supplements-Rental Housing for Lower Income Families										✓		
14.156	Lower-Income Housing Assistance Program										✓		
14.157	Housing for the Elderly or Handicapped										✓		
14.167	Mortgage Insurance-Two Year Operating Loss Loans										✓		
14.169	Housing Counseling Assistance Program										✓		
14.174	Housing Development Grants										✓		
14.178	Supportive Housing Demonstration Program										✓	✓	
14.218	Community Development Block Grants/Entitlement Grants		✓	✓				✓		✓	✓		
14.219	Community Development Block Grants/Small Cities Program		✓	✓	✓			✓		✓	✓		
14.221	Urban Development Action Grants										✓		
14.223	Indian Community Development Block Grant Program			✓							✓		
14.225	Community Development Block Grants/Special Purpose Insular Area		✓	✓			✓				✓		
14.227	Community Development Block Grants/Special Purpose Technical Assist.		✓	✓			✓				✓		
14.228	Community Development Block Grants/State's Program		✓	✓									
14.229	Community Development Block Grants/Sec. Discretionary Fund			✓			✓				✓		
14.230	Rental Housing Rehabilitation										✓	✓	
14.231	Emergency Shelter Grants Program										✓	✓	
14.232	Community Development Block Grant/Sec. Discretionary Fund Special Projects			✓							✓		
14.400	Equal Opportunity in Housing										✓		
14.506	General Research and Technology Activity			✓									
14.510	Supplemental Assistance for Facilities to Assist the Homeless			✓									
14.850	Public and Indian Housing										✓		
14.851	Low Income Housing-Homeownership Opportunities for Low Income Families										✓		
14.852	Public and Indian Housing-Comprehensive Improvement										✓		
15.142	Self Determination Grants-Indian Tribal Governments			✓									
15.143	Training and Technical Assistance-Indian Tribal Governments			✓									
15.144	Indian Child Welfare Act-Title II Grants					✓	✓			✓	✓	✓	
15.145	Indian Grants-Economic Development (Indian Grant Program)												
15.221	Cooperative Agreements for Research in Public Lands Management	✓											
15.252	Abandoned Mine Land Reclamation (AMLR) Program							✓					
15.308	Grants for Mining and Mineral Resources and Research Institutes					✓							
15.419	HCRS/NPRA Park Practice Program			✓									
15.505	National Water Research Program			✓	✓								
15.600	Anadromous Fish Conservation		✓										
15.612	Endangered Species Conservation		✓										
15.800	Geologic and Mineral Resource Surveys and Mapping		✓										
15.801	Cartographic Information, Geologic Information, Hydrologic Information		✓	✓									
15.803	National Mapping, Geography and Surveys		✓	✓									
15.804	Water Resources Investigations			✓									
15.904	Historic Preservation Fund Grants-In-Aid			✓									
15.914	National Register of Historic Places			✓		✓		✓			✓		
15.915	Technical Preservation Services			✓									
15.916	Outdoor Recreation-Acquisition, Development and Planning			✓									✓
15.919	Urban Park and Recreation Recovery Program			✓									
16.200	Community Relations Service			✓									
16.201	Cuban and Haitian Entrant Resettlement Program											✓	
16.530	Criminal Justice-Part D Formula Grants											✓	

appendix continues

Appendix C *(continued)*
Programs providing outlays in each functional policy category

Catalog Number	Program Title	Agriculture	Business and Commerce	Community Development	Disaster Prevention and Relief	Education	Employment, Labor and Training	Environmental Quality	Food and Nutrition	Health	Housing	Income Security and Social Service	Transportation
16.531	Part F-Discretionary Grants											✓	
16.532	Part E-National Priority Program Grants											✓	
16.534	Law Enforcement Assistance-Training						✓						
16.535	Law Enforcement Assistance Administration			✓								✓	
16.541	Juvenile Justice and Delinquency Prevention-Special Emphasis			✓								✓	
16.550	Criminal Justice Statistcs Development											✓	
16.551	Statistics on Crime and Criminal Justice											✓	
16.571	Public Safety Officers' Death Benefits Program											✓	
16.583	Children's Justice Act Discretionary Grants												
16.601	Corrections-Training and Staff Development						✓					✓	
16.602	Corrections-Research and Evaluation and Policy Formulation					✓							
16.603	Corrections-Technical Assistance/Clearinghouse						✓						
17.002	Labor Force Statistics		✓				✓						
17.100	Labor-Management Relations Services					✓	✓						
17.130	Labor-Management Relations and Cooperative Programs						✓						
17.207	Employment Service						✓						
17.225	Unemployment Insurance						✓						
17.230	Migrant and Seasonal Farmworkers						✓			✓		✓	
17.232	Comprehensive Employment and Training Programs						✓					✓	
17.233	Employment and Training Research and Development Projects					✓	✓						
17.234	Employment and Training-Indians and Native Americans			✓			✓					✓	
17.235	Senior Community Service Employment Program						✓					✓	
17.245	Trade Adjustment Assistance-Workers		✓				✓						
17.246	Employment and Training Assistance-Dislocated Workers						✓						
17.247	Migrant and Seasonal Farmworkers						✓			✓		✓	
17.248	Employment and Training Research and Development Projects						✓						
17.249	Employment Services and Job Training-Demonstration Programs						✓						
17.250	Job Training Partnership Act						✓						
17.251	Native American Employment and Training Programs						✓					✓	
17.301	Non-Discrimination and Affirmative Action by Federal Contractors						✓						
17.302	Longshore and Harbor Workers' Compensation											✓	
17.400	Trade Adjustment Assistance-Workers		✓				✓						
17.501	Employee Assistance Programs-Drug, Alcohol Abuse									✓			
17.600	Mine Health and Safety Grants									✓			
17.602	Mine Health and Safety Education and Training						✓			✓			
17.700	Women's Special Employment Assistance						✓						
17.801	Disabled Veterans Outreach Program						✓						
17.802	Veterans Employment Program						✓						
17.805	Homeless Veterans Employment and Training						✓						
20.005	Boating Safety Financial Assistance			✓									
20.102	Airport Development Aid Program												✓
20.103	Airport Planning Grant Program												✓
20.106	Airport Improvement Program			✓									✓
20.107	Airway Science					✓							
20.205	Highway Planning and Construction												✓
20.214	Highway Beautification-Control of Outdoor Advertising												✓
20.218	Motor Carrier Safety Assistance Program												✓
20.308	Local Rail Service Assistance												✓
20.500	Urban Mass Transportation-Capital Improvement Grants			✓									✓
20.502	Urban Mass Transportation-Grants for University Research and Training			✓		✓							✓
20.503	Urban Mass Transportation-Managerial Training Grants			✓		✓							✓
20.504	Mass Transportation Technology			✓									✓

appendix continues

Appendix C *(continued)*
Programs providing outlays in each functional policy category

Catalog Number	Program Title	Agriculture	Business and Commerce	Community Development	Disaster Prevention and Relief	Education	Employment, Labor and Training	Environmental Quality	Food and Nutrition	Health	Housing	Income Security and Social Service	Transportation
20.505	Urban Mass Transportation Technical Studies Grants												✓
20.507	Urban Mass Transportation Capital and Operating Assistance		✓	✓									✓
20.509	Public Transportation for Nonurbanized Areas			✓									
20.511	Human Resource Programs		✓			✓	✓						✓
20.512	Urban Mass Transportation Technical Assistance			✓		✓							✓
20.513	Capital Assistance Program for Elderly and Handicapped Persons											✓	✓
20.600	State and Community Highway Safety			✓									✓
20.700	Pipeline Safety												✓
20.804	Operating-Differential Subsidies		✓										
20.806	State Marine Schools		✓			✓	✓						
20.811	Research and Development Assistance		✓			✓							
20.901	Payments for Essential Air Services												✓
20.902	University Transportation Centers Program					✓							✓
21.006	Tax Counseling for the Elderly											✓	
21.300	State and Local Government Fiscal Assistance-Revenue Sharing			✓									
23.001	Appalachian Regional Development (See individual Appalachian Programs)		✓	✓									
23.004	Appalachian Health Programs			✓									
23.005	Appalachian Housing Project Planning Loan, Technical Assistance Grant			✓							✓		
23.011	Appalachian State Research, Technical Assistance, and Demonstrations			✓								✓	
23.012	Appalachian Vocational and Other Education Facilities and Operations			✓		✓						✓	
26.001	Air Carrier Payments												✓
26.003	Payments for Essential Air Services												✓
30.001	Employment Discrimination-Title VII of the Civil Rights Act of 1964						✓						
30.002	Employment Discrimination-State and Local Anti-Discrimination						✓						
30.009	Employment Discrimination Project Contracts-Indian Tribes						✓						
39.006	National Historical Publications and Records Grants			✓		✓							
45.001	Promotion of the Arts-Design Arts			✓									
45.010	Promotion of the Arts-Expansion Arts			✓									
45.013	Promotion of the Arts-Challenge Grants			✓									
45.021	Promotion of the Arts-Arts Administration Fellows Program					✓	✓						
45.023	Promotion of the Arts-Local Program									✓			
45.104	Promotion of the Humanities-Humanities Projects in Media					✓							
45.111	Promotion of the Humanities-Exemplary Projects and Humanities Programs					✓							
45.113	Promotion of the Humanities-Public Humanities Projects					✓							
45.116	Promotion of the Humanities-Summer Seminars for College Teachers					✓							
45.121	Promotion of the Humanities-Summer Stipends					✓							
45.124	Promotion of the Humanities-Reference Materials/Access					✓							
45.125	Promotion of the Humanities-Humanities Projects			✓		✓							
45.127	Promotion of the Humanities-Elementary and Secondary Education					✓							
45.130	Promotion of the Humanities-Challenge Grants			✓		✓							
45.133	Promotion of the Humanities-Interpretive Research					✓							
45.134	Promotion of the Humanities-Conferences					✓							
45.135	Promotion of the Humanities-Special Projects: Humanities					✓							
45.137	Promotion of the Humanities-Humanities Projects in Libraries and Archives					✓							
45.142	Promotion of the Humanities-Fellowships for University Teachers					✓							
45.143	Promotion of the Humanities-Fellowships for Colleges					✓	✓						
45.145	Promotion of the Humanities-Reference Materials/Tools					✓							
45.146	Promotion of the Humanities-Texts/Editions					✓							
45.147	Promotion of the Humanities-Texts/Translations					✓							
45.150	Promotion of the Humanities-Higher Education in the Humaninites					✓							
45.151	Promotion of the Humanities-Summer Seminars for School Teachers					✓							
45.152	Promotion of the Humanities-Travel to Collections					✓							

appendix continues

Appendix C *(continued)*
Programs providing outlays in each functional policy category

Catalog Number	Program Title	Agriculture	Business and Commerce	Community Development	Disaster Prevention and Relief	Education	Employment, Labor and Training	Environmental Quality	Food and Nutrition	Health	Housing	Income Security and Social Service	Transportation
45.301	Institute of Museum Services		✓	✓		✓							
47.009	Graduate Research Fellowships					✓							
47.041	Engineering Grants					✓							
47.049	Mathematical and Physical Sciences					✓							
47.051	Biological, Behavioral, and Social Sciences									✓			
47.053	Scientific, Technological, and International Affairs					✓							
47.055	Two-Year and Four-Year College Research Instrumentation					✓							
47.057	Minority Research Initiation					✓							
47.059	Visiting Professorships for Women					✓							
47.060	Research Improvement in Minority Institutions					✓							
47.063	Precollege Science and Mathematics Education					✓							
47.064	College Science Instrumentation					✓							
47.065	Advanced Scientific Computing					✓							
47.066	Teacher Preparation and Enhancement					✓							
47.067	Materials Development, Research, and Informal Science Education					✓							
47.068	Studies and Program Assessment					✓							
47.069	Research Initiation and Improvement					✓							
47.070	Computer and Information Science and Engineering					✓							
47.071	Undergraduate Science, Engineering and Mathematics Education					✓							
47.072	Young Scholars					✓							
47.073	Science and Technology Centers												
53.001	Employment Promotion of People with Disabilities						✓					✓	
57.001	Social Insurance for Railroad Workers						✓					✓	
57.004	Benefits for Rock Island Railroad Emloyees						✓					✓	
59.002	Economic Injury Disaster Loans		✓		✓								
59.003	Loans for Small Businesses		✓										
59.007	Management and Technical Assistance		✓										
59.011	Small Business Investment Companies		✓										
59.026	Service Corps of Retired Executives Association		✓				✓					✓	
59.032	Office of Women's Business Ownership		✓										
59.034	Small Business Economic Research		✓										
59.037	Small Business Development Center		✓										
64.005	Grants to States for Construction of State Home Facilities									✓			
64.014	Veterans State Domiciliary Care									✓			
64.015	Veterans State Nursing Home Care									✓			
64.016	Veterans State Hospital Care									✓			
64.023	Health Professional Scholarships-Nursing									✓			
64.100	Automobiles and Adaptive Equipment for Certain Disabilities											✓	
64.101	Burial Expenses Allowance for Veterans											✓	
64.102	Compensation for Service-Connected Deaths for Veterans' Dependents											✓	
64.104	Pension for Non-Service-Connected Disability for Veterans											✓	
64.105	Pension to Veterans Surviving Spouses, and Children											✓	
64.106	Specially Adapted Housing for Disabled Veterans										✓	✓	
64.109	Veterans Compensation for Service-Connected Disability											✓	
64.110	Veterans Dependency and Indemnity Compensation											✓	
64.111	Veterans Educational Assistance					✓						✓	
64.116	Vocational Rehabilitation for Disabled Veterans					✓	✓			✓		✓	
64.117	Survivors and Dependents Educational Assistance					✓						✓	
64.120	Post-Vietnam Era Veterans' Educational Assistance					✓							
64.121	Veterans' Job Training Act						✓						
64.124	All-Volunteer Force Educational Assistance					✓							
64.203	State Cemetery Grants											✓	

appendix continues

Appendix C *(continued)*
Programs providing outlays in each functional policy category

Catalog Number	Program Title	Agriculture	Business and Commerce	Community Development	Disaster Prevention and Relief	Education	Employment, Labor and Training	Environmental Quality	Food and Nutrition	Health	Housing	Income Security and Social Service	Transportation
66.001	Air Pollution Control Program Support							✓					
66.002	Air Pollution Fellowships					✓		✓					
66.003	Air Pollution Control Manpower Training							✓					
66.027	Unknown name, Administered by Director of EPA							✓					
66.030	Noise Pollution Control-Technical Assistance							✓					
66.418	Construction Grants for Wastewater Treatment Works			✓				✓		✓			
66.419	Water Pollution Control-State and Interstate Program Support							✓					
66.425	Drinking Water Supply-Technical Assistance							✓					
66.426	Water Pollution Control-State and Areawide Water Quality							✓					
66.428	Water Pollution Control-Professional Training Grants							✓					
66.429	Water Pollution Control-Technical Training Grants							✓					
66.430	Water Pollution Control Fellowships							✓					
66.432	State Public Water System Supervision							✓					
66.433	State Underground Water Source Protection							✓					
66.434	Safe Drinking Water						✓	✓					
66.435	Water Pollution Control-Lake Restoration Cooperative Agreements			✓				✓					
66.438	Construction Management Assistance			✓			✓	✓		✓			
66.451	Hazardous Waste Management Financial Assistance to States							✓					
66.452	Solid Waste Management Demonstration Grants							✓					
66.454	Water Quality Management Planning							✓					
66.455	Construction Grants for Abatement of Combined Sewer Overflow			✓				✓					
66.456	National Estuary Program							✓					
66.458	Capitalization Grants for State Revolving Funds							✓					
66.459	Nonpoint Source Reservation							✓					
66.500	Environmental Protection-Consolidated Research			✓									
66.501	Air Pollution Control Research							✓					
66.502	Pesticides Control Research							✓					
66.504	Solid Waste Disposal Research							✓					
66.505	Water Pollution Control-Research, Development, and Demonstration							✓					
66.506	Safe Drinking Water Research and Demonstration							✓		✓			
66.507	Toxic Substances Research							✓		✓			
66.508	Senior Environmental Employment Program						✓						
66.600	Environmental Protection Consolidated Grants-Program Support							✓					
66.602	Environmental Protection Consolidated Grants-Special Purpose							✓					
66.700	Consolidated Pesticide Compliance Monitoring and Program							✓					
66.701	Toxic Substances Compliance Monitoring Program							✓					
66.702	Asbestos Hazard Abatement (Schools) Assistance							✓		✓			
66.703	Asbestos Inspection and Management Plan Assistance							✓		✓			
66.801	Hazardous Waste Management State Program Support							✓					
66.802	Hazardous Substance Response Trust Fund							✓					
66.804	State Underground Storage Tanks Program							✓					
66.805	Underground Storage Tank Trust Fund Program							✓					
66.806	Superfund Technical Assistance Grants for Citizen Groups Grants							✓					
72.001	Foster Grandparent Program											✓	
72.002	Retired Senior Volunteer Program											✓	
72.003	Volunteers in Service to America			✓								✓	
72.004	University Year for Action			✓		✓						✓	
72.005	Student Community Service Program					✓						✓	
72.008	Senior Companion Program											✓	
72.010	Minigrant Program					✓				✓		✓	
72.011	State Office of Voluntarism									✓		✓	
72.012	Volunteer Demonstration Program			✓								✓	

appendix continues

Appendix C *(continued)*
Programs providing outlays in each functional policy category

Catalog Number	Program Title	Agriculture	Business and Commerce	Community Development	Disaster Prevention and Relief	Education	Employment, Labor and Training	Environmental Quality	Food and Nutrition	Health	Housing	Income Security and Social Service	Transportation
72.013	Technical Assistance Program											✓	
72.014	Drug Alliance									✓		✓	
72.015	Literacy Corps											✓	
77.001	Radiation Control-Training Assistance and Advisory Counseling					✓		✓		✓			
77.003	Enhance Technology Transfer and Dissemination					✓							
81.004	University-Laboratory Cooperative Program					✓							
81.007	Teacher Development Projects in Energy					✓		✓					
81.011	University Reactor Sharing and Fuel Assistance					✓							
81.023	Information Services-Exhibits, Public Speakers, and Publications					✓							
81.035	Research and Development in Energy Conservation					✓							
81.037	Research and Development-Fission, Fossil, Solar, Geothermal, Electric			✓		✓							
81.042	Weatherization Assistance for Low-Income Persons									✓		✓	
81.044	Public Education in Energy					✓	✓						
81.045	Speicial Studies and Project in Energy Education					✓	✓						
81.046	Research and Development in Biomedial and Environmental Sciences					✓	✓						
81.047	Pre-Freshman Enrichment					✓							
81.049	Basic Energy Sciences, High Energy and Nuclear Physics					✓							
81.050	Energy Extension Service					✓						✓	
81.051	Appropriate Energy Technology	✓		✓									
81.052	Energy Conservation for Institutional Buildings			✓									
81.053	Public Utility Regulatory Innovative Rates Support			✓									
81.054	Public Utility Regulatory Support			✓									
81.057	University Coal Research					✓							
81.063	Office of Minority Economic Impact Loans		✓										
81.075	Energy Graduate Traineeship Program					✓							
81.083	Minority Educational Institution Research Travel Fund					✓							
81.084	Minority Honors Training and Industrial Assistance					✓							
81.088	International Affairs and Energy Emergencies			✓									
81.094	Minority Educational Institution Assistance					✓							
83.002	State Fire Incident Reporting Assistance			✓									
83.003	Public Education Assistance Program			✓									
83.004	Technical Support Services			✓									
83.005	Arson Task Force Assistance Program			✓									
83.008	Community-Based Anti-Arson Program			✓	✓								
83.103	State Assistance-National Flood Insurance Program			✓	✓								
83.203	State Disaster Preparedness Grants			✓	✓						✓	✓	
83.400	Emergency Management Institute-Training Assistance					✓							
83.402	Emergency Management Institute Radiological Emergency					✓	✓	✓		✓			
83.403	Emergency Management Institute-Field Training Program						✓						
83.405	National Fire Academy-Training Assistance			✓									
83.406	National Emergency Training Center-Training Program				✓	✓							
83.407	State Fire Incident Reporting Assistance			✓									
83.409	Reimbursement for Firefighting on Federal Property			✓									
83.410	Community-Based Anti-Arson Program			✓	✓								
83.500	General Research, Development,and Demonstration Activity				✓								
83.501	State Assistance Program			✓	✓								
83.503	Civil Defense-State and Local Emergency Management Assistance				✓								
83.504	Other State and Local Direction, Control and Warning				✓								
83.505	State Disaster Preparedness Grants			✓	✓						✓	✓	
83.506	Earthquake and Hurricane Preparedness Grants				✓								
83.512	State and Local Emergency Operating Centers			✓									
83.513	State and Local Warning and Communication Systems				✓								

appendix continues

Appendix C *(continued)*
Programs providing outlays in each functional policy category

Catalog Number	Program Title	Agriculture	Business and Commerce	Community Development	Disaster Prevention and Relief	Education	Employment, Labor and Training	Environmental Quality	Food and Nutrition	Health	Housing	Income Security and Social Service	Transportation
83.514	Population Protection Planning				✓	✓							
83.515	Emergency Broadcast System Guidance and Assistance				✓								
83.516	Disaster Assistance			✓	✓	✓				✓	✓	✓	✓
83.519	Hazard Mitigation Assistance				✓								
83.521	Earthquake Hazards Reduction Grants		✓										
84.001	Academic Facilities Reconstruction and Renovation			✓		✓							
84.002	Adult Education-State-Administered Basic Grant Program					✓	✓						
84.003	Bilingual Education					✓							
84.004	Desegregation Assistance, Civil Rights Training					✓							
84.005	College Library Resources					✓							
84.007	Supplemental Educational Opportunity Grants					✓							
84.008	Alcohol and Drug Abuse Education					✓				✓			
84.009	Education of Handicapped Children in State Operated Institutions					✓				✓			
84.010	Educationally Deprived Children-Local Educational Agencies					✓							
84.011	Migrant Education-Basic State Formula Grant Program					✓						✓	
84.012	Educationally Deprived Children-State Administration					✓							
84.013	Neglected and Delinquent Children					✓							
84.014	Follow Through					✓						✓	
84.015	National Resource Centers and Fellowships Program					✓							
84.016	Undergraduate International Studies and Foreign Language Programs					✓							
84.017	International Research and Studies					✓							
84.019	Fulbright-Hays Training Grants-Faculty Research Abroad					✓							
84.020	Fulbright-Hays Training Grants-Foreign Curriculum Consultants					✓							
84.021	Fulbright-Hays Training Grants-Group Projects Abroad					✓							
84.022	Fulbright-Hays Training Grants-Doctoral Dissertation Research Abroad					✓							
84.023	Handicapped-Innovation and Development					✓				✓			
84.024	Handicapped Early Childhood Education					✓							
84.025	Handicapped Education-Deaf-Blind Centers					✓						✓	
84.026	Handicapped Media Services and Captioned Films					✓							
84.027	Handicapped-State Grants					✓							
84.029	Handicapped Education-Special Education Personnel					✓				✓			
84.030	Clearinghouses for the Handicapped Program					✓							
84.031	Higher Education-Institutional Aid					✓							
84.033	College Work-Study Program					✓							
84.034	Library Services					✓							
84.035	Interlibrary Cooperation and Resource Sharing					✓							
84.036	Library Career Training					✓							
84.037	National Defense/National Direct/Perkins Loan Cancellations					✓							
84.038	Perkins Loan Program					✓							
84.039	Library Research and Demonstration					✓							
84.040	Impact Aid-Construction				✓	✓			✓				
84.041	Impact Aid-Maintenance and Operation				✓	✓							
84.042	Student Support Services					✓							
84.044	Talent Search					✓						✓	
84.047	Upward Bound					✓						✓	
84.048	Vocational Education-Basic Grants to States					✓							
84.049	Vocational Education-Consumer and Homemaking Education					✓			✓				
84.050	Vocational Education-Program Improvement and Support					✓							
84.051	National Vocational Education Research					✓							
84.052	Vocational Education-Special Programs for the Disadvantaged					✓						✓	
84.053	Vocational Education-State Councils					✓							
84.055	Higher Education-Cooperative Education					✓							

appendix continues

Appendix C *(continued)*
Programs providing outlays in each functional policy category

Catalog Number	Program Title	Agriculture	Business and Commerce	Community Development	Disaster Prevention and Relief	Education	Employment, Labor and Training	Environmental Quality	Food and Nutrition	Health	Housing	Income Security and Social Service	Transportation
84.060	Indian Education-Formula Grants to Local Educational Agencies					✓							
84.061	Indian Education-Special Programs and Projects					✓							
84.062	Indian Education-Adult Indian Education			✓		✓							
84.063	Pell Grant Program					✓							
84.064	Higher Education-Veterans Education Outreach Program					✓							
84.065	Educational Television and Radio Programming					✓							
84.066	Educational Opportunity Centers					✓							
84.067	Use of Technology in Basic Skills Instruction					✓						✓	
84.069	Grants to States for State Student Incentives					✓							
84.072	Indian Education-Grants to Indian Controlled Schools					✓							
84.073	National Diffusion Network					✓							
84.075	Public Service Education					✓							
84.077	Bilingual Vocational Training					✓							
84.078	Postsecondary Education Programs for Handicapped Persons					✓						✓	
84.083	Women's Educational Equity					✓							
84.086	Handicapped Education-Severely Handicapped Program					✓							
84.087	Indian Education-Fellowships for Indian Students					✓							
84.091	Strengthening Research Library Resources					✓							
84.094	Patricia Roberts Harris Fellowships					✓							
84.097	Law School Clinical Experience Program					✓							
84.099	Bilingual Vocational Instructor Training					✓							
84.100	Bilingual Vocational Materials, Methods, and Techniques					✓							
84.101	Vocational Education-Indian and Hawaiian Natives					✓	✓						
84.103	Training for Special Programs Staff and Leadership Personnel					✓							
84.114	Capacity Building for Statistical Activities					✓							
84.116	Fund for the Improvement of Postsecondary Education					✓							
84.117	Educational Research and Development					✓							
84.120	Minority Science Improvement					✓							
84.121	Vocational Education-State Planning and Evaluation					✓						✓	
84.122	Secretary's Discretionary					✓							
84.123	Law-Related Education					✓							
84.126	Rehabilitation Services-Basic Support						✓			✓		✓	
84.128	Rehabilitation Services-Service Projects					✓	✓			✓		✓	
84.129	Rehabilitation Training					✓	✓			✓		✓	
84.132	Centers for Independent Living					✓						✓	
84.133	National Institute on Disability and Rehabilitation Research					✓				✓		✓	
84.136	Legal Training for the Disadvantaged					✓						✓	
84.138	Educational Services to Cuban and Haitian Entrant Children					✓						✓	
84.141	Migrant Education-High School Equivalency Program					✓							
84.142	College Facilities Loans					✓							
84.144	Migrant Education-Coordination Program					✓						✓	
84.146	Transition Program for Refugee Children					✓						✓	
84.149	Migrant Education-College Assistance Migrant Program					✓						✓	
84.151	Federal, State, and Local Partnerships for Educational Improvement					✓							
84.153	Business and International Education					✓							
84.154	Public Library Construction					✓							
84.155	Removal of Architectural Barriers to the Handicapped					✓							
84.157	Secretary's Initiative to Improve the Quality of Ch. 1 ECIA Projects					✓							
84.158	Secondary Education and Transitional Services for Handicapped Youth					✓							
84.159	Handicapped-Special Studies					✓							
84.160	Training Interpreters for Deaf Individuals					✓							
84.161	Client Assistance for Handicapped Individuals					✓							

appendix continues

Appendix C *(continued)*
Programs providing outlays in each functional policy category

Catalog Number	Program Title	Agriculture	Business and Commerce	Community Development	Disaster Prevention and Relief	Education	Employment, Labor and Training	Environmental Quality	Food and Nutrition	Health	Housing	Income Security and Social Service	Transportation
84.162	Emergency Immigrant Education					✓							
84.163	Library Services for Indian Tribes and Hawaiian Natives					✓							
84.164	Mathematics and Science Education					✓							
84.165	Magnet Schools Assistance					✓							
84.167	Library Literacy					✓							
84.168	National Program for Mathematics and Science Education					✓							
84.169	Comprehensive Services for Independent Living					✓							
84.170	Jacob K. Javits Fellowships					✓							
84.171	Excellence in Education					✓							
84.172	Construction, Reconstruction, and Renovation of Academic Facilities					✓							
84.173	Handicapped-Preschool Grants					✓							
84.174	Vocational Education-Community Based Organizations					✓							
84.176	Paul Douglas Teacher Scholarships					✓							
84.177	Rehabilitation Services-Independent Living Services					✓						✓	
84.178	Leadership in Educational Administration Development					✓							
84.180	Technology, Educational Media and Materials for the Handicapped					✓							
84.181	Handicapped Infants and Toddlers					✓							
84.183	Drug Prevention Programs					✓							
84.184	National Program for Drug-FreeSchools and Communities					✓							
84.185	Robert C. Byrd Honors Scholarships					✓							
84.186	Drug-Free Schools and Communities-State Grants					✓							
84.187	Supported Employment Services for Severely Handicapped					✓							
84.188	Drug-Free Schools and Communities-Regional Centers					✓							
84.189	Drug Abuse Education & Prevention Audio Visual Grant					✓							
84.190	Christa McAuliffe Fellowships					✓							
84.191	National Adult Education Research					✓							
84.192	Adult Education for the Homeless					✓	✓						
84.193	Demonstration Centers for the Retraining of Dislocated Workers					✓							
84.195	Bilingual Education Training Grants												
84.196	State Activities-Education of Homeless Children and Youth					✓							
84.197	College Library Technology and Cooperation Grants					✓							
84.198	Workplace Literacy					✓	✓						
84.199	Vocational Education-Cooperative Demonstration					✓							
84.200	Graduate Assistance in Areas of National Need					✓							
84.201	School Dropout Demonstration Assistance					✓							
84.202	Grants to Institutions to Encourage Minority Graduate Education					✓							
84.203	Star Schools Program			✓		✓							
84.204	School, College, and University Partnership		✓			✓							
84.206	Jacob K. Javits Gifted and Talented Students												
84.207	Educational Personnel Training					✓							
84.208	Native Hawaiian Model Curriculum Development					✓							
84.209	Native Hawaiian Family Based Education Centers					✓							
84.210	Native Hawaiian Gifted and Talented					✓							
84.211	FIRST Schools and Teachers					✓							
84.212	FIRST Family School Partnership					✓							
84.213	Even Start-Local Education Agencies					✓							
84.214	Even Start-Migrant Education					✓							
84.215	The Secretary's Fund for Innovation in Education					✓							
84.216	Capital Expenses					✓							
84.217	Ronald E. McNair Post-Baccalaureate Achievement					✓							
84.218	State Program Improvement Grants					✓							
84.219	Student Literacy Corps												

appendix continues

Appendix C *(continued)*
Programs providing outlays in each functional policy category

Catalog Number	Program Title	Agriculture	Business and Commerce	Community Development	Disaster Prevention and Relief	Education	Employment, Labor and Training	Environmental Quality	Food and Nutrition	Health	Housing	Income Security and Social Service	Transportation
84.220	Center for International Business Education		✓			✓							
84.221	Native Hawaiian Special Education					✓							
84.222	National School Volunteer Program					✓							
84.223	English Literacy Program												
84.224	State Grants for Technology-Related Assistance to Individuals with Disabilities			✓		✓							
84.225	Education for Homeless Children and Youth-Exemplary Grants												
84.995	Grants for Gallaudet College/Vocational and Adult Reimbursable Acts					✓	✓						
89.003	National Historical Publications and Records Grants			✓									
90.001	Bicentennial Educational Grant Program					✓							

Notes: Some programs listed in this appendix exist for only a portion of the period 1983-90. This appendix identifies the policy categories into which each program is classified. Information for policy categories is obtained from the *Catalog of Federal Domestic Assistance* (CFDA). The CFDA classfies programs into one or more policy categories. Many programs serve multiple purposes. For example, food and nutrition programs often have an educational component. Similarly housing programs often provide income security as well as shelter. Rather than attempting to assign programs to an exclusive policy category, we have retained the CFDA's multiple classifications. This means that outlays for some programs are reported in more than one policy category. Comparisons within policy categories are valid. However, it would not be valid to sum outlays across policy categories. Attempting to sum across policy categories (e.g., health and income) will over estimate the actual amount of monies allocated.

One further limitation concerning the policy classifications should be noted. Some programs that are included in FAADS are not published in CFDA. These programs are relatively few in number and tend to be temporary in nature, small in size, and often administered out of the office of the Department Secretary. Because these programs have not been catalogued in the CFDA, these programs cannot be assigned to a policy category. Consequently, the amount of monies shown in a policy category may understate the actual amount. This also means that the number of programs in this appendix is smaller than the number reported in Appendix B.

Appendix D
States in major regions

WEST	MIDWEST	NORTHEAST	SOUTH
ALASKA	ILLINOIS	CONNECTICUT	ALABAMA
ARIZONA	INDIANA	MAINE	ARKANSAS
CALIFORNIA	IOWA	MASSACHUSETTS	DELAWARE
COLORADO	KANSAS	NEW HAMPSHIRE	DISTRICT OF COLUMBIA
HAWAII	MICHIGAN	NEW JERSEY	FLORIDA
IDAHO	MINNESOTA	NEW YORK	GEORGIA
MONTANA	MISSOURI	PENNSYLVANIA	KENTUCKY
NEVADA	NEBRASKA	RHODE ISLAND	LOUISIANA
NEW MEXICO	NORTH DAKOTA	VERMONT	MARYLAND
OREGON	OHIO		MISSISSIPPI
UTAH	SOUTH DAKOTA		NORTH CAROLINA
WASHINGTON	WISCONSIN		OKLAHOMA
WYOMING			SOUTH CAROLINA
			TENNESSEE
			TEXAS
			VIRGINIA
			WEST VIRGINIA

Source: *1990 U.S. Statistical Abstract*, Figure 1.